Contemporary Issues Criticism

Volume 1

Contemporary Issues Criticism

Excerpts from Criticism of Contemporary Writings in
Sociology, Economics, Politics, Psychology, Anthropology,
Education, History, Law, Biography, and Related Fields

Dedria Bryfonski
Editor

Robert L. Brubaker
Project Editor

Gale Research Company • Book Tower • Detroit, Michigan 48226

STAFF

Dedria Bryfonski, *Editor*

Robert L. Brubaker, *Project Editor*

Bridget Broderick, Catherine E. Daligga, Lee Ferency, Thomas E. Gunton, Denise Michlewicz, Michele Roberge-Polizzi, Jane C. Thacker, Robert Bruce Young, Jr., Robyn Vernell Young, *Assistant Editors*

Phyllis Carmel Mendelson, Dennis Poupard, *Contributing Editors*

Carolyn Bancroft, *Production Supervisor*
Lizbeth A. Purdy, *Production Coordinator*

Linda M. Pugliese, *Manuscript Coordinator*
Donna DiNello, *Manuscript Assistant*

Robert J. Elster, *Research Coordinator*
Robert Hill, Carol Angela Thomas, *Research Assistants*

Cherie D. Abbey, Elizabeth Babini, Frank James Borovsky, Laura L. Britton, Ann K. Crowley,
Denise B. Grove, Serita Lanette Lockard, Brenda Marshall, Marie M. Mazur, Francine Melotti-Bacon,
Gloria Anne Williams, *Editorial Assistants*

L. Elizabeth Hardin, *Permissions Supervisor*
Filomena Sgambati, *Permissions Coordinator*
Anna Maria DiNello, Judy Kowalsky, Janice M. Mach, Mary P. McGrane, Susan D. Nobles,
Patricia A. Seefelt, *Permissions Assistants*

Library of Congress Catalog Card Number 82-9380
ISBN 0-8103-1550-5
ISSN 0732-7455

Contents

Preface 7   Appendix 619

Authors Forthcoming in *CIC* 9   Index to Critics 625

Index to Subjects 633

Authors in this volume:

5

Preface

Interpretations of recent events are as various as human possibilities, and the disciplines employed to comprehend, shape, or transform our social world are, by their natures, controversial. Commentary on current events and the ideas that inform them has burgeoned in recent years, confronting the interested reader with a vast body of material. *Contemporary Issues Criticism (CIC)* is designed to assist the reader in making evaluations of current issues, presenting significant passages from the published criticism on a variety of distinguished commentators.

The Scope of the Work

The usefulness of Gale's literary criticism series--*Contemporary Literary Criticism (CLC), Twentieth-Century Literary Criticism (TCLC),* and *Nineteenth-Century Literature Criticism (NCLC)*--suggested an equivalent need among students, teachers, and general readers interested in contemporary criticism of writing on current issues. Thus, *CIC* contains excerpts from the published criticism of contemporary works in political science, economics, sociology, psychology, anthropology, education, feminist studies, history, natural science, law, biography, and related areas. In order to provide the widest possible scope of current thought in these fields, the editors have included not only scholarly commentaries, but also articles intended for the layman and reviews of books of topical interest.

The broad range of issues and ideas presented in *CIC* can be illustrated by considering just a few of the authors included in the first volume: political theorist Hannah Arendt; conservative writer William F. Buckley, Jr.; ecologist and socialist Barry Commoner; civil rights activist Bayard Rustin; radical feminist writer Mary Daly; cultural historian Christopher Lasch; computer scientist Richard Hofstadter; Native American anthropologist D'Arcy McNickle.

Each volume of *CIC* is carefully designed to present a group of contemporary authors who represent a variety of topics, issues, and opinions. Each *CIC* author section presents an overview of critical response to that author's principal works. *CIC* is not, however, intended to provide a definitive overview of an author's career; instead, it is designed to trace the development of an author's ideas as they are expressed in his or her significant works. Furthermore, *CIC* covers only those nonfiction works which consider contemporary issues. For example, William F. Buckley, Jr.'s works of fiction, or those works by Noam Chomsky which deal strictly with the scientific/technical aspects of linguistics, would not be included in *CIC*.

The definition of contemporary is necessarily arbitrary. For purposes of selection for *CIC*, contemporary authors are those who are either now living or who have died since January 1, 1960.

The Organization of the Book

An author section consists of the following elements: author heading, bio-critical introduction, excerpts from the author's principal works, and excerpts of criticism (each followed by a citation).

● The *author heading* consists of the author's name, followed by birth date (and death date, if author is deceased). The unbracketed portion of the name denotes the form under which the author most commonly writes. If an author writes consistently under a pseudonym, the pseudonym will be listed in the author heading and the real name given in parentheses in the first line of the bio-critical introduction. Also located at the beginning of the bio-critical introduction are any name variations under which an author writes, including transliterated forms for authors whose languages use nonroman alphabets. Uncertainty as to a birth or death date is indicated by a question mark.

● The *bio-critical introduction* contains an assessment of the author's significance to his or her field or topic, a description of the author's most important works, and a summary of critical commentary on these works.

- *Excerpts from the author's principal works* are presented so that the reader may easily grasp the author's ideas and assess their merit in the light of critical commentary.

- *Criticism* is arranged chronologically in each author section to reflect the publication chronology of the author's works and to provide a perspective on any changes in critical evaluation over the years. For purposes of easier identification, the critic's name is given at the beginning of each piece of criticism.

- A complete *bibliographical citation* designed to facilitate location of the original essay or book by the interested reader accompanies each piece of criticism. An asterisk (*) at the end of a citation indicates the essay is on more than one author.

CIC includes an index to critics which will cumulate after the first volume. Under each critic's name is listed the author(s) on which the critic has written and the volume and page where the criticism may be found. *CIC* also includes a subject index. Subject headings appear alphabetically; authors who write on a given subject, along with the volume number in which they appear, are listed beneath the appropriate heading. Beginning with volume two, *CIC* will contain a cumulative index to authors.

Acknowledgments

The editors wish to thank the copyright holders of the excerpts included in this volume and the permission managers of many book and magazine publishing companies for assisting us in locating copyright holders. We extend our appreciation to the staffs of the Detroit Public Library, the libraries of the University of Michigan, and Wayne State University Library, especially Dr. Vern M. Pings, Director, Dr. Ruth J. Patrick, Assistant Director, Howard A. Sullivan, Assistant Director, and Hugh O'Connor, Interlibrary Loans of Wayne State University Library, for making their resources available to us. We are also grateful to Fred S. Stein for his assistance with copyright research.

No Single Volume Can Be Exhaustive

Since *CIC* is a multivolume work of indefinite but considerable size, neither this volume nor any other single volume should be judged apart from the concept that a single volume is but part of a larger and more comprehensive whole.

If readers wish to suggest authors they would like to have covered in future volumes, or if they have other suggestions or comments, they are cordially invited to write the editors.

Authors To Appear in Early Volumes

Abbott, Jack Henry
Abel, Lionel
Acheson, Dean
Adams, Ansel
Agnew, Spiro T.
Alexander, Shana
Alinsky, Saul
Alperovitz, Gar
Alpert, Jane
Alvarez, A.
Amory, Cleveland
Anderson, Jack
Aptheker, Herbert
Arato, Andrew
Ardrey, Robert
Arens, W.
Ariès, Philippe
Aron, Raymond
Asimov, Isaac
Atkinson, Ti-Grace
Auletta, Ken
Avineri, Shlomo
Baechler, Jean
Bagdikian, Ben
Baker, Houston A., Jr.
Baker, Russell
Banfield, Edward Christie
Baran, Paul
Barnet, Richard J.
Barrett, William
Bartlett, Bruce R.
Barzun, Jacques
Bateson, Gregory
Beauvoir, Simone de
Bell, Daniel
Berger, John
Berman, Marshall
Bernard, Jessie
Berne, Eric
Bernstein, Carl
Berrigan, Daniel
Berrigan, Philip
Bettelheim, Bruno
Bettelheim, Charles
Bird, Caroline
Blos, Peter
Blumenthal, Sidney
Boettcher, Robert
Bok, Sissela
Bond, Julian
Boorstin, Daniel J.
Boulding, Kenneth E.
Boyd, Malcolm
Braudel, Fernand
Braverman, Harry
Breines, Paul
Breslin, Jimmy
Broder, David S.
Brodie, Fawn M.
Bronowski, Jacob
Brothers, Joyce
Brown, Bruce
Brown, Dee

Brown, Michael
Brown, Norman O.
Bruch, Hilde
Brzezinski, Zbigniew
Buber, Martin
Buchwald, Art
Bukovsky, Vladimir
Bultmann, Rudolf Karl
Bundy, McGeorge
Burnham, James
Calder, Nigel
Calderone, Mary
Caldicott, Helen
Camus, Albert
Caputo, Philip
Carmichael, Peter
Carmichael, Stokely
Carson, Rachel
Carter, James Earl, Jr.
Casey, Douglas R.
Cassirer, Ernst
Castoriadis, Cornelius
Chen, Edwin
Chesler, Phyllis
Chisholm, Shirley
Cioran, E.M.
Cixous, Hélène
Clark, Ramsey
Clastres, Pierre
Cleaver, Eldridge
Coles, Jane
Coles, Robert
Commager, Henry Steele
Conquest, Robert
Cooke, Alistair
Coser, Lewis
Cousteau, Jacques
Cowan, Geoffrey
Cowan, Paul
Cox, Archibald
Cox, Harvey Gallagher, Jr.
Crick, Francis
D'Amico, Robert
Davis, Elizabeth Gould
Dawidowicz, Lucy S.
Dayan, Moshe
Degler, Carl N.
Dellinger, Dave
Derrida, Jacques
Desshusses, Jerome
Diamond, Stanley
Diop, Cheikh Anta
Djerassi, Carl
Djilas, Milovan
Donzelot, Jacques
Dorris, Michael
Draper, Theodore
Drinnon, Richard
Drucker, Peter F.
DuBois, W.E.B.
Dubos, René
Dumont, René
Dworkin, Andrea

Ehrenrich, Barbara
Ehrlich, Paul R.
Elkins, Stanley
Ellmann, Mary
Ellsberg, Daniel
Ellul, Jacques
Elshtain, Jean Bethke
Enzensberger, Hans Magnus
Erikson, Erik Homburger
Erlich, Paul
Erlichman, John
Etzioni, Amitai
Evans, Rowland
Ewen, Stewart
Fairbank, John K.
Fall, Bernard
Fallaci, Oriana
Fallows, James
Farley, Lin
Ferkiss, Victor
Feyerabend, Paul
Figès, Eva
Fine, Reuben
Firestone, Shulamith
Fishel, Weseley
Fisher, Elizabeth
FitzGerald, Frances
Ford, Gerald R.
Foucault, Michel
Frankfort, Ellen
Freedman, Gordon L.
Friedan, Betty
Frith, Simon
Fromm, Erich
Fuller, R. Buckminster
Gaddis, John Lewis
Gage, Nicholas
Gans, Herbert J.
Gardner, Howard
Gardner, Martin
Garrity, Joan Theresa
Genovese, Eugene D.
Gettinger, Stephen H.
Glaberman, Martin
Glasser, William
Glazer, Nathan
Glucksmann, André
Goffman, Erving
Goldenberg, Naomi R.
Goldman, Eric
Goldwater, Barry M.
Goodall, Jane
Goodfield, June
Goodman, Ellen
Gorz, André
Gould, Stephen Jay
Gouldner, Alvin W.
Gray, Colin S.
Greeley, Andrew M.
Greene, Felix
Greer, Germaine
Gross, Bertram
Guerin, Daniel

Haas, Ernst B.
Hacker, Andrew
Halberstam, David
Haldeman, H. R.
Hamill, Pete
Hampden-Turner, Charles
Hapgood, Fred
Harris, Marvin
Hartz, Louis
Hatfield, Mark O.
Hawkes, Jacquetta
Hayek, Friedrich August von
Hearst, Patricia Campbell
Hebblethwaite, Peter
Heilbroner, Robert L.
Heller, Walter W.
Henderson, Hazel
Hentoff, Nat
Herman, Edward S.
Hernandez, Aileen
Hersey, John
Hersh, Seymour
Hertzberg, Arthur
Hesburgh, Theodore
Hess, Karl
Heyerdahl, Thor
Hilsman, Roger
Hite, Shere
Hobsbawm, Eric
Hoffer, Eric
Hoffman, Abbie
Hoffman, Stanley
Hofstadter, Richard
Hollander, Paul
Hook, Sidney
Horowitz, David
Horowitz, Irving Lewis
Howe, Irving
Hungry Wolf, Adolf
Huntington, Samuel P.
Illich, Ivan
Irigaray, Luce
Isaacs, Harold R.
Jacobs, Jane
Jacobs, Paul
Jacoby, Russell
Janeway, Elizabeth
Janov, Arthur
Javits, Jacob K.
Jaworski, Leon
Jensen, Arthur R.
Johnson, Haynes
Johnson, Lyndon
Johnson, Sonia
Johnson, Virginia
Johnston, Jill
Joll, James
Jones, James H.
Jordan, Barbara
Jungk, Robert
Kaldor, Mary
Kalecki, Michael
Kaplan, Helen Singer

Kaufmann, Walter Arnold
Kempton, Murray
Keniston, Kenneth
Kennan, George
Kennedy, Flo
Kerouac, Jack
Kilpatrick, James J.
King, Martin Luther
Kissinger, Henry
Klare, Michael T.
Koestler, Arthur
Kohn, Howard
Kolakowski, Leszek
Kolko, Gabriel
Kolko, Joyce
Kozol, Jonathan
Krim, Seymour M.
Kristeva, Julia
Kristol, Irving
Kübler-Ross, Elisabeth
Kuhn, Thomas S.
Ladurie, Emmanuel L.
Lange, Oscar
Langer, Susanne K.
Laqueur, Walter
Lasky, Victor
Lasswell, Harold D.
Leakey, Richard E.
Lears, Jackson
Lefkowitz, Bernard
Lefort, Claude
Lens, Sidney
Lerner, Max
Lernoux, Penny
Levesque, René
Lévi-Strauss, Claude
Lewin, Roger
Lewis, Oscar
Lewy, Guenter
Libby, Leona Marshall
Lichtheim, George
Liddy, G. Gordon
Lifton, Betty Jean
Lifton, Robert Jay
Lilly, John C.
Lindbergh, Anne Morrow
Lippmann, Walter
Litwack, Leon F.
Loftus, Elizabeth F.
Lukacs, John
Lukes, Steven
Lundberg, Ferdinand
Lynd, Staughton
MacDonald, Dwight
Magdoff, Harry
Malcolm, Janet
Mandelbaum, Michael
Mander, Jerry
Mankiewicz, Frank
Mannes, Marya
Marcuse, Herbert
Martin, Malachi
Masserman, Jules H.
Masters, William
Mattick, Paul, Jr.
May, Rollo
Mayer, Martin
McCarthy, Eugene J.
McGinniss, Joe
McGovern, George S.
McIntyre, Thomas J.
McLuhan, Marshall
McNally, Dennis
Mead, Robert Douglas
Melman, Seymour

Mendes-France, Pierre
Menninger, Karl
Merton, Andrew H.
Merton, Robert King
Merton, Thomas
Meyers, Robert
Middleton, Drew
Miller, Jonathan
Miller, Perry
Millett, Kate
Mitford, Jessica
Mollenhoff, Clark R.
Moncrieff, Anthony
Mondale, Walter F
Monod, Jacques
Montagu, F. Ashley
Montgomery, David
Moody, Anne
Moore, Barrington
Morgan, Elaine
Morgan, Marabel
Morgenthau, Hans
Moyers, Bill
Moynihan, Daniel P.
Mumford, Lewis
Myrdal, Gunnar
Nader, Ralph
Neier, Aryeh
Newfield, Jack
Newman, Mildred
Niebuhr, Reinhold
Nielsen, Waldemar A.
Nitze, Paul H.
Nixon, Richard
Nizer, Louis
Noble, David
Novak, Robert
Novak, William
Nozick, Robert
Oakeshott, Michael
Oglesby, Carl
O'Neill, George
O'Neill, Nena
Orbach, Susie
Ortega y Gasset, José
Ouchi, William G.
Packard, Vance
Peale, Norman Vincent
Pepper, Thomas
Pfeffer, Richard M.
Phillips, Kevin
Piaget, Jean
Pierre, Andrew J.
Pious, Richard M.
Pipes, Richard
Piven, Francis Fox
Plummer, William
Podhoretz, Norman
Polanyi, Karl
Popper, Karl
Porter, Sylvia
Postman, Neal
Proxmire, William
Queen, Richard
Rabin, Yitzhak
Rabinowitz, Dorothy
Radosh, Ronald
Rand, Ayn
Rather, Dan
Ravitch, Diane
Rawls, John
Read, Herbert Edward
Reagan, Ronald
Reeves, Richard
Reich, Charles

Reid, Inez
Reik, Theodor
Reuben, David
Revel, Jean-Francois
Rich, Adrienne
Ridgeway, James
Rieff, Philip
Riesman, David
Robinson, Joan
Rogers, Carl
Rossiter, Clinton
Rossman, Michael
Roszak, Theodore
Rothbard, Murray N.
Rowbotham, Sheila
Royko, Mike
Rubin, Jerry
Rubin, Theodore
Rupp, George
Russell, Bertrand
Russell, Diana
Rycroft, Charles
Sadat, Anwar el-
Safire, William
Sagan, Carl
Sahlins, Marshall
Said, Edward W.
Saikal, Amin
Sakharov, Andrei D.
Sale, Kirkpatrick
Salinger, Pierre
Salisbury, Harrison E.
Sampson, Anthony
Samuelson, Paul A.
Sartre, Jean-Paul
Scalapino, Robert A.
Scheer, Robert
Schell, Jonathon
Schlesinger, Arthur, Jr.
Schlesinger, Steven
Scholem, Gershom
Schorr, Daniel
Schroyer, Trent
Scoville, Herbert, Jr.
Seabury, Paul
Selzer, Michael
Sennett, Richard
Servan-Schreiber, Jean-Jacques
Sevareid, Eric
Shalamov, Varlam
Shaplen, Robert
Shawcross, William
Shcharansky, Avital
Sheehy, Gail
Sheen, Fulton
Shoup, Laurence H.
Sihanouk, Norodom
Silk, Leonard
Silverman, Samuel
Singer, Peter
Sirica, John J.
Skinner, B.F.
Slater, Philip
Slickpoo, Allen
Smith, Robert Ellis
Snow, C.P.
Solzhenitsyn, Alexander
Sontag, Susan
Sorenson, Theodore
Sowell, Thomas
Speer, Albert
Spock, Benjamin
Stampp, Kenneth M.
Stans, Maurice H.
Steel, Ronald

Stein, Ben
Steinfels, Peter
Stephens, Mark
Stone, I.F.
Strout, Richard L.
Sullivan, William C.
Sullivan, William H.
Sulzberger, Arthur
Summers, Anthony
Sweezy, Paul M.
Swerdlow, Joel
Szasz, Thomas
Talbott, Strobe
Taussig, Michael
Tawney, Richard Henry
Taylor, Gordon Rattray
Terkel, Studs
Theobald, Robert
Thomas, Hugh
Thomas, Norman M.
Thompson, E.P.
Thompson, Hunter S.
Thurow, Lester
Tiger, Lionel
Tillich, Paul
Todorov, Tristan
Toynbee, Arnold J.
Trevor-Roper, Hugh
Tsongas, Paul
Tucker, Robert W.
Turnbull, Colin M.
Ulam, Adam B.
van den Haag, Ernest
Vanek, Jaroslav
Viereck, Peter
Viorst, Milton
Vogel, Ezra F.
Von Daeniken, Erich
Von Hoffman, Nicholas
Von Mises, Ludwig
Wald, Karen
Wallace, Michele
Wanniski, Jude
Warner, Sam Bass
Watson, James
Wattenberg, Ben J.
Weber, Eugen
Weinbaum, Batya
Weisstein, Naomi
White, Edmund
White, Theodore
Wicker, Tom
Wiesenthal, Simon
Will, George F., Jr.
Williams, Chancellor
Willis, Ellen
Wills, Gary
Wilson, Edward O.
Wilson, James Q.
Wilson, William Julius
Winner, Langdon
Wojtyla, Karol (Pope John Paul II)
Wolfe, Tom
Wolff, Robert Paul
Woodcock, George
Woodward, Bob
Woodward, C. Vann
Wright, Nathan
X, Malcolm
Yankelovich, Daniel
Yazzie, Ethelou
Young, Andrew
Zinn, Howard

Hannah Arendt

1906-1975

A German-born American political philosopher and literary essayist, Arendt ranks among the most important political thinkers of the twentieth century. In her many works she considered the central issues of the times—war, revolution, political power, totalitarianism, violence, anti-Semitism—with original, if at times controversial, insight. In *The Human Condition* (1958) she distinguished the spheres of labor, work, and action in political life, elevating political activity—specifically, the creation of a free public sphere—over economic activity as expressive of what is most valuable in human endeavor. In *On Revolution* (1963) she explored the "physiognomy of the twentieth century" in war and revolution. *On Violence* (1969) treats the distinction between power and violence, indicating the growing embrace of the latter by the revolutionary left. In her seminal *The Origins of Totalitarianism* (1951) and the controversial *Eichmann in Jerusalem* (1963) she examined the phenomenon of totalitarianism, illumining the disintegration of social life and human personality which permitted its ascendance. In all her writings Arendt sought to expand the realm of human freedom and to resist tyranny; she perceived the political thinker as a "truth-teller" who counters the lies of politicians. While her works found many detractors, they were equally admired. As Sheldon Wolin wrote: "Those who have read her writings will remember Hannah Arendt not only as a writer of remarkable insight and intelligence, but one of rare courage who took on the gravest and most dangerous problems of the times." (See also *Contemporary Authors*, Vols. 17-20, rev. ed.; obituary, Vols. 61-64.)

Excerpt from *ON REVOLUTION*

Wars and revolutions—as though events had only hurried up to fulfill Lenin's early prediction—have thus far determined the physiognomy of the twentieth century. And as distinguished from the nineteenth-century ideologies—such as nationalism and internationalism, capitalism and imperialism, socialism and communism, which, though still invoked by many as justifying causes, have lost contact with the major realities of our world—war and revolution still constitute its two central political issues. They have outlived all their ideological justifications. In a constellation that poses the threat of total annihilation through war against the hope for the emancipation of all mankind through revolution—leading one people after the other in swift succession "to assume among the powers of the earth the separate and equal station to which the Laws of Nature and of Nature's God entitle them"—no cause is left but the most ancient of all, the one, in fact, that from the beginning of our history has determined the very existence of politics, the cause of freedom versus tyranny.

This in itself is surprising enough. Under the concerted assault of the modern debunking "sciences," psychology and sociology, nothing indeed has seemed to be more safely buried than the concept of freedom. Even the revolutionists, whom one might have assumed to be safely and even inexorably anchored in a tradition that could hardly be told, let alone made sense of, without the notion of freedom, would much rather degrade freedom to the rank of a lower-middle-class prejudice than admit that the aim of revolution was, and always has been, freedom. Yet if it was amazing to see how the very word freedom could disappear from the revolutionary vocabulary, it has perhaps been no less astounding to watch how in recent years the idea of freedom has intruded itself into the center of the gravest of all present political debates, the discussion of war and of a justifiable use of violence. Historically, wars are among the oldest phenomena of the recorded past while revolutions, properly speaking, did not exist prior to the modern age; they are among the most recent of all major political data. In contrast to revolution, the aim of war was only in rare cases bound up with the notion of freedom; and while it is true that warlike uprisings against a foreign invader have frequently been felt to be sacred, they have never been recognized, either in theory or in practice, as the only just wars. (pp. 1-2)

The notion that aggression is a crime and that wars can be justified only if they ward off aggression or prevent it, acquired its practical and even theoretical significance only after the First World War had demonstrated the horribly destructive potential of warfare under conditions of modern technology.

Perhaps it is because of this noticeable absence of the freedom argument from the traditional justifications of war as the last resort of international politics that we have this curiously jarring sentiment whenever we hear it introduced into the debate of the war question today. To sound off with a cheerful "give me liberty or give me death" sort of argument in the face of the unprecedented and inconceivable potential of destruction in nuclear warfare is not even hollow; it is downright ridiculous. Indeed it seems so obvious that it is a very different thing to risk one's own life for the life and freedom of one's country and one's posterity from risking the very existence of the human species for the same purpose that it is difficult not to suspect the defenders of the "better dead than red" or "better death than slavery" slogans of bad faith. Which of course is not to say that the reverse, "better red than dead," has any more to recommend itself; when an old truth ceases to be applicable, it does not become any truer by being stood on its head. (pp. 3-4)

It is important to remember that the idea of freedom was introduced into the debate of the war question only after it had become quite obvious that we had reached a stage of technical development where the means of destruction were such as to exclude their rational use. In other words, freedom has appeared in this debate like a *deus ex machina* to justify what on rational grounds has become unjustifiable. Is it too much to read into the current rather hopeless confusion of issues and arguments a hopeful indication that a profound change in international relations may be about to occur, namely, the disappearance of war from the scene of politics even without a radical transformation of international relations and without an inner change of men's hearts and minds? Could it not be that our present perplexity in this matter indicates our lack of preparedness for a disappearance of war, our inability to think in terms of foreign policy without having in mind this "continuation with other means" as its last resort?

Quite apart from the threat of total annihilation, which conceivably could be eliminated by new technical discoveries such as a "clean" bomb or an anti-missile missile, there are a few signs pointing in this direction. There is *first* the fact that the seeds of total war developed as early as the First World War, when the distinction between soldiers and civilians was no longer respected because it was inconsistent with the new weapons then used. (pp. 4-5)

Closely connected with this perversion in the relationship between state and army is *second* the little-noticed but quite noteworthy fact that since the end of the First World War we almost automatically expect that no government, and no state or form of government, will be strong enough to survive a defeat in war. (p. 5)

The *third* fact seems to indicate a radical change in the very nature of war through the introduction of the deterrent as the guiding principle in the armament race. (p. 6)

Moreover, it is quite in line with these, as it were, paradoxical efforts that a possible serious substitution of "cold" wars for "hot" wars becomes clearly perceptible at the horizon of international politics. . . . It is as though the nuclear armament race has turned into some sort of tentative warfare in which the opponents demonstrate to each other the destructiveness of the weapons in their possession; and while it is always possible that this deadly game of ifs and whens may suddenly turn into the real thing, it is by no means inconceivable that one day victory and defeat may end a war that never exploded into reality. (pp. 6-7)

There is *finally,* and in our context most importantly, the fact that the interrelationship of war and revolution, their recipro-

cation and mutual dependence, has steadily grown, and that the emphasis in the relationship has shifted more and more from war to revolution. . . . Hence, whatever the outcome of our present predicaments may be, if we don't perish altogether, it seems more than likely that revolution, in distinction to war, will stay with us into the foreseeable future. Even if we should succeed in changing the physiognomy of this century to the point where it would no longer be a century of wars, it most certainly will remain a century of revolutions. In the contest that divides the world today and in which so much is at stake, those will probably win who understand revolution, while those who still put their faith in power politics in the traditional sense of the term and, therefore, in war as the last resort of all foreign policy may well discover in a not too distant future that they have become masters in a rather useless and obsolete trade. And such understanding of revolution can be neither countered nor replaced with an expertness in counter-revolution; for counter-revolution—the word having been coined by Condorcet in the course of the French Revolution—has always remained bound to revolution as reaction is bound to action. (pp. 7-8)

> *Hannah Arendt, in her* On Revolution *(copyright © 1963 by Hannah Arendt; reprinted by permission of Viking Penguin Inc.), Viking Penguin, 1963, 343 p.*

Excerpt from *ON VIOLENCE*

No one engaged in thought about history and politics can remain unaware of the enormous role violence has always played in human affairs, and it is at first glance rather surprising that violence has been singled out so seldom for special consideration. (In the last edition of the Encyclopedia of the Social Sciences "violence" does not even rate an entry.) This shows to what an extent violence and its arbitrariness were taken for granted and therefore neglected; no one questions or examines what is obvious to all. Those who saw nothing but violence in human affairs, convinced that they were "always haphazard, not serious, not precise" (Renan) or that God was forever with the bigger battalions, had nothing more to say about either violence or history. Anybody looking for some kind of sense in the records of the past was almost bound to see violence as a marginal phenomenon. Whether it is Clausewitz calling war "the continuation of politics by other means," or Engels defining violence as the accelerator of economic development, the emphasis is on political or economic continuity, on the continuity of a process that remains determined by what preceded violent action. Hence, students of international relations have held until recently that "it was a maxim that a military resolution in discord with the deeper cultural sources of national power could not be stable," or that, in Engels' words, "wherever the power structure of a country contradicts its economic development" it is political power with its means of violence that will suffer defeat.

Today all these old verities about the relation between war and politics or about violence and power have become inapplicable. The Second World War was not followed by peace but by a cold war and the establishment of the military-industrial-labor complex. To speak of "the priority of war-making potential as the principal structuring force in society," to maintain that "economic systems, political philosophies and corpora juris serve and extend the war system, not vice versa," to conclude that "war itself is the basic social system, within which other secondary modes of social organization conflict or conspire"— all this sounds much more plausible than Engels' or Clausewitz's nineteenth-century formulas. Even more conclusive than this simple reversal proposed by the anonymous author of the *Report from Iron Mountain*—instead of war being "an extension of diplomacy (or of politics, or of the pursuit of economic objectives)," peace is the continuation of war by other means—is the actual development in the techniques of warfare. In the words of the Russian physicist Sakharov, "A thermonuclear war cannot be considered a continuation of politics by other means (according to the formula of Clausewitz). It would be a means of universal suicide."

Moreover, we know that "a few weapons could wipe out all other sources of national power in a few moments," that biological weapons have been devised which would enable "small groups of individuals . . . to upset the strategic balance" and would be cheap enough to be produced by "nations unable to develop nuclear striking forces," that "within a very few years" robot soldiers will have made "human soldiers completely obsolete," and that, finally, in conventional warfare the poor countries are much less vulnerable than the great powers precisely because they are "underdeveloped," and because technical superiority can "be much more of a liability than an asset" in guerrilla wars. What all these uncomfortable novelties add up to is a complete reversal in the relationship between power and violence, foreshadowing another reversal in the future relationship between small and great powers. The amount of violence at the disposal of any given country may soon not be a reliable indication of the country's strength or a reliable guarantee against destruction by a substantially smaller and weaker power. And this bears an ominous similarity to one of political science's oldest insights, namely that power cannot be measured in terms of wealth, that an abundance of wealth may erode power, that riches are particularly dangerous to the power and well-being of republics—an insight that does not lose in validity because it has been forgotten, especially at a time when its truth has acquired a new dimension of validity by becoming applicable to the arsenal of violence as well.

The more dubious and uncertain an instrument violence has become in international relations, the more it has gained in reputation and appeal in domestic affairs, specifically in the matter of revolution. The strong Marxist rhetoric of the New Left coincides with the steady growth of the entirely non-Marxian conviction, proclaimed by Mao Tse-tung, that "Power grows out of the barrel of a gun." To be sure, Marx was aware of the role of violence in history, but this role was to him secondary; not violence but the contradictions inherent in the old society brought about its end. The emergence of a new society was preceded, but not caused, by violent outbreaks, which he likened to the labor pangs that precede, but of course do not cause, the event of organic birth. In the same vein he regarded the state as an instrument of violence in the command of the ruling class; but the actual power of the ruling class did not consist of or rely on violence. It was defined by the role the ruling class played in society, or, more exactly, by its role in the process of production. It has often been noticed, and sometimes deplored, that the revolutionary Left under the influence of Marx's teachings ruled out the use of violent means; the "dictatorship of the proletariat"—openly repressive in Marx's writings—came after the revolution and was meant, like the Roman dictatorship, to last a strictly limited period. Political assassination, except for a few acts of individual terror perpetrated by small groups of anarchists, was mostly the prerogative of the Right, while organized armed uprisings remained the specialty of the military. The Left remained convinced "that all conspiracies are not only useless but harmful. They [knew] only too well that revolutions are not made intentionally

and arbitrarily, but that they were always and everywhere the necessary result of circumstances entirely independent of the will and guidance of particular parties and whole classes." (pp. 8-12)

The question remains why so many of the new preachers of violence are unaware of their decisive disagreement with Karl Marx's teachings, or, to put it another way, why they cling with such stubborn tenacity to concepts and doctrines that have not only been refuted by factual developments but are clearly inconsistent with their own politics. The one positive political slogan the new movement has put forth, the claim for "participatory democracy" that has echoed around the globe and constitutes the most significant common denominator of the rebellions in the East and the West, derives from the best in the revolutionary tradition—the council system, the always defeated but only authentic outgrowth of every revolution since the eighteenth century. But no reference to this goal either in word or substance can be found in the teachings of Marx and Lenin, both of whom aimed on the contrary at a society in which the need for public action and participation in public affairs would have "withered away," together with the state. Because of a curious timidity in theoretical matters, contrasting oddly with its bold courage in practice, the slogan of the New Left has remained in a declamatory stage, to be invoked rather inarticulately against Western representative democracy (which is about to lose even its merely representative function to the huge party machines that "represent" not the party membership but its functionaries) and against the Eastern one-party bureaucracies, which rule out participation on principle. Even more surprising in this odd loyalty to the past is the New Left's seeming unawareness of the extent to which the moral character of the rebellion—now a widely accepted fact—clashes with its Marxian rhetoric. Nothing, indeed, about the movement is more striking than its disinterestedness. . . . To be sure, every revolutionary movement has been led by the disinterested, who were motivated by compassion or by a passion for justice, and this, of course, is also true for Marx and Lenin. But Marx, as we know, had quite effectively tabooed these "emotions"—if today the establishment dismisses moral arguments as "emotionalism" it is much closer to Marxist ideology than the rebels—and had solved the problem of "disinterested" leaders with the notion of their being the vanguard of mankind, embodying the ultimate interest of human history. (pp. 22-4)

I am not sure what the explanation of these inconsistencies will eventually turn out to be; but I suspect that the deeper reason for this loyalty to a typically nineteenth-century doctrine has something to do with the concept of Progress, with an unwillingness to part with a notion that used to unite Liberalism, Socialism, and Communism into the "Left" but has nowhere reached the level of plausibility and sophistication we find in the writings of Karl Marx. (p. 25)

Hannah Arendt, in her On Violence *(copyright © 1969, 1970; by Hannah Arendt; reprinted by permission of Harcourt Brace Jovanovich, Inc.),* Harcourt, 1970, 106 p.

H. STUART HUGHES

Dr. Arendt's interpretation of totalitarianism [in **"The Origins of Totalitarianism"**] is at the same time illuminating and open to serious objections. The chief of these is that like totalitarianism itself Dr. Arendt's definition has too much internal consistency. It is insufficiently flexible to allow room for local and ideological variation. On the one hand it leads her to neglect the milder forms of fascism and to concentrate on Nazism—the extreme and hence for her the most significant case. (pp. 280-81)

On the other hand, this unitary view of the totalitarian phenomenon causes Dr. Arendt to slur over the differences between German and Soviet totalitarianism. . . . For Nazism she provides a full ideological background. But in the case of Bolshevism we are left with a near void of a quarter of a century between the agitation of the Pan-Slavists and the triumph of Stalin. We are suddenly confronted with Soviet communism as the totalitarian equivalent of Nazism without any adequate account of how it got to be that way. The fate of classic Marxism in Russia, the complex process by which Pan-Slavism transformed it by fusing with it in the Stalinist credo—all this is telescoped into a few sentences. . . .

If [Arendt] had consulted some of the professional economic analyses, she might have been less ready to dismiss the first Five-Year Plan as "insanity." For Bolshevism conflicts with her definition by being *both* more totalitarian and more rational than Nazism. In Nazi Germany the average individual enjoyed more freedom than in the Soviet Union, but if he happened to be sent to a concentration camp he was probably worse off than someone meeting a similar fate in Russia. We may agree with Dr. Arendt that the police mentality is the decisive influence in both regimes. But we should like to see some analysis of the differences that have given to Soviet communism its greater resiliency and staying power.

Some critics would go on to say that it is Dr. Arendt's whole method that is at fault—that her procedure of constructing imaginary "ideal types" cannot fail to do violence to the facts. Here the present reviewer vigorously dissents. No doubt Dr. Arendt does push her data to the farthest limits of verisimilitude. . . . But this method has the virtues of its faults. It lights up in marvelous flashes of understanding the dark corners of recent history where the documents can never penetrate. In turning to new and unsuspected purposes such familiar literary masterpieces as Conrad's "Heart of Darkness," Kipling's "Kim," Lawrence's "Seven Pillars of Wisdom," and Proust's "Remembrance of Things Past," she has struck out for an uncharted domain where history and fantasy can meet on common ground. The result may be unconventional history, but it is a magnificent effort of creative imagination.

For all her exaggerations, then, Dr. Arendt has written a great book. Deeply thought-out and conscientiously documented, **"The Origins of Totalitarianism"** will take its place among the major writings of our times. The record could scarcely be more dreadful. But as she concludes her melancholy account, Dr. Arendt rises above a conventional despair. In the very futility of totalitarianism she sees hope for its eventual destruction. To the totalitarian threat to change "human nature" itself she opposes an equally total declaration of human responsibility. Her book is a moving testament of solidarity with all the "superfluous people" now living out their meaningless days in all the concentration camps of the earth. (p. 281)

H. Stuart Hughes, "Historical Sources of Totalitarianism," in The Nation *(copyright 1951* The Nation *magazine,* The Nation Associates, Inc.*), Vol. 172, No. 12, March 24, 1951, pp. 280-81.*

E. H. CARR

The nightmarish quality of ["**The Origins of Totalitarianism**"] seems to derive in part from a certain lack of historical perspective. Miss Arendt . . . has all too clearly set out to generalize the overwhelming experience of Hitler's Germany. The book is divided into three major sections—anti-Semitism, Imperialism and Totalitarianism. This is understandable in a work devoted to nazism, since the German form of totalitarianism was intimately associated with the two other phenomena. Yet these have little or no relevance to other forms of totalitarian society or to the general problem of the totalitarian menace to individual freedom.

Miss Arendt shows only a passing interest in Soviet Russia, and her remarks about it never rise above the commonplace. . . . (pp. 3, 24)

Whatever its shortcomings, however, either in its general thesis or on particular issues, the book is the work of one who has thought as well as suffered. The section on anti-Semitism is a mine of information on many unfamiliar aspects of the Jewish question. Take, for instance, the convincing demonstration that Jews played a leading role in the early stages of imperialism, but disappeared from the picture as soon as imperialism ceased to be a matter of trade and finance and became an issue of power. Or take the bitter reflection that Jews were freely tolerated in French society under the Third Republic, not because it was no longer believed that Jews were "traitors," but because society had become too cynical to object to "treason."

In a later section there is a subtle analysis of conspiratorial and secret service activities as contributory factors to the totalitarian spirit. The morbid self-effacement of T. E. Lawrence, developed in his service among the Arabs in World War I and never afterward shaken off, is treated as an illustration of the desire of the individual to become a number, to lose his identity in the service of a cause, which is one of the profoundest hidden urges toward the self-extinction of a totalitarian loyalty. . . .

Miss Arendt, her eyes fixed in fascination and repulsion on the horror of Nazi Germany, offers only slender hope for Western civilization to avoid this form of suicide. Yet the reader who shuns this conclusion can still be grateful for a disquieting, moving and thought-provoking book. (p. 24)

E. H. Carr, "The Ultimate Denial," in The New York Times Book Review *(© 1951 by The New York Times Company; reprinted by permission), March 25, 1951, pp. 3, 24.*

MARY McCARTHY

The Human Condition, which is about man's active life as a member of his species in its habitat, the earth, has the . . . faculty of surprising, then awakening suspense, and finally coming to appear clear as daylight to the initially puzzled reader. The combination of tremendous intellectual power with great common sense makes Miss Arendt's insights into history and politics seem both amazing and obvious; "Elementary, my dear Watson," the author disclaims, which is true, but only in a way—elementary to Sherlock but not to Watson. (p. 156)

The pessimism of [her] conclusions is stoic in the finest sense. Miss Arendt's essay explains what has happened and how it happened, without dismay or grievance. Nor does it offer any remedy. It only tells a story in noble language, matching its words with the action it describes. An epigraph to one of the chapters, from Isak Dinesen, declares, "All sorrows can be borne if you put them into a story or tell a story about them.'' The spirit of this maxim quickens a book that has in it a great deal more than a review can mention, for the author is full of determination to get everything in—remarks on love, friendship, and the nature of works of art, on statistics, hobbies, servants, means and ends, violence, and the ancient view of slavery, on suicide, common sense, science, and logic. It is as though she were hurriedly stuffing a trunk with all the valuables, trifles, and curios of human experience in the hope that something might survive. This hurry becomes excessive in the later sections, where technical questions of philosophy and science are packed in with too much density for the ordinary reader, but the fault is one of generosity. *The Human Condition* contains a little of everything, including the kitchen stove. (p. 164)

> *Mary McCarthy, "The 'Vita Activa' " (originally published as "Philosophy at Work," in* The New Yorker, *Vol. XXXIV, No. 35, October 18, 1958), in her* On the Contrary *(reprinted by permission of Farrar, Straus and Giroux, Inc.; copyright © 1958, 1960 by Mary McCarthy), Farrar, Straus and Cudahy, 1961, pp. 155-64.*

IRVING KRISTOL

Miss Arendt writes with passion and urgency, and she is a woman of strong political opinions. But she isn't a political thinker in [*Between Past and Future*]. She is that more valuable thing, a political philosopher. If politics is the art of the possible, then political thinking is the fusion of abstract idea with gross circumstance; it is directed and limited by political commitment. In contrast, political philosophy is (or ought to be) located at a distant remove from mere opinion; it is the contemplation of man as a political animal. It stands to political activity much as the philosophy of science stands to scientific activity: its comprehension is *post facto,* and when it is tempted to be prescriptive, it falls into presumption. True, Miss Arendt is not always immune to this temptation. Her last two essays, on American Education and Mass Culture, are full of marvellous insights into education and culture generally; yet, heedless of the crude perplexities that the educator or the journalist has to face, they are less relevant than she seems to think. But this is a trivial lapse.

Indeed, it is a lapse that may well be organically connected with her special qualities and unique virtue as a political philosopher. A former student of Karl Jaspers, she has absorbed much of the existentialist approach toward men and ideas. . . . At the same time, she is obviously much under the influence of classical German philosophy and of the later Heidegger. Thus, there is throughout these essays a tension between an almost uncanny (and exceedingly feminine) percipience and a noble, elevated (and exceedingly masculine) architectonic of ideas. I find this combination a powerful one, and so apparently do many other readers.

Miss Arendt has another source of great strength: her appreciation of the Graeco-Roman point of view, which in turn enables her to discern what it is in modernity that is specifically modern as against generically human. Her essays, at their best, liberate us from prejudices and preconceptions that we are not even aware we possess. One is not accustomed to discovering that an essay on **"What Is Freedom?"** will say something new on the subject; Miss Arendt's essay on that title is spectacularly original and provocative. This is because, instead of taking our modern liberal notion of liberty as given, and reading the hu-

man record in its light, she recaptures the Greek notion as the Greeks understood it, reestablishes it as a compelling human alternative, and then shows how the peculiar and parochial modern idea evolved. Nor is this an academic exercise (though I should say one needs some academic training in order to follow her argument). For Miss Arendt is convinced that liberty, in the modern sense, is a dying ideal, and the purpose is to remind us that the death of the liberal idea of liberty need not signify the death of liberty itself—if only we instruct ourselves, in time, of the varieties of liberty that are (in principle, at least) open to us.

Indeed, Miss Arendt is convinced that modernity itself is a dying theme, that our century is more apocalyptic than "progressive" in character. She is the Owl of Minerva (no ungallantry intended by this Hegelian metaphor!) come at dusk to gather into a supreme moment of self-consciousness and self-understanding the inchoate self-knowledge of the passing day. It is in her essay, **"What Is Authority?",** that her classical perspective and her apocalyptic sensibility unite most forcefully. Beginning with the crisis of authority in the modern world—of governmental authority, religious authority, parental authority, etc.—she distinguishes between tyranny, despotism and autonomy; demonstrates that the Greeks had neither the word nor the conception of it; that the Romans, with their superb piety toward the founding fathers ("authors"), invented it for the West; that Augustine formulated it for the Church; that the Church's idea of authority became the archetype for authority *per se;* that the shattering of religious authority has caused the whole edifice to crumble. . . . A reviewer must of necessity be timid about venturing such a judgment but I do think that the future (if there is one) will very likely treasure this essay as one of the remarkable intellectual achievements of our age. (pp. 19-20)

> *Irving Kristol, "A Treasure for the Future," in* The New Republic *(reprinted by permission of* The New Republic; © *1961 The New Republic, Inc.), Vol. 145, Nos. 2 & 3, July 10, 1961, pp. 19-20.*

W. A. SUCHTING

[In *The Human Condition* Hannah Arendt] finds a "fundamental and flagrant" contradiction running "like a red thread through the whole of Marx's thought," . . . and this leads to "patent absurdities.". . .

[However,] her interpretation of Marx is completely erroneous and . . . there is no foundation whatsoever for the "contradiction" in Marx's thought which she presents. (p. 47)

Let us see where Miss Arendt locates the fundamental contradiction in Marx's thought. It is to be found in "Marx's attitude toward labor, and that is toward the very center of his thought." . . . On the one hand, Miss Arendt says, Marx defines man as a laboring animal (in her sense of "labor"); on the other hand, he sees the task and goal of social revolution, of socialism and communism, as that of freeing men from labor. . . . But: "Emancipation from labor, in Marx's own terms . . . would ultimately mean emancipation from consumption as well, that is, from the metabolism with nature which is the very condition of human life.". . .

From this point of view Marx, far from being the prophet of the future, is, rather, simply the most consistent and comprehensive theorist of the contemporary laboring society, his ideal society—"socialized mankind"—being just a "mass society of laborers." . . . (pp. 48-9)

There can be no doubt that Marx regarded labor (*Arbeit*) and, specifically, labor by means of tools, as the feature differentiating man from the rest of the animal kingdom. The question is, then, whether Marx meant by this "labor" in Miss Arendt's sense and whether he confused it with what she calls "work."

Marx's central discussion of the "labor process" occurs in the first volume of *Capital*. He emphasizes here that he is not concerned with "the first animal-like and instinctive forms of labor," but with labor in the form which "is peculiar to man." He finds this peculiarity of human labor in the fact that the latter results in something "which, at the beginning of the process, already existed in the *worker's imagination,* already existed as an *idea.*" The human laborer "not only . . . effects (*bewirkt*) a change of form in natural objects," as animals and insects do, but at the same time "*realizes* (verwirklicht) *his own purpose*" in nature. But this is precisely the second of Miss Arendt's criteria of "work," as listed previously.

The other criterion is that of durability. But this feature, relating to the product and not to the process resulting in the product, is simply a function of time and use, purely quantitative, qualitatively homogeneous factors which cannot provide a criterion of essential demarcation, being quite accidental features of the object. The distinction between "consumer goods" and "use objects," from the point of view of durability, is a highly relative and contingent one.

It thus seems that, from this point of view at least, Miss Arendt's "work" coincides with Marx's "labor."

Miss Arendt grants, indeed, that Marx had "occasional hesitations" about his concept of labor, . . . that there exists in his work, besides the dominant concept of labor (in her sense), also that of work (in her sense). But that Marx was really not concerned with work, and only with labor, is shown by the fact that "the apparently all-important element of 'imagination' plays no role whatsoever in his labor theory," and that in the third volume of *Capital* he repeats that surplus labor beyond immediate needs serves "the progressive extension of the reproduction process."

It has just been seen that Miss Arendt's first point is simply false: in Marx's central discussion of his theory of labor it is precisely the "element of 'imagination'" that plays the *basic* role. That he does not constantly reiterate this point each time the idea of "labor" comes up is easily understandable if it is remembered that Marx was basically concerned not with the labor process in general—with those features of it *common* to *all* modes of production—but rather with the *specific* features of different historically given (and historically possible) forms of the labor process and, in particular, of course, with that at the basis of the economic system of capitalism. . . . [He] explains that, under the conditions of capitalist production, "capital and its self-expansion (*Selbstverwertung*) appears as the point of departure and the conclusion, as the motive and goal of production . . . production is production purely for the sake of *capital* and the means of production are not, on the contrary, simply the means for a constantly expanding reconstitution (*Gestaltung*) of the life-process for the *society* of producers." Miss Arendt says further, putting, as it were, the finishing touch to her argument, that "Marx remained convinced that 'Milton produced *Paradise Lost* for the same reason a silk work produces silk.'" But Marx's meaning is again misunderstood. Marx was here comparing Milton and the silkworm

not with respect to the nature of their respective labor processes (in particular, he was certainly not saying that the labor expended in the production of Milton's poem was a purely physiological process like the production of silk by the worm) but with respect to the fact that, in each case, what was produced was an immediate, spontaneous fulfilment or expression of the essential being or nature of each. This becomes obvious when the rest of the passage, quoted only in part by Miss Arendt, is taken into consideration. "It," namely *Paradise Lost,* Marx continues, "was an active manifestation (*Betätigung*) of *his* nature." In a passage of the *Oekonomisch-philosophische Manuskripte* of 1844—quoted by Miss Arendt . . . in the original German but not, however, quite accurately—Marx says that animals "produce only under the domination of immediate physical need, while man produces independently of physical need and *truly produces only when free from* this need."

So much for Miss Arendt's first point, which forms the initial step in her demonstration of a fundamental contradiction in Marx's thought. Let us now look at the second step.

We have just seen that Marx characterizes the human species by the specific type of labor process they perform. He also says in the early *German Ideology* (written jointly with Engels) that "the communist revolution . . . does away with (*beseitigt*) labor." . . . But the apparent contradiction here is very simply dissolved by recognizing that "labor" is being used in two senses, generic and specific. Marx (and Engels) did not mean that communism (*in the genuine Marxist sense of the term*) would "do away with" labor in general, in the sense that it is constitutive of the human being as such, but that it would abolish a certain sort of labor. This is quite clear from many passages. Thus, in a quite late work, the *Critique of the Gotha Program* . . . , Marx speaks of "a higher phase of communist society . . . after labor has become . . . life's prime want." And in his further words in this passage he explains briefly the sort of labor with which the above higher type is contrasted. He says that this higher mode of labor will arise (on a new social basis) "after the enslaving subordination of the individual to the division of labor, and therewith also the antithesis between mental and physical labor, has vanished," after labor has ceased to be "only a *means* of life." (pp. 49-51)

This, then, is the sort of labor and its consequences from which man is to be emancipated, according to Marx. Man must be liberated from labor that is determined only by *external* necessity, labor that is non-specific to individual men, which is devoted to the production of what is common to the needs of human beings as such, that is, the material presuppositions of their lives, "laboring that is determined by want and external utility" (*Not und äussere Zweckmässigkeit*). Thus the domain of free, properly human labor "lies beyond the sphere of strictly material production." In this domain only *internal* necessity has a place, the necessity constituted by the specific needs of development of specific individuals. In this realm of freedom, the process of development of human powers "is valued for its own sake" (*als Selbstzweck gilt*), labor becoming, to cite once more the words from which we took our point of departure, "life's prime want," the difference between "labor" time and "free" time disappearing. (p. 52)

The above analyses and explanations have attempted to show that the particular contradiction which Miss Arendt finds in Marx's thought is a result only of a fundamentally erroneous interpretation on her part. At the same time it should be clear that it is also quite false to see Marx as the theoretical prophet of the "laboring society" in Miss Arendt's sense. On the contrary, Marx was one of the most passionate critics of the state of society, some features of which Miss Arendt describes. But he was not just this; he was also one of its profoundest analysts, perhaps the deepest of all. He not only described the social phenomena in question but also attempted to explain their origins and thus to provide a key to their change. And the two tasks are not finally separable: a description which strives toward completeness eventually runs into problems of explanation. It is in this respect that Miss Arendt's exposition is so unsatisfactory, even in its positive parts. (pp. 52-3)

W. A. Suchting, "Marx and Hannah Arendt's 'The Human Condition'," in Ethics *(reprinted by permission of The University of Chicago Press), Vol. LXXIII, No. 1, October, 1962, pp. 47-55.*

MICHAEL A. MUSMANNO

There will be those who will wonder how Miss Arendt, after attending the Eichmann trial and studying the record and pertinent material, could announce, as she solemnly does in ["**Eichmann in Jerusalem**"], that Eichmann was not really a Nazi at heart, that he did not know Hitler's program when he joined the Nazi party, that the Gestapo were helpful to the Jews in Palestinian immigration, that Himmler (Himmler!) had a sense of pity, that the Jewish gas-killing program grew out of Hitler's euthanasia program and that all in all, Eichmann was really a modest man.

Miss Arendt devotes considerable space to Eichmann's conscience and informs us that one of Eichmann's points in his own defense was "that there were no voices from the outside to arouse his conscience." How abysmally asleep is a conscience when it must be aroused to be told there is something morally wrong about pressing candy upon a little boy to induce him to enter a gas chamber of death?

The author believes that Eichmann was misjudged in Jerusalem and quotes, with astounding credulity, his statement: "I myself had no hatred for the Jews." Sympathizing with Eichmann, she laments: "Alas, nobody believed him." Should anyone be blamed for lifting an eyebrow to the suggestion that Eichmann loved the Jews? At the end of the war he exclaimed: "I shall laugh when I jump into the grave, because of the feeling that I killed five million Jews. This gives me a lot of satisfaction and pleasure."

Miss Arendt defends Eichmann against his own words here, arguing that it would be "preposterous" to believe he personally slew five million people. But his guilt did not depend on personal physical annihilation. The Distict Court of Jerusalem specified: "The legal and moral responsibility of him who delivers the victim to his death is, in our opinion, no smaller, and may even be greater, than the liability of him who does the victim to death." Eichmann headed the incredibly monstrous project to exterminate cold-bloodedly a segment of the human race. (p. 1)

The disparity between what Miss Arendt states, and what the ascertained facts are, occurs with such disturbing frequency in her book that it can hardly be accepted as an authoritative historical work. (p. 40)

Another unfortunate feature of this book is that the author, an eminent scholar, should reveal so frequently evidences of purely private prejudice. She attacks the State of Israel, its laws and institutions, wholly unrelated to the Eichmann case; she pours scorn on Prime Minister Ben-Gurion. Later she speaks con-

temptuously of a man whom the Court lauded, with moving appropriateness, as "one of the just men of the world." Miss Arendt apparently did not like this elderly, gentle, snowyhaired pastor of a German Protestant church, Heinrich Grüber, because he described Eichmann, whom he knew in his allpowerful heyday, as a "block of ice" and "like marble." She perhaps saw something warm about Eichmann, because, she said, the evidence showed he was "rather decent toward his subordinates." Pastor Grüber had pleaded with Eichmann in behalf of persecuted Jews, and, for his pains, was thrown into a concentration camp where SS guards knocked out his teeth and inflicted other serious physical damage.

Miss Arendt deals rather intemperately and certainly injudiciously, with Gideon Hausner, the Attorney General of Israel, perhaps because, in cross-examining Eichmann, Mr. Hausner made mincemeat of the previously self-assured defendant. Mr. Hausner was not only an extremely able attorney general, but he is distinguished for his masterful legal ability at the world bar. The judges, who certainly knew more of Mr. Hausner than Miss Arendt, declared in their final judgment that Mr. Hausner "conducted the prosecution in all its stages as a jurist and on a very high professional level. In his brilliant opening speech which was eloquent and broad in perspective, and again in his concluding statement, he gave vent also to the deep feelings which stir the entire nation." (pp. 40-1)

Miss Arendt says that Eichmann, "to a truly extraordinary degree," received the "cooperation" of the Jews in their own destruction. This astonishing conclusion is predicated on statements of others that some Jewish leaders dealt with Eichmann, and that, in certain instances, Jews took part in police work. The fact that Eichmann with threats of death coerced occasional Quislings and Lavals into "cooperation" only adds to the horror of his crimes. . . . But none of the author's arguments in this respect can dim the luster of martyrdom of the defenseless millions who marched bravely to their doom under the guns of the most satanic force that ever defiled the earth. The Warsaw Ghetto uprising, where 56,000 perished in a last-ditch fight for freedom, shows that the Jews did not lack the stuff of courage.

Miss Arendt declares the Eichmann trial a "failure," specifying that the Court did not give "a valid definition of the 'crime against humanity.'" In point of simple optical arithmetic, the Court validly defined and described crimes against humanity not once but a dozen times. . . .

In summing up her long thesis, Miss Arendt assures the suffering world that it is possible that crimes similar to Eichmann's "may be committed in the future." And with this comforting picture assuaging the apprehensions of the reader, she adds that "no punishment has ever possessed enough power of deterrence to prevent the commission of crimes." This, in effect, says it was a terrible mistake to punish Eichmann at all!

Then, donning judicial robes, she dictates what the judges should have said when they sentenced Eichmann, if they wanted the "justice" of what was done to emerge so as to "be seen by all." They should have said to Eichmann, according to Miss Arendt, "no member of the human race can be expected to want to share the earth with you. That is the reason, *and the only reason,* you must hang." (Emphasis supplied.) In the first place, this statement would, of course, be false: there were many people who would gladly share the earth with Eichmann. There were his wife and children; there were also the thousands of bloodthirsty accomplices who enthusiastically shared Eichmann's desires to kill off "inferior" peoples. In the second place, the utterance Miss Arendt would put into the mouths of the venerable, distinguished, wise judges who tried Eichmann would make of the eight-month trial an act of sheer vengeance—instead of the meticulously fair and legally accurate proceeding which it has been recognized to be in all responsible circles, where there is a true understanding of the sanctity of law and the conscientious calm of even-handed justice. (p. 41)

Michael A. Musmanno, "Man with an Unspotted Conscience," in The New York Times Book Review *(© 1963 by The New York Times Company; reprinted by permission), May 19, 1963, pp. 1, 40-1.*

BRUNO BETTELHEIM

[The virtue of Arendt's *Eichmann in Jerusalem* is] that it views Eichmann and his trial as posing the problem of the human being within a modern totalitarian system. But in a way it is also its shortcoming: the issues are so vast that we do not seem able yet to cope with them intellectually, though her book is certainly a most serious and in part successful effort to do so.

In order to deal with totalitarianism on a human scale she had somehow to reduce it to its human basis. This she does by pursuing three basic threads of the problem: the man Eichmann; the impossibility of judging totalitarianism from our traditional system of thought, including our legal system; and the hapless victims. But so interwoven are these three issues because of the nature of the subject and the way the trial was conducted, that neither I nor Dr. Arendt can deal with them separately. . . .

[While] her book is nominally about Eichmann in Jerusalem and though the trial is discussed in a very personal, erudite, and critical way, in a deeper sense it is not even an essay on the banality of evil, as the subtitle suggests; though it is an essay on that too. Essentially it is a book about the incongruity of it all, greatest of which is the fact that by all "scientific" standards, Eichmann was a "normal" person. . . .

It is the incongruity of the murder of millions, and of one man being accused of it all. It is so obvious that no one man can exterminate millions. The incongruity is between all the horrors recounted, and this man in the dock, when essentially all he did was to talk to people, write memoranda, receive and give orders from behind a desk. It is essentially the incongruity between our conception of life and the bureaucracy of the total state. Our imagination, our frame of reference, even our feelings, are simply not up to it. (p. 23)

This, then, is a book about our inability to comprehend fully how modern technology and social organization, when made use of by totalitarianism, can empower a normal, rather mediocre person to play so crucial a role in the extermination of millions. By the same incongruity, it becomes theoretically possible for a minor civil servant—say a lieutenant colonel, to keep the parallel to Eichmann—to start the extermination of most of us by pressing a button. It is an incongruity between the image of man we still carry—rooted though it is in the humanism of the Renaissance and in the liberal doctrines of the 18th Century—and the realities of human existence in the middle of our current technological revolution. Had this revolution not permitted us to view the individual as a mere cog in the complex machinery, dispensable, a mere instrument, Eichmann would never have been possible. But neither would have been the slaughter at Stalingrad, Russia's slave labor camps, the bombing of Hiroshima, or the current planning for

nuclear war. It is the contradiction between the incredible power technology has put at our disposal, and how unimportant the individual has become just because of it. (pp. 23-4)

It is the incongruity between the banality of an Eichmann, and that only such a banal person could effect the destruction of millions. Had he been more of a man, his humanity would have kept him from his evil work; had he been less of a man, he would not have been effective at his job. His is exactly the banality of a man who would push the button when told, concerned only with pushing it well, and without any regard for who was pushed by it, or where. (p. 24)

Arendt is right not to grant the murdered Jews the sainthood of martyrs, and to view them simply as men. To those who claim they were martyrs, this is a sacrilegious position, and whoever holds that their actions may have contributed to their fate is accused of wishing to assert that the Jews were guilty—or that the Nazis were not. (pp. 24-5)

Just because we know that none of us is entirely free from guilt for what has happened, we can afford to investigate even the guilt of the victims. This Hannah Arendt tries to do around the specific event of the Eichmann trial, as others have tried to do around the concentration camp. (p. 25)

Those who will view [Arendt's book] as an account of the trial—critical, highly personal, perhaps even biased in part—will be dismayed by it because they will miss what her book has to teach. Yet to write the history of just another prominent Nazi was hardly worth her effort, nor to describe a trial that served propaganda as much as justice. If only one more miserable political criminal was being tried, then it would have seemed petty to take the court to task for the way it conducted the trial, because the accused's guilt was clear to begin with, and he admitted to it. Or why drag into her account of the trial that Jews, and even Jewish leaders, lent an unwilling heavy hand in the extermination of Jews? This had nothing whatever to do with trying the accused. His guilt was not an iota less because they did so.

Many will harp on all this because they fail to grasp the real issue. . . . [What] Arendt was talking about [in regard to Eichmann's lack of conscience] was the dreadful situation that in a totalitarian state there were no voices from the outside to arouse one's conscience. This is the important issue she deals with. . . . For us who were not Nazis, the issue is the absence of these voices, our voices. This is what makes living in a totalitarian society so desperate, because there is nobody to turn to for guidance, and there are no voices from the outside. (pp. 25-6)

Her point is that even a saintly man like Probst Grueber spoke so softly that his voice remained inaudible, and that this is the tragedy of the honest man in a totalitarian society. This is why a Pasternak remained quiet under Stalin, while the Ehrenburgs praised him.

This is also why Arendt goes to some length to discuss a different attitude toward the handing over of Jews and how it affected Nazi functionaries in countries like Denmark or Bulgaria, where there was strong resistance to it not only among the population but also among high government and church officials. She speaks of the slow erosion of doctrinaire Nazi attitudes in these Germans because they were exposed to voices that objected to Nazi morality, voices that were loud and clear enough and numerous enough to make themselves heard.

Since Arendt views the importance of the trial as revealing the nature and the still very present dangers of totalitarianism, she is critical of the legal basis of this trial. She does not accuse the judges or Attorney General Hausner because they failed in meting out justice, or for failing to conduct a trial that was as fair as one could expect it to be under the circumstances. She is critical because the court vacillated between trying a man and trying history, and to this she objects. (pp. 26-7)

[In] Arendt's opinion, which I share, [Hitlerism] was not the last chapter in anti-Semitism but rather one of the first chapters in modern totalitarianism. For this reason it is unfortunate, as Arendt stresses, that Eichmann was not tried by an international tribunal. To ensure against further chapters, as much as a writer can, Arendt tries to show the full horrors of totalitarianism, which go very far beyond those of anti-Semitism. A full understanding of totalitarianism requires that we see Eichmann as basically a mediocrity whose dreadful importance is derived only from his more or less chance position within the system.

To believe otherwise, to believe that there exists true freedom of action for the average individual within such system, is so contrary to fact that neither prosecuting attorney nor judges attempted to show that Eichmann enjoyed such a freedom. Only the extraordinary person, at great risk to himself, retains limited freedom in such a state. (p. 27)

Arendt is probably correct about the motives of the court. She believes that [questions about why the victims didn't resist] were asked to convince all Jews that there can be no strength in Jewry unless it is vested in the state of Israel. She feels that by dragging out the lack of Jewish resistance, the Israeli authorities were trying to show that no such resistance was possible because no Jewish state existed to support it. If this was the reason of the court, perhaps it was also why the same court neglected to shed light on the unfortunate and desperate cooperation of Jewish leadership with the SS.

Because, like the court in Israel, it was the misfortune of the Jews of Europe that they too saw Hitlerism as only the worst wave of anti-Semitism. They therefore responded to it with methods that in the past had permitted them to survive. That is why they got involved with executing the orders of the state; that is why the Jewish leaders and elders, with heavy hearts, cooperated in arranging things for the Nazi masters. Arendt claims, and her thesis will long be fought over, that without this collaboration Hitler could never have succeeded in killing so many Jews.

This is the part of the book that will be most widely objected to. I do not claim to know whether she is right or wrong in her argument: that if the Jewish organizations had not existed, the extermination of the Jews could never have attained such tremendous proportions. But she certainly makes her point effectively. No doubt the stories of the ghettos would have been different if most Jews and their leadership had not been more or less willing, out of anxiety, to cooperate with the Germans, if they had not opposed the small minority that called for resistance at all costs, including violent fighting back. No doubt many Jews would have been quicker to support the pitifully small fighting minority had they been told what lay in store for them by Jewish leaders who knew, or should and could have known, what fate awaited them. Many others might have tried to escape. It is another question whether more Jews could have been saved if no Jewish organizations had existed, as Arendt claims.

Here too, objections will be raised against the book. Because of her concentration on the injustice bred by totalitarianism,

Arendt at times creates an ambiguity in her evaluation of guilt. Thus on cursory reading she seems to plead that Eichmann was a victim and that Jewish leaders were heavy with guilt. In fact, Arendt saw rightly that Eichmann was not the greatest villain of all. But to say so leaves her open to the misunderstanding that she did not think him much of a villain, which she certainly thought he was. (pp. 28-9)

But again, these issues are immaterial in trying one individual for the crimes he committed. Why then did Hannah Arendt spend such a large part of her book on a discussion of Jewish willingness to cooperate and on the Jews' contribution to their own extermination?

I believe that her purpose was to paint the broader context of the trial as she saw it, which went far beyond that of anti-Semitism. This was of greatest interest to me, because it has to do with the much more important issue: how and where can an individual resist, or fight back in a totalitarian society? Jewish witnesses who testified seemed to think that nobody could, certainly not the persecuted Jews. Arendt's point—and it is well taken—is that any organization within a totalitarian society that compromised with the system became immediately ineffectual in opposing it and ended up helping it. "The gravest omission from the 'general picture' [that the court tried to paint of the extermination of the Jews] was that of a witness to testify to the cooperation between Nazi rulers and the Jewish authority." (pp. 29-30)

From this and much more Arendt concludes that, "If the Jewish people had really been unorganized and leaderless, there would have been chaos and plenty of misery but the total number of victims would hardly have been between four-and-a-half and six million people." (p. 30)

Unlike Arendt—and despite her cogent argument for an international court—I do not object to Israel's trying Eichmann, or to their trying him the way that they did, because I believe we must deal in some fashion with the Eichmanns of the world. That our legal procedures are not adequate for doing so does not mean they should go untried. . . .

Arendt seems to object to the trial as propaganda. This to me is its main justification, given the irregularities of the trial and Eichmann's having been kidnaped. . . .

So while I would recommend this book for many reasons the most important one is that our best protection against oppressive control and dehumanizing totalitarianism is still a personal understanding of events as they happen. To this end Hannah Arendt has furnished us with a richness of material. (p. 33)

Bruno Bettelheim, "Eichmann; The System; The Victims" (reprinted by permission of the author; © 1963 by Bruno Bettelheim), in The New Republic *Vol. 148, No. 24, June 15, 1963, pp. 23-33.*

NORMAN PODHORETZ

[What Hannah Arendt has done in ***Eichmann in Jerusalem***] is translate [the story of the Holocaust] for the first time into the kind of terms that can appeal to the sophisticated modern sensibility. Thus, is place of the monstrous Nazi, she gives us the "banal" Nazi; in place of the Jew as virtuous martyr, she gives us the Jew as accomplice in evil; and in place of the confrontation between guilt and innocence, she gives us the "collaboration" of criminal and victim. The story as she tells it is complex, unsentimental, riddled with paradox and ambiguity.

It has all the appearance of "ruthless honesty," and all the marks of profundity—have we not been instructed that complexity, paradox, and ambiguity are the sign manifest of profundity?—and, in addition, it carries with it all the authority of Miss Arendt's classic work on *The Origins of Totalitarianism*. Anyone schooled in the modern in literature and philosophy would be bound to consider it a much better story than the usual melodramatic version—which, as it happens, was more or less the one relied upon by the prosecution at the Eichmann trial, and which Miss Arendt uses to great effect in highlighting the superior interest of her own vision. But if this version of hers can from one point of view be considered more interesting, can it by the same token be considered truer, or more illuminating, or more revealing of the general situation of man in the 20th century? Is the gain she achieves in literary interest a matter of titillation, or is it a gain to the understanding?

Let us be clear about these questions: they cannot be answered by scholarship. To the extent that *Eichmann in Jerusalem* parades as history, its factual accuracy is of course open to critical examination. But it would be unwise to take the scholarly pretensions of the book at face value. This is in no sense a work of objective historical research aimed at determining "the way things really were." Except in her critique of the trial itself, which she attended, Miss Arendt's sources are for the most part secondary ones . . . , and her manipulation of evidence is at all times visibly tendentious. Nevertheless, a distorted or exaggerated picture drawn in the service of a suggestive thesis can occasionally bring us closer to the essential truth than a carefully qualified and meticulously documented study—provided that the thesis accords reasonably well with the evidence. The point to begin with, then, is Miss Arendt's thesis, and the problem to settle is whether it justifies the distortions of perspective it creates and the cavalier treatment of evidence it impels.

According to Miss Arendt, the Nazis, in order to carry out their genocidal plan against the Jews, needed Jewish cooperation and in fact received it "to a truly extraordinary degree." This cooperation took the form of "administrative and police work," and it was extended by "the highly assimilated Jewish communities of Central and Western Europe" no less abundantly than by "the Yiddish-speaking masses of the East." (pp. 336-38)

As for the Nazis, carrying out the policy of genocide required neither that they be monsters nor pathological Jew-haters. On the contrary: since the murder of Jews was dictated by the law of the state, and since selfless loyalty to the law was regarded by the Germans under Hitler as the highest of virtues, it even called for a certain idealism to do what Eichmann and his cohorts did. . . . Eichmann was in actual fact a banal personality, a nonentity whose evil deeds flowed not from anything in his own character, but rather from his position in the Nazi system.

This system is, of course, known as totalitarianism, and it is totalitarianism that brings the two halves of Miss Arendt's thesis together. Long ago, David Rousset, Bruno Bettelheim, and Miss Arendt herself taught us that securing the complicity of the victim is one of the distinguishing ambitions of totalitarian states, and her tale of Jewish complicity here is offered (at least on the surface) as yet another illustration of this point. Long ago, too, she and her colleagues taught us that totalitarian states aim at the destruction of common-sense reality and the creation of a new reality moulded to the lineaments of the

official ideology, and her conception of Eichmann as an ordinary man whose conscience was made to function "the other way round" is similarly set forth in illustration of the more general point. Obviously, though, this ordinary man could not have been turned into so great and devoted a perpetrator of evil if the system had not been so tightly closed—if, that is to say, there had been voices to protest or gestures of resistance. Such voices as existed, however, were in Miss Arendt's judgment pathetically small and thin, and such gestures of resistance as were displayed she finds relatively insignificant. Not only did "good society everywhere" accept the Final Solution with "zeal and eagerness," but the Jews themselves acquiesced and even cooperated—as we have seen—"to a truly extraordinary degree." Here, then, is the finishing touch to Miss Arendt's reading of the Final Solution, and the explanation she gives for dwelling on Jewish complicity: this chapter of the story, she says, "offers the most striking insight into the totality of the moral collapse the Nazis caused in respectable European society—not only in Germany but in almost all countries, not only among the persecutors but also among the victims."

An interesting version of the story, no doubt about that. But let us look at it a little more closely. (pp. 338-39)

[Since] Miss Arendt wishes us to believe that the Nazis could never have killed as many as six million Jews without Jewish help, she tries very hard to convey the impression that what the Jews themselves did in any given country mattered significantly too. And it is here that she becomes most visibly tendentious in her manipulation of the facts. In explaining, for example, why not a single Belgian Jew was ever deported (though thousands of stateless Jews living in Belgium were), she tells us how the Belgian police and the railwaymen quietly sabotaged deportation operations, and then adds: "Moreover, among those who had fled were all the more important Jewish leaders . . . so that there was no Jewish Council to register the Jews—one of the vital prerequisites for their seizure." But there *was* a Jewish Council in Belgium. There was also one in France, and Miss Arendt simply neglects to mention it. Quite right, too, for the *U.G.I.F.* made no more difference to the situation in France than the *Association des Juifs en Belgique* made to the situation in Belgium, or than any other *Judenrat* made to the situation in any other country. (p. 342)

But not only is Miss Arendt wholly unwarranted in emphasizing Jewish cooperation as a significant factor in the number of victims claimed by the Final Solution; the irony is that her insistence on doing so also involves her in making the same assumption about the Nazis that lay behind Jewish cooperation itself. This assumption was that the Nazis were rational beings and that their aims must therefore be limited and subject to negotiation. When one of the most notorious of the Jewish leaders—Jacob Gens of Vilna—declared that "with a hundred victims I save a thousand people, with a thousand ten thousand," he was saying precisely what the heads of all the major European governments had said about Hitler. (pp. 342-43)

If, then, we ask why Jewish leadership cooperated with the Nazis, the answer would seem to be that they were following a policy of appeasement, and that there was nothing in the least "extraordinary" about this. That, however, is not the answer we get from Miss Arendt; her answer is more interesting and complicated and paradoxical. A distinction must be made, she argues, between the Jewish masses and the Jewish leaders. It was "cruel and silly" of Hausner to ask why the masses went passively to their deaths, "for no non-Jewish group or people had behaved differently." But it is apparently compassionate and intelligent to ask much the same question of the Jewish leaders, even though no non-Jewish leaders had behaved differently. In any event, having raised the issue, Miss Arendt finds herself afflicted for the only time in the book with an attack of speculative diffidence and tells us nothing—literally nothing—about why so many Jewish leaders should have cooperated in the destruction of their own people and (since hardly any of them managed to survive) in their own ruin as well. "Wherever Jews lived, there were recognized Jewish leaders, and this leadership, almost without exception, cooperated in one way or another, for one reason or another, with the Nazis." *In one way or another, for one reason or another.* Period. ". . . we can still sense how they enjoyed their new power. . . . We know how the Jewish officials felt when they became instruments of murder. . . . We know the physiognomies of the Jewish leaders during the Nazi period very well." Do we, now? Then pray, Miss Arendt, what did they look like? Give her exactly thirteen lines—four and a bit each for the incredible Chaim Rumkowski of Lodz, the many-sided Leo Baeck of Berlin, and the tortured Adam Czerniakow of Warsaw—and her picture is complete. And why not? The Jews in Miss Arendt's interesting and complicated and paradoxical and ruthlessly honest version of the story are a people curiously without psychology (except of the darker sort, leading to self-destruction), and a people curiously without a history (except of the disabling sort, leading to hopeless inadequacy). When they act—whether it be going to their death, or running a country, or prosecuting a trial—a mere glance at them is enough to produce a confident judgment. And again, why not, when the judgment will almost invariably be adverse?

For what is Miss Arendt really saying when she tells us that "if the Jewish people had . . . been unorganized and leaderless, there would have been chaos and plenty of misery but the total number of victims would hardly have been between four and a half and six million people." Why, she is saying that if the Jews had not been Jews, the Nazis would not have been able to kill so many of them—which is a difficult proposition to dispute. I do not think I am being unfair to Miss Arendt here. Consider: the Jews of Europe, even where they were "highly assimilated," were an organized people, and in most cases a centrally organized people. This was a fact of their condition no less surely than sovereign nationhood was a fact of the French condition. Yet I doubt that Miss Arendt would ever take it into her head to declare that if the French people had not been organized into a nation-state, they could never have been sold out to the Nazis by Pétain and Laval. Throughout this book, Miss Arendt is very nasty about Zionists and Zionism, but the only sense one can glean from her argument is a grain of retroactive Zionist sense. The Jews, she is implying, should have known that anti-Semitism rendered their position in the Diaspora untenable, and they should therefore either have set up a state of their own or renounced their communal existence altogether. She does not explain how such renunciation could have saved them from the Nuremberg Laws. Nor does she tell us why the slaughter of Jews in occupied Russia should have been so complete even though there was no central Jewish leadership or communal organization in the Soviet Union.

But it is unnecessary to pursue the absurdities of Miss Arendt's argument on this issue, just as it is unnecessary to enter once again into the endless moral debate over the behavior of the Jewish leaders—the endless round of apology and recrimination. They did what they did, they were what they were, and each was a different man. None of it mattered in the slightest

to the final result. Murderers with the power to murder descended upon a defenseless people and murdered a large part of it. What else is there to say?

In stark contrast to the Jews, whose behavior in Miss Arendt's version of the story self-evidently explains and condemns itself, the Nazis—or anyway Adolf Eichmann—need the most careful and the most imaginative attention before they can be intelligently judged. The irony here is of course obvious, and even the Eichmann trial to some extent fell victim to it. . . . Miss Arendt also disapproves of [the] efforts by Hausner [to prove Eichmann's subjective viciousness], but her complaint is against Hausner's particular conception of Eichmann's character and not against the opportunity he gave him to speak. Far from being offended at the idea that *this self-styled nobody who had hurled into silence so many of the subtlest and most humane intellects of Europe* should have been permitted to discourse himself at such great length, Miss Arendt helps the discourse along, develops it, refines it, and in the end virtually justifies it. By this I do not mean that she defends Eichmann, as some of her critics have stupidly charged: she does nothing of the kind anywhere in her book, and she says plainly in the closing chapter that he was guilty of participation in mass murder and deserved to hang. What she does do, however, is accept Eichmann's account of himself and of his role in the Final Solution as largely true. In some sense, he *was* an "idealist"; in some sense, he was *not* an anti-Semite; and the degree of his responsibility for the murder of the six million, while sufficient to hang him, *was* relatively insignificant, and certainly nowhere near what the prosecution claimed. By building Eichmann up into a fiendish Jew-hater and a major Nazi figure, Miss Arendt believes, the prosecution missed the whole point of his crimes, of the system which made them possible, and of the lessons to be drawn for the future.

Taking Eichmann pretty much at his own word, then (except when his own word conflicts with her reading of his character), Miss Arendt treats us to a genuinely brilliant portrait of the mind of a middle-echelon Nazi and, by extension, of the world that produced him and gave him the power to do the things he did. And around this theme of Eichmann's "banality" other themes gather: the almost universal complicity of Christian Europe, and especially of the German people, in Nazism (for in diminishing Eichmann's personal responsibility for the Final Solution, she enlarges the area of European responsibility in general); and the almost total consequent unwillingness of the Federal Republic to prosecute and mete out adequate punishment to Nazi war criminals still at large and in many cases flourishing. . . . (pp. 343-47)

The brilliance of Miss Arendt's treatment of Eichmann could hardly be disputed by any disinterested reader. But at the same time, there could hardly be a more telling example than this section of her book of the intellectual perversity that can result from the pursuit of brilliance by a mind infatuated with its own agility and bent on generating dazzle. The man around the corner who makes ugly cracks about the Jews is an anti-Semite, but not Adolf Eichmann who sent several million Jews to their death: *that* would be uninteresting and would tell us nothing about the Nature of Totalitarianism. Similarly, the behavior of the Jewish leaders under the Nazis was "extraordinary," but Adolf Eichmann was ordinary, even unto banality; otherwise, he tells us nothing about the Nature of Totalitarianism. Did he have no conscience? Of course he had a conscience, the conscience of an inverted Kantian idealist; otherwise he tells us nothing about the Nature of Totalitarianism. But what about his famous statement that he would die happy because he had sent five million "enemies of the Reich" to their graves? "Sheer rodomontade," sheer braggery—to believe it is to learn nothing about the Nature of Totalitarianism. And his decision to carry on with the deportations from Hungary in direct defiance of Himmler's order that they be stopped? A perfect example of the very idealism that teaches us so much about the Nature of Totalitarianism.

No. It finally refuses to wash; it finally violates everything we know about the Nature of Man, and therefore the Nature of Totalitarianism must go hang. For uninteresting though it may be to say so, no person could have joined the Nazi party, let alone the S.S., who was not at the very least a *vicious* anti-Semite; to believe otherwise is to learn nothing about the nature of anti-Semitism. Uninteresting though it may be to say so, no person of conscience could have participated knowingly in mass murder: to believe otherwise is to learn nothing about the nature of conscience. And uninteresting though it may be to say so, no banality of a man could have done so hugely evil a job so well; to believe otherwise is to learn nothing about the nature of evil. Was Hausner right, then, in repeatedly calling Eichmann a liar? Yes, he was right, however successfully Eichmann may have deceived himself by then, and however "sincere" he may have thought his testimony was.

And the Nature of Totalitarianism? What Miss Arendt's book on the Eichmann trail teaches us about the Nature of Totalitarianism is that the time has come to re-examine the whole concept. (pp. 347-49)

[While] we can agree with Miss Arendt that, as a mere lieutenant-colonel, [Eichmann] probably did not enjoy the importance that the Israeli indictment attributed to him, neither can he have been quite so banal as she makes him out to be. After all, there *was* enough opposition to the Final Solution to have persuaded him that not everyone looked upon the murdering of Jews as a fine and noble occupation, and after all, he *was* a first-generation Nazi and an important enough one to have been trusted with a large measure of administrative responsibility for a top-priority item in the Nazi program. Now, if we are not to lose our own minds in the act of trying to penetrate into the psychology of the Nazi mind, we must be very careful to keep it clear that this item of the Nazi program—the "cleansing" of Europe, and ultimately the whole world, of Jews—was literally insane. It is one thing to hate Jews, but it is quite another to contemplate the wholesale slaughter of Jews; it is one thing to believe that no nation-state can be healthy when it contains "alien" elements, but it is quite another to decide upon the murder of eleven million people (the estimated target of the Final Solution) as a means of achieving ethnic homogeneity. (pp. 350-51)

It is in this insanity, I believe, and not in the pedestrian character of Adolf Eichmann, that whatever banality attaches to the evil of the Final Solution must be sought. And because Hitler and his cohorts were madmen on the Jewish question, there is probably little of general relevance we can learn from the Final Solution beyond what the Nuremberg trials established concerning the individual's criminal accountability when acting upon superior orders, even within a system guided by insane aims. There is, however, much to be learned from the Final Solution about other matters, and principally about anti-Semitism. When Miss Arendt speaks of the amazing extent of the moral collapse that the Nazis caused "everywhere," she must be referring specifically to the Jewish question. The will to fight the German armies did not collapse everywhere, and the will to defend democracy against the Nazi onslaught stood up well enough to triumph in the end; the only collapse that took place "everywhere" was a collapse of the will to prevent the Nazis from wiping the Jews off the face of the earth. Here again, Miss Arendt can be refuted out of her own mouth, for acquiescence in the Final Solution (as she demonstrates) was far from universal in Europe (though it may well have been nearly universal in Germany). The fact remains, however, that there was acquiescence enough to allow this insane Nazi ambition to come very close to succeeding. Nobody cared about the Gypsies because nobody ever thinks about the Gypsies—except the police. But how did it happen that nobody cared about the Jews when everyone seems always to be thinking about the Jews? The question surely answers itself, and the answer incidentally provides the justification for Ben Gurion's statement that one of the purposes of the Eichmann trial was to make the nations of the world ashamed.

Miss Arendt dislikes that statement, but no more than she dislikes every other statement Ben Gurion made about the trial. She is also unhappy with the trial itself—the fact that Eichmann was tried before an Israeli court instead of an international tribunal, the substance of the indictment, the way Hausner handled the prosecution, the way Servatius conducted the defense. The only aspect of the trial that pleases her is that the judges behaved with scrupulous regard for the interests of Justice: she is as unstinting in her praise of them as she is relentless in her contempt for Hausner and Ben Gurion ("the invisible stage manager of the proceedings"). A few of Miss Arendt's criticisms of the trial seem reasonable, but given the animus she exhibits from the very first sentence of the book, it becomes extremely difficult to look upon these criticisms as anything other than further instances of the inordinate demands she is always making on the Jews to be better than other people, to be braver, wiser, nobler, more dignified—or be damned.

This habit of judging the Jews by one standard and everyone else by another is a habit Miss Arendt shares with many of her fellow-Jews, emphatically including those who think that the main defect of her version of the story is her failure to dwell on all the heroism and all the virtue that the six million displayed among them. But the truth is—*must* be—that the Jews under Hitler acted as men will act when they are set upon by murderers, no better and no worse: the Final Solution reveals nothing about the victims except that they were mortal beings and hopelessly vulnerable in their powerlessness. And as with the victims, so with those who were lucky enough to survive the holocaust. There is no special virtue in sheer survival . . . and there is no martyrdom in sheer victimization, whatever certain sentimentalists among us may think.

The Nazis destroyed a third of the Jewish people. In the name of all that is humane, will the remnant never let up on itself? (pp. 351-53)

Norman Podhoretz, "Hannah Arendt on Eichmann: A Study in the Perversity of Brilliance" (1963), in his Doings and Undoings: The Fifties and After in American Writing *(reprinted by permission of Farrar, Straus & Giroux, Inc.; copyright © 1953, 1954, 1955, 1956, 1957, 1958, 1959, 1962, 1963, 1964 by Norman Podhoretz), Farrar, Straus & Giroux, 1964, pp. 335-53.*

GEORGE LICHTHEIM

Miss Arendt, throughout her writings and more than ever in [*On Revolution*], shows an inclination to discuss political topics in philosophical terms, and vice versa, until the distinction between metaphysics and politics is lost or dimmed in a twilight zone where it no longer seems to matter whether we are dealing with actual events, contemporary beliefs about these events, or subsequent reflections upon them by thinkers motivated by convictions and interests quite foreign to the participants. At some stage a writer has to decide whether the discussion is to be about the political realm ordinarily so called, or about the most general principles regulating human behavior. . . . To suppose, as Miss Arendt does, that "the phenomenon of revolution" can be meaningfully discussed in suprahistorical terms such as "violence," or related to mythical events ("Cain slew Abel and Romulus slew Remus"), is to obliterate several centuries of thought starting with Vico if not Machiavelli. This is not conservative empiricism but mere dogmatism—as doctrinaire as anything produced by the most extreme rationalists.

Once the discussion is brought down from the metaphysical heaven to the profane earth on which ordinary mortals dwell, the question that puzzles her—why the "disastrous" French Revolution has been so much more influential than the beneficial American one—finds a ready answer, and this quite irrespective of a circumstance to which she herself draws attention: namely that over much of Europe absolutism had established a pattern which positively cried out for violence. Setting this familiar fact aside, the French Revolution was more *radical* than the American in the fundamental sense of the term: it went closer to the roots. For example, it did away with slavery, while the American Revolution confirmed it (thereby condemning a later generation of Americans to the ordeal of Civil War). It also (for a time) did away with theology, but then even quite conservative Protestants have acknowledged that this was simply the penalty visited upon the Catholic Church for its antecedent attempt to stamp out all other forms of thought, including rival brands of Christianity. In short, the French Revolution was more "total" because the *ancien régime* was more coherent (and more despotic) than its Anglo-American counterpart.

These considerations are not irrelevant to the theme of a philosophical essay which sets out to interpret the phenomenon of revolution in the post-medieval age, with a minimum of historical reference and a maximum of emphasis on the thought processes of those concerned (notably the professional ideologists among them). Since Miss Arendt is, to put it mildly, no historian, it is no great matter that the events themselves remain in the background, or that she occasionally gets lost in unfamiliar territory, as for example, when she suggests that the Levellers whom Cromwell put down were radical democrats (they were nothing of the sort). So far as France is concerned, it may seem unkind to suggest that the Revolution (as distinct from what some people at the time said and wrote about it) is a closed book to her, but certainly the reader of Georges Lefebvre's great work on the subject will have difficulty relating his account of what actually occurred during those years to Miss Arendt's interpretation of what presumably went on in the heads of the participants—or at least the more prominent and literate among them who had the means for recording their illusions and disappointments in writing. All this is relatively unimportant, as is the somewhat confused presentation of the argument, which eschews chronology and wanders back and forth between the Greek concept of the good life (democracy = community) and the modern attempt to fashion a rule of law for people not held together by ties of consanguinity or physical cohabitation in an area small enough for all active citizens to assemble in the market place. There is, after all,

little new to be said about the problematic nature of Rousseauist (or, for that matter, Jeffersonian) notions about politics. But why are we told so little about the religious background? The fundamental fact about the American Revolution surely is that it occurred in a Protestant country with an Anglo-Saxon tradition of limited self-government. Miss Arendt makes much of the contrast between the misery of the French peasant and the relative prosperity of the American farmer; but this is merely the reverse side of the medal. No Protestant population could ever have been beaten down to the French (or Spanish or Latin American) level. Even the serfs of Prussia were not reduced to quite the existence of the peasant helotry in neighboring Catholic Poland. In the nineteenth century the landless English farm laborer had a pretty thin time, but it was the Irish peasantry that actually starved en masse. These historic circumstances are not irrelevant to Miss Arendt's work, just as it is not immaterial to the theme of her concluding chapter that in present-day Europe the two largest Communist parties are those of France and Italy (or for that matter that Hitlerism arose in Catholic Austria and Bavaria, not in Lutheran Prussia). There are of course sound practical reasons for keeping quiet about this explosive topic, notably in the United States. But a political philosopher who wields so ruthless a scalpel in dissecting the smallest logical flaw in the writings of Rousseau or the speeches of Robespierre might have been expected to cast a little light on so large and important a theme. The modern age—if one is going to talk in these terms—begins with the Reformation. Once Northern and Southern Europe had gone their separate ways (Germany as usual was partitioned), all the rest followed, at any rate if one takes the traditional view that the Dutch Rebellion and the English Civil War set the stage for the American Revolution. Is the traditional view wrong? If not, why is there no mention of Holland—the cradle of the modern world? And why the desperate attempt . . . to persuade the reader that the English Revolution of 1640-1660 was not a "real" revolution, because, if you please, the participants at first thought they were restoring the ancient order? What else did the French of 1789 think?

Practically speaking, all this is irrelevant. The French Revolution needs no defense, least of all in an age that has witness the German Counter-Revolution. What France might have become if it had not—at great cost admittedly—broken out of the medieval prison-cage can be studied in contemporary Spain. Incidentally, the endless Iberian and Latin American cycle of bloodletting over the past century and a half is much closer to what the Greeks called *stasis* than anything that has occurred in France since 1789. A writer domiciled in the United States might also have reflected upon the curious circumstance that France's relations with her former colonies—including Algeria—are decidedly better than U.S. relations with Latin America (even setting aside the distressing Cuban experience). It seems the Messianic and universalist spirit of the French Revolution, however confusing and even dangerous in the short run, is still paying dividends. This pragmatic argument should appeal to readers brought up in the decidedly unmessianic spirit of Ben Franklin. Whether it will appeal to Miss Arendt, I doubt. Her cast of mind is un-pragmatic and bears a close resemblance to that of some contemporary European ideologists. It is the more remarkable that she has found a spiritual resting place among the classic statements of the American faith in reasoned progress and constitutional liberty. (pp. 117-21)

George Lichtheim, "Varieties of Revolutionary Experience," in Partisan Review *(copyright © 1964 by Partisan Review, Inc.), Vol. XXXI, No. 3, Summer,*

1964 (and reprinted in a slightly different form as "Two Revolutions," in his The Concept of Ideology and Other Essays, *Random House, Inc., 1967, pp. 115-22).*

E. J. HOBSBAWM

The question to be asked about [*On Revolution* is whether it holds great interest for the historian or sociologist].

The answer, so far as the student of the French and most other modern revolutions is concerned, must be no. I am not able to judge her contribution to the study of the American revolution, though I suspect that it is not great. The book therefore stands or falls not by the author's discoveries or insights into certain specific historical phenomena, but by the interest of her general ideas and interpretations. However, since these are not based on an adequate study of the subject matter they purport to interpret, and indeed appear almost to exclude such a study by their very method, they cannot be firmly grounded. She has merits, and they are not negligible: a lucid style, sometimes carried away by intellectual rhetoric, but always transparent enough to allow us to recognize the genuine passion of the writer, a strong intelligence, wide reading, and the power of occasional piercing insight, though of a sort better suited, it may seem, to the vague terrain which lies between literature, psychology and what, for want of a better word, is best called social prophecy, than to the social sciences as at present constructed. However, even of her insights it is possible to say what Lloyd George observed of Lord Kitchener, namely that their beams occasionally illuminate the horizon, but leave the scene in darkness between their flashes.

The first difficulty encountered by the historian or sociological student of revolutions in Miss Arendt is a certain metaphysical and normative quality of her thought, which goes well with a sometimes quite explicit old-fashioned philosophical idealism. She does not take her revolutions as they come, but constructs herself an ideal type, defining her subject matter accordingly, excluding what does not measure up to her specifications. We may also observe in passing that she excludes everything outside the classical zone of western Europe and the north Atlantic, for her book contains not even a passing reference to—the examples spring to mind—China or Cuba; nor could she have made certain statements if she had given any thought to them. Her 'revolution' is a wholesale political change in which men are conscious of introducing an entirely new epoch in human history, including (but only, as it were, incidentally) the abolition of poverty and expressed in terms of a secular ideology. Its subject matter is 'the emergence of freedom' as defined by the author.

Part of this definition allows her, after a brief bout of shadow-boxing, to exclude all revolutions and revolutionary movements before 1776 from the discussion, though at the price of making a serious study of the actual phenomenon of revolution impossible. The remainder allows her to proceed to the major part of her subject, an extended comparison between the American and French revolutions, to the great advantage of the former. The latter is taken as the paradigm of all subsequent revolutions, though it seems that Miss Arendt has in mind chiefly the Russian Revolution of 1917. The 'freedom' which revolutions exist to institute is essentially a political concept. Though not too clearly defined—it emerges gradually in the course of the author's discussion—it is quite distinct from the abolition of poverty (the 'solution of the social problem') which

Miss Arendt regards as the corrupter of revolution, in whatever form it occurs; which includes the capitalist. We may infer that any revolution in which the social and economic element plays a major role puts itself out of Miss Arendt's court, which more or less eliminates every revolution that the student of the subject might desire to investigate. We may further infer that, with the partial exception of the American revolution which, as she argues, was lucky enough to break out in a country without very poor free inhabitants, no revolution was or could have been able to institute freedom, and even in eighteenth-century America slavery placed it in an insoluble dilemma. The revolution could not 'institute freedom' without abolishing slavery, but—on Miss Arendt's argument—it could not have done so either if it had abolished it. (pp. 201-03)

The 'freedom' which revolution exists to institute is more than the mere absence of restraints upon the person or guarantees of 'civil liberties', for neither of these (as Miss Arendt rightly observes) requires any particular form of government, but only the absence of tyranny and despotism. It appears to consist of the right and possibility of participating actively in the affairs of the commonwealth—of the joys and rewards of public life, as conceived perhaps originally in the Greek polis. . . . However—though here the author's argument must be reconstructed rather than followed—'public freedom' in this sense remains a dream, even though the fathers of the American constitution were wise enough, and untroubled enough by the poor, to institute a government which was reasonably secure against despotism and tyranny. The crux of the genuine revolutionary tradition is that it keeps this dream alive. It has done so by means of a constant tendency to generate spontaneous organs capable of realizing public freedom, namely the local or sectional, elective or direct assemblies and councils (soviets, Räte), which have emerged in the course of revolutions only to be suppressed by the dictatorship of the party. Such councils ought to have a purely *political* function. Government and administration being distinct, the attempt to use them, e.g. for the management of *economic* affairs ('workers' control') is undesirable and doomed to failure, even when it is not part of a plot by the revolutionary party to 'drive [the councils] away from the political realm and back into the factories'. I am unable to discover Miss Arendt's views as to who is to conduct the 'administration of things in the public interest', such as the economy, or how it is to be conducted.

Miss Arendt's argument tells us much about the kind of government which she finds congenial, and even more about her state of mind. Its merits as a general statement about political ideals are not at issue here. On the other hand, it is relevant to observe that the nature of her arguments not merely makes it impossible to use in the analysis of actual revolutions—at least in terms which have meaning for the historian or social scientist—but also eliminates the possibility of meaningful dialogue between her and those interested in actual revolutions. In so far as Miss Arendt writes about history—about revolutions, as they may be contemporaneously observed, retrospectively surveyed, or propsectively assessed—her connection with it is as incidental as that of medieval theologians and astronomers. Both talked about planets, and both meant, at least in part, the same celestial bodies, but contact did not go much further.

The historian or sociologist, for instance, will be irritated, as the author plainly is not, by a certain lack of interest in mere fact. This cannot be described as inaccuracy or ignorance, for Miss Arendt is learned and scholarly enough to be aware of such inadequacies if she chooses, but rather as a preference for metaphysical construct or poetic feeling over reality. (pp. 203-05)

Since the spontaneous tendency to generate organs such as soviets is clearly of great moment to Miss Arendt, and provides evidence for her interpretation, one might for instance have expected her to show some interest in the actual forms such popular organs take. In fact, the author is clearly not interested in these. It is even difficult to discover what precisely she has in mind, for she talks in the same breath of politically very different organizations. (p. 205)

Again, it is evidently *not* 'the historical truth of the matter . . . that the party and council systems are almost coeval; both were unknown prior to the revolutions and both are the consequences of the modern and revolutionary tenet that all inhabitants of a given territory are entitled to be admitted to the public, political realm.'. . . Even granted that the second half of the statement is tenable (so long as we define the public realm in terms which apply to large modern territorial or nation states, but not to other and historically more widespread forms of political organization), the first half is not. Councils, even in the form of elected delegations, are so obvious a political device in communities above a certain size, that they considerably antedate political parties, which are, at least in the usual sense of the term, far from obvious institutions. Councils as revolutionary institutions are familiar long before 1776, when Miss Arendt's revolutions begin, as for instance in the General Soviet of the New Model Army, in the committees of sixteenth-century France and the Low Countries, or for that matter in medieval city politics. A 'council system' under this name is certainly coeval with, or rather posterior to, the political parties of 1905 Russia, since it was they who recognized the possible implications of the soviets for the revolutionary government of nations; but the idea of decentralized government by autonomous communal organs, perhaps linked by pyramids of higher delegate bodies, is for practical reasons extremely ancient.

Nor indeed have councils 'always been primarily political, with the social and economic claims playing a minor role.'. . . They were not, because Russian workers and peasants did not—and indeed on Miss Arendt's argument could not—make a sharp distinction between politics and economics. Moreover, the original Russian workers' councils, like those of the British and German shop stewards in the first world war or the Trades Councils which sometimes took over quasi-soviet functions in big strikes, were the products of trade union and strike organization; that is, if a distinction can be made, of activities which are economic rather than political. In the third place, she is wrong because the immediate tendency of the effective, that is, urban, soviets in 1917 was to turn themselves into organs of administration, in successful rivalry with municipalities, and as such, quite evidently, to go beyond the field of political deliberation. Indeed, it was this capacity of the soviets to become organs of execution as well as of debate which suggested to political thinkers that they might be the basis for a new political system. But more than this, the suggestion that such demands as 'workers' control' are in some sense a deviation from the spontaneous line of evolution of councils and similar bodies simply will not bear examination. 'The Mine for the Miners', 'The Factory for the Workers'— in other words, the demand for cooperative democratic instead of capitalist production—goes back to the earliest stages of the labour movement. It has remained an important element in spontaneous pouplar thought ever since, a fact which does not

oblige us to consider it as other than utopian. In the history of grass-roots democracy, cooperation in communal units and its apotheosis 'the cooperative commonwealth' (which was the earliest definition of socialism among workers) play a crucial part.

There is thus practically no point at which Miss Arendt's discussion of what she regards as the crucial institution of the revolutionary tradition touches the actual historical phenomena she purports to describe, an institution on the basis of which she generalizes. And the student of revolutions, whether historian, sociologist, or for that matter analyst of political systems and institutions, will be equally baffled by the remainder of her book. Her acute mind sometimes throws light on literature, including the classical literature of political theory. She has considerable perception about the psychological motives and mechanisms of individuals—her discussion of Robespierre, for instance, may be read with profit—and she has occasional flashes of insight, that is to say, she sometimes makes statements which, while not particularly well-founded on evidence or argument, strike the reader as true and illuminating. But that is all. And it is not enough. There are doubtless readers who will find Miss Arendt's book interesting and profitable. The historical or sociological student of revolutions is unlikely to be among them. (pp. 206-08)

> *E. J. Hobsbawm, "Hannah Arendt on Revolution"*
> *(1965), in his* Revolutionaries: Contemporary Essays
> *(reprinted by permission of David Higham Associates*
> *Limited, as literary agents for E. J. Hobsbawm;*
> *copyright © 1973 by E. J. Hobsbawm), Weidenfeld*
> *and Nicolson, 1973 (and reprinted by Pantheon Books,*
> *1973), pp. 201-08.*

LEWIS A. COSER

Miss Arendt's main argument [in **"On Violence"**] rests on the distinction between power and violence. "Power corresponds to the human ability not just to act but to act in concert." It is collectively organized and institutionalized action, without which no society could function. Violence, in contrast, serves as a means of coercion. While power creates positive values, violence can only destroy. When men sense that they are in danger of losing power, they are tempted to substitute violence for it. . . . Yet, where violence is no longer backed and restrained by power, it results in impotence. Even though violence can destroy power, it can never re-create it. "Violence appears where power is in jeopardy, but left to its own cause it ends in power's disappearance." Miss Arendt is not deceived by the current conceits according to which power grows out of the barrel of a gun.

Miss Arendt concedes that there may be positive functions to violence. It may, for example, dramatize grievances and bring them to public attention. Yet she is at pains to warn current advocates of the politics of violence that violent means tend to overwhelm the end for which they are employed. . . .

Miss Arendt's reflections are often informed by what David Riesman once called counter-cyclical thinking. She is frequently at pains to oppose what at the moment has become a fashionable verity. This is apparent in her reflections on violence, it is even more salient in her remarks about the current racial situation. When much of liberal thought has come to be infused with guilt-ridden masochism when it comes to blacks, she has the courage and the wisdom to write, "The real rift between black and white is not healed by being translated into an even less reconcilable conflict between collective innocence and collective guilt. 'All white men are guilty' is not only dangerous nonsense but also racism in reverse, and it serves quite effectively to give the very real grievances and rational emotions of the Negro population an outlet into irrationality, an escape from reality.''

Miss Arendt's unfortunate propensity to use an esoteric terminology and to claim that previous thinkers have not made needed distinctions between the terms she sets forth, is annoying. When she says, for example, that ''our terminology'' does not distinguish among such key words as ''power,'' ''strength,'' ''force,'' ''authority,'' etc., she can be shown to be wrong by reference to most elementary textbooks in both political science and sociology. When she claims that nobody has thought of distinctions she has in mind she really means that nobody has used her own peculiar terminology. But these are minor blemishes.

Lewis A. Coser, ''In Brief: 'On Violence','' in The New York Times Book Review *(© 1970 by The New York Times Company; reprinted by permission), April 12, 1970, p. 31.*

MAX GELTMAN

On Violence seems to plough ground Miss Arendt has gone over—brilliantly—in a major work, *On Revolution*. But the subject of violence has intrigued her for a long time, and she has tried, off and on, to come to grips with it and thinks she has finally grasped the problem by separating it from the concept of power, with which it is often (and mistakenly) identified. In her words, ''Every decrease in power is an open invitation to violence.'' Which is true enough and warning enough of the need for power to reassert itself where it has to be exerted—at the seat of government. It is just here that power is most patently eroded. Whether or not her examples are the ones you and I would give, the point is that she is fundamentally sound in her observation that power is based on consent of the many—of the *polis*—of the citizenry, while violence rests ultimately on the singular capacity of the minority. . . .

When she sometimes contradicts herself, she does so in a good cause. Her examination of what went on at Columbia University, for instance, is a mixed bag. She cites reforms gained (unidentified), at the same time concluding that even here, where violence ''paid off,'' it did so ''indiscriminately, for 'soul courses,' and instruction in Swahili''—courses she finds rather demeaning to both university and students, especially to black ones. . . .

In any case, these instances are not central to her purpose, which seems to be to prove to her friends on the Left, especially the New Left, that violence is not only bad Marxism, but counterproductive *if* revolution is what one is after. Not that Hannah Arendt is unaware that even here the cure may be worse than the disease; still she is way off the mark in telling us that Marx could never have written as Sartre did: ''To shoot down a European is to kill two birds with one stone . . . there remains a dead man and a free man.'' It is true it takes a certain kind of skill to be as crude as Sartre, but Marx did counsel that ''far from opposing the so-called popular excesses, examples of popular revenge on hated individuals and public buildings . . . we must not merely tolerate these examples, but ourselves take over the leadership of them.'' (p. 472)

And here we come to a weakness in this little book. The 87 pages are bolstered by more than a hundred footnotes and fourteen pages of tightly packed notes, all designed to support her thesis that power and violence are not the same, that in fact the one rules out the other. But does it really make a difference to the hundreds of millions in China and Russia to be told that the more violent the dictatorship, the more its power-base is shrinking? Still, even if this wisdom is at best academic to the man in extreme circumstances, living in a totalitarian or tyrannical state, it is good for us in the West to learn that the difference is real and meaningful, that where power is lacking, violence prevails. It is also possible to speculate that if Miss Arendt were to rely on her insights and not so much on hearsay and quotations from Noam Chomsky, she might be able to see the Vietnam situation in a clearer light, in terms of massive violence (from *them*) and a failure of power (from *us*). Even here, however, she lacks the capacity to be insignificant.

Concluding her study, Miss Arendt returns to essentials, pointing to the disadvantages of centralization (the root and stem of all Marxology) in these words: ''Just when centralization, under the impact of bigness, turned out to be counterproductive in its own terms, the country . . . threw itself headlong, to the unanimous applause of all 'progressive' forces, into the new experiment of centralized administration—the Federal Government overpowering state powers and executive power eroding congressional powers.''

And again, she writes: ''In the United States, based on a great plurality of powers and their mutual checks and balances, we are confronted not merely with the disintegration of power structures, but with power, seemingly still intact and free to manifest itself, losing its grip and becoming ineffective.'' True, too true. Solution? Do not read Hannah Arendt for solutions, but do read her for her insights, her imagination, her fundamental understanding of the things that count in the struggle between freedom and slavery. (p. 473)

Max Geltman, ''Power and Violence,'' in National Review *(© National Review, Inc., 1970; 150 East 35th St., New York, NY 10016), Vol. XXII, No. 17, May 5, 1970, pp. 472-73.*

JÜRGEN HABERMAS

Hannah Arendt's principal philosophical work, *The Human Condition* . . . , serves to systematically renew the Aristotelian concept of praxis. The author does not rely on an exegesis of classical texts; she drafts an anthropology of communicative action. . . . Arendt analyzes the form of intersubjectivity generated in the praxis of speech as the basic feature of cultural life. Communicative action is the medium in which the intersubjectively shared life-world is formed. It is the ''space of appearance'' in which actors enter, encounter one another, are seen and heard. (pp. 7-8)

One may regard the method with which Hannah Arendt develops her practical philosophy—a method reminiscent of Alfred Schutz's social phenomenology—as inadequate; but the intention is clear: she wants to read off of the formal properties of communicative action (or praxis) the general structures of an unimpaired intersubjectivity. These structures set the conditions of normalcy for human existence, indeed for an existence worthy of human beings. Owing to its innovative potential, the domain of praxis is, however, highly unstable and in need of protection. In societies organized around a state, this is looked after by political institutions. These are fed by the power that springs from unimpaired intersubjectivity; and they must in turn protect the susceptible structures of intersubjectivity against deformations if they are not themselves to deteriorate. From this follows the central hypothesis that Hannah Arendt untiringly repeats: no political leadership can with impunity replace power through force; and it can gain power only from a nondeformed public realm. The public-political realm has also been conceived by others as a generator, if not of power then of the legitimation of power; but Hannah Arendt insists that a public-political realm can produce legitimate power only so long as structures of nondistorted communication find their expression in it. (pp. 8-9)

Hannah Arendt does not test her hypothesis against examples of the decline of great empires. Her historical investigations resolve instead around two extreme cases: the destruction of political liberty under totalitarian rule (a), and the revolutionary establishment of political liberty (b). Both investigations apply the concept of power, and in such a way that the deformations in Western mass democracies are illuminated from opposite sides. (p. 9)

The totalitarian rule of the Nazi regime historically arose on the basis of a mass democracy. This is one of the occasions that motivated Hannah Arendt to a vigorous critique of the privatism built into modern societies. Whereas the theorists of democratic elitism (following Schumpeter) commend representative government and the party system as channels for the political participation of a depoliticized mass, Arendt sees the danger precisely in this situation. Mediatizing the population through highly bureaucratized administrations, parties, and organizations just supplements and fortifies those privatistic forms of life which provide the psychological base for mobilizing the unpolitical, that is, for establishing totalitarian rule. (p. 11)

In connection with emancipatory movements [Arendt] is interested in the power of common conviction: the withdrawal of obedience to institutions that have lost their legitimacy; the confrontation of communicative power with the means of force of a coercive but impotent state apparatus; the beginnings of a new political order and the attempt—the pathos of the new beginning—to hold fast to the initial revolutionary situation, to give institutional permanence to the communicative generation of power. It is fascinating to see how Hannah Arendt traces the same phenomenon over and over. When revolutionaries seize the power that lies in the streets; when a populace committed to passive resistance confronts alien tanks with their bare hands; when convinced minorities contest the legitimacy of existing laws and organize civil disobedience; when the "pure desire for action" manifests itself in the student movement—these phenomena confirm again that no one really possesses power; it "springs up between men when they act together and vanishes the moment they disperse." This emphatic concept of praxis is more Marxist than Aristotelian: Marx called it "critical-revolutionary activity." (pp. 12-13)

Arendt stylizes the image she has of the Greek polis to the essence of politics as such. This is the background to her favored conceptual dichotomies between the public and the private, between state and economy, freedom and welfare, political-practical activity and production—rigid dichotomies which modern bourgeois society and the modern state, however, escape. Thus the mere fact that in modern times something characteristically new, a complementary relationship between state and economy, established itself with the development

of the capitalist mode of production already counts as the mark of a pathology, of a destructive confusion. . . . (p. 14)

Arendt rightly insists that the technical-economic overcoming of poverty is by no means a sufficient condition for the practical securing of political liberty. But she becomes the victim of a concept of politics that is inapplicable to modern conditions when she asserts that the

> intrusion of social and economic matters into the public realm, the transformation of government into administration, the replacement of personal rule by bureaucratic measures, and the attending transmutation of laws into decrees

necessarily frustrate every attempt at a politically active public realm. She also views the French Revolution in this dim light; and she attributes the initial success of the foundation of liberty in America to the fact that "the politically insoluble social question did not stand in the way." I cannot discuss this interpretation here. I want only to indicate the curious perspective that Hannah Arendt adopts: a state which is relieved of the administrative processing of social problems; a politics which is cleansed of socio-economic issues; an institutionalization of public wealth; a radical democracy which inhibits its liberating efficacy just at the boundaries where political oppression ceases and social repression begins—this path is unimaginable for any modern society.

Thus we are faced with a dilemma: on the one hand, the communications concept of power discloses important though extreme phenomena of the modern world to which political science has become more and more insensitive; on the other hand, it is linked with a conception of politics which, when applied to modern societies, leads to absurdities. Let us then return once more to the analysis of the concept of power. Arendt's concept of communicatively generated power can become a sharp instrument only if we extricate it from the clamps of an Aristotelian theory of action. In separating praxis from the unpolitical activities of working and laboring on the one side and of thinking on the other, Arendt traces back political power exclusively to praxis, to the speaking and acting together of individuals. Over against the production of material objects and theoretical knowledge, communicative action has to appear as the only political category. This narrowing of the political to the practical permits illuminating contrasts to the presently palpable elimination of essentially practical contents from the political process. But for this Arendt pays a certain price: (a) she screens all strategic elements, as force, out of politics; (b) she removes politics from its relations to the economic and social environment in which it is embedded through the administrative system; and (c) she is unable to grasp structural violence. Let me comment briefly on these three deficits.

War is the classic example of strategic action. For the Greeks it was something that took place outside the walls of the city. For Hannah Arendt too strategic action is essentially unpolitical, a matter for experts. The example of warfare is of course suited to demonstrating the contrast between political power and force. Waging war manifestly involves the calculated employment of means of force, whether for the sake of threatening or of physically overcoming an opponent. But the accumulation of means of destruction does not make superpowers more powerful; military strength is (as the Vietnam War showed) often enough the counterpart to impotence. Furthermore, the example of warfare seems suitable for subsuming strategic action under instrumental action. In addition to communicative action, the *vita activa* encompasses the essentially nonsocial activities of working and laboring. And since the purposive-rational employment of military means appears to have the same structure as the use of instruments to fabricate material objects or to work up nature, Arendt equates strategic with instrumental action. So she stresses that strategic action is instrumental as well as violent, and that action of this type falls outside of the domain of the political.

The matter looks different if we place strategic action alongside communicative action, as another form of social interaction (which is, to be sure, not oriented to reaching agreement but to success); and if we contrast it with instrumental action, as nonsocial action that can also be carried out by a solitary subject. It then becomes conceptually plausible that strategic action also took place *within* the walls of the city—thus in power struggles, in the competition for positions to which the exercise of legitimate power was tied. The *acquisition* and *maintenance* of political power must be distinguished from both the *employment* of political power—that is, rule—and the *generation* of political power. In the last case, but only in the last case, the concept of praxis is helpful. No occupant of a position of authority can maintain and exercise power, if these positions are not themselves anchored in laws and political institutions whose continued existence rests ultimately on common convictions, on "an opinion upon which many are publicly in agreement." (pp. 14-17)

Arendt rightly urges that strategic contests for political power neither call forth nor maintain those institutions in which that power is anchored. Political institutions live not from force but from recognition.

Nevertheless, we cannot exclude the element of strategic action from the concept of the political. Let us understand the force exercised through strategic action as the ability to prevent other individuals or groups from realizing their interests. In this sense force has always belonged to the means for acquiring and holding on to positions of legitimate power. In modern states this struggle for political power has even been institutionalized; it thereby became a normal component of the political system. On the other hand, it is not at all clear that someone should be able to *generate* legitimate power simply because he is in a position to prevent others from pursuing their interests. Legitimate power *arises* only among those who form common convictions in unconstrained communication. (pp. 17-18)

The concept of the political must extend to the strategic competition for political power and to the employment of power within the political system. Politics cannot, as with Arendt, be identified with the praxis of those who talk together in order to act in common. Conversely, the dominant theory narrows this concept to phenomena of political competition and power allocation and does not do justice to the real phenomenon of the generation of power. At this point the distinction between power and force becomes sharp. It calls to mind that the political system cannot dispose of power at will. Power is a good *for* which political groups struggle and *with* which a political leadership manages things; but in a certain way both find this good already at hand; they don't produce it. This is the impotence of the powerful—they have to borrow their power from the producers of power. This is the credo of Hannah Arendt.

The objection thereto lies ready at hand: even if the leadership in modern democracies has to periodically procure legitimation, history is replete with evidence which shows that political rule must have functioned, and functions, otherwise than as

Arendt claims. Certainly, it speaks *for* her thesis that political rule can last only so long as it is recognized as legitimate. It speaks *against* her thesis that basic institutions and structures which are stabilized through political rule could only in rare cases be the expression of an "opinion on which many were publicly in agreement"—at least if one has, as Hannah Arendt does, a strong concept of the public realm. These two facts can be brought together if we assume that structural violence is built into political institutions (but not only into them). Structural violence does not manifest itself *as force;* rather, unperceived, it blocks those communications in which convictions effective for legitimation are formed and passed on. Such an hypothesis about inconspicuously working communication blocks can explain, perhaps, the formation of ideologies; with it one can give a plausible account of how convictions are formed in which subjects deceive themselves about themselves and their situation. Ideologies are, after all, illusions that are outfitted with the power of common convictions. This proposal is an attempt to render the communicative production of power in a more realistic version. In systematically restricted communications, those involved form convictions subjectively free from constraint, convictions which are, however, illusionary. They thereby communicatively generate a power which, as soon as it is institutionalized, can also be used against them.

If we wanted to accept this proposal, we would of course have to specify a critical standard and to distinguish between illusionary and nonillusionary convictions. Hannah Arendt doubts that this is possible. She holds fast to the classical distinction between theory and practice; practice rests on opinions and convictions that cannot be true or false in the strict sense. . . . An antiquated concept of theoretical knowledge that is based on ultimate insights and certainties keeps Arendt from comprehending the process of reaching agreement about practical questions as rational discourse. If, by contrast, "representative thought"—which examines the generalizability of practical standpoints, that is, the legitimacy of norms—is not separated from argumentation by an abyss, then a cognitive foundation can also be claimed for the power of common convictions. In this case, such power is anchored in the de facto recognition of validity claims that can be discursively redeemed and fundamentally criticized. Arendt sees a yawning abyss between knowledge and opinion that cannot be closed with arguments. She has to look for another foundation for the power of opinion, and she finds it in the capability of responsible subjects to make and to keep promises. . . . She regards as the basis of power the contract between free and equal parties with which they place themselves under mutual obligation. To secure the normative core of an original equivalence between power and freedom, Hannah Arendt finally places more trust in the venerable figure of the contract than in her own concept of a praxis, which is grounded in the rationality of practical judgment. She retreats instead to the contract theory of natural law. (pp. 21-4)

Jürgen Habermas, "Hannah Arendt's Communications Concept of Power," translated by Thomas McCarthy, in Social Research *(copyright 1977 by New School for Social Research), Vol. 44, No. 1, Spring, 1977, pp. 3-24.*

JAMES M. ALTMAN

Toward the end of her life, Hannah Arendt redirected her thought inward, upon the mental activities of thinking, willing and judging. The result of that changed focus, *The Life of the Mind*, is her culminating achievement. (p. 47)

The most provocative parts of Arendt's account result from her vision of the significance of our mental activites. Expanding upon Kant's distinction between reason (our faculty for thought) and intellect (our faculty for cognition), Arendt introduces the view that the goal of thinking is meaning, not truth. This view contradicts the assumption of modern science, derived from Descartes, that the goal of thinking is clear and certain knowledge about the world. . . . [Thinking] arises out of a human need to make sense of our existence. This need remains unsatisfied by merely knowing what *is*, and therefore touches deeper chords in us than the need for the truth.

Arendt suggests that willing accords human beings a measure of divinity. . . . In Arendt's view, free human action is not dictated directly by our ideals or our desires, but originates in the inner struggle which characterizes willing. When we act, we choose to do what one pole of consciousness commands. But alternatively, we might have chosen not to do the act, as the other pole of consciousness counsels. The human capacity to interrupt the ordinary course of our individual or collective history with an utterly new sequence of actions stems from the possibility of resisting what is commanded internally by one pole of consciousness. Willing, therefore, is what enables us to start spontaneously something new and unexpected. . . . (pp. 47-8)

Arendt's account of our mental activities is most compelling where her unorthodox use of previous philosophical views is appropriate. Her approach works well in Volume One's account of thinking, since philosophers do have a privileged perspective on the thinking activity. It is less justified in Volume Two, however, since statements by professional thinkers cannot provide data for an unbiased account of willing. Arendt should have drawn her evidence from people who act in the world. This methodological error is compounded by her reliance upon the reflections of Christian philosphers concerning God's "Thou Shalt" and the "will to sin," which lack full resonance with secular readers.

Few works of philosophy published today seriously confront the Western philosophical tradition as a whole. *The Life of the Mind* has that bold ambition. At a minimum, it resembles a deep mining operation, which brings to the surface the authentic insights of a tradition which has fragmented and lost its power to guide us. Arendt intentionally preserves those treasures by reflecting upon them anew. At its best, mostly in *Thinking, The Life of the Mind* succeeds in offering us new insights to illuminate our own mental experiences and an integrative vision of their profound meanings. (p. 48)

James M. Altman, "Books Considered: 'The Life of the Mind: Vol. I; Thinking, Vol. II; Willing'," in The New Republic *(reprinted by permission of* The New Republic; © 1978 The New Republic, Inc.)*, Vol. 178, No. 8, February 25, 1978, pp. 47-8.*

LEON BOTSTEIN

[*The Jew As Pariah*] offers a new way of making sense not only of Arendt as Jew but also of Arendt's major work. In her almost exclusive attention to Jewish issues from 1933-1951, Arendt formulated the bases of her understanding of the modern world and its political and ethical dilemmas. Her grasp of the meaning and consequence of her Jewish identity, in the presence of Nazism and subsequently at the moment of the birth of the State of Israel, shaped the elements of her political and philosophical outlook on non-Jewish matters. Arendt, rather than being yet another cosmopolitan intellectual, was a uniquely Jewish thinker. (pp. 32, 34)

Arendt's attempts to grapple with the "Jewish Question" presented in *The Jew As Pariah* also cast new light on those of her works that address issues of Jewish history, the *Origins* and *Eichmann in Jerusalem*. The latter emerges as far less bizarre and incomprehensible to even the most skeptical of Jewish readers, and the supposed historical "lopsidedness" of the *Origins* begins to seem justified. I think, for example, that readers of this collection will be disabused of the notion that Arendt went to Jerusalem loaded for bear against Zionism, that she was unsympathetic to the Jews, that she reproached them for collaborating and not resisting. Indeed, I think that if the Eichmann book had been published with several of these essays, Arendt's primary concerns would have been clear from the start. How does radical evil become denatured and gain a normal banal appearance? How do average, even admirable, people become dehumanized by the critical circumstances pressing in on them? How can life in our time lose meaning and suicide become an act of affirmation? How is it that mere living and surviving can become morally problematic under conditions of extreme domination? Are Zionism and fundamental criticism of the state of Israel compatible? These fundamental themes of Arendt's thought are all adumbrated in *The Jew as Pariah*. (p. 34)

What is startling about the essays on Zionism and Israel collected in *The Jew As Pariah*, especially those written during the years of the partition and the war of independence, is the degree of practical wisdom and prophetic (from the vantage point of Camp David) judgment which shaped her vision. Arendt called for a binational state for pragmatic reasons. A Jewish state would be viewed as a foreign outpost of the West in a hostile Arab world. It would be overly dependent economically and politically on some great power, far less autonomous in international politics than it could be. The appearance of equality in the family of nations for Jews would be marred by the reality—the Jewish state as the subsidiary of a great power in a hostile local environment. Arendt thought that a Jewish state would eventually place American Jews in a domestically awkward position both as Jews and as Americans, as recent events of the years since the Arab boycott have certainly demonstrated. She predicted that the Jewish state would force Israel into investing altogether too much of its resources in the needs of an armed camp. . . . Only bi-nationalism, with a democracy and an inter-ethnic definition of citizenship with the Arabs, could satisfy both the spiritual legacy of the Holocaust and the need for autonomy for the Jewish nation in its homeland.

Only a new society which built itself on Arendt's favorite mode of political organization—small, decentralized revolutionary councils, soviets, "Räte," all similar to the kibbutz—would have satisfied her. . . . Perhaps, after peace comes to the Middle East, when cooperation between Jew and Arab emerges, Arendt's vision, the subject of contempt and ridicule in the 1950s and 1960s, will not appear so fanciful and farfetched.

As a result of *The Jew As Pariah,* it can be seen that Arendt's analysis of the Jewish dilemma provides an interpretive logic for her whole life's work. (pp. 35-6)

[These] essays should stimulate a long overdue rehabilitation of Hannah Arendt in the Jewish community, where she remains a source of embarrassment, and the object of resentment and even vicious ridicule. The visible hurt she suffered (as evident in her replies to Gershom Scholem and Walter Laqueur on the Eichmann book . . .) should be rectified, if only for those who care for her memory. Her views on European history and on Zionism, on the nature of Jewish assimilation and the mirage of emancipation were certainly singular and often jarring. . . . In her view of the Jews, Arendt was not follower, not a slogan-monger. Even in the face of open wounds, she asserted what she saw as the truth in order to stimulate virtuous action toward a just world.

These essays demonstrate Hannah Arendt's pride as a Jew. She overstated Ostjuden, for the Jew who thought that being Jewish was incidental, for that intellectual would thought fame could transform the Jew into a citizen of the world.

To Hannah Arendt, being Jewish was the decisive fact of her life as a private person and as a political thinker. It cast the mold for the thinking and willing for which she was, and will be, honored. . . . Apart from its service to the legacy of Hannah Arendt, *The Jew As Pariah* offers brilliance, eloquence, and reasoned commitment on issues where clarity and courage are in perpetually short supply. (pp. 36-7)

Leon Botstein, "Hannah Arendt: The Jewish Question," in The New Republic *(reprinted by permission of* The New Republic; © *1978 The New Republic, Inc.), Vol. 179, No. 17, October 21, 1978, pp. 32, 34-7.*

SHELDON WOLIN

The Life of the Mind is characteristically Arendtian, which is to say that there are passages of remarkable insight and suggestiveness, just as there are others that seem wrong-headed and unsupported by fact, text, or reasons. There is a majestic indifference toward the existing literature that surrounds her subject matter. She offered only a slight nod of recognition to the "philosophy of mind," the Great Totem of Anglo-American philosophers; while Freud, who had some things to say about reason, will, and consciousness, is absolutely taboo. Although these volumes, along with her other writings, deal in some detail with questions of language and speech, there is no evidence of any prior commerce with contemporary linguistics and rhetoric. Although the quest for "meaning" is singled out as the distinctive feature of thinking, a move that might lead one to suppose that she shared certain affinities with contemporary hermeneutics, she chose, instead, not to elect them. Finally, although *The Life of the Mind* is as much preoccupied by the controversy over the "active" versus the "contemplative" life as it is over any other single question, it ignores practically all of the major modern writers who have addressed it, writers of the stature of Thomas More, Machiavilli, Bacon, Hobbes, Montesquieu, Marx, and Weber.

It has to be said, also, that the book is strewn with judgments and assertions about the history of Western thought and particular thinkers that are often arbitrary, one-sided, or wrong. Thus she takes as exemplary the ancient Pythagorean description of the philosopher as a spectator who observes but does not participate in the Olympic games, and she uses it to support the ideal of a thinker who mingles with ordinary humanity and participates in a public world. Nothing is said by her about the ancient traditions that depicted the Pythagoreans as a secretive, exclusive society with a very distinct notion about reserving certain esoteric truths for an inner brotherhood. . . . Further,

although these volumes are concerned with topics which have been disputed for centuries and the approaches are mined with elaborate distinctions, counter-examples, and abandoned conceptions, she disdained even the most elementary precautions in taking up such complex matters.

The Life of the Mind is a collection of loosely related themes, not a sustained inquiry. . . . There are redeeming moments: an admiring portrait of Socrates, for instance, and an acidulous one of Aquinas. But there is no controlling and unifying impulse.

It is, nonetheless, an important work—if one can find the proper terms for understanding it, without glossing over its faults. In that vein, I would suggest, simply, that the value of the *Life* is inseparable from, even enhanced by, its shortcomings. Its excesses—an outrageous scope, magistral tone, peremptory judgments, and occasional mockery of "professional thinkers"—give its author no place to hide and, consequently, serve to dispel the first impressions of the book, namely that it is a large-scale inquiry into the nature and operation of the mind.

She has given us not a life of "the" mind, but something more personal, although not overtly autobiographical. It is a work of self-clarification and retrospection focused upon finding the right terms for the particular form of life of the author and written in awareness of her own mortality. This explains why there is so much of these volumes that will seem familiar to her readers. The same ancient authors and the same striking quotations are all here because they were the influences which had shaped the life of her mind, the stuff on which it had been nurtured. . . .

[Arendt] believed that, as a thinking subject, her own history was to be understood not in itself but in its relationship to the larger history of the "Western mind" that had begun with the ancient Greeks and had continued thereafter, undergoing successive crises and metamorphoses, and ending, temporarily, in the crisis of the "present." *The Life of the Mind* is a journey that presupposes the journey which Hegel—with whom she felt compelled to quarrel, though his influence over her was a major one—had memorialized as the *Phänomenologie des Geistes*. (p. 16)

[The present work] was written within a sharply defined tradition whose philosophical lineage runs uninterruptedly: Kant-Fichte-Hegel-Nietzsche-Heidegger. Once this is recognized, much of the seeming strangeness of her thinking is dissolved. For example, the lofty status she accorded ancient Greek philosophy simply perpetuated the judgment of Hegel, Nietzsche, and Heidegger, who were the three greatest Hellenizers in the history of post-Renaissance philosophy. But unlike Hegel and Nietzsche, who used their incomparable knowledge of the classics to open up radically new conceptions of mind and of its place in the world, Arendt's conclusions appear highly equivocal and uncharacteristically hesitant, as well as far more reluctant to break with the past. (p. 17)

The *Life* never manages to overcome a mood of resignation and it closes on the Augustinian note that "we are *doomed* to be free by virtue of being born.". . . Hannah Arendt seems tacitly to have abandoned her position of a decade ago when she had cast the thinker as a "truth-teller" whose vocational duty was to preserve the "factual truth" against the systematic deceptions practiced by contemporary politicians. At the end she seemed to want to exchange truth for meaning, fact for metaphor, truth-telling for disclosing what cannot be proven, and to argue that the freedom of the mind becomes possible when thinking is liberated from the tyranny of truth.

One is tempted to attribute this melancholy to a feeling of bereftness induced by her recognition that she had been left stranded by the last turn in Heidegger's thought. As she demonstrates, Heidegger's critique of Nietzsche's "will-to-power" ends in passivity, in a condition where the subject wills not to will, and, consequently, accepts the lot of powerlessness. But those who have read her writings will remember Hannah Arendt not only as a writer of remarkable insight and intelligence, but one of rare courage who took on the gravest and most dangerous problems of the times. A momentary flash of this memorable past is provided by a phrase she used in these volumes, "man the fighter." Perhaps this, rather than those "Hellenizing ghosts" that Nietzsche warned against, should be the epitaph to the life of her mind. (pp. 20-1)

Sheldon Wolin, "Stopping to Think," in The New York Review of Books *(reprinted with permission from* The New York Review of Books; *copyright © 1978 Nyrev, Inc.), Vol. XXV, No. 16, October 26, 1978, pp. 16-21.*

JAMES T. KNAUER

Hannah Arendt's writing on politics illuminates aspects of political action that have been little explored: politics as the expression of individual identity and political principle, politics as the creation of an intersubjectively shared life-world, politics as the creation of a uniquely human mode of being-together, political community as praxis. She directed much of her attention to the examination and elucidation of these widely ignored qualities of political action and to their public discussion within an intellectual climate largely hostile and blind to them. She was deeply troubled by the course of modern history as well as by such efforts to come to terms with that history as materialist Marxism and utilitarian liberalism. What she saw in these events and intellectual traditions was the loss of humanity. Her writing must be understood as a response to and reaction against that situation. . . . To understand and appreciate her work requires that it be read in light of these concerns.

But if her emphasis was on these largely ignored characteristics of politics, she displayed no lack of awareness of those other, more widely recognized, aspects of political action: politics as purposive action with motives and goals, politics motivated by socioeconomic interests, politics as the struggle for power. Nor did she try to purify politics by defining it to exclude these elements. What she did was choose language, focus, and emphasis as part of an effort to act against history. Why should she emphasize the instrumental aspect of all politics when her aim was to overcome its instrumentalization and trivilization? Why should she elaborate the strategic aspects of politics when her goal was to recommend politics as an activity transcending the mere struggle for power? And this is not to say that the value of her thought is limited to its illumination of those ignored aspects of politics. . . . [She] provides us with a powerful insight into the complex and subtle relationship between politics as instrumental and strategic action and politics as expression and praxis.

Arendt's work does, however, suffer from a deficiency. . . . This deficiency lies not in Arendt's concept of political action but in her rather one-dimensional treatment of economic activity. Perhaps because of her reliance on the household economics model of the *polis*, she gives insufficient consideration to the great variety of possible modes of economic organization and to their different political implications. In focusing on the negative impact of economic concerns on the political realm, she overlooks the possible positive effects of certain modes of economic organization as well as the potential humanzing of economic relations that could arise out of political association. Just as the motives and goals involved in action must ultimately be evaluated in terms of political principles, so various modes of economic organization must be evaluated in terms of their mplications for the political life of the community as Arendt conceived it. The clear implication of Arendt's work for the economic realm, I would argue, is that the realization of political freedom requires movement in the direction of a decentralized and democratic socialism with extensive worker and community control of economic enterprise. . . . And the starting point for an investigation of the relevance of Arendt's work to these matters is an appreciation of her insight into the relationship betwen politics as instrumental and strategic activity and politics as expression and praxis. (pp. 732-33)

James T. Knauer, "Motive and Goal in Hannah Arendt's Concept of Political Action," in The American Political Science Review *(copyright, 1980, by The American Political Science Association), Vol. 74, No. 3, September, 1980, pp. 721-33.*

GEORGE D. BRADEN

In this fascinating but essentially unsound book about the First Amendment [*Freedom, Virtue and the First Amendment*] Professor Berns does three things. First, he analyzes the United States Supreme Court's gyrations in First Amendment freedom of speech cases and concludes that the cases as a whole are a hopeless mishmash based upon an incorrect theory. Second, he attacks the fundamental philosophy in support of freedom of speech and, indeed, the fundamental theory of democracy. Finally, he offers a prescription for bringing order out of chaos—namely, to add "virtue" as a factor in judging freedom; in effect, to judge speech by whether it is good or bad.

The last of these is both the easiest and the most difficult to criticize. It is child's play to note, as Professor Berns himself does from time to time when analyzing parts of judicial opinions, that words of value are dangerous. . . . One man's "good" is another's "bad." On the other hand, it is most difficult to quarrel with a man who seeks as you do the Good Life. . . .

The key to Professor Berns's thesis is his attack on the fundamentals of democracy. He asserts that what the defenders of civil liberties call democracy is only a process and an empty one at that. It is empty because it is amoral, and amoral government is bad government. What Professor Berns overlooks is that we who believe in freedom, especially freedom of speech, endeavor to accommodate the moral needs of a society within narrow limits. Acts of government must be "moral," but they need not encompass all of life. . . .

If, as Professor Berns believes, most of us yearn for a good society, then our democratic government will move, in faltering steps to be sure, toward that society. We will not arrive as soon as we might if a commanding presence could channel all our efforts in the right direction. But we may arrive more surely, for the commanding presence might err. The slackness of a democratic society, the aimlessness of its movement, the tolerance for many tongues are a virtue, not a vice. Professor Berns points out that freedom to read comics is not as important as freedom to read Shakespeare. We may agree with him but still feel that our freedom to read Shakespeare is the more secure when our neighbor is free to read trash.

It is in his analysis of Supreme Court cases that Professor Berns is at his best. He demonstrates admirably the confused development of the "clear and present danger" rule and the on-again, off-again attempts by various Justices to explain why the Court should interfere in civil liberties matters whilst giving legislatures free reign in economic matters. Unfortunately, this is a surface analysis that betrays a lack of perception of the judicial process at work. . . .

This lack of perception of the judicial process is of a piece with Professor Berns's impatience with the frailties of democracy. After two hundred years of liberalism in the Western world, we seem to be no nearer to the perfect life than we were when Hobbes, Locke and Rousseau spoke. Professor Berns is all for eliminating this nonsense and going back to stern precepts of virtue and honesty and right living. With due respect to all concerned, it seems that Professor Berns wants to be the Billy Graham of political science.

George D. Braden, "Impatience with Freedom," in The Nation *(copyright 1958 The Nation magazine, The Nation Associates, Inc.), Vol. 186, No. 24, June 14, 1958, p. 550.*

LOUIS H. POLLAK

Whether or not freedom of speech holds a "preferred position" in the hierarchy of American legal values, it seems to outrank even motels and motherhood as a national symbol. Serious criticism of our country's articulate major premise is, therefore, a notable event. Especially so when the criticism takes the form of as searching and scholarly a volume as *Freedom, Virtue & the First Amendment.*

Professor Berns . . . thinks that our uncritical acceptance of freedom of speech as a national desideratum has led us into serious difficulties—for many of which the Supreme Court is chiefly to blame. . . . [The] Court's misconstruction of the Constitution—based upon a misguided adulation of freedom as an intrinsically precious commodity—is antithetic to the political requirements of a good society. . . . The First Amendment, in short, is helpful only in a good society, where people will spend its bounty prudently. . . .

Professor Berns is also persuaded that the Court has fallen into fundamental legal error in its expansive application of the First Amendment. He "suspects, but cannot yet prove, that the intention of the First Amendment was merely to outlaw previous restraints on the freedom of speech and press." . . . What Berns surmises, Sir William Blackstone was certain of two centuries ago. One would have supposed that the inadequacies of so narrow an understanding of free speech had long been manifest. (p. 163)

Berns, however, holds to the contrary, and his book suggests both the vigor and the dangerous nature of this particular heresy. . . . In a sense, however, it is not as curious that Professor Berns takes so unfashionable a view of the First Amendment as that he evinces any concern at all about the competence of the Court's performance on what Berns pejoratively describes as "the legal level." . . . For law, no matter how carefully fashioned, is in Berns's eyes an instrument of limited utility. . . . But just why law should be regarded as congenitally inadequate to the solution of the conundrums of government is puzzling.

Recognizing that we must continue to operate within the confines of that poorly designed and ineptly handled mechanism which is the First Amendment, Berns submits that "perhaps the best we can do is to interpret it to read: Congress shall make no law abridging the freedom of *good* speech." . . . Modestly stated, this is plainly enough a proposal of major dimension. It is a proposal, argued in cogent and sensitive fashion, which challenges our most cherished and possibly least comprehended institution. But the challenge to the core of America's constitutional heritage is not a hostile one—indeed, as Berns himself makes abundantly clear, it is not a product of "the so-called conservative movement." . . . Berns's book is the book of a man dedicated to democratic values and deeply troubled about how best to foster them. . . . It merits the close attention of all who cherish individual liberty—and especially of those who are certain, a priori, that Professor Berns is in error. He is in error, but in ably stating his case Berns forces on those who disagree with him a firmer understanding of the First Amendment. (pp. 163-64)

Louis H. Pollak, "American History and Government: 'Freedom, Virtue & the First Amendment'," in The Annals of The American Academy of Political and Social Science *(©1958, by The American Academy of Political and Social Science), Vol. 319, September, 1958, pp. 163-64.*

M. STANTON EVANS

[*The First Amendment and the Future of American Democracy*] is so good it is a scandal even to try to summarize it in a couple of paragraphs. . . . [It is] a first-class piece of historical scholarship concerning the complex origins and many meanings of the First Amendment. . . .

[It] seems to me definitive on the constitutional issues at stake in the battle over obscenity and pornography. What Professor Berns has demonstrated, in a nutshell, is that the Founding Fathers intended the First Amendment to be a restriction on the Federal Government only, that they left the power of controlling obscenity, libel, and other such matters to the state, and that they fully expected this power to be used. Local restraints on the likes of *Hustler,* in other words, are fully constitutional, and those who would persuade us otherwise have the tough assignment of trying to answer Professor Berns.

> M. Stanton Evans, ''Dark Horses,'' in National Review (© National Review, Inc., 1977, 150 East 35th St., New York, NY 10016), Vol. 29, No. 32, August 19, 1977, p. 956.*

WILLIAM A. STANMEYER

In [*Freedom, Virtue, and the First Amendment,* Walter Berns] showed that ''the problem of freedom cannot be understood in terms of legal rules and principles alone; it must be seen in a larger context [which requires one] to question the validity of the prevailing theory of law—the theory based on the belief in freedom as the main principle of government.'' In [*The First Amendment and the Future of American Democracy*] Professor Berns goes beyond investigation of the place of virtue in the schema of republican government; with other observers of the near-universal triumph of abstract theory over practical common sense in the Supreme Court's First Amendment jurisprudence these past twenty years, he has much at which to be distressed. Unlike others who seem tolerably content with exposing the Supreme Court's errors, he explores the likely consequences of the Court's *laissez faire* philosophy of expression: ''It is the thesis of this book that the Court, in the name of civil liberty, is steadily eroding the conditions of civil liberty, to the point where it is appropriate to wonder about the future of liberal democracy in the United States.'' (p. 367)

To assert the secular utility of virtue is not, of course, to prove it. This is not my purpose here. Rather, I raise this point because without acknowledging the importance of virtue to the political order, at least *arguendo,* the hostile critic of Professor Berns will mistake his argument and thus not come to grips with the real issues. The usual critic, to judge by the reception of Berns' earlier work, dismisses his argument because the critic has cast the problem solely in terms of liberties—how much, how far, how many ''rights'' must government recognize in its citizens. The critic rarely speaks of the wellspring or source of those rights, whether the nature of man or some ''higher law'' in the universe; for either source may easily lead to some normative limits, whether part of man's nature or imposed by a transcendant deity. The critic does not cast the problem in terms of responsibilities or duties. He does not ask such questions as: what are the legitimate limits of liberty? Can liberties be abused? What is the difference between the proper and improper use of freedom of speech? . . . What kind of citizens will we have if the law makes no attempt to encourage responsibility, morality, or civility? (p. 368)

As Berns so skillfully demonstrates in his discussion of the *Cohen, Rosenfeld,* and *Papish* cases, the Court has forgotten *why* speech was worthy of protection in the first place. Part of this amnesia is epistemological: the Court professes not to *know* whether there is a theoretical—never mind the practical, which can raise hard borderline cases—difference between good speech and bad speech. . . . (p. 369)

Perhaps his argument insufficiently stresses the fact, stated but not thoroughly elaborated, that the law is indeed a *teacher.* The system of laws as a whole expresses society's intuitive but profound judgment as to what is humane and what bestial, decent and indecent, civil and uncivil. Thus the law is the collective expression of civilization as opposed to barbarism. Where the law is silent on such matters, teaching goes on nonetheless: the lesson then is that (a) people do not know the difference, or (b) people do not care, or (c) there is no difference, or (d) the whole question is unimportant. (p. 370)

Berns will be faulted by his critics, no doubt, for making what to them is a mountain out of a molehill, and building it out of the smashed debris of the First Amendment. But the critics forget that the law is a *rule of generalization.* To permit one person to use outrageous profane language is to permit all. . . . Berns rightly observes that judges' ''contempt power'' and the honorific modes of address in a democratic parliament serve an important educative purpose. They teach respect for the modes of civilization. They embody civilization on one level. They civilize. For the Supreme Court to forget this public purpose, in the name of protecting an individual's ''right'' to offend his fellow citizens, is for the Court to cut itself adrift from the very civilized values it purports to defend. (pp. 370-71)

Through a series of quotes from Washington, Jefferson, and others, [Berns] seeks to demonstrate that the Founding Fathers' basic position on religion was that it was, as his cite from Tocqueville puts it, ''indispensable to the maintenance of republican institutions.'' . . . Thus paradoxically, while institutional religion or religion-as-institutionalized was an obstacle to the formation of the free society under law, religion-as-practiced is seen as a necessary foundation and protection to such a society. (p. 371)

[The] ''Religious Problem'' is solved, as a political matter, by relegating religion to the private realm, as long as ''piety stays within the bounds required [as Jefferson says] for peace and good order.'' But as a sociomoral matter it is not solved, as Berns concedes, since ''liberalism required both the subordination of religion and the maintenance of certain habits that religion alone could inculcate,'' *viz.,* habits of civic virtue. Here, as will appear below, it may be argued that Professor Berns resists some conclusions to which his own premises would lead. For if virtue inculcated by religion is essential to the Republic, should not the Supreme Court be praised whenever it permits a religious group to practice its faith without state interference (granted basic morality is preserved) and thereby educate its young communicants to the paths of virtue? . . .

Sympathy for Professor Berns' basic thesis—that in construing the First Amendment, the Supreme Court has lost its bearings, to the likely ultimate detriment of constitutional democracy itself—should not obscure the fact that once in awhile the Court does find its way back to port. In the case of this otherwise well reasoned study, however, the basic thesis becomes a bludgeon with which to beat the Court on all occasions, even those where the Justices showed refreshing instinct for common sense.

Such a mistake, in this writer's judgment, characterizes the treatment of the *Yoder* case. (p. 372)

In *Wisconsin v. Yoder*, Old Amish parents were criminally prosecuted for failure to enroll their children (aged 14, 15, and 15, respectively) in high school pursuant to Wisconsin's Compulsory School Attendance Law which required attendance in an accredited school through age 15. They asserted as their defense the protection of the Free Exercise Clause. They did not attack the constitutionality of the statute on its face, but solely in its application to them and to their children. The state conceded, and all three courts below the Supreme Court found, after an extensive trial, that the defendants were sincere in their religious beliefs and that the application of the statute to them interfered with the free exercise of their religion. This interference was found to be substantial and direct and, moreover, to threaten the very existence of the faith-community of Amish people in Wisconsin. The Supreme Court upheld the Amish position. . . . (pp. 372-73)

After a nod of sympathy for the piety and industry of the Amish, [Berns] states, "No doubt the Amish had good reason to believe that it would have been profoundly contrary to their way of life for their children to attend local high schools . . ." and continues with a plea that "Our sympathy for their cause should not . . . blind us to the fact that the *Yoder* decision is a palpable and unprecedented misconstruction of the Constitution, palpable because in this one respect it can be said that Old Order Amish is now an established religion in the United States (insofar as they are exempt from the operation of this law), and unprecedented because this was the first time the Court had held that one's religious convictions entitled one to an exemption from a valid criminal statute."

In one paragraph the author has managed to combine understatement and overstatement in such a neat package as seriously to distort the Amish claim. For to allow as how "the Amish had good reason to believe that it would be profoundly contrary to their way of life" to have their children attend public high schools does scarce justice to their unique problem. . . . Having understated the stakes, Professor Berns goes on, as quoted, to overstate the result: to see in it an "establishment" of, *mirabile dictu*, the Amish religion! . . . This is to turn language on its head, to coin an entirely new meaning for "establishment"; Professor Berns offers no argument for this tortured conclusion. (p. 373)

Though the Supreme Court in *Yoder* relied heavily on *Pierce* [a 1925 case that held it unconstitutional for a state to mandate that all children attend public schools for eight years], . . . Professor Berns gives *Pierce* only passing and insubstantial reference thirty pages later, in a passage dealing with other matters. . . . *Yoder* and *Pierce* may be seen as a Magna Carta for the religious family in its struggle to impart religious values and moral principles in a society increasingly one-dimensionally secular; by Walter Berns' own argument these are vital preconditions of that republican virtue which itself is an essential foundation for a free society; his hostility to *Yoder* and virtual silence about *Pierce* seem especially dissonant when juxtaposed alongside his brilliant passage on the importance of sexual integrity, an aspect of public morality which obscenity damages, for the family. . . . (pp. 373-74)

[Professor Berns] argues that the law "must also deny that religious belief, or 'conscience,' can give rise to a legitimate claim to be exempt from the rule." When pushed to its logical extreme, such a formula would render to Caesar even the things that are God's. . . . (p. 374)

To give Berns his due, the problem he has identified is not an easy one. His subsequent discussion of conscientious objection in the same chapter abundantly illustrates the difficulty and adequately points up how uneasy is the Supreme Court's solution. But to imply that the same kind of laws are at stake in the two areas is to strain analogy. Moreover, the question how "conscientious" the two really are surely must be pertinent. . . . [The] solution is not the absolutist one that the courts must never make the inquiry but rather must always insist that religious conscience conform. As a matter of consistency, too, arguing for an absolutist position ill befits one who elsewhere in the same work argues eloquently that the Court should not be absolute in always protecting "speech," but should rule against "vulgar speech" when it subverts "the public good"— i.e., should weigh competing values.

Finally, while the theory that government is "entitled to interfere" when principles, including religious principles, "break out into overt acts against peace and good order" is generally defensible, one is quite puzzled that words connoting breach-of-the-peace, physical struggle, and possibly even violence are made to describe the conduct of Jonas Yoder. . . . One must conclude that the "peace and good order" [Yoder and his children] violated was not physical; it was metaphysical. . . . For Professor Berns, "Free Exercise" appears to mean what one believes in the privacy of his own heart and, to a modest degree, what one does in formal liturgical ritual for an hour or so in church one day per week. (pp. 374-75)

This is a superb book. Its scholarship is thorough, its writing lucid, its argument stimulating. As in his earlier book and his writings about obscenity and public morality, Walter Berns reminds us of ancient truths now all but forgotten. My disagreement with his reading of *Yoder*, disproportionate in these pages to the treatment of other themes, was due to my conviction that a reviewer should not merely echo the book reviewed but spend considerable time exposing in detail what he sees as fissures in an otherwise imposing edifice. . . .

The First Amendment and the Future of American Democracy is, in my judgment, one of those rare books, like the classics by Mill and Stephen, that deserve a perennial audience. (p. 375)

William A. Stanmeyer, "Walter Berns: Philosopher of the First Amendment," in Modern Age *(copyright © 1977 by the Intercollegiate Studies Institute, Inc.), Vol. 21, No. 4, Fall, 1977, pp. 367-76.*

SAMUEL KRISLOU

In [*The First Amendment and the Future of American Democracy*] Walter Berns argues there is a need for a volume questioning the American expansion of freedom of expression as eloquent or persuasive as one of the half-dozen or so of its major defenses. That need persists.

It is Berns' argument (1) that the Supreme Court no longer follows the Founding Fathers' interpretation of the First Amendment, and (2) that their neologisms sap the very being of the republic. The first argument—which he develops at some painful length—is as surprising as would be an assertion that the Fifth Amendment (which overtly applies to crimes in which the penalty was loss of "life or limb") no longer bears its exact meaning. The second and more significant proposition is, in the main, asserted rather than argued and is virtually unsupported. . . .

By far the best part of the volume is the discussion of freedom of religion. This is a serious, well-reasoned, and even elegant argument. . . .

Berns' effort is to paint the Founders as contemporaneously permissive on doctrine and expression in religion. . . . But the persistence of blasphemy laws, as well as sectarian preference in individual states, shows how little of the modern spirit was infused into the law of the time. Berns concedes an illiberal limit to Christian sects in the Founders' attitudes, but a closer examination of reality will show their practice was so far from the needs of a pluralistic society that legal reconceptualizing was inevitable. Berns' argument about the Founders' view of personal character is historically convincing, but there is nothing in the constitutional text that legitimizes it. . . .

The section on freedom of the press and speech—Berns continuously writes as if they were isomorphic—is confused and meandering. (p. 1400)

Berns makes no effort to explain why the draftsmen of the First Amendment tossed in a new freedom of speech if they meant only to restate common-law rights or what meaning a prohibition on prior restraint could have in conjunction with speech. But he has additional difficulties: the fact is that truth as an absolute defense had persisted as the respected rule in a minority of states even in the early years. (pp. 1400-01)

In any event, Berns must and does acknowledge that the Founders' ideas evolved well past the original intent of the amendment. Apparently they were entitled to a learning experience but no one else is.

The chapter on obscenity further weakens any consistent argument on the nature of constitutional meaning that the book might have. In the absence of discussion by the Founders, Berns draws upon that great interpreter of American society—Rousseau. Even with such heroic borrowings, he can only fulminate against the Supreme Court, and suggests that a principled line can be drawn between trash and literature. But the Burger court, already floundering on just this issue, will not find here the shadow of the ghost of a hint of an idea on how to define such a standard.

The book growls to an end with a diatribe on the evils of modernity and the seductiveness of the trendy. This is supported at its climax—Berns apparently has no sense of incongruity—by a quotation from a column by Max Frankel in the *Times*. Unfortunately, Berns' talents are those of a polemicist or debater and his task calls for sterner stuff. (p. 1401)

> *Samuel Krislou, "Book Reviews: 'The First Amendment and the Future of American Democracy'," in* The American Political Science Review *(copyright, 1978, by The American Political Science Association), Vol. 72, No. 4, December, 1978, pp. 1400-01.*

CHRIS SMITH

[*The First Amendment and the Future of American Democracy*] is a scholarly conservative polemic which calls for a return to the Founding Fathers' interpretations of the First Amendment. . . . If one accepts Berns' frame of reference, parts of his book are interesting, scholarly, legal history. He supports well his thesis that Madison and Jefferson and others interpreted the First Amendment differently than Justices Warren, Black or Douglas. This is not startling, but along the way he has turned over some new facts. . . . [Basically] it seems that

Berns has really a Newtonian view of the Constitution in a world shaped and run by Darwinians. Constitutions change with conditions and like people. Merely as legal history interpreting the Founding Fathers' view of the First Amendment, the book could have been valuable. But to use history as a modern ideological weapon always seems dangerous. His last line reflects his bias; Berns states that the Supreme Court "has allowed itself to be carried about on the wind of modern doctrine." Yet, the Founding Fathers, who Berns reveres so, responded to the winds of their era too. (pp. 58-9)

> *Chris Smith, "On the History and the Present and Future Condition of the American Nation," in* The Social Science Journal *(© copyright 1979 by The Western Social Science Association), Vol. 16, No. 1, January, 1979, pp. 53-64.*

PETER GARDNER

The nub of Walter Berns's argument in *For Capital Punishment: Crime and the Morality of the Death Penalty* . . . is that the awesomeness of the death penalty reflects the horror of murder, and paradoxically, endorses the sanctity of life. In author Berns's words, the death penalty "serves to remind us of the majesty of the moral order"; its purpose is not primarily to deter but to enact justice and assuage the public anger that demands it. (p. 120)

His case is, for the most part, ably argued. However, there are obvious weaknesses. He ducks the surely very strong point, argued by foes of capital punishment, that execution involves "making a godlike judgment with no assurance that it can be made with anything resembling godlike perspicacity," by simply quoting Hugo Adam Bedau, "probably the best known of America's abolitionists," who discounts it. Most important, Berns overlooks the Christian doctrine that justice must be tempered with mercy, and the vital question of how you establish the "majesty" of the moral order in a secular age. (pp. 120, 122)

> *Peter Gardner, "Briefly: 'For Capital Punishment: Crime and the Morality of the Death Penalty'," in* Psychology Today *(copyright © 1979 Ziff-Davis Publishing Company), Vol. 13, No. 1, June, 1979, pp. 120, 122.*

GRAHAM HUGHES

[*For Capital Punishment: Crime and the Morality of the Death Penalty*] is an encomium to the Supreme Court's nodding recognition of retribution as a justification for capital punishment. . . .

Berns seems to have got hold of a few modern ideas about punishment in a muddled way and to have drawn absurd conclusions. The hopes of those who sought rehabilitation have, indeed, been dashed. Deterrence works imperfectly and unpredictably, though it has never been doubted that maintaining the criminal law and a system of punishment has an indispensable deterrent effect. . . . Berns's notion that a better understanding of the aims of punishment ought to include a revival of the death penalty is rather like going back to rubbing two sticks together because we are unhappy about nuclear power. (p. 22)

Righteous anger is certainly a recognizable and healthy emotion. But anger alone is never a good reason for doing anything bad to another person. There must be moral reasons to justify inflicting harm on people and the anger that we feel driving us to do this. Anger is not a justifier but itself needs justification. And if plain anger cannot justify any punishment then passionate anger cannot justify capital punishment. Berns's call for equivalence or even correspondence between the frightfulness of the punishment and the intensity of our anger is rooted in the rawness of the unfiltered psyche rather than in any moral theory of retribution. . . .

To say that a murderer deserves to die may be acceptable in the sense that we might not feel very grieved if he dropped dead. But to impose capital punishment is a moral judgment made in the name of an institution and crucially different from the mere absence of sorrow over a murderer's death.

Society already expresses abhorrence of murder by the process of accusation, trial, conviction, and lengthy if not permanent imprisonment. Why this is not enough for Berns and the many who think, or rather feel, as he does is unclear. In part he seems to rest on a utilitarian prediction (though he tries to pass it off as retributivist) that anything short of the death penalty does not sufficiently appease anger. When squeezed, this rhetoric yields little juice. . . .

At other times Berns appears to argue that some disharmony in the universe created by murder cries out for restoring the balance by the killer's death. This invocation of a mystical sense of blood is certainly impossible to refute. It is equally impossible to make any sense of it, except as a psychic phenomenon. Berns relies heavily on Shakespeare, whose poetic vision, he claims, particularly as expressed in *Macbeth,* validates the need for death to be answered by death. He finds this grander than what he characterizes as the base materialism of that opponent of capital punishment, Camus. That Shakespeare is a greater writer than Camus is then offered with some seriousness by Berns as a clinching argument for capital punishment.

This is absurd, but if literary champions must be put into the list we can point out that *Macbeth* is much more a reflection on guilt than a homily on the death penalty and that the only play Shakespeare wrote that is centrally concerned with capital punishment, *Measure for Measure,* is a study in insecurity, lust, and cruelty dressed in the robes of justice. Indeed, the psychopathology of rage and the vendetta was a dominant theme of the Elizabethan and Jacobean dramatists. Reading Shakespeare, Turner, Middleton, Webster, and Ford can offer only unconfortable instruction for the advocates of execution. But Professor Berns seems to have been as sparing or unperceptive in his literary reading as with his philosophical studies. (p. 23)

Berns, like Kant and many millions of Americans, just thinks eyes and teeth should be exactly exchanged and cares little about deterrence. There are of course those who would oppose the death penalty even if it could be clearly shown to be a substantial additional deterrent because they think it is morally indefensible for the state to kill people. It is not necessary, however, to take so absolute a position in order to condemn the imposition of death sentences in America as immoral and unconstitutional.

Since we are talking about killing people we may properly place the burden of proof on the advocates of the death penalty to furnish some convincing justification. As to general deterrence Berns concedes that they cannot. This leaves the possibility of utilitarian arguments in special situations such as the execution of terrorists. These arguments are speculative at best. . . .

This failure to produce any convincing arguments having to do with social benefit sufficiently collapses the case for capital punishment. But it is doubtful whether any utilitarian case could be compelling enough to outweigh the inequities and discrimination (probably ineradicable) in the imposition of death sentences in the years since *Furman.* The very statutes approved by the Supreme Court are deeply suspect on their face. The Texas law, perhaps the worst of them, allows the death sentence when the jury is satisfied that the killing was deliberate—no more than a basic element of all murders—and that there is a probability that the defendant "would commit criminal acts of violence that would constitute a threat to society."

Prediction of future violence or future harmlessness is in many cases notoriously difficult. It is in fact rare for released murderers to commit another murder, but the Texas statute not only asks the jury for a prediction of violence (rather than murder) but seemingly ignores the state's power to prevent such future acts by incarceration. It is not even clear whether the jury must find that the defendant would be violent if he were immediately released or that he would be violent if he were released from prison in twenty-five years. . . .

If the very standards for imposing the death sentence are vague and inherently unreliable (though approved by the Supreme Court), the actual pattern of sentencing raises further questions of unequal treatment. Since 1972 the percentage of blacks convicted of murder who have been sentenced to death is actually rather less than the percentage of white murderers. But that figure tells us little until we inquire into the race of the victims. (p. 24)

In Texas no whites were sentenced to death for killing blacks in 173 such cases, but death was imposed in 10 percent of the 517 cases of blacks killing whites. . . . The lesson is that if blacks are not disproportionately sentenced to death it is not because America has been gripped by a passion for equality equivalent to Walter Berns's passion for death. It is rather that killing blacks doesn't count. . . .

Professor Berns does not concern himself with such matters. Close arguments and attention to facts are not his forte. Indeed, his very short book has little to offer even about the death penalty other than incantations about purging anger and the majesty of the moral order. He does ramble on, though, about features of the legal system that he supposes are somehow connected with the death penalty. Part of the general moral rot, he tells us, is that judges are reluctant to punish criminals but rather blame society for crime. This makes one wonder if Berns has ever been near a criminal courtroom in his life. Where are these judges? Can he be talking about the ones all criminal lawyers know so well who impose the harshest sentences in the Western world?

Habeas corpus and other post-appeal procedures, according to Berns, endlessly spin out cases and postpone punishment while never showing that a murderer was not guilty. This is nonsense. . . . The purpose [of post-conviction proceedings] is to ensure that the defendant has had or will get a fair trial under the Constitution, and Professor Berns should tell us what he finds wrong with that. Finally, if the proceedings are successful (and this will be infrequent) the result is a new trial for the defendant and not his release. The suggestion that such a careful review of the fairness of a trial should be abandoned in capital cases reveals an indecently avid rush to kill people and would certainly lead, if adopted, to many miscarriages of justice. . . .

Reading Berns's book powerfully evokes righteous anger and moral indignation. His retributivist theory turns out on inspection to consist of either disguised and unconvincing utilitarian propositions or mystical calls for death that deserve psychoanalytic rather than philosophical refutation. It is chilling to be reminded that when the Supreme Court in 1976 made a casual reference to retribution as the ultimate constitutional savior of the death penalty it was to this set of disreputable arguments that it was appealing. There is in truth *no* case for capital punishment and Professor Berns at least does us the service of splendidly demonstrating this. (p. 25)

> *Graham Hughes, "License to Kill," in* The New York Review of Books *(reprinted with permission from* The New York Review of Books; *copyright © 1979 Nyrev, Inc.),* Vol. XXVI, No. 11, June 28, 1979, pp. 22-5.

FRANCIS CANAVAN

[*For Capital Punishment*] offers a calm and reasoned case for inflicting the death penalty for certain crimes. But it is an argument not so much for *capital* punishment as for capital *punishment*. Punishment is a more basic issue than the particular form it takes. . . .

[According to] Berns, the real object of the "abolitionists" is to get rid, not merely of the death penalty, but of the idea of punishment. (p. 1042)

Both rehabilitation and deterrence shift the focus of attention from the crime to the criminal: he is to be either reformed, or prevented by fear from committing crimes in the first place. But he is not to be punished. To inflict a penalty on him because the intrinsic character of his crime *merits* punishment reveals a barbaric desire for revenge unworthy of this enlightened age. (pp. 1042, 1044)

But we must come to believe again that punishment, regularly and predictably inflicted, will in fact deter, and, moreover, that crime deserves to be punished. Retribution is not a barbaric reason for punishing, it is the right reason. For only so can the community affirm the moral order on which it is based and can citizens be satisfied that justice is being done. (p. 1044)

> *Francis Canavan, "The Problem of Punishment," in* National Review *(© National Review, Inc., 1979; 150 East 35th St., New York, NY 10016),* Vol. 31, No. 33, August 17, 1979, pp. 1042, 1044.

STEVEN D. STARK

[One] thing to be said in favor of *For Capital Punishment* is that Berns has written a lucid, textbook-like account of the various arguments for and against the death penalty, as well as a short history of the modern philosophy of punishment. For anyone unfamiliar with the literature or philosophy in this field, Berns's first chapters are a good place to begin.

Having said those things, however, it has to be noted that the principal thesis of Berns's book is an appalling one: that the death penalty ought to be retained for severe crimes because it reaffirms the moral basis of our society. Berns attempts to construct a case for capital punishment primarily on grounds of retribution. . . .

Berns dismisses almost casually other theories to justify punishment, a stance which will not endear him to many who support the death penalty for reasons other than his own. As to the hotly debated question of whether the death penalty actually deters crime, Berns finds the statistical evidence con-

fusing and contradictory. This results in his making a case for the opponents of the death penalty who claim, rightly it would seem, that before anyone is executed, it should be clear that the penalty deters other lawbreakers. He writes scathingly about how the growth of the "permissive" philosophy of rehabilitation has poisoned the correctional system. Yet he ignores the fact that arguments about rehabilitation are essentially meaningless in debates about the death penalty, since in almost all cases the alternative to execution is a life sentence with little chance of parole. (p. 58)

In contrast to Berns, most legal scholars accord retribution only a minor role in any theory of punishment, and some have gone so far as to say that any punishment motivated primarily by retribution violates the Eighth Amendment's "cruel and unusual punishment" clause. These scholars realize that the Bible and Shakespeare were products of other ages and societies; sadly, the present Supreme Court has no such excuse.

What a theory of retribution has to offer a general philosophy of punishment is the idea that only the guilty should be punished and that punishment should be in proportion to the gravity of the offense. . . . [Even] if one accepts fully the dubious Berns view that retribution can be the sole justification for the death penalty, it does not follow that a theory of retribution demands the death penalty. There are retributive elements in a life prison sentence, and Berns never makes an effective argument about why it is necessary for society to express its feelings of moral outrage in the form of executions rather than life sentences. (pp. 58-9)

Berns thus ends up unwittingly making the case against capital punishment. If there is any justification for the death penalty, it must come primarily from a theory of deterrence. The fact that a proponent of the death penalty can find such little support for that theory, coupled with his own inadequate justifications for capital punishment, gives hope that the Supreme Court will someday realize that on this issue, it made a terrible mistake. (p. 59)

> *Steven D. Stark, "The Death Penalty," in* The Progressive *(reprinted by permission from* The Progressive, *409 East Main Street, Madison, Wisconsin 53703; copyright 1979 by The Progressive, Inc.),* Vol. 43, No. 12, December, 1979, pp. 58-9.

HUGO ADAM BEDAU

[In *For Capital Punishment* Walter Berns] probes the weaknesses of the case for abolition and tries to build a solid foundation for retention [of the death penalty]. It must be conceded that he has done the job about as well as it can be done. If there is a moral case for the death penalty, then in all likelihood it is the one set out in this volume. Even so, I do not think that Berns's argument persuades.

First of all, Berns presents an incomplete and highly abstract defense of capital punishment. He favors the death penalty for all traitors, many murderers, and some rapists . . . ; however, he does not condescend to try his hand at formulating a tolerably intelligible set of statutes to effect this purpose. . . . [He is] silent on prosecutorial discretion and gubernatorial clemency; yet these executive and administrative powers are decisive (as law professor Charles L. Black, Jr., has shown) in the actual operation of the death penalty as a functioning penal institution in our society. Berns has no more than a second-hand acquaintance with the voluminous research on the death penalty; he shows no evidence of having supplemented his reading with actual experience in a courtroom or prison. He expresses concern over the possible empirical connection between our racism and the use of the death penalty; but he remains optimistic that—as there is nothing inherently racist (or sexist, or classist) about the idea of capital indictments, convictions, and executions—the future will be free of the biases that have been so prominent in the past. . . . In short, Berns defends the death penalty on what he regards as moral grounds . . . in a manner that excuses him from facing up to very many of the practical questions inseparably connected to it. It is as though he seeks to win converts at the most abstract level of argument, only to become rather impatient with the necessary but boring administrative details, confident that no new grounds or accumulation of doubts at this latter stage will force reopening of the abstract argument itself. It is depressing to think that a large audience may be attracted to this style of reasoning about the moral aspects of a social problem.

The heart of Berns's argument is the belief that punishment is the proper instrument in a just society for retribution upon criminals and that certain heinous crimes deserve death. He is preoccupied throughout with the idea that the chief job of punishment is "to pay them back." . . . Berns's case for the morality of capital punishment stands or falls on the adequacy of this argument. How strong is it?

There are two main objections. One is that Berns relies throughout on a dubious premise. His argument is simply irrelevant to the extent that we do not live in a just, or nearly just, society. The truth is that our world, with its distribution of liberty, opportunity, property, and wealth, is far too unjust (and is so perceived by too many) to allow its defenders the comfort of invoking what amounts to principles of divine retribution. We are not entitled to use punitive methods whose justification rests upon conditions that only a race of moral supermen could hope to satisfy. The second objection (akin to a favorite criticism of [John] Rawls's theory of social justice) is that the premises and assumptions are tailored too arbitrarily and at too many points to yield precisely the desired outcome, so that what passes for argument on behalf of the conclusion is really an endless and elaborate pattern of priming the pump. It is this objection that strikes me as the more forceful here. Berns does not have at his disposal an adequate theory of retributive punishment; instead, he has a cluster of doctrines and principles about desert, severity, righteous indignation, and other concepts that are little more than intuitions. Against Berns's view, it cannot be repeated too often: Retribution as a principle, or set of principles, of punishment does not by itself require *any* particular mode of punishment as a criminal's just deserts, as critics and defenders of retribution from H.L.A. Hart to Andrew von Hirsch have made clear. If you believe otherwise, as Walter Berns does, then you risk embracing a version of *lex talionis* that will give you nightmares in the effort to be consistent and convincing. . . . Either way, a tolerably intelligent pattern of death statutes, indictments, convictions, sentences, and executions cannot be defended by appeal to retributive considerations alone.

On major empirical questions relating to the use of capital punishment, Berns is not a wholly reliable guide. He is altogether too impressed by Isaac Ehrlich's pioneering research, in which it was purportedly shown that actual executions achieve a murder-deterring effect. Subsequent studies by a dozen other equally skillful econometricians have failed to vindicate Ehrlich's results; Berns knows this and mentions it but is unimpressed. (pp. 450-52)

On the question of the racial impact of post-*Furman* death sentences, Berns misleads the reader. The one relevant study he cites . . . is not accurately reported and interpreted, and he seems unaware of the results of research by William Bowers published during the past few years to the effect that the race of the victim does matter: Killers of whites in Florida, Georgia, and Texas are very likely to get the death sentence, killers of blacks unlikely. . . . Berns observes that "the future of capital punishment in America will probably depend on whether it can be imposed witout regard to race and class, on white as well as black, on rich as well as poor." . . . Why he regards the future as an open question, given the current evidence, is beyond me.

In the course of his predominantly sane and tempered argument, Berns occasionally descends into regrettable exaggeration. Our rotten penal system, he claims, is "in large part the result of an attempt to avoid punishing criminals and, above all, to avoid executing them." . . . That is about as illuminating as arguing that the miseries of the aged and poor are in large part the result of current welfare programs and our refusal to practice euthanasia. Abolitionists want us, he says, to "ignore the butchery of the crimes murderers commit." . . . Berns and other retentionists presumably want us to ignore the butchery that the executioner inflicts. In either case, how to remedy or prevent more of this deadly butchery thoroughly eludes Berns just as it does his opponents. The death penalty, he believes, teaches us "the awesomeness of the commandment, Thou shalt not kill." . . . The implication, for which no evidence is given, that this lesson cannot be learned as well or at all in any other way, is armchair moral pedagogy at its worst. It is also one more instance of the moral intuitionism on which Berns relies in his argument throughout this volume. (p. 452)

Hugo Adam Bedau, "Book Reviews: 'For Capital Punishment: Crime and the Morality of the Death Penalty'," in Ethics *(reprinted by permission of The University of Chicago Press), Vol. 90, No. 3, April, 1980, pp. 450-52.*

ERNEST van den HAAG

Walter Berns fairly compiles pros and cons in this elegantly written essay [**For Capital Punishment**]. . . . I, too, am for capital punishment. But I find Berns' compilation careless and too often confused. I shall proceed synecdochically, and from minor to major objections. . . .

(1) If execution is threatened for rape, rapists are invited to murder their victim-witnesses without fear of additional punishment. (p. 470)

(2) Berns writes, "Except in the case of organic disease of the brain, there is no scientific basis for the use of the term mental illness" . . . , but also: "[some] men . . . because they are insane are not responsible for their acts". . . . Either insanity is coextensive with "organic disease of the brain," to Berns, or he is inconsistent. . . .

(3) Berns pads his account with unrelated matter, and misconstrues it. Thus Shakespeare's Macbeth is discussed . . . as though the subject were punishment rather than murder and guilt.

(4) Berns' references are erudite but erratic. His deontological argument is simplified Kant—yet that philosopher is not given the credit. His antagonist is Bentham—but he focuses on Beccaria, a comparative lightweight. . . .

(5) For Berns the death penalty need only be deserved as retribution; it need not have utilitarian benefits. But he often confuses matters by presenting actually utilitarian arguments as though arguments for a "just deserts" theory. Thus, if the death penalty is needed, as Berns asserts throughout, to express communal anger, to denounce the crime and blame the criminal, to "reward" and make the law-abiding "happy," . . . to teach respect for law and uphold its "dignity," it is a means to these crime-reducing (utilitarian) purposes. However, if the death penalty is a moral necessity, a categorical requirement of justice, as Berns believes, the mixed bag of unrecognized utilitarian arguments which he offers is irrelevant to its justification. Thus a crime may well justify anger springing from injured moral feeling. But it is hard to see how this anger in turn makes any punishment just or moral. Anger—whatever its basis—explains or motivates, but does not justify or constitute an argument for legal action, unless it be on the utilitarian ground that the anger must be legally discharged to avoid illegal action. . . .

(6) "Deterrence," Berns claims, "is incompatible with the principle of just deserts". . . . But the latter wants to "pay back" for a past act, whereas deterrence wants to prevent future acts. The principles deal with different subjects and therefore are compatible, actually even complementary. They may lead to different punishments, but Berns himself admits that they need not. . . .

(7) Following Kant, Berns regards the death penalty not as a (necessary) evil which must be offset by the good effects it produces, but as a positive good *per se* which need not be. Murderers are to be executed because they deserve to be. I cannot see how desert here is anything more than a feeling disguised as an argument. Perhaps an argument is not needed to justify acting on this feeling. Perhaps there is no argument. At any rate, I share the feeling but balk at the disguise.

Criminologists distinguish "instrumental" from "expressive crimes." Berns seems to suggest *expressive punishment* (as I would call it). I do not object—but can the expressive function of punishment be a better argument for punishment than the expressive function of a crime is for crime?

Berns could not be expected to solve the basic problems of deontological retributionism which have puzzled political philosophers for centuries. But he could have met them. Rhetoric—conservative or liberal—is of no help. (p. 471)

Ernest van den Haag, "Book Reviews: 'For Capital Punishment: Crime and the Morality of the Death Penalty'," in The American Political Science Review *(copyright, 1980, by The American Political Science Association), Vol. 74, No. 2, June, 1980, pp. 470-71.*

John W(esley) Blassingame

1940-

Blassingame is an American professor of history and chairman of Afro-American History at Yale University. In *The Slave Community* (1972) he refutes Stanley Elkins's contention in *Slavery* that the institution of slavery can be likened to a concentration camp, whose "total" character reduced slaves to a Sambo stereotype. Blassingame uses a variety of sources, including the autobiographies of former slaves, to demonstrate that black people had many different personality types. What distinguishes Blassingame from other historians of the antebellum South is his respect for the testimony of slaves. His *Black New Orleans: 1860-1880* (1973) has contributed to the ongoing re-evaluation of historical theories about slavery and Reconstruction. (See also *Contemporary Authors*, Vols. 49-52.)

Excerpt from BLACK NEW ORLEANS: 1860-1880

In the hope of developing some new insights about the [Reconstruction] period, I have chosen to examine those areas of life—education, family, religion, social and economic activities—which were of more immediate concern to blacks than politics.

At the end of the Reconstruction era the balance sheet for the Negro in New Orleans showed a bewildering set of debits and credits. While there was some contrast between the position of the Negro in 1860 and in 1880, the differences were often more apparent than real. The most important similarity of the two periods was the relative political powerlessness of the blacks. In spite of this, the Civil War and Reconstruction brought about significant changes in the Negro community in New Orleans. (p. xv)

Although the life of the New Orleans Negro was similar in some ways to that of blacks in other Southern cities, in many respects the city's Negro community was sui generis. It is obvious, for instance, that Negroes in New Orleans were far more articulate, literate, and cosmopolitan than blacks in most other Southern cities. . . . In no Southern city did Negro leaders express their racial, social, and economic philosophies more clearly or on a more sophisticated level than in New Orleans. Similarly, the diversity and size of Negro-owned businesses and the occupational structure of Negroes in New Orleans was not duplicated in other Southern cities. . . . Furthermore, there was undoubtedly more intimacy between the races in New Orleans than in most Southern cities, because Louisiana was one of the few Southern states which, only a decade after the Civil War, permitted interracial marriages, and which outlawed segregation in schools and places of public accommodations.

The importance of the findings in this study is that they provide a standard by which scholars can compare Negro life in other Southern cities. While the truly unique features of the Negro community in the Crescent City can be explained largely by its location in the most "non-American" of American cities, the group's uniqueness does not destroy the possibility of studying the features which the Negro population in New Orleans had in common with blacks in other Southern communities. This study may help to suggest some of the general patterns

Courtesy of John W. Blassingame

of the economic and social life of Negroes in Southern cities during Reconstruction. (p. xvi)

Negro social life in New Orleans was varied, rich, and in many ways a reflection of activities in the white community. This social life united the black community while at the same time accentuating class divisions. The class structure was not, however, so rigid as to preclude concerted community campaigns to eradicate such pressing social problems as the high crime and mortality rates among blacks. In spite of the oppressive conditions under which they lived, New Orleans Negroes created several impressive cultural forms and engaged in a wide variety of social activities. (p. 139)

The most important cause of social division in the Negro community was cultural differences. This area, as with wealth, education, and occupations, was to a degree linked with color and previous condition. The free mulatto was French in thought, language, and culture while the black freedman was English-speaking and Afro-American in culture. This distinction was mentioned in the newspapers more often than any other factor as a cause of class-division in the Negro community. (p. 155)

The relatively small number of wealthy Negroes, the widespread poverty and ignorance, and the discrimination in public services made it impossible for Negroes to eradicate all of the social problems facing the community. Yet they made a strenuous effort to support black orphans and to provide mutual aid in time of sickness and death. Finding sustenance for their spirit in their churches, Negroes drew upon their African and European heritage to create the spirituals and jazz, and engaged in several different kinds of social activities which helped to unite the black community. (p. 171)

Nothing is more indicative of the strange twists and turns which the color line took in New Orleans than the sexual intimacy between whites and blacks. In this area, as in many others, Latin practices belied Anglo-Saxon ideology. This is not to say, of course, that there was no painful discrimination against Negroes in public institutions and social relations. As a matter of fact, this was the customary pattern.

Most places of public resort at least occasionally served Negroes along with other customers without distinction. And, in spite of the reticence of some Negroes, the implacable resistance of some whites, the lax enforcement of some provisions of the laws, and the numerous instances of discrimination, there was undoubtedly more integration of places of public resort in New Orleans than in any other southern city (and some northern ones) during Reconstruction. This came about primarily because of several conditions: blacks had enough political power to pass and, on occasion, to enforce civil rights laws; enough of them were wealthy enough to sue businesses which discriminated against them; some whites overcame their prejudices; and Negroes used their sophisticated (almost modern) knowledge of history, logic, government, economics, and psychology to build up their own racial pride and to struggle against the degrading effects of racism and prejudice.

In New Orleans, as perhaps in no other American city, there were many cracks in the color line. Negroes frequently interacted on terms of perfect equality with whites in public institutions and in social relations. Jim Crow did not erect a monolithic barrier between the races; instead, race relations in the city presented a very complex and varied pattern of complete, partial, or occasional integration and intimacy in several areas. (pp. 209-10)

In the political area, blacks gained relatively few lasting benefits from Reconstruction. Even so, the role of blacks in New Orleans politics was distinctive in many ways. (p. 211)

Blacks were far more successful in the economic than in the political realm. Negroes in New Orleans often used the skills they had developed in the antebellum period to compete successfully against whites. The most important source of skilled labor during this period was the old free Negro class. While Negroes were prepared to compete against whites in many trades, antebellum proscriptions prevented them from developing the business acumen and accumulating the capital necessary for large-scale economic enterprises. This is clear when the complex occupational structure of blacks is compared with the small number of different kinds of businesses owned by Negroes and the relatively small amount of wealth they possessed. Again, the free Negroes, as a result of legacies from their white fathers, led in this area. Still, most Negro businesses were short-lived, small, one-owner concerns. They were strongest in those areas requiring the smallest amount of capital investment and the least cooperation from whites, particularly in those areas largely monopolized by Negroes before the war. (pp. 214-15)

The positive changes which occurred in black family life were even more encouraging than black economic successes. Although slavery had almost completely destroyed the patriarchal Negro family, it had also bequeathed some positive things to the black community. In the first place, slavery was unique among closed institutions because it permitted its members some form of family life. The form that emerged in Louisiana was the monogamous family. Since the sex ratio among slaves was balanced in Louisiana (unlike Latin America), the monogamous family became the cultural norm for Negroes during the antebellum period. Unfortunately, some of the most hellish practices of slavery were also concentrated on the family. As a result of the high rate of slave mortality and the arbitrary rule of the planters, the slave family was the most unstable institution in America. In all probability, less than 20 percent of the slave families were intact when bondage ended. (pp. 215-16)

The long, persistent campaign of Negro ministers, teachers, and editors, and of white missionaries, army officers, and Freedmen's Bureau agents, coupled with the desire of the former slaves for more stable family relations, led to a remarkable adaptation of Negroes in New Orleans to American mores regarding the family. By 1880 the Negro family had become a strong, stable institution dominated by males. As long as Negroes were able to escape from the socially disorganized central city, the family was stable. The most important contributor to family instability was the differential in the mortality rates of Negro males and females. (p. 216)

[Antebellum] patterns in race relations and the increased political power of blacks led to an almost unbelievably complex pattern in relations between the races in New Orleans during Reconstruction. While segregation was the norm, there was some integration in places of public accommodations, transportation, and social relations. Integrated schools, large-scale miscegenation, and integrated housing patterns existed at the same time that many institutions were segregated. In spite of the rhetoric of whites, there was a significant amount of integration. In spite of the rhetoric of blacks, however, segregation was the customary pattern in most areas of their lives. Two vastly different racial ideologies (with blacks insisting on equality of treatment and whites on total segregation), a large Catholic population of Latin origin, and the political power of blacks laid the foundation in New Orleans for Jim Crow's strangest career in nineteenth-century America. (p. 217)

> *John W. Blassingame, in his* Black New Orleans:
> 1860-1880 *(reprinted by permission of The University of Chicago Press), University of Chicago Press,*
> *1973, 301 p.*

CARL N. DEGLER

The slave autobiography is a rich genre containing scores of items, but historians have been loath to use them extensively because most were written to influence public opinion during the antislavery crusade and some were written completely by or with the help of antislavery whites. In the last ten years several scholars have tried to use these sources but none of them has produced a work equal in scope, imagination, judiciousness, and vigorous writing to [*The Slave Community*]. . . . It comes closer than any previous study to answering the question: "What was it like to be a slave?"

John Blassingame forthrightly confronts the objections leveled against the extensive use of slave narratives. (He uses 76 slave narratives supplemented with many other sources from whites and blacks, from North and South.) As he points out, all historians use personal and biased sources; the slave autobiographies can be analyzed and compensated for just as others are. The same applies to those who assert that slave writings are unrepresentative. Indeed, as Blassingame's book makes evident, slave autobiographies vary greatly in their portrayal of slavery, just as all usable historical sources do.

Not merely another description of the operation and nature of the slave-plantation system, *The Slave Community* provides the fullest, most balanced view of slavery from the standpoint of the slave that is to be found anywhere in the enormous corpus of historical writing on the South's "peculiar institution." Slavery comes across here not just as a cruel labor system—though it certainly was that—but also as a human institution in which blacks lived and dealt with each other as well as with whites. Blassingame sensitively portrays slave culture and life as well as the relations between slaves and their masters. His chapter on slave personalities shows that the average slave was no more a Sambo (as Stanley Elkins contended some years ago in an influential book [*Slavery*]) than he was a Nat Turner, and the typical master neither a Simon Legree nor a Robert E. Lee.

When slavery is seen from the inside in this way, it bears little resemblance to the Nazi concentration camps to which Elkins compared it. Blassingame also denies Elkins's assertion that slavery was destructive of the slave family, and he provides new evidence from the records of several thousand slave couples compiled by the Freedmen's Bureau during the Civil War. They show that more marriages were disrupted by death than by masters. In short, in Blassingame's reading, the slave family, rather than being nonexistent, was a main factor in black survival under slavery. . . .

Excellent as this book is in restoring balance and understanding to a complex and emotional subject, it is not without weaknesses. Chapter seven, for example, has a long excursion into modern psychological studies of personality, but these theoretical insights are not integrated with the historical materials in any helpful way. Sometimes, too, the author fails to exploit his sources fully. . . . Finally, in trying to counter the view that the slaves were docile, he overemphasizes the amount of overt resistance to the system, for as he recognizes in the end, the vast majority of slaves neither ran away nor rebelled. But then those two extreme forms of hostility toward slavery were everywhere and always much too dangerous to be accurate measures of the slave's true dissatisfaction with his bondage.

To write with understanding and objectivity about an institution like slavery taxes the skills of the historian as do few other subjects. No one has done the job more successfully, imaginatively and courageously than Blassingame.

> *Carl N. Degler, "What It Was Like To Be a Slave,"* in Book World—The Washington Post (*copyright ©* 1972 The Washington Post Company), October 15, 1972, p. 6.

THE ECONOMIST

To the liberal historians of American Negro slavery (ie, almost all) the "peculiar institution" presents a paradox and a problem. How can one account for its essential barbarism and at the same time for the seeming acquiescence in it of its victims?

Slave revolts were relatively few and totally unsuccessful; the slave population actually multiplied in captivity. . . .

[In "The Slave Community"] Mr Blassingame has mounted a counterattack on the Elkins thesis. This he has been able to do by concentrating to a greater degree than previous slavery historians on the slaves in their relations with each other—their roots, their culture, their family life and their religion. . . .

The central contention of the book is that the African black retained throughout and despite slavery an individual, if not a collective, identity. African influences persist, despite the shock and disintegrative effects of enslavement and migration. The institution, for all its brutality, is not really "total". It leaves the slave an area of private life and even leisure, in which the Negro family, the folk tale, the dance, the spiritual, and the practice of religion nurture a sense of identity and independence. The knowledge of and lust after freedom are kept alive. This implies, of course, a less harsh view of the realities of plantation life than many have accepted, even to a recognition, which Mr Blassingame puts forward with proper liberal modesty, of the fact that the white Southerner's religion was a moderating influence on his behaviour as a slaveowner. (He might have done more to bring out how the Southerner's sloth and inefficiency also made him a poor SS guard.) All this is shown with wide learning and good sense, plus a parade of psychological theory which serious historians can skip.

There remain problems. Mr Blassingame's reassessment still leaves partly unexplained a docility which failed to erupt into a slave insurrection even at the height of the civil war. His emphasis on indigenous Negro culture glosses over the extent to which white elements, conspicuously white religion, were absorbed into the slave's personality. His reliance on autobiographical material, though he defends it ably, necessarily entails certain limitations. Despite all this, his book is a healthy adjustment of perspective, a cool corrective of too readily accepted myths and a useful contribution to a historical debate which has a lot of vitality in it for some time to come. (p. 91)

> *"Plantation Man," in* The Economist (© *The Economist Newspaper Limited, 1973), Vol. 246, No. 6753, January 27, 1973, pp. 90-1.**

THE TIMES LITERARY SUPPLEMENT

The Slave Community: Plantation Life in the Antebellum South is to be welcomed, and its major conclusions may be endorsed. But it is also fragmentary and uneven and shows many signs of hasty compilation. It is perhaps best to be regarded as an interim report. Most if not all of Professor Blassingame's contentions have been reached by other commentators in recent years, and work on all of the subjects treated so briefly here is still proceeding. Again, more than he cares to admit, he is concerned to demolish the "Sambo" stereotype of the loyal, lazy, affectionate and child-like slave described by Professor Elkins. Yet few students of American slavery have accepted this stereotype without serious reservations.

What, then, is important in this study? Professor Blassingame asserts firmly at the outset: "The inescapable conclusion which emerges from an examination of several different types of sources is that there were many slave personality types. Sambo was one of them . . . it was not the dominant slave personality." . . .

Professor Blassingame's treatment of slave resistance and rebellion, based largely on Herbert Aptheker's pioneering though methodologically unsound work, adds little to present knowledge of the subject. . . .

Similarly, Professor Blassingame's reflections on role-playing among slaves, the purposes served by a seeming conformity to White expectations and the ways in which these expectations conflicted with White fears of the Negro, while they are sound, are hardly original. . . .

A summary of the literature on "total institutions"—armies, prisons and concentration camps—included in an appendix, is a further indication of Professor Blassingame's preoccupation with the implications and possibilities of Professor Elkins's analogy. . . .

The Slave Community raised expectations which are only partially realized. Professor Blassingame's slaves are certainly participants rather than ciphers in the multi-dimensional relationship between master and slave. A more careful, closely reasoned and extended analysis of Black responses to enslavement will, however, have to await the outcome of more sustained academic labours in the still fertile field of American Negro slavery.

> *"The Slave As Subject," in* The Times Literary Supplement *(© Times Newspapers Ltd. (London) 1973; reproduced from* The Times Literary Supplement *by permission), No. 3704, March 2, 1973, p. 230.*

GERALD W. MULLIN

Blassingame's [*The Slave Community*] is flawed by a narrow use of sources and a fascination with the plantation-concentration camp analogy and Sambo stereotype. His prose, images, and arguments reverberate with the sounds of battle against Stanley Elkins's beleaguered model. Distracted by this struggle, he allows the real issues to fall stillborn on the page in a series of unexamined generalizations: "it is not at all clear that there was a close relationship between docility and rebelliousness among slaves and their tribal origin" . . . ; "Christian forms were so similar to African religious patterns that it was relatively easy for the early slaves to incorporate them with their traditional practices and beliefs" . . . ; and "the mandatory requirements of the master—labor and obedience—were familiar to the Africans at least in the form of their former occupations and the obeisance they paid to chiefs and elders." . . .

These important and controversial statements are unsupported by systematic argument and thorough documentation. Historians of colonial New England towns (who ought to furnish the models for the next generation of studies of slavery) call this kind of history "impressionistic" and insist on the usefulness of inferring behavior and motives from what people did as well as from what they said. But *The Slave Community* has not profited from the imaginative reconstructions of the lives and societies of Plymouth, Dedham, and Andover. (p. 514)

Occasionally Blassingame argues eloquently and persuasively, particularly when he uses nonnarrative sources quantitatively (Virginia divorce petitions for the incidence of miscegenation and marriage certificates of freedmen on the extent to which owners broke up slave families). But after presenting new insights (on black family life, "mammies," conjurers, and praisehouses) to argue that slaves had lives and personalities of their own, he abruptly turns around and writes that the slave "had to be a lifelong student of the white man's moods, ideas, and actions and then conduct himself according to the changes in the white man's behavior." . . . In the end he leaves the sources of black community to talk of "guards," "bureaucrats," and closed institutions (images and concepts so out of place in the ante-bellum South), and embraces the ubiquitous Elkins wholeheartedly: "Differences in severity of treatment affected behavior on the plantation in the same way that they determined the degree of docility and infantilism in prisons, armies, and concentration camps"; "on plantations where masters and overseers were almost as morally insensitive, cruel, and sadistic as the guards in the German concentration camps, many of the slaves became docile, submissive, and Sambo-like." . . . But these opinions are not based on plantation records nor are they informed by seminal interpretations (since Elkins's in 1959) of precisely the issues with which Blassingame is concerned. . . . (p. 515)

A fundamental problem in *The Slave Community* is the uncritical use of evidence. In their own way the writers of slave narratives were elitist. Most were house servants or artisans, and "the favorites of their masters, who, in a number of cases, were their fathers." . . . But assimilation (which Blassingame recognizes in his more cogent passages) was not the only way slaves protected their culture and personalities. Viewing Nat Turner's rebellion as a revitalization movement, in the tradition of the black millenarians who emerged in the Charleston District and sea islands during the revivals of the mid-eighteenth century, helps correct the black autobiographers' assimilationist biases and their sometimes quaint and superficial views of the slave quarter and of religion—the most authentic and reliable expression of Afro-American culture.

Ignoring the indispensable variables for explaining slave community—terrain, demography, work, the extent of urbanization and planter absenteeism, and, most important, regional differences in crops and stages of development, Blassingame reduces slave behavior and culture to a question of roles and psychological characteristics. (pp. 515-16)

> *Gerald W. Mullin, "Reviews of Books: 'The Slave Community: Plantation Life in the Antebellum South',"* in William and Mary Quarterly *(copyright, 1973, by the Institute of Early American History and Culture), Third Series, Vol. XXX, No. 3, July, 1973, pp. 513-16.*

EARL E. THORPE

[Blassingame states that in *Black New Orleans, 1860-1880*] he "describes and analyzes the economic and social life" of blacks in New Orleans during the Reconstruction era, and that he "largely ignores the old and often-studied debate over politics." . . . His focus is mainly on "education, family, religion, social and economic activities—which were of more immediate concern to blacks than politics." There is a political conclusion, however, which is that the basic similarity in the condition of blacks before 1860 and in 1880 was their relative political powerlessness." . . . Although Professor Blassingame's study is not essentially political in orientation, he is rather persistently aware of the impact on black life of racism, exploitation, and oppression. . . .

In his effort to stress uniqueness in New Orleans the author occasionally appears to forget the extent to which the city fundamentally was Southern and American. (p. 138)

Although reliance on black newspapers is prominent in *Black New Orleans,* at times the sources used are too much those of white observers. . . . Chapter I, "The Negro in Antebellum

New Orleans,'' is an effort to cover more than two centuries of history in twenty-two pages. Chapter 2, ''Fighting for Freedom,'' although sketchy, makes the interesting point that, while some free Negroes early were pro-Confederacy, most blacks were enthusiastically involved in a civil war which had their freedom as a central concern. Chapter 3, ''Land, Labor, and Capital,'' treats mainly the labor system imposed by the army of occupation, a system which was often despised by blacks, and the economic activities of the city's black bourgeoisie during the Reconstruction era. Although some interesting statistics are presented in Chapter 4, ''Family Life,'' there is too much effort to resolve the debate over images of the black family which are found in the writings of such scholars as E. Franklin Frazier, Daniel P. Moynihan, and Andrew Billingsley. Chapter 5, ''Schools, Colleges and Intellectual Life,'' and Chapter 6, ''Social Life and Problems,'' are two of the strongest chapters in the book. Especially noteworthy is the information on the contributions and problems of Leland, Straight, and New Orleans universities. (pp. 138-39)

Doubtless some younger black readers will resent the frequent use of the word ''Negro,'' and some of the generalizations cannot be sustained by recent scholarship. . . . At times the author places too much of the blame for the lack of much postbellum progress by blacks on defects within the freedmen rather than mainly on the continued domination by their former owners. Still, this volume has many merits and is likely to be the best book on the subject for a long time. (p. 139)

> *Earl E. Thorpe, ''Book Reviews: 'Black New Orleans: 1860-1880','' in* South Atlantic Quarterly *(reprinted by permission of the Publisher; copyright 1975 by Duke University Press, Durham, North Carolina), Vol. 74, No. 1, Winter, 1975, pp. 138-39.*

MARION KILSON

[In *Black New Orleans, 1860-1880*] Blassingame presents a richly detailed and balanced descriptive analysis of institutional development within the rapidly growing black community of Reconstruction New Orleans. Drawing extensively upon census materials and contemporary newspaper accounts, Blassingame documents the economic roles and problems of the black community, the stabilization of black families, the growth of educational institutions, and the voluntary associational life of a community in which class differentiations correlated with cultural differences symbolized through the use of French or English. . . .

[Blassingame's book contributes] to a more complex appreciation of Afro-American society. (p. 300)

> *Marion Kilson, ''Reviews: 'Black New Orleans: 1860-1880','' in* The Journal of Interdisciplinary History *(copyright © 1975, by the Massachusetts Institute of*

> *Technology and the editors of* The Journal of Interdisciplinary History*), Vol. VI, No. 2, Autumn, 1975, pp. 299-300.*

GARY B. MILLS

Revision of *The Slave Community,* according to its new preface, was necessitated by George Bentley, a conservative, proslavery, slave pastor of a white congregation in Tennessee, whom Blassingame terms ''a mystery wrapped in an enigma.'' . . . In truth, the history of southern slavery is underlaid with inexplicable situations and individuals—black bondsmen who were property owners, petite capitalists, even slaveowners themselves. The discovery of each will continue to raise questions of how and why such existed, and Blassingame's willingness to reappraise his work in light of one man of this genre sets a commendable example.

Yet, the character of Bentley is not inconsistent with Blassingame's views in either the first or the second edition. In both, the typical bondsman emerges as a bridge between the stereotypes of Sambo and Nat, and the slave institution fluctuates between the extremes of oppression and leniency. Such a position leaves considerable room for individual enterprise such as Bentley represents.

Blassingame's revision has not changed his basic interpretations. New information reinforces some points but does not appear as diatribes against critics, as a defense, or as an apology. Specifically, the second edition includes [among other additions] . . . one new chapter (''The Americanization of the Slave and the Africanization of the South'') in which Blassingame draws parallels between southern slaves and European slaves of Arabs, Turks, and West Africans, compares the role of southern churches with those of Latin America, and examines the interaction of the races in the South.

However interesting, the additions are likely to raise new points of debate. Blassingame's discussion of southern churches as the primary agent of acculturation is confined to Protestantism. Even the comparatively small Quaker population of the South is discussed, but no mention appears of the numerous southern Catholics—despite the fact that all southern religious expressions are compared therein to the Catholic church of Latin America. (pp. 113-14)

All controversy and revision aside, *The Slave Community* remains a significant book, and the author's position that the bulk of both slaves and slaveowners lay between the stereotyped extremes should prove durable. (p. 114)

> *Gary B. Mills, ''Book Reviews: 'The Slave Community: Plantation Life in the Antebellum South','' in* The Journal of Southern History *(copyright © 1981 by the Southern Historical Association), Vol. XLVII, No. 1, February, 1981, pp. 113-14.*

Murray Bookchin

1921-

One of America's leading anarchist thinkers, Bookchin writes on politics and ecology. In *Post-Scarcity Anarchism* (1971) he argues that the "liberatory" potential of modern technology makes possible a revolution of material abundance, social renewal, and ecological harmony. Critical opinion about this work has varied: some reviewers dismiss Bookchin as a utopian dreamer, others praise the richness of his social vision. He published two early books on ecology, *Our Synthetic Environment* (1962) and *Crisis in Our Cities* (1965), under the pseudonym of Lewis Herber. One of his recent books is *The Spanish Anarchists: The Heroic Years, 1868-1936* (1977), a study of the anarchist movement in Spain prior to the Spanish Revolution/ Civil War period. Bookchin is professor of urban sociology at Ramapo College of New Jersey and has served as director of the Institute for Social Ecology at Goddard College. (See also *Contemporary Authors*, Vols. 1-4, rev. ed., under the pseudonym of Lewis Herber; and *Contemporary Authors New Revision Series*, Vol. 1.)

Courtesy of Murray Bookchin

Excerpt from *POST-SCARCITY ANARCHISM*

We normally live completely immersed in the present—to such a degree, in fact, that we often fail to see how much our own social period differs from the past—indeed from a mere generation ago. This captivity to the contemporary can be very insidious. It may shackle us unknowingly to the most reactionary aspects of tradition, be they obsolete values and ideologies, hierarchical forms of organization, or one-sided modes of political behavior. Unless our roots in contemporary life are broadened by a rich perspective, they may easily distort our understanding of the world as it really is, as well as its rich potentialities for the future.

For the world is changing profoundly, more profoundly than many of us seem to recognize. Until very recently, human society developed around the brute issues posed by unavoidable material scarcity and their subjective counterpart in denial, renunciation and guilt. The great historic splits that destroyed early organic societies, dividing man from nature and man from man, had their origins in the problems of survival, in problems that involved the mere maintenance of human existence. Material scarcity provided the historic rationale for the development of the patriarchal family, private property, class domination and the state; it nourished the great divisions in hierarchical society that pitted town against country, mind against sensuousness, work against play, individual against society, and, finally, the individual against himself.

Whether this long and tortuous development could have followed a different, more benign, course is now irrelevant. The development is largely behind us. Perhaps like the mythic apple, which, once bitten, had to be consumed completely, hierarchical society had to complete its own bloody journey before its demonic institutions could be exorcised. Be that as it may, our position in that historic drama differs fundamentally from that of anyone in the past. We of the twentieth century are literally the heirs of human history, the legatees of man's age-old effort to free himself from drudgery and material in-

security. For the first time in the long succession of centuries, this century—and this one alone—has elevated mankind to an entirely new level of technological achievement and to an entirely new vision of the human experience.

We of this century have finally opened the prospect of material abundance for all to enjoy—a sufficiency in the means of life without the need for grinding, day-to-day toil. We have discovered resources, both for man and industry, that were totally unknown a generation ago. We have devised machines that automatically make machines. We have perfected devices that can execute onerous tasks more effectively than the strongest human muscles, that can surpass the industrial skills of the deftest human hands, that can calculate with greater rapidity and precision than the most gifted human minds. Supported by this qualitatively new technology, we can begin to provide food, shelter, garments, and a broad spectrum of luxuries without devouring the precious time of humanity and without dissipating its invaluable reservoir of creative energy in mindless labor. In short, for the first time in history we stand on the threshold of a post-scarcity society. (pp. 9, 10)

In attempting to uphold scarcity, toil, poverty and subjugation against the growing potential for post-scarcity, leisure, abundance and freedom, capitalism increasingly emerges as the most irrational, indeed the most artificial, society in history. The society now takes on the appearance of a totally *alien* (as well as alienating) force. It emerges as the "other," so to speak, of humanity's deepest desires and impulses. On an ever-greater scale, potentiality begins to determine and shape one's everyday view of actuality, until a point is reached where everything about the society—including its most "attractive" amenities—seems totally insane, the result of a massive social lunacy. (p. 15)

Today, as we stand at the end of hierarchical society's development, its negative and positive aspects can no longer be reconciled. Not only do they stand opposed to each other irreconcilably, they stand opposed to each other as mutually exclusive wholes. All the institutions and values of hierarchical society have exhausted their "historically necessary" functions. No longer is there any social rationale for property and classes, for monogamy and patriarchy, for hierarchy and authority, for bureaucracy and the state. These institutions and values, together with the city, the school and the instrumentalities of privilege, have reached their historical limits. In contrast to Marx, we would have little quarrel with Bakunin's view that the institutions and values of hierarchical society were *always* a "historically necessary evil." If Bakunin's verdict seems to enjoy a moral superiority over Marx's today, this is because the institutions have finally lost their moral authority. (pp. 17-18)

Murray Bookchin, in his Post-Scarcity Anarchism *(copyright © 1971 by Murray Bookchin), The Ramparts Press, 1971, 288 p.*

WILLIAM VOGT

Mr. Herber ranges far more widely [in *Our Synthetic Environment* than Rachel Carson in *Silent Spring*] and discusses not only herbicides and insecticides, but also nutrition, chemical fertilizers (he is no organic gardener), soil structure, food additives, stresses that result from over-urbanization, our physical deterioration from excessive dependence on machines, and other side effects of civilization.

Both authors approach their subjects from a basically ecological point of view though neither . . . follows through to completely logical—or ecological—conclusions. (p. 3)

That both [Miss Carson] and Mr. Herber have written powerful indictments of those who would short-circuit ecological processes is incontestable. (p. 4)

Both authors raise issues in such a way that they can scarcely be ignored, particularly by technicians of the regulatory bodies. They (especially Mr. Herber) are sharply critical of the Food and Drug Administration, which has long—with justification—pleaded lack of funds and staff; Miss Carson castigates the U.S. Department of Agriculture for what can only be called irresponsible broadcasting of poisons. The U.S. Public Health Service, which for decades has dragged its feet on water pollution, gets off too easily. Neither writer points out that the Secretary of Agriculture is *directed,* by laws passed before the development of the new and diabolic poisons, to "control" and "eradicate" insect pests—which throws the problem right

back into the lap of the Congress. Or, to put it another way, to you and to me.

Neither author quite achieves an ecological approach by viewing these problems as a dynamic structure of dependent variables in which our economy is embedded. Could we feed 186 million "guinea pigs" without these poisons (our pestiferous "surpluses" amount to only about 5 per cent) and shall we be able to feed 350 million in the year 1999? What part do such substances play in trying to feed three billion world-wide, adding about another billion each decade? What would the control or abolition of such materials, on our approximately four million farms, do to their capital and labor input, to their social structure, and to the cost and availability of food? Both authors suggest possible alternatives, but these are not, on the whole, practices that would be feasible until after years, or even decades, of experimentation and adjustment. (pp. 4-5)

If Miss Carson and Mr. Herber are substantially correct in their facts and interpretations, and I believe that on the whole they are, a return to health and sanity will probably be roughly as complex and difficult as would have been the establishment of control over numbers and use of automobiles forty years ago. It might conceivably have been possible, before our society had become so thoroughly motor-dependent, to prevent the future hypertrophy and constipation of our metropolitan areas, the poisoning of their air, the repeated decimation of our wildlife, and the killing and maiming of far more Americans than have yet felt the icy hand of cumulative poisons. Will we move fast enough, now, to escape possible immolation in the metabolic by-products of a technology gone wild?

Both books end on somewhat hopeful notes, as is all but required by American convention, but to this reviewer it seems like whistling in the dark. If we do escape, our debt to Miss Carson and Mr. Herber will be substantial. (p. 5)

William Vogt, "On Man the Destroyer," in Natural History *(copyright the American Museum of Natural History, 1963; reprinted with permission from* Natural History*), Vol. LXXII, No. 1, January, 1963, pp. 3-5.*

THE TIMES LITERARY SUPPLEMENT

In [*Our Synthetic Environment*] Mr. Herber attempts to warn us of all the host of brand new hazards in a "synthetic world". By the time the reader has waded through the horrors of soil depletion, chemical addition to food, insecticides, antibiotics and other drugs, vehicle exhausts, atmospheric pollution, not forgetting fall-out from the Bomb, cancer from cigarettes and even the emotional strains and stresses of modern living, he is quite numbed. Paradoxically, for the first time in years, one is certain that Man will still be "living it up" around the year 2000 in an even more super synthetic environment, eating his synthetic food, drinking no doubt by then synthetic wine.

The book's lack of impact is due in part to its repetitiveness and rather clumsy construction. . . .

One might, however, have been willing to overlook such faults if some coherent ideas emerged at the end, but remarks such as ". . . a growing need to restore normal, balanced, manageable rhythms of human life—that is, an environment that meets our requirements as individuals and biological beings" are not very inspiring. What are these "balanced, normal, manageable rhythms"? As for restoring them, when did we ever achieve such intangible ideals? . . . Let us recommend

Mr. Herber to concentrate on more manageable portions of his subject in future, and hope he will present them more carefully and lucidly. There is an important job to be done in informing people of the consequences—dire and not so dire—of our ever-increasing scientific knowledge, and it is sad that this particular attempt has failed.

> *"Too Much Science?" in* The Times Literary Supplement *(© Times Newspapers Ltd. (London) 1963; reproduced from* The Times Literary Supplement *by permission), No. 3181, February 15, 1963, p. 103.*

JOHN OSMUNDSEN

Neither the best book of this sort that one could hope for, nor as bad as many that have been written, [**"Our Synthetic Environment"**] tackles the full range of the problem [of environmental pollution].

In some cases, Mr. Herber casts a current problem in a historical perspective that, while interesting and to some extent instructive, is not always relevant. And although the author seems anxious to be fair and accurate, to avoid the hysterics and histrionics of some other writers on this subject, one nevertheless gets the impression that he is at heart one of the "back to nature" boys. . . .

No one is going to stop the world so that some who would like to get off will be able to or, as with Mr. Herber, spin us backward in time. Man is here, we hope, to stay, and his very presence and the requirements for maintaining it mean that the natural environment will undergo changes, in most ways for the better, though in some ways to man's detriment. Mistakes will be made that cannot be corrected but only deplored in retrospect, for man is human after all. The best we can hope for is that he will be sufficiently aware of the risks to guard intelligently against repeating past errors or making new ones of similar nature.

And this is the best that can be said for a book such as Lewis Herber's. It does sound the alarm.

> *John Osmundsen, "Man Against Nature," in* The New York Times Book Review *(© 1963 by The New York Times Company; reprinted by permission), May 19, 1963, p. 28.*

EDWARD T. CHASE

Herber reminds us [in *Crisis in Our Cities*] that ours is now overwhelmingly an urban environment, and that air pollution, water pollution and the unholy combination of stress plus sedentary living are its hallmarks. Herber's virtually irrefutable thesis is that pollution and congestion are nearing epidemic proportions. Drastic quarantine measures are needed immediately, to be followed by lasting methods to control not only noxious automotive fumes but "unbridled metropolitan growth." . . .

The least persuasive section of *Crisis in Our Cities* concerns the health problems traceable to excessive nervous strain combined with absence of recreational exercise. Herber concludes pessimistically that only new sources of electrical power, new urban mass transit systems and some (unspecified) kind of decentralization to combat "urban gigantism" can save urban America from deterioration. (p. 19)

> *Edward T. Chase, "The Effluent Society," in* Book Week—The Sunday Herald Tribune *(© I.H.T. Corporation; reprinted by permission), May 2, 1965, pp. 4, 19.**

MURRAY POLNER

[*Crisis in Our Cities*] is valuable because it makes the problems very real. How, then, can the "crisis" be met? Herber's suggestions include barring automobiles from congested areas . . . , establishing a modest stagger system to relieve congestion on public transportation (a system which thus far has failed in most cities because all proposals have depended on the voluntary compliance of the business community) and providing much more surface public transportation (a proposal bitterly opposed by such powerful interests as the gasoline industry and the American Automobile Association). Overall, Herber considers "metropolitan planning probably the most serious single problem faced by man in the second half of the 20th century" (second only, one assumes, to the threat of nuclear war).

These recommendations are only a beginning, but they have two virtues: having identified the problems, they call for action; and even if attempted solutions result in mistakes, at least the mistakes will be on the positive side. To mark time can only invite national strangulation at the expense of ourselves and our children. (p. 1233)

> *Murray Polner, "The Urban Rat Race," in* The Christian Century *(copyright 1965 Christian Century Foundation; reprinted by permission from the October, 1965 issue of* The Christian Century*), Vol. LXXXII, No. 40, October 6, 1965, pp. 1232-33.*

TODD GITLIN

[In *Post-Scarcity Anarchism*] Murray Bookchin insists that the authoritarian Socialist position has been eroded by that very course of history which the Socialists thought they had appropriated. Far from being ahistorical or utopian, Bookchin argues, anarchism, or anarcho-communism, has become *the* logical consequence of world history, and the only credible alternative to the destruction of the planet. . . .

Let me say before going any further that his book is in many places exciting and might even be seminal. It is the closest thing I've seen to a vision both practical and transcendent. Anyone who wants to make revolution in this country should read it and reckon with it. We have so little theory, from any tradition, that speaks directly to the contemporary situation; Bookchin has occupied a vacuum, and rather deserves his singularity, which stands out vividly against the background of traditional anarchism.

In the first place, Bookchin refuses to hark back to a golden age of primitive communism as a standard by which a contemporary revolution should be judged. One of his most original essays, **"Toward a Liberatory Technology,"** gathers much evidence that decentralization of political power actually *requires* advanced technology. Cybernation makes possible the abolition of toil, and thus the integration of the individual. Steady-state power sources, sun, water, and wind, could supply the energy for subsistence and small-scale production. . . . In all these instances, capitalism perverts and retards the use of the technology which is its primary achievement.

Secondly, Bookchin is an ecologist . . . , and his apocalyptic alternative to anarchist revolution is not Marx's "barbarism" or nuclear war but ecological death of the planet. Capitalism necessarily destroys the environment as it pursues production for the sake of production and growth for the sake of growth. Unlike most ecologists, though, Bookchin points to the connection between man's domination of nature and man's domination of man and woman; historically the two developed together, and Bookchin argues they can only be eliminated together. The happy historical confluence between humanity's social needs and the needs of the planet places Bookchin in the enviable and probably justifiable position of having his revolutionary cake and eating it too. (p. 309)

Otherwise, Bookchin's essays are essentially updatings of the traditional anarchist stance. There is some history in them, not nearly enough, but perhaps that omission is outweighed by Bookchin's contemporaneity. The essential argument, parallel to a Marxist's, is that the core institutions of bourgeois life—the modern city, state, technology, central labor organization, bureaucracy, family—are played out. Whatever functions they once performed are no longer practical, even by bourgeois standards, certainly not by ecological standards, and only the "impractical" is now possible. Where Bookchin parts company with the authoritarian Marxists is in his insistence that the new order already embryonic in the womb of the old society must be decentralist and anti-hierarchical, and that "a libertarian society can be achieved only by a libertarian revolution."

But like any good Marxist he is driven to discover a revolutionary agency within the society. For him that agency is "literally the great majority of society," foreshadowed by the "decomposition" of traditional classes into a "non-class" of the anti-authoritarian and dropout young. We are now living through a prerevolutionary enlightenment in which intimations of an unalienated, integrated life are displacing the established codes; new needs are eating away at the institutions which cannot meet them. At least half a dozen times Bookchin points to the diffusion of youth culture among young workers as an omen of increasing post-scarcity consciousness. (pp. 309-10)

His own dialectic takes him to an image of a revolution which is unprecedented in that it will not reverse the power of one class over another, but eliminate it. . . .

Bookchin, like Marcuse, is more a Hegelian than a Marxist, and thus inclines toward ethereal (though holistic) formulations of "tendencies" which "reveal themselves" in this or that trend. Many of his propositions . . . dangle in tantalizing abstraction, and it is often hard to tell whether Bookchin is simply vague or actually masking confusion with historical certitude. His counterposing of catalyst against "vanguard" as the role of the conscious revolutionary needs explaining. What exactly constitutes catalysis? Aside from organizing in affinity groups, how do we proceed? How can the post-scarcity consciousness of the revolutionary young encounter the scarcity consciousness of most of the rest of the Americans? Given the penetration of bourgeois ideas into our consciousness, how, concretely, do we leap over "transition"?

Another flaw is overextrapolation, indeed overcelebration of revolutionary moments. An example: he argues that all that prevented the French workers from making the revolution in May-June 1968 was their unwillingness to operate the factories they had seized, and their inability to secure arms to protect their expropriations. Yet the alacrity with which the workers left the factories and marched back to Gaullism and the reformism of the Communist Party is not wholly explained by the failure of the revolutionary groups to pose an alternative. He

makes much of the widely quoted students' graffiti, and from them concludes that the entire failed revolution was animated by the spirit of transcendent anarcho-communism. But what are we to make of a spirit that exhausts itself so quickly? . . . Bookchin, like too many other theorists, is too easily satisfied with *assertions* rather than empirically grounded arguments. . . . Another: his celebration of youth culture, virtually to a point of (Charles) Reichian fantasy. Here as elsewhere Bookchin places great weight on a scatter of facts and hunches which will not by themselves support his summaries. One trouble is that the book is not sufficiently systematic. Bookchin's ideas are provocative, even stirring enough to have warranted rewriting into a continuous essay—which might also have eliminated his annoying repetition of ideas and even, at times, metaphors. . . .

For all Bookchin's appreciation of "the miraculous," for all his desire to unite poetry and revolution, there is too little that is either miraculous or poetic about his language. And yet the book is frequently inspiring and evocative—a tribute, I suppose, to the power of Bookchin's ideas, shrouded though they are in the jargon of a century's dialectics. (p. 310)

Todd Gitlin, *"To the Far Side of the Abyss," in* The Nation *(copyright 1972* The Nation *magazine, The Nation Associates, Inc.), Vol. 214, No. 10, March 6, 1972, pp. 309-11.*

TERRY M. PERLIN

What is missing in *Post-Scarcity Anarchism* is a confrontation with the realities of revolution. There is hardly a mention of the question of violence. Simply supporting the notion of "direct action" or, on the other hand, criticizing earlier revolutionaries for their slaughter of innocents does not confront the question of how anarchists would simultaneously seize and destroy political power.

Positing that "a basic sense of decency, sympathy and mutual aid lies at the core of human behavior" is no answer to the challenges of Freud and later aggression theorists who suggest that the masses depend on strong leadership. It is fine to expose the shibboleths of statist propaganda—and this is the chief contribution of anarchists. But creating a viable anti-politics is a more difficult task, one that Bookchin has not accomplished.

Yet a softer feeling remains after having read this book. It is the work, not of a demagogue but of an honest revolutionary, a man depressed by past failures but not yet despondent. He seems to me the political equivalent of what Herbert Read, the British art critic and anarchist, deemed the true artist: "what the Germans call *ein Rüttler*, an upsetter of the established order." (p. 540)

Terry M. Perlin, *"Radical Mavericks," in* Dissent *(© 1972, by Dissent Publishing Corporation), Vol. XIX, No. 3, Summer, 1972, pp. 538-40.*

FRANK LIPSIUS

[In *Post-Scarcity Anarchism*] Bookchin does not really know how to address the world around him. He knows what he would like to see and he criticises the General Motors of the world for not giving it to him, but he has no idea of the way technological progress should be reconciled with a break-up of overorganised aspects of society. Not only is he not sure whether he wants life simpler or more complex, but more important, he also assumes that merely taking technological research out of the hands of private industry will make it flourish all the more—and for the right cause. . . . Of course, there may not have been any technology in the first place if it weren't for the profit motive and individual enterprise—but no point in belabouring that point either. . . .

His major point is that once we foresee the end of the daily drudgery, which he blames on the distribution of scarce resources, we can reorganise the world around leisure, free love, *etc*—a combination of *Playboy* and Disneyland. . . . (p. 36)

He hates thinking of people as economic entities and he misquotes Marx. He only dimly realises that the great self-proclaimed anarchism of his type of commune movement basically lives at the sufferance of the rest of society. As long as those who escape remain self-sufficient and quiet, the great machinery of state-regulated capitalism need take no notice. In some respects these people are a *creation* of society insofar as all those who have grown into the world as unemployed and unemployable would only cause trouble if they were not shunted off to some golden glen in the shade of a sturdy oak, liberated from disgusting urban life with its two-car families, electrical appliances and leisure to watch football on television. Fie on the good life, fie! A book like this fosters the myth that the people who choose to opt out are actually reconciled to their uselessness. Bookchin does not say that drugs and eastern religions ease the drift into alienation. He merely holds out the promise of a society where we can all sit around, completely bombed out, waiting for technology to do its stuff. (pp. 36-7)

> *Frank Lipsius, "Intellectual Streakers" (© copyright Frank Lipsius 1974; reprinted with permission), in* Books and Bookmen, *Vol. 19, No. 9, June, 1974, pp. 36-9.**

THE TIMES LITERARY SUPPLEMENT

It is a disturbingly easy judgment to say that the passage of time has treated Murray Bookchin rather badly, and that the essays in *Post-Scarcity Anarchism* read a lot less persuasively today than they did in the middle 1960s; none the less, the easy judgment seems on reflection the right one. The belief that "what we are witnessing is the breakdown of a century and a half of embourgeoisement and a pulverization of all bourgeois institutions *at a point in history when the boldest concepts of utopia are realizable*" comes a lot less easily when one of those bourgeois institutions is the machinery of world trade and one of the more likely results is a great increase in starvation and misery in the Third World. Again, the cheerful belief that "an atmosphere of general lawlessness, a growing personal day-to-day disobedience, a tendency not to 'go along' with the existing system, a seemingly 'petty' but nevertheless critical attempt to circumvent restriction in every facet of daily life" affords good grounds for expecting a liberating revolution (rather than an essentially fascist backlash) is touching, but preposterous.

But Mr. Bookchin's intellectual stance is interesting, even if hard to grasp. Roughly, he is a revolutionary who professes the idealist rather than the materialist dialectic—even more roughly, he is a Bakuninist rather than a Marxist. It is the emotional tensions, the thwarting and cramping of personality, the routinization and rationalization of daily life which repel him; he is, therefore, not vulnerable to the observation that

socialist societies exhibit many of these deplorable characteristics. . . .

But the emphasis on how much we damage ourselves by seeing our existence as a series of economic problems seems to consort ill with the emphasis on ecology. It is, after all, the commonest of ecological complaints that capitalist societies are intrinsically ill-adapted to use the world's resources carefully. Mr. Bookchin wouldn't dissent; but he wouldn't regard this as any kind of threat to his own position. For he envisages a new use of largely existing technology, a use in which we shall not maintain vast conurbations and energy-hungry systems of communication. Once we throw away the city for the commune, remove the urge to dominate nature and release the desire to live in and with nature, we can live an existence in which *felt* scarcity plays no part.

Those of us who are addicted to the large, anonymous metropolis may flinch at the thought of the rural idiocy which is offered as utopia; but rural idiocy is not Mr. Bookchin's goal either. It is not the city as spoken of by Aristotle or Hegel that he despises, but the parasitic megalopolis. Indeed, it is to Athens that he looks for a partial model of what he wants—no specialization, the rotation of political tasks, the recreation of face-to-face relationships, and the abandonment of mouthpiece to earphone dealings. The problem for even the friendly sceptic, of course, is to know how many of the Athenians' virtues we can acquire without picking up the corresponding vices.

> *"Anarchist Utopias," in* The Times Literary Supplement *(© Times Newspapers Ltd. (London) 1974; reproduced from* The Times Literary Supplement *by permission), No. 3772, June 21, 1974, p. 662.*

TERRY M. PERLIN

[In *The Limits of the City*] Bookchin offers, in an admirably brief space, an historical overview of the rise of the bourgeois city. His work is based upon a viewpoint which amalgamates a critical Marxism with a Kropotkinian anarchism. A few cities in the past have been vital, socially harmonious places in which to live and work. "My purpose," Bookchin says "is to provide the reader with an idea of what the city was once like at its best, to recover high standards of urbanism all the more to question the present lack of standards in judging the modern metropolis and the society that fosters its growth."

Brief studies of pre-Columbian Mexico City (Tenochtitlan), Hellenic Athens and the medieval commune are the basis for a description of what the city can accomplish for its residents. (p. 241)

[Bookchin's] historical overview, and certainly the economic underpinning of [his] argument, owes much to Marx. Bookchin does concede in his introduction that Marx's *Grundrisse* provides a fragmentary discussion of the issues raised in *The Limits of the City*. But Bookchin rounds out the Marxist analysis by adding a psychological picture of the price paid by a purely quantitative urban growth. "The integrity of the individual depends upon its ability to integrate the many aspects of human life—work and play, reason and emotion, mental and sensuous, the private and the social—into a coherent and creative whole." The bourgeois city renders this integration impossible. Bookchin's descriptions of Los Angeles, a city of cars and only incidentally people, and of the isolation of New York City apartment dwelling are masterful case studies of the human burden carried in contemporary city life.

Bookchin admires those philosophers who have not only interpreted the world but who have advanced plans to change it. The utopian socialists Robert Owen and Charles Fourier are examined. Friedrich Engels, who, in *The Housing Question,* demanded decentralization and the elimination of the antithesis between town and country, is suggested as a source. Modern city planners, who depend more on technology than on raising the human issues of scale and values, are suitably condemned. Finally, Bookchin offers a plan for urban decentralization which combines the best features of utopianism and realism; it is not an effort to recapture an Athens lost but rather a model for creating a community in which, to paraphrase Marx, the freedom of each is a condition for the freedom of all.

Though some of Bookchin's work reminds one of the late Paul Goodman, the value of this book is that it is neither a "relevant" tract nor a "reactionary" condemnation. It is a serious piece of social philosophy that does not fear to be practical. (pp. 242-43)

> Terry M. Perlin, "Book Reviews: 'The Limits of the City'," in Science and Society (copyright 1975 by Science and Society, Incorporated), Vol. XXXIX, No. 2, Summer, 1975, pp. 241-43.

RAYMOND CARR

[Murray Bookchin] exposes his hand on every page [of *The Spanish Anarchists*]. For him Spanish anarchism not only contributed to mold a powerful and noble proletarian movement, unique in its revolutionary militancy, but in the libertarian commune of its Utopia it provided a model for the only satisfactory society of the future.

Mr. Bookchin, I take it, would agree with me that the division of the Spanish labor movement between the disciples of Bakunin and Marx was its tragedy. To Marxist socialists the anarchist militants were a gang of pistol-toting vegetarians; to the anarchists the socialists were a pusillanimous collection of authoritarian, faceless bureaucrats smelling of Marxist "German beer." Mr. Bookchin's sympathies are almost repulsively evident: every reference to the socialists is cast in a tone of contempt for their revolutionary impotence; they were "soulless" organizers of a movement that was only a mirror image of the hierarchical society it was the duty of revolutionaries to destroy. . . . Other prejudices in this book are commonplaces of anti-clericalism: village priests with "a sinister reputation for butchery," etc.

According to Mr. Bookchin, anarchism became what the liberal doctor and historian Marañon called "the most authentic expression of the Spanish revolutionary psychology" because it inherited the moral equality of the face-to-face society of the *pueblo*—the rural small-town community. Anarchists, it is argued, tried to inject its spirit of humane spontaneous cooperation into a harsh industrial society. I believe this to be a popular fallacy. It is a measure of Mr. Bookchin's misreading of rural sociology that he regards crop sharing (*aparcería*) as expressing "a rich sense of fraternity"; it was and is a richly exploitative form of land tenure. . . .

Mr. Bookchin's highly readable and perceptive study follows anarchism from its introduction into Spain in 1868 (by an Italian Bakunist who could speak no Spanish) until the outbreak of the Civil War in 1936. . . .

Throughout, Mr. Bookchin's sympathies lie with the true-red revolutionaries of the *grupos de afinidad,* small cells of anarchists held together by shared "moral instincts"; men like Buenaventura Durruti and Francisco Ascaso, bank robbers for the cause, assassins of archbishops and policemen. As for the syndicalists like Angel Pestaña and Salvador Seguí, struggling against the wild men to build up mass revolutionary unions, to the *grupos de afinidad* they weakened the revolutionary élan by compromise and ill-considered attempts to come to some understanding with the "pragmatic"—to Mr. Bookchin a word of abuse—socialist unions. . . .

Mr. Bookchin's apologia for political assassinations takes some swallowing. They did, indeed, create a "political vacuum" in the bourgeois state by knocking off three prime ministers; whether they were the expression of a "deep humanity" is another matter. Though he hints at it, Mr. Bookchin does not face up to the fact that, as Victor Serge pointed out, some anarchists operated on the frontiers of the criminal underworld or were, in Pestaña's phrase, "bully boys" running protection rackets.

I entirely accept Bookchin's . . . argument that police and military repression combined with the intransigence of the Catalan bourgeoisie to make any form of reformist socialism a dead loss during the 1920s. The violence of society induces a violent counter-society. But violence is always a vicious circle. One act of propaganda by deed could unleash and "justify" repression, enabling the military and the police to defy the civil authorities and to round up thousands of militants, removing the "moderate" syndicalists to jail and leaving the CNT at the mercy of the wild men of the action groups. Every act of police repression unleashed, in its turn, a new cycle of violence and assassination as a reprisal. (p. 22)

Some problems in history are insoluble: the testimony on collectivization is so conflicting that the truth will not come out of it. History, in this instance, will largely be the reflection of the historian's *point de départ*. This is clearly the case with Mr. Bookchin; but he is honest and scholarly enough to allow one to turn his own evidence against him.

For Mr. Bookchin the anarchist libertarian commune is not merely a historical memory; it is the model for a new counter-society. Marx was backing a loser when he put his bet on the industrial proletariat—now, as Bakunin prophesied, the passive victims of embourgeoisement. Bakunin succeeded in a semi-industrialized country like prewar Spain because he put his money on a revolution of *all* the dispossessed of incipient industrialization: the artisan struggling against the factory, the unemployed, the peasant—the marginal men whom Marx dismissed as "old shit."

Today, Mr. Bookchin argues, the revolution based on the traditional industrial proletariat is outdated, doomed to end in the ragbag of history. It is the alliance of *all* the dispossessed and alienated, the Popular Front of *all* those dehumanized by modern capitalism, that will defeat the system and set up the society of true liberty "which," as anarchism's founding father held, "does not recognize other restrictions but those traced by the laws of our nature." This is tantamount to saying that "there are no restrictions at all." It would work, provided man was naturally good and provided anarchists could strike a balance between the organizational demands of a highly complex industrial society and the simple spontaneity of the rural commune. But man is not naturally good and the libertarians, though in 1936-1937 they talked endlessly of organization and liberty, never succeeded in reconciling them. (p. 27)

Raymond Carr, "All or Nothing," in The New York Review of Books *(reprinted with permission from* The New York Review of Books; *copyright © 1977 Nyrev, Inc.), Vol. XXIV, No. 16, October 13, 1977, pp. 22, 27.**

LYNN H. NELSON

Bookchin's admitted sympathy with the Anarchists does not lead him to an uncritical eulogy [in *The Spanish Anarchists*]; he notes the failings and lack of vision within the movement, but attempts to place these faults within the social and economic context of the times and against the background of the Spanish heritage and outlook of life. Unfortunately, he fails to achieve a similar level of understanding of the forces shaping other groups within Spanish society. This is particularly true of, but not restricted to, the Carlists. As a consequence, the work is biased without being unobjective. Also, the author's interviews with exiled Spanish Anarchist leaders provide him a greater appreciation of recent events, and the quality of his narrative reflects the uneven nature of his resources. Nevertheless, he has managed to weave the complex strands of Andalusian agrarianism, Catalan industrialism, the shifting cabals of the Internationals, the idealism of Salvochea, and a wealth of other themes into a coherent network.

Lynn H. Nelson, "Europe: 'The Spanish Anarchists: The Heroic Years, 1868-1936'" (copyright by Lynn H. Nelson; reprinted by permission of the author), in History: Reviews of New Books, *Vol. 6, No. 2, November-December, 1977, p. 44.*

GEORGE WOODCOCK

[What Murray Bookchin presents in *The Spanish Anarchists*] is sound history with a strong theme and a great deal of sympathetic understanding. Mr. Bookchin is himself an anarchist, and something of a true believer, but not an uncritical one. . . .

He has his own predilections in terms of anarchist directions, and this means that when his views coincide with trends he discovers among the Spanish anarchists he can be very illuminating indeed. I have, for instance, read no better account than his of the affinity groups that were the basic units of anarchist organization in Spain, and since he is so convinced of the rightness of this kind of spontaneous and unstructured organization, it is natural that he should be acutely aware and convincingly critical of the tendencies towards centralization that arose in Spanish syndicalist organizations, whose type of industrial unionism became a mirror image of the industrial organization already created by the capitalist employers.

But, Mr. Bookchin is not a mere recounter of events or presenter of polemical points. He has a sense of the human dimensions of history, of the humane as an inevitable component of a movement like anarchism, and he weaves into the narrative of organizational changes a fascinating series of portraits of anarchist personalities. . . .

The Spanish Anarchists is not a book without faults. Mr. Bookchin is often patronizing towards his readers, particularly in his early chapters where he gives us a potted history of anarchism for the ignorant. He tends to ignore other people who have written in the field while paraphrasing their writings without acknowledgment, and where he does name one of them it is often to be belittling. . . . But though Mr. Bookchin does tend to be slighting and ungrateful to his predecessors and often simplistic in his own arguments, he has produced a needed book, which will make many readers revise considerably their views of the past of Spain and of the record of anarchism, which are complex and insufficiently understood facets of the history that has formed our age. (p. 478)

George Woodcock, "The Libertarian Virtues," in The Times Literary Supplement *(© Times Newspapers Ltd. (London) 1978; reproduced from* The Times Literary Supplement *by permission), No. 3969, April 2,, 1978, pp. 477-78.**

William F(rank) Buckley, Jr.

1925-

An American political writer, novelist, lecturer, and editor, Buckley is an eloquent and persuasive proponent of the conservative movement. He graduated from Yale University in 1950 and the next year published the controversial *God and Man at Yale*, a denunciation of Yale's faculty and textbooks for their alleged liberal and anti-religious biases. In 1955 Buckley founded the conservative bi-weekly magazine, *National Review*. In its pages, Buckley and the writers he assembled regrouped the disparate strands of the conservative movement around the tenets of cold-war anticommunism abroad and opposition to liberalism in this country. Disassociating themselves from extremist groups like the John Birch Society, Buckley and his conservative associates created a sagacious, more pragmatic conservatism palatable to a larger segment of the American public. In 1965 Buckley ran and lost in the New York City mayoral election as candidate of the Conservative party. His conservative social, political, and economic views are reflected in *Up from Liberalism* (1959), an attack on liberals and their philosophy; in *Cruising Speed* (1971), an account of a week in Buckley's life; in *Execution Eve* (1975), a collection of his journalism; as well as in numerous other books and in his syndicated columns. (See also *Contemporary Literary Criticism*, Vols. 7, 18, and *Contemporary Authors*, Vols. 1-4, rev. ed.; *Contemporary Authors New Revision Series*, Vol. 1.)

Courtesy of William F. Buckley

Excerpt from *GOD AND MAN AT YALE*

[I will now undertake] . . . a direct examination of the term "academic freedom," that handy slogan that is constantly wielded to bludgeon into impotence numberless citizens who waste away with frustration as they view in their children and in their children's children the results of *laissez-faire* education. We must determine whether freedom is violated by the administration of a private educational institution which insists upon a value orthodoxy.

The hoax to which so many of us have succumbed can only be understood after a fastidious analysis of the functions of the scholar. *We must bear in mind that the scholar has had not one but two functions, and that, further, they are not inherently related.* These pursuits are (1) scholarship, and (2) teaching. They are related solely by convenience, by tradition, and by economic exigency. This would seem clear: a man gifted in research in genetics is not thereby gifted in the art of *transmitting* to the pupil his knowledge of biology. In fact, this is periodically brought to mind in widespread student resentment at the retention by many universities of scholars who, while often distinguished in research, are miserably inept in teaching.

However, since the scholar, like his fellow-man, must earn his keep, tradition has it that in the afternoon he will utilize the university's libraries and laboratories, generally to satisfy his own desires, while in the morning he will use the classrooms to satisfy other people's desires. In short, the student pays not only for the scholar's morning work, of which the student is properly the direct beneficiary, but also, in effect, for his afternoon work, which may concern or interest the student not at all.

Now, the implications of this double role are manifold. We have in focus the methodological confusion that impedes purposive discussion of "academic freedom"; for in today's controversy, the critic is taking exception to *unlicensed teaching*, while the professors are actually basing their case on the rights of *unlicensed personal scholarship*. And while the two sides are constantly at loggerheads, they should not be at all, for both are right.

Let us remember that it is *the scholars* who have systematized the modern conception of academic freedom. They have constructed an appealing and compact philosophical package, labeled it "truth," and tossed it for enshrinement to that undiscriminating fellow, the liberal. It is understandable that the modern rationale of "academic freedom" originated with and is a product of the scholar. To the pure scholar, the bread of life is research, theory, creation. It is horrifying to him—as it ought to be to anyone who respects the individual—that anyone other than himself should seek to prescribe the method or the orientation or the findings of his research—except, of course, in those cases where he is hired to perform a specific service.

His position here is certainly unassailable. A researcher ought to be free to seek out his own conclusions, to make his own generalizations on the basis of his discoveries. To think otherwise is, at best, to think awkwardly. It is a self-contained paradox to endow a researcher or a research organization with funds and to assert simultaneously what shall come out of the investigations for which the funds are to be used. For obviously, under such a formula, there is no reason for the investigation to be undertaken at all.

But, legend notwithstanding, the proverbial longhaired professor can, at the margin, take stock of the facts of life, and these are that *research* is in large part subsidized by the consumer of *teaching*. Therefore, cannily, he distends the protective cloak of research to include his activities as a *teacher,* thereby insuring to himself license in the laboratory, which is right and proper, and license in the classroom, which is wrong and improper.

The educational overseer—the father who sends his son to school, or the trustee who directs the policy of the school—is violating no freedom I know of if he insists, let us say, that individualism instead of collectivism be inculcated in the school. Rather, he is asserting his own freedom. For if the educational overseer, in the exercise of his freedom, espouses a set of values, his is the inescapable duty and privilege to give impetus to these values in the classroom just as he does, from time to time, in the polling booth.

But, it will be objected, if no one supports the teacher of socialism, he will be out of a job; hence, in effect, will he not have been persecuted for his beliefs? Yes. Similarly, if no one votes for an incumbent, he too will be out of a job. He, too, in the realistic analysis, will have been persecuted for his beliefs. In a democracy it is proper that, in this sense, he should be. And yet we have affirmed the sanctity of independent research. There is no contradiction here. The researcher must satisfy consumer demands during those hours of his working day during which he earns his income. Research may occupy him as an avocation, as it has so many scholars. More likely, far-sighted individuals will continue to contribute funds to autonomous research. We can assume, or at least we can hope, that there will continue to be "consumers" of "untrammeled research."

Even if this is problematic, it must be affirmed that every citizen in a free economy, no matter the wares that he plies, must defer to the sovereignty of the consumer. It is of the essence of freedom that citizens not be made to pay for what the majority does not want, and there is no exception to this rule that does not entail a surrender of freedom and a substitution of minority for majority rule.

It follows, then, that where the school is concerned, the educational overseer is paying for the transmission of knowledge and values. He is not *necessarily* interested in paying for autonomous research. If he *is* interested in this activity of scholarship, let him endow a research center, (and let him not, as a man of intelligence and probity, stipulate what shall be the findings of research not yet undertaken).

[What are] . . . the sources of "new ideas" if the college came to insist, as I believe it should, on a value orthodoxy (narrower, that is than the orthodoxy to which at least Yale already subscribes). To begin with, I assume that new ideas will come in the future, as in the past, from individual research.

Who is going to pay for this research? My answer to this is, in the simplest terms, whoever wants to. Most researchers today work at their research part time. There are, though, a considerable number that work at it full time. These are subsidized, by and large, by research foundations, private corporations, philanthropists, and, in some cases, by the government. Most, I repeat, are part-time researchers whose work is subsidized by the consumers of teaching.

Let us examine the situation of Mr. John Smith, a socialist professor of economics at Yale, and survey his fate under my proposed plan. First of all, let us bar him from teaching because he is inculcating values that the governing board at Yale considers to be against the public welfare. No freedom I know of has yet been violated. We still cling to the belief in this country that, acting in good conscience, we can hire whom we like.

But before Professor Smith is discharged, let us assume that the department chairman calls him up and says: "Look, Smith, you unquestionably know economics and there is much you can teach these students. I don't believe in the values you foster, and neither do the governors of Yale. In the circumstances, we cannot conscientiously allow you to advance these values in our classrooms. But suppose you go on teaching, and you advance not your own, pro-socialist values, but our, pro-free enterprise conclusions. You are well aware, of course, what these are and what is the intellectual justification of them. This way, we can retain you. What about it?"

Now this is an alternative, horrifying as it sounds, that deserves examination. I am opposed to its being offered for reasons that will ensue. But I am not as shocked as a great many people might be, for I see similar situations, many that are applauded, in operation in the civilized world today. The civil service (particularly in England) is an outstanding case in point. Permanent public servants are supposed to help to implement the policies of the legislature, and their personal convictions are, quite properly, deemed utterly irrelevant. Such is the situation, therefore, that a civil service employee in England who considers socialism the most pernicious of all conceivable economic doctrines, might find himself, following the dictates of the government in power, drawing up plans for the nationalization of steel. He has been hired to do just this and *no freedom has been abridged so long as he is at liberty to quit his job.*

A more commonplace example can be brought forward as taking place every day in every community. A man may be skilled in masonry but he may intensely dislike working as a mason. He may prefer, let us say, to take pictures. But if no one will hire him to take pictures, and if there are consumers for masonry, he must turn to bricks, even if he is bored by the very thought of it. He must, what is more, even as the civil service worker must, perform his job well. If not, he will be fired.

Therefore, it can be argued that Professor Smith, a socialist teaching individualism, would be under no extraordinary duress. Even if he were enjoined not to publish under his own name the results of his off-hours research on the virtues of socialism (on the grounds that his hypocrisy would then become patent, and his subsequent teaching ineffective), it could be said that he would not be any the worse off than the civil service worker who would be summarily dismissed if he published an indictment of the government in power.

Nevertheless, I should be opposed to this alternative's being given to Professor Smith. I should be opposed because I believe that even though value inculcation is just a part of education, a major portion of which has to do with the relaying of knowledge, method, and so forth, it is such an important part that it must be approached with the greatest sensitivity and delicacy, and with keen and genuine enthusiasm. I have no doubt that just as there exist debaters who can uphold a resolution against which they have strong feelings and do it with the most convincing finesse and ardor, there must be many teachers who can do the same. Still and all, the knowledge of it would make me restless and unhappy, and I would advise against it.

Professor Smith is, then, relieved of his teaching duties.

His first recourse, I should think, would be to seek employment at a college that was interested in propagating socialism. But let us say that all these are already staffed. If this is the case, Mr. Smith is the victim of the kind of world he lives in, of an excess of supply over demand, and his recourse is identical with that of anyone else who plies a trade for which there are, at present, no consumers. He must move to something else until an opening turns up. At any rate, Yale is under no obligation to keep him.

Suppose, better still, that there are *no* consumers for socialist teachers? Professor Smith's fate, then, would be similar to the approaching fate of the Communist teacher. There are no bidders. He must join ranks with the teacher of companionate marriage or of fascism. If the people are to retain their sovereignty, they cannot relinquish their right to impose unemployment upon the trader in commodities or ideas for which there is no market.

No freedom has yet been abridged in the case of Professor Smith. Rather, the freedom of the consumer has been upheld.

On the other hand, suppose a foundation, or an individual, decides to subsidize Professor Smith in his research. Any number of motives might underlie such a decision. Perhaps the donor feels that as a result of the professor's criticisms, some hitherto unanalyzed shortcomings of capitalism will be exposed, and that appropriate modifications can then be made. Or maybe a foundation will feel that further research and discovery by Professor Smith will make socialism a demonstrably better system than capitalsm to live under. Either way, anyone is at liberty for any reason he likes to subsidize Mr. Smith. I repeat that in most situations only penny-wise thinking and inherent dishonesty would lead to a prescription by the subsidizer as to the outcome of research. This would be tantamount to a cigarette company's granting money for research into cancer, with the stipulation that it shall not be discovered that tobacco is in any way conducive to the spread of the disease.

But if Professor Smith found no takers whatsoever, he too would have to turn to masonry and take pictures in his spare time.

Now if the governors of Yale determined to maintain a fullor part-time research center for scholars for whose teaching there were no consumers, I should find this a reasonable decision. I should insist, on the other hand, that separate books be maintained by the Yale research center, so that a contributor to Yale should be given the clear option of subsidizing the teaching part of the University or the independent research section. It is possible that the trustees would refuse the University's facilities to some researchers for a number of reasons, but the merits of each case should be given *ad hoc* attention.

One thing is clear: it is time that honest and discerning scholars cease to manipulate the term academic freedom for their own ends and in such fashion as to deny the rights of individuals. For in the last analysis, academic freedom must mean the freedom of men and women to supervise the educational activities and aims of the schools they oversee and support. (pp. 182-90)

William F. Buckley, Jr., in his God and Man at Yale: The Superstitions of "Academic Freedom" *(copyright 1951; copyright renewed © 1979 by William F. Buckley, Jr.; reprinted by permission of Regnery/ Gateway, Inc.), Henry Regnery Company, 1951, 240 p.*

Excerpt from *UP FROM LIBERALISM*

The temptation is to measure freedom subjectively. But it is very dangerous indeed to cede to a society the right to declare what are and what are not the freedoms worth exercising. To be sure, one man may not feel free unless he can render his political views without let or hindrance. Another may put the highest value on his freedom to walk through the streets late at night. A third may care principally about his freedom to shoot ducks. Freedom belongs also to the eccentric—that much we should be quite firm about. It may be eccentric to complain about being docked a few dollars a week for social security; but how far can we go, if we deal thus cavalierly with the minority's freedoms, without changing the very nature of the voluntarist society?

What all conservatives in this country fear, and have plenty of reason to fear, is the loss of freedom by attrition. It is therefore for the most realistic reasons, as well as those of principle, that we must resist every single accretion of power by the state, even while guarding our rhetoric against such exaggerations as equating social security with slavery. The conservative rhetoric has here and there run ahead of events. Even though I myself take the gloomy view that our society is marching toward totalitarianism, I should not go so far as to say that America is not now, as societies go, free—howeverly gravely I view the restrictions on freedom implicit in, e.g., the progressive income tax, the ban on religious teaching in public schools, the union shop, the FEPC's, the farm laws, etc. Freedom is *not* indivisible. The more freedom the better, which means that some freedom is better than none at all, and more than some is better still. The conservative must, therefore, guard against the self-discrediting generalization that our society is no longer "free," while insisting, as implacably as the Liberal does every time a Communist is harassed by a disciplinary law, that not an appropriation is passed by the legislatures, but that our freedom is diminished.

The failure of the conservative demonstration in political affairs rests primarily on our failure to convince that the establishment of the welfare state entails the surrender, bit by bit, of minor freedoms which, added together, can alter the very shape of our existence.

The tendencies of Liberalism are every day more visibly coercive, as the social planners seek more and more brazenly to impose their preferences upon us. Here, I believe, is a practical distinction at which conservatives should hammer hard—the distinction between the kind of welfarism that turns dollars over to people, and that which turns services over to him. The former kind is embodied in such legislation as social security, unemployment compensation, and old age assistance. The latter in federal aid to education, to housing, to rural electrification, small business, etc.; and the proposed "insurance" programs, e.g., health, accident, etc.

In the first instance, the recipient of the money is free to allocate it according to his own lights, to satisfy his own needs and pleasures according to his own estimate of their priority. There are the obvious perils, that he will stress whiskey rather than milk, television over education; but these are the perils of liberty, with which conservatives are prepared to live. In making money grants, as distinguished from the other kind (for instance public housing subsides), the government is prevented from taking active control of industries or social services, or from having the deciding hand in the creation or development of social or service institutions. I judge this to be significant, because as long as one is free to spend the money with reference to one's desires, the government's control is at least once removed. And then at the tactical level, the longer one can hold off or slow down such grandiose ambitions of the welfarists as free health services, expanded public housing, government aid to airports, highways, schools, Olympic-game sites, the more difficult it will be to establish the necessity for the government's undertaking such enterprises. The arguments of the affluent society work in two ways: as we become richer we can indeed devote more attention to economic non-essentials. But as the people become richer we can also leave more and more to them to do out of their own resources, can we not? Surely the argument for socialized medicine in India is more compelling than the argument for socialized medicine in America. That is to say, if the relevant standard is, How many Indians, as opposed to Americans, can afford to pay their own medical bills? Granted, the question is left begging. Where is the government of India going to raise the money to pay for the hospitals, health centers, doctors, nurses and equipment we can all agree are urgently needed in India? The problem having been pondered over in the context of economic realities, the wise man will conclude that the best way to make medicine widely available is to make wealth widely available, and in turn the best way to do that is to liberate the economic system from statist impositions. (pp. 183-86)

William F. Buckley, Jr., in his Up from Liberalism *(reprinted by permission of Wallace & Sheil Agency, Inc.; copyright © 1959 by William F. Buckley, Jr.), McDowell, Obolensky, 1959, 205 p.*

Excerpt from *CRUISING SPEED—A DOCUMENTARY*

We arrive at La Seine more or less expecting that we will be dining alone with Truman Capote, but two other guests are there as we approach the table, a man and a girl, both of them tall and handsome. I recognize him, an anxiety crystallizing, as I recall our other encounter, a year ago. He and Pat had disagreed over Agnew, and Pat managed to scale her most objectionable heights, whence she takes to addressing her adversaries, "My good man," which is not the most endearing means of approaching Joe Fox, author and editor (of Truman Capote, among others)—causing, indeed, a certain tension. Well, here we are, and everybody kisses, or shakes hands with, everybody, and I do not catch, as so often happens, the name of the girl, who is young, slender, beautiful, and we sit down and order drinks. I find her a little formal; shy-type, I reason; but things move, as they tend to do with Truman, who is maybe a little bit officiously hospitable, acknowledging with his keen social intelligence that there is if not a mélange de genres— which he knows better than to contrive, unless he is feeling wicked, and this is not the night for that sort of thing—at least some impacted static there, which he intends to dissipate, and succeeds in doing so, little by little. However Truman is not altogether himself, declining, for instance—though several times urged to do so—to dilate, as under normal circumstances he would do with vivacity and passion, on his recent highly publicized ordeal. Because he had followed—or because, I forget,

he hadn't followed—his lawyer's instructions, he suddenly found himself on California's Most Wanted List for contempt of court. He had not appeared in court to give testimony on what it was that he knew, or didn't know, about a condemned prisoner whom he had interviewed in the course of producing a television special on capital punishment. Anyway, he has just come from spending ten or twelve hours in jail—a nasty resolution of judicial rectitude and executive agony, because the Reagans and Truman had become very good friends in the course of Truman's explorations into capital punishment. But it would have been unseemly for law-and-order Reagan to commute a celebrity-friend's five-day sentence. The strain of the experience is palpable, and although from time to time Truman rises buoyantly to describe this or that aspect of his tribulation, he doesn't want to recount what Joe especially wants him to tell us, and I sense that it pains him; so we let it go.

Along the way, the ladies go out to the powder room, and Truman tells me that the girl, who is called Lally, is the daughter of the late Philip Graham and of Mrs. Graham, now the publisher of the Washington *Post,* etc.—and that she was a bit hesitant about sharing an evening with me because she harbored a resentment over what I had published when her father died.

That column, *Time* Mag, when it did the cover on me, mentioned it. "In one breathtaking column, he managed to equate Henry Ford's divorce with the suicides of publisher Philip Graham and Stephen Ward, Christine Keeler's keeper. All were men, wrote Buckley, 'wanting in the stuff of spiritual survival.' Ford yanked its [projected] advertising from [*National Review*]." I tried to think back on what it was I had said, on whether I should be edgy about having said it; and I summon it up (while the ladies are out, in the fashion of John Fowles in *The French Lieutenant's Woman*). I remember writing it. It was mid-morning, drizzling, foggy, we were on my yawl, having left our anchorage at Campobello, just after dawn, in order to slide under the bridge at low tide, heading towards St. Andrews. I had to write a column and phone it in, so I turned on the radio to hear the morning's news . . .

A single radio broadcast (I wrote) brings the news of two suicides and a divorce, and reminds us that, when all is said and done, it is the individual around whom the world spins. That all our talk of empires rising and falling, of worlds torn in two, of glacial currents and galactic swoops, can seem trivial when contrasted with the fall of a titan. The radio broadcaster relegated to the end the humdrum news of atom bombs, civil rights convulsions, earthquakes in Yugoslavia, tremors in the chancelleries. His mind and the listeners' were on the divorce of Henry Ford, the suicide of Stephen Ward, and the disintegration and death of Philip Graham.

All three were men of affairs in every sense of the word. All three men of rank. All three titans in their own worlds. Ford, the scion of a great fortune, perhaps the single most conspicuous figure in modern American industry. His forthcoming divorce, particularly under the circumstances of his voluntary and explicit commitment to a religion which holds that the marriage bond is unbreakable, involves a submission to an emotional impulse which proved overwhelming notwithstanding that the eyes of the world, which sustain many famous men in time of personal tribulation, were on him. Because, as the head of his fabulous empire, Ford was, like Rockefeller, not merely a scion of wealth and power, but a scion of manners, and manners in the deepest sense reflect the stability of civilization.

Stephen Ward, a successful physician, a talented artist, a gay and vivacious courtier, was dragged down to humiliation and despair and death by the whiplash of convention; and convention, let it be said in its favor, is in the profoundest sense the underpinning of civilization.

And poor Philip Graham, the most influential publisher in the most influential city in the world, lusting after the goods of mankind according to a defective vision which conceived of macrocosmic happiness following upon the rise of Big and Benevolent Government, couldn't, in the end, find his own happiness within his own circumstances, and suffered a nervous breakdown, departing despairingly from the world he had so fastidiously mothered by living and breathing the welfare state and international big-think. For himself, his own resources were overpowered; and it is on one's own resources, and God's, that each individual must finally depend, or else he and his civilization will disintegrate.

In two cases there was a woman. In the third, there was Woman. Over and over again there is the re-enactment of Genesis, and the re-enactment of the causes of the downfall of so many of the illustrious gods of Greek and Roman mythology, for whom woman is merely the symbol, not so much of man's weakness before the cunning and wiles of the seductress, but of man profoundly and primarily in love with himself. André Malraux wrote a great novel about a man of affairs, brilliant, worldly, apparently omnipotent, who sought women because through them he found the ultimate means of making love to himself: when he embraced women he was actually embracing himself. The Protestant theologian Dean Fitch reminds us in his stunning book *Odyssey of the Self-Centered Self* that civilization has moved through several stages, and that we have recently entered upon the most acutely degenerate of them: The Age of Love of Self. For a period we loved God; then we loved rationalism; then we loved humanity; then science; now we love ourselves, and in that concupiscent love all else has ceased to exist. We are become what the philosophers called solipsists—men who recognize reality only in themselves. And when this happens, our own private little worlds, sustained only by our self-love, are easily shattered, and as they shatter we advance the destruction of our entire civilization, and race towards the Apocalypse ever so much faster than thermonuclear bombs will take us there.

The Greek dramatists knew that at the center of the weakness of the world is the weakness of the individual. How much we have forgotten in the 2,500 years from Aeschylus to Arthur Miller. The great heresies of recent times revolved around the repudiation of a plain truth. Marx instructed us that the fault lies not in ourselves but in history, that we are underlings, buffeted about by great elemental social forces which we do not dominate. Freud taught us that we should not blame ourselves for our failings, that other factors over most of which we had no control, traumatized and weakened us and made us impotent as superintendents of our own fate. The development of the philosophy of total welfarism is the political translation of the abandonment of the central idea of Christian civilization: that we are each one of us, however, crippled by burdens material and psychological, capable by the grace of God of working out satisfactory lives.

There was no misery or neglect in the development of the lives of Ford, Ward, and Graham; but they turned out to be the most miserable of men, men most seriously wanting in the stuff of spiritual survival; and because of their considerable names,

they delivered considerable blows to the tattered wall of truth that stands between civilization and total relapse . . .

So. I think again of Wilfrid Sheed's comment "Well, *that* is an ice-breaker"; and I fantasize myself rising from my chair, when the girls come back, and solemnly recanting my column in atonement; and I recognize the singular cruelty to which such as Lally are subject, and wonder whether, under reversed circumstances, I would have difficulty in fraternizing with someone who had written thus about my father; and conclude that I would not:

I realize about myself that I am, for all my passions, implacably, I think almost *unfailingly* fair: objective, *just*. This is *not* vanity, it is rigorous introspection. I could not conceive, for instance, of disparaging another man's talents simply because I disapprove the ends to which they are harnessed. Nor has this ever caused me any strain at all; indeed if it had done so, I'd be able to take such satisfaction as is due *only* to those who have to *struggle* in order to be fair. The ideologization of objectivity was brilliantly mocked by Randall Jarrell in his novel. "If [Flo] had been told that Benton College, and [her husband] Jerrold, and [her son] John, and [her daughter] Fern, *and* their furniture had been burned to ashes by the head of the American Federation of Labor, who had then sown salt over the ashes, she would have sobbed and said, at last—she could do no other—'I think that we ought to hear *his* side of the case before we make up our minds.'" That is the kind of objectivity that Kingman Brewster and the Yale students showed last spring, when they appeared to be taking the position that no murder should be investigated if there is the possibility that it was committed by a Black Panther. Not the same thing I am talking about.

And now, complacently, I cannot imagine that, reading them today, Lally, the daughter of a journalist and publisher, would find those heavy paragraphs polemically, or ideologically, horny. Still, I know that what is personally framed is more often than not personally received. A process that one once would have dared to call the feminization of criticism.

The coffee is waiting, and we drink it quickly, because Truman desires that we all should go to a place called The Sanctuary, way over on the West Side—a converted church, now a modish, super-hopped-up discothèque, psychedelic lights, blaring music, the dance floor crowded with homosexuals and lesbians and heteros, in ratio about 25-25-50, who dance with detached expression: I conjure up a vision of the Archduke Otto and his Duchess, unsmiling, frugging there, calmly, serenely, doing as the Romans do—Imperial Breeding. For all the clamor, the participants are marvelously restrained; no one accosts Truman for an autograph, or begs him to read a manuscript. We are very nearly alone in ordering our whiskeys-and-sodas: everyone else seems to be drinking Cokes, or nothing at all. I suppose that they are also smoking pot, though I am not good at detecting the smell of it. Conversation is impossible, but Truman sits there, or dances with Pat or Lally, and he seems relaxed. I find the rock working through to me, not so much overcoming the resistance that is the conservative's presumptive protection against its licentious imperative as overcoming a different order of resistance: the resistance that collapses when one is cut off, almost absolutely, from any alternative to listening to it, or better, experiencing it. You can close your eyes at The Sanctuary and spare yourself conscription by the crazy-lights that focus, distort, slither, bump, propel, reject; but the music—the sound—is sovereign, and you do not talk; you dance or sit; and there is Truman sitting, his glasses occasionally refracting the light, his expression resigned, his face reposed, while the bodies, many of them black and beautiful, writhe, the faces always silent, resisting the inordinate, orgiastic demands of the sound: a total break with the tradition of audiences of The Beatles and The Rolling Stones. I think back on the night before, Rosalyn Tureck playing the saraband, the excitement that she caused, the strain with which one listens, concentrates to hear the little, noiseless, appoggiaturas, and the idea comes to me to write this journal of a week's activity, and I wonder whether, tomorrow morning I will remember; whether anything will come of it if I do; whether anything worth the effort will come of it if I do. (pp. 175-83)

> *William F. Buckley, Jr., in his* Cruising Speed—A Documentary *(reprinted by permission of G. P. Putnam's Sons; copyright © 1971 by William F. Buckley, Jr.), Putnam's, 1971, 257 p.*

Excerpt from *EXECUTION EVE: AND OTHER CONTEMPORARY BALLADS*

Albert Jay Nock wrote a line that never leaves the memory. I paraphrase him: "I have often thought that it would be interesting to write an essay on the question: How do you go about discovering that you are slipping into a dark age?" In any such essay I think you would have to reflect on the special problems a democracy has in mobilizing public attitudes in such a way as to inform foreign policy in directions that are essentially moral. The great totalitarian systems do not have this difficulty. It sufficed that China should publicize a picture of Mao Tse-tung fraternizing with President Richard Nixon to satisfy the people that a friendly relationship with the United States was the right thing to do. Only two years ago, Chairman Mao pronounced that "U.S. imperialism is slaughtering the white and black people in its own country. Nixon's fascist atrocities have kindled the raging flames of the revolutionary mass movement in the United States. The Chinese people firmly support the revolutionary struggle of the American people." The speech in which that passage presumed was still being passed around (in several languages) while we were there. I got my copy in the hotel lobby. As easily as Mao now redirected the public on the proper attitude toward America, he could redirect it back to where it had been, as Hitler and Stalin twice changed attitudes toward each other, on either end of the Ribbentrop-Molotov Pact.

A free society cannot do this kind of thing. And America—young, inexperienced and moralistic—can do it least. When we fought hand in hand with Stalin, Churchill had said he would make a pact with the devil himself to defeat Hitler. In America, our leaders, far from thinking of Stalin as a devil, began to find great qualities in him, who before long became "Uncle Joe." Thus have the Chinese Communists been transformed, under diplomatic exigency; so that now the polls tell us that the American people, assimilating the Nixon trip, have discovered that the Chinese enterprise is "intelligent," "progressive" and "practical." To be sure, the Chinese don't do things the way we do, but their distinctive ideas on how to do things are understandable—and anyway, who are we to criticize? Who ever said we were so great?

And then too, a free society makes decisions concerning its own defenses with some reference to what it is that it seeks to defend itself against. Our own defense budget is a great extravagance—unless it is defending something that is indeed worth $80 billion a year defending, and at the risk of a nuclear war: That is the logic implicit in owning and manning 1,000 multiple-targeted nuclear Minutemen. As the differences between what we are and what we might become in the absence of an irresistible defense system diminish in our mind, so does the resolution diminish to make the sacrifices necessary to remain free—the tacit national commitment that the risk of death is better than the certain loss of liberty.

Nineteen sixty: "Do you believe that the United States should defend itself even at the risk of nuclear war?" Yes, 70 percent—of the student body of Yale University, in answer to that question.

Nineteen seventy: same college, same question—"Do you believe that the United States should defend itself even at the risk of nuclear war?" Yes, 40 percent.

Is that wrong?

Well, of course, it depends. Presumably if the people in the Dark Ages had known it was dark and why it was dark, they'd have done something about it—let in the light. As a matter of fact, eventually they did. "If the whole world is covered with asphalt," Ilya Ehrenburg wrote, "one day a crack will appear in the asphalt: and in that crack grass will grow." How will we know then that it is grass?

I have not worked that out. (pp. 41-2)

> *William F. Buckley, Jr., in his* Execution Eve: and Other Contemporary Ballads *(reprinted by permission of G. P. Putnam's Sons; copyright © 1972, 1973, 1974, 1975 by William F. Buckley, Jr.), Putnam's, 1975, 512 p.*

McGEORGE BUNDY

[*God and Man at Yale*] is a savage attack on that institution as a hotbed of "atheism" and "collectivism." As a believer in God, a Republican, and a Yale graduate, I find that the book is dishonest in its use of facts, false in its theory, and a discredit to its author. . . . (p. 50)

Mr. Buckley's thesis rests on two propositions: first, that Yale is currently anti-Christian and anti-capitalist; and second, that Yale's alumni have a right and duty to insist that it teach "Christianity" and "individualism" as he defines them. Let us consider the method and evidence with which he tries to establish these notions.

Beginning with religion, Mr. Buckley asserts that Yale has a weak department of religion, a high degree of religious apathy in the student body, and a number of un-Christian and anti-Christian lecturers in other fields. Even if all this were true, it would not make Yale anti-religious, for the weakness of religious teaching has been a national phenomenon for decades, and so has religious apathy among young men. And it is well to note that on Mr. Buckley's strict definition of a Christian such men as Jefferson, Emerson, Lincoln, and Yale's own William Howard Taft would fail to qualify.

But in fact there is no need to grant Mr. Buckley's claims. What he has done is to take the flimsiest of evidence or no evidence at all, and ignore whatever goes against his thesis. Thus on the basis of a single hearsay quotation—ripped from its context and quite unverified—he condemns as anti-religious a teacher whose profoundly religious influence I myself know from classroom experience and personal friendship. Similarly, in the teeth of the massive testimony of faculty and students alike—and quite without proof—he asserts the ineffectiveness of the saintly man who is Yale's chaplain. He makes no mention of the fact that not one of the ministers or chaplains at Yale, of any faith, agrees with his analysis; he never considers the generally agreed opinion of these and other observers that Yale is more religious than the rest of Protestant America and more religious than it was a generation ago. Most remarkable of all, Mr. Buckley, who urges a return to what he considers to be Yale's true religious tradition, at no point says one word of the fact that he himself is an ardent Roman Catholic. In view of the pronounced and well-recognized difference between Protestant and Catholic views on education in America, and in view of Yale's Protestant history, it seems strange for any Roman Catholic to undertake to define the Yale religious tradition (and Yale has thousands of Catholic alumni and friends who would not dream of such a course); it is stranger still for Mr. Buckley to venture his prescription with no word or hint to show his special allegiance.

If possible, the economic section of Mr. Buckley's attack is still weaker. A part of this attack consists of the same sort of personal "evidence" against individuals that he uses in his religious chapter. The insidious character of this sort of innuendo and quotation from lectures lies in the fact that no outsider can readily check the context in which the statements were made. Fortunately a large part of Mr. Buckley's case rests on the theory that Yale students are enormously influenced by the views of those who write their introductory textbooks in economics, and he devotes a long section to an "analysis" of the "collectivism" of four books which have been used in recent years at Yale. Here any man who has access to a library can check him up, and this "analysis" deserves detailed attention.

Mr. Buckley acknowledges that outright Marxists and Communists are exceedingly rare at Yale; he mentions none in this book. What he is attacking, and what he finds in the offending textbooks, is the more subtle menace of "collectivism," a term which remains undefined throughout his book. But let us see what he regards as evidence of this menace in the texts. First we find that these textbook writers consider nineteenth-century individualism "impractical of application" in contemporary America. This dangerous view has been repeatedly expressed by Mr. Herbert Hoover. Then Mr. Buckley complains because a quotation he has lifted discusses the excesses of capitalism (excesses which he himself admits, at least in large part); but he omits other quotations, from the same book, in which the *over-all* success of the American economic system is bluntly and vigorously asserted.

Next we find him distressed because the texts in question argue that great inequality of wealth and income should be avoided in a healthy society. Is it ignorance or trickery that leads him to neglect the fact that this "collectivist" view dates back to Aristotle, has the support of his own Church, and is roundly endorsed by the one textbook which he praises?

He then goes on to accuse the textbook writers of "egalitarianism." An inspection of the books shows that not one of the authors supports a full leveling of incomes, and among the quotations Mr. Buckley has omitted we find this: "Equality has generally been regarded as undesirable; such a goal is fundamentally inconsistent with the American focus on the advantages of aggressive private initiative based on income incentive." (pp. 50-1)

Another claim is that these texts do not defend the institution of private property. In support of this claim Mr. Buckley enters a single quotation in which it is argued that majority opinion probably does not consider "free enterprise" to be as basic a right as the four freedoms. The quotation is evidently supposed to indicate a hostility to free enterprise, and it is therefore somewhat surprising to find that the author in question went on, in a passage ignored by Mr. Buckley, to present with evident favor three detailed and practical arguments *for* the institution of free enterprise: that it works, that it is "a central causative factor in the growth of political liberties," and that it satisfies a basic human urge. This total reversal of the author's intent is a measure of the honesty of Mr. Buckley's method, and the sample could be multiplied a dozen times.

Finally, Mr. Buckley comes to the late Lord Keynes. He argues that the texts he denounces are slavish in devotion to Keynes, whereas in fact all four contain major differences from Keynes's position—just as Keynes himself constantly revised and modified his own distinctly capitalist views. The error is unimportant except that it shows Mr. Buckley's ignorance of what he is denouncing. . . .

In the end Mr. Buckley's indictment of Yale's economics texts turns out to be a self-indictment. This chapter shows him to be a twisted and ignorant young man whose personal views of economics would have seemed reactionary to Mark Hanna.

The worst is yet to come. Having made his "case" against Yale, Mr. Buckley has the appalling effrontery to urge that only those who will support his basic position should be allowed to teach subjects that relate to religion and economics at Yale. He goes on to argue that the alumni have a right and duty to enforce this view—unless they are themselves sympathetic to atheism and collectivism. His personal view of what a university should be is of course his own business, but in urging alumni control of Yale's educational policy he is absolutely wrong, both on the law and on the Yale tradition. His basic argument is that because the alumni pay the piper, they should call the tune. This argument has no more validity than a proposal that the religious teachings of the Roman Catholic Church should be dictated to the Pope by the Roman Catholic laymen who pay his bills. (p. 51)

The book winds up with a violent attack on the whole concept of academic freedom. It is in keeping with the rest of the volume that Mr. Buckley does not seem to know what academic freedom is. He leaps from one view to another, as suits his convenience, and his view of the facts depends entirely on their usefulness to his argument. . . . He totally fails to understand the vital difference between standards for hiring a professor and standards for firing him, and he has no conception whatever of the basic requirements for attracting and holding distinguished scholars. His theory seems to be that because ex-President Seymour once said he would not hire Communists, he should therefore have fired everyone who would not teach his own religious and economic views. This is one view of a free university; fortunately it is not Yale's or Mr. Seymour's.

In summary, Mr. Buckley's basic technique is that of a pretended firsthand report on the opinions and attitudes of Yale's teachers and textbooks, in which quotations and misquotations are given whatever meaning Mr. Buckley chooses to give them and not the meaning their authors intended. This method is dishonest. In addition there is a constant effort to assert that both Mr. Buckley's views and his suggestions for reform are somehow true to Yale's ancient tradition and virtues. This claim is wholly false. Mr. Buckley in fact holds views of a peculiar and extreme variety, both on economics and on the organization of a university. . . . (pp. 51-2)

No Christian or conservative should suppose that this particular book offers him either a genuine case against Yale or a useful method of advancing his views. I can imagine no more certain way of discrediting both religion and individualism than the acceptance of Mr. Buckley's guidance.

God and Man at Yale has the somewhat larger significance that it is clearly an attempt to start an assault on the freedom of one of America's greatest and most conservative universities. . . . Certainly it will put the Yale authorities to an absurd amount of trouble in making answers to questions based on a set of charges that ought to be beneath contempt. (p. 52)

> *McGeorge Bundy, "The Attack on Yale" (reprinted by permission of the author), in* The Atlantic Monthly, *Vol. 188, No. 5, November, 1951, pp. 50-2.*

PETER VIERECK

William Buckley . . . has written a book that challenges political, religious and educational liberalism. Nominally his book is about education at Yale. Actually [*God and Man at Yale*] is about American politics.

How right he is . . . to insist that man has a moral nature, that statism threatens it, that freedom depends on the traditional value-code of the West and that unmoral materialism results in a suicidal tolerance debunking all values as equally "relative." Specifically, Buckley attacks "statism and atheism" on the Yale campus. Yet what is his alternative? Nothing more inspiring than the most sterile Old Guard brand of Republicanism, far to the right of Taft.

Is there no "selfish materialism" at all among the National Association of Manufacturers as well as among the "New Deal collectivists" here denounced? Is it not humorless, or else blasphemous, for this eloquent advocate of Christianity, and unworldly and anti-economic religion, to enshrine jointly as equally sacrosanct "Adam Smith and Ricardo, Jesus and Saint Paul?" And why is this veritable Eagle Scout of moral sternness silent on the moral implications of McCarthyism in his own camp? . . .

The author irresponsibly treats not only mild social democracy, but even most social reform as almost crypto-communism. He damns communism, our main enemy, not half so violently as lesser enemies like the income tax and inheritance tax. Words will really fail you when you reach the book's final "message"—trustees and alumni should violate the legally established academic freedom to "banish from the classroom," not merely Communists, but all professors deviating far from Adam Smith.

Has a young Saint Paul emerged from the Yale class of 1950 to bring us the long-awaited Good Tidings of a New Conservatism and Old Morality? The trumpets of advance publicity imply it. However, this Paul-in-a-hurry skips the prerequisite of first being a rebel Saul. The difference between a shallow and a profound conservatism is the difference between the easy, booster affirmation that precedes the dark night of the soul and the hard-won, tragic affirmation that follows it. True: we need, as Buckley argues, more conservatism and traditional morality. Still, they must be earned by suffering and a change of heart,

not by glibly being "his class's Bright Young Man" (to quote the Yale Class History on Buckley). . . .

Not for economic privilege, but for ethical and anti-materialist reasons, some of us have preached a conservative "revolt against revolt." If the laboring mountain of the new campus conservatism can turn out no humane and imaginative Churchill but merely this product of narrow economic privilege, then we might need a revolt against the revolt against revolt.

As gadfly against the smug Comrade Blimps of the left, this important, symptomatic, and widely hailed book is a necessary counterbalance. However, its outworn Old Guard antithesis to the outworn Marxist thesis is not the liberty security synthesis the future cries for. Some day, being intelligent and earnest, Buckley may give us the hard-won wisdom of synthesis. For that, he will first need to add, to his existing virtues, three new ones: sensitivity, compassion, and an inkling of the tragic paradoxes of *la condition humaine*.

> *Peter Viereck, "Conservatism under the Elms," in* The New York Times *(© 1951 by The New York Times Company; reprinted by permission), November 4, 1951, p. 39.*

LEO R. WARD

In his little book *God and Man at Yale,* William F. Buckley, Jr., raises questions much wider and deeper than the book goes. I am concerned with some of these wider and deeper questions rather than with attacking or defending either young Buckley or Old Eli. (p. 473)

Young Buckley did not and could not, with his lack of experience, take up the problem of secularism affecting all society and all schools, including the church-related ones. But a word or two can be said for him. He is a good lively journalist and a promising publicist. Professors and whole universities abuse their power and their freedom, and impose on students. The student is licked; all he can do is lose his faith, or bite his tongue. But here is one youthful mind that would not take it lying down.

No doubt he has hurt Yale in some ways. But then Yale had first of all hurt itself and possibly hurt many students entrusted to it; not only Yale, of course, but the run of American universities. It is a tribute to one boy to say that he kept his eyes open, that he effectively resented the imposition and dishonesty and incompetence so common in schools. His book is immature and far from scientific. Yet it is good it was written, good for Yale, good for all of us. (p. 474)

> *Leo R. Ward, "Buckley's Attack on Yale," in* Commonweal, *Vol. LV, No. 19, February 15, 1952, pp. 473-74.*

ARTHUR M. SCHLESINGER, JR.

It was to have been expected that in time the effort would be made to render Senator Joseph R. McCarthy intellectually respectable. . . . [But] not until **"McCarthy and His Enemies"** came along was a full-length, custom-built, fourteen-karat job available. . . . [William F. Buckley Jr.'s and L. Brent Bozell's] first purpose is to examine the actual record and performance of Senator McCarthy, in an effort, as they would describe it, to disentangle what McCarthy actually has done from what the liberals (or, as they prefer to designate them, the Liberals) say that he has done. Their method is to analyze certain McCarthy cases, attempting to weigh the balance between truth and error in his contributions, and then to generalize from McCarthy's approach a more explicit philosophy for our times than McCarthy himself has been willing to articulate. Their deeper purpose is to administer to the liberals (or Liberals) chastisement for stupidity, self-righteousness, intellectual terrorism, and complicity in the Communist conspiracy.

The pose of the book is one of critical detachment. This enables the authors to dissent from numbers of McCarthy's specific charges or actions. But, while going through the motions of suspending judgment and considering evidence, they really accept McCarthy and his evidence at his own evaluation; this is the book's essential trick. Thus it is assumed throughout that McCarthy's genuine purpose is his stated purpose—*i.e.,* to attack Communists. Yet, when one considers the number of anti-Communists he has attacked, from General Marshall to James Wechsler, from Bernard DeVoto to Leon Keyserling, from Wilson Wyatt to Archibald MacLeish, one is compelled to conclude either (a) McCarthy's main target is liberals and Democrats, pro- or anti-communist; or (b) he is so stupid and his aim is so bad that he ought not to be in the communist-hunting business at all.

And it is hard to persuade oneself that McCarthy is stupid. The evidence would suggest rather that McCarthy is no more genuinely anti-Communist than the Communists themselves were anti-Fascist—that he is eager to exploit widespread and justified popular feelings on behalf of sensation, confusion, and himself, and that anti-Communism, like the Communists' anti-Fascism, is the pretext at hand, rather than the principal objective. (p. 15)

In their detailed analyses, Messrs. Bozell and Buckley apply the same convenient technique of assuming the truth of the charges which they are pretending to test. Thus they consistently cite Louis Budenz as a wholly reliable source. Yet they note that Budenz called Owen Lattimore a Communist, which Lattimore flatly denied; they note too that Lattimore was subsequently indicted for seven counts of perjury; but they characteristically fail to note that Lattimore was *not* indicted for false testimony in connection with his denial of Budenz's charge of Party membership. This would suggest that the Department of Justice has a somewhat lower opinion of Budenz's credibility than Messrs. Bozell and Buckley. In fact, the woods are full of people who have denied under oath Budenz's scatter-gun accusations that they were Party members; and none of them has ever been charged with perjury. Still, none of this deters our authors, who, while affecting to weigh evidence, blandly write that men and women who have roundly denounced Budenz's accusations "are *known* to one or more responsible persons as having been members of the Communist Party" (my italics), when all that is *known* is that irresponsible ex-Communists have made reckless accusations. Despite Bozell and Buckley, one would like to cling to the old-fashioned theory that there is a gap between accusation and proof. . . .

They do occasionally, as I said earlier, admonish McCarthy for extravagances of language or even of judgment. But this is done gently and with forbearance. "As regards his imputation of treasonable motives to Marshall," they mildly say, "McCarthy deserves to be criticized"; or, in calling James Wechsler a secret Communist devoted to writing attacks on himself in the *Daily Worker,* McCarthy "may have gone too far, but he is reasonable in applying a standard *different* from that applicable to persons innocent of involvement in the Communist conspiracy." Such misjudgments, in short, were natural

excesses of zeal, trifling when compared with the magnitude of McCarthy's services. Much of the time, indeed, the authors calmly transform the hurling of accusations by McCarthy into the simple and necessary "raising" of questions. (p. 16)

Messrs. Bozell and Buckley. . . , deploring occasional "ignorance or impetuosity or malice," . . . [conclude]: "But as long as McCarthyism fixes its goal with its present precision [*sic*], it is a movement around which men of good will and stern morality can close ranks."

As I read all this nonsense, it had a faintly reminiscent ring. The familiarity of the logic and tone haunted me for a moment; then I remembered the prototype. What Buckley and Bozell are doing is to write about McCarthy precisely as young fellow travelers twenty years ago were writing about the Communist leaders. The Communists then, like McCarthy now, were deemed rough and uncouth; their manners were coarse and unpleasant; their sense of evidence was defective; but, for all their vulgarity and crudeness, they were held to be alone in recognizing the true nature of the world, alone in having a sense of urgency, a stern morality, and an understanding of the necessities of history. . .

There, *mutatis mutandis,* stand Bozell and Buckley. . . . There is the same hysteria, the same sense of persecution, the same fascination with brutality and power—the same pattern of emotions, in short, and the same pattern of rationalization. Too many bright young men in the Thirties were bewitched by the extremism of Marxism. It is a grisly thought that bright young men of the Fifties are going to be equally bewitched by the extremism of McCarthyism. But it will take more than this clever and sick book to make me believe that the younger generation, whatever its capacity for nonsense, is going to enter another debauch of fanaticism. (p. 61)

Arthur M. Schlesinger, Jr., "The Pendulum of Dogma," in The Saturday Review, *New York (copyright © 1954 by* Saturday Review; *all rights reserved; reprinted by permission), Vol. XXXVI, No. 14, April 3, 1954, pp. 15-16, 61.*

GEORGE E. SOKOLSKY

[The value of *McCarthy and His Enemies* is that it states the case about Communist infiltration into the American government] much as McCarthy himself sees it. . . .

McCarthy has had predecessors in this battle and most of them were politically destroyed. Buckley and Bozell give the history of the efforts of others to clean the Communists out of Government by ordinary means and describe their failures. In this field the effort of J. Anthony Panuch, Deputy Assistant Secretary of State, 1945-1947, is significant, because had he succeeded Alger Hiss would have failed before he succeeded in diverting traditional American policy in China into a confusion of purpose which proved to be a boon to the Soviet Universal State.

Messrs. Buckley and Bozell, having cited an effort by routine means that failed, introduce the McCarthy technique, which is based on the assumption that one or a very few men can cause irreparable damage. One Klaus Fuchs can do more harm than a division of professional spies; one Julius Rosenberg penetrated two of the more guarded areas of America, Los Alamos and Fort Monmouth; one Arthur A. Adams could walk off with a sample of plutonium. Therefore the task as McCarthy has seen it, is to work on little pieces of data to find a pattern of infiltration, to discover the innocents who provide cover for the agents, to expose agent and innocent alike, thereby breaking up high organized and well-rooted apparatuses which it took great effort and time to establish.

This design Buckley and Bozell describe patiently. (p. 16)

What is lost in the battle over McCarthy personally is that, as this book proves, the facts have borne out his suspicions and that often independently of McCarthy's investigations those at whom he only glanced turn out to be caught in the uncovering of a phase of the conspiracy. . . .

Naturally, all members of a conspiracy claim innocence. If they left trails behind them they would not be conspirators. The problem is then whether such an investigator as McCarthy is to go soft as committees have done since 1937, when the country first became slightly conscious of this conspiracy, or risk an occasional error. Buckley and Bozell answer this question thus: "We are at war, and there are many strategies, many tactics, many weapons, many courses of action open to us. Our lines could be advanced by innumerable enterprises, some foolish, some proper—by assassinating Malenkov, by atom-bombing Soviet industrial plants, by subsidizing a Russian underground, by providing leadership and funds for promient European and Asiatic anti-Communists, by imprisoning violators of the Smith Act, by purging the Civil Service, and by exposing and persecuting Communist apologists in whatever occupation they are engaged. One thing is certain: Communism will not be defeated—any more than freedom was won—by postulating the virtues of democracy and of Christianity as evident truths and letting it go at that."

If McCarthy is eliminated from the technique of fighting Communism the need for fighting this aggressive effort to establish a Soviet Universal State by infiltration into governments will remain. Somebody will have to do it and by just such methods as McCarthy has employed. They are not the only methods or even the best, but in certain areas they achieve the most telling results. (p. 55)

George E. Sokolsky, "In Defense of McCarthy," in The Saturday Review, *New York (copyright © 1954 by* Saturday Review; *all rights reserved; reprinted by permission), Vol. XXXVI, No. 14, April 3, 1954, pp. 16, 55.*

WILLIAM S. WHITE

[*McCarthy and His Enemies*] is the most extraordinary book yet to come forth in the harsh bibliography, pro and con, of "McCarthyism." Measured as a literary and polemical effort, it is the most striking. . . .

[Authors William F. Buckley, Jr. and L. Brent Bozell] have written their book not as reporters who have followed the blow-by-blow contests, but rather, as "historians," who have studied the "historical" documents. One may legitimately doubt their objective approach, however, the authors have consulted with Senator McCarthy, but it is not known that they have consulted with General Marshall or any of the other "enemies" of the title.

Here, at any rate, is proof that it is the young who are infinitely the more deadly in purpose . . . of the species. Essentially what they have attempted is a defense both of Senator McCarthy and "McCarthyism" and an argument, well-written in the English language as it is, that will rather stagger those to whom that language has long expressed certain concepts of fair

play which Messrs. Buckley and Bozell seem to think either out of date or not viable in a world of great peril. They wish to make a kind of "security" that would astonish and worry traditional Conservatives.

For the kind of "security" here proposed would, in the end, and by its own definition, result in enormous insecurity for every sort of person whose notions might run counter to the youthful Buckley-Bozell political dogmas. . . .

For this sort of man, though of course in no way charged with disloyalty, had in the Buckley-Bozell view an intolerable capacity to make mistakes. Mistakes, in this book, are not tolerable when made by non-McCarthyites. When made by McCarthyites, however, and especially by Mr. McCarthy himself, they call only for a gentle chiding. We are, of course, none of us perfect; and after all, we must not forget the end in view—this sort of thing. . . .

[What is urged by Buckley and Bozell] is not only that the end justifies the means, but that a moral end justifies immoral means. "The will to morality," Nietzsche said, "is absolute immorality." Weed out—even if the good are weeded out with the evil! Sound the alarm—even if the innocent are intimidated with the corrupt! Use any methods so long as the security people are forced into a "harder" attitude. That is what it amounts to, and it is not an exaggeration to say that these authors are proposing the acceptance of a standard by which anti-communism would be defined at last by the degree of willingness to proceed in an authoritarian manner.

They find all Federal security programs to date far too soft. We must "do away with the formal hearing" for the accused bureaucrat. We must cease making "distinctions" between employees who are undesirable for security or loyalty reasons and employees undesirable for other reasons. The State Department ought to dismiss the security risk and the policy misfit the same way it dismisses an employee who is habitually late for work. And for public consumption the department ought to have a stock phrase covering all separations. . . . The risk should be thrown into a common channel with all other employees about to leave the department for sundry reasons.

Why? Well, "Conscientious security personnel are more likely to execute a hard security program *if everything has been done to lighten the consequences for the separated employee.* They feel less tempted to indulge the 'presumption of innocence' if they are no longer forced to adjudicate 'guilt;' and if the public has no longer a reason to regard separation from a sensitive agency as evidence of such an adjudication. On the other hand, the plight of the separated employee is indeed mitigated."

How many men, being habitually late to work would feel that the position had been "mitigated" by being put into this "common channel," under "a stock phrase covering all separations." And what about the conscientious security men who no longer have to indulge in a "presumption of innocence" along with no longer having to indulge in the presumption that a man is innocent until he is judged guilty?

Messrs. Buckley and Bozell find and applaud the fact that Mr. McCarthy and his followers are seeking to impose what they call a certain conformity of thought that for the time, is only directed against "Communist ideas." (p. 4)

At all events, they say that "it is still only Communist ideas that are beyond the pale," then add: "Some day the patience of America may at last be exhausted and we will strike out against Liberals." The Liberals, the authors say, are not treacherous like Communists. But they have to be reduced to political impotence because they make mistakes. Senator McCarthy makes mistakes—the authors say so. In the detailed section on the original "cases" before the old Tydings Committee, they criticize Senator McCarthy in some of these cases. Indeed, they find that "some of his specific charges were exaggerated, a few had no apparent foundation whatever." This judgement does not however tend to impeach Mr. McCarthy. The conclusion is that the action's living shame lies in the fact that the Tydings committee found his accusations a fraud and hoax. For, say Messrs. Buckley and Bozell, the McCarthy campaign forced the State Department to "take a new hard look" at some of the McCarthy "cases" and the upshot was the "separation" of 29 per cent of them through "loyalty or security channels," because earlier evaluation had not been "stern enough."

That is, the book's verdict here is that it is permissible and even singularly useful, to make attacks against the foreign office of a great anti-Communist power that are "exaggerated" or in some cases actually false if the end result is to cause the dismissal of slightly more than a quarter of those accused. (pp. 4, 20)

So, in sum, what have we here? We have a bald, dedicated apologia for "McCarthyism" made far more adroitly than Senator McCarthy himself could make it, that may well serve to clarify this issue. For the authors, enemies of the enemies of Mr. McCarthy, may have, ironically, done the Senator a disservice. McCarthyism is now on the record for all to see. They have "frozen" McCarthyism on their pages, which is an event that the instinctively fast-moving Senator may one day regret. (p. 20)

> *William S. White, "What the McCarthy Method Seeks to Establish," in* The New York Times *(© 1954 by The New York Times Company; reprinted by permission), April 4, 1954, pp. 4, 20.*

JAMES REICHLEY

[William Buckley's essays in *Up from Liberalism*] purport to be an attack on the philosophy of what he terms Liberalism (spelling it with a capital "L" to distinguish it from historic "liberalism," which he says is okay), but they are hardly that. Rather, the bulk of his argument is devoted to recounting incidents in which liberals have behaved foolishly or with malicious intent. Some of these incidents indeed reflect little credit on the individuals involved, and some of them . . . never cease to deserve retelling. But what do they prove about Liberalism, or liberalism, or any other political philosophy? It is not news that liberals sometimes fall short of the highest standards of conduct, and that some liberals are congenital scoundrels or fools. But what does this tell us about the philosophy to which these people claim allegiance? By this test the New Conservatism would be thrown out of court without further hearin. (This, of course, does not mean that the test is either fair or relevant; it seems only proper once the point has been raised, however, to mention that the New Conservatism stands to suffer far more than liberalism from any critical examination of the way in which its adherents comport themselves).

Mr. Buckley's proposition in this book appears to be that if he can prove that leading liberals are in the grip of some kind of "mania," he will thereby have demolished the liberal philosophy. The examples which he produces add up to no such proof, but even if they did, it would not follow that the liberal philosophy itself is false. It is commonplace of history that

great truths have frequently been discovered and disseminated by extremely odd people. Interestingly, Mr. Buckley himself raises this defense, correctly I think, against the attempt by some liberals to refute the tenets of conservatism by attributing them to the demented operations of "authoritarian personalities."

More significant than Mr. Buckley's argument is the light that it throws on the collapse of the movement he represents. He complains that the New Conservatives have difficulty finding liberals nowadays who will argue with them. The reason clearly is that most of the New Conservatives, like Mr. Buckley, do not appear to have much interest in arguing about the actual problems of our time—problems springing in part, it is true, from the real shortcomings of the liberal ideology—but prefer instead to challenge the good faith, character, and competence of their opponents.

> *James Reichley, "The New Conservatives' Last Gasp," in* The New Republic *(reprinted by permission of* The New Republic; *© 1959 The New Republic, Inc.), Vol. 141, No. 16, October 19, 1959, p. 27.*

RUSSELL KIRK

"Up from Liberalism" is especially telling in its indictment of the intolerance of many latter day liberals who are forever praising toleration in the abstract; and of the curious notion of "liberty" cherished by American ideologues whose hope in the Soviet Union springs eternal.

Buckley, personally a sensitive man, has hardened himself to endure the slings and arrows of what he calls "the liberal establishment."

This new book may be even more thoroughly drubbed by liberal reviewers than was his **"McCarthy and His Enemies."** It takes courage to endure indiscriminate abuse; the sort of courage which, in the long run, probably will prevail over great odds.

> *Russell Kirk, "Witty Probe into the 'Liberal' State of Mind," in* Chicago Tribune, Part 4 *(© 1959 Chicago Tribune), November 8, 1959, p. 9.*

ROBERT H. L. WHEELER

At one point [in *Up from Liberalism* William F. Buckley] says that liberal intellectuals "have tended to look upon democracy as an extension of the scientific method, as the scientific method applied to social problems," and he deplores this. This point is telling only in part. It is in general true that hopes for a "science" of society have been more closely associated with leftists in politics than with rightists. But surely not all liberals, including this reviewer, have shared that hope.

This is the key to the signal failure of *Up from Liberalism* to fulfil the promise of its title. The book is not an intellectual breakthrough beyond "liberalism" because Mr. Buckley on one hand defines as "liberals" all those whose political opinions fall to the left of those held by the late Robert Taft, (Communists excepted) and on the other defines "liberalism" in terms of such beliefs as the doctrine of inevitable progress which, as Henry F. May has recently shown, was generally discredited in this country by the end of the First World War.

If one disregards its title, however, one must add that Mr. Buckley's book scores some telling points. Almost two-thirds of it is devoted to detailed documentation of the departures from principled political conduct taken by individual liberals, including such men as Elmer Davis, Archibald MacLeish, Richard Rovere, and Joseph Rauth, during the McCarthy years. Mr. Buckley adds that at the time these facts were generally suppressed in left-of-center magazines and newspapers, and points out that this is symptomatic of the fact that ''in recent years, the discussion process in America appears to have broken down.'' A facile reply might be that in those years liberals had been forced to fight fire with fire. But Mr. Buckley's contention is strikingly confirmed by the reviews of *Up from Liberalism* which have so far appeared in the ''liberal'' press. In them this large portion of the book's content has simply been ignored, and one is forced to conclude that the profession of high political principle is not evidence of its practice, whether on the part of liberals or conservatives. (pp. 293-94)

> Robert H. L. Wheeler, ''Probing For an Intellectual Breakthrough,'' in The Yale Review (© 1959 by Yale University; reprinted by permission of the editors), Vol. XLIX, No. 2, December, 1959, pp. 290-95.

RICHARD L. STROUT

Mr. Buckley shows an affinity for some of the late [Senator McCarthy's] views. He does not think Communists should enjoy civil liberties, nor atheists teach in public schools. He is doubtful about so-called academic freedom unless it is used to inculcate ''right conduct.'' What is right conduct? In [**''Rumbles Left and Right''**] Mr. Buckley has compiled his essays and speeches to help us find the answer and the state his political views. . . .

Mr. Buckley is an American exotic of the far right, who wins some sympathy for his frankness and boldness since, in this sorry world the heterodox are always laughed at whether right or left. The difficulty is that his tone shifts. At times he seems genuinely trying to promote what he calls radical conservatism, and to make it seem smart and fashionable. But at other times he appears wilfully provocative and irritating, like a man who enjoys creating a sensation. The country needs another Mencken, perhaps, but one wonders if Mr. Buckley has the qualifications.

He subscribes to the conspiratorial view of history and to what D. W. Brogan called ''the illusion of American omnipotence.'' Red victories in Czechoslovakia, Tibet and Budapest were due, it seems, to spineless U. S. liberals, and now Cuba is the prime example. Another point of the Buckley doctrine is that the Soviets won't use the bomb. In his scheme of things, General Eisenhower was hardly more satisfactory than Mr. Kennedy. The American right wing, he acknowledges, is frequently accused of distrusting ''our leaders,'' and he replies brightly, ''nothing could be closer to the truth.''

A more politic polemicist might not have included in the same book in which he wishes away Federal aid to the poor and helpless, an account of his own genteel hobby—ocean yacht racing. But it is Mr. Buckley's expensive pleasure, it appears, to race other yachts to Bermuda, though he complains of the professionalism that is creeping into the sport.

Somehow or other Mr. Buckley, like Don Quixote, seems to have had run-ins with a great many people (the details of which he sets forth with embarrassing frankness), from the snippy waitress who wouldn't bring him his milk, to a fellow-Catholic, the editor of the Jesuit weekly, *America*, who won't have lunch with him. He summarily disposed of one liberal priest, it appears, by telling him that his ''so-called social reforms'' had been adopted in Italy ''where, nevertheless, Communism thrives.'' At one point, he criticizes a liberal encyclical by Pope John XXIII.

There is one genuinely moving and compassionate essay, **''The Last Years of Whittaker Chambers.''** Chambers becomes believable though still mysterious in this portrayal: a tragic and tortured figure who, in one leap, sprang from Communist activism to Eisenhower Republicanism. (pp. 3, 30)

The perplexed reader, viewing the phenomenon of this latter-day Don Quixote of the right, finds it hard to know what standards to apply. (p. 30)

> Richard L. Strout, ''All That Is Out of Joint and Needs Setting Right,'' in The New York Times Book Review (© 1963 by The New York Times Company; reprinted by permission), April 28, 1963, pp. 3, 30.

JOHN CHAMBERLAIN

I have often marvelled at the willingness of any embattled leftist to come within miles of Mr. Buckley. He has the deceptiveness that goes with a natural disposition to be friendly to any and all of God's creatures until they have proved themselves false to their Maker. Thus, in his *Rumbles Left and Right,* he credits Richard Rovere with the ability to be elegant in his spoofing. He admits the subtlety and scholarliness of Herbert Matthews. He accepts Norman Mailer as someone with whom he can have ''coexistence and cultural exchanges'' for years to come. He professes admiration for the ''excellence'' of Kenneth Tynan's dramatic criticism. He pays tribute to the ''sensitive'' quality of Henry Luce's journalistic ear. He thinks that Edmund Burke would have been tolerant of Dr. Robert Hutchins, and who is Bill Buckley to be less tolerant than Burke? He can spend a whole fortnight in contemplation of Murray Kempton's style and ability to express more in a sentence than any living academic sociologist can express in a 500-page book.

Nor is it merely that Mr. Buckley is a consummate master at softening an opponent up by beginning a dialogue . . . with an earned amenity. What makes him really dangerous is that even the most unreasonable of men (and in recent years we have had some darbs) must admit that Bill Buckley is reasonable. Who, indeed, can find a proper excuse to refuse debate with a reasonable adversary? Not Murray Kempton. Not the Rovere boy. Not even Jack Paar, who kidded himself that he could make Bill appear inhumane and failed.

So, one and all, they have come into the ring with Mr. Buckley only to discover that they were up against an adversary who could muster more effective combinations than Sugar Ray Robinson at the height of his pugilistic career. First, the amenity. Then another amenity. And then a bewildering salvo of light and hard blows.

Mr. Buckley can be charming because he is at peace, not with the world, but with himself. He cares more for truth than for a career as truth-teller. He has no latent bitterness to goad him into intemperate statements. If he were a politician, he would be one of those rare ones who are able to relinquish office without letting it disturb a penchant for personal gaiety. There is a sense of priorities in Mr. Buckley's convictions. On a fundamental issue he fights to the last ounce of his strength. But if it is a matter of some of the side issues of conservative politics, such as opposition to the compulsory fluoridization of city water, or fighting the application of the ''Metro'' government principle to the traffic departments of Greater Miami in Florida, or opposing the establishment of a mental hospital in Alaska, he doffs his hat to them. True, he would be entirely willing to agree that, in principle, people should be allowed to care for their own teeth rather than be compelled to drink water that may offend them. But as long as there are far more dangerous dragons to slay than the champions of fluorides in the reservoir, Mr. Buckley does not permit himself to be deflected. Castro is a greater menace to Miami than Metro government. And Soviet overflights in the Alaska regions take precedence over a mental hospital that might possibly be used as a Siberia. (p. 367)

Like Hilaire Belloc, Mr. Buckley can be the most formidable of adversaries because his convictions and rhetoric both stem from the same Christian documents. They match. But in Belloc's other manner he can be just as eloquent in praise of such wholly unpolitical things as wine, conversation, Bermuda races and the mysterious humor that bubbled up in Whittaker Chambers even in the midst of gloom. (p. 368)

> *John Chamberlain, "Won't You Come into My Parlor?" in* National Review *(© National Review, Inc., 1963; 150 East 35th St., New York, NY 10016), Vol. XIV, No. 18, May 7, 1963, pp. 367-68.*

JOHN LEO

Mr. Buckley insists that **"The Unmaking of a Mayor"** is not a non-book, and it is true that there are occasional flashes of original and highly readable prose. But about half of the 341 pages are devoted to the reprinting of campaign documents [of Mr. Buckley's unsuccessful New York City mayoral race]—editorials, letters, position papers—apparently in an effort to produce a faithful "record" of the campaign. The rest is overwritten and frequently tedious, as in the long argument attempting to prove that Goldwater is more in the Lincoln tradition than Lindsay.

The most interesting sections deal with the manhandling of Buckley by the press. Though most of us are not trained to see Buckley as a victim, his prose was, in fact, repeatedly distorted. In one instance, when he was discussing racial stereotypes ("the Jew with his crooked nose, the Italian with his accent, the Irishman with his drunkenness"), the New York Post cropped off the Irish reference and ran the rest as a racial slur.

Apropos of James Baldwin's claim that garbage was being thrown out of Harlem windows as a social protest, Mr. Buckley asked rhetorically: "Would we, by the same token, be entitled to throw our garbage out the window when John Lindsay passes by?" This turned up in The Herald Tribune as a *suggestion* that New Yorkers throw garbage out the window at Lindsay. The Tribune was consistently unable to deal with Buckley straightforwardly. Buckley's precampaign talk before the Police Department's Holy Name Society was misquoted 19 times in a single Tribune report. More damaging were the Tribune's clear suggestions of racism and admiration for the Selma police, which the text does not support.

The above distortions, and others documented in the book, ought not to be defended. But there is something to be said on the other side. Mr. Buckley has a rhetoric problem. Ideas rumble beneath the surface of his prose, and often a form of communication takes place that the transcript misses.

In his Police Department speech he managed to convey a lack of sympathy for Mrs. [Viola] Liuzzo, the civil-rights worker murdered near Selma, that no single quote can isolate. He raised the question—I paraphrase—"What did she expect?" (after all, she had been warned it was dangerous to ride alone at night with a Negro in the Selma area). To many people (the Tribune reporter included, apparently) the real message communicated here was "She got what she deserved."

Similarly, Mr. Buckley denounced a group of anti-Vietnam marchers with the words "epicene" "mincing" and "boulevardiers." The conjunction of these three words produced an idea that was not in the text, namely the suggestion of homosexuality. A long controversy followed—during which he professed (probably legitimately) to be astounded.

As Judge Samuel F. Hofstadter wrote Buckley after the Police Department talk: "God's supreme gift to man is speech. Its anatomy does not lend itself to such dissection as you now suggest—after the event." Or, to put it another way, Mark Antony, after the funeral oration, was not very well positioned to explain to Brutus that he merely referred to him as an honorable man and spoke not to disprove what Brutus said. (p. 36)

> *John Leo, "Gadfly in Fun City," in* The New York Times Book Review *(© 1966 by The New York Times Company; reprinted by permission), October 30, 1966, pp. 34, 36.*

PAUL GOODMAN

According to himself, a chief purpose of William Buckley's campaign for Mayor of New York was to defeat John Lindsay, in order to strengthen the "conservative" power in the Republican Party. . . .

[But] Buckley does not understand [the conservatism of the American people. In *The Unmaking of a Mayor* he] ridicules Mike Harrington's remark that Lindsay is a "sophisticated conservative," but he should take it more seriously. After all, Harrington learned political theory in the real school of left-wing factional debate, whereas Buckley learned his twitting at Yale. (p. 351)

In any case, Lindsay's positions *have* been sophisticated conservatism: strengthening the UN, admitting China, raising the minimum wage, strong Civil Rights, etc.—these speak for world stability, individual dignity, moderate isolationism, civil liberties, less social engineering, more public goods, and *joie de vivre*, all wrapped in a genteel respectability and paternalism. All that is lacking is agrarianism, which I hope Lindsay will come to.

A similar sophisticated conservative is Robert Theobald and his guaranteed income, whom Buckley would no doubt also consider radical. In my opinion, Burke in his prime would have approved [the social programs of these sophisticated conservatives]. Coleridge would have regarded them as the proper present conservative stability and modesty to counter liberal riskiness and expansion. On the contrary, so-called "conservatives" like . . . Buckley are wild laissez-faire radicals, unbridled technologists, punitive legalists, and international adventurers. But in our modern over-extended conditions, any cutting back, e.g. in imperialism or the abuse of technology, looks radical. And the beautiful conservative drive of community spirit seems to exist mainly in the Southern Negroes and beatniks.

The very large part of Buckley's book devoted to attacks, counter-attacks, and complaints of shabby treatment during the campaign, cannot profitably be reviewed here, at least not by me. Rather, let me use the rest of my space to comment on a few of his practical proposals for New York, which were sometimes naggingly in the area of real solutions but were usually betrayed by not being organic (conservative) enough, and were made unpalatable by being punitive ("conservative").

He proposes that welfare payments be "made available elsewhere" and he is right, for a crowded city is a poor environment for people who do not cope well, it is too complicated and expensive. And he is right when he wants to cut back on the excessive urbanization altogether. Unfortunately, he at once goes on to say "in areas established as great and humane rehabilitation centers"—which was hostilely interpreted as meaning concentration camps, the extreme of centralized social engineering. But the interpretation was accurate, for have not the Job Camps for drop-outs been just what he proposed? And they are concentration camps. Similarly, he proposes to cut back on urbanization by residency requirements, etc. Very different would be the *conservative* handling of these ideas: to combat the enclosure system (chain grocers and plantations) which compels emigration from the land; to use city capital (because that's where the money is) for rural reconstruction; to equip farms and villages to help with urban problems; and to attract people to underpopulated regions where they can cope better. The conservative attitude is not to exclude and make difficult, but to rearrange resources for everybody's advantage.

Similarly, his proposals to put able-bodied reliefers to work are punitive and wrong-headed. We should be pleased that we have available hands to do needed public work. The work should be worthwhile and the conditions excellent, so as to attract any decent person, for instance middle-class college-age youth who now go off to school too soon; under these circumstances, we could speak of jobs for reliefers.

Similarly, "The idea of private watchmen as an alternative to rising theft and assault is sound, but reimbursing the communities that hire them out of the tax funds . . . is awesomely difficult." Here again he betrays a second conservative insight by thinking repressively. What shall we say of the astounding proposition that "the primary purpose of courts of justice is to assert the demands of the public order, by meting out convincing punishment to those who transgress it"? I should have thought it was the purpose of the police to maintain the King's Peace and of the courts to secure justice; and I doubt that many penologists would agree that punishment diminishes crime, though it seems to be necessary to satisfy the thirst for vengeance.

But the conservative position, I think, would be not to maintain public (bourgeois) order at all costs, but to preserve the King's Peace according to the mores of each locality, in order to diminish tension so life can go on. For this, the simplest expedient would be not to underwrite vigilantes, but to make the municipal force consist of locals who would police misdemeanors according to local standards. (pp. 351-52)

On traffic congestion, he understands that the only solution is to cut back on the cars, and he sees that the cars are foreign to the spirit and function of cities anyway. But his expedient is merely to ban the cars at certain hours rather than organically planning toward a simpler structure with fewer cars. Thus, he cannot plan for new public transportation express busses, a system of electric taxis and—most important—a use for the streets when freed of traffic, e.g. for recreation and urban renewal without dislocation and disruption of neighborhoods. That is, he sometimes sees the obvious (which is already a rare thing), but he never thinks philosophically. Therefore his campaign was not educational.

On the same subject of traffic, he has a jolly proposal to diminish the cars by encouraging bicycles. I wonder if he knows about the White Bike movement of the Provos in Amsterdam, which has the same purpose, except that the Provos also painted their bikes white and left them unlocked to be used by anybody needing a ride, the new rider leaving them available in turn. The Provos are long-haired spirited radical youth of the type that Bill Buckley likes to call mincing, unidealistic, and too cowardly to drop napalm-bombs on children. (Incidentally, the white bikes succeeded fine till the cops arrested people for leaving private property unlocked.)

In brief, these are examples of how Buckley betrays good conservative impulses by lace curtain respectability and the attendant savagery, by petty bourgeois privatism and bourgeois cash-accounting, by literal rationalism rather than a philosophical view of the whole, and by a certain school-mistress pedantry that is all his own. On the other hand, he is often good boyish fun, which *is* conservative. (pp. 352-53)

Paul Goodman, "The Urban Crisis and the Unmaking of William Buckley," in Commonweal *(copyright © 1966 Commonweal Publishing Co., Inc.; reprinted by permission of Commonweal Publishing Co., Inc.), Vol. LXXXV, No. 12, December 23, 1966, pp. 351-53.*

HUGH KENNER

Bill Buckley is my favorite Lost Cause. A cause is lost when, like the restoration of the Austrian monarchy, it will clearly be opposed, even unto oblivion, by what Yeats called the gyres of things, and the moment is gone—it vanished, perhaps, with Jefferson—when such gifts and predilections as William Buckley's were of manifest and institutionalizable public utility.

For what definable role does the Republic offer him? Public office? Nonsense; the game is too tedious. Academic eminence? Too constricting. Some powerful person's *éminence grise?* Even positing a suitable person, he's not *gris* and couldn't be. Resident intellectual? Again, positing a suitable climate, he's insufficiently fanatical. Political theorist? But we're bored to death with theory.

So he's left to assemble a role out of odd jobs, editor, columnist, TV host, nose-tweaker of the *New York Times,* debater, campaigner, educator, author, moving so fast he's always in at least three places simultaneously; and sure enough the taxonomists whip out their notebooks, the generic category having presented itself: Entertainer!

Which is ridiculous, but how it comes about is instructive. A good place to begin is with one self-characterization: "a perfectly average middle-aged American, with, however, a jeweler's eye for political truths." He says that he said this with "calculated effrontery," as part of which effrontery I accept the "perfectly average."

But it's not the jeweler's eye we're normally allowed to hear about, it's the calculated effrontery, the principle of nothing-ever-quite-in-excess. . . .

In the great world such batrachian reticence is exceptional. The usual strategy is to admire all-out the snazzy phrase-monger, the wicked Cupid plucking from his quiver words we didn't know existed to transfix our innocence with: to hail, in short, a phenomenon of high-camp showbiz. Since politics is primarily entertainment, rhetorical flash in the vicinity of politics is just supreme entertainment: one no more expects to hear truths than to hear the beatitudes recited at Minsky's. Once nudge that tacit premise into a reader's mind, and he'll take the truths and the neon phrasings alike, as complementary effronteries, entertaining, disposable.

But grudging appreciation of how-he-says-it doesn't begin to appreciate; it misses the energy of mind that controls on their serial trajectories so many words at once, precisely out of concern for serious truths. Classic Buckley isn't neon, it isn't phrasework, it's syntactic energy, propelled by passion for complex interrelations.

The generating force of Classic Buckley whirls a long sentence, just restraining its energies, at varying velocities past two or three points of dangerous approach: "The salient economic assumptions of liberalism are socialist. They center around the notion that the economic ass can be driven to Point A most speedily by the judicious use of carrot-and-stick, an approach that supersedes the traditional notion of conservatives and classic liberals that we are not to begin with dealing with asses, and that Point A cannot possibly, in a free society, be presumed to be the desired objective of tens of millions of individual human beings."

Note the rapid concretion, "economic ass"; the stoic scholasticism of "Point A"; the node after "carrot-and-stick," where the proverb is completed but (surprise!) the sentence isn't; then the retarded pace, picking through twenty-odd careful words, suddenly accelerated at "dealing with asses"; then a glimpse of Point A again, to curve the orbit inward, and a careful deceleration through unforeseeable syntactic obligations to the point of rest, "individual human beings." Which, with its minatory *gravitas,* is where we've alighted, having careened past "ass" and "carrot" and "asses" and (twice) "Point A": nothing *quite* in excess.

Maxim: you can make phrases without meaning very much; but syntactic energy is uncounterfeitable, and nothing will propel it but that thorough grasp of your meaning which certifies to realities underlying the meaning. (p. 753)

[But Buckley has been forced to accomodate his style] to the newspaper, a low-definition medium. Much of [*The Jeweler's Eye*] consists of two-pagers, two book pages being a newspaper reader's thrice-weekly ration of opinion (with an extra paragraph for the weekender). Such pieces are written often and written fast. . . . If they were not written fast they would acquire a surface glaze from which the commuter's eye would instantly rebound; imagine being forced to empathize with that carrot-and-stick sentence, with, after a long hot day, the Long Island roadbed imposing its emetic rhythm!

What we get, typically, to assure us it's Buckley, is one rich clout or maybe two per column: "I do not enjoy spelunking in human depravity. . ."; ". . . a taboo for the maintenance of which the *New York Times* would go to the electric chair"; "'The church is a great place for all things,' said Dr. Wendt, who perhaps will stage a black mass on St. Stephen's altar next week, to drive his point home."

Phrasal, not syntactic. The energy remains, but no longer an orbital energy, simply the energy that doesn't hem and haw.

Which is to say, the political truths discerned by the jeweler's eye are isolated, affirmed, and left to carry their own conviction. The job of the columnist is to extract some substance, moral or philosophical, from a day's events. Once extracted, it carries conviction or it doesn't; there's no room, in six or eight paragraphs, to equip it with wings and a tail. (pp. 753-54)

Moreover, the newspaper's unit of attention, and hence its reader's, and hence the columnist's, is limited by inflexible convention to the single day's single event, and he who looks before and after is understood to be intellectualizing gratuitously. . . .

The Buckley enterprise is largely one of demythologization. Show how today's happening has been co-adopted by the structureless tendentiousness that passes alike for reporting and for political sentiment; if there's room, rebut; and in the interests of the reader's patience, keep it lively.

A necessary labor, though one could wish someone else were performing it; for its very conditions—the haste, the brevity, the medium—swallow up those great skills he expends on an ampler topic, and with more time for polish. A few of the longer pieces in *The Jeweler's Eye,* notably **"The Assault on Whittaker Chambers"** and **"The Approaching End of Edgar H. Smith Jr.,"** serve to confirm the persistence of those skills. One wishes for more like those two, which literally no one else could have written. One wishes their author were free to write a dozen like them a year, Simultaneously one does not want the column not to continue. And one wishes him freed from slavery to the typewriter. One wishes, as usual, for the impossible. (p. 754)

Hugh Kenner, "The Rhetoric Schlesinger Envied," in National Review *(© National Review, Inc., 1968; 150 East 35th St., New York, NY 10016), Vol. XX, No. 30, July 30, 1968, pp. 753-54.*

MARIO PUZO

The great thing about reading Buckley is that one comes to really understand why so gallant a nation as France lopped off so pretty a head as Marie Antoinette's. "Let them eat cake" is an infuriating phrase in any language and [*The Jeweler's Eye,* a] collection of nearly 100 of Buckley's newspaper columns, book reviews, magazine articles, . . . boils down to those old blue-blooded words of wisdom—with the same effect.

It can be amusing reading though, when Buckley catches the more unworldly liberals being particularly dopey: Pete Hamill attacking Truman Capote's famous party with 1930-ish irony; the tactical assault on Daniel P. Moynihan by members of the Negro left who know better; the pathetically illogical defenders of Alger Hiss.

But it is, inadvertently, more amusing when Buckley gives us what he considers the Conservative viewpoint. Conservatism certainly has its value in any society, as a belief in prudence, as a champion of individual freedom. But it is not presented in quite that fashion here.

Buckley is very strong on individual freedom. It is wrong to pass a law forbidding the sale of cigarettes, he says, no matter how much cancer is packed into each weed. But then he gets sore because his 14-year-old boy gets pornographic literature in the mail and he demands government action to stop it. In another essay, **"Let the Rich Alone,"** he argues that billionaires like H. L. Hunt should be allowed to make as much money as they please. Ten billion? Twenty billion? It doesn't matter, just let the poor guy alone. But then Buckley whirls around and says that college students should not be allowed to invite Communist speakers to address them.

Buckley wants the Federal Government to get out of the citizen's way so that local governments can solve their own problems. But he wants Martin Luther King's nonviolent protest movement suppressed, remarking in passing that he wished Hitler and Lenin had been repressed.

Mr. Buckley also has a theory that nobody should be allowed to vote unless he can prove that he will vote not for his own selfish interests but for the general welfare. Here he may be putting us on. (Buckley is a great put-on artist: he tries to make you believe that he really thinks Barry Goldwater is a more admirable human being than Eleanor Roosevelt; he reproduces some of General MacArthur's prose, which he claims will make us die happy; and he congratulates the American people for finally recognizing that Herbert Hoover was a great man.)

What gives this book a sort of special charm is that Buckley, like Marie Antoinette before him, is more innocent than malicious. His philosophy may be pure but it is surely impractical. Would a Negro fight in Vietnam for the freedoms granted him by the state of Mississippi? Would *anybody*, if Mr. Hunt has *all* the money, fight Russia and Red China to save Mr. Hunt's money and none of their own? Sure they should, as good Buckley Americans. But *would* they?

Buckley is as royally condescending to his betters as he is to the peasantry. He derides Arthur Schlesinger for talking such nonsense as that the best defense against Communism may be the social welfare state. Again this is surely innocence at work. He doesn't quite get Schlesinger's drift, which is, obviously that when a force stronger than yourself says, "Your money or your life," you hand over the money, and if you're really smart you hand over some of your money before anybody gets tough about it. It would seem unnecessary to simplify in such a fashion, but Buckley still thinks he is being begged for a handout; Schlesinger knows it's a stick-up. I do not mean to cast aspersions on the welfare state with this analogy; after all, a stickup within the legal framework of our society—via the vote, etc.—is the last word in exercising individual freedom.

Buckley is condescending even to Norman Mailer, a far more dangerous diversion. He loves Mailer as an artist, he says, because Mailer makes the most beautiful metaphors in the business, "as many as a dozen on a single page worth anthologizing." Well, that's pretty good metaphorizing. But Mailer's reaction to that kind of praise will be like that of the chorus girl who received as a birthday present from her millionaire lover a signed photograph of himself. . . .

The strange thing is that at the end of the book, through some strange, charming process, you like the author. The work did give this reader a terrible nightmare, however. He dreamed that Buckley had won his recent fight for the office of Mayor of New York City, and that the riots came in Harlem, and that Buckley set out to walk the slum streets to calm his people. Mercifully the dream ended there.

Mario Puzo, "Like Marie Antoinette," in The New York Times Book Review (© 1968 by The New York Times Company; reprinted by permission), September 15, 1968, p. 5.

C. W. GRIFFIN, JR.

[As demonstrated by *The Jeweler's Eye*, a] collection of Buckley's wit and wisdom, he is a shallow, superficial political thinker. In cold print, the illusion of the intrepid individualist cannot be sustained by the wisecracks, the clever digressions, and other sophistical techniques that suffice on television. Buckley is spontaneous and witty when ridiculing an opponent, turbid and insipid when expounding his own philosophy: "The succubi of Communism are quite numerous and eloquent enough to be counted upon to put their ghastly presences forward in effective protest against the marriage of any but the most incurable solipsist to a set of abstractionist doctrines the acceptance of which would mean the end of liberty."

Muddying the waters to make them appear deep is the only polemical strategy open to a writer defending the old familiar values and superstitions. Many of us Buckley's age (forty-three) were imbued in childhood with the same Bronze Age tribalism, medieval salvationism, and Nineteenth Century capitalism. But most educated persons so afflicted manage to chuck the barbarous burden as they grow up and think for themselves.

Buckley, however, has always been such a pugnacious partisan that his undeniably keen mind remains almost untouched by intellectual curiosity—the desire to see things unencumbered with emotional trappings.

In *God and Man at Yale* . . . , Buckley wrote, ". . . the teaching part of a college is the practice field on which the gladiators of the future are taught to use their weapons, are briefed in the wiles and strategems of the enemy, and are inspired with the virtue of their cause in anticipation of the day when they will step forward and join the struggle against error." He further attested to his "conviction that, after each side has had its say, we are right and they are wrong."

As *The Jeweler's Eye* redundantly demonstrates, Buckley has never outgrown this dogmatism. He defends Whittaker Chambers' dictum that one must choose between God and Communism ("or, some suitable variant"). Expressing his contempt for the "unreasoned hysteria" of those who warn of the horrors of thermonuclear war, Buckley writes, "If it is right that a single man is prepared to die for a just cause, it is arguably right that an entire civilization be prepared to die for a just cause. . . . if ever a cause was just, this one is, for the enemy combines the ruthlessness and savagery of Genghis Khan with the fiendish scientific efficiency of an IBM machine."

This passage reveals Buckley's absolutist mentality in all its gory glory. If one were really forced to choose between the stark alternatives posed by the Dead-Red dichotomy, to prefer the extinction of civilization to a Communist victory is infantile, egocentric fanaticism at its irrational worst. For an individual to choose a heroic death for himself is totally different from condemnation of everyone, including millions of children with no say in the matter, to a horrible, mass death. The identification of private feelings of self-righteousness with the Will of God produced the Inquisition and the barbarous, demented Crusades. (pp. 49-50)

Yet today—seven centuries after the Fifth Crusade and three centuries after the last heretic burning—this wittily disguised medieval fanaticism qualifies as Conservatism. (p. 50)

C. W. Griffin, Jr., "Medieval Buckley," in The Progressive (reprinted by permission from The Progressive, 409 East Main Street, Madison, Wisconsin 53703; copyright 1969 by The Progressive, Inc.), Vol. 33, No. 1, January, 1969, pp. 48-50.

VICTOR S. NAVASKY

William F. Buckley Jr. lost something when Eleanor Roosevelt died: his favorite target. And **"The Governor Listeth,"** his latest collection of essays, columns, revelations, forgettabilia, etc. is the poorer for it. For instance, only once does he tell us the story about how Mrs. Roosevelt said that she would not cross a picket line "under any circumstances," a proclamation which gave rise to "the most ineluctably rationalist reply" Mr. Buckley has ever known, namely, "the call—it having been ascertained that she was in residence—for volunteers to picket round the clock all the exits from Hyde Park." (p. 7)

Well, Mr. Buckley doesn't have Mrs. Roosevelt to kick around any more and so it was with some curiosity that I approached **"The Governor Listeth"** to see how he has been managing in her absence. Quite well, thank you. A brief target analysis follows:

First, he has replaced Mrs. Roosevelt, a moving target in her own right, but a square one, with three relative swingers: John Kenneth Galbraith ("who always looks like he is on leave from Mt. Olympus"), Arthur Schlesinger Jr. (whose assertion that he never signed any statement he didn't write prompted Buckley to speculate, "Suppose everyone adopted that position? Who would be left to sign Mr. Schlesinger's future statements? Nobody? Well, there's a point to be made in favor of that") and Gore Vidal, with whom Mr. Buckley is on the verge of litigation over who said what about whom.

Second, we may observe that the informed Mr. Schlesinger, the cutting Mr. Galbraith and the imaginative and bitchy Mr. Vidal are each capable of defending themselves in ways of which Mrs. R. was either oblivious or incapable; but that the badinage, rebuttal and counter-rebuttal are all calculated to bring out the best in Mr. Buckley, which is very good indeed. And indeed—aside from some hilarious bad taste excursions in the Buckley-Vidal corner—much of **"The Governor"** is graceful, civilized, witty, perceptive and, to use the adjective which follows Mr. Buckley with more frequency than any other contemporary entity save The New Yorker Magazine, urbane.

Third, a note on perspectives from the firing line. Mrs. R. was the far left of her day and Buckley was attacking from the far right. Galbraith, Vidal and Schlesinger were the enlightened center and what we have here is an inside job. It is not that Mr. Buckley has mellowed or muted his message—that the acid thrower of yesteryear has given way to court jester. Buckley can still salivate cyanide and spritz it with a tongue-flick at the mention of Alger Hiss or Judith Coplin or the Rosenbergs or Brezhnev and Kosygin, or such new lefties as Tom Hayden, although Mr. B. is as bothered by Mr. Hayden's manners as much as by his philosophy.

Rather it is that in the age of Agnew, the milieu of Mitchell, Buckley politics are quasi-establishment politics. This is not to deny that there are respects in which Chairman Bill, borrowing a tactic from Chairman Mao, has chosen to swim in the mainstream; he is in favor of a Negro for President by 1980, he was/is an attacker of the attackers of Democratic President Lyndon Johnson's foreign policy, and he is even a selective civil libertarian.

One result of this centrist geography: Not only is he engaged in civilized discourse with mainly friendly enemies but he has left President Nixon virtually alone. When one recalls his helpful perspective on the Eisenhower era ("My guess is the Communists moved with whatever caution it can be said they did between 1953 and 1960 because they hadn't the least idea what Eisenhower was talking about, and thought a little prudence might be in order") one can only join in that old folksong for conservatives: "Won't you come home, Bill Buckley/Won't you come home/ From the Establishment?. . ."

Finally, it is clear that although his self-image is amateur logician and sometimes metaphysician, his ultimate talent is as syntactician. Whether he is adumbrating Aquinas or decimating a contemporary cliché, his sentences can raise their eyebrows, he can punctuate his way out of a paper bag, he can set up a victim in parentheses and dispose of him in *italics!*

This mix—the new syntax and the old politics—in addition to exuding literary charm seems suited to Buckley's specialty: the essaylet. . . . Which is, by the way, why [**"Quotations From Chairman Bill"**] doesn't work. It is not that the bits aren't as funny as the pieces. It is simply that Mr. Buckley's syntax is his context. And the punchlines without the context are like Chambers without Hiss, Schine without Cohn, Mr. Buckley without Mrs. Roosevelt. (pp. 7, 20)

> *Victor S. Navasky, "The Sentences Raise Their Eyebrows," in* The New York Times Book Review *(© 1970 by The New York Times Company; reprinted by permission), August 2, 1970, pp. 7, 20.*

MICHAEL J. ARLEN

At times, Bill Buckley seems to be the Muhammad Ali of the Tory-Yale-Connecticut-Eastcoast. . . .

Other times, he seems more like the most debonair of our political prisoners. . . .

Buckley's new book contains both of these Buckleys, as well as a couple of others. He calls it **"Cruising Speed."** . . . The title, one imagines, is thus ironic, since the book is clearly a record of a great deal of activity and bustling around on the part of the captain. It is probably a better title than I think.

In any case, **"Cruising Speed"** is in the form of a journal. A week (late in 1970) in the life of Bill Buckley. It is a cheery, odd sort of a book, full, maybe overfull, of casual bits of detail, National Review shoptalk, anecdotes and random musings. Buckley drives (gets driven) in from Connecticut. He attends to his correspondence. He chats about associates at the magazine. He has lunch. He tells a story about Edgar Eisenhower. He goes to a concert. He discusses his lecture routines. His dog. His lawyer. Hugh Hefner. More correspondence . . . If a lot of this sounds ordinary—well, it *is* ordinary. Most people's lives are ordinary. Even Charlemagne, presumably, used to now and then putter into the kitchen, try to scramble himself an egg, and have a bit of a joke, doubtless a very imperial joke, with the cook.

What seems odd in Buckley's book isn't the ordinariness, which I think is probably what you want in a journal—that texture-of-life business all those English diarists seem to have turned out by the gross ton. What surprised me was the absence of this texture—that, when you put all the little dots together, the bits of paint, you didn't finally get much of a painting, much of a life. In a way, one can't really fault Buckley on that— because he doesn't claim otherwise. In fact, he seems pretty straight throughout about what he's doing. "I'm not hugely introspective," he keeps saying all along.

Judging by this book anyway, he certainly isn't. And, in a sense, this is attractive: after all, there isn't a scarcity of introspection on the shelves at Brentano's these days. But it's also a bit off-putting and weird. At one point, for instance, Buckley is pondering, or seems about to ponder, on the Kennedys and the Buckleys. Then: "Why are so many Irish defensive?" he suddenly mutters, or ponders. And: "How can anyone be patronising about Ireland, in the century when Ireland gave us Shaw and Joyce and Yeats, while England was defending herself primarily with American expatriates James and Eliot?" Gosh. One has the unmistakable feeling that somebody on deck is either typing too fast or thinking too slow. Or in the words of the immortal song: *"This* is Edmund Burke?"

In the end though, what I found dissatisfying about the book is what I've found dissatisfying about much of Buckley's political writing—which isn't so much his politics. (He's welcome to his politics.) It's that he seems only incidentally political. The role of reason, he preaches. Order. Roman order. Look what happened at Altamont. Avoid big government. Softness. Chaos. Chaos in fact is softness, and vice versa. And all the while, quotations from Jefferson and Hamilton. Instructions from History. The teacher on the platform keeps pointing with his pointer. "Mr. Jefferson always acknowledged . . . Hamilton insisted . . . Oliver Wendell Holmes had difficulty in . . ."

He *seems* to be saying something about our past, about our present. And, now and then, here is a segment of a voice, a register maybe, in which he does speak to us about ourselves. But mostly, it seems to me, the voice that Buckley, and much of American Conservatism, speaks to us with comes out of somewhere else, something familial, tribal, perhaps (it would not be an immense surprise) filial. This voice, for all its fluency in American history, with its harshness disguised as rationality, with its small-mindedness concealed behind flourishes and boutonnieres—speaks mostly back into itself, about itself, and only very rarely out to us, about us.

This too could be okay, certainly in a book. But I have the feeling that when Buckley talks to us about, say, American history, Hamilton, Jefferson, he too thinks that's what he's saying—something objective about Jefferson, Hamilton, and history. For myself, I'm not sure I'd pay $6.95 for even an attractive book, no matter how apt the quotations from Hamilton, in which—as intellectual center—the author comes out for such astonishments as the benefits of order against chaos, or the social uses of reason as opposed to anarchy. I'd pay a whole lot more for an ugly book by William Buckley about his journey.

I don't know where he'd start it, or where he'd end it, and I wouldn't envy him the writing of it. But it sure as hell would be something to read.

> *Michael J. Arlen, " 'Cruising Speed'," in* The New York Times Book Review *(© 1971 by The New York Times Company; reprinted by permission), September 26, 1971, p. 7.*

DENNIS HALE

No lasting judgments about Buckley's thinking can be made on the basis of [*Cruising Speed*]: It is not a work of philosophy but a documentary of a week in Buckley's life. Not a diary, exactly, and still less an autobiographical confession. As Buckley admits, he is not a man much given to public introspection. The closest thing to a surprise (to me, at least) is his fondness for the Beatles. The closest thing to a psychological clue is his description of how his father packed him off to an English

boarding school just to improve his elocution (he was not *opening his mouth* when he spoke). . . .

There is enough here to provide grounds for a question, but not enough really for a satisfying answer: the question being, What kind of conservative *is* Buckley, exactly? . . .

The Federal Constitution, which Buckley devotes much of his time to defending, is a notoriously liberal document. . . . So is the Declaration of Independence. So are most of the political philosophers this nation has produced, not to mention its politicians. Most important, for Buckley at least, the traditional working assumptions of the American business community have also been taken from that same tradition: free enterprise, a faith in science and technique, a preference for private over public government, individualism, rationalism, and the sentimental belief that things are getting better every day. Babbitt may have been stuffy, but he was not a Conservative.

Buckley has tried to escape this dilemma via Catholicism, attempting to bring to American society the kind of criticism that Chesterton brought to turn-of-the-century Britain. (p. 47)

Is William F. Buckley a conservative at all? Or is he just a liberal with an irascible temper? A liberal whose training and inclinations make him disdainful of other liberals?

The answer to that question depends in part on the answer to a more basic question: Is capitalism conservative? Or, more precisely, is the peculiar hybrid that the American economic system has become a conservative specimen or is it something else entirely?

Normally, such a question would have little meaning. As used in casual conversation, the terms "conservative" and "liberal" refer simply to preserving and changing the existing system, regardless of that system's characteristics. But Buckley does not want to be a "casual" conservative. He wants to be a conservative in the deepest sense of the word, with all of the historical associations and antecedents intact. He wants to be part of a grand tradition. He wants to be a Conservative with a capital C.

With this sense of the word in mind, Buckley and his colleagues at the *National Review* make mighty strange conservatives. For all their concern about the crisis of Western thought, for all their anxiety over our vanishing liberties, for all their scolding the New Left for its terrible manners, their program comes in the end to nothing more inspiring than dismantling the state and submitting us to the beneficence of a G.M. or U.S. Chamber of Commerce.

Aside from its other defects, this program violates the conservative tradition in two ways:

First, it has nothing of the traditonal conservative's regard for *public* liberty. . . .

Second (and this may be a too literal-minded criticism), Buckley's faith in capitalism is curious because industrialism unregulated by any notions of public good (which is a fair definition of capitalism) has been history's most prodigious waster of men and resources. It has destroyed more customs, institutions, cultures, values and people than any anarchist ever dreamed. Entire civilizations—starting with our own—have gone into its furnace to be transformed into more useful appendages of the industrial system, each time to the cheerful applause of those philosophers whose only god was the GNP.

That this furious energy has made important and valuable contributions to Western life is not to be denied. The question of the hour, though—to which Buckley is woefully indifferent—is whether we have not already gone too far toward creating a society in which industrial efficiency is the only god to whom people pay more than lip service. If we have, then William Buckley—whatever his intentions—will have to bear a large share of the blame. (p. 48)

> Dennis Hale, "Books: 'Cruising Speed: A Documentary'," in Worldview (© copyright 1972 Council on Religion and International Affairs), Vol. 15, No. 6, June, 1972, pp. 47-8.

JOHN P. ROCHE

Only an oxymoron (as William F. Buckley would say), or a numbskull (a word I prefer) would attempt a comprehensive review of [**"Inveighing We Will Go"**]. Culled from his writings over a three-year period, and dealing with all imaginable (and some unimaginable) topics, [this collection provides] a quite revealing insight into what might be called the "new Buckley." To summarize, Bill Buckley has abandoned the task of trying to formulate a coherent theory of "conservatism" and has settled for inveighing against the so-called "liberal Establishment." . . .

Buckley has left the metaphysical chores to various deep thinkers and joyously set out to smite the liberals hip and thigh. And he is good at it. No commentator has a surer eye for the contradictions, the hypocrisies, the pretensions of liberal and radical pontiffs.

"Inveighing," then, is his natural genre, and this collection shows him at his best. It is not a matter of agreement or disagreement—I suspect I disagree with every one of his major premises except his respect for the ground rules of the democratic order—but rather that, even when you wince, reading Buckley is fun. On occasion I get a bit put off by his "conceits" (in the Elizabethan sense of the word); he gets too ornate, too addicted to esoteric words and quaint formulations.

But when he is in top form, that rapier can really cut. Perhaps best of all, the venom of his early years has been watered down to a sort of genial malevolence. . . . He still is a man of strong convictions, but when he cuts loose, one no longer finds the image of a firing squad lurking in the background of his rhetoric. Keep in mind the erroneous character of his major premises, but by all means go **"Inveighing"** with Bill Buckley. (p. 40)

> John P. Roche, "'Inveighing We Will Go'," in The New York Times Book Review (© 1972 by The New York Times Company; reprinted by permission), October 8, 1972, p. 40.

DANIEL P. MOYNIHAN

[*Four Reforms*] is superbly argued. More than once I had attained that willing state of disbelief which must precede agreement with this particular polemicist, only to have him calmly put down his notes at one lectern, walk to the opposite and forthwith confirm my preceding doubts. But further in these debates with himself he has found a wider range of reference than the somewhat kinky holdouts of his early years at Yale. He is not above invoking Montesquieu, and for the things that matter most there is always Michael Oakeshott, but most of his references, and not only out of slyness, are to certified liberals, who have reacted more openly to the experience and the evidence of the 1960's. Their themes are his and deal with the subjects of his four reforms.

The first concerns welfare, about which he is far less censorious than most. . . . He simply thinks that welfare dependency is a condition to be regretted in most cases, and would like less of it. He cites a "grudging, though elegant, admission" from an Israeli professor, a socialist, who said in a television colloquy awhile back, "On the whole, those systems that have put liberty ahead of equality have done better by equality than those that have put equality above liberty." That's what Buckley thinks. Again: always has, although it has been the mode to deny his conclusions concerning the egalitarian consequences of libertarianism. (pp. 5-6)

I regret to say his welfare reform is hopeless: "Congress shall appropriate funds for social welfare only for the benefit of those states whose per capita income is below the national average." His object is to help only those who really need it. His mistake is to assume that this condition is heavily correlated with per capita income, when the truth seems almost the reverse. Social welfare is needed mostly by persons with various forms of incapacity, physical, mental, and social. These are at least as likely to be found in high income states as in low. Perhaps more so. . . .

As a second reform, he would replace the graduated income tax with a flat 15 per cent on personal income, and makes a rollicking good case. Senator McGovern, he says, was right: the present system is a scandal. Where he differs from liberals is that he doesn't think this is the result of conspiracy. Rather, he cites Hayek: In a bourgeois democracy the middle classes hold power, and everywhere use this to impose heavy taxation on the poor and on the rich. (As for the poor, he does in fact propose a modified negative income tax.) Further—and probably more important to Buckley—the present system makes cheats of us all. What republic will do that to its citizenry and expect to survive? I vote maybe on this reform. Let the economists join in.

Next, he would amend the Constitution to incorporate the Brown decision and to forbid the denial of "any relief authorized by any legislature for children attending non-public schools. . . ." He is right. The treatment of Catholic schools is a scandal of American juridical and political liberalism—the more so as those involved seem incapable of seeing this. . . .

Lastly, Buckley would abolish the Fifth Amendment and try suspected criminals with the despatch that the British attain. Here I would invoke a moderator's rule: only one Constitutional amendment to a panelist. I have no idea what the repeal of the Fifth Amendment would mean to the society except that it will be different from what any of us expect. . . . I have no desire to experiment just for the fun of finding out. Anyway, crime will recede for the same demographic reasons welfare will.

In sum: no, maybe, yes, no. Not a bad score for a neophyte reformer. And a superbly stimulating experience for this reviewer, weary beyond expression with the "eristic patter" and vulgar abuse that now so much passes for discourse on public policy. (p. 6)

> Daniel P. Moynihan, "'Four Reforms'," in The New York Times Book Review (© 1974 by The New York Times Company; reprinted by permission), January 13, 1974, pp. 5-6.

ELLIOTT ABRAMS

Four Reforms is so short that one wonders whether in writing it Buckley was not responding more to a conviction that he *ought* to write a book than to any real desire to sit down and do so. Buckley devotes only twenty-odd pages to each of his proposals, which concern welfare, aid to education, taxes, and criminal justice; this hardly provides sufficient opportunity to convert the unbelievers, and if that were Buckley's intention the book would simply be a failure. Recognizing the limitations of space, however, he has chosen a different tack. In each of four complex and highly controversial areas, he has attempted to cut through to the core of the problem with a simple, often startling, usually very conservative, proposal. The accompanying text is by and large a devastating critique of present policies, rather than a reasoned argument for Buckley's own proposals.

Buckley's four reforms may be set forth very simply: he proposes two constitutional amendments, one to repeal the Fifth Amendment and one to forbid school busing and permit aid to parochial schools; and he proposes two statutory revisions, one to replace the progressive income tax with a flat-rate tax, and one to forbid federal welfare appropriations to the richer states. The overall program is not likely to win a very high rating from Americans for Democratic Action, but in fact, little of what Buckley has to say contains much ideological bias.

His criminal-law proposal, repeal of the Fifth Amendment, is typical. The suggestion is on its face a terrible one. Upon reading the text, however, we learn that Buckley favors neither torture nor police brutality, but is instead exercised about a number of very real problems. The first is the Supreme Court's insistence on the "exclusionary rule," the doctrine that illegally seized evidence may not be received in court. The effect of this doctrine is to frustrate, on account of police or prosecutorial misbehavior, the conviction of defendants against whom there is competent and persuasive evidence. As Buckley notes, the official misbehavior itself is not punished, but the guilty are freed and society pays the penalty. It is, from the standpoint of logic, an altogether strange state of affairs, and Buckley is not alone in wondering why a less costly method could not be devised to curb abuses by law-enforcement officials. Buckley is also disturbed by the endless delays which now characterize so many criminal-court calendars, and in this area too his concern is widely shared.

Buckley's objections to the present taxation and welfare systems are not fundamentally ideological either. The Internal Revenue Code is nearly incomprehensible, Buckley holds, a circumstance which encourages people to believe it is nothing but a maze of loopholes. This is on the whole an accurate charge. Buckley's reform would entail the elimination of virtually all deductions and exemptions—a system which he claims would appear more just to taxpayers than the present, irregularly progressive, one. As to welfare, dissatisfaction with the present scheme is now so widespread that there may well be no one, even among social workers, who wishes to see it continue without reform.

Buckley, then, has little difficulty demonstrating the need for change. He is less successful in proving that his proposals, if put into effect, would solve the problems to which they are addressed. To take criminal law first, the Fifth Amendment is not in fact what is primarily responsible for the exclusionary rule or for criminal-court calendar delays. The right to counsel, for example, appears in the Sixth Amendment, and therefore any delays occasioned by the ubiquitousness of lawyers would

not disappear if "taking the Fifth" were no longer permitted. In any case, as recent and successful reforms in New York City have shown, what may be responsible for delays is poor administration of the courts, not an overly solicitous attitude toward defendants. Buckley offers no evidence that giving "Miranda warnings" has in fact reduced the number of confessions police receive, or that police effectiveness is diminished by the need to inform suspects of their rights. The FBI has followed this practice for decades, and its performance has not been noticeably impaired.

His tax proposal is likewise off the point. Buckley notes that the man in the street distrusts the endless complexity of the Internal Revenue Code, but surely one reason for dissatisfaction is the intuition that the rich are not paying their fair share. Buckley's plan would insure that the rich pay a sum certain, but would that be more or less than they pay now? Buckley never answers this, an obvious question about any tax-reform scheme; a chart he provides, however, indicates that anyone earning much over $25,000 would, under the proposed 15 percent flat rate, pay less than he does now. Since Buckley's proposal includes various forms of tax relief for the poor, one concludes that the middle class would be left with a still-heavier tax burden than today. Perhaps not—but even a 24-page discussion ought to reveal who will pay more and who will pay less.

Buckley's welfare proposal is almost bizarre. In his tax-reform chapter he suggests certain ways of lightening the burden now placed on the poor, but to the present welfare system he proposes no real alternative whatsoever, other than that Congress "appropriate funds for social welfare only for the benefit of states whose per-capita income is below the national average." Buckley's point is that federal funds are themselves derived from all states, rich and poor, and that therefore federal grants to rich states like New York constitute at least a partial subsidy of them by poor states like Mississippi. True enough, but is it not a form of tunnel vision to regard welfare funds as coming from and going to states rather than individuals? Similarly, per-capita income figures are only marginally relevant when the central issue is the distribution of income.

Buckley apparently envisions a plan whereby the federal government would make welfare payments to the poor of Mississippi while the poor of New York depended for help exclusively on the state treasury. If the New York state legislature decided to spend its money on highways, or even education, New York's poor could presumably like it or lump it—or move to Mississippi. It is not, all in all, a terribly helpful idea. If the goal is to reorganize present welfare programs and to increase aid to the poor, Buckley's proposal is, on both counts, at best a *non sequitur* and at worst a step in the wrong direction.

The chapter on education contains a superb review of the recent trials and tribulations of liberals as their dogmas have come under challenge by scholars like James Coleman, Christopher Jencks, and Richard J. Herrnstein. "Of all the dreams of American liberalism," he writes, "the dream that featured education—as the solvent of universal equality, harmony, and prosperity—was the most rudely shattered in the postwar decades." Of course, Buckley suggests no cure for this situation, since he considers it inevitable and indeed welcome. Instead, he turns to two other areas: forced busing, which he wishes to prohibit, and aid to parochial schools, which he wishes to permit. His arguments on both counts are cogent, although he is stronger on educational policy than on constitutional law, and the proposed constitutional amendment he submits is much too loosely written. (pp. 74-5)

Elliott Abrams, "Public Discourse," in Commentary (reprinted by permission; all rights reserved), Vol. 57, No. 4, April, 1974, pp. 74-8.

STEVEN R. WEISMAN

In **"Execution Eve: And Other Contemporary Ballads,"** William F. Buckley Jr. slithers venomously across the usual broad terrain of sacred and secular topics. Nobody demolishes easy targets more skillfully than he does—Jane Fonda never had a chance. Bill Buckley certainly deserves his reputation as one of the wittiest political satirists writing today. Whether you agree with him or not, it takes flair to note Senator George McGovern's sudden mid-campaign advocacy of relocating the American Embassy in Israel from Tel Aviv to Jerusalem: "Imagine discovering Jerusalem only under the triangulating guidance of the three kings, Gallup, Harris and Yankelovich."

Pungent, turgid, eloquent, repetitious, sentimental, frivolous and moralistic—Mr. Buckley is, by turns, all these things in this volume. He reveals, for instance, that his friend, E. Howard Hunt, had told him many details about Watergate in December, 1972—months before they began coming out in public. The ethics of Mr. Buckley's silence aside, his acerbic Watergate commentary doesn't seem to have been affected much by his inside knowledge in the early phases of the scandal. For the first time since he has been publishing collections of his journalism, the author also includes a lively segment from the "Notes and Asides" column of the National Review,

which he edits. A section of letters and offhand comments, it is by far the most entertaining portion of the book.

Most of the time, however, Mr. Buckley is concealing the pain and sorrow with which he evidently views the ways of the world. Occasionally he retreats into a kind of gloom and cynicism that takes the reader by surprise. "The Nobel people awarded a Peace Prize to Mr. Kissinger and Le Duc Tho for stanching the flow of WASP blood in South Vietnam," he writes at one point, in an acid comment that many on the Left might endorse. "Gooks don't count. They continue to be slaughtered at the conventional rate."

The author grieves for his countrymen—weighted down, as he sees it, with stifling Federal controls—and for the hundreds of millions abroad whose oppression marks for him the central outrage of this age. Seldom, however, does he express much pain for economic inequities, globally or nationally. Mr. Buckley effectively ridicules Senator McGovern, for instance, for being "obsessed" with a hatred of accumulated wealth—"it is a point of view that is interesting pathologically, but hardly one that should commend itself to intellectuals who think of their academic training as having emancipated them from primitive fetishism."

In another column, he states that the "problem" with protesting students is their "egalitarian ideology"—and there you have it. Mr. Buckley, a man of wealth, a man of gifts, is not going to be fooled by the false god of egalitarianism. He is, in any case, a cogent expositor of this point of view. (p. 3)

Steven R. Weisman, "Reports from Senator Jim and Brother Bill," in The New York Times Book Review (© 1975 by The New York Times Company; reprinted by permission), September 28, 1975, pp. 3-4.*

Angela Carter

1940-

Carter is a British author of novels, short stories, and feminist nonfiction. In her first nonfiction book, *The Sadeian Woman* (1978), she explores the implications for modern feminists of the Marquis de Sade's pornography. Carter's intention is to "give the old monster his due," because she believes he "put pornography in the service of women, or, perhaps, allowed it to be invaded by an ideology not inimical to women." While Robin Morgan and other critics praise her courage in posing difficult questions about sex and power, Carter's treatment of her subject has produced controversy in both feminist and literary circles. (See also *Contemporary Literary Criticism*, Vol. 5, and *Contemporary Authors*, Vols. 53-56.)

Excerpt from *THE SADEIAN WOMAN: AND THE IDEOLOGY OF PORNOGRAPHY*

Pornographers are the enemies of women only because our contemporary ideology of pornography does not encompass the possibility of change, as if we were the slaves of history and not its makers, as if sexual relations were not necessarily an expression of social relations, as if sex itself were an external fact, one as immutable as the weather, creating human practice but never a part of it. (pp. 3-4)

[Pornography] reinforces the false universals of sexual archetypes because it denies, or doesn't have time for, or can't find room for, or, because of its underlying ideology, ignores, the social context in which sexual activity takes place, that modifies the very nature of that activity. Therefore pornography must always have the false simplicity of fable; the abstraction of the flesh involves the mystification of the flesh. As it reduces the actors in the sexual drama to instruments of pure function, so the pursuit of pleasure becomes in itself a metaphysical quest. (p. 16)

When pornography abandons its quality of existential solitude and moves out of the kitsch area of timeless, placeless fantasy and into the real world, then it loses its function of safety valve. It begins to comment on real relations in the real world. Therefore, the more pornographic writing acquires the techniques of real literature, of real art, the more deeply subversive it is likely to be in that the more likely it is to affect the reader's perceptions of the world. (p. 19)

Nothing exercises such power over the imagination as the nature of sexual relationships, and the pornographer has it in his power to become a terrorist of the imagination, a sexual guerilla whose purpose is to overturn our most basic notions of these relations, to reinstitute sexuality as a primary mode of being rather than a specialised area of vacation from being and to show that the everyday meetings in the marriage bed are parodies of their own pretensions, that the freest unions may contain the seeds of the worst exploitation. Sade became a terrorist of the imagination in this way, turning the unacknowledged truths of the encounters of sexuality into a cruel festival at which women are the prime sacrificial victims when they are not the ritual murderesses themselves . . . , alike only in that

Courtesy of Deborah Rogers Ltd.

they always remain under the constant surveillance of the other half of mankind.

The pornographer as terrorist may not think of himself as a friend of women; that may be the last thing on his mind. But he will always be our unconscious ally because he begins to approach some kind of emblematic truth. . . . (pp. 21-2)

Sade is unusual amongst both satirists and pornographers, not only because he goes further than most satirists and pornographers, but because he is capable of believing, even if only intermittently, that it is possible to radically transform society and, with it, human nature, so that the Old Adam, exemplified in God, the King and the Law, the trifold masculine symbolism of authority, will take his final departure from amongst us. Only then will freedom be possible; until then, the freedom of one class, or sex, or individual necessitates the unfreedom of others.

But his work as a pornographer is more descriptive and diagnostic than proscriptive and prophetic. He creates, not an artificial paradise of gratified sexuality but a model of hell, in which the gratification of sexuality involves the infliction and the tolerance of extreme pain. He describes sexual relations in the context of an unfree society as the expression of pure tyranny, usually by men upon women, sometimes by men upon men, sometimes by women upon men and other women; the one constant to all Sade's monstrous orgies is that the whip hand is always the hand with the real political power and the victim is a person who has little or no power at all, or has had it stripped from him. In this schema, male means tyrannous and female means martyrised, no matter what the official genders of the male and female beings are.

He is uncommon amongst pornographers in that he rarely, if ever, makes sexual activity seem immediately attractive as such. Sade has a curious ability to render every aspect of sexuality suspect, so that we see how the chaste kiss of the sentimental lover differs only in degree from the vampirish love-bite that draws blood, we understand that a disinterested caress is only quantitatively different from a disinterested flogging. For Sade, all tenderness is false, a deceit, a trap; all pleasure contains within itself the seeds of atrocities; all beds are minefields. So the virtuous Justine is condemned to spend a life in which there is not one single moment of enjoyment; only in this way can she retain her virtue. Whereas the wicked Juliette, her sister and antithesis, dehumanises herself completely in the pursuit of pleasure. (pp. 24-5)

[Sade] enlarges the relation between activity and passivity in the sexual act to include tyranny and the acceptance of physical and political oppression. The great men in his novels, the statesmen, the princes, the popes, are the cruellest by far and their sexual voracity is a kind of pure destructiveness. . . . But his great women, Juliette, Clairwil, the Princess Borghese, Catherine the Great of Russia, Charlotte of Naples, are even more cruel still since, once they have tasted power, once they know how to use their sexuality as an instrument of aggression, they use it to extract vengeance for the humiliations they were forced to endure as the passive objects of the sexual energy of others.

A free woman in an unfree society will be a monster. Her freedom will be a condition of personal privilege that deprives those on which she exercises it of her own freedom. The most extreme kind of this deprivation is murder. These women murder. (pp. 26-7)

One of Sade's singularities is that he offers an absolutely sexualised view of the world, a sexualisation that permeates everything, much as his atheism does and, since he is not a religious man but a political man, he treats the facts of female sexuality not as a moral dilemma but as a political reality. (p. 27)

[Sade] was unusual in his period for claiming rights of free sexuality for women, and in installing women as beings of power in his imaginary worlds. This sets him apart from all other pornographers at all times and most other writers of his period.

In the looking-glass of Sade's misanthropy, women may see themselves as they have been and it is an uncomfortable sight. He offers an extraordinary variety of male fantasies about women and, because of the equivocal nature of his own sexual response, a number of startling insights. His misanthropy bred a hatred of the mothering function that led him to demystify the most sanctified aspects of women and if he invented women who suffered, he also invented women who caused suffering. The hole the pornographer Sade leaves in his text is just sufficient for a flaying; for a castration. It is a hole large enough for women to see themselves as if the fringed hole of graffiti

were a spyhole into territory that had been forbidden them. (p. 36)

Sade remains a monstrous and daunting cultural edifice; yet I would like to think that he put pornography in the service of women, or, perhaps, allowed it to be invaded by an ideology not inimical to women. (p. 37)

> *Angela Carter, in her* The Sadeian Woman: And the Ideology of Pornography *(copyright © 1979 by Angela Carter; reprinted by permission of Pantheon Books, a Division of Random House, Inc.; in Canada by International Creative Management), Pantheon Books, 1979, 154 p.*

PATRICIA BEER

As Angela Carter argues in the first chapter of her high-spirited book, *The Sadeian Woman,* [the Marquis de Sade] not only goes farther than most [pornographers], to become 'a terrorist of the imagination', but he really believes that society and human nature, which he shows as monstrous, *could,* in fact, be transformed, a belief which, Ms Carter thinks, is alien to the pornography of most ages, certainly to that of our own. . . .

In the non-pejorative sense of the word, Angela Carter's book is tendentious. She makes no attempt to treat Sade's writings as literature, only as pornographic literature, and as she points out 'there is no question of an aesthetics of pornography. It can never be art for art's sake. Honourably enough, it is always art with work to do.' Neither is she concerned to examine the tenets of this 'illiberal philosopher', as she calls him, intellectually. . . .

Angela Carter wishes to demonstrate that from [Justine and Juliette] descend recognisable 20th-century types of women. Justine, as portrayed by Sade, 'marks the start of a kind of self-regarding female masochism, a woman with no place in the world, no status, the core of whose resistance has been eaten away by self-pity'. Juliette, on the other hand, 'is a woman who acts according to the precepts and also the practice of a man's world and so she does not suffer. Instead she causes suffering.' . . .

Which of these two Sadeian women should we wish to be? Neither. We are not to imagine that Juliette is the one to lead us out of bondage. . . . [In] Angela Carter's words, 'a free woman in an unfree society will be a monster', and this is what Juliette is, an outstandingly wicked person. . . .

Sade emerges from this book as a slightly more admirable character than he is usually supposed to be. 'Give the old monster his due,' cries Angela Carter, and part of Sade's due is that though he gave people hell in his fantasies and, to a lesser extent, outside them too, he had glimpses and actual moments of goodness. . . .

Another part of his due, and this is very relevant to the message of *The Sadeian Woman,* is that he wished women to be free in a way that Justine and Juliette could not be, that is, in a free society where women would automatically be liberated.

> *Patricia Beer, "Sadey Ladies" (© British Broadcasting Corp. 1979; reprinted by permission of Patricia Beer), in* The Listener, *Vol. 101, No. 2605, April 5, 1979, p. 497.*

HERMIONE LEE

Few women would feel inclined to treat the Marquis de Sade with affectionate familiarity. But Angela Carter is neither ordinary nor timid, and one of the strategies of her assertive and sophisticated book [*The Sadeian Woman*] is to speak of Sade as though she had him in her pocket. . . . The tone is one of intellectual relish. . . .

There is nothing revolutionary, however, in Angela Carter's recognition of Sade's work as 'instrumental in shaping aspects of the modern sensibility'. Sade's influence on Baudelaire and Genet has always been apparent, and French structuralist criticism has for some time appreciated the extremism of his erotic philosophy. (p. 487)

Angela Carter's extension of this by now traditional praise of Sade is her claim for him as a subversive pornographer, . . . who 'put pornography in the service of women, or, perhaps, allowed it to be invaded by an ideology not inimical to women'. Most pornography, she begins by saying, is reactionary and consolatory because it deals with archetypal images which divorce sex from its social context. But sex is not universal, ahistorical, abstracted, as pornography would have it. . . . Sade is a revolutionary because, at a time of revolution, he used his aristocratic libertines in a satirical critique of exploitation: 'He describes sexual relations in the context of an unfree society as the expression of pure tyranny.' The Sadeian woman is either the political victim of sexual violence, or, whip and dildo in hand, she adopts the policies of male tyrant, and becomes a monster.

In the long (and rather self-indulgent) descriptions of Sade's fictions which take up most of this short book, Angela Carter expands on these unhappy alternatives. . . .

Angela Carter eloquently demonstrates Sade's virtues as a freethinker: the egalitarianism implicit in his enthusiasm for interchangeable rituals of domination, the revolutionary potential of his satire on the virtuous, obedient 'Christian' woman and on motherhood. But she also provides an interesting and subtle critique of Sade's intellectual limitations, which make him, in the end, the enemy of freedom. There is, first, the unresolved contradiction between his belief in moral relativity (crime is 'a matter of geography and opinion', he says in *Justine*) and his absolutist theory of innate vice and virtue. . . . [What] Sade cannot do, in his 'pornographised description of the antipathy between mothers and daughters', is to allow the mother any sexual gratification. She must only suffer, because Sade can't envisage the possibility of freedom from one's own nature, a world in which the virtuous might be free to become vicious.

Nor, secondly, can he conceive of *reciprocal* sexual relations. Pleasure, in the Sadeian universe, 'may never be shared, or it will be diminished'. The orgasm is an isolated experience: there can be no partners, only accomplices or victims. The book suddenly leaves off by saying that such 'terror of love' is the enemy to liberation; it ends with a corroborating quote from Emma Goldman: 'If partial emancipation . . . is to become complete . . . it will have to do away with the ridiculous notion that to be loved . . . is synonymous with being slave or subordinate'.

This abrupt ending is in keeping with the rather irritating highhandedness of the text, which is prone to brash formulations like 'kitschification' and which, though authoritative, has lapses into careless repetition and unfocused changes of direction. But as a concluding statement it is deeply disconcerting. A complex and ambitious analogy has been sustained between Sade's satires on sexual exploitation and the constrictive effects of a bourgeois social economy on our sexual roles and assumptions. The invocation of 'Love' as a final solution seems a breathtakingly conventional simplification, an appeal to those same immutable universals which the book has earlier rejected with so much scorn. If sex is still, as it was for Sade, a mode of power politics, then how is 'the right to love and be loved' to cut free of this? The terms of the book require that the question be answered, rather than left to us. (p. 488)

Hermione Lee, "Unfair Shares," in New Statesman *(© 1979 The Statesman & Nation Publishing Co. Ltd.), Vol. 97, No. 2507, April 6, 1979, pp. 487-88.*

RICHARD GILMAN

[To] write about pornography invariably implies a *position*.

Angela Carter's position in [*"The Sadeian Woman"*] is fierce, unaccommodating and aggressively stated: Pornography is a means of perpetuating the oppression of women because it conceives of sex purely in terms of power and thus reinforces men's pre-existing impulses toward the exercise of dominance. Moreover, pornography is the product and agency of political and social structures that themselves exist solely on the basis of power; relations between men and women will never be free, reciprocal, as long as society is organized the way it is. Miss Carter is so manifestly intelligent, so passionate in her argument, that one feels more than the usual regret at seeing her subject bring down another mind; when she is through with pornography it stands more or less untouched—mysterious, evading our convenient categories, menacing or alluring according to one's view. . . .

[Miss Carter] makes her case through a commentary on the Marquis de Sade and an exegesis of . . . "Justine," "Juliette" and "Philosophy in the Boudoir." For the most part she sees Sade in a traditional—and somewhat excessive—way, as a key shaper of "aspects of the modern sensibility; its paranoia, its despair, its sexual terrors, its . . . egocentricity, its tolerance of massacre, holocaust, annihilation." She also sees him, conventionally and with respect in this instance, as a political writer for whom sex is an expression of society's being built on force. "Relationships between the sexes are determined by history," she writes; "class dictates our choice of partners and our choice of positions."

What is rather original in Miss Carter's thinking about Sade is her idea that in the figure of Juliette he created a counterforce to the submissive woman of myth and actuality. . . .

There are a number of shrewd insights of this kind, but far too much of the book is in the grip of an iron set of biases and dubious presuppositions. For all her intelligence, Miss Carter is a rigid ideologue, fervidly feminist, furiously antireligious and against transcendence of any kind. . . .

[In] Miss Carter's case, the radical positions tend to injure both scholarship and clarity of thought. At the heart of what's wrong with her assault on pornography and her related critique of Sade is her inability or refusal to see that pornography, like any form of imagination, is an effort at compensating for finiteness, at getting past limitations. It deals with possibility, not the actual, and imaginative possibility at that. If she could see this, she wouldn't be likely to construe pornography as treating only of violence. . . .

Sade was a specialist in only one mode of pornography: sex as violence and exploitation—which naturally fits Miss Carter's thesis. . . . Though she correctly emphasizes his political motives, she fails to see how the pornography wasn't in the service of a repressive state but precisely part of a dream of a totally, impossibly free one. (p. 10)

Richard Gilman, "Position Paper," in The New York Times Book Review *(© 1979 by The New York Times Company; reprinted by permission), July 29, 1979, pp. 10, 30.*

ROBIN MORGAN

For the feminist thinker, any examination of Sade must revolve around the question: was he writing a sexual "Modest Proposal" to expose the totalitarian violence at the heart of all sexist structures, the source of tyranny itself? Or did he genuinely believe that unrestrained sexual practices, even unto murderous extremes, are liberating not only for men but for women—and if so, liberating by whose standards? (p. 31)

[Ignoring these questions] is an error Angela Carter has had the courage to avoid in [*The Sadeian Woman and the Ideology of Pornography*]. She knows that all pornography is propaganda—ostensibly propaganda for sexual activity but actually propaganda for sexist activity—since it reinforces stereotypes while denying their political origin. She understands that "pornography serves . . . to reinforce the prevailing system of values . . . ; when it does not, it is banned." . . . Furthermore, Carter recognizes that pornography assumes and propagates the notion that a brutal human nature cannot be modified by social change.

Sade's importance in the history of pornography is undeniable, not only because of the claims made for him as a philosopher, a *litterateur*, but also because he had pretensions to political theory. Carter sees him as "descriptive and diagnostic," and analyzes him as, in turn, a utopian, an atheist, an aristocrat *and* revolutionary, a self-proclaimed "feminist"—and a practicing misogynist. But Carter understates certain alarming details of Sade's life since she is at pains to prove that his writings were both Swiftian in intent and fantastical in conception—not reflections of his actual behavior. This is the only place she bends the facts to accommodate her thesis, but it is a serious flaw in the book, since current arguments exploring correlations between pornography and rape center on just that kind of frequently dismissed or hidden data.

Carter is better at dissecting Sade's so-called pro-feminism. . . . Far from any promised empowering of women, the aim is to degrade women, particularly those women whose class credentials permit even the *illusion* of power. To express sexual energy in such a setting is to collaborate in one's victimization, or to settle for a false table-turning of sexual cruelties.

Carter is at her intelligent best when unearthing Sade's true attitude toward women—not so simple a task, since his intellectual trappings of rational egalitarianism can be even more misleading than other brands of misogyny, including the opposite one—the sentimental mystification of woman as "The Other." Still, beneath all that Voltairean reason lies the cliché madonna-whore dichotomy, carried to a Manichean extreme. . . . [Neither] Justine's repressed sexuality and "honor" nor Juliette's self-indulgent libido and "reason" are viewed in a realistic social context—and neither feels a bond with other

women. Thus, at a stroke, the humanity of female persons is erased and depoliticized: the erasure, by reduction to fixed stereotypes (rather a Calvinistic *coup* for an atheist like Sade); the depoliticization, by isolating each act of suffering from every other and from the cause, patriarchal power.

Carter goes even deeper, to reveal an attitude that is, I believe, near the core of all pornography. This is the profound hatred of the mother, not in a simplistic Freudian sense, but as metaphor for disgust with life itself—with birth, nurturance, and emotional maturity. In the Sadeian world (which is tragically like our own), women are seen as possessors of the sacred womb, and so can be subjected to atrocities, since nothing can defile the sacred. (pp. 31-3)

It is as if the female capable of conception (or, for that matter, capable of *preventing* conception—but for her own purposes) were the ultimate terror, the taboo of her womb-power so great that she must be denied all other powers. If she were to be seen in her simple mortality, then not just god but the mystification of god—and of life and death—would be dead. Carter hypothesizes that this is why female emancipation frightens so many people: "It represents the final secularization of mankind."

But then, noting this "holy terror" of life and love, Carter stops. It is as if she labored for two-thirds of her book to define Sade, pornography, even patriarchy, only to confront the central question *why*—and then skim over it. Is this a failure of nerve? One might hope that a second volume would follow, picking up where this left off.

Still, even as it stands, *The Sadeian Woman* is a well-written and important, if at times frustrating, contribution to thinking about sexual politics, the reality of pornography as propaganda for violence, and the intellectual pretensions—both dramatic *and* banal—of evil. (p. 33)

Robin Morgan, "'The Sadeian Woman and the Ideology of Pornography'," in The New Republic *(reprinted by permission of* The New Republic; © 1979 The New Republic, Inc.), Vol. 181, Nos. 9 & 10, September 1 & 8, 1979, pp. 31-3.*

JAMES SLOAN ALLEN

De Sade's pornography, [as Angela Carter says in *The Sadeian Woman*], pierced the myth of sex as a natural and benign pleasure to display the inequities and cruelty underlying sexual and social relations in the *ancien régime*. At the same time, he exhibited sexual freedom as a form of social equality available to all. (p. 312)

Juliette and the many others of her type prove to Angela Carter that despite de Sade's obvious misogyny, he "put pornography in the service of women" by allowing women a sexuality and will unconditioned by culture. Although these women could not truly subvert society, Carter says, they represent the subversion of woman's traditional place in it by demolishing the oppressive—or, better, repressive—myths of woman as virgin, mother or goddess. This "final secularization of mankind," as Carter calls the ultimate female release, equalizes men and women and makes them sexually interchangeable. . . .

That Carter should equate female emancipation with a kind of androgyny is not incidental to her argument. For just as she opposes the ideology of vulgar pornography as evil mythologizing, so she denies any elemental psychosexual division between men and women: "flesh comes to us out of history," she says (betraying an unstated affinity with Michel Foucault), which means culture determines sex, sex does not determine culture, and that female emancipation will come with the death of repressive cultural myths. As feminist ideology goes, this is a rather moderate position. Were Carter more radical . . . she would not reduce sex to history and far from welcoming, would smartly recoil from de Sade's attribution to women of his own extravagant desires. And despite the intelligence of her explications and argument, which deserve praise, this moderate, historicist and androgynous position leads her to misjudge de Sade.

By merging the sexes, and assigning their conflicts to culture, Carter dims the horror of de Sade's writings, which arises from the possibility that de Sade exemplifies an unbounded male sexuality of erotic aggression and domination. His licentious women are probably not women at all, or even androgynous beings, but rather the fantasies of a sexually obsessed male. . . .

Carter's historicist feminism and taste for cultural intransigence have led her to mythologize de Sade himself. However much he might have exemplified the revolutionary spirit of his times, without a distinctly male sexuality, de Sade is not de Sade. And lest we idealize his revolutionary message, we should remember that de Sade's anthropology removed man not just from an oppressive culture but from culture altogether, and from humanity as well.

In summoning pornography to the service of female emancipation, Angela Carter has chosen a literary model who identified freedom with the most brutish of animal instincts—encompassing murder no less than lust. This freedom negates the autonomy for which the cultural revolutions of the past two centuries have been waged: self-determination and self-mastery. Reversing Freud's psychological definition of this autonomy, de Sade promised: where ego was there shall id be; here man becomes the slave not of other men but of his own irrational desires. And by dismissing as *mere* myth pornographic entertainment, psychosexual differences and traditional morality, Carter undercuts all reasons for judging de Sade wrong. She forgets that all moral ideals, including her own emancipatory hopes, belong more to myth than to history or nature. (p. 313)

> *James Sloan Allen, "Where Ego Was . . . ," in* The Nation *(copyright 1979 The Nation magazine, The Nation Associates, Inc.), Vol. 229, No. 10, October 6, 1979, pp. 312-13.*

LAURIE STONE

The patriarchal, sadomasochistic vision is the black mirror of feminism, its nightmare opposite. Pornography expresses the deepest, most primitive, and powerful reasons feminism needs to exist.

Attempts to forge an alliance between pornography and feminism are therefore hard-pressed to stay afloat logically, and [Angela Carter's *The Sadeian Woman* mostly flounders]. . . . Carter fails for the most part to justify the ways of Sade to feminism, . . . but [the book touches] core issues in the contorted relationship feminism cannot help but have with pornography. . . .

Carter is often persuasive and sometimes brilliant about the relationship between erotic violence and feminism, but because she has chosen Sade's novels and life as the context for her discussion, and because she feels she needs to connect his politics to hers, she falls into the Sade-as-radical fallacy.

Although some women in Sade's novels elect to become oppressors rather than victims (and Sade is certainly not the only creator of such women in pornographic literature), there is no "free sexuality" for any of the women in his novels. . . . [At] all times, [the] female sadists are themselves at the mercy or doing the bidding of some far more powerful man or male-dominated institution—church, law, criminal underworld. . . .

There is no doubt that feminists can study Sade's novels and discover an encyclopedia of male-hate and male-fear of women. . . .

Carter, like a number of other apologists for sadomasochistic literature, adopts the position that Sade's writing is a form of satire, a critique of the sexual politics of his age.

The thinking goes like this. Sadomasochistic novels should be read as "modest proposals," for just as Swift underscored the severity of Ireland's economic ills by advocating the fricasseeing of one-year-old Irish babies, so, too, sadomasochistic scenarios are the logical extremes of the way things really are, which implies that the writers of these books wished that things were otherwise, better, the opposite of what they depict. This view squares nicely with feminism. . . . Everything would be fine and dandy if pornography's apologists were right.

In the case of Sade, they aren't. Sade's view is deeply reactionary. . . .

Sade doesn't satirize the way of his world, he refracts it, nostalgically. His novels aren't repudiations of the system in which he grew up, they are homages to it. . . .

In Carter's effort to see humanist qualities in Sade because he was a writer (hardly anyone bothers to discover the virtues in criminals and madmen who *don't* write), she [goes] soft on Sade the man. . . .

[Carter] fails to see that Sade's sex crimes were totally consistent with everything he wrote, and that they make it very difficult to read Sade as a sexual satirist or prophet of "free sexuality." At times Carter is downright mush-brained in her eagerness to soft-peddle Sade. "Rather than his misdeeds," she writes, "it seems it was the ferocity of his imagination that led to his confinement." All well and good to say, and true, perhaps, as a motive for some of Sade's arrests, but Carter neglects to mention that Sade did not begin to write until *after* his imprisonments began.

It's too bad that Carter wrapped her often very fine thinking around Sade's fictions, because her writing is strongest when least directly tied to his. . . . [In] her most suggestive analysis, Carter posits that the whippings, beatings, and gougings of erotic violence reenact "the social fiction of the female wound, the bleeding scar left by her castration, . . . an imaginary fact that pervades the whole of men's attitudes towards women and our attitudes to ourselves, that transforms women from human beings into wounded creatures who were born to bleed."

Carter's castration theory provides one of the most credible explanations yet propounded for why strong, independent women who are revolted by real pain and forced sex are nonetheless still aroused by sadomasochistic fantasies. (p. 35)

According to Carter's reading of erotic violence as symbolic castration . . . , women's arousal may be symptomatic of something besides inchoate passivity or a genetic predisposition to yield and be dominated—the feelings which largely make feminists ashamed and conflicted. For if the images of male rage at women expressed in erotic violence (the symbolic castration of women by men) generate hatred in women (which is logical and probable), and hatred in turn generates guilt (also logical and probable), then female masochism will not be born of self-loathing but of sublimated rage. In this context, "Tie me up or I'll wind up killing you"—not "Beat me because I need to feel weak"—expresses the sentiments behind the desire for imaginary punishment.

Carter's castration theory doesn't explain masochism "away," nor does it make having sadistic and masochistic feelings any less problematic and disturbing, but it does provide a refreshing view of those emotions. As Carter's book proceeds, however, there is unfortunately very little more thinking this provocative. . . .

A good deal of what Carter says in the bulk of her book isn't new or interesting, because Sade doesn't really have that much to tell us about male fantasies of women that still seems new or interesting.

Carter would have done better to "give the old monster his due" simply by noting that Sade was, indeed, a complex character, cruel, but also capable of odd strokes of indulgence and forgiveness where revenge might have been the more expected response, and by asserting that Sade's writings have the virtue of being remarkably, obsessively confessional—if also boring and repetitious. This would have made Carter's book less boring and repetitious; it also would have reduced it to the dimensions of a long essay, which is all it should have been. (p. 36)

Laurie Stone, "The Big P" (reprinted by permission of The Village Voice *and the author; copyright © 1980), in* The Village Voice, *Vol. XXV, No. 8, February 25, 1980, pp. 35-6.**

(Avram) Noam Chomsky

1928-

Chomsky is an American linguist, educator, and author of books on linguistics and politics. The world-renowned founder of a new school of linguistics based on the concept of generative or transformational grammar, Chomsky has attracted almost equal international attention as a critic of American foreign policy. In *American Power and the New Mandarins* (1969) Chomsky criticizes U.S. intervention in Vietnam and argues that American foreign policy serves the interests of a narrow business and government elite. In *For Reasons of State* (1973) he exhaustively analyzes the Pentagon Papers, concluding that they document the real, rather than expressed, motives for America's prosecution of the Vietnam War, and that these real motives are consistent with the thesis of an imperialist American foreign policy. Chomsky links his political and linguistic studies for the first time in *Problems of Knowledge and Freedom* (1971), contending that there is a connection between the way people acquire language and the necessity and desirability of human freedom. *The Political Economy of Human Rights,* a major two-volume study of recent American foreign policy, was coauthored by Edward S. Herman and published in 1980. Chomsky's criticisms of American foreign policy and political life are quite controversial, with critics often arguing that they are overstated, when not dismissing them altogether. Nonetheless, Chomsky's stature as a scholar and intellectual has become such that Paul Robinson could write in 1979 that he is "arguably the most important intellectual alive." Chomsky is professor of philosophy and linguistics at the Massachusetts Institute of Technology. (See also *Contemporary Authors,* Vols. 17-20, rev. ed.)

Courtesy of Noam Chomsky

Excerpt from *AMERICAN POWER AND THE NEW MANDARINS*

Three years have passed since American intervention in a civil war in Vietnam was converted into a colonial war of the classic type. This was the decision of a liberal American administration. Like the earlier steps to enforce our will in Vietnam, it was taken with the support of leading political figures, intellectuals, and academic experts, many of whom now oppose the war because they do not believe that American repression can succeed in Vietnam and therefore urge, on pragmatic grounds, that we "take our stand" where the prospects are more hopeful. If the resistance in Vietnam were to collapse, if the situation were to revert to that of Thailand or Guatemala or Greece, where the forces of order, with our approval and assistance, are exercising a fair degree of control, then this opposition to the Vietnam war would also cease; in the words of one such spokesman, we might then "all be saluting the wisdom and statesmanship of the American government." If we are forced to liquidate this enterprise—in one of the two possible ways— the liberal ideologists will continue to urge that we organize and control as extensive a dominion as is feasible in what they take to be "our national interest" and in the interest of the elements in other societies that we designate as fit to rule.

As matters now stand, it appears unlikely that Vietnamese resistance will collapse. The United States seems unable to muster the military force to crush this resistance and to guar-

antee the dominance of the government and social institutions that we have determined to be appropriate. There is, therefore, some hope that American troops will be withdrawn and the Vietnamese left to try to reconstruct something from the wreckage. The course of history may be determined, to a very significant degree, by what the people of the United States will have learned from this catastrophe.

Three times in a generation American technology has laid waste a helpless Asian country. In 1945 this was done with a sense of moral rectitude that was, and remains, almost unchallenged. In Korea, there were a few qualms. The amazing resistance of the Vietnamese has finally forced us to ask, What have we done? There are, at last, some signs of awakening to the horrifying reality. Resistance to American violence and to the militarization of our own society has become, if not a significant force, at least a detectable one. There is hope that the struggle against racism and exploitation at home can be linked with the struggle to remove the heavy Yankee boot from the necks of oppressed people throughout the world.

Twenty years of intensive cold-war indoctrination and seventy years of myth regarding our international role make it difficult to face these issues in a serious way. There is a great deal of intellectual debris to be cleared away. Ideological pressures so overpowering that even their existence was denied must be examined and understood. The search for alternatives, for individuals, for American society, for the international order as a whole, has barely begun, and no one can guess where it will lead. Quite possibly it will lead nowhere, cut off by domestic repression or its "functional equivalent," to use a favorite term of the present administration: the dominance of a liberal technocracy who will serve the existing social order in the belief that they represent justice and humanity, fighting limited wars at home and overseas to preserve stability, promising that the future will be better if only the dispossessed will wait patiently, and supported by an apathetic, obedient majority, its mind and conscience dulled by a surfeit of commodities and by some new version of the old system of beliefs and ideas. Perhaps the worst excesses may be eliminated. Perhaps a way may be found to bring about a fundamental change in American society of a sort that can hardly be envisioned today. A great many people have been aroused by the Vietnam tragedy and the domestic crisis. There is a new mood of questioning and rebellion among the youth of the country, a very healthy and hopeful development, by and large, that few would have predicted a decade ago. The passionate involvement of students in the civil rights movement, in the movement to end the war, in resistance, in community organizing, already has changed the intellectual and moral climate of the universities at least. These stirrings of concern and commitment give some reason to hope that we will not repeat the crimes of the recent past. One thing is certain: we must never forget these crimes. (pp. 3-5)

> Noam Chomsky, in his American Power and the New Mandarins *(copyright © 1967, 1969 by Noam Chomsky; reprinted by permission of Pantheon Books, a Divison of Random House, Inc.), Pantheon Books, 1969, 404 p.*

Excerpt from *FOR REASONS OF STATE*

In early April 1972, Admiral Thomas Moorer, testifying before the House Armed Services Committee, explained that "if domestic restraints were relaxed the US would have the option of bombing Haiphong harbor in North Vietnam and launching amphibious assaults behind North Vietnamese lines." The domestic restraints that Moorer had in mind, according to Congressman Michael Harrington, were "the activities of the peace movement and the press."

The chairman of the Joint Chiefs of Staff is no doubt correct. There is evidence . . . that the activities of the peace movement and the work of some honest correspondents have, to some unknown degree, restrained the criminal violence of the American government in Indochina. Those who have marched and protested and resisted can compare what is with what would have been, and credit themselves with the difference. We can each of us consider what we have not done, and credit ourselves with a corresponding share of the agony of Indochina. There are not too many people who can undergo this self-examination with equanimity.

The point is more general. An American historian points out that "by 1971 it was noticed on all sides that the students at American universities, who had been rioting on the campuses two years before because of Vietnam, Cambodia, and the military-industrial complex, were forgetting almost all of their zeal and no longer found such public issues interesting." That students were no longer interested is not obvious; it is possible

that they were simply no longer willing to endure beatings, imprisonment, vituperation, and idiotic denunciations for what was in fact courageous devotion to principle. But the barely concealed hint is to the point. If their "rioting" will only cease, then aggressive wars of counterinsurgency and the diversion of scarce resources to waste and destruction can proceed without annoying impediments.

Whatever the outcome in Indochina, the framework of ideology and policy making, political culture and popular attitude, has not been substantially modified by this catastrophe, and significant changes in the system of institutions and doctrine that gave rise to it are most unlikely. We cannot lightly dismiss recent history in the hope that it will prove to be some mad aberration of little consequence for the international order that is emerging. America is weary of this war, and in the narrow groups that determine foreign policy there are many who see it as pointless, a failed venture that should be liquidated. But official doctrine nevertheless prevails. It sets the terms of debate, a fact of considerable importance. And as long as victims are designated as "Communists," they are fair game. Virtually any atrocity will be tolerated by a population that has been profoundly indoctrinated. (pp. vii-viii)

In fact, the savagery of the American attack on the people of Indochina is often condemned, but a more fundamental question is rarely raised in the mainstream of opinion. When the president comments that "you have to let them have it when they jump on you," few of the critics of his infantile rhetoric emphasize the crucial point: they are "jumping on us" in their land, not in Kansas or Hawaii or even Thailand. Successful interventions are quickly forgotten. As long as such attitudes prevail, we can expect new interventions in Southeast Asia and beyond, and if indigenous resistance is again miscalculated, then such domestic restraints as can be imposed will remain the major barrier to unlimited terror.(p. ix)

The government does not really hope to convince anyone by its arguments and claims [regarding its policies in Vietnam], but only to sow confusion, relying on the natural tendency to trust authority and to avoid complicated and disturbing issues. How can we be sure of the truth? The confused citizen turns to other pursuits, and gradually, as government lies are reiterated day after day, year after year, falsehood becomes truth.

The mechanism has been perceptively described by James Boyd in connection with the strange story of Dita Beard, Richard Kleindienst, and ITT. The evasions were "transparent and ridiculous," but that is irrelevant: "The idea is to bring the public to a point of bewilderment. . . ." The lawyer seeks "not to convince, but to confuse and weary." In the same manner, the state is content to lose each debate, while winning the propaganda war.

Shortly after the Pentagon Papers appeared, Richard Harwood wrote in the *Washington Post* that a careful reader of the press could have known the facts all along, and he cited cases where the facts had been truthfully reported. He failed to add that the truth had been overwhelmed, in the same pages, by a flood of state propaganda. With rare exceptions, the press and the public finally accepted the framework of government deceit on virtually every crucial point. Hawks and doves alike speak of the conflict as a war between North Vietnam and South Vietnam, with the United States coming to the defense of the South— perhaps unwisely, the doves maintain, and with means disproportionate to the just ends sought. It was a tragic miscalculation—the implication being that had limited means sufficed, the American intervention would have been legitimate. (pp. xi-xii)

The internal record in the Pentagon Papers reveals that United States government analysts recognized that Western intervention must destroy the most powerful nationalist movement in Indochina. But a victory of the forces of revolutionary nationalism in Indochina was regarded as inconsistent with American global objectives, and therefore it was necessary to define the Viet Minh as agents of foreign aggression, while the French were defending the independence of Indochina. The necessary premise was soon embodied in state ideology, and rarely questioned thenceforth in internal documents or official propaganda. (p. xv)

Throughout, the underlying assumption [of dominant opinion on the Vietnam war], variously expressed, is that United States intervention is uncontroversial if only it can succeed without too great a cost. Thus it is immoral for Vietnamese to resist American aggression or to come to the aid of resistance forces that cannot withstand its savagery. (p. xxi)

Nixon and Kissinger may or may not be able to achieve their ends, but they have amply demonstrated that they can exact a horrendous price for the refusal to submit. If their efforts collapse, the carnage may exceed all bounds. Limited and malicious men, trapped in the wreckage of their schemes, may be driven to unimaginable extremes of violence: The events of the past years serve as a fair and compelling illustration of what will be done by a system of centralized power, relatively free of restraints, immune from retaliation. Those who are concerned to save Indochina from further destruction will listen carefully to the chairman of the Joint Chiefs of Staff when he speaks of the domestic restraints that so distress him. And if the torture of the people of Indochina will somehow end, Americans who can liberate themselves from the grip of official doctrine will remember these words when the next Vietnam takes shape, whatever its scale.

Some believe that the Nixon-Kissinger diplomacy spells an end to the global interventionism of the postwar period, but this seems a most dubious interpretation. The new diplomacy is an effort to institutionalize the cold-war system with more rational controls. The cold war was never simply a zero-sum game, a conflict between the superpowers in which the gain of one is the loss of the other. Rather, it has functioned as a marvelously effective device for mobilizing support, in each superpower, for ventures that carry a significant cost, economic and moral. The citizen must agree to bear the burdens of imperial wars and of government-induced production of waste, a critical device of economic management. He has been whipped into line by the fear that we will be overwhelmed by an external enemy if we let down our guard. (pp. xxii-xxiii)

The cultural and institutional barriers that block the way to a more just and humane society are immense. There are, nevertheless, long-term tendencies that threaten the hegemony of coercive institutions and ideologies. It is likely that significant groups in the Third World will recognize the destructive impact of integration in the global economy dominated by the industrial powers and will organize revolutionary struggles against the imperial powers and their local associates. Or consider, as a case in point, the problem of limits of growth, now the topic of much debate. As such limits are approached, an effective technique of social control will be lost. It is not irrational for culturally determined "economic man" to accept the existing system of inequity when it appears possible that as the pie grows larger, his share will grow with it. As such possibilities decline, he no longer has such reasons for tolerating a system of injustice and may turn to a closer examination of its ideological assumptions, for example, the belief that everyone gains when a few are rewarded, or that rewards accrue to those who somehow serve the public welfare. It is possible, furthermore, that the degrading assumptions of capitalist ideology will be challenged seriously by people who recognize that there is more to life than consumption of commodities and that creative and intrinsically rewarding work, freely chosen, is a fundamental human need, along with others that cannot be satisfied in a world of competing individuals. (pp. xxvii-xxviii)

Noam Chomsky, in his For Reasons of State *(copyright © 1973 by Noam Chomsky; reprinted by permission of Pantheon Books, a Division of Random House, Inc.), Pantheon Books, 1973, 440 p.*

JAN G. DEUTSCH

Although Chomsky in his introduction [to **"American Power and the New Mandarins"**] disclaims (albeit, with reference to Vietnam) the intention of "entering into the arena of argument and counterargument, of technical feasibility and tactics, of footnotes and citations," he more than holds his own on precisely those terms. Like I. F. Stone at his best, Chomsky in these essays argues simply by adducing a mass of factual data. Whether one agrees with the conclusions drawn or not, the demonstration that his opponent has simply failed to take these facts into account amply serves to make Chomsky's point. (pp. 1, 65)

[What] is most striking about these essays is the extent to which they bear out Chomsky's reiterated claim to being both responsible and moderate. Desperately opposed to the war and wholeheartedly committed to the resistance, Chomsky begins his essay **"On Resistance"**—containing his personal reflections on the October, 1967, Washington demonstrations—by admitting his "instinctive distaste for activism."

He then describes the process by which, against his original inclination, he was led to participate in an act of civil disobedience and concludes with the warning that "we must not, I believe, thoughtlessly urge others to commit civil disobedience, and we must be careful not to construct situations in which young people will find themselves induced, perhaps in violation of their basic convictions, to commit civil disobedience." The most convincing indication of the extent to which Chomsky's wide ranging indictment of United States society and policy must be taken seriously is that a man possessed of these sensibilities should have felt compelled to undertake it.

It remains true, nevertheless, that Chomsky is least convincing on the conclusion to be drawn from the arguments he presents. That there is a lesson to be drawn from our Vietnam involvement is clear. What is less obvious is that the content of the proper lesson is that delineated by **"American Power and the New Mandarins."** . . .

[By arguing that international affairs can embody complex and painful conflicts of irreconcilable principles and interests, with American intervention in Vietnam—having no justification in legitimate principles or interests—being a rare exception to this general rule, Chomsky] presents a view of foreign affairs which undercuts the whole of his argument, for it is precisely the intention of **"American Power and the New Mandarins"** to demonstrate that Vietnam is *not* a "rare exception," that it is *not* the "accidental" blunder delineated by Schlesinger [in "The Bitter Heritage"].

Nor can Chomsky retreat—as he appears to do in his attack on Schlesinger in "The Bitter Heritage"—to the proposition that it is always illegitimate for the United States to attempt to determine the development of another nation *by military force*. For as that very essay makes clear, Chomsky regards both exploitative economic policies and the support of counterrevolutionary régimes through the provision of military assistance and the building up of internal security forces as equally illegitimate forms of intervention.

The alternative of a policy of total nonintervention, of complete isolationism, is similarly unacceptable: for—even passing by the possibility that such a stance might encourage other powers to pursue imperialist policies—Chomsky strongly indicates in **"Some Thoughts on Intellectuals and the Schools"** that one of the crucial moral issues of our time is presented "by one who enjoys his wealth and privilege undisturbed by the knowledge that half of the children born in Nicaragua will not reach five years of age, or that only a few miles away there is unspeakable poverty, brutal suppression of human rights, and almost no hope for the future . . ."

The issue, then, is not one of whether to intervene or not, but how to intervene so as to assist those groups in undeveloped countries which are struggling to establish freer and more just societies. Phrased in that way, however, the problem presented involves a considerable degree of that very "instrumentalism" to which Chomsky so strongly objects, the inevitable necessity for calculations of competing forces, of optimum strategies and likely payoffs.

As Chomsky recognizes, we have no monopoly on the evils he deplores. We are neither the first nation which, benefiting from the status quo, pursued a foreign policy that served to preserve the existing constellation of forces, nor are we alone in permitting protestations of our own benign intentions to blind us to the consequences of the policies we pursue. . . .

What makes us unique, however—the reason comparisons must necessarily prove inadequate—is precisely the fact of our preponderant military and economic strength. The fundamental difficulty, as Chomsky recognizes, is not that we are morally more evil than other nations; it is simply that there are far fewer external checks on our behavior.

If this is the problem, however, is it really so obvious that an appreciation of the limits on that power—the very position for which Schlesinger was arguing—is totally unavailing? Whether or not such an appreciation will prove sufficient for the problems ahead, it seems clear on Chomsky's own argument that it represents a very considerable and important first step toward sanity. (p. 65)

Jan G. Deutsch, "'American Power and the New Mandarins'," in The New York Times Book Review *(©1969 by The New York Times Company; reprinted by permission), March 16, 1969, pp. 1, 65.*

ARTHUR SCHLESINGER, JR.

[Noam Chomsky, in *American Power and the New Mandarins*], does not understand the rudiments of political analysis. Indeed,

despite occasional pretenses of reasoned discussion, he is not much interested in the analytical process. . . . (p. 4)

Noam Chomsky, in short, is not a political analyst at all. Like John Foster Dulles and Dean Rusk, he believes in reducing political questions to rather confident and facile moral judgments. Now the historian's rule here must be *de minimis*. A few questions, like slavery or Nazism, do qualify for unequivocal moral judgments; but, as one supposed Reinhold Niebuhr had demonstrated long since, most secular questions intermingle good and evil in problematic proportions and are more usefully handled in other than moralistic categories. Moreover, those who rush around ladling out moral judgments quickly arrogate to themselves an alarming and repellent sense of their own moral infallibility. Chomsky should remember his Chekhov: "You will not become a saint through other people's sins."

Political analysis requires a belief in the application of reason to *all* questions. Chomsky rejects this belief. It also requires a capacity to make distinctions. This too Chomsky lacks. Take the first sentence of his book: "Three years have passed since American intervention in a civil war in Vietnam was converted into a colonial war of the classic type." One may say many things about the Vietnam war; but one thing it is not is "a colonial war of the classic type"—i.e., a war in which a developed nation aims at the territorial annexation of an underdeveloped land. Indeed, Chomsky himself never claims that the United States wants to make Vietnam an American colony in the classic sense; it is just that he scorns precision in the use of language. Or, to consider another example, Chomsky calls Senator Mike Mansfield "the kind of man who is the terror of our age." If one uses language of this sort about Senator Mansfield, what words does one have left for Hitler or Stalin?

Political analysis requires in addition a reasonable sense of logic. Thus, in making his case against the Vietnam war, Chomsky mentions a newspaper photograph showing Vietnamese children in the Mekong Delta wounded by fire from American helicopters. "How many hundreds of such pictures must we see," he writes, "before we begin to care and to act?" The incident could hardly have been more horrifying; but it simply does not by itself justify political conclusions. Would the photograph of German children in Dresden or Hamburg wounded by bombs from allied planes have led Chomsky to argue that we should stop the war against Hitler? In short, logic prescribes that the case against the Vietnam war must be established—as it easily can be—on other grounds than the tragic fact of the killing or maiming of innocent bystanders. But Chomsky has no particular regard for logic.

Political analysis requires, above all, some respect for facts. This, despite a showy apparatus of footnotes and citations, Chomsky also lacks. Consider, for example, the way he deals with a President of the United States. Thus he writes:

> These words recall the characteristically direct formulations of Harry Truman, who proclaimed in 1947 that "all freedom is dependent on freedom of enterprise. . . . The whole world should adopt the American system. . . . The American system can survive in America only if it becomes a world system."

In case anyone does not get the point, Chomsky, who is rarely content with saying anything once, writes some pages later:

. . . the principles that were crudely outlined by President Truman almost twenty years ago when he observed in a famous and important speech that "all freedom is dependent on freedom of enterprise," that "the whole world should adopt the American system," that "the American system can survive in America only if it becomes a world system."

On the first occasion, Chomsky cites as his source for this "famous and important speech" a book by D. F. Fleming called *The Cold War and Its Origins*. The Fleming book refers to a speech given by Truman at Baylor University on March 6, 1947. This speech is readily available in Truman's *Public Papers*. An examination of the speech shows that Truman said none of the things which Chomsky says he said. And, while D. F. Fleming is hardly celebrated for the rigor of his scholarship, even he does not claim that Truman said them. The last two quotations, as the Fleming text makes clear, were not from Truman at all but from a book by J. P. Warburg in which Warburg was giving his own theory as to what was in Truman's mind. The first quotation does not appear on the page cited in Fleming and may well have been invented by Chomsky. (This quotation alone bears a distant resemblance to actual words of the Baylor speech, though what Truman said was essentially different: "Freedom of worship—freedom of speech—freedom of enterprise. It must be true that the first two of these freedoms are related to the third.") In the field of linguistics, Chomsky would, I am sure, be merciless on a scholar who misquoted, misattributed and made up language in order to strengthen an argument. But his contempt for political writing is evidently such that he has no hesitation in doing exactly this himself in the field of public affairs. Somewhere in the book Chomsky writes, with his usual sententiousness, "It is the responsibility of intellectuals to speak the truth and to expose lies." He must be putting us on.

Lurking in the morasses of Chomsky's prose is a perfectly serious question: that is, the relationship between intellectuals and power. He is plainly one of those who think that all intellectuals must enact the same prescribed role. This really does not make much sense. The strength of the intellectual community lies, among other things, in its diversity. According to variations in temperament and preoccupation, some intellectuals will participate in the world of power, some will criticize, some will denounce, some will cultivate their own gardens, some will, at one time or another, do all these things. A spectrum of opinion and action is indispensable if reason is to civilize power. The Chomsky notion that no intellectual should ever, ever collaborate with the state would, of course, deliver power absolutely to the timeservers and the yahoos.

But Chomsky is, as usual, something less than precise in his own conception of what the role of the intellectual should be. At various times he describes the role as that "of a dispassionate critic" or, again, that of speaking the truth and exposing lies; but his argument contradicts the first and his practice the second. Judging by *American Power and the New Mandarins*, one can only conclude that Chomsky's idea of the responsibility of an intellectual is to forswear reasoned analysis, indulge in moralistic declamation, fabricate evidence when necessary and shout always at the top of one's voice. It need hardly be said that, should the intellectual community follow the Chomsky example, it would betray its own traditions and hasten society along the road to unreason and disaster. (p. 5)

Arthur Schlesinger, Jr., "Three Cheers for Professor Chomsky—but Not Just Now," in Book World—

Chicago Tribune *(© 1969 Postrib Corp.; reprinted by permission of* Chicago Tribune *and* The Washington Post*), March 23, 1969, pp. 4-5.*

ROBERT SKLAR

[In *American Power and the New Mandarins* Chomsky] is not merely analyzing and criticizing the New Mandarin intellectuals who create American policies and misuse American power. Both explicitly and by implication he has sketched what is needed. First, to understand the failures and false claims of American social science methodology in all its institutional and political contexts, stretching back to the 19th century, and in so understanding, to overcome its power. Second, to revise our historical belief in American benevolence and righteousness toward the world, and to replace it with a more realistic assessment of America's powerful and coercive ambitions. Third, to end the elitist historians' blackout on the power and success of popular political movements in the world and especially to re-explore the anarchist challenge to the technocratic-bureaucratic mentality both of the Bolsheviks and Western capitalist countries. And finally, to build in America a philosophy of social and political power based upon human competence and self-determination.

This is an enormous agenda for thought and action. It will take more than one book and more than one mind to carry it through. The importance of *American Power and the New Mandarins* lies in its power to free our minds from old perspectives, to stimulate new efforts at historical, political and social thought. It is a long road from one book of essays to new ideas, new institutions, a new attitude toward human life; but few other books on American politics and society have given such promise of starting us on the way. (p. 374)

Robert Sklar, "The Intellectual Power Elite," in The Nation *(copyright 1969 The Nation magazine, The Nation Associates, Inc.), Vol. 208, No. 12, March 24, 1969, pp. 373-74.*

J. E. DORNAN, JR.

[For] sheer hysterical irrationalism [*American Power and the New Mandarins*] is absolutely without peer among recent critiques of United States diplomacy. . . . In the course of his diatribe, Chomsky develops a cogent brief against the "new mandarins," the behavioral scientists and technocrats of contemporary liberalism, noting at length the extent to which their gnostic expectations concerning the world's future impede the formation of intelligent public policy. Fundamentally a romantic and a utopian, however, Chomsky has allowed his hatred for the evils of the world around him to destroy his capacity to draw relevant political and moral distinctions, and thus even his valid insights lose most of their force. But in the contest for The Most Alienated Intellectual of the Year Award, this book has done more than make Chomsky the winner: he must be judged the very apotheosis of the breed.

J. E. Dornan, Jr., "Books in Brief: 'American Power and the New Mandarins'," in National Review *(© National Review, Inc., 1969; 150 East 35th St., New York, NY 10016), Vol. XXI, No. 23, June 17, 1969, p. 607.*

FRANCIS HOPE

Chomsky never quite articulates what should be the central question of [*American Power and the New Mandarins:* how did it happen that liberal intellectuals became so closely allied with state power]? There is a strong superficial link between the would-be value-free 'human sciences' and the particular form of philistinic careerism practised by American intellectuals; and indeed between that and the form of ill-informed cruelty applied in Vietnam. . . . But has imperialism produced the disciplines necessary for its survival, or has a freely chosen intellectual mistake led the academics into the wrong line of business? Are they uniquely corruptible, or a strong modern government uniquely corrupting?

Chomsky wobbles on this point. . . . (p. 770)

Chomsky finally takes his stand on old-fashioned liberal pessimism. Governments will always be bad, and the tradition of intellectual resistance should be preserved. Intellectuals in western societies have many privileges, not least that of arguing with official lies. To sacrifice that privilege, like an Arthur Schlesinger or a Writer's Union hack, for an alleged chance of improving the system is the worst sin in Chomsky's book. He is an Orwellian, a theorist of permanent opposition. Another historical diversion takes an Orwellian view of Spanish anarchism, loosely attached to the proposition that even the best liberal scholars are bound to underestimate serious revolutions. The general thesis fails to stick, and the performance on Chomsky's historical *violon d'Ingres* is too long; perhaps he is also over-eager to show that he too can smell a Stalinist rat. But the parallel with Orwell sticks in the mind: a proud defensive independence, a good plain writer's hatred of expert mystification, a doctrine of resistance which runs against the melioristic and participatory current of most contemporary intellectual life. Such men are dangerous; the lack of them is disastrous. (pp. 770-71)

> *Francis Hope, ''Free-Floating,'' in* New Statesman *(© 1969 The Statesman & Nation Publishing Co. Ltd.), Vol. 78, No. 2020, November 28, 1969, pp. 770-71.*

DENNIS H. WRONG

[*American Power and the New Mandarins*] is primarily an indictment and an anthology of agitational manifestoes. Since much of what Chomsky says is eloquent and forceful, he succeeds in drawing blood from many of his adversaries, and since his advice to the antiwar movement is frequently wise (he advised war resisters in 1967 to avoid any semblance of violence), one is tempted to overlook his errors and rhetorical excesses and simply to praise the book as a record of the partially successful campaign against the war.

But in some quarters Chomsky is being celebrated as an important and original political thinker. The extensive documentation he appends to his longer essays has impressed several reviewers as a considerable scholarly achievement, even though it is employed not to support a new analysis of American or world politics but merely to buttress the passionate moral accusations that are the substance of all Chomsky's political writings: that the United States is hypocritical and has in the past as well as the present pursued policies in Asia belying the lofty goals proclaimed by its official spokesmen, that some American scholars have justified the horrors of the Vietnam war in euphemistic terms, and that liberal intellectuals have an ''elitist'' outlook that makes them willing servants of the powerful.

Nor do Chomsky's admirers seem much concerned about inaccuracies in his assembled mass of quotations, although it seems to me more than a trifle to have twice grossly misquoted a President of the United States (Truman).

There is a time and place for the expression of moral indignation and a time and place for analysis of our situation; and the two are not identical. Nor do I assert this out of any commitment to the ''value-free'' behavioral science that Chomsky assails. (Here too he confines himself to denunciation, which hardly suffices to make him the devastating critic of positivist social science some have seen in him). But take his characterization of Vietnam as a ''criminal war.'' . . . Since Chomsky is not primarily concerned to argue that Vietnam violates the uncertain canons of international law, his epithet contributes as little to understanding the origins and nature of the war as *Daily News* fulminations against the ''criminal gang in the Kremlin'' contribute to the understanding of Soviet Communism. It is scarcely illuminating to call even the Nazis ''criminal''—Nazism perhaps represented criminality raised to the level of principle, but the qualification is crucial if we wish to understand it as a political mass movement.

This may appear to be trivial quibbling. But if this book is meant to initiate a reorientation in American foreign policy and the relation to it of the intellectual community, it would be patronizing to treat it simply as a stump crusade against the Vietnam war. Therefore it is worth exposing the exaggerations and the weaknesses in both fact and rational argument with which it abounds. Chomsky's two major arguments are that American world power is an unqualified evil and that American intellectuals have abdicated their moral responsibilities by serving its aims as a corps of ''new mandarins.'' Let us first examine his indictment of American power, for while the second accusation receives greater attention in the book and has won him prominence as a kind of Savonarola of the academic world, it is relevant only if the first charge is sustained.

Chomsky asserts that ''twenty years of intensive cold-war indoctrination and seventy years of myth regarding our international role make it difficult to face these issues in a serious way.'' Which 70-year-old myth does he have in mind? The myth of ''manifest destiny'' in the Caribbean and the Pacific? The myth of what George Kennan in *American Diplomacy* called America's ''legalistic-moralistic'' approach to international relations? The myth of Wilsonian self-determination? The myth of isolationism in the 20s and 30s? Of the Crusade in Europe against Hitler? The last seventy years have shown us many opposing myths rather than a single unchanging one. Chomsky is probably thinking of manifest destiny at the turn of the century, for later in the book he attacks in some detail American political imperialism in the Philippines and Latin America and commercial imperialism in China. Only rarely, however, does he mention the two European wars or the League of Nations and the U.N. where we obviously also played an international role. (pp. 75-6)

Chomsky opposes the war because he considers it a nakedly imperialist venture, an attempt by a large and powerful nation to impose by force a puppet government on a small nation against the wishes of the latter's citizens. Again and again he alludes to our readiness ''to pound into rubble a small nation that refuses to submit to our will,'' ''the attempt by our country to impose its particular concept of order and stability throughout the world,'' and the like. Chomsky's view is not, as some critics of American policy would have it, that out of a misguided sense of mission the United States has assumed the role of world policeman and overplayed it. To him America is as aggressively and selfishly imperialist as Japan or Britain ever were, and morally even more culpable because we are more outrageously pharisaical in our rationalizations and, in the case of Vietnam, do not have important material interests at stake such as the foreign investments, markets, sources of raw materials, need for migration outlets, or realistic concern with national security which motivated the older imperialisms. Chomsky repeatedly demands, by what *right* we take it upon ourselves to use military force to determine the political institutions of South Vietnam? His opposition to the war, therefore, derives fundamentally from his denial of any possible moral justification for American intervention in Vietnam, or indeed virtually anywhere in the world. (pp. 76-7)

[It] is striking that Chomsky barely mentions [the Cold War] . . . background to our Vietnam involvement. The Cold War he regards simply as an ideology providing a flimsy pretext for American intervention, which he prefers instead to view as continuous with the occupation of the Philippines and the landing of marines in the Caribbean earlier in the century, rather than with the great decisions of World War II and the confrontation with Russia that was its aftermath. (p. 77)

Why . . . *are* we in Vietnam? Chomsky concedes that none of the self-interested imperialist motives for which the Cold War provided a propaganda cover in Iran, Guatemala, and elsewhere were operative: in the 1930s "Japan's appeal to national interest . . . was not totally without merit" but a like appeal "becomes merely ludicrous when translated into a justification for American conquests in Asia."

Chomsky's answer is that ideology, which "can have a life of its own," has dictated American actions. Occasionally he attributes our Vietnam policy to sheer "paranoia," a manifestly irrational fear of a nonexistent "World Communism" inducing the most powerful nation on earth "to pound into rubble a tiny Asian country," etc., although he remains doubtful as to whether the fear is genuine, and thus a sign of "true" paranoia, or merely a fabricated excuse for our actions. In either case comparison with Nazi Germany would indeed be more appropriate than with the more "rational" imperialisms of the past. But, although he flirts with it, Chomsky declines to commit himself fully to so demoniacal a view of American policy and one is left wondering why, if ideology or even "ideological paranoia" also have something to do with it, he fails to examine the Cold War background to the war in Vietnam. (pp. 77-8)

I think Chomsky fails to analyze the Cold War background of the Vietnam war because to do so would inevitably temper the absoluteness of his condemnation of the United States. He would be drawn into consideration of such subjects as the Korean war . . . ; the mind of Dean Rusk fixated on the international situation of the early 50s; and how President Johnson, lacking Eisenhower's first-hand knowledge of the fallibility of generals and Kennedy's chastening experience at the Bay of Pigs, allowed the Joint Chiefs of Staff to "lead him down the garden path on Vietnam" (as Dean Acheson now reports he informed the President in early 1968 after having discovered that he himself and other top advisers had been similarly deceived).

Dwelling on these matters might suggest that American policy was no more than "criminally mistaken" rather than "merely criminal," or even that there was a partial inadvertence in our Vietnam involvement as argued by Chomsky's *bête noire*, Arthur Schlesinger, Jr. Chomsky wishes to avoid such suggestions

in order to present the Vietnam war as a morally unambiguous case of a big nation brutally coercing a defenseless small nation in a surrounding international vacuum. The purity and unassailability of such a moral verdict seems of major importance to Chomsky, as is indicated by his insistence . . . to so confirmed a dove as Stanley Hoffman that he and Hoffman, the latter's claim to the contrary notwithstanding, are in fundamental disagreement about the morality of Vietnam because Hoffman's notion of the war's immorality includes reference to the use of means that corrupt ends and entail excessive costs instead of the simple judgment that the war is immoral in and of itself.

If the war *were* a clear-cut case of brutal imperialist aggression by a great power against an isolated small country, and if American policy-makers had perceived it as such while trumping up high-sounding slogans to sell it to the public, Chomsky's charge that references to the overall costs and consequences of our policy amount to moral evasion would be entirely justified. I too oppose the Vietnam war and I agree with Chomsky that its major consequences for the Vietnamese people are not very different from what they would be if the war were no more than the crude act of American aggression Chomsky supposes it to be. But I do not agree that these consequences are the only relevant ones in evaluating the war and understanding its origins, though I think they must now be considered in themselves sufficient to obligate withdrawal from Vietnam; nor do I believe that our policy-makers are as plainly guilty of evil intentions and bad faith as they would have to be to deserve Chomsky's characterization of them as "criminal," "morally degenerate," "depraved," and the like. Nor are those critics of the war with whom Chomsky has engaged in interminable controversies, such as Schlesinger, Hoffman, and [Lionel] Abel necessarily less righteous than he, more corrupted by the relativist ethic of pragmatism, or more cowardly in their readiness to give the devil his due. Viewing the war in a larger historical and geographical context than Chomsky, they are unable to see it as the unmitigated deed of international banditry, the obvious "obscenity," that is all it amounts to in his view of it.

Chomsky's dogged persistence in debating the grounds of opposition to the war with fellow-intellectuals who have opposed it no less firmly than he is not the result of a holier-than-thou attitude. His sincerity and moral earnestness are altogether convincing. His conviction that the war must be condemned as intrinsically evil follows at least in part from his chosen role as prosecutor of the academic community, which he accuses of a new *trahison des clercs*. (pp. 78-9)

To Chomsky, behavioral science provides indispensable ideological support to a new technocratic intelligentsia deeply implicated in the excesses of American militarism; but several of his preferred examples of new mandarins, notably Irving Kristol and Daniel Bell, are, whatever their limitations, vigorous critics rather than partisans of the "behavioral persuasion" in social science. In France, where the Vietnam war is not a political issue, technocracy . . . is the subject of intense debate *within the Left* between "technocrats" and "humanists," debate of a far higher order of intelligence than the angry tirades directed by Chomsky and the New Left against our own homegrown equivalents of technocrats.

In tacit recognition of these contradictions, Chomsky broadens his attack on the intellectuals, charging them with a long-standing "elitist" bias revealed in their Stalinist sympathies in the 1930s as fully as in their more recent affiliations with

American power and their attraction to a technocratic world view. As a case in point, Chomsky turns to the treatment by American historians of the Spanish Civil War, calling attention to their neglect of the anarchist revolt in Catalonia and their acceptance of the Stalinist version of how that revolt was suppressed by the Republican government. (p. 79)

Chomsky's discussion of Spain, however, is typical of a general style of argument that is evident in his exchanges with his critics. He passes a sweeping moral judgment or makes a far-reaching generalization and then, without further elaboration or qualification, plunges into compiling a massive body of evidence on some highly specific event or situation that may or may not be directly and unquestionably relevant to the initial judgment or generalization. At the end of his assessment, he asserts that he remains uncertain about the truth of the original proposition but that the evidence he has assembled must be taken into account and seems to be at least consistent with it. (p. 80)

This approach certainly gives the appearance of being refreshingly undogmatic and open to the claims of the evidence. No doubt the most appropriate method of scholarship in a large number of fields is to measure a detailed, often technical, analysis of a particular case against the implications of an established generalization and to conclude that the generalization is either valid or needs qualification or more rigorous formulation if it is still to stand. But this case-study method hardly seems to be the best way in which to make a political argument based on historical events, for any set of particulars we refer to are likely to be interconnected and the universe from which we select our particulars is a "closed" one rather than an open one containing a potentially almost infinite number of possible cases. I don't know very much about Chomsky's field of linguistics, but I strongly doubt that moral and ideological judgments of American foreign policy in the past century can be tested or supported in the same manner that is appropriate to, say, a theory of consonantal shifts in the structure of a spoken language.

Even if Chomsky is often correct both in his overall generalizations and his detailed case studies, the hiatus between the generalization and the particular exemplification of it is too great for his argument to possess much explanatory value. For example, he may well be right in contending that intellectuals are peculiarly susceptible to elitist political doctrines and that liberal scholarship on Spain, the Leninist vanguard concept of the Party, Stalinist fellow-traveling in the 30s, and a technocratic-managerial view of industrial society are all manifestations of this elitism. (And one might add, as Chomsky doesn't, the Marcusean theory of repressive tolerance, New Left justifications of disruptive political action by militant minorities, and the hero worship of figures like Mao, Ho, and Che by student radicals.) But if all these are instances of the elitism of intellectuals, the concept explains *too much* to be very useful. The particular context in which actually or potentially elitist doctrines are put forward then becomes all-important. Thus Chomsky cleverly cites Daniel Bell's support of the Machajski theory that modern revolutions are made by intellectuals for their own ends in the name of the masses, and then chides Bell for ignoring this insight when he approvingly assigns a leadership role to the technical intelligentsia in "postindustrial society." But, without necessarily endorsing Bell's view, one should at least note that his technocratic arguments presuppose the existence of a functioning democracy which imposes definite constraints on the managerial aspirations of intellectuals

and scientists—in complete contrast to the revolutionary messianism of "discontented intellectuals" that Machajski prophetically indicted as early as 1899.

Yet in the end there is much that is attractive in Chomsky's outlook. For all the extravagance of his rhetoric, his tendency to lump together as politically insupportable a variety of things he dislikes, and his inability to sustain a general line of argument, he is largely free of the doctrinaire pettiness and polemical mean-spiritedness that so often dominates ideologues of the Left. His career as a scientist and his political sensibility remind one of the late J. Robert Oppenheimer. The Vietnam war has moved him to assume a political role, but he will probably make his presence felt on the Left long after that wretched enterprise has been concluded. (pp. 80-1)

Dennis H. Wrong, "Chomsky: Of Thinking & Moralizing," in Dissent *(© 1970, by Dissent Publishing Corporation), Vol. XVII, No. 1, January-February, 1970, pp. 75-81.*

HENRY F. MINS

[*American Power and the New Mandarins* adds up to a brilliant arraignment, a partisan analysis, and an absence of program. So far as I can see, the author, while making frequent use of the word Communist, is almost entirely unaware of historical materialism. Certain phases of recent history are vivid in his mind but he shows no signs of general historical perspective and causation. He remains on the level of ideas and ideals, taken absolutely, in a quasi-religious manner. And how is it possible that so keen a thinker, a gentle man with so blameless a heart, can arrive at such an impasse on matters which he recognizes as involving the fate of the entire human race? How can a scientist base his argument on a biased sample of materials? One is tempted to look for a systematic skewing factor and, if I am not mistaken, it lies very near the surface. The flaw is anarchism.

It comes as something of a shock to realize that the romantic creed of anarchism has not disappeared and can still appeal to a mind of Chomsky's caliber. . . . (pp. 114-15)

[The] fact is that for Chomsky no such thing as Marxism exists. It is a wraith. He agrees with various bourgeois critics that there is no Communism today. On his basis, though, there never was any Marxism. Bakunin demolished Marx's authoritarian program; Rosa Luxemburg exposed Lenin's elitist contempt for the masses. The Soviet Union represses populist spontaneity at home, and abroad seeks only its own imperialist interests. Basta. That is all there is to it. This remarkable picture, painted with remarkable unanimity by a remarkable diversity of artists, is all too familiar. I will only point out that in a book largely devoted to Vietnam, I do not find any mention of the surely relevant fact that the Vietnamese are being supplied by the Soviet Union.

It is on Vietnam as against the American invasion that Chomsky shows that he is able to make his case, and vastly improve it in the process, by citing all sides: the North Vietnamese and the NLF, the Saigon "government" and the American military command, newsmen and editorial writers of all shades, American supporters and opponents of the war, speeches in Congress and the Senate. This is scientific procedure in discussing any topic, and especially public affairs. (p. 117)

Henry F. Mins, "Book Reviews: 'American Power and the New Mandarins'," in Science and Society *(copyright 1970 by Science and Society, Incorporated), Vol. XXXIV, No. 1, Spring, 1970, pp. 111-17.*

CORNELIA NAVARI

[In *American Power and the New Mandarins* Mr. Chomsky] appears content to make a single statement and to reiterate it continually. His exposé of intellectual double-think is both sobering and tells its own story; of particular poignancy is his review of the Vietnam symposium in the August 1967 issue of *Asian Survey* where at least one academic called to advise and carry out a land reform programme was utterly confounded by the fact that agrarian reform impeded the war effort. But his quest for exposure has overtaken any attempt to analyse the phenomenon or to trace its roots. The only explanation provided for what is by Mr. Chomsky's own efforts an impressive loss of criteria is the liberal élite's predilection for being élitist and for wanting to be close to the seat of power, an explanation merely noted, with no reference deemed necessary as to why élites everywhere are not the same or why power in America is associated with loss of values. Not even the ideology of Americanism is dissected, although it is well displayed. . . . More curious still is Mr. Chomsky's examination of Gabriel Jackson's *The Spanish Republic and the Civil War*. His criticism is neither with Mr. Jackson's factual presentation nor of his source material, but that he underrates the period of spontaneous popular revolution following the Franco insurrection in July 1936. Mr. Jackson does in fact neglect it, but he does so because the purpose of the work is to elucidate the eventual fate of the Republic, during whose development the social revolution, quelled, passed off without a ripple and indeed did not inform the subsequent course of events. Mr. Chomsky's claim that Mr. Jackson is a typical liberal élitist wishing to remain untouched by popular revolution may or may not be true; the fact remains that history is a form of set-theory exercise. If events do not fit the set, the methodology of history and its internal consistency demand their exclusion. (p. 240)

Cornelia Navari, "North America: 'American Power and the New Mandarins'," in International Affairs (© Royal Institute of International Affairs 1971), Vol. 47, No. 1, January, 1971, pp. 239-40.

KENNETH J. GAVIN

Both the linguist who is interested in further explications of Chomsky's theory of language and the political analyst who is looking for new formulations in his analysis of American foreign policy will be disappointed with [*Problems of Knowledge and Freedom*]. Basically, it is not a new book at all. Most of what Chomsky says here about language and politics, he has published elsewhere before this—and at greater length. But the book is significant for other reasons: first of all, it marks the first time Chomsky has joined his linguistic and political writings under one cover; second, it attempts to outline the intellectual progression that links the theoretical linguistic insights of the MIT academic with the radical political stance he has taken in response to the United States' involvement in Southeast Asia during the past decade. . . .

[Chomsky] focuses on Bertrand Russell's philosophical attempts at *interpreting the world* and his political and social efforts at *changing the world*. In posing the question whether there is a link between Russell's philosophical and political

convictions (a question that can only strike the reader as curiously autobiographical), Chomsky suggests that common elements can be discerned in "Russell's endeavor to discover the conditions of human knowledge and the conditions of human freedom."

In his first chapter Chomsky outlines the theory of knowledge espoused by Russell in his later years—a theory that recognized the limits of empiricism and the impossibility of deducing certain principles of inference from experience. Russell's theory aimed at determining the innate principles of the mind that interact with the fixed laws of the world about us to form human knowledge. Advancing along similar lines, Chomsky argues that, if we were able to discover the innate mental structure that makes human knowledge possible, we might then be able to predict with some certainty the scope and limits of scientific knowledge.

As a linguist, language is the specific domain of human knowledge that Chomsky is most interested in. He suggests that innate and universal properties can be discovered in language that form an *a priori* mental framework within whose constraint man can understand and produce language. (Chomsky has written at length in support of the innateness hypothesis, as opposed to a behavioristic, stimulus-response analysis of language learning and human understanding in general. . . .) For Chomsky the empiricist view of human acquisition of knowledge is basically nonliberating. It is absurd, as well as fruitless, to imagine the human mind, unconstrained by any innate framework, striking out in all directions at random from the moment of birth. On the contrary, in order for the mind to realize its scope, there must be limits and restriction to which it is subject. The creativity of language is possible only within the constraints of its system of rules. It is the notion of free creation within a system of rules that Chomsky finds essential to a humanistic conception of man, and it is this belief that forms the foundation of his political insights.

In his second chapter Chomsky turns to an analysis of the political and social fabric of the United States. With Russell he believes that the aim of all social reconstruction is the "liberation of the creative impulse" in man and freedom from oppression, even when it appears in the form of what Russell called "benevolent autocracies."

The American people, Chomsky observes, have been cowed into subservience to those in power. Even the liberal university intelligentsia have been more than willing to assimilate themselves to the new military-industrial ruling class of the state, and our universities have become tools for the advancement of American self-aggrandizement. (p. 522)

Chomsky's prose is far from the dispassionate realm of academic journals. He paints a convincing, but bleak, picture of the propaganda victory that the American government has won over its own people. Russell's dream of the radical transformation of the advanced industrial societies of the West, he admits, is remoter now than ever before. Chomsky's last hope—though it does indeed sound hollow at times—seems to rest on his humanistic conception of man and his capacity for knowledge, for freedom and for building "a world in which the creative spirit is alive, in which life is an adventure full of hope and joy, based rather upon the impulse to construct than upon the desire to retain what we possess or to seize what is possessed by others."

The book, although it is aimed at a non-technical audience, is not a good introduction to Chomsky's general linguistic theory. . . . Notions such as deep and surface structure are only briefly alluded to and the necessity for a transformational approach to grammar is never adequately explained. For this Chomsky is not at fault. His goal was to highlight principles of human knowledge and indicate the priority of these principles in the reconstruction of a society. His efforts leave us with more than enough to think about. (pp. 522, 524)

Kenneth J. Gavin, "Book Reviews: 'Problems of Knowledge and Freedom'," in America *(reprinted with permission of America Press, Inc.; © 1971; all rights reserved), Vol. 125, No. 18, December 11, 1971, pp. 522, 524.*

THE TIMES LITERARY SUPPLEMENT

Instead of a synthesis of [Noam Chomsky's views, **Problems of Knowledge and Freedom**] is more a summary of his separate views on linguistics and politics, one which, moreover, seems to show that they derive from essentially different and in some ways conflicting sources. Chomsky does say in his introduction that "it is by no means obvious that a given person's efforts, in . . . separate domains, must derive from a common source or be at all tightly linked". However, since the first lecture deals with the problem of the acquisition of knowledge and belief, and the second with the public effects of the activities of certain acquirers of knowledge (acquiescent American intellectuals), it is not unreasonable to seek for a certain consistency of view in both essays. . . .

[The] second essay lacks the clarity and control of the first; it quickly develops from remarks on work as the free conscious activity of man, and on principles of education based upon Russell and Humboldt, to a generalized account of American military activity in Vietnam and attempts to control dissent in the United States. Yet linguistic constraints *restrict* the potential output of language; why, therefore, should moral and social schemata operate in a socially fruitful manner, to create free and unconstrained modes of behaviour? Centralized power, whether of Chinese or Russian communism or Western capitalism, is for Chomsky the great villain of history. Like Yeats, he is horrified by "the cruelty of governments". Yet may not innate mental schemata encourage the participation in centralized power just as easily as they could be sources of shelter from it? The powers of the mind, though inaccessible as yet to direct analysis, may be forces for tyranny and serfdom as readily as freedom.

"The Voice of the Dove," in The Times Literary Supplement *(© Times Newspapers Ltd. (London) 1972; reproduced from* The Times Literary Supplement *by permission), No. 3657, March 31, 1972, p. 359.*

RICHARD TODD

One of the interesting things about Chomsky's new collection of essays, **For Reasons of State,** is that it suggests relationships between his scholarly work and his social and political statements. Chomsky explores this question in an essay called **"Language and Freedom."** Whatever one's politics, the issues raised here are of interest and importance.

Chomsky has led a revolution in linguistics, countering what had been presumed to be the advances of the past decades. If the details of his work are abstruse, its implications are ac-

cessible. They don't lead by any sure route to Vietnam, but they do reach far beyond his academic discipline.

Chomsky disputes the behavioristic concept of language, which holds that language is simply acquired by response to external stimuli, like other, more trivial, forms of behavior. He raises troublesome questions for those who hold this view. He points out that their theories fail to explain such simple facts as a child's ability to say and to understand sentences he has never heard before; that they fail to account for the everyday genius that allows human beings to create an infinity of unique sentences. Words and rules of syntax are, of course, learned, but Chomsky maintains that the capacity for language is innate. He postulates a structure in the mind that governs our use of language, a "universal grammar" to whose rules all human language adheres.

When Chomsky is speaking of language he is always speaking of much more: of what is unique and unalterable in the human mind. That such properties exist is his fundamental claim. He thus contradicts the whole of behaviorism. This collection includes his attack on B. F. Skinner's *Beyond Freedom and Dignity,* in which Chomsky claims that much of Skinner's book is trivial and tautological. The thrust of Chomsky's scholarship works against behaviorism; and so, too, do his feelings. . . . Chomsky proposes a social science (and a society) that proceed from eighteenth-century ideas of the irreducible dignity and complexity of the human mind.

Bracing as Chomsky's social theories can be, it ought to be said that a certain ideology plays throughout these pages, which can't be derived unambiguously from his linguistic theories. Chomsky's view of an ideal society is only hazily defined, and most often in terms of what he opposes, "predatory capitalism." But it is clear enough that it rests on extremely hopeful assumptions about the prospects for human perfectibility. Chomsky is generally scrupulous in separating hopes from knowledge, and yet it seems that there are some dark possibilities he likes not to face. If you set out to map the mind, must you not prepare to find regions of malevolence?

Nevertheless, at his most impressive, Chomsky reaffirms a sense of the mystery of "human nature," a phrase he rescues from the vulgarity and quaintness into which it has fallen. (pp. 97-8)

Richard Todd, "Left, Right, Gonzo!" in The Atlantic Monthly *(copyright © 1973, by The Atlantic Monthly Company, Boston, Mass.; reprinted with permission), Vol. 232, No. 1, July, 1973, pp. 97-8.*

SIMON HEAD

The greatest value of Professor Chomsky's [**For Reasons of State** is that it provides a satisfactory answer to the question of why the United States must win in Vietnam]. . . . He shows how the psychological and geopolitical factors which have guided American policy in Indochina from the beginning are as much a part of Nixon's political psychology and behavior as they were of Johnson's or Kennedy's. Though Chomsky's analysis is mainly concerned with the pre-Nixon period (i.e., 1949-1968), the conclusions he reaches apply with equal force to the past four years and, one suspects, to the next four. . . .

Chomsky points out that [the irrationalism of America's fear of losing the Vietnam War] showed a marked increase in the early Sixties when, with the influx of a "rootless intelligentsia" into Washington, whose sole claim to power rested on nothing more than its "alleged expertise," there was "much talk of psychological tests of will, humiliation, the American image, and so on." But this horror of "loss" has also been as much a characteristic of presidents as of their acolytes. . . .

Moreover it has always been characteristic of official thinking—as Chomsky argues—that such hysterical perceptions of what is involved can coexist with a calculation of strategic interests which is more or less rational. The loss of Indochina may be a moral and a spiritual disaster, but there are also more mundane questions about real estate which cannot be ignored. For the past twenty-five years US officials have intoned with unrelieved monotony that the loss of Indochina would be followed by the loss of much else besides, the precise way in which the dominoes might fall varying according to the particular stage of the cold war one might be talking about. (p. 27)

Can these kinds of fears still exist, and continue to influence policy, when US official thinking about Chinese intentions seems to have changed drastically, and when American strategy for "ending" the war has rested on the assumption that the Chinese and North Vietnamese have different interests in Southeast Asia? The clear implication of Chomsky's analysis (and again it deals mainly with the pre-Nixon period) is that the Administration is and will continue to be in the thrall of the domino theory. Not, he argues, because the old paranoia about Chinese intentions still lurks beneath the surface cordiality of rapprochement, but for the more fundamental reason that the *real* version of the theory which has in fact guided successive administrations (including this one) has never had very much to do with Chinese and North Vietnamese aggression at all, but deals instead with events that are unaffected by what either communist power might decide to do.

All the talk about external aggression must be regarded, in Chomsky's view, not as expressions of genuine alarm about Chinese or North Vietnamese intentions, but as clever propaganda devices designed to divert attention from the real threats to US interests. These threats have always been the strength of "indigenous Communist-led movements" throughout Southeast Asia, the weakness of the pro-Western regimes they are opposed to, and the likelihood that these regimes will sooner or later succumb to local insurgents without the Chinese or North Vietnamese having to lift a finger. The US, he argues, had to fabricate the myth of a Hitlerian China because it was loath to admit that the regimes in Thailand, Malaysia, and the Philippines could not survive the trauma of a US "defeat" in Indochina. (pp. 27-8)

If there is a weakness in this argument, it is that Chomsky applies it with equal force to every stage of the US involvement in Indochina. He wants to argue that US policy makers were *never* seriously concerned about possible Chinese aggression in Southeast Asia, that they were always realistic and clearheaded about where the real danger came from, and that John Foster Dulles in 1955 was therefore as deliberate in misleading US public opinion about China as were Dean Rusk and Walt Rostow ten years later.

The difficulty here is that many of the more foolish policies followed by the Eisenhower administration in particular make sense only if we grant that there was a real, if unwarranted, fear of China and (to a lesser extent) of North Vietnam and the Soviet Union: the decision to organize the South Vietnamese, Thai, and Laotian armies on completely conventional lines; the enormous importance Dulles attached to the formation of SEATO as an alliance of great powers which would, like NATO,

"deter communist aggression"; the belief of the Eisenhower administration (and initially of the Kennedy administration as well) that the Pathet Lao and neutralist troops which marched on Vientiane during the Laotian crisis of 1960-1961 were possibly the vanguard of an advancing communist horde that would cut Southeast Asia in two, and were therefore a major threat to world peace, the source of a crisis as serious as Berlin, Cuba, the Middle East, and Vietnam itself—all were symptomatic of a highly alarmist view of communist intentions.

Moreover, in view of this genuine fear of Chinese aggression, it is an oversimplification to argue, as Chomsky does, that throughout the 1950s the prime strategic rationale for US involvement in Southeast Asia was always the need to protect the Japanese economy from the loss of Southeast Asian food, raw materials, and markets, lest the Japanese turn to the "Stalinist bloc" for other sources of supply. Though this fear undoubtedly influenced American actions, there were more straightforward military calculations which were equally important. Successful "communist aggression" in one theater would most likely be followed by more aggression in another: if Southeast Asia were lost, India and Australia would be directly threatened (thus the more fantastic versions of the domino theory) and the chances of a Soviet "move" in the Middle East or Berlin would be greater.

But whatever shortcomings it may have in explaining the past, Chomsky's thesis is of great value in making sense of the present: alarmism about Chinese intentions has faded to the point where not even Administration spokesmen bother to mouth the old familiar slogans. But the weakness of the client states is as serious as ever, and their probable reaction to "disengagement" is a major force for American inflexibility in Indochina. It is not simply that "disengagement," followed by the "loss" of the three Indochinese countries, would so encourage the insurgent movements in Thailand, Malaysia, and the Philippines that they would be carried to victory by the sheer momentum of events—though there might indeed be such fallout effects. Equally if not more important is the psychological impact such a disengagement would have on the ruling cliques in these countries. . . .

Chomsky's . . . view would seem to be that this huge reactionary endeavor [to prevent the victory of local insurgents] is irrational even according to the kind of motives which typically underlie American imperial behavior: no advantages which might now accrue from having these territories within the American sphere could possibly compensate for the strain and sacrifice involved in actually keeping them there. . . .

But of course Nixon and Kissinger are not "rational imperialists." They do not coldly add up the credit and debit sheets and decide to sell out accordingly. Though such hopeful developments as the rapprochement with China and the Soviet Union suggest a diplomacy both rational and sophisticated, nonetheless there coexists with it a more primitive view of the world which Nixon and Kissinger have constructed during their long careers as cold warriors. The cold war itself may have passed, but the categories of thought appropriate to the cold war linger on. . . .

Those who have waited eight years for the Congress to do something about the bombing of Indochina must have a nagging suspicion that things may go on much as before. They will find little comfort in Chomsky's remarkable book. (p. 28)

Simon Head, "Story without End," in The New York Review of Books *(reprinted with permission from*

The New York Review of Books; *copyright © 1973 Nyrev, Inc.), Vol. 20, No. 13, August 9, 1973, pp. 26-8.*

SHELDON S. WOLIN

The merits of [*For Reasons of State*] lie in the first four essays which deal with the Pentagon Papers and various aspects of the war in Southeast Asia. Here Chomsky displays those qualities which exemplify the finest traditions of intellectual responsibility and which have rightly earned for him the gratitude of those who have long regarded the Vietnam war as an abomination. He is relentless in tracking down official lies and exposing hypocrisy and moral indifference in the high places where the war was conceived and executed. Yet the passion of Chomsky's indictment is always controlled, and while he is harsh toward his opponents, he is never unfair or arrogant. . . . (p. 32)

Wholly admirable in exposing official deceit, Chomsky is unimpressive as a radical thinker. The reasons for this may be instructive in explaining the intellectual poverty of the American left. Stated simply, Chomsky's political writings are curiously untheoretical, which is surprising in a writer renowned for his contributions to linguistic theory. His apparent assumption is that politics is not a theoretical subject. Judging from other writings of his, he dismisses the scientific claims of contemporary social science and reasons that if no scientific theories are available for analyzing political problems, then, by definition, no theories are available for dealing with these matters. One gets the impression from reading Chomsky that if it were not urgently necessary to expose lies, immorality and the abuse of power, politics would have no serious claim upon the theoretical mind. (pp. 32, 34)

Chomsky's theoretical limitations are evident in his failure to connect the two main problems he has identified. The first involves an explanation of what American purposes were served by political and military intervention in Southeast Asia. The second is, why, having intervened, did American policymakers persist in making decisions which were increasingly irrational and morally appalling?

On the first problem, Chomsky's explanation is straightforward. An "autocracy" controls the American economy and "largely" staffs the Government. It has used its power for "the primary goal of maximizing the free access of American capital to the markets and human and material resources of the world, the goal of maintaining to the fullest possible extent freedom of operation in a global economy." It perceived Southeast Asia to be vital to "the integrated global system . . . organized by American power," and hence it sought to prevent indigenous revolutionary movements from gaining control over the processes of development in that region. The rational outcome of that determination was the ruthless destruction of people and land as well as the maintenance of reactionary and incompetent regimes.

Chomsky makes no attempt to analyze the corporate structure or behavior of the "private autocracy," but the logic of his explanation is clear enough and not without credibility. But what is the explanation for the behavior of the "technical élite"—Rusk, McNamara, Rostow, Bundy, Kissinger, et al.? Why did they traffic in domino theories, myths about the N.L.F. and various Saigon governments; why did they not only countenance the massive, senseless destruction but coldly escalate it? Here Chomsky begins to falter. Corporate imperialism has a

familiar logic that seems inapplicable to the actions of the policymakers in Washington. Other than some vague references to the "intellectual framework" of the technical mind, no explanation is offered. Chomsky's analysis is sustained almost entirely by the conviction that by exposing the "facts" and appealing to self-evident moral notions the case for radicalism has been advanced. It should be added that the Marxian premises of his analysis of imperialism are neither defended nor explained.

Chomsky's indifference toward theory means that he is disinclined to pursue unsuspected (or even unwelcome) interconnections. Thus his radicalism stops short of a critique of modern science and technology, although he will criticize individual scientists or particular uses of technology. At no point does he consider the possibility of a deep collaboration between contemporary science—with its voracious appetite for huge budgets, costly installations, bureaucratic organization—and the bureaucracies of government and industry; or of the "intellectual framework" of the Pentagon planners, with its ideology of precision, efficiency, cost-benefits analysis and game theory being the legitimate offspring of an intellectual culture which is not only technological and managerial but scientific as well. We get, instead, allusions to the irrationality of crisis managers and "institutionalized stupidity." (pp. 34, 36)

Sheldon S. Wolin, "'For Reasons of State'," in The New York Times Book Review *(© 1973 by The New York Times Company; reprinted by permission), September 30, 1973, pp. 32, 34, 36.*

DELL HYMES

[As] an anthropologist as well as linguist, I do not accept Chomsky's conception of social scientists as universally whoring after the surface features of other sciences, neglecting all fundamental problems, and taking refuge in spurious precision and trivialities. . . . There is much of this, one knows, but there is much else besides. Chomsky's notion of the social sciences may have been shaped (and warped) by close proximity to representatives of the type he describes in his own institution. . . . I agree that the [academic advisers to the American government] frequently offered spurious expertise, and that common morality should have prevailed; but there *is* such a thing as scientific expertise. Chomsky has gone a fair way to acquiring it, one essential reason for the effectiveness of his arguments. . . . (n., pp. 330-31)

Dell Hymes, "Review of Noam Chomsky" (reprinted by permission of the author), in On Noam Chomsky: Critical Essays, *edited by Gilbert Harman, Anchor Press, 1974, pp. 316-34.*

GEOFFREY SAMPSON

Chomsky's perception of the political situation in Vietnam during the years of the war (as reflected in his writings about Vietnam) was one instance of [the error inherent in methodological rationalism]. As a rationalist, Chomsky supposes that nations 'know' what social arrangements are best for them; and, as a consequence, like other socialists he has to exaggerate the degree of unanimity which existed in South Vietnam as to the desirability of a Communist victory. The truth of the matter was that some South Vietnamese wanted to see the Communists win, others hoped that the Thieu/Ky government would survive, and no doubt many wished principally that the conflict would go away; but Chomsky writes as if, except for a tiny clique of wicked profiteers or the like, South Vietnam as a whole desired a socialist revolution—which is what made it so immoral for the U.S.A. to frustrate this purpose. Since Chomsky confuses what people believe to be right with what is right, it is difficult for him to perceive a situation in which people sincerely differ. For the liberal, on the other hand, there was no paradox in the fact that South Vietnamese disagreed as to what was the better future for their country; people are as likely to make mistakes on political questions as on any others. For that matter, even if the South Vietnamese *had* been unanimous in their opinion about which side should win the war (which they certainly were not), while the liberal would be surprised at such unanimity he would not regard it as evidence for the correctness of the unanimous view. If every Vietnamese man, woman, and child had believed passionately that the best government for Vietnam was the kind of socialist government which now exists there, then certainly a liberal would examine and re-examine his grounds for disagreeing with them to see if he had not overlooked some reason why, in the circumstances obtaining in Vietnam, socialism might not after all be desirable; but, provided that he found no such flaw in his argument, the liberal would reply that every single Vietnamese was wrong, which is a perfectly possible state of affairs. It would be an interesting sociological question why an entire nation should show such bad political judgement; but, *qua* political animals rather than academic sociologists, our task is not to interpret the false political beliefs which exist in the world but to change them.

The paradoxical consequences of Chomsky's methodological rationalism become clearer still, perhaps, if we turn from the specific issue of Vietnam to the more general arena of abstract political philosophy. How can Chomsky reconcile his views with the existence of individuals who disagree with those views?

Notice, in the first place, that Chomsky does not use empirical arguments to any serious extent in his advocacy of socialism. (pp. 195-96)

Chomsky is not, at heart, primarily concerned with empirical arguments for equalitarianism, or for the other components of his political ideal. True, the argument from universals of language and psychology to politics . . . is an empirical argument. But in Chomsky's own pattern of thought this argument acts only as a confirmation of beliefs held independently; and, from the contemptuous tone of his attacks on the liberal mentality, it is very clear that he regards liberals as guilty of something much less excusable than ignorance of recent developments in academic linguistics and psychology. The main thrust of Chomsky's advocacy is purely rationalistic. If we confront social issues honestly, forsaking the devious sophistries with which we customarily defend the comfortable (for some of us) but indefensible status quo, we *know* that capitalism—economic liberalism—is wrong, Chomsky tells us; we *know* that equalitarian socialism is the only social pattern which decent men ought to be able to consider seriously. One might suggest that Chomsky's scorn for his liberal contemporaries arises from the fact that they ignore earlier empirical arguments against capitalism, which they really ought to know about even if they are excusably ignorant of Chomsky's arguments from language and psychology; but, although (as we have seen) Chomsky does from time to time allude to such arguments, they play a quite subsidiary role in his writings—I do not think that anyone who reads Chomsky could suppose that his contempt for the liberal mind is to be explained in that way. (After all, Chomsky

must know that earlier empirical arguments for socialism have all been answered by empirical counter-arguments of at least some prima facie plausibility.) What is wrong with liberals, for Chomsky, is not that they are ignorant, or incapable of working out which of two opposing arguments is fallacious, but that they are dishonest—they pay lip-service to ideas which they *know* to be false because it is convenient for them to pretend that they are true.

But if Chomsky believes that a thinker can know by introspection, more or less independently of subtle empirical argumentation, that liberalism is wrong and socialism right, then it is surely a real paradox for him that there exist other thinkers—myself, for one—who insist with equal passion that Chomsky is quite mistaken, that liberalism is right and socialism a recipe for disaster, and that the poor whose interests Chomsky has so much at heart will lose as much as anyone else by the implementation of the kind of policies of which Chomsky would approve. For the rationalist, thinkers' introspections ought not to conflict. (pp. 197-98)

I conclude, then, that no real solution is available for Chomsky's paradox. If liberalism is wrong at all, we certainly cannot know it to be wrong by mere introspection but must demonstrate it to be wrong by empirical argument. . . . (p. 199)

Geoffrey Sampson, "What We Know and How We Know It," in his Liberty and Language *(© Geoffrey Sampson 1979; reprinted by permission of Oxford University Press), Oxford University Press, London, 1979, pp. 178-209.**

A. J. LANGGUTH

If I were an editor dispatching young reporters to a first assignment as a foreign correspondent, I would ask them to make room in their suitcases for [*The Political Economy of Human Rights*] by Noam Chomsky and Edward S. Herman. Not that I agree with everything that the two professors have written. But I would hope that the central lesson of their hundreds of pages, and their 1,687 footnotes, would be clear to any neophyte: Someone is watching. Someone takes every word you write with absolute seriousness. Whenever you err, because of slackness or inaccurate sources or the pressures of time, remember that back at M.I.T. and the Wharton School of Finance, two industrious and politically committed professors are waiting to pounce upon your mistake.

It is a substantial service, the surveillance that Chomsky and Herman have extended both to government and journalism. If it is too much to expect the State Department or the Pentagon to be grateful, at least *The New York Times* and *The Washington Post* should be. Strip away the occasional, and unworthy, snideness from these books, and one finds the expectation that the United States should behave humanely and selflessly and that its press should conduct itself without a flaw. To me, the professors' exacting standards, their very intolerance, are compliments.

Each of the two volumes turns on a central thesis. "**The Washington Connection and Third World Fascism**" argues that the U.S. Government favors client states with bloody-minded dictators over Third World democracy or socialism. The second volume, "**After the Cataclysm: Postwar Indochina and the Reconstruction of Imperial Ideology**," challenges the widely held belief that the withdrawal of U.S. forces from Vietnam, Laos and Cambodia has led to wholesale Communist terror. Throughout both books runs a common theme: Not only does

Washington lie but the American press broadcasts those lies knowingly and enthusiastically.

Let someone else defend the honor of the U.S. Government. Here I would like to explore the reasons why I found the attacks on the press salubrious and challenging in some ways and willfully wrongheaded in others.

First, there is a question of method. Because neither writer is a journalist (although it appears that Chomsky has traveled through Indochina), they must depend entirely on those very reporters they so regularly scourge. They excoriate *Newsweek* repeatedly as part of what they deride as the "Free Press." Yet when they want to document the atrocities of Operation Speedy Express, a 1969 pacification effort in South Vietnam, they quote a page and a half from a *Newsweek* article by Kevin Buckley. . . .

The many quotations they use as documentation are always seen as exceptions to a generally sorry state of coverage. But in time the exceptions loom almost large enough to refute their thesis. Even Henry Kamm, whose Pulitzer Prize for reporting from Indochina the authors take as something close to a personal insult, will find himself cited as a reliable authority when his dispatches (in this case, information about the further suffering of My Lai survivors) fit the professors' argument.

It is on the matter of Indochina, in fact, and particularly Cambodia, that Chomsky and Herman become most strident. They attack—rightly, in my view—any attempt to rewrite recent history to suggest that the American involvement in Indochina was wise, decent or, at worst, a lapse from the usual beneficence. . . .

I do not dispute their doubts about refugees as reliable sources of information on the Communist "bloodbaths" after the U.S. troops left Indochina. Nor their argument that the Vietnamese have invaded Cambodia for age-old territorial reasons that have little to do with humanitarian motives. Nor their suggestion that the forced evacuation of Phnom Penh may have been an attempt to save the urban population from starvation rather than a form of repressive punishment.

But the fact of that starvation is no longer disputable, and William Shawcross, along with others, has called for an inquiry by the United Nations. Apparently Norodom Sihanouk has joined that appeal, and while Sihanouk has never been mistaken for a democrat, he managed for a remarkable length of time to keep his country at peace and his countrymen fed. (p. 181)

With all these points to concede, why then, at least to my ear, is there something tinny about the Chomsky-Herman chapters on Cambodia? Perhaps it is the unrelenting insistence that they were right about Indochina and that almost everyone else was wrong. Compared to the recent articles from Shawcross, which concerned the well-being, indeed the survival, of the Cambodian people, the passages from Chomsky and Herman represent a high degree of special pleading, which because of their obsession with our sins, ends up slighting the major issue— the present fate of the Cambodians.

They acknowledge that the Cambodia of today is in a pitiful state. Yet that concession comes glancingly and only as a prelude to further indictments of the press. For example: "The record of atrocities is substantial and often gruesome, but it has by no means satisfied the requirements of Western propagandists, who must labor to shift the blame for the torment of Indochina to the victims of France and the United States.

Consequently, there has been extensive fabrication of evidence, a tide that has not been stemmed even by repeated exposure."

In several cases, the authors are persuasive about the fabrications. (pp. 181-82)

But when one strips away their rather muddled surface of detailed examples, what does one find? The authors do not dispute that there were atrocities in Cambodia; rather, they question the scope of the brutality and whether it was ordered by the central Government or came about because of local revenge. By scaling down the casualties and treating offhandedly the Khmer Rouge reprisals against Cambodia's merchants and shopkeepers, Chomsky and Herman can conclude that events in Cambodia are probably no worse than those in France after World War II, when Nazi collaborators were summarily executed, or in present-day Timor, where political murder has gone largely unreported.

I have two objections to their tactic. First, it reminds one of the manner in which children exchange insults, So's your old man! Usually, this is a response that comes from the right: You're so concerned about Argentina, why don't you worry about Czechoslovakia for a change? How surprising to hear such talk from Chomsky and Herman. If the world press were to converge suddenly on Timor, it wouldn't improve the lot of a single Cambodian.

Even worse is the authors' implication that somehow things in Cambodia aren't really so bad, and that if there are problems, they're not the fault of those who protested against the war. Beneath the accusations and the thud of footnotes comes a steady counterpoint: Don't blame us, don't blame us. Given the urgency in Cambodia, there is only one answer to that, and it was provided by Bertolt Brecht: "First feed the face, and then talk right and wrong."

That attempt to shrug off any responsibility is the more disturbing because it is so unnecessary. Surely when the rights and wrongs of Indochina are sorted out many years from now, neither author will have much to fear. (p. 182)

Chomsky and Herman try to prove an inevitable bias of a capitalistic press against any socialistic country. There is no question that the press of the United States is big business or that its editors are executives, often middle-aged, less enthusiastic, perhaps, than their copy boys to see the prevailing system scrapped tomorrow.

But if we are expected to try to see life through the eyes of Third World peoples, to understand their aspirations and frustrations, then we should remember as well the limits on the perspective of the U.S. newspaper reader and those editors who are chosen to serve him because they share his assumptions. The press is molded less by conspiracy, warmongering and a thirst for capitalistic exploitation than by a common upbringing and temperament.

One trait of that disposition—a skepticism that is the pride of most successful editors—will always prevent the press from attaining Chomsky's political ideal. These editors will say: of course young Iranians claim to have been tortured by Savak. After all, they are politically opposed to the Shah; they may even be Communists. How can we know for sure about the torture? So at best the accusations get a few paragraphs, followed immediately by official denials.

That same skepticism prevents an editor from presenting as fact a U.F.O. sighting or a lunatic's bogus murder confession.

But in international reporting, where the best of newspapers will have only one foreign reporter covering Central and South Africa or all of Latin America, the result can be lapses—the lapses that Chomsky and Herman prefer to attribute to conspiracy.

Good reporters share their editors' wariness. Chomsky and Herman bear down hard on [Sydney] Schanberg of *The New York Times* for disregarding two eyewitness reports that were favorable to the actions of the Khmer Rouge during the evacuation of Phnom Penh. Since its mere appearance in print lends an unearned authenticity to any account, the professors, in printing this story, may persuade some readers that Schanberg purposely ignored important evidence.

But every week a reporter must evaluate dozens of conflicting stories from the misinformed, the moneyed lobbies, the cranks and the public relations offices. Without categorizing either the New Zealander or his Cambodian wife, whose pro-Khmer Rouge accounts the professors choose to trust, I would argue that Schanberg's work demonstrated an unusual skill at protecting his readers from inaccurate sources. (pp. 182-83)

When writing a history, the evidence is in; the writer must only collect the facts, weigh them and put them in an order that makes sense of them.

But who, at the beginning, knew how the Vietnam War would end? Who knows today the fate of Cambodia, except that its people are starving to death? True, a daily reporter falls back on his intuition. But in the Saigon of 1965, mine was very different from that of such knowledgeable observers as Keyes Beech of *The Chicago Daily News,* who drew on years of experience in Asia to argue for the necessity of the war. How sure could any of us be?

Better, then, to write every day only what one saw and heard and believed to be that day's scant measure of truth. Better to leave the compilation and the distillation to the professors, confident that, if you are proved wrong, they will—in their own time—let the world know about it. (p. 184)

> *A. J. Langguth, "Someone Is Watching," in* The Nation *(copyright 1980 The Nation magazine, The Nation Associates, Inc.), Vol. 230, No. 6, February 16, 1980, pp. 181-84.*

GEORGE SCIALABBA

Like that other critique of political economy, *Capital,* [*The Political Economy of Human Rights*] is both an anatomy of a system of domination, in this case America's relationship with the third world, and a dissection of the ideology that masks it, the myth of American benevolence, or in its current version, the "human rights" crusade. . . .

What is the key to American foreign policy? Here is the dirty little secret: "The deterioration in the human rights situation and the increase in U.S. aid and support each correlate, independently, with a third and crucial factor: namely, improvement of the investment climate. The climate for business operations improves as unions and popular organizations are destroyed, dissidents are tortured or eliminated, real wages are depressed, and the society as a whole is placed in the hands of a collection of thugs and gangsters who are willing to sell out to the foreigner for a share of the loot. And as the climate for business operations improves, the society is welcomed into the Free World and offered the specific kind of 'aid' that will

further these favorable developments." Other features of a "favorable investment climate" cited by Chomsky and Herman include unregulated access to minerals and other resources and easy tax and profit-repatriation laws. . . .

Besides overturning governments that resist control by American capital, there is our support for governments willing to enforce this control. . . . Since this control involves such things as conversion of agriculture to cash crops for export, creation of a large work force of impoverished ex-peasants for foreign-owned plants and plantations, guaranteed low wages as an incentive for foreign investment, and extreme austerity in social welfare programs, these governments are generally unpopular. This means repression; that is, torture.

The recitation in *The Political Economy of Human Rights* of torture statistics and torture episodes is nauseating. Details may be left for conscientious readers. But a few figures are worth quoting. According to AmnestyInternational, 35 countries were practicing torture on an administrative (i.e., regular) basis in the mid-'70s. Of these, 26 were within the American sphere of influence—recipients of military and economic aid and military and police training. Between 1946 and 1975, these countries received $36.5 billion in military aid and had over 150,000 military personnel trained by the U.S. . . .

Chomsky and Herman record many [examples of distorted reporting and interpretation of U.S. foreign policy by the media and academic scholarship], but the burden of their argument lies elsewhere. It is that the *normal* performance of scholarship and the media involves a systematic bias. Their formulation is provocative, even outrageous. They claim that, much as in totalitarian societies, our scholarship and media function largely as a propaganda system, although the mode of functioning is different. Under totalitarianism, the framework of discussion, the principles of the state religion, are explicitly promulgated. They are sacrosanct but transparent; outward dissent is illegal, but inner dissent, or mental reservation, is made easier by the blatancy of state propaganda. In the United States, the framework is unarticulated and unargued, but is nonetheless assumed by all in the mainstream—in fact, acceptance of this framework is what defines the mainstream. Dissent is legal but marginal; heretics are free to talk to each other, while among those without considerable free time and access to material outside the mainstream, the engineering of consent proceeds unhindered. The consensus is tacit but overwhelming. (p. 35)

The assumption of all "responsible" discourse about American foreign policy, the fundamental article of our state religion, is, in Chomsky and Herman's words, that "the United States is unique among the nations of past or present history in that its policies are governed by abstract moral principles such as the Wilsonian ideals of self-determination, human rights, economic welfare, and so on, not by the material interests of groups that actually have domestic power, as is the case in other societies." There is no shortage of critical analysis applied to the international behavior of other countries. It is obvious that the "groups that actually have domestic power" in the Soviet Union, or in Bismarckian Germany, set foreign policy in their own interest. But we are somehow different.

To be sure, there are voices within the mainstream that deplore this excessive idealism. These are the "realists," who argue that the limits of American power make our overriding concern for human rights and democratic values no longer affordable. Others wonder whether American moralism is a form of naivete or condescension, an attempt to graft our traditions onto complex and alien cultures. But all agree that, properly or not, "abstract moral principles" have been the soul of American foreign policy.

Occasionally it is admitted that our noble efforts have sometimes gone astray. Thus, the fact that the U.S. bears primary responsibility for turning Latin America into a torture chamber and Indochina into a moonscape is referred to (when acknowledged at all) as "ironic" and a "tragic error," the unforeseen result of "blundering efforts to do good" (Anthony Lewis), or of "good impulses transmuted into bad policy" (*The Washington Post*). Liberal critics boldly question the feasibility of this or that intervention or the prudence of supporting this or that dictator—but never the essential benevolence of American goals.

Upon this consensus Chomsky and Herman heap 800 pages of staggering documentation and ferocious scorn. Yet, their fury is controlled; there is never a suggestion of deliberate conspiracy. Again like *Capital*, the book portrays a vast, marvelously efficient system without conscious central coordination. The market organizes ordinary chauvinism: though the rules are rigged, the individual players, by and large, are honest.

An elegant theory, and it comes with a crucial experiment. The second volume of the study focuses on postwar Indochina, and especially on Western reporting about Indochina. Its thesis is that defense of the state religion requires proof that the American intervention, however destructive, was plausibly intended to prevent something worse—i.e., bloodbath and enslavement. Hence, evidence must be found, or if necessary invented, and counterevidence suppressed. And this, in part, explains the explosion of Western outrage over Cambodia's incomprehensible "autogenocide." (pp. 35-6)

All this is somewhat disorienting. The documentation . . . is staggering. But the reasoning is something more, so austere and scrupulous that its effect is almost painful. One flinches at the mechanical annihilation of complacent assumptions and gratuitous inferences, the relentless production of jarring conclusions. In a final tour de force, Chomsky and Herman orchestrate a remarkable comparison between the Western responses to atrocities in Cambodia and East Timor.

It happens that history offers a kind of controlled experiment to test the book's argument. Consider two situations of repression and mass murder, similar in many significant respects, equally worthy of exposure and protest, with this difference: In one case, the atrocities are conducted by our ideological enemies, remote from our influence, and cannot be mitigated by our denunciations; in the other, they are conducted by our clients, wholly dependent on our continuing military supplies, and therefore vulnerable to any expression of displeasure by our government or public opinion. What is the response of a morally serious person? Naturally, to protest actions that we may possibly influence and for which we bear some responsibility, i.e., the latter case. But given the Chomsky-Herman hypothesis about the propaganda function of the media, what is the predicted outcome? Exclusive concern with former case.

To explain: Indonesia is a typical subfascist client state, an "investors' paradise," according to *Le Monde*. On December 7, 1975, the Indonesian army invaded the nearby island republic of East Timor. (p. 36)

The invasion met with resistance from Fretilin, the Timorese Liberation Front. Indonesia responded with indiscriminate bombing, burning, and crop destruction. In 1977 the Indonesian foreign minister estimated Timorese deaths from the invasion at 50,000. Fretilin estimated 100,000. By early 1980 (the fighting continues to the present), refugees and Indonesian church officials put the figure as high as 200,000. Neither the United States nor any relief agency was allowed into East Timor until late 1979. . . .

The authors exhaustively review coverage of East Timor in the American press since 1975. There is next to none. What there is is so inadequate and misleading, and so nearly identical with public statements and congressional testimony by the State Department, that it is impossible to avoid the suspicion that one is the source of the other. Altogether absent, needless to say, are the thunderbolts of denunciation visited on the Khmer Rouge. Two holocausts—one visible, one invisible. The *Times*'s editorial indignation can never again sound quite real.

Commenting in another essay on the contrast between the avalanche of Western moralizing about the plight of Communist Indochina and the silence from the same quarters about suffering that cannot be exploited for propaganda purposes, Chomsky writes: "To record this miserable display in the proper terms would require the talents of a Swift or an Orwell." This is too modest: Chomsky *is* our contemporary Orwell. And not even Swift could surpass the savage indignation of *The Political Economy of Human Rights*.

Life imitates Art, or at least supplies some striking postscripts. The reception of this book has been something of a scandal. A year ago, in *The New York Times Book Review*, Paul Robinson called Chomsky "arguably the most important intellectual alive." Shortly after that assessment appeared in America's newspaper of record, the first volume of *The Political Economy of Human Rights* was published; the second volume came out in November. To date, neither has been reviewed in a single major U.S. newspaper. *Habent sua fata libelli*. The fate of this work illustrates its argument. (p. 37)

George Scialabba, "The Free World Gulag" (reprinted by permission of The Village Voice *and the author; copyright © 1980), in* The Village Voice, *Vol. XXV, No. 25, June 18, 1980, pp. 35, 37.*

LINDA McQUAIG

In this brilliant and devastating two-volume work, [*The Political Economy of Human Rights*, Noam Chomsky] and co-author Edward S. Herman . . . point to East Timor as just one example of how the Western press selects its atrocities carefully. It also selects its ideas carefully—a contention of the authors borne out by the fact that this important book has been largely ignored since its publication last fall. . . .

The most original aspect of the book . . . is its detailed analysis of the way the press has dealt with [the realities of American foreign policy]. Documenting case after case of press distortion or silence, Chomsky and Herman destroy any comfortable post-Watergate illusions about the press being tough and investigative—at least when it comes to American foreign policy.

Linda McQuaig, "Genocide in East Timor and Other Matters," in Maclean's Magazine *(© 1980 by Maclean's Magazine; reprinted by permission), Vol. 93, No. 33, August 18, 1980, p. 37.*

JAMES S. FISHKIN

We can separate a core proposition in [*The Political Economy of Human Rights*] from others that seem much more dubious. The basic point, which seems incontestable, is that there have been massive violations of human rights throughout what might be broadly termed the US "sphere of influence." . . .

One can be grateful to Chomsky and Herman for drawing needed attention to many disturbing cases without also drawing their inferences about our degree of responsibility. They infer an extent of American control and coordination comparable to the Soviet role in Eastern Europe. Their evidence for this seems to be (1) economic, technical, and military assistance, (2) US business interests, (3) State Department human rights reports which so understate the violations that "these reports are themselves solid evidence of the primary official commitment to the dispensers of terror rather than its victims."

Yet even if all this evidence were accepted (and the last will be controversial) it would add up to no more than systematic support, not control. Hence the comparison to Eastern Europe appears grossly overstated. And from the fact that we give assistance to countries that practice terror it is too much to conclude that "Washington has become the torture and political murder capital of the world."

Chomsky's and Herman's indictment of US foreign policy is thus the mirror image of the *Pax Americana* rhetoric they criticize: it rests on the illusion of American omnipotence throughout the world. And because they refuse to attribute any substantial independence to countries that are, in some sense, within America's sphere of influence, the entire burden for all the political crimes of the non-communist world can be brought home to Washington. While this indictment is shockingly overstated, we should be grateful to Chomsky and Herman for systematically documenting the most basic human rights violations in countries over which we can expect to have some influence. For while their attributions of control and direct responsibility are exaggerated, they do provide evidence for a far less moral charge in a host of cases: our complicity in acts of torture and even mass murder when these are committed by governments that we could influence in cases which are barely visible in the mass media. . . .

[The] Chomsky and Herman work—despite its overstatements and rhetorical overkill—deserves to be widely debated. (p. 38)

James S. Fishkin, "Books and the Arts: 'The Political Economy of Human Rights'," in The New Republic *(reprinted by permission of* The New Republic; © 1980 The New Republic, Inc.), Vol. 183, Nos. 10 & 11, September 6, 1980, pp. 37-8.*

Barry Commoner

1917-

Commoner is an American biologist, ecologist, author of books on ecology, and political activist. As "heir to the earth-saving mission" of Rachel Carson, Commoner calls for an end to all scientific and economic projects that pollute and impoverish the world. In such books as *Science and Survival* (1966), *The Poverty of Power* (1976), and *The Politics of Energy* (1979), he cites the dangers of pesticides and nuclear energy. He writes for the general public in the hope that popular action against ill-advised projects will result if people are fully informed. Campaigning as the Citizen's party candidate for President of the United States in 1980, Commoner ran on a platform that denounced the energy program of the Carter administration and urged the use of alternative energy sources. (See also *Contemporary Authors*, Vols. 65-68.)

Excerpt from *THE POVERTY OF POWER: ENERGY AND THE ECONOMIC CRISIS*

In the last ten years, the United States—the most powerful and technically advanced society in human history—has been confronted by a series of ominous, seemingly intractable crises. First there was the threat to environmental survival; then there was the apparent shortage of energy; and now there is the unexpected decline of the economy. These are usually regarded as separate afflictions, each to be solved in its own terms: environmental degradation by pollution controls; the energy crisis by finding new sources of energy and new ways of conserving it; the economic crisis by manipulating prices, taxes, and interest rates.

But each effort to solve one crisis seems to clash with the solution of the others—pollution control reduces energy supplies; energy conservation costs jobs. Inevitably, proponents of one solution become opponents of the others. Policy stagnates and remedial action is paralyzed, adding to the confusion and gloom that beset the country.

The uncertainty and inaction are not surprising, for this tangled knot of problems is poorly understood, not only by citizens generally, but also by legislators, administrators, and even by the separate specialists. It involves complex interactions among the three basic systems—the ecosystem, the production system, and the economic system—that, together with the social or political order, govern all human activity. (pp. 1-2)

Given these dependencies—the economic system on the wealth yielded by the production system and the production system on the resources provided by the ecosystem—logically the economic system ought to conform to the requirements of the production system, and the production system to the requirements of the ecosystem. The governing influence should flow from the ecosystem through the production system to the economic system.

This is the rational ideal. In actual fact the relations among the three systems are the other way around. The environmental crisis tells us that the ecosystem has been disastrously affected by the design of the modern production system, which has been

Queens College photo by Gene Luttenberg

developed with almost no regard for compatibility with the environment or for the efficient use of energy. . . . (pp. 2-3)

Thus, what confronts us is not a series of separate crises, but a single basic defect—a fault that lies deep in the design of modern society. (p. 3)

[The] energy crisis is so tightly linked to the crucial defects of the system as a whole as to offer the hope of leading us out of the labyrinth of interwoven crises—if we can but understand it. And we do not. This is made painfully evident by the sudden, unperceived onset of the energy crisis. For years the United States and most of the world used energy as though it were a freely given resource, its availability and uses understood as well as those of water or air. Suddenly the availability of energy can no longer be taken for granted; it has become a huge problem, strongly affecting almost every aspect of society. (pp. 3-4)

The energy crisis and the knot of technological, economic, and social issues in which it is embedded call for a great national debate—to discover better alternatives to the deeply faulted institutions that govern how the nation's resources are used. And to begin that debate, we need to understand how the ecosystem captures energy, how the production system uses it, and how the economic system governs what is done with the resultant wealth.

To penetrate the chaos that surrounds the subject of energy, there is one essential, if difficult, tool available to us—the science of thermodynamics. (pp. 4-5)

The First Law of Thermodynamics is simple enough: It states that energy can be neither created nor destroyed, so that, whatever happens to it, the amount must always remain the same. The Second Law [which states that every spontaneous process irreversibly decreases the order of the universe] is more important and more difficult to understand. It is important because it explains how work—which is the only value that energy has for us—is gotten out of the flow of energy from one place to another. It is difficult to understand because it relates this capability to several abstract and seemingly distant subjects, such as the meaning of order in the world, the nature of probability, and the one-way direction of time.

Once these unfamiliar concepts are grasped, we have a surprisingly clear path to follow. It begins with the *sources* of energy, the fossil and nuclear fuels on which we now depend, and the huge but still largely unused source—the sun. Here we need to learn why those energy sources on which we now rely are so poorly adapted to the purposes to which we put them; why they have begun to seriously disrupt both the environment and the economic system. Then we need to look at the *uses* of energy in the production system and discover why that system has been so designed as to waste energy so blatantly. Here we will find powerful links between the ways we use and misuse energy, capital, and labor. And only at that point will it become evident that our current crisis is a symptom of a deep and dangerous fault in the economic system.

[*The Poverty of Power*] is designed to trace this web of connections, in the conviction that the link between energy and the rest of our lives *can* be understood; that once it is understood, the origin of the crises can be identified; and that once this basic fault is identified, we can consider the painful but necessary steps that will, I am convinced, correct it. (pp. 5-6)

In the last thirty years many thousands of production decisions have been made in the United States. They have determined that automobiles shall be large and sufficiently powerful to travel at a rate of 100 mph; that electricity shall be produced by nuclear power plants; that we shall wear synthetic materials instead of cotton and wool, and wash them in detergent rather than soap; that baseball shall be played on plastic rather than grass; that the beneficent energy of sunlight shall go largely unused. In every case, the decision was made according to the "bottom line"—the expectation of an acceptable profit. . . . It would have been a fantastically improbable statistical accident if most or even a small fraction of these thousands of decisions, made on the basis of a hoped-for marginal increase in profit, happened neatly to fit into the pattern of a rational, thermodynamically sound energy system. Such an energy system is a social need, and it is hopeless to expect to build it on the basis of production decisions that yield commodities rather than the solutions to essential tasks; that produce goods which are maximally profitable rather than maximally useful; that accept as their final test private profit rather than social value.

Thus, the energy crisis and the web of inter-related problems confront us with the need to explore the possibility of creating a production system that is consciously intended to serve social needs and that judges the value of its products by their use, and an economic system that is committed to these purposes. At least in principle, such a system is socialism. (pp. 257-58)

[It seems unrealistic] at this moment in history, to categorically reject a socialist economy on the grounds that its political form is necessarily repressive and therefore abhorrent to the democratic freedoms that are the foundation of political life in the United States. That no existing example of a socialist society—whether the U.S.S.R., China, or Cuba—is consistent with both the economic democracy of socialism and the political democracy inherent in U.S. tradition means that wholly new political forms would need to be created. It is appropriate, in 1976, to remind ourselves that such radical political innovation is a 200-year-old, if long-neglected, tradition in the United States.

All this suggests that it may be time to view the faults of the U.S. capitalist economic system from the vantage point of a socialist alternative—to debate the relative merits of capitalism and socialism. Such a debate is now the central issue of political life in Europe, and it is perhaps time for the people of the United States to enter into it as well. (p. 262)

Here we come to the end of the blind, mindless chain of events that transformed the technologies of agricultural and industrial production and reorganized transportation; that increased the output of the production system, but increased even more its appetite for capital, energy, and other resources; that eliminated jobs and degraded the environment; that concentrated the physical power of energy and the social power of the resultant wealth into ever fewer, larger corporations; that has fed this power on a diet of unemployment and poverty. Here is the basic fault that has spawned the environmental crisis and the energy crisis, and that threatens—if no remedy is found—to engulf us in the wreckage of a crumbling economic system.

Now all this has culminated in the ignominious confession of those who hold the power: That the capitalist economic system which has loudly proclaimed itself the best means of assuring a rising standard of living for the people of the United States, can now survive, if at all, only by reducing that standard. The powerful have confessed to the poverty of their power.

No one can escape the momentous consequences of this confession. No one can escape the duty to understand the origin of this historic default and to transform it from a threat to social progress into a signal for a new advance. (p. 264)

> *Barry Commoner, in his* The Poverty of Power: Energy and the Economic Crisis *(copyright © 1976 by Barry Commoner; reprinted by permission of Alfred A. Knopf, Inc.), Knopf, 1976, 314 p.*

Excerpt from *THE POLITICS OF ENERGY*

The National Energy Plan [drafted by the Carter administration in 1978] was a statement of government policy, intended to achieve certain national goals. Like all policies, the Plan was subjective, at best a promising intention, at worst a vain hope. But to succeed, the Plan had to take certain objective realities into account. However cleverly devised, persuasively promoted, or vigorously enforced, no government policy can, after all, change the fact that oil is a nonrenewable resource which will rise rapidly in price as dwindling reserves become harder to reach. Nor can it change the fact that it costs a great deal more to build a nuclear power plant than to drill an oil well with a comparable energy yield. . . . Policy can change the national energy system, but only in harmony with certain objective physical and economic facts. (p. 24)

The basic reason for the energy crisis is that the energy sources on which we rely—oil, natural gas, coal, and uranium—are nonrenewable. (p. 25)

[All] of the harmful consequences of the nonrenewability of the energy sources on which we now depend are economic. The progressive depletion of the supplies of these energy sources results in an exponential rise in the cost of producing them, and therefore in their price. In turn, the rising price of energy intensifies inflation; it reduces the standard of living, but of the poor more than others; it hinders new industrial investments and aggravates unemployment; it intensifies the shortage of capital. The end result is a serious threat of economic depression. An energy policy that relies on higher energy prices to govern its use, that emphasizes particularly capital-intensive ways of producing energy, such as coal (as compared with oil or natural gas) and electricity, particularly from nuclear power plants (as compared with the direct burning of oil and natural gas), will intensify these economic problems. (p. 30)

It might be argued that all these economic difficulties are the unavoidable cost of solving the energy crisis. This would be true if, as the [Carter] administration has held, the answer to the crisis is conservation, and the price of energy must be increased in order to encourage conservation. However, this misrepresents the fundamental cause of the energy crisis. The crisis results from our reliance on fuels that are nonrenewable and are therefore certain to increase in price exponentially as long as we continue to produce them. To solve the energy crisis, the cost of producing energy must be stabilized, and the only way to do that is to switch from nonrenewable energy sources to renewable ones. (pp. 30-1)

[Sooner] or later the energy crisis *must* be solved. And this can be done only by replacing the present nonrenewable sources—oil, natural gas, coal, and uranium—with renewable ones, which are stable in cost. That is what a national energy policy must do if it is to solve the energy crisis, rather than delay it or make it worse. But this is a little like saying that all we need to do to cure the ills of earthly life is to enter Paradise. The real problem is whether it is possible to get there from here, and if so, how. The problem is one of transition. (p. 49)

[There] is a basic dilemma inherent in the replacement of the present, nonrenewable fuels by renewable ones. Although the continued use of nonrenewable fuels involves very grave threats to the national economy, any interruption in their flow would be even more disastrous. . . . The present, nonrenewable fuels must somehow provide a bridge to the new, renewable ones that must replace them. Thus the transition involves not only the development of sufficient supplies of renewable sources of energy, but also, at an even earlier stage, decisions about how the present, nonrenewable sources are to be produced and used. In particular, one or more of the present energy sources must be used as a "bridging fuel," to facilitate the entry of the new, renewable sources. (p. 52)

The choice of which route the nation ought to follow in the transition from the present, increasingly intolerable reliance on nonrenewable energy to a renewable energy system now lies before us. Both of the optional routes [breeder-based nuclear power and solar energy] are technically possible. . . . Both routes would be costly and both would affect much more in the nation's life than the production of energy.

Adopting the breeder-based nuclear power route involves a number of very grave questions. These include: the growing uncertainties about the safety of nuclear power plants; whether radioactive wastes can be safely stored, and if so, how; how to meet the heavy demand for increasingly costly capital for building nuclear power plants; how to cope with the resultant escalation of utility rates; what can be done about the terrifying prospects of nuclear proliferation and radioactive contamination inherent in the extensive traffic in plutonium, thorium, or uranium 233 that would be inevitable in a breeder-based power system.

The solar choice raises equally difficult, but different, questions. Some of them are: whether the oil and gas industry is able—or willing—to produce more natural gas from the known reserves and to expand gas pipelines at a reasonable cost; whether industry, the auto industry for example, is willing to invest in the large-scale production of cogenerators; how to provide the loans that consumers need to invest in collectors and other solar equipment; whether the federal government (or for that matter states and cities) would be willing to buy sufficient photovoltaic cells so that production can be expanded and the price reduced to the point of invading the conventional electric market; whether the petroleum industry will tolerate the competition from farmers' production of solar fuels and the utility industry the competition from locally produced electricity.

The social and political consequences of the choice are immense. Breeder reactors, and the intense use of coal that must precede them, would intensify greatly our present, already serious, environmental problems. The breeder route would concentrate most of the nation's energy system in the hands of either the very largest corporations or the federal government—the only institutions capable of meeting the huge cost of even a single breeder. The need to protect the system would probably bring it under the control of the military. (p. 63)

In contrast, solar energy is completely compatible with the environment. . . . Sunshine is widely distributed and is best exploited by decentralized operations, rather than by a few huge centralized plants controlled by supercorporations under military protection. Solar energy is inherently benign, and when a pump fails in a solar device there is no need to call upon the President to visit the scene in order to calm the fear of catastrophe. No form of solar energy can be turned into a huge bomb; no political fantasist or power-hungry dictator could use solar energy as an instrument of terror; no one need be tortured to recover a stolen solar device.

Is it necessary to choose *between* the two routes? Can we not follow both of them, emphasizing the advantages and minimizing the hazards of each? Unfortunately, we cannot; the two routes are inherently, intractably, incompatible. . . . The cost of either system would be so great that the nation simply could not afford to build both of them. We can take one route or the other, not both.

It is evident, then, that a choice must be made between the two routes toward a renewable national energy system; that the choice must be made now; and that it involves very grave and portentous decisions about the nation's economic, social, and political future. Although these issues clearly should have been considered in the debates on the National Energy Plan, they were not. (pp. 63-4)

It is now apparent that the United States does not yet have an energy policy explicitly designed to solve the energy crisis; nor have the momentous issues involved in establishing such a policy been subjected to legislative debate and public judgment. But we now know how to remedy this defect. To solve the energy crisis we must establish a national policy for the transition from the present, nonrenewable energy system to a renewable one. To create such a policy in keeping with the principles of democratic governance, we need to compare, in public debate, how the two possible sources of renewable energy—breeder-based nuclear power and solar energy—will affect the national welfare, and then choose between them. (p. 65)

[Many] of the serious economic problems that now confront consumers, labor, farmers, and production industries could be resolved if the nation would embark on a transition to renewable, solar energy. Consumers would be relieved of the burden of ever-rising utility rates, and of the effects of inflation generally; they would have more money to spend on other things; their standard of living would be improved. Workers would have more job opportunities in new industries, and the high levels of unemployment that are now taken for granted could be reduced. Farmers could cut production costs and increase income by producing solar fuels, helping to reverse a twenty-five-year trend which has reduced the farmer's share of the national economy. Industries in general, which all use energy, could break out of the economic grip of the energy industry, producing energy for themselves, or purchasing it from a much wider array of sources at a stable price. Everyone would benefit from a sharp reduction in the environmental degradation that has until now accompanied the production and use of energy. The country would free itself of the fear of another Harrisburg accident or worse. (p. 70)

The energy crisis—and the economic crisis that is following in its wake—is a sign that we have failed to integrate efficiently the production of energy with its use: that the links between the auto factory and the gasoline pump, between the power plant and the home, between the farm and the sun, are loose and enormously wasteful. And the solution—the solar transition—is designed to correct precisely these faults by creating links that integrate the different sources of solar energy intimately into the production processes that can best use them. That is why the solar transition means a vast improvement in the efficiency with which resources are used, in productivity and in economic output. (p. 79)

[The] solar transition offers the nation a momentous opportunity, which like the decision to abolish slavery, can rebuild the faltering economy. But it is beyond the reach of purely private governance. Society as a whole must be involved, for the solar transition is a great historic passage which only the people of the United States can decide to undertake. What stands in the way of that decision is neither technology nor economics, but politics—the politics of evasion, which, by denying that the problem exists, deprives the American people of the opportunity to solve it. (p. 80)

Once we do understand the energy crisis, it becomes clear that the nation is not poor, but mismanaged; that energy is not wasted carelessly, but by design; that the energy we need is not running out, but is replenished with every dawn; that by relying on our solar resources we can forswear the suicidal prospect of a war that would begin with oil but end with a nuclear holocaust.

The solution to the energy crisis—the solar transition—is an opportunity to turn this knowledge into action, to embark on a new historic passage. But to find our way we will need to be guided by social rather than private interests. There are many known ways—and many yet to be invented—of introducing social governance into production: national planning; local or regional planning; public utilities; cooperatives; and, if need be, public ownership on a local or national level. These measures will, of course, clash with the notion that every productive decision must be privately governed, for private profit, in order to ensure economic efficiency. But we now know from the energy crisis that the inefficiencies are located outside the realm of private governance, and are accessible only to social decisions. (pp. 81-2)

It will be difficult—some say impossible—to learn how to merge economic justice with economic progress, and personal freedom with social governance. If we allow the fear of failing in this aim to forestall the effort to achieve it, then failure is certain. But if we firmly embrace economic democracy as a national goal, as a new standard for political policy, as a vision of the nation's future, it can guide us through the historic passage that is mandated by the energy crisis, and restore to the nation the vitality that is inherent in the richness of its resources and the wisdom of its people. (p. 82)

> *Barry Commoner, in his* The Politics of Energy *(copyright © 1979 by Barry Commoner; reprinted by permission of Alfred A. Knopf, Inc.), Knopf, 1979, 101 p.*

DANIEL LANG

In **"Science and Survival,"** Barry Commoner has written a social tract dealing with the impact that science and technology exert on our daily lives. It is an enlightening and important work, so much so that its chances of reaching as wide an audience as it deserves are probably slim. . . . The tone of his book is modest and temperate throughout, even when he is being outspoken on such controversial matters as our knowledge of nuclear fallout, the use of insecticides and the efficacy of civil defense.

Indeed, it would seem the more outspoken he is, the more apparent is his instinct for fairness. . . . The reader, incidentally, to whom the author has addressed his book would appear to be the intelligent layman and, to a lesser extent, the scientist concerned with public affairs.

Mr. Commoner is appalled by the unthinking manner in which people everywhere are being exposed to hazards in the name of science. . . . The author is especially exercised by the dissemination of nuclear fallout, which he considers "the greatest single source of contamination of the planet." (pp. 3, 58)

To Mr. Commoner, these life-shortening excursions amount to unplanned and uncontrolled experiments in "environmental biology." One reason for their occurrence, he believes, is a readiness on the part of government and industry to shoot the works before weighing the consequences. Pollutants, he states, are unloosed wholesale with little or no advance balancing of risk against benefit. . . .

In Mr. Commoner's view, the indiscriminate release of nuclear fallout is one example of failure to balance risk against benefit. . . .

In large part, Mr. Commoner feels, the public owes its pollutant dangers to an official disregard or ignorance of the complexity that binds the biosphere—the community of living things in the environment. This complexity, he explains, is not merely a profound mystery awaiting solution but a matter of active value. . . .

It is difficult, within a brief space, to suggest the wealth of ideas and stimulation that **"Science and Survival"** affords, which is not to claim perfection for the book. The author tends to redundancy; here and there, he relies on hazy clichés . . . ; the section on the lethal nature of nuclear warfare is overlong; the lecturer's rhetoric sometimes dogs his writing. Far more important, though, than Mr. Commoner's writing style is his style of thinking. It is both reasonable and compassionate, his deep concern for an orderly and friendly world discernible on every page.

Unlike some colleagues, Mr. Commoner shows no condescension to laymen. In fact, he urges them to avoid a sense of mistaken humility toward scientists, their esoteric language notwithstanding. (p. 58)

> *Daniel Lang, "When Science Shoots the Works," in* The New York Times Book Review *(© 1966 by The New York Times Company; reprinted by permission), November 6, 1966, pp. 3, 58.*

WILLIAM GILMAN

[Barry Commoner] has railed often against what the nuclear scientists do to spoil our world. He does so again in [*Science and Survival*] but says nothing about what the biochemists and biologists are doing to change DNA, the molecule of heredity. Even his purely scientific criticism of their dogmas about how DNA operates overlooks the main point. As experience with atomic energy has shown, science doesn't need indisputable theory and an awareness of practical consequences before it can begin changing things. . . .

Dr. Commoner freshens his approach with a few opening pages about last year's spectacular power failures in Canada and the northeastern United States. He uses this power failure and the resulting blackout to charge, correctly enough, that automation can backfire. Thereafter, he rushes through a disorganized repetition of his previous writings against fallout, pesticides, detergents, and so forth. But again something is missing. Commoner's blunderbuss fires everywhere except at the scientific community. Science, apparently, has no responsibility to keep its own house clean. His criticism is usually aimed at a convenient "they"—the government's interferers. (p. 4)

> *William Gilman, "The Ethics of Science," in* Book Week—World Journal Tribune *(© 1966, Washington Post Co.), November 20, 1966, pp. 4, 17.*

MICHAEL CRICHTON

["**The Closing Circle**"] may be the best book on ecology ever written. It is certainly the most sober, rigorous, well-organized statement of what our environmental problems are, how we got them, and what we should do about them.

"**The Closing Circle**" is appealing first of all for its tone. . . . Barry Commoner's tone is one of near-detachment and great calm. As a result, the book is remarkable for the absence of character assassinations, for its reluctance to set timetables for disaster and for its refusal to adopt bumper-sticker solutions for environmental crises. Those readers who are tired of the usual Sierra Club blend of panic and paranoia will find the sobriety of the book a welcome relief.

Second, from a purely scientific standpoint, Commoner has a gift for explaining problems briefly and clearly without oversimplification. . . .

Third, and perhaps most unusual, the book is coherent. Environmental problems tend to be tangled yet diffused, and so are most books on the subject. . . . [The] subject matter makes . . . tight organization difficult. But Commoner has done it.

His basic thesis is not new, but it is better stated and more rigorously argued here than elsewhere. Starting from the position that most of our environmental problems appeared after World War II, Commoner analyzes the postwar period and concludes that neither population growth nor affluence is responsible for our ecological crisis. . . .

Where do the problems come from? Commoner blames the postwar growth of new technologies that break out of the natural ecological cycles: detergents instead of soap, nylon instead of wool and cotton, aluminum instead of steel, and plastic. These products cannot be degraded by existing natural processes, and many by-products of manufacturing—such as mercury compounds—are themselves serious pollutants.

Why have we shifted our postwar economy into environmentally damaging areas? In all cases, he blames industrial profit structures for our pollution problems. . . .

Commoner patiently explains that most high-profit new industries actually accumulate a debt, which is transferred either to the environment or to helpless individuals living in the environment. Yet the debt is real, and sooner or later, someone pays for it with their money or their health.

He is implacable in his economic analysis. Simple capitalism is not the villain, he finds, and socialization is not the answer. . . . To reverse present trends, "most of the nation's resources or capital investment would need to be engaged in the task of ecological reconstruction for at least a generation." In 1958 dollars, he estimates the price tag at 40 billion a year for the next 25 years.

The consequences are considerable—whole industries wiped out, and others radically restructured. Perhaps the most fundamental change required is an end to the cold-war mentality. "It is inconceivable that the United States could find the huge capital resources for the needed reconstruction of industry and agriculture along ecologically sound lines unless we give up our preoccupation with large-scale military activities—which since World War II have preempted most of the nation's disposable income."

This kind of conclusion is what Commoner means when he says that in political terms, ecology is not as safe as motherhood, but in fact represents political dynamite. In the final analysis a solution for environmental decay implies a major reordering of priorities, and a major restructuring of industrial growth.

American industry won't take this lying down; the book is certain to receive enthusiastic attack. Many environmentalists will also be displeased. For example, it is easy to argue that Commoner is soft on population. . . . His revulsion against coercion to halt population growth sits oddly with statements that industry cannot be "immune to sweeping change if it is to come to grips with the environmental crisis."

In the same way, his definition of affluence—housing, food and clothing—ignores the admittedly striking increase in leisure items, snowmobiles, campers and boats, which have a lot of destructive potential for the environment. (p. 7)

In part, these attitudes come from Commoner's hard-nosed approach. His book tends to measure the measurable, and to avoid speculation. In part, too, it comes from his desire to show that population and affluence are not the major factors in pollution—and that conclusion seems unarguable.

However one takes it, **"The Closing Circle"** is an important book on the single most important issue of our times. It is certain to produce broad impact and intense controversy. (p. 34)

> *Michael Crichton, "'The Closing Circle'," in* The New York Times Book Review *(© 1971 by The New York Times Company; reprinted by permission), October 17, 1971, pp. 7, 34.*

PETER C. STUART

The scientific establishment's complicity in the environmental muddle is precisely what makes Barry Commoner so compelling. Himself a scientist (biologist and ecologist), he retains a layman's skepticism toward science and its obedient servant, technology.

Technology, he charges in **"The Closing Circle,"** is Public Environmental Enemy No. 1. . . .

For 25 years of technological extremism, Dr. Commoner prescribes an extreme remedy.

"A major part of the new productive enterprise constructed on the basis of post-war ecologically faulty technology simply has to be rebuilt along ecologically sound lines."

The price-tag: Nothing less than the reallocation of most of the nation's capital investment resources "for at least a generation." . . .

He stops short of a blueprint for this staggering task since the necessary decisions "belong not in the hands of 'experts' but in the hands of the people and their elected representatives."

Some may be disappointed, for the book tells "why," not "how." Perhaps it's enough that a scientist alerts us to why things have gone wrong, and does it so persuasively. Few readers will ever again be able to view their technology-oriented world with detachment.

> *Peter C. Stuart, "A Throwaway World," in* The Christian Science Monitor *(reprinted by permission from* The Christian Science Monitor; *© 1971 The Christian Science Publishing Society; all rights reserved), November 4, 1971, p. 10.*

PETER PASSELL

Barry Commoner is best known for **"The Closing Circle,"** which detailed the ominous impact of modern technology on the environment. The five years since its publication have substantiated Commoner's fears, making P.C.B., vinyl chloride and red dye #2 into household words and turning the 11 o'clock news into a nightly chemistry class. What was unique about the book, however, was not the accuracy of its prophecy—others had argued the case before—but ecologist Commoner's remarkable ability to translate the conclusions of a half-dozen disciplines for those with little knowledge or interest in science.

"The Poverty of Power" attempts a more difficult task, at once predigesting the engineering and physics of the energy crisis for non-scientific palates and offering an interpretation of the causes of our energy-related economic malaise. As an analysis of the technological dimensions of the energy problem, it is a great success; one would be hard-pressed to find elsewhere so much useful information on the subject so ably presented. As a radical alternative to standard economic interpretations of the last few years of inflation and unemployment, however, **"The Poverty of Power"** is disappointing.

First the good news. In less than 200 pages Commoner manages to summarize the virtues and vices of fossil fuels, nuclear power and solar energy. He neatly demystifies the motives of the private oil companies in pressing oil and gas exploration abroad while three-quarters of United States domestic petroleum reserves still remain below ground. Another chapter coolly, if inconclusively, analyzes the environmental costs of a major effort to replace dependence on Arabian crude with dependence on Montana coal.

Even more important, Commoner exposes the fragile structure of dubious assumptions and plain wishful thinking that supports the Ford Administration's decision to go for broke on nuclear power. The book is at its best here, calmly dissecting the logic of the nuclear age. Atomic power plant operation creates small—no one is certain how small—chances of big disasters, accidents in which thousands of lives would be lost. Such pacts with the devil are not unique; the world has been coexisting with Armageddon since 1945. . . .

What is new is such careless depletion of the safety of future generations. The deadly waste products of nuclear fission must be isolated from the environment while they slowly decay. No one has devised a foolproof storage system that could last the necessary millennia. Independence through nuclear energy must thus be purchased on time: $500 billion down, a thousand lifetimes to pay. (p. 8)

Commoner makes the case for the least exploited, least hazardous and most plentiful energy source, sunlight. . . . Solar power for electricity production can't yet compete with conventional fuel, but could become viable if cost-cutting, mass production techniques can be devised. Predictably, the Federal Government is too preoccupied with the problems of nuclear breeder reactors to find out.

Were **"The Poverty of Power"** to end on this note, the reader would be saved the effort of an unrewarding essay on what Commoner believes are the inherent contradictions of capitalism. Commoner argues that the American economy is largely driven by expectations of business profit. . . . However, Commoner claims that this singular drive for profits inevitably leads to capital-intensive, energy-intensive solutions to technological problems, thereby creating shortages of capital, wasted energy sources and permanent unemployment. (p. 10)

Commoner is, of course, right that energy consumption grew faster than it ought for decades. But the cause was not some self-destructive urge built into the system. Energy was simply cheap—too cheap given what we now know about air pollution and Sheik Yamani. . . . Such reassurances are not going to make it any less burdensome to heat uninsulated New England homes or supply natural gas to inefficient New Jersey foundries next winter. The problem, however, is how to adjust, not how to save capitalism. The ruinous success of the nuclear power industry and the growth of trucking at the expense of railroads do not reveal anything about the economy other than how easy it is for the regulated to capture their regulators. And the less said about Commoner's views on chronic unemployment and the capital shortage the better.

None of this, to risk repetition, makes **"The Poverty of Power"** less valuable as a primer on the technology of energy. Read it for Commoner's lucid science; take a pass when the subject turns to economic theory. (p. 12)

> Peter Passell, "'The Poverty of Power'," in The New York Times Book Review (© 1976 by The New York Times Company; reprinted by permission), May 23, 1976, pp. 8, 10, 12.

ROY WERNER

You do not expect a book about energy to develop the case for an American evolution towards democratic socialism. Yet, it is the measure of Barry Commoner's provocative study [*The Poverty of Power: Energy and the Economic Crisis*] that its incisive analysis accomplishes that task. The reader is forced to confront individual prejudices and to consider "a production system that is consciously intended to serve social needs and that judges the value of its products by their use."

Commoner's treatment of the complex energy-environment-economic interactions is lucid and compelling. . . .

[His] chapters on various energy sources offer the most illuminating and concise information available to nontechnical readers. Only one mistake and one omission are evident. . . . In 1973, roughly 36 percent of our petroleum supply was imported—not "nearly half." Further, companies were announcing an impending energy crisis in 1971 . . . , not waiting until after the embargo to alert the public.

Economics, however, is not the author's strength. His too facile assumptions about unemployment and capital shortages belie the complexity of social science. Nevertheless, his examples challenge the "wisdom" of capitalism. (pp. 15, 17)

To Commoner, the devil behind all this is the alteration of the production system since 1945. America has gone from manure, cotton shirts, leather or wood furnishings and low-power transit to chemical fertilizers, synthetic clothing, plastic or veneer furnishings and that male ego symbol, the unnecessarily powerful automobile. We made these choices. But there is merit in the observation that perhaps the decisions were unwise. Energy problems will not be solved by "technological sleight of hand, clever tax schemes or patchwork legislation." Instead, we urgently need the great debate Commoner advocates. This book is the best single primer for that event. (p. 17)

> Roy Werner, "'The Poverty of Power: Energy and the Economic Crisis'," in America (reprinted with permission of America Press, Inc.; 1976; all rights reserved), Vol. 135, No. 1, July 10, 1976, pp. 15, 17.

ALEXANDER COCKBURN and JAMES RIDGEWAY

It should be said straightaway that [*The Poverty of Power: Energy and the Economic Crisis*] presents a more brusque and forthright explication of [the transformation of the fuel base of the economy of the United States] than has been traditional in the environmental movement, and Commoner is plainly more radical in his analysis than many of that movement's spokesmen. . . .

Commoner rounds out his profile of the energy economy of the United States with a description of capitalism in crisis—plagued by capital shortage, by falling rates of profit, and by the unemployment attendant on the development of industries powered by machines rather than men. All these ills are threaded together, in Commoner's analysis, by capitalism's irrational and ultimately inequitable uses of energy. . . .

Despite [some] concluding remarks on the possibilities of serious political change, the real significance of Commoner's book lies elsewhere. It represents a continuation and indeed revitalization of an old Utilitarian notion, namely that political problems can be solved by technical remedies. By far the most profound example of this sort of thinking can be found in the attention given to solar energy, a subject which has been of intense interest to environmentalists during the last few years. Commoner is well known for his advocacy of the development of solar energy as an alternative to nuclear power. Solar energy, as presented by its advocates, seems to offer truly remarkable solutions to most of the problems of society. . . .

[Sunlight] becomes the healing balm of the late twentieth century. Under its beneficent glow many of the evils of late twentieth-century capitalism will shrivel.

Such optimism is surely unjustified. As Commoner himself reports, the government has deliberately sidetracked solar energy. . . .

It is of central importance to understand why solar energy is crawling forward under . . . constricting conditions. The reason is surely that the policies of the government merely reflect the interests of the major energy companies; that the state is not playing any form of serious independent role in the formation and financing of an energy policy.

This is the nub of the problem. The question is how to separate the aims of the democratic state from those of private industry and make the latter responsive to the former. The environmental movement has never seen the conflict in such sharp terms. Commoner is somewhat of an exception, but most environmentalists abhor the notion of socialism in any form. . . .

Commoner's book is a political statement set largely in technical terms, and it is a clear and useful expression of the argument that the crises of late capitalism can be resolved by technical solutions. But as a practical matter the politics of technology often turn out merely to reinforce the status quo, and the question remains: who is going to impose these solutions and where are the politics to promote their imposition? As in the case of solar energy, no solution contrary to corporate interests has yet been advanced. Commoner stops short of dealing with this all-important question of political reality. . . .

Without doubt Commoner's book is a step along the way toward filling the grave need for political education of the environmental movement. But it barely states the problem: which is how the state can be extricated from corporate interests and what sort of a political movement would be needed to accomplish this immense task.

> Alexander Cockburn and James Ridgeway, "The Sunny Side of the Street," in The New York Review of Books (reprinted with permission from The New York Review of Books; copyright © 1976 Nyrev, Inc.), Vol. XXIII, No. 13, August 5, 1976, p. 44.

GERALD T. DUNNE

Thirteen years more and [*The Poverty of Power*] would be the perfect bicentennial commemoration for the revolution—the

French Revolution, for it is a superb 1789 reprise. Its ideas on property are in lineal descent from Gracchus Babeuf, who proclaimed that institution a form of theft and even homicide. Moreover, its pastoral chic faithfully echoes the milkmaids of Versailles or, better yet, the *Paul et Virginie* overtones from some *philosophe*'s salon. On the other hand, if it had appeared just a few years ago, its apocalyptic ramblings on the fundamental interrelationship of economic, ecological, and energy crises would have perfectly complemented the prose of Charles Reich and Teilhard de Chardin, especially as *Poverty* bears about the same relation to the analytics of power as *The Greening of America* does to politics, or *The Phenomenon of Man* to theology. Significantly, trendy reviewers, while plugging the book, caution avoidance of both its science and its economics, where some critical arguments—such as Commoner's extrapolation of the falling rate of profit—seem capable of inversion into an apologia for finance capitalism. One is left with no answers, but a few good questions. And indeed, if the right question is more important than the right answer, *Poverty of Power* is—quite by accident—an abrasive and uncivil contribution to the social device we know as the dialogue.

> *Gerald T. Dunne, "Books in Brief: 'The Poverty of Power'," in* National Review *(© National Review, Inc., 1976; 150 East 35th St., New York, NY 10016), Vol. 28, No. 47, December 10, 1976, p. 1367.*

JOHN MADDOX

Few will quarrel with the principle that it is not sufficient when worrying about energy economy to think of saving scraps of heat here and there. It is also necessary that the source of energy is well matched to the objectives. . . .

It is another matter whether all this can sanctify with scholarship Commoner's outbursts [in *The Poverty of Power: Energy and the Economic Crisis*] against three of the industries which have been his punch-bags for the past decade. Isn't it daft, he asks, to use nitrogen fertilisers in intensive farming, when crop rotation would allow the sun to fix nitrogen naturally? (Well, is it, if farmers really find it cheaper that way, or if land as well as energy is scarce?) Isn't it daft to use motor cars, when passenger trains give more passenger miles for a barrel of oil? (But what if there isn't a railway, and what about the luggage?) Isn't it daft to make fibres synthetically when there are natural substitutes, so to speak? (Why then, if the efficiency of the petrochemical industry is literally zero, as Commoner claims, are synthetic fibres relatively cheap?)

What Commoner is attempting in this argument is to invent his own kind of currency for describing the use we make of energy. It is an extension of the ill-discipline of 'energy accounting' that has grown up since 1974. . . .

Such passionate concern for the efficient use of energy would surely, one would have thought, have led to complaints against the fecklessness of governments, but the logic of the case seems only to sharpen the dilemma in which poor Dr Commoner finds himself throughout the book. To be blunt, he is in two minds about the role of capitalism in the modern world. Nowhere does he say outright that private corporations should be replaced by other kinds of instruments, but he does repeatedly complain that the commercial decisions of the corporations are dictated by the profit motive. . . . Commoner never says openly what he would do about corporations, but one is left with the impression that, given half a chance, he would sweep them away.

His outward ambivalence on this issue unfortunately leads him to the least convincing of his arguments—that whatever alternative sources of energy are developed (and the best part of the book is Commoner's advocacy of solar power), the high cost of the research, development and construction that will be needed for most energy alternatives will impoverish us, or our children. It is a chilling prospect, but not a real one.

> *John Maddox, "Sun User" (© British Broadcasting Corp. 1977; reprinted by permission of John Maddox), in* The Listener, *Vol. 97, No. 2494, February 3, 1977, p. 157.*

THE ECONOMIST

Professor Commoner's book ["**The Poverty of Power**"], subtitled "Energy and the economic crisis", has a valuable aim. But it is an aim that he fails to achieve in anything more than superficial terms. He sets out to show that relations between the three systems "that, together with the social or political order, govern all human activity" are deeply flawed. The three systems, he says, are the ecosystem, the production system and the economic system. The way we use energy is an excellent guide to the way they interact, and to the way in which "our current crisis is a symptom of a deep and dangerous fault in the economic system".

Professor Commoner is unquestionably right that it is impossible to consider energy in society without tracing it through the interaction of the three systems. And many of his individual views are sound. He is right, for example, to stress the importance for the whole community of the rising capital costs of conventional energy, and the shift from internal to external financing for energy suppliers. It is helpful that such a leading environmentalist can discuss the future without hysterical predictions about the imminent exhaustion of fossil fuels. He is right to stress the virtues of a flexible, decentralised approach to solar power (though hopelessly optimistic about the possible speed and expense of altering the housing stock). Where he goes wrong is to do no more than demonstrate that his three basic systems are interlinked. He fails to show clearly how the linkage works, how it grew up and what should be done to change things.

The reason for this failure is contained in the way he throws in "the social or political order" as an afterthought. There is no room for politics in his argument except as the handmaiden of some other interest. Yet the imbalance of American energy policy has been as much the result of politicians' failures as it has been of tycoons' greedy successes. Professor Commoner's political blind spot is made worse by a second set of blinkers. He ignores the experience of other industrial countries, obviously seeing them (except for a few mechanical toys, like fast passenger trains) as merely backward versions of the United States. . . . Britain and other European countries have many energy problems in common with the United States. Enough, at any rate, to rule out "the search for profit" as the root of all evil. But European, Japanese and Soviet examples are also all subtly different, as political choices have been made differently in different countries. Politics is precisely the art that links together the three "basic systems". Political choices have been wrongly made in the past, and the result in the United States may in many ways be quite as bad as "**The Poverty of Power**" suggests. But some less sketchy analysis than this aggregation of three New Yorker essays is called for. Professor Commoner knows the patient has a generalised illness—and that in itself is a step forward—but in this book he has done no more than point to the symptoms. (pp. 117-18)

"No Room for Politics?" in The Economist *(©The Economist Newspaper Limited, 1977), Vol. 262, No. 6962, February 5, 1977, pp. 117-18.*

David R. Kamerschen, "Review Article: Poverty, Power, and Pollution," in Economic Development and Cultural Change *(reprinted by permission of The University of Chicago Press; © 1979 by The University of Chicago), Vol. 27, No. 4, July, 1979, pp. 791-95.*

DAVID R. KAMERSCHEN

As with his previous two books, *The Closing Circle* and *Science and Survival,* Barry Commoner has penned a very emotional book [*The Poverty of Power*] which according to the back cover "shows the startling and frightening connection between pollution, economic stagnation and vanishing energy reserves." It goes on to call this tripartite relationship a "triple crisis." One would have hoped that the shock tactics of *Limits of Growth* genre would have gone out of style with academicians.

This is not to say that the three matters Commoner investigates are not important and worthy of study. They are. And *The Poverty of Power* contains some excellent dispassionate analysis and fact finding. But the overall impact is still one of shake and shock. . . .

While Commoner freely admits that economics lies outside his own professional training, there are certainly parts of his book that are of interest to an economist. . . .

Commoner's comments on the topic [of entropy] give new perspective and dimension to the concept. (p. 791)

His analysis of the costs and benefits of nuclear power is simple and cogent. He documents how the more complex breeder reactor was rendered obsolete by the fact that capital costs increased by more than the savings in fuel costs.

His treatment of how solar energy can be developed for cheap, abundant power is excellent. (pp. 791-92)

[Let] me describe equally briefly some of the things I do not like about [his book]. . . .

Throughout the book he tends to overdramatize the economic power of the petroleum industry.

It is true that the petroleum industry in the past has used—indeed even invented—numerous anticompetitive devices. This does not, however, mean inexorably that the petroleum industry presently possesses and/or employs monopoly power. (p. 792)

Commoner wavers alternately between praising the profit system and castigating it. At one point . . . his appeal to authority is Karl Marx! He bemoans . . . the fact that the relatively pollution-free trolley cars were sacrificed on the altar of profit. In another breath, he argues that the declining rate of profitability in the United States in the post-World War II period, especially since 1966, is a serious problem in the U.S. economy. It is gratifying that he does not, as many others do, consider oil companies to be "obscenely profitable." (p. 793)

[The] book fails to recognize fully the quite explicit tradeoff between energy and environment. A tradeoff means that if you want more of one thing you must accept less of something else. Tendentious writings promoting exclusively either of these positions are unrealistic. (p. 794)

In summary, Commoner's latest book in his trilogy should be read by serious students. I fear, however, that it is less cerebral and less validated by empirical evidence than it might have been. (p. 795)

PETER PASSELL

Professor Commoner's answer to energy inflation [in **"The Politics of Energy"**] is to turn to energy forms that are renewable. The only two within reach during this century are nuclear breeder reactors that could extend existing fission fuel supplies almost indefinitely, and, of course, solar energy. Since breeder reactors are not nice to children or other living things, the only way out is to capture the energy of the sun.

Is Barry Commoner right? His book is flawed by muddled economics. He complains, for example, that the Carter energy plan is inequitable because it asks more sacrifice from consumers than from industry. Professor Commoner's consumers, it seems, are like an independent class. They only buy things; therefore it doesn't matter to them whether businesses that supply them stay afloat, or whether anyone has a job.

Moreover, the distinction Professor Commoner makes between inflationary and non-inflationary energy sources is spurious. It is, of course, true that coal and uranium will become more expensive in the future; thus, it will inevitably pay, someday, to turn to renewable sources. But surely it won't reduce inflation today to shift from cheap non-renewable fuels if the alternative is expensive renewable fuels.

For all the problems, though, **"The Politics of Energy"** should be judged by its central thesis that we are moving too slowly on solar energy. And here the evidence favors Professor Commoner. . . . Under the most optimistic scenarios, it will be decades before the sun lights up our Christmas trees. But the promise of this environmentally benign source is so great that it simply must be given the highest priority in research on long-term solutions to the energy problem.

Peter Passell, "Energetic Proposals," in The New York Times Book Review *(© 1979 by The New York Times Company; reprinted by permission), July 29, 1979, p. 7.**

MARK NORTHCROSS

Barry Commoner does more in [*The Politics of Energy*] than just tell us that solar energy is good and nuclear energy is bad; he shows us that what we want in the way of alternative energy is not going to come from President Jimmy Carter, the energy companies, or any other appendage of the corporate establishment. The principal failing of the book may be that Commoner really does not tell us how to get around these roadblocks. However, Commoner's recent actions advocating a third party in 1980 speak louder than his words.

Barry Commoner has become a master of the rare but crucially needed art of communicating technical information to the layman. Solid analogies drawn from everyday life are essential to this kind of writing, and *The Politics of Energy* is eminently readable and enjoyable on that account. This is especially important in his book, for there are no graphics or numerical tables of any kind. Commoner, however, is so deft with numbers in his prose that he gets away with what would otherwise be an unforgivable omission. (p. 52)

[Other writers besides Commoner] have offered us a systematic vision of an economy entirely fueled by renewable energy sources, but only Commoner lets us in on the Catch-22 that neither the energy companies nor the major political parties are going to make the vision real for us. So what is the public to do? Commoner has a solution, but he soft-pedals it in his book. *The Politics of Energy* draws an analogy between our present political situation and the inertia that gripped the major political parties of the 1840s and 1850s when confronted with the issue of slavery. While *The Politics of Energy* leaves us hanging in thin air with this historical analogy, Commoner has been more forthright speaking in public. . . . Barry Commoner wants a third party by 1980, and he wants it to run a Presidential candidate.

The Politics of Energy is more than an indictment of Carter's energy program, and it is more than just another blueprint for an alternative energy future. It is an energy platform for a third party. (p. 53)

> Mark Northcross, *"An Energy Platform for the '80s,"* in The Progressive *(reprinted by permission from* The Progressive, *409 East Main Street, Madison, Wisconsin 53703; copyright 1979 by The Progressive, Inc.), Vol. 43, No. 9, September, 1979, pp. 52-3.*

SAMUEL McCRACKEN

Barry Commoner has long been a solar advocate—*The Poverty of Power* was largely a eulogy of the sun's potential—and his new book, *The Politics of Energy,* is already very influential. It makes about as strong and detailed a case for a "solar" economy as can be imagined. Yet it is fatally flawed, not only in its technical argument for solar energy, but in the ideological skeleton that lies just below the technological skin. (p. 61)

The solar scheme rests on four major developments. The first of these is the rapid deployment of solar technology for water and space heating. Commoner believes that this technology has already arrived, is now competitive, and need merely be put to work, normally in conjunction with existing systems. Additionally, there would be a rapid development of photovoltaic technology to allow the conversion of sunlight to electricity through individual installations on houses. This technology Commoner believes to be on the verge of success, requiring only mass purchases by the government in order to become economically competitive with central-station electricity. Next, we would build a new alcohol industry capable of producing some 50 billion gallons of liquid fuel a year, displacing about half of our present gasoline supply. Finally, there would be a vast new methane industry, producing that gas from various feedstocks, and shipping it around the country through a major expansion of the present natural gas network.

Commoner's analysis of the prospects for water and space heat is as rosy as it is because he compares direct solar heating with electric-resistance heating, i.e., the most expensive kind. He himself concedes this fact, but says that such heating is "very common." In reality, it accounts for only 13 per cent of all residential heating installations. (pp. 61-2)

Commoner admits that direct solar energy will never be practical as a total source of heating. But in discussing the economics of a system that integrates solar with existing sources, he appears to take no account whatever of the effect that the subtraction of the baseload would have on the economics of central electricity supply; that is, it would skim off the cream of the utilities' business—namely, the production of the cheapest part of the total demand—and leave them with the expensive peaks.

The most attractive promise of direct solar energy is the conversion of sunlight to electricity through photovoltaic cells. The obvious immediate problem in this technology, Commoner notes, is its cost. . . . A typical house with a maximum demand of 15 kilowatts would require $150,000 just for the cells. . . .

[Commoner] proposes a glittering scheme to bring these costs down to more reasonable levels. He recounts the tale of a Federal Energy Agency proposal to require the Department of Defense to purchase, over five years, a total of $440 million worth of solar cells to replace some of the military's small generators. By the end of the five years, according to the FEA study, the cost of photovoltaic cells would have plunged to fifty cents a watt. This, with auxiliaries, would bring the total capital investment for a 15-kilowatt house to over $20,000, still more than central-generating plants, and still supplied by the consumer. (p. 62)

[It is] worthwhile to consider the problems raised by [photovoltaic generation] even if it were economically plausible: the problems, as it were, of solar success.

Some of these are in the broad sense technical: they deal with measurable effects that are relevant to other forms of energy. For example, contrary to popular belief, direct solar power generates waste, not in the production of power, but in the production of its materials. . . .

Solar power also raises serious problems of efficiency. Photovoltaic generators are, from the point of view of capital investment, much the least efficient means to generate electricity. They are not available after sundown, and so have an "availability factor"—the proportion of time a generator can work—much lower than any thermal plant. Moreover, the weather and the time of day insure that a solar generator, even in daytime, almost always produces much less than its rated capacity. Its "capacity factor" is, accordingly, very much lower than that of a thermal power plant. . . .

But the technical problems of solar energy are substantially less interesting than its social ones. Lying just below the surface in most discussions of alternative energy are proposals for reshaping how we live by controlling the type and amount of energy available to us, as well as the way it is supplied to us. These are especially notable with direct solar energy. (p. 63)

[Proposals] for a major conversion to direct solar energy are at best proposals to reverse thousands of years of development by which man, through the division of labor, has made the acquisition of energy increasingly the province of fewer and fewer increasingly well-paid specialists. This is what the Commoners are decrying when they call for the decentralization of energy sources. A century ago, the American used substantially less energy than he does now, but provided much more of it through his own efforts. Now that anyone can have access to as much energy as he can pay for by pushing the right button, it was probably predictable that surfeited intellectuals would want to play at chopping wood and shoveling snow off their solar collectors. Yet it is typical of the great majority of the modern pastoralists that they seem to want to get back to nature in the most complicated and expensive way possible. Few if any mean to retire to the equivalent of an 18th-century farmstead. Rather, one is to live with the assistance of extremely costly gadgetry that will provide all the complexities of modern civilization, but with the inefficiency of time and resource that is the hallmark of the "natural" way. Unfortunately, only the few will be able to afford such "handmade" energy; the rest, one supposes, will just have to emulate 18th-century farmers.

The difficulty with direct use of the sun is that it is very expensive and requires us to adjust our way of life to fit an inferior energy source. But much of Commoner's book is concerned with indirect methods of converting solar energy—that is, with processes that store solar energy on an interim basis in devices as various as the winds, the tides, the rains, and vegetation, then "harvest" the energy thus stored by an equally various set of technologies. Such methods are hardly new— we have been burning wood for a very long time, and whether learning to call it "biomass" represents real progress one cannot say—but they have the advantage of being somewhat more adaptable to our present energy use than direct conversion of sunlight. Even so, on the scale proposed by Commoner they would require very great dislocations of the economy.

Of these, "gasohol" epitomizes alternative energy sources: even when practical in small doses (often only with substantial tax subsidies), they cannot be scaled up to provide a major source of energy. There is no reason why a farmer cannot use spoiled grain as a stock from which to distill alcohol. Mixed with gasoline, it may well be a competitive fuel—but only if sold at the bogus price that would result if the state decided to forgive the fuel tax on it. (p. 64)

The other half of Commoner's fossil-fuel replacement program is methane, which is to be generated in immense quantities— 20 quads, approximately the current production of natural gas— by a wide variety of feedstocks and piped through the land in an expanded version of the present-day natural-gas distribution system.

Commoner proposes to exploit methane largely through the use of a device called the cogenerator. . . . A cogenerator is a device that uses the inevitable waste heat from an engine for some other purpose. (pp. 65-6)

This device would no doubt be useful in the colder parts of the undeveloped world, where a noisy source of electricity and heat, subject to fairly frequent down times for scheduled major maintenance and unscheduled repair, would certainly be better

than no electricity or no heat at all. But it must be understood that for us, the future Commoner holds out is one in which our heat and electricity supply would be no more reliable than our car engines. . . .

One suspects that Commoner does not really think capitalists are as dumb as all that, but hopes that the taxpayers will be. He ends his book by surveying the political problems inhering in the grand transition. One could summarize his argument by saying that solar energy will be good for the Peepul and less good for the bosses, except those who run energy-intensive businesses. The argument takes leave of technology and shows quite clearly the trend and quality of Commoner's ideology. (p. 66)

Most of the problems inherent in the grand transition Commoner would solve by something called "social governance." It is not clear what this is a euphemism for, although Commoner does reassure us that, having survived Joe McCarthy and Watergate, we can probably survive it too. There is nothing vague, however, about another key phrase. In his last sentence Commoner calls for us to adopt as a major national goal something he terms "economic democracy." Although he does not define this term here, he did so in his earlier book, *The Poverty of Power,* where "economic democracy" is explicitly and quaintly defined as the economic system of such states as China, Cuba, and the USSR—places, as is well known, in which all economic decisions are made by individuals and popularly elected assemblies. . . .

[It] is as a political manifesto that *The Politics of Energy* makes the most sense, just as Commoner himself makes sense best not as a scientist but as an ideologue. Indeed, the whole solar movement is interesting primarily as an ideological one. Its technical slovenliness cries out to be exposed, but there is nothing new in such slovenliness on the part of enthusiasts. What is comparatively new in a democratic society is the use of technological arguments, however incompetently made, to support a call for a new vision of human life. (p. 67)

Samuel McCracken, "Solar Energy: A False Hope,"
in Commentary *(reprinted by permission; all rights*
reserved), Vol. 68, No. 5, November, 1979, pp. 61-
7.

Robert A(lan) Dahl

1915-

An American political scientist, Dahl is one of the foremost exponents of the pluralist theory of political power. His *Who Governs?: Democracy and Power in an American City* (1961) is widely considered to be a classic pluralist study, marshalling evidence to show that the community under investigation—New Haven, Connecticut—is governed by competing groups and interests. In *Polyarchy* (1971) Dahl elucidates the preconditions of democracy and the consequences for political regimes of differing levels of citizen participation in political processes. In *Size and Democracy* (1973) he and coauthor Edward R. Tufte examine the relationship of democracy to the size of political systems, searching for optimal characteristics of democratic units. Dahl is Sterling Professor of Political Science at Yale University. He was awarded the Woodrow Wilson Prize from the American Political Science Association in 1961, and the Talcott Parsons Prize for Social Science from the American Academy of Arts and Sciences in 1977. (See also *Contemporary Authors*, Vols. 65-68.)

Wide World Photos

Excerpt from *POLYARCHY: PARTICIPATION AND OPPOSITION*

Some readers might be inclined to think that differences in national regimes do not matter much: For example, one might share the view of those like Gaetano Mosca who argue that every regime is, after all, dominated by a ruling minority. As an astringent challenge to the belief that portentuous consequences for the people of a country must necessarily follow a transformation of the regime, Mosca's skepticism has a good deal to be said for it. Moreover, what appear superficially to be changes of regime are sometimes not really changes in regime at all, but simply changes in personnel, rhetoric, and empty constitutional prescriptions.

Yet few people seem able to adhere consistently to the view that differences in regimes—for example, differences between polyarchy and inclusive hegemony—are at base negligible. In fact, I have the impression that this view is most often espoused by intellectuals who are, at heart, liberal or radical democrats disappointed by the transparent failures of polyarchies or near-polyarchies; and that, conversely, intellectuals who have actually experienced life under severely repressive hegemonic regimes rarely argue that differences in regime are trivial. (p. 17)

[There] are good reasons for thinking that a transformation of a regime from a hegemony into a more competitive regime or a competitive oligarchy into a polyarchy does have significant results.

1. To begin with, there are the classic liberal freedoms that are a part of the definition of public contestation and participation: opportunities to oppose the government, form political organizations, express oneself on political matters without fear of governmental reprisals, read and hear alternative points of view, vote by secret ballot in elections in which candidates of different parties compete for votes and after which the losing candidates peacefully yield their claim to office to the winners, etc. (p. 20)

2. Broadened participation combined with political competition brings about a change in the composition of the political leadership, particularly among those who gain office by means of elections—mainly, then, members of parliament. As new groups are granted the suffrage, candidates closer in their social characteristics to the newly incorporated strata win a greater share of elective offices. (pp. 20-1)

3. As a system becomes more competitive or more inclusive, politicians seek the support of groups that can now participate more easily in political life. The response of politicians to the existence of new opportunities for participation and public contestation are manifold and have far-reaching effects. I have just described one of these: to offer candidates whom the voters feel are in some sense "closer" to themselves. Another is to adapt rhetoric, program, policy, and ideology to what are thought to be the desires or interests of the groups, segments, or strata not hitherto represented. (p. 23)

4. In any given country, the greater the opportunities for expressing, organizing, and representing political preferences, the greater the number and variety of preferences and interests that are likely to be represented in policy making. . . .

DAHL   *CONTEMPORARY ISSUES CRITICISM, Vol. 1*

5. The consequences for government policies of lower thresholds for participation and public contestation are, unfortunately, obscure. (p. 26)

We probably need to look elsewhere to find the impact of regime on policy, in particular, on the extent to which the government adopts policies that involve severe physical coercion for relatively large numbers of people. The lower the barriers to public contestation and the greater the proportion of the population included in the political system, the more difficult it is for the government of a country to adopt and enforce policies that require the application of extreme sanctions against more than a small percentage of the population; the less likely, too, that the government will attempt to do so. (p. 27)

I do not mean to argue that such massive coercion inevitably occurs in hegemonies nor, certainly, in mixed regimes, but only that the risk is significant, whereas it does not incur in polyarchies. (p. 28)

6. One could speculate about other possible consequences of differences in regimes. It is possible, for example, that over long periods of time differences in regime may have effects on beliefs, attitudes, culture, and personalities. . . . But it is also reasonable to suppose that there is a reciprocal interaction between factors of this kind and the character of a regime: if these factors affect the chances of a particular type of regime, over time the nature of the regime influences beliefs, attitudes, culture, and perhaps even personalities that are likely to develop in a country. (pp. 29-30)

It seems reasonably evident that different regimes do have different consequences. Although some people may deny the importance of these consequences, at least the advocates of polyarchy and their opponents both agree that the consequences are significantly different and important. If the consequences of polyarchy were no different from those of nonpolyarchy, or if the consequences were unimportant, there would be no reason to advocate a polyarchy rather than a one-party dictatorship— or the converse. Probably most readers will also agree that the consequences—particularly the first—are important. (p. 30)

But it is not my purpose here to make a case for polyarchy. It is enough if I have shown that important consequences will follow from reducing the obstacles to public contestation and increasing the share of the population entitled to participate. A great many people will agree, I think, not only that these consequences are important but that they are also desirable, that the benefits often (if not always) outweigh the adverse consequences, and that the net gain in such cases is well worth striving for. (p. 31)

> *Robert A. Dahl, in his* Polyarchy: Participation and Opposition *(copyright © 1971 by Yale University), Yale University Press, 1971, 257 p.*

Excerpt from *SIZE AND DEMOCRACY*

[Is] ''democracy'' related in any way to ''size''? How large should a political system be in order to facilitate rational control by its citizens? What are the comparative advantages and disadvantages enjoyed by political systems of different sizes?

Anyone who reflects on these questions will quickly discover that their apparent simplicity conceals a quagmire of complex problems. In searching for answers to the questions as we do

in [*Size and Democracy*], we shall try to confront these problems.

Let us start, then, simply by observing how very relevant these questions are today. Urbanization and the population explosion have raised the specter of uncontrolled growth at all levels of government. In the United States we are particularly concerned with the question of whether it is wise to permit cities—and metropolitan areas and megalopolises—to grow indefinitely. (pp. 1-2)

As the inexorable thrust of population growth makes a small country large and a large country gigantic, demands are often heard for bringing government closer to the people, for grass-roots democracy. Smaller units are often said to facilitate democracy better than larger units; hence the larger units must be broken up into smaller units, where grass-roots democracy is possible—regions, states, cities, towns, neighborhoods. At the same time, there are complaints that the smaller units are incapable of handling their problems, and demands are heard for larger units such as metropolitan areas, a United States of Europe, a world federation. Concerns are expressed over the size of corporations and the capacities of governments to control them—particularly the international giants.

Thus size enters into the very question of how and indeed whether democratic systems with a high degree of autonomy or sovereignty can survive in a world of great interdependence. Can local governments survive, except as agents of the national government? For that matter, can nations, especially small ones, retain much of their sovereignty? But if every unit surrenders its autonomy to the next larger unit in an ever-ascending series, is there any place left for popular control over government? At the limit, if every smaller unit were simply an agent of a world government and political participation consisted entirely of voting in elections with several billion other citizens, what meaning would be left in the word *democracy*? Conversely, if for at least some kinds of decisions decentralization and autonomy are desirable, the question persists: decentralization to political units of what size? (pp. 2-3)

It seems evident to us that among the units most needed in the world as it has been evolving lie several at the extremes: we need some very small units and some very large units. The very small units, like the Swedish communes under 8,000, once existed; but because of their inadequate system capacity they are rapidly vanishing. Very large units that transcend the parochialism and inadequate system capacity of the nation-state are evolving, but too slowly—quite possibly too slowly for human survival. If the giant units are needed for handling transnational matters of extraordinary moment, very small units seem to us necessary to provide a place where ordinary people can acquire the sense and the reality of moral responsibility and political effectiveness in a universe where remote galaxies of leaders spin on in courses mysterious and unfathomable to the ordinary citizen. At the same time that the transnational units will increase the capacity of the system to handle critical problems, and thus the collective effectiveness of a body of citizens, transnational units will also increase the ineffectuality and powerlessness of the individual citizen. As a consequence, the very small unit will become more, not less, important to the sense of effectiveness of the ordinary citizen. Yet finding space for truly significant activity in the very small unit is obviously going to be difficult.

Theory, then, needs to do what democratic theory has never done well: to offer useful guidance about the appropriate re-

110

lations among units. This problem was virtually bypassed during the classical preoccupation with the city-state; interstate relations were literally anarchic. The nation-state merely transferred that anarchy to the relations of much larger units. And federalism is not so much a theory of inter-unit relations as a set of institutions, different from country to country, conveniently anchored in the nation-state—at least up to now.

One reason why federalism has been able to deal concretely with problems arising from relationships among the constituent units is that nationalism has helped to keep down severe conflicts of loyalties within the federal system by means of a moderately clear hierarchy of loyalties. The nation was generally held to be the unit of ultimate loyalty; a layer of intermediate units—states, provinces, cantons—came next; all other units, including municipal units, were definitely subordinate to the other two. Where a hierarchy of attachments did not fully develop, or broke down, conflicts of loyalties have led to serious confrontations, as in Canada, or to civil war, as in the United States. Yet how infinitely more difficult is the problem of loyalty in a complex polity that begins to transcend the nation-state!

If boundaries can be too small or too large, depending on the problem at hand, it might be thought that a theoretical solution would perhaps be found with a system having an indefinite number of units without permanently fixed boundaries, a system capable therefore of ready and infinite adaptability. This line of speculation seems to us, however, to promise one of those solutions of little theoretical interest and less practical value. Just as a central nervous system would quickly become overloaded by a proliferation of specialized organs constantly changing in size and shape, so the costs of communication and information, and therefore of control, would become overwhelming if citizens were confronted with an indefinite number of changing units. In fact, in complex political systems these costs already appear to be so high as drastically to impair citizen effectiveness. We have long since passed the time, if it ever existed, in representative democracies when an ordinary citizen could monitor all the functions and units with a large impact on his goals and policies. Even a legislator can no longer do so, and we probably have passed the point at which a full-time chief executive can do so.

Thus one task of democratic theory may be to specify not an optimal unit but an optimal number of units with comparatively fixed boundaries. The boundaries of each unit would be too small or too large for all functions assigned to it; but the costs of a small number of units with relatively fixed boundaries would be less than the costs of any larger number of units, or of constantly shifting boundaries.

A new democratic theory will also have to clarify the powers, obligations, and characteristics of citizens and leaders, including officials, in democratic units of different types. For example, some degree of specialization of attention will certainly be required, even under assumptions calling for a considerably higher level of political involvement on the part of citizens than is true now or perhaps has existed at any time in the past. We have seen how, with increasing size, specialization becomes necessary among leaders, but citizens must, and to some extent do, also specialize. Yet indefinite specialization, like an indefinite proliferation of units, would lead sooner or later—and may already have—to so much fragmentation as to create insuperable problems of coordination. Is responsibility for looking after the general, the larger wholes, to vanish entirely, or, finally rejecting the ancient ideal of a body of citizens con-

cerned with "the general good," is this responsibility also to be lodged, knowingly, in a specialized group of citizens?

In order to catch up with the problem of the complex polity, it seems, democratic theory must (among other things) help one to decide, according to democratic or other acceptable criteria of political excellence, the optimal number of units, their characteristics, similarities, and differences, the nature of a good political life in each type of unit, and the proper relationships among them. (pp. 140-42)

> *Robert A. Dahl and Edward R. Tufte, in their* Size and Democracy *(with the permission of the publishers, Stanford University Press; © 1973 by the Board of Trustees of the Leland Stanford Junior University), Stanford University Press, 1973, 148 p.*

HARRY W. BAEHR

[In *Congress and Foreign Policy*] Mr. Dahl addresses himself to a familiar problem: can a democracy formulate and carry out foreign policies in a world of chronic crisis? Specifically, he devotes his attention to the Congress of the United States and its role in foreign affairs. The author examines the Congressman, his background, the degree to which he is actually responsible to his constituents, the effect upon him of party discipline and group pressures. He discusses the voter—his prejudices, information and interests—and decides that there is little hope of improving the quality or the extent of mass participation in policy making. And, finally, Mr. Dahl turns to the Presidency, with its trend toward leadership, which the author dissects under the provocative title: "A Constitutional Dictator?" . . .

Mr. Dahl's contentions . . . are worth careful consideration. He suggests, for example, that party discipline be fostered, a notion which is becoming popular among political scientists, but shows no signs of making headway among politicians. He believes that the sectional basis of the historic major parties is giving way to an alignment "more nearly along lines of class and status"—which he considers a prerequisite to party responsibility. And Mr. Dahl writes that a clear and meaningful party platform—necessary if either discipline or responsibility is to emerge—is becoming a practical political advantage.

Given responsible parties, Mr. Dahl thinks that Congress could set up something approaching the vote of confidence (or lack of confidence) which is a characteristic of parliamentary regimes. Concurrent resolutions, backed by a united and responsible party organization, would, he feels carry weight with the Executive. And, by the same token, once confidence in the Administration was established by collaboration with Congress, by party unity, by recourse to Congressional disapproval when necessary, the author holds that Congress could give greater latitude to the President.

This approach, based for the most part upon trends which Mr. Dahl thinks he sees and upon devices which have, in one form or another, actually been put in practice in the American government, is open to fewer objections than most treatises on the reform of Congress. One may question the reality of the trends or the precise utility of the devices, but **"Congress and Foreign Policy,"** puts forward an essentially modest and plausible thesis.

Harry W. Baehr, "Congress in Time of Crisis," in New York Herald Tribune Book Review, *July 30, 1950, p. 9.*

DAYTON D. McKEAN

A student of the American party system might feel that [in *Congress and Foreign Policy*] Dr. Dahl underestimates the effects of various features of the Constitution, such as the single-member district, upon party and Congressional behavior; for each state and district is unique, and each congressman and senator knows (or, since he won, thinks he knows) how to win in his state or district. This belief inevitably conditions his attitudes toward his party, his colleagues in committee and house, and the pressure groups which seek to persuade him to follow one or another line that affects foreign policies. Rarely does any foreign policy affect this political calculus. A senator like Byrd, with his state in his pocket, can defy them all and still look forward confidently to reelection; a senator like Lehman may have to study every vote as if it determined, as well it may determine, his reelection.

The treatment of pressure groups upon foreign policies . . . seems to this reviewer somewhat scanty. There are more of them; their interests are much more various; and the groups affect many more policies than the reader of this book might gather. "Responsible parties", writes the author, "would force such pressures to work within the parties rather than in the legislature." To be sure. But how such pressures are to be taken off the legislature and put on the parties when members of the houses are elected by their states or districts, and not by national parties, is the great and unanswered question. (pp. 617-18)

Dayton D. McKean, "Reviews: 'Congress and Foreign Policy'," in Political Science Quarterly, *Vol. LXV, No. 4, December, 1950, pp. 617-18.*

HERBERT McCLOSKY

Although modern political scholarship has paid unceasing attention to the theory and operation of democratic government, a number of questions essential to its understanding and performance remain as unsettled as ever. Where, for example, ought the power of decision to lie amid the conflicting demands of minorities and majorities? Under what conditions could a majority claim the right to enforce policies intensely distasteful to a legitimate minority? What restraints are needed if majorities, minorities, or those who govern in their name, are to be prevented from gross usurpations of power—indeed, from tyranny itself? What are the logical and empirical preconditions for the operation of a viable democracy?

These are the kinds of questions to which Professor Dahl addresses himself in [*A Preface to Democratic Theory,* a] remarkably compact and tightly reasoned new book on democratic theory. . . .

[Professor Dahl] directs his attention mainly to three theoretical models (among the several which, he points out, could have been chosen) and subjects each of them to an intensive systematic and descriptive analysis. The first, *Madisonian democracy,* represents an effort "to bring off a compromise between the power of majorities and the power of minorities, between the political equality of all adult citizens on the one side and the desire to limit their sovereignty on the other." This has been the theory most preferred by Americans, for its

emphasis on constitutional checks designed to disperse authority has seemed to them the surest defense against tyranny. Dahl finds the theory deficient both in the descriptive status of some of its assumptions and in the logic by which it is led to its conclusions. (p. 1134)

The second model examined is *populistic democracy,* which identifies democracy with political equality, popular sovereignty, and, most important, the unrestrained power of majorities. This theory, which attempts to provide a procedural rule for the perfect attainment of equality and popular sovereignty, is in reality no more than an "exercise in axiomatics," essentially lacking in empirical relevance. It is a theory plagued by numerous difficulties: e.g., it assumes that only one alternative will be preferred by a majority at any given time when in fact several alternatives may be equally preferred; it ignores the problem of intensity and would permit a small majority with weak preferences to override the desires of a large minority with strong preferences; it postulates only two goals to be maximized while others of equal importance are discounted or sacrificed; it ignores the fact that in reality a minority rules so that in practice unlimited power would be bestowed upon a few; etc.

The third model, *polyarchal democracy,* combines elements from the two preceding theories but differs from them in concentrating not on the goals to be maximized but on the common properties exhibited by democratic organizations, in order that the conditions for the existence of democracy may be meaningfully elaborated. . . . Polyarchy stresses the social rather than the constitutional prerequisites for a democratic order.

The final sections of the book assess American politics in the light of the conditions for democracy previously set forth. The American system is perceived as a hybrid, and a very successful one. Like a polyarchy, which it approximates in certain respects, it permits "all active and legitimate groups in the population [to] make themselves heard at some crucial stage in the process of decision." In this "markedly decentralized system" in which decisions are made by "endless bargaining," there is perhaps less order than in other systems, but it is nevertheless not so defective as its critics make out. It possesses great virtue, furthermore, in mediating the conflicting interests of a highly diverse population, permitting minorities of almost every description to enter into the public debate and influence the outcome. Partly for this reason it reinforces agreement and encourages moderation in a highly complex and rapidly evolving society. (p. 1135)

Some readers will doubtless find that they do not share all the views that are central to the argument. For example, Madisonian theory seems to me less vulnerable, on either logical or empirical grounds, than it does to the author. Then, too, I would assign greater importance to the role of constitutional restraints as checks against political aggrandizement and tyranny, for "social restraints" may not always be adequate: some attacks on democracy may be successfully met only by recourse to constitutional devices. More important, the argument overlooks the degree to which formal restraints help to define and maintain the social norms which eventually become "internalized." No less than the family or any other social institution, the legal arrangements serve to shape the citizen conscience.

Other disagreements could be stated, but none is sufficient to detract significantly from the importance of the book. It is a unique and unusually intelligent contribution to the literature of political science in general, and, more specifically, to a branch of the field which seems badly in need of new ways of thinking about its oldest and most traditional problems. (p. 1136)

Herbert McClosky, "Book Reviews: 'A Preface to Democratic Theory'," in The American Political Science Review *(copyright, 1956, by The American Political Science Association), Vol. 50, No. 4, December, 1956, pp. 1134-36.*

HAROLD GUETZKOW

Dahl's [*A Preface to Democratic Theory*] develops classical political theory into forms which allow it to be enriched by contemporary social theory and modern methodology. First, with admirable rigor the author formalizes the basic goals, definitions, and means-end statements of Madisonian and Populistic theories of democracy. His analysis of these two formalized systems lays bare logical inconsistencies within them and emphasizes the extent to which they tend to be axiomatic rather than real-world theories which explain American political behavior. Then he describes the "American hybrid" by constructing an ideal type, "Polyarchal Democracy." In this theory he hypothesizes that achievement of the Madisonian goal of non-tyranny by either majority or minority, with popular sovereignty and political equality, as a function of an array of both formal (constitutional) and informal (practice) conditions which exist inside the governmental processes and within the social system itself. Dahl's analysis of the conditions of consensus on political procedures and alternatives within the social organizations constituting the polyarchy makes important use of the concept of social norms. . . .

Dahl is quite clear as to whether the various issues raised by his formalization of the three theories of democracy are ethical (value-oriented), logical (consisting of interrelations among definitions and derivations), or empirical (being testable propositions about operationalized variables). . . . His use of empirical data from time to time hints at the potential which exists for empirical work in democratic theory. . . . Dahl works masterfully as a social behaviorist, while focusing the essential features of our political heritage.

Although the author, as he himself clearly understands, has only prefaced the development of democratic theory into more testable forms, his work can be built upon by behaviorists interested in political processes. It is an important step forward. A tremendous gap remains to be closed, however, between the formalized theory and the formulation of practical ways of testing it empirically. Dahl recognizes this, too, and at times seems discouraged. Little wonder that he, as political scientist, invites the "aid of our colleagues in the other social sciences."

Harold Guetzkow, "Book Reviews: 'A Preface to Democratic Theory'," in The American Journal of Sociology *(reprinted by permission of The University of Chicago Press; © 1957 by The University of Chicago), Vol. LXIII, No. 1, July, 1957, p. 121.*

HEINZ EULAU

[In *Who Governs? Democracy and Power in an American City*,] Professor Dahl's approach in studying the politics of influence in a pluralistic system with, in his own words, noncumulative or dispersed inequalities, is as plural as the political order he investigates. Three broad research strategies serve his purposes. First, a historical analysis of the transformations of New Haven's ruling groups. Second, case analyses of three arenas of policy-making—party nominations to public office, urban redevelopment, and public education. And third, a cross-sectional analysis of the distribution of resources among New Haven's citizenry. This cutting into the research pie from quite different angles is dictated by Professor Dahl's complex model of the democratic order in a competitive environment—a political system in which the politics of influence is not a zero-sum game, but a function of highly fragmented patterns of more or less direct influence, of reciprocal relations between leaders, sub-leaders and constituents, of shifting coalitions and bargaining between more or less overlapping networks of influentials who specialize in different issue areas, of varying structures of influence such as "executive-centered coalition" or "rival sovereignties," and of different and unequal distributions of those resources whose successful mobilization is the task of politics. As a result, Professor Dahl manages to escape, on the one hand, the fallacious conception which confuses the bases of influence with its scope, and, on the other hand, the equally fallacious notion that, because influence has been exerted, it is, of necessity, an all-pervasive and unified phenomenon. On the contrary, Professor Dahl shows that influence can be fragmented, both with regard to control over resources and with regard to issues, and yet can be mobilized, under certain conditions, for effective decision-making in a plural-democratic order.

With its broad-gauged theory, but middle-range empiricism, Professor Dahl's book is more than just another community study. It is a sophisticated and undogmatic treatise on democratic politics. Only in the concluding chapter does Professor Dahl take the role of the pundit who, with authority but usually with less supportive data than Professor Dahl commands, speaks about power elites, mass democracy or countervailing powers. And so we hear about *the* political stratum and *the* ordinary citizen. But fortunately, Professor Dahl is aware of the pitfalls of empirical generalization. Speaking of the function of beliefs in the engineering of consensus—"a recurring *process* of interchange among political professionals, the political stratum, and the great bulk of the population"—Professor Dahl is quick to point out that consensus is not a static and unchanging attribute, but "a variable element in a complex and more or less continuous process." (pp. 144-45)

Heinz Eulau, "Book Reviews: 'Who Governs? Democracy and Power in an American City'," in The American Political Science Review *(copyright, 1962, by The American Political Science Association), Vol. LVI, No. 1, March, 1962, pp. 144-45.*

HUGH DOUGLAS PRICE

Clearly Dahl has written a definitive account of power in New Haven [in *Who Governs? Democracy and Power in an American City*]. But has he refuted [Floyd] Hunter as decisively as Locke did Filmer? On the issue of methodology, this reviewer would say yes—"reputational analysis" is, or should be, dead. But on the substantive question of the influence of the business community, the answer is not so clear. New Haven, while typical of economically stagnant New England, is a far cry from the booming regional centers of Atlanta, Denver, Houston or Dallas, Miami, and so forth. Hunter may have "muddled through" to overstate a thesis not without relevance to those cities where rapid economic growth—which generally can come only through the businessman—is the be-all and end-all for most segments of the population, including the politicians. There remains an urgent need for "middle range theory" to relate what we are learning about different kinds of cities and different styles of politics. (pp. 270-71)

Hugh Douglas Price, "Reviews: 'Who Governs? Democracy and Power in an American City'," in Political Science Quarterly, Vol. LXXVII, No. 2, June, 1962, pp. 269-71.

DAVID ROGERS

Anyone interested in the many problems involved in studying power should read [**Who Governs? Democracy and Power in an American City**], the first of a trilogy on the power structure of New Haven. Both in historical and methodological depth the study far surpasses most previous research efforts in the field. The thorough and painstaking procedures Dahl employs to ascertain who prevails on issues of consequence in New Haven politics are in refreshing contrast to the reputational and positional methods all too frequently utilized in many community power studies. That readers may nevertheless raise questions regarding some of the author's methods and conclusions (as the present reviewer in fact does) should not prevent this from becoming a hallmark in nonpamphleteering and scholarly studies of power. (pp. 271-72)

Some fairly compelling questions are not dealt with too explicitly. Despite the excellent historical section, this reviewer would want more on the comparative implications of the study. Much of contemporary New Haven politics seems to be explained in terms of a "great man" theory with little discussion of the conditions under which such an "executive-centered" system is likely in other communities. Furthermore, with reference just to New Haven, there is no discussion as to why other issues were not included in the study. The ones selected were obviously of some significance by any criteria one chooses to adopt. But is this then a study of the total community power structure as is frequently implied? Why not take a wider range of issues, for all the expense it entails, if one is to generalize as the author does about New Haven politics. Also, we find little mention of the complex relations of the community to outside social systems, for example, state or federal governments, which may play an important role in shaping the local power structure.

Perhaps most basic of all, how much pluralism actually exists in New Haven politics? Dahl makes a most useful distinction between direct and indirect influence. From his evidence on the former, one might well conclude that at least on the three issues studied the mayor and a few lieutenants ruled the roost. To suggest that such community leaders are constrained by a concern for the zone of indifference, so to speak, of their constituents is an important question. Dahl presents some evidence on this. I wish he had presented much more. (p. 272)

David Rogers, "Book Reviews: 'Who Governs? Democracy and Power in an American City'," in The American Journal of Sociology (reprinted by permission of The University of Chicago Press; © 1962 by The University of Chicago), Vol. 68, No. 12, September, 1962, pp. 271-72.

MICHAEL HARRINGTON

"**Polyarchy**" is a scholarly investigation of the preconditions of democracy. The title refers to the existing approximations of the democratic ideal, a system with a high degree of popular participation in politics that allows the citizen to control, or contest, the conduct of government. (p. 5)

Dahl's political conclusion is that polyarchy is so difficult to achieve and is dependent upon such a maze of factors that the democrats of the advanced countries should give up their fantasies, like the early Alliance for Progress, of promoting a democratic revolution in the Third World. He argues that foreign aid should be provided by the affluent powers on the basis of "morality and compassion or rational self-interest," not "as a lever to pry democratization and liberalization out of a hegemonic regime."

Dahl's concept of preconditions is certainly basic to the modern world. From Stalin to Che Guevara, reality has cruelly revenged itself upon the idea that a sufficiently iron will can bend history to its own ends. But the way in which Dahl develops this very important insight is less than satisfactory. He studies the various factors attending the transition from hegemony to polyarchy—but not the revolutionary process which leads from feudalism to capitalism and then beyond. The various preconditions of polyarchy are thus wrenched out of their historical sequence and are not seen as functioning within an economic and social system. (pp. 5, 12)

The political implications of such an undynamic analysis are overly passive. Dahl focuses upon the constants and does not grasp the possibility of a radical transformation of the context in which they operate. If America must indeed avoid that "sentimental imperialism" (the phrase is Arthur Schlesinger Jr.'s) which proposes T.V.A.'s for the Mekong Delta, it must also realize the enormous potential in a change in aid and trade policies. An internationally administered development fund with ongoing resources not under the control of the Pentagons and State Departments of this world would not create overnight democracy in the ex-colonies. But it would make polyarchy much more of a possibility.

If "**Polyarchy**" is too negative, "**After the Revolution?**" is hopeful and intended for the New Leftist cynic rather than for the liberal enthusiast. Even though I have serious criticisms of it, I would recommend it to the thoughtful activist. It is a *realpolitik* defense of democracy in the Hobbesian tradition that explains constitutional rule as in the self-interest of the individual. And, like all theorists in this mode, Dahl misses the degree to which citizens are not simply individuals, but members of social classes with different, and quite unequal, access to power. But within this limitation, "**After the Revolution?**" provides a provocative discussion of the criteria for a democratic society. The revolutionary simplifiers of the Woodstock Nation could profit enormously from the analysis.

Moreover, Dahl has a sense of the radical uses of democratic values. General Motors, he points out, is a de facto public and social power that pretends to be a private enterprise whose legitimacy is open to challenge precisely in the name of Americanism. On an even deeper level, Dahl challenges the authoritarian organization of work within the corporation. He examines the relevance in this country of the Yugoslav experiment in self-management. But here again, his flawed method is in evidence, for the possibility of reorganizing the work place is not related to the structure of the economy itself. In Yugoslavia today, for instance, macroeconomic trends, like the growth of the private sector and the impact of market priorities, are subverting the self-management system. . . .

I disagree with Dahl's basic assumption and feel that in the most crucial cases political forms are dependent variables that economists and sociologists, not political scientists, must explain. But Dahl has collected fascinating data, and he speaks with a reasoned civility that makes dialogue possible. I cannot accept his basic approach, but I can recommend many of the uses he makes of it. (p. 12)

Michael Harrington, "'Polyarchy' and 'After the Revolution?'" in The New York Times Book Review (© 1971 by The New York Times Company; reprinted by permission), August 8, 1971, pp. 4-5, 12.

TODD GITLIN

[*After the Revolution?*] is clearly a response to the oppositional clamor [about pluralism], and a strangely ambiguous one. The title itself is a puzzle the book does not resolve: does Dahl look forward to "the revolution," or is he implying that the aftermath is a myth, or is he merely being coy? . . . His ambivalence haunts the book and informs it with the peculiar energy of a man trying to hold on to tradition yet leave it behind. On the one hand, he aims to refurbish a political theory of liberal democracy; on the other, incorporating a part of the radical critique, he wants to push past the limits of democratic theory as it has come to stultify American political discourse. The whole is unintegrated and finally unsuccessful, though in parts fascinating. But in all its ambivalence it might be a sign of a thaw in the liberal freeze—which is more than welcome, though the thaw is only beginning. (p. 117)

What shall justify authority? Dahl presents three criteria. The Criterion of Personal Choice is classical and fundamental, from Rousseau on down: simply that decisions correspond with one's personal choice. His second and third are more modern; Dahl deserves congratulations for the honesty with which he has codified two prejudices of authoritarian institutional life. His Criterion of Competence seeks "decisions informed by a special competence that would be less likely under alternative procedures." His Criterion of Economy emphasizes a decision-making procedure which "economizes on the amount of time, attention, and energy I must give to it."

About the first little need be said. It is the prime democratic principle and Dahl explores it nicely. He is properly sensitive to the need to secure minority rights by guaranteeing enclaves of autonomy within an overall system of interdependence, though he refrains from declaring whether those guarantees can in fact be granted "before the revolution." With regard to competence, Dahl resorts to the traditionally stultifying examples. Would you want the passengers to vote on the plane's or the ship's course? The patients to vote on the methods or criteria of surgery or the training of surgeons? "The fact that decision on some matter affects your interests in a vital way does not mean that it is necessarily rational for you to insist upon participating." True enough, but the trap lies in extending these analogies too far into the sphere of social decisions in general. The trap is especially well revealed when Dahl refers to the legitimate authority of parents over children; who could deny it? And yet one need not follow Wilhelm Reich in believing that all social pathology emanates from parental suppression of infantile sexuality to admit that children need guarantees against the repressive practices of the nuclear family. In society one does have the right to know the assumptions of the experts, to be aware of clashes among experts, to challenge them, and to choose other experts whose assumptions are more palatable. While Dahl fails to make this simple point, he does seem to realize that Competence can be used as an authoritarian club,

for he adds, somewhat anticlimactically: "The Criterion of Competence is politically neutral. In itself it is neither pro-democratic nor anti-democratic. Its implications for democracy depend on one's judgment about the competence of the ordinary person." Well, that all depends, doesn't it? So Dahl must finally add the most important point: "Even if it does not make sense for the ordinary man to try to take over the ship, the plane, or the operating room, it makes a great deal of sense for him to try to make sure that he can participate as much as he feels necessary in the affairs of the state."

The Criterion of Economy is more troublesome yet. Time and effort are scarce resources, and some decisions will not wait. Surely this point has been overlooked, for example by New Leftists, unencumbered by job or family, who used to like to say, "Freedom is an endless meeting." Now that it is clear that an endless meeting is merely an endless meeting, we may be sympathetic with Dahl's concern that proliferating democratic bodies would make unconscionable claims on people's time. Yet while one's time is certainly finite, one's allocation of it is not a function of eternally fixed human nature. Rather, the availability of effective and participatory democratic structures could encourage individuals to devote their time to them. There would still be limits to the spread of anyone's participation (more time devoted to the work council would mean less available for the living unit, child-care center, school, etc.), but those limits would extend beyond the boundaries of what is at present considered a "rational" use of one's time. Structures should be all the more participatory to attract participants, on the principle (which Dahl does not discuss) that, at least up to a point, the quality of decisions can be improved by engaging the widest span of people. "The only cure for democracy," as the saying goes, "is more democracy."

The second section of *After the Revolution?* is less provocative, though again an index of Dahl's growth. It begins with his Principle of Affected Interests: "Everyone who is affected by the decisions of a government should have the right to participate in that government." Straight out of early SDS. Dahl wants to temper this principle with the claims of Competence and Economy, but nonetheless he feels "it is . . . not such a bad principle to start with. It gives people who believe themselves to be seriously affected by decisions at least a *prima facie* case for participating in those decisions and puts the burden of exclusion on those who wish to press the criteria of Competence and Economy against their claims." This is as it should be. The problem is that some interests are illegitimate—most strikingly, the claims of capital against labor, the claims of highways and middle-class high-rises against poor neighborhoods—and ought not to be accorded standing. Dahl does not offer criteria for judging the weight of respective claims—that a resident's voice matters more than an intruder's, for example, and the poor's more than the unpoor. So his schema is again damaged by abstraction and a kind of atavistic recourse to moral neutrality.

Elsewhere in this chapter Dahl argues that there are advantages to representative, referendum and committee democracy, and to delegated authority, but this discussion too is crippled by abstraction. . . . Finally he turns warmly toward direct, primary or participatory democracy. . . . But he argues persuasively that the smaller, the more participatory the governing unit, the less effective it may be. "To insist upon primary democracy as the exclusive form of democracy is to condemn 'the people' to impotence." True enough, and good general advice to designers of a new order, though it is a caution that could easily become stultifying in the wrong hands. For Dahl does not balance this caution with its contrary—that institutions must be forced to deal with the concerted demands of large numbers of victimized people, not merely with too easily manageable "spokesmen." If some of him is still on the side of efficiency and the convenience of power holders, he has at least one leg over the fence and is trying to get to the other side.

This awkward posture is all the more plain in the book's final section, in which Dahl faces specific social problems and plants his principles in real soil. Problem number one: inequality of resources. The pluralist now grants—but is it news?—that "the opportunity to make effective personal choices, and hence the degree of individual freedom and opportunity, are markedly unequal in the United States." In the absence of money, sheer numbers, if properly organized, may wield a certain influence, but substantial power follows the dollar. But Dahl's emphasis on this fatal flaw in democratic theory is weakened by his separation of this problem from the next—lack of power over work. Exclusion of the public from important institutinal decisions—in other words, corporate capitalism and elite control of key institutions—*generates* inequality of resources and maintains it. The two problems must be solved together. Yet Dahl is unwilling to connect these matters with a systematic analysis of the relation between profit and wages, between control over the work process and remuneration. Instead, he steps aside with a sentence that nicely conveys the narrow framework within which he works [arguing that the American people are the greatest obstacle to democratization and the reduction of inequalities]. . . . (pp. 117-19)

Here is the recrudescence of pluralism, utterly innocent about the connection between the ruling class . . . and the, yes, bourgeois ideology which enmeshes other social sectors in accomplice roles. To blame the American people for inequality is like blaming the prisoners, the trusties, the guards and the bailiffs for the prison equally with the judges, the lawmakers, and the bureaucracies; and while that judgment is founded on a certain amount of truth, it is a partial and static truth *that can be overcome in practice* in the course of a revolutionary movement. But without a dialectical sense and a class analysis, Dahl's critique of inequality finally rings hollow. (p. 119)

Problem number two: The corporate Leviathan. One of the strongest, indeed most obvious, radical criticisms of Dahl and other pluralists was that, by riveting their attention to *governmental* decisions, they missed the most blatant hierarchies of power: corporate control over work, product, income and self-image. Dahl has absorbed the point. . . . He argues for workers' control over the decisions of economic enterprises, tempered by the rightful participation in corporate management of representatives of the public interests affected by investment, plant location, pollution, etc. (pp. 119-20)

Yet Dahl believes that the capitalism-socialism debate is "quaint and archaic." It is "foolish," he says, "to decide *a priori* that one form for governing economic enterprise is preferable to others in all circumstances." In this connection he comments on the inadequacy of the Socialist critique with its insistence on "public ownership" without troubling to formulate an anticentralist, anti-bureaucratic defintion of "public." His point is certainly well taken—too many Socialists have indeed been infatuated with central discipline and the nation-state—yet in his justified horror of Socialist centralization he concedes to the Socialist tradition only that it "helps to fill in some of the missing shades of the spectrum." The implication is that the other shades, the established ones, are legitimate. In counterposing the virtues of the market to the vices of central planning, he overlooks the possible uses of advanced two-way communications to coordinate production among different, decentralized enterprises and regions—which would avoid both the alienation and wastage of the market process and the political usurpation of central planners. Like many on the libertarian Right, Dahl confuses decentralization and the market, wholly scanting the Socialist critique of the "invisible hand" and ignoring the possibilities afforded by modern technology. His attraction for the market is more sentimental than convincing, and as for that other prime prop of capitalism, private ownership of the means of production, he has already shown its illegitimacy. What of capitalism remains to be preserved? (p. 120)

In the end, however, Dahl does hold out for genuine workers' control as against what he considers a more likely prospect, a kind of "interest group management" in which "public" representatives would serve, as Ralph Nader has urged, on corporate boards. Should this happen, the structure of power within the corporation would remain intact, and the "public" representatives would be responsible to nothing but their own consciences. But again, to imagine accountable public representatives together with workers' self-management is to imagine a sweeping social transformation in which a drive toward workers' control would be central though not sufficient. Dahl wants the result but cannot imagine the process.

Problem number three: The democratic Leviathan. Here Dahl points to problems of scale—the ungovernable megalopolis, the sheer magnitude of existing political units, which necessarily limit democratic participation. He is inclined toward an infrastructure of neighborhood government, the construction of cities of "intermediate" size, and the selection, by vote or lot, of representative advisory bodies for government officials. But while smaller functional units would certainly be indispensable in any overall reconstruction, much more is necessary. Dahl . . . ignores the potential uses of two-way media in inspiring participation and expediting referenda, and his references to the possibilities of neighborhood decentralization are curiously abstract. One wonders why he does not take the opportunity to say something about movements *in being* which seek precisely to secure neighborhood power—movements against urban renewal and for community control of police, for example. Is it a fastidious distaste for the actual workings of actual movements? Or a prejudice, at odds with his insistence on decentralized authority, tacitly assuming that reforms must be implemented from the top down? Dahl's utopian intimations, like those of Paul Goodman and others, are considerably denatured by being severed from strategy.

Eventually, Dahl calls for a vision of a new city, and that is welcome. Indeed, throughout his book he has occupied a space left free by radical default: the space of concrete utopian speculation. (pp. 120-21)

                    Todd Gitlin, "How Do We Mean To Live Our Lives?"
                    in The Nation *(copyright 1971* The Nation *magazine,*
                    The Nation Associates, Inc.), Vol. 213, No. 4, August
                    16, 1971, pp. 117-21.

AVERY LEISERSON

[*Polyarchy*] exemplifies beautifully the function of theory in disentangling the elements of a problem and understanding the relations between them, as distinct from constructing general, logically consistent theories that do not explain variations and deviant cases in the real world, or devising "practical" solutions without knowing whether or why they work. Dahl uses concepts to reveal and enlighten us as to hidden relationships in the data, rather than to gloss over or explain away factual discrepancies, contradictions, and complexities. Time and again, he punctures inflated claims and points out weaknesses in historical, economic-materialist, demographic, or psycho-cultural "explanations." He is never wholly critical, and takes great pains in each chapter to state explicitly what he has assumed, argued, concluded; what is speculative, proven, debatable, falsified, or not falsifiable. It is easy to ridicule, criticize, take advantage of such candor. We trust such a man, however, because he does not identify his analytical constructs (polarchy) with his preferences or ideals (democracy); he does not impose methodological standards upon his data that the latter will support only when forced and distorted to do so; he does not claim objective validity for a theory he believes in simply because he finds it subjectively necessary or satisfactory to assume it. In short, useful and revealing as Dahl's empirical theory of polyarchy is demonstrated to be in this study, he is the first to admit that it does not constitute the best, final, most complete, parsimonious, or "powerful" explanation of the conditions under which political systems change or are transformed from one type to another. (p. 214)

> *Avery Leiserson, "Law, Political Thought and Philosophy: 'Polyarchy: Participation and Opposition'," in* The Annals of The American Academy of Political and Social Science *(© 1971, by The American Academy of Political and Social Science), Vol. 397, September, 1971, pp. 213-14.*

ARNOLD A. ROGOW

A major difficulty with **"Polyarchy,"** as with most other efforts to construct models of complex political processes, is *not* that the data upon which it rests are non-existent, unreliable, incomplete, et cetera, but that we are never likely to acquire the necessary data in terms of which the model can be tested and significantly improved. As Dahl himself notes in a brief section titled "Some Qualifications," the data called for by most of his "conditions" are poor, fragmentary, or dubious, and even if this were not the case, the rank ordering of the seven conditions—determining which are of greater or lesser importance for one nation, much less all of them—would be extremely difficult if not impossible to accomplish. For example, in the case of the United States have egalitarian achievements been more or less important than the historical chance? For the United Kingdom does the reverse hold? Such questions not merely are unanswerable at the present time; they very likely will remain unanswerable.

A further problem with **"Polyarchy"** concerns the conditions Dahl assumes to be the crucial ones. Despite the inclusion of historical and socioeconomic variables the conditions are mainly political conditions, and to that extent neglect factors that may be far more crucial for the survival of polyarchy where it does exist, let alone its spread elsewhere. Surely polyarchy will be undermined by a continuing deterioration in the quality of life, by the accelerating decay of the urban centers, by growing violence, and by repeated and ever more serious "creditability" crises, whatever the fate of Dahl's seven conditions. What are the consequences for polyarchy of the alienation and anomie that appear to be increasing in the American polyarchy as well as those elsewhere? The closest Dahl comes to a discussion of

this question is in a chapter headed "Beliefs of Political Activists," and here much of the data for the United States, if not other countries, establishing that Americans have confidence in their political system, are, at the very least, out-of-date. One public opinion poll cited by Dahl dates back to March, 1940 (surely there must be a later survey), and the Almond-Verba five-nation study, upon which he draws extensively, was undertaken in 1959-60. Dahl writing in 1969-70 could not have known of the Pentagon Papers, but it seems a bit too cautious nevertheless to say of the Johnson years that ". . . the involvement of the United States in the Vietnam war seems to have drastically lowered the prestige of polyarchy (though not necessarily of democratic beliefs) among young people in the United States and probably elsewhere . . . a young person growing up in the United States in the late 1960's in all likelihood would not only be exposed to beliefs different from those of a young person in, say, 1950 or 1900, but the relative prestige of polyarchy, particularly as embodied in American institutions, would be lower." "Seems" to have lowered the prestige of polyarchy? Only "young people"? (pp. 617-18)

It is possible, of course, that polyarchy will continue to prevail despite endless futile wars and creditability crises, not to mention the apparently insoluble problems that afflict our cities and increasingly the suburbs. Perhaps what ultimately counts with Americans is not any of these difficulties but their indulgence of the propensity to consume more and more goods and services. Perhaps that is what it is all about: not Johnson or Nixon or Vietnam or crime or pollution or poverty but simply consumption. And if that is the case, does democracy itself matter very much? Most of us believe that it matters a good deal, but the reality for democracy may be similar to the reality for socialism as proclaimed by a disillusioned socialist some years ago. "There is no such thing as socialism," he declared, as he eyed the parties, leaders, and governments that were opportunistically proclaiming devotion to socialism. "There are only socialists." (pp. 618-19)

> *Arnold A. Rogow, "Will Polyarchy Prevail?" in* The Virginia Quarterly Review *(copyright, 1971, by The Virginia Quarterly Review, The University of Virginia), Vol. 47, No. 4 (Autumn, 1971), pp. 615-19.*

CHRISTOPHER LASCH

The chief value of Dahl's book *After the Revolution?* lies in its sustained attack on the folklore of primary democracy. It is useful to be reminded, however elementary the point may seem, that "participatory democracy" in the strict sense works, if it works at all, only in very small communities; and that because the complexity of industrial society makes it impossible for such communities to achieve complete autonomy, those who advocate direct democracy as a general program are advocating, in effect, a return to a simpler stage of social and economic organization. . . .

In the manner of one starting from the first principles of political theory, Dahl argues that democracy depends not on the direct participation of every individual but on the ability of the people to organize collectively, to make themselves heard as a body, to choose responsible representatives, to recall them at their pleasure, and in short to determine the main lines of public policy. (Clearly these things depend on the distribution of economic and educational resources.)

It is obvious that all institutions in American life are not equally democratic. "Private" corporations, academic or industrial, are not even formally democratic in their organization, unlike the state. Before arguing that they should be, according to Dahl, one must consult the "principle of competence," according to which authority should be exercised by those who are best qualified to exercise it and who understand the consequences of their decisions. . . . The argument for democracy in the state therefore depends on the proposition that "the ordinary man is more competent than anyone else to decide when and how much he shall intervene on decisions he feels are important to him." In order for this argument to apply also to the university or the private corporation, it must be shown that these institutions, although in most cases nominally private, actually embody political power, are intertwined with the state, and are public in everything but name. (p. 46)

The industrial corporation no doubt presents [a clear] case for democratization, and Dahl's discussion of this institution makes [Saul] Alinsky's talk of "proxy participation" seem shallow by comparison. There can be no question of the political character of the national and international corporation, Dahl argues: "The appropriation of public authority by private rulers . . . is the essence of the giant firm." Only a "purely ideological bias" prevents us from thinking of "all economic enterprise as a public service," in which employees and consumers, and in many cases the public in general, have as much interest as the stockholders.

How can this interest best be served? Nationalization—which Dahl identifies, perhaps too simply, as the "socialist" remedy—by no means guarantees that the public most affected by corporate decisions will be adequately protected. Workers, moreover, may lose their right to strike. A more plausible solution, but one that Dahl believes is no more satisfactory, is the gradual incorporation of consumer representatives on corporate boards. This is the strategy advocated by Ralph Nader and others—a variant of Alinsky's "proxy participation."

Dahl thinks that consumer representation, even if it were effective, would simply convert the corporation into "a system of rather remote delegated authority." It would be difficult to agree on what interests should be represented or on how they were to control their own representatives. Nevertheless this innovation, which corporations might accept in preference to more radical arrangements, "would probably be enough to deflate weak pressures for further change."

Since the alternatives seem equally unsatisfactory, Dahl has come to prefer the syndicalist solution (although he fails to acknowledge it as such): control of the corporation by its own employees. "Self-management" would "transform employees from corporate subjects to citizens of the enterprise." He recognizes the objection that the American working class may be incapable of self-management. Even more than the capitalist class, it is imbued with archaic ideas about property, which confuse property with ownership instead of defining it simply as a bundle of rights.

Dahl concedes, moreover, that the American worker regards his job "as an activity not intrinsically gratifying or worthwhile but rather as an instrument for gaining money which the worker and his family can spend on articles of consumption." . . .

Dahl thinks that these attitudes, however, might change once self-management was actually in operation. . . . Dahl believes that worker control is especially likely to be sought by workers who still view their work as a profession—that is, by the tech-

nical and professional strata themselves. At this point he abruptly drops the argument and turns to a discussion of decentralization.

His failure to press it leaves several difficulties unresolved. In the first place, he relies on "external controls, both governmental and economic," to protect the interests of consumers and the community in general, whereas one of the best arguments for worker control is that corporate employees, because they are also citizens of society as a whole, are competent not only to manage the corporation's internal affairs, with the help of professional managers, but to protect the interests of society. (p. 47)

Dahl argues that it would be "unworldly" to suppose that once the workers control an enterprise they will spontaneously act "in the interests of all." The trouble with this argument is that it pays too little attention to the political battles through which self-management will have to be achieved and to the possibility that these battles will serve as a political education for those who initiate them. Indeed it is precisely the antisocial consequences of private production that are likely to generate a movement for worker control. To Dahl's objection—"if self-management were introduced today, tomorrow's citizens in the enterprise would be yesterday's employees"—one can only reply that self-management is hardly likely to be introduced from above. It will have to be "introduced" by the workers themselves, not "today," but after long struggles in the course of which the workers' outlook could be expected to undergo changes that seem almost inconceivable at the present time.

By ignoring the political movements that would be necessary to make self-management a reality, Dahl exposes his argument to another objection, namely, that his case for worker control is curiously abstracted from current political life. If his argument for "self-management" were to carry more than the force of a political scientist's recommendation, it would have to be shown that political forces already in motion make it a real and not merely a hypothetical alternative. (pp. 47-8)

Dahl's reluctance to embark on a discussion of this question suggests a lingering belief in the separability of academic disciplines—history, presumably, can safely be left to historians, while political scientists concern themselves with an abstract model of the political process. He prefers to regard the structure of the corporation as a question "more technical than ideological," a matter "less of principle than of practical judgment." . . . The reason these formulations are evasive is that changes in the social structure will come about only when they are incorporated into the program of a political movement. Mass politics, moreover—the only agency of democratic change—contains an unavoidable admixture of ideology. Questions of principle cannot be indefinitely postponed. (p. 48)

Christopher Lasch, "Can the Left Rise Again?" in The New York Review of Books *(reprinted with permission from* The New York Review of Books; *copyright © 1971 Nyrev, Inc.), Vol. XVII, No. 6, October 21, 1971, pp. 36-48.**

HEINZ EULAU

The dilemma of democracy, as Dahl and Tufte see it [in *Size and Democracy*], is rooted in the ineluctable circumstance that every unit of government is constrained by its size (especially of population, but also of land area, natural resources, gross national product, and so on). If, as they posit, citizen effectiveness and system capacity are equally important criteria for judging the viability of a democratic polity, the intrusion of the size factor makes for democracy's dilemma: all other things being equal, the smaller the polity, the more will citizens act responsibly and competently in controlling public decisions, but the less will be the system's capacity to respond to citizen preferences. Citizen participation in collective decisions and the collectivity's ability to respond to citizen preferences are inversely related. As a result, the determination of a governmental unit's optimal size necessarily involves a tradeoff between the two criteria of democracy.

This theme Dahl and Tufte pursue with relentless logic and a good deal of empirical evidence. They pursue it at varying levels of governmental complexity—in terms of countries, of equivalent units within countries, and of local versus national units. They pursue it in terms of classical propositions about the optimal size of the polity, from Aristotle to John Stuart Mill, and they pursue it in terms of aggregate statistics and survey data. They introduce, where necessary or desirable, considerations of social and political processes, like representation, coalition politics, group conflicts, or party competition, that often confound the assumption of *ceteris paribus* so essential to theoretical clairvoyance. Where, then, do they come out?

When setting out on their investigation, Dahl and Tufte assumed, as had their predecessors, that it is possible to stipulate some "optimal democratic unit." The assumption proved illusory, and they conclude that "no single type or size of unit is optimal for achieving the twin goals of citizen effectiveness and system capacity." . . . This is so because "democratic goals conflict, and no single unit or kind of unit can best serve these goals." . . . (pp. 1301-02)

Whither, then, is democratic theory to leap? One task, Dahl and Tufte suggest, "may be to specify not an optimal unit but an optimal number of units with comparatively fixed boundaries." . . . And, leaping ahead fearlessly, the authors yet warn that "boundaries of each unit would be too small or too large for all functions assigned to it; but the costs of a small number of units with relatively fixed boundaries would be less than the costs of any larger number of units. . . ." All of which leaves me quite perplexed, for as of last count I am living in some dozen units of varying size, and though reasonably competent in these matters, I find my effectiveness as a citizen is only matched by the incapacity of these units to respond to my preferences, not the least important of which is some reduction in the costs that stem from their multiplicity. Unfortunately, Dahl and Tufte do not provide any clue about how to fix an optimal number of units that would get me out of my predicament. How few are few, and how many are many units? How does specifying an optimal number of units differ from specifying the optimal size of a single unit? And would not the optimal number of units depend on the optimal size of the subordinate or superordinate units in which a given function is performed with least cost? (p. 1302)

Heinz Eulau, "Book Reviews: 'Size and Democracy'," in The American Political Science Review *(copyright, 1974, by The American Political Science Association), Vol. LXVIII, No. 3, September, 1974, pp. 1301-03.*

LINWOOD R. WALL

[*Size and Democracy*] is both an important and timely study—important because it is an original attempt to address system-

atically the relations of size to democracy; timely, because it seeks answers to many of today's most urgent questions. (p. 207)

The authors' investigations lead them to the general conclusion: size is related to democracy but "no single type or size of unit is optimal for achieving the twin goals of citizen effectiveness and system capacity. . . . Democratic goals conflict and no single unit or kind of unit can best serve these goals. Secondly, the goal of maximizing citizen effectiveness on matters that are highly important to him can and does conflict with the effort to maximize the capacity of the political system." . . .

Although the authors' awareness of relevant scholarly literature and skillful use of empirical data are impressively arrayed in arriving at these conclusions, these are findings, as they acknowledge, which may be said to coincide with "what has been known all along." . . . But what we perhaps did not know all along or fully appreciate is the authors' equally relevant finding that democratic ideas as we have known them up to now provide no adequate guide for discovering answers to the crucial problems posed in the topic explored in the book. The authors provide us with a variety of interesting and important conceptualizations and empirical findings in searching for answers to the questions posed. In many instances, however, they are restricted by the rather severe limitations imposed by lack of suitable data for hypothesis testing. Thus, often conjecture and a high level of generalization characterize attempts to formulate definitive answers to questions or to formulate propositions affording insights into probable answers. Fortunately, the authors are aware of data limitations and are careful to acknowledge their impact on the nature of their findings. (pp. 207-08)

Linwood R. Wall, "Politics: 'Size and Democracy'," in The Annals of The American Academy of Political and Social Science *(© 1975, by The American Academy of Political and Social Science), Vol. 418, March, 1975, pp. 207-08.*

GEORGE VON der MUHLL

From the moment of its publication, *Who Governs?* elicited stronger reactions than any of Dahl's other works. These reactions fell into two reasonably well-defined phases. At first, the reception was overwhelmingly favorable. It is easy to see why. Dahl's chosen approach to his subject committed him (and his research team) to reconstructing in great detail a set of critical decisions in several different issue areas. By adopting this approach, he was able to accumulate evidence bearing directly on the demonstrated ability of the participants in each of these areas to initiate proposals later adopted as actual policy or to successfully block proposals initiated by others. The solid factual base of the research was illuminated, moreover, by explanatory propositions and conceptual distinctions formulated in sophisticatedly universal terms with Dahl's customary linguistic precision. . . . Only later, as a second generation of critics began to contemplate the possible ideological implications of these conclusions and then the methods by which they were reached, did *Who Governs?* begin to attract censure as a primary exhibit in the apologetic literature on American pluralist democracy.

That *Who Governs?* should have had so striking an impact on the discipline of political science is of some significance in itself. As the subtitle ("Democracy and Power in an American City") indicates, the book is a report on research conducted in the single city of New Haven, Connecticut. On its face, the specific findings of the study would therefore seem to have rather limited significance for those not deeply engrossed by the politics of New Haven. But since quite the opposite has proved true, there is perhaps some excuse for underlining the point. New Haven is not Floyd Hunter's Atlanta, nor is it the Lynds' Muncie, Indiana—let alone the United States of America. Criticism based on the supposition that it somehow stands for these other locales as well and that its empirical findings must be reconciled with conclusions drawn from studies of such places would seem misplaced, to say the least. The urgency of such efforts seems predicated on movement from the questionable empirical generalization that governments everywhere are only a front for overtly nonpolitical economic interests to the conclusion that any given study of government must be judged by the extent to which it unmasks such connections. Those not committed to that syllogism need experience no difficulty in entertaining the possibility that, whatever may be true of Community X, New Haven is a pluralist democracy led by multiple coalitions centering on the elected mayor (the finding reported by Dahl and his associates).

Something like this syllogism must be invoked to account for the intensity of the criticisms to which Dahl's research strategy has been subjected. For, taken on its own terms, the approach is surely more defensible than most. Instead of presupposing a unified power elite, it treats the matter as an open question to be settled by investigation; instead of employing a terminology that begs the question of whether inequalities are cumulative and stable over time in all sectors of society with regard to all issues, it disaggregates the concept of a power structure into elements that become joined empirically, if at all. Rather than collecting data on opinions as to who holds "power," it calls for direct investigation of the phenomenon through reconstruction of issues in which actors actually seek to effect their will against opposition. There is nothing in the logic of this procedure that precludes the possibility of uncovering a pyramidal pattern of power. It is consequently as misleading to call this research procedure the "pluralist" approach as it is to suggest that those who uncover a pattern of dispersed inequalities approve, as citizens, of what they have found. To call a political scientist a "pluralist" is therefore to traffic in a triple ambiguity.

More serious questions are raised by the unfortunately labeled "nondecisions" critique. For this critique is really an affirmation of the underlying logic of Dahl's research strategy, conjoined with a sharpened focus on the question of which issues are to be selected for study. On this point—clearly of paramount importance for a research strategy that proposes to draw general conclusions about the distribution of political power in a community from an examination of the terms on which specific issues are resolved—Dahl is uncharacteristically brief and unsystematic. In his 325-page report he devotes only one short paragraph to explaining and justifying his choice of the three issue areas that are to form the subject of the succeeding three chapters, which in turn form the base for the remainder of the book. The criteria for the choice seem reasonable enough (though rather too *ad hoc* to serve as much of a guide to others wishing to undertake similar research elsewhere); and if one has considerable faith (as I do) in Dahl's grasp of the dynamics of New Haven politics, one may not be inclined to question the conclusions he draws from examining this particular set. Nevertheless, we are dealing at this point with matters of faith and authority, not with the usual demanding standards of the behavioral sciences. In particular, we are obliged to assume, on the basis of fragmentary evidence,

that Dahl remained as alert as his critics to the possibility that issues of potentially crucial political importance were kept off the public (governmental) agenda altogether, or reached that agenda only after several crucial decisional premises had already been established. In as apparently open, pluralistic, and politically vigorous a community as New Haven, such a "mobilization of bias" does not in fact seem especially likely. But it is surely warranted to suggest, as David Easton has done, that the "gatekeeping" activities of the political system deserve as much attention as the management of conflict within the political arena, and that a comprehensive research strategy should systematically direct attention to both elements of the process. (pp. 1082-84)

[*Polyarchy*], despite its slender size, is breathtaking both in its scope and in the foundational character of its analysis. By any standard, it is a major contribution to the systematic study of democracy. Not since the days of Lor Bryce had any scholar dared to undertake a full-scale empirical exploration of the principal social, economic, cultural, and political conditions necessary for a democratic order, and in Bryce's time it was still possible to confine one's attention to Great Britain and its dominions, Western Europe, and a select group of nations in the Western Hemisphere. Yet Dahl's short chapters deal so directly with the leading explanations for the emergence and survival of democratic politics that one quickly comes to take for granted an enterprise that, in the range of countries considered and in the explicitness of the propositions regarding them, has in fact no real parallels in the literature of comparative politics. Much as Dr. Watson reacted to Sherlock Holmes's deductions, one marvels after the fact that no contemporary political scientist had thought to take up so obvious a project before Dahl did so himself.

For *Polyarchy* is, in its broad structural outlines, a treatise of striking simplicity. In its first sentence it poses a problem of immediately compelling interest: "Given a regime in which the opponents of the government cannot openly and legally organize into political parties in order to oppose the government in free and fair elections, what conditions favor or impede a transformation into a regime in which they can?" The remainder of the book is strictly limited to answering that question. (pp. 1086-87)

So great is the scope of the book, and so brief the compass, that some sacrifice of complexity predictably occurs. The sacrifice is far less than one might anticipate. Dahl's concise discussion of the failure of democracy in Argentina should suffice to dispel the impression that *Polyarchy* contains no more than superficial correlations of questionably aggregated variables. It is hard to think of a more pointed short discussion of the complex relationship between socioeconomic inequality and political democracy than the one Dahl offers here. Some topics do suffer more severely than others from Dahl's extreme compression—particularly the chapter on the alternative historical paths of regime transformation and the discussion of the relation of levels of economic development to the prospects for political competition. On the whole, however, *Polyarchy* must rank as one of the most impressive instances in the entire political science literature of saying much in little space.

It is inevitable that, in discussing the socio-political matrix of competitive politics in some thirty nations on six continents, Dahl should posit several disputable empirical connections. Each regional specialist will have his or her own list. It is perhaps more profitable to discuss at this point the approach Dahl employs. In essence, his strategy may be characterized as a succession of sophisticated applications of John Stuart Mill's Methods of Difference and of Agreement. Noting that polyarchal politics prevails in some countries but not in others, he seeks to account for its presence or absence by referring to the relative position of the countries under consideration on a succession of scales that middle-range theories of politics plausibly indicate to have some connection to these outcomes.

These methods have served comparative analysts very well. They may indeed be said to comprise—as Mill was wont to argue—the core of the comparative method. They invite explicit identification of the key causal and dependent variables, and explicit specification of the relationship among them. The approach tends to suffer, on the other hand, (as Mill himself quite clearly saw), from the uncertainties introduced when other theoretically relevant factors are neither totally different in all save one respect, nor totally similar in all save one. More disturbingly, it encourages examination of the variables in analytic isolation rather than as elements of organic systems.

Dahl's treatise suffers significantly from these limitations. He seldom makes use of a cumulatively refined structure of partial correlations; rather, each causal variable is separately examined in relation to his countries as part of an aggregating causal chain. Thus, in one chapter he will consider the relationship of agrarian society to polyarchy in New Zealand, Costa Rica, and India; in another, the significance of per capita income level in these countries; in a third, the degree of ethnic pluralism. But how the possibilities for competitive politics are affected in any one country by one of these variables, given the potentially synergistic effects arising from the specific levels attained by the other two in the presence of still other theoretically relevant variables, this approach does not permit us to judge. The theoretical yield from his study is therefore not so much a theory (despite the title of Dahl's final chapter) as a tabulation of loosely related propositions about conditions favoring or opposing polyarchy. It is perhaps for this reason that Dahl's analysis is at its least persuasive in accounting for such anomalies as polyarchy's lack of resilience in Uruguay, its surprising durability in pre-modern Switzerland and contemporary India, and its prospective emergence with significant modification in Mexico, Kenya, and Tanzania. More contextual forms of analysis clearly have their drawbacks as well; it may well be that *all* approaches on a global scale must remain merely searchlights in the dark. (pp. 1087-88)

[*Size and Democracy*] is a groundbreaking effort to operationalize the various politically relevant dimensions of jurisdictional "size" so as to make possible their correlation with the presence and quality of "democratic" political life. (p. 1090)

Unhappily, *Size and Democracy* falls far short of [its] goal. Little more can be positively affirmed regarding the connection between the two than before the book appeared. The reasons have more to do with the nature of the subject matter than with the limitations of the authors. Among the more prominent difficulties are the apparent unavailability at the time of directly pertinent data beyond a single study of local government in Sweden; the recurrent indications that cross-national comparisons yield less reliable conclusions than comparisons of subnational governments within one country; the useful but essentially negative finding that size alone is seldom as important as institutional, historical, and socioeconomic factors in explaining differences among democratic regimes; and the inherent problems—already referred to in the discussion of *Polyarchy*—of any single-variable causal analysis. It remains, of course, the singular merit of Dahl and his coauthor to have

carried the inquiry as far as they did on the basis of such limited and qualitatively uneven evidence. They carried through their task, moreover, with a clarity of formulation that reveals the precise obstacles to a more extended pursuit of the topic. It is not, therefore, too much to say that their ultimate failure is in many ways more instructive to contemplate than other more conclusive comparative studies. (p. 1091)

After the Revolution? . . . should be read [in the context of the political disruptions of the 1960's]. It is, of all Dahl's essays, the one most directly responsive to a specifically identifiable mood during a particular historical crisis. More, perhaps, than any other of his works, its agenda is set—on first reading, at least—by the issues of the hour. Its eye-catching cover, with its banners and headbands, is aimed squarely at an undergraduate clientele. From the question-begging title to the avuncular conclusion it serves as an emblem of the period it addresses.

Yet Dahl himself does not merely float with the stream. Despite the first-person mode of address, which often sounds alternately patronizing and irritable in cold print, *After the Revolution?* is an intensely serious short treatise for readers whom Dahl takes seriously. Its topical prolegomena lead quickly to more enduring matters. "Revolutions," Dahl notes with commendable acidity, now occur at the level of women's hemlines, but the authentically revolutionary potential of the democratic ideal can never be wisely discounted. After the latest "revolution" is over, the problem that troubled the ancient Greeks will remain with us—how to reconcile the exigencies of public governance with the belief that only those governments are legitimate that permit direct and continuous participation by the citizen in the exercise of their authority. (p. 1092)

[In] reviewing the totality of Dahl's works one notes repeatedly his nominalist tendency to make more of differences than of similarities. Rigorous and subtle in thought, and keenly sensitive to the texture of human motives and objectives, he is inclined to differentiate where others synthesize. It may seem odd to apply this characterization to a social scientist far better known for his simplified categories and diagrams than for his interest in—or flair for—contextual historical narration. Yet it accounts, I believe, for a rather predictable division of perspective between Dahl and his critics. Where they see capitalism and socialism, he sees a mixed assortment of control techniques. Where they see social structures, he writes of classless actors, or actors bearing categorical background traits, who pursue multiple objectives with limited resources. Their ruling elites become, by his criteria, contingent coalitions identified through detailed investigation of particular issues. When they treat the phenomenon of "power," he asks "over whom, with respect to what, and with what probability of compliance?" Dahl's formulations are generally by far the more logically compelling in their analytic rigor. Neither Dahl nor his critics, however, have explicitly and persuasively addressed themselves to the perhaps ultimately unanswerable problem of how to decide at what point "marginal" differences become "fundamental" similarities. Accordingly, it seems likely that Dahl's critics will continue to attach more significance than he to the structural elements defining the political arenas he chooses to investigate.

This decompositional—literally analytic—propensity is undoubtedly linked to Dahl's commitment to methodological individualism. Like the economists, whose approach to social science he quite evidently finds congenial, he is most in his element when discussing the rational responses of individual actors to a parametrically established environment. This commitment gives his work a solidity of motivational grounding and a sharpness of focus that much sociological theory so conspicuously lacks. At the same time, he has not yet found a theoretical paradigm for discussing systematically the aggregate consequences of individual choice that result in the emergence of new properties at the systemic level. In this respect his work lags behind the achievements of both classical and contemporary economic theory, and even behind the contributions of the rational behavior theorists in political science. It is partly also for this reason that he is at his least illuminating in discussing at the systemic level such phenomena as power deflation, regime breakdown and transformation, the dynamic relation between coercion and persuasion, and the like. Recently, Dahl has taken up aggregate analysis in his comparative studies of democracy; but in doing so, he has adopted a relatively conventional correlational approach that obscures many vital questions of systemic functioning.

Perhaps it is also this affinity for economic reasoning that accounts for the curious status of value formation in Dahl's works. When not altogether ignored, the binding force of a commitment to publicly defined values is either discounted without argument or reduced to a formula for realizing private preferences. Dahl's political actors pursue fixed goals derived from their personal utility curves; and while their behavior is a function of the resources available to them, of the degree to which their interests are affected, and of the manipulative skills of their competitors and opponents, they do not appear to change their course of conduct in light of an emerging understanding of their shared responsibilities as members of a collective social order. Thus the U.S. Supreme Court becomes, in one of Dahl's early essays, merely a decision-making agency whose members express preferences that may be overridden by other power groups whose vital interests are affected. Later, the relative stability of the various democracies is accounted for through configurations of interests and resources, and authority itself is discussed in terms of personal needs and individual calculations of opportunity costs. Seen in these terms, "authority" becomes scarcely distinguishable from "influence," and is exercised in much the same manner in relation to very similar objectives. Citizens are consumers who experience no schizophrenia regarding their public and private roles because they have never undergone the transformation described by Rousseau. Such an approach substitutes a welcome realism concerning enduring human motives and calculations for the question-begging terminology in which the concept of political authority is too often discussed. Its price is that of making the game of politics appear far simpler than it is.

These paradigmatic elements in Dahl's work continually inform his analysis of contemporary democracy. His nominalist sensitivities, together with his sympathy for the organizing behavioral premises of traditional economic theory, preclude his acceptance of theories of modern large-scale democracy in which the actions of democratic governments are presented as the enactment of a consensual popular will. Like Joseph Schumpeter before him, he sees the concept of a unified, rationally informed, disinterested, operational, unambiguously articulated popular will as a will-o'-the-wisp in complex societies, an artifact conjured up by populistic demagogues and dictators to cover the lack of mechanisms for authentic public consultation. Such ideational entities have no motive force within his analytic framework. Government in any modern society, he insists, is necessarily predicated, one way or another, on the enduring reality of differences of opinion and interest. Democratic governments are to be distinguished from other regimes by the legitimacy they grant to the expression of such differences, and by their commitment, in undertaking collectively binding actions that unavoidably favor some interests over others, to adhering to formulas that enhance continuing cooperation among people who do not agree.

In Dahl's view, moreover, modern, large-scale democratic (or polyarchal) government is, like other governments, a government by elites. It rests on a political division of labor in which some voices are heard more loudly than others. It is crucially differentiated from other forms of elite government by the effective guarantees it offers to oppositional elites who publicly contest the continued tenure in office of incumbent teams of leaders. For it is mainly such contests, Dahl has contended with unmistakably Schumpeterian logic, that enable citizens to make the choices necessary to enforcing some degree of correspondence between their preferences and the politics of the governing elites. Not by the values a government espouses, nor yet by its class composition, can we judge the authenticity of a democratic order, but rather by the political provisions it makes for holding governmental leaders effectively accountable to the led. (pp. 1094-95)

The centrality to Dahl's thinking of an institutional conception of democracy—of democracy (polyarchy) as an arrangement requiring political elites to seek the legitimation necessary for governance through a relatively fair and open competition for popular support—is thus beyond serious question. It is a concept that presupposes conflict rather than transcendent consensus; that focuses on actors and coalitions rather than on cybernetic equilibrations; that pays more heed to rational strategies to attain determinate goals than to unconscious psychic needs that may have been fulfilled in the process. It asserts the intrinsic importance of political institutions independently of the class interests that may at any particular time be served by the outcomes. Dahl's theoretical understanding of democracy assumes that democratic politics is more a process for implementing interests than for transforming values, and it is generally inclined to discount rather heavily the controlling efficacy of sentiments of sharing, caring, and mutual trust. As the defining contours of its principal lines of thought were already visible in *The Federalist Papers*, it will, in all probability, remain subject to the kinds of praise and criticism that that treatise on republican government has long evoked.

Dahl's choice of paradigms, and the implications of his choices, are of exceptional significance to all students of politics because . . . his outstanding contribution to the discipline is as its teacher by example. It is through the problems he selects, through the questions he asks, and through the criteria he establishes in answering them, far more than through the findings he reports or the research methods he has developed for obtaining them, that he commands our continuing attention. By and large, he has proved an admirable teacher. He has set a standard of rigor and accuracy, of universalistic theoretical speculation and relentlessly subtle and detailed analysis, that few have matched and none surpassed. In an era of esoteric specialization and turbid expression, of casual scholarship too often propelled by rancorously partisan rhetoric, these qualities cannot readily be overvalued. One must also acknowledge the limits they necessarily entail. (p. 1096)

George Von der Muhll, "Robert A. Dahl and the Study of Contemporary Democracy: A Review Essay," in The American Political Science Review *(copyright, 1977, by The American Political Science Association), Vol. LXXI, No. 3, September, 1977, pp. 1070-96.*

Mary Daly

1928-

Daly, an American theologian, philosopher, and author of books on feminism and theology, is an influential feminist theorist. Daly received her education at Catholic institutions and is now a professor of theology at Boston College. In her first major criticism of the Catholic Church, *The Church and the Second Sex* (1968), she contends that a systematic denigration of women is evident in Church doctrine and practice. She recommends, among other remedies, that the Church allow the ordination of women, and encourages women to voice their protests individually and in groups, as Daly herself did at Harvard University in 1971 by leading a walkout from a Christmas Mass. In *Beyond God the Father* (1973) Daly expresses her frustration with the Church's resistance to change and questions the usefulness of protest from within. *Gyn/Ecology* (1978), her most recent book, shows that doubt has become certainty: Daly now rejects all world religions as patriarchal and therefore inimical to women. This philosophical position is a leap from her earlier stance of loyal opposition, and has made *Gyn/Ecology* a widely read and controversial contribution to feminist theory. (See also *Contemporary Authors*, Vols. 25-28, rev. ed.)

Photograph by Gail Bryan; © 1978

Excerpt from *GYN/ECOLOGY: THE METAETHICS OF RADICAL FEMINISM*

Western society is still possessed overtly and subliminally by christian symbolism, and this State of Possession has extended its influence over most of the planet. Its ultimate symbol of processions is the all-male trinity itself. Of obvious significance here is the fact that this is an image of the procession of a divine son from a divine father (no mother or daughter involved). In this symbol the first person, the father, is the origin who thinks forth the second person, the son, the word, who is the perfect image of himself, who is "co-eternal" and "consubstantial," that is, identical in essence. So total is their union that their "mutual love" is expressed by the procession (known as "spiration") of a third person called the "Holy Spirit," whose proper name is "Love." This naming of "the three Divine Persons" is the paradigmatic model for the pseudo-generic term *person*, excluding all female mythic presence, denying female reality in the cosmos.

This triune god is one act of eternal self-absorption/self-love. The term *person* is derived from the Latin *persona* meaning actor's mask, or character in a play. "The Processions of Divine Persons" is the most sensational one-act play of the centuries, the original *Love Story*, performed by the Supreme All Male Cast. Here we have the epitome of male bonding, beyond the "best," i.e., worst, dreams of Lionel Tiger. It is "sublime" (and therefore disguised) erotic male homosexual *mythos*, the perfect all-male marriage, the ideal all-male family, the best boys' club, the model monastery, the supreme Men's Association, the mold for all varieties of male monogender mating. (pp. 37-8)

This mythic paradigm of the trinity is the product of christian culture, but it is expressive of *all* patriarchal patterning of society. Indeed, it is the most refined, explicit, and loaded expression of such patterning. Human males are eternally putting on the masks and playing the roles of the Divine Persons. The mundane processions of sons have as their basic but unacknowledged and unattainable aim an attempted "consubstantiality" with the father (the cosmic father, the oedipal father, the professional godfather). . . . Spirated by all these relations is the asphyxiating atmosphere of male bonding. And, as Virginia Woolf saw, the death-oriented military processions display the real direction of the whole scenario, which is a funeral procession engulfing all life forms. God the father requires total sacrifice/destruction.

Patriarchy is itself the prevailing religion of the entire planet, and its essential message is necrophilia. All of the so-called religions legitimating patriarchy are mere sects subsumed under its vast umbrella/canopy. They are essentially similar, despite the variations. All—from buddhism and hinduism to islam, judaism, christianity, to secular derivatives such as freudianism, jungianism, marxism, and maoism—are infrastructures of the edifice of patriarchy. All are erected as parts of the male's shelter against anomie. And the symbolic message of all the sects of the religion which is patriarchy is this: Women are the dreaded anomie. Consequently, women are the objects of male terror, the projected personifications of "The Enemy," the real objects under attack in all the wars of patriarchy. (pp. 38-9)

Radical feminism is not reconciliation with the father. Rather it is affirming our original birth, our original source, movement, surge of living. This finding of our original integrity is re-membering our Selves. . . . Radical feminism releases the inherent dynamic in the mother-daughter relationship toward friendship, which is strangled in the male-mastered system. Radical feminism means that mothers do *not* demand Self-sacrifice of daughters, and that daughters do not demand this of their mothers, as do sons in patriarchy. What both demand of each other is courageous moving which is mythic in its depths, which is spell-breaking and myth-making process. (pp. 39-40)

Women moving in this way are in the tradition of Great Hags. (p. 40)

Women choosing Hag-ocracy refuse to teach divine science to the kings of the earth, to initiate them into our mysteries. Hag-ocracy is the time/space of those who maintain a growing creative fury at this primal injustice—a fury which is the struggle of daughters to find our source, our stolen original divinity. (p. 41)

When I use the term *mythic* to describe the depths of meta-patriarchal Self-centering/be-ing, I mean to convey that the Dreadful Selves of women who choose the Wild Journey participate in the source of what the pale patriarchal myths reflect distortedly. . . . This participation is strength-giving, not in the sense of "supernatural elevation" through "grace" or of magic mutation through miracle drugs, but in the sense of creative unfolding of the Self. Metapatriarchal mythic a-mazing means repudiating saintliness and becoming wholly haggard, Holy Hags. As such, women are "wholly other" to those who are at home in the kingdom of the fathers. Dreadful women are "quite beyond the sphere of the usual, the intelligible, and the familiar." Indeed, women becoming "wholly other" *are* strange. Myth-living/loving Hags are members of the "Outsiders' Society." (pp. 49-50)

[The] attraction/need of males for female energy, seen for what it is, is *necrophilia*—not in the sense of love for actual corpses, but of love for those victimized into a state of living death. (p. 59)

[It] is a pitfall simply to reverse "penis envy" into "womb envy," for such theories trick women into fixating upon womb, female genitalia, and breasts as our ultimately most valuable endowments. Not only disparagement, but also glorification of women's procreative organs are expressions of male fixation and fetishism. These disproportionate attitudes are also demonically deceptive, inviting women to re-act with mere derivative fetishism, instead of deriding these fixations and focusing upon the real "object" of male envy, which is female creative energy in *all* of its dimensions. (p. 60)

Faced with being spooked, Spinsters are learning to Spook/Speak back. This Spinster-Spooking is also re-calling/re-membering/re-claiming our Witches' power to cast spells, to charm, to overcome prestige with prestidigitation, to cast glamours, to employ occult grammar, to enthrall, to bewitch. Spinster-Spooking is both cognitive and tactical. Cognitively, it means pattern-detecting. It means understanding the time-warps through which women are divided from each other—since each woman comes to consciousness through the unique events of her own history. It means also seeing the problems caused through space-warps—since Hags and potential Hags are divided from each other in separate institutional settings, disabled from sharing survival tactics in our condition of common isolation, spooked by our apparent aloneness. Tactically, Spooking means learning to refuse the seductive summons by the Passive Voices that call us into the State of Animated Death. It means learning to hear and respond to the call of the wild, learning ways of en-couraging and en-spiriting the Self and other Spinsters, learning con-questing, learning methods of dispossession, specifically of dis-possessing the Self of possession by the past and possession by the future. It means a-mazing the modern witch-craze, developing skills for unpainting the Painted Birds possessed through the device of tokenism, exposing the Thoroughly Therapeutic Society. (p. 318)

It is because women are known to be energy sources that patriarchal males seek to possess and consume us. This is done less dramatically in day-by-day draining of energy, in the slow and steady extinguishing of women's fire. Sparking is necessary to re-claim our fire. Sparking, like Spooking, is a form of Gyn/Ecology. . . . Light and warmth, which are necessary for creating and moving, are results of Sparking. Sparking is creating a room of one's own, a moving time/spaceship of one's own, in which the Self can expand, in which the Self can join with other Self-centering Selves. (p. 319)

In the course of this Voyage, we have seen that patriarchy is designed not only to possess women, but to prepossess/preoccupy us, that is, to inspire women with false selves which anesthetize the Self, breaking the process of be-ing on the wheel of processions. This condensing and freezing of be-ing into fragmented being is the necessary condition for maintaining the State of Possession. Condensation, or thing-ifying, makes "ownership" of Female Divinity possible, in the sense that it erases our awareness of this, our Process, and blocks our original movement. Yet it is not possible to own/possess Process itself. The confusion that is evoked in all women as a result of sensing simultaneously both the invincible reality of Female Process itself and its erasure/fragmentation in the foreground of our consciousness is the condition of being spooked. (p. 322)

The rulers of patriarchy—males with power—wage an unceasing war against life itself. Since female energy is essentially biophilic, the female spirit/body is the primary target in this perpetual war of aggression against life. Gyn/Ecology is the re-claiming of life-loving female energy. This claiming of gynergy requires knowing/naming the fact that the State of Patriarchy is the State of War, in which periods of recuperation from and preparation for battle are euphemistically called "peace." Furies/Amazons must know the nature and conditions of this State in order to dis-cover and create radical female friendship. Given the fact that we are struggling to emerge from an estranged State, we must understand that the Female Self is The Enemy under fire from the guns of patriarchy. We must struggle to dis-cover this Self as Friend to all that is truly female, igniting the Fire of Female Friendship. (p. 355)

Amazons can overcome the "sledge-hammer force" of the baffling spookers by naming them and by very explicitly analyzing/explaining their games. In this way we weave them into visibility/audibility/tangibility. We force them out of the shadows into our sight; we magnify the volume of their eerie whispers—removing their haunting inaudible mystery; we cool down their ghastly gases into puddles of liquid, so that we can bottle and label them, disable them. By this righteous objectifying of those whose intent is to objectify us we come to *know* the limits of their reality. This process is totally Other from their objectification/fetishization of Female Reality, by which they *impose* limits upon our be-ing. (pp. 408-09)

Spinning is creating an environment of increasing innocence. Innocence does not consist in simply "not harming." This is the fallacy of ideologies of nonviolence. Powerful innocence is seeking and naming the deep mysteries of interconnectedness. It is not mere helping, defending, healing, or "preventive medicine." It must be nothing less than successive acts of transcendence and Gyn/Ecological creation. In this creation, the beginning is not "the Word." The beginning is hearing. (pp. 413-14)

As Hags hear forth cosmic tapestries, re-membering the Original creation of the Goddess, there is a cacophony of cackles. Harpies harp; Hags haggle; Spinsters sputter; Crones croon; Furies fume. There is Dreadful dis-order. Some attempt to imitate/learn from the language of "dumb" animals, whose nonverbal communication seems so superior to androcratic speech. Thus, in the midst of the cackling there can be detected meowing, purring, roaring, barking, snorting, twittering, growling, howling. The noise of these solemn assemblies functions to distract the would-be invaders, baffling them. In fact, however, the tactic of distracting is not even a major intent of the singing Spinners. Our sounds are sounds of spontaneous exuberance, which the demon wardens vainly try to translate, referring to their textbooks of Demonology and Female Psychology.

Since the bafflers attempt to interpret the Crones' Chorus by the rules of the going logic, they remain baffled. Since they can hear only sounds but cannot hear hearing, they cannot break the code of the Gyn/Ecologists' Un-Convention, whose participants are hearing ever more deeply into the secret chambers of the labyrinth. Since the bafflers are only gamesters, they are unable to perceive the high creativity of Crones, which is playful cerebration. (p. 414)

> *Mary Daly, in her* Gyn/Ecology: The Metaethics of Radical Feminism *(copyright © 1978 by Mary Daly; reprinted by permission of Beacon Press), Beacon Press, 1978, 485 p.*

MYRTLE PASSANTINO

The French existentialist Simone de Beauvoir wrote a monumental study of women in 1949 entitled *The Second Sex*, in which she described a tradition of systematic oppressive antifeminism within the Catholic Church. She contended that Church doctrine makes an implicit—and deceptive—assumption about the "natural inferiority" of women that is used to perpetuate a double standard of morality in our patriarchal society. . . .

[Dr. Mary Daly] has found little to refute in Mlle. de Beauvoir's thesis. She checks it out point by point, in a book [*The Church and the Second Sex*] that is notable for its even-tempered, scholarly approach to an emotional subject, and then she goes more deeply into the historical background and present implications of the Church's attitudes toward women. . . . [The] misogynistic tendencies of the early Church have survived in various guises throughout the centuries. . . .

But antagonism toward women in general, as the author explains in a chapter called "The Pedestal Peddlars," coexists in the Church with an equally damaging fantasy of an Eternal Woman, singular, symbol of humility, selflessness and every passive virtue that can render her useful and submissive to men. High on her pedestal, she is displayed as "God's plan" for the female sex.

But, Mary Daly insists, women are not symbols—they are people. When a woman is regarded either as a subhuman possession or as a remote object of veneration, she cannot become a "developing, authentic *person*, who will be unique, self-critical, self-creating, active and searching." And a Church that does not permit this development "has deprived itself of the gift and insights of more than half its members."

This is a thoughtful, honest, provocative book. It opens some windows that Vatican II overlooked. It faces squarely all the implications of offering full equality to women in the Church. That could mean sharing the priesthood, a final step for which there is no valid theological barrier. Whether or not they can envision this possibility, Catholic women are challenged to begin working toward achieving responsible, creative partnership in a viable Church.

> *Myrtle Passantino, "Book Reviews: 'The Church and the Second Sex',"* in America *(reprinted with permission of America Press, Inc.; © 1968; all rights reserved), Vol. 118, No. 18, May 4, 1968, p. 646.*

WALTER ARNOLD

Miss Daly is hardly a roaring feminist. She expresses herself quietly, persuasively and pleasantly, if somewhat flatly. She is not the kind of writer some male had in mind when he said, "I agree with women's equality, but I don't want to read about it." If anything, **The Church and the Second Sex** is much too short. I wish the author had gone more deeply into both the historical and theological roots of the Church's attitude toward women and into the question of professional roles for women in the "new Church" and society. Dr. Daly's subject is exceedingly complex, and in less than 200 pages she barely has space to sketch it. But, then, she chose to write a kind of manifesto. (p. 26)

[The author finds] "Catholic antifeminism" reinforced by what she chooses to call the myth of the "eternal feminine," the symbol of Woman as having a special "nature," different from but complementing that of Man. This symbolism is a product of many forces, some of them having little to do with historical Christianity—platonism, chivalry, romanticism. At least half of the world's poetry and literature would be unintelligible without such a "myth." But Dr. Daly argues that what the symbol of "the real Woman" most accomplishes is the abstraction and separation of the sexes, so that there can be no real meeting between them.

Yet psychologists like Erich Fromm, who is no "pedestal peddler," have pointed out that there may be real psychological and social differences between men and women owing to their differing sexual roles. Miss Daly's view of equality is practically "asexual"; she seems to envision no differences whatever between men and women affecting their relationship, one to another, if not their role in society. Accordingly, she speaks of "partnership" rather than of "community." But her concerns in this book are typically those of the single, professional woman. I note that she quotes with approval the better side of

St. Paul: "There is neither Jew nor Greek, there is neither slave nor free, there is neither male nor female; for you are all one in Christ Jesus." Yet, certainly with regard to the sexes, this is an eschatological statement. It cannot be completely understood in terms of present realities, and is not especially helpful.

These difficulties do not prevent Miss Daly's book from being an important one as far as it goes. Her argument that the Church, by virtue of its mission, should lead in opening up the possibilities of personal fulfillment for women is irrefutable. Her "modest proposals" of practical steps, such as priestly functions for women, are imperative. If the Catholic Church would listen to what Professor Daly suggests it would add immeasurably to its "credibility" as an institution. (pp. 26-7)

Walter Arnold, "Gypped by Gender," in Saturday Review *(copyright © 1968 by* Saturday Review; *all rights reserved; reprinted by permission), Vol. LI, No. 31, August 3, 1968, pp. 26-7.*

MARY ELLMANN

[Ms. Daly] musters philosophy, theology, and psychology for a new "cosmic covenant" [in *Beyond God the Father*]. The potpourri is sometimes portentous, sometimes witty. Ms. Daly seems bold, brave, erratic, and adventurous—an eccentric Roman Catholic in theology, a sort of existentialist in philosophy. And her solution is androgyny: the mere substitution of *She* for *He*, in reference to God, will not suffice. Phallic consciousness must go, and so must all perpetuations of dualism.

But still, since the egg broke into yolk and white, it isn't clear how androgyny is meant to operate. This is, of course, a legitimate obscurity: prophets are not obliged to subdivide Utopia. On the other hand, we are not obliged to honor their speculations. I feel I need a precise account of androgynous action. For the sexes, if conceivably possible, to relinquish criticism of each other may be an androgynous benefit. But for them to become psychically indistinguishable would be dreary, if not dangerous. What would attract them to each other? . . . I would wish to keep both sexes distinct and discrete so that they can still enjoy encounters. (p. 19)

Mary Ellmann, "Women's Work," in The New York Review of Books *(reprinted with permission from* The New York Review of Books; *copyright © 1973 Nyrev, Inc.), Vol. XX, No. 17, November 1, 1973, pp. 18-19.**

DORIS DONNELY

Mary Daly usually does not tease. Coy she is not. Nor playful. Nor shy. (p. 39)

Something of a wonder, then, and a disappointment, that the bristling, forthright tone that so suited the expository style of [*The Church and the Second Sex*] is too weak and anemic for her second women's lib book, *Beyond God the Father*. Like her first book, Mary Daly's newest is tough and punchy, but times and turf have changed so that rabid *aficionados* of books, articles and every New York *Times* Op-Ed piece on women's lib like me, who seethe with fury at sexist injustice or who revel in the occasional triumphs of our sisters' struggles toward becoming human, are now looking to other women, not for fighters, but for leaders; not for muscle, but for body; not for aggression, but for passion. And passion with a flesh-and-blood body is precisely what is missing from Mary Daly's book.

More than that, Daly teases us with insights that she hints at, toys with, but does not deliver on. Certainly, a patriarchal symbol system is inadequate, but what precisely is it that women can add to our understanding of the Deity that a one-sided masculine imagery lacks? . . . [The] discussion has advanced, and we are no longer interested in repeating truisms; now comes the strenuous and creative encounter with the feminine force in creation. And Mary Daly tells us nothing new about the feminine, nothing new about who woman is—her sexuality—how woman is different so that the complementarity of an androgynous symbol system would make sense.

And more. "Why indeed must 'God' be a noun?" Daly asks. "Why not a verb—the most active and dynamic of all?" . . . [My] own juices are left unstirred by God as either noun or verb, since God makes sense and gives meaning to both only as Person. And the connections that I would have to make to confront process theology and a static metaphysic juxtaposed with noun and verb imagery is simply an unnecessary and antiseptic cerebral exercise to me.

Similarly, I find Daly's strident position for abortion lacking in credibility. . . . Like Daly, I am appalled at the simple fact that a woman faced with an unwanted pregnancy virtually has only the choice of abortion or of giving birth and raising the child. Unlike Daly, however, and awed by medical doubts concerning the potential and rights of organisms that cannot support themselves, I would opt for the energies and monies of civilized people to be directed toward the discovery and implementation of other alternatives—not only toward more refined birth control education, but, more importantly, toward a healthy psychological acceptance of unwanted pregnancies, more freedom in the adoption process and a fundamental loving posture towards life.

Mary Daly has looked forward and backward with unabashed anger, an anger which has grown more apocalyptic with the passing of time. Time has not made anger irrelevant, just insufficient. We still do not have the feminist philosophy-theology book which looks inward with secure self-respect and outward with competent love. (pp. 40-1)

Doris Donnelly, "'Beyond God the Father: Toward a Philosophy of Women's Liberation'," in America *(©America Press, 1974; all rights reserved), Vol. 130, No. 2, January 19, 1974, pp. 39-41.*

MARGARET O'BRIEN STEINFELS

Mary Daly's *Beyond God the Father* is of [the utopian] genre—Christianity without its stumbling blocks: God, Christ, sin, and salvation. It is a theological fantasy about religion freed from the patriarchal mentality. . . .

Beyond God the Father, which promises to be a fantasy about liberated men and women toward a truer understanding of the "ultimate reality," intermittently becomes a blind and ignorant assault on the sins and sinners of the past. The earthly utopia is frequently submerged, along with most of our already tenuous religious beliefs and symbols, in a wash of dubious arguments and spurious history. *Beyond God the Father* is, in fact, an unreadable book. Having read it, I find much of it unthinkable, and having thought about it, conclude that many of its positions are untenable. Those able to forage their way through the densest and darkest of prose, with as open a mind as possible and shield and buckler in place, will find themselves confronted by an enraged and furious theologian: Yahweh hath no fury like Mary Daly.

Many readers who make the journey will find a good deal that they agree with and, indeed, have read in other places. Women are oppressed. Mere human efforts to name God, be it God the father or the ground of being, are a kind of blasphemy. . . . Yet it is not for these familiar complaints that Mary Daly's book was written, will be read, and should be criticized; it is for the distinctive and sweeping claims she makes. She is not a whimpering liberal interested in the reform of Christianity and the integration of women into its power structure. She is a militant feminist in the process of "calling forth" a new religion whose marching song will certainly be "Go Down, Moses." The new religion is to be informed and inspired by the liberating experience of radical feminism; its faith-experience grows out of living in "new time" and "new space" on the margins of patriarchal society; its mission is to call forth "new Be-ing." . . . This mantle of charismatic leadership is of the same cut and design as that worn by the prophets of other liberation theologies except that instead of capitalism, racism, militarism, etc., sexism is the enemy.

The effort to decimate patriarchal religion, language, and ideas proceeds from fantasy to fantasy—that is, from utopia to absurdity—amid talk of "ovarian insights," "scapegoat syndromes," "sisterhood as antichurch and cosmic covenant," "nonsaint," "methodicide," "Christocide," "bibliolatry," "phallic morality," and "the final cause: the cause of causes," feminism. Man alone does not live by words. . . .

The big enemy in *Beyond God the Father* is, like father, like son, the former second person of the Blessed Trinity, the little man from Prague, that nefarious scapegoat, Jesus Christ. (p. 442)

An earthly utopia or Armageddon? *Beyond God the Father* is a symptom of the madness which comes from resolutely following fantasies and ideas to their final and absurd ends. Ends, in this case, which embody the imperialistic notion that liberation from oppression, of whatever kind, is an experience that must be shared by anyone who wants to maintain their membership in the human race. It leads to those boyish games of whose is bigger, my oppression or yours. It builds a system which categorizes people according to the "saved" and the "damned," the "in" and the "out," the "worthy" and the "unworthy," the "liberated" and the "unliberated." It is as absurd as it is arbitrary. It is patriarchal.

Oppression is a relative condition. While it is right to rejoice with those who are liberated from oppression (even if, as is rarely admitted these days, it is self-oppression) it does not follow that they should become our political, religious, or cultural mentors. . . . Mark Twain once demonstrated how a belief in radical equality could be combined with an abiding skepticism when he snapped back to the anti-Semites of his day, "Jews are members of the human race; worse than that I cannot say of them." We victims of oppression (women, blacks, chicanos, children and, yes, men) can do nothing better than engrave on our pulsating egos the same statement for our own category.

And if the choice between religious leaders becomes a choice between a feminist, theology professor from Boston College and a carpenter's son from Galilee, I say stick with the working class. (p. 443)

> *Margaret O'Brien Steinfels, "Earthly Utopia or Armageddon?" in* Commonweal *(copyright © 1974 Commonweal Publishing Co., Inc.; reprinted by permission of Commonweal Publishing Co., Inc.), Vol. XCIX, No. 17, February 1, 1974, pp. 442-43.*

RONALD E. SANTONI

For reasons which this book attempts to elaborate, "Few women, even among the gifted, have managed to challenge the society's prevailing vision of the 'nature of reality' with vigor, consistency, and persistence." But in *Beyond God the Father,* Mary Daly . . . does just that. The result is one of the more important works of our generation. To be sure, it is a radical critique of the structure of our consciousness and institutions, past and present; but it is more. It is a work of creation—an attempt to create theology and philosophy out of, and appropriate to, the current women's revolution, the "becoming of women." To ignore this book—even with its defects and problems—is to miss an occasion for growth as a human being. (p. 59)

As brilliant and prophetic as this book may be, it obviously is not without shortcomings. At times Mary Daly's assertions are not becoming to her discerning scholarship. And her vision seems myopic. To say the least, her apparent view that every problem of dehumanization is a product of patriarchy is questionable. Her assessment of every philosophy and theology, for example, in terms of whether it has dealt with the women's question or recognized sexism is both limiting and dogmatic. Given her wish for a "psychically androgynous being," her appeal to the "authority" of feminine experience regarding certain issues seems one-sided and dangerous. Even to suggest that a male opposing abortion is necessarily sexist—by virtue of his "privileged status" and "vested interest" in the sexual caste system—is to entertain presumption, faulty logic, and counter-objectification.

Despite its flaws—and there are more—this book penetrates the depths of our existence. It demands from us nothing less than thorough honesty and openness, hearing and listening. (p. 60)

> *Ronald E. Santoni, "Paean to Women," in* The Progressive *(reprinted by permission from* The Progressive, *409 East Main Street, Madison, Wisconsin 53703; copyright 1974 by The Progressive, Inc.),* Vol. 38, No. 5, May, 1974, pp. 59-60.

ROSS S. KRAEMER

Mary Daly's *Gyn/Ecology* virtually defies concise review. (p. 354)

Viewed from a historical perspective, Daly's philosophy exhibits remarkable affinities with the system propounded by the Christian Gnostics of the early centuries of the Common Era, although Daly does not acknowledge any explicit borrowing of Gnostic categories. The Gnostics viewed the universe as the arena for a cosmic conflict between divine souls, temporarily embedded in material human bodies, and evil archons and demons, who controlled the material realm and perpetually sought to prevent the souls from completing their homeward journey to the heavenly realm of light.

With the substitution of women for the Gnostic souls and men for the archon/demons, Daly's system, as articulated in *Gyn/Ecology,* falls rather intriguingly into place. In the beginning, women knew their creative powers and true selves, but jealous, inadequate, inferior men strove to hide this knowledge from them. To this end, they encased the souls of women in material bodies . . . which effectively prevented women from seeing their true selves within. Thus enslaved, women's souls languished while the archons ruled.

Gnostic mythology then recounted the coming of the Saviour, who was sent from the realm of light to awaken the sleeping souls; to invite them to cast off their cumbersome clothing and begin the dangerous journey home. To do so, they had to renounce all ties with earthly families and kin, to become wanderers. Mary Daly, as a radical feminist Saviour, issues a similar call. (pp. 354-55)

Gnostic gospel equated the cares of the body, including family responsibilities, with death, and the ultimate searchings of the soul with life. Daly repeatedly equates phallocratic society with death, and gynocentric society with life.

The Gnostics further distinguished levels of gnostic attainment. Daly speaks of the neophyte Searcher and the enlightened Hag or Crone, the wise woman whose long journey has brought her to a kind of salvation. The ancient Gnostic emphasis on the individual soul and its quest for merger with the divine parallels Daly's notion of the bonding of female selves. Even the language employed is similar—the Gnostics spoke of the divine sparks of light as a metaphor for the souls; Daly calls the activity of radical feminist Voyagers "sparking."

In the Gnostic cosmology, the antagonism between the Gnostics and the archons was fundamental and eternal, and arose out of the archons' fear that gnostic discovery of the truth would result in their demise, in their fall from power. In the Daly cosmology, the antagonism between the sexes is similarly primal and eternal, a function of the male fear of the creative power of women.

Daly's arguments are so structured as to be impervious to falsification. By definition, the inescapable participation of all men in patriarchal societies renders them unfit critics. Those women, particularly those who call themselves feminists, who take issue with Daly's major premises and conclusions, especially her call for total separation from the community of men, are refuted in advance by labeling them "token feminists" who have failed to see through the patriarchal deceits. Similarly, the Gnostics contended that those who rejected the Gnostic vision were still deceived by the archons. Both Daly and the Gnostics claimed that hermeneutics—methods of interpretation—were fundamental. Armed with true knowledge, Gnostics see through the deceits of the archons; radical feminists see through the deceits of patriarchy.

Daly's radical feminism shares with ancient Gnosticism not only the philosophical and logical problems of verification but also the pragmatic problems of social application. Both advocate abstinence from procreation—the Gnostics as a rejection of the material world, Daly as a rejection of heterosexual relationships. For both communities, the ultimate implication of this is self-destruction through the failure to reproduce. . . . Daly as radical feminist prophet deals with this only tangentially when she implies that radical feminism is not likely to draw large numbers of adherents. The conception of daughters to raise as feminists is not addressed, nor the dilemma of women who give birth to sons.

Despite Daly's provision for refuting contradictory evidence in advance, several substantive problems with her work should be noted. Daly accepts the existence of primal matriarchies with their attendant goddess worship, a theory whose appeal for feminist self-understanding is obvious. Yet the apparent absence of historical evidence for prior matriarchies, persuasively argued by [Sarah Bo] Pomeroy, [Joan] Bamberger, and others, cannot be dismissed simply by reference to male erasure of women's history. Daly's monolithic view of men pays insufficient attention to the equally murderous acts of men, both historically and symbolically, toward other men. . . . In her homogenization of all males, Daly has simply inverted traditional patriarchal scholarship's homogenization of women. This inversion of traditional categories characterizes much of Daly's work—if women have historically been viewed as the Other, and consequently devalued, Daly now contends that men are the Other, and also to be devalued. Thus while Daly reverses the labels and value judgments of male evaluations of gender distinctions, she appears to share with male philosophers the assumption that there are fundamental distinctions between men and women, apart from the obvious biological ones.

Gyn/Ecology is provocative, frightening, poetic, and compelling. Self-consciously radical in language and structure, it manifests affinities with other radical traditions, intentionally or not, as the comparison with Gnostic cosmology demonstrates. Moving beyond *The Church and the Second Sex* and *Beyond God the Father*, Daly's sustained analysis of the pervasive interconnections between phallocratic society and religion poses the most systematic challenge yet to those women who would attempt the reformation of traditional religions into systems reflective of true female being. (pp. 355-56)

Ross S. Kraemer, "Book Reviews: 'Gyn/Ecology'," in Signs *(reprinted by permission of The University of Chicago Press; © 1980 by The University of Chicago), Vol. 5, No. 2, Winter, 1979, pp. 354-56.*

SUSAN LEIGH STAR

Context. Since reading *Gyn/Ecology*, my nerves have been humming with new meanings for this word, seeing it as a verb for the first time. I am profoundly *contexted* by this work. Placed. Seen. With its reading, I experience newer and newer navigations of my own consciousness. Without freezing, without staticness of any sort, this book is the total confluence of method and content, of the personal and the historical, of the reach for change and the unflinching examination of suffering, that I have come to know as feminism. Where this book is, there is feminism. . . . In a deeply Un-ethical and passionately Unmoral, compassionate way, *Gyn/Ecology* Wends its way through and Webs itself across vast expanses of thought, the spatial and temporal dimensions of which are familiar to us as cohabitants of the dimension. *Gyn/Ecology* is an experience of recognition. (pp. 87-8)

In *Beyond God the Father*, Mary spoke of the need for *methodicide*—killing the gods of method in academia which have determined the shape and focus of knowledge. *Gyn/Ecology* commits methodicide at many levels. . . .

Fundamentally, her method for committing methodicide is the specification of context, of social and psychological realms out of which "knowledge" arises, knowledge which comes legitimated and delivered with the stamp of approval of patriarchal scholarship. . . .

Gyn/Ecology, by specifying more broadly and deeply than any scholarship to date, the background, origins, and assumptions of patriarchal scholarship, creates for the first time a feminist sociology of knowledge.

Mary's focus is on patriarchal scholarly legitimation of atrocities, particularly against women and including the Nazi-authored Holocaust of the Jews. (p. 88)

[*Gyn/Ecology*] shows that radical feminist method is a matter of looking again, of de-anesthetizing our numbed and battered senses, of dishabituating ourselves from patriarchal monotony in order to see their underlying strategies for gynocide. (p. 90)

In writing about atrocities, one runs a double-edged risk: that the information will either anesthetize, through the sheer numbing horror of the facts, by repetition; or that the information will be aestheticized, that is, be presented so "artistically" that one actually forgets that one is reading about/looking at human misery. What skill does it take to present page after page of this material without either anesthetizing or aestheticizing? The language, and the method, from which the book comes must pierce through *itself,* continuously, to resonate with some Other place in us than the worn perceptual structures that echo only hopelessness and despair. It must be written with a double-edged ax—*presenting hope without erasing horror. We must dwell in another frame of reference without ceasing to live here.* This is precisely what Mary does, clearly presenting and performing the choice *against* any level of consent to violence (what she calls "*sub*viving") and *for* a profound healing/creation—the spinning forth of our own truths (*surviving*). . . . [Survival] grows out of a simultaneous awareness of the *details* of normalized violence, and the *pattern/context* which makes the perpetuation of the details *possible, thinkable.* (pp. 90-1)

The restoration of context to violence is a major task for all feminists: naming names, seeing social patterns, piercing through the pseudo-rationales of patriarchal reversals. . . . (p. 91)

As an assertion of active, courageous gentleness, *Gyn/Ecology* points the way toward a new kind of survival. Surviving, in this sense, also means naming the context, the source of all forms of oppression. . . . [Many] "scholars" have overlooked the pain and torture in practices indigenous to culture other than their own in the name of "cross-cultural" relativism. In their desire not to impose the standards of one culture on another (or perhaps their inability to see women as human), they have often named practices like African genital mutilation of women as religious "beliefs and customs." Mary re-names this refusal to *see* as sexism, racism, and as an active participation in the atrocity itself. She also brings this analysis to bear on American "customs": "American women, like their African sisters, are also lulled into pain-full captivity by the prevailing beliefs and 'customs'." . . . *Gyn/Ecology* cuts cleanly through liberal mushiness to make the strongest possible statement about crimes against women: *moral relativism has no place in the face of torture.* No one nowadays would call the Nazi persecutions a "custom" based on "religious beliefs," yet, when similar things happen to women, they are often ignored, by social scientists and other scholars. Silence about gynocide *is* violent—and Mary places the responsibility for this silence, this collaboration, fully with the "scientists" who have failed to name names in the course of their studies. (p. 92)

Some of the most delightful blaspheming in *Gyn/Ecology* occurred for me in the section on therapy, or "mind-gynecology." Mary's critique of psychotherapy expands some of the earlier feminist critiques of therapy, and some of the criticisms of orthodox therapy made by the anti-psychiatry movement (those of the Radical Therapy group, for example). But Mary goes one step farther by bringing her criticisms to bear upon

all forms of therapy which come to replace originality and Amazonian creativity with categories and formulae. . . . (pp. 92-3)

Besides the process of fixating on details, and learning to classify every activity according to the theoretical model chosen by the instructor or therapist, another, more subtle process operates to create therapy as reality: the conversion of everything into a homogeneous symbol system. (p. 94)

Mary exposes patriarchal myth as the act of heuristic naming. . . . The crucial difference between patriarchal and feminist myth is . . . the difference between organic and imposed; between that which arises from and is continuously subject to the experience of the subject; and the pre-formed, other-authored directives that resonate only with gendered, nonfeminist imaginations. . . . In contrast [to patriarchal myth], feminist myth opens, unfolds.

The last part of *Gyn/Ecology* focuses on the breaking-through/celebrating of Hags, Harpies, Crones, Spinsters, and Searchers (delightful new names for the overburdened "Lesbian feminist" designation). The celebration/breaking-through incorporates a threefold process Mary calls spooking, sparking, and spinning—the exorcism of old and destructive ways of being and thinking; the interpersonal and transpersonal sparking and joining of minds and bodies of Hags, Harpies, and Crones; and the spinning-out of tapestries of creativity, in connection with each other and all of life.

In creating her web of language around the ideas of spinning, sparking, and spooking, Mary uses words that have had profound meaning for me in my life, but which I have often felt embarrassed to talk about in a "political" environment: hope, innocence, courage, gentleness, compassion, *sacredness. Gyn/Ecology* frees up some of the coopted language and silences associated with these ideals, gives them new strength.

Gyn/Ecology refuses all dichotomies of anger and gentleness, innocence and knowledge. It will be a useful tool for asking some of the basic questions about life's meanings and values that we need desperately to ask of each other and ourSelves. It has helped me to ask some of these questions in noncliched, fresh ways. (pp. 94-6)

> *Susan Leigh Star, "To Dwell Among Ourselves" (copyright © Susan Leigh Star 1979; reprinted by permission of the author), in* Sinister Wisdom, *No. 8, Winter, 1979, pp. 87-98.*

LINDSY VAN GELDER

[*Gyn/Ecology: The Metaethics of Radical Feminism*] attempts to transcend descriptive theory; it invites the reader to experience a complex intellectual and spiritual "Journey" into radical feminism.

The book is divided into three "Passages." The first is a setting down of Daly's premises and terms, including some fancy feminist footwork with language. . . . The last Passage is a spiritual guidebook and rallying cry for those who have come to understand the evils of male domination and now face a variety of pitfalls, from co-optation to madness. (p. 40)

The middle Passage—in my opinion, the heart of the book—is an analysis of Indian suttee (in which widows "voluntarily" burned to death on their husbands' funeral pyres), Chinese footbinding, African clitoridectomy, European witch-burning, and American medicine. . . . Even those readers who begin the book with a less-than-rapturous view of the gynecological profession will be struck—and radicalized—by the comparisons Daly makes between American medicine and the other seemingly more barbarous institutions under attack. All, for instance, share an obsession with "purity" from femaleness, rituals that effectively blunt the horror involved and make it appear "normal," and the use of other women to short-circuit our perception of *who* is giving the orders and for whose benefit.

Throughout, Daly combines the dispassionate skills of the scholar with a passionate feminism. . . . Still, this is not a book for everyone. Daly's theories rest on the premise that men and women are engaged in a deadly "State of War," and she notes early on that "this will of course be called an 'anti-male' book." I would not presume to ask Daly to compromise her politics; nor would I urge them on readers who might feel justifiably excluded or trivialized by the author's implicit assumption that the only true feminist is a lesbian. (pp. 40-1)

Daly is occasionally guilty of sloppy reasoning. Her views on male friendship seem almost exclusively drawn from the mindless solidarity of soldiers in combat—a tenuous control group for comparison with women. She perceives the 1975 linkup of the American spaceship Apollo . . . and a Russian craft as a male-bonding propaganda spectacle that deliberately "subliminally appealed to erotic fantasies allegedly taboo in heterosexist society." Daly here undercuts her own premise: that male culture is capable of acting out its sexual impulses. If all misogynist males *were* homosexual, we would, I submit, be living in a very different kind of patriarchy.

At the risk of sounding Yahooish, I would add that *Gyn/Ecology* is difficult to read. The first Passage, some 100 pages long, abounds with lengthy quotations from Merriam-Webster, forays into Greek and Latin derivations, invented words à la Monique Wittig, and endless puns. . . . The section may seem tiresome to women who have already thought through the limitations of patriarchal language and tiring to those who have not.

But my major criticism of Daly is that she fails to augment her frequently incisive theory with any of the how-to follow-through found elsewhere in recent feminist literature. Beyond the observation that Spinsters have learned to dress comfortably, there is virtually nothing in the third "Passage" to connect Daly's radical feminist nirvana with my real-life of children and work—much less the practical politics of *stopping* the atrocities she describes so well. It is not enough to be told to spin like a spider, or to develop the sonar of dolphins. Nor am I comforted by Daly's assertion that "Amazons can stop worrying about the false problem of numbers" since the psychic energy of even a few Spinsters can undo the patriarchal male. Feminism is not a cult, but a force to be made available to *all* women.

Living as a feminist and/or a lesbian *is* dangerous. To be dangerous to patriarchy is something else altogether, and I would very much like Mary Daly to start writing about that. . . . (pp. 41, 43)

Lindsy Van Gelder, "A Yahoo's Guide to Mary Daly," in Ms. *(© 1979 Ms. Magazine Corp.), Vol. VII, No. 8, February, 1979, pp. 40-1, 43.*

ADRIENNE RICH

Since I first read **"Beyond God the Father,"** and in many subsequent encounters with [Mary Daly] and with the growing influence of her work, I have found myself challenged and invigorated as a woman writer, as a feminist, and as a dweller in the situation of extremity she maps in **"Gyn/Ecology."** Her final chapters, especially the passages on female friendship, offer a powerful ethical message to the women's movement, questioning easy settlements, facile ideas of "community," "tolerance" or "ecstasy." In this deeply original, provocative book, outrage, hilarity, grief, profanity, lyricism and moral daring join in bursting the accustomed bounds even of feminist discourse. (pp. 10, 37)

Adrienne Rich, "That Women Be Themselves," in The New York Times Book Review *(© 1979 by The New York Times Company; reprinted by permission), February 4, 1979, pp. 10, 37.*

CARTER HEYWARD

I must confess my own bias. . . . I have some difficulty with Mary Daly. This is partly a matter of personal history in relationship to her. . . . But it also may be a matter of anxiety-laden resistance to the theological tenets of this "Female Fury," this "revolting Hag." . . .

In this essay, I am attempting to take Daly with [seriousness and appreciation]. . . . [It] may be that I am put off by Daly, in part, because in her work I encounter aspects of my own with which I am uncomfortable (such as the possibly infinite incapacity of the church to take women seriously in a fundamental way). (p. 67)

It seems to me that Mary Daly, like most traditional Catholic and Protestant thinkers, operates primarily on the epistemological assumptions of a subjective idealism. . . .

I would maintain also that Daly is creatively revolutionary. . . .

Daly is a philosopher and myth-maker first, a theologian second (if at all, according to her definition of theology as that which legitimates patriarchy). . . . It is difficult to imagine what "revolution" means for Daly apart from her own suggestion, in [*Beyond God the Father* and *Gyn/Ecology*], that she is primarily committed to the revolutionizing of women's consciousness whereby we can "transcend" the limits of patriarchy (read: world, church, culture itself), "spinning and sparking" within and among ourselves in our own Paradise. . . . (p. 68)

As a myth-maker, Daly looks like a "Bultmann-in-reverse," having come to believe that the only way to comprehend our authenticity, the Depth of our Selves, is to "mythologize" Being. In so doing, . . . Daly does not deny historical or social reality but rather subordinates it to the primacy and power of transcendence, which finds expression in prehistorical mythology. . . .

Daly is, by patriarchal standards, mindless of historical reality—out of touch with the reality of our fathers. As such, she is in touch with an aspect of reality—of human experience, of her own experience—that has, in fact, been written off, burned and beaten off, by our forefathers. To this same extent, traditional theology—especially, perhaps, "liberal" theology—does not acknowledge as valid theological data the human experiences of ecstasy, rage and visionary dreaming as expressed in mythology and yearning. . . . Nor can the case be made simply on the basis of Daly's myth-making that she is ahistorical. A myth is one historic expression of an historic reality—even if the reality is one's own dream or pain.

Given that Mary Daly is speaking of real human experience and that myth-making is not in and of itself ahistorical, in what sense might it be asserted . . . that Daly is creating a "state of mind" rather than a movement for significant social change in history?

The answer is, I think, traceable to her epistemology: Daly has chosen to remove her mind from the world and do philosophy (myth and metaethics) as a subject who is shaping her object, transcendent time-space for women. . . . Daly has chosen to be "prehistorical"—*prior* to patriarchal history (world history as created by men) both in terms of chronology and importance. She has chosen to focus—fully and finally—on the creation of a transcendent time-space for women who do not want to engage themselves in any way with the male-defined processes of world and church history.

Daly has chosen to be a women-defined woman among women for women. Noting with Simone de Beauvoir the extent to which women within patriarchy exhaust ourselves attempting to change patriarchal institutions, Daly has chosen to leave patriarchy in the only way possible—short of suicide—by "surviving." . . . Hence, she seems uninterested in social change, including movements of class and race that she perceives to be, at best, deflections and distractions from the women's revolution, and, at worst, movements dominated by patriarchal interests, methods and goals.

But this stance is made problematic for Daly by her existential roots, situated not only in Tillich's ontology of being but also in an implicit typology of "hero" as rebel, up and against the world (cf. Camus). Existentialism—the awareness of existential alienation, pain, life in the real world—sets her on the horns of a dilemma. On the one hand, such existence and awareness of it provide her with the last vestige of relationship to patriarchy (life in the non-transcendent world of men and non-feminist omen). On the other hand, it is bound also to provide the basis for her apparent contempt for men and for women whom she does not consider to be A-mazing Amazons. (p. 69)

Daly's perception of the depth of the historical problem of patriarchy and sexism is [unequivocal]. . . . She names the systemic demon, not as a theological construct, but rather as a *human agent*—*i.e., men*, creators and rulers of the patriarchal world. But she then flees inward, for a personal exorcism of the mind. . . .

Daly's sense of the *problem* [seems strong and realistic]. . . . Or, yet again, Daly perceives initially through Marxist eyes . . . and then proceeds to reject the social and historical challenge in what she sees, thereby opting for an idealist posture vis-à-vis reality as an Otherworld. (p. 71)

Daly's voice is prophetic, but she has chosen to stand outside the very community (Christianity) to whom she could most forcefully speak prophetically. Prophets get killed, and Daly has chosen survival. . . . Daly is heard to echo . . . urgently the voice of the One whom I would call "God" as God is speaking to us and means to pierce, rip and shatter patriarchy as manifest at all levels of our lives. (pp. 71-2)

[Daly] *names* the demonic work of the social construction of the patriarchal reality:

> Women's minds have been mutilated and muted to such a state that "Free Spirit" has been branded into them as a brand name for girdles and bras rather than as the name of our verb-

ing, be-ing selves. . . . Moronized, women believe that male-written texts (biblical, literary, medical, legal, scientific) are "trues". . . . Patriarchy has stolen our cosmos and returned it in the form of *Cosmopolitan* magazine and cosmetics. . . . . . .

This is the stuff that must be said—*within and to the church*. Daly may be "spinning" off into her own space of female idolatry and isolation, but her *radical naming* of the demonic destruction of women's Selves in the name of Free Spirit, *Cosmopolitan* and Christ is absolutely vital, I am convinced, to the work that [another feminist theologian, Rosemary Ruether,] is attempting to do—significant and enduring reformation of the church and meaningful restoration of the world.

What is at stake for feminist theology is no less than our Selves. Our survival is at stake, not in Daly's sense of "living above" history and patriarchal reality, but rather in the sense of *our absolute refusal to compromise or equivocate our experience of being alienated, "other," Furious Females, as the basis for our participation in the world/church*. (p. 72)

> Carter Heyward, "Ruether and Daly: Theologians Speaking and Sparking, Building and Burning," in Christianity and Crisis *(copyright © 1979 Christianity and Crisis, Inc.), Vol. 39, No. 4, March 19, 1979, pp. 66-72.*

AUDRE LORDE

Dear Mary,

Thank you for having **Gyn/Ecology** sent to me. So much of it is full of import, useful, generative, and provoking. As in **Beyond God the Father**, many of your analyses are strengthening and helpful to me. Therefore, it is because of what you have given to me in the past work that I write this letter to you now, hoping to share with you the benefits of my insights as you have shared the benefits of yours with me. (p. 94)

When I started reading **Gyn/Ecology**, I was truly excited by the vision behind your words, and nodded my head as you spoke in your first passage of myth and mystification. Your words on the nature and function of the Goddess, as well as the ways in which her face has been obscured, agreed with what I myself have discovered in my searches through African myth/legend/religion for the true nature of old female power.

So I wondered, why doesn't Mary deal with Afrekete as an example? Why are her goddess-images only white, western-european, judeo-christian? . . . Well, I thought, Mary has made a conscious decision to narrow her scope and to deal only with the ecology of western-european women.

Then I came to the first three chapters of your second passage, and it was obvious that you were dealing with non-european women, but only as victims and preyers-upon each other. I began to feel my history and my mythic background distorted by the absence of any images of my foremothers in power. Your inclusion of african genital mutilation was an important and necessary piece in any consideration of female ecology, and too little has been written about it. But to imply, however, that all women suffer the same oppression simply because we are women, is to lose sight of the many varied tools of patriarchy. (pp. 94-5)

What you excluded from *Gyn/Ecology* dismissed my heritage and the heritage of all other non-european women, and denied the real connections that exist between all of us.

It is obvious that you have done a tremendous amount of work for this book. But simply because so little material on non-white female power and symbol exists in white women's words from a radical feminist perspective, to exclude this aspect of connection from even comment in your work is to deny the fountain of non-european female strength and power that nurtures each of our visions. It is to make a point by choice.

Then to realize that the only quotations from black women's words were the ones you used to introduce your chapter on african genital mutilation, made me question why you needed to use them at all. For my part, I felt that you had in fact misused my words, utilized them only to testify against myself as a woman of color. (p. 95)

Did you ever read my words, or did you merely finger through them for quotations which you thought might valuably support an already-conceived idea concerning some old and distorted connection between us? This is not a rhetorical question. To me this feels like another instance of the knowledge, crone-logy and work of women of color being ghettoized by a white woman dealing only out of a patriarchal western-european frame of reference. (pp. 95-6)

Mary, I ask that you be aware of how this serves the destructive forces of racism and separation between women—the assumption that the herstory and myth of white women is the legitimate and sole herstory and myth of all women to call upon for power and background, and that non-white women and our herstories are noteworthy only as decorations, or examples of female victimization. I ask that you be aware of the effect that this dismissal has upon the community of black women, and how it devalues your own words. (p. 96)

I feel you do celebrate differences between white women as a creative force towards change, rather than a reason for mis-understanding and separation. But you fail to recognize that, as women, those differences expose all women to various forms and degrees of patriarchal oppression, some of which we share, and some of which we do not. . . .

The oppression of women knows no ethnic nor racial bound-aries, true, but that does not mean it is identical within those boundaries. Nor do the reservoirs of our ancient power know these boundaries, either. To deal with one without even allud-ing to the other is to distort our commonality as well as our difference. (p. 97)

> *Audre Lorde, in her letter to Mary Daly on May 6, 1979 (reprinted by permission of the author), in* This Bridge Called My Back: Writings by Radical Women of Color, *edited by Cherríe Moraga and Gloria An-zaldúa, Persephone Press, 1981, pp. 94-7.*

JOSEPHINE PAYNE-O'CONNOR

[Ross S. Kraemer, see excerpt above] fails to understand the major themes of Daly's work, claiming that it "exhibits re-markable affinities with" Christian Gnosticism and "falls in-triguingly into place" once these parallels are explored. What emerges from this enterprise is a Mary Daly disguised as a man-eating, child-hating, feminist separatist, and closet chris-tian to boot! This wild distortion would be hilarious were it not that it completely obscures the very important themes Daly addresses so successfully.

In [*Beyond God the Father*] Daly demolished the central chris-tian concepts of superior gods, lost souls, saviors, and heavens. She rejects the christian worship of death and self-denial: the view that the sacred life is the purifying struggle to overcome our evil nature to achieve deathly bliss. In *Gyn/Ecology*, Daly presents her own prophetic vision. The sacred verb, "Being," is expressed and experienced in the wild Being-between-women as and when they are authentically present to each other. (p. 340)

To the reviewer, the most enlightening theme of Gnosticism is the "primal and eternal" battle between good and evil, resolved (nonetheless) as the dormant forces of good waken to their plight, struggle against bondage, and follow their savior to the realm of light. Applying this to *Gyn/Ecology,* the re-viewer finds a commitment to the battle of the sexes and mas-sive support for feminist separatism. I, on the other hand, argue that Daly commits herself to neither of these conflicting doc-trines, but is on to something much more sophisticated.

Courageously and clear-sightedly, Daly names the root of pa-triarchal oppression of women: the destruction of the bonds between women and the fragmentation of the selves of women. This is achieved by the crippling and murder of women by token women torturers, justified by patriarchal propaganda. Thus are women coerced into consenting to our exploitation by patriarchy. The central dynamic of patriarchal exploitation of women Daly exposes as the male sin of gluttony. It is the need of the parasite male to batten on the creative energy of women. Without it he is helpless, he is passive. Hence, we can see the male need to prevent women from claiming our creative power for ourselves, and the male need to destroy the potential for autonomy in women: sisterhood.

Once we have understood this, it becomes clear that Daly would *not* recommend that women, seizing our own creative energy, squander it in continuing the male-created battle of the sexes. (p. 341)

Women who share creative energy with women are "present to women," or "woman-identified." It does not mean that we live in "total separation from the community of men" (men do not have community), nor that we "leave behind the deadly patriarchal universe" (where else is there?). Her acceptance of evidence for the prehistory, and the creative superiority, of women, leads Daly to deny the legitimacy of patriarchy and its device of female separatism. She views the "patriarchal universe" as women's domain corrupted by men, and calls to women to reclaim our heritage. . . .

The reviewer's claim that Daly prohibits procreation (especially the bearing of sons) is most bizarre. When Daly speaks to the "lesbian imagination in all women" she includes *all* women: celibate, virgin, mother, lesbian. The term "lesbian" has been least diluted by patriarchal usage and evokes, with great power, all the possibilities of celebration between women. Within the flexible unity of sisterhood, we each follow our own creative calling. Birthing is one choice. At present, it involves tem-porary union with a man, so Daly would recommend extreme caution, and no sacrifice of women's energy. But this advice is appropriate for us all who, inevitably, must Become in "alien territory." (p. 342)

> *Josephine Payne-O'Connor, "Comment on Krae-mer's Review of 'Gyn/Ecology: The Metaethics of Radical Feminism',"* in Signs *(reprinted by permis-sion of The University of Chicago Press; © 1980 by The University of Chicago), Vol. 6, No. 2, Winter, 1980, pp. 340-42.*

HELEN McNEIL

Mary Daly's *Gyn/Ecology* is about woman as victim; it seethes with rage against the societies and rituals concocted by men to kill 'the Goddess within'. Written to horrify and then to convert, it launches its attack by breaking down barriers between sociological research, mythography, feminist consciousness-raising and self-expression. *Gyn/Ecology* is an important book for its fierceness as much as for its facts, showing how we have barely begun to reassess the mythologies which mutilate women physically and emotionally. It also serves to show—sometimes inadvertently—how long it will take to articulate a feminist consciousness, a process which Daly, quoting Barbara Skerrett, says is akin to 'developing a new organ in the mind'.

Daly begins by sexually politicising language. Throughout *Gyn/Ecology,* words are punned upon, slashed apart and stitched together, and broken down into polemic etymologies. . . . Unfortunately Daly's verbal play often obfuscates her argument, forcing even what she would call a Revolting Hag Searcher, like this reviewer, to struggle just to make basic sense of passages which as often as not are about the most gross and hideous persecutions of women. Having suffered these outrages, must we now kill ourselves *reading* about them too?

In intention if not always in result, linguistic suspicion is part of the liberating process for Daly. Self-conscious alienation from male orientated language (and what language isn't?) is a necessary step towards realising what Adrienne Rich . . . calls 'The dream of a common language' of identification between women. The immediate source for Daly's slashes and sutures is Monique Wittig's *The Lesbian Body,* in which even 'je' must be slashed into j/e because its very neutrality might delude the woman writer into thinking she can forget sexual difference even for a moment. . . .

At times Daly's etymologies do look uncannily like the 'traces' and erasures in *Writing and Difference* and *Of Grammatology* by Jacques Derrida (whom Daly doesn't mention). Too often, however, Daly uses the slash lazily, to juxtapose obvious or unexamined alternatives, and her arbitrary capitalisations and words in inverted commas betray a polemic which hasn't been able to reach direct expression. . . .

Gyn/Ecology's substitution of sexual politics for ideology weakens her treatment of contemporary society. . . .

[For] Daly, society (inevitably patriarchal) often appears to exist solely to give structure to male hatred of women. *Gyn/Ecology* abjures androgyny as a goal, and mocks those women who hope for partnership with what Daly, quoting Robin Morgan, sardonically calls the 'exceptional' man. Whatever Daly's personal politics, *Gyn/Ecology* is an anti-social book. Also, despite its concluding call for women to Spook/Speak, Spin and Search, *Gyn/Ecology* is obsessed with the enemy, less a book about women than about what men do to women. (p. 514)

Helen McNeil, "Hag-ography," in New Statesman *(©1980 The Statesman & Nation Publishing Co. Ltd.), Vol. 99, No. 2259, April 4, 1980, pp. 514-15.**

Angela Y(vonne) Davis

1944-

Davis is a black American philosopher and Communist party organizer. In *If They Come in the Morning* (1971) she characterizes minority prisoners as *political* prisoners who have been victimized by oppressive political and economic conditions, and urges that they be defended by the Black Liberation Movement. In *Angela Davis: An Autobiography* (1974) she traces her life from childhood through graduate study in modern philosophy, focusing on her search for a political movement which would advance the cause of oppressed peoples. Davis considers hers a *"political* autobiography that emphasize[s] the people, the events and the forces in my life that propelled me to my present commitment" to the Communist party. In it she chronicles her imprisonment, trial and acquittal of conspiracy, kidnapping, and murder charges in connection with the 1970 Marin County courthouse shootout, placing this famous event in the larger context of black liberation struggles. Following her acquittal, Davis has continued to organize and speak around the world on behalf of the Communist party; in 1980 she was its candidate for Vice-President of the United States. (See also *Contemporary Authors*, Vols. 57-60.)

Excerpt from *IF THEY COME IN THE MORNING: VOICES OF RESISTANCE*

In the heat of our pursuit for fundamental human rights, Black people have been continually cautioned to be patient. We are advised that as long as we remain faithful to the *existing* democratic order, the glorious moment will eventually arrive when we will come into our own as full-fledged human beings.

But having been taught by bitter experience, we know that there is a glaring incongruity between democracy and the capitalist economy which is the source of our ills. Regardless of all rhetoric to the contrary, the people are not the ultimate matrix of the laws and the system which govern them—certainly not Black people and other nationally oppressed people, but not even the mass of whites. The people do not exercise decisive control over the determining factors of their lives. (pp. 27-8)

Needless to say, the history of the United States has been marred from its inception by an enormous quantity of unjust laws, far too many expressly bolstering the oppression of Black people. Particularized reflections of existing social inequities, these laws have repeatedly borne witness to the exploitative and racist core of the society itself. For Blacks, Chicanos, for all nationally oppressed people, the problem of opposing unjust laws and the social conditions which nourish their growth, has always had immediate practical implications. Our very survival has frequently been a direct function of our skill in forging effective channels of resistance. In resisting, we have sometimes been compelled to openly violate those laws which directly or indirectly buttress our oppression. But even when containing our resistance within the orbit of legality, we have been labeled criminals and have been methodically persecuted by a racist legal apparatus. (p. 28)

The political prisoner's words or deeds have in one form or another embodied political protests against the established or-

Photograph by Roy Lewis

der and have consequently brought him into acute conflict with the state. In light of the political content of his act, the "crime" (which may or may not have been committed) assumes a minor importance. In this country, however, where the special category of political prisoners is not officially acknowledged, the political prisoner inevitably stands trial for a specific criminal offense, not for a political act. Often the so-called crime does not even have a nominal existence. As in the 1914 murder frame-up of the IWW organizer, Joe Hill, it is a blatant fabrication, a mere excuse for silencing a militant crusader against oppression. In all instances, however, the political prisoner has violated the unwritten law which prohibits disturbances and upheavals in the status quo of exploitation and racism. This unwritten law has been contested by actually and explicitly breaking a law or by utilizing constitutionally protected channels to educate, agitate and organize the masses to resist. (p. 30)

The offense of the political prisoner is his political boldness, his persistent challenging—legally or extra-legally—of fundamental social wrongs fostered and reinforced by the state. He has opposed unjust laws and exploitative, racist social conditions in general, with the ultimate aim of transforming these laws and this society into an order harmonious with the material and spiritual needs and interests of the vast majority of its members. (p. 31)

The ideological acrobatics characteristic of official attempts to explain away the existence of the political prisoner do not end with the equation of the individual political act with the individual criminal act. The political act is defined as criminal in order to discredit radical and revolutionary movements. A political event is reduced to a criminal event in order to affirm the absolute invulnerability of the existing order. (pp. 32-3)

The occurrence of crime is inevitable in a society in which wealth is unequally distributed, as one of the constant reminders that society's productive forces are being channeled in the wrong direction. The majority of criminal offenses bear a direct relationship to property. Contained in the very concept of property crimes are profound but suppressed social needs which express themselves in anti-social modes of action. Spontaneously produced by a capitalist organization of society, this type of crime is at once a protest against society and a desire to partake of its exploitative content. It challenges the symptoms of capitalism, but not its essence. (p. 35)

Within the contained, coercive universe of the prison, the captive is confronted with the realities of racism, not simply as individual acts dictated by attitudinal bias; rather he is compelled to come to grips with racism as an institutional phenomenon collectively experienced by the victims. The disproportionate representation of the Black and Brown communities, the manifest racism of parole boards, the intense brutality inherent in the relationship between prison guards and Black and Brown inmates—all this and more cause the prisoner to be confronted daily, hourly, with the concentrated, systematic existence of racism.

For the innocent prisoner, the process of radicalization should come easy; for the "guilty" victim, the insight into the nature of racism as it manifests itself in the judicial-penal complex can lead to a questioning of his own past criminal activity and a re-evaluation of the methods he has used to survive in a racist and exploitative society. Needless to say, this process is not automatic, it does not occur spontaneously. The persistent educational work carried out by the prison's political activists plays a key role in developing the political potential of captive men and women.

Prisoners—especially Blacks, Chicanos, and Puerto Ricans—are increasingly advancing the proposition that they are *political* prisoners. They contend that they are political prisoners in the sense that they are largely the victims of an oppressive politico-economic order, swiftly becoming conscious of the causes underlying their victimization. (pp. 36-7)

Black people are rushing full speed ahead toward an understanding of the circumstances which give rise to exaggerated forms of political repression and thus an over-abundance of political prisoners. This understanding is being forged out of the raw material of their own immediate experiences with racism. Hence, the Black masses are growing conscious of their responsibility to defend those who are being persecuted for attempting to bring about the alleviation of the most injurious immediate problems facing Black communities and ultimately to bring about total liberation through armed revolution, if it must come to this.

The Black Liberation Movement is presently at a critical juncture. Fascist methods of repression threaten to physically decapitate and obliterate the movement. More subtle, yet not less dangerous ideological tendencies from within threaten to isolate the Black movement and diminish its revolutionary impact. Both menaces must be counteracted in order to ensure our survival. Revolutionary Blacks must spearhead and provide leadership for a broad anti-fascist movement. (p. 41)

One of the fundamental historical lessons to be learned from past failures to prevent the rise of fascism is the decisive and indispensable character of the fight against fascism in its incipient phases. Once allowed to conquer ground, its growth is facilitated in geometric proportion. Although the most unbridled expressions of the fascist menace are still tied to the racist domination of Blacks, Chicanos, Puerto Ricans, Indians, it lurks under the surface wherever there is potential resistance to the power of monopoly capital, the parasitic interests which control this society. Potentially it can profoundly worsen the conditions of existence for the average American citizen. Consequently, the masses of people in this country have a real, direct and material stake in the struggle to free political prisoners, the struggle to abolish the prison system in its present form, the struggle against all dimensions of racism. (p. 42)

Angela Y. Davis, "Political Prisoners, Prisons and Black Liberation," in If They Come in the Morning: Voices of Resistance *by Angela Y. Davis and others (copyright © 1971 by the National United Committee to Free Angela Davis, Inc.; reprinted by arrangement with The Third Press International, a Division of Okpaku Communications Corporation, 330 7th Avenue, New York, NY 10001), The New American Library, 1971, pp. 27-43.*

Excerpt from *ANGELA DAVIS: AN AUTOBIOGRAPHY*

I was not anxious to write this book. Writing an autobiography at my age seemed presumptuous. Moreover, I felt that to write about my life, what I did, what I thought and what happened to me would require a posture of difference, an assumption that I was unlike other women—other Black women—and therefore needed to explain myself. I felt that such a book might end up obscuring the most essential fact: the forces that have made my life what it is are the very same forces that have shaped and misshaped the lives of millions of my people. Furthermore I am convinced that my response to these forces has been unexceptional as well, that my political involvement, ultimately as a member of the Communist Party, has been a natural, logical way to defend our embattled humanity.

The one extraordinary event of my life had nothing to do with me as an individual—with a little twist of history, another sister or brother could have easily become the political prisoner whom millions of people from throughout the world rescued from persecution and death. I was reluctant to write this book because concentration on my personal history might detract from the movement which brought my case to the people in the first place. I was also unwilling to render my life as a personal "adventure"—as though there were a "real" person separate and apart from the political person. (pp. ix-x)

When I decided to write the book after all, it was because I had come to envision it as a *political* autobiography that emphasized the people, the events and the forces in my life that propelled me to my present commitment. Such a book might serve a very important and practical purpose. There was the possibility that, having read it, more people would understand why so many of us have no alternative but to offer our lives—

our bodies, our knowledge, our will—to the cause of our oppressed people. (p. x)

When I learned about socialism in my history classes [in high school], a whole new world opened up before my eyes. For the first time, I became acquainted with the notion that there could be an ideal socioeconomic arrangement; that every person could give to the society according to his ability and his talents, and that in turn he could receive material and spiritual aid in accordance with his needs. (p. 109)

The *Communist Manifesto* hit me like a bolt of lightning. I read it avidly, finding in it answers to many of the seemingly unanswerable dilemmas which had plagued me. I read it over and over again, not completely understanding every passage or every idea, but enthralled nevertheless by the possibility of a communist revolution here. I began to see the problems of Black people within the context of a large working-class movement. My ideas about Black liberation were imprecise, and I could not find the right concepts to articulate them; still, I was acquiring some understanding about how capitalism could be abolished. (pp. 109-10)

What struck me so emphatically was the idea that once the emancipation of the proletariat became a reality, the foundation was laid for the emancipation of all oppressed groups in the society. Images surged up in my mind of Black workers in Birmingham trekking every morning to the steel mills or descending into the mines. Like an expert surgeon, this document cut away cataracts from my eyes. The eyes heavy with hatred on Dynamite Hill; the roar of explosives, the fear, the hidden guns, the weeping Black woman at our door, the children without lunches, the schoolyard bloodshed, the social games of the Black middle class, Shack I/Shack II, the back of the bus, police searches—it all fell into place. What had seemed a personal hatred of me, an inexplicable refusal of Southern whites to confront their own emotions, and a stubborn willingness of Blacks to acquiesce, became the inevitable consequence of a ruthless system which kept itself alive and well by encouraging spite, competition and the oppression of one group by another. Profit was the word: the cold and constant motive for the behavior, the contempt and the despair I had seen. (p. 110)

Of course, the most powerful impact the *Manifesto* had on me—what moved me most—was the vision of a new society, without exploiters and exploited, a society without classes, a society where no one would be permitted to own so much that he could use his possessions to exploit other human beings. After the communist revolution "we shall have an association, in which the free development of each is the condition for the free development of all."

The final words of the *Manifesto* moved me to an overwhelming desire to throw myself into the communist movement. . . . (p. 111)

[When the Los Angeles chapter of the Student Nonviolent Coordinating Committee closed down] I tried to acquire the information I needed in order to decide whether I wanted to become a member of the Communist Party. At this stage in my life and my political evolution . . . I needed to become a part of a serious revolutionary *party.* I wanted an anchor, a base, a mooring. I needed comrades with whom I could share a common ideology. I was tired of ephemeral ad-hoc groups that fell apart when faced with the slightest difficulty; tired of men who measured their sexual height by women's intellectual genuflection. It wasn't that I was fearless, but I knew that to

win, we had to fight and the fight that would win was the one collectively waged by the masses of our people and working people in general. I knew that this fight had to be led by a group, a party with more permanence in its membership and structure and more substance in its ideology. Confrontations were opportunities to be met; problems were entanglements to be sorted out with the right approach, the correct ideas. And I needed to know and respect what I was doing. Until now all our actions seemed to end, finally, in an ellipsis—three dots of irresolution, inconsistency and ineffectiveness.

During that depressing time, I reread Lenin's *What Is To Be Done,* and it helped me to clarify my own predicament. I read Du Bois again, particularly his statements around the time he decided to join the Communist Party.

Since Frankfurt, since London, since San Diego, I had been wanting to join a revolutionary party. Of all the parties that called themselves revolutionary or Marxist-Leninist, the Communist Party, in my opinion, alone did not overstate itself. Despite my criticisms of some aspects of the Party's policies, I had already reached the conclusion that it would be the Communist Party or, for the time being, nothing at all.

But before I could make my decision I had to examine it, study it. The Che-Lumumba Club, the Black cell of the Party in Los Angeles, was the section of the Party which interested me. I wanted to know what its role and responsibilities were within the Party and how it maintained its identity and consistency as its cadres involved themselves in the Black Liberation Movement. . . . Insofar as the democratic centralist structure of the Party was concerned, the Che-Lumumba Club was just like any other club. Yet it did have a special role, originating from the fact that Black Communists in Los Angeles had fought within the Party for a club that would be all Black and whose primary responsibility would be to carry Marxist-Leninist ideas to the Black Liberation struggle in L.A. and to provide leadership for the larger Party as far as the Black movement was concerned. (pp. 187-89)

In July 1968, I turned over my fifty-cents—the initial membership dues—to the chairman of the Che-Lumumba Club, and became a full-fledged member of the Communist Party, U.S.A. (p. 189)

The more the movement for my freedom increased in numbers, strength and confidence, the more imperative it became for everyone to see it not as something exceptional but as a small part of a great fight against injustice, one bough in a solidly rooted tree of resistance. It was not only political repression, but racism, poverty, police brutality, drugs, and all the myriad ways Black, Brown, Red, Yellow and white working people are kept chained to misery and despair. And it was not only within the United States of America, but in countries like Vietnam, with the bombs falling like rain from U.S. B52's, burning and dismembering innocent children.

We wanted the culminating mass demonstration of the campaign to bring all these struggles together in a single, unified dramatization of our power. All our separate movements—political prisoners, welfare rights, national liberation, labor, women, antiwar—might generate storms here and there. But only a mighty union of them all could beget the great hurricane to topple the whole edifice of injustice. (p. 382)

At the victory party the evening of the verdict, our joy knew no bounds and our celebration no restraints. Yet in the echoes of our laughter and the frenzy of our dancing there was also caution. If we saw this moment of triumph as a conclusion and not as a point of departure, we would be ignoring all the others who remained draped in chains. We knew that to save their lives, we had to preserve and build upon the movement. (p. 397)

Fearing that some local committees might consider their mission accomplished, we decided to send out immediately a communique requesting that they all keep their operations alive. To ensure that this message filtered down to the masses, we decided that I would go on a speaking tour. While expressing our gratitude to the people who had joined the movement which achieved my freedom, I would appeal to them to stay with us as long as racism or political repression kept Ruchell, Fleeta, the Attica brothers or any other human being behind bars. (pp. 397-98)

> *Angela Davis, in her* Angela Davis: An Autobiography *(copyright © 1974 by Angela Davis; reprinted by permission of Random House, Inc.), Random House, 1974, 400 p.*

ERNEST KRAUSZ

[*If They Come in the Morning*] is, if you like, a book on American prisons; but it is that only because it is in the prisons today that the politically conscious Negro is fighting for his life and where the un-politically conscious, the framed as well as the properly convicted, are learning the meaning of true political struggle. . . .

In terms of the sociology of minorities Angela Davis's story is of the next stage beyond the ghetto; not yet, it is true, the stage of the systematic extermination-camp, but somewhere reasonably far along that road, where the Black Panthers and any other group which thinks that the lesson of Watts and all the other smouldering ghettoes is to take up arms and defend itself can be systematically eliminated.

> *Ernest Krausz, "Ghettoes and Beyond," in* The Times Literary Supplement *(© Times Newspapers Ltd. (London) 1971; reproduced from* The Times Literary Supplement *by permission), No. 3637, November 12, 1971, p. 1407.**

STEVEN V. ROBERTS

The best parts of *If They Come in the Morning* are several essays by Miss Davis. . . . Most of the remaining pages are padded with statements and letters from George Jackson, Ruchell Magee, Bobby Seale and other "political prisoners." . . . And at times, this book degenerates into stupefying radical rhetoric. . . .

In spite of the rhetoric, however, and sometimes because of it, this is an infuriating book, and rousing that sort of emotion is no small achievement. For instance, Miss Davis describes how a glaring double standard is often applied to violence by militants and police. . . .

Moreover, Miss Davis argues, the courts are often used as "instruments of oppression" against blacks—and whites—bold enough to challenge the existing order. . . .

Even allowing for exaggeration, [the cases Miss Davis cites] leave one outraged; "equal protection of the laws" rings hol-

low. But the book is maddening in another way. Its whole tone implies that the only acceptable response is an enthusiastic "right on," without any questions or doubts. The fact remains, however, that the book bristles with contradictions.

The authors repeatedly assert their independence and self-determination, yet they say that virtually all criminals are "victims" of socio-economic forces and are not responsible for their actions. They want the protection of the courts, but do not admit the right of a free society to protect itself. They talk about forging a "united front," but even the Panthers are rent by petty squabbling. . . .

In essence, then, this is a book written by revolutionaries, true believers, who can justify anything in the name of their cause. (p. 69)

> *Steven V. Roberts, "'If They Come in the Morning: Voices of Resistance'," in* Commonweal *(copyright © 1972 Commonweal Publishing Co., Inc.; reprinted by permission of Commonweal Publishing Co., Inc.), Vol. XCVI, No. 3, March 24, 1972, pp. 68-9.*

ELINOR LANGER

"Angela Davis: An Autobiography" is not so much revealing as "exemplary." Writing it was not an act of self-discovery; it was an act of political communication. Yet it is no prose poster. It takes its structure from her arrest, imprisonment, trial and acquittal and, for that reason and because the prison movement is her political work, it is sometimes the voice of Every Prisoner, a little familiar. But it is also a strong, idiosyncratic account of her childhood, youth and growth, and her choice of the Communist party as the agency through which to act. To the personal narrative she brings such precision and individuality that she reminds us out of what universal, bitter, private experiences the black movement coalesced in the first place. Her account of her involvement with the party is so plausible and fresh it turns back the burden of explanation to those who feel the C. P. is so irrelevant, drenched with the blood of history, or populated by Government agents, that anyone who would willingly join it is stupid, unserious, an agent him/her self, or fond of losing. (p. 5)

Davis's book, particularly her description of the events and discussions that were the foundation of her choice of the C.P., is a useful new look at black and radical politics of the 1960's. But her need to present her evolution as fully "objective" bothers me. Along with her need to represent herself as "unexceptional," I think it leads to distortions. She was not a typical Southern black child: Her mother worked on the Scottsboro case in the 1930's; her family always had Communist friends; she joined Advance, the Communist youth group, when she went to [Elizabeth Irwin High School in New York]. This made for attractions, comfortableness, predilections—invisible standards by which later situations are evaluated—even if they do not crudely dictate choices.

Both the anticapitalist theory she studied and the interracial Communist community to which she was accustomed must have affected her negative analysis of the American black political scene. Private factors do not invalidate the public ones, and her conclusions ought to be considered in political argument, not in ad feminem speculation. But I wish she had chosen to present herself in a slightly more rounded way. Psychologizing can undercut the political argument, true, but political autobiography can be propaganda. She would say that is an honest function, and indeed the one she chose. I think she is too large to be confined in stereotypes, even heroic ones. (p. 55)

Elinor Langer, "'Angela Davis: An Autobiography'," in The New York Times Book Review *(© 1974 by The New York Times Company; reprinted by permission), October 27, 1974, pp. 5, 55.*

IVAN WEBSTER

[*Angela Davis: An Autobiography*] is less an autobiography than a preliminary probe of her own fiber, her humble realization that she is made of stern stuff. Davis elaborates on this discovery in the context of her prison experiences, and concludes that her only possible response to our system of criminal justice is to dismantle it: she is eloquent, tough and stubborn in her moral integrity. (p. 30)

It's when she moves away from hard, stark issues that the book falters. I also heard (and heard tell of) Angela when she took to the political rostrum. While she was a generous political battler—always stressing the plight of others more than her own—as an on-the-lines rouser she was often less than stirring. The rhetoric sounded hackneyed, the terms were not fresh, and one didn't feel the riveting quality of mind that could be heard in her lectures and in her political speeches.

A similar failing, on the intellectual and analytical plane, pervades her book. She has taken a rather narrow approach, propping up this account of her life with tract-like doctrine, reprising speeches, listing political debts and settling old movement scores. She is conscious of class conflict at seven and cannily unmasking the evils of the profit motive at 15, which doesn't sound like reminiscence. Why did these things happen to *this* woman, we keep asking, and get only partial answers.

There isn't a sharp enough sense of history in these pages, either the immediate history she is surviving and trying to change, or a place in the continuum at the end of a long line of forebears. . . . She writes as if she were in a vacuum; there is no sustained discussion of how she thinks an onslaught on capitalist power ought to proceed.

She speaks as a black intellectual, but reading this book you'd never know that other black intellectuals in America have made similar decisions to ally themselves with the party and then, for reasons they've amply documented, eventually came to have serious reservations about their choice. . . . One would relish hearing her response to the critique of the role of blacks in the party by Harold Cruse in *The Crisis of the Negro Intellectual*. The book isn't mentioned; indeed she has very little to say about her reading in any case, or how she fared under Marcuse's tutelage. Instead of an exploration of the development of her political thought, she contents herself with romantic posturing—in effect, with challenging the capitalist monolith to put up its dukes, avowing that her Marxist dad can lick anybody on the ideological block.

One would have thought that if anyone possessed the theoretical equipment to provide an in-depth situation-based discussion of what the black left accomplished in the '60s and where the movement ought to go from here, it would be Davis. But her discussions, such as they are, of Carmichael, Cleaver, Newton and cultural nationalist Ron Karenga rarely grapple with these men's theory or practice. Purely, and scantily, descriptive, she offers little analysis and thus has botched a splendid opportunity.

It may be more correct to say, bypassed. I can only speculate, but I think the book is ill timed. It doesn't crackle with the convictions of a woman with a world to win. (pp. 30-1)

Ivan Webster, "Political Fury," in The New Republic *(reprinted by permission of* The New Republic; *© 1974 The New Republic, Inc.), Vol. 171, No. 20, November 16, 1974, pp. 30-1.*

JULIUS LESTER

To be born black is to know one's self as politically defined, and negatively so, before there is the opportunity to experience one's self as a person. [In *Angela Davis: An Autobiography*] Davis is eloquent as she communicates her childhood bewilderment at being an object of hate, and the book is most personal when she recounts her attempts to resist through anger, ridicule of whites, confrontations with them, and fantasies. . . .

One is left with the impression of a woman who lives as she thinks it necessary to live and not as she would like to, if she allowed herself to have desires. She seems to be a woman of enormous self-discipline and control, who willed herself to a total political identity. Her will is so strong that, at times, it is frightening. (p. 54)

Davis has used her politics to eradicate everything in her which would interfere with her commitment to revolutionary change. If there is an Angela Davis separate from the Communist woman, Davis does not know her and has little desire to do so. . . . [One] must wonder if Davis is using Marxism-Leninism to try and save the world or herself. No matter. A political ideology is unsuited for either task. (p. 55)

Julius Lester, "Young, Female, Black, and Revolutionary," in The Progressive *(reprinted by permission from* The Progressive, *409 East Main Street, Madison, Wisconsin 53703; copyright 1975 by The Progressive, Inc.), Vol. 39, No. 2, February, 1975, pp. 54-5.*

PAULA GIDDINGS

If there is a major criticism of [*Angela Davis: An Autobiography*], it is the lack of her further explanation of [her reasons for joining the Communist Party]. This part of the book is so crucial, particularly in the light of the cyclical schisms Blacks have had over this issue. . . . What were those criticisms of the Party's policies? How does she view the Party in the context of Black history? What was the significance in her mind of joining a Black collective? What have her observations been of its effectiveness since she has been a member? There is probably no one who has more resources to deal with this question. Her Marxism seemed to bloom outside of the States where, without the peculiar (and often racist) history of the American Communist Party, Marxism and Black nationalism are not necessarily diametrically opposed. But what are *her* views on that? Although one can understand her reluctance to criticize the CP, which, in its ability to organize large masses of people to her cause and make it an international issue, may well have saved her life at the most, and her present well-being at the least, one hopes that she will talk about the subject more, subsequently. (p. 95)

[After] reading the last page, one's immediate reaction is, but what have we learned about Angela Davis? The answer is a great deal. But one must understand her penchant for understatement and her style of letting significance of the events speak for themselves. . . . [She] has little desire to project herself as a singularly charismatic figure; . . . the primary purpose of her book is to illuminate the political causes and concerns central to her life. (p. 96)

> *Paula Giddings, "'Angela Davis: An Autobiography'" (reprinted by permission of the author; copyright, 1975 Paula Giddings), in* Black World, *Vol. XXVI, No. 5, March, 1975, pp. 93-7.*

JANET BURROWAY

Out of one of the luminous lives of our time Angela Davis has produced *An Autobiography* like a damp firecracker. In part, this is deliberate. She professes reluctance to tell her story at all, lest it should require 'a posture of difference, an assumption that I was unlike other women—other Black women', and in the wilful assumption that she is like other women, she has left out her identity. No *auto,* in fact; no particularising sense of her ambitions, her talents, her personal griefs and personal beauty. Worse, her determination to concentrate on the struggle against global exploitation, guilt-motivated legal systems, the spectre of fascism, etc., has led to a total exclusion of internal struggle, without which no autobiography rings true.

Her childhood in Birmingham, Alabama, passed, according to her account, in such unruffled familial accord that it might be the envy of us all, and it is striking that it is more recognisable as an American and a middle-class childhood than a Black one. . . . The shape of [her] story (including the catapult to fame) is perfectly consistent with a national myth in which Henry Ford outranks Robin Hood for heroism. The virtues involved are those of the American work ethic: self-discipline, self-reliance, familial piety and dogged optimism; and the vices are its vices: false modesty, intolerance and a political stance that is, however communist, near-Nixonian in its lack of scope. Through all this, of course, run the horrors of Black childhood in the Deep South, but unfortunately these are reported in a tone of distanced self-righteousness. Since we are not allowed to share in the personal emotions, including the less heroic ones, of the narrator, we shall not be moved. (p. 593)

What are we to do with this, essentially literary, failure?—literary because what Ms Davis has done is to take the oratorical skill of a political activist and employ it in a form for which it is embarrassingly ill-suited. She can write otherwise. When she permits herself to quote from two of her letters to George Jackson in Soledad Prison (one of them was used as evidence

against her and so public anyway), we are suddenly treated to felt flights of metaphor. But for the most part whatever is personal, passionate or sexual is skirted with a visible Victorian *moue.* . . . And whenever personal suffering can be wrenched into rhetoric, it is duly wrenched, to the frustration of our natural sympathies. . . .

Well, it is not a good book. But neither does it undo the uncompromising courage of the life. (p. 594)

> *Janet Burroway, "All American," in* New Statesman *(©1975 The Statesman & Nation Publishing Co. Ltd.), Vol. 89, No. 2302, May 2, 1975, pp. 593-94.*

GEORGE E. KENT

[*Angela Davis: An Autobiography*] is conceived to be a political autobiography, one which stresses "my overwhelming sense of belonging to a community of humans—a community of struggle against poverty and racism." Hopefully, the book would make people understand why a large number of persons feel that they have no alternative but to offer their total lives to the battle against oppression and inspire more to join the struggle. . . .

Davis places herself in the historic context of the black struggle. Part 1 registers the personal emotions but pushes an analysis of situations based upon institutional corruption and the vagaries of the capitalistic system. In this way, she guards herself from being overwhelmed by her situation as a purely individual predicament and keeps her vision clear for understanding how individuals are crushed in an oppressive system. (p. 101)

[Other] chapters are educational with respect to the resistance and elaborately thought-out strategies necessary to overcome prejudicial circumstances and unexpected events. Davis's resources in prison dramatize and underline the kinds of suffering and injustice the penal system affords for the anonymous prisoner, and the portraits of both prisoners and officials outline a discouraging picture.

Despite its single-minded emphasis upon proper ideological response, the passion with which this political autobiography is written enhances its educational objective. (p. 103)

> *George E. Kent, "The 1975 Black Literary Scene: Significant Developments," in* PHYLON: The Atlanta University Review of Race and Culture, *37 (copyright, 1976, by Atlanta University; reprinted by permission of* PHYLON*), Vol. 37, No. 1, First Quarter (March, 1976), pp. 100-15.**

Angie Debo
1890-

Debo is an American educator, historian, and author of books on western U.S. history and the American Indian. Most of her research and writing concentrate on Oklahoma, an area she came to in a covered wagon as a child and has remained in for most of her adult life. *A History of the Indians of the United States* (1970) is generally deemed her most significant book, a work termed seminal for its treatment of the relationship between Native American and white settler. Although Debo is considered an Indian advocate and writes about the Indian tribes with a great deal of sympathy and admiration, her restrained accounts such as *And Still the Waters Run* (1940) present a balanced picture of the settlement of the West. She served on the board of directors of the Association of American Indian Affairs for ten years. (See also *Contemporary Authors*, Vols. 69-72.)

Courtesy of Royce L. Craig

Excerpt from *AND STILL THE WATERS RUN*

Every schoolboy knows that from the settlement of Jamestown to the 1870's Indian warfare was a perpetual accompaniment of American pioneering, but the second stage in dispossessing the Indians is not so generally and romantically known. The age of military conquest was succeeded by the age of economic absorption, when the long rifle of the frontiersman was displaced by the legislative enactment and court decree of the legal exploiter, and the lease, mortgage, and deed of the land shark. As a preliminary to this process the Indians were persuaded or forced to surrender their tribal organization and accept United States citizenship and to divide their communal holdings into individual allotments.

Because of the magnitude of the plunder and the rapidity of the spoliation the most spectacular development of this policy occurred with the Five Civilized Tribes of the Indian Territory. At the beginning of the present century about seventy thousand of these Indians owned the eastern half of the area that now constitutes the state of Oklahoma, a territory immensely wealthy in farmland and forest and coal mines, and with untapped oil pools of incalculable value. They ruled themselves and controlled this tribal property under constitutional governments of their own choosing, and they had attained a degree of civilization that made them at once the boast of the Indian Office and living examples of the benefits of travelling in the white man's road. Their political and economic tenure was guaranteed by treaties and patents from the Federal Government, and warned by the tragic fate of all Indians who had lost their homes, they insisted upon the observance of these conditions. But white people began to settle among them, and by 1890 these immigrants were overwhelmingly in the majority. Congress therefore abrogated the treaties, and the Indians received their land under individual tenure and became citizens of Oklahoma when it was admitted to the Union in 1907.

The orgy of exploitation that resulted is almost beyond belief. Within a generation these Indians, who had owned and governed a region greater in area and potential wealth than many an American state, were almost stripped of their holdings, and were rescued from starvation only through public charity. Such treatment of an independent people by a great imperial power would have aroused international condemnation; but these Indian republics were—to quote John Marshall's famous opinion—"domestic dependent nations," and the destruction of their autonomy was a matter of internal policy. Even as a real estate transaction this transfer of property would have attracted wide attention, but the Indians had been forced to accept the perilous gift of American citizenship and they were despoiled individually under the forms of existing law; hence no writer of American history devotes even a sentence to their wrongs, students of Indian life are interested only in their inspiring achievements under the tribal régime, and their plight during the generation of their exploitation has been consistently ignored by the press.

Obviously the rapidity of the spoliation called for crude methods, in many cases even criminal methods, and the immense value of the loot exerted a powerful influence upon contemporary opinion and standards of conduct. It should not be necessary to point out that Oklahomans are no worse than their neighbors, for this is only one episode—although the most dramatic episode—in a process that constitutes an unrecorded chapter in the history of every American frontier. But the reaction of this process upon the ideals and standards of successive frontier communities is a factor in the formation of the American character that should no longer be disregarded by students of social institutions.

Fortunately the historian is not expected to prescribe remedies. The policy of the United States in liquidating the institutions of the Five Tribes was a gigantic blunder that ended a hopeful experiment in Indian development, destroyed a unique civilization, and degraded thousands of individuals. (pp. vii-ix)

> *Angie Debo, in her* And Still the Waters Run *(copyright, 1940, Princeton University Press; copyright renewed © 1968 by Angie Debo; reprinted by permission of Princeton University Press), Princeton University Press, 1940 (and reprinted by Gordian Press, Inc., 1966), 417 p.*

Excerpt from *A HISTORY OF THE INDIANS OF THE UNITED STATES*

Although these aboriginal Americans varied widely from the "western" stereotype—they did not all live in tipis, wear Sioux war bonnets, or speak one "Indian language"—yet they had many common characteristics. These have influenced their history, persist to the present day in their descendants, and form their unique contribution to the American spirit.

Notable was their adaptation to their physical environment. While the white man sought to dominate and change the natural setting, the Indian subordinated himself to it. (p. 3)

[Another] Indian characteristic [was] his love for his homeland, which amounted to a mystical identification with it. This is difficult for the white man to understand. When Garry, of the Spokanes of eastern Washington, said, "I was born by these waters. The earth here is my mother," he was not using a poetic figure of speech; he was stating what he felt to be the literal truth. Toohoolhoolzote, a chief of the Nez Percés, fighting to keep his land, said, "The earth is part of my body and I never gave up the earth." Fifteen hundred miles away in embryo Oklahoma, a region as remote to Garry and Toohoolhoolzote as the other side of the moon, Eufaula Harjo exhorted the participants in the ceremonials of the old Creek town of Tulsa, "The mountains and hills, that you see, are your backbone, and the gullies and the creeks, which are between the hills and mountains, are your heart veins." When the white man cut up this living entity with his surveying instruments, the Indian felt the horror of dismemberment.

All this, in a way not subject to analysis, was a part of the Indian's religion, for he was deeply religious. The familiar shapes of earth, the changing sky, the wild animals he knew, were joined with his own spirit in mystical communion. The powers of nature, the personal quest of the soul, the acts of daily life, the solidarity of the tribe—all were religious, and were sustained by dance and ritual.

Out of all this grew the feeling for beauty that makes the modern Indian superbly gifted in the various art forms. It is not an accident that a disproportionate number of Indians are among the great American dancers. The steps and discipline of the ballet are foreign to native experience, but the feel is there. Indian laborers are in demand as strawberry pickers in the Oklahoma Ozarks, for nobody but an Indian would arrange a box of berries with an eye to artistic effect. The beautiful penmanship of beginning Indian children is well known. (p. 4)

The Indians' eloquence in the use of language, even when clumsily interpreted, has been marked throughout their history.

Now this sensibility joined with education and skill in English usage is finding modern literary expression. (p. 5)

None of this helped the Indians in their encounter with the white man. On the contrary, their temperamental and personality traits were a handicap. Industrious and thrifty in their own way, they lacked the ruthless driving force of the invading race and they had no experience to meet it. In 1906, shortly before Oklahoma statehood, when all that new frontier was bursting with a frenzy of development and the Indians were left stranded and helpless, Pleasant Porter, the wise old mixed-blood chief of the Creeks, made a thoughtful analysis to a committee of the United States Senate. "It is a complex problem, gentlemen. . . . You are the evolution of thousands of years, perhaps. . . . We both probably started at the same point, but our paths diverged, and the influences to which we were subjected varied, and we see the result."

Even now Indian children do not want to "show off" in the classroom, and the Indian with a good job is pulled down by the needs of his numerous relatives. For 350 years an attempt has been made—a faltering attempt, but always present—to acquaint the Indians with the white Americans' economic techniques, but they have produced few business or industrial leaders. Even an organizing genius like Tecumseh depended upon emotional appeal and a mystical union with the unseen world rather than a drive for prestige.

There was one exception in many tribes—the attainment of distinction through war honors. Thus war as an exciting contest of courage and skill was a necessity. . . . But the thirst for military glory was not universal. Many tribes, like the sedentary Pueblos, fought bravely, but only in self-defense. Peace making was a highly emotional procedure involving beads and tobacco and other esoteric symbols.

In his relations with the white man the Indian had little capacity for compromise, for pliant yielding to the inevitable in order to salvage what he could. He entered into a treaty and learned its provisions and never admitted its abrogation. (pp. 6-7)

This same habit of quiet withdrawal was—and still is—used in other circumstances. The Indian wanted to be with his own people, to preserve his inner values, his cultural integrity. To this desire he owes his remarkable record of survival, the preservation of his distinctive identity, through centuries of encroachment by a more numerous and aggressive race; but it has been baffling to well-meaning "civilizers" determined to throw him into the melting pot. (pp. 7-8)

This trait accounts for the appalling loss of life when Indians were torn from their homeland. Tribes migrated voluntarily with no damage, and in times of emergency the efficiency and dispatch with which they could travel long distances is almost incredible; but any forcible uprooting carries the same dreary statistics. (p. 8)

This universality of intellectual and spiritual traits is surprising in view of the Indians' great diversity in language and physical characteristics. It is impossible to determine whether this divergence originated before they crossed from Asia to the American continent, or whether it developed during the uncounted millenniums when they settled and intermarried in small bands apart. It is readily observed wherever a fullblood group congregates, whether in church or council or dance. Within each is a uniformity of feature and body structure never found in a similar assembly of white Americans; but these groups differ widely from each other. For convenience they are usually classified according to language families known as linguistic stocks. The tribes within these larger groupings did not necessarily recognize their relationship. Although ethnologists may find traces of common beliefs and customs, these tribes were sometimes separated by great distances or even by traditional enmity. (pp. 8-9)

With so great a range of climate, topography, and flora and fauna, people conforming as did the aboriginal inhabitants of the United States to their physical background developed a great diversity of culture. It should be noted that none of them had any domestic animals except the dog, and of domestic fowls, turkeys were raised only by the Pueblos. Most of them made pottery and baskets, and many practiced agriculture—raising corn, beans, squashes, pumpkins, and tobacco, all New World products. But their practices differed widely. (p. 13)

[The] United States was inhabited by a self-sufficient people before the coming of the white man. (p. 18)

> *Angie Debo, in her* A History of the Indians of the United States *(copyright 1970 by the University of Oklahoma Press), University of Oklahoma Press, 1970, 286 p.*

STANLEY VESTAL

[*And Still the Waters Run*] tells the story of the spoliation or liquidation of [the Indian Nations called the Five Civilized Tribes].

The author is a scholar of honesty and courage, with a talent and skill, which many a literary man might envy. Her presentation is as authentic as her materials. Though the book contains a wealth of detail, it is not only readable but a solid contribution to the history of the region. . . .

Miss Debo tells her story with admirable restraint, letting the facts speak for themselves. The book demonstrates that the rights of civilized Indians were no more respected than those of "wild tribes." The property was there and the white men were determined to get it. In these circumstances there could be only one result.

Citizenship eventually aided the Indian to offer organized resistance to the process, and the New Deal for Indians is doing what it can to save what is left and repair the damage in some measure. What has been and is being accomplished along these lines is presented as fairly as the earlier tragedy. Miss Debo's book is a sound performance and will undoubtedly remain the standard book on this subject.

> *Stanley Vestal, "Despoiling the Indians," in* New York Herald Tribune, *January 5, 1941, p. 3.*

ALBAN W. HOOPES

[*And Still the Waters Run*] is a detailed study of the [history of the Five Civilized Tribes] from 1900 to the present. It contains an unrivalled wealth of information, presented in a clear, business-like manner. . . .

It is most interesting to note that the author, in common with other students of Indian affairs, regards the Collier régime as the opening of a period characterized by more satisfactory

relations between the races and with the government. "Collier was the first Commissioner who ever approached his problem from the sociological and scientific point of view . . ." . . . This may be entirely true, but it should be remembered that Mr. Collier came into office in 1933, when the Indian problem was essentially different from what it had been in 1880 or even 1900. No Indian wars faced the new administration, and the public was more friendly than was the case after Little Big Horn. Thus Mr. Collier's desire for the more exact regulation of Indian administration and the eradication of long-standing abuses found concrete expression in the Wheeler-Howard Act of 1934 . . . and the Oklahoma Indian Welfare Act of 1936. . . . One could wish for a more extended analysis of this very important legislation. A discussion of the various constitutional and legal points involved would be especially valuable.

In conclusion be it said that the author deserves commendation for her manner of presentation. The materials at hand afford an excellent opportunity to be melodramatic. Instead one finds a restrained and coldly dispassionate statement of the facts that gains force and weight as the narrative proceeds. As it stands no more severe indictment of the white man in his relations with the red has come recently under the reviewer's notice.

> *Alban W. Hoopes, "Book Reviews and Book Notes: 'And Still the Waters Run'," in* The Social Studies, *Vol. XXXII, No. 3, March, 1941, p. 136.*

LeROY R. HAFEN

[The pages of *The Road to Disappearance*] reveal the tragic story of the Creeks, from their great days as a powerful confederacy to the final destruction of their independent political identity by the Dawes Act. The tragedy is especially moving for the periods of the Red Stick War, the removal to the Oklahoma region, and the Civil War days, when the Creeks were split into Northern and Southern factions. (p. 826)

The record of the United States in its dealings with the Creeks is not one to be proud of. The breaking of promises, the defrauding, the ruthless aggression—all are marshaled by Miss Debo as a telling indictment of United States Indian policy and administration. She tells the Creek story with deep sympathy. "No white man ever fathomed their mystical love of the soil that made them regard its division into metes and bounds with a horror of dismemberment." . . . (p. 827)

> *LeRoy R. Hafen, "Review of Books: 'The Road to Disappearance'," in* The American Historical Review, *Vol. XLVIII, No. 4, July, 1943, pp. 826-27.*

MARI SANDOZ

In **"Prairie City"** . . . Dr. Debo portrays the life of a small community from its settlement in the Oklahoma land run of 1889 to the present. While the town is a composite of many places, it becomes an actuality in this story of a people learning to live together and with their land. Because the railroad is only fifteen miles away the concern is less with pioneering than with the growth of an American community. (p. 3)

While the impact of the book might have been greater if actual names and places had been used, or a strong central character created, it throws a searching light upon the American community and, through it, upon the small community everywhere. Here, in a society comparatively transparent, the student can consider modern man. He can see what happens to an unprotected minority that possesses something a stronger people wants—even the generous and humane stronger people we hold ourselves to be. He can study the effects of an economic colonial status upon a region, and the rise of tenancy with its recent refinements—whole districts with no tenants or workers who have children because the landowner is eliminating the need for schools and taxes.

No other region comparable in area or variety to the old buffalo lands offers the scientist, the historian or the novelist as complete and comprehensible a record of civilized man's incumbency upon a piece of earth. To this record the books of Dr. Debo have added a great deal. (p. 26)

> Mari Sandoz, "The Oklahoma Story," in The New York Times Book Review (© 1944 by The New York Times Company; reprinted by permission), May 21, 1944, pp. 3, 26.

STANLEY WALKER

[In *Oklahoma*] Miss Angie Debo finds the whole state fascinating. . . .

[Her] study is calm and restrained; she scorns the writers who have told melodramatic tales of poor Indians and whites and their didoes when overwhelmed by sudden riches. She goes rather light in telling of the shocking lack of ordinary probity among Oklahoma public officials, and not a single one of the state's many desperadoes gets a biography. She dismisses prohibition, which is riveted in the state's constitution and which survived a recent attempt at repeal, with only a few lines—a discussion which seems hardly adequate. She does say that teetotalism is a way of life among the great middle classes, an ideal that is generally approved, though bootlegging is an established and not always a dishonorable profession.

And yet, for all this, and within its self-imposed limitations, it is an honest and knowing book, written with a great affection. The best part of it, somehow, is the brief reminiscences of a few old-timers, little flashes which tell more than many pages of description. . . .

The Deboe study is well worth reading, notwithstanding the fact that much of it is plain description and that the criticisms are not sharp enough to suit every captious outsider. It contains much meat, but one looks in vain, and sadly, for any mention of such notable Oklahomans as Temple Houston and Moman Pruiett, the criminal lawyers; Robert Owen and Thomas Gore, the celebrated United States Senators; Sherman Bulingsley, the old Enid boy who did so much to civilize New York City, and Mrs. Thomas E. Dewey, the charming wife of New York's Governor. Oh well, we can't have everything. It's a good little book, anyhow.

> Stanley Walker, "Honest and Affectionate," in New York Herald Tribune, July 2, 1950, p. 8.

N. SCOTT MOMADAY

["**A History of the Indians of the United States**"] is a comprehensive survey, objective in style and chronological in organization. But here this combination of qualities results in a kind of prose dilemma; the compactness and continuity such a coverage required are never quite achieved. More often than not, the text seems too conscious of itself, inhibited, intimidated and confused by myriad facts and figures. (p. 46)

In the early 400 pages of Miss Debo's book we see how the familiar patterns of invasion, conquest and diplomatic administration emerge upon the geography of Progress. And familiar is perhaps the key word here. One has the sense that nothing is so appropriate to this account of the subject as the maxim that history repeats itself.

If Miss Debo's study is largely a reiteration of standard information, it is nonetheless carefully and usefully presented. What we have at last is a reference work, by and large, a grand summary of particular and historical knowledge. Moreover, there is at the end a consideration of quite recent events, a kind of survey of Indian affairs in the 1960's, on the basis of which the author is altogether sanguine about the future of Indians in this country; the final chapter is entitled "The Indians Find New Hope." There is good reason to be optimistic, certainly, and such a study as this should end upon that note. But Miss Debo's final chapter is not yet history, and the hope of which it speaks has yet to be realized. (p. 47)

> N. Scott Momaday, "When the West Was Won and a Civilization Was Lost," in The New York Times Book Review (© 1971 by The New York Times Company; reprinted by permission), March 7, 1971, pp. 46-7.*

ROBERT M. UTLEY

In *A History of the Indians of the United States* [Angie Debo as] both historian and activist combine in well-balanced proportion. (p. 125)

On the whole the presentation comes off exceptionally well. The first fourteen chapters, encompassing four centuries, a continent, and the major American tribes in all their cultural and historical diversity, is a hurried but comprehensive survey. Inevitably there are some factual errors and occasional oversimplifications—the view of the United States army, for example, is singularly one-dimensional. But there is also the knowledge and understanding resulting from almost half a century of study, reflection, and observation. The point of view is plainly sympathetic to the Indian, but the tone, unlike much modern writing about the Indian, is not stridently anti-white. These chapters form a very good survey of the sweep of Indian history through the close of the Indian wars and the beginning of the reservation period.

The last six chapters bring the story up to the present—from the Dawes Act, which started the breakup of the reservations, through John Collier's "New Deal" in the 1930s and the black years of "termination" in the 1950s, to the rebirth of hope in the 1960s. This is a story not often told in the conventional histories and rarely told anywhere with such authority and clarity. With particular emphasis on Oklahoma, which she knows most intimately, Debo once more follows the Indian down the "road to disappearance" beginning in eroding land base and ending in economic and cultural degradation. But she ends on a note of optimism that an awakened conscience of the majority combined with an emerging and articulate solidarity of the minority is at last producing a measure of justice and perhaps even atonement. (pp. 125-26)

[This] book is warmly recommended. (p. 126)

> Robert M. Utley, "Book Reviews: 'A History of the Indians of the United States'," in The Journal of American History (copyright Organization of American Historians, 1971), Vol. LVIII, No. 1, June, 1971, pp. 125-26.

ARTHUR H. DEROSIER, JR.

[In *A History of the Indians of the United States*, Angie Debo] has attempted a labor of love, a synthesis of the Indians as a factor in United States history. And she has succeeded admirably. . . .

[The book] is pure Debo pulling together a myriad persons, policies, events, and tribes into a fine, bright thread that weaves itself through four-hundred-plus years of history. Here, indeed, is the best one-volume history of the American Indians. It is "the master" capping an outstanding career with a work that will be studied and discussed as long as persons remain interested in American Indians.

There is no doubt where her sympathies lie. But she is gentle in her criticisms. Blunderers are depicted as such and not as sinister wretches out to despoil; "do-gooders" are chided for their lack of information but not for the tragic results they produced; Indians emerge as real people, not all good or all bad as others would have us believe. Although tragedy oozes from most pages, she ends on a hopeful note that offers a brighter future for Indians, if whites will only let Indians be Indians and not carbon copies of themselves. (p. 177)

> *Arthur H. Derosier, Jr., "Book Department: 'A History of the Indians of the United States'," in The Annals of The American Academy of Political and Social Science (© 1971, by The American Academy of Political and Social Science), Vol. 397, September, 1971, pp. 176-78.*

CHOICE

[*A History of the Indians of the United States* is the] best available survey of relations between the European intruders and the native Americans from discovery to the present day. . . . [The] book has more to say about what the white man did than about the Indians' development. To some degree this emphasis is warranted, because the words and deeds of the whites have been the greatest force for change among the native Americans virtually ever since Columbus. Still, the reader remains uninformed about the sources and nature of the remarkable durability and adaptability of the many Indian societies that have maintained their integrity through centuries of aggressive assaults.

> *"History, Geography and Travel: 'A History of the Indians of the United States'," in Choice (copyright © 1971 by American Library Association), Vol. 8, No. 7, September, 1971, p. 902.*

EDMUND J. DANZIGER, JR.

[*A History of the Indians of the United States*] is the best in-depth survey of United States Indian history to date. No opportunist on the publishing bandwagon, Angie Debo . . . writes with authority and conviction about the need for an intelligent Indian policy that will avoid the blunders and tragedies of the past. (p. 148)

The author's most original contributions are chapters on Alaska, where the white man has a chance to break the cycle of Indian conquest which characterized Indian history in the Lower 48, and the new hope of the 1960s. She is particularly optimistic about such self-help organizations as Oklahomans for Indian Opportunity and its programs for community improvement, work orientation and youth activities. An advocate of neither tribalism nor assimilation, she hopes to see some Indians "living happily and prospering on their own land . . . and some individuals living an adjusted life in white society." . . .

Although too much of the book focuses on Oklahoma Indians, particularly the Creeks (Debo's own research interest), she believes that their fate exemplifies Indian history. Written with liveliness and the sort of thorough scholarship we have come to expect in University of Oklahoma Press books, *A History of the Indians of the United States* is . . . a useful handbook for intelligent Americans of good will. (p. 149)

> *Edmund J. Danziger, Jr., "Book Reviews: 'A History of the Indians of the United States'," in The Historian (copyright 1971 by Phi Alpha Theta), Vol. XXXIV, No. 1, November, 1971, pp. 148-49.*

DONALD E. WORCESTER

[In *Geronimo*] Angie Debo set out to learn what sort of a man Geronimo actually was when stripped of the myths and legends that surround his name. What she found was a typical Apache warrior—a pitiless terror to his enemies, a trusted leader to his people, and an affectionate father to his family. As a prisoner of war from 1886 to his death in 1909, he also proved to be a shrewd businessman who capitalized on his name and reputation (at his death he had a bank account of about $10,000). The author, after exhaustive research and thoughtful analysis, has given us a balanced, temperate, and readable account of Geronimo the man. (pp. 363-64)

> *Donald E. Worcester, "Book Reviews: 'Geronimo: The Man, His Time, His Place'," in American Indian Quarterly (copyright © Society for American Indian Studies & Research 1978), Vol. 3, No. 4, Winter, 1977-78, pp. 363-64.*

G(eorge) William Domhoff

1936-

Domhoff is an American psychologist and author of books about politics and power. Domhoff first advanced his thesis that America's upper class is a governing class in *Who Rules America?* (1967). His books have generated considerable controversy, with critics arguing that his evidence for upper-class control of America's dominant institutions is unsubstantiated. Domhoff responds to these critics in *The Powers That Be* (1978), where he attempts to describe the specific processes through which the upper class exerts its control. Domhoff is professor of psychology and sociology at the University of California, Santa Cruz. (See also *Contemporary Authors*, Vols. 45-48.)

Excerpt from *THE POWERS THAT BE: PROCESSES OF RULING-CLASS DOMINATION IN AMERICA*

In most countries, it would be taken for granted that a social upper class with a highly disproportionate amount of wealth and income is a ruling class with domination over the government. How else, it would be argued, could such a tiny network of families possess so much if it didn't have its hooks into government? After all, isn't "power" and "rulership" inferred from various value distributions, such as those for wealth and income, which are merely the outcomes of struggles and conflicts over how the social product is to be produced and how it is to be divided? Isn't politics about "who gets what," with the "when, where and how" as subsidiary questions when it comes to the shape of the power structure?

Not so in the United States today. In a nation that always has denied the existence of social classes and class conflict, and overestimated the degree of social mobility, systematic information on the persistent inequality of wealth and income tends to get lost from public and academic debate. Besides, most social scientists, being of a pluralist persuasion, believe that many different groups, including organized labor, farmers, consumers and middle-class environmentalists, have a hand in political decisions—if not since the first years of the republic, at least since the Progressive Era and the New Deal. There is no such thing as a ruling class in America, or so we are assured by leading academicians, journalists, and other public figures.

We can begin to understand this reaction to wealth and income statistics if we realize that the predominant emphasis in American ideology is on the "process" by which things are done—democracy in government, equality of opportunity in education, fairness before the law—and not on "outcomes." The emphasis on outcomes, implying as it does a possible bias toward social egalitarianism, was anathema to most of the founding fathers, and it is anathema to the corporate business community of today. A special commentary in *Business Week* in December 1975 went so far as to charge that the new egalitarian movement of the 1970's was actually authoritarian in nature and would wreck the economic system if it were able to substitute equality of outcomes for equality of opportunity.

The emphasis on process in American thinking appears in the social sciences as a theory of power which insists that power can be known only by seeing it in action. That is, we must study the process of power, rather than infer power from outcomes. Who benefits, the very essence of a power struggle, is hardly considered. This viewpoint is epitomized in the writings of Robert A. Dahl, one of the two or three most eminent political theorists of the past two decades. In a sharp critique of sociologists Floyd Hunter and C. Wright Mills, both of whom believed on the basis of their studies that a small "power structure" or "power elite" dominated in the United States, Dahl rejected their evidence and argument because "I do not see how anyone can suppose that he has established the dominance of a specific group in a community or a nation without basing his analysis on the careful examination of a series of concrete decisions." He went on to say that he found it a "remarkable and indeed astounding fact that neither Professor Mills nor Professor Hunter has seriously attempted to examine an array of specific cases to test his major hypothesis." Not everyone, of course, has held to such an extreme emphasis on process within American social science, but enough have that it was somewhat heretical when a mainstream political scientist, William C. Mitchell, wrote in 1969: "Let us try defining power not as one who makes decisions but as who gets how much from the system. Those who acquire the most goods, services, and opportunities are those who have the most power."

Courtesy of University of California, Santa Cruz

There are philosophical and methodological difficulties with a conceptualization of power and power indicators that focuses exclusively on process. However, rather than enter into an argument over these abstract points, I am going to set aside these differences of philosophy and method for purposes of this book. I will accept the challenge presented by the dominant social-science paradigm and concentrate on the process by which the ruling class in the United States dominates government and subordinates other social classes. Putting aside the argument that we can infer power from the distributions of wealth, income, health, education and other benefits sought by members of American society, I will suggest that there are four general processes through which economically and politically active members of the ruling class, working with the aid of highly trained and carefully selected employees, are able to dominate the United States at all levels. I call these four processes:

1. *The special-interest process,* which comprises the various means utilized by wealthy individuals, specific corporations and specific sectors of the economy in influencing government to satisfy their narrow, short-run needs;

2. *The policy-formation process,* which is the means by which general policies of interest to the ruling class as a whole are developed and implemented;

3. *The candidate-selection process,* which has to do with the ways members of the ruling class ensure that they have "access" to the politicians who are elected to office;

4. *The ideology process,* which involves the formation, dissemination and enforcement of the assumptions, beliefs and attitudes that permit the continued existence of policies and politicians favorable to the wealth, income, status and privileges of members of the ruling class. (pp. 7-10)

> *G. William Domhoff, in his* The Powers That Be: Processes of Ruling-Class Domination in America *(copyright ©1978 by G. William Domhoff; reprinted by permission of Random House, Inc.),* Random House, 1978, 206 p.

ROBERT L. HEILBRONER

[In] area after area [in *Who Rules America?*], Domhoff succeeds in showing that the command posts are filled by representatives of a small, socially identifiable group. Quite properly he does not push this claim too far. There are loci of power in American life—mainly Congress, and state and local government, and certain agencies such as the FBI—where the representation of the upper class is missing and its influence, presumably, minimal. "The national upper class . . . does not control every aspect of American life," Domhoff concedes, but weighing the evidence as a whole he is led to conclude that "the income, wealth, and institutional leadership of . . . 'the American business aristocracy' are more than sufficient to earn it the designation 'governing class.'" (p. 19)

[As] far as it goes the book sheds a good deal of light on an aspect of American society where the floodlights of publicity can hardly be said to play. The designation of an "upper class" and its association with power are attributes of reality that it is well to call to our attention, if only because these attributes are politely or pointedly overlooked by most social analysts.

Yet, having made this important identification, one can legitimately ask what else Domhoff has shown.

Here the book displays two weaknesses. The first, which is perhaps inherent in his mode of analysis, is a failure to specify exactly what is meant by the "control" that the upper class wields. Take, for example, the least disputable fact—that the upper class controls the corporate economy. Certainly it is true that the upper class holds the directorships and that it receives a large share of the dividends. But what is the "control" that it exercises? The corporate economy is not a single machine to be steered at will, but rather a congeries of semi-competitive institutions whose activities impinge on each other. Certainly individual boards of directors control the course of their corporations (within the limits allowed them by pressure of the market), but it is difficult to see what is meant by the "collective" control of the upper class when each board of directors is out to undercut—certainly not to augment—the income and prerogatives of the boards competing with it.

The meaning of the key word *control* becomes even more elusive when we turn to other sectors of the nation. "Control of America's leading universities by members of the American business aristocracy is more direct than with any other institutions which they control," writes Domhoff. In so far as "control" means occupancy of certain seats (here designated as Trustees) this is undoubtedly true. But what is the limit or effectiveness of this "control"? . . . Or to turn from the university to the Federal government, it is again one thing to note that advisers and Secretaries are noticeably of upper-class background, but another to demonstrate that specific interests, policies, and decisions follow from this class domination which would not take place were another class to have those positions.

To this it may be said that the interests, decisions, and policies of the government (or of the universities, etc.) need beno more than those that generally protect the United States as a social order in which there can be an upper class based mainly on wealth—that the "control" of the upper class need consist in no more than maintaining the general compass setting that steers us toward social, economic, and political objectives compatible with the maintenance of property as the basis of the social order.

As a general historical statement this is true, and important to say. But once we have said it, the course of history is still left indeterminate. For Domhoff is careful to stress that the upper class is not a unified group with a single defined strategy or goal. It includes among its members civil libertarians as well as segregationists, hard-line anti-Communists as well as advocates of rapprochement, supporters of Eugene McCarthy as well as of Joseph McCarthy. *In a word, the identification of an upper class, and the demonstration that it occupies the seats of power, do not allow one to make essential predictions as to the future course of American national behavior.* If we withdraw from Vietnam or advance there, if we disengage from the Cold War or intensify it, if we rebuild the cities or allow them to rot, in each case and on each side we will be able to discern the "controlling" influence of the upper class. What we have, then, is an analysis that cannot be put to practical use. Mr. Domhoff's analysis cuts through much obfuscation with a sharp knife, but just when that knife is applied to the purposes for which we need it most, it loses its cutting edge. (pp. 19-20)

> *Robert L. Heilbroner, "Who's Running This Show?" in* The New York Review of Books *(reprinted with permission from* The New York Review of Books;

copyright © 1968 Nyrev, Inc.), Vol. IX, No. 12, January 4, 1968, pp. 18-21.*

GORDON TULLOCK

The simplest descriptive term for [*Who Rules America?*] is muddled. The author, who is a psychologist, refers to it as a study in sociology and it does appear that he is somewhat out of his special field in writing it. The basic question with which it concerns itself is whether the United States has a governing class. (p. 196)

Temporarily ignoring problems raised by the word "class", it is clear that all societies of which we have any knowledge have a certain portion of the population that meets this description. If we collect in any society the more prominent people in it, we will find that they have a disproportionate amount of the country's wealth, receive a disproportionate amount of the country's income, and have a disproportionate number of the members in the key decision groups of the country. Thus at this level Mr. Domhoff has a ridiculously easy problem. Later he complicates it to some extent by sneaking into his definition of the upper class in the United States the requirement that they are socially prominent (which to a large extent simply means they are in the Social Register) and his opinion that they are to a considerable extent children of people who were wealthy in the last generation. Once again, no one will quarrel terribly with the view that this is true. It is notable, however, that faced with the ridiculously easy problem of proving that to a large extent people in the Social Register are above average in wealth and are more likely to become cabinet members than is the common man, Mr. Domhoff has failed.

He does not seem to have any access to modern statistical techniques nor does he seem to have any real knowledge of what statistics other people have already collected in this area. Lastly, he has decidedly odd ideas of logic. For example, he quotes some statistics (perfectly good statistics, although perhaps not the best available) to indicate that the top one per cent of the American population have very considerably more than one per cent of the national wealth. The question then is whether this particular one percent contains most of the people in the Social Register. His method of dealing with this problem is to point out that a certain number of very wealthy men (people who would be in the upper 1/100 of 1%) are found in the Social Register. The fact that a few people in class A are to be found in Class B is not evidence that Class A contains Class B, or that there is a substantial overlap.

Thus even in the areas where what Dr. Domhoff believes to be true is obviously true he is unsuccessful in proving it. As a matter of fact, however, he believes certain things to be true which are obviously untrue. In the American society if one selects the top one per cent of the population by any criteria you wish, you will find that they are simply the top of a pyramid. One can go down the pyramid steadily and at no point find a sharp break. Dr. Domhoff in essence offers evidence of this because he discusses at some length the way in which people are introduced into what he calls the upper class. Nevertheless, he argues that the top class of society (roughly speaking, the people in the Social Register) are basically differentiated from the rest of society; that is, that there is a sharp line of demarcation between them and the rest of us. His argument for this, astonishingly, is simply that in order to be a member of the upper class you have to have quite a lot of money. It is true that in order to be in the upper income classes you have

to have a lot of money, but it doesn't follow from this that there are not a great number of people who have just a little bit less money.

He mistakes the fact that many of the people he is studying have a great deal more money than he has for the assumption that there are no people between him and these wealthy people. He even offers evidence that there are a great many potential entrants into the "upper class" as evidence that there is a clear gap. For example, it happens to be true in American culture as in many others that the newly rich have some social problems and their children do better socially than their parents. Clearly, the newly rich who have not yet been introduced into the Social Register are a group directly below but about to move into this "upper class." The fact that a very wealthy and powerful man like John D. Rockefeller is not "fully accepted" in the social world is taken by Dr. Domhoff as indicating that the power structure in our society is closed. A man with somewhat more sense of humor might mean by this that the men in the Social Register were prevented from having power by Mr. Rockefeller, but not Dr. Domhoff. (pp. 196-97)

Gordon Tullock, "A Stumble in Statistics," in Modern Age *(copyright © 1968 by the Intercollegiate Studies Institute, Inc.), Vol. 12, No. 2, Spring, 1968, pp. 196-97.*

ADOLF A. BERLE

Since the late C. Wright Mills published *The Power Elite* in 1956, unceasing endeavor has been made by one school of sociologists to identify and to define the characteristics of a class, elite, or group that assumedly governs, or "rules," America. Professor Domhoff's [*Who Rules America?*] is the ablest attempt yet made. He is not, as was C. Wright Mills, an angry propagandist, attempting to define a class he wants to destroy. He is not a neo-Marxist seeking to describe a selfish oligarchy whose liquidation he considers essential to social justice. His closing discussion—**"Is the American Upper Class a Governing Class?"** social, upper, or ruling—is immensely thoughtful and interesting. Unhappily his endeavor fails because the underlying assumption cannot be supported by Domhoff any more than it was by Mills. Evidence is totally lacking that, as such, any elite exercises power or that any "class" governs or rules—lacking, because the fact does not exist. . . .

Regrettably, despite Domhoff's lucidly written and excellently documented pages, the result falls to pieces because its basic assumption is not only unproved but invalid.

Any capable analyst can describe the qualifications and recognitions likely to be possessed by the individuals who presently "govern," "rule," or hold power, public or private, in America's myriad institutions. He can construct from them a statistical group. I think Domhoff has done better than any, though I have doubts about including the "Social Register" and "gentlemen's clubs" among the tests. But all this proves only that the statistical group falling within the description will comprise—among many nonpowerholders—the relatively few individual institutional powerholders at the time. (Many, by the way, got into the described classes, groups, or elites after, not before, they acquired power positions.) Factually, even though most powerholders fall within the described group, the described "class," "elite," "establishment," or "governing group"—as such—does not have power, does not govern, and does not rule. (p. 201)

The reason goes deeper than the "pluralism" set out by E. D. Baltzell in his *The Protestant Establishment*. To govern, to rule, or to exercise power at all requires an institution or co-ordinated institutions, organized under and held together by an idea-system, vesting power in and allocating it among stated individuals, for tacitly agreed or overtly stated purposes. Otherwise, I find only a collection of individuals, each exercising a fragment of power in disparate institutions, be they churches, universities, corporations, labor unions, or government offices. Their decisions in these disparate capacities do not reflect the will, the desire, still less the compulsive power of the statistically determined "class" or "establishment." As an ironic footnote, I find myself in Domhoff's book as one of the "rulers." While I held a sub-Cabinet office in the Roosevelt Administration, there was a degree of justification. At present, it would stump the methodology of any "leadership sociologist" to discover any "rulership" beyond my private office.

C. Wright Mills launched a persuasive though fallacious piece of propaganda. A good many sociologists fell for it. Domhoff's detachment and scholarly abilities are so great that this reviewer hopes he rapidly escapes into more profitable lines of research. (p. 202)

> Adolf A. Berle, "Book Department: 'Who Rules America?'" in The Annals of The American Academy of Political and Social Science (© 1968, by The American Academy of Political and Social Science), Vol. 377, May, 1968, pp. 201-02.

WILLIAM V. SHANNON

G. William Domhoff's **"Fat Cats and Democrats"** . . . is written in a hyped-up style and goes in for far-reaching generalizations the evidence does not support.

At least, Mr. Domhoff does not marshal enough evidence to support them convincingly. It was an interesting if rather specialized conception for a book to trace the relationship between the Democratic party's financial backers and its avowedly liberal policies. Unfortunately, Professor Domhoff . . . is much less interested in the nuances and complexities of this topic than in advancing a simple-minded conspiracy theory about American politics. But if the two-party system is a snare and a fraud, who cares about the details of how it is financed? (pp. 38, 40)

> William V. Shannon, "'Fat Cats and Democrats'," in The New York Times Book Review (© 1972 by The New York Times Company; reprinted by permission), October 15, 1972, pp. 38, 40.

JOHN R. COYNE, JR.

The subject [of *The Bohemian Grove*] is a fascinating one, its inherent interest lying in an account of the manners and morals of [rich, influential, aging American males]. What do they look like and sound like when they do what they do? How do they do what they do and why do they do it? But Domhoff misses it all. There's no texture here, no life, no fabric. . . . [What] do we get? Barely 111 pages of text (the rest of the book is padded out with a list of names and affiliations). And that skimpy text, in big type, consists almost solely of awkward paraphrases of secondary sources, primarily old Herb Caen columns and badly dated news stories and pamphlets.

> John R. Coyne, Jr., "Books in Brief: 'The Bohemian Grove and Other Retreats'," in National Review (©

National Review, Inc., 1974; 150 East 35th St., New York, NY 10016), Vol. XXVI, No. 51, December 20, 1974, p. 1476.

ANDREW HACKER

[Are the rich] a ruling class, and a national one at that? Perhaps the most prolific exponent of this view has been G. William Domhoff. . . . His most recent book, *The Bohemian Grove and Other Retreats,* carries the subtitle "A Study in Ruling Class Cohesiveness" and examines clubs, associations, and similar gathering places. When Domhoff says, "There is a ruling social class in the United States," he means to be taken literally. He is not simply saying that people in top positions bump into one another at the Council on Foreign Relations or clubs like the Links and Pacific Union. Rather, he contends, they form a distinctive stratum whose members frequent the same resorts and send their children to connected prep schools. These linkages lead to friendships and marriage, ensuring hegemony for the future. Interlocking directorates are not enough for Domhoff: he cites bloodlines and debutante parties to thicken the fusion.

Domhoff has a following, especially among younger teachers of political science who agree with his analysis and want something more recent than C. Wright Mills. Unlike Mills, however, Domhoff can be rather casual about his facts, leading to the suspicion that he may be in over his head. Take the basic question of who belongs to his ruling class. At one point he claims that its members own "25 to 30 percent of all privately held wealth in America." However James Smith's calculations indicate that to account for 29 percent of the country's holdings one must extend the list of owners to include almost four million persons. At another time, Domhoff's upper class embraces "one percent of the population," which gives us two million people, including everyone who earns $35,000 a year. At the back of *The Bohemian Grove* he lists 2,000 names (an "Appendix of Heavies") ranging from Kingman Brewster and David Rockefeller to Jacques Barzun and Edgar Bergen.

It is not easy to conceive of Domhoff's "rulers" as a class. Still, his questions are important; power in America can be understood through the people who participate in its exercise. But indiscriminately throwing statistics into a stewpot only confuses the issues.

Domhoff makes corporate executives the central members of his ruling class. I have been following his and other arguments to this effect for some time, and I still cannot see the point of giving them that label. Mills called them an "elite," a term referring to people whose power accompanies their occupancy of certain offices—bishops, generals, judges, salaried managers of public and private enterprises. Most have little in the way of property and their influence lasts only so long as they sit at a particular desk. Members of this elite are easily replaceable; in many cases it is impossible to distinguish an officeholder from his predecessor or successor. Ruling classes, in contrast, have traditionally consisted of persons who can be named and remembered. Since both individual and family property play a much smaller part in our own leading institutions, it is misleading to keep on speaking of a ruling class. For one thing, it prompts us to look for power in the wrong places. For another, it is historically inapposite. We will not understand the institutions of our times if we cling to an old conception of class rule. We do indeed have classes; but their arrangement reflects the corporate structure. (p. 10)

It is entirely possible to engage in rule without being part of a ruling class. If we assume that corporate capitalism deserves all the criticism it can get, must there be particular malefactors to receive that indictment? All this listing of names, bloodlines, and marriages implies an inability on our part to understand and deal with power in its institutional form. Apparently we cannot visualize power as exercised administratively. Instead of the edifice of Chase Manhattan, our eyes seek out Rockefellers in the flesh. Indeed we often ignore an even more powerful bank, First National City, because the name of its chairman escapes us.

Of course corporate power appears in several constellations. Some companies present themselves as being solidly established and yet "modern" in outlook, especially those that join the Committee for Economic Development and other pronouncement-making bodies. But just as the railroads got an early start through federal land grants, so entire new industries have been created by war, space, and covert contracts. This has been especially true of the more freebooting firms in the South and far West. Once public money gets transfused into Global Marine and McDonnell Douglas, taxpayers find themselves the powerless junior partners of operating executives. . . .

By concentrating on families, clubs, personalities, the criticism of contemporary capitalism is in deeper confusion than its target. Blaming "the rich" or a "ruling class" no longer makes much sense. People have sometimes shown themselves ready to direct their resentments at institutions: suspicious attitudes toward oil companies and utilities show that. Even so, it has yet to be demonstrated how deeply one can hate American Cyanamid or Rockwell International. The class struggle is easier with an enemy of flesh and blood, as we know from countries like China and Cuba, where local landlords were an everyday sight. Our own capitalism's demise seems slated for yet another postponement until its attackers find ways of rousing mass anger against an edifice whose power depends neither on the personal qualities of those who hold it nor on their membership in a ruling class. (p. 13)

> *Andrew Hacker, "What Rules America?" in* The New York Review of Books *(reprinted with permission from* The New York Review of Books; *copyright © 1975 Nyrev, Inc.), Vol. XXII, No. 7, May 1, 1975, pp. 9-10, 12-13.*

PAUL LUEBKE

Who Really Rules? is a reexamination of the issues and data presented by Robert Dahl in his classic 1961 study of New Haven, *Who Governs?* It is an unusual contribution to the community power debate in American sociology and political science in that Domhoff studies the *identical decision* which Dahl examined fifteen years earlier: the origins of New Haven's urban renewal program. As the play on Dahl's title implies, Domhoff believes that Dahl's conclusions that an elite no longer rules New Haven were wrong. In Domhoff's view, a careful study of the urban renewal decision reveals that *real* power was held by a business-based ruling class, not by elected government officials.

Domhoff's earlier work and his sympathy for the power structure conclusions of Floyd Hunter, to whom he dedicated this book, bring him into theoretical conflict with Dahl and other pluralists. Domhoff presumes that economic elites are directly or indirectly involved in government decision-making because

of their vested interest in maintaining an underlying pro-business political climate. By contrast, Dahl's associate, Nelson Polsby, stated in *Community Power and Political Theory:* "If a man's major life work is banking, the pluralist presumes he will spend his time at the bank, and not in manipulating community decisions."

Interestingly, Domhoff in *Who Really Rules?* "beats the pluralists at their own game" by interviewing economic leaders and uncovering memos that had been overlooked by Dahl. Domhoff shows that Mayor Richard Lee, whom Dahl considered the key decision-maker, developed an urban renewal plan whose major points were nearly identical to an earlier plan prepared by the New Haven Chamber of Commerce. (p. 738)

After his reanalysis of the New Haven case, Domhoff presents a thorough methodological chapter which advocates researchers' moving beyond either the decisional approach favored by Dahl or the reputational approach emphasized by Hunter. Domhoff argues that researchers should combine positional, reputational, and decisional methods to test for the presence of a powerful "class, group, or coalition." Domhoff concludes that *Who Governs?* was not a good test of community power relations because Dahl overlooked key economic elites in New Haven and did not follow political decision-making to its "institutional bases in corporations, banks, law firms, and business associations." Overall, *Who Really Rules?* is a convincing critique of *Who Governs?*

I am least impressed with Domhoff's concluding chapter, which focuses on linkages between local and national economic elites. Domhoff notes that 38 percent of New Haven economic notables are members of social clubs elsewhere in the United States, but what assurances do we have that this is typical? That Dahl sought to generalize from the New Haven case is no defense. Domhoff undoubtedly would welcome more research on possible linkages between local, state, and national elites. However, he seems to be saying that, subject to conflicting evidence, his conclusion that "New Haven has a power structure which is part of the national ruling class" probably also fits many other cities. My own research on North Carolina power structures leads me to question whether the local-national linkages in New Haven are as applicable to other middle-sized cities as Domhoff suggests. The presence of long-established financial and industrial firms and of an Ivy League university, plus the proximity to New York's corporate headquarters, possibly make New Haven atypical. (pp. 738-39)

> *Paul Luebke, "Book Reviews: 'Who Really Rules?'" in* Social Forces *(copyright © 1978, Social Forces), Vol. 57, No. 2, December, 1978, pp. 378-79.*

CLARENCE N. STONE

William Domhoff has written an important book. Although its most conspicuous characteristic is a Marxist perspective, [*Who Really Rules?*] makes contributions that are independent of its Marxist underpinnings. Domhoff provides an incisive critique (substantive and methodological) of Robert Dahl's *Who Governs?*, contributes importantly to the sociology of research, and offers a new slant on national/local political linkages. On top of this, the book is clearly and engagingly written. . . .

Domhoff makes a strong case for the view that the New Haven power structure is centered in the banks, the Chamber of Commerce, and Yale University. . . .

Domhoff thus joins other recent writers in consigning elected officials to a minor role in policy formation. . . . While Domhoff's view can be disputed, his evidence is formidable. All in all, his critique of the pluralist interpretation of New Haven is convincingly argued. However, as Domhoff shifts from critique to theoretical restatement, he is less persuasive. He plunges the reader into an icy bath of Marxism. The experience is stimulating but not addicting. . . .

[Domhoff's] general argument is that the governmental system is an instrument of the upper class, which (1) controls wealth and the corporate economy and (2) through this control dominates the media of communication and education and (3) also oversees a crucially important network of policy-planning organizations. Proposals not in the interest of the upper class thus have little opportunity to get on the decision makers' agenda. Domhoff maintains that the power structure in cities like New Haven "is part of the national ruling class.". . .

Two difficulties plague Domhoff's argument. First he equates ruling class with upper class, and he maintains that "staying 'upper' is what 'ruling' is all about.". . . But he isn't much more specific than that about what constitutes the interest of the ruling class. Since almost anything short of radical redistribution can be construed as keeping the upper class "upper," Domhoff's treatment of the interest of the ruling class is too inclusive to be helpful in analyzing political conflict and identifying class exploitation.

The second difficulty involves Domhoff's conception of systemic power and his failure to analyze in depth the relationship between the state and the corporate economy. While it is hard to disagree with his conclusion that national and local governments alike are promoters and protectors of major economic interests, his explanation of why this is the case is unconvincing. (p. 233)

Unfortunately Domhoff's fascination with ideology distracts him from other loci of business power: for a Marxist he pays relatively little attention to the underlying material situation (a stratified society in which wealth, including local government revenue, often comes through business activity). Since the main policy he examines is urban renewal, this is a particularly unfortunate neglect. . . .

Ultimately, Domhoff's argument becomes that the upper-class auspices under which policy proposals emerge determine their later character. Possibly this is the case, but the reader is left with the unsatisfying feeling that Domhoff has not dug deep enough to explain the systemic interdependence between state and economy—that, in fact, he never gets farther than the institutional level of power. Arguments about ideological hegemony do not penetrate the understructure of political inequality. Maybe various social strata operate from such unequal footings that even in an ideologically diffuse setting *without a predetermined agenda*, policy would still take on a class character. It is unfortunate, then, that Domhoff did not pursue explanations of systemic power other than ideological dominance. Still, his empirical research is richer than the theoretical position he develops. Though some will find Domhoff's version of Marxism unappealing, he confronts us all with the need to understand dimensions of power beyond the personal and situational. Whatever quarrels one may pick with him over particular points, Domhoff has provided a much-needed reexamination of community power. (p. 234)

Clarence N. Stone, "Book Reviews: 'Who Really Rules?'" in The American Political Science Review *(copyright, 1979, by The American Political Science Association), Vol. 73, No. 1, March, 1979, pp. 233-34.*

BILL BLUM

In [*The Powers That Be*], Domhoff attempts to articulate the systematic channels and mechanisms through which the American ruling class expresses and exercises its dominion. (p. 56)

As persuasive as Domhoff's account is, however, it is unlikely to go unchallenged in either academic or political circles. In the past, Domhoff's works have come under sharp attack from both the left and the right, and, ironically, for strikingly similar reasons. On the right, Domhoff has been criticized by pluralists (such as Yale political scientist Robert Dahl), who contend that the special interests that constitute the capitalist class are too numerous and too competitive to achieve the internal coherence required for genuine class rule. According to the pluralists, such interests tend to offset and cancel out one another in their attempts to secure political influence, resulting in no single social group being able to rule.

On the left, Domhoff has been criticized by a new wave of Marxian "structuralists" typified by the esoteric Greek scholar Nicos Poulantzas. Like the pluralists, the structuralists claim that the capitalist class is too variegated to achieve class rule in a direct sense. When stripped of its customarily arcane prose, the structuralist counterthesis holds that the class character of the capitalist state is determined not by the influence of corporate lobbies, foundations, and think tanks, or by the direct participation of members of the upper class in government, but by the objective functions performed by government as a protector of private property and business prerogatives. As long as basic market structures remain intact, government will necessarily operate in the interests of the corporations, even if it does not operate at their behest.

In support of their position, structuralists are quick to point out that many social reforms which have greatly benefited big business, such as the programs of the New Deal, have been enacted over the strenuous opposition of large and powerful sectors of the corporate community.

Whether *The Powers That Be* ultimately softens such criticisms is open to speculation and is of secondary importance to whatever practical impact the book may achieve. No treatise on the American power structure can be expected to tell us how to create a free and fair society, and Domhoff, to his credit, does not attempt to do so. What he does accomplish, however, is a clear-sighted and balanced examination of the complex social system we hope some day to change. The Left can only profit from his labors. (pp. 57-8)

Bill Blum, "Analysis of Power," in The Progressive *(reprinted by permission from* The Progressive, *409 East Main Street, Madison, Wisconsin 53703; copyright 1979 by* The Progressive, Inc.*), Vol. 43, No. 11, November, 1979, pp. 56-8.*

THOMAS R. DYE

Domhoff is unimpressed with the traditional pluralist argument that power can only be understood as a "process." He would be satisfied to infer power from "outcomes"—disproportionate wealth and income in the hands of the upper social class; their higher standing on a variety of measures of the quality of life; their control over major social and economic institutes of society; and their over-representation in government. But in *The Powers That Be* Domhoff explicitly accepts "the Challenge" presented by pluralists to explain the *processes* "by which the ruling class in the United States dominates government and subordinates other social classes." . . .

Domhoff's description of the special interest process fails to rise above the standard anecdotal material in trickery, bribery, conflict-of-interest, and high-pressure lobbying that one finds in many muckraking accounts. Regrettably, his description of the candidate selection process is equally commonplace: electoral rules perpetuate a banal two-party system which avoids issues, discourages participation, and allows wealthy fatcats to manipulate candidates. It is not that Domhoff is wrong in his observations, but rather that others have described these processes more thoroughly and accurately.

Domhoff's best-developed model, and most intriguing supporting evidence, are found in his description of the elusive policy-formation process. (p. 1147)

Domhoff's thinking about the ideological process is innovative, but his ideas on this topic are not as well developed as his ideas on policy formation. The ideological process is aimed at preventing the emergence of class consciousness among the masses and the development of serious alternative political programs. Individualism, free enterprise, competition, equality of opportunity, and related liberal notions are disseminated at all levels of corporate, governmental, foundation, and organizational life. Unfortunately, Domhoff decides that "the ideology network is too big to describe completely." . . . We are left with only a few interesting vignettes about the shaping of public opinion (although a short essay on the Advertising Council is a gem).

Pluralists will be enraged by this book (and so will "the powers that be," if they ever read it). It is more provocative than it is conclusive; it is anecdotal rather than systematic. But Domhoff's many fans—both Marxist and non-Marxist—will welcome its appearance. (pp. 1147-48)

Thomas R. Dye, "Book Reviews: 'The Powers That Be'," in The American Political Science Review *(copyright, 1979, by The American Political Science Association), Vol. 73, No. 4, December, 1979, pp. 1147-48.*

William O(rville) Douglas

1898-1980

An American associate justice of the U.S. Supreme Court and a writer on legal, political, and social issues, Douglas was best known for his vigorous judicial defense of individual rights. He served on the Supreme Court from 1939 to 1975, for thirty-six years a voice of liberalism whose decisions made him a champion to civil libertarians and anathema to conservatives. His opponents objected to his liberal positions and argued that he made his legal decisions solely on the basis of a few abstract moral precepts, thus showing a woeful disregard for legal precedent and analysis. Though in the beginning Douglas's decisions were written largely in dissent, by the 1960s they were in line with those of the new liberal majority on the Supreme Court. Douglas was a prolific writer on such topics as foreign affairs, legal analysis, conservation, and travel. Directed to the young, *Points of Rebellion* (1970) recalls America's revolutionary origins and warns that if fundamental political changes are not forthcoming, "the redress, honored in tradition, is . . . revolution." Douglas's concern for the environment is expressed in *The Three Hundred Year War* (1972), a chronicle of the white settlers' three-hundred-year assault on the ecology of North America. In his memoirs, *The Court Years, 1939-1975* (1980), Douglas related his career on the Supreme Court and summarized his libertarian judicial philosophy. (See also *Contemporary Authors*, Vols. 9-12, rev. ed.; obituary Vols. 93-96.)

Excerpt from *POINTS OF REBELLION*

There are only two choices [for America]: A police state in which all dissent is suppressed or rigidly controlled; or a society where law is responsive to human needs.

If society is to be responsive to human needs, a vast restructuring of our laws is essential.

Realization of this need means adults must awaken to the urgency of the young people's unrest—in other words there must be created an adult unrest against the inequities and injustices in the present system. If the government is in jeopardy, it is not because we are unable to cope with revolutionary situations. Jeopardy means that either the leaders or the people do not realize they have all the tools required to make the revolution come true. The tools and the opportunity exist. Only the moral imagination is missing.

If the budget of the Pentagon were reduced from 80 billion dollars to 20 billion it would still be over twice as large as that of any other agency of government. Starting with vast reductions in its budget, we must make the Pentagon totally subordinate in our lives.

The poor and disadvantaged must have lawyers to represent them in the normal civil problems that now haunt them.

Laws must be revised so as to eliminate their present bias against the poor. Neighborhood credit unions would be vastly superior to the finance companies with their record of anguished garnishments.

Hearings must be made available so that the important decisions of federal agencies may be exposed to public criticism before they are put into effect.

The food program must be drastically revised so that its primary purpose is to feed the hungry rather than to make the corporate farmer rich.

A public sector for employment must be created that extends to meaningful and valuable work. It must include many arts and crafts, the theatre, industries; training of psychiatric and social workers, and specialists in the whole gamut of human interest.

The universities should be completely freed from CIA and from Pentagon control, through grants of money or otherwise. Faculties and students should have the basic control so that the university will be a revolutionary force that helps shape the restructuring of society. A university should not be an adjunct of business, nor of the military, nor of government. Its curriculum should teach change, not the status quo. Then, the dialogue between the people and the powers-that-be can start; and it may possibly keep us all from being victims of the corporate state.

The constitutional battle of the Blacks has been won, but equality of opportunity has, in practice, not yet been achieved. There are many, many steps still necessary. The secret is continuous progress.

Whatever the problem, those who see no escape are hopelessly embittered. A minimum necessity is measurable change.

George III was the symbol against which our Founders made a revolution now considered bright and glorious. George III had not crossed the seas to fasten a foreign yoke on us. George III and his dynasty had established and nurtured us and all that he did was by no means oppressive. But a vast restructuring of laws and institutions was necessary if the people were to be content. That restructuring was not forthcoming and there was revolution.

We must realize that today's Establishment is the new George III. Whether it will continue to adhere to his tactics, we do not know. If it does, the redress, honored in tradition, is also revolution.

Poets and authors have told us that our society has been surfeited with goods, that our people are mostly well-fed, that marketing and advertising devices have put into our hands all manner and form of gadgets to meet any whim, but that we are unhappy and not free.

The young generation sees this more clearly than their parents do. The youngsters who rise up in protest have not formulated a program for action. Few want to destroy the system. The aim of most of them is to regain the freedom of choice that their ancestors lost, to be free, to be masters of their destiny.

We know by now that technology can be toxic as well as tonic. We know by now that if we make technology the predestined force in our lives, man will walk to the measure of its demands. We know how leveling that influence can be, how easy it is to computerize man and make him a servile thing in a vast industrial complex.

This means we must subject the machine—technology—to control and cease despoiling the earth and filling people with goodies merely to make money. The search of the young today is more specific than the ancient search for the Holy Grail. The search of the youth today is for ways and means to make the machine—and the vast bureaucracy of the corporation state and of government that runs that machine—the servant of man.

That is the revolution that is coming.

That revolution—now that the people hold the residual powers of government—need not be a repetition of 1776. It could be a revolution in the nature of an explosive political regeneration. It depends on how wise the Establishment is. If, with its stockpile of arms, it resolves to suppress the dissenters, America will face, I fear, an awful ordeal. (pp. 92-7)

William O. Douglas, in his Points of Rebellion *(copyright © 1969, 1970 by William O. Douglas; reprinted by permission of Random House, Inc.), Random House, 1970, 97 p.*

Excerpt from *THE THREE HUNDRED YEAR WAR: A CHRONICLE OF ECOLOGICAL DISASTER*

The Three Hundred Year War started in a modest way, because only axes and gunpowder were available. The wilderness was leveled in part to obtain fields for planting and to build towns. It was also leveled to obtain the great riches that came from the conversion of the eastern hemlock and great white pine into dollars. A messianic zeal accompanied this leveling, for it was part of our heritage to consider the wilderness as dangerous, if not evil, as a place filled with great hazards, which must, therefore, be laid low. That zeal extended from Plymouth Bay clear across the nation. It operates today as a force that confronts conservationists and ecologists, making them often seem un-American because they are against "progress."

The Three Hundred Year War included among its early victims the original inhabitants of the continent. They were the "heathen" who did not walk godly paths and were not imbued with godly attitudes. Yet they were, I believe, more respectful of the earth and its wonders than the newcomers whose creed and dogma showed little respect for the estuaries, sweet-waters, woods, and rivers. The leveling of the "heathen" went on relentlessly across this pleasant land. And when gunpowder and firepower had broken their organized resistance, they were still pursued. The covetous trader and speculator, yes and the politician too, euchred the Indians out of their choice lands and possessions, hounding them almost to extinction. When the Sioux hunted buffalo they killed only what they needed. But the white men sometimes took only the hides and sometimes only the tongues. "You can see that the men who did this were crazy," said the Sioux.

The Three Hundred Year War took an awful toll of our wildlife. Predatory man trapped and hunted without restraint. At first these resources seemed unlimited. But soon organized business, interested in the "fast buck," not in preservation of the wonders of this the most beautiful continent of the earth, began to specialize in extermination. (p. 5)

This chronicle concerns the age of technology, deemed by many to promise life eternal, but which has become the quick engine of complete destruction, not only of wildlife but man himself.

The wild West is only a myth. Heavy smog washes against the slopes of the Cascade Mountains. Roads are everywhere and filled with the roar of jeeps and the small motorized "tote goats." Many waters where salmon and steelhead used to spawn are now only garbage dumps. Man-made badlands are being created by the new strip mines in the Far West. We are poor caretakers of the earth.

These forces are controlled here by the powerful drive for profits. In Russia the pressures come from the consumers, who want more to eat and wear, and from the bureaucrats, who strive for promotions and medals rewarding production skills. Though there are differences between the two countries, in each the supervisory bureaucracy is cold, paralyzing, and impenetrable.

That is indeed predestined, once Materialism and Technology become the Twin Gods.

Men are a violent lot—irrespective of race or color. War, not peace, has been their emblem. Every generation has had its war; and with the passage of time the violent nature of war has increased as a result of so-called technological advances. Our efforts in Vietnam and Russia's in the Middle East underscore the point. We protest against violence. Yet the violence with which we seem to be the most concerned is violence against the police, violence of the police against people, violence of people against people, violence of people against property.

Violence against our environment is another form of destruction that implicates our very survival, and it may well be a manifestation of deep subconscious forces. Our real alma mater is the Earth, without whom we are lost. Yet man's most devastating drives are acts of aggression against her. The Wintu Indians of California said, "How can the spirit of the Earth like the white man? Everywhere the white man has touched it, it is sore." (pp. 8-9)

What we touch we are very apt to destroy. As a people we have no ecological ethic. We talk about Law and Order and we mean it when we say that burglaries, street crimes, holdups and the like must cease. But in a deeper sense we have a basic disrespect of law—unless the law restrains the other group, not our own.

The corporate world—every pressure group—is always looking for means of avoiding or even evading environmental regulations. One of their techniques is to control the agency entrusted with protection of the public interest. This influence can be venal and sometimes is. The identity of interests between the regulator and the polluter may be subtle, not corrupt. It may be found in a common ideology that laissez faire is better than government control.

We have loosed a violent tide of destruction against most of the wonders of the wilderness. Cruel overgrazing of our alpine basins has converted them to deserts. The use of dynamite to destroy the redwoods wreaked havoc on the greatest of our native wonders. The power saw, the bulldozer, and the atomic bomb have now taken its place. (pp. 10-11)

The environmental problem confronting humans has subtle connections with man's choice of violence to solve international problems and domestic problems, as well. Axes and plows are for amateurs. With bulldozers, high explosives, deep drilling, air-compression machines and the like, we have been able to speed up the destructive cycle enormously. We can now do in a decade the damage it took the ancients centuries to accomplish. (p. 13)

The Report of the President's Materials Policy Commission made in 1952 opted for "the principle of Growth," saying that "it seems preferable to any opposite, which to us implies stagnation and decay." People are beginning to wonder if "growth" may not be the long-range curse rather than the panacea.

Critics say that a "no growth" society would be repudiated by the poor as a conspiracy to rob them of the material things others have already acquired. Yet it is clear that the ravaging and raping of the earth that has gone on must stop. New amenities toward the earth must be shown by corporations as well as individuals. New amenities toward the less fortunate among us must be cultivated, as vast restructuring of society is needed. But there is no reason why the Good Life may not be enjoyed when we are in a state of equilibrium instead of in an era of roaring growth. (p. 17)

To date, our efforts on the environmental front have been largely public relations gestures. Wherever we turn—whether it be to air, water, radiation, strip mining, estuaries, wildlife, forests and wilderness, transportation, or land use—we are worse off than we were a decade ago. In spite of all the speeches, hearings, laws, and litigation, we have remained captives of old clichés. We are continuously brainwashed by press releases, by industrial advertising, and by public statements. Our priorities have been an overseas war, not the Three Hundred Year War at home. Population pressures mount; littering and

pollution remain a scourge; the powerful lobbies seem bent on destroying our last few sanctuaries.

For things to change there must be a spiritual awakening. Our people—young and old—must become truly activist—and aggressively so—if we and the biosphere on which we depend are to survive.

We can serve in that role only if we believe, with the Sioux, in "the goodness and the beauty and the strangeness of the greening earth, the only mother." (pp. 199-200)

> *William O. Douglas, in his* The Three Hundred Year War: A Chronicle of Ecological Disaster *(copyright © 1972 by William O. Douglas; reprinted by permission of Random House, Inc.), Random House, 1972, 215 p.*

Excerpt from *THE COURT YEARS, 1939-1975: THE AUTOBIOGRAPHY OF WILLIAM O. DOUGLAS*

Senator Joseph McCarthy came to the Senate in January of 1947, and remained there until his death in May of 1957. During that ten-year period he became a symbol of the intolerance which swept America during the 1950s. On February 9, 1950, McCarthy made a speech saying that there were 205 Communists in the State Department, that of these only 80 had been discharged, that the others remained, and that they were "bad security risks because of their Communistic connections." . . .

From time to time he mentioned other cases by numbers, giving credence to his representations that the government was honeycombed with Communists. For each case number he had a factual summary—vague, inconclusive but nonetheless very damning; and the total picture was one of an unsuspecting people about to be undermined by a host of subversive characters operating in government.

Actually, none of these charges proved to be true. In 1954 McCarthy was censured by the Senate. But the harm he and his ilk had done to the country was incalculable.

I knew McCarthy, meeting him through the Kennedys, who, sad to say, had helped finance his Wisconsin campaign. He was a lawyer but not one of distinction. He always greeted me in a friendly way, but his face always showed tension and anxiety. I never knew the reason for this, though I soon learned that he was an alcoholic. And in time I came to realize that he was a sick man with a very troubled psyche. He was not, of course, the first sick man to plague the world.

He often had lunch at the Carroll Arms, a restaurant near the Senate Office Building, and it was there that I would come across him. His conversation was never about the "witch hunt" but about some genuine concern he felt on foreign or economic matters. When I saw him during the days of ordeal leading to censure, he had the appearance of a hunted man, fleeing from something horrible and finding a sanctuary in liquor.

While President Truman stood up against McCarthy, he did not have the shrewdness to see that his loyalty-security program and McCarthy's techniques were cut from the same cloth. The result was a hideous perversion of the American ideal, and these two men together set loose in this country a regime of terror. People actually became frightened to espouse anything that was not wholly and utterly orthodox.

Truman did more than oppose McCarthy. To his credit, he in time protested the effort to put the government "in the thought-control business'' when we vetoed the Subversive Activities Control Act of 1950, which Patrick McCarran in the Senate and Richard Nixon in the House had eagerly promoted. The act stated that an organization would be a ''communist-front organization'' within the meaning of the act if ''the positions taken or advanced by it from time to time on matters of policy do not deviate from those of the communist movement. Such an organization would have to register and its members would be barred from obtaining passports.'' Truman in his veto put the objection in enduring words.

I was not proud of the Court's record on these loyalty cases. As I have said, it approved four to four a decision denying an employee the constitutional right to have his accuser face him and make the charge. When that issue was again presented, the Court evaded it, resting its decision on narrow technical grounds (*Peters* v. *Hobby*, 349 U.S. 331). And while the Court in other cases construed the regulations strictly in favor of the employee (e.g., *Vitarelli* v. *Seaton*, 359 U.S. 535), it never made the resounding declaration of human rights that was sorely needed. In the neighboring field of congressional investigations it often set aside convictions of contempt on procedural grounds (e.g., *Yellin* v. *United States*, 374 U.S. 109; *Russell* v. *United States*, 369 U.S. 749; *Flaxer* v. *United States*, 358 U.S. 147), and once it declared that what a person believes is protected from congressional investigation by the First Amendment: ''Abuse of the investigative process may imperceptibly lead to abridgment of protected freedoms. The mere summoning of a witness and compelling him to testify, against his will, about his beliefs, expressions or associations is a measure of governmental interference. And when those forced revelations concern matters that are unorthodox, unpopular, or even hateful to the general public, the reaction in the life of the witness may be disastrous'' (*Watkins* v. *United States*, 354 U.S. 178, 197).

But there was no carry-through that made continuing and clear the constitutional mandate that Big Brother can be concerned only with men's actions, not with their ideas.

I became alarmed about these invasions of privacy and in 1951 expressed my fears in an address called ''The Black Silence of Fear,'' which I delivered at Brandeis University.

I said that to understand what was happening, a person would have to leave the country, go into the back regions of the world, lose himself there and become absorbed in the problems of the peoples of different civilizations. When he returned to America after a few months, he would probably be shocked. He would be shocked not at the intentions or purposes or ideals of the American people, but at the arrogance and intolerance of great segments of the American press, at the arrogance and intolerance of many leaders in public office, at the arrogance and intolerance reflected in many of our attitudes toward Asia. He would find that thought was being standardized, that the permissible area for calm discussion was being narrowed, that the range of ideas was being limited, that many minds were closed to the reception of any ideas from Asia.

We carried over to days of peace the military approach to world affairs. Diplomacy took a back seat. The military approach condition our thinking and our planning.

We thought of Asia in terms of military bases, not in terms of peoples and their aspirations. We wanted the starving people of Asia to choose sides, to make up their minds whether they were for us or against us, to cast their lot with us and against Russia.

We did not realize that to millions of these people the difference between Soviet dictatorship and the dictatorship under which they lived was not very great. We did not realize that in some regions of Asia it was the Communist Party that had identified itself with the so-called reform programs, the other parties being mere instruments for keeping a ruling class in power. We did not realize that the choice between democracy and Communism was not, in the eyes of millions of illiterates, the critical choice it was for us.

We forgot that democracy in many lands was an empty word; that its appeal was hollow when made to illiterate people living at the subsistence level. We asked them to furnish staging grounds for military operations whose outcome, in their eyes, had no perceptible relation to their own welfare. Those who rejected our overtures must be Communists, Truman said. Those who did not fall in with our military plans must be secretly aligning with Russia, he thought.

After World War II the military effort involved more and more of our sons, more and more of our budget, more and more of our thinking. The military policy so completely absorbed our thoughts that we mostly forgot that our greatest strength, our enduring power was not in guns, but in ideas. In Asia we were identified not with ideas of freedom, but with guns. At home we were thinking less and less in terms of defeating Communism with ideas, more and more in terms of defeating Communism with military might and suppression of ideas. (pp. 63-6)

> *William O. Douglas, in his* The Court Years, 1939-1975: The Autobiography of William O. Douglas *(copyright © 1980 by the Estate of William O. Douglas; reprinted by permission of Random House, Inc.), Random House, 1980, 434 p.*

JAMES A. MICHENER

In an age when people are becoming afraid to speak, Associate Justice Douglas of the United States Supreme Court states in extraordinarily clear, short sentences [in **''North From Malaya''**] exactly what he thinks the United States should do in Southeast Asia. He couldn't have picked a more difficult subject, and he doesn't dodge a single one of the red-hot problems arising in that area. Few will agree with all of his conclusions, but every one must admire his energy and forthrightness. . . .

[Justice Douglas's] chapters on the Philippines and Vietnam are much the best. Those on Formosa and Korea are superficial. The Malaya chapter is a fascinating personal narrative but not a probling analysis of a complex situation. And Burma is quite as difficult for Justice Douglas to understand as for all other visitors.

I found the chapter on Vietnam a brilliant summary of difficult material. Due credit is given the French for what they accomplished as suzerains of this rare and rich land (although no mention is made of their remarkable stewardship of archeological treasures), but the sorry bankruptcy of France as leader in this part of the world is also described. Justice Douglas feels there is no hope for a continuation of French rule, although he acknowledges that for the present French withdrawal would be unwise since anti-French forces are tied to Russian communism.

Like many another observer, Justice Douglas insists that the anti-French movement was originally a movement for agrarian reform and that it degenerated into communism only when its valid claims were ridiculed by the French.

In fact, the recurrent theme of this book is that in all of Southeast Asia there must be either land reform or communism. In Vietnam and the Philippines such land reform was denied and violent communist movements resulted. Justice Douglas advises us to support agrarian revolution wherever it has legitimate claims and predicts communism if we don't. (p. 1)

It is necessary to point out that some of the Justice's main theses are contradicted by his own observations. He implies that if the French would only get out to Vietnam, if the white overlords would only leave elsewhere, a kind of general peace would settle over Asia. Well, he did not find that peace in Burma, where the overlords have left. Nor in the Philippines. Nor would he have found it in Indonesia.

Also—a minor point—the author is quite wrong when he says the Communists have no front-line trenches in Korea. . . . Some of the Marines I was with last summer will be astonished to hear that, for we could look into the trenches from our outposts or spit into them as we flew past.

This is a courageous and timely book. Although I disagree with the Justice on some points, I agree with him completely when he concludes, "If there must be a fighting war against Communism, Russia is the only nation to fight." (p. 7)

> *James A. Michener, "Justice Douglas' Challenging Report on the Troubled Asian World," in* New York Herald Tribune Book Review *(© I.H.T. Corporation; reprinted by permission), May 31, 1953, pp. 1, 7.*

HARRISON E. SALISBURY

[In **"Russian Journey"** Associate Justice William O. Douglas has put forth] several strong convictions. He believes that the desire of the Russian people for peace is intense. He also believes that the Soviet Government is anxious to avoid war but he thinks the ultimate world aims of communism have not changed.

And, what is probably most important, he has acquired a deep impression of the new strength which Soviet foreign policy has attained through the revision of tactics both at home and abroad. The United States, the justice believes, is confronted with a new situation which challenges our world leadership as never before.

Unfortunately, Mr. Douglas is more precise in his diagnosis than his prescription. His advice to the United States is a good deal like that which is sometimes given to a man who has a bear by the tail. Hang on tight, Mr. Douglas says, in effect. Eventually, the bear is bound to get tired. . . .

[It is a mistake] to suggest that Mr. Douglas has written a political analysis of the Soviet Union today and our relative position vis à vis Moscow. This book is, essentially, a travelogue—first impressions, tentative conclusions and horseback philosophizing. His book has all the merits which keen eyes and an open and reflective mind can give it. But it also suffers from the inevitable flaws of hasty generalization, and, occasionally, downright inaccuracy. . . .

The best passages of Mr. Douglas' book are undoubtedly those in which as an experienced observer of Asiatic life he describes and contrasts what he found in Soviet Asia with conditions south of the border in Iran and Afghanistan. He brings out sharply the superior living standards which have been achieved on the Soviet side of the line and the impact which they are likely to have on the underdeveloped lands to the south.

He was also able to obtain much new and interesting information on the transition through which Soviet concepts of and administration of justice are passing in the post-Stalin era. His evaluation of Soviet court procedures and the caliber of Soviet judges is much higher than many Americans might expect.

Considering its many real virtues it seems a pity that Mr. Douglas' book should be marred by a multiplicity of minor factual errors which could easily have been eliminated by more skilled editing.

> *Harrison E. Salisbury, "Observation and Opinion," in* The New York Times Book Review *(© 1956 by The New York Times Company; reprinted by permission), June 10, 1956, p. 3.*

WILLIAM M. KUNSTLER

[William O. Douglas argues in **"The Right of the People"**] that we have been beating a slow but sure retreat from the democratic ideals that are the panache of our unique system of government. He spends the greater part of his book discussing (and condemning) the assaults on freedom of speech and what he calls "the right to be let alone." As to the former, he believes that "there is no free speech in the full meaning of the term unless there is freedom to challenge the very postulates on which the existing regime rests." . . .

Almost instinctively [Douglas] senses that one of the most dangerous threats to freedom of speech is that posed by obscenity statutes. . . .

"The right to be let alone" is a potpourri of rights ranging from the privilege against self-incrimination to the protection of the home from unlawful invasion, electronic or otherwise. Because of its diversity, it is not as cohesive as the freedom of expression section, and there are several areas where, because cases involving them are presently pending before the Court, Justice Douglas is discreetly silent. This is one of the drawbacks of a book about the law in action by a sitting judge who must refrain, despite his obvious inclinations, from discussing *sub judice* matters. . . .

According to Douglas, "there is no room for censorship of any medium of expression in our society." Perhaps this conflict of practice and principle is the keynote both of his book and our times.

> *William M. Kunstler, "Our Retreat from Democracy," in* The Saturday Review, New York *(copyright © 1958 by Saturday Review; all rights reserved; reprinted by permission), Vol. XLI, No. 3, January 18, 1958, p. 14.*

WILLIAM H. EDWARDS

[*The Right of the People*] as a whole is an important book and a good book; and there is no doubt that Justice Douglas' sound heart and brilliant mind are in the right place. But what of his discretion and his sense of the fitness of things? One is a bit perplexed. Should a judge of the Supreme Court write on matters which may come before him later for decision? There are such instances here. Should a judge write of cases, recently decided by the Court, in which he dissented, and should he carry on his argument in a public lecture? If he sees fit to so do, should he not at least explain that he dissented and that his present argument is in further support of that dissent?

It is desirable that the Supreme Court be brought under the fullest scrutiny; but a member of that court has a duty, to himself, his brethren, and to "the rule of law," (does he not?), to refrain from taking embarrassing positions or positions which seem in advance to impair his complete impartiality.

By way of apology for these somewhat ungracious dubieties, one can best end with a sentence from a Supreme Court opinion. Justice Douglas quotes it with apparent approval in his first chapter. He does not say so, but it is a sentence in an opinion which he himself wrote (Craig v. Harney), and it reads: "Judges are supposed to be men of fortitude, able to thrive in a hardy climate." That will have to be this reviewer's excuse.

> *William H. Edwards, "These Rights," in* New York Herald Tribune Book Review *(© I.H.T. Corporation; reprinted by permission), January 26, 1958, p. 7.*

HOWARD ZAHNISER

[William O. Douglas in] **"My Wilderness: The Pacific West"** has related in infectiously interesting, simple and direct prose, some of the adventurous and other experiences that he has had in eleven of the still remaining islands of the once-extensive American wilderness that he has known and traveled afoot and on horseback.

Yet the book is more than a personal narrative of adventure and exploration, for it also includes throughout reflections on the values of wilderness experience to human beings and appraisals of the importance (and difficulty) of maintaining the areas within which such experiences are possible.

Thus, in a book that should be destined for wide reading, one of the most eminent members of our modern society, an Associate Justice of the United States Supreme Court, a world traveler, states in fact and opinion a strong case for preserving the wilderness that we still have—and also for seeking within it the adventure, refreshment, and inspiration which he includes among the necessities of "a full life."

Mr. Douglas has a special concern for the "restless soul who yearns to discover the startling beauties of creation in a place of quiet and solitude where life exists without molestation by man." He has perceived that "to be whole and harmonious, man must also know the music of the beaches and woods . . . must find the thing of which he is only an infinitesimal part and nurture it and love it, if he is to live." And the wilderness, he knows, is "the choice place to untangle thoughts, to slough off tensions."

"The struggle of our time," he says, "is to maintain an economy of plenty and yet keep man's freedom intact. Roadless areas are one pledge to freedom. . . . If our wilderness areas are preserved, every person will have a better chance to maintain his freedom by allowing his idiosyncrasies to flower under the influnce of the wonders of the wilderness."

Furthermore, Mr. Douglas values the wilderness not only for its stillness, its joy, its excitement, its tests of skill and endurance, but also for its meaning in ecology as the norm, "where vegetable and animal growth continues undisturbed," as the "true 'control' plot for all experimentation in the animal and vegetable worlds." And he values in the wilderness the wolf and all predators as well as other creatures. "No species should ever be eliminated," he maintains, "for man in his wisdom does not yet know the full wonders and details of the cosmic scheme."

In the wilderness "a person learns that he was born not to destroy the chain of life of which he is a part but to nourish it; that he owes respect not only to his elders but to the snow buttercup at his feet and the hoary-mantled marmot, whistling to him from a rockslide."

"We deal," says Justice Douglas, "with values that no dollars can measure."

Despite the prevalence of such expressions of opinion they do not by any means dominate the book. For it essentially is a narrative of adventure in eleven different remote and wild parts of our land. . . .

These are the adventures of a man of great courage and wide sympathy. . . .

With such values of wilderness in mind and such adventures and other experiences so deep in his memory, Justice Douglas almost inevitably concerns himself with the protective preservation of these islands of wilderness that have served him so well. . . .

Wherever he visits wilderness and especially wherever he returns after extended absence, Mr. Douglas sees danger to wilderness and need for protection. He asks the challenging question: "Do roads have to go everywhere?" He protests the threatened indignity of dams and declares that the Middle Fork "must be preserved in perpetuity." Sagebrush destruction to favor livestock, timber cutting, mechanical vehicles, and always roads are found threatening area after area, and they lead the Justice to stronger and stronger pleas for action to preserve.

Such a volume as this with the appeal of its descriptive and narrative writing . . . may indeed prove significant in helping to bring at last the needed public recognition of the value and continuing appeal of wilderness that will lead to the needed "Act of Congress" and a resulting national policy and program for the preservation of wilderness and a realization of its importance in and to our culture. In any case it makes exciting reading for all who care about the outdoors or the kind of recreation that develops and sustains greatness.

> *Howard Zahniser, "Justice Douglas Sees the Unspoiled Wilderness as a Pledge to Freedom," in* New York Herald Tribune Book Review *(© I.H.T. Corporation; reprinted by permission), November 6, 1960, p. 3.*

ROGER BALDWIN

[Justice William O. Douglas's *The Anatomy of Liberty,* a] studious plea for the rule of law in the world, is backed up by a wealth of fact and comment carrying his high authority. . . .

[Justice Douglas's book] meets very practically the need for faith in law as the alternative to nuclear holocaust. What is most needed, says the Justice, is a consensus among nations to establish the rights of man without force ("now obsolete!") in order to assure equal protection under law, domestic and global. "A world that can be circled in one hour," he writes, "is One World."

Although the book is essentially an analysis of the functions of government in relation to liberty, Justice Douglas also offers a venturesome program: first, use every existing institution to settle disputes; second, work for a "Grand Alliance with Russia" to establish rules to avoid war; and third, search for a political consensus with the Soviet-Sino bloc. For a champion of liberty in high office who has often voiced his distress over the state of American freedoms, this testament of faith in the achievement of a universal agreement on law is indeed heartening.

Roger Baldwin, "One World under Law," in Saturday Review *(copyright © 1964 by* Saturday Review; *all rights reserved; reprinted by permission),* Vol. XLVII, No. 1, January 4, 1964, p. 79.*

YOSAL ROGAT

[It] is clear that Douglas rejects the austerity and detachment traditionally imposed upon a judge. Indeed, he has come to think of himself as no mere judge, but a moralist, a political visionary, a universal philosopher. The results are appalling. (p. 5)

[*The Anatomy of Liberty* and *Freedom of the Mind*] are worth noticing only because they were written by a Supreme Court Justice and because they tell us something about current thought in the law. Douglas sees them as setting forth the general ideas behind politics and world affairs, or something of the sort: one cannot say for certain. The style wavers from junior high school civics text ("The executive power is vested in the President who has a term of four years") to commencement address ("The American political creed has as its main ingredient the sovereignty of goodwill"), from travelogue ("This I saw with my own eyes as I roamed Macedonia") to Deep Thoughts ("A goodly part of life is the arousal of sexual desires"). Passage after passage sounds like H. G. Wells gone mad: "We Aryans seem to have a special capacity for aggression. When we moved down into the subcontinent of India (about 2000 B.C.) we destroyed the great civilization of Mohenjenaro. . . . We also produced Hitler. After him came Trujillo." Banality can be found at some places in most writers, but it dominates these shrill and humorless books. One soon braces oneself for sentences like "Ideas are more dangerous than armies," or "Ideas have immortality" (not all of them, thank God) or "Outer space is a specialty of vast proportions."

These banalities are not accidental; they are part of Douglas's relentless effort to simplify our understanding of the world. In pursuit of this doubtful end, he reduces the most complex political and legal difficulties to a few abstract moral principles, and the sharpest antagonisms to a flabby and homogeneous togetherness. Politics, in particular, disappears in the larger truth of neighborliness. "It is easy to find disagreeable qualities in one's neighbor—let alone in the Russian and the Chinese. . . . We and the Russians (not to mention the Chinese) . . . are in the same fragile boat and desperately interdependent."

Some recent conservative writers have constructed what amounts to a caricature of the simple-minded liberal, a portrait so overdrawn that one can scarcely take it seriously. Douglas, however, provides an actual example of a searcher for what Michael Oakeshott has called a "short cut to heaven"; he maintains today the kind of shallow and undiscriminating radicalism attributed perhaps unfairly, to Populism. ("Banish the mysticism of inequality," Douglas quotes approvingly, "and you banish almost all the evils attendant on human nature.") Whereas

genuine Utopian thought can reveal unprecedented aspects of a new situation, new possibilities rather than traditionally acknowledged limits. Douglas's radicalism consists in simply refusing to acknowledge any obstacles to an end he desires. He merely invokes the classical villain, notably the arms industry and the press. For example, "A press can create a national mood and each has done so, with the *result* that every community the world over is now filled with suspicion" (my italics). Such an explanation obscures the complexity, and therefore the seriousness, of these problems. It also betrays the superficiality of the writer's specific charge by failing to discuss the major question it raises, namely whether "the press" or "the military" can in fact manipulate a society unless it is structurally flawed. Douglas is altogether too comfortable with unattributed symptoms.

When he emphasizes that political disputes should be settled through international law, Douglas displays the same tone of chatty confidence. . . . Douglas seems magnetically drawn to such superficial solutions. It is easy for him to assume that men can simply shuck their primal national loyalties. "Each of us is a citizen of the world," he says, and "the nation-state is obsolete." Only the blind do not see this patent truth: only the perverse prefer political conflict to universal harmony. (pp. 5-6)

When Douglas turns from international law to American Constitutional Law, which he helps to make, he displays the same unwillingness to acknowledge conflict, the same tendency to simplification, and the same universalism. ("Laws vary greatly, but the concept of Justice remains bright in every land.") Since he does not relate legal systems to the development of particular traditions and institutions, he sees only differences in the speed with which each system perceives and implements what Justice Douglas considers obvious. . . .

It is not surprising that this syncretism completely distorts the nature of constitutional interpretation. As presented by Douglas, not a single case is hard enough to perplex a right-thinking man; a case does not present a tangle of competing principles, but a single transcendent principle—for instance, free speech or religious freedom—which need only be identified for the solution to be plain. In this way, he avoids the task, so basic to legal analysis, of reconciling competing principles. Instead, he substitutes simple labels and lines: "the abuse of speech can be punished but the right itself cannot be." Unfortunately, few cases are so simple. Thus Douglas writes of free speech, "speaking [is] beyond the reach of laws." Does he then oppose laws that limit the amount of sound or of traffic obstruction caused by a speaker? Well, no. For he writes in another place "[The] state may regulate the use of its streets and parks." Or again, in Douglas's view, "the First Amendment has a broad reach and includes the exotic forms of religion." Including "exotic" religions like Mormonism? Not exactly. For "religion cannot be used to justify immoral acts and practices," and thus "the Court held that polygamy was offensive to the American community." But is offensiveness to the community a sufficient justification for repression? At a time when Communism was clearly "offensive to the American community," Douglas, often to his credit, dissented from many Court decisions that upheld laws and regulations directed at men thought to be Communists. One might expect condemnation of the polygamy ruling from someone who tries to "trace" the Bill of Rights to "the teachings of the Koran."

Douglas's homogenizing tendencies carry him beyond facile optimism and inconsistency to outright inaccuracy. It is startling, for instance, to see a reference to a law that was never enacted, and a decision that was never made.

> The Court also struck down a state law which
> reduced the vote of Negroes, Catholics, or Jews
> so that each got only one-tenth of a vote.

What does one say when a Supreme Court Justice makes up a case?

More to the point, how can such a man, trained in the law, with its scruples and its insistence on detail, become so careless? The answer lies, apparently, in indifference to the texture of legal analysis, which arises from an exclusively political conception of the judicial role. Someone who reacts only to "underlying" political choices frees himself from the restrictions not only of legal detail, but also of truth to the extent that truth inheres in detail. The lawyer never comes through in these books. As I suggested earlier, it is here that they raise significant questions. For although Douglas may be an extreme case, his political view of judicial decision is widely shared. (p. 6)

Douglas is a reductionist. He seems to think that Supreme Court Justices should answer legal questions by *correctly* applying their beliefs about the overall needs of the country, or even the world. But liberal democracies are pledged to respond more to what is thought by a few to be needed. Even if some men must, or should, be allowed to decide what is good for us it is hard to see why it should be *these* nine men. It is different when each judge mediates his political preferences through a limiting system of technical law, which creates not only the right of concealing a personal point of view (of formalism), but also the possibility of partially transcending it. "In his fetters," it has been well said, "the judge finds liberation." The work of the Supreme Court is extraordinarily hard precisely because it is neither "purely legal" nor "purely political," and making that work look easy is a certain sign of pretending that it is one or the other.

The proper exercise of judicial intelligence in any court is much more complex than Douglas suggests. Judges make difficult analogical comparisons to decide what similarities among cases (i.e., precedents) seem important. In this way they try to reconcile both the desire to apply the same law to all persons and the need to reflect changes in what seems important to society. They then try to present reasons general enough to go beyond the particular dispute and yet not so general, and not so novel, as to set in motion a great deal of unanticipated, and perhaps unwarranted change elsewhere in the law. To most conscientious judges, judging is like trying to readjust one part of a mobile without moving the rest. To Douglas it is more like distinguishing left from right. He accordingly tells us, to paraphrase Paul Freund, not about the strains of judging but only about the complacencies of voting. (pp. 6-7)

> *Yosal Rogat, "Mr. Justice Pangloss," in* The New
> York Review of Books *(reprinted with permission
> from* The New York Review of Books; *copyright ©
> 1964 Nyrev, Inc.), Vol. III, No. 5, October 22, 1964,
> pp. 5-7.*

WILLIAM F. BUCKLEY, JR.

[What] Mr. Douglas has said very simply [in *Points of Rebellion*] is that such conditions as legitimized revolution in 1776 now exist in American in 1970. He seems to be saying that George III—the Establishment—might well be given, for a little longer, a chance to reverse itself. But that is one man's judgment. Those who—for instance the Chicago Seven—believe that America has been given long enough to change its ways, and therefore advocate instant revolution, disagree with Mr. Douglas only on a matter of timing. What they advocate—violent revolution—is in Mr. Douglas' view, very simply, honored by tradition.

If that is not sufficient cause for impeaching an official of the government who has sworn to defend the Constitution and the execution of its laws, then nothing justifies impeachment. It is quite extraordinary that Congress should have got lathered up over the nickel and dime malversations of Justice Fortas, while sleeping on this one. If Mr. Douglas is not impeached, he may have proven by other means than he intended that indeed American society is irretrievably corrupt. (p. 481)

> *William F. Buckley, Jr., "On the Right," in* National
> Review *(© National Review, Inc., 1970; 150 East
> 35th St., New York, NY 10016), Vol. XXII, No. 17,
> May 5, 1970, pp. 480-81.*

ASHER LANS

In *Points of Rebellion,* the most scholarly justice of the Supreme Court . . . [presents a brief work] aimed at the "young people." The necessary restructuring of our society, to avoid "an awful ordeal" of revolution, primarily requires, in the author's view, reallocation of resources and control of the federal bureaucracy, whose proestablishment orientation too often makes government a barbecue table for fattening "special interests" rather than an institution seeking to "promote the general welfare."

The hackneyed content is partially redeemed by Justice Douglas' brevity and pungency. A valuable section describes the despotic power of "technical" agencies, such as the Forest Service and the Bureau of Public Roads, utilized in disregard of ecological, scenic and recreational values. The case for requiring administrative agencies to precede their decisions with public hearings has rarely been more forcefully demonstrated.

> *Asher Lans, "On Equality and Reform," in* The
> American Scholar *(copyright © 1971 by the United
> Chapters of Phi Beta Kappa; reprinted by permission
> of the publishers), Vol. 40, No. 1, Winter, 1970-71,
> pp. 188-90.**

RICHARD A. FALK

In *International Dissent* Justice Douglas sets forth his ideas for a new system of world order in the form of six sets of proposals, which he calls "steps" in the title and "propositions" in the text. However labeled, Douglas is after six major changes in the present arrangement of world affairs:

(1) Ending military alliances; (2) ending colonialism; (3) bringing China into the family of nations in an active way; (4) creating a corporation owned by all governments of the world to exploit the mineral riches of the oceans; (5) making a humane and serious international effort to bring the poor countries of the world into the modern age; and (6) working toward a system of world law that leads to the dissolution of the war system and to the strengthening of procedures, rules, and institutions of peaceful settlement.

These six proposals are set forth with sophistication, originality, and a firm command of the complex facts. The book constitutes an important attempt by an intelligent man who has done his homework to deal with the most difficult and menacing problems before mankind. Justice Douglas writes with a sense of "the nearness of Armageddon" and of the necessity to evolve a new system of world order in the next few decades if we are to have any reasonable prospect of avoiding "the nuclear holocaust." Such an awareness gives a sense of urgency to his prescriptions, but he is aware, as well, that the peril of the planet comes from a variety of sources, including the disruption of basic systems of ecological balance.

The legal orientation dominates Justice Douglas' outlook. . . . There is, in Douglas' view, only two choices: maintain the present world order system built around war and competition and leading to catastrophe, or rapidly evolve a new system based on peace and cooperation, and leading to gradually improving conditions of life for mankind.

In essence, *International Dissent* amounts to a recommended sequence of adjustments which, if made, would amount to the emergence over time of this more desirable system of world order. (pp. 45-6)

To some extent, Douglas combines reformist next steps in international development with remote steps that can be taken only if prevailing attitudes among the leaders of the world change drastically. He seems aware of this characteristic of his approach, but he does not do much to overcome skeptical responses—"Well, these are good ideas, but why is there any reason to believe that governments or their publics, for that matter, would be willing to move in such directions?" . . .

Douglas writes to demonstrate the reasonableness of his proposals, but if the actors in the state system were reasonable then the proposals would hardly have been necessary in the first place.

In this respect, *International Dissent* gives an up-to-date coherence to the world federalist vision, but it does not help dissolve or tell us how to dissolve the hold of the state system over other instruments of power or the popular imagination. . . .

I respond in this way to what Justice Douglas has written not in the spirit of criticism, but with a feeling of camaraderie. We need to be candid about our failures to depict the basis for change, precisely because the case is so objectively compelling. No one has yet satisfied the urgent cultural needs I am calling for. At no time in human history is it more important to organize breakthroughs that help shift world order discussion from the innocuous realms of abstract speculation to the embattled realms of practical politics. In this respect the limitations of Justice Douglas' helpful book suggest the next steps that need to be taken to reach terrain on which the most ambitious of his six changes are imaginable. We need to form world order collectives throughout the world which are as dedicated to organizing a revolution in international society as the great revolutionary movements in history have been to seizing power on behalf of a new vision of national destiny. (p. 46)

Richard A. Falk, "The Nearness of Armageddon,"
in The Progressive *(reprinted by permission from* The
Progressive, *408 West Gorham Street, Madison,
Wisconsin 53703; copyright 1971 by The Progressive, Inc.), Vol. 35, No. 9, September, 1971, pp. 45-
6.*

JOSEPH A. PAGE

"Holocaust or Hemispheric Co-op" provides a sketchy, at times repetitious introduction to the developmental problems of Latin America. Justice Douglas also offers his own, admittedly romantic solution, the formation of one vast economic cooperative comprising all the nations of the Americas, the United States included. Sandwiched somewhere in the middle of the book is a lengthy discourse on the politics, social structure and economy of Bolivia, a fascinating spot but of scant importance from the hemispheric perspective.

It has long been fashionable among commentators on the Latin American scene to invoke the spectre of the imminent blood bath, the violent revolution just around the corner. Justice Douglas is no exception. He suggests that the over-predicted explosion may occur in the next decade. Yet his alternative to the holocaust is the economic integration of the entire hemisphere, if nothing else an exceedingly long-range approach.

Other contradictions blemish the booklet. The Justice at one point recognizes that the population surplus in Latin America requires the construction of labor-saving factories. But his dream of a hemispheric co-op calls for technologically advanced machinery that would utilize little of the excess (and constantly expanding) supply of manpower.

Justice Douglas strongly criticizes the Latin American armed forces for their unswerving support of the status quo. He also advocates termination of all United States military missions south of the Rio Grande as a step toward "demilitarizing our approach to Latin America." But his chapter on Bolivia lauds the accomplishments of "civil action," a rural public-works program undertaken by the local military and its United States Army advisers. Unfortunately, Justice Douglas fails to realize that "civic action" has always been a velvet-gloved countermeasure designed to clamp down the lid on social upheaval, as well as a justification for hefty military budgets and for military participation in activities that are properly civilian.

Justice Douglas views Latin America's populists as the last best hope for the region. In noting that "it now seems pretty clear that capitalism and the bourgois [sic] mentality in America are incapable of leading Latin America out of the underdevelopment which paralyzes it," he suggests the need for some form of democratic socialism. He further states the revolutionaries who are going to remake Latin America will come from the middle class.

The reader is left to puzzle out the identity of these democratic-populist-socialist leaders, and to surmise how they will gain power. For the most part, Justice Douglas appears to be talking about the so-called "democratic left," a pro-capitalist political force which has faded since its heyday in the late 1950's. But he often points to Mexico as a paradigm of a progressive democracy—a debatable point at best—and he completely ignores the emergence of the Catholic left.

The Central Intelligence Agency is scored for its opposition to populist movements in Latin America. But this criticism is overly simplistic, since the C.I.A. has occasionally channeled support to the "democratic left" as a means to counter the threat of real socialism.

One interesting point, raised but not fully explored, is the absence of concern among Latins for problems of ecology. Although Latin governments occasionally render lip service to the need to protect the environment, they refuse to take any steps that might impede industrial growth and seem bent on repeating the mistakes of the advanced nations.

In light of the massive obstacles to the development of a prosperous, just and humanistic society in Latin America, it is difficult to fault Justice Douglas for resorting to fantasy. But his vision of a hemisphere in which all nations merge their economies in a cooperative pattern set by a technocratic élite with the help of computers contains more than a few hints of nightmare. . . .

[The] central concern of anyone wishing to help Latin America on a modest, practical level is to devise ways to affect the shaping of United States policy in Washington. To this end Justice Douglas, with his apocalyptical approach, offers no clues.

> *Joseph A. Page, "Holocaust or Hemispheric Co-op," in* The New York Times Book Review *(© 1971 by The New York Times Company; reprinted by permission), November 28, 1971, p. 48.*

THE NATION

[There] is little doubt that history will judge Douglas' opinions—and they have not all been dissenting opinions by any means—together with those of Justice Hugo Black as a major factor in preserving the liberties of the American people in the years of the cold war. . . .

Douglas is not regarded in the legal profession as a great technician, nor as one of the foremost intellects in the history of the Court. His great merit is that, as a vigorous judicial activist, he has specialized over the years in the defense of the Bill of Rights, whose provisions are under recurrent attack because they always conflict with the special interests of the moment. Every time some new subterfuge was found to undermine, however subtly, a basic constitutional right, Douglas was there to say, "Stop it!" During the period of the Warren Court this was an ongoing effort, and he has carried it over as a restraining influence on the Burger Court.

In the 1960s Douglas had a better understanding than did Black of the new life styles; this enabled him to view in constitutional perspective "long hair" cases, pornography, conscientious objection and similar issues involving behavior inherently distasteful to conservative Judges. Douglas has been able to make this identification with the young because he is himself an authentic person, authentically American in his refusal to base his views on passing prejudices. He was "doing his thing" long before that became the current fashion.

> *"Justice Douglas," in* The Nation *(copyright 1973 The Nation magazine, The Nation Associates, Inc.), Vol. 217, No. 16, November 12, 1973, p. 485.*

NAOMI BLIVEN

Supreme Court Justice William O. Douglas's autobiography, **"Go East, Young Man"** . . . , chronicles its author's rise from patches, if not rags, to eminence, if not riches. There is, however, scarcely a note of self-congratulation; this is a book at once confident and intimate. The Justice is never guarded. He records how he has changed his mind, this way and that, on any number of matters—for example, the advantages and disadvantages of earning an education through hard manual labor, as he did. And many of the topics on which he reflects are open-ended—matters that are by no means solved, such as what

appears to be the inevitable ossification of bureaucracy. Douglas has firm attachments (to the First Amendment, for one), but he does not seem to be a rigid person. He reads like the inspiring teacher he once was—he shares information, offers intellectual and moral guidance, and frequently interrupts his earnestness with good, funny stories. . . .

[The] theme of this book is grander than its author's struggle against poverty and his search for moral work; it is the conquest of fear. The Justice tells about his battles with his fears and with himself: one's own self is always one's most daunting enemy. (p. 74)

I think the most striking quality of Douglas's book—decency—is related to his fearlessness. His testing place was the American wilderness, because in his boyhood it was near at hand. One can live happily in our society without overcoming—as Douglas did—a fear of, say, cougars or heights; what is important is not to fear other people. And because Douglas does not, his book, which is at times argumentative, at times opinionated, is never bitter, harsh, or vindictive. A man who differs with the Justice does not become his enemy. And his tolerance is more than passive; it is an active, alert sensitivity on behalf of liberty—not merely his liberty but everybody's. (pp. 74, 78)

In his introduction, Douglas hopes that his book will help Americans appreciate "the great and glorious tradition of liberty and freedom enshrined in our Constitution and Bill of Rights" and persuade them to "love the continent, the most beautiful one in the whole world," and to "develop a reverence for our rich soils, pure waters, rolling grass country, high mountains, and mysterious estuaries." As most readers know, when the Justice had ceased to need the wilderness as a gymnasium he learned to love it for itself, and though I think he is unnecessarily absolute in his espousal of "forever wild" as opposed to "multiple use" conservation, he does call attention to abuses of nature that take place under the name, or behind the screen, of "conservation."

Attention to fact, to what happens when a principle is applied, was, of course, one of the characteristics of the legal thought of Justice Brandeis (there is a most beguiling account of that great man), and it is the characteristic approach of Douglas and some of his friends and heroes, Justice Black among them. In this book, there are plenty of other topics that offer Douglas a chance to remind us of the importance of examining and reëxamining the practical effects of our principles. Without such consideration, even noble ideals may degenerate into verbiage and become slogans used to extenuate wicked or dangerous doings. The author keeps stressing liberty and the First Ten Amendments partly because he has seen what awful things happen when the principles embodied in them are *not* applied. I suppose there is no people whose history does not record spasms of bad behavior in response to fear, anxiety, anger, or disappointment: the Athenians condemned Socrates after they lost a war. Douglas is not suggesting that every oddball is a Socrates, but he *is* insisting that one of our Constitution's many difficult demands is that we all, whether we are government officials or private individuals, display self-restraint and not panic to the extent of depriving any of our fellow-citizens of their Constitutional liberties. The Justice's view of what Americans must live up to may make it harder to be an American, but—or so it seems to me—if we all stick to the First Amendment, as the Justice wishes, it will also be safer to be an American. (p. 78)

> *Naomi Bliven, "Ombudsman," in* The New Yorker *(© 1974 by The New Yorker Magazine, Inc.), Vol. 50, No. 20, July 8, 1974, pp. 74, 78-9.**

L. A. POWE, JR.

The measure of Justice Douglas has been change and growth. Thirty-five years after he ascended to the bench it is easy to believe he was always a great civil libertarian, and to forget that he was the nation's expert on issues of corporate finance. The new commitment masks the old reality. Moreover, because he is so complex, with a public career so long and interests so varied, piecing together the factors influencing his judicial development is difficult, even with respect to a single area of the law. One would, of course, expect significant changes in any Justice sitting on the Court for three and a half decades; yet, Douglas has probably changed more than other Justices with lengthy tenures. Not only have his legal theories matured, but also his fundamental character and outlook have taken on new dimensions. He has broadened as an individual from the corporate finance specialist of the New Deal era to a sophisticated expert on important matters ranging from ecology and civil liberties to international relations. To be sure, this tremendous growth and development in Douglas' knowledge and perception has been reflected not only in his first amendment opinions—. . . but also in his views on other legal issues. His profound change in the area of federal tax policy, for example, has already been documented, and I have no doubt that further study will reveal significant developments in other fields as well. Only by such detailed inquiry can we piece together the totality of Justice Douglas—a man whose public life has spanned one of the most crucial periods in our history. And a better understanding of him and his imprint on this epoch will enhance our comprehension of the epoch itself.

In closing, I must emphasize that Justice Douglas' contributions to the development of the first amendment have by no means come to a halt. He continues to argue forcefully for a more vigorous application of the free expression guarantees, even in areas heretofore accepted as exempt from the constitutional command. Moreover, his broad concept of the free exercise of religion has ushered the Court to a more liberal view of religious freedom, and he continues to argue for an even more expansive interpretation of the clause. In short, Justice Douglas remains a vibrant and unwavering champion of the constitutional rights protecting private citizens from the impermissible demands of government. (pp. 410-11)

> *L. A. Powe, Jr., "Evolution to Absolutism: Justice Douglas and the First Amendment," in* Columbia Law Review *(copyright © 1974 by Directors of The Columbia Law Review Association, Inc.), Vol. 74, No. 371, 1974, pp. 371-411.*

NATHAN LEWIN

There is much that Douglas and his often controversial legal career have taught to participants in this nation's legal process—to judges, lawyers, teachers and students. The qualities of sainthood were not, however, among his lessons. He was often superficial, impetuous, demagogic, sloppy and insensitive. If one believes what his adversaries have said . . . he was also cunning and personally ambitious. But more important in public men than their private flaws are the qualities they bring to public business. Justice Douglas invested in his job enormous intelligence, independence and productivity. And he joined these virtues with universal curiosity, skepticism of government and passion for individual liberties.

Douglas believed that being a lawyer meant much more than mastering legal texts and applying analytic reasoning to the facts of cases. . . .

One need not share totally Justice Douglas' enthusiasm for raw nature (or, particularly, for the call of the loons—again remembered fondly in his farewell message to the other justices) to agree that lawyers' perspectives—particularly in this age of specialization—are much too narrow. Douglas demonstrated that it was not only possible, but desirable, to be at the peak of the profession and still remain interested, concerned and energetic in areas other than the law. Four days a week, he insisted, were enough to do the Court's business; the remainder he set aside for other things.

The breadth of Douglas' interests puzzled and annoyed lawyers. They could never anticipate what newspaper article, what book, what public event might catch his restless attention and appear, without warning, in the text of a decision or in a footnote or appendix. It was unfair, they claimed, to have Supreme Court decisions depend on statements not made part of a record and subjected to the adversary contentions of lawyers. But it was consistent with Douglas' philosophy of life and law to poke through the tidy formalities established by the legal brotherhood. Each breach was, one suspects, a deliberate reminder by the justice that life is more unruly and cluttered than lawyers would like it to appear, and that decisions which significantly affect society could not be confined by what lawyers thought relevant to their particular case. . . .

Douglas' votes were seldom limited by broad general postulates. It is remarkable, with hindsight, how often the results he reached seem right. The most consistent single principle that emerges from his constitutional rulings relates more to the role of the courts than to any particular provision of the Constitution. It was Douglas' belief, expounded in his votes and opinions, that the main job of the courts was to restrain other branches of government in their dealings with individuals. Each case in which the Supreme Court failed to correct an individual injustice or to redress a valid grievance was, by these lights, an abdication of major responsibility. (p. 8)

The concept of judicial independence was suited to Justice Douglas' temperament, and all his work on the Court was characterized by it. In an opinion dealing with the power of a panel of judges to deny a lower federal judge authority to hear and decide cases, he noted the existence of a judicial philosophy that would "make all federal judges walk in some uniform step." Never in the days when Justice Douglas walked, ran and climbed, did he do so by steps other than those that were uniquely his. (p. 9)

> *Nathan Lewin, "William O. Douglas," in* The New Republic *(reprinted by permission of* The New Republic; *© 1975 The New Republic, Inc.), Vol. 173, No. 22, November 29, 1975, pp. 7-9.*

ALAN M. DERSHOWITZ

["**The Court Years: 1939-1975,**" the] autobiography of the late William O. Douglas, one of the most remarkable jurists in Anglo-American history, raises profound questions about the role of the Supreme Court in the American system of government. . . . How, in a democratic society, can nine unelected and politically non-responsible men overrule the policy choices of state legislatures, Congress, popular referenda and Presidents? Why should judges have the last word—apart from the unwieldy and unlikely extreme of a constitutional amendment—on such emotionally laden issues as abortion, busing, pornography and even national security? Such questions lie close to the surface of all intelligent discussion of judicial review in our country. Like smoldering volcanos, they erupt periodically—usually when the Supreme Court is under attack for having rendered a particularly unpopular or controversial decision. . . .

In this memoir, Justice Douglas does not provide us with a systematic account of his 35 iconoclastic years on the world's most powerful Court. These are ragged-edged fragments and hasty over-the-shoulder glimpses. . . . Neither his own nor his colleagues' philosophy emerges in coherent fashion. But the book is still a gold mine of valuable information and perceptions. It is valuable primarily for what it tells us about the human qualities and foibles of the individuals who passed into and out of the nine high-backed chairs during Douglas's unprecedented long tenure on the Court. . . .

Douglas argues persuasively that most Justices decide momentous cases on the basis of their own predilections, personal loyalties and political preferences. (p. 9)

By his life's work, Douglas provides one possible answer to [the important question of what, if anything, distinguishes judicial decision making in highly controversial or political cases from legislature or executive decision making]. Few people in the history of our country have been as single-mindedly dedicated to the human rights of the individual in relation to government. His credo was that the Bill of Rights was designed "to take the government off the backs of the people." With a few notable exceptions, he did not allow considerations of efficiency, popularity or political loyalty to sway him. He championed the rights of every person to speak his or her mind—no matter how foul or obscene the message. He refused to bend to the pressures of McCarthyism, crime hysteria, big business, religious fanaticism or Richard Nixon. He survived four efforts to impeach him. He even resisted the seductive allure of reverse racial quotas, an expedient advocated by most of his longtime civil-rights allies both on and off the Court. Acknowledging that he once made the mistake of sustaining a classification based on race in the World War II Japanese-exlusion cases, he concluded that racial quotas—no matter how benign and well intentioned—were "a wholly un-American practice, quite inconsistent with equal protection."

It is difficult to conceive of an *elected* public official sustaining that kind of commitment to principle throughout so long a career. A government of legislators and executives dominated by considerations of efficiency and electability can afford some iconoclasts and gadflies in positions of power, or at least in positions to check and limit power. William O. Douglas was the personification of this important role.

There will never be an entirely satisfactory justification for the power of judges to overrule popular decisions. As long as judges are human beings—with passions, prejudices and politics—their rulings will not always conform to a model of principled decision making. But some judges will be able to act in a somewhat more principled fashion over a longer period of time than most elected office-holders generally do. So at least some judges can act as imperfect checks on the excesses of the other branches. It must always be remembered, however, that the allocation of such power to an unelected and life-tenured judiciary is not without its costs: Judges can be—and many are—petty tyrants with little public check on their own excesses.

During Justice Douglas's tenure on the Court, I was sometimes asked by students: "What would happen to the country if we had nine Douglases on the Supreme Court?" I always answered with a question of my own: "What would happen if we had *no* Douglases on the Supreme Court?" We have no William O. Douglas on the Court today, and despite his sometimes questionable judicial behavior and his always quixotic nature, we are the poorer for it. (p. 27)

Alan M. Dershowitz, "Inside the Sanctum Sanctorum," in The New York Times Book Review *(© 1980 by The New York Times Company; reprinted by permission), November 2, 1980, pp. 9, 26-7.*

JAMES F. SIMON

It took a dozen years on the Court for a justice's judicial philosophy to mature, Douglas once said, and he seemed slightly ahead of schedule. By the middle and late 1940s, Douglas had built on his earlier administrative and judicial experience to forge a philosophy that was markedly different in both style and substance from [Hugo] Black's, though most of his conclusions continued to coincide with his colleague's. The Douglas opinions were characterized by direct, incisive forays that cut through technical verbiage to the core legal issues. His opinions were frequently written on behalf of the "little guy," whether he was challenging a corporate president or a police sergeant.

Like [Louis D.] Brandeis, Douglas linked economic and personal freedom in one constitutional chain. He was wary of consolidated power, economic or political, believing that the public interest was best served when responsibility was spread into many hands. That was the best guarantee, he believed, that the fortunes of the people would not be dependent on the selfish interests of a few at the top of the corporate or political ladder. He abhorred economic monopoly and was just as wary of government officials who were not answerable to the people. He insisted on strict accountability to the public by corporations, government bureaucrats and policemen. When they did not meet his standards, Douglas did not hesitate to intervene.

Black was the theoretician of the activist school, reading history and the literal language of the Constitution to support his broad libertarian views. Douglas was the pragmatist, providing practical, contemporary insights to fill Black's doctrinal structure. But Douglas, unlike Black, did not feel bound by history or judicial precedent. The law survived, Douglas believed, because of its adaptability to new circumstances. What may have been a correct interpretation fifty years ago, then, might be obsolete today because the times and society's values may have changed. "It is, I think, a healthy practice (too infrequently followed) for a court to reexamine its own doctrine," Douglas wrote in 1949. (pp. 250-51)

Where First Amendment freedoms were at stake, Douglas was even more aggressive in cutting through obstructive legal language. He destroyed the Post Office Department's argument that the "smoking car" humor of *Esquire* failed to satisfy a statutory standard that a magazine be published for the "public good" (and, thus, qualify for second-class mailing privileges). Congress did not intend that the second-class mailing privilege be manipulated by . . . the Post Office Department, Douglas asserted. "What is good literature, what has educational value, what is refined public information, what is good art," wrote Douglas, "varies with individuals as it does from one generation to another. There doubtless would be a contrariety of views concerning Cervantes' *Don Quixote*, Shakespeare's *Venus and Adonis* or Zola's *Nana*. But a requirement that literature or art conform to some norm prescribed by an official smacks of an ideology foreign to our system.''

Douglas carefully scrutinized police behavior, alert to both obvious and subtle forms of intimidation. Speaking for the Court, Douglas threw out a confession of a fifteen-year-old, obtained by police officers who had worked in relays from midnight until 5:00 A.M. ''A 15-year-old lad, questioned through the dead of night by relays of police, is a ready victim of the inquisition,'' wrote Douglas. ''Mature men possibly might stand the ordeal from midnight to 5 A.M. But we cannot believe that a lad of tender years is a match for the police in such a contest. He needs counsel and support if he is not to become victim first of fear, then of panic. He needs someone on whom to lean lest the overpowering presence of the law, as he knows it, crush him.''

With each libertarian opinion, Douglas's standing among political liberals was enhanced. Among legal scholars, however, his reputation was not so sturdy. Douglas was guilty, some scholars suggested, of inattention to legal detail and indifference to precedent. It was hinted that he pandered to the general public, which did not understand or appreciate the intricacies of the law. (p. 252)

Even when Douglas agreed with a dedicated proceduralist like Frankfurter in result, his opinions often showed an impatience with tightly reasoned argument. It seemed as if he considered elaborate opinions to be unnecessary exercises in technical pedantry. (p. 253)

When Douglas paid close attention to formal legal rules, critics charged that he did so merely to achieve a desired result. That complaint was made in a case involving an unfrocked priest named Terminiello, who had delivered a speech in Chicago to the Christian Veterans of America. The speech was both stupid and vulgar. Terminiello referred to Eleanor Roosevelt as ''one of the world's Communists,'' and to Jews as ''scum.'' He also predicted that there would be violence in the auditorium where he was speaking; that was about the only accurate statement Terminiello made all evening. A protesting crowd outside got out of hand despite the efforts of police to keep their demonstration peaceful. Stones, ice picks and bottles were hurled through the doors and windows of the auditorium. Terminiello was arrested and found guilty by a jury of disorderly conduct.

Douglas, writing for a five-man Court majority, overturned Terminiello's conviction. The trial court judge's instruction to the jury was flawed—decisively flawed, according to Douglas. The judge had defined ''breach of the peace'' to the jury under the relevant state statute as conduct that ''stirs the public to anger, invites dispute, brings about a condition of unrest, or creates a disturbance.'' But speech that angered or invited dispute, Douglas reasoned, was the expression that should be protected by the Constitution's free speech guarantee.

''A function of free speech under our system of government is to invite dispute,'' Douglas wrote. ''It may indeed best serve its high purpose when it induces a condition of unrest, creates dissatisfaction with conditions as they are, or even stirs people to anger. Speech is often provocative and challenging. It may strike at prejudices and preconceptions and have profound unsettling effects as it presses for acceptance of an idea.''

How could Felix Frankfurter disagree with that inspiring defense of free speech? Frankfurter, in dissent, suggested that Douglas had ignored elementary rules of judicial analysis and procedure. The Terminiello case, Frankfurter noted, had been argued through the Illinois courts on the assumption that the charge to the jury was not to be read out of context—as Douglas had done—but in the setting in which the speech had been made. On that basis, the state court had found that Terminiello's speech had incited violent disorder. Terminiello's attorney did not even raise in the state courts the issue of the judge's instruction, and, said Frankfurter, the U.S. Supreme Court had no authority to reverse a state court's judgment on a ground that was not argued before the state courts themselves. (pp. 254-55)

But it is the Douglas opinion, not the Frankfurter dissent, that is the law today and that has become a staple for constitutional texts on the First Amendment. And that may be the most telling commentary on so many Douglas opinions.

Douglas was not writing for the *Harvard Law Review*, but perhaps it was important that he was not. For if he had played the scholarly game, delivering long, heavily documented treatises, dwelling on technical aspects of the law, he might not have reached the substantive issues that would be crucial to future generations of Americans. But he did reach those substantive issues—the fundamental right to vote in state elections, for example, and the high place of free speech in our society— and his opinions became increasingly important in the second half of the twentieth century. (p. 256)

James F. Simon, ''One Soul to Save,'' in his Independent Journey: The Life of William O. Douglas *(copyright © 1980 by James F. Simon; reprinted by permission of Harper & Row, Publishers, Inc.), Harper & Row, 1980, pp. 241-56.*

RONALD DWORKIN

Mr. Justice William O. Douglas served in the United States Supreme Court for the extraordinary term of thirty-six years— from 1939 until 1975—and he was probably more often on the right side than anyone else has been. His record in civil rights cases of all different sorts was particularly admirable. He wrote a great many important opinions and, unlike many other Justices, did almost all the writing himself. He also did much more writing off the bench than any other Justice—thirty books and dozens of speeches and articles, many about social and political justice. His enemies were the right enemies for a crusading liberal to have: he was hated by President Nixon, pursued, to the point of threatened impeachment, by Congressman Ford, and condemned on the bumper stickers of Birchers everywhere. And yet when we look back on his long and interesting career on the Court, aided by his own memoirs of those years, [*The Court Years, 1939 to 1975*], and by Professor [James F.] Simon's excellent, judicious, and admiring biography, [*Independent Journey,* see excerpt above], we find not great distinction, but two puzzles. How could he have been so unlikable a man? Why did he make so little impact on constitutional law?

Simon does not intend to draw an unattractive portrait of his subject. He ends his book with an overall flattering assessment. But I doubt many readers of Simon's evidence will share that opinion. Douglas did, it is true, have immense self-discipline and energy. . . . But always fame was the spur, and the conclusion is tempting, suggested by well over a dozen incidents, that his final and long alliance with civil liberty and the cause of the poor was based at the start not on any moral conviction or natural sympathy, but on a much cooler assessment of where, on the day, the action was.

He was, in fact, insensitive, even indifferent, to other people. . . . Even his close friendships were sometimes, so it seems, alliances with those who would join in his coarse diatribes, loaded with obscenity, against those he thought were out to get him. . . . Or sometimes with those who would feed the paranoia that led him to complain that the conference room at the Court was probably bugged, that the manuscript of his autobiography might be stolen, or that his life was in danger. He did have an attractive and continuing love of travel and of the wild. But even this sometimes seemed not so much a matter of aesthetic and physical joy but of grim satisfaction that this hard life was better than the life of the weakling urban sophisticates he despised.

Simon catches Douglas out in a variety of self-flattering but mostly unimportant fibs about his own career. But Douglas's extraordinary behavior in the Rosenberg case is much more serious than these. Douglas himself reports only his own dramatic action the day before the Rosenbergs were executed for espionage in June of 1953. The Court had already adjourned for the summer, and Douglas was about to leave for his vacation retreat in the Northwest. Before he left he issued, as a single judge acting alone, a stay against execution. But the then Chief Justice, Fred Vinson, hastily convened a session of the Court the next day (Douglas discovered this only from listening to his car radio in front of a motel in Pittsburgh, and turned around to attend) which vacated the stay by a six-to-three vote. The Rosenbergs were electrocuted the same night. Douglas allows himself, at the end of this account, a paragraph describing how "the people of this country experienced a thrill" seeing the horrible photograph of Ethel Rosenberg's moment of death in the chair. He reports that "many people in the nation felt a glow of sadistic satisfaction in viewing this picture."

But Simon reveals the astounding fact that, in the long prior history of the Court's concern with the Rosenberg case, which Douglas does not mention, he had five times voted against the Rosenbergs' requests that the Court hear arguments against their conviction. On some of these occasions his vote was decisive. Of course, as Simon observes, the Rosenbergs might still have been executed had Douglas voted otherwise, because the Court, after argument, might have affirmed their conviction. And Douglas apparently believed that the new arguments on which he based his sudden, last-moment change of heart, the day before execution, were better arguments than had been used before. "What is troubling about the Douglas record, however," Simon points out, "is that his earlier negative votes seemed so inconsistent with his whole judicial approach and philosophy. His reputation as a result-oriented libertarian justice was well documented. He had rarely based his judicial decisions on technical procedural grounds—when such grounds cut against the interests of individual defendants. And yet in the Rosenberg case, in vote after vote, Douglas seemed content to let the Rosenbergs go to their execution without even hearing a variety of legal arguments put to the Court by the Rosenberg attorneys."

Why? A cynic might argue that Douglas liked to take unpopular liberal stands only when the lion's share of the credit would go to him. In much of the earlier procedural maneuvering about the Rosenberg case, other Justices immediately assumed the lead in the battle for review . . . so that Douglas, had he gone along, would have been a soldier not the general. Only at the end, in a dramatic last-minute stay before driving off into the West, could Douglas make the cause of due process distinctly his cause. This view may be too cynical. But it would be hard to prove that it is wrong.

Douglas's failure of character might help to explain the second puzzle I mentioned. Perhaps he would have had a more profound impact on constitutional law than he did if he had not been so concerned with his immediate position in petty, pseudo battles against [Felix] Frankfurter and the others on his enemy list, or in the public's imagination abut the crusading liberal Justice. The other leading figures on the Court during Douglas's long tenure achieved much more of structural and lasting importance. (p. 3)

Douglas was certainly [Earl] Warren's intellectual master, and he was at least the equal, I think, of [Hugo] Black and Frankfurter as well. Nothing any of these greater judges did on or off the bench matches, in analytical power, some of Douglas's essays in commercial and corporate law or finance. But though several of his opinions were important as precedents for a time, they have grown less important, as all discrete opinions do, and we find very little in these opinions by way of a developed and general constitutional philosophy of the sort that Frankfurter and Black developed, or even of the inspiration that Warren achieved both in his opinions and in his administration.

Instead we find a kind of theoretical schizophrenia. When Douglas self-consciously sets out his philosophy of constitutional adjudication, as in the present autobiography, he allies himself most often to Black's textualism. He says that Frankfurter and his school, through their philosophy of a passive judiciary, rewrote the Constitution by putting their own social philosophy in place of what those who actually made the Constitution had themselves decided—which is, of course, exactly the charge that Frankfurter and the others made against Douglas. "Black and I," Douglas tells us, "took the opposite view, and in those days we spent many long hours going through the dusty volumes of Civil War history and law trying to ascertain the meanings of the drafters of the Fourteenth Amendment."

But in his actual judicial decisions, when he needed to justify overruling the illiberal decision of some state legislature or official, Douglas relied on a very different idea, an idea that Black repeatedly and caustically rejected. This is the old (but when Douglas began unfashionable) idea that individuals have certain moral rights against their government that are prior to all law including the Constitution, and that it is the office of the Justices to identify those rights and enforce them even against the will of the majority. . . .

[In his opinions Douglas] only mentioned, and never elaborated or defended, this theory of individual prelegal rights. He might have accomplished more if instead he had undertaken to defend that theory against the obvious objection made by Black and others that such rights are mere inventions by judges anxious to disguise that they are rewriting the Constitution to suit their own purposes, and from the different objection made by the Frankfurter school that the idea of such rights against the majority was inconsistent with the proper conception of democracy. But he did not do this. Nor did he undertake to explain what kind of argument he considered a good argument either in favor of some alleged individual rights, like the right to travel or the right of privacy, or against other alleged rights, like the rights to freedom of contract on which earlier judges who opposed the New Deal might have relied. Nor was he able to show, as he sometimes half-claimed, that the idea of individual rights was in fact the guiding idea of the draftsmen of the important constitutional provisions, so that the best form of textual fidelity would consist in discovering what rights people actually have even if the draftsmen themselves would not have agreed. If he had met any of these minimal intellectual responsibilities of a judge who uses the theory of individual rights to decide crucial law suits, then he would have achieved a great deal more of lasting importance than he did.

Why did Douglas never make this attempt? . . .

It is not convincing to say that Douglas would not have known how to defend the idea of rights if he had wanted to. For he several times, even in the present autobiography, indicated just where he would start. He said over and over again, in a variety of contexts, that the point of the Constitution was to get the government off the backs of the people. He took that idea from Louis Brandeis, his immediate predecessor on the Court, and though Douglas sometimes tried to disguise it, implausibly, as a piece of Blackian literalism, it was plainly, as Brandeis thought it was, the nerve of a theory of liberty that might well have served as the foundation for a theory of rights.

Nor can we say that Douglas did not develop or defend his theory because he was lazy, because his opinions were sloppy and lacked any sense of philosophical depth. He had tremendous energy and ambition, and the fact that he did not display these qualities in his opinions is not an explanation but part of what needs to be explained. He does say, as Simon reports, that he had no wish to proselytize, that his own was the only soul he wanted to save. But this is again part of what needs explaining, for Douglas was, above all, ambitious for lasting fame, and, whatever the psychological basis for (or inconsistencies in) his liberalism, he nevertheless had no doubts that it was as a liberal that he wanted fame. Why did he fail, then, to establish a distinctly liberal philosophy of constitutional law, a philosophy that at once might have organized and given coherence to the long series of his opinions, rebutted the accusation that he was interested only in the political appeal of results in particular cases, and contributed to the constitutional dialogue . . . the one important theory that dialogue now lacks? Douglas was the natural spokesman for the old liberal principle that individuals have rights against the majority. Why did he only mumble? (p. 4)

[The] most important, revealing statement [Douglas makes about his judicial philosophy] . . . is the following close to the beginning of [*The Court Years, 1939 to 1975*]. He says that at the start of his career on the Court, Charles Evans Hughes, then Chief Justice, told him something "shattering" that he later discovered to be true. "Justice Douglas," said Hughes, "you must remember one thing. At the constitutional level where we work, ninety percent of any decision is emotional. The rational part of us supplies the reasons for supporting our predilections." Douglas then adds that he had previously thought of the law as immutable principles chiseled in granite. He had not realized, as he later did, "that the 'gut' reaction of a judge at the level of constitutional adjudications . . . was the main ingredient of his decision." This discovery, he says, "destroyed in my mind some of the reverence for the immutable principles."

This passage is immediately followed by some pious, hasty, and hopelessly confused remarks to the effect that in spite of their reliance on their own "gut" reactions judges are not really creative after all. These remarks simply contradict the earlier statements (and themselves as well) and may be set aside. Nor should we accept for a moment Douglas's disingenuous claim that he was a law-chiseled-in-granite man before Hughes set him straight. Douglas taught law at the Columbia and Yale law schools in the late Twenties and Thirties, when these institutions were the seat of the only distinct legal philosophy

America ever produced, which its practitioners called legal realism. One of the central theses of that philosophy, at least in its popular form, was exactly Hughes's guts-not-reason theory of adjudication.

Douglas was not himself much of a legal philosopher in those days, but he took the realists' side in various academic battles, particularly about law school curricula, and took his closest friends from their ranks. . . . The battle over legal realism was the chief excitement in legal education in those days, and Douglas was converted to that school of jurisprudence long before his allegedly shattering conversation with Hughes in 1939. (pp. 4, 6)

[Douglas was] the first and perhaps the only true representative of [legal realism] to reach the Supreme Court. If he had been the only Roosevelt appointee, if he had had to do battle with the old guard Justices to uphold New Deal legislation in the face of their arguments that they were compelled on grounds of reason to undo what Congress had done, he would have had no trouble developing and articulating a powerful theory of constitutional adjudication. It would have been legal realism brought from the commercial law classroom into the Supreme Court, a negative philosophy fit to do negative work. But Roosevelt appointed Frankfurter and Black and Stanley Reed first, the Nine Old Men were gone, and the center of action suddenly and dramatically changed.

The crisis was reached early in a series of cases that Douglas himself describes as a turning point for him. They raised the question whether a state school board could constitutionally require all schoolchildren to salute the flag, including Jehovah's Witnesses who believed that the practice violated their religious beliefs. Suddenly legal realism, in its skepticism, recommended the result that, considered just as a result, was illiberal and authoritarian. The constitutional guarantee of freedom of religion did not provide an absolute license for any conduct required by religious belief; and "reason" could not logically compel the conclusion that a state legislature or other state institution could not require all its citizens to salute the flag. So the only genuine argument the Supreme Court could use to overturn the state's decision was that the Justices' emotions, their predilections, were different from those of the state officials, and that was not good enough.

Frankfurter reached that conclusion, and voted against the Jehovah's Witnesses, on somewhat different grounds—his theory of the proper division of powers was grounded not so much in skepticism of the visceral variety but . . . in a particular Burkean conception of democracy. In the first of the two crucial cases (*Minersville School District v. Gobitis,* 310 US 586 [1940]) Douglas and Black followed Frankfurter, whom they still considered the intellectual leader of the new Court, and the majority refused the Jehovah's Witnesses' plea.

Harlan Stone (a Coolidge appointee) was the only Justice to dissent, and Douglas may have been moved by the fact that the liberal press and institutions applauded Stone and condemned the majority decision. But it seems likely that he also sensed that, whatever realism might say, it was unjust as a matter of moral fact and not merely unappealing to him personally that small children could be forced by police power, for no very good reason at all, to do what their religious training forbade them to do. In any case, by the time the same question came before the Court again (*West Virginia Board of Education v. Barnett,* 319 US 624 [1943]), the Court reversed itself and Black and Douglas were on the other side. . . . The two Justices published a joint statement relying in part on the theory that to force Jehovah's Witnesses to salute the flag was "inconsistent with the Constitution's plan and purposes" in order to justify their change of views.

But this was hardly a realist theory—the very idea that an abstract text written more than a century and a half earlier could compel a constitutional decision of that sort by reason alone would have earned the realists' contempt in the halcyon days of their purity. Douglas had chosen what he took to be the liberal result at the sacrifice of the only legal philosophy he knew. He had begun the long process of deciding first and finding reasons later, a process that exchanged philosophical skepticism for philosophical cynicism. He had begun to write opinions that he knew would be described by the profession as careless, hasty, and contemptuous of the whole process of judicial reasoning. These opinions seemed almost calculated to provide a clear example of the claim he attributed to Hughes, that judges use reason only to rationalize their own predilections.

It is surely too simple to say, however, as his detractors do, that he was only a clever man bent on fooling the public and the profession into thinking that he had good reasons for his decisions when in fact he simply liked the results. If that had been his only aim, he was clever enough to have done a better job. The independent journey Simon describes is more complex and, perhaps, more neurotic than that. We must of course be careful to resist dramatic psychodynamic accounts of judicial behavior that the judge in question would have rejected. But Douglas did come to believe, I think, and believe with some intensity, in the idea of individual moral rights distinct from and often opposed to the will of the majority. No one who believes in a moral idea can honestly and consistently regard that idea as having no more independent objective validity than his tastes in food and drink. But Douglas also held, in his legal realism, that this idea, not being compelled by legal doctrine, was in fact just a matter of his own emotional biases, not really, at any philosophically respectable level, different from these visceral tastes.

It is perhaps not surprising that a proud man in this state of intellectual schizophrenia would refer to these rights offhandedly rather than speak out clearly and coherently for them. It is not all that surprising that he would write opinions that were, in the light of his own deepest moral sense, correct not only in result but in principle, and yet opinions that cried out to be labeled both sloppy and unprincipled. Nor is it surprising that he would posture, as he did, about how easy a Justice's work really is; oppose hiring more law clerks or reducing the Court's work load; angle repeatedly in his long career on the Court, in a job that is plainly one of the most important in the world, for a job with more executive or political power; scribble travel books while listening to oral argument on the bench; and slam his office door shut the moment the Court term ended to drive off to some wild retreat in the West. Douglas might have been a man with a guilty secret, a judge of incompatible philosophical convictions posing, mainly to himself, as a fraud. (pp. 6-8)

Ronald Dworkin, "Dissent on Douglas," in The New York Review of Books *(reprinted with permission from* The New York Review of Books; *copyright © 1981 Nyrev, Inc.), Vol. XXVIII, No. 2, February 19, 1981, pp. 3-4, 6-8.*

W. SCOTT BURKE

William O. Douglas' autobiography, *The Court Years,* reveals all too well its author's character. The book consists of the Justice's description of various events which transpired and individuals encountered during his nearly forty years on the Supreme Court, and brief comments respecting various cases which the author viewed to be most important.

The most significant feature of the book (insofar as it might reflect upon the substance of Douglas' career—his role on the court) is its extremely abbreviated explanations of the cases which came before him. Beyond these synopses he offers few substantial clues to understand his behavior on the Court; he never articulates a coherent philosophy upon which his decisions were based.

The Justice's approach is encapsulated in an aside which he alleges Chief Justice Charles Evans Hughes made to him shortly after he (Douglas) joined the Court: "At the constitutional level where we work, ninety percent of any decision is emotional. The rational part of us supplies the reasons for supporting our predilections." Douglas claims that this comment struck him like a thunderbolt; the admission that "the 'gut' reaction of a judge at the level of constitutional adjudications" was determinative destroyed his "reverence for immutable principles." . . . [There is] no doubt that Douglas' behavior on the court was not determined by judicial precedent, the words of the Constitution, or the intentions of the Founding Fathers. It is curious that so fervent a self-proclaimed defender of freedom as Douglas could see no danger in this *ad hoc* approach to judicial decision-making. If a judge need only follow his "gut" and freely distort the Constitution and precedents in order to accommodate his prejudices, there are no limits upon the Court's tyrannical power. What is to prevent some future majority on the Supreme Court from indulging the "gut" feeling that certain minorities should be liquidated or liberties eliminated, if those in control of the other two branches should share those ends? Even if events never reach such a pass, no citizen appearing before a court which makes its decisions upon "gut feel" can believe himself safe. A perception of "fairness," that decisions will be based upon principles and rules known and commonly understood in advance, is necessary if the moral authority of the judiciary is to be maintained. The "gut feel" theory of decision-making contains the seeds of the destruction of the current system of law by creating cynicism and eventual refusal to accept the Court's decisions.

The stance of the Justice on the appropriate model of adjudication appears especially perplexing when compared to his contradictory position on freedom of speech. The right of free speech, he maintained, was virtually absolute; while it was acceptable to prohibit the yelling of "fire" in a crowded theatre, limits on less clearly dangerous speech are prohibited by the First Amendment. There was no room for balancing the need for free speech against other values. . . . The Justice, forgetting the "gut reaction" theory of constitutional adjudication advocated in an earlier chapter, condemns any effort by the Court to determine the reasonableness of laws limiting free speech: "In that event they would in a sense sit as a super-legislature. Certainly, their views on reasonableness would vary quite widely. We would then have a regime of constitutional law that turned on the subjective attitudes of the Justices rather than on the Constitution. That regime would give the Court vastly more power than it would have if the Constitution were taken more literally."

The *Autobiography* is interesting reading, not because it offers any insights into the flow of political events during Douglas' years on the Court, or into the personalities of the important people with whom he came into contact—there are no such insights here—but because of its revelation of the author's character. The Justice viewed himself as resembling "The Douglas in his hall" of Sir Walter Scott's poetical invention; as "fiery and courageous," daring to challenge "the Establishment," an entity which arises frequently in this book as a target of bold defiance and scorn. If these virtues are displayed in practice by name-calling, intemperate attacks upon those disliked or disagreeing, unabashed self-promotion, and contrived justifications of one's own questionable behavior, Douglas in this book certainly proves himself their possessor in abundance. (pp. 158-59)

Douglas had great contempt for his country and its values. The Americans are hysterical, sadistic, uncivilized, feeling a perverse thrill at the administration of capital punishment. They harbor sinister "dark suspicions," are unsophisticated and childish. The United States is a modern Ghenghis Kahn, the world's most suspect and hated nation. "Main Street" constitutes an alarming threat to liberty.

This severe moralist on certain principles was perhaps not always the most scrupulous practitioner of the virtues he demands in others. (p. 160)

Douglas proves in this book that he was wholly unsuited by temperament for service on the judiciary; an intolerant zealot who, if not granted a lifetime sinecure on the Court, would almost certainly have found obscurity as a cranky law professor, perhaps contributing occasional letters to the *New York Review of Books* denouncing policies of the latest President or some benighted Latin dictator. Unfortunately, his appointment to the Supreme Court permitted him a wider forum in which to exercise his prejudices and to display unattractive personal characteristics in print and in practice. (pp. 160-61)

W. Scott Burke, "Our Betters," in Policy Review *(copyrighted © 1981 by The Heritage Foundation), No. 17, Summer, 1981, pp. 156-61.*

Richard A(nderson) Falk

1930-

An American educator, writer on international social, political and legal issues, and Albert G. Milbank Professor of International Law at Princeton University, Falk is an advocate of expanded world organization. In *This Endangered Planet* (1971) he argues that the industrial state has engendered "a crisis of planetary proportions" envisioned as "the eating away at the ecological foundations of human existence . . ."; only "stronger cooperative patterns of behavior and . . . more embracing forms of organization," he argues, can avert an ecological catastrophe. *A Study of Future Worlds* (1975) is Falk's major attempt to outline a world order to replace the current system of sovereign states. He argues that the existing world organization, lacking the ability to undertake sufficiently coordinated actions, is inadequate to the task of solving today's global-scale problems. Though citing inadequacies in some of Falk's analyses and proposals, many critics have applauded his appraisal of and systematic approach to planetary problems. Among his many organizational affiliations, Falk has been the acting director of the Center of International Studies, a senior fellow of the Institute for World Order, and a member of the advisory board of Amnesty International. (See also *Contemporary Authors*, Vols. 5-8, rev. ed.)

Excerpt from *THIS ENDANGERED PLANET: PROSPECTS AND PROPOSALS FOR HUMAN SURVIVAL*

To be a man is to be limited and mortal. To be on earth is to live within a finite and restricted environment. Life is sustained by a thin belt of atmosphere above a skin of earth crust. The life-support system based on air, earth, and water is delicate, subtly intertwined, and remarkably intricate. . . .

The rise of the industrial state, and with it, science and technology, has led us to overlook these conditions of finitude and fragility. We have come to accept theories of progress and of inevitable development that look toward an indefinite improvement of the human condition by continuous economic growth made possible by an endless sequence of technological improvements. We have identified growth and expansion with progress, and we have not acknowledged the existence of any limitations on progress. The decline of an active religious consciousness in our century has reinforced this habit of inattentiveness toward the limits and contingencies that surround our individual and collective presence on earth. In earlier periods of history the active presence of religious thought helped keep alive the distinction between the finite and the infinite.

A storm presages its coming by a variety of signals. This book attempts an interpretation of these storm warnings, giving special attention to their political significance. To take proper precautions requires that, first of all, we rediscover the reality and significance of our finitude. We need to identify and clarify the limits of our planetary existence and plan to live within those limits. The task is urgent. We may not have more than a few years to make fundamental adjustments; we certainly do not have more than a few decades. Unless we can adapt our behavior to the carrying capacity of the planet, the future of mankind will be indeed bleak—assured short-run deterioration of life circumstances, and a growing prospect of human ex-

Courtesy of Richard Falk

tinction. The stakes of this struggle are nothing less than the habitability of the planet. (pp. 1-2)

My early chapters seek to demonstrate why certain critical changes in objective circumstances make national governments increasingly incapable of solving the principal problems of mankind. The point can be developed in its most dramatic form: the present framework for problem-solving in international society increasingly imperils human survival. Such a statement can be put in a more positive form: the conditions of human existence could become safer and the quality of human life could be improved by inducing certain changes in the organization of world society. Whether to guard against extinction or to struggle for a better world, there is a need to show why and in what respects the present structures of power and authority cannot be expected to deal with the emerging problems of the planet. (p. 8)

The eating away at the ecological foundations of human existence is a useful way to envision the planetary crisis. Such a metaphor emphasizes the importance of time. To call a situation a crisis implies its urgency. We do not know and cannot know how much time is available to bring about the changes in behavior and organization needed to remove or moderate the threats.

To label a situation a crisis also implies the possibility of a favorable outcome. A crisis is a time for decision and response. The planetary crisis of survival can be dealt with, but only in the event that certain fundamental changes in attitude and organization take place. This book is mostly concerned with the international setting of the planetary crisis and concentrates upon the changes in the structure of world society that are needed. Such a focus arises from a further characteristic of the crisis: in order to be effective, change must be planetary in scope. No national society, however enlightened its government, can meet the challenge directed at its survival by independent action. National policy may hasten or defer the impact of certain disorders, but it cannot control the dynamics of the crisis. The planet is now a whole as a consequence of technological development and population increase. A coordinated response presupposes a common, or at least a convergent, interpretation of the situation by all principal governments, ideologies, cultures, and religions. At the same time we live in a world organized into contending units, where boundaries are critical organizing parameters and where power and ideology continue to be largely controlled by national governments and by institutions closely allied with such governments. (pp. 11-12)

The argument, then, is very simple. Mankind is endangered by a crisis of planetary proportions. This crisis has emerged mainly out of the interplay between a machine technology and a rising population. The dynamics of this interplay have continued for over a century and are pushing up against the carrying capacity of the earth in a variety of ways.

The political life of man is mainly organized into competitive units called states. These states do manage to cooperate for limited purposes, such as trade or tourism or to wage war against a common enemy, but the basic mode of behavior is competitive and the fundamental unit of organization is limited in its scope. An endangered planet calls for stronger cooperative patterns of behavior and for more embracing forms of organization. (pp. 13-14)

> *Richard A. Falk, in his* This Endangered Planet: Prospects and Proposals for Human Survival *(copyright © 1971 by Richard A. Falk; reprinted by permission of Random House, Inc.), Random House, 1971, 495 p.*

MATTHEW M. McMAHON

Prof. Falk can . . . be criticized as a defender of the international status quo, with general approval of America's defense policy and minimal criticism of U.S. foreign policy. However, . . . [in *Law, Morality and War in the Contemporary World*] he does attempt to develop at some length a moral basis for both law and policy in relation to the ethics of nuclear conflict and of international nuclear politics.

Prof. Falk's argument fails completely to convince this reviewer. The fault lies mainly in the secular, nationalistic basis of the norms underlying his moral views. As a student of the dominant school of positivism in jurisprudence, Prof. Falk cannot accept the natural law and says so. Yet, in the atomic age, and in the light of the plain facts of World Wars I and II, plus the present vital issue of nuclear testing, no thinking

man can ignore the consequences of positivism. This school has enshrined a force theory, and what it calls morality is pure expediency, loaded with deceptive nationalistic sentiment—worthless, if not pharisaic, and the very opposite of what even John Austen advocated.

Accepting the *pax atomica* despite its vulnerable and fragile basis (and its discreditable *conditio pacis terribilis*), the author develops an argument based largely on the organic character of the family of nations—albeit, he does not use this language and prefers to write "interdependence" of nations. He justifies the morality of atomic weaponry and atomic war according to "the traditional norms of morality." The principal moral restraint, in this view, is that force is valid, but that each nation is self-limited only to use the least amount of force necessary to accomplish its objective. This was an accepted scholastic rule, but it originated in an entirely different milieu of human affairs. Prof. Falk strongly opposes the pacifists, unilateral disarmers and all nonviolence schools, without qualification or distinction. On this grave subject, he would necessarily oppose the doctrine of *Pacem in Terris*. Apparently, he would remodel the doctrine of the just war on a pragmatic level. (p. 908)

> *Matthew M. McMahon, "'Law, Morality and War in the Contemporary World'," in* America *(reprinted with permission of America Press, Inc.; © 1963; all rights reserved), Vol. 108, No. 26, June 15, 1963, pp. 908-09.*

JUSTUS GEORGE LAWLER

[*Law, Morality, and War in the Contemporary World*] succeeds only in launching some highly conventional views.

The thesis of the work is that law must be rooted in morality. The particularities on which this notion comes to rest are probably just as unexceptionable for most reasonable men: the Cuban invasion is criticized; the United States response to the Suez invasion is praised; multilateral rather than unilateral military sanctions are advocated; and the dangers of the deterrent are recognized (though its moral implications are largely ignored). The final position is similar to that which Paul Ramsey has maintained with more cogency and precision, namely, that nuclear weapons can be used in defense against an armed attack across an international frontier, provided they are unleashed only against military targets.

One does not doubt that the author is aware of most of the major problems, the danger of escalation, of catalytic and accidental war, etc., but none of these factors receives enough treatment in the 114 pages of text to make of the book as a whole anything but a collection of highly latinized commonplaces. (p. 514)

For the most part the doctrine agrees with the natural-law tradition, and is therefore in accord with the general tenets of a Scholastic ethic. However, because Professor Falk "deprecates the application of preformed rules to behavioral choice," he believes "it is probably correct to distinguish" his view from that of the natural-law tradition. The distinction seems superfluous since the natural-law tradition as it is now being revived is not a corpus of static canons which ignore the existential situation; in fact, the role of any probabilist theory in that tradition is precisely to provide flexible standards which will be applicable to the contingencies, the behavioral choices, of a particular moment.

Professor Falk does appear to separate himself from the natural-law tradition in his definition of "legitimacy" and "justification." The former refers "to the legal status of a use of force"; the latter, to a "demonstration that a given legal status corresponds with relevant moral requirements. . . . An *essential* component of legitimacy is justification and a *usual* component of justification is legitimacy" (author's italics). Such an elaboration might be acceptable to a defender of the notion of purely penal laws; but this is a notion which has been generally and rightly discarded. The preferable distinction to be introduced here would affirm that an essential component of justification is legitimacy, the legitimacy of *codified or uncodified* law. Professor Falk's distinction is unnecessary; moreover, it could prove harmful by tending to obscure the moral roots of all law.

Without disparaging the admirable intent of this book, it may nevertheless be suggested that we have had more than enough surveys of nuclear morality which uphold the licitness of counterforce warfare and of tactical nuclear weapons. (p. 515)

> *Justus George Lawler, "Law and the Human Community," in* Commonweal *(copyright © 1963 Commonweal Publishing Co., Inc.; reprinted by permission of Commonweal Publishing Co., Inc.), Vol. LXXVIII, No. 19, August 23, 1963, pp. 514-16.*

C. G. FENWICK

[*Legal Order in a Violent World*] is a bold venture, for it deals with the fundamental problem of our times, contrasting the forces that make for law and order and setting them against the forces that tend to obstruct and destroy. It is not a mere descriptive recitation of the events of the times, but it is a careful search into the causes of the conflicting elements in international relations and an effort to find a reconciliation, or rather a means of bringing what is disruptive under control. . . .

The author also has some excellent reflections on the ways and means of attaining world order, either by revolutionary changes in the international system or by reformist methods. Unfortunately, the abstract phrasing of the essay will limit the range of its readers. For the analysis is keen, and the practical conclusions are of real value. But the style makes hard reading except for the lawyer who is already in touch with the subject. (p. 161)

[The] material is well organized, and the analysis of the conflict between law and violence is consistent throughout. Professor Falk deserves our thanks for his contribution to the great problem of the day, the urgency of which is pressing hard upon us. (p. 162)

> *C. G. Fenwick, "Book Department: 'Legal Order in a Violent World'," in* The Annals of The American Academy of Political and Social Science *(© 1969, by The American Academy of Political and Social Science), Vol. 381, January, 1969, pp. 161-62.*

ALONA E. EVANS

In *Legal Order in a Violent World*, Professor Falk examines with sophisticated insight the international uses of violence today, the problems of legal regulation of human conflict in a decentralized social system, and suggests ways of achieving his dual objectives. (p. 248)

Inevitably, a certain unevenness appears in the book, given the period of time over which the several essays were written. As the author himself points out, his discussion of disarmament predicated on the bipolarism of 1962 is not entirely *apropos* of 1968's "polycentric interpretation of international conflict." . . . Furthermore, although the various essays are broadly addressed to the same general subject matter, there is a disjointed quality about the book which suggests that it should have "collected essays" as its subtitle and that the reader should be prepared to peruse the contents selectively rather than *seriatim.* . . .

These considerations aside, Professor Falk's critical examination of the vital issues presented in the several essays makes *Legal Order in a Violent World* a valuable contribution to the current literature on problems of peacemaking. (p. 249)

> *Alona E. Evans, "Book Reviews and Notes: 'Legal Order in a Violent World'," in* The American Political Science Review *(copyright, 1969, by The American Political Science Association), Vol. LXIII, No. 1, March, 1969, pp. 248-49.*

CHARLES G. BOLTE

[*This Endangered Planet: Prospects and Proposals for Human Survival* is] a radical and realistic manual for human survival. . . . One hopes that societies and their leaders around the world take heed of this prophet, whose message, while urgent, is delivered unstridently and bolstered by scholarly evidence from such a wide range of fields as to suggest that Falk, like Harold D. Lasswell, has become a one-man interdisciplinary committee.

The argumentation is complex but the theme is simple: "The human danger is brought on by human activity." Chief among these activities is procreation. People pollution is the base for all the other pollutions that plague us. The other principal human activities that threaten human existence are diagnosed and prescribed for: the war system of sovereign nation-states, the depletion of natural resources, and the deterioration of the environment. Falk's contribution, unique so far as I know, is to bring them all together and to show their *interconnectedness.* . . . (pp. 34-5)

It is the essence of Falk's book that a drastic systems change is possible without violence. He builds a political model of a cooperative system of world order and describes a set of transition strategies that might bring it into being. He does not avoid the difficulties, including one that looms large in the vision of any observer of the present status of war/peace research: "our government takes seriously, pays well, and encourages scholars . . . to think coolly about when, how, and whether to use nuclear weapons, and expects them not to blink at the prospect." . . .

In short, Falk is full of ideas. His aim is not to outline a Utopia but to deal with the fact that "human civilization is pushing up against the limits of the earth's carrying capacity." (p. 35)

> *Charles G. Bolte, "Manual for Survival," in* The New Republic *(reprinted by permission of* The New Republic; *© 1971 The New Republic, Inc.), Vol. 164, No. 20, May 15, 1971, pp. 34-5.*

CLIFFORD HALL

[*The Status of Law in International Society* has as its purpose] to delineate the relevance of law to contemporary and future international relations. . . .

The book complements [Professor Falk's] earlier work *Legal Order in a Violent World,* but here the whole spectrum of international relations is examined, not descriptively but analytically. The jurisprudential, social and political foundations of the international legal system are reflected upon. . . . One of the central themes of the work is the necessity of developing a systematic method in the study of international law. . . . Essentially deontic in his methodology, Professor Falk's manner is nonetheless critical and realistic. The central question is held to be how the *relevance* of law to the conduct of international relations can be maintained, without sacrificing the *autonomy* of that law. To effect a 'reconciliation' between the two is the principal object of the work.

How and why does international law function as law? What are the different kinds of 'world order systems' which may be envisaged? What are the conditions precedent for change to the existing system and what is the relevance of existing procedures for change? These are some of the questions with which the author is concerned. In considering them, Professor Falk adopts a Namier-like approach. Selected parts of the spectrum are examined in order to illuminate the system as a whole. . . .

[There] is little question that *The Status of Law* represents a very significant contribution to the philosophy of international relations.

> *Clifford Hall, "Law: 'The Status of Law in International Society'," in* International Affairs *(© Royal Institute of International Affairs 1971), Vol. 47, No. 4, October, 1971, p. 811.*

SCIENCE BOOKS

There is a growing awareness among educated people that the continuation of current trends will leave the survival of man on earth in doubt. Nonrenewable resources are being rapidly depleted, pollution of the air and water is increasing, and the total population of the world is continuing its upward climb. [In *This Endangered Planet: Proposals for Human Survival*] Richard Falk has presented a well-structured, reasoned consideration of these factors which, in combination with a finite earth, make humanity's situation desperate. In contrast to many recent works in these areas, this book deals with the interrelationships among four factors rather than focusing on one factor, a process which often leads to spurious "solutions." The four principal threats to the planet are, in the author's view, 1) the war system with its constant potential for nuclear disaster, 2) overpopulation, 3) depletion of natural resources, and 4) increasing deterioration of the total environment. . . . Falk offers no pat solutions to the problem of the endangered planet, yet he is reasonably optimistic that, with a further spread of information about the danger facing the earth, humanity can put aside its differences and find a workable solution.

> *"Ecology and Community: 'This Endangered Planet: Proposals for Human Survival'," in* Science Books *(copyright © 1972 by the American Association for the Advancement of Science), Vol. VIII, No. 3, December, 1972, p. 198.*

MICHAEL LEIFER

[*The Vietnam War and International Law, Volume 3*] is undoubtedly a rich source of diverse opinion which both defends and rejects the position of the American Administration. On the Cambodian intervention, the editor, Professor Falk, argues

that it ". . . is, perhaps, the most blatant violation of international law by the United States since World War II." . . . Irrespective of the merits and demerits of the Administration's case, a striking feature of the debate on Cambodia is the extent to which legal opinions follow from differing interpretations of the available factual evidence of the events which preceded the intervention. In this respect, politics clearly dominates law. . . . (p. 171)

> *Michael Leifer, "Book Reviews: 'The Vietnam War and International Law, Volume 3'," in* Pacific Affairs *(copyright 1973, University of British Columbia), Vol. 46, No. 1, Spring, 1973, pp. 170-71.*

DON C. PIPER

[*This Endangered Planet*] is disturbing, disappointing, and not easily forgotten.

The book will disturb many readers because of the author's compelling conviction that the human race has ten to 100 years to prepare a response to the increasing threats to human survival. In general terms the threat to survival and the planetary crisis involve problems of population pressure, pollution, resource depletion, and the chance of wars of mass destruction. Although these problems may have existed in the past in varying degrees, Falk asserts that it is the technological character of contemporary society that gives the impending crisis its apocalyptic possibilities.

In viewing the planetary crisis, Falk persuasively argues that national states and the existing system of world order are wholly inadequate to meet the challenges. . . .

Although social scientists are not yet in a position to assert complete predictability in social forecasting and although any observer can probably cite evidence to support either a pessimistic or an optimistic forecast, a sensitive reader will not wish to dismiss Falk's apocalyptic scenario.

The book is disappointing because of the author's inadequate treatment of the appropriate responses to population pressure as one of the causes for planetary crisis. Indeed one might argue that the problems of population growth must be resolved before the other manifestations of the planetary crisis can be contained. Whereas Falk is articulate and persuasive in developing alternative structures for systems of world order and comprehensive in his analysis of the inadequacies of the present state system, he appears to back away from a sensitive discussion of alternatives to reduce the population pressures.

It is clear that Falk considers population pressure to be one of the causes of the planetary crisis, but he is ambiguous on the magnitude of the problem. . . . If the present population is excessive, how is it to be reduced? Falk equivocates. He rejects extreme measures such as mandatory sterilization of certain social classes or ethnic groups or the insertion of contraceptive chemicals in water supplies; but he acknowledges the inadequacy of voluntary approaches to family planning. Effective nonvoluntary population controls would appear to be doubtful in the light of the author's insistence that the world-order system be ". . . willing and able to uphold personal rights of conscience and autonomy and group rights of assembly and cultural assertion." . . .

Apart from some general humanitarian concerns, Falk's generally sensitive weaving of moral, legal, and political threads is not applied specifically to population pressures. Indeed one can suggest that it would be constructive if Falk began to think about the unthinkable. . . .

If the planetary crisis is as acute as Falk proclaims, and if one of the causes is population pressure, someone must set forth ". . . with clarity, ingenuity, and uncompromising rigor . . ." effective measures to accomplish the optimum population level. It is disappointing that Falk appears to be satisfied with outlining the difficulties of the problem. Unless he and others with similar humanitarian values engage in such thinking, strategists with ". . . a rather unusually large appetite for exploring these particular regions of unthinkability . . ." . . . may dominate the discussion to the detriment of the fundamental values he seeks to promote. (p. 371)

> *Don C. Piper, "Book Reviews: 'This Endangered Planet: Prospects and Proposals for Human Survival'," in* The American Political Science Review *(copyright, 1975, by The American Political Science Association), Vol. 69, No. 1, March, 1975, pp. 370-72.*

HAROLD TAYLOR

A Study of Future Worlds is one of the most thoroughgoing and wide-ranging investigations of world order and its future that has yet been written. It is Professor Falk's major work and combines the insight of a radical political thinker and activist with the care and diligence of a distinguished scholar.

The heart of the book lies in Falk's effort to support a world revolution while he defines in practical terms the changes necessary to bring it about. He avoids the rhetoric of revolution in favor of sober statements about attainable social goals and the means to achieve them. With an expert's knowledge of the literature and operations of the existing international system, he deals with the full range of complexity in the issues of world management.

Rather than dismissing the arguments of those who disagree with him, whether on questions of disarmament, deterrence theory, world population control, the reform of the United Nations, multinational corporations, or the relation of domestic politics to foreign policy, he is willing to entertain all their ideas. He tests them by the degree to which they encourage the reduction of mass violence and open up the possibilities for non-violent and beneficent change. Without giving an inch to anyone in his advocacy of ideal goals and a radical perspective, he writes page after page of closely reasoned analysis of the factors that must be taken into account in any effort to produce a new order. (pp. 19-20)

Richard Falk has produced a book that can serve both as a major resource of ideas for the theory of world peace and as a manual for political and social action. (p. 20)

> *Harold Taylor, "The World in a Test Tube," in* Saturday Review *(copyright © 1975 by Saturday Review; all rights reserved; reprinted by permission), Vol. 2, No. 20, June 28, 1975, pp. 18-20.*

HAROLD K. JACOBSON

[*A Study of Future Worlds*] is a challenging, maddening, frustrating, but above all an important book. (p. 154)

The book is challenging because reading it forces one to think through the crucial issues that are raised, and it provides an excellent framework and background for this exercise. Chapter 3, in which nine possible future world orders are sketched in clear, sharp, analytical terms, is a major contribution. Henceforth it will be impossible to speculate about future world politics in terms of simple projections within the Westphalian framework—that is, the system of sovereign states that has been the organizing principle for world politics since 1648. Falk's preferred world order, outlined in the fourth chapter, is a mosaic of aspects of several of the nine basic types. The key element is the development of a central guidance system. Seeing Falk's design provokes one to create one's own preferred world order.

Numerous unsubstantiated assertions give the book its maddening quality. For example . . . , Falk asserts, "The government in the United States, aware of its declining capacity to solve human problems in accordance with its own creed, acts to prevent the mass of people from comprehending the true state of affairs." Partisans of various persuasions would disagree with different parts of the sentence, but whatever one's political beliefs the mixture of contemporary rhetoric with sober scholarly analysis cannot help but be distracting. The book stresses the need to develop social indicators for assessing progress toward implementation of the values it espouses. In fact, with better use of available data Falk could have been more precise than he was.

The book is frustrating because certain crucial linkages are poorly drawn and because some analyses are never completely carried through. It is never very clear exactly how the institutions that are crucial elements in Falk's preferred world order would promote the four essential values. Growing public pressure for increased social and economic benefits is a fairly convincing mechanism for eventually bringing about disarmament and hence lessening the importance of the war system, and fear of nuclear and ecological disaster are potent forces leading in the direction of augmented central authority. Unfortunately, Falk is unable to suggest any equally convincing mechanism that would lead toward greater equity in the distribution of the gross global product. Falk deals with transnational corporations throughout the book, but in the end he remains ambivalent about under precisely which conditions these entities could contribute to his conception of a better world.

Falk argues that the first step toward the creation of his preferred world order must be the mobilization of segments of opinion, especially in the industrial countries and particularly the United States. His book is important because it will surely stimulate debate and consequently catalyze this mobilization. He viewed his book as a contribution to education, and he has achieved his purpose handsomely. (pp. 154-55)

> *Harold K. Jacobson, "Book Department: 'A Study of Future Worlds'," in* The Annals of The American Academy of Political and Social Science *(© 1975, by The American Academy of Political and Social Science), Vol. 422, November, 1975, pp. 154-55.*

ALAN JAMES

"Sensitive" international analysts, says Professor Falk [in *A Global Approach to National Policy*], have long questioned "the adequacy and durability of the state system as the basis of world order." . . . They recognize that it cannot cope with the world's presently "unmanageable" . . . problems, notably those of physical violence, insufficient social and economic welfare, social and political injustice, and ecological imbalance. They see the need for a "viable vision of the future", . . . one which takes a global perspective and so approaches problems "without reference to artificial boundaries whether of states, races, classes, or castes." . . . But their approach is not one of "utopian hope." Between this Scylla and the Charybdis of "realistic despair" . . . they propose to chart a middle course, and towards that end Professor Falk offers this book. One cannot but be impressed by his concern and compassion. One has also to say, however, that this book fails.

Its basic fault is that it is a hotchpotch. The chapters, a number of which have evidently appeared in some form before (although exact references are not given), are loosely related both to each other and to the book's alleged theme. (p. 136)

Manifestly, the people of the world are either satisfied with the present system, apathetic towards it, or are deterred from overthrowing it by their governments. They therefore have, as Professor Falk might say, to be sensitized to his perceived need for change. But his book does not present anything in the nature of a sustained, direct argument suggesting how this might be done. Then, too, it says very little about the new system which he desires. Apparently it is to be a "compromise" falling short of world government but greatly increasing the world's present "central guidance capabilities," while also diminishing "bureaucratic intrusions on individual human existence below the state level." . . . Not many will sacrifice much for so vague a goal. And, finally, even if people want change and are willing to take the author's preferred system on trust, they might well expect to be told something about how it might be reached. But here, too, Professor Falk falls short. He is very sympathetic towards non-violence, and thinks that "from a global perspective, violence creates at least as many problems as it solves." . . . Yet he says elsewhere . . . that it will probably be necessary "to evolve appropriate revolutionary tactics so as to acquire, possibly to seize, power from regressive forces associated with statism, growth dynamics, and short-term interests in profits and power." On this central question he says virtually nothing more.

These observations would be unjustified had the book under review been just a collection of some of the author's essays. But they are topped and tailed by the assertion that it is an "educational" . . . book, aiming to assist a transition to a better-ordered world. To this reviewer the link between the claim and the content is unclear. (p. 137)

> *Alan James, "Book Department: 'A Global Approach to National Policy'," in* The Annals of the American Academy of Political and Social Science *(© 1976, by The American Academy of Political and Social Science), Vol. 428, November, 1976, pp. 136-37.*

JOSEPH L. NOGEE

There are three problems posed by [Professor Falk's appeal for a global perspective on world problems in *A Global Approach to National Policy*]. First, the contours of Falk's utopia are vague. What kind of structure can replace the state system? Falk argues the need for "a supranational control to protect the general interest." This suggests a world government, but Falk acknowledges that it is unattainable under present conditions. Perhaps international organization? In one essay he refers favorably to the "quasi-legislative" competence of the General Assembly, but elsewhere he deplores the fact that the United Nations is a tool of the superpowers. We are in the end offered a "model" which increases "the central guidance ca-

pabilities of the present system of world order for functional purposes . . . !"

Secondly, Falk's analysis is not only highly subjective but places heavy reliance upon non-rational and emotional factors to produce the kinds of changes he desires. Though not rejecting the scientific method Falk finds it inadequate to produce the necessary "consciousness about the future." He therefore endorses the view of W. I. Thompson that scientific thinking must be linked with "mystical thinking." Indeed, in a footnote he cites specific songs of the Beatles and Bob Dylan as intuitive expressions of the need for drastic change and then claims that "legal and political analysis needs to be more receptive to these more literary sources of understanding." The difficulty here is not with intuition as a guide (among others) toward the truth; it is with the centrality of emotions and subjective judgments that permeates his analysis.

Finally, the intensity of Falk's polemic against the United States undermines the credibility of his argument. Approximately half the book is devoted to the "lessons" of Indochina in which the central theme is that American behavior in Vietnam was "criminal," "illegal," "madness," etc. Resistance to that policy is demanded by what he calls the principles of Nuremberg. Falk equates American influence in Central America and the Caribbean with Soviet control of Eastern Europe, suggesting even that the refusal of the United States to allow nuclear missiles in Cuba is equivalent to the Soviet refusal to permit Dubcek to pursue a liberal domestic policy. Obviously, Falk's conclusions follow from a strong anti-war ideology, though one wonders how informed he is about Eastern Europe when he asserts that Soviet troops left Hungary in 1956.

In sum, the voice of passion may identify some of the problems of international politics, but it is going to require a cooler temperament to point toward the solutions. (pp. 517-18)

> *Joseph L. Nogee, "Book Reviews: 'A Global Approach to National Policy'," in* The Journal of Politics *(copyright 1977 by the Southern Political Science Association), Vol. 39, No. 2, May, 1977, pp. 516-18.*

MORTON A. KAPLAN

[*A Global Approach to International Politics*] is an uneven collection of essays, only one or two of which represent Falk at his illustrious best. (p. 1288)

Part Two of the book presents Falk at his worst. Many distinguished scholars share Falk's high valuation of the Nuremberg trials. . . . The principle really established [at Nuremberg] was that in large wars victors try the vanquished. The danger in this, of course, is that it may make it much more difficult to limit and to terminate wars. In a nuclear age, this could produce catastrophe.

Things get even worse when Professor Falk seeks to apply the Nuremberg precedent to the trial of Karl Armstrong, who bombed the Army Mathematics Research Center at the University of Wisconsin, thus causing the death of Robert Fassnacht. Professor Falk tries to be reasonable. He points out that acts of violence will lead to acts of counterviolence; and, therefore, he believes that Armstrong should not have been entirely exculpated. However, Falk believes that the sentence should have been mitigated because Armstrong believed that he was protesting a violent and illegal war that could not effectively be opposed otherwise (a real howler in terms of democratic theory). Surely Professor Falk knows that many people believe that it is simple nonsense to argue that the war was illegal. Indeed, if any state violated international law, it was North Vietnam for, at the time of the incident in Wisconsin, the organized armies of North Vietnam were waging the war against a South Vietnam that clearly had legal personality under international law as well as a right to support from its allies. Moreover, even newspaper reporters now understand that the National Liberation Front was ruled from Hanoi by agents who were officials of the northern party.

Should the judge, prosecutor, and jury have taken this into account and perhaps have convicted Mr. Armstrong of first-degree murder under the reasonable man doctrine? Even if Armstrong believed the building to have been empty, he knew that people sometimes did work late at night and intended an explosion that could kill a person in that event.

Juries and judges do properly take into account ordinary character and motivation in arriving at sentences. To extend this principle to crucial political motivation is dangerous. Factually such extensions do occur, as in the case of the juries in Ohio that refused to convict those responsible for the atrocities at Kent State. Think how much it would damage the system of domestic law were we to write into jurisprudential philosophy the legitimacy of political sympathy in the imposition of penalties at law. It would politicize the law and legitimate its repressive use. Law may need to be tempered by moral concern, but Professor Falk's partisanship sometimes leads him to deplorable conclusions. (p. 1289)

Morton A. Kaplan, "Book Reviews: 'A Global Approach to National Policy'," in The American Political Science Review *(copyright, 1977, by The American Political Science Association), Vol. 71, No. 3, September, 1977, pp. 1288-89.*

Frantz Fanon

1925-1961

Fanon was a Martinican psychiatrist and political theorist who worked for the liberation movement in Algeria. In his writings he analyzed the psychology of racism in colonial societies and developed a theory of Third World revolution, a central tenet of which was the liberating power of violence. In his first book, *Black Skin, White Masks* (1952), Fanon examined the destructive effects of colonialism and racism on Third World people. *The Wretched of the Earth* (1961) is Fanon's passionate appeal for violent, peasant-led socialist revolutions in the Third World, aimed at shattering the psychology of oppression and bringing about social and moral regeneration. Fanon's work apparently had a limited influence on Third World revolutionaries. Ironically, his greatest audience may have been in Europe and America, particularly among American black militants and socialists of the 1960s, who referred to his *Wretched of the Earth* as "the Bible." (See also *Contemporary Authors*, obituary, Vols. 89-92.)

Excerpt from *THE WRETCHED OF THE EARTH*

National liberation, national renaissance, the restoration of nationhood to the people, commonwealth: whatever may be the headings used or the new formulas introduced, decolonisation is always a violent phenomenon. (p. 29)

In decolonisation, there is . . . the need of a complete calling in question of the colonial situation. If we wish to describe it precisely, we might find it in the well-known words: "The last shall be first and the first last". Decolonisation is the putting into practice of this sentence. That is why, if we try to describe it, all decolonisation is successful.

The naked truth of decolonisation evokes for us the searing bullets and bloodstained knives which emanate from it. For if the last shall be first, this will only come to pass after a murderous and decisive struggle between the two protagonists. That affirmed intention to place the last at the head of things, and to make them climb at a pace (too quickly, some say) the well-known steps which characterise an organized society, can only triumph if we use all means to turn the scale, including, of course, that of violence.

You do not turn any society, however primitive it may be, upside-down with such a programme if you are not decided from the very beginning, that is to say from the actual formulation of that programme, to overcome all the obstacles that you will come across in so doing. The native who decides to put the programme into practice, and to become its moving force, is ready for violence at all times. From birth it is clear to him that this narrow world, strewn with prohibitions, can only be called in question by absolute violence. (pp. 30-1)

The violence which has ruled over the ordering of the colonial world, which has ceaselessly drummed the rhythm for the destruction of native social forms and broken up without reserve the systems of reference of the economy, the customs of dress and external life, that same violence will be claimed and taken over by the native at the moment when, deciding to embody

Reprinted by permission of Grove Press

history in his own person, he surges into the forbidden quarters. To wreck the colonial world is henceforward a mental picture of action which is very clear, very easy to understand and which may be assumed by each one of the individuals which constitute the colonised people. To break up the colonial world does not mean that after the frontiers have been abolished lines of communication will be set up between the two zones. The destruction of the colonial world is no more and no less than the abolition of one zone, its burial in the depths of the earth or its expulsion from the country. (p. 33)

We must leave our dreams and abandon our old beliefs and friendships of the time before life began. Let us waste no time in sterile litanies and nauseating mimicry. Leave this Europe where they are never done talking of Man, yet murder men everywhere they find them, at the corner of every one of their own streets, in all the corners of the globe. For centuries they have stifled almost the whole of humanity in the name of a so-called spiritual experience. Look at them today swaying between atomic and spiritual disintegration.

And yet it may be said that Europe has been successful in as much as everything that she has attempted has succeeded. . . .

Europe has declined all humility and all modesty; but she has also set her face against all solicitude and all tenderness. (p. 252)

Yet it is very true that we need a model, and that we want blueprints and examples. For many among us the European model is the most inspiring. . . .

When I search for Man in the technique and the style of Europe, I see only a succession of negations of man, and an avalanche of murders.

The human condition, plans for mankind and collaboration between men in those tasks which increase the sum total of humanity are new problems, which demand true inventions.

Let us decide not to imitate Europe; let us combine our muscles and our brains in a new direction. Let us try to create the whole man, whom Europe has been incapable of bringing to triumphant birth. (p. 253)

All the elements of a solution to the great problems of humanity have, at different times, existed in European thought. But the action of European men has not carried out the mission which fell to them, and which consisted of bringing their whole weight to bear violently upon these elements, of modifying their arrangement and their nature, of changing them and finally of bringing the problem of mankind to an infinitely higher plane.

Today, we are present at the stasis of Europe. Comrades, let us flee from this motionless movement where gradually dialectic is changing into the logic of equilibrium. Let us reconsider the question of mankind. Let us reconsider the question of cerebral reality and of the cerebral mass of all humanity, whose connections must be increased, whose channels must be diversified and whose messages must be re-humanised.

Come, brothers, we have far too much work to do for us to play the game of rear-guard. Europe has done what she set out to do and on the whole she has done it well; let us stop blaming her, but let us say to her firmly that she should not make such a song and dance about it. We have no more to fear; so let us stop envying her.

The Third World today faces Europe like a colossal mass whose aim should be to try to resolve the problems to which Europe has not been able to find the answers. (p. 254)

It is a question of the Third World starting a new history of Man, a history which will have regard to the sometimes prodigious theses which Europe has put forward, but which will also not forget Europe's crimes, of which the most horrible was committed in the heart of man, and consisted of the pathological tearing apart of his functions and the crumbling away of his unity. And in the framework of the collectivity there were the differentiations, the stratification and the bloodthirsty tensions fed by classes; and finally, on the immense scale of humanity, there were racial hatreds, slavery, exploitation and above all the bloodless genocide which consisted in the setting aside of fifteen thousand millions of men. . . .

For Europe, for ourselves and for humanity, comrades, we must turn over a new leaf, we must work out new concepts, and try to set afoot a new man. (p. 255)

> *Frantz Fanon, in his* The Wretched of the Earth, *translated by Constance Farrington (reprinted by permission of Grove Press, Inc.; translation copyright © 1963 by Presence Africaine; originally published as* Le damnes de la terre, *François Maspero, 1961), Grove Press, 1965, 255 p.*

Excerpt from *BLACK SKIN, WHITE MASKS*

The explosion will not happen today. It is too soon . . . or too late.

I do not come with timeless truths.

My consciousness is not illuminated with ultimate radiances.

Nevertheless, in complete composure, I think it would be good if certain things were said.

These things I am going to say, not shout. For it is a long time since shouting has gone out of my life.

So very long. . . .

Why write this book? No one has asked me for it.

Especially those to whom it is directed.

Well? Well, I reply quite calmly that there are too many idiots in this world. And having said it, I have the burden of proving it.

Toward a new humanism. . . .

Understanding among men. . . .

Our colored brothers. . . .

Mankind, I believe in you. . . .

Race prejudice. . . .

To understand and to love. . . .

From all sides dozens and hundreds of pages assail me and try to impose their wills on me. But a single line would be enough. Supply a single answer and the color problem would be stripped of all its importance.

What does a man want?

What does the black man want?

At the risk of arousing the resentment of my colored brothers, I will say that the black is not a man.

There is a zone of nonbeing, an extraordinarily sterile and arid region, an utterly naked declivity where an authentic upheaval can be born. In most cases, the black man lacks the advantage of being able to accomplish this descent into a real hell.

Man is not merely a possibility of recapture or of negation. If it is true that consciousness is a process of transcendence, we have to see too that this transcendence is haunted by the problems of love and understanding. Man is a *yes* that vibrates to cosmic harmonies. Uprooted, pursued, baffled, doomed to watch the dissolution of the truths that he has worked out for himself one after another, he has to give up projecting onto the world an antinomy that coexists with him.

The black is a black man; that is, as the result of a series of aberrations of affect, he is rooted at the core of a universe from which he must be extricated.

The problem is important. I propose nothing short of the liberation of the man of color from himself. We shall go very slowly, for there are two camps: the white and the black.

Stubbornly we shall investigate both metaphysics and we shall find that they are often quite fluid.

We shall have no mercy for the former governors, the former missionaries. To us, the man who adores the Negro is as "sick" as the man who abominates him.

Conversely, the black man who wants to turn his race white is as miserable as he who preaches hatred for the whites.

In the absolute, the black is no more to be loved than the Czech, and truly what is to be done is to set man free.

This book should have been written three years ago. . . . But these truths were a fire in me then. Now I can tell them without being burned. These truths do not have to be hurled in men's faces. They are not intended to ignite fervor. I do not trust fervor.

Every time it has burst out somewhere, it has brought fire, famine, misery. . . . And contempt for man.

Fervor is the weapon of choice of the impotent.

Of those who heat the iron in order to shape it at once. I should prefer to warm man's body and leave him. We might reach this result: mankind retaining this fire through self-combustion.

Mankind set free of the trampoline that is the resistance of others, and digging into its own flesh to find a meaning.

Only a few of those who read this book will understand the problems that were encountered in its composition.

In an age when skeptical doubt has taken root in the world, when in the words of a gang of *salauds* it is no longer possible to find the sense of non-sense, it becomes harder to penetrate to a level where the categories of sense and non-sense are not yet invoked.

The black man wants to be white. The white man slaves to reach a human level.

In the course of this essay we shall observe the development of an effort to understand the black-white relation.

The white man is sealed in his whiteness.

The black man in his blackness.

We shall seek to ascertain the directions of this dual narcissism and the motivations that inspire it.

At the beginning of my speculations it seems inappropriate to elaborate the conclusions that the reader will find.

Concern with the elimination of a vicious circle has been the only guide-line for my efforts.

There is a fact: White men consider themselves superior to black men.

There is another fact: Black men want to prove to white men, at all costs, the richness of their thought, the equal value of their intellect.

How do we extricate ourselves? (pp. 7-10)

> *Frantz Fanon, in his* Black Skin, White Masks, *translated by Charles Lam Marksmann (reprinted by permission of Grove Press, Inc.; translation copyright © 1967 by Grove Press, Inc.; originally published as* Peau noire, masques blancs, Editions de Seuil, 1952), *Grove Press, 1967, 232 p.*

FRANZ ANSPRENGER

In [*Les Damnés de la terre*], Frantz Fanon calls on the peoples of Asia, Latin America, and especially Africa to liberate their economically backward, exploited, and colonised countries from their European, highly-industrialised masters. He gives a critical analysis of decolonisation in some parts of Africa, inspired by Africa's revolutionary war: a polemic, subjective, but intelligent and up-to-date analysis. (p. 403)

Here and there, Fanon touches closely on the painful nerves of African politics. Elsewhere, he is very far from reality. Which African peoples did he really know? Obviously only the Algerian people. Which African political leaders did he know? The French-speaking West Africans. Sékou Touré's Guinean experience certainly impressed Fanon, and many ideas of the old R.D.A. (Rassemblement Démocratique Africain) percolated into his own theoretical framework. He does not speak frequently on Kwame Nkrumah's Ghana, which he saw as an Ambassador, but some of his protests against the enervation of the Revolution and its protagonists seem to translate something of his Ghanaian impressions. The rest of Africa? Fanon had only second-hand information. There are some vague allusions to Kenya, Angola . . . , and the Congo. I don't think he can ever have read any of Julius Nyerere's speeches or writings. Fanon, even if he had lived, would probably never have been the Lenin of the African Revolution. But his is an important voice in the post-Marxist revolution of the *Tiers Monde*. (pp. 404-05)

> *Franz Ansprenger, "Reviews: 'Les damnés de la terre'," in* The Journal of Modern African Studies *(© Cambridge University Press 1963), Vol. I, No. 3, September, 1963, pp. 403-05.*

JEAN-PAUL SARTRE

[When] Fanon says of Europe that she is rushing to her doom, far from sounding the alarm he is merely setting out a diagnosis. This doctor neither claims that she is a hopeless case—miracles have been known to exist—nor does he give her the means to cure herself. He certifies that she is dying, on external evidence, founded on symptoms that he can observe. As to curing her, no; he has other things to think about; he does not give a damn whether she lives or dies. Because of this, [*The Wretched of the Earth*] is scandalous. And if you murmur, jokingly embarrassed, "He has it in for us!" the true nature of the scandal escapes you; for Fanon has nothing in for you at all; his work—red-hot for some—in what concerns you is as cold as ice; he speaks of you often, never to you. (pp. 9-10)

In short, the Third World finds *itself* and speaks to *itself* through his voice. . . . Fanon hides nothing: in order to fight against us the former colony must fight against itself; or, rather, the two struggles form part of a whole. . . . [The] unity of the Third World is not yet achieved. It is a work in progress, which begins by the union, in each country, after independence as before, of the whole of the colonized people under the command of the peasant class. This is what Fanon explains to his brothers in Africa, Asia, and Latin America: we must achieve revolutionary socialism all together everywhere, or else one by one we will be defeated by our former masters. He hides nothing, neither weaknesses, nor discords, nor mystification. . . . [The] only true culture is that of the revolution; that is to say, it is constantly in the making. Fanon speaks out loud; we Europeans can hear him, as the fact that you hold this book in your hand proves; is he not then afraid that the colonial powers may take advantage of his sincerity?

No; he fears nothing. Our methods are out-of-date; they can sometimes delay emancipation, but not stop it. . . . The settler has only recourse of one thing: brute force, when he can command it; the native has only one choice, between servitude or supremacy. What does Fanon care whether you read his work or not? It is to his brothers that he denounces our old tricks, and he is sure we have no more up our sleeves. (pp. 10-12)

Europeans, you must open this book and enter into it. After a few steps in the darkness you will see strangers gathered around a fire; come close, and listen, for they are talking of the destiny they will mete out to your trading centers and to the hired soldiers who defend them. . . . [They] ignore you; a fire warms them and sheds light around them, and you have not lit it. Now, at a respectful distance, it is you who will feel furtive, nightbound, and perished with cold. . . .

Why read it if it is not written for us? For two reasons: the first is that Fanon explains you to his brothers and shows them the mechanism by which we are estranged from ourselves; take advantage of this, and get to know yourselves seen in the light of truth, objectively. (p. 13)

Fanon is the first since Engels to bring the processes of history into the clear light of day. Moreover, you need not think that hotheadedness or an unhappy childhood has given him some uncommon taste for violence; he acts as the interpreter of the situation, that's all. But this is enough to enable him to constitute, step by step, the dialectic which liberal hypocrisy hides from you and which is as much responsible for our existence as for his. (p. 14)

Read Fanon: you will learn how, in the period of their helplessness, their mad impulse to murder is the expression of the natives' collective unconscious. (p. 21)

[Our worthiest souls] would do well to read Fanon; for he shows clearly that this irrepressible violence is neither sound and fury, nor the resurrection of savage instincts, nor even the effect of resentment: it is man recreating himself. I think we understood this truth at one time, but we have forgotten it—that no gentleness can efface the marks of violence; only violence itself can destroy them. (p. 21)

[Fanon] has shown the way forward: he is the spokesman of those who are fighting and he has called for union, that is to say the unity of the African continent against all dissensions and all particularisms. He has gained his end. If he had wished to describe in all its details the historical phenomenon of decolonization he would have to have spoken of us; this is not at all his intention. But, when we have closed the book, the argument continues within us, in spite of its author; for we feel the strength of the peoples in revolt and we answer by force. Thus there is a fresh moment of violence; and this time we ourselves are involved, for by its nature this violence is changing us, accordingly as the "half native" is changed. Every one of us must think for himself—always provided that he thinks at all; for in Europe today, stunned as she is by the blows received by France, Belgium, or England, even to allow your mind to be diverted, however slightly, is as good as being the accomplice in crime of colonialism. . . . [We] in Europe too are being decolonized: that is to say that the settler which is in every one of us is being savagely rooted out. Let us look at ourselves, if we can bear to, and see what is becoming of us. (p. 24)

> *Jean-Paul Sartre, in his preface to* The Wretched of the Earth *by Frantz Fanon, translated by Constance Farrington (reprinted by permission of Grove Press, Inc.; translation copyright © 1963 by Presence Africaine; originally published as* Le damnes de la terre, *François Maspero, 1961), Grove Press, 1965, pp. 7-31.*

CONOR CRUISE O'BRIEN

As a writer, [Frantz Fanon] is distinguished by his passionate seriousness and his frequent, penetrating insights. He is neither an easy nor a systematic writer; one feels that his writing is wrung from him by his experience. *The Wretched of the Earth* is not so much a tract or essay as a series of intellectual explosions. Experience detonates an idea; hardly has the dust settled before another idea, equally unsettling, goes up. There are almost no transitions; he writes in the implicit belief that history itself provides the element of continuity in his book. . . .

Yet Fanon's book has an unchanging central figure: that of "the colonized": *le colonisé.* . . .

There are times when he writes as if the colonial experience brought into being an entirely new kind of being, all of whose characteristics derive from colonialism. Even tribal warfare is a product of colonialism: "Collective self-destruction in tribal warfare is one of the means by which the muscular tension of the colonized releases itself." There is an element of truth in this: under colonialism and especially under settler rule—Fanon never adequately distinguishes between these two phenomena—the black man, say, will often want to hit a white man, but finds it much safer to hit another black man, and derives some relief from doing so. Nor is it necessarily a question of blacks and whites: witness the shillelagh fights of 18th-century Ireland. . . . But this is not the whole truth; for the Irish and the Africans were fighting each other before the foreigners came.

Violence is not, as Fanon often seems to suggest, a creation of colonialism. On the contrary, colonialism is a form of violence. . . .

In this respect, it seems to me that Fanon overrates the originality of colonialism. He is also inclined, I think, to exaggerate its effects and underrate the degree of continuity which exists between pre-colonial and post-colonial Africa. All African phenomena—even dancing—are to him functions of colonialism. . . . It is curious to find Fanon, of all people, falling into the kind of wild anthropological generalization characteristic of an earlier generation of European observers. (p. 674)

The truth is that *le colonisé* is far less uniform a person than Fanon's French-instilled taste for generalization leads him to suggest. . . . In [some] cases—as in Africa between the forest belt and the Sahara—large populations continued their traditional way of life, hardly touched by the colonial experience. Others have been more deeply affected, but without at all losing their sense of national identity or feeling the slightest temptation to "be" French or British. Colonial rule was often too brief to penetrate the psyche as thoroughly as Fanon assumes. (pp. 674-75)

The value of *The Wretched of the Earth* does not lie in its often fanciful generalizations but in its relation to direct experience, in the perspective of the Algerian revolution. . . . Fanon forces his readers to see the Algerian revolution—and by analogy other contemporary revolutions—from the viewpoint of the rebels. This is not the viewpoint of the European liberal, sympathetic to the aims of the revolution, but deploring its excesses and seeking a nonviolent way out. It is not even the viewpoint of a French sympathizer with the revolution like Sartre, whose introduction to this volume [see excerpt above] is mainly preoccupied with France's guilt. Fanon preaches violence, including violence against civilians, as a legitimate resource of the oppressed.

The French established and maintained their rule in Algeria by violence, including violence against civilians; the conquered have the right to use equivalent violence to end that rule; they will rightly refuse to allow their conquerors to instruct them on what forms of violence are to be considered legitimate. Fanon here touches a raw nerve in his Western readers. One of the forms of violence frequently practiced by Algerian rebels was the murder and mutilation of settlers, including women and children. . . . Before we cry out in horror at this, we might do well to consider what we ourselves implicitly condone or have condoned, by our silence. . . . [We] have murdered and mutilated, and are continuing to murder and mutilate, in Vietnam and elsewhere, far more children than the Algerian peasants ever did. But we do not call it murder when it is done from the air. And we do not feel so bad about it when the children are not white.

Fanon's position essentially is that all crimes committed by both sides in the Algerian War derive from the basic crime of a rule imposed and maintained by violence, and inaccessible to any appeal save that of violence. On the plane of generalities, I think Fanon is right. Yet personal responsibility, on both sides, inescapably remained, as the astonishing Algerian psychiatric case histories which conclude the book show. (p. 675)

Conor Cruise O'Brien, "The Neurosis of Colonialism," in The Nation *(copyright 1965 The Nation magazine, The Nation Associates, Inc.), Vol. 200, No. 25, June 21, 1965, pp. 674-76.*

ROBERT COLES

[*The Wretched of the Earth*] is a study of the political and economic nature of racism and colonialism as well as an analysis of what they both do to the minds of their victims. (p. 20)

What distinguishes this book, turns it from a blazing manifesto to an authentic and subtle work of art, is the author's extraordinary capacity to join his sharp social and political sense with the doctor's loyalty to the individual, whatever his particular worth or folly. As a result, fierce hatred—to hell with the merciless exploiters, still bleeding their victims—is qualified by an alarmed recognition that native tyranny can replace its foreign predecessor. (p. 22)

It is in the book's last section that Dr. Fanon reveals his skills as narrator and artist. Shunning any temptation to avoid confusion and ambiguity, the gray in life, he gives us instead a terrifying glimpse into the mental disorders associated with both colonialism and the revolutions that aim to end it. The crushed people are brought to life as only the novelist or clinician can do it, by detailed descriptions of their private lives, their fears and terrors. One price of rebellion, the mental pain, is revealed, as are the tortures rebellion evokes from the desperate colonial authorities, many of whom eventually collapse,

prey to their own bestiality. Fanon is impressively and painstakingly willing to see hurt and suffering on all sides, guilt everywhere, the entire population saturated with anxiety and nightmares. (pp. 22-3)

It is an awful spectacle; and in many ways the justice Fanon does to the mind of the native African under such circumstances resembles what Conrad did to the white man's in *Heart of Darkness*. Western man shares "the horror, the horror" of his nature with millions of others in all corners of the globe. Terror and madness will unite ruler and sufferer if it must come to chaos before brazen tyranny is ended. Insofar as we realize that fact, and act on what we realize, we will live safer and less corrupt lives. For all the resentment and hurt in him, Dr. Fanon had that message for us when he wrote this book, and it is a healing one. (p. 23)

Robert Coles, "What Colonialism Does" (reprinted by permission of the author; © 1965 by Robert Coles), in The New Republic, *Vol. 153, No. 12, September 18, 1965, pp. 20-3.*

A. NORMAN KLEIN

The Wretched of the Earth is in a direct line of descent from Mao, Giap and Ché Guevara. What distinguishes Fanon is the breadth of his analysis. (p. 62)

The unique flavor of his work derives in large measure from his outspoken identity with revolution. There is no pretense of academic "objectivity" or detachment. Tendentious and outspoken, Fanon strives above all to further and intensify the revolutionary aspirations of Africa's peoples; ideological commitment is his most powerful tool. (p. 63)

I propose to push Fanon's analysis back one step historically, that is, to pose retrospectively some of the issues he frames in the prospective overview of an active revolutionary engaged in attempting to construct his own future. By first examining some cultural forms of anti-colonial resistance which fall short of open, armed conflict and then moving to examples of prenationalist, anti-colonial political movements—some of which did go to war—it is possible to focus on the development of nationalist and anti-colonial ideology, the role of the peasantry in a changing class structure, and violence.

Some of the earliest developments of anti-colonial, nationalist ideology are represented by cultural forms which contain elements of almost pure protest. A variety of systems of communication are employed by oppressed people as a media for the expression of their anger and resentment. At a primitive level such cultural codes are employed by individuals or small groups to deceive, confuse and humiliate administrators, missionaries, soldiers, social scientists and others looked upon as representatives of colonial power. (p. 64)

In the colonial world the collective expression and social organization of protest have involved the incorporation of such "codes" into a wide variety of cultural forms capable of conveying explicitly political interpretations. In Mao's terminology, this is to move from "agitation" to "propaganda."

Fanon's treatment of these problems is one-sided and therefore misleading. An artistic production of Rhodesian Copperbelt miners, described and analyzed by Clyde Mitchell in *The Kalela Dance . . .* , may serve as an illustration. Here we can see an awakened understanding of the new experience of "class" differentiation, whose interpretation by dancers and audience contains the germ of real political ideology. (p. 65)

The Kalela dance illustrates some consequences of the new class structure on the activities of a popular dance team in the Copperbelt. It is performed by different teams each of which comes from a particular tribe. Each team mocks the other tribes in the audience. It taunts and derides them mercilessly, imputing to them the basest obscenity, unpleasantness and perverse sexuality. Superficially each team exalts its own tribe's virtues at the expense of the others. Surprisingly, the members of the lampooned tribe laugh as loudly as the others at their symbolic degradation. What at first glance appears to be a relatively straightforward expression of inter-tribal rivalry is, however, much more. Mitchell was struck by the fact that the dancers named "their hierarchy of officials after the hierarchies of British military or civil dignity. Moreover, the dancers do not wear tribal dress . . . ," but rather chose dapper, neat European clothing, and maintained their smartness and neatness throughout the dance. (pp. 65-6)

The Kalela dance is a bitter satire of colonial and company rule in which every figure having official status in its hierarchy is parodied and mocked. The formal structure of colonial power is completely depicted, up and down the ladder, as an object of the coarsest derision. The "stance of Empire" has been reduced to the shameless gyrations of an African dancer.

The conflict with colonialism is symbolically ameliorated in the dance, whose primary political message is to come to terms with it on its own ground. Its propaganda is not only non-revolutionary in Fanon's view, but reduces to compromise and accommodation—detracting from rather than mobilizing toward the seizure of power. This, although the examples Fanon had in mind are quite different, is one of the reasons why his psychological interpretation of primitive dance stresses its safety-valve function, i.e., as a release of pent-up feelings. . . . (pp. 67-8)

While there are elements of the Kalela dance which can quite obviously be interpreted as the letting-off of steam from accumulated primordial impulses dammed-up by the repressions of colonial society, Fanon's psychoanalytic juxtapositions are at the same time ironically inverted by the dancing miners of the Copperbelt. Politics is sublimated into sex, not *vice versa*. Sexual imagery becomes a vehicle for expressing political wants and needs. Fanon's psychoanalytic orientation plus his polar dichotomy between "culture" and "custom" block him from perceiving precisely the political content of such primitive forms. . . . "Culture" becomes the artistic summation of national aspirations. "Custom," on the other hand, is according to Fanon's usage pre-revolutionary and pre-nationalist. Its forms as well as its content are retrograde. It syphons off energies which might otherwise have been directed into revolutionary channels. The net result is, I think, an underestimation of both the artistic quality and political potential of pre-literate cultural forms.

Fanon's slighting of pre-literate "custom" is reinforced by his psychoanalytic exegesis of the overt sexuality and obscenity in many forms among primitive peoples. Collective expressions of obscenity are, for example, very widespread and are capable of conveying a wide variety of non-erotic social meanings. In concentrating on the emotional electricity of these erotic performances, Fanon seeks its primary cause in the internalized, self-destructive repression of libidinal energy which they finally free. . . . Fanon is an artist with remarkable existentialist-

psychoanalytic insights, but they have nevertheless led him to overlook some very important social and political meanings. In the case of certain ritual the eroticism of native "custom" can become ". . . a most powerful mechanism of political integration [which can generate] intense emotional energy." The Kalela dance reinforces by satire and ridicule the new inter-tribal unity along class lines of both the performers and the audience, while at the same time it ventilates many stored up feelings which might otherwise only be expressed *sotto voce*. (pp. 68-9)

Revolutionary millenarism, the earliest type of peasant war in the medieval and colonial world, poses some serious questions for Fanon's interpretation of pre-nationalist forms, his extension of existentialist-psychoanalytic reasoning to entire social and political phenomena, and finally his celebration of revolutionary violence. (p. 71)

[Millenarism] comes to typify a phase, but not necessarily a precondition through which every nationalist or anti-colonial ideology must pass, when the political goals of the revolutionary group are still part of a religious conformation under whose banners they go to war. These movements have played an important role in instituting and furthering inter-tribal and peasant cohesion against a common foe. They generated new organizations and leadership capable—no matter how mystically or fantastically attired—of sharpening and articulating not only their grievances with colonial rule, but refined strategies and tactics as well as complete programs for the construction of new societies. Millenarian-type movements have been instrumental in many areas of the underdeveloped world in contributing a particular flavor and uniqueness, the historically evolved styles of many new nationalisms. Many of the prototypic heroes and romantic political ideals of these new nationalisms are direct descendants of figures and slogans from by-gone days of peasant revolt. In Fanon's vocabulary these have become an integral part of "national culture."

Fanon, on the other hand, takes a quite different view of pre-nationalist political expressions whose religious and ideological forms are all lumped, as we have seen in the instance of primitive dance, under the heading "custom." The immediacy and urgency of Fanon's plea compel him to focus almost exclusively on the very short-run effects of pre-nationalist forms. (We might almost say on the pragmatic "cash-value" to the revolutionary movement in which he is participating.) Consequently all of his evaluations are negative. Rather than construct such phenomena as millenarism as an "earlier phase" which might contribute to the organizational and ideological underpinnings of a future nationalism, Fanon can only perceive them in terms of the demands laid down here and now by his own fully developed revolutionary and socialist nationalism. As a result all prenationalist forms (after having been denigrated to the status of "custom") can only dissipate revolutionary energy, and are retrograde and finally "dangerous." . . . (pp. 71-2)

Tactically, in the midst of an ongoing Algerian revolution, such strictures make sense. Primitive religious protests and spontaneous outbreaks would probably more weaken than enhance the effectiveness of a revolutionary peasant army and polity. If, however, we shift our perspective as Fanon does to the entire African continent and even the underdeveloped world, his evaluation becomes much less meaningful. He overlooks the political potential inherent in the content of pre-nationalist millenarisms in those parts of the underdeveloped world which exist in the past, and may still be more backward than Algeria.

Viewing at close quarters in the emergency conditions of a fully ripened revolution, Fanon cannot help but be impressed by the incompatibility of these mystical, religious forms with the objectives of his own movement. Even today, given the unevenness of ideological development in the economically underdeveloped world, might it not be a little utopian to demand full-grown nationalist responses from the various peoples of Rhodesia, South and Southwest Africa and Portuguese Africa, to say nothing of such areas as Melanesia and Bechuanaland? Does Fanon, when he warns us that "social consciousness before the stage of nationalism" is "dangerous," mean to imply that pre-nationalist protest of whatever form in these areas is *a priori,* self-destructive of "really" revolutionary, nationalist goals, which in any case may not yet have appeared?

His analysis of pre-nationalist forms is, in short, ahistoric. Such forms vary in significance and function in different historical contexts and at different levels of political and economic development.

Fanon's existentialist-psychoanalytic methods complement his short-term ahistorical overview. Rather than attempt a derivation of incentives and responses by isolating the social, economic and political variables which in each case operate to produce them, he chooses to start off with the most general effects of colonialism on the most basic biopsychological drives. His appraisals of pre-nationalist cultural forms ultimately rest on how they operate to structure and give expression to libidinal energy. When describing the function of the feud, he perspicaciously discerns its destructive and divisive role in the context of anti-colonial revolution, but at the same time limits himself to its psychological field. . . . (pp. 72-3)

Feuding—like all "custom"—is treated as one of the many mechanisms by which the native's anger at his colonial rulers is circumvented and, denied direct expression, turned inward, destroying the self rather than the original and objective source of anger and hostility. In spite of the fact that much of their work has, until recently, tended not to appreciate fully the colonialist setting of tribal life, anthropologists have nevertheless made serious contributions to our understanding of the *sociology* of the feud. When Evans-Pritchard, for example, illustrates how feud among the Nuer functions to integrate politically in groups on different levels, the implication is that feuding is much more than an individual act. Feuds do much more than "perpetuate old grudges." There is no denying that such internecine outbreaks can be very disruptive when the goal is to unite an entire people against a colonial power. The point is, however, that by consistently reducing his analysis to the level of psychological effects, Fanon tends to underestimate the techniques whereby pre-nationalist forms of protest *operate as social and political mechanisms.* . . . (p. 73)

Leaving aside questions about the importance of unconsciousness and the complex social functions of myth, magic and the domestic unit in primitive societies, when Fanon speaks of "the magical superstructure" fulfilling "certain well-defined functions in the dynamism of the libido" he assumes that entire social processes and institutions stand in isomorphic relation to psychological mechanisms of an individual personality. At the same time he is himself aware in other contexts that political and economic organisms are not directly comparable to individuals. (I think it is obvious that he intends no simple literary allusion either.) The problem comes up when he defines political and economic incentives *vis-à-vis* their relation to "libido." In fact the relationship between the complex of social, political and economic incentives to the primary drives is very

indirect and remote, even obscure. The one simply cannot be understood by reference to the other. Social incentives and "rationality" require detailed analysis of social variables. I think this becomes most obvious when we return to the questions posed by the overt eroticism and obscenity contained in so much of the ritual imagery of pre-nationalist millenarism. . . . [Fanon cannot see] the social and political meanings of these collective expressions which seem on the surface almost purely libidinal outpourings. To attempt a dissection of social, political and economical "rationality"—as did, each in his own way, both Marx and Weber—is to seek after the incipient *ideological* content of the cultural form. This requires at least some historical, structural relativism. Instead Fanon defines "rationality" in terms of a relationship between biological drives and the cultural forms which either allow or inhibit, repress or involute their expression in the setting of a war against colonialism. He therefore constantly slights the element of continuity between old ideological and cultural forms and the needs of a poet-revolutionary order. He has no way of assessing the strength and potentially positive contribution of much of the older way of life.

This raises the question of Fanon's panegyric to violence. It is a magic word in his vocabulary. Participation in armed revolutionary conflict has a positive value organizationally, ideologically, ethically and as an ultimate psychological cathartic. (pp. 73-4)

To prepare a people for such sacrifices as were necessary during the protracted war in Algeria was no easy task. It was to this end that Fanon primarily addressed himself. He was, in a word, an ideologue. *The Wretched of the Earth* is a battlecry. Modern revolutionary war demands terrific and unswerving discipline and morale on the part of the native combatants. This is especially the case since the natives are opposed from the outset by a technological-military power whose superiority is awesome. It takes a long time—how many years in China, Algeria and Vietnam?—to condition a peasant army to maintain its fighting fervor in the face of numerous tactical defeats and exacting losses. Fanon's eulogy to violence is in partial fulfillment of this task. At the same time he understood not only the final, but the immediate rewards of the fight. What heightened feelings must follow in the wake of a successful military encounter with an enemy against whom the native could previously only vent his fantasies? What internal gains are achieved when at last he is able to strike down physically and repay an enemy with some of the terror with which the native has lived all his life? What can more powerfully intensify his awareness of an identity with his fellows and nation? What more direct expression of his primal emotional energies is possible? Fanon's answers must reflect the peasant-guerrilla's feelings. He was a remarkably sensitive and trained observer whose heart went with the fighter. There is, however, quite a difference between the accurate and sympathetic description of a revolutionary soldier's motivations and psychological rewards to the elevation of these motives and rewards into an ideology, social psychology and ethics. Fanon made no such distinction.

Here his difficulties begin. It is one thing to direct and mobilize a people for the trials of guerrilla warfare; it is quite another to rhapsodize on the virtues of violence in principle. This is a theme which runs through the entire book. An acclimatization to violence and its consequences is a double-edged sword. Warfare can never be a permanent state of social existence. It is that moment when the irreconcilable antagonisms between a colonial power and a colonial people become open, manifest and violent. The most difficult tasks of the revolution begin after the barricades are dismantled. What meaning, during the period of building a new nation-state, has an ideological and psychological tribute to violence? One might point to the international and internal threats to a new revolutionary nation, which force it to maintain a state of constant military preparedness. Even so the defense of the gains of social reconstruction demands, above all, peace and not war. It seems to me that extolling violence generates a rather different set of incentives than the demand that people be prepared for rapid mobilization to defend their newly won gains. Before, the object was to take state power away from an enemy who would only yield it to superior force. Once victory had been achieved, the rewards were immediate. Now the object becomes sustained, increasing productivity and human welfare. The rewards are long-run and slow to realize. Instead of dramatic battles against an armed foe, life settles down to a day-to-day skirmish with nature. The tempo of social life must slow down and become routinized in the unremitting toil of industrialization. The psychological motivations and social and economic incentives—as well as technology and institutions—need re-tooling. How do we reconstruct the institutions of a population consciously conditioned to being rewarded by resolving its conflicts in blood? Fanon can suggest no devices by which this can be accomplished. Instead he hopes to build a new and different "man" along with the new and different society. Of what possible utility can the residues of a conscious glorification of violence be to this new man and his society? With the establishment of a new nation-state does an ideology and social psychology of violence just evaporate? They can only serve the negative function of protecting the achievements of the new nation against its foes.

In spite of Fanon's assertion of the unifying primacy of violence, the first and most obvious spur to national unity in a colonial area is the presence of an industrialized colonial power. (We must remember that not all colonial powers are industrialized nations.) Once it appears on the scene the colonial power demarks clear-cut boundaries, presents diverse populations with a homogeneous military and political authority, introduces a *lingua franca*, initiates the social and economic changes that go with industrial organization which requires a new class structure, and finally presents different groups frequently riven by traditions of feud and mutual enmity with a common political enemy. How many of the new nations of Africa are contained within boundary lines first drawn on maps in Berlin, London or Paris? In how many of these new African nations has English or French remained the official language—not necessarily because of any toadyism on the part of its leadership, but out of the simple everyday requirement of having to communicate with large groups speaking mutually unintelligible languages? Even Fanon wrote in French and not Arabic or Berber. That great exogenous factor, colonialism, has been quite independent of the will of any of its subject peoples, or of anything internal to their cultures, one of the most powerful integrative mechanisms in the underdeveloped world.

When Fanon says, "Colonialism does not simply state the existence of tribes; it also reinforces and separates them," . . . he is only looking at one side of the coin. Despite all the efforts of management and government to tribalize the Copperbelt miners [of Rhodesia], the economic process of industrialization—in itself a direct cause and consequence of colonialism in the first place—produced among the miners the unifying class allegiances which were at one and the same time eco-

nomically necessary to the operation of the mining enterprise, while politically destructive of the conscious management policy of tribalization. In urban Central Africa wage labor is the grave digger of tribal stratification and affiliation.

We have now stepped into some areas outside the provenance of Fanon's intentions. His is a book about colonialism and anti-colonial movements in the most general terms. Differences in colonial policy and practice, the consequences for the colonies of differential levels of economic development in the home countries, differences in natural resources and labor supply in separate colonial areas: these are irrelevant to him. Considering the task he set himself, they might well be. Colonialism to Fanon is the homogenized enemy, and it is Fanon's goal to homogenize the people to supplant it. His scope is so broad and his ideological demands so immediate that he confines such fine points of variation to the limbo of picayune pedantry.

On the other hand, may we not ask if Fanon's Algerian experience is really broad enough to serve as a model for the entire continent. When he addresses himself to "the African Revolution," "African Culture," "the Underdeveloped World," these differences become relevant enough. Africa is not a cultural or political-economic unity. Nor has its colonial experience been homogeneous. . . . I wonder, for example, how strictly applicable is his analysis of the privileged position of the industrial wage-worker versus the peasant in the colonial class structure, to sub-equatorial Africa today. . . . (pp. 75-8)

Were their gains the result of government and management favoritism, or did the Copperbelt miners have to fight for every inch of economic ground? If "pampered" and "privileged" in their urban enclosures, why are they constantly returning to their villages? The real question to ask Fanon is simply whether we should stop referring to them as "proletarians" the moment they go back to their crops and herds?

This is not to deny that Fanon's view has some truth, for North Africa, and West Africa especially, although the position of the wage-laborer and his relation to the peasant in the latter case is again hardly so simple as Fanon would have it. I should think that from the point of view of the strategy and tactics of revolutionary movements, such differences in political economy and changing class-structure would be critical. The contrast between Algeria and South Africa is a good one because of the similarity of objectives shared by the European colonizing populations of both, that is "the belief that it is not a settler or immigrant population with expatriate goals, but a permanent society whose racial character, material culture and morality endow it with a natural right to perpetual hegemony over a majority of non-white subordinate subjects." (pp. 78-9)

The beauty of Fanon's idealism is most compelling when he writes of the peasant and "the people." For him the meaning of the revolution consists in enriching, nurturing and bringing to fruition all their needs and aspirations. The peasant is Fanon's hero. He, as the carrier of revolution, comes to dominate the political stage. All the other social strata and "class" elements in colonial society are analyzed and evaluated in terms of their potential relation to the revolutionary peasantry which provide the leadership. . . . Fanon goes further, however, than Mao. He would extend the key role of the peasantry into the post-violent period of socialist state-building. They, and not the urban proletariat, are the element which provides the leadership and primary objectives to socialist reconstruction, and around whose activities the new socialist state must rotate.

Reminiscent of the 14th century Arabic philosopher Ibn Khaldun, Fanon is always directing his reader's attention to the contrast between the spiritual purity, revolutionary militancy and ardor of the countryside as against the vacillation, inconsistency, compromise and degeneracy of the urban centers. This dichotomy apparently continues after the military victory of the revolution. . . . (pp. 79-80)

As Fanon seems to realize elsewhere, the key to the political autonomy of any new nation in the underdeveloped world lies in its capabilities for economic development. . . . Rising productivity is a precondition to national independence. Yet, in his attachment to the peasant and his humanitarian fears of over-centralization, this is precisely what Fanon denies.

His idealism leads Fanon to unrealistic conclusions. His great alarm is for the preservation and perfection of revolutionary democracy. Mindful of dictatorship, bureaucratization and the dehumanized routinization of administrative detail, Fanon is convinced that there must be some genuinely democratic methods for achieving the desired economic ends. I am frankly pessimistic about the possibilities of Fanon's democratic socialism in the underdeveloped world. So long as the primary problem remains industrialization, some degree of political coercion to achieve this end has been required. We might simply put it that the later you industrialize the more rapidly must you do so, and the more rapidly you industrialize the less feasible become democratic solutions. . . . The not-so-simple requirements of creating a disciplined industrial labor force, on land as well as in the plants, involves in any underdeveloped country separating the peasant from his traditional routines (and perhaps "his" land as well) which were geared toward subsistence. It means acclimatizing larger and larger numbers of peasants to the rigors of a working day in the plant. It may even involve the physical dislocation of peasant populations which are re-grouped into an entirely new social organization of their productive labor. So far as I know, no peasantry has yet volunteered to sacrifice its traditional way of life in the interests of rapid industrialization. It would seem that national democracy—that is, predominantly democratic forms for an entire nation-state, rather than village or tribal democracy—is a luxury of the advanced industrial nations. Just as Fanon underestimates the positive political role of pre-nationalist ideology and culture, so does he underestimate their lasting effects on the period of reconstruction.

Fanon's illusion is that somehow the village and kin-group-rooted democracy of the Algerian peasantry can be projected over the entire structure of a 20th century nation-state. His romanticized idealization of the countryside blocks his vision of certain economic and political preconditions to national autonomy. What begins as a love for and empathy with the peasant revolutionary, produces in the end an idealism which is self-defeating. Fanon confounds the long-run social and political ends of revolutionary warfare with the immediate and individual rewards of striking down one's oppressor. It is not the violence of the overthrow of colonial power, but the exercise of a new state power in the native's self interest which gives him his freedom. Fanon so identifies with the voices of the Algerian peasantry that he refuses to recognize the possibility that no matter how truthfully, completely, sympathetically and even eloquently he expresses what they are saying, the message in itself may frequently fall short of a systematic economic and political analysis. This is his shortcoming, and his beauty. Anyone wanting to learn what the people who are fighting today's revolutionary wars in the underdeveloped world

are thinking and feeling ought not to by-pass *The Wretched of the Earth*. (pp. 80-2)

A. Norman Klein, "On Revolutionary Violence," in Studies on the Left *(copyright 1966 by Studies on the Left, Inc.), Vol. 6, No. 3, May-June, 1966, pp. 62-82.*

ROBERT COLES

Fanon took up the mentality of the oppressor in his later books; in this first one ["**Black Skin, White Masks**"] he has on his mind himself and millions of other Negroes. He wants to make his own people more self-conscious, in the best sense of that word, so that perhaps they, rather than he as a psychiatrist, will bring the white man to his senses; that is, make him do something about his guilts and the economic or political facts that continue to justify those guilts.

To achieve his purposes Fanon draws from a number of sources—his own life, his observations in the Antilles and in France, and the writings of social scientists, novelists and poets. However, since he is writing to awaken people, to inform them so that they will act, he makes no effort to be systematic, comprehensive, or even orderly. Quite the contrary, one feels a brilliant, vivid and hurt mind, walking the thin line that separates effective outrage from despair.

Right off, the reader is told not to expect still another psychological analysis of the Negro "mind" or "personality." The meaning of being black is what the author wants to spell out, but the social facts that make for that "meaning" have to be stated again and again. . . . Fanon leaves nothing undone to make his point that the black man, no matter how ingenious, adaptive or even deluded he becomes, cannot escape the history of his people.

As a psychiatrist he summons what every clinician knows about the child's early susceptibility to the fears and anxieties of his parents, and relates that knowledge to Negroes, who are predominantly poor and kept apart—as their children eventually discover and never forget. As a philosopher he calls upon men like Sartre, who have written about "the other" (be he Jew, Hun, Bolshevik or next-door neighbor) and insists that the problem of color is much more complicated than even they say. . . . As a writer he demonstrates what others have before him, how insidiously the problem of race, of color, connects with a whole range of words and images, so that black becomes associated with the dark and the shadowy, with evil, sadness and corruption, while white merges into what is light, hopeful, clean and pure.

Yet it is Fanon the man, rather than the medical specialist or intellectual, who makes this book so hard to put down. His ideas and feelings fairly pour out, and often he makes no effort to tone down his language, to sound like a detached *raisonneur,* that image so many American psychiatrists cultivate. He clearly had every chance to deceive himself, to become a prosperous doctor very much "accepted" by liberal and even doting white friends. Instead he became a fighter and a voice for the oppressed, whom he also had the courage to warn: no religious or mystical attitude, no psychological "defense" will enable the Negro to feel "secure" or "himself" until he is no longer the white man's social and economic prey. . . .

Robert Coles, "Abused and Abusers," in The New York Times Book Review *(© 1967 by The New York*

Times Company; reprinted by permission), April 30, 1967, p. 3.

RONALD SEGAL

Here already [in **Black Skin, White Masks**] are the ideas [Frantz Fanon] subsequently developed to such effect: the psychic ravages of colonialism, on colonisers and colonised alike; the betrayal of colonial revolution by mimics of the metropolitan dominion; violence as an essential instrument of liberation; the 'restructuring of the world' as the sole answer to racism.

In an incisive critique of [Othero] Mannoni's influential *Prospero and Caliban* . . . , he dismisses the argument, so congenial to the metropolitan rich and resourceful, that colonial racism is the product not of the best in European civilisation, but of the artisans, the clerks, the petty traders, the lower ranks of the civil service and army, who are the vulgar of white empire. (p. 656)

Fanon's analysis of the white racist mind is concerned principally with sexual roots. . . . I am sure that there is much truth in [his interpretation]; that the sexual sickness which whites project as the threat of the Negro's supposed superior potency, so that to persecute him is to castrate him, has a place in the development of attitudes to colour, perhaps above all among the Anglo-Saxons.

But this part of the truth Fanon spoils by over-feeding. Racism is also the exultation and excuse of power. . . .

Fanon is at his best in exploring the colonised mind: the exchange by blacks of their human meaning for the counterfeit currency of white myths; the longing to be accepted on the very terms of white superiority that inevitably make such acceptance impossible; the self-hatred, the self-contempt, the self-mutilation. (p. 657)

Ronald Segal, "Caliban Speaks," in New Statesman *(© 1968 The Statesman & Nation Publishing Co. Ltd.), Vol. 75, No. 1940, May 17, 1968, pp. 656-57.*

G. K. GROHS

[If] we try to assess the originality of [Fanon's] thinking, it becomes obvious that he is neither an existentialist, as some have assumed because of his close relations with Sartre, nor a dogmatic Marxist, in spite of his wide reading of the works of Marx, Engels, and Hegel.

His nationalism is ambivalent, because he sees it as a means of liberation, but also hopes that it will transcend its borders so that all people may co-operate in a new humanism. He is not racialist, as shown by his strong reaction to Sartre's dialectical description of *négritude* as a kind of 'anti-racialist racialism'. For Fanon, race was no category; he knew only human beings as an entity transcending all races. In one sense his theory is populist, because for him 'the people' has the ultimate authority, not the government, the party, or the leader. But this people, the nation, could itself be pluralist, and it was not difficult for him to imagine the solidarity of all oppressed men and women, whether white, yellow, or black. . . . There are nations and individuals, oppressors and oppressed, but not an oppressor race and an oppressed race. This division is too simple for Fanon.

The shortcomings of this theory lie in Fanon's proposals for the development of an independent Africa. He opts for a socialist economy against a bureaucratised and centralised dictatorship. He aims at a moderate federal state which does not break up in regionalism. But he does not show how a socialist economy can avoid bureaucracy, how the federation can avoid breaking up into its component units, or how a party which is separated from the administration can avoid being taken over by it. He does not explain how the parasitical bourgeoisie can be changed into a productive bourgeoisie; he only demands its 'liquidation'. But how can a class be abolished without being immediately succeeded by a substitute? He wants to protect minorities, but he does not explain how to destroy the prejudices of the majority against the minority.

Finally, one may question the general applicability of his concept of violence. There is much evidence that violence may be necessary in African countries which are or were dominated by white settler groups. . . . But in other countries—Ghana, Tanzania, Sierra Leone—where such groups were lacking, no violence was necessary to achieve independence and to transform the colonial economy into something approaching a 'socialist economy'. The outcome of much violent action in Europe and the U.S.A. in recent years has shown that violence as a means of revolution has to be viewed far more discriminately. It is time to think afresh about the roots, the efficiency, and the controllability of violence. This means going beyond the ideas of Frantz Fanon, which were derived to a great extent from his experiences in the Algerian war.

But, in spite of these and other shortcomings, his analysis has proved useful. . . . (pp. 554-55)

It is therefore not surprising that the books of Frantz Fanon have had a growing influence on the anti-colonial and anti-imperialist movements of the Third World. . . . (p. 555)

G. K. Grohs, "Frantz Fanon and the African Revolution," translated by G. K. Grohs (originally published as "Frantz Fanon, un Theoretiker der afrikanischen," in Kolner Zeitschrift fur Soziologie und Sozialpsychologie *(Cologne), Vol. XVI, No. 3, 1964), in* The Journal of Modern African Studies, *Vol. 6, No. 4, 1968, pp. 543-56.*

PETER GEISMAR

The Wretched of the Earth stands as a monument to Fanon's anxieties about successful liberation wars; the chapter on "The Pitfalls of National Conscience" might be considered a Communist Manifesto for the Third World outlining the false paths away from the colonial epoch. Fanon's fury is directed against the new bourgeoisies that expect to rule after independence. (pp. 192-93)

Fanon is at his best describing middle-class structure, present and future, within the Third World. As in Marx, though, his theories weaken when they broach specific methods of destroying the structure, doing away with the dictatorship of the middle class. (p. 194)

The Wretched of the Earth, as a plan for action against those who have expropriated the wars of national liberation, as a call for a second Third World revolt—against the cities and the corrupted militaries—has a disturbing lack of unity. In the midst of enumerating the perversions of decolonization, Fanon suddenly starts to describe the potentialities for renewing the revolution—without having given sufficient attention to the means of destroying the counterrevolutionary elements, the new bourgeoisies and their armies. In the whole book there are perhaps twenty pages devoted to the methods of combatting the corrupt but tremendously strong forces in control of the colonial areas today.

The plans for a rejuvenated Third World society depend on the intellectuals allied with the peasantry, a class that he has never examined with the care lavished on the new middle class. Fanon has given us a much more complete understanding of the meaning of true decolonization; his last work is most thorough in its compilation of the dangers threatening the decolonized; but there is not any thoroughgoing discussion of the rural antithesis to the urban degeneration produced by Western rule. One might return to *A Dying Colonialism* to learn of the rising expectations of the agricultural masses during the wars of liberation, but these seem to have evaporated with the evacuation of the colonial troops and declarations of independence. Fanon lacked time to put forth a detailed study of peasant class structure; it is in no way evident, from his writing, how the Third World bourgeoisie will manufacture its own doom. Today this class has a tighter control than it ever had in Fanon's time over the African and South American continents.

Then there is the crucial issue of industrialization: How is it to be carried out in the countryside? Urban concentrations of labor, material, and capital appear today as indispensable to the growth of industry; and without industry, the old colonies will always remain at the mercy of the colonizers.

Certain Marxist scholars go much further in their criticism of Fanon's writing: too many generalizations in this last book, too little precision, theory not expanded to its logical conclusions. . . . But so often these scholars forget to feel the tone of Fanon's writing; forget that he was writing to *make* a revolution, not to dissect one.

Fanon is at his best in setting forth all of the problems of decolonization—in establishing the larger program for a cultural revolution. What is amazing is that a man, propelled by such fury, could see entire political panoramas with total clarity. The older systems of class analyses, according to Fanon, have to be revised; the great criterion must be to distinguish between the exploiters and the exploited. He described the Third World rural populations, and the urban lumpen-proletariat, as the exploited; Fanon's readers have gone much further—emphasizing the unity between the American blacks and the other *damnés de la terre*. Western student activists and intellectuals have, by choice, joined the exploited; and it is by them Fanon's writing is most understood and appreciated. (pp. 195-97)

One might hesitate in attempting to evaluate Fanon's historical importance so soon after his death except that the doctor himself would have enjoyed this presumption. He was enamored of generalizing on the history of the future.

Though a great part of his life was devoted to psychiatry, Fanon will never be a major figure in the history of Western medicine. His reforms were very basic; his technical writings are interesting but not extensive or complete. (p. 198)

Fanon was too rushed to make clear the exact links between the single case examined and the general psychiatric syndrome.

The same criticism does not hold for his survey of the possibilities of creating day-care psychiatric centers that could replace large, elaborate psychiatric institutions—a way of de-

centralizing medicine along with politics. These centers could be run by a minimum of doctors supervising well-trained nurses. Nurses, Fanon showed at Blida, who would be capable of educating each other. With day-care centers, therapy could be restored to its proper social context: the patients would retain contact with families, work, and friends.

This survey was part of Fanon's major effort to improve the medical care for the masses outside of Europe by restructuring medical institutions. He was most interested in training a corps of teachers who could continue to train others to give general care to a large number of patients. The newly independent nations did not have the time or money for medical schools and doctors; numbers of well-educated nurses were immediately necessary.

In the West, quite obviously, Fanon's reputation rests on his political writings—especially *The Wretched of the Earth,* completed in three hectic spring months. The book presents most clearly the notion that we are today submerged in a surplus of wordage that has stifled radical movement. Violence, Fanon showed, has to be part of any genuine radical movement. *The Wretched of the Earth* marks, within the black civil rights movement, the change from passive resistance to active defense; Fanon's writings are of central importance to the Black Panthers, representatives of the changed politics of black America.

The white American middle class, anxious to keep informed on that which threatens them, has taken to reading Fanon too. (pp. 199-200)

But Fanon's theory has to be restored to its proper context. *The Wretched of the Earth* was never intended as a detailed analysis of economic change; it is more clearly an *outil de combat,* part of the war against colonialism. Fanon wanted to redefine the concepts of industrialization and development; the Western ideal of automobile production was not always relevant to agricultural regions; had he lived longer, he could have extended and amended his thoughts on decentralization and rural revolution.

In the spring of 1961 he had one aim: to arouse, to excite, to anger, to activate those who were being exploited. He wanted to warn of the dangers of more subtle kinds of exploitation. *The Wretched of the Earth* was just a beginning; he had become a warrior only in 1956; a socialist perhaps as late as 1960. Detailed theoretical criticism of *The Wretched of the Earth,* though enjoyable, somehow misses the point. Fanon was a brilliantly skilled revolutionary propagandist. This term ''propagandist,'' in the United States, has a sour taste to it—perhaps because Americans have developed propaganda to a degree whereby they do not recognize the extent to which they use it. In the West we are brainwashed against the use of violence in politics which works to re-enforce instituionalized injustices. Fanon popularizes the effectiveness of violence—or even the threat of violence—among the peoples who are the victims of the propaganda of passivity. He is a war correspondent from the midst of the revolution whose passion and confidence can only draw others into the battle. The oppressed are given new life when a voice as strong as his announces (in the Preface to *A Dying Colonialism*):

> This is what we want and this is what we shall achieve. We do not believe that there exists anywhere a force capable of standing in our way.

(pp. 200-01)

Peter Geismar, in his Fanon *(copyright © 1971 by Lois Silverman Geismar; permission granted by The Dial Press), Dial, 1971, 214 p.*

DENNIS FORSYTHE

Frantz Fanon stands as a great symbolic hero among militant blacks, and his ideas find responsive audiences in the Black Writers Congresses, in the ghettoes of the United States, and in most of the universities in the New World. But within academic circles, especially among sociologists, Fanon is still a controversial figure. . . . There are endless attempts to label Fanon; but surely any such attempt should be preceded by a careful consideration of his theories. On the basis of a content analysis of Fanon's books and his collected essays, the attempt here is to show that most of these labels are only partially correct: that is, when taken as a whole, in the context of colonial societies, Fanon is a "Marxist," but a different kind of "Marxist"; he is an advocate of violence, but this was based on certain fundamental assumptions; he is a psychiatrist, but he is also a sociologist and a philosopher.

The contention here is that the earlier works of Fanon, especially **Black Skin, White Masks,** embody the premises on which he embarked upon his revolutionary career. Later in his career, he began to modify these principles in the light of his recognition of Third World conditions.

Fanon began on the initial premise that he was concerned with the emancipation of all of humanity. (p. 160)

[Fanon] sought ways to facilitate "a healthy encounter between black and white." And to the extent that he accepted [one] of Marx's principles, economic determinism, he was able to envisage the conflict in "class" terms rather than "race" terms. (pp. 160-61)

This position led Fanon to adopt another fundamental principle of Marxism, the concept of alienation. "The negro enslaved by his inferiority, the white man enslaved by his superiority alike behave in accordance with a neurotic orientation." Negroes have self-hate; they are constantly trying to run away from their own individuality and to annihilate their presence. (p. 161)

Both Fanon and Marx consider revolution as the natural outcome of the dialectical processes occurring within the capitalist system, which thus contains the seeds of its own destruction. To this extent both are "determinist." (pp. 161-62)

However, Fanon following Marx, was not content merely to watch history unfold itself. Both advocated an instrumental theory of action. . . . Both Marx and Fanon tackled the philosophical issue of determinism vs indeterminism (free will). They both saw the two positions as operative; but Fanon, like Lenin, preferred the "free will" position: "There is not an objective optimism that is more or less mechanically inevitable but that optimism must be the sentiment that accompanies the revolutionary committment and the combat." . . .

In all the above respects, then, it is not difficult to see the impact of Marxism on the thought of Fanon. Yet it is misleading to describe him . . . as a "Marxist." (p. 162)

One important problem which theorists of conflict fail to deal with systematically is the relationship between class conflicts and racial conflicts, one of the most challenging areas in the field of conflict research. More than Marx's, Fanon's works reveal a constant awareness of the problem. . . .

At first Fanon's treatment of the problem of racial and class conflicts was essentially Marxian; and to the extent that he accepted the notion of "economic determinism" he subsumed racial conflicts under class conflicts. Racial conflicts and class conflicts were one and the same thing. (p. 163)

But on many occasions Fanon recognized the confounding fact that although there are many other oppressed groups, they do not suffer from the racism which is forced upon blacks, and that the poor whites are some of the most racist. . . . Later he took issue with the notion that there is a community of interests between the colonized people and the working class of the colonialist country. (pp. 163-64)

Fanon found it very difficult to resolve this dilemma—a dilemma which is so difficult as to be neglected, or to be settled by the oversimple subsumability of one under the other ("class" to "racial" loyalties or vice versa). Fanon seems to have resolved the dilemma by regarding the blacks as the "proletarian" core. (p. 164)

[There are] other fundamental respects in which Fanon departs from the Marxian view of historical development.

To begin with, whereas Marx stressed the rise of private property as the original sin in world history, Fanon stressed slavery and colonialism. It is not the rise of private property per se, but the dehumanization of blacks, the reduction of black men to the level of private property, to chattel. Colonialism has brought the black and white peoples into a relationship of uneven reciprocity. The juxtaposition of the white and black races has created a "massive psychoexistential complex." Fanon's great emphasis on the psychologically alienated traits of the colonial personality finds small counterpart in the alienated class man of Marx. Fanon's solution to the problem is largely a result of the legacies of colonialism on the "personality" of blacks and whites.

Whereas Marx's center of focus was Europe, that of Fanon is the Third World. The Third World provides the stage on which will be resolved "the problems to which Europe has not been able to find the answers." This "Colossal mass," the Third World, differs from Europe, he says, because the two-class analysis of Marx proves "totally inadequate." . . . The Third World differs also because the Marxian developmental sequence is not applicable. Here Fanon makes a major onslaught on the Marxian dialectic when applied to the Third World:

> In underdeveloped countries, then, there exists no true bourgeois, capable of creating the conditions necessary for the development of a large-scale proletariat, to mechanise agriculture and finally to make possible the existence of an authentic national culture. This means that since national capitalist development cannot occur, the colonial-Capitalist pattern of appropriate revolutionary strategies must be very different from those pursued in developed countries.

Fanon was to repeat over and over again that "the Bourgeois phase in the history of the underdeveloped countries is a completely useless phase." Furthermore, he not only idealizes the Third World, but lays greater stress on those areas in the Third World that are currently engaged in revolutionary action. (pp. 165-66)

Marx saw the proletarian class as the force to deliver the death sentence on a capitalist system. Fanon, on the other hand, favored the "Wretched of the Earth," and specifically, the dispossessed rural peasants. He stresses the revolutionary nature of the peasantry and the lumpen-proletariat, and the reactionary nature of the working classes in the Third World. . . . (p. 166)

The most important point at which Fanon departs from Marx is in his violence theory of revolution. While Marx admits the possibility of a nonviolent revolution in the cases of Britain and the United States, Fanon does not allow this possibility. . . . (p. 167)

This categorical imperative, the absolute necessity of violence, stems from certain assumptions made by Fanon about the nature of colonialism and the nature of freedom.

First, Fanon held the philosophical notion that "It is solely by risking life that freedom is obtained. Thus, reality-in-itself for-itself can be achieved only through conflict and through the risk that conflict implies." But this philosophical argument forms only a small external prop to Fanon's socio-psychological sub-structure of violence. First, he points to a perpetual tendency towards violence in colonized men. . . . Settlers keep alive in the natives an anger which they deprive of outlet. . . . Second, violence is the means to decolonize the mind, according to Fanon. "At the level of individuals, violence is a cleansing force. It frees the native from his inferiority complex and from his despair and inaction, it makes him fearless and restores his self-respect . . . those who were once unbudgeable, the constitutional cowards, the timid, the eternally inferiorised, stiffen and emerge bristling." (pp. 167-68)

Third, Fanon points to the sociological function of violence in unifying and mobilizing the people. . . .

Fanon's account of violence was given justification at yet a higher level, namely, the level of the nation. The nation is born out of the struggle, he says. This position led him to advance a theory of nationalism and internationalism which seems much more in accordance with history than that of Marx. (p. 168)

While Marx sees "Bourgeois nationalism" as a mere temporary stepping stone to, and thus antithetical to, real internationalism. Fanon posits the view that internationalism can only be based upon the solid foundation of national states, each conscious of its distinctiveness. . . .

While the Marxian dialectic could be trusted to move the urban proletariat towards an unavoidable confrontation with, and overthrow of, the capitalist system, Fanon was well aware of the self-perpetuating nature of colonial power in Africa. Thus he saw guerrilla strategies, as opposed to the bourgeois politics of political parties and trade unionism, as the only means of initiating and sustaining the violence which he regards as necessary. Like most of the new breed of revolutionaries in the Third World, he had great confidence in guerrilla warfare as the effective way to unnerve the colonialist armies psychologically. He can be recognized as one of the first advocates of what could be called the psychology of guerrilla movements. . . .

The contrast between Marx and Fanon includes their differing accounts of the post-revolutionary situation. While Marx has been criticized both for his neglect and for his idealistic and utopian vision of the "future society," Fanon was much more concrete in his account of the post-revolutionary situation, due largely to his stress on the "personality." . . . He also recognizes the unending process of struggle towards "liberation." . . . (p. 169)

In the post-revolutionary situation, Fanon does not stress complete communal ownership. Instead, he points to the all-important place of the "intermediary sector" of the economy, and argues that "if you want to progress, you must decide in the first few hours to nationalise this sector." But he warns that "this nationalism ought not to take on a rigidly state-controlled type." Fanon does not subscribe to the notion of "dictatorship of the proletariat." Though he advocates a vanguardist theory of revolution, his theory is less "elitist" than, say, that of Lenin. He saw the danger of a "bourgeois caste" developing where the "incoherent mass of people is seen as a blind force that must be continually held in check either by mystification or by the fear inspired by the police force. . . ." . . .

[The] Third World finds itself and speaks to itself through the voice of Fanon, just as Marx spoke for the impoverished urban masses in the European context. Fanon's presence was not only felt during the Algerian Revolution but his messianic and prophetic image today energizes contemporary liberation movements from French Canadian nationalism, Women's Liberation movements, to the Civil Rights movements stretching from Harlem to Africa. It might be a paradox, but a pleasing one, that although his work was concerned essentially with the liberation of the "colonised" people, his obvious "humanism" is there for all the "dispossessed" earnestly engaged in a fight against a historically oppressive system. And if it has been a paradox that blacks have turned to Marxism as if it were "theirs," whites, paradoxccally, have turned to Fanon as if Fanonism is also their refuge. (p. 170)

Dennis Forsythe, "Frantz Fanon—The Marx of the Third World" (originally a paper in a different form, "Frantz Fanon and his Relevance to the West Indies," delivered to the McGill West Indian Society on December 3, 1969) in PHYLON: The Atlanta University Review of Race and Culture, *34 (copyright, 1973, by Atlanta University; reprinted by permission of* PHYLON), *Vol. XXXIV, No. 2, Second Quarter (June, 1973), pp. 160-70.*

EMMANUEL HANSEN

For Fanon as for Marx, man is not totally determined by circumstances. Man still has the capacity and the will to go beyond the historical condition and initiate the cycle of his freedom. It is this profound belief in man and an optimistic view of history that marks Fanon's writings. It is on account of this belief that he urges the colonized to rise above their historical condition. From this it is difficult to agree with those who see in Fanon a pessimist. . . .

[For] Fanon man is freedom. But as he looks around himself, he finds that man, and particularly the black man, is not free. The question then is: Why are men, and in particular the black man, not free? This leads him to an examination of the phenomenon of alienation. . . . (p. 68)

Alienation is one of the most important themes in Fanon's thought, and he devotes a lot of space to discussing it. In fact, the whole of *Black Skin, White Masks* is a study in alienation.

His treatment of the subject, however, raises a number of questions. . . . (p. 108)

Fanon does not define the term *alienation*. He sometimes uses different words or phrases to identify the same phenomenon. He also uses *alienation* and *neurosis* interchangably. In spite of this, it is clear that when he uses the term *alienation,* or writes of the phenomenon, he has in mind some kind of separation of the person from his individuality, or from his existential condition, or from his culture or community, or from his essential self.

Fanon also assumes that alienation implies separation where unity once prevailed, and he tends to think that this unity prevailed in the pre-colonial society. . . . [However, his] image of the pre-colonial society is too general and does not bear any relation to reality. Besides, from what we know of the relations between individuals or groups in societies like Rwanda, it is extremely unlikely that alienation did not exist.

Fanon talks of violence as playing a very important part in colonial alienation. He does not define the term, and he uses it in a sense that embodies the connotations we associate with force, power, coercion, and the like. Such loose usage of such a critical term weakens its analytic utility. Another important weakness in Fanon's discussion on violence and alienation is that he does not say in what precise manner violence causes the alienation of the native. We know, for instance, that in the colonized society the violence of the colonizer was not the only form of violence, and that the colonized was also violent. How can we be sure that a particular alienation expressed by a particular person is not the result of the natives' own violence, different from the violence of the colonial regime? The only way Fanon can maintain his position is to assume that there was no violence in African society prior to the institution of colonial rule. Alternatively, he could argue that the violence of the colonial regime superseded all other forms of violence of the native. And this is the position Fanon takes. But the question is: What is it about colonial violence that makes it supersede all the other forms of violence of the native? Is it the intensity or the scale? He overcomes the problem by defining colonial rule as violence. This . . . makes sense only when we take colonial violence in its totality—structural, psychological, social, and physical. Fanon, however, in one instance of differentiating between the method of rule employed in the metropolis and that employed in the colonies insists on physical violence as the defining characteristic of colonial rule. And this . . . not only is inadequate but is also contradicted by the evidence of his **Black Skin, White Masks**. Furthermore, Fanon's attempt to explain the effect of colonial violence on the native by recourse to the Freudian concept of compensation is inadequate. African dances cannot be explained simply in terms of overcoming violence through the release of muscular tension.

Fanon's discussion on alienation is always couched in the negative, that is, it is what it ought not to be. He does not give us any picture of the non-alienated man against which we can measure the question of alienation. What is the free, autonomous, non-alienated individual? How do we know when we have achieved this status?

Fanon sometimes gives the impression that the colonized man is completely determined. If that is the situation, then de-alienation becomes an impossibility. If one is completely alienated, how can one achieve the consciousness of resistance and de-alienation? Sometimes Fanon makes it clear that alienation

is not complete: "He is treated as an inferior but he is not convinced of his inferiority." The second usage is consistent with Fanon's argument, for it is only in such a situation that the question of overcoming of alienation will be possible.

Despite the lack of conceptual clarity of the term *alienation* and the numerous problems connected with Fanon's discourse on the phenomenon, alienation is a useful concept in a discussion of the relations between the black man and the white man. It explains the totality of the black man's existence in a white-dominated world. In view of this, some of the manifestations we associate with alienation in colonial society are also noticeable among black people in the United States, though their condition may not be exactly similar to colonial relationships. The crux of the matter is that they live in a white-dominated society. Fanon's interest in alienation does not end with an analysis of the phenomenon. He is also concerned with ways of overcoming alienation. This brings us to his discussion on revolutionary violence. . . . (pp. 108-10)

Fanon's discourse on the emancipatory role of violence poses a number of problems. First, he is not as unequivocal about violence for the liberation of consciousness as he appears. . . . [It] seems that [Fanon holds] it is possible to achieve liberation of consciousness through political education or by mental contemplation. That violence is not the only way to achieve liberation of consciousness is evidenced from the experiences of Marx, Lenin, and a host of other revolutionaries. We know that Fanon himself did not play any combat role in the Algerian revolution. How did he acquire his revolutionary consciousness? Or is one to argue that it is not so much the use of violence that is critical in the emancipation of consciousness as the readiness to use violence?

Another problem with the emancipatory role of violence is that violence does not always lead to the freeing of the individual from his fears and inferiority complexes. On the contrary, it sometimes leads to neurosis and distortion of personality, as Fanon himself recognizes. (pp. 125-26)

[We] cannot avoid the conclusion that violence, even revolutionary violence, both emancipates and alienates. If that is the case, the critical question then becomes, On what conditions does revolutionary violence emancipate and on what conditions does it alienate? Are there any personalities whom it alienates? If so, on what personalities does violence act as a liberating force and on what does it act as an alienating force? The answers to these questions would provide the key to the understanding of the complex issues connected with Fanon's discussion on the emancipatory role of violence. It could be argued, of course, that the whole notion of emancipatory violence in Fanon is a myth. Although no serious critic would deny the presence of certain mythmaking in Fanon, it would be wrong to dismiss the entire argument as a myth. Besides, if the main purpose of this is to create a myth, it is difficult to understand the inclusion of material that casts so much doubt on his own myth. Is Fanon trying to warn us that however justified revolutionary violence might be, one cannot avoid the consequences of certain actions? (p. 127)

After discounting the national bourgeoisie and the urban working class, Fanon settles on the peasantry as the most revolutionary class. Why does he regard the peasantry of the underdeveloped countries as the most revolutionary? He thinks it has certain particular attributes that predispose it to revolutionary action. The peasantry, in its stern determination to maintain the social structure of the precolonial society, remains the most "disciplined element" of the population. Fanon concedes that the stubborn determination of the peasantry to maintain the social structure may sometimes give rise "to movements which are based on religious fanaticism or tribal wars." However, it is in this determination and spontaneity that its strength lies. (pp. 145-46)

The question to consider now is whether the peasant has the attributes that Fanon assigns to him and, if so, whether such attributes necessarily predispose to revolutionary action. When Fanon attributes discipline to the peasant, what does he mean? By discipline, is he referring to the propensity of the peasant to follow his leaders and chiefs; and if so, how does this constitute a revolutionary potentiality? The chiefs and leaders of the peasants are perhaps some of the most conservative elements in African society, and we would not think that a propensity to follow them necessarily implies revolutionary action. If, on the other hand, by the most disciplined element Fanon means the most strong-willed or the most fanatical, then this is a source of strength. To be a successful revolutionary, it is necessary to be fanatical as far as goals are concerned, and flexible as far as tactics are concerned. He also claims that the peasants of the underdeveloped countries, unlike the urban working class, are not individualistic and have great social solidarity. (p. 149)

Fanon also claims that the peasantry lives in close contact with his society and keeps his moral values intact. He is not alienated from his culture. He is, in a word, integrated. All the evidence we have from the sociological literature indicates that the one who is integrated is less likely to revolt or indulge in revolutionary activity than the one who is alienated and who lives on the fringes of the culture. Innovations are nearly always caused by marginal men. The integrated always have reasons to explain their adverse conditions: it is the will of the gods, or some other fatalistic reason; but the alienated is more likely to blame either himself or the one he thinks responsible for his condition, and to do something about it.

Fanon also credits the peasants with kindness, generosity, and devotion to the nation. It would be difficult to persuade anyone that kindness and generosity are either one revolutionary qualities or that such qualities predispose to revolutionary activities. It is possible that people who have shared dangers together will develop strong comradeship for each other, but this is the result of their intense involvement with each other. It is the result, not the cause, of revolutionary activity. Would the peasant extend the same kindness that he shows toward members of his ethnic and kin groups to other groups with which he would have to be in contact? The same question can be asked about the peasant's devotion to the nation. The peasant is devoted, but not to the nation. His mental horizon does not go beyond the limits of his immediate social group. The peasant is also thought to be endowed with feelings of self-confidence and moral superiority vis-à-vis the colonizer. Whereas a sense of self-confidence could be an asset for revolutionary action, it is conceivable that a feeling of moral superiority on the part of the peasant would be more likely to generate a feeling of contemptuous disregard of the colonizer than a determination to fight him.

The peasant is supposed to have a propensity for violence, and Fanon thinks this is an asset for revolutionary activity. He describes the peasants as "rebels by instinct," and those "who never cease to think of the problem of their liberation except in terms of violence." It is difficult to conceive of "rebels by instinct" as being at the same time the "most disciplined."

One may concede that the peasant has a propensity to respond with violence when his interests are threatened. The peasant base of the Mau Mau, and the recourse to arms by the cocoa farmers of Ghana to protect their cocoa trees from being cut down are cases in point. However, to show a propensity for violence to protect one's own interests is one thing, and to engage in revolutionary violence is another. (pp. 150-52)

At one point [Fanon] describes the peasants as "spontaneously revolutionary" and the "only revolutionary class," but his own model of revolutionary warfare shows clearly that it is the revolutionary intellectuals from the urban centers who desert the city and take off to the rural areas and the mountains who do the initial work of raising the revolutionary consciousness of the peasantry. All that Fanon is entitled to claim by the logic of his own argument is that the peasants constitute a potentially revolutionary class. (pp. 152-53)

The empirical evidence, then, does not seem to support Fanon when he writes, as he sometimes does, that mere participation in armed struggle is enough to revolutionize the peasant. A careful reading of the text, however, reveals that Fanon is much more careful than he is sometimes given credit for being. Participation in armed struggle has the immediate effect of releasing the peasant from his feeling of inferiority with respect to his oppressor. But for such a process of regeneration and revolutionizing to take place on a permanent basis, it must be accompanied at all times by political education. (pp. 153-54)

In sum, we can say that the attributes that Fanon gives to the peasant do not necessarily predispose him to revolutionary action. This is not to deny that the peasant could play an important role in a revolutionary movement. We know, for instance, what critical roles the peasants have played and are still playing in the revolutionary movements in China, Vietnam, Cuba, and Mozambique. The crucial question then becomes, Under what conditions do the peasants participate in revolutionary action? Also, what strata of the peasant population are most prone to revolutionary action? Fanon's inability to stratify the peasantry beyond the broad distinctions of rich and poor peasant, to assess the revolutionary potential of each stratum, and to delineate clearly the conditions under which each stratum could become predisposed to revolutionary warfare are major weaknesses in his argument. (p. 157)

Fanon's notion of the lumpen-proletariat being reformed through revolutionary violence raises a number of problems. The lumpen-proletariat, as we know already, has a strong predisposition to violence, and it does indulge in acts of violence. If it is the act of violence that purifies it, why is it not purified by the daily acts of violence that it commits? Fanon could argue that there is a difference between its daily acts of violence and revolutionary violence, which is directed against a system that oppresses it. But as we have already seen, it is possible for even revolutionary violence to produce alienation. Furthermore, Fanon states that the lumpen-proletariat could fight on either side. If that is the case, why should it fight on the side of the revolutionaries? Is it because fighting affords it the chance to express its violence, or because it becomes committed to the cause of the revolutionaries? If it fights on account of the former reason, then it is difficult to see how such participation in violence could liberate its consciousness. If, on the other hand, it fights on account of the latter reason, then it means its conversion precedes its participation in revolutionary violence. We do not deny that the lumpen-proletariat could participate in revolutionary violence, but that such participation would revolutionize it is rather difficult to conceive. (p. 166)

Fanon's argument about the lumpen-proletariat is that it has certain qualities and lives in a certain social condition that predisposes it to the use of violence. This violence could be controlled and channeled to revolutionary activities. And to the extent that Fanon considers violence a necessary part of revolution, he sees the lumpen-proletariat as potential revolutionaries. He therefore urges an alliance between it and the peasantry. The claims of critics that the lumpen-proletariat has not played any initiating or major role, or that it has often supported conservative politicians, do not invalidate Fanon's argument. A much more serious criticism that can be made of Fanon, especially in his role as a revolutionary intellectual, is his failure to stratify the urban unemployed and to assess the revolutionary potential of each stratum, indicating the conditions in which each could be drawn into the revolutionary process. And it is this sensitivity to the subtlety and complexity of the urban unemployed that gives added significance to the writings of Amilcar Cabral. One can say that Cabral carried Fanon's analysis one step further. (p. 167)

Fanon does not define his social classes, and his characterization of them is far from satisfactory. His analysis assumes a sharp class division of African society. It is not that class analysis is wrong, but it has to be refined to provide explanatory insight into the nature of African politics. In Africa, ethnicity, kinship, and patron-client relations mediate, but do not necessarily vitiate, class conflict; and any inquiry into the structure of African politics using class as an analytical category should take this into consideration. Fanon is ambivalent in his treatment of the national bourgeoisie, and his characterization of the peasantry is wanting in certain respects. His arguments for the rejection of the proletariat as a revolutionary force are based on a simplistic view of the proletariat as an undifferentiated mass; and it is the same simplistic view that leads him to characterize the entire lumpen-proletariat as revolutionary.

As much as we may find particular aspects of his thinking faulty, his argument taken in its totality has a great deal of force; and when the necessary qualifications are made to some of his statements, the core of his argument will not be found to be lacking in profundity or originality. His genius lies in his ability to discern the revolutionary potential of certain social classes previously neglected and to make a passionate agrument for a complete rethinking of the strategy for revolutionary decolonization. (pp. 167-68)

Notwithstanding the imprecise nature of Fanon's writing, he is clear about the type of society he has in mind: it is a non-repressive, non-authoritarian society; a society where men treat each other as ends and not as means to other ends; a society where men have meaningful relations with each other; in short, a society where there is no alienation. Fanon sees a socialist society as providing for this kind of ideal. For him such a society is not only possible but necessary for the underdeveloped countries if they are to avoid the mistakes of the Western industrialized countries and attain "authentic" human existence. In Fanon's view the authoritarianism and the bureaucratic socialism of the Eastern European countries are to be deprecated as much as the capitalist class oppression of Western European countries. The true end of society is the liberation of man and the expression of his "authentic" existence, and socialism provides the social and political arrangements by which this can be attained.

What then is Fanon's socialist society? Fanon does not provide any detailed description of the socialist society he has in mind. He only presents fragments here and there. (pp. 178-79)

Fanon is vague in his delineation of the features of his ideal polity. In delineating the economic features, he mentions, as a first step, the nationalization of the intermediary sectors of the economy and the organization of cooperatives. We are not given details of the subsequent steps to be taken to get the processes of production, distribution, and exchange nationalized, as his revolutionary socialism implies. His political and administrative decentralization poses problems of decision-making and coordination, and his idea of the complete identification of the individual with the society could take away from the person the individuality he so ardently desires for man. He does not say anything about representative institutions, and it is difficult to imagine how one can construct a modern society on the basis of direct democracy. He says nothing about force, coercion, or the settlement of disputes. Presumably, he does not expect any conflicts in a society of this sort, yet he has a place for the army, which must be meant then for an external enemy. We may raise many more questions about Fanon, but let us remember that he wrote with the impatience of a revolutionary fighting against an oppressive social order. In spite of the fragmentary nature of his writing, his arguments demonstrate the use of creative imagination to tackle the central problem of human existence: how to overcome the duality of man and his environment. The Christian and Hindu philosophers saw the answer in man's complete surrender to God. Fanon, like Plato, Rousseau, Hegel, and Marx before him, saw the answer in man's complete absorption in community, or, as Hegel would say, in the social substance. (p. 198)

Taking all [the] dimensions of Fanon's thought into consideration, we see that his ideas form a coherent body of thought on freedom and how it can be attained by the oppressed of the underdeveloped countries. Admittedly, other writers have dealt with some of the specific problems of oppressed people in the Third World; but what is significant about Fanon is that he not only deals with the totality of the problems within a framework that is analytically meaningful, and that commands intellectual attention, but he also raises his recommendations to the level of a general theory of social action.

To say this is, of course, not to deny that there are weaknesses in Fanon's analyses. Not even the most sympathetic critic would fail to notice the inconsistencies, contradictions, questionable premises, conclusions that do not follow from the evidence provided, and many more. These have been discussed at length in the preceding pages, and there is no need to restate them here. The important question is to consider the policy implications of Fanon's ideas. What do we learn from Fanon, and where do we go from here?

Just as Fanon argues that it is foolish for the national bourgeoisie of the underdeveloped countries to apply mechanically what they have learned in European universities to the underdeveloped countries, in the same way it would be foolish of us to try to apply Fanon's ideas without any modification.

The generality of his pronouncements calls for modifications before they are applied to specific situations. Thus, it would be wrong to seek to apply Fanon's theory of revolutionary war to the African condition, or for that matter to any condition, without any modification to suit the specific local conditions. (pp. 205-06)

It is important to remember that revolutionary theory and action should be rooted in the specific socioeconomic realities of each country.

Thus there is a lot we can learn from Fanon, but only if we make use of his ideas imaginatively and flexibly, making necessary modifications here and there to suit particular situations, in the same way that Mao made use of Marx and Lenin. It is only in this way that we shall derive much benefit from Fanon's work, and not by assigning to it the status of infallible scripture to be applied mechanically to all situations. (p. 208)

> *Emmanuel Hansen, in his* Frantz Fanon: Social and Political Thought *(copyright © 1977 by Emmanuel Hansen; used by permission of the author and the publisher; all rights reserved), Ohio State University Press, 1977, 232 p.*

BERNARD R. BOXILL

Among writers of the third world no one has as eloquently and decisively stated, and indeed at times overstated, the close connection between a people's struggle and their culture, as Frantz Fanon. He expressed his conception of culture as follows: a culture is "the whole body of efforts made by a people in the sphere of thought to describe, justify, and praise the action through which that people has created itself and keeps itself in existence."

The fundamental point of this conception of culture is that, as Fanon expresses it elsewhere, "the native poet" must "see clearly the people he has chosen as the subject of his work of art" and that, "the native intellectual who wishes to create an authentic work of art must realize that the truths of a nation are in the first place its realities. He must go on until he has found the seething pot out of which the learning of the future will emerge." Thus, a work of art is authentic when it manifests a wide, full and deep understanding and appreciation of a people's struggles and way of life, and attempts either to criticize or justify them. Only works of art which are authentic in this sense can be considered part of the culture of a people.

I think that this aspect of Fanon's analysis can hardly be challenged. The point for us is that it emphasizes the sense in which human ideals arise from the people's struggle. Unfortunately in emphasizing this point, Fanon says some misleading things. . . . I think Fanon's main point is that the artist must know intimately the struggle he intends to interpret; but to insist that the artist must "collaborate on the physical plane" implies that he can only know the struggle by being actively part of it, and this, I believe, is highly controversial even if it should turn out, in the final analysis, to be true.

To insist that the artist must "take part in action" still concedes the distinction between the artist's work *qua* interpreter and critic, and his collaboration on the physical plane. Unhappily, some of Fanon's remarks go so far as to suggest either a conflation of these two activities, or the relegation of the artist's work to a merely derivative, dependent status. . . . I think that this is true in some sense. In another sense, however, it is too uncritical. Not every habit that the people may be inclined to adopt is necessarily good and progressive, and it is not clear that unaided, they always discover their mistakes. If reflection has anything to do with life, habits and maxims that the majority would uncritically adopt must be subjected to critical analysis. (pp. 330-31)

Fanon also attacked cultural Pan-Africanism and hinted that it was based on a "racialisation of thought." Thus, . . . in rejecting the idea of a universal black culture, he too quickly concluded that its fundamental assumption is the idea of the racial basis of culture. Thus he explains the black intellectual's espousal of a universal black culture as the quite predictable response to white racism: as he puts it, since "Colonialism's condemnation is continental in scope", the black intellectual's efforts to rehabilitate himself are "logically inscribed from the same point of view" and are correspondingly continental in scope. But further, and lamentably, "The facts of negritude will not stop at the limits of the continent. The 'black world' will see the light . . ."

But having perhaps accurately divined the *cause* of the espousal of a universal black culture, Fanon seems to assume that its defense can only be maintained by what he stigmatizes as a "racialization of thought" and he writes of the "degradation" of the African Cultural society which will become clear as it elaborates the "concept of negritude." The assumption behind the belief that the espousal of a universal black culture involves a "racialization" of culture is that if the one thing which characterizes *all* black people is their common blood, then, if it is insisted that all black people have a common culture, it can only be because of the assumption that a common blood produces a common culture. (p. 331)

[Though Fanon] is influenced by Marx, he refuses to see the racial struggle in purely Marxist terms; accordingly, he rejects a cultural or even a purely economic analysis of the problem; "what parcels out the world is, to begin with the fact of belonging to or not belonging to a given race, a given *species*" he writes; and "the economic substructure is also a superstructure . . . you are rich because you are white, you are white because you are rich."

Seeing and perhaps overestimating the irrational element in race prejudice, Fanon is led correspondingly to overstress the non-rational nature of its dissolution and to recommend violence and destruction. The intellectual is relegated to playing the role of revolutionary tactician. (p. 335)

> *Bernard R. Boxill, "Dubois and Fanon on Culture,"* in The Philosophical Forum *(copyright © 1977 by The Philosophical Forum, Inc.), Vol. IX, Nos. 2 & 3, Winter-Spring, 1977-78, pp. 326-38.*

CHESTER J. FONTENOT, JR.

Fanon states quite matter-of-factly that he is not writing as an analytic social thinker, but as a creative artist. In *Black Skin, White Masks,* Fanon tells us that we should not read his book as a work of clinical psychology, but as an analysis of the psychological problems created by colonization. Though Fanon . . . states that "this book is a clinical study," he adds that "it is good form to introduce a work in psychology with a statement of its methodological point of view. I shall be derelict. I leave methods to the botanists and the mathematicians. There is a point at which methods devour themselves."

Fanon's rejection of methodologies is, in a sense, symbolic of his conscious movement from the tendency toward identification with and assimilation into European culture to the urge to assert uniqueness as one of African descent. Fanon constructs a system which, he feels, has the power to move the reader through the stages outlined above and finally into a mode which will allow the reader to participate in the insurrectionary activity he outlines in *The Wretched of the Earth*. In this sense, I want to offer that Fanon is a social visionary; that is, Fanon is not concerned with using his experiences as material for his vision which he attempts to work out in his two major books,

Black Skin, White Masks and *The Wretched of the Earth*. This implies, of course, that Fanon's vision is at least partially, but inchoately formed; the act of writing is an attempt to give shape and coherence to this vision so that it will become concrete and communicable to others. Fanon attempts to develop a vision through a critique of the past. In this case, Fanon is still working toward an ideal—not necessarily a utopia, but rather a previous notion which is incomplete and partially blurred; but, the process of writing is, in fact, the forming of his vision. . . . This blurred vision is not the product of an oversight or of a lack of methodological rigidity on the writer's part, in this case, on Fanon's part; it is intentional. (pp. 94-6)

Fanon's insistence on the present, in fact, on a constant presence which is, in a sense, antihistorical, gives his writings an aesthetic quality. Fanon sees his writings as creative insofar as he engages the reader in the dialectical process of demystifying the colonial operation, of plotting out the path the "natives" should take to expel the colonialists from their land, and of articulating the dangers and pitfalls inherent in the new society which threaten to keep the society attached to the mother country, and thus in a state of constant flux. (p. 96)

Just as Fanon's life is quizzical in that the paradoxes he faced were irresolvable, his writings are charged with the same kinds of paradoxes. These paradoxes allow Fanon's system to remain open, and they reject categorization into truth or falsehood. Any discursive statement one abstracts from the total structure is partial and incomplete.

These paradoxes are the devices of the artists, the mythmakers. They are the means by which the creative artist advances his argument. In fact, they are the only way the artist can insure that his structure has permanence, thereby frustrating those who wish to reduce his creation to a single statement. . . .

Fanon's structure must first be judged apart from his personality and the sociocultural milieu which he confronted. It must be seen as an autonomous creation, an icon, which gives off an inexhaustible number of discursive statements to those who come to it for answers. Fanon's system will not provide a clear path to the liberated society of the Third World, but it will provide us with the type of analysis needed to demystify the colonial experience. (p. 113)

Chester J. Fontenot, Jr., "Fanon and the Devourers," in Journal of Black Studies *(copyright © 1978 by Sage Publications, Inc.; reprinted with permission of Sage Publications, Inc.), Vol. 9, No. 1, September, 1978, pp. 93-114 (and reprinted as a different version in his* Frantz Fanon: Language As the God Gone Astray in the Flesh, *University of Nebraska Studies, 1979).*

GERALD E. TUCKER

The political thought of Machiavelli enjoys ubiquitous fame. Its pristine vigour is attested to by the fact that, through the past four and a half centuries, dictators and democrats have embraced its values. Yet there is no patent contradiction in this if one realises that Machiavelli deals compellingly with what *is* while not rejecting what ultimately *ought* to be; his prince is a sort of political Everyman concerned with realising the kingdom of earth.

Machiavelli, then, speaks to all practitioners of politics; his prince is not a political Hamlet, but a man of action whose stimulus lies within his existential condition. While cognisant of his historical predecessors, such a man is not enslaved by the dead hand of the past; he is spurred on by the conviction that his history and future aspirations can only have meaning in the present *potentiality* of action.

It is within this framework that Fanon's revolutionary métier may be said to find a parallel. He perceived the history of past colonial exploitation and the future aspirations of the oppressed peoples conjoined in the action of the present. To this end, the exigencies of the present defy all conventional attitudes that assume the posture of reason. These conventions, in the form of political parties, constitutions, social hierarchies, economic institutions, and religions, have usurped reason; the *ultima ratio,* for Fanon, is action, a course that can only be pursued through force and violence. (pp. 397-98)

[In] the corpus of Fanon's works there is an expressed yearning for freedom from tyranny and exploitation, and a desire for peace and community. Yet he . . . is attuned to the reality which has to be transformed. Fanon argues the futility of pleading to the better nature of the colonial overlords, in whose consciousness the reality of the situation meant the accustomed appurtenances of parliamentary government catering to the needs and comfort of a privileged few. In effect, fundamental interest could not be expected to transform itself if it meant its own destruction. . . .

In order to combat this state of affairs, Machiavelli and Fanon enquired into the nature and consequences of power. The answers, for both, necessitated an understanding of past and present configurations of power, its attainment and eventual decline. (p. 398)

Fanon, writing in the twentieth century with its greater fund of psychological insights and knowledge, advanced a more elaborate existential argument in which action in itself transforms the consciousness of the oppressed peoples of the Third World. Furthermore, the action demanded by Fanon would emanate from the masses, especially the peasants, upon whom devolved the duty of reclaiming their freedom from the European conquerors. . . .

It is contended, therefore, that the parallel between the writings of Machiavelli and Fanon is not purely arbitrary. There exists the existential *motif* which runs through the political thought of European renaissance and the emerging Third World: first, in the historical condition which informed such political writings; secondly, in the political methods prescribed; and, finally, in their implicit ethical bases. (p. 399)

Fanon throws out the challenge of a new hemisphere of politics, a new man. . . . [It] is in the realm of action that Machiavelli's prince, the symbol of the 'liberator', and Fanon's native, the energised 'wretched', must define himself and so create the new man. For Fanon, 'It is a question of the Third World starting a new history of Man'. (p. 404)

[Fanon's] 'new man' is unable to issue forth from the womb of a colonial situation without violent pangs. The truly decolonised native knows no peaceful birth. For Fanon this is so because of the psychic violation wreaked by the colonial masters.

Fanon's ethical notions are inextricably linked with the doctrine of violence; at the same time he seeks to impose the morality of his ends upon the action of his means. More telling than Machiavelli, Fanon's means are invested with the aura, the compelling human necessity, of man reclaiming himself. (p. 405)

Fanon copiously draws from a wide range of sources in order to depict the non-human condition of the black man: medicine, psychiatry, art, literature, sexuality. The inferior position of the black man has become historical reality, asserts Fanon. (p. 406)

On the moral plane Fanon's task was to bring about the transformation of the black man, the colonised. Fanon's wretched had first to see himself as a man before he could physically liberate himself. To Sartre's famous dictum that the 'Jew is one whom other men consider a Jew', Fanon extended the concept to show that the black man is a creation of the white man. Further, his etiolated condition was the product of the colonial world and its stock of self-justification: history, religion, law, morality, science, technology, aesthetics—the list is inexhaustible.

Flowing from the use of the Hegelian concept that man knows himself through contact with others, Fanon depicts the colonised natives as having been deprived of this necessary condition so vital to the development of individual and social morality. Colonised peoples have been dependent on the socially alien moralities of the historically powerful groups; every facet of their relations has reinforced this cultural dependency, and the first and final cause has been *force majeure*.

Fanon argued that from the standpoint of a revolutionary ethic of the twentieth century, any morality which permitted, supported, and perpetuated the colonial powers was by its very rôle immoral. Not only was it immoral by its own standards, as many of its own reformers recognised, but more perniciously immoral by its very attempt to claim that its order was a moral one. (pp. 406-07)

[The recognition of] a total annihilation of the black man's culture and personal identity would lead to his anguished 'realization that his destiny had been sealed before his awakening'. Viewed this way, the objectionable nature of colonial values, buttressed by the almost insuperable network of legal and physical fortifications, compelled Fanon to conclude that violence was to be the only purifying element. If the end of his political thought was to eliminate colonial dominance and its conventional morality, then there was no method open except that which was outside of such ethics. (p. 407)

Here is no question of good and evil in ordinary terms. The human tragedy importunes humanity for a solution that is denied by the very colonial presence. . . . It is important to note, however, that Fanon goes beyond the question of race, and sees morality in the very essence of man's relation to man; not just 'black' versus 'white'. . . .

Caught 'in the lasso of existence', Fanon's wretched must choose their human existence. This choice is consummated in action which can only have any meaning within the context from which it springs. Any morality or ethical appeal to reason which is not based on the human condition in its particular existential grounding loses its obligatory character for Fanon. In a *milieu* fraught with human oppression and chaos, political action receives its imprimatur from the human needs within such a context, and not from some metaphysical force. . . .

The moral basis for Fanon, then, derives from the very foundation of human relations in the Third World. He argues that political violence, at most, is no more heinous than acquiescing in colonial violence. For Fanon, the ethics of violence in a renascent Third World promotes, for all, a true spirit of community, whereas the commission of colonial violence (under the guise of stability, law, order, Christian morality, and so on) prohibits the sharing of community feelings. (p. 408)

[This] is the fundamental ethical question that must be asked of Machiavelli and Fanon; for given the success of the liberator in the initial stages of the conflict, who will be the guarantor of the moral ends? (p. 410)

Writing at a time when the one-party state was seen as the answer to the problem of modernisation in Africa, Fanon was critical of this trend and depicted it as a form of dictatorship for the aggrandisement of a dissolute and useless ruling bourgeoisie—the essence of the bad 'prince'. The republican remedy would be that 'the party should be the direct expression of the masses'. The post-independence leader must ensure the close connection between the rulers and the masses; in fact, the leaders must join the masses, reside in the countryside, and vitalise the villages.

In short, the leader must initiate the diffusion of his power and rely on the co-operation of the people. In order to ensure the success of this approach there must be 'a very rapid transformation into a consciousness of social and political needs'. Fanon is here arguing the efficacy of ideology as an agent in securing this moral community; the emergence of such a community will be the safeguard of the revolutionary ends. And when Fanon's masses are psychologically transformed, the collective action of a people engaged in violence is supposed to bring about their freedom, their moral rejuvenation. While one must question the effect of violence on the post-national state, the moral necessity of this instrument for freeing a totally subjugated people will generally be viewed as an historical act towards securing freedom. The political thought of Fanon may lack the detailed prescriptions of the Florentine diplomat; yet, it possesses a much more profound appeal to the heroic qualities of the political actor than the cold doctrine addressed to the prince.

Are the writings of Machiavelli and Fanon merely personal outpourings of disaffected invividuals, scarcely discernible outcrops on the surface of history . . .? [Could] we see in their treatment of political affairs a general approach to politics?

The argument of this article is that both writers offered a general approach to politics, and that salutary action would be informed by their ethical ends. (pp. 411-12)

The general theory adumbrated by Fanon was one in which the economic, social, and political problems of the Third World were merely epiphenomena. Colonialism was held to be the first cause from which all phenomena were to be examined and explained. Placed in the matrix of history, colonialism breeds its own destruction in the form of decolonisation. Fanon does not put history to the same use as does Machiavelli; history, for Fanon, is an unremitting force in the Hegelian-Marxist dialectic. Its movement is determined by the contradictions that inhere in the colonial situation. Yet while he explains the shaping of the Third World through the dialectical movement caused by 'the meeting of two forces, opposed to each other by their very nature', he also insists that 'the body of history does not determine a single one of my actions. I am my own foundation. And it is by going beyond the historical, instrumental hypothesis that I will initiate the cycle of my freedom. Much in the same way that Machiavelli saw the man of *virtù* pitted against *fortuna*, Fanon saw the individual asserting himself against the environment.

Like Machiavelli's prince, Fanon's leader and the masses, if they are to be successful, must also be aware of the underlying political realities. Political leadership and action must rest on a heightened human awareness, so that the moral façade of the ruling tyrants will be torn off and their oppressive inhumanity will be revealed. Fanon advocated violence for this task. (pp. 413-14)

[When] we speak of the functional rôle of violence in Fanon's political prescriptions we see it as the fulcrum upon which all other political elements are supported. It serves as an instrument by which the individual reclaims his humanity; it produces the collective will from previously dissociated ones, it energises a people who have been enervated by colonial rule; and, finally, it clears the way for the new man in a new societal structure.

A cursory glance at the symbolic expression inherent in Fanon's political thoughts reveals a theme that lends itself to the imagination, the courage, and the existential needs of all those people who perceive themselves as being oppressed: the desire for popular and responsive governments. (p. 414)

> *Gerald E. Tucker, "Machiavelli and Fanon: Ethics, Violence, and Action," in* The Journal of Modern African Studies, *Vol. 16, No. 3, September, 1978, pp. 397-415.*

Jo Freeman
1945-

Freeman is an American professor of political science who writes on feminist issues. Her "participatory history" of the American women's liberation movement, *The Politics of Women's Liberation* (1975), was one of the first books to consider the political theory behind the movement. Freeman has also edited an anthology titled *Women: A Feminist Perspective*. (See also *Contemporary Authors*, Vols. 61-64.)

Courtesy of Jo Freeman

Excerpt from *THE POLITICS OF WOMEN'S LIBERATION: A CASE STUDY OF AN EMERGING SOCIAL MOVEMENT AND ITS RELATION TO THE POLICY PROCESS*

The [women's liberation] movement manifests itself in an almost infinite variety of groups, styles, and organizations. Yet this diversity has sprung from only two distinct origins, representing two different strata of society, with two different styles, orientations, values, and forms of organization. In many ways there were two different movements which only in the last two years have begun to merge.

The first of these I call the older branch of the movement, partially because the median age of its original activists was older and partially because it began first. Its most prominent organization is the National Organization for Women (NOW) but it also contains such groups as the National Women's Political Caucus (NWPC), Federally Employed Women (FEW), and the self-defined "right-wing" of the movement, the Women's Equity Action League (WEAL). While the programs and aims of the older branch span a wide spectrum, their activities have tended to be concentrated on legal and economic problems. These groups are primarily made up of women—and men—who work, and they are substantially concerned with the problems of working women. The style of organization of the older branch groups tends to be traditionally formal, with elected officers, boards of directors, bylaws, and the other trappings of democratic structure and procedure. All started as top-down national organizations lacking a mass base. Some have subsequently developed that base, some have not yet done so, and others do not want to.

The younger branch of the movement is all mass base and no national organization. It consists of innumerable small groups engaged in a variety of activities, whose contact with one another is at best tenuous. Its composition, like that of the older branch, tends to be predominantly white, middle class, and college educated, but much more homogeneously so. (pp. 49-50)

The activities of the two branches are . . . incongruous. Ironically, the most typical division of labor is that those groups labeled "radical" engage primarily in educational work and service projects, while the so-called reformist groups are the political activists. Structure and style rather than ideology more accurately differentiate the two branches, and even here there has been much borrowing on both sides. In general the older branch has used the traditional forms of political action while the younger branch has been experimental. (p. 51)

Jo Freeman, "The Origins of the Women's Liberation Movement" (reprinted by permission of the author), in The American Journal of Sociology, *Vol. 78, No. 4, January, 1973 (and reprinted in her* The Politics of Women's Liberation: A Case Study of an Emerging Social Movement and Its Relation to the Policy Process, *David McKay Company, Inc., 1975, pp. 44-70).*

• • • • •

There were two major results from all the tensions and conflicts the movement experienced. . . . One was to create a forum for new ideas and to provide a political education for many young feminists. The other was to tear apart, slowly but surely, the reticulate interstices of the movement. (p. 142)

One reason for the movement's dissolution is that it had been limited by its own origins. A product of the counterculture and New Left, it had within a few short years expanded to the boundaries of that culture, transformed and/or integrated most of its organizations and institutions, and then turned in on itself as it had no place else to go. The new relationships and activities that were tentatively emerging in late 1972 involved many people who had not been part of the youth and student movements, whether by age or inclination.

However, these new relationships did not appear to include a new sense of direction and it is upon the rock of lack of direction that the younger branch of the movement has been floundering for so long it has practically become a way of life. There is a phoenixlike quality to the movement—different groups simultaneously dying, reforming, and emerging—so that it is hard to get an accurate reading on the state of its health. Although the resurgence of feminism tapped a major source of female energy, the structure of the younger branch has not been able to channel it effectively. Some women are able to create their own local action projects, study groups, or service centers. Most are not, and the movement provides no coordinated or structured means of fitting them into existing projects. Instead, such women either are recruited into NOW and other national organizations, or drop out of organized activity altogether. The latter rarely cease to be feminists; instead they apply their new ideas to their personal lives and individual concerns. The consequence, however, is that new groups form and dissolve at an accelerating rate, creating a good deal of consciousness and very little concerted action. To a certain extent the movement is expanding but not building; forging into new areas while failing to consolidate its gains in old. (p. 143)

The pluralistic nature of the women's liberation movement is a characteristic that has not been adequately appreciated either by the movement's participants or by its critics. The latter usually attack specific organizations for being too homogeneous in composition without realizing that the movement as a whole is becoming more and more heterogeneous. The primary means by which feminism enters new segments of the population is by the formation of new groups rather than by more women joining established groups. Black women, older women, trade-union women, office workers, etc., have all created new organizations to deal with the implications of feminism for their particular situations—even though some individuals in these groups are active in established feminist organizations. (pp. 150-51)

A broadly based organization (which few feminist groups are) is not the same as a broadly based movement (which feminism is).

The unceasing fission of the movement has been both its strength and its weakness. With the formation of each new group an entirely new segment of the female population is brought under its umbrella and a correspondingly new segment of men and women have the reality of feminist revolt brought into their everyday lives through the activities of their colleagues, friends, and relatives. Conversely, this diversity makes the possibility of a united movement more and more impossible and agreement on common issues more and more difficult. It usually means that while each separate feminist effort has the existence of the movement to give it moral strength, it lacks any powerful organization behind it to give it material strength. Apart from NOW, most feminist organizations still consist of a handful of dedicated people and a large penumbra of hesitant sympathizers. (pp. 151-52)

Jo Freeman, in excerpts from her "Women on the Move: The Roots of Revolt," in Academic Women on the Move, *edited by Alice S. Rossi and Ann Calderwood (© 1973 by the Russell Sage Foundation), Russell Sage Foundation, 1973 (and reprinted in "The Small Groups" and "The 'Mushroom Effect': A Partial Profile," in her* The Politics of Women's Liberation: A Case Study of an Emerging Social Movement and Its Relation to the Policy Process, *David McKay Company, Inc., 1975, pp. 103-46, 147-69).*

. . . . .

Regardless of the outcome of the ERA, the two-year final battle to get it through Congress had some very beneficial side effects. Primary among them was the climate it created in Congress that there was serious constituent interest in women's rights. (pp. 221-22)

The other major side effect was the establishment of liaisons between feminist organizations and congressional staff. (p. 222)

What is emerging is a network of people in various agencies of the government, feminist organizations, and other private institutions, with a personal and professional commitment to improving the status of women. While the impact of the movement on the latter has not been dealt with here, suffice it to say that feminists and feminist concerns have emerged strongly within the media, some labor unions, many educational institutions and associations, and a few other places. Together the participants in this loosely structured network are forming a policy system on women's rights. (p. 226)

While the policy system on women's rights is hardly complete, its rapid rise in part answers our original question on the relatively early, unstrenuous achievement of a good deal of policy in this area. There were a large number of "woodwork feminists" in the federal government. It could no doubt be shown that many women in the upper reaches of government had had a good deal of personal experience with sex discrimination and/ or other personal reasons for immediate interest in this issue. . . .

These women thus created a potential "policy system" which only needed the proper conditions to jell. Such conditions were provided in general by the emergence of the women's liberation movement which legitimated an interest in this area. (p. 228)

[The] ideas of a changed environment and a new policy system alone are not sufficient to explain the new policies. Women, let alone feminists, are simply just not that powerful in government or in the private sector. The reason the women's liberation movement could achieve many hard-fought legislative goals of the civil rights movement so much faster than it did was because the civil rights movement preceded it. It is not for naught that almost all the women's rights legislation involves amendments to or parallels of minority civil rights legislation. The civil rights movement broke the ground. It both created a precedent for and a model of action in the area of sex discrimination. . . .

One should be conscious, however, that coattail riding on another movement's achievements has its limits. First, those on the tails cannot usually control the direction of the coat. Many civil rights organizations have made it clear that they are very suspicious of their feminist offspring and not amenable to an easy alliance. Second, the feminist movement has several significant issues—child care, abortion, and especially the abolition of sex-role stereotypes and the traditional roles—on which there are no civil rights precedents. Here the movement will have to learn to fight its own battles, and will not find the going so easy. (p. 229)

[The] continuing centralization of power in the federal government means that it is the national feminist organizations that will have the greatest impact on policy—and be most affected by it in turn. NOW and the other older branch organizations are thriving at this point because they have been able to use the institutional tools which our society provides for social and political change. Yet the "honeymoon" is over.

The women's liberation movement caught the government by surprise, and it responded along the lines it had developed for civil rights policy. Now that the backlash has begun on several fronts, it remains to be seen whether the feminist groups can develop and mobilize their resources to maintain the momentum without getting so bogged down in the nitty-gritty politics of incremental success that they lose sight of their ultimate goals. (p. 244)

> *Jo Freeman, "The Policy Impact of the Women's Liberation Movement" and "Policy and Movement," in her* The Politics of Women's Liberation: A Case Study of an Emerging Social Movement and Its Relation to the Policy Process *(a revision of a thesis presented at the University of Chicago in 1973; copyright © 1975 by Jo Freeman; reprinted by permission of the author and Longman Inc., New York), David McKay Company, Inc., 1975, pp. 170-229, 230-44.*

JOAN PETERS

I am somewhat disappointed in *Politics of Women's Liberation*. Despite her fine documentation of the Women's Movement, Freeman's political conservatism limits her understanding of its radical portion and biases her analysis in favor of the more traditional feminist groups. . . .

The most useful part of Freeman's study is her analysis of the two major groups within the Women's Movement. . . . (p. 40)

The major problem with Freeman's evaluation of the two groups is that "immediate policy change" is her single criterion for political effectiveness. While Freeman argues convincingly that the two groups have a symbiotic relationship—the younger providing the new ideas that the older group selectively translates into political action—she sees the younger group as politically ineffectual.

This evaluation is short-sighted—a product of political conservatism. Changing laws and policies is important, but the suffrage movement should have taught us that policy change alone has limited effectiveness. Other revolutions (the Chinese, for example) show the important political function of processes such as "consciousness-raising" which do not lead to immediate policy change, but *can* result in more thorough political and social reordering.

The unconventional tactics of the younger group are, granted, difficult to examine from the point of view of traditional politics, yet their goals are clearly long range. . . . In Freeman's own terms, [their] projects can be seen as the beginning of an excellent "communications network system" created by women; one that doesn't need to be co-opted from a system inimical to its goals, against which it must constantly fight.

Freeman's single criterion blurs real distinctions in ideology between the younger and older groups, and it sells the younger short. Freeman insists that "structure and style rather than ideology . . . differentiate the two branches, and even here there has been much borrowing on both sides." Yet, some women's groups clearly feel that feminism means equal rights under the law, while other groups believe that real equality isn't possible in a capitalistic system, and that sexism is the

nucleus of this system, the primary form of oppression. (pp. 40-1)

Oddly enough, Freeman's insight into the strengths and weaknesses of the "structure" of the younger sector is both the most exciting and most questionable part of her study. She shows how the non-hierarchical and structureless pattern of organizing created a leadership vacuum which made the organization susceptible to the "star-system" and "encouraged the very kind of individualistic non-responsibility that it most condemned."

Freeman's discussion of the "gay-straight split" typifies the unevenness of her thinking. She criticizes gay women for pressuring other women to become gay, which is fair enough, but she refuses to acknowledge the oppression of lesbians as a key to the oppression of women in general. . . . As in her analysis of the younger group, Freeman does not question her own assumptions, nor does she look deeply enough into the aims of the group she is examining. (p. 41)

> *Joan Peters, "Beyond the Basics," in* Ms. *(© 1975 Ms. Magazine Corp.), Vol. IV, No. 2, August, 1975, pp. 40-1.*

CAROL ANNE DOUGLAS

Not many women have written accounts about what we have experienced in the women's movement. . . . Those of us who joined the movement in the 'seventies (almost all of us) usually have only vague ideas about the origins of our movement. . . .

Fortunately, some books help us fill in the gaps. Jo Freeman's *The Politics of Women's Liberation* is one of them. Freeman gives many details about the development of the women's movement that can help us shape our perspectives, but she does not seem to be immune from slight distortions. . . .

In addition to presenting history, the book analyzes politics from Freeman's perspective. Her basic thesis . . . is that the reformist and radical sections of the women's movement complement each other; the radical feminists conceive of new ideas and keep challenging the reformists while the reformist activists put pressure on the system to bring about some degree of change. But Freeman refuses to use the labels reformist and radical, preferring to say the "older" and "younger" parts of the women's movement. She claims that what we call radical feminists are principally engaged in educational and cultural activities while the women we call reformists engage in more distinctly political activity. In a sense, this has been true. Radical feminists do seem to spend more time publishing and creating a women's culture than putting direct pressure on the system. But her definition of the political as only those things that try to influence the policies of the governmental system is too narrow. Moreover, she ignores the political actions that radical feminists have taken. . . .

Some of her observations about the dynamics of small groups seem valid . . . but her apparent preference for the "older" branch (she belongs, at least nominally, to NOW) is regrettable. In the 'sixties, Freeman worked in what she now calls the "younger branch" of the movement, but the difficulties that she observes in this book and in [her essay] **"The Tyranny of Structurelessness"** apparently drove her like many other early feminists to the safety of an isolated position. As she herself points out, when many feminists are working individually outside of groups it may be difficult for them to be responsible to the movement. This is not an accusation that she is irresponsible—she isn't—but a wish that women who felt that they had been "burned" in past years might try working in radical groups again. Unfortunately, she does not submit the reformists to as extensive scrutiny as the radicals.

One of her less understandable analyses is her assertion that the "younger" and "older" branches of the movement do not differ ideologically, but only in style. It is true, as she says, that feminist ideology is undeveloped, but the choice to develop a parliamentary structure or a collective one must have some connection with ideology. Those of us who are trying to work collectively are not doing so because we have marvelously collective personalities, but because we think collectivity is more consistent with our frequently anarchistic values. . . .

Unfortunately, her treatment of lesbianism is . . . rather slighting. She compares lesbianism with miscegenation between whites and blacks in the civil rights days, rather than comparing it with the "black is beautiful" emphasis on relating to other members of one's own oppressed group. . . . [Generally] she does not contribute much to the discussion of sexuality.

Although radicals may be annoyed by her rather reformist politics, we can glean a great deal of information about the women's movement (both branches) and some interesting perceptions about our faults from reading this book.

> *Carol Anne Douglas, "Book Reviews: 'The Politics of Women's Liberation',"* in Off Our Backs *(copyright © Off Our Backs Inc. 1975), Vol. V, No. 7, August, 1975, p. 14.*

LYNN SHERR

"The Politics of Women's Liberation" examines how the American movement has influenced Federal policy, and how it has directly inspired laws elevating the status of women through a process that must be recognized as "playing the game"—although with some unexpected new rules. . . .

Unfortunately, Jo Freeman's observations are limited by her proximity—in time, not in sympathy—to the actual events. On the one hand, she sees that as an advantage, pointing out that such rare, early analysis keeps the information fresh, clear and "uncontaminated by hindsight." On the other hand, she acknowledges that "The women's liberation movement is just beginning to have an impact on policy and on society." (p. 38)

Since the book is based upon Freeman's Ph.D. thesis at the University of Chicago, its hypothetical nature (regarding public policy) is forgivable. That it reads like a Ph.D. thesis is less excusable. It is of enormous value to have a political scientist of Freeman's perceptions tell us what we have been doing; without its academic overtones, her six-year effort might have reached a wider audience.

To be fair, the book is very reasonable, highly objective and entirely successful in chronicling the events that led to the current women's movement. Freeman is at her strongest in reporting its origins. (pp. 38, 40)

Freeman also clarifies some of the internal conflicts: the gay-straight split of the early 1970's; the apparent middle class bias of the founders of the movement; the charges of "élitism" and "media stars" that threatened the underpinnings of a movement that likes to call itself leaderless. Her facts should set the record straight for anyone whose knowledge of women's activities comes from what she calls "the grand press blitz" of 1970. (p. 40)

> *Lynn Sherr, "'The Politics of Women's Liberation',"* in The New York Times Book Review *(© 1975 by The New York Times Company; reprinted by permission), October 5, 1975, pp. 38, 40.*

KATHRYN B. YATRAKIS

[*The Politics of Women's Liberation: A Case Study of an Emerging Social Movement and Its Relation to the Policy Process*] will make a significant contribution to the literature of the women's liberation movement. . . . Although the term "politics" is never explicitly defined and thus somewhat belies the book's title, other terms, assumptions, and hypotheses are specifically examined and developed. Freeman assumes that there is a mutual relationship between social movements and public policy, and on this theoretical base she examines the women's liberation movement. Developing the language and literature of social movements, interest groups, political organizations, and social change, the author draws her analysis from the basic economic and social conditions which created the "roots of revolt" to the present-day policy impact of the movement.

After setting the social and economic stage of revolt, Freeman attempts to explain why the first and second waves of the feminist movement were generally led by white middle-class women, particularly women in the professions, by using the concept of "relative deprivation." Freeman goes on to discuss the origins of the women's liberation movement in the general terms of social-movement theories. She develops three major propositions upon which her analysis rests. One, that a preexisting communications network was needed; two, that this network had to be cooptable [*sic*] to the new ideas of the incipient movement; and three, that a situation of strain was required. She couples these elements with a fourth, organizing effort, which together contributed to the emergence of the women's liberation movement in the mid-1960s. Within these propositions, Freeman gives theoretical shape to the movement's development. The author then examines the two "branches" of the women's liberation movement with the caveat that "structure and style rather than ideology more accurately differentiate the two branches . . .". . . . Since "ideology" is another term that has not been explicitly defined, this argument is somewhat diluted. The process of growth of the "branches," however, is effectively analyzed as the result of values and norms of the originators, internal dynamics of the organization, and environmental effects. Thus two such unlikely groups as NOW and the New York Radical Feminists can be validly discussed within one theoretical framework. (pp. 790-91)

The author has succeeded in taking the potentially unwieldly topic of the women's liberation movement and has firmly grounded it in social-movement theory. To this extent the book goes well beyond much of the literature in this area. When necessary, Freeman develops and reshapes the theory emanating from the literature to fit the reality of the movement. . . .

The author initially states her methodology as being based primarily on participant observation and suggests the advantages of this method. It would have been useful, particularly to the student, if she also indicated some of the concomitant disadvantages of this approach.

A more detailed discussion of Congresswoman [Martha] Griffiths' discharge petition of the Equal Rights Amendment would have been desirable, as well as an examination of the paradox between the enormous constituency pressure for ERA which aided its passage through Congress and the fact that the amendment, after a quick start, is now limping through the ratification process of the states. The value in Freeman's book is that she suggests a theory within which these and other problems of the women's liberation movement can be addressed. (p. 791)

> *Kathryn B. Yatrakis, "Book Reviews: 'The Politics of Women's Liberation: A Case Study of an Emerging Social Movement and Its Relation to the Policy Process'," in* Political Science Quarterly, *Vol. 90, No. 4, Winter, 1975-76, pp. 790-91.*

JOYCE T. MACRORIE

The Politics of Women's Liberation could have been a valuable hand-book and text but for one unacceptable weakness; it is unreadable.

A published thesis, it suffers from the author's fear of cheating her sources, of coming on with too much self, maybe offending someone with her hubris. She has the facts; she knows her stuff on a gut level as well as in her head. But instead of coming out with it straight, she quotes dull people, gives credit to everyone but herself, and supports, *ad nauseum,* statements that most thinking people would accept as folk knowledge. Ms. Freeman has allowed her history of the vital women's liberation movement to die by degree.

> *Joyce T. Macrorie, "Books: 'The Politics of Women's Liberation'," in* The Antioch Review *(copyright © 1976 by the Antioch Review Inc.; reprinted by permission of the Editors), Vol. 34, No. 3, Spring, 1976, p. 379.*

Edgar Z(odiag) Friedenberg

1921-

Friedenberg is an American education writer and professor of education at Dalhousie University in Halifax, Nova Scotia. In *Coming of Age in America* (1965) he argues that the educational system suppresses the individuality of adolescents and inculcates the conformist and opportunist norms of industrial society. *The Disposal of Liberty and Other Industrial Wastes* (1975) is an exploration of the social psychology of industrial society, of which a major component, according to Friedenberg, is the widespread feeling of *ressentiment*—"a free-floating disposition to visit upon others the bitterness that accumulates from one's own subordination . . .". Friedenberg maintains that the politics of ressentiment have "[assumed] a striking political importance" in the present era and pose a considerable threat to liberty. Some critics have faulted Friedenberg for overstating the tendency toward conformity in our society and for presenting a pessimistic view of the average citizen. Nevertheless, he is widely considered to be a brilliant and sympathetic observer of youth and an insightful social critic. (See also *Contemporary Authors*, Vols. 65-68.)

Courtesy of Edgar Z. Friedenberg and Dalhousie University

Excerpt from *COMING OF AGE IN AMERICA: GROWTH AND ACQUIESCENCE*

What is most extraordinary about youth today is that adults everywhere should be so worried about it. I do not mean to suggest that this concern is groundless; on the contrary. A great many young people are in very serious trouble throughout the technically developed and especially the Western world. Their trouble, moreover, follows certain familiar common patterns; they get into much the same kind of difficulty in very different societies. But it is nevertheless strange that they should. Human life is a continuous thread which each of us spins to his own pattern, rich and complex in meaning. There are no natural knots in it. Yet knots form, nearly always in adolescence. In American, British, European, Japanese, Australasian, and at least the more privileged Soviet youth, puberty releases emotions that tend toward crisis. Every major industrial society believes that it has a serious youth problem.

Adolescence is both a stage and a process of growth. As such it should proceed by doing what comes naturally. Instead, there is a widespread feeling that it cannot be allowed to proceed without massive intervention. The young disturb and anger their elders, and are themselves angered and disturbed, or repelled and depressed, at the thought of becoming what they see their elders to be. Adults observe and condemn the "teen-age tyranny" of "the adolescent society," over which they seek to establish and maintain hegemony by techniques of infiltration and control.

Adolescents are among the last social groups in the world to be given the full nineteenth-century colonial treatment. Our colonial administrators, at least at the higher policy-making levels, are usually of the enlightened sort who decry the punitive expedition except as an instrument of last resort, though they are inclined to tolerate a shade more brutality in the actual school or police station than the law allows. They prefer, however, to study the young with a view to understanding them, not for their own sake but in order to learn how to induce them to abandon their barbarism and assimilate the folkways of normal adult life. The model emissary to the world of youth is no longer the tough disciplinarian but the trained youth worker, who works like a psychoanalytically oriented anthropologist. Like the best of missionaries, he is sympathetic and understanding toward the people he is sent to work with, and aware and critical of the larger society he represents. But fundamentally he accepts it, and often does not really question its basic values or its right to send him to wean the young from savagery. (pp. 3-4)

[Every] society depends on the succession of generations, and adults usually assume that this means that their values and life style should be transmitted to the young. Youth cannot be allowed to "go native" permanently; some writers and artists may be allowed to live as beachcombers and to go on negotiating with other adults in beat and jive as if it were pidgin, but the rest have to grow up to be like their elders. When adults observe that a large proportion of youth is becoming threateningly unfamiliar and uncongenial, there is said to be a youth problem, and deliberate efforts are made to induce or compel the young to accept and participate in the dominant culture.

At this point, therefore, the position of youth is less that of a colonized native than it is that of a minority group that is gaining status and being assimilated. The plight of the adolescent is basically similar to that of an emigrant in that he can neither stay what he was nor become what he started out to be. Minority-group status occurs, and is recognized as such, only in societies that are abandoning a colonial stance and accepting the position that the lesser breeds over whose destinies they have assumed control are to be brought *within* the law and ultimately to be treated as equals. (pp. 8-9)

It would seem, then, that societies that are passing from colonialism to a period in which they recognize and accept as constituents a variety of minority groups ought to provide specially good opportunities for growing up. At such a time, there are many different ways to express fidelity in action. There is, or should be, opportunity for real social action and political commitment; for trying out roles and experimenting with new causes and foci for loyalty. (pp. 10-11)

Examples of individual integrity can still be uncovered, but they hardly set the prevailing tone of our life. The essence of our era is a kind of infidelity, a disciplined expediency.

This expediency is not a breach of our tradition, but its very core. And it keeps the young from getting much out of the diversity that our heterogeneous culture might otherwise provide them. This kind of expediency is built into the value structure of every technically developed open society; and it becomes most prevalent when the rewards of achievement in that society appear most tempting and the possibilities of decent and expressive survival at a low or intermediate position in it least reliable. Being different, notoriously, does not get you to the top. If individuals must believe that they are on their way there in order to preserve their self-esteem they will be under constant pressure, initially from anxious adults and later from their own aspirations, to repudiate the divergent elements of their character in order to make it under the terms common to mass culture. They choose the path most traveled by, and that makes all the difference. (pp. 11-12)

What is immeasurably destructive is . . . the kind of conformity that abandons the experience of the individual in order to usurp a tradition to which he does not belong and to express a view of life foreign to his experience and, on his lips, phony. For an adult this is self-destructive; for an adolescent it is the more pitiful and tragic, because the self that is abandoned is still immanent and further growth requires that it be nurtured and continuously clarified and redefined. A pregnant woman may recover, more or less, from abortion; the foetus never does.

For nearly a decade, sympathetic adults have been complaining that contemporary youth is apathetic and conforming, until new cults of nonconformity have arisen to give us what we now want and to exploit the new opportunities created by our wanting it. Many a bright young man has concealed himself strategically behind a beard and a uniform "beat" costume ill suited to his nature; and who can deny that the managers of the Hiltons of tomorrow may gain useful experience in the coffee houses of today. But actual autonomy, when it can be found, looks and sounds different. (pp. 13-14)

[The] society that prefers the kind of man who has never examined the meaning of his life against the context in which he lives is bound to believe that it has a youth problem. For its own sake, and the sake of its social future, one can only pray that it really does have.

Adolescents have very low status in our society, and serious questions about their role in it tend to turn into inquiries as to whether they are receiving adequate custodial service from their teachers, jailers, and social workers. Since, in fact, they usually are not, this is a fairly important question, and a recurrent one. When we go beyond this, however, into the basic question of why their status is low, and why they are so consistently disparaged and prevented from forming a conception of themselves strong enough to resist disparagement, we must deal with far more fundamental issues. At bottom, I suggest, is nothing less than the question of what it costs in individual freedom and dignity to provide justice and equality in a mass society. (pp. 25-6)

> *Edgar Z. Friedenberg, in his* Coming of Age in America: Growth and Acquiescence *(copyright © 1965 by Edgar Z. Friedenberg; reprinted by permission of Random House, Inc.), Random House, 1965, 300 p.*

Excerpt from *THE DISPOSAL OF LIBERTY AND OTHER INDUSTRIAL WASTES*

My central purpose in writing [*The Disposal of Liberty and Other Industrial Wastes*] has been to examine a paradox that has troubled me for as long as I have dealt with general ideas, and that has steadily become more and more important in politics. This paradox is the peculiar incapacity of the democratic, populist national state to deal generously with the less fortunate members of its population. In North America, especially, we have been taught to believe that generosity was not only economically feasible, but that it might reasonably have been expected. Our high state of technological development, it has constantly been supposed, could produce goods and services enough to provide all our people with leisure and affluence; and it has been only recently that the mounting problems of pollution and overpopulation have led us to doubt that this could ultimately be done for the entire world. Our populism was supposed to insure that the people could insist on an equitable distribution of this abundance, so that none should go in want of what they needed for a satisfying life—or at least a life filled with all that money could buy.

We now know that these were empty clichés; indeed, to say that they are has itself become a cliché. Technological development has led instead to greater concentration of wealth. All over the world, the poor become more numerous and even objectively poorer as their level of expectation rises on the waves of television. Quite adequate and convincing explanations have been offered as to why the democratic political process is unable to countervail against these destructive developments. (p. ix)

Yet none of these recent analyses of contemporary world politics deals directly with what seems to me the most remarkable, persistent and disgusting characteristic of democratic political life. This is its peculiar mean-spiritedness. "In our times, from the highest class of society down to the lowest" John Stuart Mill observed in his essay "On Liberty," "everyone lives as under the eye of a hostile and dreaded censorship." In *his* time, over a century ago. He should see us now, as millions of hardhats and other middle Americans maintain their not so silent majority vigil against blacks, poor people on welfare, pornographic books and textbooks that picture God as polyglot and the United States as one nation among many, all with problems. Middle America experienced a chastening setback in 1974, with the fall of their standard-bearer and his suite. But this is unlikely to improve their dispositions, or alter their political attitudes. In Canada, their counterparts likewise flourish, directing their efforts to the restoration of capital punishment and the repeal of the Official Languages Act. (p. x)

[It] was Nietzsche, pre-eminently, who understood the importance of the growth of spite and rancor among the lower-middling functionaries of modern society. He gave this phenomenon the name *Ressentiment,* choosing a coinage from a foreign tongue to avoid the misleading connotations already inherent in any German word he might have used. English-speaking readers still tend to see the word as "resentment," but this is crucially wrong. Ressentiment is to resentment as climate is to weather, in places like the Aleutians. Ressentiment is a free-floating disposition to visit upon others the bitterness that accumulates from one's own subordination and existential guilt at allowing oneself to be used by other people for their own purposes, while one's own life rusts away unnoticed. Rebellion, which directs the rancor at the people or institutions that actually aroused it, reduces ressentiment sharply, though at the cost of invoking further sanctions if the rebellion is unsuccessful. Acquiescence makes it worse. (pp. x-xi)

Ressentiment is the inescapable consequence of exploitation, which is why Nietzsche saw it as central to "slave mentality." It is therefore the moral responsibility of elites even more than of their victims. In a democratic state, however, ressentiment assumes a striking political importance, in which the victims of ressentiment are far more fully implicated than they would be if they had not so insistently—if misguidedly—assented to the formal definition of themselves as the titular source of political authority. However manipulated or misled the electorate in a democratic state may be by those who manage its industry and means of communication, the hand that pulls the lever on the voting machine also releases the bombs on the helpless villagers in the bombardier's path. To claim otherwise is simply to insist at the outset that the democratic process is a mammoth enterprise in political mystification. One cannot simultaneously claim political rights as one of a sovereign people and disclaim responsibility for the atrocities committed in the people's name.

In practice, unfortunately, ressentiment evades this issue, since a mass electorate in which ressentiment prevails finds it much easier to accept atrocities than public generosity. It is far less controversial politically to spend billions destroying Indochinese homes than to spend millions providing homes for unwed mothers and their children. No Indochinese victim was ever required to fill out complicated forms and wait hours to be interviewed by a bored clerk so that the bombs and napalm he could not afford to provide to his children would continue to be delivered. Though it is true that both domestic welfare-mothers and Indochinese women had reason to dread nocturnal visits by agents hoping to surprise their husbands at home. If only the American peace movement could successfully have floated a rumor that the Vietcong were *getting something for nothing*—like by selling unexploded bombs to the government of India at an immense profit and making more money than a teamster picking grapes—the war would have been over in months. The American people wouldn't have stood for it.

A ressentiment-ridden policy thus faces peculiar difficulties in dealing with the pressing needs of its less fortunate members. Though a substantial proportion of the relatively better off may be moved by compassion and by fear of revolt—in whatever combination—they cannot prevail against the ill-will of those who are outraged by the proposal of a direct subvention of the

poor. Every proposal for a guaranteed annual income is met by querulous objections that, if the income granted were large enough to insure a decent life, it would no longer be possible to get people to accept the worst and most poorly paid jobs; they'd live off the government instead. Since large entrepreneurs can easily pass rising costs on to their customers, especially if that customer is another entrepreneur or the government, they are not usually frantic about having to pay higher wages. These objections are more urgently voiced by persons who are themselves economically marginal, either as employees or as employers. And the proper answer to their objection seems to me to be "Yes, that is the intent. Nobody should have to do lousy work for lousy pay; and nobody should know that better than you, who have had to do it all your life. Avoid envy; it's a cardinal sin."

Since this answer is not politically possible; and since it is likewise impossible to ignore the plight of the disadvantaged, whose increasing alienation and desperation make them a social threat, our society has evolved an uneasy and increasingly unpleasant compromise. It defines as a social problem the poor, the young, the deviant and anybody who seems to be unable to cope—especially if other people find them disturbing. And instead of dealing directly with their difficulties and, whenever possible, giving them the money to deal with their lives themselves, our society sets up bureaucracies to rehabilitate and control them. This circumvents ressentiment; or, rather, gives it expression, since the people on whom the money is thought to be spent receive very little of it themselves; and that little under circumstances that insure that they will get no satisfaction from it. Instead, they become welded into what I call *conscript clienteles,* who provide the *raison c'être* of the cadres of professionals who are supposed to serve them; and whose services they are no longer free to refuse. It is the school children who support the school, whether or not they learn anything there or whether or not it is destructive to their self-esteem. It *could not* exist without them; they are *not allowed* to exist without it. (pp. xi-xiii)

It is not much of an exaggeration to say that the modern industrial state can spend big money only on making people miserable; to spend it on making them happy would tear it apart in jealous rage. And in this respect, the egalitarian industrial state may be more vicious than its imperious predecessor, untroubled by democratic pretensions. It has always been profitable, almost by definition, for the more powerful to enrich themselves at the expense of the weaker. But greed, pure and simple, is a relatively genial vice, and need not be insatiable. The rich and mighty enjoy what they gain at the expense of the poor; but they do not resent the poor and think of them as gaining what little they have at *their* expense. They do not ordinarily think of the poor and outcast as exploiting *them,* and fear that the poor may get a little more than they deserve. If they could, the rich would like to forget the whole thing, since it tends to spoil their day. They do not enjoy the fact of the poor's humiliation; *that,* in itself, is not the source of their wealth or prestige.

But if it is true that behind every great fortune there is a great crime, a great many more lesser fortunes are derived from the definition of certain persons as criminals and from the services and industries intended to maintain the definition and control them. It is usually true that crime does not pay, since actions that consistently do pay are redefined as lawful when their practitioners gain wealth and power; *vide* the liquor industry. And it certainly does not often pay as well as a federal judicial appointment or an executive position with a firm that provides security guards and hardware. Policemen and prison guards are not very well paid, though the former have become quite adept at making other arrangements. But they are well aware of their ceremonial function in society, not only to maintain order, but to dramatize the outcaste character of the criminal. Police do many other more useful and benign things—they are often more skilled and humane at working out the domestic troubles of the poor than professional social workers are—but they are also the visible and ceremonial expression of the ressentiment felt by the frustrated law-abiding citizen including, especially, themselves.

The prevalence of ressentiment seems to me to make it absurd and sentimental to suppose that liberty will ever be a popular cause in a modern industrial society, whether that society be socialist or liberal-capitalist. Most citizens despise the very idea of idiosyncratic and personal self-expression as the very essence of privilege, and expect the bitter disciplines of adult life to stamp such tendencies out if the schools fail to do so. And, of course, they are right. (pp. xiii-xiv)

> *Edgar Z. Friedenberg, in his* The Disposal of Liberty and Other Industrial Wastes *(copyright © 1975 by Edgar Z. Friedenberg; reprinted by permission of Doubleday & Company, Inc.), Doubleday, 1975, 196 p.*

DONALD W. ROBINSON

The manifest message [of *The Vanishing Adolescent*] is that schools today unwittingly discriminate against the socially inferior student, invade the privacy of all students, deny self-esteem in the adolescent by demanding conformity, compliance and obeisance to symbols of democracy rather than acceptance of the reality. Although [Dr. Edgar Friedenberg] implies that this state of affairs is especially characteristic of today's schools, the haunting suspicion persists that many of these conditions have been consistently improved during the very period when adolescence has been crippled.

The latent content of the book is as rich and varied as the motivations of young people, from which it derives its force and as rewarding as the reader's insights will allow. It suggests the alienation of psychologists and guidance workers from the youth they try too hard to help and the incompetence of teachers who lack dignity because they lack the pride that comes with proud possession of a respected competence. . . .

The Vanishing Adolescent, like so many of the current crop of analytical books, is more provocative than prescriptive. It is obviously the work of a man who thinks clearly, cares deeply, and writes with verve.

> *Donald W. Robinson, "'The Vanishing Adolescent'" (reprinted by permission of the author), in* The Social Studies, *Vol. LI, No. 5, October, 1960, p. 194.*

MORTON WHITE

[In *Coming of Age in America* Friedenberg] uses all the statistical means and modes at his disposal, and he discourses learnedly about autonomy and empiricism; and yet during the whole procedure his prose sparkles and his heart aches for the neglected humanist in the eleventh grade. He believes that in our mass society too many high school students have been turned into opportunists and that the sensitive adolescent intellectual has as good a chance of coming through the American high school happily as an honest man in a Madison Avenue public relations firm. . . .

No reader with a shred of feeling can help being touched by Friedenberg's concern for children who don't fit into the mould created by their dreary peers, petty principals, and petit bourgeois teachers. And who can bring himself to deny that our high schools should encourage more respect for privacy, for inwardness, and for all of the other things that Friedenberg summarizes by his use of the modish word "subjectivity"? But it is one thing to speak out movingly for all of these things, and another to write a philosophically cogent and sociologically penetrating study of the vast subject covered by this book. When Friedenberg is not accurately and delicately recording how his subjects, as he calls them, feel, but lecturing us, for example, on the nature of mass society and the evils of empiricism he is much less winning, much less persuasive, and—greatest failing of all for one of his philosophical persuasion—much less authentic.

I have written some friendly and some fighting words. Let me try to justify them. First I turn to the best part of the book. Armed with statistics, with style, and with a nice supply of irony in his soul, Friedenberg makes a striking assault on "The Structure of Student Values." . . . He invented an imaginary high school called "LeMoyen," as well as a set of six connected narrative episodes about it. . . . One of Friedenberg's most instructive episodes was called "The King's Visit," in which the students were told that the king of a country not unlike Denmark was to visit their high school, a king interested in meeting "spirited young people." They were also told that "such young people as were to be chosen should be persons to whom the school could point with pride as expressing what was finest and best about their school." Then the students were given cards which carried little descriptions of fictitious candidates, and their task was to rank them for the honor (or job) of meeting the king. Their top choice 69 per cent of the time was either one of two rather dull characters. . . .

In general, to use Freidenberg's own words, his subjects' responses to "The King's Visit" showed their dependence on external judgment as more important than self-approval and internal coherence, their suspicion of specialized personal competence unless directed and controlled by the school or the group for social purposes, and their skepticism that the King's visit could have any other purpose than good public relations. (p. 9)

He has great gifts in reporting how children feel about well-rounded people, mixers, sloppy people, and unshaven basketball players, and his observations are brilliantly formulated and cogently defended. But it is important to point out that Friedenberg does not limit himself to such homey observations about his subjects. Like so many behavioral scientists who study values, he tries to rise to a higher level on which he begins to use the terminology of philosophy, and here is where the reader begins to have a certain amount of difficulty in understanding or believing what he has to say. Here we are not completely at Friedenberg's mercy, for he is making inferences from premises and by steps that are before our eyes. The students didn't *tell* him that they didn't like Scotty Cowen because they didn't value autonomy: Friedenberg inferred that they didn't from statements which they made and which he reports to us.

I do not object in principle to such inferences, but I don't understand what Friedenberg means by the word "autonomy." Does he think that an autonomous person does what he feels like doing *without any* attention to the interests or wishes of others in his group, and that autonomy in this sense is an absolute value that his subjects are wrong not to share? Surely Friedenberg believes that sometimes when we do what we feel like doing, without attention to the interests of others, we act wrongly, and therefore that autonomy as such is *not* an unqualified good. Under what conditions, then, is it a good? Friedenberg doesn't say. (pp. 9-10)

Let me give a more crucial example of the same defect. Friedenberg criticizes his young subjects (and our society) for being addicted to empiricism, but what is empiricism as Friedenberg understands it? He thinks the students exhibited it in their reaction to "The King's Visit" because they chose as their representative someone who would make a favorable impression. They confined themselves to asserting what Kant calls an imperative of skill. If you want the king to be impressed, they seemed to say, send him Karen and Elfrieda, but don't ask us whether he *should* be impressed by drags like them. To be an empiricist in this sense, then, is to avoid ethical assessment, and more particularly, to choose a nonethical rather than an ethical interpretation of words like "finest and best" when presented with a situation in which one might interpret the words in either way.

So far, Friedenberg's analysis is very illuminating, and it is greatly to his credit that he reveals this unfortunate tendency by a masterly use of well-designed statistical techniques. But he is not content with calling the kids empiricists in his first sense. This is evident in what he says about them when they are faced with the episode called "The LeMoyen Basketball Team." Here the cards are stacked so that they *must* make a moral judgment: they can't do otherwise if they are to answer the question. So Friedenberg cannot accuse them of empiricism as previously defined, and therefore he accused them of being empiricists in another sense. What is that? When they appeal to the idea of equality of opportunity and insist that Kevin McGuire should not be kept off the team because of his race or religion, Friedenberg still condemns them because, although they appeal to a moral principle, "they don't really care whether their idea of how a democratic society works makes sense, because to them understanding something means knowing how to handle it; it does not mean being able to relate it to a larger, metaphysical whole." Now Friedenberg has his poor subjects coming and going. To avoid his disapproval, they must not only construe all value questions as moral questions when they have the choice, but when they answer moral questions they must be able to relate their conclusions to "a larger metaphysical whole." Does Friedenberg tell us what he means by this dark saying? Not at all, and so by the time we and Friedenberg leave LeMoyen's corridors together we begin to worry about his power to guide us through the clouds of sociology and philosophy that loom ahead.

Indeed, we begin to suspect that Friedenberg may not know what he is talking about in the higher realms, and such suspicions are more than confirmed by later chapters in which he begins to talk about the highest aims of education. Earlier, when he is being so lofty about the empiricism of the students and deplores their failure to establish contact with larger metaphysical wholes, the reader may think that Friedenberg is some kind of rationalist who wants children to be taught how to forge a logical link between their moral judgments and ontological structures, as the saying goes. But when we come to the last chapter we find this kind of scholastic logic-chopping is as far from Friedenberg's mind as it could possibly be. The argumentative boy is no gentleman. What Friedenberg wants to cultivate is inwardness and subjectivity. Hence his sociological hauteur about IQ tests. . . . Now it may be that "lower status" children are penalized by I.Q. tests but I cannot agree that amateur juvenile seers are disadvantaged by having to understand "abstract symbolism."

As the clouds lift a bit we can see the lack of originality in Friedenberg's theorizing. Building on a well-worn tradition in nineteenth-century thought, he thinks that our mass society has encouraged the empiricism of bureaucrats and the "abstract symbolism" of shopkeepers in the name of equal opportunity. And so, in conformity with an anti-intellectualist, romantic stereotype that I find indefensible, he sees middle-class boys calculating, experimenting, climbing, never evaluating, avoiding metaphysics, and paying no attention to their inner lives. Therefore, in another familiar move, Friedenberg decides that we must play both ends against this middle class. We must revive the amateur, the gentleman, with his humanity and trustworthiness, his sense of style and personal integrity, his taste for intimacy and his contempt for calculation. But where, in this society, shall we find him? Mainly in the slums, says Friedenberg in a burst of inverted snobbery that allows him to have and eat his cake of custom. Friedenberg will beat Madison Avenue, as a knowing New Yorker might say, by joining Madison Street. But as one who knows a good deal about Madison Street I can testify that while humanity, integrity, and trustworthiness certainly flourish there, they do so in about the same degree as they do on most other residential streets of the world. And even with due attention to what he says about Dr. King and the late Medgar Evers, I cannot take seriously Friedenberg's statement that "one hardly ever encounters examples of aristocratic bearing among any . . . contemporary Americans" besides Negroes. Nor can I take seriously his proposal that we set up federally supported boarding schools for "culturally deprived" children who show signs of becoming gentlemen in his sense while other more conventional adolescents continue in public and private schools. I see no objection to giving special encouragement to the distinguished of all kinds, whether they be sensitive, bright, or both, but it seems grotesque to form a special institution for those who seek primarily to "understand the meaning of their lives and become more sensitive to the meaning of other people's lives" while their contemporaries are segregated in other schools, presumably doing geometry, physics, and social studies as they learn about space, time, and mass society.

What is to be said in a more general way about all of this? For one thing, that Friedenberg's own intellectual limitations and his prejudices in favor of *Gemeinschaft* are mirrored in his educational ideals. What he can't do, namely reason analytically, he demotes; and what he can do, namely respond sympathetically, he promotes. But just as inwardness is not enough when one wants to be a philosopher of education, so the cultivation of inwardness is not the only or the highest aim in educating the young. I am sure that we have sinned in our failure to develop a respect for intimacy in our children, but I am also sure that we have sinned in our failure to develop their power to think. I am not talking about power in physics and mathematics. I mean the ability to reason clearly and consecutively about matters of the greatest human importance. I deny therefore that what we need today is only or mainly to resist the depredations or inwardness conceived as narrowly as Friedenberg conceives it, for modern society has victimized the mind in a more thorough way. It has not only discouraged those (in and out of high school) who want to understand "the meaning of their lives and become more sensitive to the meaning of other peoples' lives and relate to them more fully," but also those who want to think coherently and honestly about politics, literature, religion, history, science, law, and, of course, education. Therefore, if we want to battle effectively against the encroachments of mass society we must try to protect not only the poet against the philistines, but also, to put it simply, the philosopher in us all. (p. 10)

> Morton White, "Rites of Passage," in The New York Review of Books (reprinted with permission from The New York Review of Books; copyright © 1965 Nyrev, Inc.), Vol. IV, No. 10, June 17, 1965, pp. 9-11.

EDWARD WEEKS

In his search [in *Coming of Age in America*] for the values which adolescents of today hold dear, Dr. Friedenberg is repeatedly dismayed by "the averageness and well-roundedness" which they esteem. But I wonder if this is really any different from what seniors in 1915, whether at Battin or at Yale, would have had in mind when they voted for the Man Most Likely to Succeed. Again, I think he underestimates the tendency of students in the face of awe-inspiring sociologists to cover up and to give the safe answer rather than the daring one. . . . [One] must season these findings with one's own salt. Dr. Friedenberg is forthright and at times naïve in proclaiming his own values. He postulates the desirability of having a more aristocratic standard in the school, which is all very well, but his citation of modern gentlemen is absurdly limited. When he says, dogmatically, that "schools are not primarily instruments for the redress of social and economic grievances," he protects himself with "primarily" but seems to overlook what the high school has become ever since we began filling the melting pot.

Even so, there are plenty of shocks in this book for the conscientious parent, and not least from the interior picture of the high school which emerges. It is appalling to think of so much repression and regulation: the steel cage that descends on the cafeteria, lunch over, through whose gate at the sound of a buzzer the students file to their classrooms, the almost punitive locking up of the toilets, and the snooping for any trace of tobacco or sex; the rules devised for the convenience of the teacher rather than for the improvement of the pupil. All this cannot help breeding defiance. I do not share the Doctor's fear that automation will exterminate the middle class, but on his evidence I quite agree that the American high school is a poor substitute for good parents. (p. 122)

> Edward Weeks, "The Peripatetic Reviewer: 'Coming of Age in America'," in The Atlantic Monthly (copyright ©1965, by The Atlantic Monthly Company, Boston, Mass.; reprinted with permission), Vol. 216, No. 2, August, 1965, pp. 121-22.

RICHARD KLUGER

Friedenberg's weakness [in *Coming of Age in America*], it seems to me, is precisely [this]; he convinces us that his analysis of adolescent value patterns is essentially correct, but he does not convince us that he understands why they prevail. It is not enough to hark back to his theme of conformity as "a moral mandate" . . . , for while there is some truth in the notion that America has won its "position of leadership and dominance by carefully subordinating personal and ethnic disparity to the interests of teamwork," there is a countervailing and hardly less valid argument that we got where we are because enough intrepid and enterprising souls dared to dream hugely, work tirelessly and live dangerously. "Rugged individualism" was once part of our folklore. The pertinent question here is what has happened to that radiant credo. It is a question begged by this book.

Certainly he does not convince me, as I think he means to, that the principal culprit in the evanescence of individualism is the American system of compulsory education, its misguided administrators and its badly educated teachers "with minds of really crushing banality." Their crime is what they do to "subjective" youngsters—the kind of kids, says Friedenberg, who "want to discover who they are" while "the school wants to help them 'make something out of themselves!' They want to know where they are; the school wants to help them get somewhere. They want to learn how to live with themselves; the school wants to teach them how to get along with others. They want to learn how to tell what is right for them; the school wants to teach them to give the responses that will earn them rewards in the classroom and in social situations." The implication plainly is that these ends are in conflict, that the conflict is ruinous, and that the purposes he ascribes to the school are inappropriate. Yet these public values war with the private impulses in each of us—during our school years as before and after them—and we live out our lives trying to reconcile them. Friedenberg has described nothing more or less sinister than the collision of id and superego at the foundation of Freudian thought. The schools are no more culpable as an enforcer of acquiescence than any other institution in our society. . . . (p. 30)

Clearly, Friedenberg is one of the Good Guys, but the terrain he cultivates throughout this book is very soggy. He passionately hopes, for example, that the Negro will not consent to be homogenized as part of our spiceless, suburban middle class, for the Negroes are a "people whose moral vision has been . . . preserved and sharpened by exclusion from opportunities for self-betrayal as well as self-advancement." The notion that cultural deprivation inspires loftier moral vision may be acceptable as theology, but as pertinent social criticism it is, to say the least, highly arguable. (p. 31)

> Richard Kluger, "The Pied Piper of Davis, California," in The New Republic (reprinted by permission of The New Republic; © 1965 The New Republic, Inc.), Vol. 153, Nos. 6 & 7, August 7, 1965, pp. 30-1.

ROBERT COLES

In this strong-minded and often brilliant book ["**Coming of Age in America**"], Edgar Friedenberg warns that, for all our concern, the hypocrisy and callousness of the market place or the political arena have saturated the schools. It is not easy to read Mr. Friedenberg; he has an unsettling willingness to speak sharply about what he sees, even when to do so is to raise doubts about the cherished values of the American middle-class and the purposes of our system of compulsory public education. (p. 6)

I think Mr. Friedenberg's book weakest . . . in its almost unqualified emphasis on the school's power to compel acquiescence. The author largely ignores the complicated interplay of individual psychological growth and *its* needs for social organization.

Though Mr. Friedenberg acknowledges his admiration for Erik Erikson, he might well have drawn more heavily on his extraordinary work, and for that matter, the excellent psychoanalytic literature on youth and adolescence. . . . There are, after all, thousands of American youth whose lives, past and present, put into question some of Mr. Friedenberg's fears. . . . (pp. 6, 29)

Life in this nation is simply not as grim and empty as some critics insist. And human beings are very complicated and very unpredictable. The schools are but one part of life. Any critic of the schools must somehow account for the large number of young people who do conform to admittedly shameful trends in our classrooms and go on to live genuinely kind, useful and thoroughly imaginative lives. . . .

Edgar Friedenberg is also concerned that we see the fatal consequences to our children of our various public sins. At times he has strained too hard; nevertheless, his intention is that the hearts of more youths be sustained. One can only hope that such a spirited voice—in many ways to very angrily, fervently, and morally American—will be heard over the land. (p. 29)

> *Robert Coles, "That They May Become All That They Can Be," in* The New York Times Book Review *(© 1965 by The New York Times Company; reprinted by permission), August 15, 1965, pp. 6, 29.*

JONATHAN KOZOL

If there is any reason at all for hesitation in praising ["**Coming of Age in America**"], it might be only the unusually romantic wistfulness with which Mr. Friedenberg singles out and idealizes the Negro as some sort of still unspoiled and still uncorrupted child. His terror at the thought of Negro assimilation into the stream of those common values which he has just been describing is understandable enough, but it leads him—in the book's last chapter—into passages of naive panegyric which would somewhat embarrass, I think, even that very minority population with which he is most centrally concerned.

Despite such moments, however, the book as a whole remains one of the most insightful condemnations of American education that I have ever read. The essays are eclectic, not wholly unified, and at times intemperate, but they are consistently eloquent and they rise on many occasions above the level of conventional "social science" to something like an inspired social tract.

> *Jonathan Kozol, "Are They What Adults Make Them?" in* The Christian Science Monitor *(reprinted by permission from* The Christian Science Monitor; *© 1965 The Christian Science Publishing Society; all rights reserved), September 9, 1965, p. 7.*

MICHAEL VINCENT MILLER

I am not taking issue with Friedenberg's thesis [in **Coming of Age in America**] that high school students learn to think along utilitarian and public relations lines. His research results for the most part do bear out this thesis. But if it is true that the responses of the group being tested are conditioned by expec-

tations that the tests themselves create, then these results do not add very much to what is said elsewhere in the book. Friedenberg the social critic, who dominates most of **Coming of Age in America,** seems to me far more perceptive and interesting than the Friedenberg who puts in an appearance as a professional research sociologist. (p. 255)

> *Michael Vincent Miller, "The Journey to Identity," in* The Nation *(copyright 1965 The Nation magazine, The Nation Associates, Inc.), Vol. 201, No. 12, October 18, 1965, pp. 254-55.*

D'ARCY McNICKLE

One problem in reading Friedenberg is that he sets off so many firecrackers, often in a single sentence, that one can't always be sure of the target area, or who may have taken a blast from an occasional round of live shot. However, there are enough clean hits on target [in **The Dignity of Youth and Other Atavisms**] to compel respect for the marksmanship. The one bull's-eye that is repeatedly smacked dead center with every manner of missile is the public high school. And since we are interested here in contrasting the process by which young people enter adult society in a tribal folk world, and in an industrial urban world such as America has become, we have in the Friedenberg volume a set of observations which should persuade Indians to stay with their drum-beating, and nontribal Americans to run, not walk, to the nearest exit. . . .

In general, he finds that compulsory school laws—which are justified on the grounds that popular government can only succeed where there is an educated citizenry—limit the freedom of the growing child and subject him to needless hostilities, without actually providing for his education. The age limit is an artificial device which is not correlated to any achievement level, and there is no remedy for failure of the school to provide services of a minimum quality. If the student withdraws from school because his needs are not being served, he becomes an offender, and probably an alien as well.

That schools do fail to meet the needs of their students is part of the general argument. The failure is at different levels. It may be failure in content. . . .

But the more pervading failure derives from policy and value concepts. . . . American public schools, for various reasons, some of which are political and some having to do with the status motives of teachers and administrators, are not designed to function at [a] creative level. They pursue instead a goal of fixing "a common pattern of values and responses among adolescents from a diversity of class and ethnic backgrounds"—the melting-pot response to cultural diversity. . . .

The disquieting thought that emerges from this analysis . . . is that the failure of the school to respect and nurture individual strengths must result in the production of adults whose growth stopped short of full potential. And yet, as adults in a democratic society, these are the electorate, entitled, quoting from Ortega y Gasset, "to give force of law to notions born in the café. . . . The commonplace mind, knowing itself to be commonplace, has the assurance to proclaim the rights of the commonplace and to impose them wherever it will."

In trying to find a way around so awkward a development, Friedenberg backs himself into a corner from which no exit is visible, unless he has a trap door to be revealed in a later publication. (p. 366)

D'Arcy McNickle, "Two Ways to Grow Up," in The Nation (copyright 1966 The Nation magazine, The Nation Associates, Inc.), Vol. 202, No. 13, March 28, 1966, pp. 365-66.*

THE TIMES LITERARY SUPPLEMENT

Professor Friedenberg, more Laingian frequently than his subject [in **R. D. Laing**], . . . brings us to the ultimate impossibility of everything with the cheeriness of one of those radio astronomers foreseeing the universe sucked into a black hole of antimatter. . . .

A brief and lame conclusion suggests that the counter-culture may offer an answer to the dilemma; lame because, as Professor Friedenberg's logic must surely recognize, a counter-culture can only exist by having something to counter. If it became *the* culture, the same problems of management and government would arise; nor would the British, alienated or otherwise, surrender without bloodshed their suburban semis for communes or their pubs for pot. These entertaining fantasies of Professor Friedenberg's, which take his author's insights and prophecies to ruthlessly logical extremes, would not bring a reader who was new to Laing any closer to his real meanings. What in fact do the key concepts, alienation and inauthenticity, actually mean for Laing himself? What are we alienated from, and how is life to be lived authentically?

"The Human Sickness," in The Times Literary Supplement *(© Times Newspapers Ltd. (London) 1974; reproduced from* The Times Literary Supplement *by permission), No. 3751, January 25, 1974, p. 71.*

ROBERT BOYERS

[**R. D. Laing**] is a speculative work that tells us little about Laing that we did not already know. Nevertheless it is an instructive and lively little book that attempts to think about a whole range of cultural issues that continue to fascinate many of us. Friedenberg uses Laing as an occasion to ask a variety of questions about the relation between personal authenticity and social responsibility, about psychiatry as a potentially life-denying normative institution, and about the blight that is mass democracy American-style. Here and there Laing disappears from view, and the thread of the argument seems to have been lost; but Friedenberg's book is a relatively genial polemic, speculative and argumentative by turns; it is difficult not to appreciate the tact and generosity of Friedenberg's approach.

The book asks important questions and implicitly directs a vague response, but its very commitment to tactfulness and a genial counterculturalism prevents it from pursuing its arguments. In the first place the author is "hung up" (Friedenberg's impression) on being fair to his subjects, so that even when he persuasively reveals disastrous omissions and misrepresentations in Laing, he draws back almost at once from what he has said as though the issue were of little moment. This happens so frequently that one suspects the operation of a principle. . . .

We expect brilliant social critics like Friedenberg to suggest that their counterculture comrades have failed to address the essentials implicit in their own arguments. Laing's position is compromised by his refusal to ask the kinds of questions Friedenberg raises. At one point Friedenberg goes so far as to indicate, briefly, that Laing's identification with his patients is itself a risky enterprise, though clearly admirable in purely human terms. . . . Having said as much, Friedenberg drops

the point once again and leaves his reader uncomfortable at the prospect that the book will not return to it.

The dissatisfaction with Laing to which Friedenberg gives voice finally goes a good deal beyond Laing, though his work is a suitable focus. . . . (p. 20)

As a champion of the counterculture, Edgar Friedenberg has long wished to proclaim the benefits of autonomy, but his understanding of social dynamics has always prevented him from arriving at rude or hysterical generalizations. Thus, though he wants to embrace Laing, to participate in an open combat with the dominant forces in the culture, he recognizes all too well the difficulty of espousing freedom under conditions that demand constraint, and frequently reward people substantially for the sacrifices they make.

There is no doubting the fact that Friedenberg understands the weaknesses in Laing's entire canon. There is, for example, his disciplined intuition that ultimately it is impossible for most men to will the kind of freedom Laing would have them struggle for—in Friedenberg's view, men in culture necessarily respond to severe constraints whether or not they have been officially conditioned to. Group membership confers a variety of advantages and problems, and there is no use in pretending that one can deliberately decide what kinds of freedom he will have. (p. 21)

Laing doesn't hesitate, in his own books, to quote from Marx, Marcuse and others, but one feels he does not sufficiently understand what is meant by necessity, that the unavoidable is a condition of social life which no amount of liberated willing can altogether alter. These are facts of life that Friedenberg understands well. Had he insisted on such facts throughout his book, he'd have accomplished more than the modest probing and pointing no serious reader can fail to commend, and avoided the sentimental identification with Laingian counterculturalism toward which his book finally tends. In drawing back from the painful consequences of his own brilliant insights, Friedenberg demonstrates anew how hard it is for men of good sense to resist the transcendental and libertarian impulses American writers have for so long enthusiastically entertained. (p. 22)

Robert Boyers, "Counterculturalism," in The New Republic *(reprinted by permission of* The New Republic; © 1974 The New Republic, Inc.), Vol. 170, No. 20, May 18, 1974, pp. 20-2.*

WILSON CAREY McWILLIAMS

[There] is a great deal to be said in support of Friedenberg's analysis [in **"The Disposal of Liberty and Other Industrial Wastes"**], especially his willingness to trace the roots of our malaise to industrialism and the very structure of modernity itself. However, despite the sweeping nature of his critique, Friedenberg's political vision is curiously orthodox. (p. 31)

When all is said and done, Friedenberg comes down again on the side of the nation-state and political democracy, despite his criticism of both. He suggests only that classes and groups abandon any concern for the "common good" and speak solely for their interests. Compromises will be arranged by politicians, and definitions of the "public welfare"—which Friedenberg agrees must sometimes override "particular liberties"—will presumably be left to the "élite." But this argument reproduces the American political orthodoxy of the last quarter-century, the "group theory of politics," with its emphasis on pluralism, the "end of ideology" and a state restricted to the role of "broker." The good society, to Friedenberg, consists of the interplay of self-interests combined with a rather romantic, but wholly individualistic idea of "liberty." And both are about as radical, in America, as James Madison and Ralph Waldo Emerson.

Whatever his abilities as a critic, Friedenberg shows little genius as a moralist. He is eloquent both in pointing out that an "equality of opportunity" only masks the inequality, indignity and *ressentiment* which are its results, and in calling for "moral equality" instead. But Friedenberg has never posed as an egalitarian, so one's suspicions are increased when he comments that while moral equality is an "*a priori* assumption" it "is not, and is not held to be, an inalterable condition." This sounds rather like "All animals are equal, but some are more equal than others."

Indeed it is. Moral equality for Friedenberg means that all people are entitled to "what they need" for their "self-realization." But not all people will get the same things—some people *need* privilege and others do not—nor will these "morally equal" human beings be able to decide what they need. (pp. 31-2)

Friedenberg is rightly concerned to hold the majority responsible for offenses in which it participates or to which it acquiesces, but he seems unaware that the poor, the criminal, and the outcast yearn for a dignity based on a sense of contribution—and feel deprived of a right to be *held* responsible. Welfare with less bureaucracy may be more humane; it is still welfare. To be permissive, or to tolerate lower class behavior intended to provoke, shows not a devotion to liberty, but indifference and contempt.

Although Friedenberg is ready to proclaim the incapacity of the majority, he is nevertheless disturbed that mental patients are deemed incapable of judging their own best interests; and in relation to narcotics he declares that "it is not necessary to control the sale of poison to potential addicts—only its surreptitious administration to the unwary." Yet he would disdain the same argument being applied to mass advertising or the market economy. Friedenberg has one line ready, however: drugs liberate the mind from repressive society. "Pushing drugs on kids in 1975 is rather like teaching blacks to read in 1855." One wonders how many addicts Friedenberg has ever seen, or whether he would argue that the British opium traders advanced the liberty of the Chinese against Manchu oppression.

Like Friedenberg's rather confused arguments about crime and criminals, these arguments suggest a somewhat indifferent and contemptuous compassion. Friedenberg says that while the excesses, hatreds and violence of the majority may be "understandable," they are still "intolerable." So, one would think, is crime, political terrorism, or the auto-anesthesia and self-destructiveness of narcotics. That Friedenberg does not draw the parallel only indicates that, despite his disclaimers, he does feel the middle and working classes should be held morally responsible for their plight. His concern for the poor and the outcast, however paternal, hints at an underlying belief that they must be excused when understood because no more can be expected of them. Friedenberg's embrace dehumanizes as it enfolds.

This is not the first time that the unfortunate have suffered at the hands of their self-proclaimed friends. In fact, Friedenberg's book is itself a lengthy example of bourgeois *ressentiment,* characterized by an indignation so extreme as to lack moral discrimination.

At its best, the bourgeoisie can do better than that. Friedenberg wishes that Bob Cratchit, in Dickens's "A Christmas Carol," had angrily rejected Scrooge: this would have made the tale "far more moral." Friedenberg does not seem to care that Cratchit would have been sacrificing the welfare of his family for a moment's verbal satisfaction. He seems even less aware that self-sacrifice can be just as authentic—or more authentic—than self-assertion. Freedom, for the liberal tradition, is mastery, and Friedenberg speaks with the voice of that heritage; the old aristocracy, which he professes to admire, knew that self-sacrifice is near the essence of nobility.

"The Disposal of Liberty" illustrates the fact that in any society as democratized as America any criticism of the public is a criticism of oneself. (p. 32)

> *Wilson Carey McWilliams, "'The Disposal of Liberty and Other Industrial Wastes',"* in *The New York Times Book Review (© 1975 by The New York Times Company; reprinted by permission), October 12, 1975, pp. 31-2.*

ROBERT LEKACHMAN

Musing on Friedenberg's vision of his society [in *The Disposal of Liberty and Other Industrial Wastes*], one which approximates in cordiality H. L. Mencken and Gore Vidal, I find myself muttering, to my own astonishment, that things can't really be that bad in the home of the occasionally brave and the land of the partially free. The public, despite the Mayaguez spasm, has not reacted to American defeat in Indochina by clamor for victory elsewhere. In state after state, the politicians are decriminalizing marijuana. As Andrew Levison pointed out in his useful *The Working Class Majority*, despite the stereotypes (happily embraced by Friedenberg), blue collar workers were no more belligerent on Vietnam than the general population, nor by the usual measures any more authoritarian in attitude. And although Ford's pardon of Nixon badly confused the civics lesson that Congress was administering during Watergate, some residual decency must have stirred the psyches of that huge section of the Nixon majority which turned against their hero as the extent and variety of his perfidy gradually dawned upon them.

I'd best stop right here before Friedenberg turns me into an unlikely American patriot. With most of this polemic's details, I in fact agree. Unlike Friedenberg, I retain a little hope in the working class and even the AFL-CIO.

> *Robert Lekachman, "Half a Hope Is Better Than None" (© 1975, The Washington Post), in* The Guardian Weekly, *Vol. 113, No. 18, November 2, 1975, p. 20.*

STEVEN DEUTSCH

In [*The Disposal of Liberty and Other Industrial Wastes*] Edgar Friedenberg develops themes which he has examined in prior work on youth and schools and the shaping of values and behaviors in American society. I have appreciated his work and learned from it. As an essay it is provocative and well done. We learn a lot from it, and it is full of useful and challenging ideas. Yet I believe it falls short in its political sociological analysis.

The book is addressed to exploring the inability of the modern industrial society to deal with the perpetuation of an underclass and the resulting *ressentiment*—the projection of bitterness by victims onto others (illustrated by poor whites in West Virginia burning textbooks which examine ways in which they themselves are victimized in the society). He argues that freedom is absent in all societies, yet the book is essentially an indictment of corporate capitalism. (pp. 332-33)

[While] he discusses authority throughout this book, he does not address the range of work and evidence to support the challenges to the legitimacy of authority in Western societies. He argues that Milgram's studies revealed contempt for authority rather than respect for it, and he states that people who respect authority are more sensitive to its abuses. . . . Is this really the case? Is the erosion of legitimacy of authority tied to respect or contempt for authority? Friedenberg's assertions cry out for further discussion, documentation, and debate.

A major point of the book is to examine the social psychology of mass behavior. He attacks the masses more than the elites in this society. He wants to explore the "good Germans" thesis, why "the people are participating in the repression of what they ought to know" . . . and what leads to the abandonment of their will. This discussion is exciting and insightful; it is the outline of solid political sociology. But it fails to give a structural analysis of *why* the masses have come to this point, how the dynamic works, and what the sources of challenge have been. He approaches a [Seymour Martin] Lipset viewpoint on working class authoritarianism . . . but does not take us far enough along to critically view the processes that impinge on the working class, the evidence of resistance, or the challenges. He explores the relationship between economic growth and the conception of liberty but then asserts that economic depressions lead to greater reverence for authority. . . . [Why] does Friedenberg fail to see the working class response to its condition expressed in industrial sabotage, wildcat strikes, ghetto riots, oppositional electoral politics, and the many, many indicators which suggest something other than reinforcement for traditional sources of authority? Perhaps this is partly due to the time in which the book was written (he refers to July 1973 in some places, Nixon's resignation in others), and it would be important to see how Friedenberg might respond to the events and literature of the past few years.

Sometimes I think he asks the wrong question; for example, he ponders why "the movement, as such still [has] no proud constituency and especially no *conservative* constituency." . . . But the point is that these were movements for social changes, not conservation, even though some "fundamentalist" values such as the Bill of Rights were espoused. (pp. 333-34)

Other times Friedenberg is wonderfully insightful and in a few words makes solid points. When he talks about "the state [as] both the guarantor of liberty and its enemy" . . . and the "loss of authority by the state cannot but enhance the legitimacy of the giant corporations" . . . he is making keen arguments and projections. Similarly his analysis of the role of the state as "the source of nearly all the violence in the world" . . . is connected quite brilliantly to his observation that "in democratic mass societies severe social conflict is usually a form of class conflict." . . . I just wish that his excellent metaphors and illustrations (such as the politics of social control with airport security and marijuana as cases in point) were matched by some structural analysis that documented the process of *ressentiment* and mass political social psychology. Furthermore, I wonder if the concluding line of the book is the real Friedenberg as cynic? Or is he a cynic? Has the disposal clogged and is there a challenge to legitimacy of authority that speaks to liberty? (p. 334)

Steven Deutsch, "Book Reviews: 'The Disposal of Liberty and Other Industrial Wastes'," in Contemporary Sociology *(copyright © 1978 American Sociological Association), Vol. 7, No. 3, May, 1978, pp. 332-34.*

THOMAS BUTSON

[Edgar Z. Friedenberg] can't understand Canadians and their ways of doing business. . . .

[It is the] supremacy of Parliament that most disturbs Mr. Friedenberg. In **"Deference to Authority,"** he points out quite rightly that Canada's Bill of Rights is a feeble document, subject to the whims of successive Parliaments, that Parliament itself is subject to the policy of the Government—that is, the Cabinet—and that the Canadian Supreme Court is not the constitutional review board that John Marshall and his legal descendants created in the United States. (p. 13)

In Canada, Government operates not, as Mr. Friedenberg's title suggests, by undue deference, but by trust. The Ottawa Government is formed from the party with the largest number of-seats in the House of Commons or from a coalition of parties that can maintain a majority in the House. . . .

It is equally mistaken to deduce from their adoption of parliamentary government that Canadians are unnaturally deferential to anyone in authority. By the same token, it is a mistake to cite, as Mr. Friedenberg does, statistics purporting to show that Canadians put an abnormal number of miscreants behind bars. Canadians can, and often do, cite those same statistics to argue that Detroit, Houston and—yes—New York are unsafe at almost any pedestrian speed precisely because Americans don't lock up enough muggers and murderers.

What exactly does Mr. Friedenberg mean when he complains that there is not enough violence in Canada, or deplores the lack of graffiti on Canadian walls or the fact that Canadians rely too much on ombudsmen or coroners to redress official wrongs? If he is saying that Canadians have been hypocritical in their treatment of Indians and nonwhite minorities, he is right. If he is saying that the Royal Canadian Mounted Police abused their mandate when they burned down a barn suspected of housing a Quebec separatist cell, he is right. If he is saying that Canadians have troubles with Quebec political nationalism or Albertan economic nationalism, he is right. Even Pierre Elliott Trudeau would agree.

But if he is saying, behind his screen of jarring puns and word plays, that Canadians are misguided because 200 years ago they declined to follow the republican ideas exported to Lower Canada by Ben Franklin through the power of a printing press and by Benedict Arnold at the point of a gun, he is mistaken. After all, a written constitution is no inalienable guarantee of liberty. Just ask Andrei D. Sakharov. (p. 48)

Thomas Butson, "The Case of Canada," in The New York Times Book Review *(© 1980 by The New York Times Company; reprinted by permission), May 18, 1980, pp. 13, 48.*

J. M. CAMERON

Friedenberg seems continually astonished [in *Deference to Authority: The Case of Canada*] that Canada is not the United States. It is more deferential, more secretive, quieter, less litigious, concerned more with good government than with the rights of individuals; above all it lacks a written constitution and a foundation document in which inalienable rights are inscribed. Sometimes it is almost as though he cannot credit that men and women with two eyes, a nose, and a mouth, and speaking North American English, can exist happily under such conditions. Rightly, he sees the sovereignty of Parliament, a doctrine derived from Britain, as the fundamental principle of Canadian law and politics; but he is a little scandalized by the principle according to which Parliament can do anything that is not naturally or logically impossible, that is, that it can do anything except change the laws of physics and what happened in the past. (p. 31)

Canadians lack the conviction, deep (so Friedenberg believes) in the American political consciousness, "that the state and its apparatus are the natural enemies of freedom." He even believes that this Canadian defect is reflected in Canada's preferences and achievements in the arts. He rightly picks out ballet as an art form in which Canada excels. But this is "the art that provides least opportunity for spontaneity or improvisation. . . . As a form . . . it is peculiarly unsuited to exploring the implications of human experience, just as it is peculiarly suited to expressing the feelings associated with such experience."

This may be true, though the theory of art assumed strikes me as disputable. But when he goes on to state that as an art form ballet is "in its North American context . . . inherently counter-revolutionary," this is surely an unnecessarily twiddly piece of decoration stuck onto his argument. . . . (pp. 31-2)

[One] of Friedenberg's most powerful themes [is] the widespread Canadian habit of secrecy, defended up to the last possible moment by the law, and then, when the secret is no more, the acceptance of the immunity of authority from the consequence of its misdeeds. This is abundantly illustrated by the proceedings of the McDonald Commission of inquiry into the conduct of the Royal Canadian Mounted Police, by the proceedings and by such of the evidence as has been published. It became known, and this led to the establishment of the commission, that the RCMP had for many years, and especially during the Quebec political crisis of 1970, engaged in illegal activities. . . .

Friedenberg argues, and I think he is right, that the point of the McDonald Commission was to shield delinquent members of the RCMP from the legal consequences of their acts, and that this confers on them a quite different status from that of private citizens who are without reluctance prosecuted for similar breaches of the law. . . .

The Canadian presumption, Friedenberg argues, is that public officials are concerned with the common good and may do with impunity what would get a private citizen into trouble with the law. The RCMP is, in fact, still a sacred and venerated institution in Canadian life; and it was striking that the Progressive Conservatives, in their short time of office, quite lost that concern for civil liberties the case of the RCMP had persuaded them to show while they were in opposition.

We may allow that Friedenberg has made a strong case . . . for his view that Canada is a deferential society, in which those in authority are presumed to have good intentions when they do something illegal or morally off-color, in which the proceedings of government are impenetrable by the common man, and in which the legal and constitutional arrangements are such that men lack or have a weak hold upon the notion of the inalienable rights of man. He repeatedly tells us that in practice the difference between Canada and the United States isn't very great, but that somehow the social atmosphere of Canada is, as it were, thicker, more cloying, even perhaps relatively boring. I see what he means by this. But I think the case for a written constitution, rights expressed in legal formulas, and the rest, as against an unwritten constitution and parliamentary sovereignty, is less powerful than he wants it to be. (p. 32)

J. M. Cameron, "Aimez-vous Canada?: 'Deference to Authority: The Case of Canada'," in The New York Review of Books *(reprinted with permission from* The New York Review of Books; *copyright © 1980 Nyrev, Inc.), Vol. XXVII, No. 12, July 17, 1980, pp. 31-2.*

Milton Friedman
1912-

Friedman is a prominent American economist and recipient of the 1976 Nobel Prize in Economics for his work in monetary economics and consumption theory. He is an advocate of the quantity theory of money, contending that the aggregate amount of money in circulation has a determinative influence on the national economy. As such, he opposes the emphasis that Keynesian economics places on regulation of tax rates and governmental spending. Friedman gained public attention in the sixties for his iconoclastic monetarist theories, and as professor of economics at the University of Chicago, brought national prominence to a new center of economics known as the Chicago School. A classical liberal in the nineteenth-century mold of Adam Smith, Friedman believes in the laissez-faire principle of creative cooperation between individuals in a free-market system and fears the baleful effects of discretionary government power. These concerns are expounded in *Capitalism and Freedom* (1962), written with his wife, Rose Director Friedman, which argues that competitive capitalism, a system of economic freedom, is a necessary condition for political freedom. In *Free to Choose* (1980), also written with his wife, Friedman continues his attack on the proliferation of governmental programs, offering such alternative proposals as a negative income tax to replace the welfare system and a voucher plan to improve the educational system. Critics favoring interventionist government policies have attacked Friedman's application of free-market analysis to social programs for its refusal to use government as a tool for translating gains in technology and economic growth into reduced poverty and increased social justice. However much one agrees or disagrees with the social policy conclusions Friedman draws from his economic analysis, most would agree with Arthur Kemp that few economists "have had as great or greater impact on professional economic thought in the twentieth century." Friedman has been a contributing editor for *Newsweek,* has acted as economic advisor to Richard Nixon and Barry Goldwater, and was formerly president of the American Economic Association. (See also *Contemporary Authors,* Vols. 1-4, rev. ed.; *Contemporary Authors New Revision Series,* Vol. 1.)

Courtesy of Milton Friedman

Excerpt from *CAPITALISM AND FREEDOM*

In a much quoted passage in his inaugural address, President Kennedy said, "Ask not what your country can do for you—ask what you can do for your country." It is a striking sign of the temper of our times that the controversy about this passage centered on its origin and not on its content. Neither half of the statement expresses a relation between the citizen and his government that is worthy of the ideals of free men in a free society. The paternalistic "what your country can do for you" implies that government is the patron, the citizen the ward, a view that is at odds with the free man's belief in his own responsibility for his own destiny. The organismic, "what you can do for your country" implies that government is the master or the deity, the citizen, the servant or the votary. To the free man, the country is the collection of individuals who compose it, not something over and above them. He is proud of a common heritage and loyal to common traditions. But he

regards government as a means, an instrumentality, neither a grantor of favors and gifts, nor a master or god to be blindly worshipped and served. He recognizes no national goal except as it is the consensus of the goals that the citizens severally serve. He recognizes no national purpose except as it is the consensus of the purposes for which the citizens severally strive.

The free man will ask neither what his country can do for him nor what he can do for his country. He will ask rather "What can I and my compatriots do through government" to help us discharge our individual responsibilities, to achieve our several goals and purposes, and above all, to protect our freedom? And he will accompany this question with another: How can we keep the government we create from becoming a Frankenstein that will destroy the very freedom we establish it to protect? (pp. 1-2)

How can we benefit from the promise of government while avoiding the threat to freedom? Two broad principles embodied in our Constitution give an answer that has preserved our freedom so far, though they have been violated repeatedly in practice while proclaimed as precept.

First, the scope of government must be limited. Its major function must be to protect our freedom both from the enemies outside our gates and from our fellow-citizens: to preserve law and order, to enforce private contracts, to foster competitive markets. Beyond this major function, government may enable us at times to accomplish jointly what we would find it more difficult or expensive to accomplish severally. However, any such use of government is fraught with danger. We should not and cannot avoid using government in this way. But there should be a clear and large balance of advantages before we do. By relying primarily on voluntary co-operation and private enterprise, in both economic and other activities, we can insure that the private sector is a check on the powers of the governmental sector and an effective protection of freedom of speech, of religion, and of thought.

The second broad principle is that government power must be dispersed. If government is to exercise power, better in the county than in the state, better in the state than in Washington. If I do not like what my local community does, be it in sewage disposal, or zoning, or schools, I can move to another local community, and though few may take this step, the mere possibility acts as a check. If I do not like what my state does, I can move to another. If I do not like what Washington imposes, I have few alternatives in this world of jealous nations. (pp. 2-3)

[*Capitalism and Freedom*'s] major theme is the role of competitive capitalism—the organization of the bulk of economic activity through private enterprise operating in a free market—as a system of economic freedom and a necessary condition for political freedom. Its minor theme is the role that government should play in a society dedicated to freedom and relying primarily on the market to organize economic activity. (p. 4)

It is widely believed that politics and economics are separate and largely unconnected; that individual freedom is a political problem and material welfare an economic problem; and that any kind of political arrangements can be combined with any kind of economic arrangements. The chief contemporary manifestation of this idea is the advocacy of "democratic socialism" by many who condemn out of hand the restrictions on individual freedom imposed by "totalitarian socialism" in Russia, and who are persuaded that it is possible for a country to adopt the essential features of Russian economic arrangements and yet to ensure individual freedom through political arrangements. [My] thesis . . . is that such a view is a delusion, that there is an intimate connection between economics and politics, that only certain combinations of political and economic arrangements are possible, and that in particular, a society which is socialist cannot also be democratic, in the sense of guaranteeing individual freedom.

Economic arrangements play a dual role in the promotion of a free society. On the one hand, freedom in economic arrangements is itself a component of freedom broadly understood, so economic freedom is an end in itself. In the second place, economic freedom is also an indispensable means toward the achievement of political freedom. (pp. 7-8)

Viewed as a means to the end of political freedom, economic arrangements are important because of their effect on the concentration or dispersion of power. The kind of economic organization that provides economic freedom directly, namely, competitive capitalism, also promotes political freedom because it separates economic power from political power and in this way enables the one to offset the other. (p. 9)

Fundamentally, there are only two ways of co-ordinating the economic activities of millions. One is central direction in-

volving the use of coercion—the technique of the army and of the modern totalitarian state. The other is voluntary co-operation of individuals—the technique of the market place.

The possibility of co-ordination through voluntary co-operation rests on the elementary—yet frequently denied—proposition that both parties to an economic transaction benefit from it, *provided the transaction is bi-laterally voluntary and informed.*

Exchange can therefore bring about co-ordination without coercion. A working model of a society organized through voluntary exchange is a *free private enterprise exchange economy*—what we have been calling competitive capitalism. (p. 13)

The basic requisite is the maintenance of law and order to prevent physical coercion of one individual by another and to enforce contracts voluntarily entered into, thus giving substance to "private". Aside from this, perhaps the most difficult problems arise from monopoly—which inhibits effective freedom by denying individuals alternatives to the particular exchange—and from "neighborhood effects"—effects on third parties for which it is not feasible to charge or recompense them. (p. 14)

So long as effective freedom of exchange is maintained, the central feature of the market organization of economic activity is that it prevents one person from interfering with another in respect of most of his activities. The consumer is protected from coercion by the seller because of the presence of other sellers with whom he can deal. The seller is protected from coercion by the consumer because of other consumers to whom he can sell. The employee is protected from coercion by the employer because of other employers for whom he can work, and so on. And the market does this impersonally and without centralized authority. (pp. 14-15)

The existence of a free market does not of course eliminate the need for government. On the contrary, government is essential both as a forum for determining the "rules of the game" and as an umpire to interpret and enforce the rules decided on. What the market does is to reduce greatly the range of issues that must be decided through political means, and thereby to minimize the extent to which government need participate directly in the game. The characteristic feature of action through political channels is that it tends to require or enforce substantial conformity. The great advantage of the market, on the other hand, is that it permits wide diversity. It is, in political terms, a system of proportional representation. Each man can vote, as it were, for the color of tie he wants and get it; he does not have to see what color the majority wants and then, if he is in the minority, submit.

It is this feature of the market that we refer to when we say that the market provides economic freedom. But this characteristic also has implications that go far beyond the narrowly economic. Political freedom means the absence of coercion of a man by his fellow men. The fundamental threat to freedom is power to coerce, be it in the hands of a monarch, a dictator, an oligarchy, or a momentary majority. The preservation of freedom requires the elimination of such concentration of power to the fullest possible extent and the dispersal and distribution of whatever power cannot be eliminated—a system of checks and balances. By removing the organization of economic activity from the control of political authority, the market eliminates this source of coercive power. It enables economic strength to be a check to political power rather than a reinforcement. (p. 15)

In the 1920's and the 1930's, intellectuals in the United States were overwhelmingly persuaded that capitalism was a defective system inhibiting economic well-being and thereby freedom, and that the hope for the future lay in a greater measure of deliberate control by political authorities over economic affairs. The conversion of the intellectuals was not achieved by the example of any actual collectivist society, though it undoubtedly was much hastened by the establishment of a communist society in Russia and the glowing hopes placed in it. The conversion of the intellectuals was achieved by a comparison between the existing state of affairs, with all its injustices and defects, and a hypothetical state of affairs as it might be. The actual was compared with the ideal. (p. 196)

The attitudes of that time are still with us. There is still a tendency to regard any existing government intervention as desirable, to attribute all evils to the market, and to evaluate new proposals for government control in their ideal form, as they might work if run by able, disinterested men, free from the pressure of special interest groups. The proponents of limited government and free enterprise are still on the defensive.

Yet, conditions have changed. We now have several decades of experience with governmental intervention. It is no longer necessary to compare the market as it actually operates and government intervention as it ideally might operate. We can compare the actual with the actual.

If we do so, it is clear that the difference between the actual operation of the market and its ideal operation—great though it undoubtedly is—is as nothing compared to the difference between the actual effects of government intervention and their intended effects. Who can now see any great hope for the advancement of men's freedom and dignity in the massive tyranny and despotism that hold sway in Russia? (p. 197)

Let us look closer to home. Which if any of the great "reforms" of past decades has achieved its objectives? Have the good intentions of the proponents of these reforms been realized?

Regulation of the railroads to protect the consumer quickly became an instrument whereby the railroads could protect themselves from the competition of newly emerging rivals—at the expense, of course, of the consumer.

An income tax initially enacted at low rates and later seized upon as a means to redistribute income in favor of the lower classes has become a facade, covering loopholes and special provisions that render rates that are highly graduated on paper largely ineffective. . . . An income tax intended to reduce inequality and promote the diffusion of wealth has in practice fostered reinvestment of corporate earnings, thereby favoring the growth of large corporations, inhibiting the operation of the capital market, and discouraging the establishment of new enterprises.

Monetary reforms, intended to promote stability in economic activity and prices, exacerbated inflation during and after World War I and fostered a higher degree of instability thereafter than had ever been experienced before. The monetary authorities they established bear primary responsibility for converting a serious economic contraction into the catastrophe of the Great Depression from 1929-33. A system established largely to prevent bank panics produced the most severe banking panic in American history.

An agricultural program intended to help impecunious farmers and to remove what were alleged to be basic dislocations in the organization of agriculture has become a national scandal that has wasted public funds, distorted the use of resources, riveted increasingly heavy and detailed controls on farmers, interfered seriously with United States foreign policy, and withal has done little to help the impecunious farmer. (pp. 197-98)

Social security measures were enacted to make receipt of assistance a matter of right, to eliminate the need for direct relief and assistance. Millions now receive social security benefits. Yet the relief rolls grow and the sums spent on direct assistance mount.

The list can easily be lengthened. . . .

There have been some exceptions. (p. 199)

[But if] a balance be struck, there can be little doubt that the record is dismal. The greater part of the new ventures undertaken by government in the past few decades have failed to achieve their objectives. The United States has continued to progress; its citizens have become better fed, better clothed, better housed, and better transported; class and social distinctions have narrowed; minority groups have become less disadvantaged; popular culture has advanced by leaps and bounds. All this has been the product of the initiative and drive of individuals co-operating through the free market. Government measures have hampered not helped this development. (pp. 199-200)

Is it an accident that so many of the governmental reforms of recent decades have gone awry, that the bright hopes have turned to ashes? Is it simply because the programs are faulty in detail?

I believe the answer is clearly in the negative. The central defect of these measures is that they seek through government to force people to act against their own immediate interests in order to promote a supposedly general interest. They seek to resolve what is supposedly a conflict of interest, or a difference in view about interests, not by establishing a framework that will eliminate the conflict, or by persuading people to have different interests, but by forcing people to act against their own interest. They substitute the values of outsiders for the values of participants; either some telling others what is good for them, or the government taking from some to benefit others. These measures are therefore countered by one of the strongest and most creative forces known to man—the attempt by millions of individuals to promote their own interests, to live their lives by their own values. This is the major reason why the measures have so often had the opposite of the effects intended. It is also one of the major strengths of a free society and explains why governmental regulation does not strangle it. (p. 200)

The preservation and expansion of freedom are today threatened from two directions. The one threat is obvious and clear. It is the external threat coming from the evil men in the Kremlin who promise to bury us. The other threat is far more subtle. It is the internal threat coming from men of good intentions and good will who wish to reform us. Impatient with the slowness of persuasion and example to achieve the great social changes they envision, they are anxious to use the power of the state to achieve their ends and confident of their own ability to do so. Yet if they gained the power, they would fail to achieve their immediate aims and, in addition, would produce a collective state from which they would recoil in horror and of which they would be among the first victims. Concentrated power is not rendered harmless by the good intentions of those who create it.

The two threats unfortunately reinforce one another. Even if we avoid a nuclear holocaust, the threat from the Kremlin requires us to devote a sizable fraction of our resources to our military defense. The importance of government as a buyer of so much of our output, and the sole buyer of the output of many firms and industries, already concentrates a dangerous amount of economic power in the hands of the political authorities, changes the environment in which business operates and the criteria relevant for business success, and in these and other ways endangers a free market. This danger we cannot avoid. But we needlessly intensify it by continuing the present widespread governmental intervention in areas unrelated to the military defense of the nation and by undertaking ever new governmental programs. . . . (pp. 201-02)

I believe that we shall be able to preserve and extend freedom despite the size of the military programs and despite the economic powers already concentrated in Washington. But we shall be able to do so only if we awake to the threat that we face, only if we persuade our fellow men that free institutions offer a surer, if perhaps at times a slower, route to the ends they seek than the coercive power of the state. (p. 202)

> *Milton Friedman with Rose D. Friedman, in their* Capitalism and Freedom *(reprinted by permission of The University of Chicago Press; © 1962 by The University of Chicago), University of Chicago Press, 1962, 202 p.*

Excerpt from *FREE TO CHOOSE: A PERSONAL STATEMENT*

The story of the United States is the story of an economic miracle and a political miracle that was made possible by the translation into practice of two sets of ideas—both, by a curious coincidence, formulated in documents published in the same year, 1776.

One set of ideas was embodied in *The Wealth of Nations,* the masterpiece that established the Scotsman Adam Smith as the father of modern economics. It analyzed the way in which a market system could combine the freedom of individuals to pursue their own objectives with the extensive cooperation and collaboration needed in the economic field to produce our food, our clothing, our housing. Adam Smith's key insight was that both parties to an exchange can benefit and that, *so long as cooperation is strictly voluntary,* no exchange will take place unless both parties do benefit. No external force, no coercion, no violation of freedom is necessary to produce cooperation among individuals all of whom can benefit. (pp. 1-2)

The second set of ideas was embodied in the Declaration of Independence, drafted by Thomas Jefferson to express the general sense of his fellow countrymen. It proclaimed a new nation, the first in history established on the principle that every person is entitled to pursue his own values. . . . (p. 2)

Economic freedom is an essential requisite for political freedom. By enabling people to cooperate with one another without coercion or central direction, it reduces the area over which political power is exercised. In addition, by dispersing power, the free market provides an offset to whatever concentration of political power may arise. The combination of economic and political *power* in the same hands is a sure recipe for tyranny. (pp. 2-3)

Smith and Jefferson alike had seen concentrated government power as a great danger to the ordinary man; they saw the protection of the citizen against the tyranny of government as the perpetual need. . . . To Smith and Jefferson, government's role was as an umpire, not a participant. (p. 4)

Ironically, the very success of economic and political freedom reduced its appeal to later thinkers. The narrowly limited government of the late nineteenth century possessed little concentrated power that endangered the ordinary man. The other side of that coin was that it possessed little power that would enable good people to do good. And in an imperfect world there were still many evils. Indeed, the very progress of society made the residual evils seem all the more objectionable. As always, people took the favorable developments for granted. They forgot the danger to freedom from a strong government. Instead, they were attracted by the good that a stronger government could achieve—if only government power were in the "right" hands. (pp. 4-5)

Emphasis on the responsibility of the individual for his own fate was replaced by emphasis on the individual as a pawn buffeted by forces beyond his control. The view that government's role is to serve as an umpire to prevent individuals from coercing one another was replaced by the view that government's role is to serve as a parent charged with the duty of coercing some to aid others.

These views have dominated developments in the United States during the past half-century. They have led to a growth in government at all levels, as well as to a transfer of power from local government and local control to central government and central control. The government has increasingly undertaken the task of taking from some to give to others in the name of security and equality. One government policy after another has been set up to "regulate" our "pursuits of industry and improvement," standing Jefferson's dictum on its head. . . . (p. 5)

These developments have been produced by good intentions with a major assist from self-interest. Even the strongest supporters of the welfare and paternal state agree that the results have been disappointing. In the government sphere, as in the market, there seems to be an invisible hand, but it operates in precisely the opposite direction from Adam Smith's: an individual who intends only to serve the public interest by fostering government intervention is "led by an invisible hand to promote" private interests, "which was no part of his intention." (pp. 5-6)

The experience of recent years—slowing growth and declining productivity—raises a doubt whether private ingenuity can continue to overcome the deadening effects of government control if we continue to grant ever more power to government, to authorize a "new class" of civil servants to spend ever larger fractions of our income supposedly on our behalf. Sooner or later—and perhaps sooner than many of us expect—an ever bigger government would destroy both the prosperity that we owe to the free market and the human freedom proclaimed so eloquently in the Declaration of Independence.

We have not yet reached the point of no return. We are still free as a people to choose whether we shall continue speeding down the "road to serfdom," as Friedrich Hayek entitled his profound and influential book, or whether we shall set tighter limits on government and rely more heavily on voluntary cooperation among free individuals to achieve our several objectives. (p. 6)

In the United States, in Great Britain, the countries of Western Europe, and in many other countries around the world, there is growing recognition of the dangers of big government, growing dissatisfaction with the policies that have been followed. This shift is being reflected not only in opinion, but also in the political sphere. It is becoming politically profitable for our representatives to sing a different tune—and perhaps even to act differently. We are experiencing another major change in public opinion. We have the opportunity to nudge the change in opinion toward greater reliance on individual initiative and voluntary cooperation, rather than toward the other extreme of total collectivism. (p. 7)

The key insight of Adam Smith's *Wealth of Nations* is misleadingly simple: if an exchange between two parties is voluntary, it will not take place unless both believe they will benefit from it. Most economic fallacies derive from the neglect of this simple insight, from the tendency to assume that there is a fixed pie, that one party can gain only at the expense of another. (p. 13)

Adam Smith's flash of genius was his recognition that the prices that emerged from voluntary transactions between buyers and sellers—for short, in a free market—could coordinate the activity of millions of people, each seeking his own interest, in such a way as to make everyone better off. It was a startling idea then, and it remains one today, that economic order can emerge as the unintended consequence of the actions of many people, each seeking his own interest. (pp. 13-14)

In today's world big government seems pervasive. We may well ask whether there exist any contemporaneous examples of societies that rely primarily on voluntary exchange through the market to organize their economic activity and in which government is limited to . . . [certain] duties.

Perhaps the best example is Hong Kong—a speck of land next to mainland China containing less than 400 square miles with a population of roughly 4.5 million people. The density of population is almost unbelievable—14 times as many people per square mile as in Japan, 185 times as many as in the United States. Yet they enjoy one of the highest standards of living in all of Asia—second only to Japan and perhaps Singapore.

Hong Kong has no tariffs or other restraints on international trade (except for a few "voluntary" restraints imposed by the United States and some other major countries). It has no government direction of economic activity, no minimum wage laws, no fixing of prices. The residents are free to buy from whom they want, to sell to whom they want, to invest however they want, to hire whom they want, to work for whom they want.

Government plays an important role that is limited primarily to . . . four duties interpreted rather narrowly. It enforces law and order, provides a means for formulating the rules of conduct, adjudicates disputes, facilitates transportation and communication, and supervises the issuance of currency. It has provided public housing for arriving refugees from China. Though government spending has grown as the economy has grown, it remains among the lowest in the world as a fraction of the income of the people. As a result, low taxes preserve incentives. Businessmen can reap the benefits of their success but must also bear the costs of their mistakes. (pp. 33-4)

It is often maintained that while a let-alone, limited government policy was feasible in sparsely settled nineteenth-century America, government must play a far larger, indeed dominant, role in a modern urbanized and industrial society. One hour in Hong Kong will dispose of that view.

Our society is what we make it. We can shape our institutions. Physical and human characteristics limit the alternatives available to us. But none prevents us, if we will, from building a society that relies primarily on voluntary cooperation to organize both economic and other activity, a society that preserves and expands human freedom, that keeps government in its place, keeping it our servant and not letting it become our master. (p. 37)

Milton Friedman and Rose Friedman, in their Free to Choose: A Personal Statement *(copyright © 1980, 1979, by Milton Friedman and Rose D. Friedman; reprinted by permission of Harcourt Brace Jovanovich, Inc.), Harcourt, 1980, 338 p.*

FRANK R. BREUL

[Friedman] classifies himself with the Philosophical Radicals who learned their economics from Smith, Malthus, and Ricardo and their politics from Bentham. The essence of his theory [in *Capitalism and Freedom*], therefore, is that laissez faire should be the means of reducing the role of the state in economic affairs and thereby enlarging the role of the individual. The list of present-day governmental activities that he would discard as violations of individual freedom and as unwarranted encroachments by the state is impressive, to say the least. Among the programs he would eliminate immediately are farm price supports, legal minimum wages and maximum prices, the progressive income tax, peacetime conscription, national parks, fair employment practices acts, right-to-work laws, public schools, and the monopoly of the post office in carrying the mail. (p. 201)

Many of the programs that Friedman would so nonchalantly give up are dear to the hearts of all modern progressives. This reviewer, after reading the Introduction and a few chapters, made ready for battle and even looked forward with pleasure to refuting each ancient argument. But when he came across this statement he had some second thoughts: "The heart of the liberal philosophy is a belief in the dignity of the individual, in his freedom to make the most of his capacities and opportunities according to his own lights, subject only to the proviso that he not interfere with the freedom of other individuals to do the same." That is, of course, the basis of Western political philosophy. It is identical to the premise on which we base many of the programs that Friedman would eliminate.

The temptation is to accuse Friedman of laying an ideological smoke screen to hide a Spencerian contempt for the underprivileged and dispossessed. But it soon becomes apparent that such an accusation would be entirely false. This book is written by a man of good will who has a strong social conscience and who believes sincerely that attempts at reform during the past fifty years have done more harm than good. His approach is positive instead of negative. He is not suggesting that all the reforms of the last half-century be repudiated, with nothing to take their place; in each case he offers a substitute that he believes will fulfil the objectives of the discarded program yet will maximize individual freedom and minimize coercion by government. His arguments follow logically from his premise of the desirability of enhancing the freedom of men; his recommendations are consistent and without political bias. . . . Unlike his predecessors of the nineteenth century, he does not insist that the unfettered working of the free-enterprise system will eventually eliminate poverty or that poverty is a condition which must be tolerated in order to achieve the well-being of the greatest number. Instead, he believes that poverty must be eliminated, but not in the coercive, paternalistic manner of today. (pp. 201-02)

The classical economists with whom Friedman would like to be identified were nurtured on the poor-law debates of the late eighteenth and early nineteenth centuries. . . . Since that time economists have given little attention to the problem of alleviating poverty, but rather have concentrated on the way the economy can be organized to raise the nation's productivity to the point at which there would be no poor. . . . Few have faced up to the implications of the fact that, even in most prosperous times, our economy has not provided jobs for all and that our present income-maintenance programs are so inadequate and inequitable as to constitute a national disgrace. As a result, few suggestions for changes in our methods of caring for those without sufficient incomes take into consideration the dynamics of the total economy. Let us hope that Friedman has set a precedent and that other economists will take part in the twentieth-century poor-law debate. (pp. 206-07)

> *Frank R. Breul, "'Capitalism and Freedom': An Essay Review," in* The Social Service Review *(reprinted by permission of The University of Chicago Press; © 1963 by The University of Chicago), Vol. XXXVII, No. 1, March, 1963, pp. 201-07.*

ABBA P. LERNER

[*Capitalism and Freedom*] is largely a defense of liberalism against "liberalism"—that is, . . . of nineteenth-century European liberalism's concern for individual freedom against twentieth-century American "liberals." . . . [Milton Friedman characterizes the latter] by their readiness to rely on the state for the furtherance of welfare and equality.

Although Friedman is no more against welfare than the "liberals" are against freedom, he seems to have reacted so strongly against the failure of many "liberals" to understand the nature, the merits, and the potentialities of the market system, and their consequent tendency, in or out of season, to cry "there ought to be a law," that he tends to cry "never, never pass a law—well hardly ever!" In this he is buttressed by a deep political pessimism about the inevitable corruption of even the best-intentioned government action by narrow partisan interests. The result is that although he erects his system on an unimpeachable framework that all "liberals" as well as all liberals would accept—recognizing that a case may be made for government intervention whenever the market system fails to work satisfactorily by reason of monopoly or "neighborhood effects" (divergence between private and social benefits or costs)—his pessimistic antigovernmentism leads him to some strange extremes.

Thus, he is against fair employment practices legislation (FEPC) because by admitting the government into that area one opens the way to unfair employment practices legislation like the Nuremberg laws (UEPC?). . . . His treatment of racial and other discrimination as a matter of taste whose gratification is legitimate (however bad the taste) would be applicable, and not merely elegant, if the resulting supply of black, white, and mixed schools or housing had no great "neighborhood effect" in depriving Negroes of reasonable facilities. His displeasure with the Keynesian concentration on fiscal policy (a result of

its development at a time when monetary policy was not working well or was being worked very badly) leads him to declare the belief that "a rise in government expenditures relative to tax receipts, even when financed by borrowing, is *necessarily* expansionist" . . . to be based on one or the other of two extreme assumptions; either a liquidity elasticity of infinity (the liquidity trap) or an investment elasticity of zero (collapse of confidence). But although one of these extreme assumptions is required for the belief that *monetary policy* is completely ineffective, neither is really necessary for the belief that expansionary *fiscal policy* "is *necessarily* expansionist." All that is needed is the rejection of the opposite extreme assumption of an unchangeable velocity of circulation. . . . Nevertheless, he concludes that the belief that expansionary fiscal policy can relieve depression is "economic mythology." . . . (pp. 458-59)

And yet in spite of these and a few other extravagances, *Capitalism and Freedom* is an important and valuable book. . . . For the book powerfully demonstrates an impressive number of ways in which both freedom and welfare could be increased by a fuller utilization of the price mechanism. In some cases this could be achieved by freeing the price mechanism from governmental or private hindrances that have outlived any justifications they may once have had; in other areas, like education, by developing new institutions (for providing security of investment in human capital) that would permit the competitive price mechanism to begin to operate in them. Annoyance with Friedman's antigovernment complex should not be permitted to obscure the legitimacy and the persuasiveness of his plea for permitting private enterprise to compete freely with government enterprise in such activities as schooling or mail delivery, or his arguments against price supports, tariffs and import restrictions, output restrictions, rent and wage controls, and the ICC's perversion from combating railroad monopolies to enforcing general transportation monopolies. He provides a beautiful analysis of the American Medical Association's self-virtuous conspiracy against the American public. Particularly welcome is his treatment of the control of money, even though it suffers from his inability to credit governmental authority with the power to learn to avoid even "inexcusable" misjudgments, and his chapter on international trade and financial arrangements, where he deserves special praise for his unflinching courage in demonstrating how any compromise on the unpopular cause of flexible exchanges endangers all the popular aspects of free trade and sentimental internationalism. (p. 459)

The antigovernment extravagances that I have perhaps overemphasized in this review are to be deplored less for the (to my mind) bad advice to which they lead than for their inhibitory effect on potential readers of an important book that will provoke much thinking and rethinking. (p. 460)

> *Abba P. Lerner, "'Capitalism and Freedom'," in* The American Economic Review *(copyright American Economic Association 1963), Vol. LIII, No. 3, June, 1963, pp. 458-60.*

LEON H. KEYSERLING

Despite considerable pretense to the contrary, Professor Friedman's [*Capitalism and Freedom*] sheds no light on economic problems as such. Instead, his conclusion as to each specified economic program is deduced from a general formulation that the most important thing in the world is "freedom." In turn, this "freedom" is said to depend above all upon limiting the functions of government as closely as possible to protecting the individual "both from the enemies outside our gates and from our fellow-citizens: to preserve law and order, to enforce private contracts, to foster competitive markets."

I think that this general formulation, as used by the author, is inconsequential or misleading. To illustrate, some of the key statements in the formulation are just as valid if turned completely about. (p. 195)

Dr. Friedman says that "by relying primarily on voluntary cooperation and private enterprise in both economic and other activities, we can ensure that the private sector is a check on the powers of the governmental sector and an effective protection of freedom of speech, of religion, and of thought." In the American context, there is at least equal merit in the opposite proposition that centralized governmental power is essential to prevent private action, or decentralized state or local action, impairing freedom of speech, religion, or thought.

Next, the book suggests that, instead of the progressive income tax, there should be substituted a flat 23.5 per cent tax on all personal incomes. This, it is said, would avoid the type of intrusion involved when government imposes an income tax rate ranging from 20 to 91 per cent. But I cannot see where government intrusion would be any less if it were decided that a $5,000 a year family could as well bear a 23.5 per cent tax rate as a $200,000 a year family, contrasted with the prevailing decision that a higher tax rate upon the $200,000 family is more compatible with simple justice and economic common sense.

Dr. Friedman then argues against the view that corporate officers and labor leaders have a "social responsibility" going beyond the interest of their stockholders or their members. He says that this view "shows a fundamental misconception of the character and nature of a free economy." I suggest that this increasing sense of "social responsibility" is one of the most heartening things happening in America. To frustrate it would, under current and foreseeable domestic and world-wide conditions, lead inexorably to an appalling concentration of governmental action. (pp. 195-96)

Referring to the ravages of the Great Depression, Dr. Friedman implies that the initial downturn would have been held to moderate proportions, and corrected in reasonably short order, but for the mistakes made by the Federal Reserve System in trying to do something about it. It was not the free market, but rather public authority, that went wrong. In other words, if a great fire catches us with an inadequate fire department, the remedy is to do away with fire engines, instead of preventing people from throwing lighted matches around in a paper factory.

The most profound development in the world today is the determination of free people to use the concerted action of free government, along with other action, to translate the new technology into reduction of poverty, elevation of living standards, and enlargement of social justice. A set of prankishly-employed theorems, which seeks to place road blocks across these desires of free people, is, in my view, largely nonsense. It is not dangerous nonsense only because too many free people have too much good sense to listen to it. (p. 196)

Leon H. Keyserling, "Book Department: 'Capitalism and Freedom'," in The Annals of The American Academy of Political and Social Science (© 1963,

by The American Academy of Political and Social Science), Vol. 350, November, 1963, pp. 195-96.

PAUL A. BARAN

Friedman's radicalism is tame indeed. It is not likely to cause much anguish among the have's or to produce much enthusiasm among the have-not's. The account of the syndrome with which our society is afflicted is not very comprehensive, the diagnosis is not very deep, and the remedies prescribed attack nothing but the symptoms. . . .

What nevertheless renders [*Capitalism and Freedom*] novel and interesting are the differences which it discloses between the position of the modern heir to the liberal tradition and that of many whose heritage he is claiming. Thus John Stuart Mill would have hardly been content with Friedman's notion of freedom—the absence of interference with and the coercion of the individual on the part of the government. Much as he valued this "negative" freedom, the "positive" freedom of man's access to opportunities for self-realization, growth, and all-sided development constituted in his view an integral and indeed indispensable part of liberty. (p. 593)

Or consider the problem of monopoly. Traditionally, monopoly based upon large accumulation and control of productive resources was thought of by liberals to be a threat to the free market and, worse still, a mortal danger to the democratic process and a source of corruption and perversion of democratic government. . . . But Friedman, spellbound by the government, the growth of which is in itself a reflection of the far-reaching monopolization of the economy, sees none of it. "The most important fact about enterprise monopoly," he writes in 1962, "is its relative unimportance from the point of view of the economy as a whole. There are some four million separate operating enterprises in the United States. . . . In almost any industry that one can mention, there are giants and pygmies side by side." Indeed in every industry there is a DuPont and a drugstore, as in many a water there are sharks and sardines "side by side." (pp. 593-94)

If the government is controlled by vested interests, as in the case of the regulatory commissions to which Friedman rightly objects,- nothing but nepotism, corruption, and disregard for public interest can be expected. If the government were of the people, by the people and for the people, and—having socialized the sources of private wealth and private pressures— were free to devote its energies to the furtherance of the interests of society as a whole, it could perform wonders in raising the material and cultural welfare of man.

The building of such a society is obviously more difficult than letting things alone, advocating inconsequential reforms, and accepting every outcome as an inevitable and inexorable verdict of Providence. But as Friedman himself so well says, "supposed difficulty in administration is a standard defense of the status quo against any proposed change." It is a pity that Friedman has traveled so far away from radicalism and has placed his prodigious abilities so unreservedly in the service of conservatism—both in the etymological sense of preserving what is and in the political sense of opposing the only available possibility of attaining a more human, more rational—and more liberal—economic and social order. (p. 594)

Paul A. Baran, "Book Reviews: 'Capitalism and Freedom'," in The Journal of Political Economy (*reprinted by permission of The University of Chicago*

Press; copyright 1963 by the University of Chicago), Vol. 71, No. 6, December, 1963, pp. 591-94.

JEANNETTE P. NICHOLS

[In *A Monetary History of the United States, 1867-1960* Milton Friedman and Anna Jacobson Schwartz maintain that] monetary policy has been so persistently misdirected and ill-timed that it (rather than inherent instability of the private economy) produced the Great Depression and failed to counter recessions. Policy should follow rigid rules, achieving an automatic, contro-cyclical fluctuation, and should include a 100 percent reserve scheme. The money stock should be increased from three to five percent annually, or in roughly equal proportion to the rate of growth in output. . . . To indicate that instability of the money supply always accompanies severe economic instability, he utilizes two statistical types of evidence. The first is a series for the six severe contractions since 1867—1873-1879, 1893-1897, 1907-1908, 1920-1921, 1929-1933, and 1937-1938—each showing an "appreciable decline" in the money stock. For each period of stable *growth* since 1867—1882-1892, 1903-1913, 1923-1929, and 1948-1960—the statistics show a high degree of stability in "year to year change" in money stock. In the second type of evidence—used to indicate that changes in business conditions *emanate from* changes in the quantity of money, rather than vice-versa—Federal Reserve restrictions are tabulated. (p. 102)

The conclusion reached from this second set of evidence is far the more vulnerable of the two; the animadversions on the Federal Reserve are too dogmatic and severe; it has had to share responsibility with the Treasury Department, fifty-one commercial banking systems and numerous other lending and regulatory agencies, public and private. Do the authors mean that it has harmed America more than did nineteenth-century wildcat banking?

Historians can admit the usefulness of the statistics but may question the simplicity of their interpretation. Suppose that the rigid rules of monetary policy had existed in the periods delineated, could not the same kind of statistical tabulations have been generated nevertheless? Do not the statistics tend to minimize the influence of disparities in growth, as between regions and occupations, and the presence of nongrowth factors? Can not concentration on figures tend to underestimate the history of the background facts? Might the costs of transition outweigh their benefits?

A mechanical view of life which may have worked well to the middle of the nineteenth-century is outmoded. Four of the most powerful worldwide phenomena presently at work certainly postpone any real-life test of Friedman's theories: the emphasis upon rapid economic development, the phenomenal expansion in government activities, the accumulation of variables in statistics, and historic trends likely to throw new light upon all historical developments.

This modern support for the quantity theory of money seems to this reviewer to neglect the fluidity pervading twentieth-century existence. (pp. 102-03)

Jeannette P. Nichols, "Book Reviews: 'A Monetary History of the United States, 1867-1960'," in The Journal of American History *(copyright Organization of American Historians, 1964), Vol. LI, No. 1, June, 1964, pp. 101-03.*

C. B. MACPHERSON

Milton Friedman's *Capitalism and Freedom* . . . is now apt to be treated by political scientists as the classic defence of free-market liberalism. As such it deserves more notice from the political theorists' standpoint than it got on publication, when its technical arguments about the possibility of returning to laissez-faire attracted most attention. Whether or not *Capitalism and Freedom* is now properly treated as the classic defence of the pure market theory of liberalism, it is at least a classic example of the difficulty of moving from the level of controversy about laissez-faire to the level of fundamental concepts of freedom and the market. (p. 95)

In addition to arguing that competitive capitalism is a system of economic freedom and so an important component of freedom broadly understood, Professor Friedman argues that capitalism is a necessary condition of political freedom (and that socialism is incompatible with political freedom). And although he is more concerned with freedom than with equity, he does argue also that the capitalist principle of distribution of the whole product is not only preferable to a socialist principle but is in fact accepted by socialists. (p. 96)

Professor Friedman's demonstration that the capitalist market economy can co-ordinate economic activities without coercion rests on an elementary conceptual error. His argument runs as follows. He shows first that in a simple market model, where each individual or household controls resources enabling it to produce goods and services either directly for itself or for exchange, there will be production for exchange because of the increased product made possible by specialization. But "since the household always has the alternative of producing directly for itself, it need not enter into any exchange unless it benefits from it. Hence no exchange will take place unless both parties do benefit from it. Co-operation is thereby achieved without coercion." . . . So far, so good. It is indeed clear that in this simple exchange model, assuming rational maximizing behaviour by all hands, every exchange will benefit both parties, and hence that no coercion is involved in the decision to produce for exchange or in any act of exchange.

Professor Friedman then moves on to our actual complex economy, or rather to his own curious model of it:

> As in [the] simple model, so in the complex enterprise and money-exchange economy, co-operation is strictly individual and voluntary *provided: (a)* that enterprises are private, so that the ultimate contracting parties are individuals and *(b)* that individuals are effectively free to enter or not to enter into any particular exchange, so that every transaction is strictly voluntary. . . .

One cannot take exception to proviso *(a)*: it is clearly required in the model to produce a co-operation that is "strictly individual." One might, of course, suggest that a model containing this stipulation is far from corresponding to our actual complex economy, since in the latter the ultimate contracting parties who have the most effect on the market are not individuals but corporations, and moreover, corporations which in one way or another manage to opt out of the fully competitive market. This criticism, however, would not be accepted by all economists as self-evident: some would say that the question who has most effect on the market is still an open question. . . . But political scientists need not await its results before passing judgment on Friedman's position, nor should they be tempted to concentrate their attention on proviso *(a)*. If they do so they are apt to miss the fault in proviso *(b)*, which is more fundamental, and of a different kind. It is not a question of the correspondence of the model to the actual: it is a matter of the inadequacy of the proviso to produce the model.

Proviso *(b)* is "that individuals are effectively free to enter or not to enter into any particular exchange," and it is held that with this proviso "every transaction is strictly voluntary." A moment's thought will show that this is not so. The proviso that is required to make every transaction strictly voluntary is *not* freedom not to enter into any *particular* exchange, but freedom not to enter into any exchange *at all*. This, and only this, was the proviso that proved the simple model to be voluntary and non-coercive; and nothing less than this would prove the complex model to be voluntary and non-coercive. But Professor Friedman is clearly claiming that freedom not to enter into any *particular* exchange is enough. . . . (pp. 97-8)

One almost despairs of logic, and of the use of models. It is easy to see what Professor Friedman has done, but it is less easy to excuse it. He has moved from the simple economy of exchange between independent producers, to the capitalist economy, without mentioning the most important thing that distinguishes them. . . . What distinguishes the capitalist economy from the simple exchange economy is the separation of labour and capital, that is, the existence of a labour force without its own sufficient capital and therefore without a choice as to whether to put its labour in the market or not. Professor Friedman would agree that where there is no choice there is coercion. His attempted demonstration that capitalism co-ordinates without coercion therefore fails.

Since all his specific arguments against the welfare and regulatory state depend on his case that the market economy is not coercive, the reader may spare himself the pains (or, if an economist, the pleasure) of attending to the careful and persuasive reasoning by which he seeks to establish the minimum to which coercion could be reduced by reducing or discarding each of the main regulatory and welfare activities of the state. None of this takes into account the coercion involved in the separation of capital from labour, or the possible mitigation of this coercion by the regulatory and welfare state. Yet it is because this coercion can in principle be reduced by the regulatory and welfare state, and thereby the amount of effective individual liberty be increased, that liberals have been justified in pressing, in the name of liberty, for infringements on the pure operation of competitive capitalism.

While the bulk of *Capitalism and Freedom* is concerned with the regulatory and welfare state, Friedman's deepest concern is with socialism. He undertakes to demonstrate that socialism is inconsistent with political freedom. He argues this in two ways: (1) that competitive capitalism, which is of course negated by socialism, is a necessary (although not a sufficient) condition of political freedom; (2) that a socialist society is so constructed that it cannot guarantee political freedom. Let us look at the two arguments in turn.

The argument that competitive capitalism is necessary to political freedom is itself conducted on two levels, neither of which shows a necessary relation. (pp. 98-9)

The first, on which Friedman properly does not place very much weight, is a historical correlation. No society that has had a large measure of political freedom "has not also used

something comparable to a free market to organize the bulk of economic activity." . . . "The nineteenth century and early twentieth century in the Western world stand out as striking exceptions to the general trend of historical development. Political freedom in this instance clearly came along with the free market and the development of capitalist institutions." . . . Thus, for Professor Friedman, "history suggests . . . that capitalism is a necessary condition for political freedom." . . .

The broad historical correlation is fairly clear, though in cutting off the period of substantial political freedom in the West at the "early twentieth century" Friedman seems to be slipping into thinking of economic freedom and begging the question of the relation of political freedom to economic freedom. But granting the correlation between the emergence of capitalism and the emergence of political freedom, what it may suggest to the student of history is the converse of what it suggests to Professor Friedman: i.e., it may suggest that political freedom was a necessary condition for the development of capitalism. Capitalist institutions could not be fully established until political freedom (ensured by a competitive party system with effective civil liberties) had been won by those who wanted capitalism to have a clear run: a liberal state (political freedom) was needed to permit and facilitate a capitalist market society. (p. 99)

Passing from historical correlation, which "by itself can never be convincing," Professor Friedman looks for "logical links between economic and political freedom." . . . The link he finds is that "the kind of economic organization that provides economic freedom directly, namely, competitive capitalism, also promotes political freedom because it separates economic power from political power and in this way enables the one to offset the other." . . . The greater the concentration of coercive power in the same hands, the greater the threat to political freedom (defined as "the absence of coercion of a man by his fellow men"). The market removes the organization of economic activity from the control of the political authority. It thus reduces the concentration of power and "enables economic strength to be a check to political power rather than a reinforcement." . . .

Granted the validity of these generalizations, they tell us only that the market *enables* economic power to offset rather than reinforce political power. They do not show any necessity or inherent probability that the market *leads to* the offsetting of political power by economic power. We may doubt that there is any such inherent probability. What can be shown is an inherent probability in the other direction, i.e., that the market leads to political power being used not to offset but to reinforce economic power. For the more completely the market takes over the organization of economic activity, that is, the more nearly the society approximates Friedman's ideal of a competitive capitalist market society, where the state establishes and enforces the individual right of appropriation and the rules of the market but does not interfere in the operation of the market, the more completely is political power being used to reinforce economic power.

Professor Friedman does not see this as any threat to political freedom because he does not see that the capitalist market necessarily gives coercive power to those who succeed in amassing capital. . . . He sees the coercion possible (he thinks probable) in a socialist society where the political authority can enforce certain terms of employment. He does not see the coercion in a capitalist society where the holders of capital can enforce certain terms of employment. He does not see this because of his error about freedom not to enter into any particular exchange being enough to prove the uncoercive nature of entering into exchange at all.

The placing of economic coercive power and political coercive power in the hands of different sets of people, as in the fully competitive capitalist economy, does not lead to the first checking the second but to the second reinforcing the first. It is only in the welfare-state variety of capitalism, which Friedman would like to have dismantled, that there is a certain amount of checking of economic power by political power.

The logical link between competitive capitalism and political freedom has not been established.

Professor Friedman argues also that a socialist society is so constructed that it cannot guarantee political freedom. He takes as the test of political freedom the freedom of individuals to propagandize openly for a radical change in the structure of society: in a socialist society the test is freedom to advocate the introduction of capitalism. (pp. 99-101)

His case that a socialist state as such cannot guarantee political freedom depends on what he puts in his model of the socialist state. . . . In one [model], the government is the sole employer and the sole source from which necessary instruments of effective political advocacy (paper, use of printing presses, halls) can be had. (p. 101)

Accepting this as a proper stipulation for a socialist model, [one] question to be answered is: does the monopoly of employment itself render the government incapable (or even less capable than it otherwise would be) of safeguarding political freedom? Friedman expects us to answer yes, but the answer is surely no. A socialist government which wished to guarantee political freedom would not be prevented from doing so by its having a monopoly of employment. Nor need it even be tempted to curtail political freedom by virtue of that monopoly. A government monopoly of employment can only mean (as Friedman allows) that the government and all its agencies are, together, the only employers. A socialist government can, by devolution of the management of industries, provide effective alternative employment opportunities. True, a government which wished to curtail or deny the freedom of radical political advocacy could use its monopoly of employment to do so. But such a government has so many other ways of doing it that the presence or absence of this way is not decisive.

It is not the absence of a fully competitive labour market that may disable a socialist government from guaranteeing political freedom; it is the absence of a firm will to do so. Where there's a will there's a way, and for all that Friedman has argued to the contrary, the way need have nothing to do with a fully competitive labour market. The real problem of political freedom in socialism has to do with the will, not the way. The real problem is whether a socialist state could ever have the will to guarantee political freedom. This depends on factors Friedman does not consider, and until they have been assessed, questions about means have an air of unreality, as has his complaint that Western socialists have not faced up to the question of means. (pp. 101-02)

[In Chapter 10, Friedman] sets out the ethical case for distribution according to product, as compared with "another [principle] that seems ethically appealing, namely, equality of treatment." . . . Distribution according to product he describes, accurately enough, as the principle "To each according to what he and the instruments he owns produces." . . . : to be strictly

accurate this should read "resources" or "capital and land" instead of "instruments," but the sense is clear. This is offered as "the ethical principle that would directly justify the distribution of income in a free market society." . . . We can agree that this is the only principle that can be offered to justify it. We may also observe that this principle is not only different from the principle "to each according to his work," but is also inconsistent with it (except on the fanciful assumption that ownership of resources is always directly proportional to work). Professor Friedman does not seem to see this. His case for the ethical principle of payment according to product is that it is unthinkingly accepted as a basic value-judgment by almost everybody in our society; and his demonstration of this is that the severest internal critics of capitalism, i.e. the Marxists, have implicitly accepted it.

Of course they have not. There is a double confusion here, even if we accept Friedman's paraphrase of Marx. . . . Certainly the implication of Marx's position is that labour (though not necessarily each individual labourer) is entitled to the whole of the value it creates. But in the first place, this is, at most, the principle "to each according to his work," not "to each according to what he and the instruments he owns produces" or "to each according to his product." In the second place, Marx accepted "to each according to his work" only as a transitionally valid principle, to be replaced by the ultimately desirable principle "to each according to his need." (p. 105)

Ignorance of Marxism is no sin in an economist, though cleverness in scoring off a travesty of it may be thought a scholarly lapse. What is more disturbing is that Professor Friedman seems to be satisfied that this treatment of the ethical justification of different principles of distribution is sufficient. Given his own first postulate, perhaps it is. For in asserting at the beginning of the book that freedom of the individual, or perhaps of the family, is the liberal's "ultimate goal in judging social arrangements," he has said in effect that the liberal is not required seriously to weigh the ethical claims of equality (or any other principle of distribution), let alone the claims of any principle of individual human development such as was given first place by liberals like Mill and Green, against the claims of freedom (which to Friedman of course means market freedom). The humanist liberal in the tradition of Mill and Green will quite properly reject Friedman's postulate. The logical liberal will reject his fallacious proof that the freedom of the capitalist market is individual economic freedom, his undemonstrated case that political freedom requires capitalism, and his fallacious defence of the ethical adequacy of capitalism. The logical humanist liberal will regret that the postulate and the fallacies make *Capitalism and Freedom* not a defence but an elegant tombstone of liberalism. (p. 106)

C. B. Macpherson, *"Elegant Tombstones: A Note on Friedman's Freedom,"* in Canadian Journal of Political Science (© *Canadian Political Science Association and/et la Société québécoise de science politique 1968), Vol. 1, No. 1, March, 1968, pp. 95-106.*

ROBERT LEKACHMAN

The grand theory of the return to the days of Eisenhower the Good is provided by Milton Friedman [in *Monetary vs. Fiscal Policy: A Dialogue*]. . . . Here as in his massive and highly influential *A Monetary History of The United States 1867-1960,* Mr. Friedman advocates a monetary, as opposed to a fiscal, interpretation of American business-cycle history. In his view, the Federal Reserve System through its usually mistaken policies has played a crucial role in creating recessions and inflations. Greatly to oversimplify a highly controversial position, the monetary school is convinced that what counts in explaining the level of economic activity is not aggregate demand for goods and services (the gospel according to Keynes) but changes in the quantity of money (currency plus bank deposits) which is controlled by the Federal Reserve System. Accordingly, the clue to economic stability is not to be found in fiscal policy—which ought simply to be regulated according to the public's preferences between private and public goods—but in properly conducted monetary policy which in itself is capable of generating steady growth and high employment. . . .

Although [Walter W.] Heller holds his own quite successfully in his dialogue with Friedman, and the Chicago school, fortunately, has not converted the entire profession, Chicago teachings are quite clearly consistent with the inclinations of a conservative, noninterventionist President. . . .

[There is danger] in the retreat from an activist conception of the federal government's role in economic affairs. In America social change comes slowly, seldom, and inadequately. But when it comes at all, it is almost invariably as the consequence of Presidential initiative. Activist fiscal policy goes hand in hand with activist social policy. The new emphasis upon monetary policy accords admirably with the new quietism of social policy. I hope we all survive until 1973. (p. 84)

> Robert Lekachman, *"Economic Revisionism," in* Commentary *(reprinted by permission; all rights reserved), Vol. 48, July, 1969, pp. 81-2, 84.**

THE TIMES LITERARY SUPPLEMENT

[Milton Friedman] is known to the world as belonging to the school of laisser faire; on occasion he has carried his doctrines in this regard to extreme lengths. . . .

He has applied his doctrines to the topic of money, with which [*The Optimum Quantity of Money*] is concerned. He has held that big mistakes have been made by the Federal Reserve System, notably in 1930 and 1931, but also continuingly in more recent months. He holds accordingly that, rather than give a central bank discretionary power, one should have some simple rule for the issuance of money, such as maintaining its quantity permanently static or expanding it regularly at some predetermined percentage a year. This would be to abandon the idea that a central bank can serve a useful function by ironing out the business cycle, an idea that has been prevalent in the United States from the early days of the Federal Reserve System, and of which there were traces in England as early as the nineteenth century. Professor Friedman's idea is that, with human fallibility, positive policies will be subject to recurrent error, and that on balance, however well-intentioned, they will do more harm than good. He often reverts to the view that there is a continuing and varying time-lag between various policy measures and their effects, which makes correct policy formation difficult, if not impossible. He also holds that varying policy from time to time gives rise to fluctuating expectations about the future, which do more harm than the policies do. . . .

Basing himself on the idea that there should be an "optimum" quantity of money—but is that really so?—he has developed a fresh theory. This is of a complex and even "tortured" character; the reasoning is fine-spun and the reader will find

[the title] essay one of the most difficult in the book to understand and assess. . . .

Professor Friedman starts his new essay by making a number of highly unrealistic assumptions. Any author is entitled to do that. But, before modifying them, so as to bring his theoretical structure a little closer to the facts of real life, he is already saying: "our simple example embodies most of the basic principles of monetary theory". In this "example" the increase in the supply of money falls like manna from heaven. But in fact the way in which money is provided may influence the subsequent disposal of it. He assumes that individuals spend the whole of their windfall on consumption and do not dispose of it in other ways. At this early stage, however, he makes the point, which is important throughout the book, that in choosing how much money to hold, individuals have regard to the purchasing power of their holding rather than to its nominal amount. Thus far the rate of interest has played no part, and some may think that his treatment of interest in later passages is not altogether satisfactory. . . .

[At] one stage he introduces the concept of a "natural" level of unemployment. One may search in vain for a definition of this concept. If it can be given a meaning which has a realistic relation to the facts of life, and is not based on some arbitrary and fine-spun assumption, it would clearly be one of great importance. . . .

The intellectual calibre of [*The Optimum Quantity of Money*] is high. Professor Friedman's work needs challenging; to do this, analysis by someone of comparable calibre—and that is hard to find—would be needed. Furthermore the task of analysis would take even the most able mind a considerable period of time. The book is a challenge to potentially capable economists not to have their heads so deeply buried in problems, the main characteristic of which is that they can be solved by a computer. Professor Friedman's book suggests that there is still scope in economics for pure thinking as such.

> "Very Much Laisser Faire," in The Times Literary Supplement (© Times Newspapers Ltd. (London) 1970; reproduced from The Times Literary Supplement by permission), No. 3555, April 16, 1970, p. 407.

WILFRED BECKERMAN

[Milton Friedman] believes that changes in the money supply have important effects on the way the economy behaves. But the nature of these effects is not always understood by many of his political converts. . . .

Of course, none of the professional protagonists in the debate pretend that the way changes in the money supply affect the rest of the economy is simple, although the Friedmanites do not believe it is quite as complex as did Keynes. But there are . . . aspects of the monetarist doctrine which do not seem to be really in dispute and yet which are of great importance from the policy point of view.

First, the extent to which 'money matters'—as the monetarists believe—is largely a question of whether one is talking about the long run or the short run. Even the layman can grasp the idea that if changes in the supply of money are offset by changes in the demand for it, there will not be much effect on its 'price' (which, for present purposes can be loosely regarded as what the rate of interest is). . . . The essence of Keynes's view that an increase in the supply of money would not help much reduce the mass unemployment that existed in the 1930s (when he was writing about these problems), was that an increased supply of money would be taken up by increased demand for money holdings, so that interest rates would not fall much. If, in addition, investment is not sensitive to changes in short-term interest rates, the link between changes in the money supply and changes in investment and hence the level of income and output, is further weakened.

The Friedmanites would claim that, in the longer run, the various short-term influences on the demand for money would cancel out or lose their potency and that long-run interest rates would eventually adjust to changes in the money supply. Also, investment is held to be more sensitive to interest changes than in the Keynesian models.

Now, there is a wide area of agreement that the choice between these two theories should depend on which of the two conflicting pairs of assumptions is true. Is the demand for money stable, and investment very responsive to changes in interest rates, as Professor Friedman would maintain, or the opposite? . . . [It] is difficult to interpret the evidence and the disputes are not yet fully resolved. But it is not clear how far the remaining technical disagreements really matter. For the limitations on Milton Friedman's theories from the policy point of view do not seem to depend on the points at issue but on features of his theory which are hardly in dispute.

First, the monetarists have never claimed that changes in the money supply would have an *immediate* effect on prices and output. Although they believe that people adjust their expectations and behaviour more rapidly than did Keynes, Friedman has always accepted that the effects of money on production and prices would only be felt after 'long and variable lags'. And this does not encourage one to resort to monetary policy as a means of solving problems at some indeterminate date in the future. (p. 540)

How far monetary restraint would stop inflation is, of course, not something to which Keynes needed to pay attention at the time he was writing. The most eminent living Keynesian, Lord Kahn, has recently stated that 'It can be readily conceded to the monetarists that an increase in the quantity of money though not the *cause* of inflation, is a necessary condition'. . . . [But] he emphasised that the costs of beating inflation by monetary restraint would be very much greater than through some effective incomes policy. (pp. 540-41)

Now, Milton Friedman makes no secret of his view—as in his newly revised textbook (*Price Theory* . . .)—that trade unions do not cause inflation but that they do determine the 'natural level of unemployment', i.e. the level at which the economy would settle if the authorities would follow his policies and thereby achieve stable prices in the long run. In his system of thought this 'natural level of unemployment' would be higher the more powerful are the trade unions and, hence, the more imperfections and obstacles to the free working of the market mechanism. But to argue, as does Milton Friedman, that, given union power and behaviour, we have inflation because governments try to run the economy at acceptable levels of unemployment (as distinct from arguing that, given the social desire to maintain an acceptable level of unemployment, unions behave in a manner that leads to inflation) is, in Hazlitt's famous phrase, a 'distinction without a difference'. Restraint on the money supply would probably stop inflation in the end, though, at best, through leading to politically quite unaccept-

able levels of unemployment and a far greater and more lasting collapse of investment than anything we have seen so far.

The only way, therefore, that inflation can be brought under control without such consequences is by changing the manner in which unions operate. This—as was clearly seen by Keynes—is a political problem, not an economic problem. . . .

If Nobel prizes are awarded according to the intellectual power of the recipients and the extent to which they have stimulated research and analysis in their fields (and why should they not?) Milton Friedman certainly deserves one. If they are awarded according to the extent to which the recipients have correctly analysed some aspects of the phenomena they have studied, he may still deserve one, but it is not yet possible to be sure about this. But nobody should think that its award to Professor Friedman constitutes universal recognition that his theories provide simple new tools of policy that can be used in a democracy. (p. 541)

> *Wilfred Beckerman, "The Value of Milton Friedman," in* New Statesman *(© 1976 The Statesman & Nation Publishing Co. Ltd.), Vol. 92, No. 2379, October 22, 1976, pp. 540-41.*

JAMES TOBIN

[Milton Friedman's Nobel prize for economics] was certainly merited. Of the many reasons I will mention only four. In his 1945 study of professional incomes, with Simon Kuznets, Friedman was a pioneer in developing and applying the fruitful idea of "human capital". In 1957, Friedman showed how the distinction between permanent and transient income resolved puzzles in consumption and saving statistics for whole economies and for samples of households. His monumental monetary history (in 1963, with Anna Schwartz) is an indispensable treatise packed with theoretic insights and policy analysis as well as historical and statistical narrative. Today nobody can consider trade-offs between unemployment and inflation without confronting the "natural rate of unemployment". Although others had anticipated the idea, Friedman's version, in his brilliant 1967 American Economic Association presidential address, is the classic statement. . . .

Friedman's over-riding objective is to minimise state compulsion of private individuals—to pay taxes, serve in armies, attend designated schools, sell or buy at prescribed prices, belong to trade unions and in general refrain from mutually agreeable contracts with other citizens. He would minimise both the economic size of the public sector and the scope for government activities. Freedom from state coercion is the ultimate political value, and competitive markets transform the self-interested economic actions of individuals into social benefits.

Friedman, like Adam Smith, has not lacked vulnerable mercantilist targets like tariffs, import quotas, foreign exchange restrictions, farm price supports, rent controls, minimum wages and interest rate ceilings. The notion that governments should intervene to raise the prices of what deserving voters sell, or lower the prices of what they buy, is a durable political fallacy. Friedman is at his best showing—sometimes with exaggerated certainty—that these are inefficient remedies and often even damage the groups whose plights are the rationalisation for the policies. Most economists of all persuasions basically agree.

Nevertheless, many of us are sceptical of Friedman's other claims for the superiority of unfettered market outcomes. There are several reasons.

First, Friedman pays little attention to market imperfections and failures. He is not a notable supporter of government efforts to preserve or promote competition or to improve consumer information. He does not, for example, seem bothered by the possibility that firms will, even from miscalculation of long-run self-interest, market hazardous products or provide unsafe working conditions. He has no solution except voluntary agreement among the parties for the "externalities"—pollution, environmental damage, congestion—that are an increasing feature of economic life. To economists less obsessed with the view that government is the coercive enemy of freedom, government seems the natural agency for arriving at the complex social compacts needed.

Second, Friedman's hard libertarian line is little tempered by egalitarian sentiment. Henry Simons, an early Chicago apostle of laissez-faire, advocated progressive income taxation to accomplish, directly and efficiently, the redistributions which motivate misguided intervention in specific markets. Friedman advocates less progressivity. And though he is rightly credited with the negative income tax device, his proposal was a modest one designed largely to clear the decks of other transfer programmes.

Third, Friedman is unwilling to trust the institutions of representative democracy to determine the size of the public sector and the allocation of resources of public goods. He vigorously supports constitutional limitations on state expenditure and taxes. Somehow the preferences of citizens as voters are not accorded the same respect as their preferences as individual consumers. (p. 94)

Friedman has never provided a convincing theoretical foundation for his policy prescription. A doctrine which enthrones the stock of money as the sovereign determinant of money, income and prices might be expected to offer a clear conceptual basis for a sharp distinction of "money" from its substitutes and for ignoring systematic and random variation of monetary velocity. Instead Friedman relies on a series of simple empirical correlations between money stocks, variously defined, and money income aggregates or price levels.

These correlations cannot erase significant variations of velocity. In any case causal inferences from such correlations are hazardous. Statistical relations of money and income are based largely on observation when central banks, according to Friedman's own criticism of them, supplied money to accommodate the economy's demands. As recent experience already suggests, past correlations may be unreliable when money stocks are used as controls. Moreover the extraordinary non-policy shocks suffered by the world economies in recent years may be nature's ironical response to the fashionable faith that stable policy means stable economy.

Monetarism converts long-run equilibrium conditions into short-run policy recommendations. Natural rate theory says that no permanent reduction of unemployment can be gained by accepting higher inflation. Yet anti-inflationary policies entail, as the current travails of the world economy exemplify, severe and protracted social costs in lost output and employment. These "transitional" costs do not weigh heavily in the value scales of monetarists, though Friedman acknowledges them more squarely than many of his evangelical followers. Given their free market ideology, he and they will not entertain wage and price controls or other incomes policies as alternatives or complements to anti-inflationary monetary restrictions. Here the two crusades converge. If they triumph, democratic capitalist economies will suffer high unemployment and slow real growth for some years to come. (p. 95)

> *James Tobin, "The Nobel Milton," in* The Economist *(© The Economist Newspaper Limited, 1976), Vol. 261, No. 6947, October 23, 1976, pp. 94-5.*

SIDNEY WEINTRAUB

"Free to Choose," written with his wife Rose, is published in conjunction with Professor Friedman's public-television series of the same title, a balancing sequel of sorts to John Kenneth Galbraith's book and television show, "The Age of Uncertainty." Predictably, while Professor Galbraith was often concerned with the defects of the market system, the Friedmans extol its triumphs and virtues.

Early on, the authors try, by quotation and reference, to enlist Adam Smith and Thomas Jefferson in their cause, arguing that "economic freedom is an essential requisite for political freedom." Unfortunately for the Friedmans' case, there are ambiguous strands in Jefferson. And Adam Smith's grand doctrine of the organizing power of the principle of self-interest—the strongest, though not the noblest motive—lends itself to sordid abuse: the self-interest of cheaters, criminals and various con artists can violate the general interest. (p. 9)

The Friedmans hail the important functions performed by the price system. Few economists, regardless of ideological persuasion, would dispute its merits; only some "crazies" could think that a complex social order could dispense with its services. The serious disputes arise over its efficiency in an era of big firms and oligopolies. The authors still see prices as a sensitive register of demand and cost pressures. Professional opponents see prices instead as lethargic and abused through corporate distortion.

Clear, cogent, sure and humorless, **"Free to Choose"** is sweeping and surgical in cutting up economic absurdities perpetrated by government agencies since the New Deal. (pp. 9, 34)

The Friedmans castigate the consumer movement in a lively chapter replete with some very dubious assertions, such as this: "the shoddy products are all produced by government or government-regulated industries.". . .

There is some vintage Friedman on inflation theory: the price explosion is all very simple, the authors say, for it is entirely a matter of excess money supplies—"too much money." On this problem, which colors all issues today, I think Professor Friedman's recommendations are a surefire recipe for disastrous stagflation, meaning simultaneous unemployment and inflation. His views have helped sustain our mad assault on the laws of arithmetic, with money incomes jumping by about 10 percent per annum, while productivity has grown by meager amounts. In **"Free to Choose,"** no attention at all is paid to this issue. If unions—or *all* of us—acted totally on his diagnosis, we should *all* ask not for 8 or 10 percent more in wages per annum but for 100 or 1,000 percent more, and then denounce the Federal Reserve for inflation! I think this is mischievous doctrine; most of our stagflation troubles stem from our having taken Professor Friedman's views too seriously, and from our administrative officials having acted upon them, over the last dozen years. . . .

Unlike Professor Galbraith, the Friedmans have hardly a word to say about the gargantuan corporation, with its minimal solicitude for ends other than profits and its not infrequent corruption of the political and economic process. Gross and grotesque discrepancies in income shares also get hardly a mention in **"Free to Choose."** The authors' myopia is most pronounced in their failure to discern that the self-interest that they venerate for market outcomes is also at work in the electorate's pressure on its representatives to do something on its behalf, and in the legislators' responses. . . .

A volume by Professor Friedman is always noteworthy for its clarity, logic, candor and unequivocal stand on political implications. **"Free to Choose"** conforms to those standards. . . . But to close out this century, I am skeptical of its message, and I would be wary of all its proposed constitutional amendments. (p. 35)

> *Sidney Weintraub, "Adam Smith Agrees," in* The New York Times Book Review *(© 1980 by The New York Times Company; reprinted by permission), February 24, 1980, pp. 9, 34-5.*

KENNETH J. ARROW

[Friedman is] fond of quoting, "there is no such thing as a free lunch." In policy terms, this means that every policy change is bound to do some harm somewhere. Yet in his popular writings there is little sense of qualification. In [*Free To Choose*] and in the earlier *Capitalism and Freedom* . . . , there is very little suggestion that their very large redirections of policy could possibly have any negative consequences. Government regulations of all sorts—occupational licensing, social security, public education—are all to be committed to the bonfire. There is no sense that there may be real losses as well as possible gains to these drastic changes. (p. 25)

To be sure, the Friedmans do note, at least in the case of regulation and licensing, that there are special interests that lose. And there is an especially harsh passage about physicians' self-protection, dating back to the Hippocratic oath. But why are "special interests" not worthy of protection in the Friedmans' view? Surely not because there is some concept of a "general interest." Though the Friedmans do not disavow such a notion or even discuss it, one may confidently assume from the texture of their discussion that overall social objectives play no role in their thinking.

What are the criteria by which the Friedmans judge whether government actions are good or bad? The clearest statement I could find comes at the end of the chapter on social security, welfare, and health policy:

> The waste is distressing, but is the least of the evils of the paternalistic programs that have grown to such massive size. Their major evil is their effect on the fabric of our society. They weaken the family; reduce the incentive to work, save, and innovate; reduce the accumulation of capital; and limit our freedom.

Apart from the weakening of the family, these criteria reduce to economic efficiency and freedom.

The concept of freedom, though it appears in the title of the book, is not analyzed. The commonplace idea that poverty is in many ways a restriction of personal freedom is not even mentioned. Implicitly, there are several not completely compatible strands in the Friedmans' analysis. As the title suggests, the Friedmans advocate an emotional libertarianism. No action is valid which is not the outcome of voluntary action and

agreement. . . . This position does not rest on economic efficiency at all. Still, the Friedmans' training as economists cannot be shed so easily. Economic progress matters a good deal to them, and economic success is a major argument for laissez-faire. They are also aware that economic theory shows that the market cannot always be successful in achieving efficiency, for there are externalities, such as pollution, with which it does not deal. (p. 26)

The question of criteria of judgment assumes particular force when the Friedmans deal with income distribution. They explicitly and strongly repudiate equality of outcome. But their reasoning is less clear. Part of the argument is that fair allocations are hard to define; but the difficulties of defining freedom are not even mentioned, let alone admitted as an argument against some attempt to achieve freedom. "The key point" is the conflict between egalitarianism and freedom. Here, indeed, the Friedmans point to Russia, China, and the Cambodia as evidence of the evils of egalitarianism, though elsewhere we are told that Russia and China are very inegalitarian. The vigorous efforts at egalitarianism in the United Kingdom, the Netherlands, and Sweden have of course led to no reduction of freedom, but they go unmentioned.

Several times, the Friedmans argue that equalization will destroy all incentives. . . . [They] are fond of using basketball players as an example of rewards to unusual skills, [and they] also add Marlene Dietrich's legs. In fact, however, entertainment and sports figures constitute a very small fraction of those with incomes over $100,000 per year, probably less than one percent, a statistic the Friedmans don't acknowledge. The argument really is an elementary textbook example of false logical reasoning. From the sensible proposition that individuals will not undertake risks or engage in especially demanding occupations without some reward, they slip over into the proposition that any reduction in income inequality will destroy all incentives. (pp. 26-7)

Their lack of interest in the distribution of income appears heartless when (in another context) they observe, "persons with lower incomes on the average have a shorter life span than persons with higher incomes."

If one turns to the arguments the Friedmans do make, rather than the problems they do not face, a repeated theme is the relation between free markets and economic growth. Broadly speaking, there can be no argument that the relation has been historically strong. But the Friedmans certainly overstate the case. When convenient, "freedom of markets" is interpreted very strongly and literally; but at other times countries with quite strong state intervention are placed in the free enterprise world. As they say, the United States and the United Kingdom grew rapidly in the 19th century with virtually no state intervention. But France, Germany, Japan, and czarist Russia (which had rapid growth from 1900 to 1910) had high tariffs, government-owned railroads, and state-controlled banking systems. Among developing countries, Hong Kong is the glory of the Friedmans' account and does indeed serve as an advertisement for free enterprise. But the prosperity of Taiwan and South Korea has been based on very considerable government planning and intervention. Indeed, stripped of the socialist rhetoric which the Indian government has (decreasingly) used, there would be little to choose in the degree of government intervention between South Korea and India, which is a prime example in the Friedmans' case against planning. It is true that South Korean controls, for example over investment, have been much more in accordance with economic principles than India's; but that hardly justifies a blanket indictment of planning as a barrier to growth. . . .

The Friedmans' reading of economic history is in general rather cavalier. There are many ugly aspects to balance the economic gains of the 19th century, on which the authors place such great stress. There is no reference to the strikes in railroads, steel, and especially mining, with their brutal suppression. The strains suggested by these episodes deserve at least some comment. In the United Kingdom and on the European continent, the memories of this period have created a permanent working-class hostility, which in Britain has led to the postwar drive toward egalitarianism, which the Friedmans so deplore, and on the Continent to the continued strength of the Communist parties, the greatest threat to freedom of any kind.

It may be expected that there are no references to the social reality of classes in this work, and that is true with one exception: the Friedmans have borrowed from Irving Kristol his *bête noire*, the "new class" of bureaucrats, academics, and journalists. This group may indeed have its influence, exaggerated though it has been, but to claim that its advocacy is motivated by self-interest is basically a crude and false argument. An expansion of the welfare system will increase employment for some part of the new class, but unless their sense of class solidarity is much stronger than anything the Friedmans would concede to any other group, they will lose on the whole through higher taxes. They are indeed paid above the average, and their advocacy of egalitarianism at their own expense can only be ascribed to self-interest by the most tortured reasoning. (p. 27)

The Friedmans realize that one of the great charges against free enterprise is the instability of the system, the recurrent business cycles that culminated in the Great Depression. There is a detailed analysis of the last, in which the chief blame is placed on the policies of the Federal Reserve system with respect to the money supply and to the subsequent bank closings. . . . No competent critic doubts that Federal Reserve policy indeed added to the severity of the depression. But the reader should be warned that the sole emphasis on incompetent monetary policy as the cause of the Great Depression is disputed by serious scholars, who point to other factors. It must be noted that the really bad turns in monetary policy did not come until the end of 1930, by which time the recession was already very severe. When one adds that the Great Depression, while the worst in capitalist history, had some very serious precursors, notably in 1893 and 1873, and fluctuations of a smaller amplitude were continuous, the conclusion is hard to avoid that instability of a considerable magnitude is endemic in the free enterprise system, even with a stable monetary policy.

The strength of the Friedmans' critique of active policy does not lie in general principles or broad sweeps of history. It lies in the itemization of government failures: industrial regulation that is primarily in the interests of the special groups regulated, inefficient post offices, disappointing schools, welfare "messes," the failure of public housing. . . . These failures are in part real, and the Friedmans are not wrong in suggesting that the pursuit of social goals is very apt to be carried on much less efficiently than the pursuit of one's own self-interest. They do not question the theoretical need for internalization of externalities, as in pollution, but argue that the arrangements are bound to be inefficient (actually, they are rather muted on this particular argument, and nowhere flatly assert that the social gains do not exceed the costs). They are strongly opposed to

testing drugs for efficacy but do not seem to question testing them for safety.

In short, the critique tends to be selective. They are very ingenious at suggesting alternative policies for some problems, such as the voucher system for elementary education, the negative income tax to replace welfare, or the abolition of licensing for physicians. But when advocating comprehensive changes, it is important to consider the effects on the entire system. (pp. 27-8)

I agree with specific planks in the Friedmans' program, but I remain disappointed at the lack of guiding principles, the casual recommendation of sweeping changes without consideration of their systematic effects, and the one-sided selection of evidence and problems. (p. 28)

> Kenneth J. Arrow, "Books and the Arts: 'Free to Choose'," in The New Republic *(reprinted by permission of* The New Republic; © *1980 The New Republic, Inc.), Vol. 182, No. 12, March 22, 1980, pp. 25-8.*

ROBERT L. HEILBRONER

The first message [of *Free to Choose*] is forceful and clear. It is a ringing endorsement of economic freedom and political liberty, and a warning about the dangers of continuing on our present course. . . .

[*Free to Choose*] has the ring of self-evident truth and self-confidence, a tone of conviction that is quickly communicated to the reader. Indeed, what strikes one at first is the apparently overwhelming logic, the unanswerable evidence in favor of the Friedmans' case. Take, as an initial instance, the contrast of Japan in 1867 and India in 1947 which they introduce early into the book. Was there not a striking similarity in the initial starting points of the two nations? "Both were countries with ancient civilizations and a sophisticated culture. Each had a highly structured population. Japan had a feudal structure . . . , India had a rigid caste system. . . . Both countries experienced a major political change that permitted a drastic alteration in political, economic, and social arrangements. In both countries a group of able, dedicated leaders took power . . . , determined to convert economic stagnation into rapid growth. . . ." (p. 3)

Yet look what happened. Japan rose to be a formidable economic power, with a high standard of living and widespread political freedom. India remained economically stagnant and even lapsed into brief dictatorship, which it may do again (the Friedmans warn). What, then, explains the difference? "We believe the explanation is the same as for the difference between West and East Germany, Israel and Egypt, Taiwan and Red China. Japan relied primarily on voluntary cooperation and free markets. . . . India relied on central economic planning."

The argument sounds convincing, until one begins to think about what has been left out: the long traumatic Indian experience with British imperialism for which the Japanese have no counterpart; the linguistic fragmentation of India, compared with the homogeneity of Japanese culture; the Japanese descent into dictatorship in the 1930s. The Friedmans leave out also the huge injection of American capital into Japan after World War II. . . .

They leave out, in short, a vast array of elements that would muddy the clarity of their exposition. What appears to be a clear-cut demonstration, properly simplified to present a bold case, becomes in fact a case built on selected and omitted evidence that, were it used by an ideologue of the left, would unhesitatingly be described by the Friedmans as shameful. And it is not just in the contrast of India and Japan that we find this kind of argument. The contrast between East and West Germany makes no mention of the drain of resources out of East Germany by Russia. In discussing the difference between Israel and Egypt they do not consider the respective skills and training of the two populations or the critical infusion of philanthropic capital into Israel. The juxtaposition of Taiwan and mainland China omits the fact that the market system of pre-communist China collapsed.

This same one-sided argument characterizes much of their policy diagnoses and prescriptions. Their espousal of the voucher system, for example, pays no heed to the critics' fears that such a system would convert our public schools into dumping grounds for all students who, for whatever reasons, would not be acceptable to private educational institutions. Their attack on the regulated industries effectively returns us to the aegis of free-market forces which is precisely the environment from which we fled into government regulation in the first place. Their confident call for a curb on the money supply to halt inflation ignores the growing body of professional skepticism with the monetarist position. . . .

In the face of such arguments, a critic can only throw up his hands. Some of the Friedmans' specific proposals appear to me to be shrewd and worth consideration, but not on the basis of the winnowed evidence or shabby arguments they have advanced on their behalf. *Free to Choose* is to serious economic and political debate what fundamentalist preaching is to Bible scholarship. (p. 4)

[Let me] turn to a few basic ideas that seem to underlie their thinking. The first of these is their view of the historic role of capitalism itself with respect to "human nature." To the Friedmans, capitalism represents a stage of history in which a propensity of deep, almost primordial, strength is finally accorded its rightful place and scope. This is the propensity for material betterment that provides the motor strength of capitalism and—as a consequence of competition—its built-in regulating device. Adam Smith certainly held such a view of history, calling the market economy the stage of "perfect liberty," and the Friedmans continue to rest their social philosophy on that belief.

There is, however, an opposing view. It is that the market system, far from representing the fruition of a long-blocked propensity, is the product of a violent process of social displacement during the seventeenth and eighteenth centuries that culminated in an unstable and unwelcome structure of social and economic relationships. That is the view of such observers as Burke and Coleridge and Ruskin, not to mention Polanyi, Veblen, and Marx. From this standpoint, the market system is only a passing episode in the human drama, a tumultuous and creative era in which the economic sphere was temporarily lifted above the matrix of political and social forces that normally contain and control it.

From this perspective, I think, we get a clearer picture of the contrast between market and nonmarket societies that figures so large in the Friedmans' book. . . . Capitalism builds and it also undermines. It satisfies wants but creates new ones even more rapidly, so that capitalist societies are marked by a perpetual craving, not a sense of contentment. Capitalist societies create political freedoms and simultaneously fear the implications of applying the democratic creed to the economic sphere.

Thus capitalism is far more dynamic, more restive, more self-contradictory than the Friedmans would have us believe. Their view of the market system is naïve, grasping one part of its nature, blind to others.

Closely associated with this simplistic view of the market system is their conception of economic freedom. A key word here is one the Friedmans use often: "voluntary." The hallmark of a market system, as they describe it, is that its members cooperate voluntarily, and therefore with enthusiasm and efficiency. . . . [But] the exchange of labor on the marketplace—the core activity of the market system—is not quite so natural or so unambiguously voluntary as the Friedmans make it out to be.

This restricted view of economic freedom of course affects their argument. As they use the term, economic freedom means the right to pursue one's livelihood in the marketplace, and the allied right to enjoy as little public restraint as possible in that pursuit. But once again, there is another view. Economic freedom can take the form of laws that set men free from the pressures of the marketplace, for example by enabling them to demand a legal minimum wage, or to go on welfare rather than perform distasteful work. We may not like the effects of minimum wages or welfare provisions, but it is wrong to deny that they also provide freedom of a kind to those who benefit from them. So too, economic freedom can appear as the ability of individuals to achieve collectively ends they cannot attain singly: labor unions make men free to impose their desires, which they would not be free to do without them. (p. 6)

The Friedmans of course recognize that unions can win special benefits for their own members, but they call our attention to the constraints they impose on others. It never seems to occur to them that the rights of property and of managerial prerogatives also enhance the freedom of some and limit the freedom of others. As with their conception of capitalism, the Friedmans' use of the word freedom is oversimplified and abstract.

A third idea also displays a curiously narrow view. This is the Friedmans' approach to equality:

> Much of the moral fervor behind the drive for equality of outcome comes from the widespread belief that it is not fair that some children should have a great advantage over others simply because they happen to have wealthy parents. Of course it is not fair. However, unfairness can take many forms. It can take the form of the inheritance of property—bonds and stocks, houses, factories; it can also take the form of the inheritance of talent—musical ability, strength, mathematical genius. The inheritance of property can be interfered with more readily than the inheritance of talent. But from an ethical point of view, is there any difference between the two?

The answer to this question is that there is indeed a difference, and moreover a difference that must surely be known to the authors. It is that we do not attach any moral significance to unfairnesses determined by nature, whereas we do attach such significance to those determined by society. No one considers it *morally* wrong that one person is handsome and another ugly, but everyone holds it to be morally wrong when two people have incomes which, when compared, offend sensibilities or violate conventions. This is true whether those incomes are equal or not. We are morally outraged when a gangster makes as much as a law-abiding citizen and when a useless citizen has more than a useful one. Thus the moral issue is not that of equality of outcomes at all. It is the character of the arguments that we adduce in favor of, or against, any kind of social determination, be it access to justice, work, income, or whatever. The Friedmans have failed to alert their readers to this obvious moral distinction. They must not be discomfitted, then, if their readers, on hearing it, conclude that their mentors are not altogether reliable moral guides. (p. 8)

Robert L. Heilbroner, "The Road to Selfdom," in The New York Review of Books *(reprinted with permission from* The New York Review of Books; *copyright © 1980 Nyrev, Inc.), Vol. XXVIII, No. 6, April 17, 1980, pp. 3-4, 6, 8.*

E. J. MISHAN

In important ways [*Free to Choose*] is a popular version of the more fastidious but no less cogently argued statement of his views elaborated in Friedman's *Capitalism and Freedom* (1962), views that have all but dominated the philosophy and methodology of the University of Chicago's economics department. . . .

[The remarks which follow] are guided by attention to two questions. First, is it reasonable to believe that significant social improvement can result from implementing the programme of the radical conservatives as it appears . . . ? Second, is there much likelihood of its overriding objective, reduction in government power and a consequent increase in individual freedom, being realized in the near future? . . .

The very simplicity of the remedy proposed—reducing the rate of increase of the money supply—seems to have exerted a hypnotic power on monetarists which has all but suspended their critical faculties. Such monetary theory as exists takes on dimensions of time and magnitude only from an interpretation of the statistical evidence of recent history, a history in which economic, social, and institutional conditions are unlike those that have prevailed since the 1970s. Thus both the extent of the unemployment and the extent of the duration necessary to reduce the rate of inflation to a tolerable figure are matters of sheer speculation. . . .

Central to the economic writings of the radical conservatives is the importance of individual choice. Their case for reducing government intervention in housing . . . and for increasing choice in the areas of education, pensions, and medicine . . . turns heavily on this point. And their case is strengthened when augmented by proposals for direct money transfers to the poor as entailed by Friedman's scheme for a "negative income tax".

Once we turn to the goods bought in the shops, however, the arguments depending on free choice are less compelling. Although on political grounds and, possibly, on cost-reducing grounds, a more competitive market may score high marks, a consequent expansion in the range of consumer goods is not a decisive social benefit for a number of reasons.

A growth in the existing assortment of goods in today's advanced economies is unlikely to be of much social value. Indeed, extension of the proliferation of brands and models can reach a level beyond which more bewilderment than satisfaction is created. . . .

Moreover, since a person is not only a consumer but also a worker or producer, small and ephemeral gains to consumers in substituting one relatively expendable good for another can inflict substantial losses on workers who may, in consequence, remain for some time without employment or be forced to part from neighbourhood friends in a familiar community and seek less congenial work elsewhere. By extension, the consumer advantages from freer international exchange diminish according as the pattern of demand becomes subject to impulse and fashion. . . .

On the question of the free flow of labour between countries, the radical conservatives do not take a clear position. . . . [At] a time when illegal immigration from poor to rich countries is becoming one of the touchier domestic and international issues, it is becoming painfully evident that a sustained net immigrant inflow not only adds to the congestion and disamenity in town and city but assumes a threat to cultural identity, aggravates community resentments, taxes the ingenuity and patience of the police, and deflects the political resources of the nation. . . .

For the Chicago School . . . pragmatic considerations give way to doctrinal ones. Invoking a number of restrictive suppositions, economists may conclude that unhindered migration of labour raises world income. And by transcending the bounds of mere national interest, Friedman would extend the principle of equality of opportunity to encompass untrammelled freedom of movement for every citizen of the planet. Provided only that they were not eligible for welfare, he would favour the removal of all restrictions on immigration into the United States.

Be that as it may, it is when persons are regarded not only as consumers and workers but also as citizens who are submerged in an increasingly man-made environment that the hope of expanding individual choice by the simple expedient of enlarging the area of the market seems to be foredoomed. For whatever additional choice may be gleaned from a larger market is likely to be swamped by the trend towards a reduction in the choice of the physical and social environment, a reduction of choice that is largely the consequence, since the turn of the century, of the growth of what economists call "spillovers"—those unwanted side-effects, incidental to the legitimate production and use of man-made goods, that are familiar to the public as pollution, noise, congestion and other pervasive hazards and disadvantages.

The radical conservatives are, of course, amply aware of the public's absorption with the phenomenal increase in these spillovers over the past two decades since scarcely a day passes without some alarming report about the discovery of an unsuspected hazard or the accidental escape of some toxic gas. . . . [They] draw heavily on the implications of property rights and on the concept of reorganization costs in contending that, for the most part, the market can indeed cope efficiently despite the incidence of spillovers. (p. 965)

[The] Chicago School writers [observe that] once proper account is taken of these unavoidable reorganization costs, implementation of any of the proposed pollution reducing strategies is likely to inflict a net economic loss on society. Indeed, from the logic of this providential consideration, there has been fabricated a presumption that reorganization costs do indeed exceed the apparent benefits of curtailing pollution whenever the pollution in question is observed to remain uncurtailed.

Comforting though such doctrine is to the fraternity of radical conservatives, it does not stand up to scrutiny. First of all, an extension of property rights will not, of itself, suffice to prevent overuse of a scarce resource. (pp. 965-66)

Second, the virtue most persistently claimed for the market, individual choice, resides in its ability to "decompose", so to speak, what would otherwise be packages of goods, or of goods-cum-bads—packages that, for example, could result from state decree or popular vote—into their constituent ingredients, among which, at their market prices, the individual is then free to choose. It is revealing to regard environmental spillovers in this light. Thus, if a person complains of traffic or aircraft noise, remarks about the impressive growth of travel opportunities are not to the purpose. Our individual may have little use for the new facilities offered to the general public. And if he does decide occasionally to use them it is only because he realizes that whether he does so or not makes no difference to the noise he will have to suffer. Certainly he has not agreed to the provision of new travel opportunities in exchange for the increase of noise. He simply has no choice in the matter. . . .

What the radical conservative fails to perceive is that this reduction of individual choice arising from the growth of spillovers is formally identical with the reduction of individual choice arising from the introduction of government welfare services which he is so eloquent in denouncing. For the introduction of a public good consists also of a good-cum-bad package—the good being the service provided, the bad being the tax—that each citizen is compelled to accept on the terms set by the government. Nor does the institution of property rights alter this conclusion for the more significant spillovers. If the rights to an air-shed over several hundred square miles were to be auctioned, it is almost certain that industry within the area could outbid the few thousands families who would suffer once the industry used the air as a dump for its waste gases. . . .

Indeed, this conclusion remains valid even where some ideal effluent tax is imposed so that an "optimal" level of pollution is produced by an industry.

Third, it cannot too often be repeated that whatever the methods used to curb the growing array of spillovers, there can be no general presumption of a balance of social advantage arising from the economic activities associated with them. This is particularly true when the train of adverse consequences comes to light tardily so that by the time the worst is known and society realizes, say, that it was far better off prior to the introduction of the activity in question, it also realizes that it has become too costly to return to the *status quo ante*. . . .

Fourth, and no less important, are the repercussions over time of the changing products of technology on the institutions and hence on the character and, ultimately, the viability of Western civilization. Whether such crucial and far-reaching consequences ought to be grouped under the umbrella term spillovers is, perhaps, an interesting taxonomic question. But however resolved, the fact remains that they do not lend themselves to formal economic analysis. Nor do they feature prominently on the agenda of the radical conservatives. Yet in some all-encompassing balance of well-being they surely outweigh the more mundane advantages that are thought to flow from the operation of free markets. . . .

True, those advocating an extension of the market sector of the economy do not claim that a well-functioning market is a panacea for all social infirmities. But neither do they spend time stressing its limitations; for instance, that the market is wholly indifferent to the moral quality of the society it serves. It can serve a slave economy as faithfully as a free one. So far as economic efficiency or consumer choice is concerned, it can work as well, or perhaps better, within an authoritarian regime as within a democratic one. And though we may accept, on Friedman's authority, that "There is no inconsistency between a freemarket system and the pursuit of broad social and cultural goals" . . . , the claim cannot be pitched higher: for there is no lack of evidence in the modern world to confirm the fact that a free market has no noticeable tendency to diffuse good taste or to maintain standards of excellence among the populace. . . .

We may conclude tentatively that if we are concerned, in the main, with individual freedom of choice, *a fortiori* if we are concerned with the social good, it would be naive to place such hope in the expansion of competitive markets. But is it reasonable to anticipate a significant expansion of the market sector at the expense of the public sector of the economy, and if so, would it entail some worthwhile increase in personal freedom?

Reflections on the direction being taken by modern technology beget scepticism. Certainly, those innovations based on silicon chips, on microfilm, and on computer technology generally, which have multiplied the capacity for the rapid processing, organization, storage, and retrieval of information, act to extend the efficient size of the industrial, commercial, or government unit that can be centrally controlled. In increasing the effective economies of size, they also extend the reach of government control.

What is more, these same innovations make it technically feasible to accumulate detailed and personal information about millions of citizens, an opportunity that governments and private agencies will find difficult to resist. . . .

No less important in this respect are those innovations either of consumer gadgetry that spoil the amenity of others, or else of industrial processes that produce a variety of toxic wastes or of synthetics that enter the food chain. Both kinds of innovation create new social hazards and conflicts of interest within the community. Inevitably, then, both produce a public demand for government regulation and control. . . . [The] vigilance necessary for reasonable standards of safety will require security measures that only restrict personal freedom.

A less obvious factor, though one that could be decisive, tending to promote government control is the social phenomenon we euphemistically refer to as "permissiveness". . . .

[On] the face of things, this permissive society is also a providential development, whereby the modern technically sophisticated economy, under a constant institutional compulsion to expand, may be kept going. For the expansion of modern industry depends directly on whetting and enlarging the appetite of the consuming public so as to enable it to engorge a growing volume and variety of goods. Clearly, a public whose appetite is restrained by established norms of propriety or traditional notions of good taste will not serve. The ideal public for modern industry must be one that is both promiscuous and insatiable—the qualites *par excellence* of the permissive society. For a society in which "anything goes" is *ipso facto* a society in which anything sells.

To where does this tend? A new "own-ethic" society, one in which each citizen guides his actions by reference to his own privately constructed conscience, must surely weaken the foundations of the free enterprise system. After all, the pride in personal rectitude, which carries over into business dealings, into the relations between employer and employee, is also an essential part of what we might call the moral infra-structure of a well-functioning capitalist system.

But the spread of the permissive ethic may not only threaten the efficient functioning of business and, indeed, of government; more important, it may pose a direct threat to the maintenance of law and order, and thus to personal freedom itself. In a society in which ideas of right and wrong become increasingly ephemeral, self-serving, and diverse, the citizen, fearful of the resulting rise in anarchy and violence, is readier to surrender to the police powers of search, arrest, and control, that are incompatible with contemporary notions of personal freedom.

Friedman, observing the political manifestations in America of the public's resentment against tax burdens and against bureaucratic incursions into the everyday life of people, is sanguine enough to entitle the final chapter of his new book, "The Tide is Turning". . . . Once we raise our sights above the prospects for the market sector to take in other and more startling phenomena—the world's teeming population and its current overspill into the rich but vulnerable West, or the social conflicts and dangers associated above with rapid technical innovation—there is no cause for complacency about the direction of the gathering tide.

On reflection, it transpires that the intimate relation between capitalism and freedom, so ably argued and so convincingly illustrated by . . . Friedman . . . turns on two tacit preconditions: the existence of a benign technology and the existence of a moral infrastructure. As indicated, however, modern technology has become environmentally and socially disruptive, while the emergence of the permissive society, seemingly so opportune for the survival of post-war capitalism, also perverts the moral order without which a free society cannot endure.

If there is public alarm today about the power and size of governments, there is no less public alarm about the unfolding consequences of modern technology and, for that matter, much more public alarm at the post-war trend of violence and terrorism. . . . For no expansion of material prosperity can alter the fact that life is a pathetic thing if people, emerging from behind the bolted doors of their homes and cars, have to creep about the streets in continued fear of physical assault.

Well may Friedman demur in that last chapter of his. Perhaps his mind was momentarily ruffled by the ominous thought that the permissive society could indeed be the precursor of the totalitarian state. (p. 966)

> *E. J. Mishan, "Chicago, with Reservations," in* The Times Literary Supplement *(© Times Newspapers Ltd. (London) 1980; reproduced from* The Times Literary Supplement *by permission), No. 4040, September 5, 1980, pp. 965-66.*

DONALD J. YANKOVIC

[This] review will first examine the Friedmans' message in the context of the debate [which *Free to Choose*] has aroused and then offer a critique from the point of view of one who teaches economics. . . .

Robert Heilbroner's review [see excerpt above] . . . takes the Friedmans to task for "one-sided" argumentation, for offering "simplistic" views of the market system and the concept of economic freedom, and a "narrow" view of the concept of equality. With respect to the method of argumentation, the book is subtitled "A personal statement" and the authors clearly indicate that their purpose is to persuade readers to embrace a certain set of principles. To accomplish this the presentation is selective and incomplete. . . .

The Friedmans' view of the market system as providing for economic growth and for improving the well-being of the bulk of the population is contrasted by Heilbroner with the view that it "is the product of a violent process of social displacement . . . that culminated in an unstable and unwelcome structure of social and economic relationships." That there is a trade-off between freedom and security is well known, and the balance is generally struck differently by those on different rungs of the economic ladder. (p. 568)

Heilbroner's point about the "narrow" concept of equality articulated in Chapter 5 seems to be misplaced. He focuses on the statement that "The inheritance of property can be interfered with more readily than the inheritance of talent. But, from an ethical point of view, is there any difference between the two?" . . . Heilbroner answers yes, ascribing greater moral offensiveness to inequalities created by society. One could agree with Heilbroner, of course, and still agree with the Friedmans that the best course of action to remedy the resulting outrages to our moral sensibilities (arising from either source of inequality) is to have the freest possible society so that these inequalities do not become institutionalized.

In his *London Times* review [see excerpt above] . . . E. J. Mishan reflects on whether it is reasonable to believe that any "significant social improvement" would follow from the adoption of the Friedmans' proposals and whether these proposals might be implemented in the near future. He is pessimistic on both questions, believing that public apprehensions about the dangerous effects of some technologies, together with the apparent increase of ruthless fanaticism and violence, will give rise to ever increasing demands for the hand of government in society.

How should these issues be approached? . . . Technology, of course, always wears two faces, and calls forth the cultivation of many new individual and social skills to mitigate its possible malevolent effects. (pp. 568-69)

The Friedmans offer a sound prescription for improving the economic well-being of the bulk of the population by widening the range of individual choices. The problem of what to do about the "evils that remain" is still with us. . . .

The society characterized by economic and political freedom presents both opportunities and responsibilities to its citizens, and there is always a price to be paid. The fact that some will abuse freedom is not a condemnation of the market system or a proof of its evil; rather, it is an evil that it cannot prevent—on the grounds that the evils of despotism are worse.

If we are to help our students shape a vision of the good society (and live in the real one), two things must be done. First, we must teach them how to protect themselves from others who would abuse freedom. *Free to Choose* is a great help here. It reminds us that there are many protections for us, in our various economic roles, in the market itself. It also reminds us that when we turn to government for protection, good intentions can lead to perverse results. (p. 569)

Second—and every bit as important as the first—we must be prepared to go on to teach about virtue; that is, about how to protect others from the consequences of our own actions when we enter the marketplace. As teachers of economics we can, through example and exhortation, show our students that treating others as mere objects for personal gain will invariably give rise to calls for limiting economic freedom.

Here again *Free to Choose* is an excellent text. The litany of government regulations is also a litany of areas where gross abuses have entered the marketplace. Whether self-protection and competition in markets, or the regulatory instruments of government are most appropriate to deal with these evils are areas of controversy. Reasonable men of good will can be expected to disagree. The book provides an excellent point of view for considering this issue. (pp. 569-70)

> *Donald J. Yankovic, ''Book Reviews: 'Free to Choose: A Personal Statement','' in* The Journal of Economic Literature *(copyright © 1981 by The American Economic Association), Vol. XIX, No. 2, June, 1981, pp. 568-70.*

John Kenneth Galbraith

1908-

A Canadian-born American political economist, educator, editor, writer on political and economic issues, and novelist, Galbraith has profoundly influenced American economic theory. A major accomplishment has been his translation of difficult economic theories into language understandable by the general public: his dry wit and ability to synthesize complex ideas have made such books as *The Affluent Society* (1958) and *The New Industrial State* (1967) popular successes. He has been called by Paul A. Samuelson the "non-economist's economist." Galbraith was influenced by the economic theories of John Maynard Keynes, whom he credits with his own conversion to economics. Galbraith was the American Ambassador to India from 1961 to 1963, served as an advisor to Presidents Kennedy and Johnson, and was the Paul M. Warburg Professor of Economics at Harvard University from 1959 to 1975. (See also *Contemporary Authors*, Vols. 21-24, rev. ed.)

Wide World Photos

Excerpt from *THE AFFLUENT SOCIETY*

The final problem of the productive society is what it produces. This manifests itself in an implacable tendency to provide an opulent supply of some things and a niggardly yield of others. This disparity carries to the point where it is a cause of social discomfort and social unhealth. The line which divides our area of wealth from our area of poverty is roughly that which divides privately produced and marketed goods and services from publicly rendered services. Our wealth in the first is not only in startling contrast with the meagerness of the latter, but our wealth in privately produced goods is, to a marked degree, the cause of crisis in the supply of public services. For we have failed to see the importance, indeed the urgent need, of maintaining a balance between the two.

This disparity between our flow of private and public goods and services is no matter of subjective judgment. On the contrary, it is the source of the most extensive comment which only stops short of the direct contrast being made here. In the years following World War II, the papers of any major city—those of New York were an excellent example—told daily of the shortages and shortcomings in the elementary municipal and metropolitan services. The schools were old and overcrowded. The police force was under strength and underpaid. The parks and playgrounds were insufficient. Streets and empty lots were filthy, and the sanitation staff was underequipped and in need of men. Access to the city by those who work there was uncertain and painful and becoming more so. Internal transportation was overcrowded, unhealthful and dirty. So was the air. Parking on the streets should have been prohibited, but there was no space elsewhere. These deficiencies were not in new and novel services but in old and established ones. Cities have long swept their streets, helped their people move around, educated them, kept order, and provided horse rails for equipages which sought to pause. That their residents should have a nontoxic supply of air suggests no revolutionary dalliance with socialism.

The discussion of this public poverty competed, on the whole successfully, with the stories of ever-increasing opulence in privately produced goods. The Gross National Product was rising. So were retail sales. So was personal income. Labor productivity had also advanced. The automobiles that could not be parked were being produced at an expanded rate. The children, though without schools, subject in the playgrounds to the affectionate interest of adults with odd tastes, and disposed to increasingly imaginative forms of delinquency, were admirably equipped with television sets. We had difficulty finding storage space for the great surpluses of food despite a national disposition to obesity. Food was grown and packaged under private auspices. The care and refreshment of the mind, in contrast with the stomach, was principally in the public domain. Our colleges and universities were often severely overcrowded and underprovided, and the same was even more often true of the mental hospitals.

The contrast was and remains evident not alone to those who read. The family which takes its mauve and cerise, air-conditioned, power-steered and power-braked automobile out for a tour passes through cities that are badly paved, made hideous by litter, blighted buildings, billboards and posts for wires that should long since have been put underground. They pass on into a countryside that has been rendered largely invisible by commercial art. (The goods which the latter advertise have an absolute priority in our value system. Such aesthetic considerations as a view of the countryside accordingly come second. On such matters, we are consistent.) They picnic on exquisitely packaged food from a portable icebox by a polluted stream and go on to spend the night at a park which is a menace to public health and morals. Just before dozing off on an air mattress, beneath a nylon tent, amid the stench of decaying refuse, they may reflect vaguely on the curious unevenness of their blessings. Is this, indeed, the American genius? (pp. 221-23)

> *John Kenneth Galbraith, in his* The Affluent Society *(copyright © 1958, 1969, 1976 by John Kenneth Galbraith; reprinted by permission of Houghton Mifflin Company), revised edition, Houghton Mifflin, 1969, 333 p.*

Excerpt from *THE NEW INDUSTRIAL STATE*

In the past, leadership in business organization was identified with the entrepreneur—the individual who united ownership or control of capital with the capacity for organizing the other factors of production and, in most contexts, with a further capacity for innovation. With the rise of the modern corporation, the emergence of the organization required by modern technology and planning and the divorce of the owner of the capital from control of the enterprise, the entrepreneur no longer exists as an individual person in the mature industrial enterprise. Everyday discourse, except in the economics textbooks, recognizes this change. It replaces the entrepreneur, as the directing force of the enterprise, with management. This is a collective and imperfectly defined entity; in the large corporation it embraces chairman, president, those vice presidents with important staff or departmental responsibility, occupants of other major staff positions and, perhaps, division or department heads not included above. It includes, however, only a small proportion of those who, as participants, contribute information to group decisions. This latter group is very large; it extends from the most senior officials of the corporation to where it meets, at the outer perimeter, the white-and blue-collar workers whose function is to conform more or less mechanically to instruction or routine. It embraces all who bring specialized knowledge, talent or experience to group decision-making. This, not the narrow management group, is the guiding intelligence—the brain—of the enterprise. There is no name for all who participate in group decision-making or the organization which they form. I propose to call this organization the Technostructure. (pp. 73-4)

The planning system has brought its supply of capital, and in substantial measure also its labor supply, within its control, and thus within the ambit of its planning. And it has extended its influence deeply into the state. Those policies of the state that are vital for the planning system—regulation of aggregate demand, maintenance of the large public (if preferably technical) sector on which this regulation depends, underwriting of advanced technology and provision of an increasing volume of trained and educated manpower—are believed to be of the highest social urgency. This belief accords with the needs of the system. And the influence of the technostructure of the mature firm extends to shaping the demand for its particular product or range of products. Individual members of the technostructure identify themselves with the design, development and production of items purchased by the government as the technostructure identifies itself with the social goal, say, of an effective national defense. And the members of the technostructure adapt design, development or need for items procured

by the government to what accords with their own goals. These goals reflect, inevitably, the needs of the technostructure and of its planning.

Paralleling these changes, partly as a result and partly as a cause, has been a profound shift in the locus of economic and political power. The financier and the union leader are, relative to others, dwindling influences in the society. They are honored more for their past eminence than for their present power. The technostructure exercises less direct political power than did the antecedent entrepreneur. But that is because it has far more influence as an arm and extension of the public bureaucracy and in its effect on the larger climate of belief. The scientific, technical, organizational and planning needs of the technostructure have brought into being a large educational and scientific estate. And, while the commitment of the culture, under the tutelage of the planning system, to a single-minded preoccupation with the production of goods is strong, it is not complete. Rising income also nurtures a further artistic and intellectual community outside of the planning system. (pp. 330-31)

If we continue to believe that the goals of the planning system—the expansion of output, the companion increase in consumption, technological advance, the public images that sustain it—are coordinate with life, then all of our lives will be in the service of these goals. What is consistent with these ends we shall have or be allowed; all else will be off limits. Our wants will be managed in accordance with the needs of the planning system; the policies of the state will be subject to similar influence; education will be adapted to industrial need; the disciplines required by the planning system will be the conventional morality of the community. All other goals will be made to seem precious, unimportant or antisocial. We will be bound to the ends of the system. The state will add its moral, and perhaps some of its legal, power to their enforcement. What will eventuate, on the whole, will be the benign servitude of the household retainer who is taught to love her mistress and see her interests as her own, and not the compelled servitude of the field hand. But it will not be freedom.

If, on the other hand, the planning system is only a part, and relatively a diminishing part, of life, there is much less occasion for concern. Aesthetic goals will have pride of place; those who serve them will not be subject to the goals of the technostructure; the planning system itself will be subordinate to the claims of these dimensions of life. Intellectual preparation will be for its own sake and not for better service to the planning system. Men will not be entrapped by the belief that apart from the goals of the planning system—apart from the production of goods and income by progressively more advanced technical methods—there is nothing important in life.

The foregoing being so, we may, over time, come to see the planning system in fitting light as an essentially technical arrangement for providing convenient goods and services in adequate volume. Those who rise through its bureaucracy will so see themselves. And the public consequences will be in keeping, for if economic goals are the only goals of the society, it is natural that the planning system should dominate the state and the state should serve its ends. If other goals are strongly asserted, the planning system will, one can hope, fall into its place as a detached and autonomous arm of the state but one responsive to the larger purposes of the society.

We have seen wherein the chance for salvation lies. The planning system, in contrast with its economic antecedents, is intellectually demanding. It brings into existence to serve its intellectual and scientific needs the community that, all should hope, will reject its monopoly of social purpose. (pp. 413-14)

> John Kenneth Galbraith, in his The New Industrial State *(copyright © 1967, 1971, 1978 by John Kenneth Galbraith; reprinted by permission of Houghton Mifflin Company), revised edition, Houghton Mifflin, 1978, 446 p.*

NORMAN MacKENZIE

[In *American Capitalism*] Mr. Galbraith offers . . . a "pump-priming" programme as his answer to those who ask if the U.S. can afford peace. But he completely fails to understand that the point of the question is not the technical feasibility of a Keynesian prescription, but its political feasibility. He blandly asserts that Congress would vote the funds, though his assertion rests more on faith than argument. Swept away by his obsession with the virtues of monopoly capitalism, he never stops to ask whether the big corporations would accept the social implications of this domestic programme, which would be far less attractive to them than a continuation of rearmament and inflation on the scale of recent years. It may be better than a slump. But is it better than things as they are?

It is all very well for Mr. Galbraith to resent suggestions that American capitalism is now propped up by armament expenditure. But he himself argues that the fear of depression in the United States is greater than the fear of war. . . . If this is true, then it is at least fair to argue that many Americans may prefer rearmament—which means full employment as well as inflation—to the prospect of another depression. Why risk the loss of present comforts merely for the assurance that any slump could be cured by hypothetical economic medicines? They are medicines, moreover, that the most important patients might well refuse to swallow. If Mr. Galbraith had really faced that issue, he could not have presented this sophisticated apologia for American monopoly capitalism with such complacency. (p. 458)

> Norman MacKenzie "The New Formula," in The New Statesman & Nation *(© 1952 The Statesman & Nation Publishing Co. Ltd.), Vol. XLIV, No. 1128, October 18, 1952, pp. 457-58.*

GEORGE H. HILDEBRAND

[*A Theory of Price Control*] is less a *theory* of price control than it is an interpretation that blends history with *ad hoc* reasoning. The treatment is not general, hence theoretical, in the sense of a refined system of models within which the influence of key variables can be examined. Ends themselves are not really compared, and for any given end the merits of various alternative means are not adequately explored. However, the subject is relatively new, and these things may not be entirely reasonable to ask. Having asked them, I should elaborate.

An adequate theory of price controls ought to consider the *timing* of their introduction. If the shift to war economy begins in depression, at what point, if any, should the controls be imposed, and in what form? If the shift begins in full employment, then should price controls be applied at once, or during, or after reallocation? And again, in what form?

Granted, next, that we want "maximum" production in wartime, overfull employment follows. It also follows that we cannot then have a monetary policy that penalizes strategically situated sellers for uneconomic prices and wages. Instead, we inflate the whole system further, to finance a higher price level without sacrificing production. Here Galbraith calls for concealing the inflation with price control, rather than allowing it to take the open form. His reason is that he fears the effects of inflation (open) upon "the values and amenities of economic life.". . . I agree with him. Yet in all candor price controls do not prevent inflation. They hide it. And in the considered judgment of some economists, price controls, too, threaten the survival of a free society, though in wartime their use might be viewed as a temporary surrender of certain liberties made necessary for the survival of liberty itself.

Yet the place of price controls in a war economy itself is not self-evident. Several questions require investigation. To what extent does the adoption of price control depend upon the extent of the reallocation required? Why is it preferable, say, to the use of multiple currencies in free markets? Or to one currency, free prices, and direct allocations only?

What is the basis for assuming that price control will probably yield a better economic performance than could be had under open inflation? Does the answer depend upon the probable rate of increase in the price level under open inflation? Or does the issue turn upon incentives? During the war, much was said about "equality of sacrifice." Is there greater equality of sacrifice under price control than in open inflation? Is it true that equality of sacrifice has greater force as an incentive for production than would market-determined rewards (suitably taxed) under free prices?

Consider, next, limited mobilization. Here Galbraith predicts a monetary policy that will yield full employment. To full employment he couples monetary equilibrium. Then he predicts rising wages and prices, citing the "interaction" of wages and prices. What is the cause of this "interaction"? Is it the "power" of certain sellers, treated as an independent variable? If so, the argument confuses the parts with the whole. To me it is fantastic to say that these selected groups can themselves determine the whole level of prices and wages. If money supply is held constant, the upward push of particular wages and prices will be checked. Either these sellers will experience declining sales and employment (elasticity of demand); or, if they are mainly situated at points of increasing demand because of rearmament, then demands elsewhere must decrease. Either way, a moderate buffer of unemployed resources is created.

To say, therefore, that wages and prices by "interaction" can generate inflation is to confuse an effect with a cause. What the proposition really means is that monetary expansion is to be practiced, to accommodate the aggressive sellers. If so, there will be a general pull of excess demands, which will operate to raise the level of prices and wages all around. The real cause is monetary policy. As the cause, it is a variable for theory, capable of hypothetical manipulation. Political "necessities," if they exist, are irrelevant for analysis. The duty of the economist is to link causes with effects.

Last, if the purpose of price controls is to *keep down* prices and wages during transition to preparedness, they are not likely to work. The imperatives of a wartime society are not there to sustain them. And if by a miracle they were to work, the resulting distortions would make little economic sense.

Galbraith has given us two cases in which he believes price control is desirable: war economy and limited mobilization. There is also a third for which price control is being advocated. Its outlines are now becoming clear, in the year following completion of his manuscript. In deference to its ingenious founders, I shall term it the "Oxford approach," though in this country it has been developed by equally capable politicians, acting either from design or pragmatic opportunism.

The "Oxford approach" has nothing to do with war or limited mobilization. It begins with the idea of perpetual full employment at any cost. It calls for price control as a method for transferring incomes from the relatively unorganized majority to well-organized minorities who are immensely strong politically—the members of certain favored unions, and, of course, the farmers. The technique is to control prices in different ways: to hold down some, while pushing up others. This is to be done by state intervention. The policy calls for systematic expansion of money supply. With suitable legislative and adminstrative exemptions, this draws up farm prices. At the same time, employment is kept full. It also calls for highly virtuous *downward* control of the prices of manufacturers and distributors. This permits some squeezing of profits, which are partially converted to wages for the favored unionists. The transfer is effected by government wage control *upwards*. Government wage-raising is achieved by setting up a wage control board whose task is to rationalize large wage increases, which then acquire patriotic sanction. To this may be added, where necessary, direct coercion of one part to collective bargaining (Presidential attacks on profits plus seizure of the industry).

I humbly suggest that economists interested in price control ought to give thoughtful study to this case, or program, or collection of policies. Investigation might turn up some real dangers to a free society that are lurking in the background.

If all of this were defended simply on the ground that farmers and unionists are better than other people, at least it could be understood and even debated. But the wonder of it all is that the losers themselves seem to favor it. Most of them firmly believe that the program is necessary: (1) to fight inflation (it promotes it); (2) to overcome poverty (it increases it); (3) to obtain more equal incomes (it makes them more unequal). All of which suggests the wisdom of Professor Knight's lament that man is essentially a romantic animal, hence a political one. (pp. 988-90)

> George H. Hildebrand, "Industrial Organization, Public Regulation of Business: 'A Theory of Price Control'," in The American Economic Review, Vol. XLII, No. 5, December, 1952, pp. 986-90.

DANIEL BELL

[In *American Capitalism*] Galbraith has skillfully developed a realistic theory of political economy, more suitable than the old competitive one to a world of economic behemoths. And yet, Galbraith is enough of a Keynesian to know this is not enough. . . . The need . . . is for some form of centralized government decision, namely in the area of fiscal policy so as to influence the total demand for goods through taxation or government spending. "If the Keynesian formula is workable, then the last of the major reasons for alarm over American capitalism dissolves."

Yet the book fails in a singular manner. It never answers its own question: *why* are the business community and the left captives to a description of reality that no longer exists; *why*, in effect, is the myth more compelling than the reality? To reply, as Galbraith does, by supplying a truer picture of the reality is merely like telling a neurotic that his fears are groundless; they may be, but the answer cannot convince the neurotic of the fact until the sources of the fear are laid bare. The sources involve an examination of some dialectical processes which raise the question not only of the new nature of capitalist reality, but some quite new challenges to its survival. (pp. 609-10)

Curiously, the problems caused by a permanent war economy Galbraith avoids almost completely. (p. 611)

> Daniel Bell, "The Prospects of American Capitalism: Today's Economists' Somewhat Rosier View," in Commentary (reprinted by permission; all rights reserved), Vol. 14, No. 12, December, 1952, pp. 603-12.*

ROBERT L. HEILBRONER

Much of [*The Affluent Society*] will appear as so much heresy to the defenders of the current economic morality, and all the more so because, like all dangerous heresies, so much of it is good sense. The general reader will relish a book whose style is polished and witty, but the professional will feel its sharp barbs. Hence no doubt the book will be subjected to much technical criticism. Let us hope that this will not take place at the expense of a more probing criticism of the basic issues which this book raises. One of these is the moral problem of how an Affluent Society may be prevented from becoming merely a Rich one. A second is the efficacy of Mr. Galbraith's reforms to offset the inertia and the vested interests of a powerful social structure. A third is what form of social cohesion can replace our troublesome but useful absorption in Production. It is a measure of Mr. Galbraith's achievement that it raises questions of this magnitude and importance.

> Robert L. Heilbroner, "Economist's Provocative Challenge to Certain Cherished Beliefs," in New York Herald Tribune Book Review (© I.H.T. Corporation; reprinted by permission), June 1, 1958, p. 3.

MICHAEL D. REAGAN

Three [objections to John Kenneth Galbraith's arguments in *The Affluent Society*] for which answers are not readily apparent occur to this reader. The first is that productivity outruns needs today only in terms of the domestic market. From a world view, all our output and more *could* be invaluable to Asian-African people—and South Americans! What Galbraith means by his attack is that the problem of *consumer* goods has been solved for *America*, but he states his case in a way to neglect the qualifications. Perhaps overstatement was necessary to make the case effectively.

A second objection is that he disposes too easily of the problem of poverty in America. Granted that improved social balance would in the long run be of greater value to the poor than avoidance of a sales tax, it seems hyperbolic to say that "In the affluent society no useful distinction can be made between luxuries and necessaries." "Affluent" is a middle- and upper-income label. It does not, even in America, apply to the twenty per cent of families whose average income is below $3,000.

For these families, food and clothing are not "opulent expenditures," and a sales tax which fails to distinguish such items from the outboard runabouts of the seven-thousand-dollar family strikes me as inconsistent with the rest of his program.

Finally, the greater success of national than of state and local politics in taking the long view makes one doubt the likelihood of obtaining sufficient taxes of any kind from state legislatures and city councils. The liberal influence which would approve Galbraith's social program is much stronger in national politics. For this reason a federal grant-in-aid program seems a more hopeful, if a more cumbersome, arrangement.

These criticisms are at most qualifications upon a stimulating and persuasive argument. A more refreshing examination of the stereotypes of both liberal and conservative economic thought has not appeared in many a year. (p. 547)

> *Micheal D. Reagan, "Private Wealth and Public Poverty," in* The Nation *(copyright 1958 The Nation magazine, The Nation Associates, Inc.), Vol. 186, No. 24, June 14, 1958, pp. 546-47.*

THE ECONOMIST

"**The Affluent Society**" is penetrating, fresh, knowledgeable, humane, and—though it gets off to a slow start—entertainingly written. It is also perverse, muddleheaded, provincial and dangerous. The society which Professor Galbraith analyses has a number of other characteristics besides affluence. Its industry is no longer typically competitive, but oligopolistic; so is its labour market. Partly as a result, its consumers' "needs" are not autonomous, but dependent on the ever-intensified pressure of advertising, seconded by consumer credit. Also as a result, it is highly unstable and subject to creeping inflation. Because of the "dependence effect"—the pumping-up of consumer needs to match output—it has an inadequate margin either for defence or for technological progress; and its public services, from street-cleaning to university teaching, are starved and unconsidered. These evils persist because, in matters of economic theory, public policy, and social ethics, the Affluent Society continues to be guided by a "conventional wisdom" applicable only to an age of mass poverty.

[The] central notion of "affluence" remains vague. At what level of income per head does it replace poverty and make the "conventional wisdom" obsolete? When the generality of consumers have three square meals a day and shoes all round? Or a bedroom apiece? Or indoor plumbing? Or a car? Was America "affluent" in the 1900s, the 1920s? Is Britain "affluent" today? There is no hint of an answer; no hint, either, that the necessary changes in the "conventional wisdom" may be a matter of less and more, of shifting balance and emphasis, corresponding to the gradually changing preoccupations, the gradually altering relative urgencies, and the differing problems, of an evolving society. To Professor Galbraith the conventional wisdom is now, whatever its past usefulness, merely bunk; and indeed, by equating it almost exclusively with the pronouncements of the nineteenth-century classics and with the more dinosaur-like noises emitted by the National Association of Manufacturers, he does succeed in making it sound not merely obsolete but repulsive. The Affluent Society, he says, should cast it aside; stop worrying about efficiency, avoidance of waste, incentives, and the sanctity of consumer choice; concentrate on stability of prices and employment—with controls for the one and featherbedding for the other, as necessary—and impose a sales tax on private spending in order to finance the public services, defence, and the kind of investment, especially in education, whose market value is too remote to interest private business.

Is "social unbalance"—the starving of public services . . . necessarily the fruit of "conventionally" guided affluence, or, simply, an American weakness? Never an eye does he cast across the Atlantic for an answer. How practicable a long-run remedy for inflation is price control? Again, a look abroad might have helped, but none is taken. More important, is it really justifiable to assume that all improvements in the private standard of living, once primary needs are met, are of the "dependent" kind, generated by the productive process itself and by implication never missed if never achieved? Rude plenty is one thing; civilisation—meaning not more and more chromium nor even more and more comfort, but the opportunity for human development beyond the merry-peasant level—is another. . . . Still more important, can even America embark on a massive campaign to correct "social imbalance" and simultaneously neglect efficiency, decry incentive, and provide feather beds all round? True. Professor Galbraith's programme includes a diversion of resources to fundamental research, eventually fruitful in production; but the productive gains from fundamental research are apt to be just the kind that depend on adaptability, mobility, the smashing of existing productive patterns, and all the discomforts of dynamic change. (p. 928)

"**The Affluent Society**" . . . is, by implication, about advanced societies in general; and plenty of people in Britain, the second most affluent of the major economies, will find his arguments congenial. "They shall be simple in their lives, And splendid in their public ways"—how attractive an ideal. How unimportant, how delusive, is consumers' freedom. How detestable, how soul-killing, is the competitive rat-race. How humane an enterprise is the provision of feather beds. One has heard this sort of thing before; one will even without Professor Galbraith's encouragement, assuredly hear it again. The truth is that while America, the world's economic pace-setter, can slacken off without sacrificing more than the gains which sustained effort would have brought, Britain has long ago lost the pace-setter's privilege; its alternatives are not a strenuous but rewarding dynamic progress or a reasonably comfortable stagnation at present levels of "affluence," but dynamic progress or decay and collapse. This may be extremely regrettable; the ideal Subtopia, screamed over by jet airliners, redolent of frying oil, peppered with fluorescent display signs, threaded by processions of near-immobile cars between endless avenues of Jacobethan villas, falls some way short of the New Jerusalem. But if the alternative is not the New Jerusalem but something like the Jarrow of the 1930s, even Subtopia is preferable. "**The Affluent Society**" may, on balance, make very salutary reading in its native land. In Britain, it may only encourage delusion. (p. 929)

> *"The Price of Affluence," in* The Economist *(© The Economist Newspaper Limited, 1958), Vol. CLXXXVIII, No. 6004, September 20, 1958, pp. 928-29.*

R. H. S. CROSSMAN

In *The Liberal Hour* [Galbraith] returns more than once, and with ever increasing unease, to the [theme of *The Affluent Society:* namely, elaborating and suggesting remedies to the endemic problems of inflation and the chronic imbalance between public and private affluence]; and, as if convinced at last that his first cure was inadequate, comes up with two new and suprisingly drastic remedies. His chapter 'Inflation: What It Takes' is characteristic of this new, more radical mood. First, in a few pages, he analyses the problem with the sardonic lucidity of which only he is capable. Then, when we are dazzled by his brilliance, he coolly tells us that the way to control inflation is through State intervention. In semi-monopolies such as steel, where wages and prices are both regularly increased without any comparable increase of productivity, the State should step in and regulate both. This, from someone who turns down the extension of public ownership to the great monopolies as politically impractical and an inroad on freedom, is a little breathtaking!

His attitude to defence spending seems to me equally Utopian. Having rightly asserted that the USA is not economically dependent on arms orders, he is faced with the problem of what should replace defence spending if peace broke out. [He argues that this transition requires careful planning and a clearly specified alternative to arms expenditures.] . . . But the real question is whether the government of a western Affluent Society which is now carrying a vast defence budget *can* spend the same amount on 'a clearly specified alternative'. . . .

Of course I am not suggesting that Galbraith's remedies are economically unsound. Yet they seem to me irrelevant, because they are abstracted from political reality. If politics is the art of the possible, they are just not politics. Indeed, these essays only confirm my impression that, despite the revolutionary implications of his analysis, Galbraith remains, in the strictest sense of the words, a liberal economist; and the title of this little book is aptly chosen to explain how a man who is so rigorous and extreme in theory yet manages to remain the confidant of successive Democratic candidates. Like his predecessors, Hobson and Keynes, the two most subversive thinkers of our century, Galbraith shields himself from the logic of ideas by studying economics in isolation from politics and power. . . .

The result of this uncritical attitude is an astonishing naivety of political analysis. The very man who has exposed the nature of oligopoly in the modern economy remains blind to the role of even more formidable concentrations of power in democratic politics. In the Galbraithian philosophy, the pursuit of happiness is still regarded as the main motive of western democracy. That the pursuit of power as an end in itself has become the dominant force in the twentieth-century State is a concept too unorthodox and too vulgar for him to take very seriously. Like Keynes, and for the same reason, he writes of Marxism and other ideologies as superstitions, too silly to discuss seriously, and dismisses as unreal those factors in the situation which cannot be resolved into their economic components. It was the role of Hobson, while detesting Communism, to provide Lenin with the ideas which could be vulgarised into a revolutionary myth that destroyed the whole system of colonial imperialism. It may well be that Galbraith has already performed a similar historical role by providing the prolegomena to any modern socialist theory of capitalism, while remaining, in his political attitudes, staunchly anti-socialist. How often in history it is the bastard ideas, whose paternity the author firmly denies, that shake the world.

R.H.S. Crossman, "Economics in Isolation," in New Statesman *(© 1960 The Statesman & Nation Publishing Co. Ltd.), Vol. LX, No. 1545, October 22, 1960, p. 616.*

RAYMOND J. SAULNIER

["**The New Industrial State**"] is a tightly organized, closely reasoned book, notable for what it says about the dynamics of institutional change and for certain qualities of its author: a sardonic wit, exercised liberally at the expense of conservatives, and unusual perception. That the latter in fact produces slightly out-of-focus images of reality (the key to understanding Mr. Galbraith) makes it, in a way, all the more interesting.

Although the book's theoretical structure is formidable, its architecture is not particularly novel. . . .

But novelty isn't everything: one can make a decent case for the proposition that it is more important to be right than different. The critical question is whether Galbraith's building-blocks are sufficiently strong to support his structure. This reader thinks they are not. It is not that what he says on specific issues is completely wrong. Rather, what he says is just true enough to be plausible, but not true enough to make a convincing case. In the end, what Mr. Galbraith presents is a shaky edifice. (p. 2)

The crucial question in evaluating [Galbraith's theory] is whether corporate enterprise and government have in fact achieved the degree of control he attributes to them. It is not enough to say they have achieved important control; the question is whether the process has gone far enough to have produced the institutional transformation his theory implies.

In the first place, is the consumer the manipulated, accurately forecastable, somehow faceless figure he is pictured as being, buying what he is told to buy at prices and in amounts that suit the convenience and security of the technostructure? Without meaning to underrate the adman's successes, I suggest that there is little in experience or logic to support this view. If advertising had the power here alleged, would a product ever lose its market position, let alone fail altogether? But the record is full of fatalities; indeed it is rare that a product, design or style, no matter how much advertising money is spent, does not at some point fall from favor. By some beneficent law of nature, admen consume admen.

Second, there is no evidence that corporate enterprise has achieved meaningful financial independence. In the years 1960-65, corporations went to market for one-third of their capital requirements; and last summer a good many treasurers got a quick course of instruction in the virtues of liquidity.

Third, the familiar concept of separation of corporate ownership from control, a piece of now-conventional wisdom that is a key building-block in Galbraith's structure, is actually quite obsolete. It misses entirely the hawk-eye surveillance of corporate management by institutional investors and security analysts, all surrogates of the individual shareholder and, Galbraith notwithstanding, still very much interested in profit maximization. As for comfortable independence, it would be difficult to name a figure on the American scene, political personages not excepted, more closely monitored than the head of a large corporation.

Fourth, contrary to what Galbraith states or implies, there is no convincing empirical evidence of a trend toward greater concentration in markets . . . ; there is no basis for asserting that a market with only a few large suppliers (an oligopoly) cannot be intensely competitive, and no *a priori* reason why oligopoly cannot be economically efficient.

Finally, is the technostructure, through its alliance with government, protected against cost increases, and assured of never-failing aggregate demand? Was not 1966 the year the wage guideposts collapsed? And has it not been demonstrated in the past nine months that even with military expenditures approaching $75-billion a year, there is still a risk of recession? It is part of the now-conventional wisdom that the state can prevent such mishaps, but there they are—accompanied, moreover, by budget deficits that could exceed $25 billion a year and a payments imbalance that threatens both the international monetary system and the nation's gold supply.

What it all comes to is that the U. S. economy is not as neatly buttoned-up as Mr. Galbraith's book would lead one to believe. He disarms potential critics with occasional displays of modesty. . . . But his argument is basically dogmatic. Its elements are sufficiently out of focus to produce a distorted over-all picture.

This is not to deny there is a risk that our economy, in its relation to government, will evolve into the near-monolithic shape implied by Galbraith's theory. But if it does, I doubt it will do so by the route he has sketched. Unfortunately, there is more than one road to the monolithic society. A possibility altogether too likely is that basically inflationary fiscal and monetary policies will be persisted in, will invite more and more pervasive regulation of prices and profits and will in the end amount to a suppression of private undertakings. (pp. 36-7)

But this is another story; for the moment, it is pertinent only to repeat one's admiration for Mr. Galbraith's considerable intellectual achievement. **"The New Industrial State"** deserves the widest possible attention and discussion. It will provoke much argument among economists; it may well inspire graduate schools of business to ask new questions about what they are doing; and, hopefully, it will provide a conversation-piece in executive dining rooms. All in all, a constructive result. (p. 37)

> *Raymond J. Saulnier, "The Shape of Things," in* The New York Times Book Review *(© 1967 by The New York Times Company; reprinted by permission), June 25, 1967, pp. 2-3, 36-9.*

ROBERT L. HEILBRONER

To my mind, Galbraith is an economist of considerable merits, who seeks to infuse economics with a social relevance that is, on the whole, egregiously missing from most of its current output, particularly from that of the Chicago school. At the same time, I believe that the celebrated style, far from being an expression of Galbraith's power and boldness, is in fact his fatal weakness. (p. 16)

[A fundamental difficulty with *The New Industrial State*] lies, I think, in the level of abstraction of the work, which hovers between a very generalized schema and an empirical study, and is not quite either. As a result it suffers on the one hand from the absence of the solid empirical demonstration that would convince us of the conceptual validity of the technostructure as the new power center of capitalism, while on the other it is not quite reduced to the fundamental level of generalization that served to make Schumpeter's theory of capitalism so impressive.

Take, for example, the central contention of the book—that the strategic group within the economic system has shifted from the possessors of wealth to the possessors of collective expertise. I do not doubt that Galbraith is right in stressing this basic trend and in assigning its cause to the fundamental forces of

technology and science. The trouble is that this tendency is treated as if it were already an accomplished fact, and this is doubtful. It is my belief that even in the most "mature" corporations (i.e., those in which the technostructure is most clearly visible), there is still a final level of decision-making power that is lodged firmly at the top, and this top upon examination often turns out to be a small group of powerful stockholding interests or their representatives. The technostructure may propose, but in the end it is the Directors, or a small number of top officers, who dispose.

Thus the technostructure is much too diffuse a term to describe hierarchies and groups within which there continue to reside all-important distinctions of power. Further, it masks the fact that there is going on within American capitalism a contest between the forces of science and technology and the older forces of wealth and ownership. I believe, with Galbraith, that the future lies with the ascendency of the professional elites, but the tension between the Old Guard and the New needs to be brought to the fore—not hidden behind the undifferentiated screen of the technostructure.

I am not convinced either by Galbraith's prescription for social reform. Surely if history teaches us anything it is the futility of appeals to the educated elite. . . . If, as Galbraith so boldly (and I think correctly) maintains, the "imperatives of technology and organization" will shape society, then he must have the courage to carry his theoretical model into the future, whatever its course. It was precisely this that gave to Schumpeter's analysis its power, for he unflinchingly extended the implications of his analysis to the end, even though he disliked the conclusions to which it led. Galbraith's model is important and original, and by comparison with the pale stuff of so much contemporary economics, powerful. But his grand outline is weakened by an unwillingness to press home his analysis to its bitter conclusion—a conclusion touched on lightly in the vision of a self-perpetuating and self-serving Industrial System, but then blurred by conclusions that are, I believe, just "another hortatory exercise."

This final reluctance to allow the model to reach its ultimate destination may well be related to the curious problem of Galbraith's style. (pp. 18-19)

The much envied style is aphoristic, terse, above all mocking. . . . [But] Galbraith's mocking irony causes him in the end to avoid a clear moral commitment with regard to the problems he raises.

Is such commitment necessary? "The economy for its success requires organized public bamboozlement," writes Galbraith flatly. The word "bamboozlement" is the clue. Any other—"deception," "fraud," "untruth"—would amount to a declaration of war. "Bamboozlement" allows an issue of the most searching importance to be passed over in a mood of raillery. The next sentence in the text reads: "And at the same time it nurtures a growing class which feels itself superior to such bamboozlement and deplores it as intellectually corrupt." Galbraith is himself a member of that class—and, indeed, in his public life has lived up to his own prescription in speaking out for ends and ideas that differ considerably from those of the technostructure. Yet in this book, as indeed in his previous books, his position *vis à vis* the society he criticizes remains essentially ambiguous. Rather than producing clear judgment, the moral power of his argument is, finally, dissipated in wit. (p. 19)

> *Robert L. Heilbroner, "Capitalism without Tears," in* The New York Review of Books *(reprinted with*

permission from The New York Review of Books; *copyright © 1967 Nyrev, Inc.), Vol. VIII, No. 12, June 29, 1967, pp. 16-19.*

KENNETH E. BOULDING

[*The New Industrial State*] will not disappoint Mr. Galbraith's numerous admirers. It goes to work like a grindstone on a very important problem of our society, shooting off innumerable aphorisms and sparks of wit as it grinds. If the wit occasionally verges on the arch, and the aphorisms seem occasionally to be a little labored, what is missing perhaps is what the author himself describes in his introduction as "the note of spontaneity which comes into my writing in the fourth or fifth draft." These minor irritations aside, however, this is a book with something to say and it says it well, as we could expect, and it is a worthy addition to its predecessors. (p. 2)

[Galbraith's analysis] is very interesting and very exciting. One cannot help wondering, however, whether Galbraith has not produced another myth, if not a new conventional wisdom, to replace the myth he is attacking. Galbraith's thought, like that of Veblen, whom he somewhat resembles in his aphoristic style and half-suppressed moral fury, is a spotlight turned with peculiar intensity on a particular problem, and especially on particular weaknesses of the social structure. The aphoristic style itself suggests the spotlight character of the thought behind it, for the aphorism is an intense insight into a fragment of the whole. What Galbraith lacks, and what Veblen lacked also, is a systematic understanding of the totality of social relationships. This lack is highly excusable. There is an intolerable intellectual arrogance in the great systematizers, like Ricardo, Marx, Max Weber and Talcott Parsons, and though, having a touch of this myself, I am inclined to regard it with a somewhat tolerant eye, one is grateful to Galbraith for having avoided it. Behind the not infrequent arrogance of his style one detects a genuine humility of spirit. This is attractive, and on the whole Galbraith has avoided the great trap of mistaking insights for systems. Nevertheless, whether Galbraith himself systematizes or not, his insights will be taken for a system and as a system they are incomplete.

Take, for instance, his attack on the notion of the self-regulating market. He certainly visualizes his "revised sequence" as a very fundamental change. Quite apart from the fact that he exaggerates the power of persuasion of the advertisers (the Edsel after all was not the only unsuccessful product of the technostructure), he fails to appreciate the fundamental distinction between market-oriented organizations on the one hand and organizations like the state which depend fundamentally on coercive power. . . .

[Classification] of organizations by what might be called their input-output environment is also of great importance, and Galbraith seems quite insensitive to this. The Wisconsin dairy farm and General Motors are alike in that they exist primarily in a market environment. They derive their revenue by selling things and they produce their revenue by buying things and transforming them into things to sell. This is very different from the environment of the national state and still more of the Department of Defense, which obtains its revenue not by selling things in the market but by cashing in on taxes collected under the threat of imprisonment and distraint.

What I am complaining about here is that Galbraith does not adequately distinguish what I have elsewhere called the "exchange system" from the "threat system" and this leads him to confound things which are dissimilar and to distinguish things which are similar. Thus, I would argue that the distinction between the defense-oriented corporation, such as Lockheed Aircraft or Republic Aviation, which sells almost all of its output to the Department of Defense and a consumer-oriented corporation, such as General Motors and General Electric, is far more fundamental than the distinction between small and large consumer-oriented corporations, at least in regard to their input-output environment. While I would argue very strongly therefore that there is a military-industrial complex comprising perhaps 10 per cent of the economy, I would also argue that the gap between that part of the consumer-oriented economy which is dominated by the large corporation, and that part which is not, is much smaller than the gap between the military-industrial complex and the rest. It seems to me therefore that Galbraith has drawn his lines of distinction at the wrong place and that this confuses the important issues.

Galbraith is not only insensitive to the distinction between the exchange and the threat systems, he is also insensitive to that whole area of social life dealing with such matters as status, identity, community, legitimacy, loyalty and love, which is coming to be called the "integrative system." He seems to be attacking the legitimacy of the large corporation, yet he never really discusses how things gain and lose legitimacy in society except by indirection. His David is in fact a humble servant of Goliath. The educational and scientific estate has little unity; it is a weak integrative system; it does not command any intensity of feeling, and it has proved extremely vulnerable—as in Nazi Germany—to popular uprisings of folk malevolence.

The truth seems to be that Galbraith is trapped by his own membership in the intellectual sub-culture and he has very little appreciation of the complexities of the system of legitimation. He completely discounts, for instance, the churches, a great natural ally in his attack on the technoculture. Today the church is almost the only effective countervailing power against the overriding legitimacy of the state, and it certainly has a wider base in the population on which to build its legitimacies than does the educational and scientific estate, to which it docs not really belong. It is only the church, or perhaps one should say the sect, which stood out against Hitler in Germany while the universities, the corporations and the trade unions went down like ninepins, and the same might well be true in the United States. One-and-a-half cheers, therefore, for Galbraith's insights, reserving the remaining one-and-a-half for a more careful analysis of the total dynamics of society. (p. 12)

Kenneth E. Boulding, "Milking the Sacred Cow," in Book Week—The Sunday Herald Tribune *(© I.H.T. Corporation; reprinted with permission), July 16, 1967, pp. 2, 12.*

HARRY MAGDOFF

One of the most appealing features [of Professor Galbraith's argument in *The New Industrial State*] is the unity and consistency of the economic theory supplied—the end result, it seems, of Galbraith's long search for what is rational in an irrational society. But what emerges is as much a rationalization as a rationale of the business system. This may be due to the method of analysis itself, in the way the rational is separated from the irrational. The structure and operation of the modern economy is seen to be objectively determined; hence it is logical and inevitable. The irrational features arise from the goals of the industrial system, which are subtly interwoven with the goals of society as a whole. And since these goals are in the realm of ideas, they are amenable to change and improvement.

Galbraith's selection of technology as the key to a rational explanation of gigantism and planning may strike a responsive chord in the reader living in the atomic, electronic and space age. But does it fit the facts? Was it technology that dictated the origin of the Standard Oil Company? Is it the complexity of manufacture that induces oligopoly in the cigarette, soap, detergent and chewing gum industries, in each of which four companies control from 70 per cent to 90 per cent of the market? Or perhaps it is the mystery of technique that requires the extent of market control that exists in meat, ice cream and flour mill operations, where eight leading companies control 40 per cent to 50 per cent of each market?

While the procedure of isolating specific causes is used for the sake of dealing with reality, it may often result in a graceful side-stepping of the more vital aspects of reality. Take, for example, the appearance of hardheaded realism in the statements: "The industrial system has not become identified with weapons competition by preference or because it is inherently bloody. Rather, this has been the area where the largest amount of money to support planning was available with the fewest questions asked." The reader is thus directed to the significance of military orders as the source of corporate identification with foreign policy. But by the same token, the examination of any other interest of the industrial system (Galbraith's term for the dominant giant corporations) in U.S. pacification and control of foreign lands is eliminated. The avoidance of such an issue seems quite strange in a book devoted to proving the vital need of the giant corporations to control their sources of raw materials and to achieve persistent growth of sales. One would imagine that if control over sources of supply is an imperative for the corporation, then the latter might have more than a vague curiosity about the stability and security of their foreign properties from which life-giving raw materials come: iron ore, bauxite, copper, lead, zinc, manganese, tantalum and columbium (for jet engines and gas turbines), and lest we forget, oil.

In addition, the imperative to grow and control markets has been pushing the larger business organizations beyond the domestic borders. Thus, of the 500 largest corporations, 386 had notable foreign operations. A score or two of the large companies have a third or more of their total assets abroad; some eighty of these firms derived 25 per cent or more of their sales and earnings from overseas. Sales of foreign-based U.S. manufacturing firms have increased more than five times since 1950. In 1965, it has been conservatively estimated, earnings on foreign investments amounted to more than 20 per cent of after-tax profits of domestic non-financial corporations.

Perhaps, then, there is more than a mild interest by the corporate organizations in U.S. foreign policy and its military complement as a convenience in sustaining a comfortable business environment. In Galbraith's analysis, though, the irrationality of the cold war and militarism is an unfortunate accompaniment to the rational need of industry for government support of domestic markets; as such, it is unrelated to the persistent needs for business expansion and control.

Even more striking is the separation of the situation of the Negro and of poverty from the framework of analysis. It is hardly the case that Galbraith is indifferent to the social evils of our time; he could properly insist that the main purpose of his tract is to contribute to the removal of the evils. The issue is the diagnosis. Implicit in his diagnosis is the assumption that

such evils are things apart from, and surely not a product of, the industrial system. For example, " . . . the poor, by any applicable tests, are outside the industrial system. They are those who have not been drawn into its service or cannot qualify"; the unemployed are "those who are currently unemployable by the industrial system." Hence, the solution to poverty is to be found largely in better education and "better *cultural* accommodation to the industrial system."

This sort of thinking reflects the common observation that there are job opportunities for certain skills, especially during the overheated period of the economy. But it does not square with the historical tendency of the industrial system to require less labor relative to the labor force. . . . It is hardly reasonable to assume that the industrial system would have supplied a significantly greater number of jobs if there were more technically educated and "culturally accommodated" persons available.

By separating out social evils as things apart from the industrial system, Galbraith avoids confronting the issue of whether the industrial system operates in such a way as to create "culturally unaccommodated" pockets. Thus, he notes the pattern that Negroes are the last to be hired and the first to be fired. But he does not in the least recognize that this very industrial practice, whereby the Negro serves as a cushion of reserve labor, is an essential ingredient in a long and entrenched process in which lack of "cultural accommodation" evolves.

Nor, by the same token does Galbraith take into account any interdependence between the success of the industrial system and poverty. He affirms the role that profits play in securing corporate power, but ignores the influence of profits as a contributor to poverty and a barrier to the elimination of poverty. Profits are needed for research to create artificial obsolescence; they are needed to finance mergers for better market control. Naturally, prices and costs must be consistent with these and other profit imperatives. In turn, such necessary costs and prices become the measuring devices—the standards—to determine what is economically feasible and efficient. This much will undoubtedly be granted by our author. But he does not concern himself with the consequences that these are the very standards by which the corporation decides to invest abroad and also decides not to invest in the economic development of underdeveloped city and farm areas of the United States. Similarly, there is no consideration of the conflict between the cost-price-profit arrangements of existing institutions and, on the other hand, changes in the structure of industry to produce goods which meet social needs and, say, a program of industrialization and land reform to revitalize the urban ghetto and the rural South.

The absence of an appreciation of the influence of profit making on poverty may be a by-product of the author's concentration on his theory of corporate motivation. According to this theory, the modern corporation is more interested in rapid growth of sales than in the growth of profits. Unexplored in the book is the question whether one is feasible without the other or whether there is any conflict between these aims during a long cyclical upswing. (pp. 246-47)

In his reform program to replace the cold war, Galbraith does introduce a note of realism that will seem strange to the Keynesian community. The more orthodox Keynesians, especially the right wing, maintain that the economy could adjust quite readily to disarmament with simple fiscal adjustments; in particular, with a sufficient tax reduction. Progressive Keynesians, on the other hand, claim that tax-rate changes will not be effective regulators in the absence of very large public expenditures. Hence, the way to handle the impact of disarmament is to counterbalance with large public works—housing, hospitals, schools. Galbraith, though, goes much further than even these left wingers. He is all for social-welfare spending and believes it should be carried on for its own sake. But it won't do the trick because it won't feed the giant corporations with the right kind of stimulants.

To keep business solvent and sustain the economy without cold war, he proposes government sponsorship of substitutes that are roughly equivalent in scale and technical complexity to military items; for example, high-speed land and air communications, ocean-floor explorations and climate alteration. Valuable as these suggestions may be, we should recognize that they too may not be adequate. It will probably take too much time for the research and development before production can begin; more than that, they may not even then result in sufficiently large scale repetitive operations to keep the wheels of the industrial system turning. What is really needed is an ingenious scheme which could continuously depreciate our stock of bombs, missiles, airplanes, tanks and navy ships and, at the same time, stimulate the need for periodic replenishment of these stocks with new models—all this without anyone getting killed. Did someone propose a declaration of war against Mars? (p. 248)

> *Harry Magdoff, "Rationalizing the Irrational," in* The Nation *(copyright 1967 The Nation magazine, The Nation Associates, Inc.), Vol. 205, No. 8, September 18, 1967, pp. 246-48.*

MICHAEL HARRINGTON

[In] a book which must be ranked as one of the most significant works of social thought in this generation [*The New Industrial State,* John Kenneth Galbraith] has provided a brilliant, reasoned analysis which substantiates many of the most bitter charges that have been made against the [liberal] movement. . . .

[*The New Industrial State* contains] an extraordinarily lucid analysis of the planned, privately collectivized, and state-supported system of production which obtains in this mythically free-enterprise land. There were thinkers before Galbraith who caught the broad outlines of this trend—Rathenau, Schumpeter, and Keynes being among the most notable—but it is Galbraith's achievement to have presented in detail its economic, political, and even its cultural structure. The unacademic conclusion of his documented argument is that liberalism, and the nation, must strive for the growth of an Ungross National Product. (p. 77)

Galbraith's program operates on three distinct levels, ranging from the immediately practical to the reluctantly prophetic. It deals with the "lacunae" of planning and the abolition of the cold war; the transformation of the quality of life; and the evolutionary socialization of the corporation. (p. 78)

Galbraith's program, while very much in the liberal tradition, involves important new departures. Only a few liberals in recent years have dissented so emphatically from the myths of the marketplace or been able to stress so cogently the need for truly massive public intervention and planning in areas like mass transit, housing, and land use. Disarmament activists, of course, have long talked of the domestic effects of the cold war, but they have been wont to reduce complicated consid-

erations of political, economic, and military pressures to a charade of material interests. Galbraith's account of the defense sector is much more sober, and his recognition of the difficulties of a transition to peace much more realistic, than the usual run of peacemongering analyses.

I feel, then, that the analytic sections of *The New Industrial State* (and these sections make up the bulk of the book) are more probing than anything I have read on this subject in years, and that its proposals for immediate, practical change, and for the middle-distance transformations of the quality of human life, are excellent. If I devote the rest of this essay to a critical look at the shortest and most speculative portion of the book, it is not for reasons of utopian nitpicking. Galbraith has every right to be wary of proclamations about the Future of Man. His premises are, of course, liberal; mine, however beleaguered, are those of a radical who belongs to the liberal community. Yet I think that by focusing upon a distant area of subtle difference I can raise some important questions which touch on tomorrow's strategies as well as on the more remote problems of the 21st century.

In Galbraith's scenario, first of all, it is the educational and scientific estate which must take the lead in putting the industrial system in its rightful, subordinate place. Such a move will, of course, provoke the opposition of at least part of the system. But this hostility, Galbraith continues, may well be mitigated by basic trends within the society. (p. 79)

Galbraith is no Candide. He recognizes that right, justice, truth, and beauty may lose out to the religion of efficiency, production, and corporate power. Yet I do not think he takes sufficient account of tendencies which do not simply frustrate his hopes but work actively against them—for there is a strong evolutionary trend toward subordinating the social good to private purpose. This gloomy possibility, which must be given the unfortunate weight it deserves, is not adequately recognized by Galbraith for what it portends. . . .

Galbraith redefines and updates the anomaly which fascinated Marx and Keynes. The corporation, he says, is "capitalism without control by the capitalist, . . . socialism without control by the society." But it is precisely the second half of his formula which is subversive of his optimism. The corporation was not revolutionized into socialism, as Marx hoped, nor was it evolutionized into benevolence, as Keynes predicted. On the contrary, the "natural" inclination of this institution seems to be toward a brutal and anti-social egotism. This is no less true now that the crude definitions of profit have been modified and motives made to seem much less crass. (p. 80)

Indeed, the motives of the technostructure are generally more complicated than Galbraith suggests. . . . [As] an institutional entity, as a whole, the corporation is motivated much in the style of the obsolescent individual entrepreneur. (p. 81)

[The] data about corporate profit-seeking and tax-avoidance make me question Galbraith's confidence in wage-price guideposts. In the early period of the Kennedy-Johnson boom, when unemployment was high enough to make the unions relatively weak, the companies took as much as they could get, which was a lot. Then, when an inflationary danger appeared, in part because of the way business had behaved, the executives—in what is by now a familiar domestic comedy—lectured labor on its responsibilities and told the government to be thrifty.

But perhaps the most summary point to be made about the anti-social habits built into the very structure of the industrial system has nothing to do with money. Even when an enterprise is not concerned with a maximum profit, even when it is run by cultivated and idealistic men, it remains a center of power. . . . Non-pecuniary motivation, in short, may only change the reasons for irresponsible behavior, not the behavior itself.

But if, then, the new industrial state is even more resistant to reform than Galbraith suggests, what hope is there? The answer lies seemingly far afield. Galbraith, as noted earlier, is cautious about entering into speculative debate over vague, distant possibilities. Yet he knows that the industrial system is transitory, and he has the intellectual daring—rare in these days of the "end of ideology"—to consider alternative social systems. So as a socialist I find it much to his credit that he has written a critique of socialism. Most American social thinkers are so complacent that they do not even know that the issue is relevant.

Galbraith's basic argument against the socialist claim to the future is that it seeks to transform a capitalism which no longer exists. In the days of the entrepreneurial corporation, he maintains, it made sense to propose that the workers' representatives, or the state, should take over the functions of the owner-manager. The capitalist performed relatively simple, straightforward tasks and these could be done just as well democratically. However, the industrial system changes all that: "The technical complexity and associated scale of operations that took power from the capitalist entrepreneur and lodged it with the technostructure, removed it also from the reach of socialist control." (pp. 81-2)

It is the thesis of *The New Industrial State* that there are "lacunae" of planning in areas outside of the system proper, like housing and transportation. In these cases, Galbraith is forthrightly in favor of massive governmental planning and intervention. But he seems to be saying tacitly that where the industrial system is already engaged in planning, one need only impose some decent values from without. Once again, I suspect him of oversimplifying power relationships. For if the corporate concentrations are left to themselves, they cannot help but constitute a countergovernment and a counterplan. And whatever one thinks of the question of nationalized enterprise, it seems to me necessary to add to Galbraith's program a proposal for federal economic planning that would be subject to democratic debate and decision. This is the only way to establish a basic social context in which all of the relevant technical choices can be made. (This does not mean the abolition of capitalism, although it could, in my opinion, be a step in that most happy direction.)

If my analysis is correct, then the tasks posed by Galbraith are even more difficult than he makes them seem, for the corporations will undoubtedly launch a very determined institutional resistance to reforms of this sort. This leads to a slightly different perspective on political tactics than the one presented in *The New Industrial State*. (p. 82)

In [*American Capitalism*], unions were seen as a major force against corporate autocracy. Now labor is described as a numerically dwindling movement which does more to rationalize the work situation than to challenge the values of the system itself, and hence as a negligible force in the task of accommodating the technostructure to the needs of society.

The manpower patterns upon which Galbraith bases his analysis are familiar enough. In the mid-50's, white-collar workers became more numerous than blue-collar workers, causing a decline in the organized percentage of the labor force, whose proportion of (traditionally) "organizable" jobs was thereby

reduced. So the unions have entered a period of stagnation and there is no sense in looking to them as dynamic participants in the movement to break the ideological monopoly of the industrial system.

In making this argument, however, Galbraith ignores what might be described as the newest example of countervailing power. One of the most significant labor developments in recent years has been the growth of the American Federation of Teachers. The AFT has won election after election and, even when defeated, has usually managed to transform the rival National Education Association into a de facto union. The changing manpower patterns are thus not quite so gloomy as Galbraith suggests, especially if one is looking, as Gus Tyler has pointed out, for collective bargaining tendencies rather than mere increases in union membership. (pp. 82-3)

Thus far, the mood of collective bargaining has not extended to the lower echelon of the technostructure itself. And yet, as office- and committee-work becomes more and more rationalized, it is possible that these people will be affected by the same spirit which now animates the teachers. Were this indeed to happen, the industrial system might be challenged from within, particularly if the nation were to realize, as Galbraith hopes it will, that the stockholders of the big companies receive princely rewards for performing no economic function whatsoever.

I am not here proposing some kind of corporatist utopia. Collective bargaining organizations can develop their own forms of egotism and national determination of basic economic priorities needs to be established in any case. Yet trade unionism—taking the term in its broadest sense—could well make an enormous contribution in the struggle for alternatives to the industrial system. Indeed, Galbraith recognizes this point in one very important area, but he does not generalize from it. There is a very special danger that the university will be decisively dominated by corporate values. And clearly the educational and scientific estate must have its independent base—its Yenan, its Sierra Maestra—if it is to fulfill the political role which Galbraith imagines for it. In this perspective, the battles in recent years among students, faculties, and administrations cease to be mere quarrels over individual rights and take on deep social significance. They become one of the preconditions for reform in the nation as a whole. . . .

"Engine Charlie" Wilson unwittingly stated the motto of this Third New Deal when he appeared before the Senate in 1953: what is good for General Motors is good for the United States of America. The industrial system, as Galbraith documents it, plans so effectively that it is able to impose its values upon both the state and the society. Therefore the liberal political movement must counterplan. The techniques which have succeeded so spectacularly in creating a lopsided, discriminatory affluence can be put in the service of an Ungross National Product. The famous American knowhow can be directed to unmet social needs like housing, public transportation, and the dilapidated public sector. The country can decide to find a less terrifying way to subsidize research and development than through the arms industry. Considerations of beauty and social consequence can be politically programmed into economic calculations, the boundaries between work and leisure can be redrawn to suit human needs, the university can be turned into something better than a technological trade school. All this is the stuff which liberal dreams are made of. It is Galbraith's achievement, in offering American liberalism a new beginning, a summons to go beyond the consensus which it helped to create to have made the realization of those dreams seem possible once again. (p. 83)

Michael Harrington, "Liberalism According to Galbraith," in Commentary (reprinted by permission; all rights reserved), Vol. 44, No. 4, October, 1967, pp. 77-83.

SCOTT GORDON

Galbraith's analysis of the American economy is constructed upon his conception of the legal and organizational nature of the modern industrial firm. The essentials of this conception derive from Berle and Means' classic of thirty years ago, *The Modern Corporation and Private Property*. . . . *The New Industrial State* may render good service in bringing, once again, to the attention of a wide audience one of the most momentous facts of the modern age, the emergence of the corporation as a primary social institution.

Galbraith's concept of the "technostructure," however, overstresses the monolithic nature of the corporate managerial system, and it is more likely to become a cliché than a useful tool of analysis. The decentralization of modern managerial organization indicated by Peter Drucker's *The Concept of the Corporation* has no reflection in *The New Industrial State*, though this development is, one would think, of the utmost importance in appraising the corporation's role as an economic and social institution. Galbraith also has little to say about other important modern developments, such as the growth of the conglomerate-type corporation and the phenomenal rise of pension funds as actual and potential owners of corporate stocks. In short, *The New Industrial State* does not enter upon an examination of the important recent and current developments in corporate evolution. (pp. 638-39)

The corporation here appears as a very strange organism indeed. It controls completely all the important elements of its environment. It has no need to accommodate itself to any exogenous circumstances: it is able to mold these to suit itself. Such a corporation would be like no organism, biological or social, that ever was, for it would encounter no constraints upon what it wishes (for is impelled) to do, which is to grow. Theoretically, we should observe all major industrial firms growing infinitely large, each of them—moreover, instantaneously! . . . It is not sufficient simply to say that "of course" rabbits or ants or humans or General Motors cannot overrun the earth, eliminating all other organisms. One must discover the mechanism that prevents this from happening. Scientific explanation is an essay on the constrained maximum; no less so when we examine the growth of firms. But the Galbraithian firm knows no constraints. (p. 639)

The "countervailing power" thesis of *American Capitalism* might be invoked here, but Galbraith does not employ it in the analysis of *The New Industrial State,* and nothing else is introduced that might play a similar explanatory role. We are left with a microeconomics *sans* Walras—a particular equilibrium analysis in which the equilibrium is nonsensical.

This points to the main defect of Galbraith's conception. He deals with the organization of the individual firm, but he says nothing about the organization of the *economy*. (pp. 639-40)

On the question of the determinants of consumer wants, he is . . . astoundingly naïve. He seems to believe that it is the affluence of America that has made wants susceptible to manipulation and that in poor societies wants are natural or, as he puts it, "original" with the individual. Every gothic spire in Europe, every temple in India, certifies the power of dominant social institutions in achieving major manipulations of income allocation, even in very poor societies. Any anthropologist could tell him how far removed from the "original" are the consumption patterns of even the most primitive peoples who live on the edge of existence.

The opposition Galbraith draws, in both *The Affluent Society* and *The New Industrial State,* between the natural wants of the poor and the culturally attenuated wants of the rich cannot be sustained. As a basis for a philosophy of distributional equity, it is the weakest of foundations; as an explanation of "social imbalance"—why we live in a society of clean houses and dirty streets—it is not penetrating. But that does not mean that the underlying issue—the cultural determination of wants—is unimportant. Eighty years ago, Alfred Marshall, who created so much of the modern economics which Galbraith deplores, noted that as civilization advances, wants are more and more the *results* of economic activity rather than the causes of them. The point is fundamental. It is hard enough to view economic theory as an exploration of the logic of allocating given resources to the satisfaction of given wants in a world where neither wants nor resources will stand still. In a world in which the wants change *as a result of* our economic efforts to satisfy them, economic theory is faced with subtle and difficult problems and, moreover, problems which will not remain within the boundaries of "positive" economics.

A great deal of Galbraith's writing may be viewed as hinging on this question. In a sense, there is an economic sociology or, as Marshall would have put it, an "economic biology" contained in his theory of technological determinism. But it does not seem to me that the issue is examined in Galbraith's books with the profundity of thought or scholarship it deserves and requires. In his specifics, Galbraith sticks to the most hackneyed theme of modern social literature—the power of advertising. His general stance is also an old and dusty one—the degradation of man by the economic system. His writing recalls the bitter plaints of the Victorian romantics—Carlyle, Dickens, Ruskin, and others—who looked upon the youthful face of industrialism and found it a monstrous evil. Galbraith looks upon it in its "maturity," and though his reaction is more urbane, it is essentially the same cry. The machine has been installed in the garden; the human birthright is being sold for a mess of GNP; the economic mechanism does not feed man but feeds upon him, and calmly spits out the bones. A century ago Ruskin admonished, "There is no wealth but life," and Galbraith echoes, "What counts is not the quantity of goods, but the quality of life." (pp. 641-42)

It is a great and lyrical theme, one of the most emotive in romantic literature, and it has always enjoyed a good market. . . . But the argument is essentially wrongheaded. If there is anything that deserves to be called "conventional wisdom" with all the derision that Galbraith has so firmly attached to that phrase, it is the idea that there is an inherent conflict between the satisfaction of material wants and the needs of the cultivated spirit. Material welfare and the "higher" humanism are complementary, not competing, things. The civilized sensibilities flourish where there is economic plenty; and the more the better, even when it is devoted in part to automobiles and television sets. The common man is not a noble primitive who has been spiritually pauperized and morally enslaved by material progress; he has in fact been freed and elevated by it. There is much more distance to go along this road, even in the "affluent society" of the United States. (p. 642)

Galbraith leaves us with a void. He offers no alternative system of economic analysis or even the sketch lines of one that might be built. (There was a suggested approach in *American Capitalism,* the first and best of Galbraith's major works, but it has not been developed in the subsequent books.) (p. 643)

It is always hazardous to declare what the Muses will in time decree; the history of economic and social thought is filled with many surprises. But it seems quite certain to this reviewer that Galbraith's work will not be the foundation of a new school of economics and that its impact on social thought in general is unlikely to outlast the immediate consciousness of the author's contemporaries. But immortality has many circles, and Galbraith's name is now firmly fixed on the high middle ranges where dwell the spirits of the effective gadflies of an age. His books will be of scholarly interest to the library moles of the future who will use them in their attempts to understand the complex intellectual agitation of a society that is powerful beyond measure and yet is cataleptic with doubt and fear. (p. 644)

> Scott Gordon, *"The Close of the Galbraithian System," in* The Journal of Political Economy *(reprinted by permission of The University of Chicago Press; copyright 1968 by the University of Chicago), Vol. 76, No. 4, July-August, 1968, pp. 635-44.*

DAVE M. O'NEILL

Although [*Economics and the Public Purpose*] contains some important insights, it also contains an insufferable amount of arm-chair theorizing. Unfortunately this eventually leads to a host of highly controversial policy recommendations which, if Galbraith's theories are wrong, would be downright dangerous.

Galbraith's important insight is to see the possibility of a significant influence of corporate wealth and organizational structure on governmental operations and decision making in advanced technological societies. (p. 402)

Galbraith, however, does not bother to pursue any serious empirical work on this specific issue. He is after much bigger game. Instead he devotes the first two-thirds of the book to the frenzied development of an all-encompassing theory of social and economic development. From this theory Galbraith then proceeds to derive a wide range of suggestions for reform. Some of them represent no more than benign (although hopelessly pompous) exhortations to private individuals to change their life styles. However, most of them are very controversial programs for the government to enforce—high levels for the legislated minimum wage, minority-and sex-hiring quotas, permanent wage and price controls, socialized medicine, etc. (p. 403)

How should someone, especially someone who is not strongly committed to Galbraith's particular set of social values, feel about the general validity of this model? More important, should one seriously consider the policy recommendations he derives from it? One way for the non-true believer to assess the model is to see how consistent it is with broad empirical facts and how well it explains them relative to alternative theories.

Expenditures on health care and education for example, two major industries in the "market system," have grown enormously in recent years. Indeed the entire service sector has grown more rapidly than the goods-producing industries. At the least these facts put the burden of proof on Galbraith to show some direct evidence on the mechanisms by which the technostructure dominates consumer wants.

Or consider the notion that the planning system somehow "holds back" the growth of earnings and incomes in the market system by determining the prices at which it sells its products and purchases its intermediate goods. What are the relevant facts on this issue? How much of the market system's final output and purchases are transacted with monopolistic firms in the planning system? The education and health care industries appear to deal largely with consumers and other firms in the market system. Galbraith does not bother to present one scrap of data on this question.

Also we are told that the salary of a Lee Iacoca is sixty or seventy times that of a blue-collar worker not because of his relative productivity, but because of the power of the technostructure. But what of a Joe Namath? How is this denizen of the market system able to behave like the president of General Motors? Unfortunately for Galbraith, the hated neoclassical model easily explains both cases. They both represent situations in which wages are being determined almost exclusively by competition among demanders since the talent is in such scarce supply.

But one could go on ad infinitum. For example, Galbraith's analysis and recommendations about the minimum wage just ignore the voluminous empirical evidence that has been accumlating on how it has serious adverse effects on teen-agers. In sum it is this reader's opinion that, at present, there exists no convincing empirical basis to support Galbraith's theory and that therefore his policy recommendations can hardly be taken seriously.

Galbraith might be more influential if he would spend less time attacking the neoclassical model and more time developing some solid empirical support for his own theory. (pp. 403-04)

> Dave M. O'Neill, *"'Economics and the Public Purpose'," in* Political Science Quarterly, *Vol. 89, No. 2, June, 1974, pp. 402-04.*

MARY DOUGLAS

[J. K. Galbraith's argument in *Economics and the Public Purpose*] is very much the recipe as before. There is nothing surprising now in the argument that countervailing powers be wielded by the state against the over-powerful corporations. Seen as an anthropological work, even the omissions are not surprising. Anthropology claims to be comparative but often finds the comparative project hard to carry through. The ordinary reader would like to know how the planning system fares in Germany or Scandinavia. Why should the countervailing power all come from the state? Galbraith asserts unceremoniously that organised labour is easily bought and silenced by the planning system. From this particular outpost of Europe the case would need closer arguing. Can it not be envisaged that the unions themselves, now national, might soon rise to the same multinational level as the planning system? What would happen then? Seen as an economist, it is not surprising that he has very mixed feelings about consumption. The author wishes the individual consumer to be free to consume what he likes, without imposing too much servitude on his wife, and without choosing luxuries; not too much food, not too much television, not cheap undignified travel. The puritanical streak points to a weakness in economic theory which the author himself has not discerned. Economists cannot imagine why people need goods. Somewhere between goods which sustain life and health and the spiritual arts of civilisation, painting, sculpture and ballet, there lies a mass of unnecessary goods, demand for which they are at a loss to account for except that it is whipped up by advertising. But just try telling the great flour-milling combines that their advertising can make people eat more bread. Galbraith himself falls into a central weakness of economic theory, its failure to see the consumer as a social being fulfilling autonomous intentions of his own. Because of this theoretical gap the economist who undertakes the general anthropological task of surveying the institutional background of public purposes is hamstrung at the outset. Any anthropologist knows that goods trace social relationships. Therefore understanding of the affluent society is blocked until the main characteristics of these relationships be established. Without any sociological theory of the purposes which the individual consumer needs to fulfil with the goods he buys, the critic is stuck with a rag-tag and bobtail list of public concerns. Clearly a new general theory is needed. Galbraith's strictures on economics and society testify to his good heart; but the general theory he promises is still unbroached.

Looking back one sees that the weakness of this book is that its two predecessors were strong in drawing attention to trouble spots. The disappointing thing is that they never initiated a theoretical reform. It is easy to knock economic theory. Most economists do it every day. More difficult is to devise a better tool of analysis for the measuring and comparing that economists try to do. Yet this is the urgent problem. The short, staccato sentences which were once well chosen for delivering shocks sound strangely in a book with no surprises. The old machinery of charm is creaking; the prophet is rambling. His readers know now that the problems he reveals are more grave than his prescriptions suggest. (p. 806)

> Mary Douglas, "Puppet Consumers," in New Statesman (© 1974 The Statesman & Nation Publishing Co. Ltd.), Vol. 87, No. 2255, June 7, 1974, pp. 805-06.

THE ECONOMIST

["**The Age of Uncertainty**" adds nothing to Professor Galbraith's] reputation as critic, polemicist or intellecual leader. It lacks originality and appears to be based largely on secondary sources. It is not even all that well written. The best parts are a series of autobiographical fragments scattered through it. . . . But the book is chiefly intended to be about economists and economic history. Thus this reader is told something of Smith, Ricardo, and Malthus, but this is at more or less the level of "every schoolboy knows". For the general reader there are at least half a dozen books on the history of economic thought which he will find more interesting and more useful. . . .

[We] are given a long chapter on Marx. Here . . . the emphasis is placed on the story of his life rather than on what he wrote, despite Professor Galbraith's insistence on the importance of ideas. Indeed, the opportunity is missed to discuss the fascinating question of whether the impact of Marxism as a set of ideas can be explained by, or is compatible with, Marxism. The chapter on Lenin is possibly more satisfactory, although again the story is much more an account of the man and what he did and did not do. Professor Galbraith does, however, make the crucial point that Lenin's role in the revolution was rather limited. . . .

The chapter on Keynes is a poorer account of the man and his theories than is to be found in several other easily accessible books. It tends to exaggerate the extent to which Keynes himself was outside public affairs in the 1920s and 1930s. It is a pity that Professor Galbraith does not draw the reader's attention to present day controversies on British economic history of the 1920s and 1930s and the causes and consequences of the return to the gold standard. . . .

Nonetheless, in his discussion of Keynes Professor Galbraith does raise a question fundamental to current economic policy-making. He argues that if full employment is reached by Keynesian methods, direct action is required to offset the inflationary activities of corporations and trade unions. He concludes: "this does not leave the market system intact as Keynes, the conservative, had intended. It is a portent of radical change that not many wish to face". . . .

"**The Age of Uncertainty**" was written in association with a television series. It is full of pictures, the point of most of which it is impossible to determine. Perhaps that is why it is such an unsatisfactory effort. But altogether we are left with an overwhelming sense of failure, of how much more all this effort and talent could have achieved.

> "Stray Thoughts," in The Economist (© The Economist Newspaper Limited, 1977), Vol. 262, No. 6966, March 5, 1977, p. 130.

GEOFFREY BARRACLOUGH

The reasons why the calculations of the Eisenhower administration [regarding the eradication of world poverty] were so disastrously wrong are cogently set out in [*The Nature of Mass Poverty*]. Members of that administration were bemused, in the first place, by the alleged imperatives of the cold war and misled by the false analogy of the Marshall Plan. They deceived themselves about the real causes of poverty, assuming that what worked for the United States and for Western Europe would work in the totally different circumstances of Asia and Africa. The surprise is not that it didn't, but that anyone thought that it would. But, as Professor Galbraith puts it, "if action is imperative"—and in Mr. Dulles's opinion the Soviet economic offensive made action imperative—it was necessary to "make the cause fit the action." Or, since what the United States had to offer was capital and technology, lack of capital and technology must be the cause of backwardness. "The remedy included the diagnosis."

The essence of Professor Galbraith's argument, supported by his experience as ambassador in India, is that this way of proceeding was bound to produce a wrong diagnosis. On that score we can go with him most, if not all, of the way. As a critic, Professor Galbraith writes with his customary verve and wit; but it also has to be said that his book is more persuasive on the negative than on the positive side. For my taste at least, it reads a little too much like an elegant academic exercise, rather than a confrontation with the real world which, any day now, may blow up in our faces.

Professor Galbraith's central thesis is that there is an inbuilt tendency in poor countries to "accommodate" to poverty, and that this makes nonsense of many current prescriptions. (pp. 30-1)

[Professor Galbraith argues that] action if it is to be effective, should concentrate not on [those mired in "absolute poverty"], but on the "non-accommodating" sectors of the population:

on those, in other words, who flee the countryside for the city, who leave agriculture for industry, and above all on those who opt with their feet, abandoning Mexico (for example) for Texas or Bangladesh for Birmingham, England. These, Professor Galbraith assures us, are the people "best prepared for rescue." It sounds, for my taste, a little too much like a new variant of the notorious "lifeboat" solution.

Professor Galbraith, it will be seen, has little use for the currently orthodox development strategies. Land reform is frustrated by "the equilibrium of poverty"; industrialization is "an unpredictable design," "highly uncertain" both in "time and magnitude." His own solution, produced rather like a rabbit from a conjuror's hat, is migration. We have, apparently, to envisage millions of people crossing frontiers, legally or (more probably) illegally; and all will be well—or, at any rate, a lot better. . . .

It is a surprising argument, to say the least, and it would take another essay, as long as Galbraith's, to analyze its assumptions and its alleged historical justification. But that is scarcely necessary because, all other criticism apart, it is surely obvious enough that migration can at best touch the margin of the problem. If, for example, the population of India is approximately 600 million, how many millions of Indians would have to emigrate before there was any significant impact? And what is the practical possibility of emigration on this scale? Mr. Callaghan and Mrs. Thatcher know the answer; and so, no doubt, does George Meany.

Part of Galbraith's argument is that Callaghan and Thatcher are wrong. In other words, that the prosperity of Western Europe—and the same applies to the United States—is (or was) due to the import of Turkish, Yugoslav, Spanish, Puerto Rican helots. And that it was good for them. . . . "The economy," Professor Galbraith writes, "grows with the labor force." This, no doubt, is economic orthodoxy; but what about when, as at present, the economy obstinately refuses to grow? Then, Professor Galbraith tells us, employers "cut their labor forces." In other words, the Turks etc. go home. A nice solution for European businessmen and American agribusiness, but not much of a solution to the question of poverty in the underdeveloped third (and fourth) world.

In the end, it is true, Professor Galbraith hedges his bet. Migration, he concedes, is not the "only" or even the "principal" solution. The trouble is that, if you subtract this "old and evident answer," all you are left with in Galbraith's analysis is the conclusion that mass poverty is "a tightly integrated phenomenon"—or, in plain English, a complicated, many-sided problem—which, besides being a platitude, is no answer at all. Or at least it is not an answer that is going to still the rising discontent in the underdeveloped world, and its demands for action. Professor Galbraith's book is urbane and civilized. The question is whether the time for urbanity and civilized detachment is not running out. (pp. 31-2)

For me, the most memorable statement in Professor Galbraith's book is a quotation from C. T. Kurien. Mass poverty, Kurien says, "is a reflection of the total malfunctioning of the economic order." His words raise an issue which Professor Galbraith deftly sidesteps. But we must not expect the poor countries and their leaders to do likewise. Their demand for a New International Economic Order may, or may not, be muddled and inconsistent, as Western economists argue. That is not the point. The point is that it is there as a challenge, today, tomorrow and the day after. (p. 32)

Geoffrey Barraclough, "'The Nature of Mass Poverty'," in The New Republic *(reprinted by permission of* The New Republic; © *1979 The New Republic, Inc.), Vol. 180, No. 12, March 24, 1979, pp. 30-2.*

BILL BLUM

Beyond the two truisms that poverty tends to last until disrupted and the poor develop outlooks of grim resignation, *The Nature of Mass Poverty* lacks depth and clarity. Galbraith never seriously attempts to explain why certain parts of the world have been successful in eradicating poverty and why others have not. Indeed, in his brief treatment of this question, he can only combine the old theories of exploitation, capital shortage, climate, and overpopulation in a curious and indecisive blend. In the end, one senses that Galbraith has confused the conditions of poverty with its causes.

Galbraith's treatment of the impact of socialism and the role of Western imperialism in the Third World is particularly weak. Virtually no attention is given to the relationship between multinational corporations and underdeveloped nations, a feature which operates to sanitize the phenomenon of mass poverty and to absolve the United States and other western countries of any responsibility for the plight of the world's poor.

In the final analysis, Galbraith can be applauded for the stand he takes on the volatile issue of world migration. . . .

Galbraith makes . . . compelling arguments in favor of today's migrants. Far from being a source of unemployment, crime, and disease (as they are so often depicted by the media), today's migrants, be they the "illegal aliens" of the American Southwest or the "guest workers" of Western Europe, enrich their second homelands just as their predecessors did at the turn of the century. . . .

If his views help in any way to ameliorate this country's brutal treatment of the "illegal alien," Galbraith may not achieve the theoretical advance he had hoped for in the field of political economy. But he will have made a solid and unexpected contribution to the eradication of a national disgrace—an accomplishment, no doubt, of equal worth. (p. 56)

Bill Blum, "Poverty and Aliens," in The Progressive *(reprinted by permission from* The Progressive, *409 East Main Street, Madison, Wisconsin 53703; copyright 1979 by The Progressive, Inc.), Vol. 43, No. 8, August, 1979, pp. 54-6.*

ROBERT W. WHITAKER

For those of us in the less automatically publishable part of the population, *Annals of an Abiding Liberal* is not exactly a book. But then, it is not necessary for one of the faithful of the liberal Establishment to actually write a book in order to have it published. So Galbraith put together some of his articles and speeches, and here we have it: umpteenth book, same pulpit, same congregation.

Then again, one might well question whether a book *could* have been written under this title. One may not be justified in stating flatly that a man of the author's imaginative powers could not have found enough to say to write a new book about liberalism, but it is not too much to suspect. For a generation, the media and the publishing industry have been saturated with liberal opinions on every subject and every problem, real and invented. At this point, there is really nothing Galbraith can say about liberalism beyond the mind-deadening declaration that, whoever else may desert it, he will remain true to the faith he helped to father. As for *Annals of an Abiding Liberal,* its content is its title. (p. 107)

Galbraith's boring recitation of liberal theory is not only outdated, but largely irrelevant. It is not liberal theory, but liberal practice, which has reduced the ranks of its unapologetic adherents to a handful of last-ditchers. Even socialist theory is not what crippled the Swedish economy. Galbraith makes the point that wage and price controls are a regular part of the economic policy in European countries that are doing very well. But European price controls have a limited destructive potential because they are based on clear and limited objectives: national prosperity and protection of the country's currency. In America, such powers would be exercised by the same Establishment that conducted the War on Poverty and the escalation and rout in Vietnam. (pp. 107-08)

To liberal theory in practice, Galbraith vouchsafes not a paragraph. Aside from the dates on his reminiscences, nothing appears in *Annals* that could not have been produced by a liberal graduate student in the 1930s; forty years of this theory in action are ignored. *Annals* is an intellectual return to the womb. . . .

Galbraith is a good writer, but this book, weighted down by the tediousness of the beginning and the apologetic nature of the remainder, is not one that good writing alone can save. Its title is its epitaph—which, unlike most epitaphs, accurately describes what lies beneath. (p. 108)

> Robert W. Whitaker, "Abide with Me," in National Review (© National Review, Inc., 1980; 150 East 35th St., New York, NY 10016), Vol. XXXII, No. 2, January 25, 1980, pp. 107-08.

ARCH PUDDINGTON

[One] of the principal aims of *Annals of an Abiding Liberal* is to debunk what Galbraith calls the "conservative majority syndrome," the notion, recurring at regular intervals during the past decade or so, that "conservatism is the wave of the American future."

It is fitting that Galbraith should take up this challenge, since he is responsible for conceiving or popularizing many of the more controversial liberal policies and ideas. (p. 83)

Galbraith has assumed the role of intellectual "point man" for what some call the New Class or New Politics movement, but which he prefers to describe as the "educational and scientific estate." Many of his writings are devoted to building a case for both the inevitability and desirability of this grouping's dominance in government and economic affairs.

As ideologue of the educational and scientific estate, Galbraith is often willing to assert opinions which the estate's rank-and-file draw back from for fear of being called irresponsible or elitist. . . .

Elitist sentiment oozes from his account of a 'round-the-world tour, replete with observations on the fine food, excellent conversation, beautiful and interesting women, and sumptuous accommodations which made the journey an altogether memorable one. Although Galbraith derives great enjoyment from mocking the "rich and powerful" (probably the most recurrent

phrase in the book), he himself has acquired a strong taste for a style of life that comes only with wealth and high influence.

More disturbing in this regard is his benign view of totalitarian societies, and their effect on individual men and women. Galbraith is a leading proponent of the "convergence" theory—the idea that the differences between Communist and Western democratic societies are steadily diminishing through a process of economic interdependence. Galbraith maintains a certain ambiguity, one suspects purposely, as to whether Communist-capitalist convergence constitutes a narrow phenomenon of raw economics, or applies as well to political and civil rights. Whatever the case, life inside Communist society, for Galbraith, may not be as free or pleasant as we in the West are accustomed to, but then it's not all that bad either. . . .

Galbraith remains oblivious to the human tragedy that always seems to follow in Communism's wake. During his 'round-the-world tour, Galbraith visits Bangkok, where, as in the other cities on his itinerary, he attends meetings with political leaders, journalists, academics, and policy-makers. Yet if we are to believe Galbraith's account, the events in Indochina since the fall of Saigon, momentous events for Thailand, were hardly discussed at all. Galbraith does offer a personal observation, reflecting with satisfaction that the dominoes—Thailand, Malaysia, Indonesia, Singapore—have not been toppled by the Communists. He adds that the "strategic theorists who gave us the domino doctrine . . . took for granted that the Communist example would be persuasive," a remark that is characteristic of the misrepresentations which run through Galbraith's writings about Communism. Persuasion, after all, was never the issue; the issue was Vietnam's willingness to use its military might. Certainly the fears expressed then have been little allayed by Vietnam's subsequent conduct in Laos and Cambodia.

Aside from this, we get nothing at all about Indochina: the flight of the boat people, Cambodian genocide, Vietnam's invasion of Cambodia are ignored, even though at the time of Galbraith's Thailand visit, October 1978, Thai refugee camps were bulging with Cambodians fleeing both Pol Pot and the invading Vietnamese. Pol Pot's butchery was drawing the fire of Senator McGovern, and the expulsion of the boat people was well under way. This rather incredible omission is no doubt largely due to Galbraith's unwillingness to come to grips with his past view that life in a Vietnam run by the Communists would differ little for the average Vietnamese from life under what Galbraith once called the "repressive, obscene, and incompetent dictatorship" of General Thieu. But there is another, deeper issue at work here, and that is Galbraith's refusal to draw the obvious connection between the unprecedented human misery in Indochina and the kind of social order, a Communist one, that its rulers are determined to forge at any price.

Galbraith himself believes that for the average person, democracy is preferable to authoritarianism, but he does not believe that the degree of difference between them is as great as those who cling to the "conventional wisdom" about Western society would have it. After all, he argues, repression and the manipulation of the masses through advertising is built into the industrial societies of the West; as he has written elsewhere, "in modern capitalism too there is an inherent conflict between organization with its discipline and the individual." Moreover, to insist stubbornly on pointing out the darker aspects of Communist society is to invite the Galbraith treatment of amused disdain. One never opposes Communism out of genuine revulsion against its systematic forms of oppression; one is rather a captive of a "global strategic" mindset, a craven apologist for the Pentagon, or a smug defender of the economic status quo in the capitalist world. Critical thought and anti-Communism do not coexist in Galbraith's world.

Galbraith believes that the Left faces two fundamental challenges in the immediate period ahead: the first is to devise a workable model for a new, publicly controlled structure of corporate governance; the second is to train a cadre of talented and forceful men and women to manage nationalized entities. He offers a blueprint for the public corporation of the future which would transfer authority from private boards of directors to new mechanisms to be dominated, not surprisingly by the leading members of Galbraith's educational and scientific estate.

Galbraith's plan would eliminate private stockholders. The corporate board of directors would be replaced by a "board of public auditors," a majority of whose members would be appointed by the state, with the remainder coming from the upper ranks of management. Public members would be "men and women of strong public instinct" whose principal responsibility would be to insure that policies of the corporation served the public good. (pp. 85-6)

Specifically excluded from representation on the new public boards would be trade unionists, the one group which might be thought to have the most justified claim to a participant role in corporate management. The explanation is that union members would really not be affected by the policies set down by the public board since daily operation of the corporate entity would continue to lie within the province of management. One suspects, however, that Galbraith's dim opinion of codetermination-type arrangements is largely a manifestation of his overall view of trade unions as insufficiently enlightened to promote corporate conduct that conforms to the "public good." He would prefer to reserve the new places of corporate power for his educational and scientific estate, whose members would oversee the policies of the public corporation as well as handle the daily routine of management. Meanwhile, under the Galbraith model, the role of unions would be doubly diminished since collective bargaining, the foundation of trade-union strength in the U.S., would be handed over to the government officials who determine wage-price guidelines.

Galbraith acknowledges that the members of his enlightened estate are concerned about corporations because "that's where the power is." But he seems to find it inconceivable that the estate might be moved by common material interests or entertain cultural values antithetical to the interests and values of the majority. And although other groups would have a voice in public affairs, Galbraith would redraw the rules so as to make that voice a relatively powerless one. In the meantime, members of the estate would reign supreme, setting wages and prices, determining economic priorities, reorienting foreign policy, setting down the rules of whom to hire and admit to universities.

Most people would object to the entrenchment of this technocratic hierarchy in society's commanding heights, just as the majority has in the past often rejected the ideas Galbraith put forth and the candidates he endorsed. Unfortunately, the educational and scientific estate has more than once demonstrated its ability to achieve its goals despite the expressed wishes of the majority—quotas and certain foreign-policy decisions being prime examples. Galbraith would have us believe that he speaks for people who have been unfairly and foolishly excluded from the machinery of power; in fact, Galbraith is the ideological spokesman for a class, or estate, which has a good deal of power, and wants much more. (p. 86)

Arch Puddington, "Idealogue of the New Class," in Commentary *(reprinted by permission; all rights reserved), Vol. 69, No. 3, March, 1980, pp. 83-6.*

MICHAEL BLISS

Some critics feel that [John Kenneth Galbraith] is out of touch [with current economic developments]; while there may have been a social imbalance ("private affluence and public squalour") in Herbert Hoover's or Dwight Eisenhower's America, surely the gigantic growth of government in the 1960s and 1970s has righted the balance, possibly even created a new imbalance in the other direction. . . .

It is not entirely fair to accuse Galbraith of not adjusting to the times. Quite apart from the new material and revisions in succeeding editions of *The Affluent Society* and *The New Industrial State*—apart, too, from the way in which past experience, as in wartime, has a lot to tell us about such "agonizing new problems" as inflation—it is clear that Galbraith is still adjusting his system. His admissions at Yale of the problems of property taxes and poor public administration were cases in point. So is an argument he is toying with about the propensity to "senility" in certain large organizations, such as Chrysler and Massey-Ferguson. Galbraith may be on the verge of having to adjust his whole system to account for the unexpected vulnerability to competition—i.e., to the market—of a rather large number of North American corporations.

The clearest demonstration of Galbraith's flexibility and relevance is a little book he published in 1979 called *The Nature of Mass Poverty*. These several lectures . . . are packed with original and provocative insights. "The greatest sleeper I ever wrote," Galbraith calls the book, which has gone into innumerable editions and translations. Its central argument, that about the only way to attack mass poverty is to encourage emigration and create literacy, bears little relation to any of the main themes of Galbraith's earlier works. His enthusiasm for population movements, which may not be unrelated to his own migration and indifference to the nation state, is no more shared by his old friends on the political left than by his enemies on the right. He is attacking everybody's conventional wisdom about mass poverty.

For all his agility and capacity still to surprise, Galbraith has pretty well made his contribution to twentieth-century economic thought. It will not be considered a "mainstream" contribution, at least not in the conventional sense of the term. Despite having joined the American political establishment, and notwithstanding his year's presidency of the American Economic Association in the early 1970s, Galbraith stayed firmly outside and to the left of the main currents of modern economics. History may well judge him to be a mainstream socialist economist (Galbraith says he dislikes all labels, but has no strong objections if people care to call him a socialist; he has called himself one on occasion). Or it may see him as an American original, a brilliant iconoclast. (p. 27)

Michael Bliss, "The Unconventional Wisdom of John Kenneth Galbraith" (copyright © 1981 by Michael Bliss; reprinted by permission of the author), in Saturday Night, *Vol. 96, No. 5, May, 1981, pp. 17-28.*

ROBERT SKIDELSKY

Something of [an] unplanned, and clearly undesired, obsolescence has afflicted Galbraith. The last President to use his drafts on economic policy was Lyndon Johnson in the mid-1960s. Galbraith was then in his late fifties. Serviceability to government might seem an odd criterion for judging intellectual worth. Yet it was a criterion which the statist liberal intellectuals of Galbraith's generation had made peculiarly their own. Brought up on the New Deal, the Keynesian Revolution, and government service in the Second World War, their intellectual investments were geared to problem-solving by means of deliberate state action. Collapse of faith in the state left them high and dry. . . .

Of course, Galbraith is far too individual, and considerable, a figure to be bounded by the conventional pieties of his generation. At a time when most economists were obsessed with increasing the quantity of material goods, Galbraith in *The Affluent Society* . . . foreshadowed the later concern of environmentalists with the quality of life. At a time when American neo-liberals were busy selling Keynes to Kennedy, Galbraith was writing *The New Industrial State* which showed how great corporations were manipulating the state for their private good. These two important books, however, did not break with the neo-liberal faith that, in the last analysis, the forces of industrial society could be channelled by an intellectual élite towards its vision of the good life.

Above all, Galbraith stands out by his style. The style is very much the key to the man. Its chief characteristics are wit and irony. The Galbraith style serves many purposes and explains many things about his relationship with the American establishment and the nature of his influence. Galbraith, like Keynes, is the subversive insider, showing up the folly of the "secular priesthood" from a commanding position at the centre. But whereas Keynes's popular style was shaped by his hatred of incompetence, Galbraith, one feels, was moved more by the need to affirm superiority and placate the resentment engendered by the affirmation. Irony offered the ideal mode. The point was made that we were ruled by dunderheads, but in a manner which would amuse even the dunderheads. Above all, criticism was deflected into laughter. In this latter aspect, Galbraith's prose—objectively as the Marxists would say—has served a conservative purpose. Irony is the enemy of passion. (p. 901)

The Affluent Society . . . launched Galbraith on his career as best-selling author. The adjective itself, as well as the phrase "the conventional wisdom", became part of the radical chic of the decade. The idea of the book was not as new as Galbraith thinks. There would soon come a time, Keynes had argued in 1930, when society would have to accommodate its psychology and social structure to plenty, not scarcity. Galbraith simply said this time had arrived, at least in America and the advanced capitalist world. Instead of keeping the industrial machine growing by constantly creating new material wants through advertising, the time had come to pay attention to the quality of life—the environment in which people lived, the creative use of leisure. This readjustment would require a different "social balance" between private and public outlays. Galbraith feels now that he greatly underestimated the "public costs of congested existence in the modern metropolis". *The Affluent Society* undoubtedly captured a mood in both America and Britain. The premise of prosperity became the starting-point of the American theorists of counter-culture in the 1960s: Marcuse, Roszak, Charles Reich. Children of plenty revolted against the "surplus repression" which turned them into corporation executives. In Britain, the book's message was used to dignify industrial decline. Britain's poor economic growth, it was fashionable to suggest, had less to do with obsolete machinery, poor labour relations, low expectations, than with a mature concern for civilized values. However, prophets of the imminent arrival of the stationary state have had a poor track record in prediction, and Galbraith seems to be no exception. There are too many poor still left; and the rich are too greedy. . . .

[*The New Industrial State* is Galbraith's] most ambitious, and systematic, attempt to describe contemporary capitalism as it is, rather than as reformers say it should be, or as it is depicted in textbook models of perfect or imperfect competition. . . . More impressive than Galbraith's detailed argument was his vision of the modern economy as a set of interlocking security systems radiating out from the large corporations to control, on the one hand, their suppliers and customers, and on the other, the state. The distinction between microeconomics and macroeconomics was abolished. . . .

Galbraith's picture of American capitalism has been subjected to intensive criticism, economic as well as political. The imperatives of technology, it is said, do not necessarily dictate an increase in the size of firms. Technical change may favour products made by relatively small firms; or smaller, more flexible, firms may be readier to innovate than the giants. The statistical evidence for increasing concentration has been disputed. Even today, firms with fewer than 500 workers employ nearly 60 per cent of the American work force. Galbraith himself was moved to redress the balance of his account in a later book, *Economics and the Public Purpose* . . . , which sought to explain the survival and resilience of the "market sector" of modern economies. A second type of criticism, which to some extent applies to all Galbraith's "popular" books, is that his analytical approach is insufficiently historical, descriptive, or theoretical, to yield adequate generalization. For a European reader his work focuses rather parochially on the American experience. Take, for example, his view that Keynesian policy is to be seen as an accommodation by the state to the needs of corporate planning. How well does this fit the British case? Finally, Galbraith has been attacked from both sides of the political spectrum—a comfortable position to be in. A point often made by economic liberals is that international competition coupled with trust-busting can be used to keep domestic economies sufficiently competitive and efficiently unplanned. To the extent that monopoly conditions have nevertheless developed this is a result of state policy, not technological imperatives; policy which can be reversed. Galbraith himself accepts an opposite criticism from the left: "It is on the state that the public must rely for the assertion of the public interest. The state, however, is extensively under the control of corporate power." So how is the public interest to be secured? Galbraith admits he "faced but did not resolve" this contradiction.

It was in the 1960's that the statist liberals came into their political inheritance in both the United States and Britain—only to fritter it away with astonishing speed. . . .

In this débâcle of liberal hopes, Galbraith, at least, played a fairly minor, and honourable, part. . . .

Galbraith's star shone brightest in the 1950s. By the 1970s his place as the West's favourite guru had been taken by Milton Friedman, the apostle of monetarism, who voiced the new mood of disenchantment with big government. Disillusion with the results of monetarism is already setting in; in the 1980s we may expect new prophets of hope and despair to rise and fall in ever more rapid succession. The truth is that, inadequate as it was, there is no viable democratic alternative to the vision of the statist liberals—at least in the mature capitalist states. Thatcherism is too divisive, Bennism too claustrophobic. Intelligence, style, humanity, wit—these were the values Galbraith stood for. They may not be enough to win a better world; but they are necessary ingredients of one. (p. 902)

Robert Skidelsky, "Prophet of the Liberal State," in The Times Literary Supplement *(© Times Newspapers Ltd. (London) 1981; reproduced from* The Times Literary Supplement *by permission), No. 4088, August 7, 1981, pp. 901-02.*

George F. Gilder

1939-

Gilder, an American writer and conservative social critic, is regarded as an intellectual spokesman for the new right in Republican politics. A former associate editor of *The New Leader* and a contributing editor for *National Review*, Gilder writes on various topics including urban poverty, the sexual constitution of society, and economics. In addition, he has written speeches for Richard Nixon and both Nelson and David Rockefeller. In *Sexual Suicide* (1973), a book sharply criticized by the women's movement, Gilder argues that social and economic stability is founded upon traditional sex roles. As a proponent of supply-side economics in *Wealth and Poverty* (1981), Gilder praises the entrepreneur as the creative force behind capitalist society and argues that fostering a healthy economy by reducing taxes and federal spending will ultimately benefit all Americans. Although *Wealth and Poverty* is given much credence by the Reagan administration, liberal Democrats and minorities charge that economic revival attained at the expense of social programs will merely increase the disparity between rich and poor. (See also *Contemporary Authors*, Vols. 17-20, rev. ed.)

Photograph by Barclay Hudson

Excerpt from *SEXUAL SUICIDE*

Nothing is free, least of all sex, which is bound to our deepest sources of energy, identity, and emotion. Sex can be cheapened, of course, but then, inevitably, it becomes extremely costly to the society as a whole. For sex is the life force—and cohesive impulse—of a people, and their very character will be deeply affected by how sexuality is managed, sublimated, expressed, denied, and propagated. When sex is devalued, propagandized, and deformed, as at present, the quality of our lives declines and our social fabric deteriorates. (p. 1)

Gay liberation, pornographic glut, and one-night trysts are all indices of sexual frustration; all usually disclose a failure to achieve profound and loving sexuality. When a society deliberately affirms these failures—contemplates legislation of homosexual marriage, celebrates the women who denounce the family, and indulges pornography as a manifestation of sexual health and a release from repression—the culture is promoting a form of erotic suicide. For it is destroying the cultural preconditions of profound love and sexuality: the durable heterosexual relationships necessary to a community of emotional investments and continuities in which children can find a secure place.

The inflation and devaluation of sexual currency leads to a failure of marriage that subverts the entire society. The increasing incidence of divorce, desertion, illegitimacy, and venereal disease produces a chaotic biological arena. (p. 5)

All these social problems are ultimately erotic. The frustration of the affluent young and their resort to drugs, the breakdown of the family among both the rich and poor, the rising rate of crime and violence—all the clichés of our social crisis spring from, or reflect and reinforce, a fundamental deformation of sexuality.

The chief perpetrators of these problems are men: Men commit over 90 percent of major crimes of violence, 100 percent of the rapes, 95 percent of the burglaries. They comprise 94 percent of our drunken drivers, 70 percent of suicides, 91 percent of offenders against family and children. More specifically, the chief perpetrators are *single* men. Single men comprise between 80 and 90 percent of most of the categories of social pathology. . . . Together with the disintegration of the family, they constitute our leading social problem. For there has emerged no institution that can replace the family in turning children into civilized human beings or in retrieving the wreckage of our current disorder.

Yet what is our new leading social movement? It's Women's Liberation, with a whole array of nostrums designed to emancipate us. From what? From the very institution that is most indispensable to overcoming our present social crisis: the family. They want to make marriage more open, flexible, revokable, at a time when it is already opening up all over the country and spewing forth swarms of delinquents and neurotics, or swarms of middle-aged men and women looking for a sexual utopia that is advertised everywhere, delivered nowhere, but paid for through the nose (and other improbable erogenous zones). At a time when modernity is placing ever greater strains on the institutions of male socialization—our familes, sports, men's organization—the women's movement wants to weaken them further, make them optional, bisexual, androgynous. Most of the books of the feminists speak of the need to "humanize" (emasculate?) men. (pp. 5-6)

In the most elemental sense, the sex drive is the survival instinct: the primal tie to the future. When people lose faith in themselves and their prospects, they also lose their procreative energy. They commit sexual suicide. They just cannot bear the idea of "bringing children into the world." Such people may indulge a lot in what they call sex. But it is a kind of aimless copulation having little to do with the deeper currents of sexuality and love that carry a community into the future. (p. 8)

The crucial process of civilization is the subordination of male sexual impulses and psychology to long-term horizons of female biology. If one compares female overall sexual behavior now with women's life in primitive societies, the difference is relatively small. It is male behavior that must be changed to create a civilized order. Modern society relies increasingly on predictable, regular, long-term human activities, corresponding to the female sexual patterns. It has little latitude for the pattern of impulsiveness, aggressiveness, and immediacy, arising from male insecurity without women—and further enhanced by hormonal activity. This is the ultimate and growing source of female power in the modern world. Women domesticate and civilize male nature. They can destroy civilized male identity merely by giving up the role. (p. 23)

[It] is female power, organic and constitutional, that is real—holding sway over the deepest levels of consciousness, sources of happiness, and processes of social survival. Male dominance in the marketplace, on the other hand, is a social artifice maintained not for the dubious benefits it confers on men but for the indispensable benefits it offers the society: inducing men to support rather than disrupt the community. Conventional male power, in fact, might be considered more the ideological myth. It is designed to induce the majority of men to accept a bondage to the machine and the marketplace, to a large extent in the service of women and in the interests of civilization. (p. 24)

Women control not the economy of the marketplace but the economy of eros: the life force in our society and our lives. What happens in the inner realm of women finally shapes what happens on our social surfaces, determining the level of happiness, energy, creativity, and solidarity in the nation.

These values are primary in any society. When they deteriorate, all the king's horses and all the king's men cannot put them back together again. (p. 25)

[The] feminists, as well as the *Playboy* philosophers and the *Joy of Sex* technicians, are profoundly wrong—wrong about both love and sex. Like the musicologists who try to reduce Bach to algebra, they miss the point; collectively they are promoting in the United States an epidemic of erotic and social disorders.

They fail to understand the real sources of sexuality and love or the crucial role of sex both in individual personality and in civilization. They are thus subverting and stifling real sexuality and love, and are undermining civilized society. It is chiefly the common sense and conservative instincts of non-intellectual Americans that are retarding this fashionable movement of feminists, sexologists, male chauvinists, and pornographers, all of whom imagine themselves as conflicting forces but who

can be seen objectively as collaborators in a Sexual Suicide Society. (p. 32)

Without a durable relationship with a woman, a man's sexual life is a series of brief and temporary exchanges, impelled by a desire to affirm his most rudimentary masculinity. But with love, sex becomes refined by selectivity, and other dimensions of personality are engaged and developed. The man himself is refined, and his sexuality becomes not a mere impulse but a meaningful commitment in society, possibly to be fulfilled in the birth of specific children legally and recognizably his. His sex life then can be conceived and experienced as having specific long-term importance like a woman's.

The man thus can integrate his immediate physical sensations with his highest aspirations for meaning and community. The sex act itself can become a civilizing human affirmation, involving his entire personality and committing it, either in fact or in symbol, to a long-term engagement in a meaningful future. (p. 35)

George F. Gilder, in his Sexual Suicide *(reprinted by permission of Georges Borchardt, Inc.; copyright ©1973 by George F. Gilder), Quadrangle/The New York Times Book Co., 1973, 308 p.*

Excerpt from *WEALTH AND POVERTY*

The belief that the good fortune of others is also finally one's own does not come easily or invariably to the human breast. It is, however, a golden rule of economics, a key to peace and prosperity, a source of the gifts of progress. (p. 9)

The golden rule finds its scientific basis in the mutuality of gains from trade, in the demand generated by the engines of supply, in the expanded opportunity created by growth, in the usual and still growing economic futility of war. On this foundation have arisen most of the world's economic gains since the times of Smith and Hume. . . . But it is a belief that is always in danger of erosion and attack.

A prominent source of trouble is the profession of economics. . . . [Adam Smith] stressed the productive powers, but his followers, beginning with David Ricardo, quickly became bogged down in a static and mechanical concern with distribution. . . . The focus on distribution continues in economics today, as economists pore balefully over the perennial inequalities and speculate on brisk "redistributions" to rectify them.

This mode of thinking, prominent in foundation-funded reports, best-selling economics texts, newspaper columns, and political platforms, is harmless enough on the surface. But its deeper effect is to challenge the golden rule of capitalism, to pervert the relation between rich and poor, and to depict the system as "a zero-sum game" in which every gain for someone implies a loss for someone else, and wealth is seen once again to create poverty. As Kristol has said, a free society in which the distributions are widely seen as unfair cannot long survive. The distributionist mentality thus strikes at the living heart of democratic capitalism. (pp. 9-10)

Statistical distributions, though, can misrepresent the economy in more serious ways. . . . For example, the share of the tobacco industry commanded by the leading four firms has held steady for nearly thirty years, but the leader of the 1950s is now nearly bankrupt. The static distributions also miss the simple matter of age: many of the people at the bottom of the charts are either old, and thus beyond their major earning years, or young, and yet to enter them. Although the young and the old will always be with us, their low earnings signify little about the pattern of opportunity in a capitalist system.

Because blacks have been at the bottom for centuries now, economists often miss the dynamism within the American system. The Japanese, for example, were interned in concentration camps during World War II, but thirty years later they had higher per capita earnings than any other ethnic group in America except the Jews. Three and one-half million Jewish immigrants arrived on our shores around the turn of the century with an average of nine dollars per person in their pockets, less than almost any other immigrant group. Six decades later the mean family income of Jews was almost double the national average. Meanwhile the once supreme British Protestants (WASPs) were passed in per capita earnings after World War II not only by Jews and Orientals but also by Irish, Italians, Germans, and Poles (which must have been the final Polish joke), and the latest generation of black West Indians.

It is a real miracle that learned social scientists can live in the midst of these continuing eruptions and convulsions, these cascades and cataracts of change, and declare in a tone of grim indignation that "Over the last fifty years there has been no shift in the distribution of wealth and income in this country." (pp. 10-11)

Conservatives surely, above all, have long known and warned that real poverty is less a state of income than a state of mind and that the government dole blights most of the people who come to depend on it. The lesson of the period since 1964—a lesson so manifest it cannot be gainsaid—is that conservatives, if anything, understated their argument. In the time since the war on poverty was launched, the moral blight of dependency has been compounded and extended to future generations by a virtual plague of family dissolution. (p. 12)

As the 1980s began, a similar myopia distorted the vision of economists and social scientists appraising the condition of the middle and upper classes in the American economy. Again scrutinizing their distribution charts, they could maintain that the years of inflation since 1973 have brought "no significant shifts," as Lester Thurow wrote in *The Wall Street Journal,* "in the distribution of economic resources either across sectors (government, business, and labor) or among individuals (rich vs. poor, black vs. white, etc.)." . . .

Now it is certainly true that no catastrophe remotely comparable to the one that struck the blacks has troubled the upper and middle reaches of American society. But their decline in wealth and welfare is just as surely real. It is the statistics of rising gross national product and rising real household incomes that seriously misrepresent the conditions of American life. (p. 13)

Capitalism begins with giving. . . . The capitalists of primitive society were tribal leaders who vied with one another in giving great feasts. Similarly, trade began with offerings from one family to another or from one tribe to its neighbor. The gifts, often made in the course of a religious rite, were presented in hopes of an eventual gift in return. The compensation was not defined beforehand. But in the feasting process it was expected to be a return with interest, as another "big man," or *mumi* as he was called among the Siuai in the Solomon Islands, would attempt to excel the offerings of the first. (p. 21)

Helen Codere describes potlatching, a similar sequence of work and saving, capital accumulation and feasting, performed among the Kwakiutl of the northwestern United States: "The public

distribution of property by an individual is a recurrent climax to an endless series of cycles of accumulating property—distributing it in a potlatch—being given property—again accumulating and preparing." The piles of food and other gifts and ceremonial exchanges could mount to dumbfounding quantities. . . .

These competitions in giving are contests of altruism. A gift will only elicit a greater response if it is based on a understanding of the needs of others. In the most successful and catalytic gifts, the giver fulfills an unknown need or desire in a surprising way. The recipient is startled and gratified by the inspired and unexpected sympathy of the giver and is eager to repay him. In order to repay him, however, the receiver must come to understand the giver. Thus the contest of gifts leads to an expansion of human sympathies. The circle of giving (the profits of the economy) will grow as long as the gifts are consistently valued more by the receivers than by the givers. . . .

By giving a feast, the *mumi* imposed implicit debts on all his guests. By attending it, they accepted a liability to him. Through the gifts or investments of primitive capitalism, man created and extended obligations. These obligations led to reciprocal gifts and further obligations in a growing fabric of economic creation and exchange, with each giver hoping for greater returns but not assured of them, and with each recipient pushed to produce a further favor. This spreading out of debts could be termed expanding the money supply. The crucial point is that for every liability (or feeling of obligation on the part of the guest), there was a previous asset (meal) given to him. The *mumi,* as a capitalist, could not issue demands or impose liabilities or expand money without providing commensurate supplies. The demand was inherent in the supply—in the meal. (p. 22)

That supply creates its own demand is a principle of classical economics called Say's Law. It has come to be expressed, and refuted, in many interesting technical forms. But its essential point is potlatching. Capitalism consists of providing first and getting later. The demand is implicit in the supply. Without a monetary economy, such gifts were arrayed in expectation of an immediate profit in prestige and a later feast of interest, and they could be seen as a necessary way to escape the constraints of barter, to obviate the exact coincidence of wants and values required by simple trading. In most cases, the feasts and offerings were essentially entrepreneurial. They entailed the acquisition of goods at a known cost with the intention of acquiring in exchange—in this case, over an extended period—goods of unknown value. As devices of savings and investment, they depended for success on the continued honesty and economic returns of all members. (p. 23)

Capitalist production entails faith—in one's neighbors, in one's society, and in the compensatory logic of the cosmos. Search and you shall find, give and you will be given unto, supply creates its own demand. It is this cosmology, this sequential logic, that essentially distinguishes the free from the socialist economy. The socialist economy proceeds from a rational definition of needs or demands to a prescription of planned supplies. In a socialist economy, one does not supply until the demands have already been determined and specified. Rationality rules, and it rules out the awesome uncertainties and commensurate acts of faith that are indispensable to an expanding and innovative system.

The gifts of advanced capitalism in a monetary economy are called investments. One does not make gifts without some sense, possibly unconscious, that one will be rewarded, whether in this world or the next. . . . The essence of giving is not the absence of all expectation of return, but the lack of a predetermined return. Like gifts, capitalist investments are made without a predetermined return. (pp. 24-5)

The ultimate strength and crucial weakness of both capitalism and democracy are their reliance on individual creativity and courage, leadership and morality, intuition and faith. But there is no alternative, except mediocrity and stagnation. Reason and calculation, for all their appeal, can never suffice in a world where events are shaped by millions of men, acting unknowably, in fathomless interplay and complexity, in the darkness of time. (p. 27)

When government gives welfare, unemployment payments, and public-service jobs in quantities that deter productive work, and when it raises taxes on profitable enterprise to pay for them, demand declines. In fact, nearly all the programs that are advocated by economists to promote equality and combat poverty—and are often rationalized in terms of stimulating consumption—in actuality reduce demand by undermining the production from which all real demand derives. Buying power does not essentially "trickle down" as wages or "flow up" and away as profits and savings. It originates with productive work at any level. This is the simple and homely first truth about wealth and poverty. "Give and you will be given unto." This is the secret not only of riches but also of growth.

This is also the essential insight of supply side economics. Government cannot significantly affect real aggregate demand through policies of taxing and spending—taking money from one man and giving it to another, whether in government or out. All this shifting of wealth is a zero sum game and the net effect on incomes is usually zero, or even negative.

Even a tax cut does not work by a direct impact on total disposable incomes, since every dollar of resulting deficit must be financed by a dollar of government debt, paid by the purchaser of federal securities out of his own disposable income. Even in the short run real aggregate demand is an effect of production, not of government policy. The only way tax policy can reliably influence real incomes is by changing the incentives of suppliers. By altering the pattern of rewards to favor work over leisure, investment over consumption, the sources of production over the sumps of wealth, taxable over untaxable activity, government can directly and powerfully foster the expansion of real demand and income. This is the supply side mandate. (pp. 45-6)

> *George Gilder, in his* Wealth and Poverty *(copyright © 1981 by George Gilder; reprinted by permission of Basic Books, Inc., Publishers), Basic Books, 1981, 306 p.*

TOM WICKER

One of the few encouraging developments from the Republican debacle of 1964 has been the new intellectual ferment that now centers on the plight of the Grand Old Party. What should it do to recover a strong and useful place in American politics? . . .

Two remarkable Republicans, George F. Gilder, and Bruce K. Chapman, . . . have now made, in **"The Party That Lost Its Head,"** an invaluable contribution to that ferment. Unfortunately, they have not solved the major Republican problem, and their stimulating book shows by sad contrast that the ferment is still on the outside looking in.

For example: the young authors propound a thoughtful program for Republican regeneration both *of* and *in* the cities—a "conservative approach," as they call it—that would concentrate less on the bulldozer and public housing and tackle the whole range of urban problems. This, they believe, is also the proper path toward renewed Republican ability to win elections in the cities, where the votes are.

The problem is that the authors do not really suggest any practical means by which Republicans can adopt and execute such a policy. . . .

Mr. Gilder and Mr. Chapman (and others trying to point the way to restored Republican eminence) confront a nearly insoluble dilemma. The national party they have to work with—that is, its officeholders in Congress—evinces little if any realization that it has been on the wrong track for many years, and offers more of the same old Eisenhower-Nixon-Goldwater mélange of standpat. And, since a political party, unlike a corporation, has no board of directors and executive officers to impose sound policy and decent administration on it, there is no easy or even visible way to develop a new Republican approach, much less win its general acceptance in the party.

Nevertheless, these authors have many useful things to say, and they say them with verve and nerve. . . .

They castigate and document Republican indifference to intellectuals and the fatal Republican fascination with "the Southern strategy" and its inevitable handmaiden, white supremacist politics. They are equally scornful of me-too thinking among Republican progressives—and make the striking argument that it is the Democrats who are in danger of becoming the prisoners of ideology through their single-minded reliance upon massive Federal action as the antidote to all problems.

Few escape the Gilder-Chapman broadside. Barry Goldwater, in an analysis long needed, is seen as less a Republican than the creature of evangelistic right-wing extremism. (p. 14)

They lambast the axiomatic Republican notion, expressed *ad nauseam* at any G.O.P. gathering one cares to attend, that the way to victory, even in the Democratic cities, lies in the twin virtues of "organization" and "unity." Neither can be effective, they argue, until there is something or somebody attractive enough to organize for and unite around. The solution, as they see it, is in an "ideological regeneration" of the party, the application of the old Republican traditions of free enterprise, individual liberty and restrained government in a sensible way, not to the hobgoblins of the past, but to the problems of the day.

They argue, for instance, that Democratic emphasis on economic expansionism (the theory of aggregate demand) to create new jobs, alleviate poverty and absorb the rising work force will fail because automation and technology will eliminate jobs as fast as others can be created. Among other things they urge as Republican alternatives is advocacy of the shorter work week, which they place squarely in line with traditional Republican principles. (pp. 14, 16)

What the party needs most is leaders, men who will provide or evoke from others the ideology, the programs, the ideas that are needed.

No ideology ever made a President of a weak or inarticulate man who adopted it; but a man who wants to be President, who knows the country he seeks to lead and what he must do to win its confidence, will be creating and voicing his ideas and approaches, changing and adapting them, at every step of the way. That is how a winning political "ideology" is made. That is what American politics is all about. And if Bruce Chapman and George Gilder, impressive as their ideas are, think they are going to put the Republican party back in power merely by imposing an ideology on it, they are going to be as sadly disappointed as the right-wingers who tried to do just that in 1964. (p. 16)

> Tom Wicker, "The G.O.P.'s Future," in The New York Times Book Review (© 1966 by The New York Times Company; reprinted by permission), May 15, 1966, pp. 14, 16.

WALTER DEAN BURNHAM

Written by two young journalists . . . of intellectual liberal Republicanism, [George Gilder and Bruce Chapman, *The Party That Lost Its Head*] is part analysis, part sectarian tract. Its polemics, couched in a style of evangelistic fervor, mixed metaphors and occasional journalistic clichés, are probably primarily of interest to those within the party lodge—though the bitterness encountered here makes an outsider wonder how the GOP will ever be able to make a 1968 nomination which all of its sects can support.

The analysis is extremely interesting in places, but ultimately suffers from a superficiality common to most American political literature: it tends to be content to identify specific villains (individuals or groups), and hence to overlook broader and more impersonal systemic processes which are shaping party destinies. For example, the discussion of our enormous urban problems leaves the impression that they are largely the fault of the Democrats and cities which somehow consume themselves as if they were not made by human hands or inhabited by human beings. Surely there are more fundamental issues here—issues going to the heart of the socio-economic system and the human relationships engendered by it. (p. 559)

Still, this book is worth reading on at least two counts. In its first half it provides exceptionally interesting "inside" material on the 1964 debacle, while in its second half its authors do make a serious attempt to provide a programmatic justification for the existence of liberal Republicanism as a separate political entity. There can be no question that Democratic welfare-warfare-state liberalism—partly because of the ineffectiveness of Republican opposition—has become sterile and drearily unimaginative. At least some of the urban mess, after all, is the Democrats' fault. Federalism could be put to far more balanced and constructive uses, and even if it be true that much of the blame rests with reactionary obstructionism in the state legislature, it cannot be said that Washington has really been terribly concerned about the problem. The Far Right is just as neolithic as the authors say it is, and their observations—interspersed among the polemics—make useful reading.

How was it possible for 1964 to occur at all? At the outset it should be remarked that the title of this book lays a false scent across the trail. How could a party lose a head when it has not had one in the memory of the past generation? If by "head" we mean the existence of a top party leadership which has both mind and *esprit,* the GOP has had only three in this century: Theodore Roosevelt, Herbert Hoover and Wendell Willkie. . . .

In modern times—and especially since the advent of the New Deal—the Republican party has developed a notorious aversion to dynamic executive leadership and the life of the mind in politics. One of the best jokes of the 1964 campaign was that Barry Goldwater was running not for but against the Presidency. But in this, at least, he differed less from the "mainstream" of his own party than is often supposed. When one looks elsewhere at Republican candidates—Dewey and Nixon in particular—one finds failures of nerve, will and intellect which fatally damaged their chances of election. On the whole, the record of the GOP in this century has been one of persistent Whiggery on the national level—a Whiggery which is of course directly and functionally related to the major interests it seeks to protect, a Whiggery which has caused more than one observer to comment that it acts more like a pressure group than a party. . . .

Which brings us to the strange case of President Eisenhower. There are no peculiarities in the man: he is the perfect exemplar of the apolitical military hero, a William Henry Harrison who lasted eight years in office instead of one month. What is strange is the extent to which a mystique has been developed around him by liberal Republicans. It is no less wrong to think of Eisenhower as a "leader" of this wing of the party—much less that he had anything to do with its ideology, as the authors seem to think—than it was politically wrong for grown men in 1964 to try to stop Barry's legions by a thunderbolt from Gettysburg. The Eisenhower administration represented in fullest form the contemporary Republican instinct of non-leadership and a mass politics of pure personality. (p. 560)

The authors of *The Party That Lost Its Head* seem to have swallowed heavy doses of the Eisenhower elixir. This gives us a clue to the nature of liberal Republicanism. This wing of the GOP is a descendant of the Mugwumps, the "gentle reformers" of the 1880s and 1890s. Like the modern-day GOP liberals, these reformers were disproportionately concentrated in the East; they were solid members of the White Anglo-Saxon Protestant middle classes; they were heavily weighted with intellectuals and professional people; they were profoundly hostile to the political party as a social institution. Vaguely benevolent toward the urban proletariat and deprived ethnic minorities, they advocated and sometimes carried out reforms so long as none of the basic institutions of society was even remotely threatened in the process. . . . They were ultimately destroyed as a political force, . . . but ultimately destroyed because their mild reformism had become irrelevant to politics in an age of mature corporate capitalism.

It remains at best unclear whether our latter-day Cleveland Democrats will escape a similar fate. The realignment of the parties, underway for a generation, shows no signs of abating in the long run. As it continues, and problems which Americans have ducked for decades finally have to be resolved, liberal Republicans will increasingly be called on to justify their separate existence in American politics. This the authors have tried to do. The extent to which they have fallen short of their goal reveals the magnitude of the task ahead. So does the present condition of the Republican party. (pp. 560-61)

> Walter Dean Burnham, "'The Party That Lost Its Head'," in Commonweal (copyright © 1966 Commonweal Publishing Co., Inc.; reprinted by permission of Commonweal Publishing Co., Inc.), Vol. LXXXIV, No. 20, September 2, 1966, pp. 559-61.

CHARLES O. JONES

[*The Party that Lost Its Head: The Republican Collapse and Imperatives for Revival*] purports to analyze the present difficulties of the Republican Party and to offer a blueprint for elevating a near-permanent minority party to majority status. . . . Regretfully, however, I must report that in my opinion this book is more destructive than constructive. Able young phrasemakers have misused their talents to impugn the judgment, honesty, and motives of their peers. Virtually no Republican leader, liberal or conservative, escapes. Presumptiveness and impertinence abound. If one could see the constructive purpose in such a distorted rendering of Republican Party politics, the effort could be accepted for that reason. But, in my opinion, the authors have allowed vindictiveness to influence, perhaps even dictate, their descriptive analysis of recent party history. It is too much to ask that the reader separate revenge from fact. . . .

Though the book is fairly discursive, it is possible to identify several themes which hold it together. First and foremost is that Barry M. Goldwater and his right-wing strategists *conspired* to win control of the Republican Party. Most of the Goldwater people, it is asserted, were outsiders who relied on subterfuge to undermine the party. . . . [What] Gilder and Chapman call conspiracy, I call plain, old-fashioned pre-convention politics. There is nothing new about winning the nomination as the Goldwater strategists won it. In fact, until very recently that is the way it was usually done. I think it is probably a dumb way to do it these days if you want to win the general election, but I don't see anything conspiratorial about it. . . .

A second theme is related to the first. Goldwater was successful because of the ineptitude of the normal Republican leadership. Congressional leaders, governors, national party leaders, President Eisenhower, all stumbled about when they ought to have been working closely together. But the leadership is to be condemned for more than their ineptitude in heading off Goldwater. According to the authors, they have also failed to develop a reasonable Republican program and discouraged those who tried to do so. Surely Gilder and Chapman do not expect efficiency and unity from a minority party in America. Regrettable or not, minority party politics in this country is just not very monolithic.

The result of the Goldwater coup, and the ineptitude of the progressive leaders, is a seriously split party which is unbalanced to the right. The third theme suggests a way out. What the Republican Party needs is an ideology. Party leaders and party professionals have stressed organization and unity in the past but that emphasis will not result in majority party status for Republicans. (p. 1029)

Gilder and Chapman provide "an ideology for Republicans" at the conclusion of their book. It would include a "revitalized federalism" on the domestic level—not unlike that recently outlined by President Johnson. It would include patching up several urban programs which have been poorly conceived and poorly administered. It would include reasonable approaches to the many problems related to technology. It would include reform of the draft and attention to the problems of educating large numbers of people. It would include a more dynamic role for the opposition party in foreign policy.

I find myself in almost total agreement with this excellent, if occasionally "me-too," summary statement of programs and goals for Republicans. But I reject the conclusion that this is the first statement ever issued on these subjects. The fact is

that many Republican research committees and coordinating committees have issued similar statements over the past 20 years—and continue to issue them today. (pp. 1029-30)

There is a fourth theme in this book which is much less obvious—even, I think, to the authors. Gilder and Chapman talk about *the* Republican Party as though it existed somewhere—at a specific address in a specific city—and had a "head" to lose. Decentralization is a characteristic of American political parties which is well-known—at least to most students. It causes more mischief for the minority party than the majority party but that is the result of many factors—not just the ineptitude of party leaders. What is the remedy? Apparently, according to Gilder and Chapman, to get all Republicans subscribing to an ideology and then to develop an organization strong enough to achieve the goals stated in the ideology. Goldwater tested the authors' formula in 1964. Surely one lesson of the 1964 election is that ideological "tidying up" can only result in resounding defeat.

There is no pat formula for a minority party becoming a majority party in this country. It is probably true that the Republican Party is more likely to win control of the government as a result of what the Democrats do than anything they may do. Not that many Republicans should not continue to rethink party goals and organization. They should do so and are doing so. (p. 1030)

> Charles O. Jones, "American Government and Politics: 'The Party That Lost Its Head: The Republican Collapse and Imperatives for Revival'," in The American Political Science Review *(copyright, 1966, by The American Political Science Association), Vol. LX, No. 4, December, 1966, pp. 1029-30.*

DAVID GUTMANN

[George Gilder's *Sexual Suicide* provides only] a small sample of the potential "masculinist" counterattack to Women's Liberation, but a review of [its] arguments will give as good an idea as any of sentiments in the silent male majority. Then, too, an examination of the counterattack may provide insight into the nature of the original provocation, and hence into the real agenda in the current argument between the sexes. . . .

[*Sexual Suicide*] deals with the topic of male aggression, with particular emphasis on the consequences for women when they provoke that aggression. . . . [Gilder asserts] that the male endowment of aggressive energy is biologically rooted; that it is a major pivot of sex distinctions; and that it is a critical issue for societies and individuals. (p. 59)

Gilder sees aggression not as a relatively discrete and boundaried social-scientific variable, located within the individual human unit, bonded to the neuro-endocrine systems, and constant and fixed in its goals, but rather as something at once more protean and more diffuse: it is a potential for human relatedness; it is also an aspect of male sexuality; and it is shaped by the intense encounters which it stimulates. Gilder's main point . . . is that male sexuality and aggression in the forms that they usually take are not the inflexible products of a biological drive but are reciprocal to the sexuality of women. . . . [Male] striving for patriarchy and dominance is not inevitable, but rather represents a disciplining and focusing of male aggression, in large part sponsored by women, toward socially productive uses.

For Gilder, man is not a natural patriarch. Left to himself, "to the normal circuits of male sexuality," man—perhaps like the primitive hunter—alternates between ferocity and apathy, raping, hacking, and boozing one day, then sleeping it off until his rising lust for mayhem and fornication drive him into action again. . . . Gilder's model of "natural" man seems to be abstracted from disorganized societies—from the inner-city ghettos, the shanty-town *barrios* and *favellas*, the urban fringes of Indian reservations, all those environments in which the bases of male attainment have been undercut, where men are "castrated" by social circumstances and by their women's contempt, and where they have slouched off and left the women to raise the children they have aimlessly fathered. Gilder, in other words, shares with some feminists the view that men are naturally bums; but unlike the feminists, he believes that it is women's mission, consistent with their self-interest, to civilize men, to subordinate "male short-term interests and psychology to the long-term interests of female biology"—a biology that is organized toward the raising of viable children.

In Gilder's view, men are not imperial animals . . . ; to the contrary, they are extremely vulnerable to women's judgment of their sexual performance, and they are mortified by the all-important role of women in procreation. They can maintain their sexual potency and tame their wild aggression only if women give them a great deal of compensatory recognition. Women have to convince men that they have a vital and unique role, as protectors and providers, in procreation and child-rearing. They must also validate the male need to set up exclusively masculine wild-life preserves—politics, warfare, sports, secret societies—in which men can build up their threatened self-regard. And since what preserves the male ultimately preserves the female, women must also concede the prestige of such "sexist" business: they must honor and admire superior male performance in activities that largely exclude women. If women fail to validate the more restrained and bourgeois versions of masculinity, then domesticity itself will become a threat and men will fall back to seeking their manhood in the barroom, in drunken, murderous brawls, in casual sex, and in the kind of work—in mines, ships, and lumber camps—that takes them far from family and fatherhood. Feminists have claimed that unisex, and the breakdown of sex distinction in marriage, will "liberate" men and turn them into tender comrades and lovers—mother and father rolled into one; instead, Gilder asserts, unisex will bring about more and more of the *truly* exploitative male types who are already filling the urban world today—the ambisexual rapists, pimps, and junkies. . . . In Gilder's view this outcome, when it becomes the norm for men, represents social catastrophe; fornication may actually increase in volume but all the *civilized* deployments of male sex and aggression—toward the protection of women and children, toward productive labor—will be undone. The result is the "Sexual-Suicide Society," one that will brutalize men and oppress women far beyond anything that either now endure.

Feminists will undoubtedly be enraged by Gilder's ideas, seeing them as a form of blackmail, bitter confirmation of what they have all along been maintaining is the male attitude toward women: "Adore me or I'll kill you." Similarly, Gilder's praise of women as a civilizing force will be seen as a piece of Victorian hypocrisy designed to flatter women into loving their chains. Interestingly enough, however, the tone if not the message of Gilder's book is close . . . to the feminist literature he deplores. Like the feminists, Gilder has an ambivalent if not a downright low opinion of men, and he agrees with them that male morale requires much female self-effacement. Like them,

too, Gilder judges every instance of social practice by its quotient of "sexism": does it or does it not support clear sex differences, the prestige and dignity of the bourgeois male life style? And like the feminists, but of course taking the opposite side, he believes that one is either part of the solution or part of the problem. Thus, if equal pay for equal work without regard to sex undercuts the prestige of men as breadwinners, then Gilder is against it; similarly with the Pill, Aid to Dependent Children, and the Open Marriage. These are all aspects of sexual suicide.

In sum, to the feminist claim that male aggression is not authentic, that, since there are no *intrinsic* differences between the sexes, it is only social pressure which artificially inflates male, and reduces female, aggression, [Gilder responds]: the superior male endowment of aggression is natural and intrinsic, and women should be careful not to become the rivals of men. . . . [Gilder] believes that in the face of female rivalry men will abandon the status struggle without at the same time giving up their aggression, which will erupt in the more dangerous and primitive forms of violent crime and brutal or exploitative sex. (pp. 60-1)

> *David Gutmann, "Men, Women, and the Parental Imperative," in* Commentary *(reprinted by permission; all rights reserved), Vol. 56, No. 6, December, 1973, pp. 59-64.**

JUDITH ADLER HENNESSEE

One reads this elaborate, Freud-haunted apology for patriarchy [entitled **"Sexual Suicide"**] with a depressing sense of déjà vu. Whether men invent a mythology that makes women superior or inferior, the end result is likely to be the same—women belong in the home.

Through some mystical medieval process (a strong religious flavor permeates the book, parts of which read as if they had been dictated by the Vatican), George F. Gilder has decided that women are morally and sexually superior to men, which is rather like saying that apples are superior to bananas. . . .

Stripped to the bare bones, it is Gilder's thesis that sexism is inevitable in a civilized society and that women should just relax and enjoy it. Actually, enjoy is probably the wrong word. In this rigid, biologically determined world, shot through with misogyny like a streak of insanity in the family, there is no room for pleasure. Life is real, life is earnest, and its goal is procreation. Sex, love and even marriage for any other reason are utterly without redeeming social importance.

Men are the problem, according to the author. They are basically superfluous, and some sort of cultural role must be manufactured for them to make them equal to women, who achieve creativity and profound fulfillment through having children, breast feeding them and nurturing them. It's *Kinder, Küche, Kirche* all over again, with one big difference—what Freud did for the penis, Gilder is doing for the womb. Mere paternity does not make men equal within the family, the only place it counts. Men need something of their own in compensation. It is the ineluctable job of women, the caryatids of the world, to "induce men to submit their short-time sexual horizons to long-time female sexual patterns"—to socialize men into supporting and providing for the family. (p. 36)

Since men do not work for money but "to affirm their masculinity," the author states, equal pay is a terrible threat to them. It kicks away one of the props in their precarious endeavor, and leads us further along the road to the "Sexual Suicide Society," where male activity will degenerate into "the vain pursuit of power." If male sex patterns prevail, men will become dominant in society. They will drop out, become violent, hedonistic and homosexual: homosexuality is a "disease" that Gilder seems to feel is almost as catching as a cold. Women will be demeaned and "become a subordinate class," and we will find ourselves living in a technocratic police state. I'm not sure whether the police are going to be men or women.

This breakdown in our "sexual constitution" is being brought about by a combination of forces, but chiefly by women's liberation. Some of the most passionate sentences in the book are devoted to vilifying feminism, with scattered distortions of it here and there. Its proponents are "virulently anti-American," and they exhibit a "prurient obsession with rape," among other things; but worst of all is its Equal Employment Opportunities Commission take-over of the machinery, which ought to be used only for black males. The ghetto is the exemplar of our sexual crisis: The black problem is not primarily racism but "a failure of male socialization."

There's much, much more, and there is simply no excuse for it. To uphold social injustice in the name of biological mysticism is outrageous arrogance. By now we are all aware that women's role stereotypes are as culturally contrived as men's, and that what we don't know about sex would fill an encyclopedia. At a time when women are discovering their own sexuality, Gilder makes the egregious error of professing to understand and define it for them.

There are dozens of statements in this book that are preposterous, as well as oversimple generalizations that contain a germ of truth but veer off wildly into fantasy. One searches in vain for some understanding of the individual need for self-fulfillment. Of course men work to support their families—among other reasons. The drive for money and power, the ultimate aphrodisiac, can hardly be attributed to domestic concerns, nor can it be written off merely as unconscious expressions of the need to have children. They are valid forces in themselves. Human behavior is too complex to be narrowed down to a single cause.

But even if one accepts the Freudian premise that sexuality is the root of everything and that social ills are really sexual ills in disguise (I do not), there remains a simple but devastating contradiction at the heart of the book. The things that Gilder is warning against happened a long time ago. Male action and aggression have degenerated into "the vain pursuit of power" that Gilder deplores. What else is Watergate? And they were all good husbands and providers. Female sexual patterns have been dominant for centuries, but females have not. For all their erotic power over men, guaranteed to keep them superior, women have been a subordinate class for at least 5,000 years. And it is precisely in those countries where women are limited strictly to the home, the "center of human activity," that they are most demeaned. When the home ceased to have an economic function, it also ceased to be the center. The center moved out into the world, leaving women stranded on their pedestals.

Women's liberation, that great "menace" to civilization, hasn't brought on any of these things. The kind of society Gilder celebrates has done it, and men are also uneasy with their prescribed masculinity. . . . The real problem is achieving a humane society in which neither sex is sacrificed to the biology of the other. Turning back the clock is an exercise in futility. (pp. 36, 38)

Judith Adler Hennessee, "What We Don't Know about Sex Will Fill an Encyclopedia," in The New York Times Book Review *(© 1973 by The New York Times Company; reprinted by permission), December 9, 1973, pp. 36, 38.*

MORTON A. KAPLAN

In a slashing attack on the excesses of the feminist movement, George Gilder [in *Sexual Suicide*] shows how this offshoot of comforting liberalism fits the needs of those upper-middle-class "fat cats" who dominate such mutual-support societies. . . .

The essential core of Gilder's book is the assertion that there is a basic sexual constitution to society and that our effort to rationalize it out of existence will produce sexual suicide. . . .

This is an interesting and provocative thesis. As a counterpoint to the unisex myth and the belief that biology does not matter either in personal relationships or in the cementing of society, it almost surely points in the direction of truth. Neither man nor society is infinitely malleable. . . . The enthusiasm of the feminists for simple solutions is surpassed only by the general state of ignorance concerning the working of society.

Unfortunately for our state of mind, Mr. Gilder cannot simply be proclaimed the victor in the intellectual debate. His insights are often profound, his apothegms often brilliant, and his flair for argument strong. Yet one finds no humility on his part in the face of our enormous ignorance concerning society and politics. Every sentence is uttered with Jovian authority. Mr. Gilder even contradicts himself with authority, as in his early assertion that the male, unlike the female, requires constant sexual conquest and his later assertion that this behavior is produced in social situations that frustrate him and interfere with his sense of identity.

Mr. Gilder is certainly not anti-intellectual, for his argument is reasoned. Yet, as with the feminists he attacks, one senses a desire to convert the reader rather than to engage his intellect. Are parts of the argument less well supported by evidence than others? Mr. Gilder does nothing to suggest that this might be the case. . . . The bibliography in the rear of the book is long, and, where Mr. Gilder does marshal evidence, he shows that he can read better and think more clearly than most of his opponents; on the whole, however, we are left more with Mr. Gilder's conclusions than with the analysis that produced them. (p. 1419)

From an altitudinous point of view, the feminist attitudes make no sense. But, even if we accept the argument that the desire by important percentages of females to seek occupations previously defined as male rests on a fundamental misunderstanding of the real importance of different roles in society, no such intellectual arguments are likely to prevail as long as our current value structure leaves many women deeply dissatisfied in their current roles.

I agree with many of Mr. Gilder's incisive comments on the silliness of our current welfare system, on the inherent clash of interests between the feminine and racial movements, on the absurdity of the drug culture and the liberal response to it, on the dangers in the abortion movement—and not merely to the sexual constitution, as Mr. Gilder puts it, but to more fundamental values as well. But again these views are bound to be largely academic until we come to terms with those features of our current social system and value structure that produce these aberrations. . . . However much I doubt that the crisis of our society is entirely sexual in origin I do not doubt that we are suffering a deep trauma that is somehow related to our individualistic utilitarianism and to the shallowness of our conception of community. Mr. Gilder's book argues strongly against the damage that feminism will do to community, but treats sexuality in a narrow sense as the key variable. In this sense, it continues to indulge in the individualistic fallacy.

As a provocative polemic, designed to stimulate debate, Mr. Gilder's book is effective, and as social commentary, its insights touch deep wounds in our society. (p. 1420)

> *Morton A. Kaplan, "On the Sexual Constitution,"*
> in National Review (© *National Review, Inc., 1973;*
> *150 East 35th St., New York, NY 10016), Vol. 25,*
> *No. 51, December 21, 1973, pp. 1419-20.*

BARRY M. DANK

Sexual Suicide is an overtly polemical and emotionally laden book. Gilder views American society as being on the verge of social disintegration, and the cause of the débacle is the Women's Liberation Movement, whose ideas are undermining the sexual constitution of American society. (p. 418)

Although Gilder writes as an avowed moralist, he most often presents his arguments in a quasi-sophisticated, anthropological-sociological framework. This will undoubtedly explain the popularity of this book—an emotional critique of the Women's Movement in a "scientific" context. His application of anthropological studies to modern technological societies is highly naive. His sociological reasoning tends to be teleological and often unsupported by systematic empirical data. His excellent analysis of the situation of the lower-class black male is marred by his emotional rhetoric, so characteristic of most of the book. (pp. 418-19)

> *Barry M. Dank, "'Sexual Suicide',"* in Contem-
> porary Sociology *(copyright © 1974 American So-*
> *ciological Association), Vol. 3, No. 5, September,*
> *1974, pp. 418-19.*

M. J. SOBRAN, JR.

[*Naked Nomads*] concentrates on single men themselves, who, taken all in all, are a bad lot. Only 13 per cent of the population, they commit 90 per cent of the violent crime. They lead the league in suicide, mental illness, alcoholism, drug addiction, venereal disease, you name it; the Bureau of the Census backs Gilder up dramatically. Single women aren't even close when it comes to suffering and inflicting misery.

But the statistics, decisive as they seem to be, are only a point of departure for a penetrating essay on the male psyche. Gilder agrees with some feminists that men need women far more than women need men; the feminists' error, so to speak, is not that they are wrong, but that they don't know how right they are. In their denunciations of men they have hit on a truth they would rather exploit than explore. Men *need* the acceptance and approval of women; *crave* the assurance of vows of fidelity, children, and a role of their own to guarantee themselves a place in a fruitful future. If the state of a mother without a husband is economically precarious, that of a man without a woman is psychically so. These complementary facts conspire to encourage a marital balance of nature that is threatened when, for instance, a government weakens the male role by assuming the responsibility for single mothers. Making women

self-sufficient may seem a worthy goal; but it inevitably makes men superfluous, thereby generating myriad social problems. . . .

But this is only one of the lines of argument taken by this dauntlessly original thinker, who is unabashed at reaching traditional conclusions. He says things that were never before necessary to say, and it may be a long time before anyone else says them as well.

> *M. J. Sobran, Jr., "Sanity and the Sexes,"* in Na-
> tional Review (© *National Review, Inc., 1975; 150*
> *East 35th St., New York, NY 10016), Vol. 27, No.*
> *17, May 9, 1975, p. 517.*

EUGENIA SHANKLIN

Gilder [in *Naked Nomads*] has what I think is an unconscious talent for voicing the dissenting view; few among us worry much about the "depopulation crisis" he foresaw in *Sexual Suicide,* and fewer still will be moved to pity the plight of the male at the hands of the "female conspiracy." Even amidst the virulent critics of the women's liberation movement, Gilder was probably unique in sensing a female conspiracy aimed at undermining the roots of Western civilization. Gilder does not so much state his case as whine about it, statistically and anecdotally; his point is that women are the cornerstone of society, by virtue of their ability to settle men into orderly groups of hard-working drones. Should women suddenly refuse this role in the service of their own liberation, then the devastating consequences for men will become apparent, consequences only hinted at now by the statistics on mental illness, low income, and other disorders suffered by single men. Curiously, the women's movement has a natural ally in Gilder; they might consider subsidizing him. When he attempts to make a case for women receiving less money than men for the same work, the absurdities emerge far more readily than when the refutation is presented by rhetoric and polemics. (p. 864)

> *Eugenia Shanklin, "A Tide in the Affairs of Women,"*
> in American Anthropologist *(copyright 1976 by the*
> *American Anthropological Association; reproduced*
> *by permission of the American Anthropological As-*
> *sociation), Vol. 78, No. 4, 1976, pp. 861-65.**

M. J. SOBRAN, JR.

Gilder has written a kind of narrative case study [in *Visible Man*] of one young man whose life seems powerfully to confirm, vividly to illustrate his thesis about our "sexual constitution." Part of that thesis is that men need to earn, need to be needed, and that the welfare system, benevolently intended to make poor mothers independent, has also the unintended effect, subversive of the sexual constitution, of making their men unnecessary. This fosters male dependence on women, and actually has created a class of welfare predators who compete, often violently, for the fleeting favors of welfare women. Gilder sees the problem of the young black criminal as far less racial than sexual.

The case of Mitchell "Sam" Brewer, hero of *Visible Man,* shows how it works. Sam, a black youth who has come north to Albany with his mother, is the product of one of her serial liaisons. He has no responsible male role models; he has experienced women only as providers for him. Nonetheless, he *knows better;* and he has a rudimentary, but weak and ill-supported, ambition to be a provider himself. He begets a couple of children on a couple of girlfriends, but finds himself at their mercy: they don't need him. He has nothing to offer they can't get elsewhere.

Ironically, he comes close to a more-or-less stable relationship whose prosperity inheres in its illegality. He impregnates a third girl, an under-age white runaway named Bev. Technically she is jailbait. Yet this also means that she is ineligible for welfare, and he stays with her and takes care of her. . . . The affair is precarious to begin with, and it is fatally threatened by the approach of Bev's 16th birthday, when she will be eligible for welfare and is tempted to move out on Sam. His troubles culminate in a charge of rape. . . . The prospective sentence is 25 to life. . . .

It would be nice to say that this close shave taught Sam his lesson and propelled him, chastened, toward a sober and industrious life. It doesn't work out that way. We see him falling back into his old habits of drunkenness and general shiftlessness, spurning the opportunities available to him. . . . And this points up the technical failure of *Visible Man*.

Sam's backsliding shouldn't come as a shock. Throughout the book, however, Gilder shows us how things must have looked to him, without really showing us how Sam himself looked. Bev and the minor characters are more clearly drawn from without; but with Sam, we are encouraged to enter his situation without getting a clear sense of what makes poor black *him* react, finally, so differently from the way white prosperous *we* would have reacted. We can figure it out in various ways; Gilder's theory itself helps. But the book should have done more to make this come alive. It shouldn't be necessary to fall back on deduction. . . .

For all its flaws, *Visible Man* is lively and wise; and haunting. It sees the all too "visible man" with genuine imagination; and so, hereafter, will its readers. (p. 1033)

M. J. Sobran, Jr., "Dispensable Man," in National Review *(© National Review, Inc., 1978; 150 East 35th St., New York, NY 10016), Vol. 30, No. 33, August 18, 1978, pp. 1032-33.*

MICHAEL NOVAK

[*Visible Man* is] about a particular form of racism, the racism of our cultural elites, "the worst racism in America, black or white—the respectable kind—that will acknowledge blackness if it is holding a gun or applying for food stamps, a racism that claims as somehow 'white' the essential values of any modern economy or ordered society." . . .

George Gilder cuts through many fashionable evasions. . . . [He] limits himself to seeing as straight as he can the expereince of one young black male in Albany, New York, an impressive young man with an excellent record in the military, a clearly recognized talent as an artist with a state agency, a restless lad, stormy, often violent, tried (and acquitted) on a charge of raping a white woman. Gilder wanted to understand this young man's life and the culture he is part of. He spent hundreds of hours interviewing him—practically, at times, living with him—and interviewing dozens of others who made up part of his world. (p. 122)

Sam did what several hundred other black men in Albany did; he moved in with a woman. The day she became 16, Bev and her teenage friends (without Sam) celebrated: Bev now qualified for Aid to Families with Dependent Children, and the child she had borne to Sam assured her of $1044 per year in food stamps; Medicaid, worth in her accident-prone world about $2000 per year; $179 per month in rent subsidy ($2148 a year); and another $2000 in welfare. Sam, after taxes, was bringing home several hundred dollars less than on his job. He quit his job, and their new, larger apartment was taken out in her name—so she could qualify for AFDC. Although Bev was white, about half the other women in Albany that young black males like Sam moved in with—men too proud to collect welfare under their own names—were black. . . .

Gilder and Sam eventually took a long trip to South Carolina, to Greenville, to try to make contact with Sam's natural father. (p. 123)

In the end, Gilder's tale suggests the theme of fathers and sons—and of women deprived of stability, of children without fathers, of sons without certainty about the roles of son, father, breadwinner, husband. Oddly enough, the relation of father and son appears not to be related to poverty as we might expect. Gilder compares figures for Greenville and for Albany, Sam's two homes. In Greenville there are 19,145 blacks (1970) and in Albany, 14,132. Poverty was much worse in Greenville, but there were far more female-headed families with small children in Albany. Median black income in Albany was 20-percent higher, the proportion of black families in poverty 45-percent lower. But Greenville's black men were more often married, and far more often stayed with their women and children, than Albany's did. Greenville had 17 percent more black husband-wife families, in proportion to size. It had only half the number of female-headed households that Albany had.

Poverty, Gilder concludes, cannot be the cause of the abandonment of wife and children by men. Greenville had 50 percent *more* black poverty, and 50 percent *less* abandonment of women and children. The disparity between the two cities can also be dated. Before the mid-1960's, female-headed families were no more common in Albany than in Greenville. The disparity began precisely with the "war on poverty" in Albany.

Gilder examines statistics for rural counties in Carolina even poorer than Greenville. Though their poverty is greater, so is family stability. The correlation is not between the abandonment of family and poverty, but between abandonment and *welfare* poverty. In 1969, 40 percent of Albany's poor blacks were on welfare; only 18 percent of Greenville's. The 650 black welfare families in Greenville received only $676 per year. The families of Albany—like Bev and Sam—received closer to $6,000 per year; rational behavior leads many to the choice they made: quit work, live off welfare. Yet Sam could not survive that way.

"We must face the fact that today it is the North, Northern liberals—in a spirit of charity, fatally corrupted by a spurious sense of guilt—who are enslaving blacks," Gilder concludes. . . . The North has fashioned its own plantations: government offices. And its own system of total dependence: welfare. It may have demoralized and destroyed a higher proportion of brave, good, sound young persons in a few short years than a generation of slavery did. It definitely appears to have injured the black family more than slavery did. (p. 124)

Michael Novak, "Enslaving Souls," in The Public Interest *(© 1979 by National Affairs, Inc.), No. 56, Summer, 1979, pp. 122-25.*

ANDREW KLAVEN

Staunch capitalists and staunch socialists suffer from the same defects: a crafty blindness to human nature, and a secret aversion to human freedom. So, George Gilder's *Wealth and Poverty* is rendered nonsensical not by its methodical defense of what is known as conservative, supply-side economics, but by the moral hogwash on which that defense is based.

Gilder asserts that capitalism is a moral system based on a "golden rule" of giving. But examined closely, the reasoning behind that assertion runs something like this: Capitalism is moral because it rewards work, family, and faith in God; work, family, and faith in God are moral because—well, look how rich you get when you have them. Therefore, Gilder concludes, "Equality, bureaucratic rationality, predictability, sexual liberation, political populism, and the pursuit of pleasure . . . are . . . inconsistent with the disciplines and investment of economic and technical advance." If we remove the word "moral" and replace it with "to Mr. Gilder's liking," the whole argument begins to make more sense. (pp. 74-5)

> Andrew Klaven, "Book Briefs: 'Wealth and Poverty'," in Saturday Review *(copyright © 1981 by* Saturday Review; *all rights reserved; reprinted by permission), Vol. 8, No. 1, January, 1981, pp. 74-5.*

ROGER STARR

"Wealth and Poverty" offers a creed for capitalism worthy of intelligent people. Mr. Gilder has written the kind of good book that alternately astonishes the reader with new and rather daring insights into familiar problems and bores him with long, tract-like passages to support them, particularly on "supply-side" economics, which is concerned with the problems of encouraging production instead of the difficulties of distribution. At times, he offers startling anthropological data and references to elaborate studies of the business cycle over hundreds of years. At times these same areas seem irrelevant to his case. . . .

[At] the core he provides . . . a sense that on crucial matters of human value, capitalism offers a system of economic arrangements more congenial than the alternatives, not simply because the alternatives are less pleasant, but because they are based on a mistaking of the conditions of human life.

The book constitutes a defense-in-depth, a series of arguments in favor of capitalism, which must be breached, if at all, one at a time. . . .

As for capitalism itself, Mr. Gilder points out as his first defense that it is based on a sounder economics than its rivals. It explains the basic issue of economic life: what makes men productive. Capitalist economics recognizes that the questions of distribution that have occupied so much time in the critiques of its detractors, are subsidiary to the basic problem of production: Without it, there is nothing to distribute.

For those who doubt that the tax concessions of "supply-side" economics will really stimulate production as much as promised, Mr. Gilder offers an ethical defense based on anthropological verities. In primitive societies, he says, the accumulation of goods was not a selfish activity in the narrow sense. Rather, it was based on the "gift relationship" that inspired certain men to accumulate property so that they could give it away to their fellow tribesmen. The gift was prompted not by a contractual expectation of reward, but by hope itself, though held under the shadow of risk of failure. . . . I find Mr. Gilder's account of the gift relationship interesting, but am unable to draw a connection between it and the rise of industrial capitalism centuries later on the other side of the globe. Experts may do better.

Mr. Gilder, however, explains that systems like socialism base their production on the certainty of a limited future, believing that all great innovative discoveries and inventions have already been made. Socialists, he says, are motivated by a spirit antithetical to the gift relationship in which one proffers what one knows in the hope of getting something unheard of, unknown, in return. He claims that the mercantilist tradition made the same error that socialists make, assuming that wealth is tangible and limited, while in fact, he argues, true wealth is intangible, consisting of the fertility of the human imagination that can be liberated only by a leap into the unknowable future.

Those who clamber over this ethical line find themselves facing what might be called Mr. Gilder's biological defense. He describes capitalism as consonant not only with the higher, more ethical human possibilities, but with mankind's essential nature. Poverty, he tells us, can be overcome only by a human society that has accepted three basic relationships, activities, states of mind. They are work, family and faith. . . .

What comes on the reader unexpectedly in this third defense of capitalism, is the extraordinary importance Mr. Gilder attaches to the persistence of faith:

> Faith in man, faith in the future, faith in the rising returns of giving, faith in the mutual benefits of trade, faith in the providence of God are all essential to successful capitalism. All are necessary to sustain the spirit of work and enterprise against the setbacks and frustrations it inevitably meets in a fallen world. . . .
>
> (p. 10)

[Capitalism] poses the dangers of inherited wealth and other temptations to undermine the principle of work, and there are capitalists who mistake the nature of their system and undermine its most constructive values in the course of seeking to maximize their benefit from it. But Mr. Gilder claims that the hazards of socialism and crucially moderated capitalism (he never truly defines how much pure capitalism may safely be modified) are greater. The indolence, underachievement and sapping of faith in the future do not simply reduce the productivity of the economic system, they corrode the people who are part of it.

Finally, to skip several of the defense perimeters, Mr. Gilder argues that capitalism works because it does not seek to evade the notion of risk. It accepts the possibility of failure as an intrinsic element in human life and encourages people to live fruitfully in the shadow of failure. He claims as a "good" the very quality of *chance* that current egalitarian writers argue plays too important a role in deciding who gets what in a capitalist society. [He] argues that the acceptance of chance as a determining factor in human life is the necessary precondition of freedom, which Mr. Gilder regards as higher good than equality. When a society as a whole tries to eliminate chance, it must project the patterns of its past into the future because they constitute the only certainty, and those patterns are clung to long after they have lost their natural markets, long after they have stopped responding to human needs.

Now all of this may be as persuasive as it is elegant in its comparison of two social orders—capitalist and socialist. It seems to me stronger as a defense of the capitalist himself than of the system that gives him scope and then, as Mr. Gilder puts it, hates him for the wealth he has achieved. Mr. Gilder seeks, perhaps for the benefit of those who grew up when American capitalists were identified ineluctably as robber barons, to explain the work the capitalist entrepreneur undertakes. (pp. 10, 37)

Undoubtedly, those who assembled economic power to make an industrialized society possible had to develop the unpleasant characteristics that their critics have described. . . . But it is really of no more ultimate significance to decry the capitalist personality than to recall the gift relationship of the Kwakiutls to praise their generosity. The test of the value of capitalism is whether the society made possible by it improved the conditions of life for the vastly increased population that their industry made possible. And then there is the second test: whether an alternative economic arrangement can improve on the defects of capitalism without even more grossly undermining its achievements. On this point it seems to me that Mr. Gilder is on the most secure ground in arguing that capitalism can be defended. The mildest criticism of the existing socialist states is that they have not released the immense flow of human energy that their advocates predicted would follow the end of private ownership of factories.

For a moral philosopher, which Mr. Gilder considers himself, it is not enough to deal with failure; one must also confront the problem of evil. Why, if capitalism is on balance so fruitful, has it been modified into a condition of low productivity and stagnation? Mr. Gilder rejects the regression from the entrepreneurial stage to the bureaucratic stage as the inevitable result of a society's aging. Instead, he blames the progressive income tax, claiming that he would rather pay for the excess costs of a modulated capitalism by inflation than by continuing the tax rates that discourage entrepreneurial energy. . . .

He theorizes that the economics of the "Laffer curve" will make possible increased productivity without increasing inflation by providing a higher flow of tax revenues at lower rates because the lower rates will stimulate greater economic activity. Reviewers are not expected to pass judgment on predictions of this kind. Perhaps Mr. Gilder is right . . . and capitalism will be retrieved from the evils of the progressive income tax. But even if he is wrong, the book stands as an eloquent defense of the capitalist high ground and the human values that capitalists, despite their bad manners and admitted defects, managed to embody to the benefit of their fellows. (p. 37)

> Roger Starr, "Guide to Capitalism," in The New York Times Book Review (© 1981 by The New York Times Company; reprinted by permission), February 1, 1981, pp. 10, 37.

THE ECONOMIST

Like so many of those who preach that lower taxes will bring such bountiful prosperity that the government's tax revenues will actually go up as tax rates come down, Mr. Gilder [in *Wealth and Poverty*] is an amateur economist. He regards this as a plus. Professional economists, he reckons, are so programmed by their training, their charts, statistical tables and econometric models, just as sociologists are by their data printouts, that "novelty, creativity, imagination and surprise—the elusive variables of all our lives—are left out"

Maybe so. But it does mean that Mr. Gilder calls for a huge leap of faith when he dismisses Mr. Lester Thurow's "The Zero-Sum Society", which grapples with the world as it is,

and asks us instead to contemplate the world as it might be now that the supply-siders have discovered the philosopher's stone to solve all our stagflationary problems.

What is his evidence? His proof negative—well, socialist countries like Sweden are obvious failures, are they not? Well, actually, no. Objectively, Sweden has one of the highest living standards in the world. Subjectively, the quality of life (a low crime rate, an absence of poverty, a well-educated population and so on) is exceptionally high in Sweden as well. His proof positive—President Kennedy's tax cut increased both economic activity and tax revenues, did it not? Well, yes, but back in those days nobody had heard of Opec, the dollar was still mighty, America had no inflation to speak of, the federal budget was in near-balance. . . .

What has gone wrong since? Mr. Gilder finds abundant reason to believe that the American welfare state long ago passed its points of diminishing and counter-productive returns, that the insurance features of American society now so overbalance the risk features that everyone—rather than just the direct victims of hardship and change—feels anxious and insecure. For him, the moral hazards of current programmes are clear. . . . Disability insurance in all its multiple forms encourages the promotion of small ills into temporary disabilities and partial disabilities into total and permanent ones.

Programmes of insurance against low farm prices and high energy costs create a glut of agricultural commodities and a dearth of fuels. . . . All means-tested programmes (designed exclusively for the poor) promote the value of being "poor" (the credential of poverty) and thus perpetuate poverty. "To the degree that the moral hazards exceed the welfare effects, all these programmes should be modified, usually by reducing the benefits."

Most of this is within the mainstream of the American supply-siders. Where Mr. Gilder swims away from many of the others is in his old-fashioned morality. Men and women ought, he believes, to concentrate on their traditional roles: mothers on child-rearing, fathers on bread-winning. (p. 87)

The monogamous marriage and family is good, he thinks, for the economy, too. . . . The work effort of married men increases, it is said, with their age, credentials, education, job experience and birth of children, while the work effort of married women steadily declines. His conclusion is that "these sexual differences alone, which manifest themselves in all societies known to anthropology, dictate that the first priority of any serious programme against poverty is to strengthen the male role in poor families".

Mr. Gilder wants a counter-revolution in values in the economic sphere as well. The main thrust of his sermon is to win converts to his belief that the good fortune of others is also finally one's own. The religious analogies come easily. In writing his capitalist manifesto, Mr. Gilder seeks to give capitalism a moral basis by demonstrating that money-making is really about giving rather than taking. (pp. 87-8)

This capitalist bible-punching makes absorbing reading. . . . Its fascination . . . lies in Mr. Gilder's skill in engineering a confluence of two increasingly powerful but previously separated currents of thought on the American far right—the ideas of the supply-siders in economic policy and the secular parts of the social policy pushed by the so-called Moral Majority. Blessed, it seems, are the money-makers: for they shall be called the fathers of capitalism. Blessed are the sleek: for they shall inherit the earth. (p. 88)

"Blessed Are the Money-Makers," in The Economist (© *The Economist Newspaper Limited, 1981), Vol. 278, No. 7175, March 7, 1981, pp. 87-8.*

CHRIS GOODRICH

[*Wealth and Poverty*] is a highly intelligent and often arrogant defense of the capitalist system, seeing it as the best thing since coolie labor. Scorning what he calls the "apologist" capitalism school represented by Friedman, Gilder writes that the "redemptive morality" of capitalism can save us, once we recognize that the system is essentially "altruistic." Although Gilder occasionally sounds like a Madison Avenue snake-oil pitchman, his argument is well-reasoned and, for the most part, sensible. The major problem is that Gilder's heart—if he has one—is in the wrong place.

"Capitalism begins with giving," he writes, because the businessman risks his own time and money for an uncertain reward. Gilder compares the system to an Indian potlach: an ambitious tribesman gives feasts and gifts to his fellows in hopes of gaining their support (Gilder fails to note that this is also called "bribery"). He may lose all his goods through this generosity—or "altruism," in Gilder's peculiar definition—but if not he has attained power and, perhaps, more gifts. He is now a successful capitalist, his pals and acquaintances are happy, and the cycle of hard work, risk, and expansion of the economy continues.

The most obvious flaw in Gilder's reasoning is one he brings up himself and immediately dismisses, calling it "the illusory limits of growth." Potlaches do not, in fact, grow forever: they are classic pyramids, failing as soon as the flow of new blood or new products comes to an end. Gilder contends that this will never happen in capitalism. His belief in growth is nearly mystical, apparently based on the fact that mankind has always—so far—broken through technological bottlenecks and has always had low men on the totem pole. . . . Capitalism is in trouble now, he believes, because high taxes prevent businessmen and entrepreneurs from risking their capital, thus arresting growth and creating even more poverty. . . . The "materialist fallacy," he continues, encourages unhealthy stasis because it fosters "the illusion that resources and capital are essentially things, which can run out, rather than the product of human will and imagination which in freedom are inexhaustible."

Gilder is right to emphasize the unquantifiable factors which affect economics, such as will and imagination, but he is myopic when it comes to many of man's negative qualities—such as greed and laziness (these he blames principally on the welfare system). (p. 11)

What may be most irksome about *Wealth and Poverty* is that it ignores such obvious facts highlighted by [Adam] Smith. Smith warns us in *Paper Money* to be wary of economists, because they make too many rational assumptions; but he might well warn us about Gilder as well, for making too many blustering, hazy assumptions. A cornerstone of Gilder's capitalism is faith, and it certainly is the key to successful entrepreneurship, but did the possibility of *too much* faith, *too much* unreason, ever cross his mind?

Faith in capitalism, free market or not, led indirectly to the creation of OPEC, and the investing boon of the 1920s, too,

was grounded on the assumption that the stock market would *never* crash. It was supposed to keep on growing forever, much like Gilder's ideal, self-fueled economy. (pp. 11-12)

The irony is that Gilder's economic theory creates its own seductive traps. The major tenet of Reaganomics is the dominance of the "supply side": "the very conscience of capitalism," Gilder contends, is "the awareness that one must give in order to get, supply in order to demand." It is the product which is the motive force, not the needs or demand of the consumer, so what the producer must do is *create* demand. . . . For those already wealthy, who can afford to keep up-to-date and in style, no problem; for the poor there is little hope of catching up. . . .

Gilder does have sympathy for some segments of the poor: he calls immigrant laborers "a great American capital asset." They work hard, doing jobs that most Americans—with their Madison Avenue shaped sensibilities—won't do. Gilder believes they too can improve their lot through his matchbook cover success program, but of all those who solder printed circuit boards in Silicon Valley, how many actually do "succeed"? The American Dream is comatose, if not dead, for many of them; and though better off, probably, than in Indochina, they are absorbed into an unforgiving system in which to spend is to be, in which some shadowy carrot—the need to compete and be better off than your neighbor—is always dangling before them. For many, hard work seems a way to go nowhere fast—except, of course, on the never-satisfying treadmill of consumerism and planned obsolescence. Gilder regards the welfare programs many disillusioned people opt for as "new forms of bondage and new fashions of moral corruption": but it may well be, instead, that these programs are among the many ways by which capitalism is destroying itself, following a natural path predicted by Marx—the creation of the alienated worker. . . .

Adam Smith recalls in *Paper Money* the scene in *Peter Pan* in which Tinker Bell seems to be dying. Peter asks the audience to believe that Tinker Bell will recover, badgering it to "Say you believe! Clap your hands if you believe!" The audience invariably responds, for to do otherwise is to ensure that the show cannot go on. George Gilder seems to be the most fervent applauder and booster of capitalism around—a self-appointed voice in the wilderness—and seems to have forgotten that Tinker Bell does not live on encouragement alone. Unlike Smith, who has at least examined the disease, Gilder is merely making noise; and, should the end in fact arrive, he will be unpleasantly surprised. (p. 12)

Chris Goodrich, "How to Succeed in Business without Really Thinking," in San Francisco Review of Books (*copyright* © *by the* San Francisco Review of Books *1981), March-April, 1981, pp. 11-12.*

MICHAEL WALZER

Wealth and Poverty is a diatribe and a panegyric. It is a diatribe against egalitarian reformers, welfare bureaucrats, social workers, academic radicals, upper-class "defectors," liberal editorialists, fashionable publishers, civil rights workers, and feminists—above all, feminists, who turn out to be the deepest and most dangerous enemies of capitalism. It is a panegyric for entrepreneurs, businessmen, risk-takers, investors, the thrifty poor, and aggressive males—above all, aggressive males, the true source of capitalist wealth. Gilder believes that welfare only makes the poor poorer, sinks them in the mire of dependency and moral decay. If they are ever to escape, what they need above all is "the spur of their poverty." (Why there were ever poor people in the dim years before the welfare state is, on his view, very hard to understand: the spur of their poverty is the one thing the poor have always had.) What the wealthy need, by contrast, is more money. Their spur is greater and greater wealth—low taxes and capital gains. All the complex ills of the US economy today come down to this: we take too much money from successful businessmen, and we give too much money to the poor. . . .

[Gilder] does have a great deal to say about entrepreneurs, whom he admires, above all, because they don't rely on the government. They take risks and strike out on their own. . . . Though two-thirds of all new business ventures collapse within five years . . . the will to succeed is indefatigable. Some 400,000 small businesses are started annually, and these brave initiatives are the crucial source of innovation and growth in the capitalist economy and of mobility in capitalist society. . . .

Indeed. It is great fun to see the petty bourgeoisie thus returned to the stage of history, and I am entirely sympathetic to the effort to bring them back. But all this makes for a small part of the capitalist story, and Gilder is reluctant to tell the rest. He is uneasy with big business, corporate bureaucracy, old wealth. He doesn't like efforts to reduce the risks of economic life, to stabilize markets, fix prices, control innovation. But this sort of thing is surely central to the internal development of capitalism. . . . [Entrepreneurs] are prepared to take risks, but they have no romantic attachment to danger, and faced with what Gilder calls "the iron rule of gambler's ruin," they will do the best they can to improve the odds. And the best they can clearly includes the enlistment of governmental support. Big government may sometimes be, as Gilder has it, the enemy of entrepreneurial success, but it is by no means the enemy of successful entrepreneurs. It is more likely to be their instrument. But of capitalism as a system of power, Gilder again has nothing at all to say.

He writes only melodrama. The compassionate state cuckolds poor men, and the confiscatory state robs wealthy men. The liberation of women is paralleled by the "war against wealth." Gilder's presentation of tax statistics is quite extraordinary. By his calculations, rich Americans appear to be more heavily taxed than any of their counterparts in the Western world. Contrary to all the evidence of our senses, it is simply impossible to make money in the United States today. . . .

When Gilder recommends "diligence, discipline, ambition, and a willingness to take risks" to the poor, however, he assures them that it is still possible to do well in business and even to put together, after taxes, a small fortune. In this mood, he is full of success stories. Though he loves to talk about risk, there are no accounts of failure in *Wealth and Poverty*. But of course small businessmen do fail, even at increasing rates, and this has a great deal to do with the success of large-scale capitalism and very little to do with governmental intervention or with what Gilder tells us is the currently fashionable hatred of money-making and of moneymakers ("the racism of the intellectuals"). (p. 3)

What is missing from Gilder's book is any serious or sustained account of democratic politics. In a sense, democracy must always be a danger in his world. Where there is risk, people will seek security, protection against the endless explosions of capitalist energy. And politicians, so long as they must look toward re-election, will be eager to provide that security. Hence

the welfare state, old age pensions, unemployment compensation, and so on. . . . But the state, in the hands of egalitarian reformers, welfare bureaucrats, and so on, creates, he says, a vast and counter-productive system of over-insurance. The health of American capitalism requires a balance between security and risk, solidarity and competition. But that balance is long gone, security and solidarity have triumphed, and Americans, especially poor Americans, have been robbed of the opportunity to test "the miraculous prodigality of chance."

I doubt that many American workers faced, say, with plant closings and large-scale lay-offs will recognize this portrait of our welfare state. It is a great deal shabbier in its treatment of the poor than Gilder acknowledges. But whatever degree of welfare we have achieved constitutes a democratic response to capitalism, and I cannot imagine any democratic way of restoring the discipline of hardship to which he is so ardently committed. Most of us are not heroes. Of course, the poor can be punished; there may well be, there apparently arc, temporary electoral majorities in favor of doing that. But the long-term curtailment of the welfare state is radically unlikely without political repression. Within the limits of democracy, if there is to be hardship, there must also be a more equal sharing of risks and opportunities. It is in this direction that democrats might look for an alternative to "over-insurance." . . . For [Gilder], democracy is little more than a cowardly escape from the rigors of entrepreneurial life. . . .

[The] whole purpose of the book is a defense of capitalism through grandiose inflation of entrepreneurial activity. . . .

Gilder is full of what I suppose is male aggressiveness and what I am sure is entrepreneurial energy. But he is not full of new ideas. For all his talk of innovation, for all his embrace of fashionable theories (above all, his spiritualized version of supply-side economics), what he finally has to offer is Horatio Alger and Life with Father. His book is indeed a gift—to Reaganite intellectuals and politicians. He suggests that they imagine themselves as noble adventurers and heroes of the providential order when all they want to do and all they are going to do is apply the spurs: more poverty for the poor, more wealth for the wealthy. (p. 4)

Michael Walzer, "Life with Father," in The New York Review of Books *(reprinted with permission from* The New York Review of Books; *copyright © 1981 Nyrev, Inc.), Vol. XXVIII, No. 5, April 2, 1981, pp. 3-4.*

IRVING KRISTOL

Perhaps the most important single quality of George Gilder's *Wealth and Poverty* is its tone. It is buoyant, exuberant even. . . . It is nice to see the idea of a free-market economy freed from the dialectical prison of orthodox economic theory, with its grim emphasis on the rational allocation of scarce resources, and to have that idea again associated with a vision of economic growth, as distinct from a scholastic analysis of distribution.

This association permits Gilder to recapture Adam Smith's original and revolutionary insight—that such economic growth permits everyone to "better his condition." One might say that Gilder has restored, not only the optimism of Smith, but what, for want of a better term, we might call his "populism." As a result of this reorientation, it is once again possible to think of capitalist economics as being the specific and legitimate property of "the party of hope." . . .

[Capitalism] is about *economic growth as the consequence of entrepreneurship,* of all kinds, at all levels. Modern economic thought has little interest in entrepreneurship, which it ignores or takes for granted, because entrepreneurship cannot be calculated into the kind of economic aggregate that fits into the economist's sophisticated equations. It is no accident that the major proponents of what we call "supply-side economics" have had their origins outside (or at the margins of) the academic profession. . . .

There is one important point, however, on which I have to register a strong disagreement with Gilder. That is his pseudo-anthropological analysis of economic activity as inherently and ineluctably giving birth to a viable morality. It is certainly true that successful commercial activity is more often than not organically connected to the cultivation of such virtues as diligence, trustworthiness, prudence, the ability to defer gratification, etc. These are solid bourgeois virtues, if essentially utilitarian virtues, celebrated by merchants and businessmen for many, many centuries. . . . But they do not add up to a complete moral code that a society can base itself on. Not only are certain virtues neglected—where is charity? physical courage? patriotic self-sacrifice?—but a purely commercial code of ethics does not enable us to cope with those all too many instances when circumstances conspire to ruin us, regardless of our virtuous practices. Life *is* unfair, and only a morality embedded in a transcendental religion can cope with that fact. (p. 414)

A market economy can provide us with economic growth and individual liberty—but it cannot prevent us from abusing our affluence or our liberty. It can at best offer us a vision of human decency, not of human perfection. And it certainly cannot offer us consolation amidst disaster, reassurance as to the meaningfulness of life when our bourgeois virtues do not avail us. Gilder . . . seems to lack a religious sense. He sees so vividly into economic reality that he is blinded to other, no less important aspects of reality. That is a serious flaw. (p. 415)

Irving Kristol, "A New Look at Capitalism," in National Review (© *National Review, Inc., 1981; 150 East 35th St., New York, NY 10016), Vol. XXXIII, No. 7, April 17, 1981, pp. 414-15.*

J. A. PARKER

[*Wealth and Poverty*] is particularly significant coming right now, as President Reagan is attempting to implement a program of budget-cutting together with reduced taxes. The Reagan program has been attacked by self-appointed "black leaders," who argue that it is insensitive to the needs of minority-group members. In fact, however, it is the welfare-state philosophy, which has dominated our thinking in the post-World War II period, that has done the greatest harm to black Americans and other minorities.

Discussing "the nature of poverty," Gilder quite properly shows how our current welfare system provides disincentives to work and victimizes minorities in the nation's inner cities. . . .

Gilder correctly challenges the idea that black poverty is caused by racism and discrimination. This analysis, presented repeatedly by those black "leaders" who urge expensive government "compensatory" programs (of which they will be the major beneficiaries), is largely self-serving. It is, beyond this, superficial in the extreme. As Gilder argues, such an analysis "slanders" white Americans and "deceives and demoralizes"

blacks. In addition, it leads to the false view that "blacks cannot now make it in America without vast federal assistance, without, indeed, the very government programs that in fact account for the worst aspects of black poverty and promise to perpetuate it." . . .

The institutionalization of affirmative action, welfare, and other benefits which, in many instances, pay more than work has given rise to the view that wealth and hard work are unrelated. We have, in effect, priced work out of the market for those to whom living on a government dole has become a way of life. This liberal philosophy, Gilder writes, includes the assumptions "that wealth can be taken for granted rather than produced by toil and thrift; that life is supposed to be easy and uncomplex; that its inevitable scarcities, setbacks, and frustrations are the fault of malevolent others; that good intentions should be worth their weight in gold and good credentials should convert instantly into power and glory without sordid interludes of productive competition and struggle."

The philosophy Gilder is presenting, while sharply criticized by the Black Congressional Caucus, the Reverend Jesse Jackson, and the NAACP, is quite similar to that expressed by Malcolm X. (p. 415)

Bayard Rustin, director of the A. Philip Randolph Institute, said that the welfare-state philosophy inherent in the various "wars on poverty" is an "immoral bag of tricks" amounting to a new form of slavery. He stated that "the problems for Negroes, Puerto Ricans, and poor whites . . . is that America has no commitment to turn muscle power into skills."

Now that racial discrimination is illegal—and while we must be vigilant in enforcing the Civil Rights Act of 1964—the fact remains that black Americans cannot advance in a declining economy. The enemies of black economic progress are all those who advocate a "no-growth" philosophy, those who have, through a variety of regulations and tax policies, placed American business in a virtual straitjacket, and those who have kept blacks out of the marketplace through a form of discrimination which remains legal, namely government licensure. . . . In addition, black teenagers cannot work because the law refuses to permit businessmen to pay them their real value, insisting instead upon a minimum wage which prices them out of the job market.

In a word, the enemy of black economic progress is white liberalism, the maze of rules, regulations, and debilitating welfare programs which—although they may have been motivated by high ideals—have had a wholly negative effect. The way to ease poverty, as Gilder understands, is, on the one hand, to remove the disincentives of the dole and, on the other, to stimulate investment and business expansion which will produce new jobs.

Make-work programs such as CETA, which so many black "leaders" are so vocal in defending, are harmful to the poor in the long run. Gilder points out that they prevent resources from being invested in the creation of real, productive jobs. (pp. 415-16)

Those of all races in American society who wish to understand the nature of wealth and the causes of poverty would do well to read [*Wealth and Poverty*]. (p. 416)

J. A. Parker, "The Nature of Poverty," in National Review (© *National Review, Inc., 1981; 150 East 35th St., New York, NY 10016), Vol. XXXIII, No. 7, April 17, 1981, pp. 415-16.*

ADAM MEYERSON

With its unabashed defense of capitalism, its attack on the excesses of the welfare state, its emphasis on both religious faith and the family, and its argument for supply-side cuts in marginal tax rates, *Wealth and Poverty* is . . . the best single book for understanding many of the economic and social ideas influencing the domestic policies of the Reagan administration.

The first section of *Wealth and Poverty* is a defense of capitalism against what Gilder sees as three sets of enemies: egalitarians, whose redistributive tax policies stymie the creative potential of entrepreneurs; pessimists, who think unplanned market economies are incapable of handling all the resource scarcities and uncertainties of the modern world; and half-hearted proponents of capitalism, who prefer capitalism to other economic systems but nevertheless see it as morally vacant or, worse, centered on greed.

The great folly of the egalitarians, Gilder argues, is to view wealth as a "zero-sum game." Together with classical economists for the last two centuries, Gilder contends that there are mutual gains from trade and that one of the keys to prosperity is "the belief that the good fortune of others is also finally one's own." But in a departure from classical economics that owes much to the work of Joseph Schumpeter, Gilder sees entrepreneurial innovation as the driving force in economic advancement. What disturbs him most about egalitarian tax policies is that they rob entrepreneurs of the venture capital they need to bring new goods and services to market. (pp. 77-8)

Gilder's rationale for cutting marginal tax rates is not to "defend established privilege" or make the rich richer. . . . It is to induce the rich to invest more productively in the U.S. economy—whether through their own efforts or, more likely, by financing entrepreneurs.

A critical assumption here is Gilder's notion that the world—and in particular the U.S. economy—is full of opportunities for entrepreneurs to exploit once they have the incentive and the wherewithal. Unlike many of the Cassandras who dominate economic writing, Gilder does not worry about the depletion of natural resources. Wealth, he argues, consists in people's "morale and ingenuity," not in physical resources, which is why Japan, Taiwan, and Hong Kong, with virtually no resources but their populations, are rapidly advancing while Saudi Arabia with all its oil billions is still an underdeveloped country. . . .

Gilder's most ambitious defense of capitalism is his effort to ground it in religious faith and altruism. Most defenders of capitalism—from Adam Smith to Irving Kristol—have accepted as a given that the system is propelled by the self-interested profit motive. Not Gilder. For him, "capitalism begins with giving." . . . [The] modern entrepreneur "gives" his energy, his imagination, his organizational ability. He willingly sacrifices his time and capital in order to provide a new good or service, even though he knows his rewards are uncertain.

To make sacrifices in the face of this uncertainty, says Gilder, the entrepreneur must be motivated by some kind of faith. . . . Successful capitalism requires not only "faith in man, faith in the future, faith in the rising returns of giving, faith in the mutual benefits of trade." It also requires "faith in the providence of God."

In the second section of the book, a critique of U.S. welfare programs, Gilder borrows from the insurance industry the metaphor of "moral hazard," the "danger that a policy will encourage the behavior—or promote the disasters—that it insures against." . . . [He] worries that the panoply of welfare benefits now available—AFDC, Medicaid, food stamps, housing grants and subsidies, social, legal, and child-care services—make it economically irrational for many poor people to work.

In place of existing welfare programs, Gilder proposes "a disciplined combination of emergency aid, austere in-kind benefits, and child allowances—all at levels well below the returns of hard work." In short, he wants to make welfare dependency much less attractive; "in order to succeed," he contends, "the poor need most of all the spur of their poverty." Here too, as in his discussion of wealth, a critical assumption is that opportunity abounds for those who are willing to work hard. Gilder is convinced that racism has largely been eliminated from U.S. job markets, and that there are plenty of attractive job opportunities, especially in small businesses. He dismisses the "dual labor market" theories of many economists and social critics who argue that the menial jobs usually available in restaurants, garment manufacture, and other small businesses offer few opportunities for either security or advancement. (p. 78)

In the third and most timely section of the book, Gilder argues that high marginal tax rates combined with inflation are sapping the American economy of its productive potential. When state and local taxes are added to the federal take, Gilder contends that the vast majority of American households face marginal tax rates of at least 50 percent—meaning that "most Americans could expect to keep less than half of any additional earnings they might choose to seek." This tax burden is a powerful disincentive to work, savings, and other taxable economic activity. Gilder argues that the combined burden of marginal taxes and inflation has fallen most heavily on income from productive investments—and that the U.S. government has therefore been "massively and persuasively telling its citizens and corporations to disinvest in the productive capital of America."

Instead, Americans have been investing in tax shelters and housing. . . . One of the principal purposes of supply-side tax cuts would be to encourage the rich to put more of their capital at risk—instead of spending it on themselves.

Unlike many supply-side enthusiasts, Gilder does not try to deny that marginal tax cuts might be inflationary. But he reminds his readers that inflation rates were fairly high in Japan during that country's most dramatic period of continuous economic growth. The difference was that the tax incentives in Japan encouraged greater capital formation. For just that reason Gilder is willing to place a higher priority on tax cuts—particularly as they affect savings and investment—than on reducing inflation.

Given the scope and ambition of *Wealth and Poverty*, it is hardly surprising that Gilder's arguments are not always consistent, and not always persuasive. If, for example, "faith in the providence of God" is so crucial to entrepreneurship, one wonders why it should also be necessary to cut marginal tax rates. Perhaps entrepreneurs require both faith *and* incentives—though this would suggest that faith is contingent on a demonstration of success. In any case, Gilder does not fully address the relation between faith in the future and the rational calculation of likely risks and rewards as each of them applies to entrepreneurship.

Moreover, even if faith in a higher morality is a practical necessity for entrepreneurship, this is not the same thing as saying that capitalism itself is ethical, nor does it justify capitalism on religious grounds. (pp. 79-80)

Despite its flaws, however, *Wealth and Poverty* remains one of the most significant, and gracefully written, works of political economy in years. Hardly a page fails to provoke thought or to challenge some conventional assumption. (p. 80)

Adam Meyerson, "The Spirit of Enterprise," in Commentary *(reprinted by permission; all rights reserved), Vol. 72, No. 1, July, 1981, pp. 77-80.*

ERNEST van den HAAG

[Gilder's *Wealth and Poverty*,] in stressing the economic advantages of capitalism, . . . has also brilliantly articulated what most people feel inchoately about government's efforts to improve on the system. The economy would be much more productive with fewer regulations and less taxation—so much more that a tax reduction might stimulate supply more than demand, dampening inflation by increasing production.

With lower taxes there would be increased political pressure to reduce government expenditure, much of which is unproductive or even counterproductive. . . .

Gilder is most persuasive in describing the efficiency, the equity, and the freedom provided by capitalism. Unfortunately, he does not think that these are enough to justify capitalism. Gilder also insists on a moral, metaphysical, and historical justification.

For openers, he insists that businessmen are motivated by—hold on to your hats—altruism. This idea seems more original than accurate. All societies rest on mutual solidarity and altruism as well as on self-interest. . . .

Gilder's zeal to give a moral pedigree to the activities of businessmen leads him into treacherous historical and metaphysical waters, in which his valuable ideas nearly drown. In the course of defending economic freedom, he tells us that physicists "concede freedom for microscopic particles," wherefore social scientists should not "begrudge it to human beings." Particles may be unpredictable but they are not "free" since they do not make decisions—unless Gilder has altogether anthropomorphized them. Human beings must be in some measure predictable (otherwise social life as well as social science would be impossible). But that hardly deprives them of freedom. It is the use people make of their freedom that experience permits us to predict. (p. 151)

Gilder does no better with history than with metaphysics. He believes that society has always been hostile "on every continent and in every epoch . . . to its greatest benefactors, the producers of wealth." Indeed there has always been envy and ambivalence. But the social hostility Gilder writes about is quite recent. Specific historical events—the legacy of the 1930s—shook confidence in business and changed the climate of opinion. The people who had elected Coolidge or Harding or Hoover were not hostile to "the producers of wealth." Gilder cannot see capitalism, and the hostility to it, as a historical phase. Indeed he believes that "the reason capitalism succeeds is that its laws accord with the laws of mind" and that it has "faith in the compensatory logic of the cosmos." Besides not making much sense (the cosmos has regularities at best, not logic, and there is nothing "compensatory" about them), this timeless cosmic view leads one to wonder why capitalism has not always existed everywhere. Has the cosmos changed lately? Or our faith in its "compensatory logic"?

About the nature and genesis of capitalism, Gilder writes, "The essence of productive work under capitalism is that it is altruistic." It "begins with giving." . . . (pp. 151-52)

Gilder labors to justify the equating of gifts and investments, on which, incredibly, he insists throughout—how could it have escaped him that he was skating on no ice? He argues that "the essence of giving is not the absence of all expectation of return but the lack of a predetermined return." Hence, presto, investments that lack a predetermined return are gifts and "capitalism begins with giving." If the meaning of "return" is extended enough, it will cover everything. Even a charitable donation may have a psychic "return." But when I invest in real estate or in a business, I expect more than a psychic return. I expect to get my principal back and to get a satisfactory material return. This distinguishes an investment from a gift. If the return is not predetermined, the investor takes a risk—for which he expects to be rewarded. Risk taking is not gift giving. To be sure, many investments are made with little realistic chance for any return. But when I buy tickets in a lottery, or invest in any business, however risky, I am not making gifts. I hope to win, or gain. That I may be irrational does not make me altruistic.

It is true that others may benefit from my investments, as they may from my gifts. Benefit is the *intention* of the donor of a gift. But it is merely an effect of the investment of my capital. . . .

Like Gilder, I believe that capitalists do more good than intentional do-gooders. But they do so by producing for profit. Gilder reverses the mistake of those hostile to capitalism. They infer bad effects from the "selfish" profit motive of capitalists; he infers "altruistic" motives from the good effects of capitalism. He is as wrong as they are. The true merit of capitalism is that it makes gratification of self-interest—the profit motive—socially useful. . . .

[But it] is effects, not motives, that matter to the system. And the effect of capitalism is that one gets rich, not by robbery and oppression, as so often in pre-capitalist times, but by producing and selling what people want. George Gilder shows superbly how useful businessmen are in this. He should have stopped there. (p. 152)

Ernest van den Haag, "Sense and Nonsense about 'Wealth and Poverty'," in FORTUNE *(© 1981 Time Inc.; all rights reserved), Vol. 104, No. 1, July 13, 1981, pp. 151-52.*

Paul Goodman

1911-1972

An American novelist, poet, psychotherapist, educator, lecturer, and writer on social, political, and cultural issues, Goodman is widely considered to have been one of mid-twentieth-century America's most thought-provoking social critics. Characterizing himself a "conservative anarchist," Goodman vigorously criticized the centralism and bureaucracy of modern society and proffered his vision of a decentralist, anarchist polity. He made numerous and often innovative proposals for social reform, advocating the decentralization of social and political institutions; the revival of civic and community life; the permitting of a free, natural sexuality; the encouraging of self-reliance; and the redirecting of our social energies to the fulfillment of practical human needs. Goodman was intensely concerned with the problems of young people in society; his *Growing Up Absurd* (1960) established him as a prophetic voice of youthful unrest and a forceful critic of American life. Theodore Solotaroff calls *Growing Up Absurd* the "single book that helped dispell the prevailing atmosphere of complacency and conformity" of the Eisenhower Age. Goodman's last book, *Little Prayers and Finite Experience* (1972), is an autobiographical summation of his life, politics, and ideas. Goodman's detractors call his proposals "simplistic" or "utopian," arguing that they are unrealizable barring a revolution. Many people, however, admire the independent radicalism and wide-ranging intellect reflected in his work. Kingsley Widmer's respectful assessment of Goodman's career seems not untypical: "As a man of letters, in the Enlightenment sense now so rare, he ... thought and wrote and acted contentiously and suggestively on all he could of finite society and life. It was a valuable effort, not to be defined by any particular ineptness, and we could use more of it." (See also *Contemporary Literary Criticism*, Vols. 1, 2, 4, 7, and *Contemporary Authors*, Vols. 19-20; obituary, Vols. 37-40, rev. ed.; *Contemporary Authors Permanent Series*, Vol. 2.)

The New York Times

Excerpt from *GROWING UP ABSURD: PROBLEMS OF YOUTH IN THE ORGANIZED SYSTEM*

In every day's newspaper there are stories about the two subjects that I have brought together in this book, the disgrace of the Organized System of semimonopolies, government, advertisers, etc., and the disaffection of the growing generation. Both are newsworthily scandalous, and for several years now both kinds of stories have come thicker and faster. It is strange that the obvious connections between them are not played up in the newspapers; nor, in the rush of books on the follies, venality, and stifling conformity of the Organization, has there been a book on Youth Problems in the Organized System.

Those of the disaffected youth who are articulate, however—for instance, the Beat or Angry young men—are quite clear about the connection: their main topic is the "system" with which they refuse to co-operate. They will explain that the "good" jobs are frauds and sells, that it is intolerable to have one's style of life dictated by Personnel, that a man is a fool to work to pay installments on a useless refrigerator for his wife, that the movies, TV, and Book-of-the-Month Club are

beneath contempt, but the Luce publications make you sick to the stomach; and they will describe with accuracy the cynicism and one-upping of the "typical" junior executive. They consider it the part of reason and honor to wash their hands of all of it.

Naturally, grown-up citizens are concerned about the beatniks and delinquents. The school system has been subjected to criticism. And there is a lot of official talk about the need to conserve our human resources lest Russia get ahead of us. The question is why the grownups do not, more soberly, draw the same connections as the youth. Or, since no doubt many people *are* quite clear about the connection that the structure of society that has become increasingly dominant in our country is disastrous to the growth of excellence and manliness, why don't more people speak up and say so, and initiate a change? The question is an important one and the answer is, I think, a terrible one: that people are so bemused by the way business and politics are carried on at present, with all their intricate relationships, that they have ceased to be able to imagine alternatives. We seem to have lost our genius for inventing changes to satisfy crying needs.

But this stupor is inevitably the baleful influence of the very kind of organizational network that we have: the system preempts the available means and capital; it buys up as much of the intelligence as it can and muffles the voices of dissent; and then it irrefutably proclaims that itself is the only possibility of society, for nothing else is thinkable. . . . (pp. ix-x)

But it is in these circumstances that people put up with a system because "there are no alternatives." And when one cannot think of anything to do, soon one ceases to think at all.

To my mind the worst feature of our present organized system of doing things is its indirectness, its blurring of the object. The idea of directly addressing crying objective public needs, like shelter or education, and using our immense and indeed *surplus* resources to satisfy them, is anathema. For in the great interlocking system of corporations people live not by attending to the job, but by status, role playing, and tenure, and they work to maximize profits, prestige, or votes regardless of utility or even public disutility—e.g., the plethora of cars has now become a public disutility, but automobile companies continue to manufacture them and persuade people to buy them. (pp. xi-xii)

We live increasingly, then, in a system in which little direct attention is paid to the object, the function, the program, the task, the need; but immense attention to the role, procedure, prestige, and profit. We don't get the shelter and education because not enough mind is paid to *those* things. Naturally the system is inefficient; the overhead is high; the task is rarely done with love, style, and excitement, for such beauties emerge only from absorption in real objects; sometimes the task is not done at all; and those who could do it best become either cynical or resigned. (p. xiii)

Paul Goodman, in his Growing Up Absurd: Problems of Youth in the Organized System *(copyright © 1960 by Paul Goodman; reprinted by permission of Random House, Inc.), Random House, 1960, 296 p.*

Excerpt from *LITTLE PRAYERS & FINITE EXPERIENCE*

Paradise is the world practicable. I do not mean happy, nor even practical so that I can make it work, but simply that I can work *at* it, without being frustrated beforehand. A task to wake up toward. If I work at something, I am happy enough while I am doing it—I don't think about whether or not I am happy. And if I have worked at it, if I have tried, I sleep well even if I have failed.

This is a very modest criterion of paradise. To many people (how would I know?), there might be no reason to call such a world miraculous rather than the nature of things. For instance, John Dewey, who must have been a happy man, describes the nature of things as pragmatic through and through. But though I have faith that there is a world for me, I am foreign in it, I cannot communicate my needs, I do not share the customs, I am inept. So it is like a new world, I am as if resurrected, when the world is practicable. Therefore, until that moment, I put a premium on patience and fortitude.

The difficulties of the world, said Kafka, are mathematical. Given the spreading of space in all directions on a plane, it is infinitely more probable that our paths will diverge than converge. That you will be out when I phone and I will be out when you ring my bell—indeed, as Kafka points out, I was on my way over to your place. If several conditions are necessary for success, and each is moderately probable, the likelihood of their combination is wildly improbable. At every relay the message is distorted, and we did not speak the same

dialect to begin with, but just enough of the same language so that we thought we were communicating. An unexpected stress, a lapse of attention, makes me vulnerable to other stresses, breakdowns, and accidents, so the rate of mishap is exponential. You get a flat tire and pull over, and step out over the edge and break a leg. These are the facts of life, no?

They are the facts of life for those who cannot abstract, who have only concrete and finite experience, like Kafka and me. We cannot take the vast numbers of possibilities as collective facts to manage, assigning them the infinite numbers Aleph, Beth, and Gimel. We cannot soar off the ground covered by our own two feet in order to survey the landscape. Since we have no values except in the tendency of what we are doing, we cannot make a plan of action to a far goal; we have no such goal, just the reality that we are dissatisfied. Then except by the miracle that events happen to converge in my poor Here Now and Next, my world is impracticable.

Fortunately, I have low standards of what is excellent as happiness.

In my politics—anarchist, decentralist, planning to leave out as much as possible, strongly conservative of simple goods that in fact exist—I have hit on a principle: Given the mathematical improbability of happiness, for God's sake don't add new obstacles.

In my morals, the cardinal sin is waste.

Consider the logistics of sexual satisfaction, a major part of happiness for most of us. Starting with the odd notion of sexual intercourse as a way of reproducing species, there is a rough carpenter's logic in dividing the human males and females equally, 50-50, to maximize the couplings; and then to attach a strong instinctual drive so that the animals will seek one another and persist in accomplishing the complicated operation of approaching, getting an erection, finding the hole, being receptive, and so forth. But a desire that is attached can become detached. The 50-50 possibilities are immediately drastically reduced by notions of beauty, inevitable childhood nostalgias and tabus, insecurities caused by factors that have nothing to do with sexuality, fetishism of other poles and holes. Since it is a complicated mechanism, Murphy's Law will certainly hold: if the parts can be put together wrong, they will be. And the machine has to operate in the frame of the rest of life and social life: being hungry and sleepy, sick, maimed, hampered by institutions and laws, poor and disadvantaged. Of course, since nature always operates with prodigal generosity and calculated waste, with a factor of safety in the thousands and millions, in spite of everything the human species is reproduced. The chances of personal happiness are trivial.

I have had half-a-dozen too brief love affairs (I am past 60), and in every case our virtue was to be practical, seizing chance opportunities, creating no obstacles, having no ideas in our minds, and trying hard to make one another happy. Or put it this way: I offer myself all at once as a package, with the absurd conditions of my ineptitude, my fantasies, my perverse needs, and my crazy hope. I must be either frightening or ludicrous. But the one who became my lover was not put off and took me at face value. *Then* we were practical. And I say proudly, when we could not continue indefinitely as is the essence of love, the causes of our separation were not our doing, they were mathematical. (pp. 105, 107, 109, 111)

Paul Goodman, in his Little Prayers & Finite Experience *(copyright © 1972 by The Estate of Paul*

Goodman; reprinted by permission of Harper & Row, Publishers, Inc.), Harper & Row, 1972, 124 p.

ALBERT GUÉRARD

There is one paramount issue today: planning or chaos—with war as an unhappy medium. The Goodman brothers [Percival and Paul] believe in planning, city planning, community planning. They are among the Children of Light. . . .

[In their book **"Communitas"** there] is a good summary of modern plans, liberal enough not to damn Sitte and his cult of the picturesque plaza, daring enough to consider the Radiant City, the Voisin Plan, antiquated. The brothers' own plan is arresting. In the center a cylinder a mile in radius, twenty stories high; rail and bus terminals in the basement, shopping and amusements on the first seven floors, light industries on the next six, offices on the last seven; an airport on top; hotels on the six-mile ribbed outer wall. Then a mile-wide ring for the university—rather a formidable campus. Beyond, residential quarters, arranged in squares which are complete home communities. Naturally, the scheme is only a "paradigm," as they call it. It has points.

Their sociological pattern is simplicity itself. Instead of pump priming, subsidies, relief, and all the devious ways of a mixed economy, let's frankly make minimum subsistence in food, clothing, and shelter a community responsibility. With modern technology these essential needs could be satisifed with a small fraction of mankind's total effort. All the spare time, all the unspent energy, could be devoted to luxury, where private enterprise would have a magnificent field. Dare we face the possibility of allowing men to die of hunger or cold? No. Then we might adopt the Goodman idea: on a sure communistic foundation rear as splendid a capitalistic edifice as you please. This, I am afraid, is a little too sane to appeal to our present rulers. All that they will see, in this witchhunting season, is that **"Communitas"** has no fewer than eight letters in common with communism.

Albert Guérard, "Children of Light," in The Nation, *Vol. 164, No. 20, May 17, 1947, p. 574.*

SVEND RIEMER

The spoken language and the language of architectural design are combined in [*Communitas*] in an attempt to explore the task of community planning. The authors commit themselves to a form of discussion which they term "neo-functional." While functionalism emphasized the appropriateness of architectural means to a given set of ends, the function of planning is broadened here to encompass a critical evaluation of the ends themselves. The architect-planner, thus, is challenged to consider the way of life that is suggested in his design. According to the authors, the planner cannot be concerned, only, with current social conditions. The potentialities of physical design offer new vistas of possible social reorganization. New means are not to be adapted to the status quo; they carry in themselves the germs of unprecedented social experimentation. To make planning truly democratic, however, the public will have to be presented with clear alternatives for purposes of discussion, arbitration, and final decision.

This publication is welcome as a first step in the direction of closer contacts between physical design and social science. Very wisely no final solution to the dilemma of modern community and city planning is proposed by the authors. They recognize, however, the need for more penetrating discussion of the interrelationship between available means and the social ends which might prove to be desirable to the community. In the pursuit of this task they apply a method which we would like to call ideal-typical construction. They confront the reader with three paradigms of possible community life. These different ways of life and of making a livelihood are not held out to the public as rigid and mutually exclusive alternatives. They represent models of thought rather than comprehensive utopian schemes. Neither of these alternatives will ever be achieved in full detail. But the authors manage well in educating the reader to think in terms of internally consistent patterns of life and to relate them to different comprehensive schemes of community planning.

There is the city of efficient consumption; there is the community plan which aims at the elimination of the artificial separation between productive and consumptive functions which characterizes the outlay of the modern American city; and there is, finally, a rather fantastic scheme in which the authors have jumped over the border of common sense as far as the treatment of our social and political problems is concerned. They propose a division of our economic organization into one sphere of productive and consumptive activities which is left in the hands of private enterprise and concerned with luxury goods. Completely separated from the market economy, they visualize a segment of highly regimented security economy providing for all citizens a minimum standard of living free of charge. As a paradigm, this scheme is not without its fascination. We may ask ourselves, however, whether the authors are not spoiling their chance of making a needed contribution to a sincere discussion between social scientists and architects by giving free rein to playful imagination instead of coping with acute planning problems which are more closely tied to existing social conditions. (p. 232)

Svend Riemer, " 'Communitas: Means of Livelihood and Ways of Life'," in The American Journal of Sociology, *Vol. LIII, No. 3, November, 1947, pp. 232-33.*

MILTON L. BARRON

Problems, Goodman stresses [in *Growing Up Absurd*], test and criticize the society in which they occur. We live increasingly in a society in which little attention is paid to the object, the function, and the need, but much is given to role, procedure, prestige, and profit. Growing up calls for adequate objects in the environment to meet the needs and capacities of the young. But American society, its affluence notwithstanding, lacks opportunities and goals that make growth possible and invites instead the development of delinquents, beatniks, and cynical conformists. For boys more than girls, it is difficult to grow up, to be useful and make something of oneself, when our economic "rat race" alienates the young, when the absence of patriotism and faith deprives them of purpose, and when the general social attitude toward sexuality is inconsistent. It is hard for a social animal to grow up, continues Goodman, when space, time, clothes, opinions, and goals become so preemptive that young people cannot establish individuality and experience genuine novelty, surprise, and spontaneity. . . . It is hard to grow up with nothing to be or do.

Goodman's argument is that all these social and cultural inadequacies are the accumulation of what he calls the "missed" and "compromised" revolutions of modern times, falling most heavily on the young. Children and adolescents need a coherent and simple society in which to grow up, but a missed revolution makes obsolete the system that persists, and a compromised revolution shatters but does not replace the standards and community that once were. Delinquency is one response by the young, a compulsive proving and identifying behavior which asks for what society will not legitimately give at this time—manly opportunities to work, self-esteem, adequate space and schools, sex without shame and fear, and loyalty to community and country. Under our present system, the recourse instead is to curfews, ordinances against carrying knives, threats against parents, and more police and reformatories. Thus, official policy works to increase delinquency rather than to remedy it. (pp. 47-8)

By the author's own admission, the book is a gloomy and exaggerated portrayal that omits all the positive features in American society. It is cogent but, unlike [Vance] Packard's books, it disdains most empirical evidence. Perhaps this is because Goodman has been willing to share culturology with social scientists without ever bothering to learn their research techniques or accept many of their findings. To him sociologists and the others are merely part of the highly organized system itself and do not like to think that rebellion or the initiation of fundamental change are social functions. Goodman does not know the difference between the case history and the questionnaire. He ignores all sociological studies of social classes, relying instead on his own incredible three-fold scheme: the organized system (comprising the subclasses of workers, organization men, and managers), the poor, and independents. He is for spontaneity and individuality in one part of his book, and elsewhere he favors a community life that is "planned as a whole, with an organic integration of work, living and play."

Yet the author has succeeded eloquently in making his point, the same point once made by the conservative Coleridge, and we had better heed it before it is too late. Quite simply it is this: to have citizens, you must be sure that you have produced men. (p. 48)

Milton L. Barron, "A Criminogenic Culture," in Saturday Review *(copyright © 1960 by Saturday Review; all rights reserved; reprinted by permission), Vol. XLIII, No. 45, November 5, 1960, pp. 47-8.*

SAUL MALOFF

Growing Up Absurd is all prose, lively, eccentric, colloquial prose, twisted to [Goodman's] own odd shape, fanciful, scattered, digressive as the best talk often is; full of feeling, raging, lyrical, caustic, scathing, roaring mad; imaginative, even reckless, fertile of ideas and crazy salvationist schemes which make remarkable good sense. There is nothing objective here; it is all intensely personal.

In a way, the title is misleading, creating, as it does, the impression that the book is about the process of growing up, which it is not. Goodman is interested not in the process itself but in its end, in what the boy has around him to grow up to. Sartre speaks somewhere of an absurd world as one without ends of meaning and value; and it is in this sense that young people—juvenile delinquents and junior executives, poor and rich, hipsters and squares—grow up absurd. To describe the depredations and empty wastes of that absurdity, to convey the

look and the feel of it, and to reclaim its appalling cost is the burden of the book.

Goodman has the artist's eye for the right detail, the revealing instance, the surprising and illuminating juxtaposition; a reliance upon lived and felt experience; and a passionate heart. After the abstractness, the deadness, of so much of academic sociology, it is exhilarating to find a critic who begins and ends with people, who keeps the human person at the center of his vision so that we see not the "dynamics of society," but the figure itself. That is his method, to walk through the landscape and point, to show the ends toward which we compel people to grow up. (p. 17)

This is not simply another example of the criticism of "mass culture" in a "mass society"; . . . Goodman shares certain of its premises but ranges far beyond them, is more radical. His theme is that "*Growth, like any ongoing function, requires adequate objects in the environment* to meet the needs and capacities of the growing child, boy, youth, and young man, until he can better choose and make his own environment. It is not a 'psychological' question of poor influence and bad attitudes, but an objective question of real opportunities for worthwhile experience." He does not so much attack as dismiss the "psychology of adjustment" by facing it with what seems to him the crucial and dismantling question: adjustment to what? The "to what" is the substance of the book. . . . (pp. 17-18)

If one sees less to hope for from alienated youth than does Goodman, indeed if one sees Goodman's hope as desperation, well, that's no great matter. He is, in the year 1960, unashamedly utopian, storming for excellence. If his terribly exacting demands do not receive the most urgent attention we can summon, it will be because we are staring fixedly at nothing much, because we cannot respond to demands. (p. 18)

Saul Maloff, "Assault on the Pointless Life," in The New Republic *(reprinted by permission of* The New Republic; *© 1960 The New Republic, Inc.), Vol. 143, No. 21, November 14, 1960, pp. 17-18.*

DAN JACOBSON

Growing Up Absurd is not intended to be a theoretical work of social criticism. On the contrary: it is presented as a direct report on the author's own experience and that of others—felt, pondered over, and understood. And it is precisely for this reason that it does not seem to me frivolous or 'literary' to say that *Growing Up Absurd* fails because it is so very badly written. (I am not talking here of minor ineptitudes and inelegances of expression, though these can be counted in their scores.) Mr. Goodman tries hard to be earthy, slangy, brisk, and intimate with the experience he is concerned to describe; but over almost everything in the book there hangs a fog of remoteness and abstraction, which conceals and smothers whatever life is supposed to be beneath it. . . .

The truth is, of course, that no rigorous theoretical essay could possibly support such bumpy, lumpy, repetitive catalogues [as abound in this book]. How much less, then, can a book whose purpose it is, in the first place, to give us the very quality of modern life as people have inwardly experienced it, and secondly to remind us of the values of . . . 'utility, quality, rational productivity, personal freedom, independent enterprise, human scale, manly vocation, or genuine culture.' *Growing Up Absurd* is altogether more depressing, and depressing in more ways, than the author intended it to be.

For even where Mr. Goodman does see cause for hope, and tries to give us the grounds of his hope, as in his discussion of the Beat Generation, his matter remains curiously thin and unconvincing. In fairness, it must be said that the chapter devoted to the Beat Generation is one of the better in the book. Mr. Goodman is quick to penetrate Beat pretensions; but he does so without malice or self-satisfaction. And he comes to the conclusion that the Beats have managed to achieve 'a simpler fraternity, animality and sexuality than we have had, at least in America, in a long, long time.' Now whatever one may think, in the abstract, of this particular trio of abstractions, one would like to believe that Mr. Goodman is telling some kind of truth here. But he offers us so little evidence for his assertion, one just does not know how to take it. Indeed, the actual evidence all seems to go the other way. . . .

[When] it comes to talking about the positive values that Mr. Goodman perceives in Beat life, to the proffered sexuality, for example, we have, lamely, 'My impression is that . . . Beat sexuality is in general pretty good . . . if inhibition is relaxed and there is courage to seek for experience, there ought to be good natural satisfaction.' This is not really very persuasive or informative. And a similar lack of persuasive force characterises the author's descriptions of Beat fraternity. (p. 407)

In discussing the juvenile delinquents, Mr. Goodman has some acute, compassionate things to say: he points out, for example, that one of the compulsive motives for delinquency is the need to be caught and punished. However, once again Mr. Goodman is driven to assert that some vague, undefined, superior virtue is inherent in 'the fatalistic self-destruction of the kids,' though the evidence he offers for this assertion is even more tenuous than that offered on behalf of the virtues of Beat living. In fact, his definition of the virtue he has in mind, and his evidence for it, consist of nothing more than an obscure and unsatisfactory account of the works of Jean Genet.

Mr. Goodman is not afraid to condemn almost entirely the 'successful doings' of his society; but he is, it is quite clear, afraid to condemn in the same wholesale way those whom he believes to be in rebellion against that society. Reading this book one cannot help feeling that the author is looking around desperately for some kind of community with which he can identify himself; and though the Beats and the delinquents appear weak and cramped to him, he nevertheless clings to them—for if 'these crazy young allies,' as he calls them, are not on his side, who is? But surely anybody who is really disturbed about the mess we are in, and who wants to do something about it, should be prepared to accept his own isolation with more stoicism. The critic of society must certainly try to find friends, colleagues and an audience; he must try to work through existing institutions or to establish new ones. But the search for allies is not his business. (p. 408)

Dan Jacobson, "Crazy Young Allies," in The Spectator (© 1961 by The Spectator; reprinted by permission of The Spectator), Vol. 206, No. 6926, March 24, 1961, pp. 407-08.

THE TIMES LITERARY SUPPLEMENT

Mr. Paul Goodman, in **Growing Up Absurd**, which is especially concerned with the provision for and attitude towards male youths in American cities, begins by explaining that what young people want is satisfying work. This, of course, is a tautology. He then goes on to define satisfying work as that concerned with satisfying the basic human needs of food and shelter.

Is he then making a warrantable or a utopian statement? Would it merely be nice if this was the kind of work that satisfied young men most, or is there some hard evidence that, given a choice of occupations, farmwork—Mr. Goodman is positive that it must not be work in food factories—and building in a craftsmanlike way—Mr. Goodman is positive that building amid corrupt labour practices will not do—are preferred above other means of gaining a living? There is at least some evidence to suggest that without the consolations of a Wordsworthian outlook farmwork is almost the least favoured job, not only by contemporary youth in America but by youth in all civilized communities as soon as other choices become available.

Our own puritan heritage may too readily lead us, without further questioning, to agree with Mr. Goodman's wholesale condemnations of a society that holds up to youth the material life as the best life and makes no provision for healthy outlets for natural sexual urges—though Mr. Goodman does not specify precisely what these would be. We all of us pay at least lip-service to the superiority of spiritual over material values, and almost no one, not even the people Mr. Goodman inveighs against, would openly condemn the goals he sets—for instance, free expression of minority opinion, development of genuine agrarian and city cultures, true fraternity between classes, brotherhood of races and so on. But it is a long time since St. Paul observed that we do not always seem able to do the things we know we ought to do, and utopian blueprints that postulate a change of heart as a necessary prerequisite are not really useful. . . .

This is not to say that books such as Mr. Goodman's do not have some value, for it is always better to inveigh against wrong than to ignore it, and these muddled but sincerely worried outcries may be the precursors of some good and useful work.

"Why Do Lions Not Eat Straw?" in The Times Literary Supplement (© Times Newspapers Ltd. (London) 1961; reproduced from The Times Literary Supplement by permission), No. 3083, March 31, 1961, p. 204.

SAUL MALOFF

Usually, [Goodman's essays] are epistles of the philistines, written in the heat of feeling in response to some public controversy, expressing with a sense of urgency some publicly relevant idea, directed toward the correction of some folly or wickedness. Roughly, they fall into these categories: psychology and sociology, urbanism and technology, education, literature and literary criticism, esthetics, and art; but within each of them, in Goodman's hands, almost anything goes, his mind bounds and plays, constantly uncovering unsuspected possibilities. . . .

The measure of Goodman's inventiveness and élan is that such a book [**Utopian Essays and Practical Proposals**] should be an almost unfalteringly interesting one. And in fact the witty and ironic title is not a dodge for concealing the randomness of a collection: it is an accurate description of the contents and intention, and in the face of proliferating moral and political dilemmas before which there is a public feeling of futility and despair. . . . (p. 24)

Whatever the problem, Goodman is intent upon the same question: What tends to block, restrict, limit human freedom, joy, creativity? What tends to release, free, liberate? Always, for his purpose of criticizing society and life to the end of improving it, he is animated by a steady vision of a good—that is, rational, *human*-society, a coherent community, a style, and quality, of life that is fully human, and humanizes. That is the sense in which he is utopian.

Yet his utopianism has nothing to do with dreaminess: it is wonderfully hard-headed, pragmatic, inventive, problem-solving, ingenious; he is a persistent participant in the life around him. That is the sense in which he is practical. Indeed it is with "spite," with an almost malicious joy that he poses problems in which we are hopelessly entangled, going from bad to worse, managing cruelly or stupidly or both—and offers alternatives which are often beautiful in their simplicity and reasonableness. (pp. 24-5)

The center of Goodman's thinking is always the human person and the community he might live in; not reckless production and synthetic demands created by advertising, but efficient planned production and consumption based on a technology *selected* to achieve this end. He is marvelously persuasive that we can, that the alternatives are at our disposal. Instead, we call alternatives "utopian," in the mocking pejorative sense; and appoint commissions to search for "national goals," as if "goals were not implicit in concrete activity," as if ends had nothing to do with means. What we are really objecting to, often, when we say that ideas are utopian though they seem feasible and even useful is that "they propose a different style, a different procedure, a different kind of motivation from the way people at present do business." Structure, folkways, style, procedure, motivation are precisely what Goodman would change by a politics of direct action, direct intervention, for these go straight to the heart of the matter; and he reveals, in the sudden and sharp angles of his vision, a style of thinking about our dilemmas which we would be fools to ignore, or ignore by merely praising. (p. 25)

Saul Maloff, "Epistles to the Philistines," in The New Republic *(reprinted by permission of* The New Republic; © *1962 The New Republic, Inc.), Vol. 146, No. 9, February 26, 1962, pp. 24-5.*

DONALD BARR

It should be possible for every school, for every teacher, *both* to present very urgently the needs and claims of the world *and* to protect very gently the lovely idiosyncrasy of the child. But Mr. Goodman does not see it this way [in *Compulsory Mis-Education*]. To him, it is an issue. Essentially—with a few qualifications, mostly rhetorical—he is a libertarian, and he argues for the simon-pure—one might say the simple-simon-pure—developmental view.

There are moments when he seems to glimpse some trace of truth or importance in the scholastic view. There are some fine paragraphs . . . on teaching science, in which he speaks of making "a great number of citizens at home in a technological environment, not alienated from the machines we use." He speaks wisely of the current notion that schools should not try to teach "middle-class culture" to the poor but should develop the merits of the virile and sociable "culture of poverty"; Goodman answers that this notion is good for the teacher's technique but bad as a philosophy: "The philosophic aim of education must be to get each one out of his isolated class and

into the one humanity. Prudence and responsibility are not middle-class virtues but human virtues . . ." Finally, however, he repudiates the style, the procedures and the moral impetus of scholastic programs.

He ridicules the new concern over "drop-outs," arguing naughtily that in the present state of the schools the drop-outs may be showing good judgment, and arguing cogently that the high unemployment rate among drop-outs may be an artifact—employers arbitrarily and irrelevantly demand the high-school diploma. He favors big educational budgets, including Federal aid—so long as they are not given to the hacks and hypocrites who now run our schools. He sees the insidious anti-intellectualism of our massive, automated testing programs. He takes the disguise of jargon off "programmed instruction," exposing its reductive presumptions and showing it to be an ugly caricature of the scholastic approach—but at that he thinks it a fair likeness. He sees that, for many children—perhaps most—the longer the schooling, the duller the mind. He sees children learning to march before they learn to walk, learning to conform hypocritically and then learning to conform sincerely, learning to express everything but rage and pain and fear and love and joy. These things are there to be seen.

He is extraordinarily sensitive to children and adolescents. . . . [He] describes the origins of defiance and embarrassment. It has a brilliant authenticity. But throughout the book, one continually feels an oscillation between gullibility and almost paranoid suspicion. Paul Goodman can accept, without any critical activity whatever, the mystique of small classes; his whole praxis is based on the silly notion that the group overwhelms the individual by sheer numbers. But the same Paul Goodman sees bad education as "interlocked" with "the system," and "the system" as the private enterprise of certain "dominant economic and intellectual groups" using "the mass-media" to enforce psychological obedience. This is his myth. It is an expression of what seems to be a purblind resentment of all authority.

For him, good education must be voluntary; school attendance should be voluntary; classroom attendance should be voluntary; classroom activities should be voluntary. He writes diatribe rather than dialectic because he simply cannot perceive the creative side of authority. He cannot see its importance to the child as an emblem of completed growth. He cannot see its importance as reassurance: children are always probing for the limits of the world's concern; they are frustrated and lost if no one will say "No" to them, and they need to know if a "No" is genuine; they test this in ways that may hurt them a little, just as they poke at a loose tooth.

Paul Goodman cannot see the exquisite cruelty of yielding, yielding and always yielding, tolerating, tolerating and always tolerating, understanding, understanding and always understanding. The child wants the respect of serious and heartfelt resistance. He wants his little opacities respected. He wants his "sins" respected as sins. How can he be free if he is not free to be "bad"?

For all its blindnesses, however, this partisan, partial, useful little book deserves to be pondered.

Donald Barr, "Simple Simon Says, Hands Off of Eyes," in Book Week—New York Herald Tribune *(© 1964, The Washington Post), September 27, 1964, p. 4.*

EDGAR Z. FRIEDENBERG

Goodman is a poet . . . and *Compulsory Mis-Education* exactly fits Marianne Moore's definition of a poem as "an imaginary garden with real toads in it." As a gardener, he is unimaginative. There is too little planning and diversity among his plots. But he is trustworthy in what really counts in gardening. Goodman understands growth, and cares about it; knows which poisons and harassments will stunt it and are therefore literally intolerable. (p. 10)

Where Goodman is unscientific, and thereby limited, is in treating his observations anecdotally, rather than as examples of classes of events whose theoretical relationships are not yet fully established—that is, as data. The consequence is that his work seems as predetermined in its course as a sermon. Virtually everything he says about adolescents or the schools could be confirmed by an honest observer, and I believe he is also generally right in his interpretation of what he sees. But his style seems to brook no alternative consideration of what the facts might mean. Certainly, it suggests none. Reading him is rather like listening to a crusading public health official of the last century, demanding that prison camps be cleaned up so as to reduce the frightful incidence of pellagra. People did die horribly of pellagra in such camps, and their death was caused by the squalor in which they were confined. Morally, it is an insignificant detail that the efficient cause of their death was dietary deficiency rather than infection. But theoretically it is highly significant; and unless one is prepared to stop and notice the indications that it might be so, one can learn no more about the disease or a good many others. (p. 12)

> Edgar Z. Friedenberg, "The Education of James Conant and Paul Goodman," in The New York Review of Books (reprinted with permission from The New York Review of Books; copyright © 1964 Nyrev, Inc.), Vol. III, No. 7, November 19, 1964, pp. 10-12.

ROBERT L. HEILBRONER

[With *People or Personnel*] Paul Goodman has written an important book, about which I have thought harder than any other book I can remember reading for a long while. I think it likely that his book will strike a live nerve, not only on the campuses where Mr. Goodman is already a considerable culture hero, but in Washington, and along Foundation Boulevard. I would be happy if it did, for the book offers suggestions for social improvement that are worth following up, and it forces its readers to reconsider ideas that no longer seemed worth the bother of fresh examination. At the same time I offer these warm commendations, however, I must add that I also find a grave weakness in the book—a weakness that will in the end, I believe, severely limit its applicability and the degree of esteem it will permanently merit.

Mr. Goodman would be the first to admit that the central theme of his book is not new. It is a *cri de coeur,* in the grand tradition of humanistic dissent, against the stupefying bigness, the sapping but self-sustaining routine, the quantitative victories bought at the price of qualitative defects, typical of contemporary society. At the same time, it is also a plea, in the same venerable tradition, for a society refashioned so as to leave more space, more choice, more chance for engagement for individual man. The operative principle—at once the problem and the lever for change—is the technical organization of society. . . .

A strength of Mr. Goodman's book is that he also knows [the limits of decentralization], and is not hesitant to urge more centralism in some areas than we have now—for instance in the standardized production of the basic necessities of life. . . . But the point is that Mr. Goodman is not a doctrinaire organizational Leveller nor an arts-and-crafts enthusiast with a Mission. He is aware that contemporary society requires central direction and coordination in many of its activities. The case he wishes to make is that its centralism need not be, as is now so often the case, a mere yielding before routine, and that decentralized forms of organization may find application in many areas of society now needlessly consigned to bureaucracy. . . .

[Wherever] it can be done—and it is refreshing to discover how many overlooked possibilities there may be—Mr. Goodman presses for the small over the big, for the informal over the formal, for the neighborly over the impersonal. In education and cultural enterprises as well as in business and government he is committed to the notion that "personnel"—the units of humanity administered within large-scale organizations—can become people only if they are given an environment scaled down to the point at which an individual's effort again becomes a recognizable entity. . . .

After so much praise, I must be candid enough to admit that I have my misgivings about some of these suggestions. There is a certain anecdotal quality to Mr. Goodman's style of thought—an instance, casually tossed out on one page, becomes an anchor of reference a few pages later. And there is at least one matter in which I find myself taken aback by his air of assurance: Mr. Goodman's suggestions in regard to economic development are about at the *Reader's Digest* level: give them some good advice and the basic tools and they'll do the job, but don't corrupt their healthy cultures by sending in "the high standard and elaborate capital" of a technologically advanced civilization since this can only result in cultural corruption and disruption.

If the same cavalier over-simplification of complex problems pervaded other suggestions, then his book would be only a brochure of deception. But I do not think this is the case. At any rate, Mr. Goodman disarms me with his frankly experimental approach, and he convinces me that a great deal of what he suggests is worth a serious try. I hope that those who run the poverty programs, education programs, foundation programs and all the other programmatic efforts to improve our quality of existence will take this much of the book to heart.

If it were no more than just a collection of recipes for organizational innovation, I would stop here. But there is a deeper message in Mr. Goodman's tract to which I must now direct some less affirmative words. For Mr. Goodman is not really content just to introduce a few breathing spaces into a suffocating society. At bottom, he wishes to refashion society on the grand scale, to write his program for humanism large. (p. 12)

In [Goodman's] society the necessaries of life will be regularized and produced with the smallest possible quantum of social labor time (which may be very small indeed), and made available on some equitable basis to all. By way of integrating this necessarily centralized flow of production with opportunities for individual effort, Mr. Goodman shows a nice ingenuity—he suggests, for instance, quadrennial competitions for automobile design, after which the new standardized line is again turned out at minimum cost until the next occasion for competitive redesign. . . . But social life really begins above this sector of assured and guaranteed social sustenance in the much larger decentralized one—here are the small shops, the truly private enterprises, the community health and recreation projects, the vast and varied enterprise of education, the provision of social service for the very young and the very old.

I have no fault to find with this landscape, which might be a much better place in which to grow humanity than the one we have now (although I suspect the amount of centralism needed to run even a modest subsistence sector might be larger than we are likely to imagine). Rather, what concerns me is whether such a society lies within the evolutionary limits of our own society—and if it does not, what degree of responsibility attaches to the man who writes the travel folder about it. Not to mince words, I do not think it does lie within our present evolutionary capabilities. The private ownership of the massive means of production, the hegemony of the market and the structure of incomes (particularly upper incomes) that rests on this market, the legal network of contractual obligations of a capitalist system—all this would have to go before the subsistence sector could be accomplished. To put it differently, a whole new social order, based on the public control over basic industrial output, on strict planning in the industrial sector, and on the institution of some new form of economic controls over the individual would have to precede Mr. Goodman's society. The old-fashioned word for the passage beyond one set of property, legal, and social arrangements into another was *revolution*. But nowhere does Mr. Goodman suggest that this might have to be the price we would have to pay for admission to his Promised Land. (pp. 12-13)

What is presented as a serious social goal by Mr. Goodman is not seriously related by him to the society we must change, with its unscalable walls, its impregnable forts, its powerful defenses. Thus, what is given to us as something within reach is not really within reach at all—or rather, not without an effort of will and an assault of politics that are not ever mentioned, much less weighed. In the end this is what robs Mr. Goodman's tract of lasting significance. It is a handbook for small-scale social experiment, which is a very excellent thing, but not a guidebook for profound social change, which is what it would like to be. (p. 13)

> *Robert L. Heilbroner, "Utopia or Bust," in* The New York Review of Books *(reprinted with permission from* The New York Review of Books; *copyright © 1965 Nyrev, Inc.), Vol. IV, No. 7, May 6, 1965, pp. 12-13.*

MICHAEL HARRINGTON

[For all his] tough-mindedness and existential pragmatism, Goodman makes a political assumption [in *People or Personnel*] which comes out of the American tradition of innocence and optimism: that since his proposals are more moral and efficient than the prevailing methods, the executives and wielders of power will surrender to the force of his argument. What this ignores is that a great deal of centralist enterprise is highly profitable, and therefore, from the profit taker's point of view, quite rational.

Goodman's discussion of the industrial psychologists is a classic instance of his naïveté in this crucial regard. The industrial psychologists, he writes, are "decentralist by disposition and have taught a wisdom opposite to the time-motion studies of 'scientific business management.'" The original scientific

business managers regarded the worker as an object to be calculated like a machine. Then Elton Mayo came along, and in his famous experiments demonstrated that the people on the assembly line responded to human attention and concern, and what was more important, responded in terms of increased productivity. He thus defined nonmaterial incentives which could be used to forward the basic aim of the scientific business managers: maximum production.

In a society dominated by Paul Goodman's values, Mayo's revelations could have been put to humane and exciting use. But that is hardly what the corporations have done. They have simply hired psychologists and sociologists to make their control of the production line even more scientific. (pp. 90-1)

In short, so long as concentrated economic power determines how change is to proceed, the most radical and rational ideas can be assimilated to the most irrational purposes. And even at this moment, a shrewd centralist executive may be studying his Goodman, trying to find out how he can extract a decentralist technique and put it to work for this own centralist ends. The basic need, therefore, is a political movement which can offset concentrated economic power and a social setting in which Goodmanesque ideas can be placed in the service of Goodmanesque ideals. In *People or Personnel*, Goodman does not face up to this point. . . .

It would be wrong to close this analysis . . . on a sour note. The analyses in *People or Personnel* are rewarding in their own right. More than that, they provide some clues about why the generation which revolted at Berkeley, which marched in Washington, and which challenged the sovereign state of Mississippi is responsive to the marriage of Zen, Tao, and Camus with William James and John Dewey. Goodman and his audience are the first existentialists of affluence. (p. 91)

> *Michael Harrington, "On Paul Goodman," in* The Atlantic Monthly *(copyright © 1965, by The Atlantic Monthly Company, Boston, Mass.; reprinted with permission), Vol. 216, No. 2, August, 1965, pp. 88-91.*

CHRISTOPHER LASCH

[*People or Personnel*] tends to divorce the idea of politics from the idea of power. [Paul Goodman's] analysis of what is wrong with American society is as convincing as ever, and it is hard not to sympathize with his plea for decentralization and a return to "community"; but how are these things to come about? By putting off the politics of power, according to Goodman, and putting on the politics of love; by learning to live "communally and without authority"; by working "usefully" and feeling "friendly." As so often happens in American radicalism, power and authority themselves are defined as the source of evil. Politics then becomes non-politics; for politics is not "feeling friendly" but that which has to do with power.

Goodman has heard these arguments, of course, and he can reply that the "psychology of power" is itself a "neurotic ideology." So it is, when it becomes an ideology; but an understanding of the neurotic obsession with power should not be used to rule out power, arbitrarily, as a subject of political analysis. Ruling out power simply means that Goodman's proposals become subject not for political discussion at all, if politics is concerned with the institutional relationships among groups of people, but for psychology. Having analyzed the evils of centralization—a political question, because it involves the distribution of power—Goodman prescribes not political solutions but therapy. As Robert L. Heilbroner has pointed out, he does not call on anyone to give up power; he only asks them to give up the psychology of power—an appeal that is not so disturbing as Goodman likes to think. (pp. 116, 118)

Goodman writes feelingly of the sense of powerlessness that pervades American society, but it does not seem to me that the antidote for a sense of powerlessness is to be told that "nothing less will serve" than ringing down the flag. If we can't have peace without a revolution, then we are powerless indeed. (p. 120)

Christopher Lasch, "'People or Personnel: Decentralizing and the Mixed System'," in Commentary *(reprinted by permission; all rights reserved), Vol. 40, No. 5, November, 1965, pp. 116, 118, 120.*

MARTIN DUBERMAN

"All confessions," Erik Erikson has written, "want to settle a curse." Perhaps he might have added all *valuable* confessions. The basic trouble with Paul Goodman's **"Five Years"** is that its central theme, his homosexuality, is revealed not to settle the curse but to glamorize it.

He does once refer to his sexual drive as "a false cultus-religion," but this single reference aside, he is remarkably undiscerning (especially for a professional therapist) about the causes, dimensions and costs of what he likes to call his "search for Paradise." Like Gide, that other stoneblind diarist of the homosexual life, Goodman's revelations seem to be interior but in fact concentrate on surfaces, on describing symptoms rather than confronting their meaning. There is far too much comment, and in rhetoric far too romantic, about his "long, long years" given "to trying for love," about his "animal vitality," about how "in many big ways," including his sexual "hunting," his style makes more sense than what he sees around him.

One episode that Goodman recounts captures well the diary's essential tone: he sees an "attractive fellow" on the beach but then notices, with "no small frustration," that the man is with his wife. The wife smiles at Goodman who, "pursuing my New Policy of immediate impulse, of saying it out and having it out," says to her, "'Stop grinning at me. I don't lose any love on *you*. Why don't you fly a kite and lose yourself, so him and me can be men together . . .?'" But the husband, "the booby," feels he has to protect his wife, and so the New Policy proves unsuccessful. Goodman's comment on the incident is a fair sample of his self-awareness: "What could I have seen in such a stupid, hen-pecked type . . .?"

In response to such encounters and comments scattered throughout **"Five Years,"** the uncomfortable feeling mounts that Goodman's "candor" is motivated less by courage than conceit, is marked less by honesty than self-aggrandizement. When he tells us of his "simplicity, humility, humanity," when he remarks that he is "careless of reputation, insult, hurt feelings, appearances, social success," it seems almost redundant to add that he must be careless of self-knowledge as well.

The inadvertent self-portrait that emerges from **"Five Years"** is of a man indulgent of his frailties. Goodman apparently believes that whatever is part of him, is, by definition, valuable. Even those elements in his personality that ordinary insight might label pathology, he attempts, by the employment of symbol and metaphor, to convert to heath—no, to merit. Thus

he connects his homosexuality, even its obsessional aspect, with his career as rebel, experimenter, nonconformist.

Since these attributes, in turn, are part of the catechism of higher virtue (at least to the young—Goodman's constituency), his sexual behavior is promptly rescued from question or denigration. By linking his private life with his public stance as Outsider, Goodman has guaranteed that his homosexual revelations will be taken as additional proof of his "courage," that he will be still further elevated in the pantheon of contemporary heroes.

When, in a passage meant to be summary, Goodman writes, "I have been corrupted by the freedom of the spirit, by too much study of works of truth and beauty, by not paying any mind to the popular culture, by not taking seriously the spurious politics," the effect, in the absence of any redeeming irony, is distasteful in the extreme. One may agree, on the evidence of this diary, that Goodman has indeed been "corrupted," but, on the same evidence, that the causes have eluded him—perhaps because the search for self-understanding has never yet been successfully combined with the search for notoriety.

I would not presume to discuss Goodman's homosexuality, nor his motives for revealing it, had he not by publishing his diary, all but demanded such speculations. By insisting that we accompany him on his round of the docks, on his endless pursuit of erections and orgasms, he has forced his private life on public attention. There is immense grandiosity in this—it is assumed we *must* be interested in all that relates to him—and also, finally, immense sadness—the kind we feel when watching an unloved child jump through every hoop, employ every device of shock, to gain attention, and to affirm its own existence.

It comes as a relief to turn to Goodman's other new book, **"Like a Conquered Province"** . . . and to concentrate on his role as public commentator. In one sense a reading of **"Five Years"** is good preparation for **"Like a Conquered Province,"** for the private diary makes clear one facet of Goodman's thought not hitherto so apparent: he views both himself and his society a-historically. Just as in the diary the present patterns of his own life are unconnected to his past (except a bare reference now and then, to having been "fatherless"), so in the essays historical allusion tend to be *pro forma*, with current social conditions unrelated, organically, to earlier developments.

Goodman's refusal to be burdened or impressed by the weight or value of past experience, is one of his major strengths as a public moralist. He encourages us to believe that there is no encumbrance that cannot be ignored or thrust aside. We can do what we will—with our own lives, with our society—because the immediate moment carries overriding power and importance, while the "givens" (our instincts, our traditions) exercise limited dominion only. (p. 3)

Goodman feels that Americans "are both too decent to succumb to fascism and too spirited to remain impotent clients of a managerial elite." Although he believes that we are "on a bad course," he also believes that we will avoid a Roman success abroad and a police state at home. He places chief hope for such an escape in the mounting tide of protest from the young, protest that will produce new forms of experimentation and, ultimately, a reconstruction of values and institutions.

In the essay **"Counter-Forces for a Decent Society,"** Goodman makes a persuasive case for the view that such a reconstruction is already under way. The Supreme Court has been extending civil liberties; there has been a notable shift in public opinion away from moralism and Puritanism; there has been a renewal of social consciousness in the church; there has been an explosion of experimentation in the arts. . . .

At the same time there are other, parallel developments that jeopardize these hopeful prospects and that Goodman (at least in these essays) minimizes: the growing alliance between big government, big business and the military; the continuing (probably increasing) dominance of our economy by the supercorporations; the deadening authoritarianism of most of our educational system; the religiosity and conformity of our people; the banality of our culture.

Moreover, Goodman's chief grounds for optimism—the radical movement among the college-age population—seems to me an unsure quantity, and his prediction that the movement "will certainly increase even more rapidly in the next years," far too sanguine. Perhaps, on the contrary, it may already have crested. . . .

Goodman's argument is further weakened by the superficiality of some of his analyses and the occasional flipness of his prose. He seems to have little patience for the intricacies and contradictions of argument, with the result that shallow statement too often substitutes for careful inquiry. . . . And the informal, easy quality of Goodman's style, often so attractive, can degenerate into a slick banality reminiscent of the ladies' magazines. . . .

"Like a Conquered Province" is not vintage Goodman; most of it he has said before, and often better. But even a second-rate performance by Goodman, the public philosopher, is far more digestible than the exhibitionism of his private diary. (p. 45)

> Martin Duberman, *"The Private Man and Public Prophet," in* The New York Times Book Review *(© 1967 by The New York Times Company; reprinted by permission), June 11, 1967, pp. 3, 45.*

THEODORE ROSZAK

Touched with his usual charitable spirit, [Paul Goodman's] *The New Reformation* is a model of intelligent ambivalence: certainly the most discriminate discussion of our dissenting youth culture yet to appear.

Goodman's purpose here is to play Erasmus to the young, whom he likens in their impetuous moral outrage to the sixteenth-century Protestants. The comparison has its limitations, but Goodman develops its perceptively, neatly paralleling the thickly corrupted Catholic Church of Luther's day with the careerist, militarized leviathan the modern industrial state has become.

He rightly discerns that the attack of the young upon the technocratic establishment is essentially a clash of religious sensibilities. Technological society has become the new whore of Babylon, wielding its vast research and development facilities like the veritable sacramental powers. It promises us an earthly New Jerusalem, but produces much unconscionable waste and fearsome violence. So the alienated young, gifted with justified disgust, lean toward wholesale repudiation of its ideals and institutions as fanatically as Luther cast out the Church's moral theology of works. . . .

The historical analogy weakens at this point, for Luther's heresy was in the way of loyal opposition: an appeal backward to the Christian kerygma literally preserved in scripture. But to what tradition does Goodman feel the new Protestants trace back? Or does he feel they can legitimately trace back to *anything* outside the scientific tradition, which he vastly admires? Yet, in the midst of religious famine, what can the young find within the tradition to feed the hungry?

Here we have a decisive difference between the Reformations Old and New. "In the end," says Goodman, "it is religion that constitutes the strength of the new generation." Yes . . . but the Word is not to be had from science even at its pristine best. . . .

What concerns Goodman most—in his Erasmian stance—is that the new Reformers are assuming many an ugly and foolish aspect of late. Their intolerance for real evils carries over into an indiscriminate rejection not only of science and technics, but of intellect and culture generally. What a sad sign of the times it is that Goodman must go to the trouble he does here to vindicate (against the McLuhanites in large part) the values of literature. Of *literature!* But it is a fine apology—and a necessary one. For the self-congratulatory gaucherie he chastises is all there: It fills most versions of the underground press and much avant-garde theater. . . .

So, for those young having the ears to hear, Goodman makes the brave defense of "Culture with a big C." It is a wise discussion, especially where it touches on science and technology, on their imperative need to become "prudent, ecological, and decentralized," on their historical glories and their possibilities of nobility within the tradition of a principled professionalism. Here we have the voice of an authentic conservatism; not the familiar conservatism that propagandizes for corporate or ecclesiastical elites, but instead a "neolithic conservatism" whose instincts are anarchist and whose politics aspire to be "decentralist, anti-police, anti-party, anti-bureaucratic, organized by voluntary association, and putting a premium on grass-roots spontaneity."

There is nothing in Goodman's thinking that is not subtle and many-sided; so he offers little I would criticize except for what I take to be his emphasis here and there. I cannot, for example, agree with him that moon-rockets are the "cathedrals" of our time in anything more than a sarcastic sense of the word (which he does not intend) or that these space ventures are "something unquestionably to be done and worth doing." They seem to me a sad distraction from less preposterous ways of being human and heroic. And besides, the Faustian aspirations of our technician-elites are becoming—for all the rest of us—pathetically vicarious. I feel, too, that it goes too far in the celebration of science to declare Newton's mathematics of planetary motion "even more beautiful than the Evening Star itself." How can that be? But doubtless 99 per cent of America would agree. Numbers are fast becoming the only realities most people know—and probably few have seen the poet's much-praised star since the smog set in.

There is also a curiously ethnocentric flavor to the book—as if the culture Goodman thinks our youth must properly claim as "their own" extends no further than that of the West since Newton . . . or perhaps since Aristotle. But not all our young are illiterate and philistine. Rather, many have begun to find their "inspiration and grandeur" in other quite respectable cultural traditions that also need to be conserved, especially those of the primitives and the eastern mystics. . . .

Goodman's book is a superb educational effort. But one cannot help being gloomy about its reception at the hands of those ever more a-cultural young who most require its counsel. They are apt to conclude—simply and stupidly—that Goodman is just no longer on "their" side. As if saving the society were all a matter of leading cheers for the team. Let us hope they will muster the good will to see how real is their critic's concern for the health of their souls, the strength of their cause.

> *Theodore Roszak, "A Radical Defense of Culture,"
> in* Book World—The Washington Post *(© 1970 Postrib Corp.; reprinted by permission of* Chicago Tribune *and* The Washington Post*) Vol. IV, No. 20, May 17, 1970, p. 6.*

EUGENE GOODHEART

Goodman's ambivalent view of the youth revolt [in *New Reformation*] strikes me as absolutely right. He sympathizes with the attempt to loose authoritarian and rigid educational structures, but he is revolted by the mindless hostility to the tradition of humane letters, which has its own instructive radicalism if the young would only care to listen and learn. The implicit McLuhanism in all versions of youth protest has created an ideological impatience with anything that requires long periods of reflection. Goodman is sensitive to the commercialism of the counter-culture, which is closer to the mainstream culture of television and advertising than it is to any genuine radicalism. (p. 85)

> *Eugene Goodheart, " 'Unless I Can Think Up an Alternative or Two'," in* The Nation *(copyright 1970 The Nation magazine, The Nation Associates, Inc.), Vol. 211, No. 3, August 3, 1970, pp. 84-6.*

JAN B. GORDON

[These] *Notes of a Neolithic Conservative* are a strange parody of Luther's theses; non-negotiable demands for decentralized administration; the adaptation of the vernacular as an aid to escaping the jargon of an excessively technocratic society; the right of every man to worship in the way he sees fit (read: "Do your own thing"); and an end to the corruption of the industrial-military-university troika. But the dangers posed by the first Reformation are also present in Goodman's analogy. The abstract universalizing and isolation of individuals, an economism that destroys genuine community and real wealth by polarizing evidence of election, the fractured leadership that results in a multiplication of the original schism into numerous religious sects—all make for a limited success of the movement.

On balance then, Goodman's latest book is comparatively more restrained in his advocacy of youth; whereas in the late '50s he had referred to the young as his "crazy allies," *New Reformation* calls attention to their intolerance and the blatant contradictions in the economic philosophy of the New Left. (p. 152)

Goodman, for all his astuteness, seems trapped in the "either/ or" logic of the old left rather than the "being/and" thinking of today's young people and it is the radical juxtapositions that make the current radical so distant from him. . . . Goodman's request for some viable political philosophy from the New Left is a request for purpose from an increasingly tribalized society which is willing to pay the price of internal contradiction to preserve a fragile unity of being.

To those detractors who would accuse Paul Goodman of fuzzy-liberalism, *New Reformation* appears the private papers of a conservative out of the Jeffersonian mold. (pp. 152-53)

Goodman's bias, as it has always been, is pluralistic. Instead of the few national goals of a few decision-makers, he opts for a manifold of goods in many activities of life and many professions and interest groups each with its own criteria for excellence. (p. 153)

Goodman's proposals should not go unchallenged. There is a tendency to equate decentralization with smallness in his work, in spite of the evidence that small education and the typical small business is often a nest of inefficiency with no guarantee of a quality product. One suspects that internal competition in science or education or business can only be carried on by firms that have reached a certain size; the model of pluralism is more likely to be General Motors than Studebaker. Hence the return of the small school *per se* is not sufficient to achieve the reformation that Goodman requests without a shift in consciousness.

There is also a confusion in the two goals of Western education in his thought: the organic ideal which insists that the self must be allowed to grow with as little interference as possible and which assumes an analogy between human development and plant development and the other scheme, which envisions growth as a dialectical process through the mediation of various interlocutors and, above all, through progressive encounters with a series of imaginative models. Nature does not always provide the second, even to the eyes of shepherds.

But Goodman's *New Reformation: Notes of a Neolithic Conservative* would be an exciting document, even if one disagrees with some of its author's premises. Almost novelistic in structure, the book moves from the environment in which our sciences and professions breathe, to the educational structures which feed them, and finally, to the increasingly private confessions of its author. The movement of *New Reformation* is part of the humanistic journey to decentralization. (p. 154)

> *Jan B. Gordon, " 'New Reformation: Notes of a Neolithic Conservative'," in* Commonweal *(copyright ©1970 Commonweal Publishing Co., Inc.; reprinted by permission of Commonweal Publishing Co., Inc.), Vol. XCIII, No. 6, November 6, 1970, pp. 152-55.*

KINGSLEY WIDMER

Paul Goodman's last book [*Little Prayers and Finite Experience*] . . . was not his best work. But Goodman has been, I believe, one of our more provocative and important social critics and moralists. And even this final mishmash shows some of that. For Goodman was right in his typically awkward little verse that says of himself that he had "the gift of earnest speech / that says how a thing is"—and how many things ought to be. . . .

The double role, littérateur and social critic, ran through all of his life. Of his two dozen published volumes, about half are "literary" (poems, plays, stories, novels, confessions). It is the other half of his writings, where important social subject and unusual earnestness overcome difficulties of style, which were, and remain, valuable. Recall such useful essays as *Communitas* and its imaginatively utopian yet very specific and pertinent thinking about "city planning" and communal forms. And *People or Personnel,* an incisive argument for "decentralization" in many of our overpowered and dehumanizing institutions which yet treats with considerable subtlety and balance the issues of moving toward a "mixed" institutional order of greater freedom and variety and life quality.

Perhaps Goodman's literary awkwardness and social perceptiveness complement each other. In *Finite Experience,* he several times speaks of his "extraordinary ineptitude." For the practice of a craft, such as literature, that may be damaging, but for the practice of social wisdom, such as compassion for the perplexities of the young, that may be essential. The great myth of the festering "wound" and the compensatory "bow" also applies to social thinkers. . . .

Goodman was an early and seminal opponent of the liberal prejudice that we can resolve our problems with more schools and schooling—the mirror image of the reactionary bigotry that imagines we can eliminate our social problems with more police and policing. He had a just horror of our endless custodial busywork and mandarin aggrandizement and humanly wasteful academicization of the lively. Historically, Goodman has been a key figure in carrying earlier American progressive education, run aground in programmed submissiveness and bureaucratic vulgarization, to the "new school" and "deschooling" educational reformers of the present. . . .

Such an anti-schooling view of education, paradigmatic for Goodman's other social views, aimed at a rather Jeffersonian vision of people living in sturdy and creative independence in viable communities. In education, as in economics and politics, decentralizing was the crux: "localism, ruralism, face-to-face organization," all based on a pluralistic sense of "natural rights." (p. 21)

His insistence on a "politics within limits" appeared drastic to the conventional Left and Right alike in its demands for a modest and humanly proportioned social order. With some quaintness, he eventually came to identify his views as "conservative anarchism." . . . Like many anarchists, he was angrily preservative in temper, though it becomes increasingly hard to find things to preserve, and humble in hopes. As he writes in *Finite Experience,* "idolatry makes me uneasy. I don't like my country to be a Great Power." But the inverted megalomania of much of the New Left, which took him up but also put him back down in the 1960s, was no adequate alternative: "I am squeamish about masses of people enthusiastically building a New Society," and "One must not manipulate real people because of an abstract idea." Right or Left, he was against manipulation and domination, which these days made him far more negative and alienated than suited his temperament.

"Our mistake is to arm anybody with collective power." Authentic politics, then, is resistance to and reduction of collective power and control. Unlike many libertarians, Goodman did not base this on a benign view of human nature. On the contrary, he thought people will often be, and have a right to be, "crazy, stupid or arrogant." Society should be so organized as to admit such possibilities. Still, when not empowered and driven to impose on others, or resentfully destroy them, most people may be able to arrive at some useful work, affectionate relationships and some small happiness. Large ambitions and powers and institutions interfere with this. Big and centralized organization "guarantees stupidity" about tangible life because it must, for its manipulations, abstract away from it. (pp. 21-2)

Goodman's political counters to this, as well as his positive social goals, were small scale. He disliked generalized moveements that would impose a "positive morality," or destructive "spite." He had, perhaps, an excessive optimism about the political effectiveness of radical efforts at "secession," "autonomous communities," "passive resistance" and the general good effects of independent honesty and intelligence and work. This is part of his earnestness which, even if mistaken, is mostly admirable. He lacked the usual political man's cynicism. And he lacked the saving irony which is the usual defense, and withdrawal tactic, of the literary intellectual. He may be criticized for not having an adequate political means to his goal of a responsively finite socio-political order. But who has? And in the meantime he did have an active, and exceedingly decent, individual and small-group morality of resistance.

Goodman's views were also conservative in another, and less radical, way; he was, for reasons never clear to me, no egalitarian. Perhaps this was another result of the "inept" not only admiring those of special skills—the "professional" with his guild community—as he did, but a willingness to allow them excessive prerogatives and perquisites. But, he commented, this should not be confused with what is now "mistakenly called 'conservatism,'" which destructively reduces all vocations and moral and aesthetic and communal goods to the economic marketplace, itself increasingly abstracted and manipulated away from concrete human needs. General Motors is not Adam Smith's nail manufactory, and the mad glut of extravagant American automobiles on strangling freeways is neither rational economy nor reasonable transportation. (pp. 22-3)

Perhaps partly because of what he called his "ineptness" at dealing with the larger world, and perhaps partly from a poet-pose of detachment, Goodman, with what he liked to call his "dumb bunny" proposals for doing things more simply and directly and humanely, had an expert nose for the rationalized irrationalities of our gigantism. Not only in schooling and production and urbanization and military manias but in ways of thought. Unlike most humanists, he had an abiding devotion to physical science. . . . He did not believe that science was "value-neutral" but saw it in practice as a heroic secular form of the "Calvinist virtues" of self-discipline, austerity, humility and vocation.

A similar sense of Enlightenment finiteness marks his concern with other intellectual activities. Art should be personal and communal ritual, clear and ordered, with an Aristotelian beginning, middle and end. The philosophical mind should not create metaphysical and ideological systems but should carry out the Kantian duty of criticizing the applied professions and faculties of knowledge, in a kind of permanent opposition. In religion . . . his views were equally "finite." He was willing to allow for small gods and personal and communal "creator spirits." But, he says, he "never experienced that All is One or that everything is connected." Apparently big religious claims also "guarantee stupidity" and are indifferent to tangible life in society.

Aware as he is of impending death, the underlying theme of Goodman's prayer-poems, philosophical notes, aesthetic marginalia and social criticism I take to be the comment that, logically, "the chances of personal happiness are trivial." There's no good human use in disguising that truth, but there is also none in resigning oneself to worsening it. We must do what we can to make that condition more communally bearable. In a characteristic sentence in *Finite Experience,* he says that his social criticism always aimed to "diminish intermediary services that are not directly productive or directly enjoyed." Quite possibly, life was ultimately a waste, but further wasting it was the ultimate sin. Spiteful stupidity, wars, coercive governments, big bad institutions, pretentious arts, mean schooling, repression of affectionate sex, enforced anxiety and competition, and general human alienation, were all a terrible waste.

The early Paul Goodman was a Left-Freudian, artistic vanguardist and radical anarchist. After a surprising, and rather fortuitous, degree of public success in his middle age—partly with the aid of his New York intellectual coterie—he became rather more an Enlightenment moralist, though still aptly scoring our manias of gigantism. That his views, early and late, seemed peculiar to many, may be less to his discredit than to theirs. I don't mean to deny his humorless oddness—evident in his publicized bisexuality, in his awkward style that mixed the pedantic and the outrageous, and in a personal manner of arrogant humility and egotistical simplicity, which I, too, found irritating—but it was an earnestly intelligent and often insightful peculiarity. I doubt if Paul Goodman ever realized just how eccentric and inept he was, and how peculiarly distant from mainstream America. But he had the courage of his confusions. As a man of letters, in the Enlightenment sense now so rare, he fortunately did not confine himself to "poet" but thought and wrote and acted contentiously and suggestively on all he could of finite society and life. It was a valuable effort, not to be defined by any particular ineptness, and we could use more of it. (p. 23)

Kingsley Widmer, "The Conservative Anarchist of 'Politics within Limits'," in The Nation *(copyright 1973 The Nation magazine, The Nation Associates, Inc.), Vol. 216, No. 1, January 1, 1973, pp. 21-3.*

GEORGE LEVINE

[Paul Goodman's last book, **"Little Prayers and Finite Experience"**] has the virtue of telling us a lot about him, though really not much more than his other books have revealed in passing. It is the kind of autobiography he was best equipped to write, requiring a personal voice talking to somebody, but being essentially about ideas; not the story of his life, not a summing up, but a rambling through his beliefs, obsessions, limitations, pains, sexual hungers, knowledge. It is an attempt to account for himself to an audience of students who wanted to know how he "went about" being. This may seem a little pretentious (though the point will be recognizable to anyone who has read **"Growing Up Absurd"**), but pretentiousness—except perhaps an occasionally excessive attempt to be direct, honest, concrete, earthy—was not Goodman's mode. He was right to assume that he had earned the right to talk about himself in this way, having lived a life of remarkable integrity, and having written a good deal without which we would be poorer. (p. 4)

This isn't one of those fortuitous conclusions to a career in which a rationalist suddenly sees the light and turns to God. For a long time, Goodman had been identifying the crises of our time as religious. In earlier books he talked about the way modern society has deprived the young of the power to believe in anything outside themselves and, consequently, in themselves as well. They have no work that might enspirit them, no models (outside popular culture) to emulate, no communities to care about. In this sense, they have no faith. Goodman's own faith was his work as a writer. . . .

Thus in **"Finite Experience"** Goodman was doing the same job he had worked at for two decades. He had only one subject, he said in **"Utopian Essays and Practical Proposals"** (1962), "the human beings I know in their man-made scene." His work was to make life satisfying for human beings, largely by demonstrating that their social world is man-made and, therefore, man-changeable. The resources for change, he insisted, are in man himself.

Goodman's writing is touching because this faith in human possibility had always been manifest in its very texture. The writing is the faith because it is a kind of work—not the communication of a message, a means to an end, but a way of being in the world, an action. His prose has rarely been beautiful (it is striking how unbeautiful his fiction is), but the nonfiction has a life that grows from Goodman's almost physical sensitivity to the presence of his audience, and from an awareness of what he calls, in **"Speaking and Language"** (1971), the double life of words. Every speech must be ambiguous because it is almost impossible to tell "what of the meaning . . . comes from the experience and what meaning has been added" by the speaking. For various reasons, explained in his brilliant work in **"Gestalt Therapy"** (1951)—the only emotionally engaging textbook I know—Goodman always preferred to live with that duality. "If you want to make sense," he wrote in his dedication to **"The Structure of Literature"** (1954), "you had better take all important factors into account." And what could be more important than the self speaking and the self listening?

At its extreme, this view makes it difficult to distinguish rational argument from autobiography or dialogue. And it has evoked much criticism of Goodman from "experts." But who would prefer the value-free objectivity of the language of bureaucrats and social scientists. . . .

Goodman's dislike of "objectivity" is the substance and the subject of most of his writing, and he picks it up again in the short section on gestalt therapy in this last book. . . .

For me, the most satisfying aspect of Goodman's work is in precisely [his] power to connect the psychological with the social, to recognize the human in everything. His emphasis on the importance of "primary experience" leads him to his peculiar politics of communitarian anarchism. For him, politics was the activity of attempting to "remedy institutions that hinder experience from occurring." As he puts it here, "There is no politics but remedial politics; often the first remedy is to take 'Society' less seriously, and to notice what society one has." "Society" is not real. It's an abstraction that gets between us and the community we need in order, simply, to be. It keeps us from "noticing."

These attitudes allowed Goodman to anticipate the terrible malaise of the last decade and made him, for a while in the early sixties, a prophet to the young. Not trapped by abstractions, he could explain to us all what was happening and why, and he could creatively attack the various institutions that were trapped. For each institution he made "Utopian" proposals—that is, "practical" ones. He wanted us to ignore impractical obstacles erected by the institutions themselves and take each problem as it affects us directly. He regarded arguments that his proposals for radical change were impractical, that we must compromise and face facts, as psychologically and sociologically neurotic.

In his brilliant and characteristically erratic **"Utopian Essays and Practical Proposals"** (1962), he argued that we have attempted to solve our problems by doing nothing more than more of the same—as the present frightening moment in our history seems to confirm. . . . By now this should be old hat, but it isn't. Clearly, whether or not Goodman's particular proposals are usable, his general proposal that we need a radical reconsideration of the way we go about solving problems is accurate.

He argued, long before reforming liberals were willing even to consider it, that the central practical problem of our society is how to handle bigness—how to avoid waste and fragmentation and dehumanization without centralization, which, by definition (we have discovered rather later than Goodman), increases these things even while it attempts to remedy them. . . .

Goodman so passionately loved youth, energy and sexual vitality, and saw them as so essential to any real change, that he allowed himself to believe that the various political, communitarian, rebellious activities of the young in the sixties would lead to the kinds of reform he wanted. But in **"New Reformation"** (1969), he says, "In 1958 I called them 'my crazy young allies' and now I'm saying that when the chips are down, they're just like their fathers."

Yet **"New Reformation"** sounds like the same old Paul Goodman, as does **"Little Prayers and Finite Experience."** Some of the new difference might be accounted for by the disintegration of the youth movements toward hippiedom or the left that we are still watching (with exactly that sigh of relief that would have enraged Goodman); some by the dogmatic intolerance of those whose rejection of the "system" has hardened irrevocably. But one can see, with the clarity of hindsight, that Goodman's and youth's mutual disillusion was inevitably built into Goodman's way of being. (p. 5)

Goodman's anarchism is in a way the ultimate laissez faire. It implies a deep faith in human powers of creative adjustment, a willingness to risk the dangers that come with the absence of system, and trust in other humans. In fact, among Goodman's Utopian proposals he includes the encouragement of conflict within communities: "Conflict," he says, "is not an obstacle to community, but a golden opportunity, *if the give-and-take continue, if contact can be maintained.*"

But this is hardly revolutionary. Marxists would argue that Goodman's anarchism implies that he too was trapped in the tradition of bourgeois individualism—the cause of the trouble, not the way out. "Practical" politicians would argue that you can't change the system by invoking individual responsibility and encouraging individual growth. Goodman wrote and acted as if you could. Wanting community, he worked at it by dealing with particular problems, but he couldn't believe that any institution—even one created by a revolution from the left—could improve the texture of individual life, of social and sexual intercourse, except by making itself go away. You can't be a revolutionary theorist and reject objectivity, abstractions and even theory itself. Marx, Lenin and Mao couldn't help him because Goodman wanted not more system but less. And so he has been attacked as a bourgeois reactionary by the young who expected something different.

In addition, like a good radical tory, Goodman had enormous respect for history, for language, for tradition, for science. In **"Like a Conquered Province"** (1967) he rejects the Ludditism of the fighters against technology. "Knowledge," he said, "must be pursued for its own sake, as part of the human adventure." His point has always been not that we should turn away from technological development, but that science and technology should be humanized. Scientists and engineers should engage themselves morally in their work and be responsible for it. Again, the attack turns out to be aimed not at the activities themselves but at the false idea of objectivity which has institutionalized and dehumanized them.

Another aspect of his radical toryism was manifest in **"Growing Up Absurd,"** which contains (though most of us must have missed it the first time around) the last praise of patriotism I can remember from a serious writer. The problem, Goodman asserted over and over again, is that the young, seeing that none of the traditions around them seem worthy of respect, find it difficult to believe that there ever were or could be any.

Again, the last book Goodman published in his lifetime, **"Speaking and Language,"** is a "Defence of Poetry." It is partly an attack on scientific linguistics, which Goodman thinks of as another example of false and deadly objectivity, but it is also an assertion of the values of the past, and of language intelligently, sensitively, carefully used. And it is thus, also, another implicit attack on the young, who, Goodman believed, in their disrespect for language and for the past, are as guilty of reifying abstractions as their parents, and hence as dangerous. Perhaps Goodman thought that with sensible rebellion would come some sensible faith: some of the bitterness and anger of the last books reflects his awareness that it has not come.

But it would be wrong to think that Goodman's career ended with an old man's reaction from youth. He had lost none of his envy of, his love for the young—though the accidental death of his son must have helped lead to his disillusion. He attacked the young for the same reason he had supported them, because he cared for—even lusted after—them, and he knew, as he says in "New Reformation," that "they *are* the ball game."

Simple rejection was not his style. He never went in for polarities, and his writing is about sharing, about getting beyond dualisms of self and society, man and nature, I and Thou. We exist only insofar as we are in creative contact with the people and things around us. "You are what you eat," and what you see and feel and smell and touch.

As Goodman understood, accepting his way of thinking and being entailed danger; but risk is the price of growth—and of creative adjustment. Still, it is difficult not to play the role of the neurotic conformist in Goodman's scenario—the person who rejects his proposals because they just don't seem practical. (pp. 5-6)

Goodman, even in his death, remains an outsider. At one point, he quoted Ruskin as saying, "I show men their plain duty and they reply that my style is charming." That was Goodman's fate too. But unlike Ruskin, Goodman managed to stay sane, if also ineffectual. Maybe his Utopias are coming; probably not. But I confess to a quiet longing after them myself and to gratitude to Goodman for imagining them for me. He has taught me a lot about myself, about my world and about possibility. In **"Five Years,"** in some few of his poems, in most of his essays, he has put me in touch with a man. I for one will miss him. (p. 6)

George Levine, "Paul Goodman, Outsider Looking In," in The New York Times Book Review *(© 1973 by The New York Times Company; reprinted by permission), February 18, 1973, pp. 4-6.*

GOODMAN

JOSEPH EPSTEIN

How seems [*Growing Up Absurd*] now? Not quite the same [as ten years ago], it turns out. Fish and visitors, said Franklin, begin to stink after three days; radical writing dependably rots after a decade. Right off there is, as one rereads it today, an odor of datedness about *Growing Up Absurd:* ". . . the problems I want to discuss in this book," Goodman writes in his opening chapter, "belong primarily, in our society, to the boys: how to be useful and make something of oneself. A girl does not *have* to, she is not expected to, 'make something' of herself." Perhaps one cannot blame Goodman for not including the women's movement in his vaticinations. One can blame him, though, for the tremendous jumble of his book. So many statements in it are made *ex cathedra*. . . . Frequently Goodman will clinch an argument with a quotation from the earlier work by that noted authority—Paul Goodman. Arguments often lead nowhere; subjects founder in obscurity, as when, talking about the community culture of the Beats, Goodman writes that they would do well to ponder, as a model, "the Balinese dances." As befits its anarchist author, *Growing Up Absurd* may be one of the few books organized along anarchist lines; that is to say, without any organization at all.

The language of *Growing Up Absurd* was a compound—compost?—of the purest psychobabble overlaid by sociological barbarisms. No one who so regularly cited himself as an artist ever wrote so poorly. "Depersonalized" was a big item in his vocabulary, as was "structure." He could refer to one's "own meant world"; "needs" were inevitably "felt"; and it nearly goes without saying that he was for "growth," "dialogue," and "feelingful sex." True, such phrases were not then the clichés they have since become, but they served the same purposes, then as now, of evasion, obfuscation, and self-deception. But Goodman's book contains clichés of thought as well as of language. "Community" was one he regularly fell back upon, as in this dubious statement in *Growing Up Absurd:* "children of all classes are equally deprived of the human community." . . . He availed himself of the even more commonplace clichés of social criticism, complaining of freeways, suburbs, supermarkets; and at a higher level of generality, though certainly no deeper a level of penetration, of Wall Street and Madison Avenue and Hollywood.

Paul Goodman was famously eclectic, which seemed to give him the authority to speak out in several different voices. At one point, he spoke as a psychologist; at one point, as a literary critic; at one point, as a city planner . . . ; and always as an artist ("Consider the case of the artist," he writes, "my own."). While the variety of Paul Goodman's accomplishments seemed to make him more appealing in his role as a social critic, the harsh fact is that he was not a very incisive psychologist, an original city planner, an interesting literary critic, or a good novelist, poet, or playwright. That he did all these things is impressive, but as Samuel Johnson once said, "A horse that can count up to ten is a remarkable horse, not a remarkable mathematician."

Although many of the notions in *Growing Up Absurd* anticipated those of the New Left later in the 1960's, as Goodman's vaporous language anticipated the therapeutic view of life still much in the air today, there remains a sense in which Paul Goodman was not himself conventionally doctrinaire. "I have felt the power of my disinterestedness," he wrote, "since indeed I have no ax to grind and don't want anybody's money." To come on as he did well above the ruck, all disinterest and deep feeling, was surely a great part of the appeal of Paul

Goodman. . . . He was very good, in the same vein, at conveying the sense of squandered energies and their cost. Goodman had his voice, his characteristic tone, and when served up in an unadorned syntax, shorn of clotted language, it could be very winning. (pp. 71-2)

Allied to Goodman's sadness at the prospect of waste was the Rousseauism that was one of the major motifs in everything he wrote. Almost everywhere in Paul Goodman's work not men but institutions are at fault. In literary matters, to cite an almost comical example, Goodman felt that the problem with our novelists is not that they are inferior in understanding society but that society is not good enough for them: "The burden of proof is not on the artist but on society." Who is to blame is always left rather vague in Goodman. . . .

Goodman's method was to criticize existing arrangements, always making sure to suggest alternatives: decentralize here, organize from the bottom up rather than the top down there, change an existing law elsewhere. Some of his alternatives were interesting, some superficial, some silly. But were these alternatives made in the name of a large vision? Socialism, strictly speaking, was not the name of Paul Goodman's desire. What, then, was?

In his brief foreword to *Five Years,* Goodman writes: "When I speak of 'psychology' I am speaking about 'society.'" The two, for him, were interchangeable. When Goodman spoke of "repression," he did not mean the word metaphorically, a borrowing from psychological discourse to be put to political or social uses. He thought that people were quite literally repressed, their natures twisted and thwarted by life in modern society. The roots of this repression were psychological, even if its consequences were political. . . .

The sexual element in Paul Goodman's work was more than merely pronounced. He never hid it. His admirers—myself of a decade ago among them—simply never wished to recognize it. The fact that Paul Goodman was a roughhouse homosexual—"trade's trade," as he once described himself—was not in any case considered a fit topic for polite intellectual talk. (p. 72)

Goodman felt that his homosexuality gave him a certain edge as a writer. "As one grows older," he wrote in an essay entitled **"The Politics of Being Queer,"** "homosexual wishes keep one alert to adolescents and young people more than heterosexual wishes do. . . ." He was also, to put it gently, sexually highly charged: "There have been few days back to my 11th year when I have not had an orgasm one way or another." Among his admirers, there was a tendency to treat Paul Goodman's homosexuality as peripheral, perhaps as imbuing him with a greater hunger for social justice, but otherwise not really central to his chief concerns. He was, in this view, a cogent critic of modern American life who *happened* to be homosexual. . . .

Having practiced homosexuality, did Goodman preach it? Not explicitly, though he was an ambassador for sexuality generally. . . . [What] is implied in so much of Goodman's writing, is that if we had better sexuality, we would have better community. Thus his young men in *Growing Up Absurd* are often violent as a result of repressed homosexuality. Everywhere the enemy is repressed sexuality. . . . For Goodman, the "coercive society" was one that not alone repressed sexuality but also failed to encourage it. The good society, for Goodman, started at the groin.

Many of the things Paul Goodman asked for in his essays and books of the 1960's have now come about, and with rather pitiful consequences; and this as much as anything, when one rereads him today, diminishes his stature. In *Growing Up Absurd,* he complained, for example, that "the powerful interests have the big presses." He should be alive today to read the New York *Times* and the Washington *Post.* In **"Pornography, Art, and Censorship,"** an essay first published in . . . 1961, he complained about "the forbidden topic, the mockery of sacred public figures." He should be alive today to read the novels of E. L. Doctorow and Robert Coover, the journalism of Garry Wills and Gore Vidal. He believed that if the legal restrictions were lifted from pornography, it would "ennoble all our art," "humanize sexuality," have "beautiful cultural advantages." He should be alive today to walk the 42nd Street of every large American city. He believed in decentralizing everywhere, getting back to the land and artisanship. He should be alive today to see the squalor of youthful communalism, the triviality of boutique culture. One could go on. Many of the things Paul Goodman asked for have come about—and with the result that he now seems a voice a good deal overvalued in his own lifetime. (p. 73)

> Joseph Epstein, *"Paul Goodman in Retrospect,"* in Commentary *(reprinted by permission; all rights reserved), Vol. 65, No. 2, February, 1978, pp. 70-3.*

John L(angston) Gwaltney

1928-

Gwaltney is an American author of books on anthropology and associate professor of anthropology at Syracuse University. Blind since infancy, Gwaltney met some skepticism as a graduate student in Columbia University's department of anthropology regarding his ability to conduct field research. Margaret Mead suggested he study the Yolox Chinantec people of Mexico, who were in a region where blindness is a constant threat, since he "doesn't have to worry about losing his sight." The field work resulted in his first book, *The Thrice Shy* (1970), which won Columbia's Ansley Dissertation Award. Subsequently, Gwaltney has conducted ethnological research among black Jews in Harlem, American Indians, and Jamaican Maroons. His second book, *Drylongso* (1980), presents 42 out of the 300 interviews he conducted with black Americans in the 1970s. The title means "ordinary" in Black English; the intent of the book is to present the histories of members of the "core black culture," men and women holding responsible jobs and solid positions within their communities. One of the messages that comes through in this book, according to its black author, is that "you would have to believe in unicorns not to believe that racism exists in this country—and that most political actions are invested in it." (See also *Contemporary Authors*, Vols. 33-36, rev. ed., and 77-80.)

Courtesy of John L. Gwaltney

Excerpt from *THE THRICE SHY: CULTURAL ACCOMMODATION TO BLINDNESS AND OTHER DISASTERS IN A MEXICAN COMMUNITY*

Calamity has been a superordinate element in Yoleño history since the founding of the pueblo. Centuries of living in the shadow of impending disaster which they are powerless to avert have made most Yoleños deferential, skeptical and extremely accommodative before nature and nature's God.

Onchocerciasis, with its attendant possibility of blindness, is only the most bizarre of a host of catastrophies which assail the pueblo. . . . Poisonous snakes, pneumonia and a host of respiratory furies, measles, lethal lightning storms, malaria, numerous other acute chronic diseases, whooping cough, floods, droughts, fires, venomous lizards, earthquakes, hurricanes, hunger and a running land feud are all established expectations and have conditioned the Yoleño to expect the worst.

This traditional, ongoing body of calamitous precedence and its resultant ingrained predisposition toward negative anticipation exert a profound influence upon village character and is the aspect of their history with which villagers are primarily concerned.

A climate of catastrophy made the Chinantec a wary conservative. Centuries of submission, grinding poverty and a high death rate have eliminated optimism as a serious factor in Chinantec personality. Unalloyed optimism simply does not play any serious part in the thinking of most villagers. Both experience and custom dictate an attitude of deferential but profound skepticism toward altruism, natural benignity and divine love. Divine authority is regarded as the most compelling source of coercion.

Villagers are assiduously devoted to the detection of interested motives in human interaction. This pessimistic evaluation of human motives approaches the fantastic when villagers are speculating about human behavior beyond their customary experience. (pp. 154-55)

Persons of all degrees of sympathy and integrity are the vehicles of innovation in the village. And Yoleños are the thrice shy children of oft bitten fathers. (p. 156)

There is a marked tendency to reckon time and to remember important events coincidentally with natural disasters or grievous personal misfortune. (p. 158)

The traditional defense is phlegmatic compliance to the mandate of divine, natural, parental, and communal authority. There is an ingrained communal conviction that much more is required of anyone to whom much is given. The dominant Chinantec personality defense is a sierra variation of the old Army Game, in which eccentricity is tantamount to volunteering.

This cultural inclination to ask little of God, the stranger, and their paisanos, and to expect the worst from all three is probably a prime element in the resistance encountered by medical and paramedical personnel of the Mexican Government's National Campaign against Onchocerciasis.

The Chinantec have devised their own means of meeting all stressful agencies in their calamitous context. These traditional responses to particular stressful agencies are intended not to control or eradicate but to restore a balance, however adverse. (p. 159)

Yoleños do not conceive of man as being the measure of all or even most things. There is a customary conviction that anonymity or, failing that, accommodation before God, nature and the powerful stranger is the best that can realistically be expected in this world. (p. 160)

> *John L. Gwaltney, in his* The Thrice Shy: Cultural Accommodation to Blindness and Other Disasters in a Mexican Community *(copyright © 1967, 1970 Columbia University Press; reprinted by permission of the publisher), Columbia University Press, 1970, 219 p.*

Excerpt from *DRYLONGSO: A SELF-PORTRAIT OF BLACK AMERICA*

[*Drylongso*] is the product of an anthropological field study conducted in the early 1970's in more than a dozen northeastern urban black American communities, and of my own experiences and observations as a member of such communities. . . . I share the opinion commonly held by natives of my community that we have traditionally been misrepresented by standard social science.

This book is a self-portrait of what I call core black culture. It consists of personal narratives that were offered in contexts of amity, security and hospitality. All who contributed did so with the plain intent of presenting ourselves as we think we are. . . . This is not, therefore, another collection of street-corner exotica but an explication of black culture as it is perceived by the vast majority of Afro-Americans who are working members of stable families in pursuit of much the same kinds of happinesses that preoccupy the rest of American society. Almost all of the men and women whose thoughts are represented in this volume think well of themselves and are well thought of by their relatives, friends and neighbors. Their feelings of personal and communal satisfaction are rooted in the astonishing reality of their civil, principled survival in spite of the weight of empire that rests upon their backs. In black culture, as in any other, there are those who can and those who cannot "get it together." *Drylongso* is the creation of those who can. (p. xxii)

Core black culture has traditionally esteemed good talk and profound dialogue. It has sustained a variety of forms of oral discourse from 'fending and proving—the art of clandestine theological exegesis practiced by slaves—to non-veracious forms, such as woofing and sounding. Black culture proceeds upon the premise that "the truth is the light," but it is equally aware that "the truth is a razor," so people were at pains to render meticulous narratives. . . .

Those who were gracious enough to donate life histories took it for granted that proper understanding of the material is indispensable, and many quite specifically alluded to the danger of outsiders imposing their own meaning on their life histories. (p. xxv)

The narratives in this book are loosely arranged so as to illuminate main themes, but certain narratives overlap chapter headings because that's how people talk and think. However spontaneous these narratives may seem, they are never ad hoc or slapdash. The thinking which informs this volume proceeds from men and women of ripe judgment. Almost all the people I listened to have examined their lives, the life and the nature of humanity. Their contributions were informed by that discernment which has enabled them to survive with dignity in a caste-like conquest environment. Their reflections and observations were offered as statements in which theme and development are manifest. . . .

From these narratives—these analyses of the heavens, nature and humanity—it is evident that black people are building theory on every conceivable level. An internally derived, representative impression of core black culture can serve as an anthropological link between private pain, indigenous communal expression and the national marketplace of issues and ideas. These people not only know the troubles they've seen, but have profound insight into the meaning of those vicissitudes.

Core black culture is more than ad hoc synchronic adaptive survival. Its values, systems of logic and world view are rooted in a lengthy peasant tradition and clandestine theology. It is the notion of sacrifice for kin, the belief in the natural sequence of cause and effect—"Don't nothin' go over the devil's back but don't bind him under the belly." It is a classical, restricted notion of the possible. It esteems the deed more than the wish, venerates the "natural man" over the sounding brass of machine technology and has the wit to know that "Everybody talking 'bout Heaven ain't going there." (p. xxvi)

The sense of nationhood among blacks is as old as our abhorrence of slavery. Black nationhood is not rooted in territoriality so much as it is in a profound belief in the fitness of core black culture and in the solidarity born of a transgenerational detestation of our subordination. The tradition which is so vital in shaping black culture was founded and fostered by those slave foreparents who are so widely respected for their refusal to accept, in their hearts, the Euro-American definition of them as things. (p. xxvii)

White people loom large in the narratives because racist subordination is the ramified goad that black people must deal with. Given the negative conditioning of the Afro-American historical experience, it is astounding that so many black people are prepared to deal with white people as individuals. . . .

Taken in the mass, white Americans are responsible for the inegalitarian social order which creates black power disadvantage. A hypothetical color-blind conqueror who reduced the whole earth to bondage would bulk large in the thinking of all of us. On both the personal and the societal level, it is cultural and natural nature for us to devote more than scant attention to the architects of so much of our misfortune. (p. xxviii)

The reputation for sound-mindedness and responsibility enjoyed by the people I worked with is founded on the readily apparent integrity of their lives. The thinking of the authors of this book is more than crude data. Proceeding from the bedrock of their respective personal experiences, they speak about the climate of communal coexistence in terms which are plainly analytical. . . .

To the extent that the prudent masses of black people are interested in anthropology at all, that preoccupation is almost exclusively concerned with rectification of the record. The record, that is, what anything actually *is,* is infinitely more important than the *intent* of anything. Black Americans are, of course, capable of the same kind of abstract thinking that is practiced by all human cultures, but sane people in a conquest environment are necessarily preoccupied with the realities of social existence. (p. xxix)

Principled survival in a familial and communal context, complicated by the iron inconsistencies of caste, is a preeminently analytical process. It demands a virtuosity at option sorting and general improvisation which places an often mortal premium on profound thought. It is this kind of indigenous analysis that I call "native anthropology." In the sense that Frantz Fanon used the term, "native" means subordinate, dark and poor. The consideration of perspectives, philosophies and systems of logic generated by populations which are usually expected to produce only unrefined data for the omniscient, powerful stranger to interpret could augment the vital elements of diversity and accuracy which are prime prerequisites of a truly post-colonial anthropology. (p. xxx)

> *John Langston Gwaltney, in his introduction to* Drylongso: A Self-Portrait of Black America, *edited by John Langston Gwaltney (copyright © 1980 by John Langston Gwaltney; reprinted by permission of Random House, Inc.), Random House, 1980, pp. xxii-xxx.*

LEONA GROSSMAN

It is possible to approach this review from several different viewpoints because [*The Thrice Shy: Cultural Accommodation to Blindness and Other Disasters in a Mexican Community*] reflects so many of the fundamental issues that face the behavioral and social sciences at this time. The fabric of traditionalism, the resistances to change, the intricate relationship between social institutions and personality, and the ecological explanation for social structures are some of the areas of speculation that this book raises. The author has chosen to define his stance through his subtitle. (p. 469)

The Thrice Shy gains in fascination as one becomes aware that the researcher himself is blind. His auditory initial encounter with the pueblo, the rhythms of the environment, the constant canine din that announces the stranger, and the specific sound patterns that reflect Chinantec culture are new experiences for the sighted reader. In an appendix there is a detailed discussion of his orientation to the field and a description of methodology. One fails to detect how blindness made any appreciable difference in his entering the field. As a matter of fact, it may have put the researcher at some advantage in creating rapport with the blind population of Yolox and their child-guides, who acted as willing informants.

The author uses the interesting device of interspersing his text with running excerpts from taped field interviews. There is vigor and beauty, ranging on the poetic, in these passages. He has selected them with great sensitivity to reflect the basic themes of his study: the hard realities of an uncertain world, the philosophical abandonment to fate, the grim resignation to abject poverty, the suspicion of anyone outside the family. (p. 470)

> *Leona Grossman, "Book Reviews: 'The Thrice Shy: Cultural Accommodation to Blindness and Other Di-*

sasters in a Mexican Community'," in Social Casework *(copyright © 1971 by Family Service Association of America), July, 1971, pp. 469-71.*

THOMAS CRUMP

[*The thrice shy: cultural accommodation to blindness and other disasters in a Mexican community*] is essentially a report of the author's fieldwork in San Pedro Yolox, a poor, isolated, inaccessible *municipio* in that part of the southern Mexican province of Oaxaca known as Chinantla. Any work of this kind involves somewhat intractable problems of presentation, terminology and style. As to presentation, the author must decide whether he is writing primarily for middle-American specialists, in which case he can take for granted not only such matters as the formal political organisation of rural Mexico or the general topography of the *sierras,* but also a wide acquaintance with the kindred literature. Here Professor Gwaltney is uncertain, and this is reflected in his terminology. His use, variously, of English and Spanish terms—county, *pueblo, cabecera,* village, *barrio*—is confusing to the reader, and his erratic references to the *ayuntamiento* as the 'Honorable Authority' remind one only of Pooh-Bah. At the same time it is nowhere made explicit that the first language of Yolox is Chinantee and no indigenous term is given for any local institution.

The individual adjustments within the local society required by the high incidence of blindness due to endemic *onchocerciasis,* a flyborne, filarial infection, which purports to be the main theme of this book, is the subject of a single chapter of 17 pages. The 'other disasters', poisonous snakes, thunderstorms, earthquakes, and so on, occur throughout middle America, and combine to give the people of Yolox a characteristically pessimistic view of life, in which the physical surroundings are 'very ugly'. Such theoretical analysis as there is runs aground in uneasy sociological jargon, characterised by neologisms such as 'microtranshumance'.

In contrast, the narrative style is pleasing, but it is more that of a travel book. . . . [Professor Gwaltney's] descriptions of Yolox and its people are sensitive, humble and evocative, so the real merit of his book is the feeling that it gives of an Indian community in middle-America. But with so little recognition of other studies in its field, and a treatment of its own material which, anthropologically speaking, is lightweight, it cannot expect a significant place in middle-American scholarship.

> *Thomas Crump, "Book Reviews: 'The Thrice Shy: Cultural Accommodation to Blindness and Other Disasters in a Mexican Community',"* in Man *(© Royal Anthropological Institute 1971), Vol. 6, No. 3, September, 1971, p. 514.*

GEORGE A. COLLIER

The image of the thrice shy, those negatively reinforced by unrelenting reality into fatalism and apprehensive resignation, is the theme by which Gwaltney, himself blind, characterizes contemporary life style in San Pedro Yolox, the only Chinantec community to receive monographic treatment in more than a decade. (pp. 37-8)

A sensitive analysis of the attitudes and life style associated with marginality fleshes out the study's topical structure. Endemic Onchocerciasis is not the only burden borne by the village; the scarcity and infertility of farmland result in both seasonal and catastrophic food shortage, and mortality from illness is high. To these the reaction is one of purposelessness and fatalism that accepts misfortune as divine retribution for social transgression or as simple bad luck.

[The assets of *The Thrice Shy*] are threefold: First Gwaltney lucidly reviews the meaning of *Chinantla*, confusing because of its non-coordinate geographic and ethnic reference. Second, his discussion of social institutions lends life to several features attributed to the Chinantec: non-territorial *barrio* groupings linked with *mayordomias*, the institutional age-grading of adolescents, the feuding and disputes over land tenure, and the mechanisms of civil government linked to obligatory public service. Most compelling is Gwaltney's sensitive treatment of villagers' attitudes, values, and philosophy from both normative and subjective expression in their statements, gossip, and actions.

The book's defects are traditional to Mesoamerican ethnography's narrowness of scope. Too much attention is given to San Pedro Yolox as an entity and too little to its place in broader economic and political fields. . . . [Gwaltney's] passing mention of villagers' continued contact with *émigrés*, of the explicit association of the national Onchocerciasis eradication program to educational and other public health agencies, and, indeed, of the ease of his own placement in San Pedro Yolox by prominent Mexican anthropologists are all suggestive of local-level and regional political linkages which are not discussed at all. Finally, submarginal economic conditions, malnutrition, and high rates of mortality and disability from disease are endemic to much of rural Mexico and do not offer problems of adaptation unique to this community, yet the adaptive mechanisms of other areas are ignored.

Despite these defects, *The Thrice Shy* is pleasantly written. Withal, it is a sensitive and welcome addition to the sparse literature on the Chinantec. (p. 38)

> George A. Collier, "'The Thrice Shy: Cultural Accommodation to Blindness and Other Disasters in a Mexican Community'," in American Anthropologist (copyright 1972 by the American Anthropological Association; reproduced by permission of the American Anthropological Association), Vol. 74, Nos. 1 & 2, 1972, pp. 37-8.

DAN CRYER

Inside *Drylongso,* which purports to be majestic oral history in the tradition of *Working* or *All God's Dangers,* there is an eloquent book trying to get out. Black people too ordinary to make headlines or get into trouble, people of stable jobs and stable families . . . have poured out their souls to black anthropologist John Langston Gwaltney. And they say a great deal that is worth hearing, mostly about the troubles they've seen. . . . (p. 36)

What prevents this earnest book from being a good one is Gwaltney's refusal to impose professional judgment on what his interview subjects tell him. Despite the book's title, Gwaltney will not let them be ordinary. He introduces each as a paragon of folk wisdom, as if suffering and survival have made their every utterance a gem of truth. He records silly comments as well as penetrating ones, giving equal weight to both. The interviews run on too long; clarity and focus are lost in a blizzard of words.

Perhaps the purpose of oral documentation of this sort is purely to record the beliefs of a people, truthful or otherwise. But their credibility is undermined by Gwaltney's florid introductions, which puff up the interviewees (and read like unintended parody of James Baldwin). . . . (pp. 36, 38)

What kind of veracity . . . should we ascribe to the outlandish notions found on page after page of *Drylongso*? Whites, it is said, "don't know how they feel about anything until they consult their leaders or a book" . . . ; all white children are spoiled; their minds are warped by seeing their parents in the nude; whites "teach their children to urinate in the same glass they drink out of." . . .

Gwaltney is trying to educate an America that still prefers to deny the reality of black culture and black rage. But his unwillingness to edit his material makes it harder to accept the unwelcome truths that his book undeniably contains. (p. 38)

> Dan Cryer, "Brief Reviews: 'Drylongso: A Self-Portrait of Black Americans'," in The New Republic (reprinted by permission of The New Republic; © 1980 The New Republic, Inc.), Vol. 182, No. 23, June 7, 1980, pp. 36, 38.

DARRYL PINCKNEY

In *Drylongso* John Langston Gwaltney . . . has created a remarkable work, one that illustrates the power of testimony, the importance of bearing witness. . . .

Drylongso is an attempt to correct some of the misinterpretations in conventional social science and to present a truth more profound than that conveyed by statistics. . . .

The people [interviewed] talk of their lives and of their feelings with a force more commonly associated with fiction. The drama of their condition and the intensity of their beliefs give a greater significance to the stories told. This is not a mere compilation of individual statements. What emerges in these fascinating narratives is that the problems of race in America have not been resolved at all. . . .

Something in the direct and brutal way people in this volume express their political opinions recalls the defiance and mocking tone of Malcolm X's speeches in *By Any Means Necessary*. . . .

Much of what is said in *Drylongso* will seem incomprehensible, overly bitter, and even racist to white readers. . . .

There are numerous, richly expressed examples of a kind of folk wisdom in this volume. . . . There is much emphasis placed on the positive features of black characteristics. However, there are some illuminating passages on the prejudices and provincialism among blacks regarding interracial relationships. . . .

Gwaltney, like Zora Neale Hurston and Oscar Lewis, has effaced himself, but it is his dedication to his subject matter that inspires this document. The people interviewed were his family, his friends, friends of friends, which may account for the rising, orotund quality of his prose. Perhaps there will be some criticism as to how representative the sentiments expressed in this book truly are. Nevertheless, *Drylongso* will stand as an imaginative and provocative rendering of the tragedy and comedy in the Afro-American vision of life.

> Darryl Pinckney, "'The Problems of Race in America Have Not Been Resolved at All'" (reprinted by

permission of The Village Voice *and the author; copyright © 1980), in* The Village Voice, *Vol. XXV, No. 33, August 13-19, 1980, p. 37.*

MEL WATKINS

Despite the grossly exploitative nature of television shows such as "Real People" and "That's Incredible," it's obvious that, beyond pandering to the public's fascination with *real*-life exotica, there is considerable merit in documenting ordinary people's behavior and their attitudes about their environment. Authors such as Studs Terkel and books such as "The Children of Sanchez" have demonstrated the literary as well as the sociological merit of such an approach. John Langston Gwaltney's **"Drylongso,"** despite some drawbacks, should take its place among the most illuminating of these books. . . .

[The] central question asked [the respondents] by Professor Gwaltney . . . was what in their opinions is the difference between black and white Americans. While often critical of blacks, most of those interviewed thought blacks were more honest and less "hateful" than whites. They felt that whites were more powerful ("they have the mojo and the sayso") but generally less moral than blacks.

Individual replies differ but, not unexpectedly, taken together they reveal a deep-seated contempt for and distrust of whites. (p. 534)

Revealing, amusing, authentically folksy and sometimes joltingly blunt—except for some novelistic depictions—**"Drylongso"** is probably the most expansive and realistic exposition of contemporary mainstream black attitudes yet published. Not that it doesn't have its flaws. Professor Gwaltney's introduction and his brief descriptions of the respondents are peppered with phrases that wed black dialect and sociological jargon in a most awkwardly flamboyant manner: a riot, for instance, becomes "federal suppression of a black urban insurgency." And the glossary contains entries such as, "two-cent slick—Pyrrhic perspicacity." But, even given these stylistic slips and the presence of a few narratives that never transcend narrowly subjective concerns, Professor Gwaltney has assembled an enlightening array of interviews. (p. 535)

Mel Watkins, "'Drylongso'," in The New York Times, *Section III (© 1980 by The New York Times Company; reprinted by permission), September 2, 1980 (and reprinted in* Books of the Times, *Vol. III, No. 11, 1980, pp. 534-35).*

DAVID ROEDIGER

Gwaltney divides [*Drylongso*] into eight chapters, each of which centers on a theme. Although such expansive reminiscences inevitably embrace many topics, the themes of nationalism, slavery, color distinctions, authority, welfare, sex, work, relations among the generations, and transcendence describe the central thrust of each chapter. A probing introduction binds the narratives together and presents the author's conviction that his research captures the essence of an Afro-American "core culture" characterized by a strong sense of communal responsibility, a spirit of toleration, an abiding conviviality, an awareness of past and present oppression, a confidence in the "fitness" of the black community, and rich language so unfamiliar to most readers that the book begins with a lengthy glossary. (p. 53)

The texts, in the tradition of black autobiography from the slave narratives to Nate Shaw's *All God's Dangers* to the writings of W.E.B. DuBois, James Baldwin, Paul Robeson, and Malcolm X—from ballads to the blues—are vivid, personal, poetic, and true.

Drylongso is easily read but full of hard lessons. Its contents argue against any blanket celebration of ghetto life. . . .

These testimonies tell of continuing exploitation, of a deep distrust of politics, of an ongoing conviction that blacks constitute a separate community, and of a persistent feeling that "the business of white men is to rule." That such sentiments are elegantly phrased by thoughtful men and women whom we come to know in all their full humanity only heightens their impact. (p. 54)

David Roediger, "Black Americans Talking," in The Progressive *(reprinted by permission from* The Progressive, *409 East Main Street, Madison, Wisconsin 53703; copyright 1980 by The Progressive, Inc.), Vol. 44, No. 11, November, 1980, pp. 53-4.*

Jürgen Habermas
1929-

Habermas is a German social philosopher and a leading representative of the Frankfurt school of neo-Marxist critical theory. One of his major accomplishments, presented in *Communication and the Evolution of Society* (1979), has been to supplement the Marxist theory of historical materialism with a theory of "communicative action." Habermas argues that Marxism has unduly emphasized the connection between the development of productive forces and the evolution of thought and behavioral norms. Normative structures, in his view, "have an internal history": they are rooted in our very capacity to communicate and have evolved independently of productive processes. Habermas reasons that our capacity to communicate presupposes our mastery of the ability to justify our utterances in terms of the norms of truth, sincerity, and moral correctness. From this base he outlines a theory of the progress of "moral-practical insight" and locates the source of human alienation in distorted communicative patterns. In *Toward a Rational Society* (1970) Habermas investigates the potential of student unrest to challenge the legitimating ideology of capitalist society; in *Knowledge and Human Interests* (1968) he attacks the philosophical premises of positivism and emphasizes the importance of the "self-reflection of the knowing subject"; and in *Legitimation Crisis* (1973) he synthesizes the thought of Talcott Parsons and Karl Marx in his exposition of the integrating and disintegrating forces extant in the functioning of the advanced-capitalist state. Although Habermas is often criticized as having a dense, opaque, and imprecise writing style which undermines his goal of non-distorted communication and human enlightenment, he is generally recognized as one of contemporary Europe's most important social thinkers.

Courtesy of Suhrkamp Verlag

Excerpt from *TOWARD A RATIONAL SOCIETY: STUDENT PROTEST, SCIENCE, AND POLITICS*

A new conflict zone, in place of the virtualized class antagonism and apart from the disparity conflicts at the margins of the system, can only emerge where advanced capitalist society has to immunize itself, by depoliticizing the masses of the population, against the questioning of its technocratic background ideology: in the public sphere administered through the mass media. For only here is it possible to buttress the concealment of the difference between progress in systems of purposive-rational action and emancipatory transformations of the institutional framework, between technical and practical problems. And it is necessary for the system to conceal this difference. Publicly administered definitions extend to *what* we want for our lives, but not to *how* we would like to live if we could find out, with regard to attainable potentials, how we *could* live.

Who will activate this conflict zone is hard to predict. Neither the old class antagonism nor the new type of underprivilege contains a protest potential whose origins make it tend toward the repoliticization of the desiccated public sphere. For the present, the only protest potential that gravitates toward the new conflict zone owing to identifiable interests is arising among certain groups of university, college, and high school students. Here we can make three observations:

1. Protesting students are a privileged group, which advances no interests that proceed immediately from its social situation or that could be satisfied in conformity with the system through an augmentation of social rewards. The first American studies of student activists conclude that they are predominantly not from upwardly mobile sections of the student body, but rather from sections with privileged status recruited from economically advantaged social strata.

2. For plausible reasons the legitimations offered by the political system do not seem convincing to this group. The welfare-state substitute program for decrepit bourgeois ideologies presupposes a certain status and achievement orientation. According to the studies cited, student activists are less privatistically oriented to professional careers and future families than other students. Their academic achievements, which tend to be above average, and their social origins do not promote a horizon of expectations determined by anticipated exigencies of the labor market. Active students, who relatively frequently are in the social sciences and humanities, tend to be immune to technocratic consciousness because, although for varying

motives, their primary experiences in their own intellectual work in neither case accord with the basic technocratic assumptions.

3. Among this group, conflict cannot break out because of the extent of the discipline and burdens imposed, but only because of their quality. Students are not fighting for a larger share of social rewards in the prevalent categories: income and leisure time. Instead, their protest is directed against the very category of reward itself. The few available data confirm the supposition that the protest of youth from bourgeois homes no longer coincides with the pattern of authority conflict typical of previous generations. Student activists tend to have parents who share their critical attitude. They have been brought up relatively frequently with more psychological understanding and according to more liberal educational principles than comparable inactive groups. Their socialization seems to have been achieved in subcultures freed from immediate economic compulsion, in which the traditions of bourgeois morality and their petit-bourgeois derivatives have lost their function. This means that training for switching over to value-orientations of purposive-rational action no longer includes fetishizing this form of action. These educational techniques make possible experiences and favor orientations that clash with the conserved life form of an economy of poverty. What can take shape on this basis is a lack of understanding in principle for the reproduction of virtues and sacrifices that have become superfluous—a lack of understanding why despite the advanced stage of technological development the life of the individual is still determined by the dictates of professional careers, the ethics of status competition, and by values of possessive individualism and available substitute gratifications: why the institutionalized struggle for existence, the discipline of alienated labor, and the eradication of sensuality and aesthetic gratification are perpetuated. To this sensibility the structural elimination of practical problems from a depoliticized public realm must become unbearable. However, it will give rise to a political force only if this sensibility comes into contact with a problem that the system cannot solve. For the future I see *one* such problem. The amount of social wealth produced by industrially advanced capitalism and the technical and organizational conditions under which this wealth is produced make it ever more difficult to link status assignment in an even subjectively convincing manner to the mechanism for the evaluation of individual achievement. In the long run therefore, student protest could permanently destroy this crumbling achievement-ideology, and thus bring down the already fragile legitimating basis of advanced capitalism, which rests only on depoliticization. (pp. 120-22)

Jürgen Habermas, "Technology and Science as 'Ideology'" (originally published under a different title in Technik und Wissenschaft als 'Ideologie', *Suhrkamp Verlag, 1968), in his* Toward a Rational Society: Student Protest, Science, and Politics, *translated by Jeremy J. Shapiro (translation copyright © 1970 by Beacon Press; reprinted by permission of Beacon Press), Beacon Press, 1970, pp. 81-122.*

Excerpt from *KNOWLEDGE AND HUMAN INTERESTS*

If we imagine the philosophical discussion of the modern period reconstructed as a judicial hearing, it would be deciding a single question: how is reliable knowledge (*Erkenntnis*) possible. The term "theory of knowledge," or "epistemology," was coined only in the 19th century; but the subject that it retrospectively denotes is the subject of modern philosophy in general, at least

until the threshold of the 19th century. The characteristic endeavor of both rationalist and empiricist thought was directed likewise at the metaphysical demarcation of the realm of objects and the logical and psychological justification of the validity of a natural science characterized by formalized language and experiment. Yet no matter how much modern physics, which combined so effectively the rigor of mathematical form with the amplitude of controlled experience, was the model for clear and distinct knowledge, modern science did not coincide with knowledge as such. In this period what characterized philosophy's position with regard to science was precisely that science was accorded its legitimate place only by unequivocally philosophical knowledge. Theories of knowledge did not limit themselves to the explication of scientific method—they did not merge with the philosophy of science.

This was still the case when modern metaphysics, which was already organized around the problem of possible knowledge, was itself subjected to doubt. Even Kant, through whose transcendental-logical (*transzendentallogisch*) perspective epistemology first became conscious of itself and thereby entered its own singular dimension, attributes to philosophy a sovereign role in relation to science. The critique of knowledge was still conceived in reference to a system of cognitive faculties that included practical reason and reflective judgment as naturally as critique itself, that is a theoretical reason that can dialectically ascertain not only its limits but also its own Idea. The comprehensive rationality of reason that becomes transparent to itself has not yet shrunk to a set of methodological principles.

It was with the elaboration of a metacritique that subjects the critique of knowledge to unyielding self-reflection, with Hegel's critique of Kant's transcendental-logical inquiry, that philosophy was finally brought to the paradoxical point of not altering its position with regard to science but abandoning it completely. Hence I should like to put forth the thesis that since Kant science has no longer been seriously comprehended by philosophy. Science can only by comprehended epistemologically, which means as *one* category of possible knowledge, as long as knowledge is not equated either effusively with the absolute knowledge of a great philosophy or blindly with the scientistic self-understanding of the actual business of research (*Forschung*). Both equations close off the dimension in which an epistemological concept of science can be formed—in which, therefore, science can be made comprehensible within the horizon of possible knowledge and legitimated. Compared with "absolute knowledge" scientific knowledge necessarily appears narrow-minded, and the only task remaining is then the critical dissolution of the boundaries of positive knowledge. On the other hand, where a concept of knowing that transcends the prevailing sciences is totally lacking, the critique of knowledge resigns itself to the function of a philosophy of science, which restricts itself to the pseudo-normative regulation of established research.

Philosophy's position with regard to science, which at one time could be designated with the name "theory of knowledge," has been undermined by the movement of philosophical thought itself. Philosophy was dislodged from this position by philosophy. From then on, the theory of knowledge had to be replaced by a methodology emptied of philosophical thought. For the philosophy of science that has emerged since the mid-nineteenth century as the heir of the theory of knowledge is methodology pursued with a scientistic self-understanding of the sciences. "Scientism" means science's belief in itself: that is, the conviction that we can no longer understand science as *one* form of possible knowledge, but rather must identify knowledge with science. The positivism that enters on the scene with Comte makes use of elements of both the empiricist and rationalist traditions in order to strengthen science's belief in its exclusive validity after the fact, instead of to reflect (*reflektieren*) on it, and to account for the structure of the sciences on the basis of this belief. Modern positivism has solved this task with remarkable subtlety and indisputable success.

Every discussion of the conditions of possible knowledge *today,* therefore, must begin from the position worked out by analytic philosophy of science. We cannot return immediately to the dimension of epistemological investigation. Positivism has unreflectively leaped over this dimension, which is why it generally has regressed behind the level of reflection represented by Kant's philosophy. To me it seems necessary to analyze the context in which positivist doctrines originated before we can take up the current discussion. For a future systematic investigation of the basis in human interests of scientific knowledge cannot abstractly restore epistemology. Instead it can only return to a dimension that was first opened up by Hegel through the radical self-critique of epistemology and then once again obstructed.

In opposition to Kant, Hegel was able to demonstrate the phenomenological self-reflection of knowledge as the necessary radicalization of the critique of reason. But he did not develop it logically, owing, I believe, to his preoccupation with the postulates of the philosophy of identity (*Identitätsphilosophie*). Marx, whose historical materialism really required the movement of Hegel's self-reflection, misunderstood his own conception and hence completed the disintegration of the theory of knowledge. Thus positivism could forget that the methodology of the sciences was intertwined with the objective self-formative process (*Bildungsprozess*) of the human species and erect the absolutism of pure methodology on the basis of the forgotten and repressed. (pp. 3-5)

Positivism marks the end of the theory of knowledge. In its place emerges the philosophy of science. Transcendental-logical inquiry into the conditions of possible knowledge aimed as well at explicating the meaning of knowledge as such. Positivism cuts off this inquiry, which it conceives as having become meaningless in virtue of the fact of the modern sciences. Knowledge is implicitly defined by the achievement of the sciences. Hence transcendental inquiry into the conditions of possible knowledge can be meaningfully pursued only in the form of methodological inquiry into the rules for the construction and corroboration of scientific theories. True, Kant had also tacitly adopted from contemporary physics a normative concept of science. Leaving aside the point that this assumption already contradicts the intention of an unprejudiced critique of knowledge, Kant took the form of modern science as the starting point of an investigation into the constitution of possible objects of causal-analytic knowledge. Positivism loses sight of this dimension, because it conceives of the fact of modern science not so much as eliminating the question of the meaning of knowledge in general but as prejudging its answer. Positivism certainly still expresses a philosophical position with regard to science, for the scientistic self-understanding of the sciences that it articulates does not coincide with science itself. But by making a dogma of the sciences' belief in themselves, positivism assumes the prohibitive function of protecting scientific inquiry from epistemological self-reflection. Positivism is philosophical only insofar as is necessary for the immunization of the sciences against philosophy. For methodology by itself does not suffice; it must also prove itself as epistemology or, better, as its legitimate and reliable executor. Positivism stands and falls with the principle of scientism, that is that the meaning of knowledge is defined by what the sciences do and can thus be adequately explicated through the methodological analysis of scientific procedures. Any epistemology that transcends the framework of methodology as such now succumbs to the same sentence of extravagance and meaninglessness that it once passed on metaphysics.

The replacement of epistemology by the philosophy of science is visible in that the knowing subject is no longer the system of reference. From Kant through Marx the subject of cognition was comprehended as consciousness, ego, mind, and species. Therefore problems of the validity of statements could be decided only with reference to a synthesis, no matter how much the concept of synthesis changed with that of the subject. Explicating the meaning of the validity of judgments or propositions was possible through recourse to the genesis of conditions that are not located in the same dimension as that of the contents of the judgments or propositions. Questions about the conditions of possible knowledge were answered with a universal genetic history. Each history reports on the deeds and destinies of a subject, even where it is through them that the subject is first formed. But the philosophy of science renounces inquiry into the knowing subject. It orients itself directly toward the sciences, which are given as systems of propositions and procedures, that is, as a complex of rules according to which theories are constructed and corroborated. For an epistemology restricted to methodology, the subjects who proceed according to these rules lose their significance. Their deeds and destinies belong at best to the psychology of the empirical persons to whom the subjects of knowledge have been reduced. The latter have no import for the immanent elucidation of the cognitive process. The obverse of this restriction is the development through which logic and mathematics become independent, self-sufficient formal sciences, so that henceforth the problems of their foundations are no longer discussed in connection with the problem of knowledge. As the methodology of research, the philosophy of science presupposes the validity of formal logic and mathematics. As autochthonous sciences these in turn are severed from the dimension in which the genesis of their fundamental operations can be made the subject of inquiry.

Once epistemology has been flattened out to methodology, it loses sight of the constitution of the objects of possible experience; in the same way, a formal science dissociated from transcendental reflection becomes blind to the genesis of rules for the combination of symbols. In Kantian terms, both ignore the synthetic achievements of the knowing subject. The positivistic attitude conceals the problems of world constitution. *The meaning of knowledge itself becomes irrational*—in the name of rigorous knowledge. In this way the naive idea that knowledge describes reality becomes prevalent. This is accompanied by the copy theory of truth, according to which the reversibly univocal correlation of statements and matters of fact must be understood as isomorphism. Until the present day this objectivism has remained the trademark of a philosophy of science that appeared on the scene with Comte's positivism. Transcendental-logical inquiry into the meaning of knowledge is replaced by positivistic inquiry into the meaning of ''facts'' whose connection is described by theoretical propositions. Ernst Mach radicalized this manner of posing the question and developed the philosophy of science on the basis of a doctrine of elements that is supposed to elucidate the facticity of facts as such.

Positivism so lastingly repressed older philosophical traditions and so effectively monopolized the self-understanding of the sciences that, given the self-abolition of the critique of knowledge by Hegel and Marx, the illusion of objectivism can no longer be dispelled by a return to Kant but only immanently— by forcing methodology to carry out a process of self-reflection in terms of its own problems. Objectivism deludes the sciences with the image of a self-subsistent world of facts structured in a lawlike manner; it thus conceals the a priori constitution of these facts. It can no longer be effectively overcome from without, from the position of a repurified epistemology, but only by a methodology that transcends its own boundaries. The beginnings of this sort of *self-reflection of the sciences* can be found in the works of Charles Sanders Peirce and Wilhelm Dilthey. The pragmatist and historicist critiques of meaning emerged from the contexts of the methodology of the natural and cultural sciences respectively. Nevertheless, Peirce (1839-1914) and Dilthey (1833-1911), contemporaries of Mach (1834-1916), were each in his way still so much under the spell of positivism, that in the end they do not quite escape from objectivism and cannot comprehend as such the foundation of the knowledge-constitutive interests toward which their thought moves. (pp. 67-9)

The reduction of theory of knowledge to philosophy of science first effected by early positivism was interrupted by a counter-tendency exemplified by Peirce and Dilthey. But the self-reflection of the natural and cultural sciences only interrupted the victorious march of positivism and did not stop it. Thus the knowledge-constitutive interests that had been discovered could be immediately misunderstood in a psychologizing manner and succumb to the critique of psychologism on whose basis modern positivism has been established in the form of logical empiricism and which has determined the scientistic self-understanding of the sciences up to the present.

The connection of knowledge and interest that we have discovered methodologically can be explained and preserved against misinterpretation through recourse to the concept of an *interest of reason,* developed by Kant and especially by Fichte. But the dimension of self-reflection cannot be rehabilitated as such by a mere return to the historical phase of the philosophy of reflection. Therefore the example of psychoanalysis will serve to demonstrate that this dimension reappears on the foundations laid by positivism. Freud developed an interpretive framework for disturbed and deviant self-formative processes that can be redirected into normal channels by therapeutically guided self-reflection. However, he viewed his theory precisely not as systematically generalized self-reflection, but as strict empirical science. Freud did not take methodological cognizance of the characteristic that distinguishes psychoanalysis from both the empirical-analytic and exclusively hermeneutic sciences. Instead, he attributed it to the peculiarity of analytic technique. Thus Freud's theory remains a scrap that the positivist logic of science since has vainly tried to digest and that the behaviorist research enterprise has tried in vain to integrate. But the hidden self-reflection that is the source of trouble cannot be conceptualized in this manner. Nietzsche is one of the few contemporaries who combine a sense for the import of methodological investigations with the ability to move light-footedly in the dimension of self-reflection. But Nietzsche, a dialectician of the Counter-Enlightenment, places the highest importance in using the form of self-reflection to deny the power of reflection. In so doing, he surrenders the knowledge-constitutive interests, of which he is well aware, to psychologism. (p. 189)

Jürgen Habermas, in his Knowledge and Human Interests, *translated by Jeremy J. Shapiro (translation copyright © 1971 by Beacon Press; reprinted by permission of Beacon Press; originally published as* Erkenntnis und Interesse, *Suhrkamp Verlag, 1968), Beacon Press, 1971, 356 p.*

Excerpt from *LEGITIMATION CRISIS*

The mode of functioning of the advanced-capitalist state can be adequately conceived neither through the model of an unconsciously acting executive organ of economic laws that are still spontaneously effective, nor through the model of an agent of the united monopoly capitalists that acts according to plan. Involved as it is in the production process, the state has altered the determinants of the realization process itself. On the basis of a class compromise, the administrative system gains a limited planning capacity, which can be used, within the framework of a formally democratic procurement of legitimation, for purposes of reactive crisis avoidance. In this situation, the collective-capitalist interest in system maintenance is in competition, on the one hand, with the contradictory interests of the individual capital groupings and, on the other, with the generalizable interests, oriented to use values, of various population groups. The crisis cycle, distributed over time and defused of its social consequences, is replaced by inflation and a permanent crisis in public finances. Whether this replacement phenomenon indicates a successful mastery of economic crisis or only its temporary displacement into the political system is an empirical question. In the final analysis, the answer depends on whether capital expended so as to be only indirectly productive does attain an increase in the productivity of labor, and on whether the distribution of the growth in productivity of labor, and on whether the distribution of the growth in productivity in line with functional requirements of the system is sufficient to guarantee mass loyalty and, simultaneously, keep the accumulation process moving.

The government budget is burdened with the common costs of a more-and-more-socialized production. It bears the costs of imperialistic market strategies and the costs of demand for unproductive commodities (armaments and space travel). It bears the infrastructural costs directly related to production (transportation and communication systems, scientific-technical progress, vocational training). It bears the costs of social consumption indirectly related to production (housing construction, transportation, health care, leisure, education, social security). It bears the costs of social welfare, especially unemployment. And, finally, it bears the externalized costs of environmental strain arising from private production. In the end, these expenditures have to be financed through taxes. The state apparatus is, therefore, faced simultaneously with two tasks. On the one hand, it is supposed to raise the requisite amount of taxes by skimming off profits and income and to use the available taxes so rationally that crisis-ridden disturbances of growth can be avoided. On the other hand, the selective raising of taxes, the discernible pattern of priorities in their use, and the administrative performances themselves must be so constituted that the need for legitimation can be satisfied as it arises. If the state fails in the former task, there is a deficit in administrative rationality. If it fails in the latter task, a deficit in legitimation results. . . .

A rationality deficit can arise because contradictory steering imperatives, which cause the unplanned, nature-like development of an anarchistic commodity production and its crisis-ridden growth, are then operative within the administrative system. Evidence for this modified-anarchy thesis has been supplied by Hirsch, among others, using examples from the administration of science. The thesis has a certain descriptive value, for it is possible to show that the authorities, with little informational and planning capacity and insufficient coordination among themselves, are dependent on the flow of information from their clients. They are thus unable to preserve the distance from them necessary for independent decisions. Individual sectors of the economy can, as it were, privatize parts of the public administration, thus displacing the competition between individual social interests into the state apparatus. The crisis theorem is based now on the reflection that growing socialization of production still adjusted to private ends brings with it unfulfillable—because paradoxical—demands on the state apparatus. On the one hand, the state is supposed to act as a collective capitalist. On the other hand, competing individual capitals cannot form or carry through a collective will as long as freedom of investment is not eliminated. Thus arise the mutually contradictory imperatives of expanding the planning capacity of the state with the aim of a collective-capitalist planning and, yet, blocking precisely this expansion, which would threaten the continued existence of capitalism. Thus the state apparatus vacillates between expected intervention and forced renunciation of intervention, between becoming independent of its clients in a way that threatens the system and subordinating itself to their particular interests. Rationality deficits are the unavoidable result of a snare of relations into which the advanced-capitalist state fumbles and in which its contradictory activities must become more and more muddled. (pp. 61-3)

> *Jürgen Habermas, in his* Legitimation Crisis, *translated by Thomas McCarthy (translation copyright © 1975 by Beacon Press; reprinted by permission of Beacon Press; originally published as* Legitimationsprobleme im Spätkapitalismus, *Suhrkamp Verlag, 1973), Beacon Press, 1975, 166 p.*

DONALD CAPPS

Knowledge and Human Interests may . . . be read as an illumination, through a historical excursion, of the philosophical poverty of contemporary scientific theory, both natural and social—the reading which Habermas himself invites. On the other hand, the book may also be read as an interpretation of the shift within philosophical thought from traditional epistemology to hermeneutics. In this regard the juxtaposition of Dilthey and Freud, especially the analyses of their complementary approaches to the interpretation of written and otherwise recorded texts, is most instructive. So for those interested in current discussions of the problem of hermeneutics, this book is virtually must reading. One might quarrel with certain aspects of Habermas' interpretations of the figures he treats. And the style is at times almost too leisurely, lending itself to unnecessary repetition and laboring of points. But such criticisms are rather pedestrian when applied to a work which so ably exemplifies Dilthey's recognition of the importance of "personal virtuosity" in the hermeneutic art. (p. 1143)

Donald Capps, "Hermeneutic Virtuosity," in The Christian Century *(copyright 1971 Christian Century Foundation; reprinted by permission from the September 29, 1971 issue of* The Christian Century*), Vol. 56, No. 6, September 29, 1971, pp. 1142-43.*

JERZY J. WIATR

In his discussion of student protest and the problems of university democratization [in *Toward a Rational Society*], Habermas starts with two assumptions. First, the students' protest is not directed primarily against the defects of the university, despite the fact that they "regard the campus as nothing but a training ground for the mobilization of troops." . . . The students' protest reflects a potential, and as yet not articulated, general discontent with the *status quo*. Second, the university system has become obsolete, conservative, and anachronistic; it has to be changed. Habermas advocates, therefore, the formation of "joint commissions in which professors confer unrestrictedly with instructors and students about all demands regarding university policy." . . . More important, Habermas criticizes the general pattern of Welfare State capitalism and points out that radical students question the very ideology of career achievement built into the system. He shows that the isolation of student protest results from the conservatism (and anti-Communism) which has prevailed in West-German social and political life during the past two decades. . . . Therefore, without closing his eyes to the mistakes and outrages of the student movement, he calls for deep understanding of the sources and consequences of the students' protest. Quite correctly, he takes a strong stand against those who concentrate on pointing to the extravagances of the radical students without looking into the problems that lie below the surface of the university disturbances. So far, so good. However, when Habermas presents his positive recommendations, he leaves the reader in the lurch. "The only way I see to bring about conscious structural change in a social system organized in an authoritarian welfare state," he says, "is radical reformism. What Marx called critical-revolutionary activity must take this form today. This means that we must promote reforms for clear and publicly discussed goals, even and especially if they have consequences that are incompatible with the mode of production of the established system." . . . If so, what is specifically Marxist in this position? And what is new about it? I am not at all sure that the controversial issue is reform of the system, even reform that is "incompatible with the mode of production of the established system." When class struggle has disappeared from the analysis—and Habermas' concept of technological change explains why it did—his call for radical reformism becomes vague or indistinguishable from what is being advocated by the progressive wing of the establishment.

The deepest revision of the traditional Marxist approach comes in Habermas' analysis of technological change in modern capitalism. He believes that "capitalist society [has] changed to the point where two key categories of Marxian theory, namely class struggle and ideology, can no longer be employed as they stand." . . . He thinks that state-regulated capitalism suspends class conflict, which therefore becomes latent. In my opinion, this view—similar to, albeit less extreme than, some of Marcuse's theories—puts too strong emphasis on phenomena that are characteristic for the present situation of a relative stabilization of capitalism. Moreover, class struggles in France in the late sixties demonstrated how misleading all theories of disappearing (or, to use Habermas' terminology, suspended) class conflicts are. As the result of these assumptions about the character of class conflicts in contemporary capitalism, Habermas' proposals for a new ideology are worded in "above-the-class" terms. "The reflection that the new ideology calls for must penetrate beyond the level of particular class interests to disclose the fundamental interests of mankind as such, engaged in the process of self-constitution." . . . Since most of the proposals are worded in such general terms, it is not at all easy to say whether or not one agrees with Habermas' critique of technocratic consciousness . . . and other aspects of contemporary capitalism. He certainly makes profound observations on the consequences of technological change in capitalist society. Far from being enthusiastic about it, he shows its deep impact on the social and political structure of the capitalist system. However, when it comes to perspectives for action, he reiterates the idea that the student movement is the only significant protest potential in advanced capitalist society—at least for the time being. I seriously doubt whether this over-emphasis on student potential does not obscure the real picture of the social forces, particularly class forces, that are at work in the present-day capitalist society, as they were decades ago. It may be unfair to cite very recent developments as evidence in this sort of argument, but is it not true that the American student protest in 1970 showed signs of decreased potential and *élan*? If so, how is it compatible with predictions that point to the students as the main, if not the only, revolutionary force in advanced capitalist society?

In concentrating on differences, I have not given equal weight to the strong elements of the book. There is no doubt in my mind that Habermas' essays belong to the best political and philosophical literature, that they are very well written, full of new ideas. If they provoke disagreement, they serve their purpose. (pp. 373-75)

> *Jerzy J. Wiatr, "Book Reviews: 'Toward a Rational Society'," in* Science and Society *(copyright 1971 by Science and Society, Incorporated), Vol. XXXV, No. 3, Fall, 1971, pp. 373-75.*

LEWIS A. COSER

If I understand [Jürgen Habermas aright in **Knowledge and Human Interests**], and this is by no means made easy by the involuted complexity of his exposition, he means to provide with this book the grounds for a thorough attack on the philosophical basis of positivism. Positivist thought, he contends, severs knowledge from interest, and erects a barrier between descriptive and prescriptive statements. In consequence, claims the author, "the conception of theory as a process of cultivation of the person has become apocryphal. Social theory is possible only as the self-reflection of the knowing subject." In self-reflection, knowledge for the sake of knowledge is wedded to the interest in achieving autonomy and responsibility; it is a movement of self-emancipation. Hence positivism, which excludes such reflection as illegitimate and defines the meaning of knowledge by what the sciences do, stands in the way of the emergence of a truly humane social theory. (pp. 507-08)

The last part [of **Knowledge and Human Interests**], which is mainly devoted to a discussion of Freud's mode of analysis, is the highpoint of the book. Faced with a thinker who formulated his thoughts with exemplary clarity, Habermas here abandons his murkiness of exposition and writes with cogency. Though Freud's mental equipment was rooted in an obsolescent physiological scientism, Habermas contends, Freud was led through his analytic practice to conceive of a mode of inter-

pretation that found its justification in a process of enlightenment of the patient. Psychoanalysis has therapeutic results only if the patient overcomes blocks to consciousness; the patient is aided through self-reflection to appropriate lost portions of his life history. The psychoanalyst, by making it possible for the patient to replace id drives by ego awareness, makes himself the instrument of the patient's knowledge. In a similar way, I presume, Habermas conceives of the social theorist of the future as an agent of human emancipation who will stimulate the awareness of the subjects he studies. His critical thrust will aim to enlighten humanity through self-conscious reflection about the burdens and distortions of capitalist culture.

Professor Habermas seems unaware of the fact that a contribution to the self-emancipation of mankind has loomed very large on the agenda of many of those "positivists" he so despises. But that, plainly, is another story. (pp. 508-09)

> *Lewis A. Coser, "Book Reviews: 'Knowledge and Human Interests'," in* Political Science Quarterly, *Vol. 87, No. 3, September, 1972, pp. 507-09.*

TRENT SCHROYER

Habermas's reconception of Marx implies that increasing restrictions on communicative interactions have sustained the material constraints placed on the development of the forces of production by capitalism. This is manifest in the progressive adjustment of all institutions to the innovating private economic sector. Capitalistic power and privilege is thus maintained on the one hand by the degree to which the truth of capitalist ideology is beyond doubt, and on the other the extent to which socialization processes are reified in a technological milieu. Habermas further points out the extent to which scientism has provided a model of institutionalized rationality which facilitates acceptance of the existing structure as legitimate.

Despite these advances, Habermas has not demonstrated their relation to Marx's critique of political economy. Is the communication theory, which achieves a normative foundation in the rational idealizations of human communication (thereby grounding a cultural Marxist critique in a manner different from other members of the Frankfurt School), presented by Habermas as the new conceptual basis for critical theory? An affirmative answer would imply that Marx's value theory has been superseded and that the economic criticisms of it are viable. Although Habermas claims that the quantitative formulations of Marx's work cannot express the surplus created by the unique potentials of a scientistic production system, he does not really refute Marx. (pp. 164-65)

Insofar as Habermas has replaced one normative foundation with another he has completed a moment of critical theory which has never been developed. Both Marx and Habermas have formulated normative foundations for one moment of the dialectic of social evolution. We are confronted therefore not by a sublation but by Habermas's dialectical completion of the basis by a critical theory of society. It is not either Marx or Habermas but Marx *and* Habermas that make possible a critical dialectical theory.

Another area in which Habermas could be said to transcend Marx is in his conception of the relation of science to social liberation. Habermas, and other cultural Marxists, have shown how the reproduction dynamic of late industrial society in general (i.e. both advanced capitalist and "socialist" societies) necessitates the scientific-technical strata that generates the new rationales and techniques which both stimulate economic growth and make further ideological control possible. These groups, while not constituting a necessary and sufficient "class" for the activation of change, are increasingly in a pivotal strategic position within the dynamic of late industrial society. Embedded in the social norms that bind the scientific community to its projects, and in their basic *telos* of the discovery of truth, there is a revolutionary potential for the recognition of domination. The need for rational discourse about the objectivistic and scientistic dogma of established science is legitimated by the norms of open scientific communication. The turning around of a small part of the scientific community to recognize the ideology of amorality and the pseudo-neutrality of state use of science would release new types of research and could create new alignments between science and society.

The consequences of the scientific community's consciousness of domination cannot be anticipated, but a possible result is the creation of models of liberated social development that would enable other institutions and/or groups to emancipate themselves from unnecessary domination. Habermas's work reveals that liberation from the contraints of block utilization of productive forces for social needs is not enough. Emancipatory struggle must be broader than Marx imagined and it must increasingly involve the self-liberation of persons from the "ego-identities" that are emerging from a scientized civilization. Social emancipation requires self-emancipation from the social costs of late industrial society, not only in the overproduction and underutilization of societal potentials, but also the transformation of life styles into so many types of adjustment to rationales which foreclose communicative interaction. Habermas's reconceptualization of the relation of critique to communicative practice adds to the interpretive scope of critical theory and to the realization of a theory of emancipation.

In the end, however, there is something very muted about Habermas's utopian ideal that suggests why Marx remains essential. The ideal speech situation is a purely formalistic concept. Whereas Marx conceived of the use-value concept (an essential component of the utopian ideal of communism) as a historical actuality, Habermas's formalistically derived ideal has no components that express historical relations. There is no part of this utopian ideal which can express the mode of realization that Marx's ideal of use-value did in its ideal of an "organic" relation between production, distribution, and the mediation between universal and individual needs. Habermas's ideal depends upon the community of scientists to measure and assess the historical specifics of distorted communication and this seems to imply that no other function need be performed by critical theorists. No doubt Habermas would use this difference in defense of his ideal by pointing to the objectivism of such notions as use-value and he would then be able to show the totally non-objectivistic nature of the ideal speech situation. There is a sense in which the utopian moment of critical theory requires a recognition of the emancipatory potentials of reconstructed histories. This doesn't entail the working out of detailed plans of strategic action but only the identification of the potentialities inherent in a given historical configuration and those aggregates of people who seem to be most directly associated with these objective possibilities. To put this another way, Habermas's concept of the dialectic between domination and emancipation stops short of an adequate realization of its utopian moment. While trying to maintain critique strictly within the limits of reason, Habermas also fails to include the needs of people who are able to see the possibility of enlightenment only in everyday activity.

Habermas's theory of enlightenment is therefore too Hegelian. Like Hegel, he makes the assumption that the logic of historical development is moving toward greater actualization of freedom, or non-repressive communication. Human consciousness is extended as the scope of world history widens; like Hegel the development of human enlightenment moves ever forward. Perhaps Habermas's passion for reason is here, like Hegel's, the result of a life of reason that sees all existence as the manifestation of a comprehensive system.

Until we have completed a reconstruction of the social evolution of mankind along the lines suggested by Habermas's theory of cognitive interests, we are still dependent upon the most comprehensive theory of the historical tendencies that we have—that of Karl Marx. Perhaps this will remain so. But it does not stop us from reconstructing the objectivistic aspects of Marx's work along the lines established by Habermas's metatheory. (pp. 165-68)

> *Trent Schroyer, "A Reflexive Philosophy of Critical Theory," in his* The Critique of Domination: The Origins and Development of Critical Theory *(reprinted by permission of George Braziller, Inc., Publishers; copyright © 1973 by Trent Schroyer), Braziller, 1973, pp. 105-73.**

DUNCAN MacRAE, JR.

[*Theory and Practice*] centers on several dilemmas in the relation between theory and practice. Theory connotes abstract and detached knowledge or discourse, not aimed at particular applications. Practice embraces a diversity of activities, from social engineering to institution building, and from revolution to particular choices among actions. Some major dilemmas follow:

1. How does knowledge depend on action? The engineering model (Aristotle's *techne* as opposed to his *praxis*) conceives of knowledge as developed in monologue rather than dialogue, independently of discourse or action, and then applied. Conversely, Hegel's observation that "the owl of Minerva flies only at dusk" implies that understanding emerges only after the event. A Marxian model, however, sees certain kinds of practical knowledge as emerging only in the course of action.

2. Is the calculated prediction of human behavior consistent with virtue and enlightenment? Habermas concludes with a warning of "an exclusively technical civilization, . . . devoid of the interconnection between theory and praxis . . . [and] threatened by the splitting of its consciousness, and by the splitting of human beings into two classes—the social engineers and the inmates of closed institutions." . . . Following Leo Strauss, he sees the political philosophies of Machiavelli, Hobbes, and Thomas More as calculating means to ends in the manner of modern social science, but departing from the cultivation of virtue characteristic of the classical Greek *polis*. Virtue was encouraged through a "discursive formation of the will" which Habermas also sees as characteristic of earlier bourgeois democracy, but undermined or "scientized" in later capitalist society through the action of the mass media. Psychoanalysis exemplifies an asymmetrical communication, which can be replaced only afterward by reciprocal enlightened discourse.

3. Through what means can enlightened public opinion be formed? In a Marxist perspective, Habermas sees enlightenment taking place in the working class, which then "virtually" represents the bourgeoisie who are themselves incapable of understanding. But the general principle of virtual represen-

tation might also be claimed by governments issued from revolution, in their attitudes toward "capitalist remnants"—even though Habermas disavows Stalinism. Hegel is cited, . . . though not approvingly, as favoring disproportionate representation for higher strata. But Habermas continually stresses dialogue, discourse, and reciprocity rather than manipulation. Some of the less penetrable prose on Hegel even seems reminiscent of George H. Mead, when a relationship between a "generalized other" and the formation of universal law of norms is established.

Habermas's examples are drawn from major historical changes such as the French Revolution. For example, he compares the role of natural law as a principle of justification in the French and American revolutions. He notes that for the French natural law provided a basis for constructing entirely anew on abstract principles, while for the Americans it was simply Paine's "common sense" and the assertion of rights existing since time immemorial in Britain. This contrast leads Habermas to contrast the arbitrary base of Rousseau's social contract with the claims of truth by earlier advocates of natural law. He sees contemporary positivistic discourse, however, as completely reducing the basis of decisions to arbitrary and unreasoned claims.

Although the scope of Habermas's erudition is impressive, it is paradoxical that he does not deal in this book with concrete contemporary examples. "Practice" in a literal sense is not restricted to choices of regime or of revolution. The general themes of the book might well be developed in connection with applied social research in urban or welfare policy, the use of social indicators, evaluation, and other more pedestrian problems. For even if an existing social order should be fundamentally deficient, and if it should be replaced by another, these dilemmas would confront the alternative order. It would be odd if we could direct our practical intelligence only to major changes and not to minor ones. (pp. 1078-79)

> Duncan MacRae, Jr., "Book Reviews: 'Theory and Practice'," in The American Journal of Sociology (reprinted by permission of The University of Chicago Press; © 1975 by The University of Chicago), Vol. 80, No. 4, January, 1975, pp. 1078-79.

NEIL J. SMELSER

The largest part of [*Theory and Practice*] is a number of wide-ranging historical investigations of various philosophers, whose thought is interpreted within the framework of "critical sociology" developed by Habermas and others associated with the Frankfurt school in the past several decades. . . .

Early in the book Habermas makes a distinction which is fundamental to his effort to mediate theory and praxis. He distinguishes among (1) "critical theorems" of knowledge, which are assessed according to the canons of scientific inquiry; (2) "processes of enlightenment," which involve the insightful grasp of knowledge in relation to the real experience of human groups; and (3) "the selection of appropriate strategies, the solution of tactical questions, and the conduct of the political struggle." These three aspects of experience stand in intimate relation to one another. Indeed, right action—the proper relation between theory and praxis—is defined as "the experience of an emancipation by means of critical insight into relationships of power, the objectivity of which has as its source solely that the relationships have not been seen through." Thus right action involves knowledge, enlightenment, and prudent decisions. The three aspects, however, cannot appropriately be

reduced to or isolated from one another. Most of Habermas' criticisms of past and present systems of thought, in fact, note that they have committed one or the other of these errors.

Though Habermas regards Marx's diagnosis of bourgeois capitalism as outdated by modern social and political trends, his line of analysis is Marxist in the senses that his focus is on removing "externally imposed compulsion," justified by dogmatic ideologies; and that compulsions are overcome by purposive group actions based on true consciousness or enlightenment. He is also much influenced by the psychoanalytic principles that insight is gained by the breakdown of "systematically distorted communication" and that this insight leads to the "emancipation from unrecognized dependencies." Habermas points to the parallels between the relation of "theory to therapy" in Freudian thought and the relation between "theory and praxis" in Marxist thought.

Habermas finds most contemporary sociology lacking on several grounds. Some of its categories—for example, the concept of role—while precise, cannot comprehend the variability of the historical process. More important, he argues that sociologists, wrongly committed to a posture of "value-neutrality," are blind to the sociopolitical consequences of their activity, in particular to the fact that sociology is becoming "an applied science in the service of administration." These deficiencies may be overcome only if sociologists become critical, strive for insights about their own role in the social process, and put an end to their fictional disembodiment from society. My feeling is that Habermas underestimates the extent of critical thinking among contemporary sociologists. Many are deeply concerned to enlighten about social evils and many reflect continuously on their own relation to society, though perhaps not in the ways Habermas has in mind.

One point of pervasive uneasiness I feel in reading Habermas' critical sociology is that important underlying assumptions of that sociology themselves appear to remain uncriticized. I have in mind his conviction that the fundamental social evils in the world are human dependencies, and his belief in the potency of critical enlightenment and right action to overcome those evils.

> Neil J. Smelser, "Book Reviews: 'Theory and Practice'," in Social Forces (copyright © 1975, Social Forces), Vol. 53, No. 4, June, 1975, p. 650.

Z. BAUMAN

[*Legitimation Crisis*] has few, if any, equals among sociological writings of the last decade or two. No other book . . . has set for itself tasks of similar dimensions: to bring together an exhaustive phenomenological analysis of the conditions of social and systemic integration in general, and the empirical (though highly generalised) description of the historically specific, modern society.

Perhaps the most unlikely bridge to be built in *Legitimation Crisis* is between Marx and Parsons, long considered as irreconcilable poles of sociological thinking. Marxian theory has been adopted by modern sociology as, above all, an explication of conflict and structural crisis. Parsons's sociology has been cast into the mould of an equally one-sided theory of systemic stability and integration. Their contingent, rather than essential, aspects have been thereby magnified out of all proportion, and the two sociologies, or rather their popular images, seemed hopelessly out of touch with each other. Thanks to Habermas's novel approach, one can see how the two theories can actually engage in a meaningful dialogue. (p. 147)

Reading carefully through Habermas's rather involved argument one can conclude that the difference between the organisation principles of, respectively, liberal-capitalist and post-modern societies, boils down to the changing role of state administration. In the liberal-capitalist system, the principle of organisation is "the relationship of wage labour and capital"; and the market, through which the integration of the system as a whole is being achieved, takes over, as well, socially integrative tasks. Ideology of rational-natural law and utilitarianism, which supplies the liberal-capitalist society with its legitimation, "is itself built into the economic basis—namely, the exchange of equivalents." Hence the direct link between human motivations and the system integration; the steering problems manifest themselves, in the circumstances, in minor battles and major wars between classes; above all, in wage labour questioning the legitimacy of capitalist rule.

Not so in the post-modern society. Here, "the state actually replaces the market mechanism." Steering becomes an administrative problem; hence the contradictions of the systemic imperatives take on a directly political form; this time, however, not the form of class warfare. With evident, though unacknowledged, help from Deutsch and Easton, Habermas classifies crises which can arise in the new situation as those of output (administration, confronted with conflicting demands, is incapable of taking the rational course) and input (administration, forced to follow the imperatives of the system, fails to secure the required level of mass loyalty). It seems that the administration can choose between the devil and the deep blue sea, but can hardly avoid both. Still, the management of society is now seen as a conscious action and, therefore, the avoidance of crises "is thematised as the goal of action." With the new organisational principle in operation, imperatives of the system can assert themselves only through actions of the members of administration. So the provision of mass loyalty becomes the major worry of the administration, and crises, if they break through to the surface of political events, take on the form of the inefficacy of legitimation and correlated motivation.

Legitimation Crisis is, unlike previous works by the same author, multi-thematic; the many threads are woven in a delicate tissue whose subtle pattern might be easily impaired by rash treatment. The book requires diligent study. One hopes that it will become a focus of prolonged discussion, in the course of which foundations of a unified, empirically grounded theory of the modern western society can be laid. In this context, however, it is a pity that the phenomenological analysis of system imperatives is not the only inspiration Habermas derived from Parsons. The other one is his new tendency to couch his propositions in unnecessarily complex, hermetically sealed jargon. Enlightenment and emancipation through a discourse in which "there are only participants" have been the major concerns of Habermas. But this book, whatever its potential importance for the self-understanding, and therefore emancipation, of modern man, is a failure as an overture to a discourse reaching beyond the inner circle of pundits. (pp. 147-48)

> Z. Bauman, "Marx to Parsons" (© New Society; reprinted by permission of the author), in New Society, Vol. 38, No. 733, October 21, 1976, pp. 147-48.

LEWIS COSER

Habermas sees his work as grounded in a tradition of critical enlightenment. Freudian psychoanalysis serves him as an ex-ample. He is not particularly interested in Freud's substantive theorizing, but believes that the Freudian approach yields most from it when it is conceived as a method to overcome "systematically distorted communication" through a critical dialogue between analyst and analysand. Both collaborate to arrive at a reconstruction that is free from distortion of the patient's life history. Only if and when this reconstruction has been consensually validated, when the patient has appropriated the undistorted view of himself that emerges from the dialogue, has enlightenment been reached.

Taking his cue from the structure of psychoanalytical therapy, Habermas then contends, more generally, that a great deal of current and past human misery and alienation has its roots in distorted communicative patterns. Hence, he argues in the first part of [*Communication and the Evolution of Society*], what is needed is the development of "universal pragmatics," able to identify and to reconstruct the universal conditions of possible understanding between human actors. Undistorted truth between human actors can only be attaned when not only language but also speech is purged of distorting elements so that fully communicative competence can be attained. The notion of communicative competence closely parallels Chomsky's notion of linguistic competence. But while Chomsky wants to explain the skills of each particular language user, Habermas is concerned with the skills that underlie the dialogical utterances of interacting speakers. As Norbert Wiener once put it (with much greater clarity than Habermas), "Speech is a joint game by the talker and listener, against the forces of confusion." Habermas assumes, counterfactually, an ideal speech situation in which complete understanding has been achieved, and uses this as a baseline against which barriers to communicative patterns can be measured. His is a consensus theory of truth which has, at the same time, a critical edge in as far as it rejects all elements, such as coercion and ideological distortion, which interfere in the rational pursuit of dialogical communication.

In later portions of this volume, Habermas supplements his theory of communicative distortions and their overcoming by borrowing from Piaget and his Harvard disciple Kohlberg a theory of the ontogenetic stages of moral development. Here he argues that the ability to make autonomous moral judgments, far from being "given," arises only in the last stage of a person's moral development which starts with an egocentric view, in the early years, and proceeds by several stages, through communicative interactions with others, to reach a flexible, autonomous and post-conventional maturity. Pushing beyond Piaget and Kohlberg, Habermas then proceeds to argue that a fully mature and autonomous ego development can only be attained in an emancipated society of the future that does away with blocked communications and distorted forms of human interaction.

The next two chapters of the work constitute an ambitious attempt to develop a novel theory of human evolution. This theory is meant to supplement historical materialism, but seems, in fact, largely to supplant it. Stressing parallels between individual (ontogenetic) development and the evolution of the human race, Habermas argues that Marxism, by putting undue emphasis on the development of productive forces and productive relations, has failed to take into account the evolutionary maturation of structures of thought and of norms of behavior. "I am convinced," he writes, "that normative structures do not simply follow the path of development of productive processes . . . but have an internal history." Though aware of the pitfalls that have attended previous attempts to draw parallels between individual and social development, Habermas contends nevertheless that it is possible to find "homologous structures of consciousness" in the history of the individual and of the species. Social evolution is conceived as a learning process which involves both technical/cognitive and moral/practical aspects, the stages of which can be described structurally, and ordered in a developmental logic. To simplify: the human race on the road to emancipation follows roughly the stages that Piaget and Kohlberg describe for the individual.

In assessing Habermas's contribution as a whole, one is forced to comment on his extremely involved, turgid, and imprecise style. The elephantine heaviness of his presentation and the fogginess of his argumentation owe nothing to the great expository tradition of Marx, or of Heine and Nietzsche. Instead, this author, who puts such store in the emancipatory potential of language, is given to an academic jargon cultivated in the German academy which has shielded the arcana of the professoriat from the instrusive gaze of the vulgar. Habermas writes about enlightenment in a most unenlightening manner.

As to the substance of his thought, definitive judgments would be premature. Habermas has stressed that his present writings are only the first fruits of a much larger intellectual program for the future. Much of what he has to say seems at present less than persuasive. The parallels between ontogeny and phylogeny, for example, run counter to the findings of most specialized scholars in this area. Nevertheless, what makes Habermas so appealing is his continued attention to the "big questions" that most academics eschew in their quest for narrow, but fully documented, results. One can only wish that he might manage in the future to demolish the formidable linguistic barriers that he has erected between his discourse and his audience, so that he can contribute to that enlightenment he so ardently wishes to provide. In any case, nothing that he writes should go unattended. His is a significant voice that needs to be listened to, even if it sometimes seems to speak in riddles. (pp. 630-32)

> Lewis Coser, "The Uses of Language," in Partisan Review (copyright © 1980 by Partisan Review, Inc.), Vol. XLVII, No. 4, 1980, pp. 630-32.

THOMAS HEENEY

Habermas' first move [in *Communication and the Evolution of Society*] is an analytical *deconstruction*: He takes the theory of historical materialism apart in order to rebuild it in a more satisfactory way. His reconstruction of the received tradition of terms and critical insights is at once a clarification and a critique of the heritage of Marxian dialectical analysis of our material conditions as historical beings. Habermas makes this deconstruction or interpretation of historical materialism appear unproblematic, through selective citations and by continually deferring for another time his argument on key theoretical *topoi*. In fact, his "reading" of historical materialism is quite controversial. But even more interesting is his apparent shift in emphasis away from political and social theory, especially the notions of the "public sphere" and the "bourgeois public," discussed in previous works, and toward a "developmental" and "reconstructive" communication theory of society. The categories used to undertake this reconstruction are brilliantly, though only provisionally, integrated concepts and assumptions borrowed from the Frankfurt legacy of critical social theory, psychoanalysis, and cognitive-developmental psychology.

Habermas is undeniably a most difficult thinker to read. Even fellow members of the Frankfurt school, such as Leo Lowenthal and the late Herbert Marcuse, have confided to me that they find his work "very difficult." Thinkers such as this provide respectable work for a small cadre of interpreters. And the irony, which is not lost on the members of the school themselves, is that the intellectual industry of the Frankfurt school interpreters has almost made a popular commodity of the very works that critique the tendency in advanced capitalism to turn everything into neatly packaged and easily consumable products.

> Thomas Heeney, "Book Reviews: 'Communication and the Evolution of Society'," in The Quarterly Journal of Speech (copyright 1980 by the Speech Communication Association), Vol. 66, No. 3, October, 1980, p. 347.

MICHAEL ROSEN

Communication and the Evolution of Society is particularly significant . . . for in it Habermas returns to the topics dealt with in *Knowledge and Human Interests,* his major book of the 1960s. It is now possible to see how he has met the difficulties facing that earlier work.

There were three main elements in the account of philosophy and social theory developed in *Knowledge and Human Interests*. First, that philosophy is concerned with the recovery of meanings—social meaning that has become concealed from the society that generated it. Second, that the process of bringing these meanings to light has an emancipatory moral and political dimension. And, third, that this provides the key to the understanding of social development; societies represent a series of stages in a movement towards autonomy and self-awareness.

If the picture which these elements form—of a society coming to know itself by recovering the traces of its own activity—seems thoroughly Hegelian, then this is no accident; Hegel has always been the absent presence (as they used to say in Paris) informing Habermas's work. But, equally, Habermas has always claimed to be a *materialist*. This commits him to achieving any Hegelian results he may want by unquestionably non-Hegelian means. He can make use of none of the Idealist doctrines about self-positing *Geist* or Absolute Knowledge which frame Hegel's own treatment of history.

This requirement is at the root of *Knowledge and Human Interests*'s difficulties. For, corresponding to each of the book's three main elements, Habermas invokes concepts derived from Hegel: the meaning which is to be repossessed results, he says, from a process of *synthesis;* it is recovered by *reflection;* and the social development which incorporates it is a *Bildungsprozess* (a "self-formative process"). The challenge was, then, to demonstrate that these concepts could be made to function independently, without reliance on their original Idealist context. . . .

It is most striking, therefore, that the Idealist terminology has been entirely eliminated from *Communication and the Evolution of Society*. Philosophy still aims at the recuperation of lost meaning, but the doctrine of meaning which the book draws on has been purged of any resonances of Hegelian *Geist*. Society Habermas now defines as a "symbolically prestructured segment of reality", open to understanding because it has been "produced according to rules". Philosophical reconstruction is to "explicate the meaning of a symbolic formation in terms of the rules according to which the author must have brought it forth''.

Evidently, this equation of meaning with production according to rules is crucial. It guarantees that—in principle, at least—we can know what we have made. Yet it seems to me a mistaken, even ideological, thesis and, regrettably, Habermas gives no argument in its support. The omission is the more notable for the fact that precisely the opposite claim is so deeply rooted in the German tradition. German philosophy, perennially in revolt against "formalism", attached the highest importance to art and to the poetic use of language just because these were activities, indisputably significant, which escaped the compass of formal systems of rules.

I am also unconvinced by the claims that Habermas makes regarding specifically moral rules, the "universal presuppositions of communication" which form "the core of a universal ethics of speech". Habermas argues that, starting from the commitment which every speaker enters into by the fact of engaging in discourse, we can arrive at general principles to test the validity of norms of action. At the highest level, the speaker is committed to a principle which acknowledges the equal claims of each individual's true needs.

Here again the argument seems incomplete. What remains to be shown is that this principle concerning true needs, even if we do adopt it, is sufficiently specific to provide guidance in cases of moral perplexity. . . . Unless Habermas can prove that the principle of needs is precise enough to be able to resolve moral dilemmas, he is open to the classic objection to universal moral principles: we reject them, not because we would endorse the contrary principle, but because their formality makes them empty.

These then are two reasons why I follow *Communication and the Evolution of Society*'s rich philosophical, psychological and sociological discussion with scepticism as well as admiration. But the serious-mindedness with which Habermas elaborates his programme is beyond praise. His tenacity (and, it must be admitted, his tortuous prose) remind one inevitably of Kant. It was Kant who wrote that to be *konsequent* was "the highest obligation of a philosopher". Habermas epitomizes this commitment.

Michael Rosen, "The Recuperation of Meaning," in The Times Literary Supplement *(© Times Newspapers Ltd. (London) 1980; reproduced from* The Times Literary Supplement *by permission), No. 4052, November 28, 1980, p. 1362.*

ROGER S. GOTTLIEB

[*Legitimation Crisis*] fails to provide any serious account of how criticisms of the existing social structure are to be made effective in changing that structure. (p. 290)

Habermas fails to clarify how [the universal presupposition of an ideal speech situation] functions in a society marked by hierarchy, domination, and 'systematically distorted communication.' Do people actually hold this presupposition? Then how does class society continue to exist? Is it an intellectual construct in the struggle with positivism, part of the attempt to show that social norms are subject to rational justification? Then how is it, any more than other such constructs, to be made operative in social life? It is this dilemma which Habermas fails to confront.

Also, it should be noted that Habermas's position here—that the 'crisis' is not an economic breakdown but a wholesale rejection of the legitimacy of the ruling institutions—is similar to much of the 'classical' Marxism which he often takes as his enemy. Whatever disputes there might be about Marx's own position, Marxists as different as Lenin, Luxemburg, Trotsky, and Gramsci all denied that economic crises lead automatically or unproblematically to socialist revolutions. But they, as opposed to Habermas, emphasized the need for revolutionary struggle to make good the realizations of critical reflection.

Habermas's stress on legitimation also ignores a very basic fact: people can believe that the major institutions of society are illegitimate and still not rebel. A legitimation crisis must be combined with a sense of confidence, with a willingness to act, and with political organization. If this combination does not exist, then a widespread rejection of the legitimacy of the ruling institutions can, as in the contemporary United States, be combined with equally widespread cynicism, passivity, and despair. (pp. 291-92)

[In *Communication and the Evolution of Society*] Habermas fails to address directly what might be taken as the central claim of traditional historical materialism: that an analysis of the mode of production abstracted from normative structures can provide the key for an explanation of the development of society as a whole. Until Habermas relates his 'reconstruction' of historical materialism to this claim, it will be unclear whether he is asserting that normative structures are causally autonomous.

I suspect that Habermas seeks to replace historical materialism, considered as a theory of history, with a transcendental logical developmental schema which functions normatively rather than predictively. In doing so, he has retreated from the ambitions of the original theory. Now this 'Hegelian turn' of replacing social history with transcendentally justified schemas, turning a (supposed) science or social history into a (supposed) science of norms, may be justified by the failure of the most crucial of Marxism's predictions: that the working class would overthrow advanced capitalism. But Habermas is not as clear as he might be about the transformation he has effected. After this transformation, historical materialism no longer offers good grounds for believing that certain historical developments will occur. Rather, our knowledge is limited to knowing which developments would be good ones if they did occur.

This rich volume . . . holds insights for anyone concerned with linguistics, social theory, ethics, or political philosophy. It once again enables the reader to confront a synoptic view which both draws on diverse sources (e.g., Austin, Searle, Apel, Piaget, Marx, Godelier, Offe, Kohlberg) and remains uniquely that of Habermas. Despite my admiration for the power and intelligence of Habermas's work, I must conclude with two more brief critical comments.

First, there is an unfortunate abstractness in Habermas's fairly rigid distinction between communicative action (oriented toward understanding) and strategic action (oriented toward control of other people). He initially characterizes communicative action as seeking "reciprocal understanding, shared knowledge, mutual trust, and accord . . ." . . . , but later claims such action is successful if the hearer is simply able to "understand and accept the content uttered by the speaker in the sense indicated (e.g., as a promise, assertion, suggestion) . . . ." . . . The second description is much weaker than the first, and would seem to include, for example, a master giving orders to a slave. Habermas does not seem to realize that communicative action can take place within a broader scheme of strategic action—that we may seek understanding in order to deceive or oppress, as well as to reach "mutual trust and accord." Without a clarification of this point, it is hard to see how the norms presupposed by communication function as a foundation for ethical principles and social norms.

Second, Habermas's 'Hegelian turn' toward using quasi-transcendental principles derived from a theory of communicative action to justify a theory of progressive stages of human development is subject to some of the same criticisms which Kierkegaard and Marx made of Hegel. Habermas for the most part ignores the antirationalist arguments of the existentialist tradition. It is questionable whether an account of sincerity, goodness, and justice can be adequate if it ignores issues of existential choice, authenticity, and self-deception raised by philosophers such as Kierkegaard and Sartre. In Kierkegaard's words, we may again be confronted by a somewhat 'absent-minded' thinker who has included everything within his system but an account of his—or any other individual's—subjective relation to it. Finally, Habermas's model of human development as a learning process tends to obscure the class relations which institutionalize opposition to the growth of 'reasoned argument.' His tendency to turn social problems into problems of deficient cognition (albeit cognition in the realm of 'moral-practical' knowledge) suggests that he has abandoned, rather than reformed, reconstituted, or grounded, the Marxist tradition of which he was originally a part. (pp. 294-95)

Roger S. Gottlieb, "The Contemporary Critical Theory of Jürgen Habermas," in Ethics *(reprinted by permission of The University of Chicago Press), Vol. 91, No. 2, January, 1981, pp. 281-95.*

DIETER MISGELD

[In *Communication and the Evolution of Society* Jürgen Habermas makes it] clear that he has a program of social science *research* in mind. . . . Habermas is true to his early interest in reconstructing Marxian social theory as a systematic theory of history with practical intent that is "empirically falsifiable." (p. 585)

[In the first three chapters] Habermas takes bold steps toward reformulating the project of a critical social theory by (a) making a case for communicative action, the "type of action aimed at reaching understanding" . . . as the fundamental form of social action, and (b) proposing the reconstruction of normative structures and of their institutional representations. This proposal takes its bearings from the study of the development of moral reasoning structures in the child (Piaget, Kohlberg). It follows from this that critical social theory aims at the elaboration of a theoretical model for the explanation of rationality structures in society. It uses developmental studies of the cognitive/moral features of the socialization of individuals as indicating the possibility of these explanations.

For Habermas, critical social theory becomes a "reconstructionist" science. The latter is neither purely explanatory in the sense of a causally explanatory empirical science nor interpretive, as the "hermeneutic" orientation sometimes claimed by the author might suggest. A "reconstructionist" science identifies and describes fundamental systems of rules by relying

on interpretively generated or "intuitively" preunderstood data. It is applied to the reconstruction of the competence to raise validity claims (communicative competence) in the employment of speech acts (Habermas calls this reconstruction "universal pragmatics"). It is also applied to the reconstruction of structures of moral reasoning and of the corresponding identity formations of the person as developmental processes. In the latter case, existing theories provide "formal conditions for a developmental logic" . . . that can be integrated into an action theoretic framework. They lack as yet, according to Habermas, an identification of the relevant causal mechanisms to accomplish this. A reconstructionist science, however, requires this corroboration; without corroboration it can designate only "the range of variations" . . . of rationality structures, as the range is indicated specifically by a structural description of various institutionally represented communicative modes. They are described in their essential purity in language theoretical discussions informed by the philosophy of speech acts and theoretical linguistics (i.e., Chomsky). All that remains from the earlier tradition of critical theory is a willingness to employ abstract categorical investigations in conjunction with nonpositivist or nonempirical social science in order to locate structural problems of "late" capitalism, especially with respect to the analysis of individual and collective identity formations.

In the end Habermas brings these considerations to bear on a "reconstruction of historical materialism." . . . Here the central heuristic device consists in the claim that homologies can be found between "ego-development and the evolution of worldviews." . . . Studies of ego-development are suggestive for this purpose because they seem to show how there are normally irreversible levels of learning: social progress becomes conceivable after all, but only if we concede that levels of learning differ in social development, depending on whether they mean "progress of learning ability" . . . in the dimension of "objectivating knowledge" (knowledge as it enters into the organization of production and of production relations) or in the dimension of "moral-practical insight." . . . This is an interesting claim. Labor and interaction function as two distinctive categories designating two separate sets of institutional relations, a theme underlying all of Habermas's work. The conclusion is interesting as well because it makes any "economist" reduction impossible in the theory of ideology.

Those who regard the analysis of the development of moral-practical insight and of structures of rationality represented in worldviews as merely subsidiary to the primary tasks of Marxism (political economy) will have little sympathy for Habermas's claims. Those who have understood the project of critical theory to consist in the analysis of the collective beliefs that suppress critical reflection will understand the point of these investigations. Both groups of readers should carefully consider why Habermas breaks with some basic tenets for social theorizing held either by Marxists or critical theorists. The not-yet-fully-graspable project of a reconstructionist science is constitutive of this break. Critical questions ought to address it, for in this text the basic schemata of Habermas's metatheoretical explorations have been stated more clearly than ever before. (pp. 585-86)

Dieter Misgeld, "Book Reviews: 'Communication and the Evolution of Society'," in Contemporary Sociology *(copyright © 1981 American Sociological Association), Vol. 10, No. 4, July, 1981, pp. 585-86.*

Michael Harrington

1928-

A political activist, educator, editor, and writer on social, political, and economic issues, Harrington is regarded as America's foremost democratic socialist. His best-known work, *The Other America* (1962), confronted Americans with the problems of "the invisible poor": those trapped in poverty in an affluent nation. Harrington's book was considered a major catalyst in reshaping attitudes towards poverty on the domestic level, bringing it to a position of primary concern and study throughout the Kennedy and Johnson Administrations. Subsequent works have analyzed capitalism from a democratic socialist perspective. In *The Accidental Century* (1965) Harrington writes of the gap between our technological potential and our social and political consciousness, which remain tied to capitalism. Harrington describes how this impasse may be overcome in *The Twilight of Capitalism* (1976), where he contends that a crisis-ridden capitalism, unable to "tolerate its own success," will eventually yield to a collectivist society. Harrington is a controversial writer, with his detractors most frequently criticizing him for a lack of depth, naiveté, and a convoluted writing style. (See also *Contemporary Authors*, Vols. 17-20, rev. ed.)

Photograph copyright © 1982 by Fred W. McDarrah

Excerpt from THE OTHER AMERICA: POVERTY IN THE UNITED STATES

The United States in the sixties contains an affluent society within its borders. Millions and tens of millions enjoy the highest standard of life the world has ever known. This blessing is mixed. It is built upon a peculiarly distorted economy, one that often proliferates pseudo-needs rather than satisfying human needs. For some, it has resulted in a sense of spiritual emptiness, of alienation. Yet a man would be a fool to prefer hunger to satiety, and the material gains at least open up the possibility of a rich and full existence.

At the same time, the United States contains an underdeveloped nation, a culture of poverty. Its inhabitants do not suffer the extreme privation of the peasants of Asia or the tribesmen of Africa, yet the mechanism of the misery is similar. They are beyond history, beyond progress, sunk in a paralyzing, maiming routine.

The new nations, however, have one advantage: poverty is so general and so extreme that it is the passion of the entire society to obliterate it. Every resource, every policy, is measured by its effect on the lowest and most impoverished. There is a gigantic mobilization of the spirit of the society: aspiration becomes a national purpose that penetrates to every village and motivates a historic transformation.

But this country seems to be caught in a paradox. Because its poverty is not so deadly, because so many are enjoying a decent standard of life, there are indifference and blindness to the plight of the poor. There are even those who deny that the culture of poverty exists. It is as if Disraeli's famous remark about the two nations of the rich and the poor had come true in a fantastic fashion. At precisely that moment in history where for the first time a people have the material ability to end

poverty, they lack the will to do so. They cannot see; they cannot act. The consciences of the well-off are the victims of affluence; the lives of the poor are the victims of a physical and spiritual misery.

The problem, then, is to a great extent one of vision. The nation of the well-off must be able to see through the wall of affluence and recognize the alien citizens on the other side. And there must be vision in the sense of purpose, of aspiration: if the word does not grate upon the ears of a gentile America, there must be a passion to end poverty, for nothing less than that will do. (pp. 158-59)

> *Michael Harrington, in his* The Other America: Poverty in the United States *(reprinted with permission of Macmillan Publishing Co., Inc.; © Michael Harrington 1962), Macmillan, 1962, 192 p.*

Excerpt from THE ACCIDENTAL CENTURY

The chasm between technological capacity and economic, political, social, and religious consciousness—the accidental revolution, in short—has unsettled every faith and creed in the West. This has led many people to a sense of decadence. The theories that express this mood relate to every aspect of human life. They embrace psychology, religion, ethics, and art, and there are important things to be seen from each of these specific vantage points. But in a complex way, the accidental revolution is party to every one of these developments.

The result of this process, the summary paradox, is that these most conscious and man-made of times have lurched into the unprecedented transformation of human life without thinking about it. And in a sense, this century, this scientific, technological, and utterly competent century, has happened accidentally. (p. 41)

Practically every ethical, moral, and cultural justification for the capitalist system has now been destroyed by capitalism. The idyll of the free market, risktaking, inventiveness, the social virtue of making money, all these have been abolished by the very success of capitalism itself. In some cases, most particularly in the United States, this contradiction between rhetoric and reality has led to the appearance of an atavistic "conservatism" which seeks to repeal the modern world. As a social and economic program, this is preposterous; as a political movement, it might threaten the very peace of the earth.

But, most basically, the problem of the cold decadence of capitalism is not that it represents the decline of the values and ideologies of the past. It is that this system will transform itself without really noticing the fact, and that the businessman as revolutionist will corrupt, not simply himself, but the society of the future as well. (pp. 108-09)

Western technological ingenuity is now subverting Western economic, political, and social assumptions. That has been the case for the whole of the century, but in the fifties and early sixties it was not so obviously expressed in the collapse of dynasties and nations. As a result, some were able to overlook a revolution, but it continued just the same. In the fairly immediate future, this process will probably become dramatic once again.

The old-fashioned ideology of the poor predicted that the political and economic context of Western capitalism would prove incapable of containing, much less mastering, its own technological revolution. The old-fashioned movement of the poor proposed to take over the direction of this rampant technology and apply reason to its uses as well as to its inventions. There are inconclusive signs that both the ideology and movement of the Western poor have irretrievably lost their force. And there is no successor utopia with an appeal to the hearts and minds of millions.

If this trend turns out to be decisive, then machines, under the control of antisocial geniuses or dictators, will guide the revolution. The conditions of life will be as utterly changed as Marx or any prophet had ever predicted, only without the participation of the majority of the people. The West would then stumble into an unprecedented environment, and the ideal of the autonomous and choosing man will become a memory, like Eden.

Or, it could be that the technological revolution will create new revolutionists. (pp. 142-43)

The West, which more than any other part of the globe learned to cope with starvation and gradually to conquer it, faces the distinct possibility that abundance—its long-dreamed utopia, its Cockaigne—will be the decadence of some of its most cherished values and that it will take more ingenuity to live with freedom than it did to subsist under necessity. (p. 244)

The social revolutions of the past were all accidental, that is, they did not conform to the images the revolutionists projected. But that gap between dream and reality was a function of the general ignorance and level of consciousness. It was life itself that was sad. Today, the problem is not in our stars but in our philosophy. The revolution is happening precisely because society has become so intentionally and carefully competent. History can no longer be blamed; it is man who is in doubt. . . .

If the accidental revolution is to be made conscious and democratic, that will happen in the course of an involved, complex process. It is no longer a question of "seizing" power, for that metaphor implies that the existing power is suitable to the new purpose if only the proper hands are laid upon it. It is rather a problem of transforming power, of changing it, of making new institutions. (p. 296)

> *Michael Harrington, in his* The Accidental Century *(reprinted with permission of Macmillan Publishing Co., Inc.; copyright © Michael Harrington 1965), Macmillan, 1965, 322 p.*

Excerpt from *THE TWILIGHT OF CAPITALISM*

In the middle seventies, every capitalist nation in the Western world found itself in a crisis more serious than any that had occurred since the Great Depression of the 1930s. In Britain, which had pioneered and named the welfare state, there was talk of the collapse of the system. Even in the United States, still the strongest power in the world, the serious, established men of power began to speculate publicly on whether a simultaneous depression-inflation might not rend the very fabric of democracy itself.

And yet, most people in the West did not think that these events had anything to do with the capitalist economy as such. They seemed, rather, to be the product of external and fortuitous circumstances—of the cartel of the Organization of Petroleum Exporting Countries (OPEC), which had quadrupled the price of oil between 1973 and 1974, of the increasing demand for food on the world market, and so on. These accidents, including the vagaries of the weather which affected the harvests and thereby the market, were indeed important, and one could hardly blame capitalism for them. But if capitalism could not be held reponsible for circumstances beyond its control, it was reponsible for what it made of them. (p. 205)

It is the argument of Part II of [*The Twilight of Capitalism*] that it was and is the structure of capitalist society that turned the historical accidents of the 1970s into calamitous necessities. The West carefully helped to fabricate its own bad luck. Moreover, this extraordinary process can be understood only in the light of the themes developed by Karl Marx in *Das Kapital* and, above all, in its first chapter.

That last proposition must seem absurd on its very face. *Das Kapital* was written about a mid-nineteenth-century economy, which is as distant from the 1970s as the nuclear reactor is from the steam engine. And Chapter I of that book, we know, is a conscious and extreme simplification of that relatively simple system. What could Marx's Hegelian definitions of use value and exchange value, his theory of the fetishism of commodities, have to do with our world? This anti-Marxist point should be particularly persuasive, since capitalism has been profoundly modified by the welfare state. . . .

The extraordinary fact of the matter, as the next five chapters will demonstrate, if that this welfare state, which has indeed effected profound modifications of the capitalist structure and is even potentially anticapitalist, still follows the basic logic described in *Das Kapital*. (p. 206)

I do not want to suggest for a moment that the crisis of the 1970s is a final breakdown of the system, its *Götterdämmerung*. I fully expect it to recover from this cruel and unnecessary depression. The event is only a moment in a complex process of decline and fall that will certainly go on for some time to come and just as certainly will end with the collapse of the bourgeois order. (p. 320)

[Even] in prosperity, and indeed because of prosperity, the contradictions of this system are at work.

For the explosive fact of the matter is that capitalism cannot tolerate its own success. The system, for all its Keynesian transformations, is fundamentally hostile to full employment; it is wracked by its own booms. (p. 322)

Crises, as Marx understood, performed the irrationally rational function of making a contradictory system once again workable. Only, a point has been reached where, for political reasons that apply to the right as well as the left, [the method of using high unemployment to restore] "equilibrium" can no longer be used. In tinkering with, but by no means abolishing, the machinery of capitalist crisis, governmental intervention has created structural tendencies toward inflation. (pp. 330-31)

[The] secret history of the crisis of the seventies reveals that, first of all, an antisocial socialization of the economy in behalf of the corporations perpetuates and aggravates, rather than resolves, the contradictions of capitalism. Secondly, it shows that the capitalist mechanism of boom and bust continues in a moderated, and sometimes politically exacerbated, form and that the system thus sickens from its own success. Thirdly, these new expressions of the intrinsic instability of bourgeois society have, since 1973, been magnified by the effect of an oil cartel whose effectiveness is, in considerable measure, a result of the fact that American energy planning followed capitalist priorities for a generation.

In short, a fundamental Marxist insight allows one to fathom dimensions of the events of the seventies that are not at all visible on their surface. It is not technology or industrialism or the "bad luck" created by oil-rich sheiks that has brought us to the incredible pass of this decade. Rather, it is the capitalist use—or, more precisely, inherent misuse—of resources that is reponsible for our plight. (pp. 333-34)

That human life will be radically transformed in the medium range of the future cannot be questioned any longer, because that future has already begun. All that is in doubt is the most crucial of issues: Whether this collectivist society which is emerging even now will repress, or liberate, men and women. I conclude, then, with an "if"—but then, in this era to be even provisionally hopeful is to affirm—if the best of what humans have achieved is to prevail, which is to say, deepen, in the unprecedented environment that is already beginning—if all men and women are to be free in a just society—then, the spirit of the new Karl Marx must be our comrade in the struggle. (p. 341)

> *Michael Harrington, in his* The Twilight of Capitalism *(copyright © 1976 by, Michael Harrington; reprinted by permission of Simon & Schuster, a Division of Gulf & Western Corporation), Simon & Schuster, 1976, 446 p.*

HARVEY J. BRESLER

[In *The Other America*, Michael Harrington] considers separately—among others—the victims of technological change, the farm-poor, the alcoholics, the very poor among our intellectuals (yes, even the beatniks), those whom poverty has maimed psychically, and the ethnic and racial minorities of which the Negro is the tragic prototype. He discusses at length and with feeling the plight of the aged, itself a huge statistic. (p. 266)

[Mr. Harrington] has thoroughly studied his source material; his statistics are grimly impressive and his scholarship is sound. What about his proposed remedies? Certainly they recognize that the dimensions of the problem are so great that only the federal government can afford to tackle them. . . . But, as Mr. Harrington points out, our present cost of policing the social misery generated by poverty, of preventing poverty from exploding into something worse (as if there were anything worse!), already mounts higher than we realize. . . .

This book contains sober proposals for tackling some of the other components of poverty in this country. These square well with the thinking of men like Galbraith, one of the intellectual stewards of the New Frontier. . . .

Is there any real hope that we can abolish poverty in America? Not without something to galvanize the conscience of our too-affluent society. (p. 267)

> *Harvey J. Bresler, "The Poor Are Still with Us," in* The Nation *(copyright 1962 The Nation magazine, The Nation Associates, Inc.), Vol. 194, No. 12, March 24, 1962, pp. 266-67.*

A. H. RASKIN

Behind the glittering facade of America's "affluent society" lies a ghetto of loneliness and defeat populated by the poor. . . .

This is the angry thesis of ["**The Other America,**"] Michael Harrington's study of poverty in a nation that prides itself on having built the highest standard of living in the world and on having done most to assure economic justice for all its people. . . . His book is a scream of rage, a call to conscience. . . .

His study is not meant as a dissent from the thesis so illuminatingly expounded by John Kenneth Galbraith in "The Affluent Society" that our economic thinking must now be geared to solving the problems of opulence rather than those of want. Mr. Harrington cheerfully embraces the Galbraith notion that today's poor are the first minority poor in history, the first poor not to be seen and thus the first poor the politicians can afford to ignore. But he has no sympathy for Mr. Galbraith's belief that what we have left in the way of poverty can be overcome by an individual case approach or by attacking "islands" of unemployment or social neglect.

His skepticism stems from a conviction that the structure of our welfare state, with its hitching of public and private social-security systems to wages, is calculated to provide the least help for those who need it most. He estimates—and the basis for his estimates is likely to draw violent challenge from less impassioned analysts—that 40 million to 50 million Americans now live as internal aliens in a society bent on forgetting their existence. (p. 5)

Handicapped by lack of schooling and lack of skills, they stand not to benefit by automation and other industrial progress but to experience a deepening of exile. Not only do they not share in the fruits of the higher productivity improved technology permits, but they find themselves further disadvantaged by the freeze-out of the unskilled and semi-skilled work on which they once relied.

To Mr. Harrington, there is a culture of poverty that makes the poor different from the rich in ways that transcend money. . . .

He writes with sensitivity and perception as well as indignation. The Council of Economic Advisers might say, with justice, that he has overdrawn his case as to both the size and intractability of the problem. That is no indictment. The chroniclers and celebrants of America's upward movement are plentiful; it is good to be reminded that we are still a long way from the stars. (p. 26)

> A. H. Raskin, "The Unknown and Unseen," in The New York Times Book Review (© 1962 by The New York Times Company; reprinted by permission), April 8, 1962, pp. 5, 26.

DWIGHT MACDONALD

In the admirably short space of under two hundred pages, [Michael Harrington in **"The Other America"**] outlines the problem [of poverty in America], describes in imaginative detail what it means to be poor in this country today, summarizes the findings of recent studies by economists and sociologists, and analyzes the reasons for the persistence of mass poverty in the midst of general prosperity. It is an excellent book— and a most important one.

My only serious criticism is that Mr. Harrington has popularized the treatment a bit too much. Not in the writing, which is on a decent level, but in a certain vagueness. There are no index, no bibliography, no reference footnotes. In our over-specialized culture, books like this tend to fall into two categories: Popular (no scholarly "apparatus") and Academic (too much). I favor something intermediate—why should the academics have *all* the footnotes? The lack of references means that the book is of limited use to future researchers and writers. A pity, since the author has brought together a great range of material.

I must also object that Mr. Harrington's treatment of statistics is more than a little impressionistic. His appendix, which he calls a coming to grips with the professional material, doesn't live up to its billing. "If my interpretation is bleak and grim," he writes, "and even if it overstates the case slightly, that is intentional. My moral point of departure is a sense of outrage. . . . In such a discussion it is inevitable that one gets mixed up with dry, graceless, technical matters. That should not conceal the crucial fact that these numbers represent people and that any tendency toward understatement is an intellectual way of acquiescing in suffering." But a fact is a fact, and Mr. Harrington confuses the issue when he writes that "these numbers represent people." They do—and one virtue of his book is that he never forgets it—but in dealing with statistics, this truism must be firmly repressed lest one begin to think from the heart rather than from the head, as he seems to do when he charges those statisticians who "understate" the numbers of the poor with having found "an intellectual way of acquiescing in suffering." This is moral bullying, and it reminds

me, *toutes proportions gardées,* of the habitual confusion in Communist thinking between facts and political inferences from them. "A sense of outrage" is proper for a "moral point of departure," but statistics are the appropriate *factual* point of departure, as in the writings of Marx and Engels on the agony of the nineteenth-century English working class—writings that are by no means lacking in a sense of moral outrage, either.

These objections, however, do not affect Mr. Harrington's two main contentions: that mass poverty still exists in the United States, and that it is disappearing more slowly than is commonly thought. (pp. 82, 84)

> Dwight Macdonald, "Our Invisible Poor," in The New Yorker (© 1963 by The New Yorker Magazine, Inc.), Vol. XXXVIII, No. 48, January 19, 1963, pp. 82-132.*

HERBERT J. MULLER

I think Harrington insists too much [in *The Accidental Century*], tending to blow up every problem into a "crisis." Even so I find his book refreshing as well as provocative. He has a keen eye for paradox and a flair for epigram. For an alarmist he is on the whole uncommonly reasonable . . . , keeping his head and keeping it where it ideally belongs, above a warm heart. And in view of the complacent, conservative temper of America today, the fondness for "challenges" that don't rock the boat, I assume that we can do with more "radicals" like Harrington.

This conservatism, however, suggests some reservations about his familiar account of the cultural, spiritual "crisis" of unbelief, which has been going on for a century. Here he sometimes lapses into such cliches as that "no one really seems to believe in anything," whereas one might argue that we have suffered more from an excess of "true believers," or from too little doubt about the national consensus. In any case, he reports only a "magnificent decadence" in modern literature, reflecting the breakdown of Western society, and adds that the insights of a few geniuses cannot compensate for the bewilderments and sufferings of countless millions. But his own humanistic faith appears in critiques of the limited insights of Nietzsche and Dostoevsky, who as prophets have been considerably overrated because they predicted calamity. (pp. 1,16)

Harrington emphasizes the test now being forced by automation. Will [the corporations] give priority to the social problems it is creating: the many displaced workers left with useless skills, the growing need of forcing many people not to work, the need of providing liberal education for all? He is sure they won't. He sees no evidence that big business can be trusted on its own to subordinate the calculus of gain to ethical or social considerations, or in particular that the great advertising industry—now socializing taste in the interests of private profit— can be trusted to educate the public in civilized uses of the leisure automation will bring. I make out more signs of a growing enlightenment in business leaders, some recognition of the challenge he poses. Still, he is surely right in insisting on this challenge, and on the tardy, uncertain response to it. . . .

Harrington declares that at least the potentials of a great movement exist in the racial minorities and the poor, a revived labor movement, the liberal middle class, and immediately the liberal wing of the Democratic party. Actually, none of them shows any signs of going in for socialism. He might therefore look more closely into the reasons why it no longer seems dynamic, why most of the socialist parties in Europe look pretty tired, and why on the other hand the "revolutionists" he hopes to stir up are unlikely to be as reasonable and humane as he himself is. In particular he might reconsider his premise that our "present course" is leading to "a decadence that will be simply a death." This has been a course toward a mixed economy, combinations of private and government enterprise, in which socialist ideals have had considerable influence, and which has been by no means so "accidental" as he insists. . . .

In the foreseeable future, at any rate, I think that those who share Harrington's basic ideals can hope for no more than a continuation of this course, at best somewhat faster, more enterprising, and more intelligent. In America it will almost certainly continue to disappoint mere liberals too. But I do not think that our technological crisis is quite so desperate as he assumes, or our society quite so decadent. I see somewhat more reason for hope in the growing consciousness of our revolutionary situation, to which he here makes a lively contribution. (p. 16)

> Herbert J. Muller, "Rocking the Boat," in Book Week—The Sunday Herald Tribune (© I.H.T. Corporation; reprinted by permission), August 22, 1965, pp. 1, 16.

LEONARD REISSMAN

Western civilization, according to Harrington [in *The Accidental Century*], has stumbled into a revolutionary, but accidental, transformation pushed on by technology and science. The old ideology, inherited from the social critics of the last century, helps us not at all to explain that transformation occurred because capitalism did not develop as predicted. Instead of a volcanic eruption fed by inner contradictions, capitalism has produced a "cold decadence" by destroying morality and creating a collective society for private profit. The altered situation demands an altered philosophy if the West is to use its superior technical competence to control the future. The ideology Harrington visualizes is socialism, which means a "profound economic and social deepening of democracy."

The book exhibits a kind of precocious naïveté. . . . I could not agree more with Harrington's thesis, including his vision for a humane future that could be possible "if people can freely and democratically take control of their own lives and society." Yet, this is not a popularity contest in which we applaud only for our side. It takes more than sincerity, which Harrington possesses and more than a literate statement of the problem, which Harrington has written. What is required is the application of the scientific competence that Harrington rightly believes we possess.

Specifically, we need to move the argument along by valid, logical, and sustained reasoning. . . . How, for example, have American institutions been converted to support the new collective capitalism without staggering waves on the surface of that good old entrepreneurial capitalism? What are the forces that have created the accidental revolution and allowed it to take place at all? Competent intellectuals in a competent society should try to supply some answers.

Perhaps this demand burdens Harrington unfairly because no one else seems to be answering those questions either. Yet, that is no reason to avoid the deeper questions in favor of the utopian vision, as Harrington seems to do here. . . . One way to move closer to the "deepening of democracy," I am saying,

is to lay some of the hard responsibilities for social analysis on the intellectuals. (pp. 183-84)

> Leonard Reissman, "Book Department: 'The Accidental Century'," in The Annals of The American Academy of Political and Social Science (© 1965, by The American Academy of Political and Social Science), Vol. 362, November, 1965, pp. 183-84.

WILLIAM V. SHANNON

In "**Toward a Democratic Left**," Harrington has returned to the mode of ["**The Other America**"]. He is once again the brilliant pamphleteer, making use of some fundamentally Marxist ideas and some piercing insights of his own to provide an exceptionally lively description of current social problems, both domestic and international. . . .

Harrington does not contend here for full-scale public ownership but he does argue for a much larger role for the public sector. Only government can bring to bear the resources and enforce the correct priorities to wipe out slums, find jobs for the underemployed and unemployed, provide efficient mass transportation, and reconstruct large cities as livable communities. (p. 1)

The case for more government spending and more government planning is worth reading in this political season when most of the leading politicians . . . are agreed that private corporations, aided by a few tax incentives and government-guaranteed bonds, can rebuild slums, solve unemployment in the ghetto, and achieve a new social harmony.

Harrington asks hard questions about this proposed social role for corporations: "The naive faith that corporate interest and common good usually coincide is simply not supported by the evidence. . . ." What is really needed, he argues, is more democratic debate and more effective popular control over huge government-spending programs that have produced unplanned, untoward social effects. . . .

If there is to be a much greater element of conscious political choice in the planning and spending of Federal money, Americans will have to liberate themselves from what Harrington terms the politics of "utopian pragmatism," the belief that all is for the best in this best of all continent-sized political muddles where every contending force converges toward the center and every issue gets compromised.

Having achieved the intellectual triumph of making radicalism once again seem fresh and pertinent to national issues, Harrington is equally effective in his undoctrinaire approach to international problems of political violence and economic underdevelopment. . . . The great challenge of the underdeveloped world is to enable hundreds of millions of people to move out of poverty without going through the totalitarian ordeal of forced savings and forced industrialization. Harrington is not sanguine, but he shows why the present mixture of private investment by the West, modest foreign aid and foreign trade as now conducted is not likely to rescue the underdeveloped countries. (p. 37)

> William V. Shannon, "How to Remake a Country," in The New York Times Book Review (© 1968 by The New York Times Company; reprinted by permission), May 19, 1968, pp. 1, 37.

DANIEL BELL

Harrington subtitles [*Toward A Democratic Left*], ambiguously, "A Radical Program for a New Majority." But what is the program? There is some rhetoric: ". . . . society [must] dictate to the Gross National Product rather than the other way around, the change must be conscious and democratic," whatever that means. And there is one general proposal: The President shall be obliged to make to the nation a periodic Report on the Future. The report shall project the basic choices, and estimate both the economic and social costs of alternate programs. "The report shall state a Social Consumption Criterion which will *clearly* measure the impact of *every* department of public expenditure on the *social standard of living*." . . .

This is an unexceptionable suggestion. And, in fact, such an effort, though less grandiose, is under way. . . .

I have italicized some of Harrington's words because I would be grateful if he could clarify their meaning. I suspect that he has little sense of the enormous conceptual difficulties in defining exactly what one would mean by a "social standard of living," let alone an "adequate social minimum," "decent housing," and other nice-sounding phrases. For these goals are not attained by rhetoric.

But given Harrington's, and our, ambitions—to eliminate poverty, provide liveable cities, clean up the environment, raise health levels, expand educational opportunities, and the like—the chief question remains: How do we do it? . . .

[Despite] the subtitle, there is *no* program in this book. The gap between the intellectual and the technocrat, indeed, is that the former has little notion of how to turn *ideas* into a *program*. . . . A program is an "economic good": One has to specify institutional arrangements, to say who is to do what.

And even when one has finally set up a program, there is the further problem of operation. (p. 22)

The worst government programs are those stressing detailed planning and detailed administration—such as price control and rationing, public assistance and public housing—because their very detail creates rigidities that make them unworkable or invite abuse. If there is any further lesson to be learned from these experiences, it is that a social program can work best when the government sets guidelines, policy, and standards, but leaves the administration and operation to a wide variety of decentralized units.

Some of these operational units may be private enterprises. And why not? They have the organizational skills, the experience and flexibility, and they even have a motive. . . . Harrington looks darkly on the entry of private industry into the operation of government-financed social programs, because they are in it "for profit" (a strange accusation, since Harrington relies for his economics on John Kenneth Galbraith, and one of his chief arguments in *The New Industrial State* is that stability, not profit, is the principal motivation of big business today).

But if one adopts a test of performance, rather than ideological purity, it may well be that such profit is cheaper for the society than the lagging progress and heavy-handed bureaucratization of governmental enterprises. . . .

The point of all this is that, short of Utopia, a society has to provide a large number of varied incentives, and usually monetary ones, to induce individuals and firms to act, especially for the realization of social programs, where there is little or no immediate economic payoff. One has to avoid the ideological fetishes which, in *a priori* fashion, rule out schemes simply because they do not square with the ideology. . . . The test, necessarily, has to be performance—within the framework of the social goals that we have agreed upon.

My feeling, then, is not that Harrington's book is wrong, but that it is irrelevant. He wants to stand on Pisgah and point to the future while, like every radical ideologue, clinging to his perch and staving off the other ideologues who are trying to shove him off the mountain so that *they* can point the way. Everybody wants to be the prophet. But how does one get from Pisgah to the Promised Land? That is a much more mundane task, and there are few people working on laying out the road, let alone building it. (p. 23)

> *Daniel Bell, "How Do We Climb Down from Pisgah?" in* The New Leader *(© 1968 by the American Labor Conference on International Affairs, Inc.), Vol. LI, No. 11, May 20, 1968, pp. 22-3.*

CHRISTOPHER LASCH

The trouble [with *Toward a Democratic Left*] is that Harrington's analysis stops short of the conclusion to which it logically leads. He is correct in saying that there are no new social forces automatically evolving toward socialism (which is what "democratic planning" comes down to). Presumably this means that radical change can only take place if a new political organization, explicitly committed to radical change, wills it to take place. But Harrington backs off from this conclusion. Instead he seems to predicate his strategy on the wistful hope that socialism will somehow take over the Democratic party without anyone realizing what is happening. He admits that "there is obvious danger when those committed to a new morality thus maneuver on the basis of the old hypocrisies." But there is no choice, because radicals cannot create a new movement "by fiat." It is tempting, Harrington says, to think that the best strategy for the Left might be to "start a party of its own." But this course would not work unless there were already an "actual disaffection of great masses of people from the Democratic Party."

At this point, however, one has to ask whether large defections from a liberal to a socialist party would be likely to occur in the absence of a socialist alternative. People do not defect from existing parties unless there is some place to defect to. Until the Left creates "a party of its own," defectors will have no place to go, except perhaps to occasional third-party movements based on single issues. . . .

Radical change, as Harrington himself makes clear in refuting theories of the automatic evolution toward socialism, can only come about through radical consciousness. But how is this consciousness to be created except through a political organization which embodies it, and which dares to call things by their proper names?

It is true, as Harrington says, that "before raising the barrier of a new party . . . there must be some reasonable expectation that significant forces will join it." There is of course no immediate prospect that a majority of Americans would join a socialist party. In order to arrive at an accurate assessment of what this prospect means, however, one must realize that the object of a radical party is not primarily to win elections, to register a protest vote, or to influence the major parties, as American third parties have traditionally done, but to introduce socialist perspectives into political debate, to create a broad consciousness of alternatives not embraced by the present system, to show both by teaching and by its own example that life under socialism would be preferable to life under corporate capitalism, and thus *in the long run* to fashion a new political majority. (p. 4)

> *Christopher Lasch, "The New Politics: 1968 and After," in* The New York Review of Books *(reprinted with permission from* The New York Review of Books; *copyright © 1968 Nyrev, Inc.), Vol. 11, No. 2, July 11, 1968, pp. 3-6.**

GARRY WILLS

[Michael Harrington's starting point in **"Socialism"**] is the twin demand made upon man by the visionary and the realistic tasks. Utopias are practical, he argues, for without a dream man's practical efforts are not directed to a unified goal. Yet, paradoxically, the utopia must be kept distant in order to be practical. Pretending that the utopia has been realized, or can be achieved by one last desperate push, has been the rationalization for tyranny all through this century. . . .

Harrington's model for the blend of visionary sweep and practical adaptation is Karl Marx. He argues that Marx has not been properly understood because critics have not shared the dual nature of all his thought. . . .

Harrington gives us a fresh reading of Marx, defending as realism what has been called determinism, and as moral paradigm what has been called ideology. Marx was proposing an ideal to man's freedom, not imposing a system from outside it. His objection to capitalism was moral, not merely utilitarian: his view was not simply that it couldn't work, but that it shouldn't be allowed to work. Harrington notes the similarity between his view and the medieval condemnation of usury. . . .

In Harrington's eyes, it is the major crime of the socialist regimes that they tried to force the pace of history, not cooperating with time's processes but taking "sudden drastic leaps into the future." In Marx's eyes, the left's task is not just to make a revolution by any means, but to forge a people worthy and able to live the revolutionary ideals. That is the key to the whole process, the one step that can never be bypassed. Harrington is, therefore, merciless in his judgment of those who tried to run "Marxist" revolutions without a proletariat as their vehicle of change. . . .

Harrington's analysis, subtle and admiring, becomes at times hagiographical—as in the long apologia for that unfortunate phrase "dictatorship of the proletariat." ("Marx did not mean dictatorship when he said dictatorship.") But a deeper flaw lies in Harrington's very orthodoxy, the fact that where other men stay true to Marx in their fashion, he insists on staying true to Marx in Marx's fashion. For Harrington, no force but labor can be true heir to the vision. This makes much of the last part of the book an elaborate attempt to trace a constantly thwarted, constantly reasserted revolutionary élan in the union movement. He sees a true left emerging beneath, through, and despite the false left. (p. 1)

[In] his realistic critique of fuzzy idealism he goes too far. As his master did. Marx was as much a moralist as Adam Smith; but both men felt moral ideals could only find permanent social footing on the ground of self-interest. In that sense, even Marx's social vision was based on the satisfaction of individuals—first as a class (hence the need for predatory war on any smaller class whose overthrow would sate a larger class) and then as a social whole.

Yet community has been, and can be, based on other considerations than the economic satisfaction of individuals comprising it. . . . [But] it is easy to dismiss them as unimportant in the modern world. This means that their force is exercised in unexamined (hence uncontrollable) ways.

For instance: Vietnam and the cold war in general, arose more from motives of an aberrant religio-patriotic crusade than out of strict calculations of economic advantage. . . .

Henceforth, to learn from Marx (a continuing task of the modern world) will be to learn, as well, from Harrington. He poses the essential problem of our politics—that man has socialized everything except himself—and he suggests many practical ways to ameliorate that problem even while we keep dreaming of its solution. He has met his own test, of staying central to real needs while being "eccentric" in judgment from a sane detached viewpoint. (p. 18)

> *Garry Wills, "'Socialism'," in* The New York Times Book Review *(© 1972 by The New York Times Company; reprinted by permission), April 30, 1972, pp. 1, 18.*

ROBERT COLES

[*Socialism*] is a powerful and convincing statement, broad in its command of facts, deep in its examination of various economic and political systems, tempting in its analysis of man's psychological capabilities, as they emerge, given favoring circumstances, in the larger world we refer to collectively as "the society"; and finally, it is a statement that can sometimes become unnerving to many of us—because of the implied questions that come across repeatedly in the author's narrative, though he is too kind and tactful to force them upon us. (p. 26)

The questions have to do with fundamentals, of course, nothing less than the economic and moral basis of the nation's institutions: the profit motive, the nature of capitalism and its connection with imperialism—the old-fashioned kind, but also the more sophisticated kind, wherein corporations rather than armies enter those "foreign lands." By the same token, the questions are personal. What kind of children *can* we bring up, . . . if in the clutch every boy and girl eventually gets to learn that he or she either controls or is controlled, either works day in, day out for wages others set at their convenience or takes in profits as they accumulate, with no obligation to do anything in particular for anyone, including those whose work in the first place made the whole thing possible? Socialists answer that a transformation of capitalist society is necessary. They say that individualistic economic forces have to be brought under social control, and until that happens . . . the basic nature of the society will persist: a relative handful owns a lot, whereas the large majority of people have a kind of "enough" that never even remotely approximates, either politically or economically, what those few on top and near the top claim as a right. (p. 27)

Much of Harrington's book is taken up with a thoughtful and conscientious analysis of . . . how a number of socialists, especially Marx, have regarded the world, with its various and unequal continents, nation-states, and within them, classes. There is no doubt that Harrington has his own point of view, his own belief that certain thinkers were right and others were wrong, and sometimes evil. The evil ones transformed Marxist thinking and potentially socialist political efforts into repressive political leviathans of the worst kind, and that outcome clearly haunts the author. That is why he constantly writes of *democratic* socialism. . . .

Harrington takes pains to emphasize the moral and activist side of Marx, which better than any intellectual and logical precocity, made for a kind of analysis rich in its capacity for irony and ambiguity. If, as he puts it, the "talmudic reading" of Marx that Lenin and others have made such a prominent part of the 20th century has done the man's ideas a gross injustice, several chapters in this book at least set things straight for the record. But there is more to this book than that. The author is not yet another sectarian polemicist. He is at once a serious scholar, an impassioned social critic, and a man right in the middle of a struggle now being waged in America—between those who want to hold on to what is (and what they have) and those who believe this nation's wealth and power ought to be used and shared by its working people in a thoroughly different way than is now the case. (p. 28)

Michael Harrington believes he knows what is fair and honorable for his fellow man, has spelled it out in more than one book, and no doubt every day of his life will make sure his considerable intelligence and energy go toward achieving not a New Jerusalem but a society so set up that more people than ever before live in reasonable security and dignity, live free of want or the threat of want. (p. 29)

Robert Coles, "An American Prophet," in The New Republic *(reprinted by permission of* The New Republic; © *1972 The New Republic, Inc.), Vol. 166, No. 23, June 3, 1972, pp. 26-9.*

DENNIS H. WRONG

Separating the wheat from the chaff in the 150-year history of socialism as Utopian aspiration and political movement, Harrington necessarily devotes a great deal of space [in *Socialism*] to demonstrating its indissoluble connection with democracy. . . .

Harrington is fully aware that the preservation and extension of democracy may make it impossible to fulfill the dream of an instantaneous "expropriation of the expropriators," followed by a total transformation of social and economic relationships, in the relatively affluent capitalist Western societies. Yet he does not resign himself to accepting "piecemeal reforms" within the limits of welfare-state capitalism; he recognizes that the ideal of full-fledged socialism can serve as a guide to proposals for reform and keep those moved by it from complacently accepting limited gains.

Harrington seeks to ground the inseparability of socialism and democracy in Marx himself. He carefully notes the shifts, nuances and changing historical contexts of Marx's developing views, acknowledging the occasional warrant for Leninist or Blanquist conceptions of the seizure of power by determined minorities, but maintaining that the mature Marx increasingly adopted a social democratic view of the transition to socialism. One feels occasionally that Harrington is guilty of what he criticizes in others: treating Marx's writings "as a scripture to be ransacked for holy precedents." One cannot be certain of what Marx, or any other man who antedated them, would have thought about the various authoritarian "Socialisms" that have emerged in this century out of the disorders of shattered precapitalist social orders. Still, in drawing fully on Marx himself

and on the best contemporary Marxist scholarship (particularly on George Lichtheim), Harrington succeeds in persuading us that Marx became a convinced democrat in his own time and place. (p. 15)

Dennis H. Wrong, "Reviving the Socialist Tradition," in The New Leader *(© 1972 by the American Labor Conference on International Affairs, Inc.), Vol. LV, No. 14, July 10, 1972, pp. 15-16.*

JOHN KENNETH GALBRAITH

["**The Twilight of Capitalism**"] is an important and extremely interesting book. . . . Harrington is a lucid writer, able to say plainly and exactly what he means. But he has little sense of architecture; the structure into which the ideas build is very diffcult to grasp, possibly because it doesn't much exist.

The first half undertakes to rescue Marx from the vulgar interpretations of Marxists and non-Marxists alike. This includes a lengthy reexamination of the Marxian conceptions of capital, value and surplus value as also of capitalism. He defends Marx against the charge of narrow materialism, holds that his moral system extended to include ethical and spiritual values—a kind of spiritual materialism. He argues similarly against a narrow view of Marx's commitment to economic determinism. . . .

The second half of the book develops the inherent contradictions of capitalism in their modern setting. No one needs to be a Marxist to find them compelling. The contradictions consist in the powerful and righteous impulse of the executives of business corporations, of bankers, the affluent in general, aided frequently by the most reputable of economists, to urge what is most destructive of capitalism and to resist what might save it. . . . Whatever might lead to a more equitable distribution of income, whether in private revenues or public services, and thus temper dissent and dissatisfaction is strongly resisted and abetted by solemn though highly convenient doctrine.

Thus arguments about a prospective shortage of capital are adduced out of the conservative imagination in support of steps that would make income distribution worse. . . .

There is a similar attack with similar effect on the welfare activities of the Federal Government. This is in the name of Government economy but in further development of the contradiction an exception is made for those outlays that are important for the large corporations and most notably for arms. . . .

Harrington remains committed to the democratic faith and method. So presumably he continues to believe that these contradictions can be resolved by the force of public opinion and popular power. His evidence, on the whole, is to the contrary but that, without doubt, was the best way to leave matters.

John Kenneth Galbraith, "'The Twilight of Capitalism'," in The New York Times Book Review *(© 1976 by The New York Times Company; reprinted by permission), May 23, 1976, p. 3.*

JAMES RIDGEWAY

Harrington's most interesting and probably controversial contention occurs in the second part of ["**The Twilight of Capitalism**"] (entitled "**The Future Karl Marx**") in which he applies his version of true Marxism to the problems of contemporary America. It is often argued on the left that the state is an instrument of capital, acting as a sort of central brokerage for corporate interests by granting subsidies, doling out contracts, removing revenues from one sector of the economy and pumping them into another. Harrington believes that the state is not a mere instrument of the corporation, but rather that it has a tenuous independence. . . .

[He contends] further: "The welfare state government is not itself the initiator of most production within the economy. The corporations do that. However, that same government is increasingly charged with arranging the preconditions for profitable production."

Harrington says the state can and has instituted beneficial reforms from the top down. It is not necessary, although it is helpful to have a thrust from a mass political base. He cites reforms in the 1960s, including Medicare, LBJ's poverty program. . . . and Social Security benefits as examples.

There are several problems with this. In the first place, Harrington's examples of independence and reform all are initiated within the legislative sector of the government. . . . But, in fact, the most important actions of government occur in the executive sector, where instances of beneficial social change are few and far between.

Second, I can't believe Harrington wants seriously to argue that the poverty program constituted any sort of meaningful reform. At the time, the poverty program always seemed to be more a measure of pacification than anything else. (p. 44)

Medicare is a far more interesting example, and certainly represents a step in the direction of national health insurance, of one sort or another. As a practical matter, Medicare was the vehicle for reorganizing the medical industry, where political power came to be shared among insurance companies, drug manufacturers, doctors and hospitals, the Social Security Administration, and most important, the Blue Cross organization. . . . The idea that Medicare illustrates "independence" of the government is hard to believe.

Or take another example: the pricing of natural gas. . . . [In 1954] the Supreme Court ordered the Federal Power Commission to regulate the prices of gas paid producers by the interstate pipeline companies. Ever since then the industry has fought to escape regulation of gas. (pp. 44-5)

But as the companies have fought their way through the FPC, the courts, in a display of independence, have thrown them back. . . . Even within the executive branch of the government, where the White House, FPC commissioners, Interior Department functionaries all have dutifully argued the line for big oil, lesser bureaucrats, including a group of staff economists at the FPC, have opposed the industry view. . . .

Now here surely is precisely the sort of independence of the state that Harrington talks about. In one of the most crucial areas of all economic activity, an area that influences literally millions upon millions of citizens, the state can be seen to have a "life of its own."

So what? As a practical matter this "independence" is a mirage, a facade behind which the administration, in response to industry pressure, goes right ahead and slowly pushes up the price of natural gas. . . .

The fact is that the state's "independence" crucially depends on the abilities of organized labor, acting for the most part in the Congress, to implement change, or as is more and more the case, to hold the line against erosion of New Deal style measures already in existence. . . .

At any rate, whether one agrees or disagrees with Harrington, **"The Twilight of Capitalism"** is extremely useful, and well worth reading. (p. 45)

James Ridgeway, "Marx Sparks Sharks' Larks" (reprinted by permission of The Village Voice *and the author; copyright © The Village Voice, Inc., 1976), in* The Village Voice, *Vol. XXI, No. 30, July 26, 1976, pp. 44-5.*

SIDNEY HOOK

Karl Marx has been revised many times and in many different ways. Harrington in [*The Twilight of Capitalism*] has the unique distinction of revising Marx by the cool assertion that Marx "misunderstood" himself, and therefore "misrepresented" Marxism to the world. . . . He dedicates himself to restating Marx's genial insights free of the blundering and inept words in which Marx obscured them. . . .

Were Harrington's book not so long and labored, one would be tempted to interpret its first part as an elaborate spoof. But since he is obviously serious and humorless, his procedure must be characterized as intellectually scandalous. He performs not a lobotomy on Marx but a brain transplant, substituting for Marx's closely knit grey matter a diffuse Hegelian mess. (p. 34)

Harrington dismisses the entire Preface [of Marx's *Critique of Political Economy*] in which the mode of economic production is given primary but not exclusive causal importance, as the most vulgar expression of vulgar Marxism. . . . Rather [Harrington focuses on an unpublished manuscript by Marx which he claims] asserts that the culture of a society is an "organic whole" in which all parts interact (dialectically, of course!) and mutually determine each other. The mode of economic production on this view is no more basic or ultimately determining than the mode of dress, war or marriage. . . .

Having dubbed Marx's Preface an indiscretion of his mature years, consistency requires that Harrington judge *The Communist Manifesto* an indiscretion of Marx's earlier years since it formulates the theory of historical materialism in even simpler terms. He must also jettison Marx's analysis of class. For Marx defined a class fundamentally by its role in the mode of production. Since Harrington denies that the mode of production played a decisive role in slave and feudal societies—he is somewhat ambiguous about capitalist society—he must regard Marx's statement that "The history of all hitherto existing society is the history of class struggles" as another absent-minded aberration. . . .

Aware of the extremism of his operation on Marx, Harrington makes a desperate effort to save the characteristic Marxist emphasis on the mode of production by distinguishing between "the determinant" and "the dominant." The economy is always "determinant"; it is "dominant" only under capitalism. However in any genuinely organic system, causally this is a distinction without a significant difference. . . .

Harrington takes the human body as a paradigm of an organic system. Human society is far from being as organic because of the greater influence of physical factors on it. Even in the human body not all aspects are "dialectically" interrelated. But regardless of the degree of interrelation it is downright silly to ask, what is the most decisive or dominant or determinant aspect in the functioning of the body—its digestive, nervous, circulatory, reproductive or skeletal system? Only in relation to some problem or difficulty or purpose is such a question meaningful and answerable. Similarly with society. The relevant causal factor is that which must be altered or controlled to achieve a desirable result. (p. 35)

There is hardly a page in Harrington's book that does not invite correction or critical comment. In general whenever he ventures into philosophy, he is in water over his head. Although he seems to have taken a crash course in Hegel to help him understand Marx, he fails to see the difficulties and defects of the Hegelian logic which is an ontology rather than a theory of inquiry or scientific proof. . . . He disregards Marx's explicit statement that he was "coquetting" with Hegel's terminology, that his findings were derived "scientifically," independently of Hegel, and therefore must be judged by the historical, empirical evidence.

It is precisely that critical assessment of Marx's theories in the light of the empirical evidence that Harrington wishes to avoid. Although he admits that some specific predictions of Marx, and especially their timing, were disastrously wrong, he still fervently affirms the validity of Marx's analysis of capitalist development. . . . No matter how long the twilight years of capitalism drag on, darkness will surely fall. He is not so confident as Marx was that it will be followed by a true socialist dawn. That is definitely to his credit. . . .

Rejecting the classical Marxist positions on historical materialism and the class struggle, Harrington clings all the more fiercely to Marx's theory of surplus value and the economic analysis of *Das Kapital*. His argument is somewhat obscure: he seems to believe that because Marx was aware of the contradicton between the first and third volumes of *Kapital* that therefore there is no contradiction. . . . Where Marx speaks of the workers' "growing mass of misery, oppression, slavery, degradation, exploitation," Harrington insists that Marx was referring only to the *relative* difference in income and standards of living between workers and capitalists. On Harrington's view of Marx's meaning, even if workers were to enjoy real wages and fringe benefits of $50,000 annually in uninflated dollars, so long as there were a small group of millionaires, the workers would still be degraded paupers and Marx's account of their lot true. . . .

The second half of [*The Twilight of Capitalism*] is an attempt to show that the welfare state in no way refutes Marx's economic predictions. It merely postpones the inevitable day of reckoning. Harrington insists that the welfare state in the United States and elsewhere is still a capitalist society. In one sense it is. But it is also true that the size of the public sector, the power of free trade unions, the scope of regulatory agencies, makes capitalist society of 1976 more different from that of 1876, than 1876 is from 1776. (p. 36)

The second section contains some well founded criticisms of current tax and energy policies. Their failure is attributed to the capitalist nature of the welfare state. To establish this Harrington abandons the notion of society as an "organic" totality in which there is reciprocal causation among plural factors and reverts to reliance upon the "primary" or ultimate cause—the capitalist structure—that cannot explain differential, specific effects. . . . Regardless of the problem, it seems as if it is always capitalism that in the last analysis is responsible for our failure to solve it. But since welfare state capitalism is certainly compatible with tax, energy and income policies that more equitably redistribute the burdens of the recession, if only enough citizens can be persuaded of it, capitalism cannot be the decisive factor in explaining the choice among policy alternatives . . . .

Harrington's analysis is as enlightening as the observation on the death by lung cancer of a heavily addicted smoker, that his death was not merely the result of his addiction but also of "the profound limitations" of the human organism.

A scientific approach to social as well as medical problems deals only in proximate causes. The limitations of capitalist society are much more modifiable than those of the human organism. (p. 37)

Sidney Hook, "Books Considered: 'The Twilight of Capitalism: A Marxian Epitaph'," in The New Republic *(reprinted by permission of* The New Republic; © *1976 The New Republic, Inc.), Vol. 175, Nos. 6 & 7, August 7 & 14, 1976, pp. 34-7.*

IAN MAITLAND

The task Harrington sets himself is to provide a fresh interpretation of Marx and to apply it to elucidating the "secret history" of capitalism's recent crises. Accordingly, over half [*The Twilight of Capitalism*] is taken up with a close exegesis of Marxist texts. . . .

Harrington's Marx is an expurgated version, which is to say he is a Social Democrat. He has been purged of all his grosser mechanistic tendencies. But in the process of sanitizing him, Harrington has left Marx curiously bloodless and vacuous. . . . (p. 963)

Harrington's argument is that the greatly enlarged role of the state in Western society has not altered that system's basically capitalist character, but has aggravated its natural propensity for crisis. In capitalism (i.e., wherever the economy is dominated by private institutions) the state is automatically co-opted by corporate interests. . . . And his evidence for the proposition that the welfare state has been pressed into the service of corporate interests is strained: what possible corporate priority is served if whites make greater use of Medicaid than blacks, or New York than Alabama?

On a deeper level Harrington's book is intelligible less as another socialist manifesto than as a romantic assault on the technocratic values he feels are dominant in Western culture. He is especially severe on the mentality that enthrones economic criteria at the expense of social priorities—in Harrington's scheme the two are always antagonistic, never cooperative—a mentality characterized by terms such as profit, efficiency, productivity, the "flawed concept of the GNP," and so on. . . .

It should be remarked that a deep vein of cultural snobbery runs through Harrington's attack on economic values, as it does through much middle-class radicalism. After all, he is denouncing values shared by a large majority of the working class, and, what is more, he is calling them dupes for holding those values. This sort of socialism springs not from a sympathy for the worker and his aspirations but from a profound alienation from him.

In these pages "capitalism" is judged and found wanting by the standards of "democratic socialism," a concept which is realized in no contemporary society and which Harrington never analyzes. By insisting that the problems of capitalism are peculiar to it and by taking for granted its benefits, Harrington excuses himself from saying how his alternative would improve on its solutions. (p. 964)

Ian Maitland, "How Is a Marxist Like a Penquin?"
in National Review (© National Review, Inc., 1976;
150 East 35th St., New York, NY 10016), Vol. XXVII,
No. 33, September 3, 1976, pp. 963-64.

LEWIS A. COSER

In Part I [of *The Twilight of Capitalism*] (and in a series of appendices) Harrington attempts to extract the valid core of Marxist doctrine and to distinguish it from what he considers the many past and contemporary fallacies concerning Marx's essential message. In this endeavor he states that Marx himself and the Marxists "made a major contribution to the misunderstanding of Marxism". . . . Perhaps. But if, as the author avers, Marx "conceptualizes society as an organic whole in which the economic, the political, the sociological and the cultural so interpenetrate one another that they cannot be explained in and of themselves" . . . , then it becomes unclear what distinguishes the Marxian vision from that of a great number of other thinkers. The proletariat, the main actor in the Marxian drama, is all but absent in Harrington's account.

Curiously enough, the most distinctively relevant element of the Marxian canon for Harrington is the labor theory of value and the theory of surplus value developed in the first volume of *Das Kapital*. Yet it is precisely that aspect of the Marxian doctrine which has been rejected even by economists . . . who are otherwise most sympathetic to the Marxian vision. Be that as it may, Harrington's Marx is essentially the theorist of capitalist exploitation, and the analyst of the anarchy of capitalist productive relations with their built-in cycles of boom and bust and their dehumanizing effects not only on the working class but on society as a whole. He is a determinately democratic thinker whose spirit has been perverted by most of those who purport to speak in his name, be it in the East or in the West. There is much here with which one may well agree while yet failing to be fully persuaded by Harrington's sometimes rather involuted attempts to save Marx from his critics. . .

Despite Harrington's undoubted erudition and vast knowledge of both primary and secondary sources of Marxism, one cannot help but feel that he is more at home in his polemical discussions of the present predicaments of American capitalism. Here his social passion and his commitment to the notion of a more equalitarian, more fraternal, and more democratic society serve him well. His documentation of, among others, the American government's collusion with the oil companies both at home and abroad, the government's subsidies to giant agribusiness interests, or the inequities of our tax system is devastatingly effective. His claim that much of what goes by the name of the welfare state, far from bringing about greater equality, has in fact favored the upper classes, sounds convincing indeed. Yet it would seem that these impassioned pages owe as much to the American muckraking and reform tradition as they owe to classical Marxism. Surely many non-Marxist economists and sociologists would agree with Harrington that ours is still a capitalist, profit-oriented society whose largely unplanned development continues to be marked by social and economic crises. (pp. 701-02)

Lewis A. Coser, "Book Reviews: 'The Twilight of Capitalism'," in Political Science Quarterly, Vol. 91, No. 4, Winter, 1976-77, pp. 701-02.

LEWIS S. FEUER

"The spirit of the new Karl Marx must be our comrade in the struggle," writes Harrington [in *The Twilight of Capitalism*].

The "new Karl Marx" turns out to be Michael Harrington's personal philosophy as buttressed by those quotations from Marx that fit; those that don't are either ignored, explained away as statements by Marx made when, for reasons unknown, he was engaged in misrepresenting Marxism. . . . (p. 46)

Harrington especially rejects the "deterministic Marx," the "vulgar Marxism," "mechanistic" and "schematic." Stalin, he asserts, wanted a deterministic Marx for political reasons. . . . But Marx's theory, says Harrington, was not "a deterministic economic construct." The purely scholarly difficulty for Harrington is that Marx, in his first preface to *Das Kapital*, in 1867, did write of his book as helping a nation to get "on the right track for the discovery of the natural laws of its movement"; laying bare "the economic law of motion of modern society" would thus help make the transition easier. (pp. 46-7)

Mr. Harrington is . . . generally mindful, as he states it, that there is no "neat" relationship between philosophical theory and political practice. But he does not note that Marx throughout his life . . . affirmed precisely such a relationship. (p. 47)

In Harrington's eyes . . . the Marxist standpoint toward reality is privileged. Marx's political commitment, he holds, opened his eyes to realities that a "bourgeois" couldn't perceive. We might ask: What realities did he perceive that such bourgeois as [John Stuart] Mill and [Benjamin] Disraeli failed to note? As a theologian, Harrington might have told us of the Marxist sin of pride; for the privilege of the "proletarian" standpoint also may carry its penalty; Marx failed to see things that others did. . . . Similarly, Harrington sees rationality in planning, a matching of supply to demand, when theory and experience alike show that their gross mismatching is far more likely.

Apart from the search for the "new Marx," Mr. Harrington's book is a sustained polemic against the welfare state, which, he argues, is national planning subordinated to capitalist priorities. . . . He proposes to give its "secret history" (a classical Marxist phrase). Franklin Roosevelt, he holds, was a cynic and inaugurated the New Deal mostly as a "conscious attempt to stave off radical change". . . . Again we are confronted with the pride-primed assumption that only Marxists could conceivably have the people's welfare at heart. . . . Occasionally Harrington graciously concedes that the welfare state is not a "conscious, almost conspiratorial" tool of the corporations; it turns out that he means it's an unconscious tool rather than a conscious one, which given the Marxist concept of ideology as shaped by unconscious economic motives is a minor amendment. . . . Harrington wants to pump a socialist content into the welfare state. Naturally he indicts the multinational oil corporations for having made the American economy so dependent on Arabian oil. But let us suppose that these corporations had been nationalized in the manner of the Anglo-Iranian Oil Company or the Soviet companies operating in Czechoslovakia. Is the record of socialist imperialism better than the capitalist? (p. 47-8)

Dialectical is the key word that irrupts continuously in Mr. Harrington's paragraphs. Its function seems, however, primarily an ecstatic one. I gave up after a while enumerating its different senses. . . . [We] are driven to the conclusion that Harrington has a dialectical theory of *dialectic*, that is, the word never has the same meaning twice from paragraph to paragraph. This verbal flux might have pleased Heraclitus, but the scientific ("bourgeois"?) reader may think that it contravenes scientific logic.

The word *whole* has likewise an ecstatic significance for Harrington, whose usage seems prescientific. For the question one asks about any given system is: How interdependent are its elements? . . . The language of functions and parameters can express the variations in the types of systems; the language of "wholes" cannot. Harrington argues that an "organic whole" differs from a "system" insofar as it includes the action of the observer. But it was precisely such systems-theorists as Niels Bohr who clarified the bearing of the observer on the observed entities and relations; Bohr's principle of complementarity told scientists to drop the notion of explaining the "whole." Harrington shares the antipathy of Lukacs (and Marcuse) to mathematics as the "[bourgeois] paradigmatic science for all thought." This, however, was precisely what Marx believed, unlike the latter-day irrationalists.

Economic determinism, Harrington warns us, can lead to "paranoiac" misinterpretations of history. . . . Alas, this propensity has been a pervasive trait in all the Marxist parties, factions, and sects. . . . It is doubtful that Marxists are saner than their rival ideologists. (p. 48)

> *Lewis S. Feuer, "Mendicant Friar of the Revolution," in* The Humanist *(copyright 1977 by the American Humanist Association; reprinted by permission), Vol. XXXVII, No. 1, January-February, 1977, pp. 46-8.*

DANIEL BELL

Michael Harrington begins *The Twilight of Capitalism* with the startling premise that Paul Samuelson, Joan Robinson, Louis Althusser, Erich Fromm, Hannah Arendt, Raymond Aron, and I, in one way or another, have misinterpreted, misunderstood, and even misquoted Marx and that he will present not just a possibly better or more comprehensive reading but, to quote him, the "authentic Marx," the "real Marx" (and presumably, then, the only rational Marx). . . .

This is surely an extraordinary claim. How could so many well-known and even distinguished scholars mislead themselves and thus their readers? It turns out on closer examination that Harrington believes the real culprits were Marx and Engels themselves. . . . (p. 187)

Actually, in his crude attempt to "whitewash" Marx, Harrington is unfair to Marx and to the genuine intellectual questions he wrestled with all his life, which led him often, even if understandably, to vulgar statements as well as to different and more complex formulations. Like all of us to this day, Marx was seeking to resolve a number of inherently irreconcilable dilemmas in the epistemology and sociology of the social sciences. (p. 189)

The point is that on no single theme associated with Marx's name—historical materialism, class, the crises of capitalism—is there a single unambiguous definition of a concept. Marx never used the phrase "historical materialism" (it was coined by Engels; Engels never used the phrase "dialectical materialism," which was invented by Plekhanov); and the famous statement that it is not the consciousness of men that determines their existence but their existence that determines their consciousness is vague, mechanistic, and even contradictory. "Class" is defined variously. . . . (p. 190)

Harrington wants to correct the "vulgar Marxists" who see society in terms of a substructure and superstructure and see the politics and culture of a society as always "determined" by the economic elements or even the mode of production itself. Society is an "organic whole," "in which the economic, political and social interact reciprocally upon one another." . . . Thus, "When one conceptualizes society as an organic whole in which the economic, the political, the sociological and the cultural so interpenetrate one another they cannot be explained in and of themselves, then there is no room for a completely independent discipline of economics or political science or sociology or aesthetics."

One rubs one's eyes in astonishment. This is like saying that, if one sees "nature whole," there is no possibility of independent disciplines such as physics, chemistry, geology, astronomy, or the like. But the real confusion is compounded because Harrington nowhere defines what he means by "society" or what are its boundaries in space and time. If one talks, as Harrington does, of "capitalist society," are prewar and postwar Japan; the Weimar, Nazi, and Federal Republics of Germany; and the United States all part of an "organic whole"? (pp. 190-91)

Harrington is confusing a "system" with a "society." Any system has mutually interacting elements, and capitalism as a socioeconomic system (e.g., commodity production) is an aspect of these different societies; but the political systems are largely at variance because they do not derive from the socioeconomic. And the different components such as the technological and the cultural have completely different historical rhythms; so again, what is "organic"? . . .

The central dilemma for Marx was that he thought the "mode of production" (a conceptual abstraction) *constitutive* of society, as Darwin's theory of evolution was constitutive of biological development or Newton's laws of motion constitutive of the universe. Harrington writes that for Marx "economics is, by its very definition, a bourgeois discipline." This is not so. For Marx—and this was the rock of his belief—economics was the *material embodiment* of philosophy. . . . (p. 191)

Harrington's second effort to provide a "new Marx" is to rehabilitate the "law of value" against its economic despisers such as Paul Samuelson. But if the first effort is highly focused, the second has no focus at all. It is quite evident that Marx's idea of value is independent of price, because he sought a system of constants in which, to use the technical jargon, microeconomics (the individual decisions of buyers and sellers) could be aggregated into a macroeconomic, or system, model. Harrington seems to be completely unaware of that problem. His discussion of the law of value repeats the motif of soapbox oratory that, when a worker works an eight-hour day, some hours are "gratis" or surplus value; his central point is that, since the system is unplanned, there is bound to be a cycle of boom and bust. (How planners would know what the people want, without markets, remains undiscussed.)

Harrington spends much time on the so-called transformation problem—how values become converted into market prices—yet seems totally unaware of the question of aggregation. And the crux of that issue is whether capitalism necessarily has to break down. (p. 192)

The point I want to make is that Harrington's exposition is a cheat. It pretends to discuss the "law of value" but ignores the entire technical literature on the problem, from its comprehensive exposition in Paul Sweezey's *Theory of Capitalist Development* (reformulating Bortkewicz) down to the profuse literature of the present day.

The same cheat is repeated on a more elaborate scale in part 2 of the book. In a chapter entitled "Introduction to a Secret History," Harrington claims, "It is the argument of Part II of this book that it was and is the structure of capitalist society that turned the historical accidents of the 1970s into calamitous necessities." But nowhere does Harrington employ, in coherent or more than offhand remarks, any of the Marxian tools or any of the specific theories of crises in order to explain the situation of the 1970s; he merely states repeatedly that the unplanned nature of capitalism leads to crises. Most of the chapters are taken up with polemics seeking to show that the United States government has intervened more directly to help corporations than other social groups, that inequality has not been substantially reduced, that the neo-conservatives are wrong in their judgments about the welfare state, and so on. All of these points are debatable, but I do not want to be deflected from the central question, which is, What specifically does this "new Marx" tell us about contemporary society that is genuinely new? The answer is nothing. (p. 193)

I have said Harrington's book is a cheat. That is a serious charge. Yet it derives from his method. On a theoretical level, it derives from the most serious violation of Marx's own method, which is to treat ideas historically. In constructing his "authentic Marx," Harrington makes a pastiche in which passages from [Marx's] *Economic-Philosophical Manuscripts* are joined with passages from [Marx's] *Capital*, etc. This is a lawyer's brief or a theological mode, but not true to the way a man's ideas develop. He compresses passages in order to make Marx seem more foresighted than he was. (pp. 194-95)

The notion of an "authentic Marx" is inherently absurd. No protean thinker can ever be given a single, unambiguous reading. (pp. 195-96)

> *Daniel Bell, "Review Essay: The Once and Future Marx," in* The American Journal of Sociology *(reprinted by permission of The University of Chicago Press; © 1977 by The University of Chicago), Vol. 83, No. 1, July, 1977, pp. 187-97.*

RICHARD C. LEVIN

[Michael Harrington, in *The Twilight of Capitalism*, presents a] subtle and comprehensive analysis of the relationship of economics and politics in contemporary capitalism.

Harrington has a twofold purpose, and his book is divided accordingly. His first aim is exegesis: he argues that Marx has been widely misunderstood, by Marxists and non-Marxists alike. . . . Harrington insists that Marx did not advance a theory of economic determinism in which the dynamic forces in the economic "base" completely determine the development of the political and cultural "superstructure." Rather Marx viewed society as a complex totality, an organic whole in which economic, political and ideological forces interact reciprocally, yet a whole to which the mode of production imparts "a pervasive lighting . . . a special atmosphere.". . . . Harrington could have undoubtedly strengthened his case had he examined more carefully Marx's historical writings, such as those treating the 1848 uprisings, the ascension of Louis Napoleon, and the Paris Commune, in which Marx's acknowledgment of the "relative autonomy" . . . of political and ideological forces is readily apparent.

While Harrington rightly criticizes crude formulations of economic determinism as reductive and misleading, his position is not wholly satisfactory. . . . [If] the dynamic of technolog-ical forces and class relations within the mode of production is not conceived as the ultimate determinant of historical development, but merely as a "pervasive lighting" coloring the whole of social reality, one must ask whether Harrington's Marx really has a distinctive theory of historical development, or even of capitalist development. (pp. 755-56)

Despite this shortcoming, Harrington's discussion of Marx has much of value. While not profoundly original, it is by and large a balanced and sensible reading of Marx, and its chief virtue is its clarity and simplicity. . . . While Harrington rarely probes deeply, neither does he rely on the obscure Hegelian rhetoric so prevalent among Marxist writers. Indeed, I know of no better broad-brush introduction to Marxian social theory.

In the second part of his book, Harrington attempts to analyze in the spirit of Marx the role of the welfare state in modern capitalism. The exercise constitutes an application of Marxist methodology only in the loosest sense, in part because Harrington's conception of Marxist methodology places so much emphasis on its openness and flexibility. Save for his discussion of the ideological elements in the language of political actors and contemporary social theorists, it is difficult to understand in what sense Harrington has given us more than a sensible, perceptive empirical analysis of the character and significance of the welfare state.

In Harrington's view, the contemporary state is no mere tool of the ruling class. . . . Rather, as in the vision of pluralism articulated by liberal political scientists, policy is formed through competition among interest groups. In Harrington's view, mass organization by labor, blacks, or other minority interests can have significant political and economic consequences; the obstacle is that the capitalists hold the trump cards. Thus, pressures for reform come from below, but reform is typically co-opted from above and deflected to suit the interests of the powerful. The outcome is ambivalent. On the one hand, capitalism contains the forces seeking to alter the real distribution of power and wealth in society; on the other hand, the price of containment is the enlargement of the role of the state, which, given its relative autonomy, renders the system susceptible to further pressures for reform. (p. 757)

> *Richard C. Levin, "Perspectives on Contemporary Capitalism," in* The Journal of Economic History *(copyright 1977 by The Economic History Association), Vol. XXXVII, No. 3, September, 1977, pp. 755-61.**

J. RON STANFIELD

The central theme of [the first part of Michael Harrington's *The Twilight of Capitalism*] is that Marx has been sadly misinterpreted by foes and friends alike. The potential reader is allowed some skepticism owing to the parade of "what Marx said" and "what Marx really said" books. However, Harrington avoids the tone of this parade even if he must reasonably be said to be marching in it. Moreover, much is to be said for a new addition to the parade given the fruitful discussions within and without Marxism which have taken place in the last few decades. (pp. 217-18)

Harrington begins with the fundamental insight of Marx's social economics, that it is not simply the production of goods and services that must be examined, but more importantly, the reproduction of society. . . . He goes on to explore the relation of the Marxist economic categories base and superstructure to one another and fairly convincingly refutes any inevitablist, reflexive, and technological or economic determinist interpretation of Marx. . . . Harrington adroitly demonstrates the insensitivity of orthodox economics to Marx's work. . . . [In his treatment of Marx's "spiritual materialism"] Harrington comes off as both the hard bitten liberal, sympathetic but rather cynical about high ethical ideals, and as the passionate humanist scathingly rejecting determinism. . . . Harrington [in the final chapter of Part One] establishes himself as a Marxist social theorist of the first rank. His scholarship is demonstrated by such insights as his recognition of the "Introduction" to the *Grundrisse* which Marx wrote in 1857 as a profound methodological statement. . . . Harrington thus carries on the finest tradition of Marxism, that of the competent scholar and zealous political activist. For this reason alone, that it establishes one of a handful of important political leaders on the American left as a scholar in his own right, this is an important book.

But it is also important for Part Two. . . . [The] main task of Part Two [is the] demonstration that the liberal welfare state remains capitalist and will remain so until dealt with as such. . . . Harrington denies the contention of disillusioned liberals, neoconservatives, that the welfare state failed in the 1960s due to some inherent limitations of its ideals or of human nature. Obviously, the purpose is to clear the way for the conclusion that it is the underlying capitalist reality that subverts the ideals of the welfare state. (pp. 218-19)

Harrington as political chronicler . . . is somewhat less satisfying to this reviewer than Harrington as dissector of Marxist theory. . . . Still, Harrington is both a Marxist theorist and political commentator; and if the two parts do not quite form a unified whole, they are nonetheless two good parts. (pp. 219-20)

> *J. Ron Stanfield, "Book Reviews: 'The Twilight of Capitalism'," in* Review of Social Economy, *Vol. XXV, No. 2, October, 1977, pp. 217-20.*

JOHN LEONARD

[In **"The Vast Majority"** Michael Harrington] is writing a book about "the cruel innocence" of Americans whose worldwide economic arrangements are designed to preserve the gap between the rich and the poor, those who eat steak and those who eat rice. And yet he keeps biting himself on the neck. If I, he seems to be saying, if I—full of good intentions, socialist pieties and all the latest facts and figures—can go dull at the wretchedness of what I see, what hope is there? . . .

At first [Harrington's] method seems arbitrary and annoying. The self intrudes. Who cares whether Mr. Harrington took his tennis racquet to Bombay or why he feels more at home with Julius Nyerere than with Robert McNamara? Get on, please, with your argument.

Then we realize that Mr. Harrington is in despair. His despair is that he will fall into despair; that the situation is so bad that his own brand of humane democratic socialism may be inadequate; that the alternatives are quietism or terrorism, a status quo or a Stalin. He intrudes to prove his sincerity. He wants desperately to believe that our labor movement is more idealistic than it is, and that there is an enlightened capitalist self-interest to which the third world can appeal. He is a man putting his very sinew on the line.

His argument is that "Northern"capitalist expansion has so changed the world that the "South" is never going to be able to expand, or take off, in the same way. Because of trade

relations, capital reinvestment, research and development programs, new technologies and general flimflam, "they" aren't even going to catch up with "us." Moreover: Why should they? We waste. Our cultural vitality consists of hundreds of varieties of cereals differentiated only by advertising. Nevertheless: Too many of them are starving for a liberal stomach to stand or swallow. . . .

What, then, is to be done? After explaining that the birth rate isn't really the problem; and that natural resources and labor productivity are not the problem, and that climate and genes are not the problem, either—although cultural "coherence" may be—Mr. Harrington is modest. He proposes increasing and then stabilizing prices paid for third world commodities, more aid from the "North," the forgiving of debts, help in industrialization, a world treasury and, ultimately and extravagantly, a world government and global economic planning. . . .

There is such an outlet in Nairobi. We aren't as good as Mr. Harrington thinks we are. Some consciences don't even wheedle. But if we make it up from scum to something like a principle, we will be standing on the shoulders of people like Mr. Harrington.

> *John Leonard, "Food and Conscience," in* The New York Times *(© 1977 by The New York Times Company; reprinted by permission), November 21, 1977, p. 35.*

ROBERT LEKACHMAN

[**"The Vast Majority"**], by turns perceptive reportage and passionate social analysis, records impressions of brief visits to India, Kenya, Tanzania and Mexico. Analysis and travel diary are part of the author's determination to rescue Americans from their willful ignorance of the many ways in which our national policy contributes to the continuing destitution of most of the world's population.

In India during Mrs. Gandhi's mercifully terminated experiment in authoritarian rule, Harrington broods on the Stalinist temptation to replace inefficient democratic forms with state propaganda and police coercion, the better to drive the reluctant citizens of a backward society into the modern world. Although he is himself a socialist and a democrat . . . , he searches his heart and discovers there, momentarily, the same impatience with the corruptions of capitalist democracy as perhaps animated Indira Gandhi. It seems that, in a degraded form, Stalinism echoes the Platonic dream of benign, omniscient guardians of the state. A little more observation of Indira suffices to persuade him that Mrs. Gandhi, in taking away Indian liberties, did not pay in the coin of coherent, central planning and suppression of corruption.

Stalinism is not the remedy for global poverty, but what is? Capitalism, American-style? Not for Harrington. He agrees with neo-Marxist condemnation of the United States as an imperialist power "at the center of a complex, structured and interdependent system, historically and presently suffused with capitalist values and priorities, which massively reproduces the injustices of a world partitioned among the fat and the starving." It helps matters very little that most Americans are utterly unaware of the degree to which multinational corporations distort developing economies in their own interest. Many poor countries must import food not only because there are more mouths to feed, but also because so frequently multinationals have diverted native agriculture from home-consumed foods to cash export crops like coffee, beef, sugar, cotton and cocoa. As in Brazil, often cited as a success story of capitalist development, rapid growth has been accompanied by steady decline in average living standards. The Green Revolution that has for the most part benefited landowners and prosperous farmers has foundered because of reliance on petroleum-based fertilizers and expensive farm equipment ill suited to poor countries.

Harrington is bitterly skeptical about the proposition popular in respectable business and political circles that the developing countries will solve their problems by showing proper hospitality to foreign capital. . . . As Harrington accurately observes, Kissinger and his allies rely upon the classic principle of comparative advantage. Poor countries are allotted raw-material production and labor-intensive manufacturing. Their rich trading partners get the sophisticated, high-productivity technology and the bulk of the gains from specialization that are at the center of economists' demonstrations that everybody wins from free trade.

Marxist and non-Marxist radical analysts have their their limitations. They are good at diagnosis and terrible at therapy. Harrington is troubled by the complete dearth of practical proposals. He cites Christian Palloix, a French Marxist, who concluded a two-volume study of the world capitalist economy with the candid admission that his theory was "purely negative." Since socialist revolution is implausible, and Harrington's world community of nations utopian, something must be done today to feed the hungry and clothe the naked.

Thus, with resignation Harrington comes back to an exploration of what can be done within the limits of market capitalism. Noting the actual moderation of Third World demands, he thinks that the poor will fare better if their cries for commodity stability are heeded, . . . and if the United States vastly expands its foreign aid, now running at less than half the standard suggested by the United Nations. Here too, Harrington realistically notes that it is hard for average Americans to support more foreign aid when their own jobs and incomes are in peril. The prerequisite to more liberal foreign policies is full employment at home.

Like everything Michael Harrington writes, this sensitive evocation of the plight of the world's poor is animated by a rare combination of compassion, civility toward opponents, introspection and analytical skill. (pp. 12, 45)

> Robert Lekachman, *"The Other World,"* in The New York Times Book Review (© 1977 by The New York Times Company; reprinted by permission), November 27, 1977, pp. 12,45.

JOHN GREENWAY

The Vast Majority is Michael Harrington's eighth book. All achieve a supernally consistent quality. . . . In this account of his "journey to the world's poor"—some two billion people by his body count—he demonstrates that his grasp of geopolitics is as firm as that of the folksinging Appalachian hillbilly who explained to the song-collecting professor that his next ballad was about a son of the Virgin Queen Elizabeth named King Napoleon, who led an army of Kentuckians south by canoes across the Alps to capture a group of cities in Moscow called "The Bonny Bunch of Roses-O."

Harrington returned from his Third (and Fourth) World tour with the revelation that we Americans, not satisfied with having invented the plagues of profit, poverty, oppression, capitalism, nationalism, colonialism, multinational capitalistic economic imperialism, slavery, well-poisoning, pollution, genocide, anthropology, and procrastination, devised out of our surfeit of innocent maliciousness such things as Tanzanian fanaticism, filariasis, schistosomiasis, prostitution in Tiajuana (sic), chewing gum for beggar children in Mexico City, and a socioeconomic system "that makes children leprous in Bombay, furrows the foreheads of women in Kenya, and turns Indians in Guatemala into drunkards." (p. 161)

[It] is no kindness to Harrington to look at him seriously. His curious admissions ("I want to write with a passionate objectivity"; "I am a contradictory, compromised, and somewhat baffled person"; "I want now to briefly face up to the tensions within me"); his hatred of America, embedded in his very soul; that pathologically melancholy face, unchanged across the years, except for the furrows deepening in his forehead; his graceless prose; the agenbite of inwit and acedia characteristic of apostate Catholics—all show him to be a Hofferian True Believer without a god, faith, or master, one whose commitment is only to fouling his own nation's nest.

He professes socialism, yet in this book he admits that philosophy cannot work without the prosperity only capitalism can supply, and that his wished-for abolition of capitalism would mean the destruction of his beloved Third World. (pp. 161-62)

> John Greenway, *"Biting Sticks,"* in National Review (© National Review, Inc., 1978; 150 East 35th St., New York, NY 10016), Vol.XXX, No. 5, February 3, 1978, pp. 161-62.

ANDREW SILK

[Self-doubt] is at the center of Michael Harrington's *The Vast Majority: A Journey to the World's Poor.* In journals of short trips to India, East Africa and Mexico as well as in a long theoretical discussion of underdevelopment, he writes of the painful conflict of a Western radical. . . .

[The] limitation of self-consciousness hampers Harrington's theoretical discussion of underdevelopment. He is not at home enough in the Third World to be able to bring his theory close to the poverty he has traveled through. Instead he uses the discussion to explore his own problematic position within the American Establishment—as a man who attempts to influence the mainstream, but is sympathetic to Marxist analyses.

He writes to expose what he calls the "cruel ignorance" of many good and caring Americans who assent to a system which helps create and sustain Third World poverty. . . .

Harrington is at great pains to distance himself from the "vulgar Marxists" who see the work of all multinationals as demonic. Yet at the same time, he is on unfamiliar ground, and often does little more than give his own reaction to the writings of neoclassical and neo-Marxist economists as well as Marx himself. It is hard to figure out where he stands. . . .

The Marxist theory of underdevelopment, much of which Harrington endorses, maintains that the expansion of capitalism results in the continuation of Third World poverty and forces deformed development in those countries. At times, Harrington appears to believe that there is little to stop the further immiserization of Third World countries aside from a violent struggle against capitalist domination of the world economy.

Yet he does not call for such a global confrontation. Instead, he urges mild reform: greater aid to the Third World, a cancellation of Third World debts, and an increase in the prices of commodities produced there (p. 123)

But no sooner does he suggest these reforms than Harrington gives in to his radical suspicions. By enabling the existing relationship between First and Third Worlds to work more equitably for a while, the reforms may perpetuate the system and in the long run produce a greater crisis.

Harrington finally appears as frustrated by the intellectual challenge of the Third World as he is by the emotional challenge. . . .

This feeling of desperation results from Harrington's failure to respond to the Third World on its own terms. He bases his analysis too much on Western guilt for he sees the Third World largely as our poor step-child. There may be a distorted truth in this. But Americans will only be able to rescue themselves from their cruel ignorance when they begin to see the underdeveloped world as it sees itself—as an independent people fighting internal struggles and looking for internal solutions. (p. 124)

> Andrew Silk, *"The Perils of Compassion," in* The Nation *(copyright 1978* The Nation *magazine, The Nation Associates, Inc.), Vol. 226, No. 4, February 4, 1978, pp. 123-24.*

MICHAEL LEDEEN

In *The Vast Majority,* Michael Harrington . . . purports to offer an analysis of global inequality; . . . and a "remedy" for the current world system. . . . The villain of the piece, to no one's surprise, is the United States, indeed "the people of the United States," who in their "cruel innocence" are the keystone of this entire repressive and exploitative edifice.

In Harrington's view, Americans are responsible for the suffering of the world's poor because they participate in the capitalist system, which has committed the grave sin of imposing a "growth process" on the Third World from without, instead of permitting underdeveloped countries to evolve naturally and organically. As if this were not enough, the growth process itself turns out to be a sham, because it is based on nothing but the desire for profit on the part of external capitalist forces led by multinational corporations. As a result, the Third World has no hope of reaching the standard of living of the developed West, because even when it achieves high levels of productivity, its wealth is drained off into the capitalist world—largely into the U.S. marketplace. . . .

Now, there is a case to be made for spreading the wealth around the world more equally, and Harrington recognizes that the case is essentially moral. Unfortunately, the moral argument can be stated in a line or two. . . . Harrington has written some two hundred fifty pages of incoherent, pretentious, and contradictory nonsense. . . .

The central thesis—and the central weakness—of the book is the claim that misery is due to capitalism. If there is one subject that any self-respecting socialist ought to have mastered, it is this. But Harrington, despite his numerous protestations against vulgar Marxism, remains the slave of a rigidly mechanistic view of both the history and the contemporary practice of capitalism. Worse still, he has gotten many of his categories confused, and repeatedly confounds bourgeois society with capitalism, the growth of cities with the industrial revolution, and accident with what Hegel used to call "the cunning of history." (p. 86)

Harrington's treatment of capitalism derives from the American radicalism of the 60's, according to which anything America and American businesses do is "capitalism" or "imperialism," and the underdeveloped societies are the innocent bodies upon which it is done. This model runs throughout *The Vast Majority,* even though there are moments when Harrington himself realizes that he has got it all wrong. (p. 87)

Harrington . . . has chosen to ignore the central fact about the Third World: its exquisitely totalitarian political structure. This is a curious omission for a democratic socialist, who ought to know that the problem of distribution cannot be dealt with until there is a *democratic* revolution. For if you do not have political democracy, national wealth will not be distributed throughout the population. Thus, until the poor within a country have enough political power to compel the wealthy to share with them, even a massive influx of money and "infrastructure" will not solve the problem of poverty. One need only look at the behavior of the Saudi royal family—several thousand strong—to grasp the fatuousness of the argument that sharing the wealth of the capitalist North will bring about a more equitable distribution of resources in the [Third World] South. Harrington is so obsessed with the notion of America's responsibility for world poverty that he refuses to see what is right there under his nose: the responsibility of the ruling classes of the Third World.

Harrington conveniently overlooks another central fact about the demands for the New Order: most of the countries asking the United States and Western Europe to contribute to their welfare are dedicated to the enfeeblement of the West. Significantly, there is little discussion in the book of the successful Arab oil embargo and attendant price rise, for to have dealt with these would have compelled Harrington to recognize that the Arab countries, which are not investing billions in the capitalist North, should themselves be asked to make massive investments in the South, where the petroleum price increases have sounded the death knell for most development plans. Instead, we find a tortured discussion of American grain policies at home and abroad. (pp. 87-8)

It is useless to approach these problems through the myths of a bygone day, and it is ludicrous that the source of such mythmaking should be a writer who passes for a major American social critic. (p. 88)

> Michael Ledeen, *"To Have & Have Not," in* Commentary *(reprinted by permission; all rights reserved), Vol. 65, No. 3, March, 1978, pp. 86-8.*

LORNA HAHN

[*The Vast Majority: A Journey to the World's Poor*] is a maddening book. Maddening because [Michael Harrington], a leading American Socialist, flays people of the industrial world for behaving in ways he himself admits are natural or inevitable, while ignoring or indulging many faults and frailties of the less fortunate. Maddening because, although a good number of his points are bolstered by a wealth of documentation drawn from Marxist as well as non-Marxist sources, others cry for some elaboration or demonstration. Maddening because in addition to soundly structured arguments, we are given easily-toppled straw men. And maddening because the conditions Michael Harrington describes with convincing compassion are so real, so perdurable and, as he implies, so defiant of solutions.

The villain is "a global system of injustice that warps or destroys the minds and bodies of hundreds of millions of human beings." . . .

That, of course, is hardly news. What is new and worth reading are some of Harrington's views as to why most schemes that appear likely to help the Third World constitute little more than "the development of underdevelopment" and the reinforcement of existing evils. . . .

Realistically and judiciously, Harrington does not attribute the perpetuation of international injustice to deliberate individual or governmental malevolence, but rather to the system in which, consciously or unwittingly, we are all ensnared. He also declares: "The worst thing that could happen to the Third World during the next 25 or 50 years would be a catastrophic collapse of Western capitalism." And he rightly notes it would be good business for the U.S. to make sure the poorer countries do not become so pauperized that they can no longer provide resources and markets.

But surely Harrington is being unrealistic in repeatedly exhorting the wealthier countries to sacrifice and to restructure their ways on terms geared basically to the needs of the poor—especially since, as he observes, some of their own leaders care less than we do about who starves. He is on weak ground as well when he condemns Western capitalists and analysts for looking upon the status quo to be "Utopia." No one, including the individuals he cites, really holds that view. At worst, the various arguments of the defenders of present conditions boil down to the contention that nothing better can be done. Others, meanwhile, have been striving for genuine improvements in the living standards of the poor—and actually achieving success in several quarters—without risking radical upheavals that could prove dangerous for all concerned. (pp. 22-3)

[He cautions that India, Mexico and East Africa should be viewed in terms of their] own history and values, not broad or self-serving generalities. He does not, though, go on to attack endemic Third World practices that do so much to impede cohesive development . . . and can at least to some degree be corrected. Nor does he heed his own advice about respecting cultural differences when he suggests that in India, where the Prime Minister proudly and publicly drinks his urine, we should be appalled that the poor urinate and defecate in the streets and rivers and should take steps to change this. . . .

Harrington can be maddening. Nonetheless, his book is valuable and should be read because it also contains much that will get people mad for the right reasons and contribute to his unchallengeable objective: to improve the lot of the poor. (p. 23)

Lorna Hahn, "Missing the Full Story," in The New Leader *(© 1978 by the American Labor Conference on International Affairs, Inc.), Vol. LXI, No. 6, March 13, 1978, pp. 22-3.*

ANDREW HACKER

Harrington's [*The Twilight of Capitalism*] is primarily an homage to Marx. It is a rereading of the master, showing a sympathy that manages to avoid sycophancy. His purpose is to find modern meaning in Marx, acknowledging that anyone who has

been dead for 94 years may need a little help from his friends. Harrington begins with the laudable premise that Marx was neither blind nor obtuse. To those prone to intone that "Marx failed to see" something apparent to just about everyone else, Harrington shows that he was perfectly well aware of whatever it was he is supposed to have overlooked. What we end up with may be less Marx himself than a disciple's interpretation of his mentor. . . . Harrington's achievement is to retain Marx as an instrument for understanding contemporary American capitalism. We may need other tools as well. But the Marxian foundation has fewer fissures than many think.

I wish that Harrington had extended his exegesis one step further, to the interfaces where technology and psychology meet. . . . If we are to reach the socialism Harrington hopes for, then we must know how today's capitalist culture is schooling us for a new form of citizenship. (p. 679)

Andrew Hacker, "American Politics: 'The Twilight of Capitalism'," in The American Political Science Review *(copyright, 1978, by The American Political Science Association), Vol. 72, No. 2, June, 1978, pp. 678-80.*

RAYMOND PLANT

There are many good and useful things in [*The Twilight of Capitalism*] although, taken as a whole, it is something of a disappointment. The first part expands and defends a humanistic reading of Marx, and this is done very well. . . . Indeed, if one wished to refer students to a synoptic but manageable discussion of issues in the contemporary interpretation of Marxism one could not do much better than suggest Part I of Harrington's book. The second part is an attempt to discuss the history of capitalism since the Second World War and in particular features such as current recession and the impact of social policy in the light of the position developed in Part I. . . . The aim, however, is to show that the current crisis in capitalism and the relative failure of social policy is structural to capitalism, but here the argument really draws far too little in detail from the Marxist perspective outlined in the earlier part of the book. I wonder whether this failure is symptomatic—the humanization of Marx may have the effect of making a number of his crucial concepts so vague as to render them of dubious use in rigorous economic and social analysis.

Raymond Plant, "Books: 'The Twilight of Capitalism'," in Political Studies *(© Oxford University Press 1978), Vol. 26, No. 2, June, 1978, p. 301.*

KENNETH J. ARROW

[*The Twilight of Capitalism*] is a deeply felt, carefully thought out, awkwardly expressed argument that Marx's analysis of capitalism is still of great value and in fact supplies the key to understanding the present situation. . . .

Harrington is almost ecumenical among Marxist sects and rival viewpoints, Stalinism and the bureaucratic collectivism of the Soviet Union alone falling outside the pale. He displays understanding and appreciation of most of the current Marxist writers; I doubt if the word "brilliant" has ever been used so often in a book not dealing with diamond cutting. (p. 118)

The book is divided into two parts; the first seeks to interpret Marx correctly and appropriately, the second to apply Marxist analysis to the current economic and political situation.

The first part is largely devoted to critical analysis of Marx's words and actions and to the comments of others on them. The theme, if I may desperately simplify, is that the model of society envisaged by Marx is much less rigid than usually contemplated. (p. 119)

As part of his theme, Harrington denies the contradiction between the humanist Marx of the 1844 manuscripts and the scientific Marx of *Capital*. The latter was simply examining in great detail the economic basis for the alienation of human labor in the capitalist system; but the aim is still the achievement of the unified man.

I am no scholar of the Marxian corpus and cannot evaluate the extent to which Harrington represents correctly Marx's views. (pp. 119-20)

The more specific analyses of the current situation in the second part of the book are more valuable as criticisms than as positive contributions to understanding. It is not that there are not many good pieces of analysis. That the welfare state is a continuation of capitalism and not a new society, that the claims of those who see postindustrial society as a remarkable revolution are exaggerated are well argued. Harrington sees the effects of the new interventions for economic stability as continuing the old views that business determines the priorities of society. He does . . . not allow for the effects of competition in at least somewhat shaping the economy's priorities towards the public's needs. . . . As for health care, one would be hard put to defend the proposition that insufficient resources are being put into that area; even the distribution of the system's benefits has been greatly equalized by the welfare state, through Medicare and Medicaid.

Harrington is usually very fair in his implications; only once did I detect what I would regard as a misleading use of data. He notes . . . that the proportion of tax reductions (in the period 1964-1973) going to the poor was less than the proportion of tax returns (and *vice versa*) at the opposite end of the scale. This means that the *dollar amounts* of tax reduction were lower at the low end than the upper. But a little arithmetic will show that the *proportionate reductions* were much greater. I don't think the phrase "pampering the rich and slighting the poor" is a complete characterization. (p. 122)

Harrington's book is well worth reading. It defies easy summary, because many of its most illuminating remarks are made incidentally. It is more a development of a point of view than a genuine theory. (p. 123)

> *Kenneth J. Arrow, "The Economy and the Economist," in* Partisan Review *(copyright © 1979 by Partisan Review, Inc.), Vol. 46, No. 1, 1979, pp. 113-26.**

ROBERT LEKACHMAN

[In his treatment of contemporary economic adversity in *Decade of Decision*,] Harrington concedes that a possible outcome of our crisis of soaring energy prices, persistent (and increasing) unemployment, sluggish growth in gross national product, and pervasive inflation, is a version of corporate planning. There is an alert, self-confident and intellectually sophisticated wing of the business establishment . . . which accepts national economic planning in its own interests and realistically expects to control the planning process. . . .

As might be expected, the corporate style of national planning emphasizes high profits, cooperative Presidents and Congresses and "responsible" unions. . . . Harrington represents the interests, often at odds with corporate priorities, of blue- and white-color workers, as well as those of his first constituency, the poor. . . .

[Business] is the strongest of American interest groups, the source both of jobs for individuals and prosperity for their communities. As Harrington tells the tale, the responsibility for stagflation is truly corporate, the consequence of its investment and location policies and its resistance to national policies which might alleviate both inflation and unemployment. . . .

Harrington argues that Americans have tolerated a great deal more inequality of income and even more of wealth than is required in order to promote investment and individual effort. By his telling, American extremes of wealth and destitution are ascribable to our heritage of racial, class and sexual prejudice and to the failure, under corporate influence, of Congresses and Presidents of either major party to pursue with genuine enthusiasm full-employment policies.

As Harrington reminds his readers, the pursuit of full employment is a frustrating activity. (p. 309)

Some valuable pages in this volume explain why full employment is vital, a primary target for unions, women, minorities and young workers and a danger to be averted by the corporate sector and its allies. . . .

In Harrington's tactical handbook, full employment is the immediate issue capable of uniting unions, professional workers, minorities, women and intellectuals. If all goes well for the left, full employment as an issue will translate into the growing realization that its achievement requires public control of the corporate sector—the taming of private economic power. Harrington is eclectic about the means of control, a spectrum that covers stronger public regulation . . . and partial or complete nationalization of vital industries like energy and important services such as health care. . . .

In the end, two criteria apply to a polemic like *Decade of Decision*. In the first place, how persuasive is its analysis? By this test, Harrington does extremely well. He has identified the likeliest possibilities for this decade—corporate planning or democratic socialism. But as Harrington is candid in saying, he is an advocate as well as an analyst. The second criterion applicable to his book, then, is how effective is the call to action here sounded? Harrington has convinced and mobilized me, but then I was convinced and mobilized even before I read this volume. Presumably we must wait a few years to see how many of Harrington's fellow citizens actually are converted and then, still harder, inspired to lift themselves out of political apathy into effective organization. (p. 310)

> *Robert Lekachman, "Planning in the 1980s," in* The Nation *(copyright 1980 The Nation magazine, The Nation Associates, Inc.), Vol. 230, No. 10, March 15, 1980, pp. 309-10.*

JAMES FALLOWS

Although written with considerable economic erudition, [*Decade of Decision*] is essentially a political manifesto. Like others of that genre, it is far more acute and convincing when analyzing what is wrong today than in saying, specifically, what else we should do. Harrington dissects modern-day capitalism to reveal its familiar problems: an economic distribution in which one half of one per cent of the people own one quarter of the total national wealth. . . .

This analysis is most effective when Harrington argues against the two basic planks of the capitalist creed: that economic inequalities are essential to inspire discipline and hard work, and that the invisible hand of free enterprise will point to wiser solutions than the clumsy fist of centralized control. To the first, Harrington retorts that today's inequalities are only coincidentally connected to effort and skill. . . .

To the other part of the credo, Harrington says that we don't face a choice between planning and the free workings of the market. Things are going to be controlled one way or the other, he says; it's only a matter of deciding how and by whom. . . . The economy is already planned, Harrington says, but the plan is that of "corporate statism," in which a big, unresponsive public bureaucracy follows the wishes of a big, irresponsibly selfish private one.

When it comes to solutions, we are suddenly on spongy terrain. The book is full of proposals for detailed policy changes . . . but on the largest questions it steps up several levels of abstraction, toward the realm of pie in the sky. For example, after analyzing the deterioration of many northern industrial cities, Harrington concludes: "So the only way the nation will get a decent, liveable urban environment is through national planning." Well, okay—but by whom, and by what standards, and in what way? . . .

Removing gross economic inequalities, as Harrington prescribes, would certainly change some of the pressures on decisions—but will it really bring us that much nearer consensus on what the goals of our planning should be? . . .

The insights and understanding of this book make it valuable reading, even for those, like me, who remain unconvinced. Harrington's greatest glory is his commitment to participatory democracy, political and economic; more specifics on the where and how would earn him his readers' thanks.

> *James Fallows, "Condition Critical: America in the '80s," in* Book World—The Washington Post *(© 1980, The Washington Post), March 23, 1980, p. 5.*

GAR ALPEROVITZ and JEFF FAUX

[Michael Harrington's *Decade of Decision*] is a polemic designed to stiffen the backbone of liberalism by reminding us of the simple errors and foolishness of the conservative program, and of our obligation to continue the evolution of progressive thought and action toward a more democratic and just society. (p. 28)

Harrington's central argument is that the issues facing the American economy do not involve "policy" so much as the structure of the system itself: our system is one in which the major investment decisions that shape the future for all of us are made on the basis of private rather than public costs and benefits. The point should be obvious. Private corporate investment decisions are by far the major determinants of the economic context we live in. . . . To be sure, there is room here for argument. We think Harrington overemphasizes the importance of recent changes in industrial concentration in creating modern stagflation and underemphasizes the way new global resource problems and international rivalries interact

with concentration in key industries. He is right, however, about the main point—that the structure of American investment policy is at the heart of our economic problems. (pp. 28-9)

Street demonstrations against poverty and the government programs that followed were based on the common assumption that the problem lay in the people rather than in the system. . . . [The] demand for social justice was transformed into a quest for "affirmative action" in which a few blacks and women were given a boost up the competitive ladder. But so long as the number of places on the ladder did not increase, some people had to be out of work. (p. 29)

The long struggle to open up the educational system to minorities is an instructive case in point for Harrington. . . . [By] focusing primarily on the school, Harrington argues, [minorities] were doomed to failure because the schools themselves functioned simply as part of a labor market dominated by the corporate desire to expand the supply of skilled labor. (pp. 29-30)

It was not that minority leaders and liberals were ignorant of the links between corporate power and the educational system. But they accepted the central assumption that the growth of the US economy would guarantee a steady expansion of opportunities for which they could successfully compete. They hoped that the "ladder" would always be an upwardly moving escalator. This hope was dashed in the rolling economic crisis of the 1970s. . . .

In analyzing the crisis, Harrington skewers the fashionable fetishes of ex-liberals and neoconservatives about balanced budgets, capital shortages, and tax incentives. He is especially harsh on the efforts of comfortable academics to define unemployment and poverty away with statistical sleights of hand. . . . The goal Harrington urges is democratic control over the nation's basic economic resources—a goal, he hastens to add, that can be pursued only in small steps at a time.

Harrington believes—and we agree—that the unsettling conditions of the new economic era create possibilities for a political movement based on a progressive coalition of the poor, the disadvantaged, and the increasingly impoverished middle class. If this "progressive" coalition is not formed, a reactionary one inspired by a meanspirited corporate socialism that pits workers, races, sexes, and regions against one another is likely to emerge out of the trauma of the economic crisis. . . .

Beginning with the thesis that the American people are conservative in ideology but liberal in practice (i.e., against government in general but for most of the services that government provides), Harrington comes at the question programmatically. He advocates price controls on monopolies; sectoral policies like national health care and rationalized farm production and income support programs; control by workers of their own pension fund investments; tax reforms; and reform of the welfare and educational systems.

These are not extreme demands. Most conventional economists will admit the wisdom of using public authority to control prices in the absence of competition. . . . Neither singly nor collectively will these reforms dramatically change the system. But Harrington believes that they will begin to chip away at the power and maneuverability of corporate America. . . .

Still, a laundry list of programs does not a long-term strategy make. There remains the question of ideology and vision. Harrington's political caution tells him that the best we can hope for in the 1980s is "the emergence of a revived liberalism . . . much more socialistic even though it will not, in all probability, be socialist." Yet it was precisely the narrow disparate goals of incremental liberalism that contributed to its demise. (p. 30)

Harrington does not duck the question of long-term strategy. But neither does he explore it in any depth. Mainly he seems to jump over it. . . . He ends by identifying the core conceptual issue—the need for some centralization in order to construct a workable, decentralized planning system. But what the elements of such a system might look like—and how they might serve to help build a political strategy that takes us beyond the difficulties of the 1960s—are questions Harrington does not develop beyond broad generalizations.

Harrington is clearly on the right track, and his book is useful in its critique of conservative nostrums and its cataloging of progressive structural reforms. He is also right that a revived American liberalism can succeed only if it is willing to face the issue of democratic planning, with all of its contradictions and difficulties. (pp. 30-1)

Harrington's book is important, therefore, because it demonstrates that a close look at the difficulties facing the country—and the myriad local responses to them—shows that preconditions for serious political changes lie beneath the surface of the crisis. (p. 32)

> *Gar Alperovitz and Jeff Faux, "Books and the Arts: 'Decade of Decision',"* in The New Republic *(reprinted by permission of* The New Republic; © *1980 The New Republic, Inc.),* Vol. 182, No. 19, May 10, 1980, pp. 28-32.

GEORGE McKENNA

Here we are in the 1980's and capitalism, as crisis-prone as ever, seems to be holding on and even breathing a new air of legitimacy supplied by some of its former critics. Harrington is still waiting for Godot, but now a new, uncharacteristic tone has crept into his writings: sourness. In his latest book, *Decade of Decision,* Harrington continues to insist that America suffers from irreparable "structural" flaws, and yet—Harrington comes to this conclusion most reluctantly—so powerful are the "myths" and "illusions" of capitalism that the American people don't seem ready for socialism. (p. 312)

Harrington has not yet abandoned hope, and his book contains a scattering of proposals for nudging us closer to socialism. He suggests putting workers on corporate and pension fund boards, forcing banks to invest in marginal neighborhoods and adopt minimum quotas for loans to women and "minorities," increasing inheritance taxes, forcing corporations to answer to new government agencies before they can relocate their factories, making the rich pay higher taxes and giving the money to the poor in a federalized welfare system, and so on. Some of these proposals may be innocuous, some are almost certainly mischievous, but none merits discussion here, for Harrington himself hardly discusses them. Some get a page or two of exposition, others a few paragraphs. His heart doesn't seem to be in them, and the reason is obvious. He knows just how familiar they all are. What he says of his urban proposals might apply to the others as well: "Almost all of them are already part of the program of the democratic Left and have been so for a long time. Too long a time."

The weariness of this book is the price it pays for its lack of introspection. For the most part Harrington seems unaware that

Americans are turning their backs on the programs of his "democratic Left" because they know that those programs always end by creating swarms of new bureaucrats of very doubtful fidelity to the purpose of their programs. The most convincing parts of Harrington's book are those showing the corruption of government agencies set up to regulate business and manage the economy. Yet Harrington proposes as a solution more agencies of various kinds, more power in the hands of elites who will of course *claim* to speak for "the public." Not until the last page of the book does Harrington take account of socialism's own "structural" contradiction. He observes that George Wallace created his populist constituency out of Americans who regarded government as a distant "them," a corps of technocrats contemptuous of ordinary people. Harrington concedes that Wallace was on to something. He twisted the truth, "but there was a truth there." Very well, "what, then, should one do?" Unfortunately, Harrington has exactly two paragraphs left to answer the question, so of course he doesn't answer it. Instead, there is a little uplifting rhetoric about "a transformation of the social and economic conditions of the planet," followed by the hope that "bewildered America" may yet come to its senses and accept his programs for "the elimination of poverty and racism at home and the possibility of eliminating it [*sic*] around the globe, decent health and respect for the environment, disarmament and the participation of the people in the decisions that shape their lives, and all the rest." The goals are as familiar as his methods for achieving them. When it has reached the point where he can finish off the litany with "and all the rest," then we know that there is weariness here, too.

No one can possibly guess what Harrington will write after this book. He knows, too well, that America "is psychologically individualistic, more so than any other advanced country," but he cannot bring himself to consider that this intractable individualism might be a good touchstone for testing the grand schemes of reformers. Consequently, there seems to be no place else for Harrington to go, and nothing else to say. He has exhausted his store of ideas and, from what can be gathered in *Decade of Decision,* gotten himself into a bad mood. The best restorative would be a long hiatus of silence, humility, and self-doubt—a decade, perhaps, or at least a few years, of hesitation. (pp. 313-14)

> *George McKenna, "Socialist Blues,"* in Modern Age *(copyright © 1981 by the Intercollegiate Studies Institute, Inc.),* Vol. 25, No. 3, Summer, 1981, pp. 312-14.

WILLIAM B. LOGAN

Two decades after *The Other America,* his influential study of poverty in the United States, Michael Harrington meditates on the plans of America's resurgent right: "They recognize the same crises I do, yet the future they project is a past that never worked." His forthright new essay—twined with Bob Adelman's striking documentary photographs—[*The Next America*] is a ruthless critique of the recent past. Yet it is remarkable for its evenhandedness. . . .

[Harrington] shows how the hedonism of the Sixties was not just the product of a flaw in our character. "Hedonism," he writes, "became an essential dictate of public policy." Conspicuous consumption was a patriotic act; "dropping out" was a rebellion dependent on the fantasy of eternal prosperity. When the Seventies' recessions came, everybody suffered.

This socialist analysis of our recent crises makes excellent sense. What distinguishes the book from mere polemic, however, is its personal, almost intimate tone and its lively, quirky commitment to certain American successes. Trade unions, social security, even Disney World—phenomena usually dismissed by the revisionist intelligentsia—find a sympathetic commentator in Harrington. Though his optimism occasionally cloys, Harrington has something of the rare talent once claimed for another social critic, Alexander Pope: He shows common sense in strong, beautiful, uncommon lights.

William B. Logan, "Books: 'The Next America'," in Saturday Review *(copyright © 1981 by* Saturday Review; *all rights reserved; reprinted by permission), Vol. 8, No. 8, August, 1981, p. 54.*

Douglas R(ichard) Hofstadter

1945-

Hofstadter is an American computer scientist and author. In *Gödel, Escher, Bach: An Eternal Golden Braid* (1979) Hofstadter places Kurt Gödel's Incompleteness Theorem at the center of his exploration of the implications of self-reference and isomorphism for human creativity. To Hofstadter, the existence of self-reference within a closed system is what makes human consciousness possible, yet he also believes that somehow we can transcend the seeming limitations of our brain and psyche through Zen. Described in the *Village Voice* as "the *Ulysses* of soft-science books" for its all-encompassing subject matter and its word play, the book won the 1980 Pulitzer Prize for nonfiction. Hofstadter is an associate professor of computer science at Indiana University, Bloomington. (See also *Contemporary Authors,* Vol. 105.)

Excerpt from *GÖDEL, ESCHER, BACH: AN ETERNAL GOLDEN BRAID*

The "Strange Loop" phenomenon occurs whenever, by moving upwards (or downwards) through the levels of some hierarchical system, we unexpectedly find ourselves right back where we started. . . . Sometimes I use the term *Tangled Hierarchy* to describe a system in which a Strange Loop occurs. As we go on, the theme of Strange Loops will recur again and again. Sometimes it will be hidden, other times it will be out in the open; sometimes it will be right side up, other times it will be upside down, or backwards. "Quaerendo invenietis" is my advice to the reader.

To my mind, the most beautiful and powerful visual realizations of this notion of Strange Loops exist in the work of the Dutch graphic artist M. C. Escher, who lived from 1902 to 1972. Escher was the creator of some of the most intellectually stimulating drawings of all time. Many of them have their origin in paradox, illusion, or double-meaning. Mathematicians were among the first admirers of Escher's drawings, and this is understandable because they often are based on mathematical principles of symmetry or pattern . . . But there is much more to a typical Escher drawing than just symmetry or pattern; there is often an underlying idea, realized in artistic form. And in particular, the Strange Loop is one of the most recurrent themes in Escher's work. (pp. 10-11)

Implicit in the concept of Strange Loops is the concept of infinity, since what else is a loop but a way of representing an endless process in a finite way? And infinity plays a large role in many of Escher's drawings. Copies of one single theme often fit into each other, forming visual analogues to the canons of Bach. . . . In some of his drawings, one single theme can appear on different levels of reality. For instance, one level in a drawing might clearly be recognizable as representing fantasy or imagination; another level would be recognizable as reality. These two levels might be the only explicitly portrayed levels. But the mere presence of these two levels invites the viewer to look upon himself as part of yet another level; and by taking that step, the viewer cannot help getting caught up in Escher's implied chain of levels, in which, for any one level, there is always another level above it of greater "reality", and likewise, there is always a level below, "more imaginary" than

Photograph by Mary Ann Carter

it is. This can be mind-boggling in itself. However, what happens if the chain of levels is not linear, but forms a loop? What is real, then, and what is fantasy? The genius of Escher was that he could not only concoct, but actually portray, dozens of half-real, half-mythical worlds, worlds filled with Strange Loops, which he seems to be inviting his viewers to enter.

In the . . . Strange Loops by Bach and Escher, there is a conflict between the finite and the infinite, and hence a strong sense of paradox. Intuition senses that there is something mathematical involved here. And indeed in our own century a mathematical counterpart was discovered, with the most enormous repercussions. And, just as the Bach and Escher loops appeal to very simple and ancient intuitions—a musical scale, a staircase—so this discovery, by K. Gödel, of a Strange Loop in mathematical systems has its origins in simple and ancient intuitions. In its absolutely barest form, Gödel's discovery involves the translation of an ancient paradox in philosophy into mathematical terms. That paradox is the so-called *Epimenides paradox,* or *liar paradox.* Epimenides was a Cretan who made one immortal statement: "All Cretans are liars." (pp. 15,17)

But how does it have to do with mathematics? That is what Gödel discovered. His idea was to use mathematical reasoning in exploring mathematical reasoning itself. This notion of making mathematics "introspective" proved to be enormously powerful, and perhaps its richest implication was the one Gödel found: Gödel's Incompleteness Theorem. . . .

The proof of Gödel's Incompleteness Theorem hinges upon the writing of a self-referential mathematical statement, in the same way as the Epimenides paradox is a self-referential statement of language. But whereas it is very simple to talk about language in language, it is not at all easy to see how a statement about numbers can talk about itself. In fact, it took genius merely to connect the idea of self-referential statements with number theory. Once Gödel had the intuition that such a statement could be created, he was over the major hurdle. The actual creation of the statement was the working out of this one beautiful spark of intuition. (p. 17)

No one knows where the borderline between non-intelligent behavior and intelligent behavior lies; in fact, to suggest that a sharp borderline exists is probably silly. . . . Computers by their very nature are the most inflexible, desireless, rule-following of beasts. Fast though they may be, they are nonetheless the epitome of unconsciousness. How, then, can intelligent behavior be programmed? Isn't this the most blatant of contradictions in terms? One of the major theses of this book is that it is not a contradiction at all. One of the major purposes of this book is to urge each reader to confront the apparent contradiction head on, to savor it, to turn it over, to take it apart, to wallow in it, so that in the end the reader might emerge with new insights into the seemingly unbreachable gulf between the formal and the informal, the animate and the inanimate, the flexible and the inflexible.

This is what Artificial Intelligence (AI) research is all about. And the strange flavor of AI work is that people try to put together long sets of rules in strict formalisms which tell inflexible machines how to be flexible.

What sorts of "rules" could possibly capture all of what we think of as intelligent behavior, however? Certainly there must be rules on all sorts of different levels. There must be many "just plain" rules. There must be "metarules" to modify the "just plain" rules; then "metametarules" to modify the metarules, and so on. The flexibility of intelligence comes from the enormous number of different rules, and levels of rules. . . . Without doubt, Strange Loops involving rules that change themselves, directly or indirectly, are at the core of intelligence. Sometimes the complexity of our minds seems so overwhelming that one feels that there can be no solution to the problem of understanding intelligence—that it is wrong to think that rules of any sort govern a creature's behavior, even if one takes "rule" in the multilevel sense described above. (pp. 26-7)

I have sought to weave an Eternal Golden Braid out of these three strands: Gödel, Escher, Bach. I began, intending to write an essay at the core of which would be Gödel's Theorem. I imagined it would be a mere pamphlet. But my ideas expanded like a sphere, and soon touched Bach and Escher. It took some time for me to think of making this connection explicit, instead of just letting it be a private motivating force. But finally I realized that to me, Gödel and Escher and Bach were only shadows cast in different directions by some central solid essence. I tried to reconstruct the central object, and came up with this book. (p. 28)

All the limitative Theorems of metamathematics and the theory of computation suggest that once the ability to represent your own structure has reached a certain critical point, that is the kiss of death: it guarantees that you can never represent yourself totally. Gödel's Incompleteness Theorem, Church's Undecidability Theorem, Turing's Halting Theorem, Tarski's Truth Theorem—all have the flavor of some ancient fairy tale which warns you that "To seek self-knowledge is to embark on a journey which . . . will always be incomplete, cannot be charted on any map, will never halt, cannot be described."

But do the limitative Theorems have any bearing on people? Here is one way of arguing the case. Either I am consistent or I am inconsistent. (The latter is much more likely, but for completeness' sake, I consider both possibilities.) If I am consistent, then there are two cases. (1) The "low-fidelity" case: my self-understanding is below a certain critical point. In this case, I am incomplete by hypothesis. (2) The "high-fidelity" case: My self-understanding has reached the critical point where a metaphorical analogue of the limitative Theorems does apply, so my self-understanding undermines itself in a Gödelian way, and I am incomplete for that reason. Cases (1) and (2) are predicated on my being 100 per cent consistent—a very unlikely state of affairs. More likely is that I am inconsistent—but that's worse, for then inside me there are contradictions, and how can I ever understand that?

Consistent or inconsistent, no one is exempt from the mystery of the self. Probably we are all inconsistent. The world is just too complicated for a person to be able to afford the luxury of reconciling all of his beliefs with each other. Tension and confusion are important in a world where many decisions must be made quickly. (pp. 697-98)

Science is often criticized as being too "Western" or "dualistic"—that is, being permeated by the dichotomy between subject and object, or observer and observed. While it is true that up until this century, science was exclusively concerned with things which can be readily distinguished from their human observers . . . this phase of science was a necessary prelude to the more modern phase, in which life itself has come under investigation. Step by step, inexorably, "Western" science has moved towards investigation of the human mind—which is to say, of the observer. Artificial Intelligence research is the furthest step so far along that route. Before AI came along, there were two major previews of the strange consequences of the mixing of subject and object in science. One was the revolution of quantum mechanics, with its epistemological problems involving the interference of the observer with the observed. The other was the mixing of subject and object in metamathematics, beginning with Gödel's Theorem and moving through all the other limitative Theorems we have discussed. Perhaps the next step after AI will be the self-application of science: science studying itself as an object. This is a different manner of mixing subject and object—perhaps an even more tangled one than that of humans studying their own minds. (pp. 698-99)

Does Gödel's Theorem . . . have absolutely nothing to offer us in thinking about our own minds? I think it does, although not in the mystical and limitative way which some people think it ought to. I think that the process of coming to understand Gödel's proof, with its construction involving arbitrary codes, complex isomorphisms, high and low levels of interpretation, and the capacity for self-mirroring, may inject some rich undercurrents and flavors into one's set of images about symbols and symbol processing, which may deepen one's intuition for the relationship between mental structures on different levels.

Before suggesting a philosophically intriguing "application" of Gödel's proof, I would like to bring up the idea of "accidental inexplicability" of intelligence. Here is what that involves. It could be that our brains, unlike car engines, are stubborn and intractable systems which we cannot neatly decompose in any way. At present, we have no idea whether our brains will yield to repeated attempts to cleave them into clean layers, each of which can be explained in terms of lower layers— or whether our brains will foil all our attempts at decomposition.

But even if we do fail to understand ourselves, there need not be any Gödelian "twist" behind it; it could be simply an accident of fate that our brains are too weak to understand themselves. . . .

Barring this pessimistic notion of the accidental inexplicability of the brain, what insights might Gödel's proof offer us about explanations of our minds/brains? Gödel's proof offers the notion that a high-level view of a system may contain explanatory power which simply is absent on the lower levels. (p. 707)

Gödel's proof suggests—though by no means does it prove!— that there could be some high-level way of viewing the mind/ brain, involving concepts which do not appear on lower levels, and that this level might have explanatory power that does not exist—not even in principle—on lower levels. It would mean that some facts could be explained on the high level quite easily, but not on lower levels *at all*. (p. 708)

What might such high-level concepts be? It has been proposed for eons, by various holistically or "soulistically" inclined scientists and humanists, that *consciousness* is a phenomenon that escapes explanation in terms of brain-components; so here is a candidate, at least. There is also the ever-puzzling notion of *free will*. So perhaps these qualities could be "emergent" in the sense of requiring explanations which cannot be furnished by the physiology alone. But it is important to realize that if we are being guided by Gödel's proof in making such bold hypotheses, we must carry the analogy through thoroughly. . . . If our analogy is to hold, . . . "emergent" phenomena would become explicable in terms of a relationship between different levels in mental systems.

My belief is that the explanations of "emergent" phenomena in our brains—for instance, ideas, hopes, images, analogies, and finally consciousness and free will—are based on a kind of Strange Loop, an interaction between levels in which the top level reaches back down towards the bottom level and influences it, while at the same time being itself determined by the bottom level. . . . The self comes into being at the moment it has the power to reflect itself.

This should not be taken as an antireductionist position. It just implies that a reductionistic explanation of a mind, *in order to be comprehensible*, must bring in "soft" concepts such as levels, mappings, and meanings. In principle, I have no doubt that a totally reductionistic but incomprehensible explanation of the brain exists; the problem is how to translate it into a language we ourselves can fathom. Surely we don't want a description in terms of positions and momenta of particles; we want a description which relates neural activity to "signals" (intermediate-level phenomena)—and which relates signals, in turn, to "symbols" and "subsystems", including the presumed-to-exist "self-symbol". This act of translation from low-level physical hardware to high-level psychological software is analogous to the translation of number-theoretical statements into metamathematical statements. Recall that the level-

crossing which takes place at this exact translation point is what creates Gödel's imcompleteness and the self-proving character of Henkin's sentence. I postulate that a similar level-crossing is what creates our nearly unanalyzable feelings of self.

In order to deal with the full richness of the brain/mind system, we will have to be able to slip between levels comfortably. Moreover, we will have to admit various types of "causality": ways in which an event at one level of description can "cause" events at other levels to happen. Sometimes event A will be said to "cause" event B simply for the reason that the one is a translation, on another level of description, of the other. Sometimes "cause" will have its usual meaning: physical causality. Both types of causality—and perhaps some more—will have to be admitted in any explanation of mind, for we will have to admit causes that propagate both upwards *and* downwards in the Tangled Hierarchy of mentality. (pp. 708-09)

The important idea is that this "vortex" of self is responsible for the tangledness, for the Gödelian-ness, of the mental processes. People have said to me on occasion, "This stuff with self-reference and so on is very amusing and enjoyable, but do you really think there is anything *serious* to it?" I certainly do. I think it will eventually turn out to be at the core of AI, and the focus of all attempts to understand how human minds work. And that is why Gödel is so deeply woven into the fabric of my book. (p. 714)

Douglas R. Hofstadter, in his Gödel, Escher, Bach: An Eternal Golden Braid *(copyright © 1979 by Basic Books, Inc.; reprinted by permission of Basic Books, Inc., Publishers), Basic Books, 1979, 777 p.*

BRIAN HAYES

In ["**Gödel, Escher, Bach: An Eternal Golden Braid**"] Professor Hofstadter yokes together [Kurt] Gödel, Johann Sebastian Bach and the Dutch artist Maurits Cornelis Escher, and a substantial part of his book is dedicated to showing that this is not such an unlikely team of oxen. Escher is the easier case: his drawings (like the paintings of René Magritte, which are also discussed) have an obvious connection with verbal and mathematical paradox. (p. 13)

Escher and Bach are only the beginning of Professor Hofstadter's Shandean digressions. He traces connections that lead from Gödel's theorem to Zen, where contradiction is cherished; to the social insects, where it is not clear whether the ant or the entire colony should be regarded as the organism; to television cameras pointed at television screens. . . . He constructs a quite elaborate analogy between the incompleteness theorem and the transmission of genetic information encoded in the nucleotide sequences of DNA; here the self-reference of the theorem is comparable to the self-replication of the molecule. Most of all, he is at pains to present the implications of Gödel's proof for theories of the human mind (and of artificial intellects). In the mind the entire procedure of the Gödel proof seems to be repeated: A large but mechanistic, rule-following system, when it grows complex enough, develops the capacity for self-reference, which in this context is called consciousness.

Professor Hofstadter's presentation of these ideas is not rigorous, in the mathematical sense, but all the essential steps are there; the reader is not asked to accept results on authority or on faith. Nor is the narrative rigorous in the uphill-hiking sense, for the author is always ready to take the reader's hand and lead him through the thickets. . . . But Douglas Hofstadter's book is [an] . . . ambitious project. It is also a . . . pretentious one. (pp. 13, 18)

> *Brian Hayes, "This Head Is False," in* The New York Times Book Review *(© 1979 by The New York Times Company; reprinted by permission), April 29, 1979, pp. 13, 18.*

MARTIN GARDNER

For laymen I know of no better explanation than [*Godel, Escher, Bach: An Eternal Golden Braid*] presents of what Gödel achieved and of the implications of his revolutionary discovery. That discovery concerns in particular recursion, self-reference and endless regress, and Hofstadter finds those three themes vividly mirrored in the art of Escher, the most mathematical of graphic artists, and in the music of Bach, the most mathematical of the great composers. The book's own structure is as saturated with complex counterpoint as a Bach composition or James Joyce's *Ulysses*. (p. 16)

> *Martin Gardner, "Mathematical Games," in* Scientific American, *Vol. 241, No. 1, July, 1979, pp. 16, 18-24.*

PETER WILSHER

[One] of the many puzzles about this extraordinary, exhilarating book [*Gödel, Escher, Bach: An Eternal Golden Braid*] is just where a conscientious librarian should file it. In its 777 intricately cross-cultural pages, there is ample justification for a place under music, philosophy, computer science, art, theory of numbers, biochemistry, formal systems, artificial intelligence, Zen, linguistics and the creative use of paradox. . . . But what, as the conscientious librarian must ask, is it About? And what did this Gödel actually do to get his name at the top of the masthead? . . .

The relevance of Gödel here is that his Incompleteness Theorem has been advanced (sometimes very aggressively) to 'prove' that the mechanisation of brain function—whatever success may have been achieved with various specialised, but essentially elementary automata—is inherently impossible. Hofstadter is not so sure, and his doubts, set out and explained in a series of dazzling expository devices, make up the substance of this splendid *tour de force*. He is fascinated by the phenomena of isomorphism, where one set of ideas is mapped on to another, apparently completely different, and by self-reference, where thoughts and concepts appear to loop back on themselves, like nested flashbacks or plays-within-a-play. With a small cast of characters . . . he constructs a highly ingenious, not to say tricky, collection of dialogues which together manage to explore and illuminate some of the most baffling problems of logic, language and symbolic communication, which lie at the heart of the debate about the nature of thought.

At the same time, he contrives to make a large number of rather good jokes. . . . [In] oblique ways he coaxes and inveigles the non-scientific, the non-musical, the innumerate and the illogical into arcane mental regions that they could normally never hope to penetrate.

For once he has used his Crabs and his Anteaters to provide the conceptual equivalent of waterwings, he has no hesitation in towing his pupils out into deep water. Hooked by Hofstadter, they will find themselves trying to keep afloat in very elevated intellectual company—Quine and Tarski, Cantor and Fermat, Watson and Crick, and the Masters of Zen. It is a measure of the book's easy versatility that it is as eloquent and convincing on *koans* (as an attempt to transcend the dichotomy of thought) as it is on the genetic code (as a working example of self-reproducing entities): and that may well be its real achievement—not that it resolves the argument over artificial intelligence, but that it leaves you feeling you have had a first-class workout in the best mental gymnasium in town.

> *Peter Wilsher, "The Mental Gymnasium," in* New Statesman *(© 1979 The Statesman & Nation Publishing Co. Ltd.), Vol. 98, No. 2534, October 12, 1979, p. 558.*

WALTER KENDRICK

Douglas Hofstadter's *Godel, Escher, Bach* could only have been written by a scientist. Worse than that, a computer scientist—one of those pale, enigmatic creatures who are always rushing off to program something at five in the morning. It has all the maddening qualities of conversation with such a specimen: no sense whatever of when a point has been sufficiently made (. . . the book is monstrously too long), a stupefying habit of translating everything into equations (if he'd said "Let this equal that" one more time, I'd have thrown the book out the window), and a more-than-elephantine whimsy that would justify homicide to any court in the land. Yet it also has qualities that we humanists may have started with but that most of us have lost—sincere and lively wonder at the beauty of the mind, genuine awe at the magnificence of its products, unjaded enthusiasm for art and artists alike.

Escher, Godel, Bach is the *Ulysses* of soft-science books. A product of the bifurcated '70s, soft-science translates the commonplaces of hard-core science into language that a nonscientist, even a hard-core humanist, can understand. . . .

EGB's greatest accomplishment is to show that the austere and frigid world of pure mathematics is by no means as remote from the two worlds of art and music as the humanist in the street believes it to be. The three worlds are, in fact, isomorphic—one of Hofstadter's favorite words—which means that, viewed from a standpoint outside any one world, all three can be seen to have the same shape or form. They can be meaningfully "mapped onto" one another, and recursion is the key feature they share. . . .

[It's] the second greatest accomplishment of *BEG* to make such an abstruse formulation [as Godel's Incompleteness Theorem] clear to even a reader who fled from math after high school. . . . [Before] you're halfway through *GBE* you'll find yourself actually understanding Godel's Incompleteness Theorem, or at least believing that you do.

I won't tell you how Hofstadter turns this trick; I can't. But Godel's Theorem isn't the only mystery of mathematics that he unravels for the common reader. He also leads that poor soul through such labyrinths as the propositional calculus, recursive transition networks, and typographical number theory. It's some excuse for the book's burdensome repetitiveness and crushing length that these abstruse matters require painstaking step-by-step exposition to make them clear. Like the most patient of tutors (or like a slightly mad grad student who won't let go of your arm), Hofstadter guides his uninitiated reader through level after level of the mathematical funhouse, not only explaining its layout but also conveying a sense of the wonder and the beauty that do, in fact, reside there.

Hofstadter's own specialty is what he calls AI—Artificial Intelligence—and much of his book is devoted to the profound question of whether it will ever be possible to program a computer to operate in what most of us would think of as a uniquely human way—that is, intelligently instead of just mechanically. The question never gets a final answer, but more interesting than any answer is the process of moving toward one, exploring the structure and functions of the human mind. . . . (p. 48)

This is the style of *BGE:* a nervous jumping from one isomorph to another, mounting steadily higher in abstraction and complexity, until it shimmers away in gasps of awe and flurries of exclamation points. In this, the book's style imitates its subject, since in any recursive system the greatest danger is that of infinite regression. . . . In manmade recursive systems like those of sophisticated computers, the process is made to "bottom out" somewhere; but it can only be a matter of faith, as it is of Hofstadter's, that the recursions of the real world, too, must have a stop—either in the hard-rock physical ground of things or at the other end, in the upward limit of all recursions that could go by the name of God.

God is invoked by name in only one small part of *EGB* and there in a fanciful context, but the book is in one sense Hofstadter's "religion," as he tells us, and it is animated throughout by an awe at the wonders of Nature that can truly be called religious. Religion is a personal matter, of course, and Hofstadter never preaches; he only expounds. But for all its abstractness and addiction to mathematical formulas, *GEB* is an intensely personal book in every way. Not only is it Hofstadter's religion, it's his life's work as well. . . .

It may seem unfair or irrelevant to consider any book, particularly a scientific one, as a symptom of the mind that produced it. Ever since the New Criticism, we humanists have been taught that it's a sin to treat works of art that way, and the stalwart objectivity of most scientific works would seem to discourage such treatment absolutely. Yet as Hofstadter tells us, it's the chief earmark of intelligence that it can jump out of any system, breaking free of one set of rules to see that system as an element in a larger structure with rules of its own. . . . [Just] as Hofstadter repeatedly teases his readers with little puzzles that can only be solved recursively, so too his persistent personal presence encourages us to break out of *GBE* and speculate on the dazzling and quirky mind from which it came. . . .

Hofstadter's flights of fancy aren't quite as tedious as they seem in summary. They're always more or less related to the expository chapters of the book, and often an abstruse concept can be more easily grasped when it's explained through characters and situations than when it's merely stated. It's inevitable, too, I suppose, that a book about self-reference should be self-referential, yet the gaudy structure of *EBG* not only drags the reader's attention away from the book's subject to the strange mind of Douglas Hofstadter, it also wrenches the book from its comfortable soft-science context and throws it among works of literature, where we humanists lurk, scalpels ready.

It would be easy to mock Hofstadter for his artistic naivete . . . ; to dismiss the whole enterprise of *BGE* as the presumptuous extravagance of a very young man who'll calm down when he grows up. More to the point, however, would be the response a generous-jaded humanist might make: The discovery of self-reference throughout the universe is hardly the source of joy that Hofstadter takes it to be. Art has known about self-reference for a very long time, and lately it's come to look more like a prison than a setting-free. (p. 50)

Science, I used to think, was the last refuge of reference. . . . *GEB* has gone far toward demolishing that naive faith of mine, forcing me to think of scientists as troubled, like me, by humanistic problems. I wish Hofstadter hadn't done that.

For the most part, however, Hofstadter's book is securely grounded in a referential faith. Even when his subject is self-reference he manages to treat it referentially, and whenever he self-refers he's only playing. . . . [Even] Godel's disturbing theorem, which seems to drive reference from its last resort, was only, Hofstadter tells us, the working out of "one beautiful spark of intuition." Intuition—the spark from an object to a subject, proof that both exist and are separate. And though there may be beauty in self-reference, the profounder beauty lies there.

Hofstadter seems to know this, and though the upshot of his book might be to abolish referentiality altogether, still he clings to it in spirit if not in fact. Yet a strange unease permeates *EBG,* a haunted awareness that, just as intelligence can jump from any given system into a higher one, so too it should be able to jump out of the universe that *GBE* seems to define. Not just from the book to the man who wrote it, but all the way out—beyond both reference and self-reference to some third and higher thing. And the book contains an escape route that would lead one away from both—the escape route of Zen.

"I'm not sure I know what Zen is," says Hofstadter early on. "To me Zen is intellectual quicksand—anarchy, darkness, meaninglessness, chaos." Yet Zen is also "humorous, refreshing, enticing." . . . He never gets over his initial distress and delight. Zen haunts his book like a sweetly mocking ghost, promising a leap out of everything that is, yet never revealing how that leap can be made. And when he neatly loops his book together at the end, Zen still stands outside, still smiling. (pp. 50, 52)

Walter Kendrick, "The 'Ulysses' of Soft Science" (reprinted by permission of The Village Voice *and the author; copyright © 1979), in* The Village Voice, *Vol. 24, No. 47, November 19, 1979, pp. 48, 50, 52.*

EDWARD ROTHSTEIN

If Gödel's theorem shattered a sort of dream, it seems as if Hofstadter [with *Gödel, Escher, Bach: An Eternal Golden Braid*] is intent on creating another one, a dream filled with wordplay and association in which Gödel plays a metaphorical role. Such a dream could have dissipated into chaos; but instead the book is exhilarating, challenging, valuable, and frustrating. Hofstadter writes directly and playfully for the lay reader, explaining the most abstract and wide-ranging arguments in short sections of great virtuosity. He is sophisticated in his understanding of the systems he explores and is adventurously speculative about their limits. But the book resists simple evaluation; it is at once surprisingly subtle and annoyingly naïve, exuberantly clever and embarrassingly silly. (p. 34)

Hofstadter gives a convincing mathematical argument why the mind is as limited as a machine. But more importantly, it is one of the themes of *Gödel, Escher, Bach* that while there may be a formal system underlying all mental activity, the mind somehow transcends the formal system which supports it.

Once the underlying formal system is powerful enough to reflect itself, even on the most elementary levels, Hofstadter argues, a new dynamic enters into the brain. Hofstadter makes an extended comparison between the brain and an ant colony; the complex organization of the ant colony displays a strategy and awareness while the individual ants seem to play the parts of neurons. . . .

The method of argument used in Gödel's proof becomes more important for Hofstadter than its limiting result. The proof's usage of codes, its creation of mappings, its mixing of levels, and dizzying self-reference, all seem to Hofstadter to carry metaphorical implications for the activity of intelligence itself. . . . "Indirect self-reference" is one of the richest and most vivid of his conceptions; it is, he argues, a crucial process of our minds when we correct ourselves, solve puzzles, engage in interpretations. Without some ability to refer back to our own mental activity, and to transform it, intelligence itself would be impossible. . . .

[If] consciousness can emerge out of a formal system of firing neurons, then so too, Hofstadter seems to argue, will computers attain human intelligence. (p. 37)

Hofstadter is frequently persuasive about the potentials of AI [Artificial Intelligence] if only because of his insights into the processes involved in solving problems. In fact, his own intelligence is so interesting and lively that one feels such a mind would succeed in mirroring itself in its activities in some way, even in attempting to do so literally in a computer program.

"Indirect self-reference," a character called the Author says in one of Hofstadter's dialogues, "is my favorite topic." He does not only want to discuss it in its various forms—in Gödel's proof, in intelligence, in the cell—he wants to create it in the text as well, create a literary model, turn the entire book into "one big self-referential loop." . . . Hofstadter playfully and immodestly hints at . . . "unending subtleties" that might appear in the "many levels of meaning" in his own work. "By seeking, you will discover," he quotes Bach.

Much of what is to be discovered, however, has more to do with Escher than with Bach. Escher's drawings are often amusing tricks or puzzles, exploiting self-reference, level interaction, and figure/ground play. They are coolly intriguing, unsettling at times, but are, for the most part, propositional tricks in picture form. Similarly, Hofstadter is attracted to verbal trickery; he hides acrostics, anagrams, puns, and self-referential jokes throughout the text. (pp. 37-8)

Many of Hofstadter's discussions . . . confuse profound insights with the most banal ones. (p. 38)

[Seemingly trivial] links become a serious problem because the book is concerned directly with the nature of links, or "maps," between formal systems. The book is strongest in its explications of formal systems, in its discussions of Gödel, the brain, the computer, the cell. Hofstadter then uses various formal devices for connecting the systems he discusses. Texts and ideas are pared down to a syntax; maps and charts identify the most diverse objects through their shared structure. Such identifications, Hofstadter believes, contain suggestive meanings. . . . But Hofstadter's "maps" can . . . be outrageously silly. . . . [In] identifying characters' initials with DNA's bases, or his book with the *Musical Offering,* he is punning on the lowest "structural" or "syntactic" level, and it is difficult to

imagine such mappings having the higher significance Hofstadter implies they have. Formalisms outside mathematics must be filled out with interpretations before they are cavalierly mapped; the mapping may touch only on the most trivial aspects of the structure.

The difficulty, then, lies not in creating formal parallels but in judging interpretations, not in the syntax but in the semantics. Curiously Hofstadter has no illusions about this. He discusses varying significances and the limitations of formalism quite clearly. But though he will talk generally about the complexities of language or music or beauty, he is much more at ease in expounding formalisms. . . . [He] treats Bach on [a] trivial level, implying that the same self-reference that lies at the heart of Gödel's and Escher's work is also the source of Bach's greatness. But every formal observation Hofstadter makes about Bach can be made of more contemporary composers who are explicitly formalists. . . . Yet Hofstadter in this book suggests no way of discussing the significant differences between such music and Bach's.

Hofstadter, we come to see, does not have much to say about how musical meaning may arise from musical form, nor about how to approach similar problems of meaning in language or the arts. He has great insight into formal systems and procedures of intelligent reasoning, but he does not succeed in overcoming the limitations of his own formal inquiry, even though the transcendence of merely formal inquiry is one of the main concerns of his book.

Hofstadter hopes to demonstrate transcendence by establishing correspondences involving self-reference between Gödel's proof, the cell, and the mind. He intends to reveal similar structures, to show that what holds in one system may well hold for another, to argue that unpredictable consequence may come into play when formal systems reach a certain level of complexity: Gödel's string may be produced, life may emerge, and intelligence may be created. But these correspondences are rough and metaphorical, and are more assertive than convincing. In order to show how such systems might reach inventiveness Hofstadter himself would have to articulate a theory of meaning that he seems to be reaching for, one that goes beyond a formalist notion of "exotic isomorphism." He would have to move from syntactic, structural, and formal links of varying value and depth to a consideration of the semantics of language and art. (pp. 38-9)

[The] question of the infinite regress . . . recalls Wittgenstein's questioning: why should one be compelled to accept a logical conclusion? Hofstadter would answer that there is always an "inviolable substrate" in the cell, in the mind, in the computer—a formal system which is the limit of infinite regress, the end of all searches for grounding one's knowledge.

I don't see why we should accept this solution: a logical problem of infinite regress is not solved by reference to "hardware." I prefer one of Hofstadter's other formulations: "You can't go on defending your patterns of reasoning forever. There comes a point where faith takes over." And so, finally in this book, it does. Hofstadter has faith that AI will succeed in its quest. . . . Hofstadter does not minimize the difficulties, but they seem formidable. . . . Researchers in AI hope they will never have to model the physiology of the brain; they concentrate upon the workings of the mind, attempting to mirror its features. But this project seems just as enormous. The achievement of AI's project would mean that one would have a program, a finite set of instructions, that would give a literal structure of the human mind, a "string" of statements in which one could read a universal grammar of creativity. Such a project is probably of the same order of difficulty as the search for the secrets of life itself.

But in some sense this dream of AI is the archetypal dream of much of contemporary inquiry. It is not to find a "universal language" whose syntax would reveal the truth of the world—Gödel proved such a language to be impossible—but to find a "universal hermeneutics" that would reduce the fullness of the world to an underlying syntax, to basic "structures," and that would, conversely, be able to read the complexity surrounding us in these basic strings. . . .

"In a way," Hofstadter confides at the beginning, "this book is a statement of my religion." It clearly sets a transcendent goal which may always lie infinitely far away, but Hofstadter's enthusiasm, boldness, and intelligence so engage us that if by the end we seem no closer to that goal, we have nevertheless been enriched by where we have been. (p. 39)

> *Edward Rothstein, "The Dream of Mind and Machine," in* The New York Review of Books *(reprinted with permission from* The New York Review of Books; *copyright © 1979 Nyrev, Inc.), Vol. XXVI, No. 19, December 6, 1979, pp. 34-9.*

RUSSELL HARDIN

Gödel, Escher, Bach is a discussion of Gödel's proof and various (not always clearly) related issues in the nature of mind. It is written in the style of the new journalism (with greater emphasis on the journalist's telling than on what is told), as though by a child of Salinger's Glass children whose large intellect has limited control over his adolescent enthusiasm. The result is a very long book . . . which is variously intelligent, learned, clever, silly, and pretentious and not so variously self-indulgent. . . .

Hofstadter is a computer scientist, a point which is not intended to be an academic equivalent of an ethnic slur but rather to suggest what is the predominant interest of his book: the problem of calculability as it bears on computers and the human mind. On these issues he is remarkably informative in that he discusses with clarity a rich array of others' works, albeit chiefly works by computer scientists and information theorists. (p. 310)

Too much of the more nearly serious part of the book shares the worst traits [of the humorously intended "dialogues"]. . . . Puns pass as insights. Eclectic jumbling of references (as to Gödel, Escher, and Bach) provides the substance for the puns. . . . At its best, perhaps, the result is contentful metaphor. But after reading a few hundred pages, one may begin to hope with Browning that "the best is yet to be." Alas, false hope, and many of what seem on first reading to be Hofstadter's best insights tarnish under scrutiny.

This book was failed by its editors, who should have inducted Hofstadter to render it down below a quarter of a million words. Then, its clever presentation of Gödel's proof for nonspecialists, which is now scattered through several chapters, might be more widely read (along with much else that is valuable). (pp. 310-11)

> *Russell Hardin, "Book Reviews: 'Gödel, Escher, Bach: An Eternal Golden Braid'," in* Ethics *(reprinted by permission of The University of Chicago Press), Vol. 90, No. 2, January, 1980, pp. 310-11.*

ERIC WANNER

[Douglas Hofstadter and Daniel Dennett] have assembled something quite different from the usual AI [artificial intelligence] fare. *The Mind's I* is not a description of the various beasts in AI's current menagerie. Rather, it is a collection of philosophical ruminations, sci-fi fantasies, imaginary dialogues, and other entertaining oddities, including [Alan M.] Turing's original essay [on whether or not computers can think] and excerpts from both authors' recent books (*Gödel, Escher, Bach* by Hofstadter and *Brainstorms* by Dennett). The announced purpose of this inspired hodgepodge is to chew over some of the deep metaphysical questions that lurk just below the surface of AI—questions like, "What is the mind? Who am I? Can machines think?" But there is also a private agenda, namely, to defend artificial intelligence from claims that it will forever be artificial—that intelligent machines, no matter how well they pass Turing's test, will nevertheless lack something, whether that something is soul, or sentiment, or intentionality, or self-awareness, or consciousness.

Like the fictional King Zipperupus in Stanislaw Lem's "The Princess Ineffabelle" (also included in *The Mind's I*), most of us would staunchly resist the chance to have our mind rehoused in a computer, no matter what immortality or other advantage awaited us. Evidently, we believe that something essential would be lost. Hofstadter and Dennett are out to reassure us that, in principle at least, that need not be so. (pp. 104, 106)

[Hofstadter and Dennett ask], "What is consciousness *for*, if perfectly unconscious, indeed subjectless, information-processing is in principle capable of achieving all the ends for which conscious minds were supposed to exist? If theories of cognitive psychology can be true of us, they could also be true of zombies, or robots, and the theories seem to have no way of distinguishing us. How could any amount of mere subjectless information-processing (of the sort we have recently discovered to go on in us) add up to or create that special feature with which it is so vividly contrasted?"

The answer that Hofstadter and Dennett give to this question is complicated, but it can be boiled down without too much damage to two steps:

Step 1 concerns self-representation. Any representational system complex enough to pass Turing's test will need to contain a representation of itself. Although self-representation risks an infinite regress and leads to other conundrums explored by Hofstadter in *Gödel, Escher, Bach,* still, any intelligent machine will have to know something about what is on its own mind. Any unselfconscious machine would fail Turing's test in a flash. That much is clear.

Step 2 concerns the nature of self-consciousness. Just how would an intelligent machine think about itself? Any complicated system—a hurricane, for instance, or an ant colony, or a brain—can be thought about at different levels. The lowest levels—those involving the air molecules, or the ants, or the neurons—may exhibit the basic workings of the systems, but there will be many things such systems accomplish: flooding Miami, building nests, or having ideas, things that can only by described at higher levels. And such higher-level descriptions will generally be uninformed (and uninformative) about the levels below them. We can, for instance, predict that a given hurricane will spare Miami without referring to the nature of air molecules. Similarly, there are ways of thinking about thought that make no reference to neurons or to any of the lower-level mechanisms that make thought possible. Hofstadter and Dennett propose that it is just this upper-level thinking about thought that characterizes human self-consciousness. As usual with upper-level thinking, it is blind to the lower levels. We are really just intelligent machines, even though we protest that we are possessed of a quite unmechanical consciousness.

The authors imagine a hypothetical reader wondering, at this point, "'Is the suggestion then that I am my body's dream? Am I just a fictional character in a sort of novel composed by my body in action?'" Hofstadter and Dennett want us to get more comfortable with affirmative answers to these questions. "But," they add, "why call yourself fictional? Your brain . . . cranks along, doing its physical tasks, sorting the inputs and the outputs without a glimmer of what it is up to. . . . It is creating you in the process, but there you are, emerging from its frantic activity *almost* magically."

That—drastically compressed—is the Hofstadter-Dennett solution to the age-old problem of consciousness. The ghost (consciousness) just emerges from the machine (the brain or the computer) "almost magically." Perhaps we should understand Hofstadter and Dennett's argument as a demonstration that there is nothing *necessarily contradictory* about AI's understanding of intelligence and our own insistence on consciousness. If so, they may have made the point. But if that almost magical emergence is rephrased as a prediction about the future of AI, then I, for one, am skeptical. Will it really be the case that all those programmers at Yale and Carnegie-Mellon and M.I.T. will go on writing their subroutines for reasoning and talking and learning, and then one day, when the subroutines are put together, the resulting program will insist—just as stubbornly as we do—that it is conscious? It could happen, but I don't think Hofstadter and Dennett have said anything to convince me that it will. And, come to think of it, even if such a consciousness-claiming computer did spring into being, how would we decide whether its consciousness was just like ours? Aren't we right back where we started from—at Turing's test? I wonder. (pp. 106-08)

> *Eric Wanner, "I Am a Computer," in* Psychology Today *(copyright © 1981 Ziff-Davis Publishing Company), Vol. 15, No. 10, October, 1981, pp. 104, 106-08.**

PETER WILSHER

I started off by finding the format [of *The Mind's I*] rather irritating: a chunk of Borges, followed by a page or two of commentary, then a bit of science-fiction originally published by the Buddhist Society and more commentary; and so on through the book. But gradually the point of the annotated-anthology structure begins to emerge, and to justify itself. For it is the Hofstadter-Dennett purpose here not so much to dazzle the reader with cerebration but to engage him, as far as this is possible through the medium of a plain, old-fashioned book, in a debate—or rather, in a many-sided symposium where all and sundry can have their say.

The topic, of course, is the nature of you-ness and me-ness, him-ness and her-ness. What, if anything, is unique and invariant about this body, this brain, this combination of heredity and experience that makes up the entity you claim to regard as yourself? (p. 22)

[The] best thing in the book is from Hofstadter himself, in the style that made *Gödel* a runaway best-seller. His **'Conservation with Einstein's Brain'** takes the form of an extended dialogue

between Achilles, an eager but intellectually somewhat flat-footed pursuer of enlightenment, and the subtly seditious Tortoise, whose dubious pleasure is to impale the unsuspecting on the sharp spikes of his logic. On this occasion he invites Achilles to consider the thesis that Einstein's brain could, at any rate in principle, be encoded within the pages of a book. Each page—and there are around one hundred billion of them, but still a finite number—contains the necessary mathematical detail of one individual neuron, and the electrical impulses needed to cause it to fire. With a set of tables setting out how such a firing affects other neurons along the chain, this surely provides a complete, cell-by-cell account of the apparatus that conceived $E = mc^2$ and the General Theory of Relativity. By programming its response to aural inputs you could even (could you not?) conduct a conversation with it. But it is not Einstein, it is a book modelling, or mapping, Einstein. What would be the effect if you left it out in the rain, and a few pages became illegible or blew away? What would be its status if you lost the instructions on how to use it? And if you republished it in paperback, how many Einsteins would you have? And which, perish the thought, is the 'real' one?

Hofstadter and his co-editor offer no answers. If their own book has an overriding message it is, 'Just think about it'. (p. 23)

> *Peter Wilsher, "You-ness," in* New Statesman *(© 1981 The Statesman & Nation Publishing Co. Ltd.), Vol. 102, No. 2643, November 13, 1981, pp. 22-3.**

HOWARD GARDNER

[What Douglas R. Hofstadter and Daniel C. Dennett have done in *The Mind's I*] is collect 27 heterogeneous essays drawn from a variety of disciplines and perspectives. With one exception, the essays are followed by "Reflections": short commentaries by one or both of the composers which place the essays in a wider context, and often suggest additional implications or readings. (p. 32)

Despite the mix of authors, disciplines, and degrees of abstruseness, certain common devices, themes, and problems run through the book. Several of the writers present "Gedanken experiments" (thought experiments), in which, say, a mind is transplanted from one body to another, a brain is analogously transplanted, a brain is rewired, a brain is converted into a set of passages in a book, or a robot simulates a person. There is pervasive preoccupation with those organisms and machines which challenge our notions of what persons, thoughts, and minds are (and what they aren't): chimpanzees which talk or don't talk, bats which resemble or are different from human beings, computers, gods, robots, and even the grim products of attempts at genetic engineering.

One has the feeling that Ripley's Believe It Or Not, the proceedings of the National Academy of Science, the American Philosophical Society, and the latest science fiction thrillers have all been trapped between two covers.

Does this *potpourri* add up to a clear set of messages? Hofstadter and Dennett seem to be making the following points:

1. Materialism has carried the day. There are no ghosts or spirits in the organism. And yet it is perfectly proper and scientifically respectable to talk about minds and selves.

2. It is possible to create machines which think. In fact, human beings may be considered such machines. The Turing test,

where an observer must, in effect, judge whether he has been conversing with a computer or a person, serves as a fair measure of success in creating thinking machines.

3. An intelligent system, or machine, like a human being must be able to rearrange or "reconfigure" its thought processes.

4. The existence of minds is by no means restricted to certain arrangements of brain cells. For instance, computer programs can embody mental processes. What is critical for mental activity to occur is simply certain arrangements of elements.

5. The notion of mental representation is central in the cognitive sciences. A representation consists of structures that in some way can mirror the world and that can modify their modes of operation to reflect changes in the world. Thus a computer, but not a television set, qualifies as a representational system.

6. It is legitimate, though tricky, to talk of selves and consciousness in minds, be they organic or "merely" mechanical. Legitimate invocation of these attributes may occur when a representational system achieves a certain level of complexity which includes the capacity to represent its own capacities and attributes. As essayist Richard Dawkins puts it, "perhaps consciousness arises when the brain's simulation of the world becomes so complex that it must include a model of itself."

7. Work in the cognitive sciences should incorporate various levels of analysis as well as the particular perspective from which a phenomenon is observed. In evaluating simulations of mental activity, for example, one needs to take into account such factors as the physical material out of which a simulation is constructed, the degree of accuracy of the simulation, the physical size of the simulation, the nature of the simulating mechanism, and the speed of that mechanism.

While these points come through with some regularity and clarity, Hofstadter and Dennett are also inveterate collectors of puzzles and paradoxes. Among those which they revisit are the tricks which language can play on an individual; the problems encountered when one shifts levels of analysis without being aware of it; the difference between internal consciousness (how one feels oneself) and external consciousness (the problem of the existence of "other minds"); the subtlety of the line between fictive and "real" states; and finally, the question of who creates—the scientist, the programmer, the novelist, or God.

These, then, are Hofstadter's and Dennett's preoccupations, their reasons for choreographing this book. Yet in fact it is not easy to figure out just where the editors stand on the issues, I have noted, which I had to extrapolate from the texts. For some reason, Hofstadter and Dennett are reluctant to put their cards on the table. The book is replete with disclaimers. We read "This thing speaks for itself." "It is hard to say." "We'll leave this one for you to ponder on." "Right or wrong, the ideas are worth thinking about." "We will leave answers implicit." Rather than succumbing to "handwaving" without evidence, Hofstadter and Dennett embrace the opposite sin of "headshaking."

Part of the problem may be ambivalence about audience. Naturally the editors want to reach the largest possible readership, but that is difficult to accomplish with a collection of this sort. . . . I don't want to suggest that the book is solemn or overly

technical; much of it is fun to read and highly provocative. Yet I suspect that few readers will be satisfied. The authors can't decide whether they are seducing bright freshmen or challenging advanced graduate students. Novices will fail to understand large sections of the text, while those steeped in the cognitive sciences will search in vain for original material.

Just as it is difficult to figure out what the editors wish to propound, it is difficult to ferret out what they are against. Despite their claim that they will offend both spiritualists and materialists, their discussions are, in fact, highly eclectic and catholic. There is no discussion of the philosophical objections which might still be raised against rampant mentalism, nor is there a critique of the artificiality of most research in contemporary experimental cognitive psychology. Indeed, the only place in the book where Hofstadter and Dennett give their own views is in their uncharacteristically lengthy and contentious reflection on John Searle's essay, "Minds, Brains and Programs." In this essay, Searle, a philosopher of language at the University of California at Berkeley, challenges the "strong" claims of the artificial intelligence movement. In his view, computer programs cannot legitimately be said to understand anything. (pp. 32-3)

In Searle's view, "genuine" understanding can only emerge in organisms which have intentionality, and the ability to have and carry out intentions may depend on being a certain type of protoplasm. The notion that intelligence can be embodied in an artificial symbol-manipulating computer strikes Searle as absurd. This criticism obviously cuts to the heart of this collection and so Dennett and Hofstadter detail their grievances against Searle. But I must admit that I found Searle's presentation more compelling than Hofstadter and Dennett's various attempts to undercut it. Perhaps this is because, unlike Hofstadter and Dennett, Searle has minced no words in saying exactly where he stands on central issues in the cognitive sciences.

On the whole, then, incompleteness pervades the Hofstadter-Dennett collection. Certainly this smorgasbord is enjoyable to read and it is valuable to have these articles collected together. Moreover, Hofstadter and Dennett's own Socratic-style dialogues and reflections are among the very finest in the book. But the whole is not greater than the sum of its parts. In putting together such a collection, Hofstadter and Dennett have added to a pile of books of a kind that is becoming increasingly common: collections of provocative ideas which readers are expected to synthesize for themselves. . . . On rare occasions such a compilation can be successful: in his *Organization and Pathology of Thought* (1951), David Rapoport, the gifted clinical psychologist, wrestled with several texts by other authors and ended up producing a classic of his own. But most "readers" remain just that, not integrated works; and *The Mind's I* is simply not in Rapoport's class. (p. 33)

The Mind's I does tell us many things. But by abdicating the possibility of creating a genuinely novel synthesis, Hofstadter and Dennett have provided less than we have the right to expect from two such unusually talented cognitive scientists. (p. 34)

Howard Gardner, "The New Science of Cognition," in The New Republic *(reprinted by permission of* The New Republic; © *1982 The New Republic, Inc.),* Vol. 186, No. 8, February 24, 1982, pp. 32-4.*

G(odfrey) H. Jansen

1919-

Jansen is an Anglo-Indian nonfiction writer and journalist now living in Cyprus. He is the author of *Militant Islam* (1979), a controversial book that attempts to identify for westerners the social, political, and religious fundamentals of Islam. Jansen has served in the Indian diplomatic corps and currently is Middle East correspondent for *The Economist*.

Excerpt from *MILITANT ISLAM*

[A] survey of the prospects of militant Islam in countries across the expanse of the Muslim world reveals that those prospects, on the whole, are good and getting better. Thus, militant Islam is in position, though in a somewhat secondary and passive role in Libya and Algeria. It already actively wields power, wholly or very substantially, in two large and important countries, Iran and Pakistan, even though in both it is the focus of controversy and challenge. It is very well placed to come to power in even larger and more important countries: in Egypt and the Sudan in the near future, and in Indonesia in the not too distant future. It seems certain to make gains in Tunisia and Morocco. It is in countries like Saudi Arabia and Turkey that its future seems most problematical. Just as the frontier of Islam, as a religion, is moving steadily outwards and southwards in Black Africa, so too the spiritual or ideological frontier of militant Islam progresses steadily towards the Islamic state. And just as Islam, historically, has been extremely tenacious in holding on to any new territory acquired, so too any gains made by militant Islam will almost certainly be for the most part irreversible: one cannot conceive of either Iran or Pakistan ever again becoming completely secular states. The onward march of militant Islam is that much more assured not only because of the lack of an alternative but also because there are signs of a possible accommodation with its chief opponent.

That opponent is Westernizing nationalism, also the main antagonist of communism, which it has successfully rebuffed in Afro-Asia. Will it be as successful in halting the advance of militant Islam in Indonesia, Turkey or Egypt? There is the fact that, so far, the Westernizing nationalists, both the civilian politicians and the military men, have not succeeded in solving the fundamental, essentially economic, problems of their countries. Perhaps because of this observable failure we see civilian Westernizing nationalists, especially in Iran but also in Pakistan and to some extent in Turkey, moving back to their roots. The same is true of some of the Westernized military men—General Zia in Pakistan, General Nasution in Indonesia, Colonel Boumedienne in Algeria. On the other hand many of the religious reformers accept the importance of controlled Westernization—men like Ayatollah Telegani in Iran, Sadik Mahdi in the Sudan, and Natsir in Indonesia.

Apart from these evidences of mutual rapproachment the religious reformers must set about trying to reach a serious and long-term accommodation because nationalism as a political emotion is still an immensely strong force in Afro-Asia, perhaps even of equal strength to Islam. The time does not yet seem ripe for supranational or anti-national Islamic political structures—on the basis of the caliphate, or of pan Islam or of

the world-wide umma, the Muslim community. . . . But, as a first step, should not Mecca itself be ruled by a regime somewhat nearer the Islamic ideal than is the present one there?

So also Islamic nationalists need not push their nationalism towards exclusive chauvinism but, as an initial relaxation of nationalism, move towards regional arrangements. . . . (pp. 197-99)

What has been objectionable to reformist Islam about nationalism has not only been its narrowness and divisiveness but its Westernized exponents. Both these objectionable features are being indigenized and diluted. Also, several of the reformist movements—the brotherhood, Masjumi and the Jamaat—have strongly advocated that type of nationalism called love of country or patriotism, so that on every side the lines of opposition between Islam and nationalism are being blurred. Indeed a form of Islamic patriotism could become a median position between strict nationalism and supranational all-umma utopianism.

We now come to the crucial question in this assessment of the future possibilities of militant Islam, the primary question which has been pushed into second place by the headlong pace of developments in the Muslim world: does militant Islam have the answers to the political, economic and social problems of the Muslim countries?

Its political answer, as given in the form of the ideal constitution of the Islamic state is to place all, or almost all executive power in the hands of a single man, a modern caliph, and having democratically given him despotic powers to hope that he will be and remain 'a just despot'. This seems like asking too much from human nature, for it is a historical fact that 'power corrupts . . . ' . . . . If in the ideal Islamic constitution the legislature is decidedly inferior to the executive, the judiciary is supposed to be independent and therefore equal to the executive. But for how long will an almost all-powerful despot, however just, tolerate an independent judiciary? So militant Islam's answers to the terrible problem of power is not so much a solution, more a calculated risk. One thing is certain—the man of religion with the gun can and should never be anything more than a transitory phenomenon.

The real test of militant Islam's relevance or competence will be its handling of the economic problems of the Muslim countries. Here it is on surer ground than in the political sphere. It is, by now, well known what these problems are, and that they are common to all Afro-Asian countries; thus the Islamic solutions to them have also been extensively studied. . . . So there is no dearth of Islamic ideas on economic problems. There is still less of a dearth of money, because the oil-rich Muslim states have shown a commendable readiness to share their wealth with their less fortunate Muslim brethren. What is needed, and so far has been in very short supply in rich countries like Indonesia, Iran and Saudi Arabi, is character: drive linked to dedication and honesty. These qualities the Islamic reformist groups are well able to supply; for even in lax societies like Indonesia and Egypt it is agreed that the members of these movements are noteworthy for possessing just such qualities of character. This is why they have been both envied and feared.

As a solver of social problems the Islamic state begins with two initial disadvantages. Governments based on or closely associated with religions are automatically associated with the right of the political spectrum; hence, despite active wooing, the failure of the Jamaat and the brotherhood to make much headway with the trade unions in Pakistan and Egypt. But perhaps Algeria for the Sunnis and Ayatollah Telegani of Iran for the Shiahs have done something to shift the image of political Islam towards the left. This is important because the basic trend in Afro-Asia is towards the left, and it is also industrializing with trade unions becoming more powerful.

The second disadvantage is massive: the fact that Islam puts one half of the human race, women, into a subordinate position to the male half—no amount of apologetics about respect for women, protection of their just rights and so forth can get around this basic and unjust discrimination. It is firmly embedded in Islamic practice because it is there in the Koran, as are the canonical punishments.

This brings us to a consideration of what sort of Islam can provide the enduring basis for militant Islam, both before and after it comes to power in a Muslim country. As such a basis Islam will constantly run into problems and contradictions and self-contradictions if it clings to two dogmas—an old one, that every single word in the Koran is of divine inspiration, and a newer one, that Muhammad is the most perfect human exemplar and is above all or any criticism. Militant reformist Islam can be solidly based only on a reformed Islam. Because,

so far, new unorthodox Islamic thinking on political, economic and social problems has gone along with a touching but inconsistent loyalty to orthodox theology, militant Islam has tended to fall between two stools. Any real reconstruction of religious thought in Islam needs to be based on the principle that the area of unquestioned revealed truth needs to be narrowed, but not diluted. (pp. 199-202)

The gates of ijtihad, of independent judgement, need to be flung wide open. Till that happens and Muslim thinkers begin to think the unthinkable, and to publish their unthinkable thoughts, they will continue to spend far too much time, as they do at present, putting forward unconvincing apologies for Islam on such issues as the position of women and the canonical punishments. Islam has bigger and better tasks ahead of it: Toynbee has indicated two tasks for which he believed Islam was peculiarly fitted—the solution of the problems of racial discrimination and of alcoholism. But Islam would do better to devote itself to such tasks, after it has done the essential rethinking of its essential nature, and the reformation of thought, rather than indulging in flexing its military muscle as when in January 1979 it was announced that forty-one Islamic nations had spent $40 billion on their defence forces, had 3.5 million men under arms, and owned more thanks and aircraft than NATO excluding the USA; and that all this military might could be pooled in a single Islamic armoury. But there is not going to be another Poitiers or another Vienna.

Such boastings can best be excused as expressions of youthful vigour. And indeed it is this very vigour of Islam, its youthful militancy, the generation gap between it and an ageing Christianity, that is itself productive of misunderstanding. . . . But militant Islam *is* certain of the truth of its beliefs, and it believes that it *does* really know the truth. Like its militant Protestant predecessors it is not going to relax or to be particularly tolerant. And it will not cease from mental and spiritual and material strife till those beliefs govern the destinies of every Muslim country. (pp. 203-04)

G. H. Jansen, in his Militant Islam *(reprinted by permission of David Higham Associates Limited, as literary agents for G. H. Jansen; © G. H. Jansen 1979), Pan Books, 1979, 224 p.*

LUCY MAIR

In one or other capacity [G. H. Jansen] has attended most of the conferences at which the new states of the post-war world have sought to agree upon and define their common interests. His delightful irony . . . [in *Afro-Asia and Nonalignment*] deserts him only when he is reciting the stereotyped mythology of the colonial era. The ideas of Afro-Asia and non-alignment are shown to be competitive, not complementary. Afro-Asia is the spirit of Bandung, non-alignment that of Belgrade. It is easy to define an Afro-Asian, less easy to identify a non-aligned nation. Non-alignment as Nehru understood it was the pursuit of an independent foreign policy. By this criterion, Mr. Jansen argues, many of the participants in conferences of the non-aligned should not have been there. Who was invited depended in practice on the attitude of the host country and the organisers. In Mr. Jansen's view the Third World was most effective when at Geneva 77 poor countries stood together to assert their interests at the conference on world trade. 'In future,' he predicts, 'the only non-aligned or Afro-Asian conferences that have any real value will be those dealing with economic questions.' His record of these conferences is invaluable, and sometimes very funny.

Lucy Mair, "The Third World," in New Statesman (© 1966 The Statesman & Nation Publishing Co. Ltd.), Vol. 72, No. 1846, July 29, 1966, p. 171.*

WERNER LEVI

[In *Non-Alignment and the Afro-Asian States,* the American title of *Afro-Asia and Non-Alignment,* G. H. Jansen] gives the history of the rise and decline of [the movement toward Afro-Asian solidarity], describing its highlights in considerable detail and including in his survey the often neglected non-official efforts of the Communists and the Socialists to strengthen and exploit some sense of solidarity. As a journalistic essay, the book is excellent and of a high intellectual standard. As an analysis of an interesting political phenomenon it remains incomplete. Though the author approaches his subject in a laudably dispassionate, liberal, and critical manner he is satisfied with the more obvious and by now fairly well known explanations of the "movement's" eventual failure, such as the breakthrough of individual national interests or the pretensions and illusions of individual national leaders. There is no attempt to go into the deeper reasons which might be found in the nature of the international political system itself or in the general prerequisites for the cooperation and integration of sovereign national units.

At the end of a story of failures, the author makes some surprising assertions, among them that "truly defined" non-alignment will survive if backed by armed force. Or that the Afro-Asians have "incontestably" saved the peace, especially between 1949 and 1953. Such conclusions, not born out by the substance of the account, may result from the author's wish not to leave his reader or himself in too deep a pessimistic mood. (p. 379)

Werner Levi, "Book Reviews :'Non-Alignment and the Afro-Asian States'," in Pacific Affairs (copyright 1967, University of British Columbia), Vol. XXXIX, Nos. 3 & 4, Fall and Winter, 1966-67, pp. 378-79.

CECIL V. CRABB, JR.

Many of Jansen's assertions and insights [in *Non-alignment and the Afro-Asian States*], it must be said, are timely and illuminating. He has a clear sense (which some proponents of neutralism clearly lack) of the semantic confusion surrounding the concept, of its inherent flexibility (if not ambiguity), and of the impact of the international political environment upon its essential meaning. He sees that it can and does accommodate, under one diplomatic credo, an often bewildering multiplicity of national viewpoints and politics, which are in some cases antagonistic.

Jansen makes no attempt to eschew value judgments; his own intimate association with Indian viewpoints frequently colors his evaluation, particularly when he discusses India's recent and traumatic encounter with Red China. Understandably, if regrettably, his grasp of Asian attitudes and objectives surpasses his knowledge of the Arab and African worlds. Yet sometimes his assessment of even Indian diplomatic behavior is misleading and oversimplified. This author ought to know better than most students, for example, that on numerous occasions Prime Minister Nehru rejected Gandhian non-violence

as a viable principle of statecraft. And in several instances, Jansen is much less prone to give other neutralist nations the benefit of the doubt than he is when dealing with New Delhi's policies and behavior.

The author concludes what is, on balance, a highly critical evaluation of neutralist behavior with the assertion that the non-aligned nations have amassed a record of "solid achievement" and have amply "justified" their attachment to this diplomatic posture. Perhaps they have. In fact, I am inclined to believe Jansen is right. But this verdict—so out of harmony with most of what is said or implied in preceding pages—is both a surprising and intriguing judgment. It is not a conclusion following logically from his own study. The reader is bound to wonder how the author himself arrived at it and why. (p. 299)

Cecil V. Crabb, Jr., "Book Reviews: 'Nonalignment and the Afro-Asian States'," in Political Science Quarterly, Vol. 82, No. 2, June, 1967, pp. 298-99.

BARBARA SMITH

[Godfrey Jansen] has written at high speed a splendidly timely book ["**Militant Islam**"]. He demolishes a wall of Christian myths about an Islam red in tooth and claw, and then proceeds to introduce the non-Moslem to the demanding, enveloping nature of the Islamic faith. His style is gently erudite, felicitously phrased and sufficiently controversial to keep the adrenalin flowing. . . .

Islam draws no dividing line between spiritual and material life: there is no equivalent to the Christian injunction to give unto Caesar the things that are Caesar's. To the true believer every aspect of public and private life is or should be governed by religious doctrine. What has happened, as Godfrey Jansen explains concisely, is that the assertion of Islam's relevance to politics and to law has broken through the weakening structure of several Moslem states at the same moment, culminating spectacularly in the Iranian revolution. . . .

Mr. Jansen argues that the Christian reaction, in particular, is based on atavistic fears and hatreds. Witness, he says, the western emphasis on canonical punishment: on flogging, amputating and decapitating; on the vision of strange bearded men in robes and turbans, the blood dripping from the stumps of their victims' amputated hands. This concentration on the crueller side of the movement goes beyond the automatic shock-horror response of sensation-seeking newspapers; it is also, says Mr. Jansen, the continuation of a pattern set before Crusader times but clearest in that period. This ancient hostility between Christian and Moslem is not dissipated by western Islamists, many of whom dislike the men and the faith they study; the time is long overdue, writes Mr. Jansen, who is Indian, for oriental Islamists to come to the forefront of oriental Islamic studies.

With the advent of the theological regime in Iran, outsiders have suddenly been made aware that there are two main branches of Islam: Sunni and Shia. Mr. Jansen deals fairly briskly with the doctrinal differences between the two but explains the essential difference that makes it immediately plain to Christian readers: the Shia Moslems believe, rather like Roman Catholic Christians, that the earthly community should be led by an Imam (or a Pope) who acts as mediator between the human and the divine; the Sunni believe, rather like Protestants, that a man can stand directly before God without need for an intercessor. But it is Islam's fortune, writes Mr. Jansen, that its Sunni believers are so much more numerous than its Shias;

this, until now, has largely spared the Moslem world the wars in the name of religion that have ravaged Christianity.

Islam is strongest in traditional societies. But Godfrey Jansen argues that neither urbanisation nor modernisation have yet shaken the faith's strong simplicities. Islam is adaptable to new needs; it is also realistic. "Muhammad himself set the tone of down-to-earth practicality, for when asked by a bedouin, 'Shall I let loose my camel and trust in God?' he gave the answer: 'Tie up your camel and trust in God'." This book is full of such glancing enlightenment as the author, with the lightest of hands, explores the mysteries of the Moslem faith.

> Barbara Smith, "True Believers," in The Economist (© The Economist Newspaper Limited, 1979), Vol. 273, No. 7102, October 13, 1979, p. 113.

JIM HOAGLAN

[G. H. Jansen] begins as if he intends a quick but full portrait of a global religion [in *Militant Islam*], one that he argues is unique for its totality and present vitality. He produces instead a series of intellectual snapshots that quickly flip past.

Jansen's sketch of Islam differs sharply with Western conceptions of the religion. He argues that the 10-century decision to slam shut "the gates of *ijtihad* (independent judgement)" to believers, thus confining Islamic belief to the Koran and a few other texts, left the religion sparse in doctrine yet supremely flexible and pragmatic in form, able to be adopted easily in Africa, Asia and elsewhere in the Third World.

Secondly, he argues that the religion is only now entering its "vigorous early middle age." . . . On his time-line, Islam stands now at the point Christianity had reached "a century away from the climactic summation of Aquinas, within half a century of the poetic summation of Dante and of the terrors and ecstasies of the Black Death." The impulse for the Reformation was just beginning.

A challenging point, worth being weighed against the view that there is a general resurgence of fundamentalism in religion as all of our lives become vastly more complicated and we seek certainties. Jansen, however, quickly walks away from his point, a pattern he repeats throughout the book. When he asserts that "Islam has become anti-American" because of U.S. support for Israel and that since 1955 American students of the Middle East have in turn become anti-Islamic, he offers no further explanation or exploration of the monumental consequences of such judgements.

Jansen does, however, give good detailed reporting on the Moslem brotherhoods of various nations and on the explosive content of their increasing political activity. (p. 1)

Surprisingly, he describes serious weaknesses in the totalitarian Islamic systems established in Pakistan by General Zia al Haq and in Iran by the Ayatollah Khomeini, whom Jansen describes as "a perfect example of the Peter Principle"—a good opposition leader totally out of his depth in power. (p. 2)

> Jim Hoaglan, "Islamic Culture of Scimitars and Minarets: 'Militant Islam'," in Book World—The Washington Post (©1980, The Washington Post), January 20, 1980, pp. 1-20.

J. B. KELLY

[Mr. Jansen sets out in *Militant Islam*] to enlighten us about the true nature of Islam and in so doing to demonstrate that the hostility between the Christian West and the Moslem East emanates almost wholly from the Western side. Barely is he out of the starting gate, however, and almost before he can utter his first cry of "Allahu Akbar!," than he is off and running around the old, familiar, anti-imperialist track, already churned up by the hooves of a thousand polemical hacks before him.

The West, so Mr. Jansen feverishly informs us, has held the Moslem East in fear and contempt for centuries. It has oppressed and exploited the Moslem peoples, occupying their lands, depleting their natural resources, denigrating their religion, and generally debasing their lives. Most pernicious of all has been the West's cultural imperialism, which has among other things destroyed the structure of traditional Moslem education and put nothing of comparable value in its place. (According to Mr. Jansen, the European imperial powers founded no universities in the territories they ruled, an accusation that will raise a few eyebrows in India, Pakistan, Malaysia, and Africa.) The *ghazis*, shock troops, of this cultural offensive, it seems, have been the Western scholars of Islam, whose attitude toward their subject is one of dislike, if not downright antipathy.

All this, it need hardly be said, is a travesty of the history of Western relations with the Moslem world. Mr. Jansen, who has an engaging line in half-truths, evasions, and distortions, shows about as much respect for historical accuracy as the student mobs of Tehran show for the principles of international law. . . .

The explanation for Mr. Jansen's avoidance of . . . potentially embarrassing topics would appear to lie in his own animosity against Western Christendom, an animosity which informs nearly every page of his book and which expresses itself, among other ways, in his categorization of Christianity as a religion unsuited to black Africans, in his ridiculing and vilification of the labors of Christian missionaries, in the silence he observes about the slave hunts conducted in the Sudan by successive rulers of Egypt, in his traducing of the aims and methods of the former British administration in the Sudan which wiped out slave-trading, and in his perverse allocation of blame for the massacre a decade ago of thousands of black Christians in the southern Sudan not to the Moslem government in Khartoum but to the Christian missions in the south. (p. 27)

Mr. Jansen, as we shall have occasion to note more fully later, is very free with his sneers at and aspersions upon Western scholars of Islam, whom he accuses of displaying bias and ignorance in their writings. On the evidence he affords here of his own defective knowledge of Islam and Islamic history, he would do well to hold his tongue. He equates the division between Sunni and Shi'i Islam with that between Protestantism and Roman Catholicism, a misconception that qualifies—to employ a phrase of Mahatma Gandhi—as a Himalayan blunder. He alleges that because of the Sunni ascendancy, Islam, unlike Christianity, "escaped the destruction of wars made in the name of religion and it escaped the erosion of spiritual values that is bound to result from such wars. . . . In fact, inter-Muslim wars have been surprisingly few." In fact, as a closer acquaintance with Islamic history would confirm, sectarian conflict has marked the course of inter-Moslem relations since the early years of Islam: three out of the first four caliphs, after all, met their deaths by an assassin's hand. And if no erosion of spiritual values has taken place in Islam, why, may one ask, have there been so many movements of revival and reform?

The other elementary errors and omissions in Mr. Jansen's book, which there is no space here to list, are of a similiar kind. (pp. 27-8)

Never once in his protracted diatribe against the West for its antagonism to Islam does Mr. Jansen allude to those provisions of the *shari'a,* the law of Islam, which divides the world into the *dar al-Islam,* "Moslem territory," and the *dar alharb,* "hostile territory" (of which Christendom is the principal constituent); and which go on to declare that between the two entities there can exist only a condition of continuous warfare, which, while it may be interrupted by truces, can never be terminated. Again, in taking the Western world to task for becoming unduly exercised over the so-called "canonical punishments," i.e. beheadings, amputations, floggings, stonings to death for adultery, and so forth, he indignantly asserts that these penalties are only inflicted by "the political exploiters of Islam," those professional politicians and generals in Moslem countries who, "not knowing the deeper truths of their religion," resort for motives of expediency to the Islamic system of punishment. In so doing, he argues, "these secular Islamic leaders . . . give Islam a bad name and give militant Islam an even worse name." Whether Mr. Jansen likes it or not, these punishments are those prescribed by the *shari'a,* and they will be implemented by any Moslem government that is true to the letter of the law of Islam. As for those "secular Islamic leaders" who do not know "the deeper truths of their religion," would he number among them the Ayatollah Khomeini and his fellow divines? Or the late King Faisal of Saudi Arabia and his successor, King Khalid, neither of whom has hesitated to enforce the Koranic penalties whenever the occasion required it? Far from being mere secular rulers, successive Saudi monarchs have borne the title of *imam* of the Wahhabi sect of Islam. But Mr. Jansen tells us nothing of these matters: they tend rather to spoil his case. (p. 28)

With advocates like Mr. Jansen, Islam has little need of detractors. His pious avowals that Islam is a religion of compassion ring rather hollow when set against the economic distress caused to the poorer countries of Asia and Africa by the huge increases in the price of oil imposed by the Moslem oil-producing states in recent years—a subject on which Mr. Jansen maintains a discreet silence. There is a hollow ring also to his reiterated claim, the central thesis of his book, that the militancy now being exhibited by Islam is in reality nothing more than a "sincere" and "laudable" attempt "to square the conduct of public life with the principles of religion." "The one encouraging factor for Muslim reformers today," he asserts, "is that the attempt is now being made more seriously and intelligently than ever before and in more than one country at the same time." Where exactly is this "sincere," "laudable," and "intelligent" Moslem reformation taking place? In Libya, where a sinister buffoon holds his people in thrall while acting as the paymaster and instigator of terrorism in a dozen countries? In Iraq, where the Sunni Ba'athist junta, allied to the Soviet Union, keeps the Shi'i majority of the population in subjection? In South Yemen, where a Marxist dictatorship, itself securely under the Soviet thumb, has turned the country into a large concentration camp? In Iran? In Afghanistan? To ask such questions is not to be anti-Moslem, as Mr. Jansen would doubtless have it, but to act in the spirit of free inquiry which is at the heart of modern Western civilization. If independence of thought and an aversion to cant are held to be synonymous with inveterate hostility, then there is little hope of understanding between Christendom and Islam. (p. 29)

J. B. Kelly, "Books and the Arts: 'Militant Islam'," in The New Republic *(reprinted by permission of* The New Republic; © *1980 The New Republic, Inc.), Vol. 182, No. 4, January 26, 1980, pp. 27-9.*

FOUAD AJAMI

Mr. Jansen earnestly tries to understand Islam on its own terms, and here and there [**"Militant Islam"**] does accomplish something. It provides a useful historical narrative of the encounter between Islam and the West and the bloody and shifting boundary they have shared over the centuries. It reminds us in the West of the passion that Islam provokes because of the West's claim to a monopoly on truth; it provides an antidote to the sure smugness that order and rationality are wholly on one side, fundamentalism and incoherence on the other.

Although Mr. Jansen tries hard to understand, his method ultimately fails him. He has attributed to the scripture more importance than it deserves; he has seen and heard the professed devotion of Moslems to Islam, but he has missed their bewilderment, their confusion, the ways in which rival groups profess and put forth wholly contradictory notions of Islam. He has seen men held by a religious doctrine only to miss the way they hold and manipulate it; he thus errs in his assessment of how far they can go with it.

Mr. Jansen is convinced that "Islam retains its grip on the total life of the members of its community," that "Islam is so entirely a living faith today precisely because it is a totality, legislating the totality of man's earthly activities, and not just his social needs." From such a premise, and writing as we all do now in the shadow of the Iranian upheaval, Mr. Jansen reaches an equally "pure," unequivocal, fixed conclusion: that Islam will push steadily "towards the Islamic state." Moslems tried other things—secular nationalism, liberalism, Marxism—and now "*faute de mieux* militant Islam is on the threshold of political power." In the Moslem movements he covers, there is always the "same steely core" and the "steeliness" is all the tougher not only because the fundamentalist groups involved are "engaged in the high and holy task of infusing the principles of a higher religion into workaday politics, economics, and social affairs" but also because the religion in question "happens to be Islam which is quite uncompromising in the totality of its claims for authority over all aspects of the life of man."

There is enough drama in the world Mr. Jansen covers for him not to need such a caricature. If there is one thing that is missing from Mr. Jansen's world view, it is a tolerance for ambiguity, for moral and cultural paradoxes—which is the one thing needed to approach a world split right down the middle, where different cultures and eras exist side by side. . . .

No one knows what an Islamic estate would or would not do, would or would not look like. Ideas and systems—liberal, Marxist, Moslem, whatever—become a cover for power, an apology for decay. Behind the labels lurk the struggle for power and the fears and ambitions of men. Reality devours the scheme, and men are left insisting that it was "only" betrayed or disfigured by greed or incompetence. Or they are left using the "forms" of a particular civilization—its methods of punishment, its rituals, its outward displays of devotion—as a smoke screen behind which they engage in sordid or banal affairs. In Pakistan, for example, nauseating Islamic piety serves as a cover for military dictatorship. The outward militancy is there, but at the core lies not "steeliness" but the familiar mix of avarice, ambition, incompetence—a society in stalemate. These are things that we know all societies are subject to. When we don't write about them in our discussions of Pakistan, Iran or other faraway lands, it is because we insist on regarding them as militant, as exotic. . . .

It is not that these societies are totally "like us," for that assumption is also a dead end. But we are sure to lose sight of the troubles and phenomena we are dealing with if we insist on the idiosyncratic, on shadows or gripping images. In today's folklore, Islam is militantly anti-Western. But what are we to make of the "love" for America expressed by Pakistan's ruler, Zia ul Haq, or his bid for American aid, his inviting show of America's muscle and will? Where is the "true" Islam: in Khomeini's view of things or in Sadat's, in Saudi Arabia or in Qaddafi's Libya? "Militant" Islam is one form; bourgeois Islam of the bazaar and the middle classes is another; reactionary Islam is yet another. Some read socialism into Islam, and we should not be surprised when their adversaries find in the same Islam high regard for private property and inequality. There is no happy conclusion to the drama of politics, no short cut to the city of justice.

It was Iran that supposedly showed us the militancy of Islam; it is Iran that may be throwing us off the right track, playing into our stereotypes. And appropriately enough, it is Iran that is providing a denouement to the "militant Islam" hypothesis, to the Islamic utopia that tantalizes the true believer and frightens those in the West who worry about the receding of "civilization." (p. 6)

Fouad Ajami, "Islamic Ideas," in The New York Times Book Review *(© 1980 by The New York Times Company; reprinted by permission), March 2, 1980, pp. 7, 29.**

Donald C(arl) Johanson
1943-

Maitland A(rmstrong) Edey
1910-

Photograph by Tocky Run

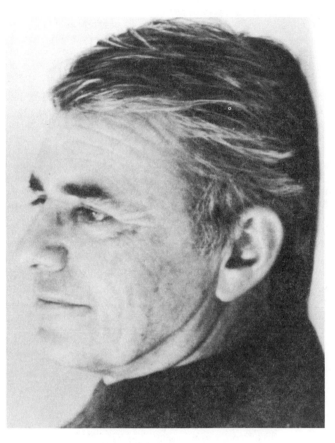

Courtesy of Maitland Edey

Johanson and Edey are an American paleoanthropologist, educator, and museum curator and an American editor and free-lance writer, respectively, who coauthored *Lucy: The Beginnings of Humankind* (1981). A description of Johanson's discovery of the oldest bipedal anthropoid yet discovered, a nearly intact, almost four-million-year-old female skeleton he named Lucy, their book presents this important anthropological breakthrough in colloquial language designed to entertain and inform a popular audience. Sprinkled throughout the account are passages detailing Johanson's feuds and rivalries with fellow anthropologist Richard Leakey, with whom he disagrees on evolutionary theory. Johanson is a professor of anthropology at Case Western Reserve University and Kent State University. (See also *Contemporary Authors*, Vols. 57-60 for Edey.)

Excerpt from *LUCY: THE BEGINNINGS OF HUMANKIND*

''Lucy?''

That is the question I always get from somebody who sees the fossil for the first time. I have to explain: ''Yes, she was a female. And that Beatles song. We were sky-high, you must remember, from finding her.''

Then comes the next question: ''How did you know she was a female?''

''From her pelvis. We had one complete pelvic bone and her sacrum. Since the pelvic opening in hominids has to be proportionately larger in females than in males to allow for the birth of large-brained infants, you can tell a female.''

And the next: ''She was a hominid?''

''Oh, yes. She walked erect. She walked as well as you do.''

''Hominids all walked erect?''

''Yes.''

''Just exactly what is a hominid?''

337

That usually ends the questions, because that one has no simple answer. Science has had to leave the definition rather flexible because we do not yet know exactly when hominids first appeared. However, it is safe to say that a hominid is an erect-walking primate. That is, it is either an extinct ancestor to man, a collateral relative to man, or a true man. All human beings are hominids, but not all hominids are human beings.

We can picture human evolution as starting with a primitive apelike type that gradually, over a long period of time, began to be less and less apelike and more manlike. There was no abrupt crossover from ape to human, but probably a rather fuzzy time of in-between types that would be difficult to classify either way. We have no fossils yet that tell us what went on during that in-between time. Therefore, the handiest way of separating the newer types from their ape ancestors is to lump together all those that stood up on their hinds legs. That group of men and near-men is called hominids.

I am a hominid. I am a human being. I belong to the genus *Homo* and to the species *sapiens:* thinking man. Perhaps I should say wise or knowing man—a man who is smart enough to recognize that he is a man. There have been other species of *Homo* who were not so smart, ancestors now extinct. *Homo sapiens* began to emerge a hundred thousand—perhaps two or three hundred thousand—years ago, depending on how one regards Neanderthal Man. He was another *Homo*. Some think he was the same species as ourselves. Others think he was an ancestor. There are a few who consider him a kind of cousin. That matter is unsettled because many of the best Neanderthal fossils were collected in Europe before anybody knew how to excavate sites properly or get good dates. Consequently, we do not have exact ages for most of the Neanderthal fossils in collections.

I consider Neanderthal conspecific with *sapiens,* with myself. One hears talk about putting him in a business suit and turning him loose in the subway. It is true; one could do it and he would never be noticed. He was just a little heavier-boned than people of today, more primitive in a few facial features. But he was a man. His brain was as big as a modern man's, but shaped in a slightly different way. Could he make change at the subway booth and recognize a token? He certainly could. He could do many things more complicated than that. He was doing them over much of Europe, Africa and Asia as long as sixty or a hundred thousand years ago.

Neanderthal Man had ancestors, human ones. Before him in time was a less advanced type: *Homo erectus*. Put him on the subway and people would probably take a suspicious look at him. Before *Homo erectus* was a really primitive type, *Homo habilis;* put him on the subway and people would probably move to the other end of the car. Before *Homo habilis* the human line may run out entirely. The next stop in the past, back of *Homo habilis*, might be something like Lucy.

All of the above are hominids. They are all erect walkers. Some were human, even though they were of exceedingly primitive types. Others were not human. Lucy was not. No matter what kind of clothes were put on Lucy, she would not look like a human being. She was too far back, out of the human range entirely. That is what happens going back along an evolutionary line. If one goes back far enough, one finds oneself dealing with a different kind of creature. On the hominid line the earliest ones are too primitive to be called humans. They must be given another name. Lucy is in that category.

For five years I kept Lucy in a safe in my office in the Cleveland Museum of Natural History. I had filled a wide shallow box with yellow foam padding, and had cut depressions in the foam so that each of her bones fitted into its own tailor-made nest. *Everybody* who came to the Museum—it seemed to me—wanted to see Lucy. What surprised people most was her small size.

Her head, on the evidence of the bits of her skull that had been recovered, was not much larger than a softball. Lucy herself stood only three and one-half feet tall, although she was fully grown. That could be deduced from her wisdom teeth, which were fully erupted and had been exposed to several years of wear. My best guess was that she was between twenty-five and thirty years old when she died. She had already begun to show the onset of arthritis or some other bone ailment, on the evidence of deformation of her vertebrae. If she had lived much longer, it probably would have begun to bother her.

Her surprisingly good condition—her completeness—came from the fact that she had died quietly. There were no tooth marks on her bones. They had not been crunched and splintered, as they would have been if she had been killed by a lion or a saber-toothed cat. Her head had not been carried off in one direction and her legs in another, as hyenas might have done with her. She had simply settled down in one piece right where she was, in the sand of a long-vanished lake edge or stream—and died. Whether from illness or accidental drowning, it was impossible to say. The important thing was that she had not been found by a predator just after death and eaten. Her carcass had remained inviolate, slowly covered by sand or mud, buried deeper and deeper, the sand hardening into rock under the weight of subsequent depositions. She had lain silently in her adamantine grave for millennium after millennium until the rains at Hadar had brought her to light again. (pp. 18-21)

Lucy always managed to look interesting in her little yellow nest—but to a nonprofessional, not overly impressive. There were other bones all around her in the Cleveland Museum. She was dwarfed by them, by drawer after drawer of fossils, hundreds of them from Hadar alone. There were casts of hominid specimens from East Africa, from South Africa and Asia. There were antelope and pig skulls, extinct rodents, rabbits and monkeys, as well as apes. There was one of the largest collections of gorilla skulls in the world. In that stupefying array of bones, I kept being asked, What was so special about Lucy? Why had she, as another member of the expedition put it, "blown us out of our little anthropological minds for months"?

"Three things," I always answered. "First: what she is—or isn't. She is different from anything that has been discovered and named before. She doesn't fit anywhere. She is just a very old, very primitive, very small hominid. Somehow we are going to have to fit her in, find a name for her.

"Second," I would say, "is her completeness. Until Lucy was found, there just weren't any very old skeletons. The oldest was one of those Neanderthalers I spoke of a little while ago. It is about seventy-five thousand years old. Yes, there *are* older hominid fossils, but they are all fragments. Everything that has been reconstructed from them has had to be done by matching up those little pieces—a tooth here, a bit of jaw there, maybe a complete skull from somewhere else, plus a leg bone from some other place. The fitting together has been done by scientists who know those bones as well as I know my own hand. And yet, when you consider that such a reconstruction may consist of pieces from a couple of dozen individuals who may have lived hundreds of miles apart and may have been separated from each other by a hundred thousand years in time—well, when you look at the complete individual you've just put together you have to say to yourself, 'Just how real is he?' With Lucy you know. It's all there. You don't have to guess. You don't have to imagine an arm bone you haven't got. You *see* it. You see it for the first time from something older than a Neanderthaler.''

''How much older?''

''That's point number three. The Neanderthaler is seventy-five thousand years old. Lucy is approximately 3.5 million years old. She is the oldest, most complete, best-preserved skeleton of any erect-walking human ancestor that has ever been found.'' (pp. 22-4)

> *Donald C. Johanson and Maitland A. Edey, in their* Lucy: The Beginnings of Humankind *(copyright © 1981 by Donald C. Johanson and Maitland A. Edey; reprinted by permission of Simon & Schuster, a Division of Gulf & Western Corporation), Simon & Schuster, 1981, 409 p.*

BOYCE RENSBERGER

[In "Lucy"] Dr. Johanson and Mr. Edey put forth the fascinating conjecture that bipedalism was linked to the origin of pair bonding and the nuclear family. This theory, developed by C. Owen Lovejoy, a Kent State University anthropologist, starts with the observation that if the earliest proto-humans were anything like apes, they reproduced very slowly. For example, the period of time required for a chimpanzee female to reach sexual maturity and rear two offspring (that is, replacements for herself and a mate) is 21 years; each baby chimpanzee needs five to six years of nurturing, which the female chimpanzee provides without the assistance of the male.

This system works in a food-rich tropical forest, but such environments began shrinking many millions of years ago as global climates turned more sharply seasonal. The ape population has been decreasing ever since. One species' hardship, however, is another's evolutionary opportunity. The way was open for a new, apelike animal that could evolve some means of reproducing faster or surviving longer. According to Dr. Lovejoy's theory, the crucial event was monogamous pair bonding, in which the male helped gather food for his family. Since the newly seasonal environment put food sources farther apart, the best foraging method would have been to split up, gather food and bring it back to share at a home base. Bipedalism arose, so the theory goes, because it allowed proto-humans to carry more food. (pp. 1, 28)

The discovery of Lucy also led to a redrawing of the hominid family tree. In 1979, Dr. Johanson—with the collaboration of Dr. Timothy White of the University of California at Berkeley, who had found similar fossils in Tanzania—proposed that Lucy and similar specimens represented a previously unrecognized species of human ancestor. They called it *Australopithecus afarensis*.

These anthropological breakthroughs figure prominently in "Lucy," but the book is also the latest volley in a no longer very friendly rivalry between Dr. Johanson and Richard Leakey, the Kenyan anthropologist. Mr. Leakey's recent books, "Origins" and "People of the Lake," contain some of the factless flights of evolutionary interpretation to which Dr. Johanson and many other paleoanthropologists object. Though

the feud has involved bitter personality clashes, Dr. Johanson sticks largely to the scientific issues here, in particular Mr. Leakey's apparent unwillingness to change his own story of human evolution in the light of new evidence. . . .

The book does have its annoying moments. Particularly obvious are certain lapses of humility. Dr. Johanson speaks of his fossils as "an unparalleled collection" and says that his ideas "if accepted, would affect the way all paleoanthropologists would have to look thereafter at the pattern of human ancestry." Strictly speaking, of course, Dr. Johanson is right. And given the nature of the events they describe, it is possible to excuse some of his sweeping statements: He calls the time he and his colleagues discovered an unprecedented collection of at least 13 hominid skeletons in one spot "one of the most extraordinary days in the history of paleoanthropology." It's true: it appears that all 13—men, women, and children—were members of a single family struck down by some unknown catastrophe. (The collection has been dubbed the "First Family.") On the other hand, Dr. Johanson is disarmingly willing to acknowledge his own scientific errors. He concedes a number of mistakes in his early scientific publications and admits that he was too hasty in reaching certain conclusions. He even says that he wishes he could withdraw an entire paper.

On balance, "Lucy" is a fascinating, candid and scientifically reliable account of one of the most compelling scientific investigations ever undertaken—the effort to understand how human beings evolved. (p. 28)

> *Boyce Rensberger, "About To Be Human," in* The New York Times Book Review *(© 1981 by The New York Times Company; reprinted by permission), February 22, 1981, pp. 1, 28.*

MICHAEL BISHOP

Lucy has a distinctly autobiographical flavor. And, despite the author's conscious, even conciliatory, effort to keep the needle of self-deflation at hand, the book does not *completely* escape the toils of puffery and smugness. I do not see how it could. The "I" in the narrative is Donald Johanson (coauthor Edey selflessly extinguishes his identity in this pronoun), and at the heart of the book lies the gritty, absorbing chronicle of his four fateful seasons at Hadar, a stiflingly hot desert of ridges and wadis in Ethiopia's Afar Triangle. Here, between 1973 and 1977, Johanson and a team of highly trained French and American specialists made the discoveries—the first hominid knee joint, Lucy, an entire hominid band nicknamed the First Family—that elevate Johanson to a status comparable to that of "paleoanthropology's certified supernova, Richard Leakey." Although by no means a grandstander, Johanson clearly enjoys keeping such company, and he has earned the right. This book explains how and why. (pp. 4-5)

One of the peculiar, oddly engaging aspects of *Lucy* is Johanson's seeming tendency to talk past the reader at his famous rivals in Kenya. These passages, although ostensibly aimed at a general audience, read like snippets of a passionate private letter alternately reasoning, cajoling, exhorting, and teasing the Leakeys out of the hidebound errors of their ways. Let me cite a fairly subtle example. Late in the book Johanson reports that a journalist investigating his and White's collaborative work on Lucy and the First Family had been put in mind of the partnership of the Noble laureates James Watson and Francis Crick in riddling out the double-helix structure of DNA.

"In fact," Johanson smoothly comments, "there was a geneticist, Rosalind Franklin, working at the same time they were, who all on her own nearly broke the DNA problem several times. She came *so close,* but she had nobody to talk to. She needed that last push—another mind. She never got it. Tim and I, in having each other, had been extraordinarily lucky."

These sentences contain a puckish, or maybe infuriating, implication. Richard and Mary Leakey may be two people, but they cleave to the Louis S.B. Leakey line. Like Rosalind Franklin, they require a perspective other than their own. Indeed, they might have made the taxonomic breakthrough engineered by Johanson and White if only they had had another mind to prod them out of the bunker of their own preconceptions, hangups, and biases. Johanson wants to be that mind.

How to censure, or resist such winning chutzpah? Easily, perhaps, if your name is Leakey—but I cannot help feeling that Johanson will not desist until his Kenyan counterparts have raised their tight hands and repeated solemnly after him, "I love Lucy . . ." In any event, this is an exciting, informative, mind-rocking, and important book. (p. 5)

> Michael Bishop, *"Lucy in the Mud with Footprints,"* in Book World—The Washington Post *(© 1981,* The Washington Post*), March 15, 1981, pp. 4-5.*

MATT CARTMILL

Johanson and Edey have written an uncommon sort of book to explain Johanson's finds and what they mean. . . . [*Lucy*] is partly a professional memoir, partly a compressed history of paleoanthropology, and partly a popular treatment of current knowledge and guesses about human evolution. These three strands of the book loop in and out of each other in a fluid and ingratiating way that is obviously the work of a professional writer who knows his stuff. The scientific exposition is fascinating, thorough-going, and easy to follow; even complete novices will find themselves picking up a surprisingly detailed understanding of everything from potassium-argon dating to the importance of the ectosylid in identifying fossil horse teeth. The authors have seized on the increasingly popular gimmick of using dialogue to put across technical points in colloquial language. This works well as long as the reader doesn't start wondering how on earth Johanson got a verbatim transcript of a chat Clark Howell had with Louis Leakey in 1965. The passages recalling the history of paleoanthropology are a delight to read. (p. 94)

Johanson and Edey's book shows us some of [the rivalries among people who work on fossil hominids] from Johanson's point of view, and the descriptions of his antagonists are not flattering. Richard Leakey, for example, is introduced as an "obscure bushwhacker" who spurned a university education to become a white hunter and safari guide, stumbled across Koobi Fora in a snit while evading distasteful work at another dig, and barred Tim White from Koobi Fora when he dared to voice a dissenting opinion about the date of the 1470 skull. Happily, Johanson can take it as well as dish it out. Even Richard Leakey would probably relish the quotes from White describing Johanson as "a nail-polish salesman . . . who wears Gucci loafers and Yves Saint Laurent pants." Nevertheless, Richard and Mary Leakey, Solly Zuckerman, Jon Kalb, and four or five other anthropologists are going to get no pleasure out of reading this book.

The rest of us will. In the present dark days, when impassioned ignoramuses across the country are marshaling their forces to get Noah's ark put into the Constitution, a book like this of enormous value. Entertaining and informative without being condescending, it will give any fair-minded reader an enlightened understanding of the vast mass of minutely detailed evidence that underlies our knowledge of human evolution, and of the hard physical and intellectual work that has gone into piling up that evidence. Evolutionary biologists, whose currently intense arguments over theoretical fundamentals have hamstrung them in fending off the onrush of the Bible-thumpers, should welcome a book like *Lucy.* It puts across the excitement and headaches of studying human evolution and does the job with conviction, accuracy, and pizzazz. This book needs to be on our new President's bookshelf. (p. 95)

> Matt Cartmill, *"Lucy in the Sand with Footnotes,"* in Natural History *(copyright the American Museum of Natural History, 1981; reprinted with permission from* Natural History*), Vol. 90, No. 4, April, 1981, pp. 90-5.*

JOHN LEONARD

[*Lucy*] is fascinating on various levels. It is, first of all, a portrait of the paleoanthropologist as a young man, lucky and brash. Such is Mr. Johanson's self-regard that he can quote unflattering descriptions of himself and still chuckle: "The smooth young hotshot," shooting off his mouth; "a nail-polish salesman, a real operator," perhaps careless and naïve; suspect, as any anthropologist should be suspect "who wears Gucci loafers and Yves Saint Laurent pants" and has a craving for sweets.

The man who said those nasty things about Mr. Johanson, Timothy White, is now his colleague. Together, they have challenged "the paleoanthropological establishment," which is to say, the Leakeys, Louis and Mary and their son Richard. Mr. Johanson is particularly envious of Richard, "the certified supernova" of paleoanthropology whose formal education, we are told, stopped in high school. He and Mr. White rushed into print with a brand-new "tree of man," anxious to stake their claim "before anybody else had a chance to do it," a clause Mr. Johanson himself italicizes. They were looking over their shoulders, as James Watson was looking over his shoulder in "The Double Helix": Linus Pauling might be gaining on him.

This isn't science at its most dignified, but it certainly entertains. So do the passages devoted to work away from the dig— the cleaning and sorting and dating, the sifting of volcanic ash and the major surgery on besalt. (p. 210)

I do wish, though, that Mr. Johanson and his collaborator had worked a little harder on their prose. Here is what they say about an important discovery: "It is impossible to describe what it feels like to find something like that. It fills you right up. That is what you are there for. You have been working and working, and suddenly you score." A simple "Eureka!" would suffice. (p. 211)

> John Leonard, *"'Lucy',"* in The New York Times, *Section III (© 1981 by The New York Times Company; reprinted by permission), February 19, 1981 (and reprinted in* Books of the Times, *Vol. IV, No. 5, May, 1981, pp. 210-11).*

RUSSELL H. TUTTLE

With *Lucy,* Johanson and Edey have created a new genre: a captivating, informative book of which authorship may not be coveted because it contains bold commentaries that will unnecessarily offend a number of colleagues. It is a spicy potpourri of exceptionally lucid expository scientific writing, tattling exposé, novelized conversations and events, nostalgia, and wishful thinking. The idiom is decidedly middle American. The book is oddly reminiscent of *20/20* and *60 Minutes.* . . .

Considering that the authors mostly iterate readily accessible biographical anecdotes, one expects a high degree of accuracy [in the sections relating the historical backdrop of the Hadar discoveries and their aftermath]. This is not always to be found. For instance, Johanson and Edey state . . . that Louis Leakey "felt so strongly that Teilhard de Chardin was guilty" of perpetrating the Piltdown hoax that "in 1971 he refused to attend a symposium honoring" him. Yet we know from [Sonia] Cole's biography of Leakey (*Leakey's Luck* . . .) that he forthrightly expressed his opinion to the organizers of the conference, was thanked for his candor, and attended the meeting despite his poor health. Hurtful hearsay, more suitable for an *International Inquirer,* is also conspicuous in the historical sections of the book, as when Leakey, the son of English missionaries, is purported to have uttered American profanity upon first seeing "Zinj." . . .

The heart of the volume lies in its second two-fifths. Here we share the thrill of discovery, the tensions from working in the midst of political turmoil, the tedium of the laboratory, the uncertainties about reactions of colleagues to one's ideas, and the changes of mind that are part and parcel of paleoanthropology. Johanson is refreshingly candid about what he now perceives to have been errors in his initial classification of the Hadar fossils and his co-workers' dating of them geochronologically. . . .

The accounts of potassium-argon dating . . . and of the craniodental features that indicate the extent to which the Hadar hominids resemble African apes, other Plio-Pleistocene hominids, and humans . . . are excellent. But again we find friends romanticized (Loring Brace is handsome . . . , Bill Kimbel is a giant, and Bruce Latimer is a tawny blond All-American . . .) while rivals are vilified. Mary Leakey incurred the authors' invective because she refused to endorse *Australopithecus afarensis* from her field camp. One wonders what reputable scientist would co-author a taxonomic paper without first studying the entire hypodigm and, if not expert about the materials, being led point by point over the diagnostic features with proper comparative materials at hand. If Richard Leakey sends Johanson the bottle of wine he *now* owes him, Johanson had better test it before he tastes it.

I can recall at least five professors at the University of Chicago who contributed to Johanson's formal training in paleoanthropology, dental anthropology, osteology, and primatology. He mentions only two of them. One is effusively extolled and the second is immortalized as a *bête noire extraordinaire.* Perhaps the others are lucky to have escaped recollection.

The latter chapters of *Lucy* are salted with factual errors. For example, not all chimpanzees are dark-skinned . . . ; gibbons and siamangs do not have shrunken, short, and weak lower limbs . . . ; and all estrous baboon "girls" do not "appeal to all the boys." . . .

From a strictly scientific point of view, the weakest part of the book is . . . where the authors repeat Lovejoy's . . . theory about the evolution of bipedalism. There is a growing consensus among experts on the evolution of anthropoid locomotion that arboreal vertical climbing had a good deal to do with the emergence of hominid bipedalism. This is ignored totally in favor of a somewhat tortuous argument relating to special K-selection, pair-bonding, monogamy, and carrying food and youngsters to keep the group upright. Lovejoy is bound to have his own hands full as feminists pursue him for some implications of the theory. The sort of monogamy that I think he is describing is more for the birds. The few primates that are monogamous are skeletally quite monomorphic, whereas the Hadar hominids appear to have been very dimorphic.

In *Lucy,* the long, curved toes of the Hadar hominids are explained as adaptations to "strong" walking on rough stony ground and mud, where gripping would be useful. . . . It is perhaps more probable that the creatures were still partly arboreal. Whether feet like those from Hadar could have made virtually human footprints like those at Laetoli is also moot.

Russell H. Tuttle, "Paleoanthropology without Inhibitions," in Science *(copyright © 1981 by the American Association for the Advancement of Science), Vol. 212, No. 4496, May 15, 1981, p. 798.*

JOHN BINTLIFF

No one is spared systematic character demolition [in *Lucy*], except, suspiciously, those whom Johanson is closest to. The core of the book is the demolition of the Leakey family, and if we want to understand the reasons for their 'exposure', and that of their predecessors, clues litter the book. Almost all famous fossil-hunters are presented as self-centred, ready to use any devious trick to step into the scientific limelight and push others into the shadows. Such behaviour is apparently the only way to the top when funds are limited and expeditions expensive. Whenever Richard Leakey enters the story, we are reminded of his 'supernova', 'glamorous' public image, the leading field researcher when Johanson is still a nobody. Johanson, with generous assistance from the Leakey family, aims to blow all his funds on a brief gamble in the remote Hadar region, praying that world-beating fossils will emerge. By unbelievably good fortune he finds the largest, oldest and best preserved collection of early hominids to date, including the three-and-a-half million-year-old Lucy. Revelling in the welter of publicity, Johanson sees himself on a par with the Leakeys, and finally as their better. Richard Leakey, meanwhile, is having trouble with the dating of his most famous finds, making them much later than the Hadar. A new Johanson-White theory claims that the Hadar hominids are the true source population from which all later varieties, such as Leakey's, derive—a direct fossil one-upmanship. There remains, however, an intriguing tale here of the flesh and blood behind the severe academic papers reporting early man discoveries. And, it must be admitted, the Johanson-White evolutionary tree does look more plausible than that of the Leakeys. (p. 53)

John Bintliff, "Tales and Tell-Tales, of Famous Men and Famous Bones" (© British Broadcasting Corp. 1981; reprinted by permission of John Bintliff), in The Listener, *Vol. 106, No. 2719, July 9, 1981, pp. 53-4.*

Herman Kahn

1922-

An American mathematician, political scientist, futurist, and the director of the Hudson Institute, Kahn is the author of several influential books in which he predicts military, economic, and political alternatives for the future. An early, controversial work, *On Thermonuclear War* (1962), states that a thermonuclear war between the United States and the U.S.S.R. could have a number of possible results, only one of which is mutual annihilation. Given proper planning and depending upon the course of the war, Kahn posits, there could be a large number of survivors with a tolerable chance for a normal life. This position caused a furor among many critics, who claimed that by minimizing its horror, Kahn was making thermonuclear war ponderable and therefore more likely. More recent works such as *World Economic Development* (1979) have advocated continued world economic growth as the path to unprecedented affluence and an eventual postindustrial world. Some critics have dismissed Kahn's scenarios—accompanied as they are by numerous qualifications and caveats—as fanciful or of limited utility. Others, however, contend that his forecasts are of ground-breaking importance to policy makers and students of social change. (See also *Contemporary Authors*, Vols. 65-68.)

Excerpt from *ON THERMONUCLEAR WAR*

Contemporary phrases, used by both experts and laymen in describing war, expressions like "balance of terror," "thermonuclear stalemate," "suicidal war," "mutual annihilation," "inescapable end of civilization," "destruction of all life," "end of history," "live together or die together," and "nobody wins a suicide pact," indicate a widespread inclination to believe that thermonuclear war would eventuate in mutual annihilation as the result of almost any plausible turn of military events. (p. 9)

A thermonuclear war is quite likely to be an *unprecedented catastrophe* for the defender. Depending on the military course of events, it may or may not be an unprecedented catastrophe for the attacker, and for some neutrals as well. But an "unprecedented" catastrophe can be a far cry from an "unlimited" one. Most important of all, sober study shows that *the limits on the magnitude of the catastrophe seem to be closely dependent on what kinds of preparations have been made, and on how the war is started and fought.* (pp. 10-11)

Actually, when one examines the possible effects of thermonuclear war carefully, one notices that there are indeed many postwar states that should be distinguished. If most people do not or cannot distinguish among these states it is because the gradations occur as a result of a totally bizarre circumstance— a thermonuclear war. The mind recoils from thinking hard about that; one prefers to believe it will never happen. If asked, "How does a country look on the day of the war?" the only answer a reasonable person can give is "awful." It takes an act of iron will or an unpleasant degree of detachment or callousness to go about the task of distinguishing among the possible degrees of awfulness.

But surely one can ask a more specific question. For example, *"How does a country look five or ten years after the close of war, as a function of three variables: (1) the preparations made before the war, (2) the way the war started, and (3) the course of military events?"* Both very sensitive and very callous individuals should be able to distinguish (and choose, perhaps) between a country which survives a war with, say, 150 million people and a gross national product (GNP) of $300 billion a year, and a nation which emerges with only 50 million people and a GNP of $10 billion. The former would be the richest and the fourth largest nation in the world, and one which would be able to restore a reasonable facsimile of the prewar society; the latter would be a pitiful remnant that would contain few traces of the prewar way of life. When one asks this kind of question and examines the circumstances and possible outcomes of a future war in some detail, it appears that it is useful and necessary to make many distinctions among the results of thermonuclear war. (pp. 19-20)

[If] we have a posture which might result in 40 million dead in a general war, and as a result of poor planning, apathy, or other causes, our posture deteriorates and a war occurs with 80 million dead, we have suffered an additional disaster, an *unnecessary* additional disaster that is almost as bad as the original disaster. If on the contrary, by spending a few billion dollars, or by being more competent or lucky, we can cut the number of dead from 40 to 20 million, we have done something vastly worth doing! The survivors will not dance in the streets or congratulate each other if there have been 20 million men, women, and children killed; yet it would have been a worthwhile achievement to limit casualties to this number. It is very difficult to get this point across to laymen or experts with enough intensity to move them to action. The average citizen has a dour attitude toward planners who say that if we do thus and so it will not be 40 million dead—it will be 20 million dead. Somehow the impression is left that the planner said that there will be *only* 20 million dead. To him is often attributed the idea that this will be a tolerable or even, astonishingly enough, a desirable state!

The rate of economic recuperation, like the number of lives saved, is also of extreme importance. Very few Americans can get interested in spending money or energy on preparations which, even if they worked, would result in preindustrial living standards for the survivors of a war. . . . [Our] analysis indicates that if a country is moderately well prepared to use the assets which survive there is unlikely to be a critical level of damage to production. A properly prepared country is not "killed" by the destruction of even a major fraction of its wealth; it is more likely to be set back a given number of years in its economic growth. While recuperation times may range all the way from one to a hundred years, even the latter is far different from the "end of history."

Perhaps the most important item on the table of distinguishable states is not the numbers of dead or the number of years it takes for economic recuperation; rather, it is the question at the bottom: "Will the survivors envy the dead?" It is in some sense true that one may never recuperate from a thermonuclear war. The world may be permanently (i.e., for perhaps 10,000 years) more hostile to human life as a result of such a war. Therefore, if the question, "Can we restore the prewar conditions of life?" is asked, the answer must be "No!" But there are other relevant questions to be asked. For example: "How much more hostile will the environment be? Will it be so hostile that we or our descendants would prefer being dead than alive?" Perhaps even more pertinent is this question, "How happy or normal a life can the survivors and their descendants hope to have?" *Despite a widespread belief to the contrary, objective studies indicate that even though the amount of human tragedy would be greatly increased in the postwar world, the increase would not preclude normal and happy lives for the majority of survivors and their descendants.* (pp. 20-1)

> *Herman Kahn, in his* On Thermonuclear War *(copyright © 1960 by Princeton University Press; reprinted by permission of Princeton University Press), Princeton University Press, 1960, 651 p.*

Excerpt from *WORLD ECONOMIC DEVELOPMENT: 1979 AND BEYOND*

A century from now, much relative poverty and perhaps even major pockets of absolute poverty will probably still persist. The arithmetic (but probably not geometric) gap between the richest 10 percent and the poorest 10 percent of the world's people will almost certainly be greater than today. But unless the future is marred by a major nuclear war or other disaster, almost all of humanity will be materially better off. The traditional grinding absolute poverty, famine, pestilence, disease and incapacity, illiteracy, and backbreaking toil, all of which

have been humanity's lot throughout history, should be almost gone, and with luck for once and for all. What the majority of people will do in such a world is an open question and may be a serious problem. The opportunities for both good and evil will be enormous. If all goes well, the centuries to come could well be when humanity's true history begins. (pp. 15-16)

Almost everybody agrees with Sophie Tucker, that "it is better to be rich than poor." In discussing the possibilities of how affluence and technology can be used to improve human life we have increasingly been drawn to the concept . . . of what we call the Marriage of Machine and Garden. The concept of the Garden comes out of some well-known American and European literature that extols the virgin forest and the rural, agrarian, or wilderness areas of North America that were formerly untouched and were often regarded as a refuge or earthly Garden of Eden for Europeans. At the same time, however, the United States is also the most technologically advanced nation in the world; hence the Machine.

Some historians suggest that it is useful to view American history as a continual struggle between the pastoral, rural, or wilderness ideal and the rapid, almost ruthless, industrialization and urbanization of the continent. Sometimes the two themes fought; sometimes they merged into a single whole; sometimes they settled for an uneasy truce. We visualize Garden society as a modernization of the rural, pastoral ideal, a possible future society whose ideology is directed toward maintaining a high quality of life but that shows little change and technological dynamism. . . . [A] very attractive life style that might characterize almost any of the eventual possibilities of modernization would be such a marriage. It may also be a part of the transitional society that is still far from achieving the ultimate goals of modernization.

This is just one of a number of potentially attractive scenarios for the use of affluence and technology. Yet, incredibly, such scenarios or images of the future are increasingly rejected as unfeasible or even undesirable. The economic growth scenario, for example, seems to us attractive. Yet instead of enthusiasm for more economic growth, opposition to growth is mounting. Neo-Malthusians argue that the world's resources are insufficient to support continued expansion of gross world product and population. They contend that even if resources were available, pollution, ecological imbalance, or management problems would lead to disastrous consequences. We believe that we and others have answered this thesis effectively. Therefore, we do not deal with it further except to identify specific serious problems that could result from the limits-to-growth movement rather than from the finite size of the earth.

Others argue that humanity's output is already adequate. These numerous opponents of growth believe that the transition to "the good and the beautiful" can be accomplished now. Actually, gross world product will expand enormously as developing countries accumulate capital and technical expertise and become mass consumption countries. The world economy will first become super-industrial rather than post-industrial. In 1978, for example, there were almost 300 million cars in a world of about 4.25 billion people. If current trends continue, there will be about a billion cars in the year 2000, but the number of people on earth should increase by less than 50 percent. A similar doubling or tripling (or more) can be expected for other consumer durables, as well as for the output of energy and other resources.

It is this super-industrial aspect of our long-range scenario that is being most questioned today on grounds of both desirability and feasibility. We do not maintain that great tragedies cannot happen, including the collapse of civilization. We do argue that no basic technological and economic barriers preclude our scenario. Such barriers may exist, but they have not as yet been demonstrated. (Bad luck or bad management, of course, can always cause trouble.)

We firmly believe that despite the arguments put forward by people who would like to "stop the earth and get off," it is simply impractical to do so. Propensity to change may not be inherent in human nature, but it is firmly embedded in most contemporary cultures. People have almost everywhere become curious, future oriented, and dissatisfied with their conditions. They want more material goods and covet higher status and greater control of nature. Despite much propaganda to the contrary, they believe, almost certainly correctly, that it is technologically and economically possible for them to achieve these goals. (pp. 21-4)

> *Herman Kahn with the Hudson Institute, in his* World Economic Development: 1979 and Beyond *(copyright © 1979 by Herman Kahn; reprinted by permission of Westview Press), Westview Press, 1979, 519 p.*

JEROME SPINGARN

["**On Thermonuclear War**"] is most assuredly a landmark in the literature of military strategy and power-oriented diplomacy. . . .

It is one of Kahn's great virtues that he has considered opposing points of view with tolerance and respect as well as incisive argumentation; his opponents owe him no less sophisticated consideration.

This book is tremendously valuable for its virtuosity in method. In analyzing questions, Kahn uses techniques of mathematics, physics, genetics, economics, sociology and political science. Above all, the work is valuable because the author has taken off the blinders of self-deception and has faced up to the stark realities of thermonuclear war. (p. 3)

> *Jerome Spingarn, "Picking Up the Pieces," in* The New York Times Book Review *(© 1961 by The New York Times Company; reprinted by permission), January 1, 1961, pp. 3, 32.*

GEORGE G. KIRSTEIN

[In *On Thermonuclear War* Herman Kahn] feels, and this reviewer agrees, that discussion of thermonuclear war should be as widespread as possible in this country. He believes that, as a prerequisite of such discussion, we must "create a vocabulary that is both small enough and simple enough to be learned, precise enough to communicate and large enough so that all important ideas that are contending can be comfortably and easily described." (p. 34)

The author encourages debate on his concepts of strategy, but he warns that these debates will have little value unless the participants are at least as sophisticated . . . as present policy planners, including Mr. Kahn. He feels that the ultimately dangerous debaters are those "men of good will," usually intellectuals, who believe that you can just sit down with the

Russians and come to agreements. Men who believe that may exist outside the author's imagination, but I have not met them. I have met and share the opinions of those who believe that bargaining, compromise, and the gradual elimination of points of conflict and the sources of mutual terror are far more promising methods than the ones which occupy Mr. Kahn's mental processes, as augmented by the computers available to him at the RAND Corporation. For the position Mr. Kahn takes, it seems to me, is the ultimately unsophisticated one.

He warns in his text that it is imperative for the researcher in this field to ask the "right question." Yet he never asks the basic question as to why we should be concerned with preserving a species of animal which can weigh coolly the concepts set forth in this book. If *On Thermonuclear War* were concerned with the destruction of 100 million or more dogs, anti-vivisection societies, sportsmen and dog lovers generally would raise a howl of protest which would deafen even the "decision makers." But because the subject matter is the incineration, poisoning and starving of women, children, and perhaps a few combatants, this book has been hailed as the important work of a thoughtful and dedicated man, and recommended for reading by the country's leaders from the President down. That it deserves wide reading, I agree, for it is the ultimate example of the fruits of the support which our officialdom is extending to its chosen scholars. If survival is to be bought at Mr. Kahn's price, the question must arise, is it worth it? To Mr. Kahn it is, to me it is not.

No one knows how many of Mr. Kahn's predictions as to the strategy which we or our opponents will adopt in the forthcoming thermonuclear war will be borne out by experience. The author devotes one entire chapter to guessing whether the survivors of thermonuclear attack will envy the dead, and of course concludes that it will still be thought good to be alive. Perhaps the majority of readers will take heart from this book's thesis that the next war will not be as devastating as the "idealists" would have us believe. It had the reverse effect on me. I can understand and respect career military officers who have chosen the "honorable profession of arms" as a way of life, often at a sacrifice in comfort and emoluments, and who are subsequently assigned the duty of formulating war plans to meet all eventualities. But Mr. Kahn is a physicist, a scholar and a civilian. To be blunt, his book made me ashamed that we are fellow countrymen. (pp. 34-5)

> *George G. Kirstein, "The Logic of No Return," in* The Nation *(copyright 1961 The Nation magazine, The Nation Associates, Inc.), Vol. 1920, No. 1, January 14, 1961, pp. 34-5.*

NORMAN THOMAS

Mr. Kahn [in *On Thermonuclear War*] deserves the most attention from those of us who believe: (1) that universal disarmament down to a police level under a strengthened U.N. is our sole valid hope of a decent existence for our race and (2) that such a state is less impossible to achieve than the arms control systems offered to us as a means of survival in war if not of avoidance of war. . . .

[Mr. Kahn] writes at length and interestingly concerning various sorts of arms control that are necessary to acceptance of thermonuclear war and discusses a way of alleviating its catastrophic consequences; however, he takes pains to say that it by no means need lead to disarmament. But it will be very difficult to live in a world of the future unless there are implicit agreements on behavior, and explicit agreements as well, which will apply to the conduct of nations in war. Such hopes for arms control do not contemplate a stable deterrent. (p. 18)

Part of Mr. Kahn's hope for rapid recuperation [from a nuclear war] is based on the fact that "the human fertility rate is high." Which suggests that in the business of persuading us how possible it will be to accept even thermonuclear war Mr. Kahn and the Rand Corporation have so far overlooked a bet. They should team up with Professor Heinz von Foerster, of the University of Illinois, who in *Science* for November 4th argued that without some controls we shall by excessive growth suffocate our race by 2026. What control of population would be more effective than a war of the magnitude Mr. Kahn is so sure that a large proportion of us could survive? (I hate, however, to think how popular Mr. Kahn's proof of power to survive nuclear war will be with the Chinese Communists. If we—or some of us—can survive, how much more can they? Kahn will be their answer to Khrushchev.)

It is at first hard to understand the obvious satisfaction these chess players, and their numerous kibitzers at well-financed conferences, get in this weird game. It is the national power, not humanity, that counts. It is that which never must be checkmated or destroyed. The pundits don't any longer bother to dwell on ideal values thus preserved. They do not feed us with old illusions that the next great war will surely be the last. They do not expect to destroy war by war. They deal with war's deterrence or prosecution in military terms regardless of the policies, our own as well as our opponents', that may lead to it or avoid it. Recurring wars are to them simply a fact of history that a nation on which the mantle of greatness has fallen can hardly expect to avoid forever.

On reflection one can understand that this game of high military strategy has its own fascination, especially if one can train one's self to think in terms of nations and statistics, not human beings. It appeals to our basic conservatism, our acceptance of the time-honored institution of war, which our race has indeed hated but yet cherished for the profit, the power, the glory it has brought to victors. Moreover, we players and onlookers alike are worshippers at the shrines of anarchic national sovereignties, which have always demanded sacrifices of blood.

Besides these general considerations there are many exceedingly tangible reasons why very influential sections of our population should want, not a shooting war, but a continuous cold war in which they find profit, prestige, and jobs. How good it is for our powerful military services, the third of all our scientists and engineers who are committed to the arms race, and the five million workers who are wholly and directly engaged in it (the figures are President Eisenhower's) to be able to rationalize this employment as the only way to serve the national security if not the world's peace. Have not the wise theorists assured them that disarmament is impossible and talk about it dangerous save for such lip service as may quiet the fearful and the deluded?

Thus far I have been accepting without argument the general soundness of Mr. Kahn's emphatic conclusions that the next great war need not mean annihilation or even such misery and despair that the survivors will envy the dead. On the basis of his own facts, figures, and speculations—combined with his omissions—I have grave doubts. For instance, Mr. Kahn does not discuss the suggestion of a former high official in the Pentagon that part of the furnishings of Mr. Rockefeller's shelters should be submachine guns with which the *pater familias,*

gathering his own family in his own shelter outside the reach of blast and fire, can keep from being overrun by frantic people far from their own hiding places. He assumes too easily a possible "moderate" first attack and at least a breathing space after it. He is too confident of the will and capacity of a nation to carry on after the slaughter in a matter of hours of all its principal cities and the death of twenty to forty millions of its people. He does not discuss at all adequately the psychology of alarm in a world at war, where individual soldiers or spies can carry on their person, if they are ready to die for their country, chemical, bacteriological, and even nuclear weapons of appalling destructive power. He recognizes, but scarcely gives sufficient weight to, the brutal stupidity of great wars. He expects too much common sense in combatants crazy enough to risk war in the nuclear age. He should remember how caustic is the British authority General J. F. C. Fuller in his "Military History of the Western World" on the stupidity of all governments in prolonging World War I, in which they all lost. Along these and other lines Mr. Kahn's and similar arguments need a closeness of examination that the Rand Corporation is unlikely to finance.

My immediate contention is that the American public—if it can be persuaded to stop, look, and listen—would not find Mr. Kahn's condition of survival at all tolerable. The people might begin to identify with the twenty to forty million dead, or have a more imaginative association with the misery of the survivors. They may give more weight than Mr. Kahn docs to his admission that his war, which we could survive, would make the world "more hostile for human life for 10,000 years." (pp. 19, 33)

In other words, the people, aroused to Mr. Kahn's own picture, may begin to wonder if universal disarmament under a strengthened U.N. may not be less difficult to achieve and maintain than stable arms control. Granting that such disarmament would require certain measures of inspection and policing, and provision of some alternatives to war, could it not more easily be made relatively more secure, and we safer, under the world's acceptance of its importance to life, than under any of the conflicting forms of deterrence and arms control that our theorists present?

But what is shocking in all this arms theorizing is the underlying assumption, without argument, that our national power in the world is in terms of human values worth a war that we might survive so perilously, or that any real, human values can be preserved or won by it. India won freedom from England by Gandhian methods of nonviolent resistance and lost much of its value by popular resort to the old methods of violence in loyalty to competing religions. Has the lesson no meaning for us all? Some of the world's problems most acutely affecting the peace and well-being of mankind arise from the demand of exploited masses for economic betterment. Neither Khrushchev's answer nor ours can be given by missiles, and Khrushchev's apparent greater eagerness than ours for universal disarmament is a positive advantage to him. He could afford to circularize many of our discussions of "arms control" in Latin America to his advantage.

Mr. Kahn and his fellow theorists have done something to convince me that a substantial part of the human race may survive World War III; they have not convinced me that mankind deserves to survive if it is capable of the horrors of destruction for which we prepare ourselves at such material and spiritual cost. And why? Merely that we may begin again the cycle of recuperation and preparation for new slaughter in the strife of garrison states worshipping at the altars of National Power. (p. 33)

Norman Thomas, "Roads That Bypass Peace," in Saturday Review *(copyright © 1961 by* Saturday Review; *all rights reserved; reprinted by permission), Vol. XLIV, No. 5, February 4, 1961, pp. 17-19, 33.**

FRED GREENE

On Thermonuclear War is the result of massive research and thought, rich in concrete illustrations and valuable speculation about the future. However, . . . it is open to question in its analysis of our present situation on many counts, four of which will be discussed here. Can we really protect ourselves? Can we obtain Credible First Strike Capacity in this missile age? Are the negotiations proposed too dissociated from world politics to be useful? What are the immediate practical effects of [Mr. Kahn's] thesis?

Mr. Kahn's argument—that we could go beyond the mere avoidance of war and still survive—rests on a civil-defense study whose optimistic conclusions may have been valid for the late 1950's but already appear dated. It presupposes an attack primarily by bombers, and explosives totaling 20,000 megatons (2000 bombs averaging 10 megatons). Staggering as these totals seem, they are far below what a superpower *can* and would attain if he planned to attack us. In casting doubts on the invulnerability of mobile missiles, Mr. Kahn himself assumes attacks of 100-megaton bursts. What would this do to recuperative rates, ability to limit thermonuclear attacks, or negotiate settlements? What effect will new Chemical-Bacteriological-Radiological weapons, now just over the horizon, have on our ability to check disease in crops, animals, or humans? Civil defense preparations may be more vital than ever, but they will not offer the hopeful outlet that Kahn seeks in case of disaster.

Mobile, invulnerable missiles play a great role in his post-1965 analysis, but Kahn seems to have been unprepared for their current rapid development. As a result he does not give them the consideration they deserve but seeks instead to downgrade their invulnerability, presumably because we see in Polaris and Minuteman a cure-all. Yet secure missiles present grave problems since, with enemy missiles safe, they must focus on cities for blackmail or counter-threat. Again, civil defense and abundant missiles are vital, but as palliatives. We know that states must suffer tremendous destruction, for an angry combatant, perhaps American, can respond to an assault by continual or delayed firing from secret caches. How can blackmail pressure be checked save by the deterrent threat of unlimited war? And what happens to a credible first strike capability if, for example, we know Russia possesses invulnerable strategic forces and threatens to overrun Europe? Are we not then driven back to old-fashioned deterrence?

The author is also unjustly harsh with British advocates of finite deterrence, though they do assume too easily the preservation of a balance of terror. He superimposes an American perspective on an island state whose compactness, nearness to Russia, and relatively weak technology deny it the advantages his own system requires. Nor is he accurate in holding that finite deterrence has dominated American strategic thinking in recent years. Our Air Force gained pride of place during the 1950's, to develop a great kill capacity at the expense of other weapons. The development of a Russian counterforce and the evolution of missile technology may have eroded its power,

but the people and Congress still favor massive striking forces. In all likelihood strategic missiles plus active air defense will continue to get highest priority.

His concentrated thermonuclear perspective at times gives the study an apolitical tinge. He judges most Soviet moves by their degree of "provocation" (*i.e.* the extent to which they may drive us to consider a nuclear response), or as testing actions short of war. Yet the Russians may be focusing on the immediate political objectives at hand, seeking to avert war or even tone down the thermonuclear threat. Each outlook requires a different preparation for and response to crisis and we cannot assume that strident provocation and threat lie behind each Russian move, nor cite Soviet classics selectively to prove our point. In fact, how long can Russia play at thermonuclear games when each successful industrial plan makes its cities more prosperous and more vulnerable? Their vaunted dispersal through Eurasia may soon turn all cities into isolated, distinct targets. What would become of Russia if its European or Chinese neighbors stay neutral during an American-Russian exchange?

Equally difficult to envisage are his related recommendations for NATO specialization and arms control. For us to devote ourselves to great weapons while Europe provides ground forces is to advocate a degree of specialization that would strain even a federation, let alone an alliance that is up for renewal in eight years. He calls upon the nations to yield some sovereignty but weakens his case by asking our allies to become utterly dependent upon us. His arms control amounts to a "US-SU" combine, with all others compelled to renounce modern weapons. This admirable solution for the super-powers rests on the assumption that all else must bend before the present bipolar power structure and technological danger. But the others, from prudent Briton to fanatic Chinese, object vigorously. To pin our hopes on an American-Russian co-dominion over arms makes the disarmament case appear hopeless.

Effective limited war forces, with minimum dependence on nuclear power, play an important role in the author's scheme to deal with moderate or limited crisis. Yet he believes that our strategic force must deter all major thrusts including many that are not directed against our homeland. However, if missiles do become invulnerable, a counterforce strategy geared to eliminate the enemy's strategic force will lack credibility, just as SAC did in the 1950's when it bore the dual burden of deterring total and limited wars. In addition, by the time we provide for an adequate strategic arm, passive and active defense, and space exploration, limited-war forces will sorely lack funds even in an expanded budget.

We may now have to recognize that "limited war" is a grossly inaccurate term for the projection of our forces over oceans, during a diplomatic crisis, in trying combat conditions, and under threat of global conflict. This, rather than the massing of strategic power was our greatest problem in the 1950's. Yet Kahn favors the withdrawal of our troops from abroad in time of peace though to Europeans they prove the firmness of our commitment. He also labels as "dreams" any thoughts of projecting them abroad in a central war. His flexible war plans revolve around our thermonuclear forces. Yet the mobilization and deployment of conventional forces during a crisis but prior to an attack may deter war, or it may sustain our wartime negotiations and postwar settlements. (pp. 16-17)

Fred Greene, "Beyond the Balance of Terror," in The New Republic *(reprinted by permission of* The New Republic; © *1961 The New Republic, Inc.), Vol. 144, No. 9, February 27, 1961, pp. 16-17.*

PAUL JOHNSON

[A] new science, or rather pseudo-science, has been developed by the Rand Corporation. This attempts, with the help of an army of young civilian 'experts' and batteries of electronic computors, to answer two basic questions. First, which is the best 'posture' (in terms of the number, type and disposition of strategic weapons) the West *should* adopt to deter Russia—or, alternatively, to minimise and so survive an attack? Second, what is the most effective way (in terms of money, manpower and technical resources) this posture *can* be adopted? The main conclusions of the Rand Corporation are summarised in [Herman Kahn's *On Thermonuclear War* and Charles Hitch and Roland McKean's *The Economics of Defence in the Nuclear Age*], which deal respectively with the strategy and economics of nuclear policy.

I call the work of the Corporation a pseudo-science for the simple reason that its exponents have no means of verifying their conclusions by experiment. Apart from the two bombs dropped on Japan, they do not know what really happens when nuclear weapons are used. True, their writings have a scientific veneer. The US Air Force provides them with elaborate data about 'weapons systems'. They make extensive use of computors (Mr Kahn, who has what seems to me an unhealthy affection for these machines, believes that if von Moltke had possessed enough computor-man-hours in July 1914, and so had been able to re-cast his rigid railway time-tables, the First World War might have been avoided). Nevertheless, these studies are essentially works of science-fiction.

Indeed, they bear a strange and comforting resemblance to medieval philosophy. The schoolmen believed that the world would soon be destroyed by God; their problem was to discover a system of belief and a code of morals which would permit the human race to survive this catastrophe and pass safely to the other side. All aspects of knowledge came within their ken, and they built up massive cosmologies of intricate and satisfying symmetry. So long as their fundamental assumption was accepted, their conclusions were inevitable and relevant: the details of the tortures inflicted on the damned became an important question, which could be debated with profit. Unfortunately, the assumption itself could not be proved; it could only be believed.

The schoolmen, however, were relatively harmless. They argued fiercely among themselves, and occasionally burnt each other at the stake; but they did little damage to the community as a whole. There is no evidence that their conclusions on statecraft or public morality influenced medieval governments in the slightest. In one sense the work of the Rand-men is likely to be equally futile. I find it hard to believe that western defence planners—those who actually take the responsibility for decisions—will be any the wiser for reading these two books. For both break down, inevitably, as soon as they try to give practical answers to concrete problems. . . .

But if the new schoolmen, like their predecessors, fail to influence the men at the top, they may do a good deal of damage lower down. Ambitious young politicians who have yet to experience the sobering reality of taking life-and-death decisions could be—and, I believe, have been—corrupted by such books. They possess an intellectual ruthlessness which appeals strongly to men learning—or yearning—to wield the levers of power. Mr Kahn, for instance, believes that by 1970 we could build what he calls a Doomsday Machine, capable of destroying life on this planet, adding—a masterpiece of unconscious irony— 'I have been surprised at the unanimity with which the notion of the unacceptability of a Doomsday Machine is greeted'. Throughout his book he is at pains to emphasise not only the possibility of nuclear war, but its desirability in certain circumstances, and what he terms the 'acceptability' of casualties running into millions. We must find, he says, 'an alternative to peace'. These mental attitudes, expressed in a vocabulary whose very awfulness has a certain magnetism, undoubtedly strike a chord among some western politicians who have come of age in the Cold War.

They appeal also to able young officers with intellectual pretentions. There are now a good many western staff-officers with some sort of scientific training. The impact of pseudo-scientific doctrines on these men, whose moral reflexes have been blunted by the exigencies of the Cold War, can be disastrous. . . . For them, books like these should be treated as pornography, within the meaning of the act; otherwise we may all be factored into oblivion.

Paul Johnson, "The New Schoolmen," in New Statesman *(© 1961 The Statesman & Nation Publishing Co. Ltd.), Vol. 61, No. 1574, May 12, 1961, p. 754.**

STEFAN T. POSSONY

There is indeed much to talk about [regarding nuclear strategy in *On Escalation, Metaphors and Scenarios*], and the conversation is always scintillating and often brilliant. Still, it might have helped if Kahn had looked at what the Communists are saying. (p. 601)

Kahn admits that he has committed the "besetting sin of most U.S. analysts" of having "attributed to the Soviets a kind of military behavior that may in fact be appropriate only to U.S. analysts—and not at all relevant to Soviet conditions and attitudes." Fortunately, things are looking up, for "as part of a general Hudson Institute program, several theories of escalation are being developed that seem consistent with Soviet ideological and political assumptions and with Russian national and military traditions and conventions." As a starter, a highly unconvincing "hypothetical" Soviet escalation ladder is presented. Not much will be gained if the Hudson program is restricted to reading what American sons of Russian Mensheviks have to say about Bolshevik strategy. But if Kahn's crew were to immerse themselves in Lenin, Stalin, Mao Tsetung and Truong Chinh, to such an extent that they understood the inner secrets of Communist strategic thinking empathetically, the trouble could be cured.

Kahn's present escalation models apply to opponents of a more or less identical type. Obviously, the models must change if, for example, one side is constantly eager to liquidate the struggle, while the other is engaged in a protracted conflict and considers each crisis as a step on an escalation ladder that is visualized in a time framework rather than in terms of violence. It is equally obvious that the models must change if we assume that one side is struggling to preserve social continuity and evolution, while the other aims to "smash" existing institutions and states and may be conditioned to inflict mass casualties.

Kahn opposes the diffusion of nuclear weapons with an argument that ignores many of the really crucial problems; he does not even try to see the point of view of our NATO allies. Nor is he very illuminating about alternate courses of action. However, and now happily I turn to the satisfactory portions of the book, he does a superb job in presenting an original proposal for the gradual deployment of American anti-ballistic-missile systems. He is just as good in discussing civil defense, stressing the merits of evacuation as a practical and indispensable measure.

The real topic of this book is how crises can be managed by increasing the military effort, the level of violence, and the threat to the opponent; how to continue a "competition in risk taking" up various ladders of growing violence and danger; or, as the case may be, how to de-escalate international crises toward safer intensities. Kahn's philosophy is that we should learn how to use force, coercion, violence, and threat in a reasonable and effective manner. He has done a masterly job of distinguishing the various "rungs" on the escalation ladder and illustrating multiple options that would be available on each of these rungs. There is no question that Kahn has suggested many concepts and measures through which the United States could improve its ability to manage the Cold War. More important still, he has indicated types of United States strategic behavior which could prevent the degeneration of the Cold War into a full-fledged nuclear war.

Modern conflict, in several aspects, may be compared to the relatively "bloodless" wars of maneuver that occurred during the Renaissance; whenever feasible, we should conduct the struggle according to this model. The notion that use or non-use of nuclear weapons constitutes the most important, if not the only real "fire-break" on the escalation ladder is effectively debunked. Kahn criticizes American war planning, and rightly so, for neglecting the possibilities of long war. He argues that if there are fixed peacetime budgets, "a greater degree of effectiveness can be achieved by increasing the emergency-readiness and mobilization characteristics of systems than by increasing their capability in being." He proposes a badly needed distinction between offensive and defensive deterrence. In passages which reconcile this reviewer to virtually all of his "besetting sins," Kahn emphasizes the imperative necessity for the United States to resume the serious study of strategy and tactics. He specifically opposes the asinine theory that since nuclear war, regardless of what tactics are used, would be annihilative, "tactical theory" is irrelevant. (pp. 601-02)

For the United States the strategic problem remains how to deter escalation by the opponent and at the same time ensure that we retain options to escalate *unilaterally* whenever we deem more forceful measures to be unavoidable. Kahn points out correctly that mere military superiority does not suffice to ensure "escalation dominance." Unfortunately, he fails to develop the crucial question of how the United States can acquire and maintain a reliable capability of dominating escalation. Yet without this capability, the Free World has no assurance of survival.

Kahn is provocative, informative, and witty. He is a good phrase-maker. He is also absolutely honest and, for the most part, constructive. And he excels at his real job, which is to build abstract models for the benefit of the strategists. (p. 603)

Stefan T. Possony, "A War of Maneuver," in National Review (© National Review, Inc., 1965; 150 East 35th St., New York, NY 10016), Vol. XVII, No. 28, July 13, 1965, pp. 601-03.*

RONALD STEEL

Herman Kahn had to learn that there is a delicate line between shaking people out of their apathy and shocking them out of

their pants. He applied the lesson in his second book, *Thinking About the Unthinkable,* and seems to have taken an overdose in [*On Escalation—Metaphors and Scenarios*], his latest study of atomic unthinkability. What we have now is not only a more mellow Herman Kahn, but a cautious, and even a benign one— a veritable expurgated version of his former outrageous self. To be sure, many of the old elements are still there: people are optimistically trooping off to their civil defense drills, Russia and America are blasting each other with atomic bombs, and nations are bounding back to their former levels of prosperity in double-time. Even that Strangelove monstrosity, the "doomsday machine," makes a return bout, and at virtually bargain basement prices (between $10 billion and $100 billion) although it is now dismissed as impractical and "not likely to affect international relations directly." But the old gusto is gone, and with it some of the gems that made the first book such a landmark of (unintentional) sick humor—like the unforgettable comment of one blast victim to a vomiting fellow-victim suspected of malingering: "Pull yourself together and get back to work! You've only received a ten-roentgen dose!"

Instead of such hearty stoicism, Kahn now admits that nuclear war will be no bed of roses. Which doesn't, however, make it impossible. Or even unlikely. Like Clausewitz, on whom he seems to model himself, he wants us to consider how force, even nuclear force, can be used for political ends. Deploring our reluctance to use force sparingly for limited objectives, and then to use too much force once our emotions are aroused, he preaches a "cool, restrained and moderate willingness to threaten or use force." And in the atomic age, force means atomic weapons.

A primer on nuclear arm-twisting *On Escalation* is not designed to shock but to instruct—to show how we can use our atomic weapons and still, perhaps, come out alive. Or at least kicking. Based on the premise, unexceptionable in the abstract, though deceptive in the specific, that "a very undesirable peace might have consequences . . . worse than those of many wars—even [some] thermonuclear wars," it tells us how to avoid such an undesirable peace by being willing to wage certain kinds of atomic war. Rather than merely thinking about the unthinkable, Herman Kahn now speculates on how we can do the unthinkable—and maybe even get away with it.

Escalation, in Kahn's definition, is a "competition in risk-taking," not unlike the adolescent game of "chicken" in which the players try to gain prestige and humiliate their opponents by taking dangerous risks. Like chicken, it is no game for the faint-hearted, for as Kahn observes, "when one competes in risk-taking, one is taking risks. If one takes risks, one may be unlucky and lose the gamble." And when one gambles with nuclear weapons, he might have added, there may be no return bout. Why, then, play the game at all, the unromantic might ask? Why not reach agreements without threatening to use force? Why not "reason together," as a President impervious to other people's reason keeps suggesting? Because, as Kahn tells us, "if either side desperately desires to make a settlement without harm or risk of harm, it is likely to get a very bad bargain."

Having thus admirably defined *Real-politik* as a global chicken-playing, Kahn constructs an escalation ladder by which nations can work their way up a series of forty-four graduated rungs from ordinary cold war unpleasantness to all-out nuclear oblivion. (pp. 8-9)

Adding increasing doses of nuclear weapons a little bit at a time, like oil into mayonnaise, Kahn is attempting nothing less than a demystification of nuclear war. Escalation becomes the means by which it is possible to open the atomic cupboard and take some of the small bombs off the shelf. In a world of atomic stalemate, limited nuclear battles are offered as the alternative to "all-out spasm war or peace at any price." By taking the mystery out of nuclear war, Kahn transforms the traumatic into the ordinary. Which is why there was such an outburst of horror when his earlier books were published. We do not want nuclear war to be demystified, because we fear that the more ordinary it seems, the more likely it will be to occur. For most people, its unthinkability is the only guarantee of its improbability.

Once nations think they can get away with just a "little" nuclear war, won't they be in for as big a surprise as the girl who thought she could be just a little bit pregnant? Even Kahn seems to sympathize with those who fear "that the more both sides believe in the possibility of nuclear bargaining . . . the more likely it is that such bargaining will be tried and that it will escalate." But his answer (and it is not such a bad one) is that nations are going to engage in escalation anyway, so they might as well do so with some knowledge of the risks involved, rather than in total ignorance. . . .

[His] is not the counsel of a monster, but of a man deeply troubled by the implications of his own analysis and the uses to which it is likely to be put by those responsible for making political decisions. As an escape hatch from this nuclear nightmare, Kahn counsels arms control which would limit options and thereby reduce the dangers of escalation open to sovereign states. Although so long as states are sovereign, it seems unlikely that they would forego the temptations that escalation provides. Failing such self-restraint, the only other hope is some form of world government—which Kahn vaguely espouses, but for which he sees little prospect except as the result of a nuclear Armeggedon. (p. 9)

> Ronald Steel, "Up the Doomsday Ladder," in The New York Review of Books (reprinted with permission from The New York Review of Books; copyright © 1965 Nyrev, Inc.), Vol. IV, No. 12, July 15, 1965, pp. 8-10.*

NEVILLE BROWN

Some space [in *On Escalation*] is devoted to a rather casual advocacy of the creation of a European Strategic Force sufficiently large and varied to conduct a slow-motion exchange with the Soviet deterrent. Kahn thus displays a certain lack of awareness of the most important implication of his own study. It is that the differences in power and status within the nuclear club itself are sure to remain sufficiently profound to limit the value of nominal membership. Bomber Command might well be able to inflict heavy damage on the USSR if used in full retaliation for a single all-out nuclear strike. But a series of well-planned partial attacks could reduce those who direct it to impotent confusion. As much would be true of any 'European' force for many years to come. In fact, no deterrent could expect to stand up to those of Russia or America until it had become approximately as large and variegated. Peking, please note.

Herman Kahn has not even tried to show how an armed clash between the superpowers themselves could effect anything more conclusive than a bloody stalemate. . . . (pp. 364-65)

> Neville Brown, "Strategic Man," in New Statesman (© 1965 The Statesman & Nation Publishing Co.

Ltd.), Vol. 70, No. 1800, September 10, 1965, pp. 364-65.*

MICHAEL HOWARD

It is . . . in their discussion of the controlled use of nuclear force [in *On Escalation*] that Mr. Kahn and his colleagues break most fresh ground and where they are likely to provoke the most controversy. . . .

[Mr. Kahn tells us that] nuclear war is unfortunately not unthinkable, and we must bring to its consideration the same sustained intelligence that we would to any other field of human activity—such as torture, one wonders gloomily? If Mr. Kahn sometimes loses touch with his audience the blame surely lies not in the fertility of his imagination but in the petrified barrenness of our own. (p. 25)

In [*On Escalation*] the complex nature of world politics is ruthlessly simplified into a stark confrontation between East and West. . . . Mr. Kahn's massive and subtle reasoning is devoted to analyzing the strategic confrontation of these two powers alone; the only two capable of fighting the kind of wars he has in mind. It must constantly be remembered, in reading his study, exactly how specialized it is, and how large is the area both of strategy and of politics to which Mr. Kahn's concepts are very largely irrelevant. But perhaps we may look forward to further volumes in which these areas are given the same impressive treatment. (p. 26)

> Michael Howard, "Thinking about War," in The Bulletin of the Atomic Scientists: a magazine of science and public affairs (reprinted by permission of The Bulletin of the Atomic Scientists: a magazine of science and public affairs; copyright 1965 by the Educational Foundation for Nuclear Science, Inc.), Vol. XXI, No. 8, October, 1965, pp. 25-6.*

POUL ANDERSON

Get [*The Year 2000*]. Read it. Think about it. The matter concerns you in the most fundamental way.

This does not mean that my enthusiasm is unqualified. On the contrary, I shall have to express several major disagreements and caveats. But here we are offered the ideas of some very able professional thinkers (*nota bene*: thinkers, not "intellectuals") about the world that we are to live or die in through the next generation. You may not like the ideas, but you had better not ignore them. . . .

In considering the remainder of our century, Herman Kahn and Anthony Wiener have avoided both [prophecy and prediction]. They make no claim to prophetic insight, nor do they hold that anything they foresee is bound to occur. Rather, they suggest various logical possibilities. But they treat each of these with much greater thoroughness than even the best predictors have been wont to do. The result is an often disturbing, always important examination of what we may face. . . .

What [Kahn and Wiener] do is, first, to use historical perspective and scientific-technological extrapolation to construct a "standard world" in which their "surprise-free" forecasts have come true. The description is generalized rather than going into particulars. (p. 90)

One of the best things in the whole book is a thoughtful discussion of how far alienation may go as a direct result of social-technical developments, what forms it might take and what might perhaps be done to alleviate it.

To be sure, the projection involves some highly debatable suppositions. For instance, the authors frankly take it for granted that economics will be managed along Keynesian or post-Keynesian lines, and that this will not lead to collapse. They do not consider the possibility of other kinds of collapse either, e.g. in China or India, though some think these catastrophes have already begun to happen. But then, the standard world is not presented as *the* future, only as a basis for further inquiry.

On that basis, several "canonical variations" are shown, ranging from an essentially stable situation where problems are being coped with, to different kinds of advanced social disintegration. The latter depictions make the book especially valuable, in that they show how the nightmares may come to pass if nothing is accomplished by way of prevention. . . . The cool, rational treatments of such "scenarios" make them all the more monitory.

Paradoxically, that reasonableness may be the principal flaw in the book. No doubt it was unavoidable if the purpose was to be achieved. But it requires unspoken assumptions—e.g., that Communist countries are countries in the traditional sense, with needs and deeds not too alien to ours—which are quite false to fact at present and, I think, will remain so for a long while at best. This vitiates a certain amount of the ensuing discussion.

You will also be put off by occasionally slipshod grammar and proofreading, and by phrases like "those oriented to the cultural heritage—whether they are unschooled conservatives or liberal, literary intellectuals." But these are trivia. In the long run, Kahn and Wiener are on our side. (pp. 90-1)

> *Poul Anderson, "In One More Generation," in* National Review *(© National Review, Inc., 1968; 150 East 35th St., New York, NY 10016), Vol. XX, No. 4, January 30, 1968, pp. 90, 92.*

KENNETH E. BOULDING

It is at the level of culture, values, community, and legitimacy—what I have elsewhere called the integrative system—that the Kahn-Wiener theory [set forth in *The Year 2000*] is at its weakest, even though there are some interesting discussions in this area. It is pretty clear, however, that Kahn and Wiener regard it as extraneous, something less fundamental than the economic or the military system. This may be a great mistake. I have come to the conclusion that the dynamics of the integrative system, and especially of legitimacy (the acceptance by the individual of his own acts and those of others), dominate all other social systems, and that neither exchange capability (wealth) nor threat capability (power) are capable of organizing society unless they are legitimated. To put it another way, if we lose legitimacy we lose everything. The idea that the integrative system has a unity and dynamic of its own—that there is, in other words, an "integrity" as there is an "economy"—is quite foreign to most thinking today. We tend to assume, for instance, that wealth and power legitimate themselves, which sometimes they do and sometimes they do not. My last word, therefore, is to recommend to the Hudson Institute, which sponsored this book, the study of the dynamics of legitimacy, which could throw more light on the future than almost anything else they might undertake. (p. 37)

> *Kenneth E. Boulding, "'Prognostics': A Guide to Present Action," in* Saturday Review *(copyright © 1968 by Saturday Review; all rights reserved; reprinted by permission), Vol. LI, No. 6, February 10, 1968, pp. 36-7.*

NIGEL CALDER

The opinions of the authors of *The Year 2000* appear at first sight humane enough—they would moderate man's Faustian impulses to overpower the environment and would reduce the centralisation of political power. With a rather spurious and distracting veneer of methodology, Herman Kahn and Anthony Wiener speculate about technological and social change in the next three decades, on the basis of familiar forecasts, but they are largely concerned with global politics and the rise and decline of nations. The 'scenarios' for radical alteration of the international scene include, inevitably, Herman Kahn's 'thinkable' nuclear wars. Much as one may mistrust the outlook of the American think-tanks, whence this book comes, it is hard to quarrel with their right to exhibit possibilities, without necessarily recommending them. Their exposition of a 'long-term multifold trend'—a 13-point list of apparently inexorable tendencies in Western society, none particularly novel but impressive when put together—is itself sufficient to make this book a significant addition to the growing non-fictional literature of the future.

That said, it remains unhappily true that the deceptively free-ranging style of Kahn's speculation does not allow him, or apparently his colleague, to escape from explicit or hidden assumptions about the supreme importance of the survival and success of the United States, in the face of all kinds of global challenges. They allow that American 'morale and prestige' could in fact be eroded—a mechanism they cite is by withdrawal from Vietnam!—but one is left with the impression that no price is too high to avoid such an outcome.

I have always been mistrustful of attempts to dress up the forecasting of human affairs as a science. It is an art to be cultivated, certainly, perhaps even to be aided by computers, but a science, never; any philosophy freshman could show why not. In any case, why strive for objectivity and consensus about how the future *will* be, when we ought to be arguing strenuously about how it *should* be? (p. 552)

> *Nigel Calder, "Depressing Futures," in* New Statesman *(© 1968 The Statesman & Nation Publishing Co. Ltd.), Vol. 75, No. 1937, April 26, 1968, pp. 552-53.*

DAVID BRUDNOY

[In *The Emerging Japanese Superstate* Herman Kahn] predicts that by the year 2000 or thereabouts, Japan will have surpassed America and the Soviet Union and have the largest gross national product in the world. And, he suggests, it is not unlikely that Japan will become a military superpower, maybe even *the* superpower, as well.

Mr. Kahn assumes that Japan's current economic growth rate of 10 per cent per annum will continue unabated, and that all additional factors—e.g., economic growth rates in the other major powers—will remain constant as well. Extrapolations are always dicey affairs, and Kahn's prediction sounds especially fantastic; *fabulous* might be the better word. . . .

Mr. Kahn's *Emerging Japanese Superstate* is a remarkable achievement: a book encompassing and occasionally bettering the descriptive analyses in a variety of well-chosen sources; a study so shrewdly suggestive that, if given the careful attention it deserves, it will certainly be recognized as the most important examination of today's Japan in recent years, and one which should become the focus of intense debate for some time to come. It is really two books, one descriptive, the second predictive. (p. 1216)

The predictive portions of this book are by their very nature less amenable to precise evaluation than are the descriptive chapters. Any Japanologist will immediately recognize a gap between the soundness of Kahn's portrait of Japan as she is and the tentativeness of his projection for tomorrow. *If* Japan's growth rate continues as at present; *if* Japan overcomes her "nuclear allergy" and becomes a nuclear power at the time and in the manner Kahn thinks will be most conducive to her development; *if* there is no nuclear Armageddon or even another Sino-Japanese war; *if* there is no phenomenal technological breakthrough in either the Soviet Union or the United States or, for that matter, in some other country, which could somehow cut seriously into Japan's access to raw materials; *if* all this and more—then perhaps the Japanese Century will indeed replace the American Century within three decades.

Mr. Kahn succeeds admirably in his stated goal of opening up rather than settling discussion. Even if his extrapolation is assumed to be fanciful hypothesis at best—and such a cavalier dismissal of his main point would be foolish—*The Emerging Japanese Superstate* will be acknowledged as invaluable to anyone interested in Japan, and as a book which should be read straightaway by anyone concerned with geopolitics. Moreover, as a teacher of Japanese studies who has long searched for the one volume which could bring together the best scholarship on contemporary Japan and present it in a cohesive, comprehensive manner, I can state flatly that Herman Kahn has written precisely that book. (pp. 1216, 1218)

> *David Brudnoy, "The Japanese Century?" in* National Review *(© National Review, Inc., 1970; 150 East 35th St., New York, NY 10016), Vol. XXII, No. 45, November 17, 1970, pp. 1216, 1218.*

CHALMERS JOHNSON

Is "futurology" a science? On the basis of [*The Emerging Japanese Superstate*] written by Herman Kahn, a self-described "professional futurologist," I think not. It is possible that Kahn's futurological wager will prove to be correct, but if so it will be because he made a lucky guess, not because he knows what he is talking about. Kahn and his Hudson Institute associates are deeply impressed by the growth of the Japanese economy over the last 15 years, and they believe that it is likely to continue to grow at close to the present rate (12.6 percent increase in real GNP during fiscal year 1969) for the next two to three decades. On the basis of that projection, they conclude that Japan will become something called a "superstate" during the 1990's—a configuration that is never adequately described but that presumably means a nation-state capable of having a commanding influence on the course of international events because of its great economic and therefore, potentially, military power.

The chief interest in such a prediction lies not in its assertion but in its demonstration: What are the facts, trends, extrapolations, and projections that make the prediction believable?

Here, I submit, Kahn is not only in trouble, he is putting on an inexcusably bad act. . . .

Regrettably, this book is the 1970's social science equivalent of the 1950's Los Angeles and San Francisco Zen books: Americans now write about the "Japanese Economic Miracle" . . . in the same way they used to write about achieving *satori* (Buddhist spiritual enlightenment) on the Hollywood Freeway.

Kahn makes lots of little errors: the Dodge Plan currency reform was made in 1949, not 1951—that is, before the Korean War began, which makes a difference. . . ; Japan's alleged "greater moderation, care, and even love of the environment" is laughable in view of the fact that the country acknowledges it has the worst environmental pollution problem of any industrialized nation; his statement that there have been no fatalities in Japan's student riots, except for Miss Kamba in 1960, is inaccurate; and his assertion that "the Japanese have a hinterland in Non-Communist Pacific Asia of possibly 200 to 300 million people, many of whom they will simply incorporate, by one device or another, into their economic superstate even while not moving them geographically" . . . reveals that he is ignorant of both the history and the current nature of East and South Asian politics. Neither China, nor India, nor Indonesia, nor Japan is large enough (in any sense) to dominate its neighbors, but each is too large not to entertain secret (or not so secret) thoughts about trying to achieve a dominant position. Some East Asian nations are beginning to show slight glimmers of understanding of this fact of life.

Kahn's real problems, however, are not with factual errors. They lie rather with matters of tone: old-fashioned American racism, intellectual arrogance ("I am much more concerned . . . that the anti-nuclear sentiment in Japan is so precarious that the influence of a foreign commentator [Kahn] may upset the balance" . . . , and a belief that glibness can compensate for slipshod analysis ("In discussing these possibilities I do not wish to imply that there will necessarily be clarity or real unity and consensus on any or all of these issues. However, neither would I like to preclude that possibility." . . .)

Slipshod analysis is particularly evident in his heavy reliance on Ruth Benedict's 25-year-old treatise *The Chrysanthemum and the Sword*, which he calls "perhaps the best book" in the entire field. In the postwar period, two schools of thought have emerged concerning the values and social structure of modern Japanese society. One, composed primarily of domestic Japanese social critics, stresses the bureaucratization of the modern Japanese state and alleges the existence of a ruling stratum in Japan, which either cajoles or forces the population to do what this elite wants it to do. The other school, beginning with Ruth Benedict and today composed primarily of domestic idealists and foreign, chiefly American, historians and sociologists, stresses that peculiar and highly specific Japanese values—above all those inherited from the feudal tradition—predispose the Japanese people to do what their leaders tell them to do. Obviously, both schools of thought are partly correct, and the best interpretations of Japanese society, foreign or domestic, incorporate both. (p. 467)

Kahn, on the other hand, argues that most Americans accept the tenets of the first school—which is demonstrably untrue with regard to American writing on Japan—and he opts for the second. In so doing he is insensitive to the logical difficulties of beginning a study of social phenomena with a blanket assertion about values rather than making them a residual or final variable. Assertions concerning values, like Freudian psychology, can be used to explain (away) anything. For example, Kahn argues, "It is the basic thesis of this book that the Japanese differ from Americans and Europeans in many important ways." . . . In other words, Japan has enterprise unions, consensus politics, and intense corporate loyalty because that's just the way the Japanese are. An equally serious fault in his discussion of Japanese values is that, although all Japanese adults (and Kahn himself) distinguish between Japanese who were socialized before the end of World War II and those who came of age only in the postwar world, his reliance on Benedict's book, which was published in 1946, compromises his assertions about the present generation. (pp. 467-68)

Chalmers Johnson, "Forecast," in Science *(copyright © 1971 by the American Association for the Advancement of Science), Vol. 171, No. 3970, February 5, 1971, pp. 467-68.**

W. BASIL McDERMOTT

The Year 2000 strives to be something more than a handbook for future-watchers. It is primarily a book searching for a general theory of change. A major irony is that its very concern with the dynamics of change eventually leads one to believe that the real purpose was to reveal why such a theory cannot be constructed. What we have instead is a vast number of "reflections" on the problems of change, or, as the cynic might put it—101 ways things can go wrong. . . .

There is a subtle ploy in which all future-watchers are prone to indulge. It goes something like this: Make a general proposition and then subsequently, imperceptibly, even unknowingly perhaps, begin qualifying the statement until it becomes rather meaningless or trivial at best, or contradictory at worse. (p. 65)

One walks away from such qualifications wondering what anyone can profitably have to say about any aspects of the future. And this I think raises a more basic question about the nature and the purposes of *The Year 2000*. Just what purposes should futurist thinking serve? To the extent that Kahn and Wiener do not diligently pursue the probable consequences in any one area of any given change, or the inter-relationships of different kinds of change, then very little is gained in presenting a "framework for speculation on the next thirty-three years," as the subtitle of the book indicates. The way in which these issues are tackled in this book renders one incapable of making judgments about what one might do, where one might start, or which areas are deserving of more thought than others. This, in turn, is related to the pervasive implicit assumption to which most of us are victims, namely, that the future (or life) is something that happens to people rather than something we are constantly creating simply by how we are now living. If the world is out of control as is deeply implied in most futurist writing, then precisely what shall we do with our lives? Kahn and Wiener do not address themselves directly or sufficiently to such issues and probably would balk in embarrassment at the suggestion that somewhere in *The Year 2000* a major discussion should have been devoted to a more explicit development of their preferences for the future, their reasons for these preferences, and what means they might be willing to support in furthering such goals, plus a consideration of the implications and probable consequences of such choices. The malaise one discovers in *The Year 2000* stems in great part from a crisis in value judgments about the alternative futures we ought to be creating. (pp. 65-6)

W. Basil McDermott, "Thinking about Herman Kahn," in The Journal of Conflict Resolution *(copyright © 1971 by Sage Publications, Inc.; reprinted with permission of Sage Publications, Inc.), Vol. XV, No. 1, March, 1971, pp. 55-70.*

ROBERT E. BURNS

In what is likely to be its most controversial projection, *The Next 200 Years* foresees continuing economic growth that will not lead to the rich getting richer while the poor get poorer, as some gloomier prognosticators predict. Kahn does not agree that the gap between "the rich" and "the poor" or the nations so categorized will disappear. But he looks for a growth rate that might, for example, be one third for the wealthier, developed nations over a given period of time while the poorer, developing nations might realize an economic growth of 100%. . . .

Kahn, Brown and Martel are also bullish on the future of energy sources, of raw materials including food and on our ability to maintain a liveable environment, both near-term and in what they describe in one of the book's most interesting chapters, the difficult long-term environment, "maintaining the earth's fragile envelope."

While Kahn and his colleagues do not entirely disregard the causative influence of non-economic or non-material forces, their projections do seem to assume that the needs and desires of economic man are inexorable and unlikely to be significantly influenced by "higher" motives. It is hard to fault this assumption when the projections concern people living at the subsistence level or in exceptionally meager circumstances. People who are habitually hungry are likely to look to their needs for food before seeking nobler, less physical goals. (The need for myths and even the persistence of religious faith among some of our world's most abjectly poor should not, however, be ignored.)

Nevertheless, the Hudson Institute team does not seem to allow much room for the influence in the next 200 years of poets, prophets and especially saints. While the influence in our time of such as Mahatma Ghandi, Martin Luther King and Ralph Nader is clearly small when compared with the non-human forces of supply and demand, it has surely made a difference in our society. And if we extend the period under consideration a century into the past, the influence of Marx, Darwin and Freud has been tremendously significant.

I hope that I have not given the impression that the scenario sketched in *The Next 200 Years* is not carefully documented and carefully reasoned. . . . While he presents a thesis that is obviously unacceptable to many and one that, like a lawyer's brief or a debater's argument, is one-sided and hardly self-correcting, the reader has little reason to doubt that Kahn would be equally persuasive in public debate with the best of those who disagree with his conclusions. His research is formidable and it would take an enterprise equal to his to gainsay it. (p. 74)

Robert E. Burns, "Books: 'The Next 200 Years'," in The Critic *(© The Critic 1976; reprinted with the permission of the Thomas More Association, Chicago, Illinois), Vol. 35, No. 1, Fall, 1976, pp. 73-5.*

THE ECONOMIST

The basic criticism that can be made of [*The Next 200 Years*] is that by writing in terms of 2176 Herman Kahn and his fellow authors virtually by-pass all the fearsomely difficult political and economic phases of transition through which the planet must pass if it is to get what could be, technologically and scientifically, a conceivable future. The result is that there is little to help the policymakers or pressure groups or teachers to make up their minds about decisions today or even before the year 2000. Unemployment, inflation, the likelihood that disease, not choice, is lowering the birthrate, inappropriate technologies—not one of these urgent present issues is examined. The Kahn vision is conceivable. But the route thither is anyone's guess.

> *"Janus Kahn?"* in The Economist *(© The Economist Newspaper Limited, 1977), Vol. 263, No. 6972, April 16, 1977, p. 123.*

FRANK B. GIBNEY

In **"The Japanese Challenge,"** the Hudson Institute's Herman Kahn and Thomas Pepper, old hands at dramatizing the soaring potential of Japan, now offer some cautionary speculation about what may happen to the Japanese if they amend their philosophy of growth and neglect to build up their domestic structure. (p. 12)

[Kahn and Pepper argue] with considerable conviction that Japan can only become the true postindustrial society of its planners' dreams by stepping up the engines of growth, not by letting them idle.

There is some logic to his thesis. A drive to improve housing and general living conditions at home would certainly raise the levels of Japanese industry and diminish the constant temptation for Japanese companies to keep exporting in the face of continuing domestic recession caused by unused plant capacity and by the consumer's reluctance to discard his habit of saving. (Most Japanese still save almost 25 percent of their income.) . . .

They rightly note that one result of past concentration on capital investment is "today's sharp imbalance between the wholesale and consumer price increase and the extremely high prices the Japanese consumers must pay for the commodities of daily life." Their ingenious argument includes imaginative plans for hillside cities, retirement villages and other innovations.

There is some question as to whether either Japan or the outside world could support a domestic rebuilding program of the same intensity as the "double-your-income" drives of the growth years. Yet what Messrs. Kahn and Pepper have to say about the lack of momentum in Japanese society today, and its fading sense of achievement, cannot easily be dismissed. (p. 42)

> *Frank B. Gibney, "Success Story,"* in The New York Times Book Review *(© 1979 by The New York Times Company; reprinted by permission), June 10, 1979, pp. 12, 42-3.**

ROBERT LEKACHMAN

Provided one avoids taking too seriously Herman Kahn's scenarios of the future, his extrapolation of shaky statistics into the 21st and 22d centuries, his analogies to the Zealots, Maccabees, Sadduccees and Slavophiles among others, and his numerous lists of such exotica as "Fourteen 'New' Emphases and Trends in U.S. Values" and "Thirteen Traditional Levers," [**"World Economic Development"**] . . . can be enjoyed as an entertaining exercise in the popular sport of futurology.

Although the text is repetitious, poorly organized, grandiose in tone (Mr. Kahn is addicted to the imperial "we") and immodest in its claims, it is also imaginative, intellectually playful and abundantly provocative of argument. (p. 9)

> *Robert Lekachman, "Futurologists,"* in The New York Times Book Review *(© 1979 by The New York Times Company; reprinted by permission), August 5, 1979, pp. 9, 21.**

EDWIN O. REISCHAUER

All in all Kahn's program [for economic growth in Japan presented in **The Japanese Challenge**] is not very convincing. Though condemning the old Japanese "religion" of industrial growth at any price, he himself sounds like its last true believer. His whole plan seems to be only a variant of Tanaka's ill-timed "restructuring of the Japanese archipelago," which ran afoul of pollution and crowding problems and then the energy crunch. I for one am happy that Japan's economic future is not in Kahn's hands but in those of more cautious and pragmatic Japanese politicians, bureaucrats, and businessmen, who seem to be handling the Japanese economy quite ably, while keeping Japanese society and politics on an extraordinarily even keel. (p. 35)

> *Edwin O. Reischauer, "'The Japanese Challenge': The Success and Failure,"* in The New Republic *(reprinted by permission of* The New Republic; *© 1979 The New Republic, Inc.), Vol. 181, No. 7, August 18, 1979, pp. 35-6.**

THE ECONOMIST

[Herman Kahn's analysis in **World Economic Development: 1979 and Beyond**] of what is and has been happening [regarding world economic growth] is convincing, infuriating, easily pinchable by us jackals of journalists, but then unfortunately turns incomprehensible just as it graduates from being today's cute summary of widely misunderstood trends into becoming some parts of tomorrow's future conditional. This is because, as Sam Goldwyn once said, it is difficult to make forecasts, especially about the future. Mr Kahn has brilliantly pioneered the futurological style of presenting alternative scenarios so that observers can progressively check which seems the nearest to the one they are currently moving through, but he dreams up so many alternative lifestyles for the future so fertilely that, by the time he is talking about a possible Skinnerian utopia as well as his beloved basic longterm multifold trend and 13 traditional levers, even his proof-readers have not understood what he means. . . .

[The] first six chapters [of **The Japanese Challenge**] are one of the best explanations ever published of Japan's extraordinary economic success and of its new economic problems now (overcapacity in the traditional industries, end of the investment dynamic and the need to restructure industry as South Korea and others advance).

Unfortunately, the clinching chapter 7, which details Mr Kahn's recommended new policy for Japan, seems to rely on yelling Yonzenso like banzai. Because Japan's meaningless and sensibly disregarded third plan (called Sanzenso) is universally regarded as wet, Mr Kahn wants a Yonzenso (or fourth plan) which should try to rush Japan temporarily into a 12% a year economic growth rate so as to use up overcapacity and stir new investment, while rightly relying on heavy imports to keep the cost of living down. The shape of his Yonzenso turns out to demand heavy new government spending on infrastructure and especially on private housing. But one reason for Japan's economic success is precisely that government spending, which in Asia is often corrupt, has been kept low. (pp. 120-21)

"Kahn and His Banzai," in The Economist *(© The Economist Newspaper Limited, 1979), Vol. 272, No. 7097, September 8, 1979, pp. 120-21.*

STEVEN A. SCHNEIDER

With the world economy facing its most serious crisis since the Great Depression, futurologist Herman Kahn tells us [in *World Economic Development*] that if we simply allow "natural" economic forces to operate, then 200 years from now nearly everyone will be rich. Unfortunately, Kahn fails to make a convincing case that the growth he projects will occur. And, while he maintains that the record to date is encouraging, that conclusion is undermined both by problems in his analysis and by his own discussion of the current economic situation.

Much of the book consists of argument by assertion. Where problems get in the way of Kahn's optimistic scenario, they are assumed away. We are told that the resources needed for rapid long-run economic growth are available and that by the year 2000 we can have "nearly unlimited and economical quantities of clean energy from renewable or inexhaustible resources." But there is no evidence in the book supporting either claim.

While Kahn trumpets the relatively huge rates of economic growth achieved in certain middle-income countries, particularly South Korea and Taiwan, he fails to examine the impact that economic growth has had on the bulk of the population of these countries. Throughout the book, economic growth and per capita income are the measures of success, while the distribution of that income is never examined.

Kahn also tends to prefer cultural explanations to structural ones. While he notes the special characteristics that facilitated economic growth in Taiwan and South Korea—high levels of United States aid, the fear of external attack, and the role of these countries as export economies—he tends to dismiss these factors, emphasizing instead the fact that these countries have a neo-Confucian culture, one that emphasizes hard work, seriousness, institutional identification, etc. This analysis leads Kahn to the conclusion that other countries could emulate the success of these countries by simply emphasizing the right cultural values. What he fails to recognize is that much of the success of South Korea and Taiwan has been due to their role as low-wage centers for export industries and that only a limited number of countries can assume this role in the world economy. (pp. 20-1)

The book also contains much that is extraneous. The first part is devoted mainly to the development of a framework and concepts, which contribute little to the analysis in part 2. The reader learns that there are three systems of truth, four phases in the fine arts, six degrees of belief, thirteen traditional levers, and fourteen new emphases. But this is pedantry rather than erudition. And rather than making a genuine contribution to knowledge, much of the book is simply a verbose and pseudoscholarly rendition of themes regularly found in the business press or at any conference of corporate executives. (p. 21)

Steven A. Schneider, "Social Change" (reprinted by permission of the author), in Sociology: Reviews of New Books, *Vol. 7, No. 1, November-December, 1979, pp. 20-1.**

Russell Kirk

1918-

An American historian, political theorist, novelist, journalist, and lecturer, Kirk is one of America's most eminent conservative intellectuals. His works have provided a major impetus to the conservative revival that has developed since the 1950s. *The Conservative Mind* (1953), one of Kirk's early books, describes conservativism as a living body of ideas "struggling toward ascendancy in the United States"; in it he traced the roots and canons of modern conservative thought to such important predecessors as Edmund Burke, John Adams, and Alexis de Tocqueville. Kirk has also been a trenchant critic of the decline of academic standards in American universities: *Decadence and Renewal in the Higher Learning* (1978), in particular, is a forceful denunciation of the "academic barbarism" which he states has replaced the traditional goals of higher education—wisdom and virtue—with the fallacious ones of "utilitarian efficiency," relaxed admissions, and innovative forms of education. The result, in Kirk's view, is that "the higher learning in America is a disgrace." Kirk's detractors have sometimes been skeptical of the charges he levels against liberal ideas and programs, accusing him of a simplistic, one-sided partisanship. His admirers, on the other hand, point to the alleged failure of liberal precepts—in particular those applied in the universities—as evidence of the incisiveness of Kirk's ideas and criticisms. (See also *Contemporary Authors*, Vols. 1-4, rev. ed.; *Contemporary Authors New Revision Series*, Vol. 1; *Authors in the News*, Vol. 1.)

Courtesy of Russell Kirk

Excerpt from *DECADENCE AND RENEWAL IN THE HIGHER LEARNING: AN EPISODIC HISTORY OF AMERICAN UNIVERSITY AND COLLEGE SINCE 1953*

The American public, by and large, has forgotten—or else never knew—that the ends of education are wisdom and virtue. The average American has looked upon education as a means to material ends: the way of practical success, social advancement and general jollity. Although these may be desirable aspirations, they are not the true objects of the higher learning. They may be achieved through *training* (as distinguished from *education*), through personal endeavor of a kind not scholastic, and through a state of mind like that of Democritus, the laughing philosopher. But these goals are not primary concerns of real colleges and universities.

The Americans, Tocqueville says, tend to neglect the general for the particular: that is, to shy away from theory. A pragmatic attitude dominated the United States before the term "pragmatism" was coined among us. When a people achieve great power and corresponding responsibilities, nevertheless, there occurs urgent need for reference to first principles. That time is upon us. No longer do all Americans take for a sign of health the impulse for compelling young people to "adjust" to modern society, without reflection. If the time is out of joint, conformity to vulgar errors is sin and shame.

Any society depends for the mere mechanics of its functioning, as for much else, upon the maintenance of a high level of imagination and integrity among the people who make decisions, small or great. And any society depends for the foundation and scaffolding of intellectual life, as for much else, upon the accumulated wisdom of our intellectual and moral patrimony. The decay of the higher learning among us has diminished that imagination and our understanding of that patrimony.

Perhaps a grand act of will—or rather, a series of such acts, preceded by serious reflection on the part of many of us—may yet redeem higher education in this country. Some people suggest that we may have to abandon established "Education", as a kind of ideological infatuation or mass-production business offering next to nothing for mind and conscience. Let the usurpers have it, these critics say. The awakening of imagination, by the discipline of the intellect, may have to be undertaken by new independent associations, in defiance of the educationist establishment.

That may be so; yet possibly there remains to us hope for the reformation of college and university. Decadence is not inevitable, so long as a tolerable number of men and women retain the elements of reason and the will to survive. Has the higher education in America been a democratic triumph or an egalitarian disaster? Neither, as yet—although in recent decades we have been sliding toward the latter consummation.

If the choice had to be made, Eliot wrote once, it would be better to educate well comparatively few people than to school everybody shoddily; for in the former circumstance, at least we should possess some competent leadership. An egalitarian disaster has not yet occurred in this country only because in fact we have not yet wholly abandoned the older understanding of education as an intellectual means to an ethical end. No democracy can endure if it rests upon intellectual apathy and indifference.

We have succeeded in sending a great many people to college and university; we have not succeeded in educating most of them. We have fallen into grave error by attempting to convert college and university into cauldrons for brewing equality of condition. We have not developed so effective a system of popular instruction as Switzerland has, nor yet so admirable a system of higher education as Britain used to have. The typical product of our colleges and universities is mediocre in mind and spirit—no triumph, as yet no disaster.

But the times demand more than mediocrity. Our failure to quicken fallow minds accounts for many of our national difficulties, now formidable. Our public men tend to lack moral imagination and strength of will: our cities turn ugly and violent because vision and courage are lacking. Mediocrity in a pattern of education may not be ruinous in itself, and yet it may contribute gradually to private and public decadence. Mediocre appeals for excellence will not suffice, in the absence of sincere and vigorous educational reform.

Despite our prodigious expenditure of energy and money upon schooling, we have accomplished little toward clearing the way for the human potential in America; nay, we have obstructed that way in our higher learning. (pp. 341-42)

[Short of new institutions] and as yet nobody has done anything to bring them into existence—we must make what we can of present establishments. Who at Behemoth State University aspires to any such abstract ends as wisdom and virtue? Yet if those with power in the educational establishment remain unconcerned for wisdom and virtue, the ethos of sociability and material aggrandizement must evaporate, perhaps quite swiftly—leaving a vacuum to be filled, conceivably, by force and a master.

Livy, a great historian in a decadent time, once was much read in America. "Of late years," Livy wrote of the perishing Roman Republic, "wealth has made us greedy, and self-indulgence has brought us, through every form of sensual excess, to be—if I may put it so—in love with death, both individual and collective."

Close parallels may be drawn with our age, and sometimes the death-wish seems to be operating in the American higher education. Yet even as Livy wrote that sentence, the Augustan age of renewal was taking form about him, and would carry on the civilizing mission of Rome for some centuries.

So it may come to pass with us in America. From causes in part explicable, in part mysterious, sometimes civilizations are reinvigorated. We Americans possess the resources for such a fullness of the higher learning as bloomed in the age of Augustus, and for more than that. Either we will become Augustans in the dawning age, I suspect, or we will take the road to Avernus.

It may be that Americans are not addressed to vanity, but instead are meant to strive imaginatively toward the human potential. If, pulling down our vanity, we are to make ourselves

Augustans—why, an urgent necessity, not to be denied, is the recovery of the higher learning. (pp. 343-44)

Russell Kirk, in his Decadence and Renewal in the Higher Learning: An Episodic History of American University and College since 1953 *(copyright © 1978 by Russell Kirk; reprinted by permission of Regnery/Gateway, Inc.), Gateway Editions, 1978, 354 p.*

FREDERICK D. WILHELMSEN

Mr. Russell Kirk, in *The Conservative Mind,* has gone farther than anyone writing in English today in the work of restoring to the educated consciousness the full inheritance of the word "conservative."

Mr. Kirk's theme is the conservative mind, within the Anglo-American tradition, from Burke to Santayana. Working inductively from the thought of a host of varied and sometimes opposed thinkers, the author attempts to find a common conservative philosophy and attitude that runs through Burke, Adams, Coleridge, Randolph and Calhoun, Tocqueville, Bronson, Disraeli, Newman, and others.

He locates the beginnings of modern conservatism in Edmund Burke and the reaction against Jacobism and the spirit given birth by the French Revolution: the spirit holding, for first principles, the perfectibility of man and the necessary progress of human society; the contempt for tradition, coupled so paradoxically with both the religion of reason and the Romantic worship of emotion and impulse; the desirability of political levelling; the passion for economic and social collectivism.

Opposed to these liberal dogmas—the dogmas that largely made the modern world—conservatism, according to Mr. Kirk, summed itself up in six canons: (a) "belief that a divine intent rules society as well as conscience;" (b) affection for the "variety and mystery of traditional life;" (c) the conviction that "civilized society requires orders and classes;" (d) the persuasion that freedom must languish unless built on the foundation of property; (e) faith in the politics of prescription; (f) the recognition that change, if it would be fruitful, must be in close continuity with the historic social forces that have formed the corporate conscience.

This conservative canon is stamped with the genius of Edmund Burke, who saw human society as an order appointed by Providence, growing slowly with the ages into maturity, carrying into the present the accumulated wisdom of generations, expressing itself in a rich diversity of social and economic classes each bearing its own unique burden, and all working together toward the common good: a good fulfilled and achieved only on the condition that each man, village, town, profession, and class maintains itself distinct and apart.

The politics of prescription—Burke's trademark—grew out of a deep sense of veneration and reverence. Mr. Kirk indicates, with great penetration, how Burke's distrust for the abstract "natural rights" of the Revolution was born of his love for the complexity and mystery of human life, and for the sacredness of the person.

In Mr. Kirk's opinion, the essentially practical and humanist program of Burke was carried forward by conservatives who fought a long battle through a century and a half full of triumphs for the opposition best represented by Utilitarianism, Liberalism, Benthamism, and Socialism. From Coleridge, through the "Tory Democracy" of Disraeli, and beyond to the rethinking of conservatism by Mallock, the forces of tradition have yielded point after point to the enemy, so that today English Toryism is no longer the exclusive party of the "country" as opposed to the "town."

Paradoxically enough, the limitations of the author's analysis of the English scene reveal themselves to the reader only after he has followed his discussion of American conservatism. Beginning well with a consideration of John Quincy Adams' insistence on Liberty under the Law, Mr. Kirk goes on admirably to dissect the myth of Hamiltonian "conservatism." It was the commercial and centralizing policy of Hamilton that eventually blurred the essential conservatism of the American Constitution—an instrument forged by men convinced that freedom lay in the decentralization of political and economic power.

Up to this point, Mr. Kirk's handling of American conservatism is not only admirable; it is masterful. But his failure to treat the whole tradition of American Agrarian Democracy, from Jefferson to the Populists, leaves his thesis incomplete and possibly in jeopardy.

If conservatism today is marked everywhere, as he holds it to be, by its opposition to the mechanized universe of the great modern city, if conservatism resolutely sets itself against the "social engineers," the "democratic planners," the "salvation through leisure time" sociologists—if conservatism, in short, opposes the whole depersonalized civilization in which we live, then a study of the conservative mind ought to consider one of the main forces that opposed this new world through a whole century of combat.

The Jeffersonian tradition was such a force . . . (pp. 278-79)

Mr. Kirk has marshalled an impressive list of American and British conservative thinkers: men who are reacting against the collectivist universe on battlegrounds ranging from party politics to religion. The question I would ask him and all conservatives is this, what is the key to the spirit conservatism is fighting? Unless that spirit be understood in its very essence, the fight is in vain.

Until Mr. Kirk leads his investigation into this ground I am afraid his restoration of the conservative heritage will remain incomplete. (p. 279)

> *Frederick D. Wilhelmsen, "To Recover a Concept and a Tradition," in* Commonweal *(copyright © 1953 Commonweal Publishing Co., Inc.; reprinted by permission of Commonweal Publishing Co., Inc.), Vol. LVIII, No. 11, June 19, 1953, pp. 278-79.*

FRANCIS BIDDLE

When we examine the content of most conservative thinking described in [*The Conservative Mind*] the vagueness of its substance and the confusion of its ideal emerge with greater emphasis, set against [Alexis de Tocqueville's] analysis. Put very simply, most of it dates. Take, for example, Mr. Kirk's summary of conservative principles. The assertion that conservatives believe that divine guidance must rule a civilized society implies that liberals are excluded from sharing such a faith, and indicates that those who would preserve the society which they have enjoyed, in most cases as members of a privileged group, assume that God is on their side without taking the trouble to discover whether they are on his. They distrust the skeptical, in essence the critical approach which the liberal

welcomes, because it challenges the authority which the conservative admires as long as it is exercised by members of his own class. But the liberal does not reject faith in divine guidance but believes that faith is a matter of individual judgment, and has no place in a democratic state of which an essence, culled from the bitter experience of religious wars, is that State and Church should function each in its sphere, and that what is God's should not be rendered to Caesar—at least the American essence. For even if belief in divine intent rules society—which may be doubted in the contemporary world—the discovery of that intent remains a human task, necessarily involving human disagreement.

Nor do I believe that affection for variety as distinguished from uniformity is an attribute confined to the conservative heart. The marrow of the liberal faith, of the individualism which Mr. Kirk so dislikes, was the freeing of the individual from the bondage of authority and misery which had been his usual lot without much variance along the generations. That at least was the ideal of the men who fought the Revolution and wrote the Constitution even if their successors have not achieved a closer reality. (pp. 17-18)

The conviction that civilized society requires orders and classes, I am disposed to leave to the conservative. It really comes down to a preference. . . .

I cannot put our world against any other period and say flatly men were then happier, the essence of life was richer and more beautiful. But such a reflection need not defer one from recognizing the tendencies toward uniformity and mechanism which threaten us today. And even if they result from the levelling processes of modern society, the equalitarianism which Mr. Kirk so generously detests, I am not prepared to admit that the extreme poverty and extreme riches of an earlier world, the very basis of the class society which Mr. Kirk's Conservative would have us restore, is a price worth paying. . . .

The men whom Mr. Kirk discusses are an extraordinarily diversified and interesting group. Yet sometimes their dish of conservative thought tastes curiously flat, without much spice or variety. The eighteenth century philosophy of a class society, built on a world which has long since disappeared, against the background of a secured leisure and an accepted hierarchy, dates like some smooth performance of *Candida* or *The Cherry Orchard*. It has the nostalgic unreality of so much of contemporary American intellectual conservatism, of T. S. Eliot, that "partisan of a graded society," of Allen Tate, of Peter Viereck, who seems to have little to offer to nourish or cultivate the wasteland which surrounds them.

They can see the forces of an unlimited industrialism at work in a civilization caught in a mechanical spin; but they can suggest no substitute of philosophy or of symbols, blaming democracy for men's sins against the spirit, hating the "barbarian nomads," as Eliot calls them, largely because they have ventured to overrun those preserves which in the world they would like to reconstruct were reserved for the elite. Unless you blame democracy for the discovery of modern power, to equate it with the destructiveness of that power is like thumbing your nose at the Universe because you don't like it. (p. 18)

> *Francis Biddle, "The Blur of Mediocrity," in* The New Republic *(reprinted by permission of* The New Republic; *©1953 The New Republic, Inc.), Vol. 129, No. 4, August 24, 1953, pp. 17-19.*

CLINTON ROSSITER

[*The Conservative Mind*] must certainly be acknowledged one of the most valuable contributions to intellectual history of the past decade. (p. 868)

Professor Kirk's stand for conservatism is staunch and uncompromising. It is refreshing to meet an historian of political and social ideas willing to go on record with statements like these: of Emerson—"His specific political notions are almost shocking—frightening in the first instance for their perilous naïveté, in the second instance for their easy indifference to uncomfortable facts"; of Babbitt's *Democracy and Leadership*—"perhaps the most penetrating work on politics ever written by an American." . . . It should be said in the author's behalf that he never fires one of these broadsides without carefully training his guns. His scholarship is manifestly of the highest order.

In dealing with this subject, especially in dealing with it in so clear and committed a spirit, Professor Kirk has laid himself open to serious attack. Limitations of space do not permit a full catalogue of possible chinks in his armor, but certainly it would seem proper to point out what may well be the most serious defect of the book: the implicit assumption, occasionally made explicit but never really supported by conclusive evidence, that all our present discontents may be traced back to the forces of lustful, shallow, irreligious liberalism loosed upon the West by the French Revolution. The historian of ideas has a deep obligation not to put too much faith in the power of ideas. (p. 869)

[The] so-called "new conservatism" of the postwar period takes on new substance and meaning with the publication of this splendid book. (p. 870)

> *Clinton Rossiter, "Reviews of Books: 'The Conservative Mind: From Burke to Santayana'," in* The American Political Science Review *(copyright, 1953, by The American Political Science Association), Vol. XLVII, No. 3, September, 1953, pp. 868-70.*

PETER GAY

No one will begrudge Mr. Kirk his admiration for Burke and Tocqueville [as expressed in *The Conservative Mind*]. No one who is familiar with radical or liberal doctrines will deny their frequent naïveté, their occasional philistinism, or their unjustified faith in the beneficial results of tinkering with political machinery. Indeed, the conservative emphasis on the mysterious variety of the human animal has served and can serve as a welcome correction for the shallowness of the traditional liberal theory of man. It has been a long time since the contributions of conservative doctrine to political thought have been summed up as well as they have in *The Conservative Mind*.

But Mr. Kirk's main thesis—that the various forms of liberalism have been responsible for the troubles of modern society and that conservatism alone can be the great healer—is, I believe, not borne out by history. Nevertheless it is a position that is urged upon us with increasing frequency. While conservatives have talked of dignity and continuity and respect for man, radicals have fought for humane legislation and against nihilism. (Indeed, the most serious charge which can be leveled against our contemporary American conservatives is their failure to distinguish themselves from, and to crush, the Nihilists in their own ranks.) It is a commonplace that modern society

is mass society, but its grossness is hardly the work of socialists or their allies. True, the lines can never be sharply drawn—some liberal movements have been guilty of cruel insensitivity . . . , while some conservatives like Shaftesbury have championed the cause of humanity. Radicalism may often have failed to take into account the irrational factors in man which conservative anthropology stresses (and stresses unduly), but the very omissions have permitted radicalism to set up critical postulates without which little social progress would have been possible.

Mr. Kirk's difficulties in attempting to resurrect conservatism as an ideology emerge most clearly in his treatment of individual authors. He praises such writers as Paul Elmer More (whose phrase—"To the civilized man the *rights of property are more important than the right to life*"—he quotes with approval. . .), and Irving Babbitt, in whom, Mr. Kirk holds, "American conservatism attains maturity". . . . But recent scholarship has pointed out again and again the fundamental vulgarity of Mr. Babbitt's criticism—for instance his substitution of personal attacks on his archenemy Rousseau for an attempt to understand Rousseau's work. Mr. Kirk, somewhat lamely, tries to find a political explanation for the low esteem in which Babbitt is now held—he cites the attacks on him by "writers of the Left" . . .—but such a defense is hardly impressive.

Conversely, Mr. Kirk is compelled to attribute to his adversaries opinions to which they certainly never subscribed. "Dewey's postulates", he writes, ". . . are simple and quite comprehensible. He commenced with a thoroughgoing naturalism, like Diderot's and Holbach's, denying the whole realm of spiritual values: nothing exists but physical sensation, and life has no aims but physical satisfaction. He proceeded to a utilitarianism which carried Benthamite ideas to their logical culmination, making material production the goal and standard of human endeavor . . .". . . . (pp. 586-88)

In thus attempting to prove the existence and the moral and intellectual respectability of a conservative ideology, Mr. Kirk has only succeeded in doing the opposite. . . . (p. 588)

> *Peter Gay, "Reviews: 'The Conservative Mind from Burke to Santayana'," in* Political Science Quarterly, *Vol. LXVIII, No. 4, December, 1953, pp. 586-88.*

HENRY M. WRISTON

It is sad to be critical of a book which supports one of my lifelong ideals, and which contains so much valuable analysis of the nature and limitations of academic freedom. However, [*Academic Freedom*] is a "conservative" tract; its theme is that doctrinaire liberals will destroy freedom. They worship Democracy, a concept tolerable only in its modified form of "constitutional, representative, political, traditional American democracy." This contrasts with Demos, "a false god, or at best a god with feet of clay," with whom Truth "generally is unpopular." That sort of Democracy is a "utopian collectivism, in which everyone shall be just like everyone else."

"If academic freedom is to be preserved through this dark time, the work must be done by men of conservative bent." The validity of the idea rests upon "natural rights" under which academic freedom is a separate, specific sort of freedom, not just one phase of the broader concept. "If theorists deny the reality of natural law, logically they must deny the reality of academic freedom." "Religious conviction remains an indispensable support to academic freedom.'' The scholar is a ''Bearer of the Word,'' dedicated to Truth. It may be remarked, parenthetically, that the author's altar should be inscribed ''to an unknown God.''

The book does not pretend to deal with academic freedom either historically or systematically, though it appeals both to history and to philosophy. But it is written with passion. When dissecting an opponent, even some he ''admires,'' the author uses a scalpel. He points out words used loosely, he seizes upon flaws in logic with avidity—in criticism he is a precisionist. But when he has a point to make he writes with his fist. His discussion of truth is in the manner and style of Donnybrook—the more heads he can break the greater his satisfaction. He praises quiet contemplation in a loud voice.

He says many wise things, has many clear insights, penetrates shams, and reveals the hollowness of slogans. Then he is carried away by passion into dogmatic assertions and examples that do not fairly illustrate. . . . Mr. Kirk depends too much on caricature and accentuates evils until the good seems lost. He makes naïve and uncritical use of statistics of violations of academic freedom. Nor is he always careful of facts. . . . (pp. 608-09)

The author has a gift for the sort of extravagant generalizations he deprecates in others. . . .

When constructive suggestions are offered, the evils have been so overdrawn that the remedies seem feeble. (p. 609)

After so much about the dominance of false philosophy, mass indoctrination, the ''professor-employee'' bullied by presidents and deans, caring too little about freedom, it is astonishing to come upon an optimistic note: ''The real scholar and the real teacher, men broadly tolerant because they have convictions from which to tolerate error, quietly dignified because they know themselves to be Bearers of the Word, still *compose the majority in our Academy*.'' This is near the end; what preceded would not have led the reader to anticipate that conclusion. (p. 610)

> *Henry M. Wriston, ''A Conservative View of Academic Freedom,'' in* The Yale Review *(© 1954 by Yale University; reprinted by permission of the editors), Vol. XLIV, No. 1, September, 1954, pp. 608-10.*

RAYMOND ENGLISH

[''**A Program for Conservatives**,'' Russell Kirk's] second blast on the conservative trumpet . . . , is intended to give intellectual expression to the prevalent sober revulsion from complacent and disintegrated liberalism.

The present book is necessary and most welcome. It turns the reflected light of Burke's undying wisdom (and not a little of Burke's emotive style) upon the contemporary scene, illuminated and socialistic doctrines. Mr. Kirk's business is not with politics in a narrow sense—for ''politics is indeed the preoccupation of the quarter-educated''—but with the whole range of social and personal morality and morale.

Thus he devotes ten of his twelve chapters to the problems of the Mind, the Heart, Social Boredom, Community, Social Justice, Wants, Order, Power, Loyalty and Tradition. The program that emerges is one for moral and intellectual regeneration through the conversion of men of goodwill to prudence and the principles of love, piety, prescription, beauty, natural order and honor—''the unbought grace of life.''

''The first task for the imaginative conservative,'' however, ''is the hard duty of frank criticism,'' and Mr. Kirk deals faithfully with the smug and sentimental intellectual fashions that have contributed to our demoralized culture. . . .

Perhaps the main weakness of his book is its failure to provide adequate constructive leadership for the new mood of the new brood.

More serious is a certain doubt that arises as to whether Mr. Kirk is truly a moderately pessimistic conservative prepared to come to terms with a distracted world or an uncompromisingly pessimistic reactionary. His Jeffersonian hatred of cities and industrialization, for example, seems either more or less than conservative; so does his detestation of contemporary culture, a detestation which expresses itself in such phrases as ''something is dreadfully wrong with modern society.'' Uncomfortably significant, too, are the dramatic opening comparison of the challenge of our time to the ''Gorgon's Head'' that petrifies all who look it in the face and the extreme statement concerning America's recently acquired international power—''We have employed it abominably.'' Despite his profound insights, Mr. Kirk fails to face two central facts: America's situation as the leader of a civilization in danger and the ineluctable role of the modern state. The omissions are doubtless intentional, but they detract from the value of the book as a prescription in another sense than the Burkeian. One cannot help feeling that Mr. Kirk is a gloomy and learned diagnostician rather than a physician for our ills, but his diagnosis is one we cannot afford to neglect.

> *Raymond English, ''The First Job Is Criticism,'' in* The New York Times *(© 1954 by The New York Times Company; reprinted by permission), November 21, 1954, p. 30.*

ERWIN W. GEISSMAN

Russell Kirk's [*Academic Freedom*] is a stimulating new examination of the problem [of academic freedom]. This is one of those questions which cannot be discussed without prejudice, but at least Mr. Kirk's prejudice is one from which we have heard little during the past generation. . . .

[Mr. Kirk's] presentation is urbane and intelligent, sound rather than profound, exploratory rather than definitive. He is concerned with academic freedom as a fact in the history of the academy, not as a moral or statutory right. The liberties of the academy are ''the product of custom and moral prescription, rather than of positive law.'' So be it, and may all right-thinking men deem them so.

Academicians must be bearers of the word. Their first obligation is to truth. Academic freedom is their freedom to seek the truth. Mr. Kirk's favorite enemies of this freedom are state coercion, statutory control, mass criteria, and the intellectual leveling of the professional educationist. The very selectivity here reflects Mr. Kirk's own political and educational prejudices. I mean nothing pejorative; I share most of Kirk's educational prejudices, but I do not mistake them for dogma. Education in a free society presents enormous practical problems and these are not going to be talked out of existence by a univocal extension of our political or philosophical views. But it is well that we recognize that the legitimate freedom of the academy can be limited from many different directions.

Mr. Kirk's particular prejudices lead him to emphasize dangers which are usually neglected, and this is all to the good. We should remember, though, that the problem in the concrete is one of human adaptability rather than of political or social commitment. Experience of the academy should teach Mr. Kirk that admirers of Edmund Burke can rank among the most arbitrary and small-minded members of the academic community. . . .

Academic freedom must not be confused with the human rights of teachers. Mr. Kirk avoids this confusion but it is not clear that he realizes that these subjects, though independent, cannot be entirely separated in discussion without practical confusion. The integrity of the academy cannot be maintained unless there are methods available for the removal of the incompetent, the idle, and the humanly perverse elements from the teaching profession. On the other hand we will never have true academic freedom while the bulk of our teachers are expected to bring up their families in conditions of genteel poverty which are made all the more insecure by professional obligations to maintain at least some pretense of gentility.

Mr. Kirk's illustrations are interesting in themselves but they tend to concentrate attention on the least important aspect of the problem. Instances in which the genuinely competent scholar is dismissed for unworthy reasons are few and will probably become even fewer at respectable academies. (p. 187)

I would disagree with the way in which Kirk handles the problem of academic freedom and politics. The primary function of the academy is not pure research but education. The teacher should ideally be an example of the educated man—not merely an expert but a whole man. This involves engagement of varying kinds, and avoidance of engagement is frequently what makes the research specialist a hopeless dud as an educator. The range of the individual academician's interests and the amount of time and effort he expends on his duties as citizen cannot be determined by theoretical judgments on the totality of his professional engagement to the pursuit of truth. . . .

In fairness to Mr. Kirk it should be remembered that he does not pretend to an exhaustive examination of the subject of academic freedom. As a discerning essay from a particular point of view, his book should be a source of profitable discussion in the common rooms of our academies, even though there are some unfortunate instances of carelessness in documentation. . . . [They are minor instances] but they may serve to remind us that the truth which is held out as an ideal to the academic community is not be confused with anything so mundane as scholarly accuracy. (p. 188)

> Erwin W. Geissman, "A New Look at the Pursuit of Truth," in Commonweal (copyright © 1955 Commonweal Publishing Co., Inc.; reprinted by permission of Commonweal Publishing Co., Inc.), Vol. LXII, No. 7, May 20, 1955, pp. 187-88.

FREDERICK D. WILHELMSEN

Beyond the Dreams of Avarice is presented by its author as "the random vaticinations of a social critic." Its matter contemporary; its manner, Georgian. Its temper is that of a confident, even imperious reaction. . . .

When commenting on American life today, Kirk seems at his best in "**The Age of Discussion**"—an analysis of the decline of the literate journal in America—and in "**The Ethics of Censorship**"—a penetrating judgment not only of official but also of the unofficial censorship exercised by publishing houses, universities, librarians and government officials. He judges this censorship to be directed more often against the friends of tradition and religion than against their enemies. (p. 375)

Kirk's "**Notes From Abroad**" reveal him as a man of an essentially poetic temper. Until his critics can firmly grasp this quality they will never understand him. It misses the mark to attack him, as he has been attacked, for trying to conjure up an American Tory tradition that never existed. The real question in weighing Kirk's thought is why a conservative tradition does appeal to him. . . .

For such a man, loving the things he knows, the only reaction to the impersonal world of the mass state can be one of contempt and defiance. . . .

There is a test, I think, by which Kirk's achievement and influence can be measured. Imagine our having been told five years ago that a man who writes casually of the regiments which were opposed at Killiecrackie, who recounts with relish the legends of the Clanranolds, who models his style on the periods of Burke—imagine our having been told that this man would rise up as a leading figure in American letters in the Atomic Age. That it happened at all speaks well for the toughness of the tradition Mr. Kirk has championed and made his own. (p. 376)

> Frederick D. Wilhelmsen, "Contemporary Criticism in the Georgian Manner," in Commonweal (copyright © 1956 Commonweal Publishing Co., Inc.; reprinted by permission of Commonweal Publishing Co., Inc.), Vol. LXIV, No. 15, July 13, 1956, pp. 375-79.

MARY M. CLARKE

[Mr. Kirk states that *Beyond the Dreams of Avarice* is] concerned with viewing the modern age "in the perspective of the past." He looks at contemporary culture with a constant awareness that he and the moderns, though he indicates they may not realize it, participate in "that great continuity and essence which is the civil social order we have inherited from a hundred generations."

Our civil social order is now showing, in Mr. Kirk's opinion, signs of advanced decay. He contends that avarice, the passion of the age, is accepted as a virtue by reformers, proletarians and established interests. As the restraint of religious and moral principles relaxed, as we forsook our moral traditions, in his theory, the desire for material improvements first swelled, then was fed, and now in large measure has been satiated. When we completely satisfy our lust of acquisition, he asks, will we rush into an Age of Gluttony in which we will wallow in well-fed security? If we do sink into gluttony, according to Mr. Kirk, if all our lusts are gratified, one lust will still inevitably remain to be fulfilled: the lust after power. To escape the boredom of a world of surfeited lusts, man will accept the carnage demanded by this lust after power and Armageddon will have arrived.

To stop this destruction of the human in man, the author urges a return to religious and moral principles. . . . Modern liberalism shows the faults of sterile rational ideology, Mr. Kirk argues. Following its secular dogma to the logical conclusion, he maintains that liberalism has become an "uninspired collectivism," ruled by "squalid oligarchs" in the name of "democracy" and "progress" and "security."

On the other hand, Mr. Kirk says, true conservatism realizes that society cannot be perfected by an ideology, or by any set of reasoned principles. Man must be obedient to a transcendent order, to a natural law. The nature of man is complex and flawed; human problems are intricate. Human longings and desires are not to be gratified on this earth, and, since man's nature is not changeable, no scheme for an earthly Utopia can survive. Knowing all this, Mr. Kirk's conservative realizes that he must strive for possible and prudent solutions to the world's troubles rather than seek to establish, by means of a doctrinaire ideology, a plan for a future of perfection. (pp. 473-74)

As always, Mr. Kirk offers a pert style and is eminently readable. Since the book is a combination of previously unrelated articles, however, it suffers in some measure from a repetition of ideas and occasionally of phraseology. Mr. Kirk's critics once again will be able to complain that he contrasts the best of conservatism with the worst of liberalism. They also may resent the choice of Bentham as the major spokesman of the liberal creed. In treating his English topics, and more particularly, in criticizing the innovations of the Labor Party, Mr. Kirk tends to surrender to a nostalgia in which the picture of the former social and political situation in Great Britain is distorted.

A relentless flogging of the evils of liberalism and a static reverence for things past already have trapped some "new" or "renewed" conservatives. Let us hope that Mr. Kirk, who concedes he is aware of these blind alleys, can avoid them. (p. 474)

> *Mary M. Clarke, "Other New Books: 'Beyond the Dreams of Avarice',"* in Catholic World *(copyright 1956 by The Missionary Society of St. Paul the Apostle in the State of New York), Vol. 183, No. 1098, September, 1956, pp. 473-74.*

PAUL KINIERY

[In *The American Cause*] Russell Kirk does his best to blast [liberal] ideas out of the minds of his readers. Some will consider him disgustingly sane and conservative and Christian. He states plainly that every person has a soul, a distinct essence, that is precious to God. He maintains that all men are brothers in a mystical, spiritual kinship in Christ. He affirms that man has a dignity that is conferred upon him by God, and that without God, there can be no human dignity. If God is denied, he reminds us, "then men and women merely are bitterly competing little organisms, with no moral obligations to one another." He explains in detail why Communism does make an appeal to some people, but he is sympathetic to those who have been ensnared by its false promises. Regarding the Communists, he observes: "For love, they substitute hatred; for the uncertainties of a free society, the certain slavery of a Communist society." If you are not a Communist, you will like this book which puts into hard-hitting words many of your thoughts and convictions about the gift that is represented by life in the United States.

> *Paul Kiniery, "Other New Books: 'The American Cause',"* in Catholic World *(copyright 1958 by The Missionary Society of St. Paul the Apostle in the State of New York), Vol. 187, No. 1117, April, 1958, p. 74.*

DAVID SPITZ

[A reading of Russell Kirk's *The American Cause* reveals that there are still some who think that an appeal to tradition is also an appeal to God], and who invoke the guidance of our ancestors on a highly selective and arbitrary basis.

Kirk is, in fact, much less of a traditionalist than he is a believer in God. He *uses* tradition but does not respect it. This is why, despite his seeming genuflections to the past, he ignores those elements in it that do not advance his argument. He quotes approvingly that crusty old aristocrat, John Adams; he does not mention Paine or Parker or Thoreau; and when he cites Jefferson it is primarily to explain him away—to argue, or at least to assert, that Jefferson did not mean what people have taken him to mean when he denied that the United States is a Christian nation and affirmed that all men are created equal. What Kirk really reveres is the "divine intelligence," though it is not altogether clear whether this intelligence is to be found in God or in Kirk's hero, Edmund Burke; and since, as Kirk believes, the United States *is* a Christian nation, he is concerned to spell out those beliefs "which are at the heart of the American cause"—the fatherhood of God and the brotherhood and dignity of man.

Now Christians and some others can no doubt subscribe to these beliefs without agreeing as well to the particular moral, political and economic principles that Kirk derives from them. For these principles—once we get away, as Kirk cannot, from God the stern judge but loving Father and the sins of His tormented servants—show Kirk to be not merely a man divided but a man who is tragically uninformed.

It is unfair, I suppose, to compare *The American Cause* to Kirk's earlier books, for in these, as a true (i.e., Kirkean) conservative, he was a critic of America, a Jeremiah wailing at the wall; and now he is a defender of the American faith. But the man beneath the armor cannot always conceal his true identity, and what the defender affirms the conservative often denies. The result is a potpourri in which conservative doctrines and American beliefs and practices dwell discordantly together. (pp. 326, 328)

How shall we explain this book? Clearly, on the basis of some of his earlier writings, Kirk is too sensitive a person not to be aware of some at least of his flagrant distortions: repeatedly, for example, he resorts in *The American Cause* to a double standard of judgement, condemning the Communists whenever their practices depart from their professions but justifying the Americans whenever they do the same on the ground that such inconsistencies are merely the normal differences between imperfect man and ideal society. What accounts for this performance, I suspect, is that Kirk is here trying to rally Americans, particularly the military—"it is a compliment to an American soldier to ask him to die for the ashes of his fathers and the temples of his God"—to the support of a cause in which he does not altogether believe.

For this reviewer, however, precisely because the American cause is in its commitment to democracy a noble cause, it merits a noble defense; and this can be achieved only by one who sees that cause for what it is, and who can condemn those who attack it both from within and from without. (p. 328)

> *David Spitz, "Confusion of Principles,"* in The Nation *(copyright 1958 The Nation magazine, The Nation Associates, Inc.), Vol. 186, No. 15, April 12, 1958, pp. 326, 328.*

FRANCIS W. COKER

[In *The American Cause* Kirk argues] that most Americans today cannot defend their ideas and interests against "the grim threat of collectivism." For proof of this "perilous condition," he points to the behavior of American prisoners of the Korean War. . . . Kirk paraphrases [a Senate sub-committee] report as concluding that "failure of our educational system to provide proper instruction in history, politics, economics, and other subjects was a principal cause of the bewildered and shameful conduct of the majority of American prisoners."

Regarding such conduct as symptomatic of a general decline in American intellectual and moral valor, Kirk offers his book as an effort to recover for Americans the long-run beliefs that "secure our order, our justice, and our freedom.". . .

Kirk offers corrections for what he believes to be prevalent present-day misconceptions about democracy and civil liberties. Our Constitutional founders did not intend to establish a "pure" democracy or a "classless" society. The "aristocracy" they rejected was essentially that of hereditary titles and privileges. "Classes," they understood, are inevitable—in the sense of natural groupings of citizens according to their varying abilities and services. They understood the need for political leadership by men of superior intelligence, education, and political acumen. They therefore balanced the influence of superior wealth, professional achievement, and intellectual force with the influences of free popular opinions, mixing democracy and aristocracy, with safeguards against abuses from either source. Moreover, they did not, Kirk says, intend to establish a "centralized democracy." (p. 1141)

Kirk's discussion of our economic principles is devoted chiefly to praise of our "free economy" of "private enterprise" and "freedom of competition." Our economic freedom, he declares, supports all our other freedoms—"bound together inseparably" with our political freedom, and "not altogether separated" from "freedom of religious opinion." . . . He warns against the devices of "zealots" who, speaking in the name of "social justice," really advocate a "regimented," "servile," "totally planned" economy, in which "all people" are to have "equal share in the world's goods." He finds it necessary to tell us that "pure equality" is "impossible."

The last two chapters describe and refute Communist attacks on our system: our "materialism," "crass concentration on private profits" gained from "labors of the poor," our "imperialism," and our general cultural decay. Any readers who have serious doubts as to our superiority, in policy and doctrine, to the Communists should be helped by Kirk's comparisons. This reviewer, however, has doubts about the justice and usefulness of some of Kirk's other comparisons and appraisals.

Kirk does not take time to point out that our free economy has required various sorts of governmental aids and restraints to keep it stable and efficient; that, from colonial times on, we have had a "mixed economy," with changing mixtures; that demands for governmental intervention have come from various groups of energetic citizens, speaking variously in terms of special practical needs and of general principles of social justice, and from our ablest statesmen, from the beginnings of our national independence—none demanding, however, a totally planned economy or an equal sharing of goods for everybody.

This reviewer believes that Kirk should reconsider his confident judgments (judgments which he represents as fully borne out by the Army and Senate sub-committee reports) on the conduct of the majority of imprisoned American soldiers in Korea. [The Senate sub-committee's conclusion that mitigating circumstances make assured judgments of the soldiers' behavior questionable] seems a better judgment than Kirk's sweeping condemnations—which are hardly needed as introduction to "an honest description" of traditional American beliefs about freedom and order and justice. This is not to say that there was nothing seriously wrong in the soldiers' responses and nothing seriously wrong in our national failure to prepare them to resist the indoctrinators by defending our convictions and interests with clear understanding and a strong will. But Kirk seems excessively selective in identifying our special sinners and their sins. He places the responsibility chiefly on our teachers. The Senate sub-committee places primary responsibility on our "parents, churches, and schools"; and perhaps we should also include, in such lists, our journalists and public speakers, and our authors and reviewers of books. (pp. 1142-43)

Francis W. Coker, "Book Reviews: 'The American Cause'," in The American Political Science Review *(copyright, 1958, by The American Political Science Association), Vol. LII, No. 4, December, 1958, pp. 1141-43.*

THOMAS MOLNAR

[*The Intemperate Professor*] offers a fundamental critique. Freud and Marx (and Sartre and Mannheim, etc.) have spoiled us with their insistence that no psychological or social analysis is complete without peeling off common sense and rationality layer after layer. What we find under the Ego, or the superstructure of respectability or ideology, is, according to them, the real reality, even though the profane may not recognize it. The profane, indeed, accept the conclusion because they stand in awe before the Expert, distrusting their own eyes rather than contradict him.

Kirk, it seems to me, is not tempted by this microscopic view of men and institutions. He is confident that we *can* know physical things and social phenomena without making them wither in the cognitive process. He does not try to simplify in the manner of laboratory social scientists, who apply to man what they learn about rats, and he writes effortlessly where others use jargon. (p. 275)

There is considerable courage in writing about institutions, individuals, groups, or notions like wealth and beauty as they appear on the level of observation, or as, in the light of events, they live and die. It is the very opposite of the fashionable method; it starts from the singular and the conscious, and its criterion is the traditionally accepted rational standard. Of course, it is less spectacular than the bulky studies devoted today to all problems from civil rights to the spanking of children. On Kirk's pages we do not read of hidden historical forces, of collectively reacting classes, of social determinism or the ever-present subconscious. We read of people and institutions as bearers of culture, hence as responsible agents. If there is decadence, Kirk implies, we need not look for hidden sociological poisons but for conscious individuals who make the wrong decisions or for institutions that fail in their tasks.

The essays in this book are, indeed, devoted to the ultimate guarantors of civilization: the church, the school, the integrity of teachers, the creators and patrons of culture, the humane milieu, the businessmen trading goods, and the purveyors of the more subtle products of the mind. When Kirk describes the conformist clergymen or the "inhumane businessmen" (come to think of it, they're much the same!), his concern is not with a class but with a cultural type, not with an abstraction determined by "factors," but with men too indolent to live outside the mould. The cumulative effect is a quiet but persistent critique of the prevailing ideology. Not so much a radical critique in the sense of exposing the roots, as one proceeding by description of the Liberal environment in its poverty of imagination, its oversimplifications—and its victims. (p. 277)

> *Thomas Molnar, "The Fault, Dear Brutus," in* National Review *(© National Review, Inc., 1966; 150 East 35th St., New York, NY 10016), Vol. XVIII, No. 6, February 8, 1966, pp. 275, 277.*

WILLIAM C. HAVARD

Like most of us, Kirk is at times open to charges of indulging in moral cant, of rationalizing untenable preconceptions, and of indiscriminate selection in marshalling empirical evidence to support his position. But the reader is never in doubt as to what his position is. The theme which gives coherence to the pieces in *The Intemperate Professor* is his view of the underpinnings of modern western civilization. Civilization, as he sees it, rests on three great bodies of principle and conviction: Christian faith, the humanism revealed in great literature from the classical period onward, and social and political institutions ground in the concept of ordered liberty. . . .

For the most part the threats [to culture with which Kirk is concerned] take the form of a denial in ideology or in practice of the foundations on which these attributes of culture rest—the failure to live up to or the explicit rejection of the standards that Kirk sees as generically characteristic of liberal education, religion, the aesthetic articulation of a sense of community, and the legitimate uses of wealth. Kirk is most bothered by the illiberality of liberal professors, lack of emphasis on humanistic learning in the colleges, the confusion of science with technology, the secularized insipidity of the religious establishments and their congregations (his survey of contemporary American Protestantism may well be the best selection in the book), the dehumanization of both the pursuit and the use of wealth among American businessmen, and the conformity and ugliness of a (planned?) commercial civilization which simultaneously stresses anarchic liberty and unqualified equality.

Ritualistic liberals cannot easily abide Russell Kirk, and even humane liberals may be somewhat cynical about the extent to which his exaggerated Burkean posture and antiquarian romanticism can be reconciled with his apparently Riccardian views on property and economic policy. But if he sometimes conjures up absurd pictures of knightly American corporation presidents exhorting boards of directors arrayed in cowls or academic regalia, he is also capable of calling attention to our faults, our limitations and our hypocrisies. As a quondam political scientist he is especially adept at probing the peculiar vanities and sins of omission and commission of our particular band of sectarians. We may not always like what he has to say, but he says it with grace and wit, and the substance of his essays is, at the least, worth quarreling with. (p. 714)

> *William C. Havard, "Book Notes and Bibliography: 'The Intemperate Professor and Other Cultural Splenetics'," in* The American Political Science Review *(copyright, 1966, by The American Political Science Association), Vol. LX, No. 3, September, 1966, pp. 713-14.*

HARRY CARGAS

Russell Kirk has got to be wrong when he says [in *Enemies of the Permanent Things*] that the first duty of our men of letters and our teachers is "conservative in the larger sense of that adjective," that their work, their end, is to "shelter and promulgate an inherited body of learning and myth." This implies that "the truth" is a fixed body of known dimension. I rather wish our writers would work to discover new truths and amplify the old so that they may not become stagnant clichés.

Dr. Kirk's ideas, of course, are not to be dismissed as irrelevant. He is certainly one of the important contemporary conservative thinkers. His insistence that it "ought to be the moral imagination which creates political doctrines, and not political doctrines which seduce the moral imagination" almost sets the tone for his latest book. Somewhat unfortunately, the title of these essays does so better. It signifies a negative approach to much of the world on which Kirk comments. . . .

Possibly because of his overwhelming respect for the "good" of the past, Dr. Kirk, in these pieces of politics and literature, allows little time for treatment of the present. He does discuss Eliot, Ehrenberg, Orwell, Voegelin, Riesman and others (including Ray Bradbury in a very perceptive chapter). But he seems to do so only to prove something about the past and not to indicate relevance or irrelevance for the present.

He sees all kinds of threats in those seeking improvements, and his labels of them (they are ideologues, rationalistic liberals, political totalists, neoterists) indicates to me an unwillingness to dialogue and an unawareness of what sober modern liberalism attempts. . . .

Kirk fears anyone who supports a doctrine of progress. He finds "grimly amusing" some of the talk about abolishing poverty, since Christ told us that the poor we will have always with us. . . .

There is much else in the book, of course, much that is valuable to readers of any political persuasion. I have been selective because I have been disappointed in Kirk's disregard for modern thought. He refuses to come to grips with evolution, the military-industrial complex, racial discord, ecumenism. The contemporary forward moving world does not seem to make an impression on Dr. Kirk. Was it the Russell Kirks that Teilhard had in mind when he wrote, in *Science and Christ:* "The learned may smile, or be angered, to hear us speaking of progress. . . . But have they the faintest suspicion, these men, that their skepticism will end logically in making the world unintelligible, and in destroying our capacity to act?"

I guess my question to Dr. Kirk is simply this: "What does it mean to act?"

> *Harry Cargas, "Book Reviews: 'Enemies of the Permanent Things'," in* America *(reprinted with permission of America Press, Inc.; 1969; all rights reserved), Vol. 120, No. 20, May 17, 1969, p. 596.*

FREDERICK D. WILHELMSEN

Russell Kirk, that latter day Dr. Johnson of conservatism, centers his *Enemies of the Permanent Things* around his understanding of what constitutes norms. "A norm means an enduring standard. It is a law of nature which we ignore at our peril. It is a rule of human conduct and a measure of public virtue." The author does not see a norm as necessarily following from philosophical first principles, although he does not deny the role philosophy plays in the discovery of norms. Kirk's insight into the normative is thoroughly analogical: standards capable of forming the keel of the barque of humanity are hewn out of wood found in many forests of the human spirit. Norms are established by custom, by a traditional living out of historical existence in which each generation forms a new skin built upon the sinews of its predecessors. (p. 862)

Avoiding the pitfall of equating the good with the merely old, Russell Kirk roots his thesis firmly in the classical and Christian inheritance of natural law, a law elevated and transfigured in the fires of Revelation. Custom and natural law are joined by the imaginative insight of the seer in constituting a trinity of sources from which mankind produces that civility without which life degenerates into a barbarism worse than mere animality.

Kirk's conviction that literary knowledge is precisely *that*, knowledge, is demonstrated in part two of his book. Kirk tells us unabashedly that he believes that "the aim of great books is ethical—to teach what it means to be a man." . . . Convinced that the health of a society is generally in proportion to the vigor of its letters, Dr. Kirk finds his heroes in men like Max Picard who sang silence, Tolkien who revived fantasy, and Ray Bradbury who turned science fiction to moral and therefore human ends. (pp. 862-63)

Kirk, unlike this reviewer, interprets American liberalism as largely imported from nineteenth-century English and German models. In any event, his discussion of American federalism and of its profoundly conservative roots is among the more interesting studies found in this work. Distinguishing territorial democracy from plebiscitary, Kirk argues that they are antithetical and that the drift towards the latter in our day portends an even further centralization of governmental power in Washington. This power would have to collapse under its own weight because of the impossibility of ruling a nation so enormously complex from one fixed geographical center. Kirk demonstrates his contention most effectively, in my opinion, in his discussion of local control of schools by boards appointed by and directly responsible to parents. In all cases, Kirk is the friend of diversity in unity, of analogy, and the enemy of any rationalist structuring of society around the principle of mass production. . . .

All friends of civilization are in [Dr. Kirk's] debt for his having written a profoundly urbane and elegant critique of the enemies of the permanent things. In truth Russell Kirk is the Dr. Johnson of a movement towards restoration which has nourished all of us, even those of us who believe today that we must move into a world which will be so radically new that it will require a surgery whose instruments are older than conservatism while being paradoxically younger than anything thus far known in the past four hundred years of Western experience. (p. 863)

> *Frederick D. Wilhelmsen, "A Standard for Public Virtue," in* National Review *(© National Review, Inc., 1969; 150 East 35th St., New York, NY 10016), Vol. XXI, No. 33, August 26, 1969, pp. 862-63.*

DONALD ATWELL ZOLL

It is not merely an obvious affection for Edmund Burke that links Russell Kirk with the eighteenth century. His emergence in the arena of contemporary letters reveals the transmigration of an eighteenth century spirit, the revival of the literary grace and versatility of the century of the high baroque. He person-

ifies the still lively *arete* of a more leisurely age, the urbane versatility of the literati of the era of Addison and Steel, Swift, Pope, Chesterfield, Johnson and Burke. (p. 112)

[For] all his rhetorical skill and his no mean flair for dialectical argument, a certain almost cavalierish sense of gallantry pervades [Kirk's] work, an intense sense of the civilized protocols. (pp. 112-13)

It is not irrelevant to comment on Kirk's unusual range of literary interests or his stylistic preference, since the heart of his social philosophy is ultimately aesthetic. His historical commentary, quite apart from his literary criticism, shows that his elemental judgemental criterion is an aesthetic one; those whom he admires most in the history of social thought are those imbued with an intense aesthetic orientation and a corresponding artistic talent. . . .

Russell Kirk is, in fact, a premier figure in the twentieth century revival of aesthetic conservatism, a repudiation of vulgarity in terms of both life-style and the procedures of politics. (p. 113)

[In] a very considerable area, Kirk is an immensely sophisticated writer, a fact he is occasionally quite ready to exhibit. His learning is wide-ranging and comports in every way to his own humanistic ideals. . . .

On the other hand, he is often thrust into speculations which, like those of Burke once more, would benefit from an amplified philosophical rigor. (p. 129)

Kirk's invocation of the authority of the philosophical tradition is not without its problems. The history of philosophy, as a discrete part of the "social accumulation," cannot be adequately conceived, in my view, as a compendium of "eternal truths." If that were the case, the philosophical enterprise could be largely restricted to a continuous reassimilation of past philosophical reflection. (pp. 129-30)

Kirk has, I think, a somewhat extravagant estimation of the *kerygma* of philosophy, and this leads him, as well, to a likely overmodest conception of the more immediate potentialities of the philosophic method. The risk in Kirk's historicism consists, it seems to me, in being insufficiently daring in conjecturing about the ramifications of his teleological commitment. If purpose is emergent in process, one cannot assume a rigid formalism regarding the ways in which purpose is clothed in actuality. (p. 131)

Additionally, a defense of "the permanent things" may entail more than the reiteration of a literary-ethical tradition; it may require an exploration of the ontological order upon which Kirk's "norms" appear to rest. The absence of this investigation, the presentation of a rigorous ethic, for example, in Kirk's work is not by itself a crucial omission, if one recognizes a division of labor in which Kirk's role as a social critic is acknowledged. By the same token, his work might well be strengthened in its cogency by a more forthright survey of the interconnections between his social viewpoint and its philosophical antecedents. What occasionally appears as too facile in his analysis would take on greater impact.

It may be, too, that Kirk's frequent hostility to science and empiricism in general may be misplaced. He too easily assumes that science and its methods are identical to the parody of them presented by his positivistically-oriented foes. His social criticism and corresponding recommendations, resting as they do upon theological, historical and literary insights, would be more formidable if buttressed by the empirically-derived evidences of contemporary science. He is not fully aware, perhaps, to what extent such evidential reflection would be conducive to the defense of the "permanent things" or the revival of the "moral imagination." He is distrustful, with some reason of course, of the sterile reductionistic tendencies of naturalism, but he does not fully appreciate, I believe, the enormous philosophical implications inherent in investigations of the natural order that have been undertaken within the decade. (pp. 131-32)

Kirk, as much as any man among us, is aware of the richness of human culture. No one, certainly not I, could argue against the thesis that any valid normative evaluation of that culture rests largely upon ethical and aesthetic determinants. He has every right to assert the significance, even the authority, of these attainments as necessary to civilization. Indeed, Kirk is, among other things, a defender of civilization in a most meaningful fashion. Thus, his far from superficial pertinence is to vividly remind us of the standards of our culture and to alert us to the dangers of mediocrity and ethical compromise. His own "authority" arises from his undeniable familiarity with these standards—even if they do not comprise either all of the "permanent things" or are only symbolic constructs of them. His eminent value lies not in philosophic speculation, but in a stewardship of some, perhaps the major part, of the civilized heritage. (p. 132)

Kirk is often content to defend a premise by reference to its compatibility with Christian principles or concepts. I am not prepared to dispute his theology, some of which I construe I would be in agreement with, but I am troubled by the adequacy of supporting what I take to be essentially secular concepts with theological justifications. (p. 133)

A large part of Kirk's indictment of contemporary social life lies in its retreat from rationality, its emotionalistic disdain for prudence and circumspection. That is certainly a very customary conservative counsel, but it may be remembered that this conservative cast of mind is not only the product of piety, but also the result of skepticism, a skepticism that not only holds back from the ideological illusions, but also from the more simplistic ramifications of religion itself. The urbanity which Kirk both admires and personifies acts as a brake upon religious enthusiasm, especially in its mystical manifestations. I do not think it is possible to reconcile the Anglo-Saxon conservative ethical and political tradition that he celebrates . . . with a palpable religious mysticism, but I equally believe that this is a growing tension in his thought. . . .

Kirk's critics assume a doctrine of cultural inevitability, melioristic or otherwise, which he, quite validly, elects to reject. His main purpose is *conservation*, hardly a reactionary point of view. It may not be quite realistic to argue for the return of the horse and the abolishment of automobiles, aesthetic preferences aside, but it is surely rational and realistic to insist that automobiles be prevented from poisoning us to death. The continuity and preservation of artifacts are not quite the same as the conservation of values. (p. 134)

To some degree, Kirk has made a career out of being intellectually unfashionable, but he has . . . demonstrated that in his sense of normative alarm he has been more relevant than his detractors. He seems on the verge of enjoying a certain fashion at last. It is a curious testimonial that some of the New Left, Kirk's ideological opponents, have chosen to call themselves "humanists."

In a broad view, Kirk, in the 1950s, reintroduced the broken web of historical social conservatism by the deceptively simple device of describing it and declaring it to be yet lively. This feat, no less of courage than of intellect, may have historic implications for the principal reason that it may yet be influential in channeling the resentment against the ideological drift of liberalism into forms both humane and restorative. Moreover, Kirk's brand of social conservatism provides an arresting contrast to the social Darwinistic tendencies of much contemporary Rightwing thought. (pp. 134-35)

The problem for Kirk . . . is how to preserve diversity in uniformity—how to insure the prerogatives of the individual without denying the preeminence of the community. From another perspective, if order, as Kirk maintains, is the first concern and responsibility of government, it is difficult to construe governments as having the limited discretion attributed to them by the nineteenth century liberals. Kirk's response, at base, is the assertion of individual difference and creativity within the perimeters of an objective, theocentric order. For him, individual freedom is not egocentric, but consists of possibilities for transcendence dependent upon a primal obedience to the ethical substance of universal order.

The tenability of this conception of freedom aside, its evocation creates a wholesome leaven against the primacy of egocentrism and the methodical adulation of selfishness that has shattered the *homonoia* of our age.

Russell Kirk's writings underscore the eradicable significance, not only of the continuity of moral wisdom as contained in the majestic works of literature, but also of the most rudimentary forms of social inter-action. Like Santayana, their stylistic urbanities aside, Kirk's social philosophy is ultimately a defense of simplicity, an ability to see the moral import in common experience, the final dignity, the joys of the elemental experiences that loom behind the "winds of doctrine." The strength, finally, of Kirk's humanism lies in its ability to connect in ethical, aesthetic and spiritual terms the glories of racial attainment with the prosaic obligations and satisfactions that are the universal lot of men. The defense of standards is thus blended with the indispensable elements of compassion, of mutuality, of sensitivity to the tragic predicament. (pp. 135-36)

Donald Atwell Zoll, "The Social Thought of Russell Kirk," in The Political Science Reviewer *(© Intercollegiate Studies Institute, Inc., 1972), Vol. II, Fall, 1972, pp. 112-36.*

MALCOLM MUGGERIDGE

In the face of [the alarming increase in violent crime], what Professor Russell Kirk has done [in ***The Roots of American Order***] is to go back to the beginning and see how order first established itself and developed in North America . . . Nothing could be more salutary. . . .

If a tree is sick, it is to the roots that we must go to find the cause. Likewise with a society that is sick. Thus, to understand how order has broken down we need to know how it came about in the first place. Then there is a possibility of applying a corrective. I cannot imagine how this so essential task of referring back to the origins of order as it has existed in North America could have been more lucidly, unpretentiously, unpedantically and yet informatively executed than by Professor Kirk. His book is exactly what people need to read, and he has made it easy, even pleasurable, for them so to do. . . .

Professor Kirk begins with Jehovah and the Mosaic code, which, via the Old Testament, came to North America with the first colonists. Then he goes on to the new dispensation of love expounded in the New Testament, which, as its originator explained, did not supersede or abolish the Mosaic law, but rather fulfilled it. For the Pilgrim Fathers this was not just something they accepted, but the very dynamic which sent them on the hazardous journey across the Atlantic in the first place. They were often monstrously untrue to it, certainly, in establishing themselves in the New World—notably, in their dealings with the indigenous inhabitants and reliance on imported slaves; but still, when they came to declare their independence and write their constitution, their words and intentions contained authentic echoes of the beginnings of Christendom, in Galilee, and as carried by the Apostle Paul to Rome itself, thence to spread throughout the empire. Also, of Greco-Roman culture and polity; medievalism and its Schoolmen, the Renaissance and the Reformation—all strands in the fabric of order the founders of the Republic instituted in North America. And, of course, more particularly, the influence of England, whence they came, and of the colonial regime under which they lived prior to independence.

All this is gone into by Professor Kirk with unostentatious scholarship, and in great, but not excessive, detail. Throughout there is the recurrent warning note that if these roots of order deep in America's and Christendom's past are allowed to wither, it cannot be long before the whole structure of what is called Western Civilization as it exists today comes tumbling down.

> *Malcolm Muggeridge, "Books: 'The Roots of American Order'" (copyright © 1975, Esquire Publishing Inc.; used by courtesy of the magazine), in* Esquire, *Vol. LXXXIII, No. 2, February, 1975, p. 20.*

ROBERT W. HOFFERT

[*The Roots of American Order*] is, in important respects, unsatisfying and unsatisfactory. Kirk intends to chart the "roots" of America's "order." Yet, there is never an adequate joining of the roots and the order. The roots are described with great care and detail. The order is treated as if self-evident, because immutable. The relationship between the two is, presumably, intuitively obvious. Kirk's message is a charade: a guessing game which instructs us via tableaux and indirection. Thus, to appropriate the book in a fuller sense, the reader must construct a suitable syntax to animate the image units provided. The grammatical key to this work is one man's reading of the conservative tradition in America, two hundred years after independence. (pp. 640-41)

Kirk's heavy rhetoric against reason and ideology is especially ironic since he only offers us a rationalistic tract in the history of ideas. There is a neglect, salutary or not I wouldn't guess, of identification for most primary source quotations. More substantively, Kirk is unwilling to ask hard questions and to come to terms with the implications of his own assertions: e.g., consider the relationships between personal order and social order, "order" and social class, and liberty and equality. Most troubling of all, Kirk's vision is consistently flat, unidirectional, and exclusionist. Does scripture provide such easy chronologies? Does Hooker summarize the Reformation for America? Can Locke be displaced as well as dethroned? What confidence can we have in the summaries of Hume when his position vis-a-vis American independence is so totally misstated? Are British and American common-law perspectives

undifferentiated? How tight must we squint our eyes to see the Declaration of Independence as a conservative document, the Constitution as an organic convenant, and to have the *Federalist* and the Articles of Confederation drop from sight altogether? What is the relationship between classical liberalism and Kirk's conservatism with regard to representative government, checks and balances, separations of power, liberty, private property, individualism, free enterprise, stability, toleration, and continuity?

In important respects, Kirk offers a confession of faith rather than a rigorous historical or philosophical analysis. If you come to it as a believer, you'll be overwhelmed. But how can you respond as an infidel? Yet, respond you must. The heuristic stimulation of this book is enormous, as is the danger that it may be swallowed whole. Solace may come inadvertently. The seeds of this harvest may succumb to the sterility of their own purity of breed. (pp. 641-42)

> *Robert W. Hoffert, "Book Reviews: 'The Roots of American Order'," in* The American Political Science Review *(copyright, 1977, by The American Political Science Association), Vol. 71, No. 2, June, 1977, pp. 640-42.*

RICHARD B. HOVEY

[The subtitle of Russell Kirk's *Decadence and Renewal in the Higher Learning*] is *An Episodic History of American University and College since 1953*. And so it is—although "episodic" is too deferential a word for his careful structuring, substantial documentation, and readable and sometimes witty prose. (p. 417)

To those concerned about our culture's crises, the record is disheartening. For anyone seeking acquaintance with the recent history and hullabaloo, fads and follies, waste and corruption on our campuses, the breath-taking acceleration of decline in academic values, Russell Kirk is a sharp-eyed and all-too-convincing guide. Whether or not we agree with him on every issue, reading him is *de rigueur*. One reason is that academe has become a major industry. . . . "In a single year," we learn, "America spends more upon higher education than all the people of the world, throughout history, had spent upon the higher learning down to the time of the Second World War."

The problem is not merely inflation of populace and money. The crux is that the absurd and dire muddleheadedness of our educators and leaders has plunged us into miseducation. Their gargantuan enterprise is based on two fallacies: that "the only really justifiable function" of the college and university is to "promote utilitarian efficiency": and the hyper-democratic notion that almost everybody should and has the right to attend college. The consequences: "On the whole—to express myself mildly—the higher learning in America is a disgrace." As to the big state universities (where the majority of our collegians go), they are "beyond reformation." . . .

Kirk concentrates his fire on "Behemoth University," his name for our mammoth public institutions. Their actual purpose is to "give the public what the public seems to desire": offering "career education"; training specialists; granting the boon of "amorphous humanitarianism"; rendering "community service" through researching *ad hoc* techniques to solve or ameliorate all of society's present-day problems; and affording diversions for the millions of students in the lonely crowd. Thus, in the past quarter-century has Behemoth U. swelled in importance. . . .

Given such a momentum, the strengthening and centralizing of power for the governance and operations of Behemoth U. brought to the fore a rapidly multiplying and new breed of administrators: the managerial experts. Few of these had achieved repute as scholars; few had extensive experience in teaching—the root of such traditions being readily cut. The managers were neither academic leaders nor spokesmen for education. Their function was to maintain the show of efficiency among their underlings and willy-nilly to be responsive to and co-operative with the state capital and Washington. They had only one model to follow: the ethos of big business and big government. In a word they were bureaucrats. (p. 418)

What temporarily jammed the cogs and wheels was of course the hippies' outbreak. Surely, opposition to the Vietnam War was one big factor. But the rebellion of the youthful "counter-culture" was worldwide, a phenomenon no historian has as yet explained. Dr. Kirk naturally deplores the chaos, destructiveness, vandalism, and violence which erupted. Interestingly, though, this conservative admits a "sneaking sympathy" with the motivation of some of the rebels. Although their cry for relevance and do-your-own thing was mindless, they were not merely attacking administrators. They had also become disappointed in their teachers. The young were seeking, at least subliminally, real authority—if only to challenge it. So they probed for some "solidity." Instead, they found in their mentors only flabbiness. . . . To the youngsters' very real though never articulated question, "How shall we live?" their courses and their teachers had no answer. For Kirk, the campus disorders are "evidence of the unsoundness of American higher education."

Rightly, he puts a share of blame on the professors. Too many of them had long been enervated by "permissive liberalism," by a stance of moral neutrality, by professing "no standards, nothing worth fighting for." Professorial Pyrrhonism—or new style Situation Ethics—taught the student radicals that "violent if meaningless action was a release from depressing awareness of the greater meaninglessness" of their predicament.

The persisting result of the eruption has been to make the learning process more than ever "student-driven" rather than "value-driven." . . . Students, no longer probationers in college to acquire maturity but now our-customers-and-we-must-give-them-what-they-want, the policy has become to lower standards, discard requirements, further fragment the curriculum, and multiply the variety of attractively marketed courses. (p. 419)

I go along with Russell Kirk, say, eighty percent of the way. The values he upholds as to "wisdom," "tradition," and the ends and means of liberal education I also subscribe to. My own peregrinations, however, lure me to challenge some of his points.

His heart's dream is the little liberal arts college. In my five years on such a campus—which had two chapels!—most of even my better students were curiously unteachable. Their "moral imagination" never fired, they seemed already to have the answers. In "Two Cheers for Behemoth University" (*Modern Age,* Spring, 1979), Professor Stephen J. Tonsor has questioned this Kirkean nostalgia. Tonsor speaks of students who "served time in their late adolescence and imbibed the prejudices of their particular Protestant sect and their economic and social class." Precisely what I encountered. Am I anti-religious to note that Dr. Kirk's belief leads him to assert that "secular dogmas necessarily are harsher far than religious dog-

mas"? Has he overlooked the Inquisition? Galileo? Salem's 1692 witchcraft mania? or what that Tory, Anglican cleric Swift satirized with his Big Endians and Little Endians in Gulliver's account of Lilliput?

Next, Dr. Kirk prescribes that we "must go to the roots of culture." He himself does not quite go there. A reader unaware that Kirk's prolific publications prove the reach of his historical learning might get the impression here that the forces destructive of the higher learning are of recent origin. He writes as if he would ignore Richard Hofstadter's 1963 study, *Anti-intellectualism in American Life,* wherein we learn not only how long and strong has been this negative tradition but also how vigorously some fundamentalist sects contributed to it.

Next, I must enter some demurers as to the author's views of professordom. As if there was nothing in it either anti-intellectual or against the constitutional guarantees for every citizen, Dr. Kirk glosses over the damage done by the smear-raids and loyalty oaths of the Joe McCarthy period. The long-range effects were to demoralize and further intimidate what is perhaps the most timid of all the professions. Nor have I, through the decades, met, or known about, more than a tiny handful of colleagues of the sort he labels "intemperate dogmatists" of a "secular" ideology, Marxist or otherwise. The overwhelming majority have been and are, simply, specialists—so wrapped up in their own specialties that anything like a view of where their particular discipline fits into a larger pattern or like a vision of what the higher learning is or might be is uninteresting to them and beyond their ken. Given their fretful and sometimes picayune individuality, it is difficult in the extreme for professors to get together over any common concern. (pp. 419-20)

Bafflingly, Dr. Kirk, it seems, would keep them so—even if, *mirabile dictu*! they might attain a consensus of sorts on a non-self-defeating philosophy of education he could approve of. For collective bargaining stirs dread in him, and the possibility of professorial unionizing is his bugbear. His nightmare is the destruction of academic freedom, with professors herded about by Hoffa-like bosses. (p. 420)

Unless I grossly misinterpret his over-all reasoning, the author here leads us to an almost abysmal dichotomy. He posits a powerless professor: "Freedom and power stand in eternal opposition." Nor am I garbling by quoting out of context. For Dr. Kirk defines the scholar as "a man who professes to have given up the claim to power over men in favor of the service of truth." How in the academic-bureaucratic power-structure such a person is to prevent being squashed, to secure conditions adequate for meeting his responsibilities, and to speak out the truth, Russell Kirk does not say.

He nevertheless rejects pessimism: "Because the state of the academy scarcely could grow worse, it may grow better." Part II of the book he titles **"Conceivable Renewal."** Yet it is significant—perhaps ominous?—that these latter pages total 106 as against the 243 of his jeremiad. Maybe it is temperament. I at any rate cannot share his optimism. His recommendations are straws in the wind, desperate remedies, pious hopes. . . . Surely the humanities, as originally defined, are in a *danse macabre.* For, the culture which brought them into being in academe and which, for the West, originated in the Renaissance has come to an end. A new (dis-)order is upon us. One reasonable hope is that here and there in scattered cells—one thinks possibly of medieval monks in their scriptoria—will be the few to keep alive the light of books in time-proven devotion to the study of history, philosophy, and literature.

In his finale Dr. Kirk quotes Livy on the collective death-wish of the Roman Republic, to remind us that at that moment the Augustan Age was being born. Small comfort: that age lasted only six decades. And though its greatest poet sang the dream of empire, is it not Virgil's melancholy over the doubtful destiny of the race which these days is the more compelling? (pp. 420-21)

Richard B. Hovey, "Academe—and the Abysm?" in Modern Age *(copyright © 1979 by the Intercollegiate Studies Institute, Inc.), Vol. 23, No. 4, Fall, 1979, pp. 417-21.*

PHILIP F. LAWLER

"Were I to indulge my taste for Jeremiads, I might succeed in outwailing the New Left people at the Ivory Tower's western wall," Russell Kirk reports midway through [*Decadence and Renewal in the Higher Learning*]. To tell the truth, Kirk *has* indulged his taste for jeremiads—*Decadence and Renewal,* yes, but mostly decadence. Only in the last forty pages does the author get around to outlining his program of reform for higher education (an equal space is devoted to the prior question of primary and secondary schooling), and even then he cannot avoid the impulse to instruct by negative example, showing contemporary American schools as models of what *not* to do. Nor is Kirk's tone optimistic. The book is divided into two major sections, entitled "**Progressive Decadence**" and "**Conceivable Renewal**." The renewal is "conceivable," not actual, in most cases, or even likely. (p. 146)

Unfortunately, Kirk is laboring at a disadvantage. He has been writing trenchant criticisms of the American educational Establishment for twenty-five years, and for twenty-five years he has been right. He has advanced the same sound arguments in dozens of books, articles, and columns (to say nothing of speeches), for a quarter-century. So while the evidence continues to pour in to support his charges, and while the academic hierarchy continues blithely to ignore them, Kirk can only pound away at the same neglected points. Even he, with his distinctive stylish prose, has trouble inventing original ways to convey the same truths. The thesaurus boggles.

So the arguments here are not really original. The unifying themes are ones that Kirk has developed more fully elsewhere: purposelessness, intellectual disorder, and gigantism in higher education; enfeebled primary and secondary schooling. Ceaseless repetition has polished Kirk's arguments, and when he does tackle a theoretical question he eviscerates the pat educationist dogmas with striking efficiency. But this is a primer, not a philosophical tract. The reader comes away with a wealth of anecdotes and insights and a list of books that Kirk commends for further research. (He gives insufficient notice to his own books; *Academic Freedom,* his earliest effort in the field, is indispensable.) Through it all, the reader profits from Kirk's inexhaustible store of information, accumulated in the course of a long career as an educational critic. (p. 147)

Kirk does mention specific remedies in his call for renewal, and he cites a number of laudable programs. But he keeps coming back to the same basic point: a true university must be a community "suffused with reverence." Amen. (p. 149)

Philip F. Lawler, "The Educational Wasteland," in Policy Review *(copyrighted © 1979 by The Heritage Foundation), No. 10, Fall, 1979, pp. 146-49.*

Joyce A. Ladner

1943-

Ladner is an American professor of sociology at Hunter College, author, and contributing and advisory editor of *The Black Scholar*. In *Tomorrow's Tomorrow* (1971) Ladner depicts black womanhood as a sociohistorical phenomenon and urges black women to go beyond white definitions in developing their own self-concept. *Mixed Families* (1977) is a study of transracial adoption in which Ladner concludes that there is little danger of "cultural genocide" from white parents adopting black children provided that the number of such adoptions remains comparatively small and prospective parents are screened for sensitivity and self-awareness. Some critics contend that *Mixed Families* merely presents material without further analysis and thus fails as a product of systematic social work, while others regard it as a scholarly contribution to family sociology and black American experience.

Courtesy of Joyce A. Ladner

Excerpt from TOMORROW'S TOMORROW: THE BLACK WOMAN

[*Tomorrow's Tomorrow*] is not attempting to resolve the problems of Black womanhood but to shed light on them. More than anything else, I feel that it is attempting to depict what the Black woman's life has been like in the past, and what barriers she has had to overcome in order to survive, and how she is coping today under the most strenuous circumstances. Thus, I am simply saying, "This is what the Black woman was, this is how she has been solving her problems, and these are ways in which she is seeking to alter her roles." . . . My primary concern here is with depicting the strength of the Black family and Black girls within the family structure. I will seek to depict the lives of Black people I knew who were utilizing their scant resources for survival purposes, but who on the whole were quite successful with making the necessary adaptive and creative responses to their oppressed circumstances. I am also dealing with the somewhat abstract white middle-class system of values as it affects Blacks. (pp. xx-xxi)

Certain historical as well as contemporary variables are very important when describing the young Black woman. Her cultural heritage, I feel, has played a stronger role than has previously been stated by most writers in shaping her into the entity she has become.

Life in the Black community has been conditioned by poverty, discrimination and institutional subordination. It has also been shaped by African cultural survivals. From slavery until the present, many of the African cultural survivals influenced the way Blacks lived, responded to others and, in general, related to their environment. Even after slavery many of these survivals have remained and act to forge a distinct and viable set of cultural adaptive mechanisms because discrimination acted as an agent to perpetuate instead of to destroy the culture.

I will illustrate, through depicting the lives of Black preadolescent and adolescent girls in a big-city slum, how distinct sociohistorical forces have shaped a very positive and practical way of dealing and coping with the world. The values, attitudes, beliefs and behavior emerge from a long tradition, much of which has characterized the Black community from its earliest beginnings in this country.

What is life like in the urban Black community for the "average" girl? How does she define her roles, behaviors, and from whom does she acquire her models for fulfilling what is expected of her? Is there any significant disparity between the resources she has with which to accomplish her goals in life and the stated aspirations? Is the typical world of the teen-ager in American society shared by the Black girl or does she stand somewhat alone in much of her day-to-day existence?

In an attempt to answer these and other questions, I went to such a community and sought out teen-agers whom I felt could provide me with some insights. I was a research assistant in 1964 on a study of an all-Black low-income housing project of over ten thousand residents in a slum area of St. Louis. (pp. xxiii-xxiv)

I spent almost four years interviewing, testing . . . , observing and, in general, "hanging out" with these girls. (p. xxiv)

I feel that the data is broad in scope and is applicable to almost any group of low-income Black teen-age girls growing up in any American city. (p. xxv)

The total misrepresentation of the Black community and the various myths which surround it can be seen in microcosm in the Black female adolescent. Her growing-up years reflect the basic quality and character of life in this environment, as well as anticipations for the future. Because she is in perhaps the most crucial stage of psychosocial development, one can capture these crucial forces—external and internal—which are acting upon her, and which, more than any other impact, will shape her lifelong adult role. Thus, by understanding the nature and processes of her development, we can also comprehend the more intricate elements that characterize the day-to-day lives of the Black masses. (pp. xxv-xxvi)

There are basically three periods that relate to the Black woman that will be included in this analysis: (1) the African background; (2) slavery; and (3) the modern era. In discussing the Black woman from a historical perspective, it is important to know that there is no monolithic concept of *the* Black woman, but that there are many models of Black womanhood. However, there is a common denominator, a common strand of history, that characterizes all Black women: *oppression*. (p. 4)

Black women in contemporary American society have been influenced by the conditions which characterize the history of Black people in Africa and the New World. The "matriarchy" has become a popular symbol that is used by many to describe Black womanhood, although this label is probably most often invalid. Today Black women play highly functional and sometimes autonomous roles within the family and society because the same economic and social conditions which allowed for the emergence of a female-dominated society during slavery still perpetuate this type of family structure. The female-headed household is assumed to be the predominant family form although less than one quarter of all Black families in the United States are headed by a woman. (pp. 27-8)

Given the highly unsuitable conditions to which the Black family has been subjected, one would expect the number of female-headed households to be considerably higher. (p. 28)

The highly functional role that the Black female has historically played has caused her to be erroneously stereotyped as a matriarchate, and this label has been quite injurious to Black women and men. It has caused a considerable amount of frustration and emasculation within Black men because it implies that they are incapable of fulfilling the responsibilities for the care and protection of their families. It has also caused certain added responsibilities to be placed on the shoulders of the Black woman because the larger societal expectation of her was in conformance with this stereotyped conception.

In recent years the Black woman has almost become a romantic, legendary figure in this society because the vast conceptions of her as a person are largely dictated by these stereotypes. . . . It is ironic that as the Black woman was romanticized for her so-called superior strength, at the same time she was criticized because she was labeled as a perpetuator of "bastardization" and the Black man was systematically excluded from meaningful participation in the society.

The dualism which characterizes the way in which the Black woman is perceived by the dominant society (the towering pillar of strength and an "immoral" person who cannot approximate the white woman, who has become the adorned symbol of femininity in American society) is responsible for many of the conflicts and problems she must endure. She has been forced to accept the images of what the larger society says a woman should be but at the same time accept the fact that in spite of how she strives to approximate these models, she can never reach the pedestal upon which white women have been put. Until recently this was the source of a considerable amount of anxiety in many Black women, but the new thrust toward Black consciousness and Black identity have allowed for the development of an internal set of standards by which many Black women have begun to judge themselves. (pp. 29-30)

Many of the tensions and conflicts which the girls in this study experienced are reflected more profoundly in the interpersonal relations between adult males and females. (p. 284)

The strong roles which Black women have traditionally played are now coming into sharp focus amid the controversy over whether or not she should basically be a *passive supporter* of Black men or should continue to *assert her individuality* and make the contributions to the Black community that she has always proved capable of making. Many Blacks have already redefined the woman's role to be that of the *passive,* non-assertive individual, whose major function is to be supportive of her spouse (defined in this context as husband or boyfriend). The justification for this position is that manhood is defined in terms of strength and it is assumed that Black men cannot find their places at the top of the family hierarchy if women continue to maintain the aggressive roles which many of them fulfill. Some base this on the African polygynous model, in which women assume the more passive roles. Others maintain that all of the Black institutions will eventually have to change if they are to remain relevant to its people and this redefinition of the male-female relationship is only one such change to anticipate. The counterposition is that Black men must assert their masculinity in spite of the traditional role Black women have played. The assumption is also made that the full resources of both sexes are vitally needed and women must not, unfairly, be asked calculatedly to submit themselves to all the demands of Black men. (pp. 284-85)

What is clear, however, is that an alteration of roles between Black males and females must occur. The traditional "strong" Black woman has probably outlived her usefulness because this role has been challenged by the Black man, who has demanded that the white society acknowledge his manhood and deal directly with him instead of using his woman—considered the weaker sex—as a buffer. The cowardice which characterized the relationship between the larger society and Black women has come to an abrupt end. I am not suggesting that the distinctive positive character of Black womanhood forged by centuries of oppression should be abolished. Obviously there is much to be preserved from this model because of its highly functional as well as humanistic value. I am proposing, however, that the stereotyped "Sapphire" ("Sapphire" is the name applied to the typical *strong* Black woman) cannot continue to operate in the traditional manner but must make the necessary adjustments that will allow for the full development of *male and female*. Black women must utilize those survival techniques in the larger struggle for the liberation of Black people. Even the middle-class Black woman must redefine her role. No longer must she view herself as an independent professional woman devoid of the burdens of race prejudice and discrimination, simply because she had the opportunity to be socially mobile. Her destiny is intricately related to those of poor women, and her commitment to survival must also be the same.

Black women must join all Black people in the process of defining who they are, what their goals are to be, who their prophets and heroes—past and present—are and what the strategies of survival will be. . . . (pp. 285-86)

In many ways the Black woman is the "carrier of culture" because it has been she who has epitomized what it meant to be Black, oppressed and yet given some small opportunity to negotiate the different demands which the society placed upon all Black people. Thus, she can be considered an amalgam of the diverse components which comprise Black culture: the pains and sorrows as well as the joys and successes. Most of all, it was she who survived in a country where survival was not always considered possible. As we return to the lives of the adolescent girls presented in this study, we must be aware that their lives cannot be viewed in an isolated context—in the context of a slum area in St. Louis, Missouri—but rather within the national and international context of neocolonialism and its disastrous effects upon oppressed peoples. (p. 287)

These girls, like Black girls throughout America, will enter womanhood in an era when the demands for commitment to the fight for survival will be more necessary than at any other time in recent history. They will be forced to engage themselves in those serious tasks which will ensure the survival of Black people against extermination. Unfortunately, they will not have the luxury of living the carefree life of many of their middle-class counterparts. Perhaps it will be the strength of their forebears which will allow them to triumph! (p. 288)

> *Joyce A. Ladner, in her* Tomorrow's Tomorrow: The Black Woman *(copyright © 1971 by Joyce A. Ladner; reprinted by permission of Doubleday & Company, Inc.), Doubleday, 1971, 296 p.*

Excerpt from *MIXED FAMILIES: ADOPTING ACROSS RACIAL BOUNDARIES*

[*Mixed Familes*] is about white Americans who adopt black children and about the controversy the adoptions created. It delves into the private lives of these couples, examining why they adopted and what their experiences have been. It examines the kinds of goals the adoptive parents have for their children and their expectations of the child's motivational and intellectual capacity. Do the parents' expectations of their black children differ from those of their white children? What are the parents' attitudes regarding their black child's racial identity?

This book also records and examines the reactions of grandparents, other relatives, friends, and neighbors, as well as the relationship between adoptive and biological children. It explores the roles these parents, their children, and other significant persons play and how they influence the developing black adopted child. Of critical importance too, it looks at the role the adoption agency plays in the family drama. (pp. ix-x)

Transracial adoption, as will be shown, is an extremely complex phenomenon. Such complexity defies simplistic explanations and pat solutions.

I first became interested in transracial adoption in 1969 when I noted the increasing amount of human-interest coverage given the phenomenon in newspapers, magazines, and on television. The question of motivation particularly intrigued me. Why were more and more whites adopting black children? (pp. x-xi)

In 1971 I heard the first organized rumblings against these adoptions by black social workers. They bitterly criticized adoption agencies for not recruiting black parents and seriously questioned the ability of white people to rear black children. (p. xi)

Supporters of transracial adoption have often exalted the adopting parents by pointing to their virtues. They have been referred to as charitable, good-hearted, decent, and noble. Some think they are more concerned with child welfare than the average parent. In my pursuit for clarification, I sought to find out if these parents lived up to such lofty descriptions and, if so, *why* they chose this rather risky path. . . .

Also I wanted to find out to what extent these children were merely pawns in a quasiconspiratorial system involving "decent" white parents, insensitive or racially biased adoption agencies, and dissenting, hostile black social workers. Were the children only incidental to a political and ideological confrontation being waged between blacks and whites? Indeed, I wondered if these children were being lost in the tug-of-war between these antagonistic groups. (p. xvii)

I realized that I should also hear the point of view of the black social workers who had expressed vehement opposition. It was also necessary to focus on the people who create adoption-agency policies, because they bore the responsibility for turning these children over to white parents instead of black ones. . . . How important was their notion that whites are incapable of transmitting a *black* identity to black children? This fundamental problem had widespread implications for the adoption of foreign children and children whose ethnic backgrounds were different from their parents—for example, native American, Asian American, Chicano, and Puerto Rican. The question was: Could *any* child of a different race, nationality, or ethnic group develop into an emotionally healthy individual with a strong and positive sense of identity if he or she is reared by parents outside his or her ancestral group? (pp. xvii-xviii)

Transracial adoption became a social problem when, on the one hand, adoptive parents and adoption agencies and, on the other, black social workers and black nationalists enunciated two fundamentally different sets of values. The values in conflict are racial integration, espoused by the adoptive families, and black autonomy, a preliminary step to the development of cultural pluralism, advocated by black social workers and their allies. (pp. 81-2)

[Transracial] adoption is a rapidly declining phenomenon whose chances for being revived are dim. . . .

Therefore, the more important concern is what the future will be like for those children who have already been adopted, and secondarily, what the prospects are for those black youngsters who will be adopted in the future. Beyond the controversy over transracial adoptions and the social policies lies the basic consideration of what is in the best interests of the child. This very important element has often been obscured, as the various forces have become embattled in a bitter confrontation and power struggle. The interests of the warring adults—adoptive parents, agencies, and black social workers—have been served to the detriment of the child's welfare. (p. 281)

I firmly believe that every child is entitled to a *permanent* home and parents. The permanency that the home offers enables the child to develop a secure sense of self, a stable identity, and the confidence that will enhance his or her ability to function, to perform adequately, and to meet the challenging tasks in life. There is an abundance of evidence that suggests that children who grow up in institutions and foster care frequently do not develop adequately psychosocially because of lack of permanence in their lives, which often leaves lifelong scars. (pp. 281-82)

The outcomes of those children who have already been adopted poses many serious and challenging concerns. While few parents have had serious problems as a result of adopting a black child, they nevertheless look to the future, especially adolescence, with great hesitancy. Even the more idealistic parents acknowledge that the problems will increase as their black child begins to interact more with the outside world on his or her own. (p. 282)

At some point, the average child can be expected to exercise some kind of defensive tactics in his or her behalf.

This is what the black social workers refer to as survival skills, an attribute they feel every black child should have to cope with racial discrimination. On the other hand, it can be a temptation for such parents to interpret each incident their child encounters as having racial overtones, when this is not always the case. Parents must be cautious that they maintain a balanced view and not err too much in either direction—that of being oblivious to racial considerations, nor overly sensitive so that they view their child's entire existence through the prism of race. (p. 284)

It is important that white parents expose their black children to a variety of role models in all walks of life. It is necessary for these black youngsters to see black "success" models, as well as people functioning in ordinary roles. Children should be exposed to and interact with blacks—adults and children—instead of being aware of their existence vicariously, through children's story books on black heroes, eating "soul food," and on other indirect ways.

Many parents feel that if they love their adopted child and provide for his or her physical needs, then there should be no serious problems ahead. The notion that love is sufficient is indeed naïve. That most of the parents who adopt these children love them is probably indisputable. But whether they understand what their differential needs are and will be as they grow to maturity is a more important question. Are they willing to transform their white suburban middle-class lifestyles to accommodate the child's needs, which, ultimately, are their own needs? (pp. 288-89)

I fully recognize that there are many whites who are capable of rearing emotionally healthy black children. In fact, some of the parents in this study appear to be handling this sometimes difficult task quite well. Such parents, however, must have an abundance of positive characteristics that one rarely finds in a married couple. They must be idealistic about the future but also realistic about the society in which they now live. To deny that racial, ethnic, and social class polarization exists, and to deny that their child is going to be considered a "black" child, regardless of how light his or her complexion, how sharp their features, or how straight their hair, means that these parents are unable to deal with reality, as negative as they might perceive that reality to be. On the other hand, it is equally important for parents to recognize that no matter how immersed they become in the black experience, they can never become black. Keeping this in mind, they should avoid the pitfalls of trying to practice an all-black lifestyle, for it too is unrealistic in the long run, since their family includes blacks and whites and should, therefore, be part of the larger black and white society. (p. 289)

Adoptive parents need to be exceptionally strong, well-adjusted, independent-minded, confident individuals who are more prepared for failure in their childrearing than are birth parents. The added dimension of transracial adoption is obvious. It requires courage, commitment, independence, and sensitivity to undertake this awesome responsibility in bringing up a healthy black child. . . .

Ultimately, the future of transracially adopted children, as with all children in the society, is inextricably linked to the future of the American people. Their growing-up years can be as problem-free or as problematic as the majority of Americans decide. The racial attitudes and behavior as well as their attitudes toward adoption itself will, more than anything else, determine these children's outcomes. (p. 290)

> *Joyce A. Ladner, in her* Mixed Families: Adopting
> across Racial Boundaries *(copyright © 1977 by Joyce
> A. Ladner; reprinted by permission of Doubleday &
> Company, Inc.), Anchor Press, 1977, 290 p.*

TONI CADE BAMBARA

What we have in *Tomorrow's Tomorrow: The Black Woman* . . . is a solid piece of scholarship, . . . moving and vital and eminently sensible. What we get is a perceptive discussion of Black womanhood, not a trotting out of all the fixed socio-historical something or others, but talks with young girls who speak on and live out what it means to grow up Black and female in a country that regards neither with any special fondness. . . . And, what we get is a sharing of a trained sociologist's discovery that the tools, techniques, and premises of her training are riddled with that very disease we are striving to counter, contain, halt, obliterate—racism. . . .

[In *Tomorrow's Tomorrow* Ladner] must juggle what she knows and understands to be for real and what she's been trained to regard as importance or truth. And herein lies the crux of the drama, the tension that permeates the book—though she modestly and professionally keeps her own discoveries subordinate to the girls and their stories—the clash between the society in which she(we) has been socialized and the framework in which she's been trained. Fortunately, she can think and see better than she's been trained, so what results is a rejection of the social sciences as "pure" mystique that trains "objective" specialists to go into the bush to study dirty natives or quaint folks or fabulous savages. And with it—the superiority premises, and the whole colonial relationship between the researcher and the subject (read "object"). And what results is a re-embracing of the idea that ourselves are and must be an occasion for serious inquiry by us and in our own interest.

Tomorrow's inquiry . . . [centers] on the intricate network of influences (familial, peer, societal, *etc.*) that bombard the young girl. And the counters and stratagems she devises to get over from day to day—her inner strength. Her coming of age. (p. 82)

What Ladner manages to accomplish is to assert a something we have always known but have to learn over and over again for some bizarre reason. And that is that "Black womanhood has always been the very essence of what American womanhood is attempting to become"; that the variety of peoplehood models within our own community should encourage us, not only to deplore, but to resist, the alien voyeurs who would hustle us for doctorates or government appointments or whatever the case. . . .

[She lays to rest] an awful lot of the notions about being a Black woman that so overload the image circuit that a whole lot of us get shorted out fore we can even see the light. And she does it simply by listening and looking and remembering and raising questions and listening again. Seems so sensibly simple. So what results—is a whole new set of things to consider and from a whole new perspective. The sections on teenage pregnancy, for example, open up a whole new avenue of thought that makes it impossible, or at least difficult, but mostly fruitless, possibly stupid—to refer to unwed motherhood, or whatever the labels, as a syndrome, or a self-destructive act. . . . Whole new set of things to consider. Not only about single motherhood but about womanhood in general. (p. 83)

> Toni Cade Bambara, "Books Noted: 'Tomorrow's Tomorrow: The Black Woman'" (reprinted by permission of the author; copyright, 1971 Toni Cade Bambara), in Black World, Vol. XX, No. 12, October, 1971, pp. 82-3.

ANN CHANDLER HOWELL

[*Tomorrow's Tomorrow: The Black Woman*] attempts to focus, with a very pronounced view of the role of white racism, on the processes by which low-income black girls approach and become black women. [Joyce Ladner], a black woman, makes it quite clear that her position is biased, bringing with her a sensitivity to the problems confronted by blacks and reaffirms that blacks have demonstrated an amazing capacity to survive in a "white racist society." She asserts (as have numerous others) that blacks are the sum of neocolonial brutalization and, given this condition, their emerging socially defined deviant behavior patterns are in fact creative adaptations, implying a well-adjusted group. It is noted that this work is a conscious endeavor to "break away from the traditional" methods employed in social science research of blacks, and a concerted effort is made to counteract negative interpretations of black family life and its members. . . .

The author reports her source of data was the life histories and responses to open-ended questions concerning "attitudes and behavior that reflected approaching womanhood," in tape sessions, of a "randomly selected" group of thirty adolescent girls between the ages of thirteen and eighteen in [a low-income housing project in St. Louis, Missouri]. . . . One gets the impression that these interviews, quoted in pearl fashion throughout the book, are feeble efforts to support the author's feelings reported in the book's conclusions. Indeed the sentiments in the introduction and conclusions are the major contribution of the work. . . .

The author chose to begin with a brief discussion of black womanhood from a historical perspective, including its African background, modifications through slavery, and contemporary adaptations. Coherence in this chapter is absent as there emerges no thread of continuity in essence to lend credence to the position that African heritage had had any marked impact on the modern black female.

Part two deals with certain features of "growing up black" where emphasis is placed on the significant role of the peer group and extended family in attitude development. Much is made of the problems of the "unprotected" black child and the shortness of childhood with the black child experiencing little or no adolescence. Credit for the survival of these children is given to their "inner resourcefulness" (a definition of which remains wanting).

The third section of the book deals with the problem of "racial oppression and the black girl." Questions of "self-hatred," negative identity, and self-esteem are considered with a rejection of earlier studies in the literature based on psychiatric interviews. These clinical studies are considered invalid because they are based on small nonrepresentative numbers, a criticism one might visit upon this project! I think the author is correct, however, in suggesting that the terminology employed in research dealing with blacks be considered from a black view point. (p. 561)

Chapters four and five of the work are concerned with defining womanhood and images of black womanhood. The topics here are diverse and their inclusion tends to contribute little in the way of providing insight into black womanhood in general. The author admits she was unable to find any "single route to becoming a woman" in this area. A string of quotes provides little support for the arguments advanced in Ladner's editorial conclusions. One could certainly take exception to the contention that there exists a "tradition" gearing a black female to aspire to being the "hard-working backbone of the family and for having children." The questions of viable alternatives and passive acceptance of their roles are not addressed.

In chapters six and seven the matter of "becoming" a woman is considered. Subdivided into onset of menstruation, learning "about boys" (interpersonal relationships), emancipation from parental controls, premarital sex, becoming a mother, marriage, contraception, and abortion, these chapters are laden with conflicting interpretations and exaggeration. The author would have us believe children are a highly valued entity, a strong emphasis being "placed on one's being able to give birth," with pregnancy testimony to womanhood. . . . "Black humanism" makes contraceptive techniques and abortion unacceptable to the black female who is said to consider sex a natural behavior, pregnancy a probable outcome! Further, we are asked to accept the notion that fears and ignorance have only slight influence in their expressed attitudes. Again the question of viable alternatives to demonstrated behaviors is absent as well as an investigation of certain realities (midwives in the community, number of black children abandoned annually, placed in agencies, etc.). (pp. 561-62)

I would suggest an inquiry in these areas needs address itself to the emotional and social needs of the girls. Ownership or possession of a child and its meaning for existence was not explored. It has been my experience (in a large metropolitan community), that young black girls when asked to relinquish rights to a child born out of wedlock question the right of ownership. For many of these girls the baby was the only thing they could call their very own and was the primary factor in retention of the child. A significant percentage, when asked why they risked pregnancy expressed a need for someone to "love"—the child, not necessarily the sex partner; perhaps implying an absence of emotional gratification in their environments (primarily one-parent households)? These responses did not generally reflect "positive adjustment." Further, the implication on the part of the author that there are no promiscuous black females is simply foolhardy! . . .

[This] is a book limited in sociological generalizations and utility, but does provide some insight into low-income black womanhood, not all black womanhood. The subject continues to await a more detailed and systematic investigation. Nevertheless, it does provide a descriptive base of information which may serve to make it useful for building future scholarly theory as it emphasizes a need for new definitions and perspectives in black experiences. Numerous unsupported statements, editorial comments, and the lack of analytical evaluations restrict the value that this work might have had. (p. 562)

Ann Chandler Howell, "Book Reviews: 'Tomorrow's Tomorrow: The Black Woman'," in Journal of Marriage and the Family (© copyright, 1972, by the National Council on Family Relations; reprinted by permission), Vol. 34, No. 3, August, 1972, pp. 561-62.

CAROL L. ADAMS

The contributions made by Ladner in *Tomorrow's Tomorrow* fall into three general, although not mutually exclusive, categories: (1) the emergence and definition of a black conceptual framework; (2) the destruction of stereotypic myths about blacks in general, and black women in particular; (3) the recognition of some social characteristics about black family life and black women traditionally overlooked by social scientists. In a sense, it is the first accomplishment which makes the other two possible. . . .

Essential to the methodology Ladner employs here is the idea that blacks must formulate their own definitions and concepts of social phenomena from a perspective untainted by the ethnocentricity and cultural arrogance of those who seek to compare aspects of black culture to the white middle-class model. This process is referred to as *decolonization*—"the refusal to allow the oppressor to define the problems and solutions of the Oppressed." . . . (p. 456)

With the advancement of the idea that a different set of moral codes regulates the sexual behavior of black people, the author questions the validity of the "moral-immoral dichotomy" in which sex is framed by the dominant society. Ladner suggests that the attitudes of low-income black people are certainly more realistic, more human. Within this context, another concept viewed as inappropriate when studying the black community is "illegitimacy." She observes that the low-income black community holds an inherent value that no child can be "illegal." The child is seen as having the right to exist and representing the fulfillment of womanhood, thus neither the mother nor the child is degraded and stigmatized. (pp. 456-57)

Central to the author's interpretation of the black condition is her realization of the effect of the American social system, through its institutional racism, on the black community. Ladner contends that the contemporary black community is a *product* rather than the cause of American social policy. . . .

Ladner attacks many of the dominant stereotypic notions about blacks which are propagated and perpetuated by its scholars and philosophers, for instance:

1. The allegation that the black community is inherently pathological is denounced as the invention of members of the dominant society who seek to obtain a "superior" status by creating an "inferior" class.

2. The charge that black people suffer from an inability to defer gratification is seen as stemming from the Protestant ethic of self-denial which white society itself "deviates" from in its preoccupation with materialistic goods as manifested in patterns of conspicuous consumption.

3. The notion of black self-hatred or low self-esteem is viewed not as an idea that emerges from blacks themselves but as a concept falling "within the realm of institutional subjugation that is designed to perpetuate an oppressive class". . . .

4. The more prevalent myth abounding in social science literature about the black woman is that which depicts her as a matriarch and an emasculator of black men. From this perspective, the strength and the resourcefulness of the black woman is portrayed as a negative thing and researchers once again point to the "pathologies" of the victim. . . . Ladner does not pretend that there are no frustrations in the relationships between black men and women, but places the locus of these tensions in external forces impinging upon the black community rather than on the defects of the black woman. . . .

Repeatedly, the author emphasizes the need to acknowledge as a positive force the strength and stability which enabled blacks in this country to survive. (p. 457)

[She] advances the notion that black women are now serving as role models for white women who are beginning to question such things as the institution of marriage, the concept of illegitimacy, and the general moral code traditionally associated with this society. It is interesting to note that much of the behavior characterized as deviant when practiced in the black community is now being sanctioned by the majority groups and thus becoming "legitimate." (p. 458)

Carol L. Adams, "Book Reviews: 'Tomorrow's Tomorrow: The Black Woman'," in The American Journal of Sociology (reprinted by permission of The University of Chicago Press; © 1972 by The University of Chicago), Vol. 78, No. 2, September, 1972, pp. 456-58.

DAVID C. ANDERSON

How are [the black or racially mixed children adopted by white couples in the 1960's] faring in this more cynical decade, a harsh season for the nuclear family in any case? To find some answers, black sociologist Joyce Ladner conducted interviews with 136 adoptive families in six states. [**"Mixed Families"**] offers few surprises—some of the families justify the early enthusiasm for interracial adoption; others vindicate the black social workers' angry response.

In the end, Miss Ladner asserts, "there are many whites who are capable of rearing emotionally healthy black children," but, she adds, the task requires courage, commitment and sensitivity, focused especially on the black child's need to develop a strong identity. . . .

But these conclusions, while sound and somewhat reassuring, are not an adequate response to the more trenchant questions: Are the good intentions of sensitive white parents enough to help a black child ride out the emotional storms of adolescence? And can they give him the self-assurance, the good sense, the strength of soul he will need to survive as a black in a society that now shows few signs of realizing the old ideals that caused him to be raised by whites?

To these questions there can be no final answers for another several years, but the enterprising Miss Ladner hints at some anyway, by tracking down older black children and some of the few black adults who have grown up in white homes. These case histories make up the most interesting chapter of her book. (p. 12)

One cannot generalize from [these few case histories], of course, but by their functioning, [the successful adoptees] do affirm the deep belief of many white couples who choose to raise black children: Relations between parent and child aren't supposed to be perfect; instead, they are richly complicated, molded by imponderable forces great and small. (p. 27)

> *David C. Anderson, ''Black Kids, White Homes,'' in* The New York Times Book Review *(© 1977 by The New York Times Company; reprinted by permission), August 14, 1977, pp. 12, 27.*

WILLIAM FEIGELMAN and ARNOLD R. SILVERMAN

[*Mixed Families*] offers a useful, up-to-date, and complete summary of pre-existing literature on transracial adoptions. One might expect that this book could be very useful to the prospective transracial adoptive parent or to an agency worker unfamiliar with this area. The profiles of various transracial adopting parents are most interesting, particularly the interviews with the transracial adoptees.

Yet, for social scientists and those deeply concerned with this policy question there is little new here. Much of what is presented has been said many times before in earlier studies. As a product of systematic social science research, the work leaves much to be desired. There is a notable lack of analysis of much of the case study materials. All too often Ladner merely presents the interview material without comment or further reflection. . . .

It is clear from the case study material offered that some of the families deal quite effectively with their black child's racial identity, some deny their child's blackness altogether, and some adopt a variety of intermediate positions. Unfortunately, Ladner does not use her data systematically to identify the characteristics of those families who are adept at dealing with their child's black identity and those who are not. This is a central question both in making transracial placements and in understanding majority/minority relationships. Clearly, Ladner has both the data and the facility to deal with this question. One is surprised and disappointed to see that she has not extended her analysis.

She ultimately embraces a position that all groups interested in transracial adoption would unequivocally agree with—namely that first efforts should be made to expand the scope of black adoptions in the black community. (p. 304)

One imagines that black social workers are seen as an important audience for this book. Ladner disagrees with the notion of transracial adoption as a form of cultural genocide. She feels that for the relatively small numbers of children involved with it, it poses no realistic threat to the integrity of the black community.

Her overall assessment of transracial adoption is that it is inherently problematic. Although the evidence presented in her text, both anecdotal and otherwise, suggests few serious adjustment problems among the members of her sample, Ladner remains ambivalent about transracial placements. She acknowledges that under certain conditions interracial placements may work out well. She includes the following conditions as important: when an interracial child is the first choice placement of the prospective adoptive parents, when whites have extensive interracial experiences, when they live in integrated neighborhoods, and when parents become involved in community organizations where there are other blacks. All these factors, Ladner believes, are associated with better adjustments. These are interesting hypotheses. It is a shame, indeed, that Ladner

did not marshall her data more effectively to systematically explore these and other notions. It would have produced a far more substantial yield. (pp. 304-05)

Ladner's long term prognosis for transracial adoption is that it will be diminishing in the years ahead. We think this view is not demonstrated. Clearly, the opponents of transracial adoption have effected substantial reductions in domestic transracial placements over the last few years. Yet, the incidence of transnational interracial adoptions has steadily continued to mount. The most recent figures on domestic transracial adoption suggest that placements are slowly beginning to rise again.

Those who see transracial adoptions decreasing in the future in response to the antagonistic reactions of minority communities may have overestimated minority opposition. A recent survey taken in a midwestern city . . . indicated that a substantial majority of blacks were not opposed to transracial placements, and were in favor of them when the alternative was institutionalization. . . .

[The] future portends increasing numbers of fertile couples will be actively seeking transracial placements in an attempt to establish newer and more harmonious family forms, modes that are more consistent with their religious and social values. Also, present demographic trends and the resulting shortages of white adoptable infants do not show any signs of abatement. This is likely to lead ever enlarging numbers of infertile couples to consider the idea of adopting transracially. Thus, the above trends lead us to anticipate that transracial adoptions will continue to be a minor, yet persistent, feature of the American family scene for some time to come. (p. 305)

> *William Feigelman and Arnold R. Silverman, ''Family and Intimate Lifestyles: 'Mixed Families','' in* Contemporary Sociology *(copyright © 1978 American Sociological Association), Vol. 7, No. 3, May, 1978, pp. 301-05.*

DORIS Y. WILKINSON

With the probing insight of a skilled ethnographer and the sensitive introspection of a humanist, [in *Mixed Families*] Ladner uncovers the uniqueness of intra-familial dynamics and the politico-social matrix which permeate transracial families. (p. 305)

Black autonomy and racial integration represent prevailing value perspectives in contradistinction to each other. Articulating the black autonomy ethos are those who perceive whites adopting black children as motivated by a perverted wish to remedy alleged black community pathology. They define transracial adoption as a cultural genocidal conspiracy. Ladner, on the other hand, disagrees. . . . She does not feel that ''an estimated fifteen thousand transracial placements'' will undercut growing racial pride nor damage measurably the black family institution. . . . I think, however, it is too early to give credence to either claim. Black social workers and others who assert that adopting across racial terrain does not alter a racist social order are quite right.

Mixed Families . . . makes a major contribution to Family Sociology and our understanding of the myriad of black experiences in America. It is well written, scholarly, exceedingly readable, and a relevant product. I strongly recommend it not only for its highly informative content but also because it demonstrates the skilled management of bias and consequently an objective treatment of so sensitive a topic as adoption across racial boundaries. (p. 306)

Doris Y. Wilkinson, "Family and Intimate Lifestyles: 'Mixed Familes'," in Contemporary Sociology (copyright © 1978 American Sociological Association), Vol. 7, No. 3, May, 1978, pp. 305-06.

MARTI WILSON

Joyce Ladner's book, *Mixed Families: Adopting Across Racial Boundaries,* is a study of transracial adoptions whose aim, as stated in the introduction, is "to provide some insight into this complex and controversial approach to family formation." . . .

Unfortunately, Ladner does not provide an in-depth critical analysis of the issue of adoptions in a racist society, nor does she give enough consideration to the question of how the adoption of a black child by a white family affects the social and psychological development of the child.

In some cases the book appears to be an attempt to build a case for the adopting of black children by whites. . . .

Ladner comes to . . . conclusions [apparently supporting transracial adoption] in spite of the fact that many white adoptive parents admit that they considered adopting a black child only after they were informed that there were no white babies available. Ladner never deals with this point.

In a capitalistic system, the law of supply and demand reduces adoptable children to a commodity status. Children of color appear in newspaper, magazine ads and even in T.V. commercials tempting the anxious consumer to step up and buy. In a consumer oriented economy, white children become the brand name products and the Third World child represents the "no-name" brand. The question of psychological damage to the child never becomes an issue. The attitude seems to be: What the hell, at least the kid will have a home. The State has one less child to support and the adoption agency is rewarded with one more happy customer.

But what about the child? To study transracial adoptions without some discussion of how children are perceived by the society and the status of children in the U.S.A., as a whole, is to view the issue (of transracial adoption) out of context. (p. 82)

It was disturbing to this reader to find that the major question, when searching for reasons families adopt across racial lines, was never asked, i.e., are there underlying reasons why people adopt children of different ethnic groups and if so, are these reasons sound?

Because of the complexities of transracial adoptions, it would be important to know whether the prospective adoptive parents, other children in the family and the potential adopted child have a positive attitude about the adoption. An even more important question is whether this factor alone can be used as a basis for determining the success of the placement? Another crucial question that is not raised is: Would white children ever be placed with black adoptive families, if these families so requested? Presuming the answer to be no, from that point could emerge an in-depth investigation into the politics of transracial adoptions, more appropriately called: White Adoptions of "Coloreds." (pp. 82-3)

Mixed Families plays a very important role in the controversy because the author fully explores the pros and cons of the argument, and it is perhaps the only book which deals with this important topic in such a comprehensive manner. Ladner does an excellent job of discussing the problems inherent in blacks adopting and the biases in the traditional adoption agency's rules and procedures. The eligibility requirements which infringe upon the black cultural norm include untimely scheduling of interviews, fertility tests, high income level and home ownership criteria. The combination of these requirements and the white middle class attitudes which permeate them are used as a measuring stick for placing black children.

Recently, however, there have been some changes in the adoption policies and criteria for eligibility largely due to the efforts of a group of black social workers and child advocates. The New York Chapter of the National Association of Black Social Workers has developed a program to "recruit" black adoptive families and work to change child care agency policies and state laws that make it difficult for blacks to adopt. . . .

Although Ladner's book has numerous drawbacks, the strength of *Mixed Families* lies in the fact that it approaches the question of integration from a new perspective, and heightens the level of dialogue on the subject of cross racial adoptions. (p. 83)

Marti Wilson, "'Mixed Families: Adopting across Racial Boundaries'," in The Black Scholar (copyright 1979 by The Black Scholar), Vol. 11, No. 2, November-December, 1979, pp. 82-3.

R(onald) D(avid) Laing

1927-

A Scottish psychiatrist, psychoanalyst, author of books on psychiatry, and educator, Laing is a pioneer in the study of the experiential dimension of psychosis. In contrast to the mainstream of the psychiatric profession, which considers psychosis a disease in need of treatment, and which thereby analyzes symptoms and behavior, Laing has sought to understand the experiences of those categorized as insane on their own terms. Laing concludes in *The Divided Self* (1960) that the bizarre, seemingly incomprehensible behavior of psychotics is in fact an understandable response to an unlivable situation; furthermore, he begins to question the sanity, from an ideal viewpoint, of "normal" experience. Going even further in *The Politics of Experience* (1967), Laing argues that our society is inherently alienating and its people "estranged from (their) authentic possibilities"; he decries the "madness" of normal life and announces the "liberating" potential of psychosis. Though Laing's views have made him popular with young radicals, a number of social critics, and a minority within his profession, he has many detractors. He is commonly faulted for romanticizing the psychotic, for falsely denigrating normal experience in favor of a spurious and mystical "liberation," and for providing a simplistic and misleading account of social processes. Many critics agree that Laing's most recent works have added little to his previous insights.

Excerpt from *THE DIVIDED SELF*

A man may have a sense of his presence in the world as a real, alive, whole, and, in a temporal sense, continuous person. As such, he can live out into the world and meet others: a world and others experienced as equally real, alive, whole, and continuous.

Such a basically *ontologically* secure person will encounter all the hazards of life, social, ethical, spiritual, biological, from a centrally firm sense of his own and other people's reality and identity. It is often difficult for a person with such a sense of his integral selfhood and personal identity, of the permanency of things, of the reliability of natural processes, of the substantiality of natural processes, of the substantiality of others, to transpose himself into the world of an individual whose experiences may be utterly lacking in any unquestionable self-validating certainties.

This study is concerned with the issues involved where there is the partial or almost complete absence of the assurances derived from an existential position of what I shall call *primary ontological security:* with anxieties and dangers that I shall suggest arise *only* in terms of *primary ontological insecurity;* and with the consequent attempts to deal with such anxieties and dangers. (p. 40)

Generally, it is evident that what we shall discuss here clinically is but a small sample of something in which human nature is deeply implicated and to which we can contribute only a very partial understanding.

To begin at the beginning:

Biological birth is a definitive act whereby the infant organism is precipitated into the world. There it is, a new baby, a new biological entity, already with its own ways, real and alive, from *our* point of view. But what of the baby's point of view? Under usual circumstances, the physical birth of a new living organism into the world inaugurates rapidly ongoing processes whereby within an amazingly short time the infant *feels* real and alive and has a *sense* of being an entity, with continuity in time and a location in space. In short, physical birth and biological aliveness are followed by the baby becoming existentially born as real and alive. Usually this development is taken for granted and affords the certainty upon which all other certainties depend. This is to say, not only do adults see children to be real biologically viable entities but they experience themselves as whole persons who are real and alive, and conjunctively experience other human beings as real and alive. These are self-validating data of experience.

The individual, then, may experience his own being as real, alive, whole; as differentiated from the rest of the world in ordinary circumstances so clearly that his identity and autonomy are never in question; as a continuum in time; as having an inner consistency, substantiality, genuineness, and worth; as spatially co-extensive with the body; and, usually, as having begun in or around birth and liable to extinction with death. He thus has a firm core of ontological security.

This, however, may not be the case. The individual in the ordinary circumstances of living may feel more unreal than real; in a literal sense, more dead than alive; precariously differentiated from the rest of the world, so that his identity and autonomy are always in question. He may lack the experience of his own temporal continuity. He may not possess an overriding sense of personal consistency or cohesiveness. He may feel more insubstantial than substantial, and unable to assume that the stuff he is made of is genuine, good, valuable. And he may feel his self as partially divorced from his body.

It is, of course, inevitable that an individual whose experience of himself is of this order can no more live in a 'secure' world than he can be secure 'in himself'. The whole 'physiognomy' of his world will be correspondingly different from that of the individual whose sense of self is securely established in its health and validity. Relatedness to other persons will be seen to have a radically different significance and function. To anticipate, we can say that in the individual whose own being is secure in this primary experiential sense, relatedness with others is potentially gratifying; whereas the ontologically insecure person is preoccupied with preserving rather than gratifying himself: the ordinary circumstances of living threaten his *low threshold* of security.

If a person of primary ontological security has been reached, the ordinary circumstances of life do not afford a perpetual threat to one's own existence. If such a basis for living has not been reached, the ordinary circumstances of everyday life constitute a continual and deadly threat.

Only if this is realized is it possible to understand how certain psychoses can develop.

If the individual cannot take the realness, aliveness, autonomy, and identity of himself and others for granted, then he has to become absorbed in contriving ways of trying to be real, of keeping himself or others alive, of preserving his identity, in efforts, as he will often put it, to prevent himself losing his self. What are to most people everyday happenings, which are hardly noticed because they have no special significance, may become deeply significant in so far as they either contribute to the sustenance of the individual's being or threaten him with non-being. Such an individual, for whom the elements of the world are coming to have, or have come to have, a different hierarchy of significance from that of the ordinary person, is beginning, as we say, to 'live in a world of his own', or has already come to do so. It is not true to say, however, without careful qualification that he is losing 'contact with' reality, and withdrawing into himself. External events no longer affect him in the same way as they do others: it is not that they affect him less; on the contrary, frequently they affect him more. It is frequently not the case that he is becoming 'indifferent' and 'withdrawn'. It may, however, be that the world of his experience comes to be one he can no longer share with other people. (pp. 42-5)

Excerpt from *THE POLITICS OF EXPERIENCE*

Few books today are forgivable. Black on the canvas, silence on the screen, an empty white sheet of paper, are perhaps feasible. There is little conjunction of truth and social "reality." Around us are pseudo-events, to which we adjust with a false consciousness adapted to see these events as true and real, and even as beautiful. In the society of men the truth resides now less in what things are than in what they are not. Our social realities are so ugly if seen in the light of exiled truth, and beauty is almost no longer possible if it is not a lie.

We live in a moment of history where change is so speeded up that we begin to see the present only when it is already disappearing.

It is difficult for modern man not to see the present in terms of the past. The white European and North American, in particular, commonly has a sense, not of renewal, but of being at an end: of being only half alive in the fibrillating heartland of a senescent civilization. Sometimes it seems that it is not possible to do more than reflect the decay around and within us, than sing sad and bitter songs of disillusion and defeat.

Yet that mood is already dated, at least insofar as it is not a perennial possibility of the human spirit. It entails a sense of time, which is already being dissolved in the instantaneous, stochastic, abrupt, discontinuous electronic cosmos, the dynamic mosaic of the electromagnetic field.

Nevertheless, the requirement of the present, the failure of the past, is the same: to provide a thoroughly self-conscious and self-critical human account of man.

No one can begin to think, feel or act now except from the starting point of his or her own alienation. We shall examine some of its forms in the following pages.

We are all murderers and prostitutes—no matter to what culture, society, class, nation, we belong, no matter how normal, moral, or mature we take ourselves to be.

Humanity is estranged from its authentic possibilities. This basic vision prevents us from taking any unequivocal view of the sanity of common sense, or of the madness of the so-called madman. However, what is required is more than a passionate outcry of outraged humanity.

Our alienation goes to the roots. The realization of this is the essential springboard for any serious reflection on any aspect of present interhuman life. Viewed from different perspectives, construed in different ways and expressed in different idioms, this realization unites men as diverse as Marx, Kierkegaard, Nietzsche, Freud, Heidegger, Tillich and Sartre.

More recent voices in the United States continue to document different facets of our fragmentation and alienation, whether it is the exposure of sham, the spatialization and quantification of experience or the massive economic irrationality of the whole system.

All such description is forced to describe what is, in the light of different modulations of what is not. What has been, what might have been, what should or might be. Can we describe the present in terms of its becoming what it is not-yet—a term of Ernest Block's, so frightening, so ominous, so cataclysmic, that it is sometimes easier to see the present already darkened by the shadow of a thermonuclear apocalypse, than either to envisage further declensions from that from which our nostalgia absents us, or to see a redemptive dialectic immanent in the vortex of accelerating change.

At all events, we are bemused and crazed creatures, strangers to our true selves, to one another, and to the spiritual and material world—mad, even, from an ideal standpoint we can glimpse but not adopt.

We are born into a world where alienation awaits us. We are potentially men, but are in an alienated state, and this state is not simply a natural system. Alienation as our present destiny is achieved only by outrageous violence perpetrated by human beings on human beings. (pp. xiii-xv)

> *R. D. Laing, in his* The Politics of Experience [*and*] The Bird of Paradise *(copyright © R. D. Laing, 1967; reprinted by permission of Penguin Books Ltd.), Penguin Books, 1967, 156 p.*

THE TIMES LITERARY SUPPLEMENT

[In *Sanity, Madness and the Family* R. D. Laing and A. Esterson] have a new approach to the perennial problem of schizophrenia. They are psychoanalysts who believe that the condition or mode of behaviour which psychiatrists call "schizophrenia" is an intelligible response to certain kinds of family situation rather than an "illness". . . .

The striking feature which emerged from [the authors' interviews with the families of twenty-five female schizophrenics] was the difference between the way in which the schizophrenic person regarded herself and the way in which her parents and other members of the family regarded her. Schizophrenics appear to be compliant and "good" children; but their inner life is usually totally at variance with their external demeanour, and, in a number of examples, there appears to have been no support within the family for the schizophrenic person's true identity.

Whether or not the author's views are enough to account for the whole phenomenology of schizophrenia must be considered doubtful. For although they produce much evidence in their interviews of grossly contradictory parental attitudes which must undoubtedly have baleful effects upon the children, it might be supposed that such contradictory attitudes are common enough not to be sufficient cause alone to produce a schizophrenic child.

Nevertheless this is a most valuable and stimulating piece of research, and one which deserves most careful study and extension.

> *"Schizophrenic Studies," in* The Times Literary Supplement *(© Times Newspapers Ltd. (London) 1964; reproduced from* The Times Literary Supplement *by permission), No. 3253, July 2, 1964, p. 568.*

ROBERT COLES

As a psychiatrist I [find R. D. Laing's writing in *The Politics of Experience*] quite literally stunning. I am overpowered by the challenges he dares make to what has become a rather conventional profession, very much the property of (and a source of solace to) the upper middle-class American, this century's *civis Romanus*. To Laing, we psychiatrists are something else, too: willing custodians, who for good pay agree to do the bidding of society by keeping tab on various "deviants," and in the clutch "taking care" of them—the double meaning of the verb being exactly to the point.

There seems to be something seriously wrong with Dr. Laing: he doesn't believe that the educated, literate and often enough psychoanalyzed Americans and Englishmen who read his books are without exception alert, vital and honest people. As a matter of fact he asserts that they commonly are the dead rather than the quick, well behaved rather than alive. In a word, they do not experience—"life," one another, the ridiculous and the sublime that the world offers so freely. (p. 26)

[*The Politics of Experience*] is organized around a discussion of "experiences," whether they be called psychotherapeutic, schizophrenic, or transcendental. Even more, he asks the reader to experience this book, to meet rather than understand at a distance the mind of R. D. Laing—a doctor, a writer, a human being trying to live enthusiastically and suffer honorably. What troubles Laing, however, is his conviction that he will fail, that deaf ears and blind eyes are everywhere, particularly among those who declare books "interesting" and those who "treat" what they call "syndromes." Intellectuals, he feels, turn the writer's passion into academic capital, ideas that come and go. Psychiatrists convert the experience of talking with another person, sweating it out with him, into one more icy, abstract "process."

We have, then, a psychiatrist who doesn't seem to distinguish between sanity and madness. On the contrary, he appears to be worried about us, the "well adjusted" men and women that society values so very much. He sees us educating our children "to lose themselves and to become absurd, and thus to be normal." Then he adds: "Normal men have killed perhaps 100,000,000 of their fellow normal men in the last fifty years." (pp. 26-7)

Laing also despairs, and tells why in this book. We are in the same sinking ship, oppressor and victim. Men of success live haunted and frightened by the climb they have made over the minds, bodies and rights of others. What they did to their neighbor can be done to them—and that goes for nations as well as individuals. As for the "failures," they have their "problems" too, everything from hunger to the sense of worthlessness "we" make sure "they" feel. Laing devotes a whole chapter to "us" and "them," to the ways we cut off others, deny them in desperate spite the humanity we ourselves have lost. He also insists that psychiatrists have allowed themselves to be separated from their patients, to categorize them rather than learn from them and with them, to use "the economic metaphor," so that one hears physicians talk of emotions "invested" and "objects" gained or lost. In sum, because of their emphasis on "function," on getting people "going" or "adjusted" (to what?) Laing views his colleagues as captives of their own amoral pragmatism.

Dr. Laing is no glib and smart-aleck critic, masquerading as a psychiatrist. He has a good deal of clinical research to his credit, much of it done with schizophrenics and their families. . . . He sees schizophrenia as a "special strategy that a person invents in order to live in an unlivable situation." He does not know why some people (rather than others) feel so utterly, decisively thwarted, but he wants insanity understood as an effort to reach out, to break out; and further, he wants it understood as potentially something more, something "transcendental." Madness is not only confusion and loss, an inner world of ideas, voices, shapes and impulses asserting itself like never before; madness is a radical departure, and Laing sees it as "potentially liberation and renewal."

It is refreshing to read his discussion of insanity, even if one does not accept his viewpoint completely. He is not out to blame anyone, or call people thinly disguised (psychiatric) names. He isn't hammering away at the weakness, the morbidity, the deviance of people. Nor does he glorify or romanticize madness; he wants to understand it, to see it for the universal and quite human condition that it is. He knows what many of his colleagues think, how they scan minds for "disorders of thinking" and sign commitment papers, one after another, so that patients—they are sick, sick, sick—will get "treatment." He asks what kind of treatment, and from whom. Will the psychiatrist under the best circumstances be someone highly trained but ultimately condescending, more interested in getting the patient to be like others than in finding out where he himself is going, and would like to go? (pp. 27-8)

[Since Dr. Laing realizes that in every society children are subjected to some kind of conformist restraint], the reader must ask why he as a psychiatrist objects so strenuously to what he knows to some extent is inevitable. As a matter of fact the book's real value stands or falls on whether the author makes his criticisms unqualified to the point of irrelevance. Will we hear once again, and from a psychiatrist this time, that children are by nature *only* sensitive, kind or honorable, and destined to remain so were it not for the thieves and cheats who teach them and rule them, let alone bring them into the world? Are we to understand that things have to be pulled inside out, that madness is sanity and sanity the worst kind of madness? Are the murky existentialist words going to replace the dumb psychiatric ones—say "authenticity" for "mental health"? Do we have yet another author who tears down everything around with a certain vindictive relish but has not a damn thing to offer the millions who don't read him, who live outside of his coterie and whom he can only grant the scorn of his pity?

In my opinion, Laing comes off very well on such questions. He acknowledges the demonic and chaotic in man, and he does not try to make a religion out of psychosis. ("Certain transcendental experiences. . . . I am not saying, however, that psychotic experience necessarily contains this element more manifestly than sane experience.") In other words, he holds to the *reality* of madness, but insists upon its integrity—and so emerges as only a man, with precisely that "status," a knowing and searching human being rather than a self-important doctor.

Unquestionably, he is thoroughly dissatisfied with what 20th-century industrial society does to the minds of people; and he is equally unhappy with the way psychiatrists generally manage to avoid facing sticky and controversial problems like that one. He will not have his profession used to "cure" those who dare question social or political absolutes, and even more radically, he is willing to find madness—in some cases—a necessary way station or a point of departure in a spiritual voyage all too few people care or dare to make, particularly since if they do the middle-class world will shun them, mock them and when they make enough "trouble," cart them off.

At the end of the book Laing demonstrates what he means by offering us first a "case-history" and then in a chapter called "The Bird of Paradise," his own flight of fancy and terror. These last pages do not read easily, and at times I could not understand what was before me, which may be the author's point about me, you, and him—that in today's world we barely can hold on to the senses we are still permitted, let alone call them ours or convey their "meaning" to others. In any event the book as a whole presents an exceptionally courageous psychiatrist who is willing to plumb his own depths and challenge head-on the hypocrisy and duplicity of his own profession and the larger society of which it is so prominent a part. I can only hope that he will be heard and heard respectfully. . . . Nor do I think Dr. Laing deserves the eager company of the psychoanalytically disenchanted, a growing minority in America today. It seems to me that he is trying to give the essence of Freud's journey . . . a particular kind of historical, political and philosophical perspective. I do not think he means to deny the validity of the analytic method; quite the contrary, it has enabled much of his vision. The point anyway is not to pit views against one another, but find whatever coherence possible out of them all—without resort to ideological squabbles. Freud called himself a conquistador, and if the bookkeepers and bureaucrats have now descended upon the psychoanalytic "movement" in droves to claim his mantle, all the more reason for a man like Laing to stand fast as the psychoanalyst he is.

When I finished this unusual and troubling book, I thought of Bob Dylan and the loneliness he has described squeezing at people, the things they do to distract themselves, and the obligation to be compassionate that anyone who would criticize them must feel. I think that Laing shares a similar sense of horror, a similar spirit of generosity, and not always do we find in one man that range of sensibility. (pp. 28, 30)

Robert Coles, ''Life's Madness'' (reprinted by permission of the author; © 1967 by Robert Coles; in The New Republic, *Vol. 156, No. 19, May 13, 1967, pp. 24-8, 30.*

ROLLO MAY

The directness and single-minded honesty with which Ronald Laing [asks what it means to be human is what makes *The Politics of Experience*] so refreshing and compelling. (p. 37)

What is refreshing and exciting in Laing is not his glorification of the irrational—of which he is sometimes accused by psychiatrists and psychologists who preach adaptation—but his frank challenge: "Adaptation to what? To society? To a mad world?" To Laing the height of irrationality is adjusting to what is called "normal"—to a world of Vietnam, a world in which cities not only poison their citizens physically through air pollution but shrink the individual's consciousness, a world in which "machines are already becoming better at communicating with each other than human beings with human beings. The situation is ironical. More and more concern about communication, less and less to communicate."

Laing's constructive contribution has been to blend the interpersonal theory of Harry Stack Sullivan with an existential, phenomenological foundation. (p. 38)

I do not agree with a main criticism of Laing—that he glorifies schizophrenia. Rather, he humanizes it. In this humanizing, Laing's words have in them the ring of Blake and Dostoevsky in literature, and of Sullivan in psychiatry.

Nevertheless there remains a real problem in Laing's work. If, with respect to psychic problems, he rejects the concept of "illness," what criteria, what norms does he have as alternatives? What structure does he propose that he, and the rest of us, build upon? His writings, which in this book have a somewhat fragmentary character, may well be misunderstood and misused as a justification for mere "feeling" or anti-intellectualism. Or his work may be taken as indicating that if the truth is not readily at hand by our rational methods, LSD and other drugs will open the magic doors to new truth. . . .

Laing himself is no anti-intellectual; he thinks with dedication and profundity. But the tension in consciousness of holding together such different streams of thought and science—the task that Laing essays—is great indeed. And consequently the tendency to slide into anarchy or go off on disintegrating tangents is also great. Laing has developed a framework in his ontological bases, and taken important steps toward a science of interpersonal relationship. We can hope he will be able to continue building on both, for he has much to give. (p. 39)

> *Rollo May, "The Frontiers of Being Human," in*
> Saturday Review *(copyright © 1967 by* Saturday Review; *all rights reserved; reprinted by permission),*
> *Vol. 50, No. 20, May 20, 1967, pp. 37-9.*

THEODORE SOLOTAROFF

Laing's relatively brief career has been marked by a steady expansion of interests from the clincial to the social and by a personal development from the detachment of the analyst to the passionate inwardness of the critic and lately of the prophet. "Detachment" is not quite the right word, though. Laing's first book, *The Divided Self,* is for all of its calm, dispassionate tone, one of the most moving accounts of madness I have ever read as well as the clearest. Its strength derives from Laing's insistence on viewing his schizoid and psychotic patients as persons rather than as cases. He explains their behavior as an effort to preserve their lives in a world that has been made unlivable for them by their early formative relationships—relationships that have bred an anxiety that pervades their existence as thoroughly as coldness pervades the existence of an Eskimo. This state of "ontological insecurity" creates a terrible logic; to preserve his small sense of aliveness, reality, and integrity, the person constructs a "false self" that draws attention and threat away from his "true self" and also enables him to function to the extent that he can in the real world. At the same time, however, this splitting of the person's being progressively worsens the problem that it sought to manage by depriving the "true self" of any sustenance save that of fantasy and by making the functioning of the false self increasingly compulsive and artificial. This basic dilemma spawns a variety of subsidiary ones, and when the torments of the division become intolerable, the schizoid person will decide either to murder his self or abruptly begin to act out his true self despite everything. Either decision is likely to produce a psychosis.

All of which is meant to describe not a "disease" but rather a state of radical privation (and a desperate struggle to cope with it) that is all too human. Laing beautifully fleshes out this analysis by descriptions of the character and experiences of his patients that are to the usual case histories what Hamlet is to those scholarly disquisitions on his motives. Indeed, Laing's portraits of "David," "an adolescent Kierkegaard played by Danny Kaye"; of "Peter," an apparently robust young man who was at home only with dogs, who lived, as he put it, "on the fringe of being," and who was "driven by a terrible sense of honesty to *be* nothing"; of "Marie," a girl suffering from acute contactlessness who cured herself by going for a week to see *La Strada*—these and others form a gallery in *The Divided Self* of the radically abused and injured victims of the common life that not only demonstrate Laing's theories about the integrity of madness but also make the book a deep literary experience.

In a recent preface to a new edition of *The Divided Self,* however, Laing expresses a dissatisfaction with the book: "I was already partially falling into the trap I was seeking to avoid. I [was] still writing . . . too much about Them and too little of Us." Much of his intervening work, particularly that in *Reason and Violence,* which he wrote with David Cooper and directly under the influence of Sartre, has sought to relate the sources of individual alienation not only to the family background but also to the broader social norms that govern the relations between the individual and others. In his new book, *The Politics of Experience,* Laing has reached the extreme position to which many younger intellectuals are being driven today by the manifest brutality and absurdity of these norms. . . . (pp. 218-19)

The Politics of Experience thus goes well beyond the Freudian resolution of civilization and its discontents. Laing argues that society is not only sexually and instinctually repressive but also that its steady barrage of pseudo-reality alienates us from our senses and sense, impoverishes and destroys our experience. This "condition of alienation—of being asleep—of being unconscious, of being out of one's mind, is the condition of the normal man. . . . If our experience is destroyed, we have lost our own selves."

The Politics of Experience is both a technical and prophetic exploration of the processes of this destruction: of what we do to each other and to ourselves as alienated beings. There are the defense mechanisms that keep the Other off, that protect us by means of self-mystification from the fear and trembling of what little freedom to be ourselves and to relate positively to others survives. Such mechanisms, as Laing keeps insisting, are not merely personal but trans-personal: in insidiously aggressive ways they distort the Other's experience and turn him into a thing. Similarly, Laing wishes us to realize that the largest sum of these trans-personal alienating mechanisms is the society, the state. How much alienation, for example, is being inflicted at present both on the Vietnamese and on ourselves by those mystified defense mechanisms with which we are "containing Communism"? "In order to rationalize our industrial-military complex," Laing says, "we have to destroy our capacity to see clearly any more what is in front of, and to image what is beyond, our noses. Long before a thermonuclear war can come about, we have had to lay waste our own sanity."

Such assertions are, of course, prevalent today. Contemporary politics makes apocalyptics of us all. The question is how much authority Laing's picture of our alienation carries. *The Politics of Experience* suffers from being made up of papers that were originally intended for special audiences, whether those that read psychiatric journals or the *New Left Review.* As a result, the writing tends to be often baldly assertive and elliptical and often lacks the rigorously sustained development of his ideas that one finds in *The Divided Self.* But, more crucially, I think Laing has fallen victim to the kind of literary terrorism that our chronic desperation encourages: what might be called the "signaling through the flames" school of writing. The trouble is that desperation is not enough. We are all desperate. The notions of freedom on which Laing grounds his analysis of man—good existentialist that Laing is—require that we be responsible for the attitude we bring to the experience of fragmentation, contactlessness, violence, that we try to hold together the whole man in ourselves, in all his abiguities, even as he is being daily torn apart. In a sense we are, as Laing says, "all murderers and prostitutes . . . no matter how normal, moral, or mature we take ourselves to be," just as we are all, to a greater or less degree, schizoid. But we merely begin to mystify ourselves, and to foster further alienation, when we try to substitute these definitions for our experience of being in the world. The ugliness of one feeling does not cancel out the decency of another, just as the dehumanization of children in one household does not mean that pre-psychotics are also being created next door.

The overwhelming problem that all sensitive men face today is to maintain their balance, and not to con themselves by believing, as Laing says he does, that the worst has already happened. Curiously enough, the most convincing pages of *The Politics of Experience* are those devoted to the sanity and spirituality of "madness," rather than those that seem devoted to driving the rest of us out of our "wretched minds." Which is perhaps only to say that Laing writes best when he writes from the integrity of his own experience and eschews the temptation to make a total, vague, and baiting politics of it. (pp. 220-21)

> Theodore Solotaroff, "The Uses of Madness," in Book Week—The Washington Post (© 1967 Postrib Corp.; reprinted by permission of Chicago Tribune and The Washington Post), July 9, 1967 (and reprinted in "The Red Hot Vacuum" and Other Pieces on Writing in the Sixties, Atheneum, 1970, pp. 217-21).

DAVID INGLEBY

[*Self and Others*] is a 'new and revised edition' of [a book] first published in 1961, but it will be a great pity if its appearance is neglected on that score: for Laing has not simply rewritten, but painstakingly rethought, the whole book. It would be missing the point to say that the result is a better book (though it is, both in readability and construction): the point is that it is a different book by a different author. For by a familiar delayed-action process, the ideas Laing originally put together have forced new implications on their author, challenging the very framework in which they were first expressed.

Most importantly, it now appears that Laing was seriously led astray before by imagining that he was what he appeared to be, a psychiatrist: his earlier exploration of the unconscious 'social phantasy systems' in which people are for the most part immersed was not simply narrowed, but actually led off the scent, by being conducted as a psychopathological exercise. (Even if Laing himself was not so misled, he still remains for most people primarily a man who writes about schizophrenics.) To be sure, Laing always questioned the nature of the 'reality' which psychotic patients are supposed to be 'out of touch with': but actually to examine the 'reality' of normal people with the critical severity customarily reserved for deviants is an activity totally at variance with the psychiatrist's role in society—a species of grave professional misconduct.

Laing's repudiation here of the last vestiges of the psychiatric stance has, however, inevitable self-destructive consequences. To question socially accepted notions of reality is (to the extent that one lives and breathes in this reality) to dismantle the vehicle of one's own thought: hence, having refocused his microscope at this level, Laing discovers through its lens many of his own habits of thought. This, of course, is why the book had to be rewritten: and one suspects that the process is far from complete. (pp. 733-34)

[We] find Laing still using concepts of identity ('true' and 'false') quite freely—he speaks assuredly, for example, of 'the obligation one has to oneself, to be oneself': but for Laing to use concepts like identity straightfacedly, when he feels obliged

to bracket them off with quotation marks in other people's usage, points to an unresolved conflict of meaning. In the end, one feels that Laing's revision was doomed to incompleteness: a man can only imperfectly separate himself from the system of social thought in which he is brought up, and there are logical as well as psychological barriers standing in the way of any such critique from within.

By comparison with this shift in the focus of Laing's analysis, the other noticeable changes in the book are of secondary importance, though still significant. In the first place, Laing has worked out some inevitable conflicts between the twin disciplines on which his work is founded, psychoanalysis and phenomenology. If phenomenology sets out to understand people's behavior in terms of their experience of the world, while psychoanalysis places unconscious phantasy at the root of this experience, what is the experiential status of phantasy itself? In this revision, Laing is careful to dissociate himself from the psychoanalytic idiom of 'unconscious experience', whereby 'too many, not all, psychoanalysts plunge right in and out of a revolving door at the threshold of phenomenology'. In attempting to sort out this morass of concepts, however, Laing plunges into another revolving door—and stays there going around in circles: since analytical philosophy is what Laing gives every appearance of trying to do in Chapter I, it seems odd in such a scholarly book that no recourse is had to philosophical psychology of the analytical variety.

The last revision to comment on here is perhaps the most welcome. By countless alterations and rearrangements, Laing has subtly transformed the book's whole style: and this change is as much part of his altered stance as the book's revised content. Having ceased to be the psychiatrist, Laing has adopted a lucid prose style in contrast to which much of the earlier version now appears mannered, aloof, and unnecessarily opaque: this change of style also betokens a change in his relationship to his audience, and a shift in our intellectual climate (where such ideas as Laing's, being no longer alien or exotic, can now be presented without such façades of technicalities).

Not many writers, one imagines, would have what it takes to 'revise' a book, in Laing's sense of the word. (p. 734)

> David Ingleby, "Revisionist," in New Statesman (©1969 The Statesman & Nation Publishing Co. Ltd.), Vol. 78, No. 2019, November 21, 1969, pp. 733-34.

MARSHALL BERMAN

[In **"The Divided Self"** R. D. Laing] has "decoded" the language of schizophrenics, and transmitted some of what they are trying to tell us. Much of what they are saying, he makes clear, is "existential truth"; and very often it is a truth that we do not want to hear.

How do schizophrenics get that way? In recent years there has been much evidence that it may be essentially genetic and hereditary. Laing neither accepts nor rejects this hypothesis. He believes, however, that if schizophrenia did not biologically exist, our culture would invent it. So many people seem inexorably driven to it, trapped in environments which destroy their sense of identity before it has any chance to develop.

Laing brings to life a great variety of these insulted and injured people. . . .

Laing's attempt to get at the "existential truth" of what his patients are saying leads him to investigate the context in which they are saying it. In **"The Divided Self,"** and further in **"Sanity, Madness and the Family, Volume One: Families of Schizophrenics"** . . . he focuses on family structures, and analyzes brilliantly the psychic pressures they generate. . . .

Under such pressure, out of total insecurity, the individual constructs a network of defenses, which Laing calls a *false-self system*. The purpose of a false-self system, he explains, is to split the self off from all its activities. Thus the self is "uncoupled" from the body: the body becomes merely one object among other objects in the world, the core of a "false" self; the "true" self is felt as something detached, disembodied, hidden within.

Thus the true self is protected from participation in the life of a world that is set up to destroy it. From now on the self will be purely a spectator; it will observe, judge and criticize whatever the body, that alien object, happens to be experiencing or doing, but it will not get involved. It will leave no fingerprints or footprints in the world. It will be a stranger in a strange land. Divided, the self may be able to stand; united, it will surely fall.

"But the tragic paradox," writes Laing, "is that the more the self is defended in this way, the more it is destroyed. The apparent eventual destruction and dissolution of the self in schizophrenic conditions is accomplished not by external attacks from the enemy (actual or supposed), from without, but by the devastation caused by the inner defensive manoeuvers themselves." If the shut-up self cannot be enriched by outer experience, its whole inner world will become more and more impoverished; it will find even less living space within its citadel than it had outside. Inner life will be felt as empty, cold, dry, impotent, desolate, worthless, dead; the self will suffocate within its own walls. Worse: the false-self system will be felt as a fifth column, a base for the enemy; every move, every breath comes to be controlled and directed by hostile, destructive forces—by a mother or father, by the authorities, by "Them"—that are continually closing in. The self grows desperate to break out. But outside it sees only the malignant power structure that drove it inward in the first place. There is nowhere for the individual to go. So he goes mad.

"The Divided Self" vibrates with the excitement of discovery, a discovery that resonates far beyond the hospital gates. Laing is steeped in modern literature and existentialist philosophy. He is aware, and he makes us aware, how much of our whole modern sensibility and awareness is rooted in the radical doubt and anxiety that permeates schizophrenics' whole lives; he evokes the alienation they feel with a vividness that strikes a sympathetic chord in all of us. Their dread of nameless threats embedded in everyday life, their sense of aloneness and emptiness, of the precariousness of a person's being—all this is fundamental to our culture. Laing points it out in Baudelaire and Kierkegaard and Dostoevsky, in Kafka and Eliot and Yeats, in Beckett and Genet. (p. 2)

[Laing asserts boldly in **The Divided Self**] that, from its deepest roots, our whole society is mad. Indeed, he suggests, the only difference between his schizophrenic patients and "normal" men is that his patients know that they are mad, while normal men deceive themselves into thinking that they are sane. . . .

[Laing's most recent writings] focus on the dilemma of psychiatry in a sick society. In **"Self and Others,"** Laing generalizes the conceptual scheme he developed in **"The Families of Schizophrenics"**: all social relationships, it appears, are closed "fantasy systems" whose members are alienated from themselves. Some members of these systems (few? most? all? Laing is very abstract here, and the reader is left to infer the worst) are placed in "untenable positions," in which "it is impossible to leave and impossible to say." They are physically up against the wall.

The members of any social fantasy system are taught by "Them," the authorities, to believe that "the box," the system, "is the whole world." It follows from this premise that the only way to get out of the box is to "step off the end of the world"— to go mad; and Laing has shown us how fearful going mad can be. Hopefully, the authorities are wrong. If they are wrong, then there are (in principle) ways for the self to get out of the box and to live sanely and happily in the world. But what if the authorities are right? What if the box *really* is the whole world? Then madness, terrifying as it may be, is the only way for the self to survive. And Laing seems to suggest that everyone should indeed go mad.

Is the self really so totally boxed in? Laing does not make a very good case to back up his drastic indictment: his discussion of our social system is disappointingly abstract, moralistic, derivative, unconvincing; his feeling for ambiguity and contradiction, his sense of tragedy, seem to disappear. Our common sense tells us to dismiss Laing's indictment out of hand, and probably our common sense is right. And yet, having once said this, it is hard not to feel uneasy. Laing's view of society may strike us as paranoid, even schizophrenic; but it is a paranoia that strikes deep, and it creeps imperceptibly into our minds. . . .

Can madness really be a way back into ourselves? We must take very seriously Laing's argument that it can. It can, he says, if we go mad only for awhile, and only under very carefully controlled conditions. Then madness can propel us out of the box, and can liberate all the feelings that the box has kept locked up. Thus "the cracked mind of the schizophrenic may let in light which does not enter the intact minds of many sane people whose minds are closed." Madness may bring to the surface all our repressed fear, rage, hatred, violence and despair; but this opening up can also release all our repressed hope and love and creativity, all our buried feeling for life. We must let go, Laing believes, because only if we lose ourselves can we authentically find ourselves. . . .

The life and energy of Laing's vision—in his practice as well as his books—creates a little more open space for the self in the world. It is this that so many respond to. In a time when the open spaces are being closed off fast, Laing can at least give us a start in the direction we need to go. To have made such a start may be, in the end, the best thing the 1960's can leave to the hard times ahead. (p. 44)

Marshall Berman, "'The Divided Self' and 'Self and Others'," in The New York Times Book Review *(© 1970 by The New York Times Company; reprinted by permission), February 22, 1970, pp. 1-2, 44.*

NORMAN N. HOLLAND

R. D. Laing is but the latest . . . medicine man [using psychoanalysis or quasi-psychoanalysis to turn guru, and his nostrum in *The Divided Self* and *Self and Others*] combines a bit of mysticism with a touch of Marx in an engagingly anti-military, anti-imperialist program one can hardly disagree with.

But one can't derive it from schizophrenia, either, even with Laing's marvelous eloquence and sensitivity. . . .

Frankly, I think that to anyone who has loved a schizophrenic, suffered with or through one, or who has even walked through a chronic ward, [Laing's analysis] is cruel and vicious nonsense, but, I suppose, I may be doing Laing an injustice. He has aided some people, and nobody working with schizophrenics can claim more, for cures are sporadic, unpredictable and not understood. Laing, however, claims much more: a total understanding of the origins of the disease and its benefits as a psychedelic experience. . . .

[One] can justly doubt any account of the disease that neglects the genetic and chemical factors obviously present or, much more irresponsibly, the agony, nightmare and even suicide so many victims suffer. Less mesmeric workers like Searles or Bion, to name but two, will do more in the long run for the schizophrenic than Laing's existential flights of fancy which make more of an invitation to schizophrenia than a cure for it.

I am prepared to take Laing seriously as a dedicated therapist, but when he turns ontologist, he poses quite another set of questions, those of a metaphysic or a poetry. Why does his Mary Baker Eddy stance appeal? Why, at this troubled moment, does a writer on schizophrenia become a general seer? Why, for example, have my graduate students (in English, naturally) taken most seriously for three or four years now this psychiatric writer little heeded and very often . . . not even heard of by professionals? Laing is evidently saying something the student generation wants to hear. What is it, and why do they want it? (p. 569)

Orality is good, Laing is saying, and that is what youth wants to hear. Oral traits permeate youth culture: the deliberate blurring of the boundaries of self through hallucinogens, groupsex, unisex, and commune; the verbal blurring of distinctions in speech, among them the revolutionary violence of mouth and bullhorn; the feeling of a timeless "Now" filled with joys out of one's own mind; the re-creation in new social settings of love-hate encounters with parent-substitutes perceived as "power" (the strike as tantrum); the narcissistic belief in oneself and one's mates as unaggressive and perfectible; the masochistic joy when others (cf., *Easy Rider*) prove by their distrust and anger their contrasting fallibility. . . .

[Laing] is not important for what he says so much as for who listens. He speaks for the blurrings of youth culture, as in the kind of paradox he loves: "A little girl of seventeen in a mental hospital told me she was terrified because the Atom Bomb was inside her. That is a delusion. The statesmen of the world who boast and threaten that they have Doomsday weapons are far more dangerous, and far more estranged from 'reality.' . . ." If we put the moral issue aside, the psychological line stands out sharply: the statesmen are acting phallicly, the girl orally.

Laing, speaking to his oral admirers, wants to blur the boundary out of existence, while an Agnew, say, speaking for *his* phallic constituency, wants to make it a Maginot line. Neither guides us any more truly than a TV commercial, but Laing is the guru at issue here. Dr. Laing may help his particular patients, but Preacher Laing offers only total immersion in already troubled waters. (p. 570)

Norman N. Holland, "Medicine Man," *in* The Nation (*copyright 1970* The Nation *magazine,* The Nation Associates, Inc.*), Vol. 210, No. 18, May 11, 1970, pp. 569-70.*

WILLIAM F. LYNCH

[R. D. Laing's argument in *The Divided Self* and *Self and Others*] about madness versus society is powerful but complicated.

The kind of human being Laing, or any psychologist worthy of his salt, wants is one who is thoroughly separated out from the world (ontologically secure in his autonomy) and solidly, reasonably related to the world. These two factors, autonomy and relationship, do not destroy each other but interpenetrate and help to create each other. But much of Laing begins to be understood with great clarity as we follow his study of the corruption of these two great forces (of the inner and outer life) and their tragic polarization. . . .

It is these sharply conceived images of an empty inner life and a mechanical outer life within a conforming and technological culture that are now making it possible for Laing's books to re-emerge as symbols and explanations of present social woe and many madnesses. He has done a particularly forceful job in his description of the ways in which the false and external self becomes more and more extensive in its operations. Instead of achieving that new autonomy without which we cannot live, it moves more and more into a destructive form of autonomy which really means separation from any form of true self and alienation from true inwardness; it becomes more and more dead and mechanical. And surely there must be an inward rage and terror present underneath. So the man goes from being good, to being bad, to being mad. Madness is being described as an existential solution to an existential situation. It is also the search for the 'bright gold,' for the pearl at the bottom of the sea. (p. 484)

I have two quite radically different judgments on the work of Laing. The first is that from the very first occasion of coming upon him some years ago he emerged as a sharp and exciting thinker whom I recommended to others. I still do.

My second judgment is that these two books, especially *The Divided Self*, now stand in dire need of supporting volumes or else they are in danger of becoming sources of polarization, cliche and stereotype themselves. If we use the topology of the outer false self and the inner empty self too indiscriminately, if we do not break this topology down into all kinds of separate problems, and if we extend the wasteland image of the world to the point of paranoia, as we have, then we may be doing the popular but not the scientific thing. On the one hand this mad world is indeed driving us mad; on the other hand it is our mad selves that have made the mad part of the world. We are again in the middle of the perpetual quarrel between Pascal and Rousseau.

Again, I for one do not like this decisive distinction between false self and true self. We need a better mix in our time than that and it is hard to say which is the more unendurable with false selves or true selves.

Finally, a word about madness as a solution. There are many forms of madness that are not worth talking about. They are chosen as a solution, but solve nothing. But the creative and frightening return to an inward life that will restore the sense of self as a preface to social reality is what R. D. Laing is really talking about; of course it is the great need, really solving everything. I wish that he would responsibly write several more books on the various forms of this madness. He has it in him to do it. (pp. 484-85)

William F. Lynch, "Books: 'The Divided Self' and 'Self and Others'," in Commonweal *(copyright © 1970 Commonweal Publishing Co., Inc.; reprinted by permission of Commonweal Publishing Co., Inc.), Vol. XCII, No. 20, September 25, 1970, pp. 484-85.*

JAMES S. GORDON

[In **"Knots,"**] Laing continues to explore some of the themes that have been prominent in his work since 1958. The emphasis is on disorders of human communications and feelings, their origins in the family, and their tortured, mutually unsatisfactory elaboration in later relationships. But in **"Knots,"** Laing has abandoned his ordinarily graceful prose for highly condensed poems, the knots of the title. Poetry, the most personal of the literary arts, is used as a medium for highly formal philosophical and psychological descriptions which themselves delineate intensely personal experiences.

The knots are "patterns . . . of human bondage," descriptions of the bonds (or binds) that people—parents and children, lovers, friends, therapists and patients—put each other and themselves in. They are meticulously constructed, often hilariously and painfully recognizable. But they do not yield easily. Several readings—preferably aloud—are sometimes not enough. Each reader, after their initial dizzying resistance is overcome, will probably untie them differently. . . .

Sometimes the small knots proceed in a developmental sequence. . . .

The large knot of which [the small knots are] a part climaxes in a series of variations on the theme of differentiation between the self and the world, the "me" and "not me," the "mine" and "not mine." The formal logic seems hopelessly complex, its component propositions mutually contradictory. But the impossibility of logical explanation of this earliest stage of human development is in a creative tension with the process itself. . . .

The roots of interpersonal relations are seen to dwell in the same soil as religious mysticism. One feels the connection between the infant's struggle to define what is inside his body and what is outside and the mystic's strenuous denial of this separation, but both these pursuits are seen as "webs of *maya*" against a more remote background. Everything that Laing has described, everything that has gone before, as well as what follows, may be illusory. . . .

Ultimately, descriptions which have delighted the reader and compelled him to mental gymnastics yield to that which cannot be described. The most basic human experiences and all the precise and elegant forms Laing has used to convey them—words, logic, music—have arisen out of formless silence. . . .

In his earlier work Laing guided the reader to understanding. In **"Knots"** he compels him to experience. The surface brilliance of phenomenological description gives way to the vortex of contradictions which make up the unconscious. To grasp this dense and difficult book one must be willing to follow Laing in his spirals of descent. If **"Knots"** is to yield, one must yield to the knots.

James S. Gordon, "'Knots'," in The New York Times Book Review *(© 1970 by The New York Times Company; reprinted by permission), December 13, 1970, p. 6.*

DAVID MARTIN

The main methodological prescriptions of Laing are broadly of a kind with which the present writer is in sympathy. (p. 184)

Perhaps Laing's [methodological] position is best summarised in his own remark that one does not *have* schizophrenia, in the same way as one has the measles, one *is* schizophrenic. . . . Laing argues that at a certain point in the process of explanation some psychoanalysts cease to make their observations within the context of mutual exchange between persons and assume a one-sided superiority of objective external judgment towards the condition of the patient as if he were a mere biological organism. Both the personal relationship and 'the person' disappear.

There are several different points encapsulated here, and some confusion. For example, there is no necessary relation between stepping into an objective role for the purpose of 'judgment' and losing the reciprocity of a relationship. Indeed, there must be *some* assumption of superiority which the analyst will take up in his role as specialist in psychological dynamics, otherwise he is simply interacting with the other person. This need not be the almost absolute assumption characteristically made (say) by a consultant in relation to biological disease, since the patient is always himself experienced in what it is to be a human and often acquires insight comparable in kind if not usually in degree to that possessed by the analyst. The patient may even, in particular instances and in relation to particular aspects, have superior insight.

Presumably Laing is not objecting to the assumption that on the average and at the margin the psychoanalyst is more experienced and in a sense more objective than the patient, and therefore must on occasion step back for a 'review' on the basis of that experience, objectivity and detachment. Moreover, a doctor may recognise how marginal the superiority of his experience and how frail and partial his objectivity while not wanting to trumpet the fact to patients who are often specialists in using such admissions as means of avoiding whatever fragments of the truth the analyst has managed to acquire. He may also legitimately restrict the degree of reciprocity and involvement which he allows himself, since he, too, has to survive.

Yet there are real dangers here to which Laing points, though it is regrettable that some of his criticisms are not more specific. (pp. 185-86)

[Presumably Laing is] saying that reductionist assumptions lurking in the medical mind lead doctors to resort more frequently than is appropriate to drugs and to physicalist methods of dealing with particular problems, such as pre-frontal surgery and electric treatment. Occasionally he bothers to state this position in a qualified and commonsense form, but at other times the assault on his own profession must seem so extreme as to prevent fellow-doctors hearing what he has to say. (p. 188)

Laing's second main point with respect to methodological prescription concerns the relevance of the social context in interpreting individual psychology. This leads in two different directions: one is to establish the relevance of social context in any explanatory model of behaviour and the other involves a philosophical issue insofar as the positivistic abdication from value judgments prevents one seeing how the psychoanalyst is in his whole mode of operation expressing and executing the values of society. . . . This is an important point, however much overstated.

The point about the relevance of the social context is also genuinely helpful, but it suffers like almost all psychiatric excursions into sociology from excessive universalism. Let us take Laing's wholly acceptable remark about men qua men ultimately being free, choosing as well as 'chosen'. He both asserts this as a universal truth about the human person as such and refers to the nature of capitalist society as being a near-universal social context in which that freedom is deformed. Unless he appeals to contemporary communist society as *not* implicated in such deformations, which seems an unlikely and certainly an unpersuasive recourse, he is saying that developed society as such is a universal context within which freedom is distorted. Indeed, where he appeals to an alternative type of society he actually looks back to periods notorious for their deformation of the possibility of freedom, actually postulating in one instance a decline over the past thousand years. Since he firmly indicates no concrete milieu where deformations do *not* occur, one suspects that his category of society is not limited at all, even when it appears to have special reference to capitalist society: it is society *tout court* in all its historical manifestations hitherto which is at fault. *Vide* Freud. Thus we have two universals, the universality of freedom and the universal repressiveness of society as such.

Now it is worth asking here whether men are more or less free according to the *variations* in their social milieu, within societies as well as between them. (pp. 188-89)

I would agree with Laing that freedom is a universal option of humanity, but I would also want to know whether that affirmation, as stated by Laing, takes adequate account of the variation in its availability. At what levels of analysis is it universal, at what levels variable? (p. 190)

The points just made have been related to the variable cultural context of personal freedom and of institutionalised liberty, but they also can relate to Laing's general attempt to bring the social context into account as contributing to explanation of psychological phenomena. Laing does, of course, speak of the socialisation provided by the family, and very occasionally by the school, as agents of the general socialising process emanating from global society. But he gives almost no impression whatever of the hierarchy of status and class, the processes of aspiration, of mobility and peer-group formation, and all the vastly differentiated milieux in terms of cultural pattern from one area to another, town and country, north and south. He may describe very well a highly generalised social process such as the mechanisms of gossip and scandal by which everybody is caught up in a situation which thereby acquires its own autonomous momentum because each person is primarily concerned about what the other thinks. But while he refers to persons and to groups and to society, there is little particularised social and historical location through which the universal processes have to be channelled if they are to be truly explanatory.

This is perhaps more a complaint about psychiatry as such than about Laing, but it does indicate why the jeremiads and lamentations in which he engages refer so much and so indiscriminately to '*the* society', '*the* family', '*the* school' and so on. Since he seems not personally to have rejected the family, this suggests that some families in certain circumstances are better than others. The question is: which? By always referring to institutions in general, his work is a triumph of masterful evasion. (p. 191)

[One] must turn to a group of ideas and attitudes which provide a bridge passage between [Laing's] psychiatric stance and his politics: they are contained in the notion of the 'mystification of violence'. For Laing, a central element in the broader task of 'demystification' is an attempt to 'demystify' violence, and the essence of this task is to recover access to that direct experience which socialisation so succesfully violates and destroys. Socialisation, for him, is the local agent of that canalised institutional violence which is located in central government and which stalks society cloaked in the language and unspoken assumptions of the mass media. Socialisation is the first and primal violence against the person which can only be met by projecting violence on to others, acting violently towards them and justifying oneself by attributing violence to them. *It is this view of socialisation which links the experience of the family to politics, psychiatry to global issues, approaches to upbringing and pedagogical method to Vietnam.*

For people of this mind, all delimitation of issues, all academic division of scholarly labour, and all attempts to view phenomena objectively from a variety of specialised perspectives at different analytic levels, are part of a policy of divide in order to rule. There can be no taking apart of Humpty-Dumpty even in order to put him together again: the question is, as Humpty-Dumpty himself said, 'Who is master?' The appeal of this to the kind of young person looking for quick global answers, impatient with the requirements of careful study, and armed with a drifting paranoid suspicion of all authority, is obvious. The psychology of identifying a malevolent 'Them', which he describes, is unusually well developed in his followers.

Global accusation [as found in Laing], like libel and rumour, is easy: refutation, like art, is long and difficult. There is no answer to a grain of truth eked out by indiscriminate misrepresentation except a disciplined understanding. It would take too long; but one can at least begin by pointing to the central assumption, derived from Rousseau, that man as man is originally innocent, and civilisation, especially modern civilisation, the focus of original sin. Incidentally, it is interesting that this assumption links Laing with another large success in the field of commercial publishing: the type of egregious ethological speculation represented by [Desmond Morris's] *The Human Zoo* and *The Naked Ape*. In short there are those who see human institutions as dykes canalising a raw, variable, morally ambiguous human potential into the fructifying ways of civilisation, and those who see those institutions as barriers to a flood of inherent generosity, innate humanity and abounding creativity. Laing is of the latter.

That said, it is instructive to look more closely at what appears to be a very confused discussion [in *The Politics of Experience*] . . . which Laing conducts concerning socialisation, violence and value judgments. What he says is this. First, socialisation, including moral and political socialisation, is a violence against personal experience because it is socially derived and imposed rather than individually achieved. Now it is not clear how else moral perspectives can be derived in the first instance except from society, and it is even less clear that people do not, as they mature, partly transform what is so derived into a personal and critical perspective. Secondly, Laing argues that to regard animals and humans in a given scientific context as (e.g.) biochemical complexes is equivalent to a denial of their true nature as animals and persons; and such a context prevents those who adopt it from an ethical response when violence against men and animals is perpetrated.

Now there is a tiny grain of truth here, which is that a person specialising at a given level of scientific interest such as biochemistry may become so professionally deformed as to forget that what he studies is also a human being, may indeed refuse to acknowledge that in principle results may need to be reassimilated within a wider view which includes the specifically human. Humpty-Dumpty may lie shattered on the floor. It may even happen that such an attitude enters into a scientist's general moral perspective. But it happens to a certain degree to certain people, and the extent to which it does would require extensive documentation; unfortunately the techniques of the propagandist asserting the primacy of his 'genuine' human experience do not allow so wasteful an expenditure of intellectual energy in the cause of mere verification. It is more economical and more effective to say, 'Meanwhile Vietnam goes on.' And here, of course, one encounters a cheapness of effect which in Laing goes with this kind of intellectual economising. The situation in Vietnam is too appalling, the issues too confused, the murderous intent on both sides too typical of war at almost and times, for it to be used as a catch-all riposte by those too lazy or too frenetic to engage in honourable argument.

In any case, a more appropriate intellectual economy might have been employed, since what is being said is even more simple than appears. Laing is claiming that his value judgments are rooted in his genuine experience as a human being, whereas those who disagree with him are the deluded facsimiles of oversuccessful socialisation. He has not adequately considered the possibility that—to quote him from a different context—his opponents may be people like himself, dressed differently. They, too, may be human. (pp. 196-98)

This is the framework, these the plausible half and quarter-truths which are major keys to the syndrome of attitudes found in Laing. They are allied to a stress on the need for transcendence, which is in part a range of experience akin to mystical illumination which modern society is held to inhibit and denigrate and which is also an ability to see beyond the confines of one-dimensionality to another mode of social life. Since this is important, any exposition must include some reference to the religious elements found in Laing: our alienation from ecstasy and the problem of an original sin uniquely focused in capitalist society. . . . The crucial point for criticism of Laing is the contrast between his politics of experience and the experience of politics. (p. 200)

[Laing's] basic themes are simply found on a larger scale in *The Politics of Experience:* white western society, its governmental system, its methods of upbringing, its science and its scholarship are part of a tissue of delusion which is responsible for stereotyped divisions into 'us' and 'them', and is to blame for violence and counterviolence. We think 'they' are to blame; not at all, it is we who are to blame in the world. This is a simple diagnosis, easily achieved by standing an equally simple diagnosis on its head. The basic stratagem of this style of thinking is: if you want to know what to believe, find out what is the current consensus and turn it upside down; that way you won't necessarily be right but at least you won't inevitably be wrong. If, in addition, you hope for a hint as to what is right, listen to those whom society stigmatises as abnormal. They've got something.

As one proceeds to document the Laingian position one can hardly help noticing two characteristics in his own work which illustrate his own analysis of what constitutes a fundamentally irrational view of the world. One is the simple stereotyping of 'us' and 'them', encapsulated in vast assertions about what people in western societies think: a grandiose simplification of all issues achieved by stigmatising whole societies as solidary

elements in 'the Enemy'. No evidence is cited, just projections about what people in the disapproved societies are projecting about 'them'. This looks like an unfortunate example of the spiral perspectives in which Laing is himself a specialist. The other characteristic is the repetition on the macro-scale of what he describes as inherent in the experience of schizophrenia on the microscale. All other types of society *except* his own have some kind of ontological root, something which may be admired, some kind of right to exist. Only that which is his own constitutes a kind of delusion, a mass of subhumanity, suffering from ontological weightlessness. There is in Laing's writing not a single word suggesting that any virtue inheres in what is his own inheritance. So total a rejection, so wholehearted a separating out of the self from the body of society, so extraordinary a fear of becoming re-attached to it by fiendish subtleties, looks like a curious analogue of the self hating what is most truly its own. Perhaps the condition could be called macro-schizophrenia. (pp. 201-02)

Essentially the politics of experience are no adequate guide to the experience of politics; a denunciation is not a viable policy. It is this fact that should be the basis of any critical appraisal of the type of politico-religious awareness found in Laing. (p. 204)

[Laing] does not explicitly embrace irrationalism, and indeed he uses the word "irrational' to stigmatise institutions and activities of which he disapproves. However, in such instances he rarely tells us what he means by 'irrational' and one can only assume he uses the word simply as a stand-in for emotional disapproval. He can certainly be considered an irrationalist in that he finds rational and argued discussion of religious questions uncongenial, and insists that the essence of religion is ecstasy. And while it would be better to regard ecstasy as supra-rational rather than irrational, there is in Laing's whole style a *substitution* of ecstasy for argument and a disinclination to build up a sequence of ordered points, supported by carefully collected evidence, qualified in respect of this issue or that.

His method consists in random accusation and sloganised virulence, which destroys the possibility of genuine discussion. Patient refutation has to build up on a basis of carefully verified evidence, has to define its terms (whereas Laing simply prefers to use them) and eventually to build up a cumulative impression, usually in terms of more or less, of marginally this rather than that. Such a method cannot compete with a rhetorical either/or, with grossly simplified alternatives, with slogans used as an excuse for not thinking. You cannot talk with a man who throws his sincerity at you and who persistently implies that you and every other person who disagrees with him is a racialist, an anti-semite and a crass authoritarian. (p. 205)

Laing will not engage in rational argumentation because that is not the way converts are made. Laing is also an irrationalist in the sense that he proposes no means to achieve his vision, apart from offering vague hints about psychic subversion in the middle-range type of institution, such as the school and the university. He proposes no policies, articulates no alternatives, raises no queries about viability, weighs no costs and advantages, assesses no immediate and remote consequences. For obvious reasons: if he did, the whole visionary edifice would collapse like the baseless fabric of a dream. (pp. 205-06)

David Martin, "R. D. Laing" (© 1970 by Maurice Cranston; reprinted by permission of the author), in The New Left: Six Critical Essays, *edited by Maurice Cranston, Bodley Head, 1970 (and reprinted by The Library Press, 1971), pp. 179-208.*

ALAN TYSON

[The terms that Laing employs in *The Divided Self*] to describe his patients—terms such as self (whether true of false, embodied or unembodied, divided or undivided), security and insecurity, self-consciousness, reality and unreality, inner and outer—are for the most part close to popular speech and far removed from psychiatric jargon; but more importantly for him they are the language of *experience*—one of Laing's key words—and not merely of observation, description, classification, or categorization. (In another context he criticizes psychiatrists for seeming to be more concerned with a patient's behavior than with his experience.) Moreover they are terms of intrapersonal or interpersonal experience rather than of "it-processes." The latter two-thirds of the book—the schizoid and schizophrenic case histories—can be taken as a demonstration of the advantages in using this kind of language when attempting to make the experiences of such patients intelligible.

Within these chosen limits this demonstration is brilliantly successful. The memorable vignettes with which the book is crammed—of James, David, and of Peter, whose complaint was that "there was a constant unpleasant smell coming from him," of the more flamboyantly mad Joan and Julie, self-described as "the ghost of the weed garden"—distinguished the book as something of a landmark in descriptive writing on the fragmented personality, and in any event as an astonishing and admirable performance for a man of twenty-eight.

Particularly moving, perhaps, is the sense of pain that these case histories convey. The defensive maneuver, whereby, as Laing describes it, the self is divided, aims at preserving the "true self" while offering to the world both as ambassador and hostage a compliant persona (the "false self"). But the loss of integration is evidently extremely painful to bear. Most painful of all, it would seem from the case material, is the feeling of being split into a mind and a body, usually involving an identification with the mind and an alienation from the body. It is not perhaps surprising, in view of the widespread distribution of schizoid character traits, that the clinical material of *The Divided Self* evoked a cry of recognition from thousands of readers who felt that the dimensions of their own sense of alienation had been charted for the first time.

There are, of course, hazards in linking the structure of one's theory so closely to the inner experience of going or being mad. Although, as I have hinted, Laing's comments on the difficulties of finding language in which patients are to be discussed are often acute, they appear to be part of a less plausible attack on abstractions in general; he seems to have a horror of any abstraction that is not immediately intelligible in the language of the patient's inner experience. There may indeed be dangers in abstraction or reification, as he suggests, but there are also dangers in anthropomorphizing, as psychoanalytic theoreticians know. In his attempts to make even the apparently most bizarre statements that patients make about themselves meaningful in some way, Laing is led rather dangerously in the direction of saying that their statements are in a certain sense true. (pp. 3-4)

Within the limits set by the size of [*Sanity, Madness and the Family*] the presentation is exemplary. There is no doubt that for most readers these eleven families, with their stifling atmospheres, their subtle emotional blackmail systems, their killing by kindness, become palpable, so that the deforming pressures to which the daughters were exposed are easy to grasp. And by the end of the book most readers will have gained the impression that Laing and Esterson are offering an explanation

of what went wrong: that these parents, through their insensitivities, their pathological phantasy systems, and their anxieties, first drove and then kept their daughters crazy. But is this what Laing and Esterson are saying? Apparently not; in the Preface to the second edition they state, or restate, that their aim was a much more modest one:

> We set out to illustrate by eleven examples that, if we look at some experience and behavior without reference to family interactions, they may appear comparatively socially senseless, but that if we look at the same experience and behavior in their original family context they are liable to make more sense.

The sense of anticlimax, which I cannot believe I am the only reader to have felt on meeting these words, as well as an unfamiliar note of bluster in the new Preface, suggest that Laing and Esterson have been forced into a partial retreat, possible from criticisms that there were flaws in their techniques for fostering scientific objectivity (their lack of a control group, for example). The material that they have presented in this highly original study seems at any rate much more fertile than the conclusions that they are prepared to draw from it (p. 4)

Besides being diffuse [*The Politics of Experience*] is an intemperate book. No doubt it will be said—as Laing himself says in the Preface—that things have now come to such a pass as to justify the stridency. There is certainly a fashionable element in the denunciations, whether they are addressed to the institutions of society, the "often fibrillating heartland of senescent capitalism," or to the human beings who inhabit it: "we are all murderers and prostitutes." Occasionally the language becomes dithyrambic; here is the voice of the bard in best Messianic-Ossianic vein. . . . There is not much sustained argument in the book. If indeed the deforming, inimical agents are not to be seen in one's unaccepted, repudiated impulses, or in parental misattributions, or in particular mystifying, confusing patterns of family interaction, but are produced by the nature of modern society itself, this is a much harder process to exemplify, illustrate, and indeed to identify, though it is easy enough to roar against. Society, Laing claims, has processed us all on Procrustean beds.

But are these deforming influences of society at large to be found in every family, and in the pressures exerted by every institution? Laing does not really bother to clarify this. He seems indeed to believe that man is born in original innocence but is irremediably maltreated by everything that shapes his growing up. Continuing to live in a society is only a daily renewal of this distortion, deformation, alienation.

He talks rather airily of realizing the extent of our alienation as "the essential springboard for any serious reflection on any aspect of present interhuman life," but—apart indeed from some murmurs against the psychiatric profession, certainly not *wholly* unjustified—he does not say how this is to be done. The family, psychiatry, capitalism are vaguely attacked. There seems to be a confusion of various myths and fables, such as the myth of Primeval Innocence, or an updated version of the Emperor's New Clothes in which Laing, speaking for the innocence of childhood, declares that the Emperor is really wearing a strait jacket.

These and other myths are worth examining for it seems to me that the mythopoeic element in Laing is the source both of his diffuse appeal and of the difficulty that is often experienced in getting him into focus. The views that are implied by the impetus of much of Laing's writing (though I am left in some doubt how far Laing still holds them)—that most psychotic behavior is intelligible and meaningful within the sphere in which the patient has to operate; that a psychotic breakdown can be in itself a means to recovery; that the statements of psychotics about themselves are in a profound way true; that society itself literally traumatizes its children into psychosis, just as in one of his earlier formulations (later abandoned) Freud conceived of fathers as literally seducing their daughters into neurosis: these seem to me to be romantic myths which contain a strong wishful element and have just enough truth in them to prevent that distressing fact from being easily recognized. Some of them are at any rate no worse than their antagonistic positivist myths (e.g., that all "psychiatric" or emotional disorders will be found to have a biochemical cause). I wish however that they had not been confounded in Laing's work with other, more trite, observations and aspirations, such as that life in an industrial society is often frustrating to personal development, or that doctors should treat their patients more humanely, and so forth.

In any case it is often possible to be impressed with a point that Laing is making without the necessity of being stampeded into sharing all his conclusions. . . .

If will be a pity if [Laing's] impressive but at the same time exasperating gift for aphorism and paradox, and his sense of how to appeal to the *Zeitgeist*, should tempt him to abandon the more tedious tasks of rendering his views clearer and more sharply argued and of resolving some of the ambiguities that undoubtedly lurk in them. For I cannot myself think it entirely coincidental that someone who has written so sensitively about the forcing of people into unacceptable, untenable positions should seem to find himself so often misunderstood by those he is trying to reach; nor would I have thought it a very gratifying position to be acclaimed, as surely Laing is acclaimed, by another, more popular, readership that is unable to render a convincing account of his views. (p. 6)

Alan Tyson, "Homage to Catatonia," in The New York Review of Books *(reprinted with permission from* The New York Review of Books; *copyright © 1971 Nyrev, Inc.), Vol. XVI, No. 2, February 11, 1971. pp. 3-4, 6.*

RICHARD SENNETT

In a moment of anger in ["**The Politics of the Family and Other Essays**"], R. D. Laing writes, "Our own cities are our own animal factories; families, schools, churches, are the slaughterhouses of our children; colleges and other places are the kitchens. As adults in marriages and business we eat the product." These charges may all be true, but they are tiresome, written in such a way that the reader turns them off. The strongest impression I have after reading "**The Politics of the Family and Other Essays**" is that Laing has substituted an easy rhetoric of accusation and condemnation for the struggle to understand people's feelings that dignified his earlier work. (p. 2)

The writings of R. D. Laing have moved from early books which put forth a complex, painful vision of the human oppression involved in the phenomenon society labels "insanity" to books which replay all the early themes in such a fashion that the reader feels he is in a closed and stuffy room. Laing's thought has disintegrated dramatically in the last four years, but it is unworthy of him simply to itemize that decline. For

what has happened to him shows why it is not just a matter of words that makes contemporary words of anger stale. . . .

[The power of "**The Divided Self**," lay in R. D. Laing's] ability to catch the rationality behind seemingly irrational behavior, a logic he revealed by making the reader see through the eyes of someone labeled schizophrenic. Laing did not "explain" schizophrenia as a disease; he showed how schizophrenia was a perfectly logical way of coping with impossible, longstanding situations in a person's family or immediate society. . . .

In the course of [his early] books Laing came to think that parents are no more to blame for posing the child insane demands than is the child for responding insanely. Forces out of their personal control make them hurt the child; few of the people in families of schizophrenics, Laing remarked, ever *want* to create sickness; they *have* to, they are driven souls. Who then is responsible?

Laing came to believe that everyone and no one is. Society makes insanity, he argued; sanity is a condition in which people are willing to obey social rules, even if the commands are inhumane and irrational. The rebels are labeled insane. That little girl is a rebel in her acts because she didn't try to paper over a contradiction; she tried to respond as honestly as she could to the demands made on her, and her show of honesty prompted others to think she was sick. . . .

By the time Laing wrote "**The Politics of Experience**". . . it seemed logical that he would become a social analyst, a man whose experience as a psychiatrist would give him, and his readers, new insights into how society organized repression. But these insights were not forthcoming. Rather than follow the logic of his own anger and become a social critic, he chose to make his patients, whom he had formerly seen as dignified in their suffering, into heroes. He dealt with society only by clinging to those people who were its victims and whose actions, if not intentions, showed they were fighting back.

This tendency to cling to the victim as hero took hold of Laing in two ways. Everthing he saw in his consulting room, all his intellectual associations and allies, made him think that traditional psychiatric logic, positing "rational" standards of behavior, was a sham, was really a tool for keeping dissidence down. If Laing were to become a social critic, if he began to ask why society brought into being these human traumas, wouldn't he run the risk of becoming one of "them," wouldn't his gifts of sensitivity and originality fall prey to the deadness of that sane world? There is a failure of nerve here, a fear of putting himself in enemy territory, but it is complex and humane because it is a fear of losing his own humanity. . . .

Laing's sympathy for his mentally ill patients is enmeshed in the same contradictions that led to a crisis between black and civil-rights workers, but he has gone a step further. Laing has come to see madness not just as an act of rebellion, but as an act of "liberation," of "waking up," of a "freeing" of the individual from society's constraints. Rebellion and liberation are separated by a simple matter of fact: a liberation ends the causes of the distress that makes people want to rebel. Laing, however, has turned this around, and looks at madness as a liberation in which the individual reorganizes the world on his or her own terms, so that society can be shut out. But why then are mentally ill people ususally in great and unending pain? (p. 3)

All the essays [in "**The Politics of the Family and Other Essays**"] are ostensibly concerned with the role of the therapist intervening in family crises.

I should say at once that the reader who was moved by **"The Divided Self"** will find in these essays of a decade later a few pages with the old force. (p. 40)

Sadly, the few passages with the old fire are sandwiched between dead prose. . . . Laing can no longer write clearly unless he is showing someone being hurt.

Laing cannot talk about the theories and intellectual constructs surrounding mental illness with the same imagination and originality with which he talks about the mentally ill patient because he won't permit himself to. All of Laing's own powers of originality are concentrated on speaking *for* the patient; but the patient, as Laing elsewhere argues so strongly, is not the maker of his own illness. What can Laing use to confront the tormentors? Examples of their practices gone wrong. But there is no way of explaining what has gone wrong other than by using their terms. He sounds like Doctor Laing, pompous and boring, because it is he who made the split between doctor and human being, for fear he would not have the strength to confront the doctors without his patients to hold on to.

Making the victim a proxy for his own anger forces Laing's thoughts about victimization itself into a pedestrian mold. In **"The Politics of the Family"** he argues that there is a triangle composed of blind authority, the invasion of intimate feelings, and "waking up" through mental illness. From the moment of their birth men are contaminated by others, ultimately by society. Laing draws a "map" of this invasion, but the countryside and the routes of invasion have all been laid out before by Freud, David Rappoport and Alfred Adler—none of whom gets much credit. Laing argues that nuclear war and genocide are connected to schizophrenic feelings without drawing the connections at all. How can this psychiatrist help us if outside the consulting room his great gifts of intelligence go dead, and he mechanically and woodenly repeats the ideas of others? This failure of intellect is especially disturbing since the behavior Laing perceived in his consulting room could not be adequately explained by the older theories.

This invasion from the outer world, Laing says, is blind, unintentional: each person or social group wounds others only hoping to protect itself. I believe this, but I don't understand why. Laing believes it, and doesn't think it matters why, because "why" gets us too far away from the "reality that is the patient."

So when Laing talks of waking up, of liberation, he ends at an impasse. If this is a vicious and insane world what are men to do? How are they to wake up? The analysis of schizophrenia on which Laing's work rests is that people are forced into what society calls insane behavior when they try to take the world seriously; it is the essence of his argument that you do not become insane by some willful act or failure of your own. . . . If I, a sane man, want to wake up, and I can't will myself into mental illness, what am I to do?. . .

The conversion of his patients into "models" of behavior inhibits Laing from talking about three issues. The first is himself. . . . A humanistic psychiatry does not have to bear the burden of autobiography or confession, yet Laing cannot talk about himself openly in the detail he feels entitled to talk about his patients. When he uses "I" in this book, it usually is in terms of putting himself in the place of a suffering patient.

Laing thinks of himself as an existentialist. . . . But as a writer he has become the worst of existentialists, one of the "spec-tators" Sartre so detests. How can a writer be an existentialist when he discounts himself?

Secondly, Laing talks about how emotions get twisted, but seldom talks about what emotions there are in the heart to twist. A reader who wants to find out about the range of feeling involved in human trust, in friendship, in sensuous pleasure, will not find it in Laing. **"The Divided Self"** described an idea of "ontological security" in which men felt able to take a wide variety of risks; the books since **"The Politics of Experience"** show a writer who can imagine only one.

This is to say, finally, that Laing has lost that capacity to dream which is necessary in any enduring radical vision. . . . Because Laing now has lost the power to dream and make his readers dream and desire, his catalogue of abuses is losing its power to anger (pp. 40-1)

When Laing crossed [the barrier between himself and his patients] and began to live through others, he went dead inside, could not speak of himself as probingly as he could speak for his patients, lost the power to create anger at the world which held them both so harshly in its grip. I wish I knew where it would lead to think out the realities of our lives as persons who are not dramatically suffering, but I do know that until we stop this presumptuous sentimentality, until uncertainty and curiosity about who we are ourselves return, we will become increasingly bored with our own "causes" and tolerant of the society that brings them into being. (p. 41)

> *Richard Sennett, "'The Politics of the Family and Other Essays'," in* The New York Times Book Review *(© 1971 by The New York Times Company; reprinted by permission), October 3, 1971, pp. 2-3, 40-1.*

EDGAR Z. FRIEDENBERG

[R. D. Laing has] concluded that the only essential distinction between persons deemed schizophrenic and other persons lay in the unconscionable demands life, through the agency of their families, [has] laid on them and the devastating though appropriate response they had made to such demands. Granted equally destructive demands, any of us might have responded the same way, or in ways even less adaptive.

This is true, certainly; but it leaves something important out of account. . . . For life is in some degree for all of us an adversary proceeding; and in a society whose basic unit is the mononuclear family, parents are always in some degree adversaries to their children. And an adversary proceeding is always conducted to some degree in a double bind of the kind Laing finds characteristic of human relations in the homes of his most schizoid patients. The judge is always predisposed toward the prosecution, though perhaps not decisively so, since both are part of the establishment that maintains stability and order. . . . And a defendant who points this out is, unless the circumstances are truly exceptional, in contempt of court; for it is indeed unlawful to insist that the judge is, by virtue of his very position as pillar of the establishment, inherently biased. The authority of the courts depends on their putative neutrality, which may not be questioned on structural grounds; particular abuses may be cited and, if proved, result in a new trial in which both prosecution and defense will behave more circumspectly. The defense is forbidden to argue, however, that the court system is inherently biased because of its own place in the political and social structure. To admit this argument is to risk invalidating the courts, thereby preventing them from discharging their fundamental function of invalidating socially threatening defendants. (pp. 6-7)

In an adversary proceeding, as in life, much of the unavoidable discomfort stems from the fact that witnesses may not choose the questions they will answer. And the very essence of successful cross-examination is the selection of questions that destroy the witness's credibility by disrupting his view of the world, so as to make sure that the judge and jury and if possible he himself will be led to reject his view of reality, thus rendering his testimony worthless. This is much more than a matter of showing that a witness is lying. A really effective trial lawyer can often manage to leave the court with the impression that the witness is too caught up in his own limited world view, confusions, and hostilities for it to even matter whether he, himself, believes his own testimony.

This, precisely, is what Laing asserts that the families and psychiatrists of schizoid patients do to them, while their alleged schizophrenic symptoms are evidence of their efforts to maintain their own integrity under such sustained and often brutal attack. . . . [This] does not mean that nothing distinguishes psychotics from other persons; on the contrary, it means that something must. Not all of us go to pieces on the witness stands of life. Most persons who come to be adjudged psychotic were reared in homes with siblings who managed to cope, at whatever costs to themselves, with the demands made on them and retain some measure of autonomy; or, at least, avoid the catastrophic loss of autonomy involved in hospitalization. *Why* this should be so is not, to be sure, Laing's question. But that is no reason why it should not be one of ours. It is an important question; and one which Laing's rejection of scientifically controlled observation makes it very difficult to answer. (pp. 7-9)

[Laing's thesis is] that "the standard psychiatric patient is a function of the standard psychiatrist and of the standard mental hospital." His case for this proposition seems, ultimately, irrefutable; the mental patient, in the hospital as in his family, finds himself barred from communication, even though capable of it, by virtue of the low status assigned him. Laing explicitly maintains that the psychiatric interview that serves as the basis for commitment to the institution is, in Harold Garfinkel's phrase, a "degradation ceremony," which formally initiates the person into his subhuman role as patient.

But if one grants the truth of this, then Laing's relatively successful efforts to communicate across the brutally blasted gap between the normal and the certifiably insane must be viewed in the light of this truth, too. The gap between the normal and the psychotic is not a less dangerous abyss because it is largely artificial—any more than the gap between blacks and whites is less real and threatening because it is a social artifact. Quite the contrary. A natural barrier may be a nuisance and an obstacle that serves no man's interest; breaching it is then a technical problem only. But barriers that are established and maintained at great cost and with manifestly destructive consequences to some, if not all, of the people divided by them are highly charged parts of the social dynamism. And they are erected in such a way as to threaten most effectively the people confined on the low-status side of the barrier, who understand this very well. (pp. 10-11)

Ultimately, as Laing came to realize, what is required is not more humane and responsive psychiatry so much as Mad Liberation. It is certainly true, as Harry Stack Sullivan noted in the admirable and much quoted phrase with which he ushered the psychotic into our world, that "we are all more simply human than otherwise"; and Sullivan had a strong and acknowledged influence on Laing's thought. Even so, why apologize for idiosyncrasy? What merit can there be in claiming to share a species with so sane a man as Lieutenant William Calley? Meanwhile, whatever madness may be, and however it may come to be defined, there is relatively less ambiguity about the phenomenon of social subordination.

The function of social subordination in the molding and subsequent definition of the psychotic is crucial to any understanding of Laing's conception of mental illness. I have mentioned his use of Garfinkel's conception of the "degradation ceremony" to characterize the psychiatric admissions interview. He makes greater and equally appropriate use of the work of Erving Goffman, who undertook a year of menial work in a St. Elizabeth's mental hospital to do the field work necessary for *Asylums* and came, like Laing, to see the role of mental patients as defined by a process of stigmatization. Yet Laing does not come to grips with the implications of social subordination for his work; at any rate, his disdain for methodological rigor as itself a form of violation of the people whose lives he is seeking to understand keeps him from taking account of its effects. (pp. 11-12)

[Laing fails to ask important questions about schizophrenia] such as what predisposed these persons to madness, rather than other members of their households and comparable households, rather than their sisters, for example. This is the sort of question that *does* require scientifically controlled study, and one whose answer might possibly strengthen Laing's view of schizophrenia as an ascribed stigma rather than an objectively pathological state.

His disdain for a comparison between the victims and the survivors of the psychopathogenic situations he describes seems to be due to an assumption that such a comparison could only result in meaningless psychological nitpicking, which would distract attention from his insistence that what is going on is a process of aggressive social degradation rather than psychiatric diagnosis. Laing is interested in what those deemed schizophrenic are trying to tell us about the meaning of their lives, so he dismisses at the outset those *not* so deemed. A comparative study would involve him in a frustrating search for psychological differences that he is convinced do not exist. This conviction, moreover, is an expression not of sheer dogmatic stubbornness but of insight. For Laing, convinced as he is, and with good reason, that he understands why his "schizophrenic" patients act as they do, a controlled scientific comparison between them and those who, though often just as alienated, have escaped stigmatization would be futile. To demand this could be like insisting on a series of carefully controlled bacteriological comparisons between the organisms found in the saliva and bloodstream of scurvied and normal individuals, when scurvy is already known to be a consequence of dietary deficiency and not infection. (pp. 14-15)

Laing's dismissal of controlled comparison as a technique for studying the schizophrenic process probably has done a grave disservice to his own formulation. For it is unlikely that the major factors distinguishing the two groups would be found to be psychological. They are much more likely to be social, especially if Laing is right. One would expect such comparisons to reveal many more instances in which individuals with similar low status and no hiding place, though very different personalities, had been diagnosed as schizophrenic than in which individuals with similar personality structures but very different status had been so classified. . . . Had Laing, therefore, undertaken to do what his critics suggested, he might well have obtained unassailable evidence that psychiatric diagnosis is little more than a process of social manipulation. (p. 16)

[Laing's] way of writing about [his patients] has increasingly suggested a greater degree of identification with them—so great, indeed, as to jeopardize his willingness to assess the role they might be playing in contributing to their own misery and existential plight.

Assessment, his position clearly implies, is not of much value to those deemed mentally ill—or, rather, it is almost certainly harmful and usually hostile as well as a part of the process that has made them what they are. What is needed instead is understanding, acceptance, and especially *authenticity* of response from the physician, who must, above all else, prove trustworthy as a person. Authenticity is a key concept in Laing's view of healing. (p. 21)

[An authentic response] must, however, under some circumstances, cause not only pain—which may indeed be essential to growth—but real therapeutic difficulties. For if one assumes that what people need most is the genuine and authentic response of their fellows one must ignore the strength and prevalence of evil in the world. Laing does not deny that there are evil men abroad—the experiences of his patients prove that—but like all existential therapists he does in principle deny that what is worst in men is basic or original and fully authentic. To the degree that our growth and humaneness have not been warped or stunted, each of us will be able to and will wish to support the growth and humaneness of others. This is a very appealing doctrine; but it is not self-evident and not demonstrably true. (pp. 22-3)

What is finally lacking in Laing's view of the levels of reality in human personality is, I believe, an essential respect for evil and cruelty as just as real and human as love and growth. (p. 24)

> *Edgar Z. Friedenberg, in his* R. D. Laing, *edited by Frank Kermode (copyright © 1973 by Edgar Z. Friedenberg; reprinted by permission of Viking Penguin Inc.; in Canada by the author), Viking Penguin, 1973, 118 p.*

JULIET MITCHELL

The progress of Laing's work has been from an analysis of the split individual, through a study of the individual divided from, and against, others, to others against the individual within the small unit of the family, to each against each in microsocial personal relationships (i.e. marriage) and to the two sides of the macrosocial political world of Them and Us, East and West, Black and White, etc. This movement is the logic of his preoccupation with division and distinction; from *The Divided Self* to

> All distinctions are mind, by mind, in mind, of mind
> No distinctions no mind to distinguish.

Man's separateness, his alienation from his own 'true' self and from 'real' others, is encapsulated for Laing in the predicament of the schizophrenic who is scapegoated—i.e. made more alienated, therefore incarcerated in incomprehension: private autism and public mental hospital.

In the early work, the schizophrenic's 'madness' is found to be an intelligible response to certain mad-making social pres-

sures; in the middle work the mad-making social pressures come to seem the real madness; by default, the schizophrenic's response has moved from being intelligible to being 'normal'; in the late works the schizophrenic's 'madness' has become the true sanity from which the vast majority of people are divorced. Many critics have decried Laing's descent/ascent into mysticism, but it is clearly the completely logical progress of his preoccupations. (pp. 277-78)

Laing reflects the current political dichotomies of East and West. He virtually parodies them with his TV imitations of 'goodies and baddies'. He believes that divisions plague us all. His remedy, he tells us, is to cease to have divisions. It is quite logical, for after all, the only thing you can do if you are trapped in a reflection is to invert the image. (p. 278)

[Laing's] notion that 'madness' is an intelligible response runs parallel to his ascription that people drive each other mad in an insane effort to establish their own normality and to confirm the distinction between 'them' and 'us'—here the 'sane' and the 'mad', which is often synonymous with the 'good' and the 'bad'. . . .

With madness and sanity on this sort of continuum and only falsely posed as polarities by those whose sanity depends on such distinctions, it is inevitable that Laing should, to some degree, right the balance. And this he does. In his case-studies of schizophrenics and their families, we find him constantly making such remarks as, of the Blair family, 'But the whole family seems to have been very odd', or of the relationships of one patient's mother and grandmother, 'we shall see . . . how extraordinary this bond is'. The point is that in establishing the patient's 'normality' Laing is forced, despite his intentions, *by his own methodology* to say someone else is abnormal. As he is not searching for any other 'cause' of psychosis than that of the present-day social interaction in which the patient is engaged, it is necessary for him to remove the onus of categorization from the classified patient and place it on someone else. Despite his original plea to stop categorizing, ultimately all he can ask for is either more, or differently directed, classifications. (p. 280)

And for want of new terminology, Laing has in fact had to redeploy the old, so he will conclude of the hospitalized schizophrenic girl, Lucie Blair's, *parents:* that *if* what Mrs Blair says of Mr Blair is true, then the father is probably psychotic; if it is not, then the mother is; or, more likely, both of them. By now one must ask: if the parents are mad, who drove them that way? (Their parents?) Or, alternatively, if 'madness' is, as Laing claims, a false description in the malign pursuit of differentiation, it is no 'truer' to label a parent 'psychotic' than it is to do this to its child. The family becomes 'extraordinary' to make the patient's response 'ordinary.'. . . (p. 281)

Laing, to remove the denigratory value judgement from the classified schizophrenic, has to transfer it to the others. Wishing not to fall into the trap of making distinctions, he can in fact not avoid them, only transpose them. It is this dilemma, I believe, that eventually leads him out of social analysis into mystic celebration.

However, in showing how normal 'abnormality' is and how 'peculiar', 'extraordinary', etc. 'normal' social interaction is, Laing, as his concept of a 'science of persons' demands, has inevitably himself fallen into the trap (or release) of producing studies of people in which one cannot distinguish types of problems or behaviour. This is the concrete dimension to his theoretical project of showing psychosis vanish into its social intelligibility. (p. 282)

It seems that in a wish to make all intelligible Laing sometimes either merely see-saws the structure so that normal-abnormal change places, or all, in an undifferentiated way, becomes either normal or abnormal, and crucial extraordinary details are overlooked. (p. 283)

Freud's theory of the significance of transference-love in the therapeutic situation has been reversed by Laing. In any case analysis susggested that only a neurotic, not a psychotic, could become involved in such a transference. Freud's patient co-operates in the cure because he transfers the good feelings that he once had for his parents on to the analyst—and wants to please him as he once wanted to please his parents by working hard at his own self-understanding. The patient repeats anew—as a memory—his infantile predicament, but this time works through it consciously. Laing on the contrary is not concerned about the patient's love for the therapist, it is the therapist who must be able to empathize with and show compassion for the patient. This therapist thus *really* replaces the kindly parent and presumably the patient is comforted. Despite appearances, the behaviour and character of the doctor has gained in importance and that of the psychotic has diminished. Exit analyst, enter guru. (pp. 283-84)

Juliet Mitchell, "Rebel with a Cause," in her Psychoanalysis and Feminism *(copyright © 1974 by Juliet Mitchell; reprinted by permission of Pantheon Books, a Division of Random House, Inc.), Pantheon Books, 1974, pp. 277-84.*

ROBERT J. ANTONIO

Even though it has substantial theoretical content, Laing's position towards madness has not gained wide intellectual legitimacy. Furthermore, it is misunderstood and misinterpreted by those who consider him to be a guru. The group who perceives him in this way probably includes both his strongest advocates and his most severe critics. Part of the reason for the problem is that Laing has not written an integrative treatise in which he explains his position in its full development. (p. 15)

Laing believes that madness *should not* be categorized as an illness. . . . Laing views treatment based on the medical model to be a societal response to control normative violations. Unfortunately, such treatment may have violent, destructive and counterproductive consequences for the mental patient. . . .

Laing's concern with the treatment of the mad goes far beyond the process of institutionalization. He suggests that the psychiatric enterprise, because of its medical orientation, tends to treat the behavior of the patient as the mindless discharge of a disease rather than as the result of the volitional acts of the person. Because they are considered pathological, these behaviors and the processes that supposedly underlie them must be altered or eliminated through medical intervention. According to Laing, this means that the personal world of the troubled person, and the meaning system on which it is based, is mortified through psychiatric invalidation.

Laing sees the greatest weakness of medically oriented psychiatric treatment to be that it directs attention away from what he believes to be the actual source of psychological problems. Contrary to what some of his critics say, Laing *does* characterize the mad as having problems in operating in the everyday world. However, he does not see the problems to be the result of intra-individual pathology and internal breakdown. Instead Laing views them to occur because of difficulties in the realm of 'interexperience'. In short, he believes that madness results from disturbances between people, rather than from disorders within individuals. He argues that this position is supported by much research, including his own, from which he concludes that all schizophrenics exhibit disturbed patterns of communication that constitute a reflection of, and reaction to, the disturbed and disturbing interactional context of his or her family of origin. (p. 16)

Laing suggests . . . that, when madness is treated as a medical problem: 'The heart of the illness then resides outside the agency of the person. That is, the illness is taken to be a process that the person is subject to or undergoes, whether genetic, constitutional, endogenous, exogenous, organic or psychological, or some mixture of them all.' The mad person's behavior is dehumanized. It is seen to be a product of the disease, rather than a product of the person. It is reduced to unmotivated action, devoid of meaning, governed by forces that are beyond the person's control. In contradiction to this position, Laing believes that the behavioral patterns that are supposed to be symptomatic of madness are actually *adjustments* to highly disturbing interpersonal relations. Thus, the behaviors that are characterized as dysfunctional, disordered, meaningless products of disease come to be seen as desperate attempts to cope with a fractured social reality. Although they are not easily understandable, they have meaning, order and even function within the personal world of the actor. To understand them we must look into the person's existential world, and into this world's relation to the experience of others. According to Laing, medically oriented psychiatry, with its pathological lens and intra-individual focus, operates to deepen, rather than lessen, mystification about this complex system of meaning. Laing argues that there is something essentially wrong with the medical approach that suggests that conformative behavior is adjustive for the organism, while deviant behavior is maladjustive and pathological. Health becomes synonymous with acceptance of, and conformity to, the existing social system, no matter how destructive that system may be to the person.

Laing not only criticizes the imputation of pathology to madness, he also questions the very nature of normalcy. He suggests . . . that the condition and the behavior of the 'normal' man in contemporary society demands that we reconceptualize sanity. . . . (pp. 16-17)

Laing believes that the traditional definitions of sanity and madness have little meaning. Furthermore, he suggests that those who use conformity as a measure of mental 'health' neglect to ask questions about the nature of the reality that the person is supposed to conform to. . . .

The 'normal man' belongs to groups whose members enforce conformative behavior and experience through reciprocal concern. Members act on the basis of what they think others in the group would think of proposed lines of action. . . .

Group members assume that others in the group are always concerned about their behavior. Acting on this assumption, they govern their lives in accordance with what they think others think of their activity. Questions about the desirability or destructiveness of the activity are forgotten in the process. . . . (p. 17)

Built into Laing's disturbing characterization of social organization in contemporary Western society is the idea that it can be transformed. He argues that that social structure consists of patterns of social relation, and does not have objective, material existence. . . . If man accepts this reality as the proper and natural order of things he will probably not attempt to change it. This form of pattern maintenance is cheap and effective, for the police force is in the mind. Each believer passively accepts the social order and controls his own behavior so that it conforms to society's dictates. Laing implies that this is a prime form of social control in almost all societies. In treating social structure as a projected-introjected reification he implies that it can be changed, but only after man shakes his thinglike conception of it. (p. 18)

[Laing treats the reification of human experience] as a major source of social control that inhibits change by limiting man's activity so that it is consistent with ideology and supportive of his society's infrastructure. Laing sees the present condition of man as being built upon a reified, shared hallucination called reality, in which man exists in a state of collusive madness that we call sanity. . . . Laing's depressing picture of the reified world of the normal man is tempered by the belief that man created it, and that man can change it. He asserts . . . that '*We* are the veil that veils us from our self.' (p. 19)

Laing's characterization of normal alienation represents a marriage of [Husserl's] concept of natural attitude and [the Marxian concept of] false consciousness. The normally alienated man experiences the world in a highly reified fashion. It is taken for granted as paramount reality, unchanging and absolute. He does not reflect upon the rules, relations and events of the social world. Instead, he just accepts them and adjusts to them as he does the rain or cold. Ironically, the more intense the condition of normal alienation, the more likely the person will not be cognizant of it. (pp. 19-20)

In order to fully understand Laing's normal alienation, we must grasp the dialectical conception of man in which it is embedded. The roots of this conception lie in Marx's assertion that man's uniqueness lies in his potential for self-fulfilling praxis. Central to this activity is his ability to impose order on the world by synthesizing diverse and meaningless elements of experience into meaningful wholes, or *totalizations*. . . . Man's action in the world depends upon the way he organizes and constitutes reality. Reality emerges from man's totalizing activity. The success man has in accomplishing his projects is largely dependent upon his ability to organize his perception and action on the basis of totalizations, or what we call ideas. For these to be effective tools, they must be allowed to be responsive to the time and the situation. In fact, man must constantly question and eventually negate his totalizations through continuous inclusion of new information that challenges their definition and ultimately transforms their very nature. After negation and reintegration, new and more useful totalizations emerge. However, these must also be negated, for totalizations are profoundly historical entities that eventually outlive their usefulness. Man's ability to transcend his condition springs from the circular movement (thesis-antithesis-synthesis-thesis) of his dialectical totalizing activity. . . . Man goes beyond his present condition through a constant process of tearing down and rebuilding his constructions. It is in this process that he exposes the defining quality of his humanity, the ability to become.

Totalizing activity is drastically reduced in the case of the normally alienated. The set of totalizations through which the world is organized ceases to develop and grow. The normally alienated reify these totalizations, experiencing them as ahistorical, external and unchangeable entities. Man's own constructions become inert facts, which are external to him and

over which he has no control. Being blind and held captive by ideas, he loses his grasp on the ideal, and with it the ability to negate and transcend his condition. As a result, man is reduced to a pattern-producing automaton who helplessly lives the nightmare his ancestors created. In short, normal alienation refers to a state of arrest in the process of dialectical growth. Man is bereft of his humanity to the degree that this process of becoming is slowed or stopped. (p. 20-1)

[The] normally alienated reap benefits from their conformity: they receive social support that validates their conceptions of self; they experience a comforting sense of ontological security; and they can cope in the social world. On the other hand, the mad, who live outside the natural attitude, no longer share this intersubjective world of validating others, but instead confront head-on the forces of invalidation and stigmatization. They cease to communicate, for they are trapped, alone, in the boundless space and endless flow of sensation that constitutes internal consciousness. Drawn inward, sensitized to the rich complexity of these internal events, they are no longer willing to cope with the social world that is radically external to their experience.

Critics have accused Laing of romanticizing madness. However, he never disputes the desirability of returning from this state. On the contrary, he understands the fear and isolation of madness and has dedicated his life to leading people back from it. In fact, the major thrust of Laing's criticism of psychiatry focuses upon its inability to succeed at this task. He . . . asserts that psychiatric intervention (as it is practiced), with its labeling and pseudo-therapeutic techniques, actually retards, rather than speeds, the return from madness. Laing argues that these practices are an impediment to the 'natural healing' process that he believes would restore sanity if madness were allowed to run its course. Laing deserves to be thoroughly criticized for his choice of terminology. First, by referring to a 'healing process' he slips into agreement with the medical model that he is attempting to attack. Secondly, he reifies this process by calling it 'natural'. However . . . these problems are not insurmountable since they result from poor terminology and incomplete conceptualization, rather than inherent contradiction.

The trip back from madness is a crucial, but underdeveloped, element in Laing's thinking. To Laing, healing means escape from total immersion in the inner world of madness. It means regaining the ability to share intersubjective meaning, to communicate, to experience ontological security and to cope with the social world. However, Laing does *not* suggest that this represents a return from a pathological state to a healthy state. By conceptualizing this as a natural process, he implies that the signs of madness and breakdown should not be repressed as symptoms of disease, but should be allowed to unfold as the first step in a dialectical transformation. (p. 21)

Questions must be entertained about the possibility and nature of dealienation in Laing's scheme. Laing does not provide a detailed description of the absence of alienation, although it is implied throughout his later work as an achievable alternative to normal alienation. This unalienated state is difficult to conceptualize, because it refers to an ideal condition. To extend Laing's position without contradicting its basic framework, one would have to say that total dealienation is not achievable unless man's alienative social environment is transformed. However, Laing makes no pretense about having a masterplan for achieving this massive, collective revolutionary task. Thus, even the positively reintegrated madman is not free of alienation. Does this mean that contemporary man is trapped in the stultifying listlessness of normal alienation?

The problematics suggested above can be avoided if we conceptionalize alienation in terms of a continuum ranging from complete alienation to a complete lack of alienation. The former is characterized by arrest, where all totalizing activity has ceased. Completely alienated men lack the ability for creative innovation, are totally determined and are pawns of both history and the environment. Their world is totally reified, for even '. . . their very own thoughts and feelings, in their most intimate interstices, are the outcome, the resultant, of processes which they undergo.'. . . The opposite extreme on the continuum is characterized by constant totalizing activity and dialectical growth. Completely unalienated men have an unlimited capacity for innovation; they are free, and both history and the environment are their servants. In short, they are, to the optimum degree, materially comfortable and spiritually fulfilled. The empirical existence of either of these polar types is less important than man's struggle to move toward the latter unalienated state. Laing's conception of positive reintegration implies just this kind of dialectical movement. The positively reintegrated person is not mystically transformed into a totally unalienated, self-fulfilled individual, despite an alienative social environment. Instead, he has only started to become, to embark on what could be the first of a series of negations and transformations towards the ideal.

Laing . . . asserts that the reality of mental illness can only be understood '. . . within the larger context of the civic order of society—that is, of the *political* order, of the ways persons exercise control and power over one another'. He suggests that the treatment of the mad is politically motivated and is related to the preservation of the existing social order and power structure. However, he never completely explicates why it is necessary for society to exert forceful control over those expressing the symptoms of madness. Granted, the mad break rules; but their deviation seems, at least superficially, to carry few direct political implications. Why, then, is social reaction so swift and powerful, even when the behaviors do not seem to be politically destructive? (pp. 21-2)

[Laing] suggests that the mad experience a sense of ontological insecurity. This involves a profound and pervading sense of uncertainty and distrust in the reality of their life-world. . . . The mad undergo a radical suspension of belief and desiccation of the natural attitude. More importantly, they often communicate this doubt through verbalizations about their experience or through violation of assumptive rules, that foundation of the very substance of belief.

The effects of the communication of doubt should be considered theoretically. Remember that Laing adheres to the Marxian view of social control, which considers the reified knowledge of the natural attitude to be necessary to the perpetuation of the institutional arrangements that generate it. If maintenance of the natural attitude supports institutional arrangements, then dereification or suspension of the natural attitude can be threatening to the ongoing stability of these arrangements. Laing . . . suggests that the '. . . human scene is a scene of mirages, demonic pseudo-realities, because everyone believes everyone else believes them'. Because this scene is founded upon the human imagination and consensual validation, it is always vulnerable to exposure as a collective fiction. The madman threatens reality by striking at its core, its unquestionable foundation, the assumptive world. He breaks the circle of deception by communicating through his words and deeds that 'the emperor

has no clothes'. He rips away the thin veil of legitimation and reality stands naked as a cruel hoax. (pp. 22-3)

Laing's assertion that the harsh treatment of the mad is politically motivated now becomes understandable. It is political not only because it imposes harmful restrictions on the victim, but also because it is an important part of the broader process of ideologically based social control of consciousness. The madman is subversive to the political order. His subversive powers lie in his ability to communicate doubt in the knowledge system that supports the societal infrastructure. He is living proof that alternative realities can be created that negate the supposed 'natural order of things'. In his role of destroyer and creator, he escapes society's first line of defense in the social control of consciousness. This consists of internal controls implanted in him in socialization (embodied as superego, generalized other, self-conscience). The madman stirs a crisis of belief which, like communicable disease, can become an epidemic. He becomes a potential 'destroyer of worlds' and the threat he represents must be quelled. Society, then, hardens its second line of defense, external control. It acts swiftly against the transgressor to maintain the world of belief and to protect the sleep of the normally alienated. (pp. 23-4)

Laing's conception of an alternative psychiatry is one that would be oriented to the elimination, rather than the perpetuation, of normal alienation. It would be, by definition, a subversive institution geared to exposing the sources of mystification and reification, to fashioning positive reintegration from the debris of breakdown, to encourage personal and social transformation, and finally to free consciousness from repressive social controls. Such a psychiatry may be impossible to realize in the existing social order, for its practitioners would be even more subversive than the madmen they treat and therefore subject to the same social controls. They would be vulnerable to the same devastating forces of invalidation used against the mad. Such practitioners would probably be labeled mentally ill themselves. . . .

Beyond its substantive contribution, Laing's work is important because it represents a significant and potentially productive departure from traditional empirical social science which has, to this point, failed miserably in dealing with the most serious problems of our times. Laing argues that contemporary empirical social science at best makes descriptive statements about alienated reality, rather than defining the forces that lead to alienation. This often deepens mystification because this alienated reality tends to be treated as unchangeable objective facticity. (p. 24)

Social science that proceeds only by the concatenation of empirical generalizations can do little more than present a series of snapshots about what is or what was. As Laing has shown us, the greatest problem is normal alienation, not madness. This alienation is best expressed in the gap that exists between what man is and what man could be. A social science that focuses in a descriptive, noncritical way on what was and what is tells us little about what man could be. Contemporary social science contributes to the processes of reification and alienation since it produces descriptions that are presented as Reality and sometimes even acted upon as if they are Reality. Thus, the metamorphosis, the science that has the potential to transform society, becomes that which contributes to its preservation in its present form.

Laing's work is significant because it suggests an alternative. It represents critical social science that refuses to be mystified by appearances and is dedicated to the elimination of both alienation and the ideological determinants that perpetuate it. This implies a social science that approaches the problem of change by searching out and exposing the sources of reification throughout the social structure (as Laing did with the case of mental disorder). This involves reorientation of social science, for it should not only concern itself with what man was and is, but also with *What Man Could Be!* (p. 25)

> *Robert J. Antonio, "The Work of R. D. Laing: A Neo-Marxist, Phenomenological Interpretation," in* The Human Context *(© 1975 The Chaucer Publishing Co. Ltd.), Vol. 7, No. 1, 1975, pp. 15-26.*

BRUNO BETTELHEIM

[In *The Facts of Life* R. D. Laing describes himself as having entered the world] under the influence of sex-denying, puritanical, deeply religious parents who seemed to have hated each other. If that is how Laing experienced the ordinary world in his early years, little wonder that he wishes to have no association with it. One of the defenses against being deeply rejected from birth on is to wish to believe that such is man's ordinary fate. . . .

If a person has encountered deep rejection even before birth, he wonders how his uterine life may have been, and how it may have influenced him; and he wishes to be reborn—by somebody who deeply desired him. So the longest section of Dr. Laing's book is devoted to speculations about intra-uterine experiences, their nature, meaning and consequences. Much of the rest of the book tells about the need for rebirth among schizophrenics, and how Laing has observed this to happen. . . .

In viewing such metaphorical birth [as is experienced by some schizophrenics]—as happens also in many initiation ceremonies, which are also symbolic rebirths—as a real rebirth, Dr. Laing is trying to turn a metaphor into reality. This possibility is present whenever we are confronted with deep unconscious processes, and hence it is a danger and a temptation inherent in psychoanalysis against which the psychoanalyst must guard himself, if he is not to be drawn into the delusions of his patients. Entering into a patient's delusions prevents the therapist from helping the patient to give up his delusions for a much less poetic and fantastic, much more pedestrian but useful and safe life in reality. . . . Dr. Laing seems tempted to embrace [this] danger. (p. 12)

> *Bruno Bettelheim, "'The Facts of Life: An Essay in Feelings, Facts and Fantasy'," in* The New York Times Book Review *(© 1976 by The New York Times Company; reprinted by permission), May 30, 1976, pp. 5, 12.*

G. M. CARSTAIRS

Probably the most controversial sections in [*The Facts of Life*] will be those in which the author speculates about the possibility that our earliest formative experiences are not, as Melanie Klein would have us believe, the fantasies of our first year of life, but much earlier than that. After musing upon the truly extraordinary capacity for storing genetic information shown by the single fertilized ovum which becomes the ancestor of all the millions of cells in an adult's body, Laing toys with the idea that somehow—no one knows how—a primordial aware-

ness may already reside in that single cell and its immediate descendants.

He claims that many of the archetypal myths of mankind can be interpreted as a reliving of the fertilized ovum's journey down the fallopian tube, its coming to rest in a more or less unwelcoming endometrium, and its life within the womb, ending with the traumatic experience of childbirth. These fanciful ideas have been aired before, by Francis J. Mott and Otto Rank; but Laing is perhaps the first to suggest a profound emotional relationship, rudely interrupted at birth, between the fetus and its placenta: "It seems to me more than likely," he writes, "that many of us are suffering lasting effects from our umbilical cords being cut too soon."

These ultra-speculative ideas are presented in passages which take the forms of free or of concrete verse, as if they were too whimsical to be expressed in prose. . . .

Could we indeed [be haunted by our intra-uterine experiences]? These passages are calculated to separate the true believers, unreservedly willing to suspend disbelief, from those who still adhere to reality-testing. The wilder speculations can be read as metaphors, or flights of imagery; but Laing seems to intend (or half-intend? it is not quite clear which) that they be taken literally, as no doubt they will be by the most credulous of his many admirers: but not, I suspect, by the majority of his readers—and perhaps not even by Laing himself.

His epilogue is a moving statement of his groping uncertainty. He avows certain deep-seated convictions—"but authorised by what or by whom?". . . .

[Laing] brings us very near to what William James discerned as the root of all religious experience: an inner sense of incompleteness, and a striving to put it right. Perhaps R. D. Laing is at the threshold of an illumination? Meanwhile, his willingness to share his perplexities and his deepest concerns will ensure a lively response to this very personal, and necessarily inconclusive, statement of where he now stands.

> *G. M. Carstairs, "The Sense of Incompleteness," in* The Times Literary Supplement *(© Times Newspapers Ltd. (London) 1976; reproduced from* The Times Literary Supplement *by permission), No. 3898, November 26, 1976, p. 1474.*

STANLEY MOLDAWSKY

[*The Facts of Life*] is a collection of [Laing's] musings and speculations about life, Birth, sexual information, and the parent-child relationship. It is of general interest to follow a psychiatrist's thoughts and share his speculations and wonder a bit. However, it does not offer much to the psychoanalyst in the way of further understanding of the analytic situation nor does it offer any systematic way of understanding personality development. It is another attempt at idealizing the craziness in us and that is essentially what is new in this book. What is good in this book is not new—and what is new is not good. (p. 228)

> *Stanley Moldawsky, "The Facts of Laing," in* Contemporary Psychology *(copyright © by the American Psychological Association), Vol. 22, No. 3, March, 1977, pp. 227-28.*

THOMAS SZASZ

I think it's in *The Politics of Experience,* in 1967, that [R. D. Laing] first alludes to his interest in 'empty white sheet(s) of paper': 'Few books today are forgivable. Black on the canvas, silence on the screen, an empty white sheet of paper, are perhaps feasible.' His recent books, such as *Facts of Life, Do You Love Me?* and *Conversations with Children*, contain lots of 'empty white sheets'. Unfortunately, not all of the pages of his most recent books are clean sheets; some are soiled by printer's ink.

According to Laing, *Conversations with Children* is an 'anthology' of his conversations with his own children, which he considers important because 'no similar anthology of dialogues with children has been published.' He claims that the 'anthology' is authentic and accurate. Since it's a record of conversations, the implication is that it is a verbatim, or near verbatim, account of what was said by each speaker. 'I have added nothing,' says Laing. 'I am responsible for deletions, and I suppose, inevitably, some inadvertent omissions. But I have made no additions, no embellishments.' How, then, did Laing obtain such a faithful record? 'No tape recorder was ever used,' he hastens to explain. 'The conversations in this anthology were written down by me from memory over a six-year period as part of a journal I keep. They are all recorded from memory.' Well, either Laing has a fantastic memory or his claim concerning the absolute authenticity of these conversations is a lie.

How does Laing justify publishing such an ostensibly intimate diary of his children's babblings (or babblings he attributes to them), thus making a part of their private world public? He knows, of course, that doing so constitutes an invasion of their privacy. But publishing such 'intimacies (of) family life' was permissible, he tells us, because it 'is done with the full accord of my wife—and the children.' That self-justification reveals the full measure of Laing's utter contempt for an ethic of respect for persons grounded in contract. The children on whom he so generously bestows the right to contract range in age between three and eight. If a father took sexual liberties with children of that age and then told us that they (and their mother!) consented to it, we would regard his self-justification as adding insult to injury.

Why did Laing write this book? Having written several books about the unhappy communications characteristic of other people's families, Laing felt ready, he says, to present 'the other side of the story . . . the language of the happy dialogue of intelligent beings . . . ' Where was he going to find such 'beings'? In his own family, where else? (p. 72)

What are we to make of *Conversations with Children?* It's not really a book; it only looks like one. Therein, perhaps, lies the answer to the question I posed. The book is a joke, a put-on. Intoxicated with himself, Laing is playing not only before his audience but also with it. His seemingly multi-faceted personality has now fused into a single role—namely, that of clown. Peter Mezan, who knows Laing personally, has actually characterised Laing in such a way: 'In the mind's eye, under the magical sign of the caduceus, stands a gaunt, pixielike man in the garb of prophet—acid at his right hand, revolution at his left, his head haloed with the clear light of an Oriental paradise, his eyes intimating madness—crushing beneath his avenging foot the serpent of the Western rationalist tradition. . . . In a single evening I have seen him run the gamut of emotions, taking on one distinct person after another, even changing sex, and in each one appearing to be wholly himself.'

How ironic, but how fitting. Laing, the clown, the Marcel Marceau of psychiatry. . . . [Laing] has a good nose for business—in particular, for selling his dramatised impersonations of himself. So far he has sold himself as student of schizophrenia, theoretician of anti-psychiatry, charismatic healer of madness, existenial philosopher, New Leftist social critic, guru of LSD, Buddhist monk, and radical critic of the family. Now he is posing as devoted paterfamilias, basking in 'happy' communications with his children. (p. 73)

Thomas Szasz, "Pilgrims' Regress" (reprinted by permission of the author), in The Spectator, *Vol. 241, No. 7838, September 23, 1978, pp. 72-3.**

JACK NESSEL

I have always admired the voluptuous language and rhythms of the Hopkins sonnet that begins "No worst, there is none," although the poem suffers from the absence of any context for its cosmic despair. The reader has to fill in from his own experience an appropriate notion of what could be so monstrous as to warrant the judgment that nothing is worse. My own candidate, at the moment, is the just-published collection of sonnets and adages by the radical psychiatrist R. D. Laing, [*Sonnets*]. (p. 97)

Jack Nessel, "Briefly: 'Sonnets','' in Psychology Today *(copyright © 1981 Ziff-Davis Publishing Company), Vol. 15, No. 2, February, 1981, pp. 97,99.*

Christopher Lasch

1932-

An American historian and professor at the University of Rochester, Lasch has united political radicalism and cultural conservatism in his analyses of American society. One of his major concerns is to examine how capitalism and its progressive allies have dismantled traditional institutions and values in service to the creation of a bureaucratic, consumption-oriented society. Lasch's much-discussed *The Culture of Narcissism* (1978) traces the social and psychological effects of the shift from entrepreneurial to bureaucratic capitalism. Though some critics have questioned Lasch's use of Marxist analytical concepts and have criticized his neglect of empirical evidence, many agree that he sheds new light on the current crisis of American culture. (See also *Contemporary Authors*, Vols. 73-76.)

Excerpt from *THE CULTURE OF NARCISSISM: AMERICAN LIFE IN AN AGE OF DIMINISHING EXPECTATIONS*

As the twentieth century approaches its end, the conviction grows that many other things are ending too. Storm warnings, portents, hints of catastrophe haunt our times. The "sense of an ending," which has given shape to so much of twentieth-century literature, now pervades the popular imagination as well. The Nazi holocaust, the threat of nuclear annihilation, the depletion of natural resources, well-founded predictions of ecological disaster have fulfilled poetic prophecy, giving concrete historical substance to the nightmare, or death wish, that avant-garde artists were the first to express. The question of whether the world will end in fire or in ice, with a bang or a whimper, no longer interests artists alone. Impending disaster has become an everyday concern, so commonplace and familiar that nobody any longer gives much thought to how disaster might be averted. People busy themselves instead with survival strategies, measures designed to prolong their own lives, or programs guaranteed to ensure good health and peace of mind. (pp. 3-4)

After the political turmoil of the sixties, Americans have retreated to purely personal preoccupations. Having no hope of improving their lives in any of the ways that matter, people have convinced themselves that what matters is psychic self-improvement: getting in touch with their feelings, eating health food, taking lessons in ballet or belly-dancing, immersing themselves in the wisdom of the East, jogging, learning how to "relate," overcoming the "fear of pleasure." Harmless in themselves, these pursuits, elevated to a program and wrapped in the rhetoric of authenticity and awareness, signify a retreat from politics and a repudiation of the recent past. Indeed Americans seem to wish to forget not only the sixties, the riots, the new left, the disruptions on college campuses, Vietnam, Watergate, and the Nixon presidency, but their entire collective past, even in the antiseptic form in which it was celebrated during the Bicentennial. (pp. 4-5)

To live for the moment is the prevailing passion—to live for yourself, not for your predecessors or posterity. We are fast losing the sense of historical continuity, the sense of belonging to a succession of generations originating in the past and stretching

Wide World Photos

into the future. It is the waning of the sense of historical time— in particular, the erosion of any strong concern for posterity— that distinguishes the spiritual crisis of the seventies from earlier outbreaks of millenarian religion, to which it bears a superficial resemblance. Many commentators have seized on this resemblance as a means of understanding the contemporary "cultural revolution," ignoring the features that distinguish it from the religions of the past. (p. 5)

The contemporary climate is therapeutic, not religious. People today hunger not for personal salvation, let alone for the restoration of an earlier golden age, but for the feeling, the momentary illusion, of personal well-being, health, and psychic security. Even the radicalism of the sixties served, for many of those who embraced it for personal rather than political reasons, not as a substitute religion but as a form of therapy. Radical politics filled empty lives, provided a sense of meaning and purpose. (p. 7)

Today Americans are overcome not by the sense of endless possibility but by the banality of the social order they have erected against it. Having internalized the social restraints by means of which they formerly sought to keep possibility within civilized limits, they feel themselves overwhelmed by an annihilating boredom, like animals whose instincts have withered in captivity. A reversion to savagery threatens them so little that they long precisely for a more vigorous instinctual existence. People nowadays complain of an inability to feel. They cultivate more vivid experiences, seek to beat sluggish flesh to life, attempt to revive jaded appetites. They condemn the superego and exalt the lost life of the senses. Twentieth-century peoples have erected so many psychological barriers against strong emotion, and have invested those defenses with so much of the energy derived from forbidden impulse, that they can no longer remember what it feels like to be inundated by desire. They tend, rather, to be consumed with rage, which derives from defenses against desire and gives rise in turn to new defenses against rage itself. Outwardly bland, submissive, and sociable, they seethe with an inner anger for which a dense, overpopulated, bureaucratic society can devise few legitimate outlets. (p. 11)

Plagued by anxiety, depression, vague discontents, a sense of inner emptiness, the "psychological man" of the twentieth century seeks neither individual self-aggrandizement nor spiritual transcendence but peace of mind, under conditions that increasingly militate against it. Therapists, not priests or popular preachers of self-help or models of success like the captains of industry, become his principal allies in the struggle for composure; he turns to them in the hope of achieving the modern equivalent of salvation, "mental health." Therapy has established itself as the successor both to rugged individualism and to religion; but this does not mean that the "triumph of the therapeutic" has become a new religion in its own right. Therapy constitutes an antireligion, not always to be sure because it adheres to rational explanation or scientific methods of healing, as its practitioners would have us believe, but because modern society "has no future" and therefore gives no thought to anything beyond its immediate needs. Even when therapists speak of the need for "meaning" and "love," they define love and meaning simply as the fulfillment of the patient's emotional requirements. It hardly occurs to them—nor is there any reason why it should, given the nature of the therapeutic enterprise—to encourage the subject to subordinate his needs and interests to those of others, to someone or some cause or tradition outside himself. "Love" as self-sacrifice or self-abasement, "meaning" as submission to a higher loyalty—these sublimations strike the therapeutic sensibility as intolerably oppressive, offensive to common sense and injurious to personal health and well-being. To liberate humanity from such outmoded ideas of love and duty has become the mission of the post-Freudian therapies and particularly of their converts and popularizers, for whom mental health means the overthrow of inhibitions and the immediate gratification of every impulse. (p. 13)

> *Christopher Lasch, in his* The Culture of Narcissism: American Life in an Age of Diminishing Expectations *(reprinted by permission of W. W. Norton & Company, Inc.; copyright © 1979 by W. W. Norton & Company, Inc.), Norton, 1978, 268 p.*

ALFRED KAZIN

History is haughty to writers not of the first quality; to crusading intellectuals who write their names in causes—programmatic intellectuals, idealistic, liberal, radical, utopian—it can be dev-

astating. Mr. Lasch [in *The New Radicalism in America, 1889-1963*] sees modern American radicalism as the expression of intellectuals, and these intellectuals as typically rebels against their own middle-class backgrounds; by the time he gets through analyzing the careers of Jane Addams, Randolph Bourne, Mabel Dodge Luhan, Lincoln Steffens, and on a smaller scale those of Walter Lippmann, Reinhold Niebuhr, Sidney Hook, Dwight Macdonald, Arthur Schlesinger, Jr., and Norman Mailer, one recognizes the full extent of the snub, the classical stare of non-recognition, which one generation administers to another. I have been awaiting for some time a rejoinder to the veterans of the Thirties by a young historian born in the Thirties—and here it is, cool as you please, brilliantly thought out and sharply written, scholarly yet committed and open. This is a book to take seriously. Mr. Lasch is a careful and self-dependent thinker, he has no newer radicalism to offer but does have a great many subtle observations to make about the old, and his keen sense of the limitations of politics in our era of the bigger and bigger state tells a great deal about the overriding sense of American limitations from which this book arose. . . .

Mr. Lasch is perfectly sure that his detailed account of the personal unrest behind so many idealists does not constitute an "explaining-away" of their earnestly held beliefs. But since the whole point of his biographical method is to refute the older and more usual thesis that his subjects were more sensitive than others to social outrage, his sense of what really happened when the "new" intellectuals from the genteel middle class came into contact with suffering in the big cities is that these intellectuals experienced a "cultural crisis played out against the increasingly audible sounds of revolution."

What was achieved by this cultural crisis does not impress Mr. Lasch. Mabel Dodge Luhan and other American leaders of the first Freudian generation were unable to understand, even when they were in contact with D. H. Lawrence in America, that Lawrence's prime interest was in writing. The "religion of experience" was deep in these intellectuals who felt "different" from the bustling extroverts around them. . . .

Mr. Lasch is very good on this religion of experience, which has never been more intense than in our post-genteel age, but which remains the same series of defiant gestures, from the first Freudians to the latest Reichians, against what theoretically excludes the intellectual from the "vital" and "dangerous" and "real." But Mr. Lasch does not fairly show the provincialism and moral anxiety against which so many fine writers in the Middle West rose seventy years ago, and which they made their subject. . . .

Mr. Lasch has his advantage over the sociologist who works in samples and categories; he does not have the advantage that the historian of the times has. He does not admit the past as an historical dimension, an objective presence; he is too intent on showing the comparative shallowness and abstractness of the intellectuals' revolt against it. One can grant him everything he says about American intellectuals who were not artists and thought that they could enlist even politics in the service of cultural improvement—ridiculous in the Eighties, even more ridiculous now. What Mr. Lasch does not do, however, is to show the actual prohibitions, gentilities, sterilities, and complacencies against which the "new" intellectuals arose at the turn of the century. (p. 3)

Mr. Lasch's criticism is that the intellectuals tried to supplant this culture by abstract slogans and "progressivism" in politics and education; he is surely right. American intellectuals have produced all the radicalism we have; visitors like George Lichtheim think that American "liberalism" does not exist outside the colleges and universities. This liberalism-radicalism is, however, bound to the society that has produced it—never more so than today, when among the middle-aged and now prosperous children of the depression, Russia serves as an alibi for complacency about their condition, while among the newer, or hipster radicals, obviously the children of affluence, the fear of being left out of *anything* leads Norman Mailer to "force himself into the thick of the Patterson-Liston fight."

What I like about Mr. Lasch's tough and acute last chapter—on hipsters airily *méchant*, ex-Communists still morally obsessed by Russia, New-Frontier "realists," and Washington "young executives" stupefied by the inescapability of money and the access to power—is that he relates the polemicists, the abstractionists, the cold-war philosophers, the hipsters, and the new computer-age intelligentsia squarely to the realities of American life and the frustrations created by the omnipresent state. He does not nag the radicals occupying position A from the newly acquired self-righteousness of position B. He is, in fact, pretty hopeless. . . . He says clearly that the supposed alliance between Kennedy and the intellectuals rested, among the intellectuals, on enthusiasm for the money, the chic, the power, the "style" that became the obvious mark of success. ". . . intellectuals not only admired these things, they associated them with *intellect*." Intellectuals have in many sectors attained the status of a privileged class, are now jealous of their recognized position in the social order, especially as the trained specialists who alone can handle the vast apparatus of systematized data on which both business and government depend under the pressure of technological revolution, expanding population, and the indefinitely prolonged emergence of the cold war. The intellectuals of the mass media, of Broadway, of the universities, are really talking about themselves when they talk about "society."

It was about time that someone made a categorical definition of the stake that so many intellectuals now have in the inequalities of our society, in the perpetuation of the cold war, in the often trivial but protected differentiation of professional functions; about time that someone held the mirror up to American intellectuals and showed us the extent to which we are implicated in our wars as in our prosperity—for it is also us, and not just President Johnson and General Taylor, that other people are thinking of when they level the charge that is unintelligible to most American intellectuals—"American imperialism." Mr. Lasch is able to make his definition convincingly. He is a scholar, and likes the truth. He does not come out of this book politically superior to other people. American radicalism is what American society, mass society, and the all-powerful state have made and are making of our intellectuals. (pp. 3-4)

> *Alfred Kazin, "Radicals and Intellectuals," in* The New York Times Book Review *(© 1965 by The New York Times Company; reprinted by permission), May 20, 1965, pp. 3-4.*

NORMAN BIRNBAUM

Christopher Lasch has written a subtle, disturbing and important book. A composite portrait of the American intellectual from the end of the nineteenth century to the Kennedy administration, [*The New Radicalism in America, 1889-1963*] is also an essay on the place of intelligence in modern society.

Lasch's historical method is psychological, and his psychology is an amalgam of biographical and social analysis. . . . [He] identifies the symptomatic aspects of the lives of his subjects, the personal crises which are idiosyncratic versions of common difficulties.

But the strength of the work is, perhaps inevitably, a source of weakness. History is here recounted like a late bourgeois novel, a curious *Bildungsroman* whose hero—the American intellectual—seems unable ever to reach maturity, compelled indefinitely to repeat the follies of his youth. Lasch maintains the unity of his own critical thought by insisting upon the traits common to his subjects. A fully achieved portrait is the result, but the era's inner movement comes rather short. In the end, he has very little to say about the changes in our circumstances; living history turns out to be, disappointingly, not entirely alive and moving.

The "new radicalism in America," Mr. Lasch feels, is less a fixed doctrine than a set of attitudes, a system of preconceptions—fundamentally, a critique of the quality of American life. (p. 463)

Lasch's diagnosis of a collective intellectual unconscious has a therapeutic purpose. He'd prefer intellectuals to adopt a mode of thought which is detached from immediate political considerations, critical and true to the pursuit of culture. Unfortunately, Mr. Lasch's prescription is exceedingly vague. It is appreciably easier to see what he dislikes than to imagine what he favors. (p. 464)

Lasch attributes the intellectuals' malaise to a specific historical development, the emergence of a mass society in which they as a group were only one of many fragments. In contrast to his descriptions of particular persons and events, his larger historical analysis of the source of the intellectuals' discontents is quite unconvincing. He is uncertain whether capitalism, industrialism or mass society is responsible for the intellectuals' plight, and these highly schematic terms are not used anywhere critically.

There are, however, many good things in this book: remarks on the intellectuals and the cult of publicity; reflections on youth, age and wisdom; thoughts on sexuality and personal relationships generally. (A sketch of the intellectuals' attachment to the Kennedy administration is very amusing and highly instructive.) There are also some very striking failures to seize some obvious opportunities for enlarging our self-knowledge as intellectuals.

Lasch seems confident that religion in America is relatively unimportant in the recent progression of its intellect. He is right to be skeptical about the conventional notion that a secularized Protestantism accounts for the morality of social reform. Yet the despair of an earlier generation may have been due to something profoundly repressive in the Protestantism to which they were heirs. (He does acknowledge this might be the case for Bourne.) It isn't plausible, further, for an author to evoke New York's role as the center of American intellectual life while ignoring the eastern European Jewish immigration. . . . Lasch also says nothing about Catholicism. . . . Lasch is quite silent about a problem which is still pertinent: the American intellectuals' relationship to Europe. . . . The American intellectual today, despite his travels, is less cosmopolitan than his predecessor of a generation ago—with serious consequences for the detachment and suppleness of his thought. Lasch's method, which concentrates on continuity, allows him to ignore important breaks in historical pattern of this sort.

Yet another break is mentioned by Lasch, but he skirts it. He begins his book by identifying the intellectuals as a special class in a fragmented society, ends it by noting that a technical intelligentsia in the service of power now has an enormous stake in the maintenance of society. By his own criteria, the technical intelligentsia are not necessarily intellectuals. The latter think; the former worry about "on-going research." The polarization of American intellectual life between the programmer and the hipster is one historical variant of a general problem. Perhaps the problem is more vexed in America because of the absence of a deeply rooted tradition of humanism. At any rate, Lasch's brief for rational criticism assumes what remains to be proven—that rational criticism is in contemporary America politically practicable.

Lasch emerges very well in one respect. He remarks that succeeding generations of American intellectuals have almost invariably abused their predecessors (and that some of those now aged forty-five or older have taken to abusing their successors, as well). His own treatment of our forebears is remarkable for its restraint, dignity and discrimination. . . . I wonder, however, what he thinks of the new Narodniki from the American middle class, the allies of the southern Negro, the volunteers for the Peace Corps—and of those who have refused military service in Vietnam. The new organization of American power implicates the educated young in its exercise from the very beginning. But if it has provoked something like a qualitative change in consciousness, the compulsive cycle Lasch sees has been broken. (pp. 464-66)

> Norman Birnbaum, "The Radical Circle," in Partisan Review (copyright © 1966 by Partisan Review, Inc.), Vol. XXXIII, No. 3, Summer, 1966, pp. 463-66.

P. P. ARDERY, JR.

In one of the five loosely related essays that make up [*The Agony of the American Left*], the author casually refers to Franklin Roosevelt as an "enlightened conservative." Such a bizarre reading of the political spectrum tends to befuddle. Unless one suspends one's own more conventional political framework, too many of Christopher Lasch's polemics are without bite, too many of his insights without clout. For example, the third essay in this volume is a shrill documentation and denunciation of the anti-Communism of some liberals. Those readers not sharing the author's radical bias are likely to plod quizzically through the angry phrases and then, at the end, ask, "So?" But Lasch at his best is not a partisan writing for fellow partisans but a near-pure analyst, the best the New Left has produced to date. And the last two essays . . . are brilliant, objective critiques of the black and student revolutionary movements. The one theme common to all five essays is the failure of ideology, this being the agony of the American Left. Our radical intellectuals have always looked to Lenin or Mao for their philosophical underpinnings, but the ideas of both men have consistently failed to gain a foothold on American soil because, says Lasch, they're irrelevant to conditions in the United States. . . . Lasch would construct a new socialist ideology, almost from scratch. The New Left can become a serious revolutionary movement if it follows the course that Lasch is beginning to chart. Conservatives should read his book to learn where the Left may be headed, thus to head it off.

> P. P. Ardery, Jr., "Books in Brief: 'The Agony of the American Left'," in National Review (© National

Review, Inc., 1969; 150 East 35th St., New York, NY 10016), Vol. XXI, No. 19, May 20, 1969, p. 501.

JOHN McDERMOTT

The Agony of the American Left is at once intellectually lucid and politically opaque. The distinction, I recognize, is an odd one and difficult to explain but it holds nevertheless. Each of the five essays collected in this volume contains an unusual wealth of insight into the history of the American Left and its recurring (and, Lasch feels, highly abortive) efforts to reform our society. . . .

Yet, for all the illumination, a political opaqueness still remains. It stems, I think, from Lasch's almost unremitting failure to perceive the current Left movement in this country as a political movement per se giving expression to profound social and economic grievances. Instead Lasch . . . insists on portraying today's radicals as animated by moral or cultural (or even) generational protests only marginally related to American politics and social life. Accordingly, the tempered political judgment which characterizes his treatment of earlier American movements such as the Socialist Party before World War I, or even American society today, is put aside when he reaches the New Left and we must settle instead for unrestrained and unenlightening polemic. (p. 797)

[The sophisticated and effective political activities of the New Left] are inexplicable if one characterizes the Movement, as Lasch often does, as a loose collection of morally "alienated" people which deals not with real issues but with "leftist fancies," led by its "more demented" elements who must be "recall[ed] to their senses (those that ever had any)."

When the views of a writer of Lasch's caliber overlap those of, say, Max Lerner, Sidney Hook, Eric Sevareid, Richard Nixon, or the education editor of *The New York Times*, it is a matter which obviously requires more than passing explanation.

Lasch argues forcefully that the United States is now a post-industrial society, a society in which the problems of poverty, economic deprivation and regimentation to industrial discipline have been or can be solved for the vast majority of Americans. By contrast, in post-industrial society poverty and its kin have become endemic for a minority (mostly black) who are excluded from mainstream America. Simultaneously, mass education removes large numbers of young people

> at a critical period in their lives and for a considerable time from the productive process and . . . from institutional ties to the rest of society. . . . As marginal members of society students as a class, like Black people, are more likely than other classes to be attracted to perspectives highly critical of society, particularly when they are faced with "integration" into society in the form of the draft. This is the basic sociological condition that gives rise to the student Left and the "new radicalism" in general.

It is this perspective, more than anything else which makes Lasch concentrate on the zanier, less responsible and less pleasant elements of the Movement, which make him read its anti-academic clericalism as anti-intellectualism, its combativeness as nihilism, and its contempt for procedural liberalism as incipient totalitarianism. . . .

I fear that a misperception about a very tiny point leads [Lasch] to very large and erroneous consequences. Youth or students *as a class* are not marginal to post-industrial society and they are not created as its by-product. There are no such classes in pre-industrial or even classical industrial society. In both cases, one goes directly from childhood to adulthood without an intermediate stage. The significance of "youth" and "students" in contemporary American society follows from the need of advanced technological society to give very broad technical and scientific training to great masses of people, while at the same time acculturating them to an extraordinarily restricted political, social, personal and work life. (pp. 798-99)

One is not using a metaphor when one speaks of students being turned out like industrial products. It's the simple truth. The university is now one of the main consumers of the nation's capital investments (much of it in the form of tuition). Its open-market structure has been replaced by a managed economy, and the organization of its productive process, the division of its labor, and the specifications on its end products have been thoroughly rationalized. Some institutions, such as Harvard and Berkeley, even offer quality control.

Such changes in the university, the *details* of which Lasch describes quite brilliantly, are not aptly characterized by his concept "post-industrial." In fact, analogous changes are now going on throughout American society. . . . Whereas formerly only hard goods were the subject of industrial production, now the production of students, research, health care, social services, residence and transportation systems, culture and even lower echelon managers is increasingly becoming capital intensive, management intensive and rationalized at every stage. The processes of industrialization, formerly experienced by a relatively small segment of our population, are now permeating the society as a whole. . . .

[The] Movement is the beginning of the American people's response to a new wave of industrialization masquerading under the name of technological progress. Industrial society has not ended; in a real sense it has hardly begun.

Lasch's main contribution in these five essays is his dissection of the causes and effects of the American intellectuals' isolation from mass movements in this century. Especially in his essay on the Congress for Cultural Freedom . . . he shows how their elitism and power worship—the latter usually disguised as "pragmatism" or "realism"—have created a profound and destructive intellectual, moral and social chasm between them and the political movements of the Left which have had such hopeful beginnings in the past and whose failures are symbolized in the title of his book. The problem has been and remains the problem of being intellectuals not *to* the Movement but *of* the Movement, not its clergy but its staff, not its organizational commissars but its intellectual cadre. More pointedly, there is no sense in demanding that the Movement have a program here and now. Such a program is now shaping itself as our people, long politically dormant, look at their society with a critical eye, learn its realities in sometimes ill-focused but always instructive struggles, and come to recognize what they want and what they don't. Left intellectuals should add their considerable talents to that process, and not be content to chafe at its slowness. High on the agenda is the task of building an adult movement on the Left of a size and strength commensurate to that of the students, co-belligerent with them, and capable of shaping the radical program Lasch demands. It is a job hardly begun and, despite my critical observations, it is a job to which, I feel, this book makes substantial contribution. (p. 799)

> John McDermott, "Politics of the Movement," in The Nation (copyright 1969 The Nation *magazine,* The Nation Associates, Inc.), Vol. 208, No. 25, June 23, 1969, pp. 797-99.

DAVID MARQUAND

The central message of **The Agony of the American Left** is that the pragmatic, problem-solving liberalism of the progressive movement, the New Deal and the New Frontier has now broken down: and that nothing has yet appeared, or is likely in the foreseeable future to appear, to take its place.

Despite the rather querulous tone in which it is put, and the crude, neo-Marxist assumptions which underlie part of the argument, the first part of this message seems to me convincing. It is surely beyond dispute that more is wrong with American society than a series of discrete 'problems' to be 'solved' in the traditional pragmatic fashion. (p. 773)

If pragmatic liberalism is bankrupt and the revolutionary rhetoric of Black Power and the New Left a false dawn, where is the American Left to look instead? At this point, Mr Lasch's critical faculties suddenly desert him. The obvious alternative to liberal pragmatism on the one hand and revolutionary romanticism on the other is a revitalised and much more radical Democratic party, mobilised around a coherent programme of social reform. Mr Lasch considers this alternative, though only in a few unsatisfactory pages at the end of his book, but rejects it on the grounds that it would amount to nothing more than 'welfare liberalism', and that 'welfare liberalism' cannot eliminate the contradictions of American capitalism.

The crucial assumption on which this whole argument is based is that there are, in fact, contradictions at the heart of modern American capitalism which cannot be resolved without a total transformation of the whole system. But as Mr Lasch himself points out in his critique of the Black Power movement, the available evidence points in exactly the opposite direction. The real tragedy of the Northern negroes—and the same applies to the other disaffected minorities—is that they are economically marginal: that the capitalist system can get on perfectly well without them, and therefore has no need to pay any attention to them. When Marx talked about the contradictions of capitalism he did not mean that capitalism was nasty and immoral. He meant that it was doomed to collapse, and that it was doomed not by its failures but by its successes. This is simply not true of American capitalism today. The blacks, the poor whites and the alienated students of modern America are not a Marxian proletariat; and a political movement based on the assumption that they are would have failed before it had begun.

In his more sensible moments, Mr Lasch evidently realises this himself, but he cannot bring himself to face the implications. In his capacity as a historian, he recognises that one of the perennial weaknesses of the American intellectual Left has been its refusal to face the realities of American life and its tendency to analyse American problems in terms which have no relevance to American history. In his capacity as a social theorist he then proceeds to fall into exactly the same trap himself. Part of the reason, at any rate, is that he is a victim of the classic American gap between the radical intelligentsia and the labour movement. That gap, it seems to me, is still the greatest single obstacle to social progress in America. It is a tragedy that a critic of such sensitivity and intelligence as Mr Lasch has done so little to bridge it. (pp. 773-74)

> *David Marquand, "A Radical Dilemma," in* New Statesman *(© 1970 The Statesman & Nation Publishing Co. Ltd.), Vol. 79, No. 2046, May 29, 1970, pp. 773-74.*

KLAUS J. HANSEN

[Sensitivity] is one of Lasch's great strengths. He also has a very subtle mind and, at his best, the kind of historical imagination that reminds us of Richard Hofstadter. It is for these reasons that through his best essays in [*The World of Nations*] he has sustained a critique and a vision of the American past that follows consistently from Vico's text: "the world of civil society has certainly been made by men, and . . . its principles are therefore to be found within the modifications of our own human mind. Whoever reflects on this cannot but marvel that the philosophers should have bent all their energies to the study of the world of nature, which, since God made it, He alone knows; and that they should have neglected the study of *the world of nations* or civil world, which, since men had made it, men could hope to know."

Lasch's purpose, of course, is not only to "know" in the academic sense, in the fashion of the monograph, but to explain. In a brilliant essay on **"The Origins of the Asylum,"** for which we can forgive him much that follows in the first section, he points to the ironic "limits of liberal reform." In a second section, on **"Alternatives to Liberalism,"** he warns us that outmoded, nineteenth-century notions of "revolution" can be no solution to the problems generated by modern industrial society. Lasch is equally skeptical of the neo-romanticism of the New Left and of the prophets of the "counterculture." Though he calls himself a socialist he sees the limits (and limitations) of Jack Newfield, Michael Harrington, and George McGovern. Marx, to him, is still the essential bedrock for a socialist perspective. And yet, Marx failed to address himself to the problem that Lasch sees as central to the solution of our current impasse, "the need to distinguish between 'culture' and 'ideology'." . . .

Lasch thinks it ironic that the anti-Marxist purveyors of the notion of a "post-industrial society" are likewise unable to make that distinction. Before we can go about remaking the "world of nations" we must clearly understand what we *can* do, and what we *want* to do. Lasch still believes that man is basically a rational being. If a cynic may argue that the wish is the father of the thought, Lasch's humane intelligence, which illuminates this work and makes its whole greater than the parts, provides evidence to prove the cynics wrong. (pp. 412-13)

> *Klaus J. Hansen, "Reviews of Books: 'The World of Nations: Reflections on American History, Politics, and Culture'," in* Pacific Historical Review *(© 1974, by the Pacific Coast Branch, American Historical Association), Vol. XLIII, No. 3, August, 1974, pp. 412-13.*

GEORGE GILDER

We can be sure that Christopher Lasch would not like us to weigh too carefully the Marxist buncombe with which he disguises, for the consumption of academia, this marvelously reactionary book on the family [*Haven in a Heartless World*].

Let us merely observe in passing that he depicts the medical, social welfare, and "child development" bureaucracies that beset and threaten the modern home—always at the behest of the political Left—as characteristic implements of "capitalism." He also claims that the shallow behaviorist sociology behind this invasion of the family is somehow inconsistent with the aims and insights of Marxism, itself the most influential of all behaviorist formulas. His arguments on these points, however, are too complex and unintelligent to be worth repeating in a review of this otherwise shrewd and brilliant critique of the pretensions of modern social science.

Where once in the human city a cathedral towered, and later the halls of legislation loomed, there now stands a hospital as "the symbolic center of society," the cathedral of the therapeutic state. It is not a simple vendor of medicine. To Lasch, the hospital, with its reach into the realms of public health and mental hygiene and its association with the "helping professions" of social welfare and education, symbolizes the dispossession of parents by vendors of "expertise" and special knowledge. . . .

This secular expertise, according to Lasch, gains its force from the regnant ideology of social science. This ideology views human beings as almost entirely the products of their environment: human ciphers ruled by Society, as interpreted by social scientists and as embodied in the institutions of social therapy—creatures whose natural spontaneity and kindness are perverted only by the morbid intensities, expectations, and sex-role transactions of the family. (p. 220)

Even if there are warps of caricature in his depiction of the experts, Lasch is essentially right about the inner logic and observable effect of their ascendancy. The authorities on child-rearing, for example, remain today in almost complete confusion on the subject, with new fashions and theories emerging so often that any mother who tried to follow them would tie herself and her children in knots. . . .

[The] invasion of the home is explained not by its benefits, nor by any necessary collapse of parental effectiveness, but chiefly by the drive for power of a new class of professionals. Obviously, the analogy to capitalism founders here, since industrialization conferred spectacular material benefits that, according to Lasch, even provide the basis for a new and better form of society; while the usurpation of the family by the expert, Lasch suggests, leaches out of the contemporary personality the "imagination and energy" needed to exploit the new opportunities.

Lasch believes that democratic politics depend on the maintenance of the family, not merely as "a haven in a heartless world" but also as the matrix of individuals with conscience and character, immune to manipulation by the state. Much of his book, therefore, is devoted to a tenacious and resourceful defense of Freud's theory of an individual unconscious, turbid and irrational, unreachable by social policy, but malleable in the intense inner heat of familial sexuality and conflict.

It is a theory not only of individual psychology but also of cultural transmission and social change. Only the patriarchal family, says Lasch, can dependably enact the oedipal drama by which the conflicts of the unconscious are tamed and transcended in the forms of conscience and super-ego—the individual expressions of civilization. . . .

State coercion, Lasch contends, is the inevitable, ironic harvest of the liberal drive for a rational and therapeutic order. Attempting to reduce family life to mere companionship, recreational sex, and reciprocal services—all devoid of the profound and passionate workings of real sexuality and love—the social therapists destroy the essential mechanisms both of civic responsibility and of constructive change. Such families, Lasch persuasively shows, leave all the compulsive rages of the unconscious unresolved, until they emerge in the crimes and psychological disorders characteristic of a society in which neither love nor discipline can be long sustained and the rise of despotism is just a matter of time.

Today, however, the chief resistance to the invasion of the "doctors" comes not from the bastions of psychoanalysis—the defenders of the Freudian unconscious—but from the reawakening of religion in America. Religion is the patriarchal corrective that can still flourish redemptively whenever the familial father is pushed aside. The chief flaw of Lasch's difficult but rewarding book is its entrapment by the claims and limitations of secular psychoanalysis, against which could be made a complementary case in religious terms just as true as his own splendid refutation of contemporary social science. (p. 222)

George Gilder, "The Therapeutic State," in Na-
tional Review (© National Review, Inc., 1978; 150
East 35th St., New York, NY 10016), Vol. 30, No.
7, February 17, 1978, pp. 220, 222.

DAVID BRION DAVIS

Lasch's subject [in *Haven in a Heartless World*] is the "tradition of sociological study, which still defines the issues that inform most of the current commentary on the family." More specifically, his book is a commentary on the ways in which academic and clinical social theory has reinforced and interacted with the institutional structures of corporate capitalism. . . .

His book will provoke howls of common anger from many otherwise opposing camps, since he boldly takes on Marxians and anti-Marxians, neo-Freudians and feminist anti-Freudians, Parsonians and anti-Parsonians, Moynihanians and anti-Moynihanians, and he directs his fire at most of the major American anthropologists, sociologists, and neo-Freudian analysts of the past sixty years. . . .

There can be little question that Lasch is unnecessarily combative and often given to exaggeration and reckless generalization. Yet he also seeks, with admirable clarity, to understand and revise a cumulative body of criticism. His excesses spring not only from a Jeffersonian "hostility against every form of tyranny over the mind of man," but from a conviction that the worst and most subtle forms of such tyranny are those that are made to appear natural, inevitable, or invisible as a result of deliberate mystification or of massive intellectual conventions. It will be most unfortunate if the serious flaws in Lasch's book encourage easy misreading or indignant dismissal. For there is no more brilliant exposure of the collective self-deceptions of a "therapeutic" society in quest of psychic security. (p. 37)

Lasch's central theme . . . is that critics, commentators, and therapists of all persuasions have helped to strip the family of its last shreds of privacy and autonomy, rendering it vulnerable to the full onslaughts of hucksterism and market manipulation. The same forces that had earlier impoverished work and civic life, in this bleak view, have now made family members "un-

able to provide for their own needs without the supervision of trained experts." . . .

[A serious problem with Lasch is that sometimes he] writes like a critic who views his subject from the outside, employing Freud and Marx to portray a highly interdependent, self-limiting system which serves the interests of a privileged class and which develops efficient mechanisms for neutralizing dissent. At other times Lasch writes like a neo-Populist who has merely substituted social scientists and the "helping professions" for Wall Street bankers and railroad magnates. In the latter mood Lasch comes across as a besieged participant and victim, threatened by a strange alliance of marriage counselors, home economists, psychiatrists, social workers, sex therapists, "educators and social reformers," "planners and policymakers," to say nothing of the violent, young, and narcissistic pseudo-radicals who are egged on by the professionals.

If Lasch stops short of indulging in fantasies of conspiracy, which in this case would veer perilously close to those of the extreme right, he does obscurely equate his homogenized enemy with the "state," with "capitalists," and with the "same forces" responsible for most of the misery of modern Americans. Both of Lasch's perspectives presuppose significant connections between the control of socialization and the aggrandizing structures of corporate power. But Lasch as external critic exposes the mystifications that contribute to homeostasis; Lasch as the embattled moralist rails against an irreversible fall from grace. (p. 38)

Lasch's great achievement, in directing a dazzling burst of light upon dangerous illusions, is not diminished by the distorted shadows he casts on our past and future. His indispensable contribution is the argument that public concern for the plight of the family has commonly masked efforts to subject the family to new forms of outside influence, usually in the interest of marketing new services and products. Yet it needs to be stressed that by locating the origins of the decline of the family in the relatively recent past, Lasch falls into an uncritical nostalgia for a golden age when the functions of the family formed "an integrated system" insulated from the intrusions of a heartless world.

The nostalgia is misleading on two counts. Most of the issues Lasch discusses were visible long before the Civil War, when "interventionists"—ranging from the Boston Prison Discipline Society to public school reformers—were already proposing, for example, that families adopt the system of surveillance and calculated privation that had supposedly proved effective in penitentiaries. If it is objected that few families actually followed the advice offered in sermons, childbearing manuals, popular magazines, and lyceum lectures, one must answer that Lasch says nothing about the number of parents and children currently victimized by the "helping professions." Lasch's theory of unilinear decline also overlooks the misery, shame, violence, humiliation, and ignorance of the "premodern" family. Far from encouraging the notion that each individual is the "autonomous creator of his own destiny," such families were typically dominated by the terrors of Calvinist or Catholic conceptions of sin. Moreover, in defiance of historians, these supposedly "premodern" patterns have shown a stubborn unwillingness to become extinct. For good or ill, the American family has been far less volatile, conformist, and changeable than has social theory.

When one elongates the historical perspective, the future of the family appears less bleak than Lasch would have it. Since the "invasion" he describes has been under way for nearly two centuries, we would have nothing left to invade if history had moved, as he seems to presuppose, in a single direction. But this is only to say that the model of a continuous decline shares the defects of the model of continuous progress, of which, of course, it is the mirror image. (pp. 38-9)

David Brion Davis, "The Invasion of the Family," in The New York Review of Books (reprinted with permission from The New York Review of Books; copyright © 1978 Nyrev, Inc.), Vol. 25, No. 2, February 23, 1978, pp. 37-8.

NATHAN GLAZER

[Haven in a Heartless World] is chiefly an attack on the state for the myriad ways in which it impinges upon the family, the sort of attack one might have expected from a conservative or traditionalist, but hardly from a representative of the radical Left. Professor Lasch does not, let it be said, take the easy route of condemning only the bourgeois state while exculpating the socialist or Communist state. If nothing else, he is consistent in apparently demanding no public intervention whatsoever into the private realm of the family, no matter what political arrangement prevails. How he maintains his position as a radical while upholding this view is an interesting question, and one which tells us much about the style of radical scholarship today.

Professor Lasch looks with skepticism on just about every liberal reform that has ever been made in the area of child welfare and family life. He manages to sound sarcastic even when writing about the abolition of child labor, or the advent of compulsory education, and he is scarcely more forgiving of those reformers who sought to remove children from the jurisdiction of criminal courts. . . . In all these cases, Professor Lasch is presumably defending the rights of parenthood against the incursions of arrogant outsiders, and perhaps with some justice. But he seems almost willfully indifferent to the fact that children have benefited enormously from these reforms. . . .

But it is not the reformers alone who incur Professor Lasch's scorn. He is no less critical of the liberal sociologists of "marriage and the family" who in his view looked on with equanimity while the role of the family continued to dwindle, and as its authority was stolen away. What is more, he seems to be half-blaming them for this development, though it is hard to understand how these hapless representatives of one of the least influential branches of an uninfluential discipline could have had much effect on anything. Indeed, Professor Lasch has a consistent problem in this book of confusing what has actually happened to the family with what people said was happening, or what they might have wanted to happen. Thus, he exaggerates, to my mind, the role of the "helping professions"—psychologists, psychiatrists, family sociologists, etc.— in shaping family life in the 20's and 30's, a period during which they allegedly appropriated the parental function. . . .

Christopher Lasch is a Freudian, and as such is strongly committed both to the truth and to the desirability of Freud's model of psychological development within the family. He rejects out-of-hand the criticism that the family as described by Freud, with its basis in the Oedipus complex, was historically and socially conditioned, rooted in the particular circumstances of turn-of-the-century Vienna, and hence irrelevant to our own concerns. Professor Lasch maintains to the contrary that the Freudian family dynamic is applicable to all societies at all times, that it is grounded not in any given social structure, but rather in biology itself. It is not the Viennese family, or the 19th-century family, or the middle-class family, or the bourgeois family that Freud was describing, but rather the family, a fundamental biological reality, and to tamper with it is accordingly to court disaster. (p. 51)

At this point in Professor Lasch's analysis we begin to understand how the pessimistic and apparently conservative views of Freud on human destiny can be enlisted in the cause of radical hope: he sees in the family a kind of cradle of the revolution, a source of energy for later resistance against despotism, but only when the family's natural dynamic has not been undercut and subverted by the Meads, the Fromms, and the Horneys, with their optimism about the human condition, or by the ministrations of mental-health enthusiasts and liberal family sociologists, with their claim that scientific progress can modify the harshness of repression and mitigate the pains of achieving adult sexuality. . . . What Professor Lasch seems to be saying here, in effect, is a more sophisticated version of the old radical notion that for things to get better, they must first get worse, and a little mitigating reform is a dangerous thing.

In fact, his skepticism about the benefits of gradual change reaches back to a point well before the bourgeois family came into being. Just about every change that has ever been made in family arrangements seems to have been for the worse in his opinion, possibly including even the creation of the bourgeois family itself. The attractiveness to Professor Lasch of the pre-industrial past that was undermined by capitalism, industry, science, and the rise of the professionals keeps breaking through. He sounds on occasion as though he were defending even its darkest aspects. Thus, he writes at one point that "the attack on disease was part of a general attack on pre-industrial customs. It went hand in hand with the suppression of public executions, the movement to institutionalize the insane, and the campaign to replace domestic riot and licentiousness with domestic bliss. . . ." If this does not precisely constitute advocacy of disease, public executions, or public baiting of the insane, it certainly suggests that the author is not happy with what replaced them. The promised "domestic bliss" turns out to have been a fraud, first of all because the therapeutic professionals in Professor Lasch's view simply did not know as much as they claimed to.

Here he adds his voice to the growing radical critique of the professions—both that of medicine and the lesser examples— attributing their rise during the modern period not to any increase in knowledge but only to a desire for power and monopoly modeled on analogous developments in the world of capitalist industry. Just as capitalist methods of production undermined the competence of the workers, so did the professionals' invasion of the family undermine the sense of competence of parents—and with deplorable results for the family: the father, weakened, yielded to the mother who, in turn, unable to cope, called upon the fraudulent assistance of so-called professionals in family management. The parents, increasingly helpless, could do nothing but stand by and watch as their children, far from prospering under their new freedom, incurred a variety of psychic ills from homosexuality to impotence—paying the price for disruption of the natural, biologically-based family configuration.

Having followed him this far, I will not even try to explain how Professor Lasch manages to tie all this in with capitalism, for his explanation, if we can call it that, has more in common with incantation than with analysis. Mainly, it seems to consist of invoking, at points both appropriate and inappropriate, such phrases as "the machinery of organized domination," "the manipulative spirit . . . ascendant in business life," etc., etc. Unfortunately, Professor Lasch shares with many other contemporary radical theorists the tendency to use extravagant and irrelevant terminology to suggest connections which simply make no sense at all between capitalism and all sorts of other unrelated social developments. (p. 52)

So taken up is Professor Lasch with theorizing that he manages to ignore the concrete actualities of state intervention into the affairs of the family. He has almost nothing to say, for example, about the massive intervention that is inevitably involved in providing welfare, food subsidies, Medicaid and Medicare, child-care programs like Head Start, as well as the large variety of other state services which expanded so enormously during the 60's and whose impact on children and the family we are perpetually trying to gauge. It would seem that anyone concerned with how the state, wittingly or unwittingly, has affected the family, would have to enter into the history, intentions, and unanticipated consequences of these programs, but Professor Lasch is virtually silent on the subject. Instead, we are numbed with grand but obscure phrases such as "the socialization of reproduction" and the "proletarianization of parenthood." They suggest that the writer, struggling with his conservative instincts, is trying to save his radical credentials by ivoking the proper spells. (pp. 52-3)

Nathan Glazer, "The Rediscovery of the Family," in Commentary *(reprinted by permission; all rights reserved), Vol. 65, No. 3, March, 1978, pp. 49-56.**

EDGAR Z. FRIEDENBERG

[*Haven in a Heartless World* never establishes] that family life, marriage, and relations between parents and children have indeed suffered . . . ravages recently at the hands of liberal praxis and ideology. Most of what we know of families other than our own comes not from "studies" but from biography, novels, and drama; and these can hardly be said to verify that the perils of family life have grown steadily greater and the satisfactions correspondingly less. . . .

It seems regrettable that Lasch should have chosen to base his work on the proposition that family life now faces ruin, since his basic argument does not depend on it anyway. That argument cannot, I think, be faulted and it deals with issues of the most fundamental moral and social importance. (p. 554)

By yielding to the temptation to develop his book into a conventional jeremiad of a kind less perceptive authors have written often enough in the past, Lasch forfeits an opportunity to cap his impressive but finally incoherent analysis with an attempt at a really creative intellectual synthesis; one can almost hear the ghost of Hegel, which likes to see historians make it, gnashing its teeth in spectral rage. For what Lasch's thesis finally suggests is that super-ego failure, whatever its causes may be, seems especially crucial today because it has spread to the families of the ruling classes, who have lost their nerve and with it their legitimacy.

As Lasch might have said, had he been the first to think of it, the best lack all conviction while the worst are filled with passionate intensity. But that doesn't mean that the superego is dead and that everything is therefore permitted; merely that

conscience is making cowards of the wrong set, at least from the viewpoint of tradition. Historians, surely, have seen *that* happen before; that's how the Christians took over Rome and the Stalinists went marching through Georgia. The Puritans aren't dying out; they're just changing their habits to suit a different brotherhood. Puritans, are not however, necessarily harbingers of a moral renaissance; and I would be grateful, on that account, for the expression of a little grief for the passing of the much-despised hedonists. As we join hands to sing "Kampuchea the Beautiful," let us not forget how much nicer Acapulco Gold is than plain old Pol Pot. And how much less dangerous to your health. (pp. 555-56)

Edgar Z. Friedenberg, "Reviews of the Literature: 'Haven in a Heartless World: The Family Besieged','" in American Journal of Orthopsychiatry *(reprinted with permission; copyright 1978 by the American Orthopsychiatric Association, Inc.), Vol. 48, No. 3, July, 1978, pp. 553-56.*

FRANK KERMODE

[Professor Lasch's argument in **"The Culture of Narcissism"**] sounds pretty hopeless, and however much one agrees with some of the diagnosis, the cure is both unpromising and unappealing. Professor Lasch believes that many of our ills are related to the removal from our society of visible sanctions; by sparing the rod we spoil not only the child but ourselves. The danger here, I think, is precisely that the introjected archaic parent also favors terror. In early modernism we had several instances of the way in which a desire for order and discipline may be transformed into support for political terror. You may begin quite abstractly, like the art historian Wilhelm Worringer, and argue for the benefits of closed, hierarchical societies; but already with his disciple, T. E. Hulme, the argument is associated with a cult of violence, and a generation later Hulme's friend Wyndham Lewis was ready to welcome Hitler.

And what is to be offered to ordinary people when their dismal pleasures have been taken from them? The right to be poor, to be beaten in childhood, constrained by a savage penal system, compelled to suffer through an unhappy marriage, to be openly instead of covertly exploited, and to die young? For those conditions are as much a part of the relevant past as sobriety, ambition and discipline. And most of us, given a choice, would stick to what we've got. Because women may be exigent about orgasm, do we want a world in which most of them hardly know what the word means? For all that one agrees with Professor Lasch about the debasement of sports, do we want the great performers to return to wage slavery? And is their experience really so unusual? The painters made it in the 16th century, the actors in the 18th; no longer artisans or vagabonds, they were valued performers. And so with ballplayers now; their success is concededly accompanied by many less agreeable signs of corruption, but you could find people ready to argue that the same is true of the success of the painters and actors.

Perhaps the world has changed less than Professor Lasch believes. He condemns the modern painters for their insistence on formal qualities, their flaunting of illusion; yet they are only doing what Velázquez did before them, though they may be more interested than he was in the theory of what they are doing. For ours is an age of theory, and much of the situation Professor Lasch deplores may arise from an unduly heavy feedback of theory into practice. Historians lose confidence in history partly because the theory of history turns out to be so complex, and history so hard to distinguish from lying. It might even be argued that we have a more honest understanding of our intellectual plight than our predecessors, and that this accounts for our mistrust of simple rules and remedies. We are bound to be skeptical, of renovation as well as of decadence. But one thing we do know: there is no going back. We cannot destroy television, prohibit contraceptives, restore the work ethic, and if we did we should hardly be better off. What Professor Lasch has done—with somber force and occasionally with gloomy wit—is to provide us with a black survey of the way we live now, and leave us to use all our resources of theory and skepticism to make the best we can of it. (pp. 26-7)

> Frank Kermode, " 'The Culture of Narcissism'," in The New York Times Book Review (© 1979 by The New York Times Company; reprinted by permission), January 14, 1979, pp. 1, 26-7.

JACKSON LEARS

The Culture of Narcissism takes a number of Lasch's recent essays, adds some new material, and reworks the whole into a continuous argument. In broad outline, the book is a powerful indictment of the nonmorality promoted by consumer capitalism, drawing on a wide variety of evidence; it is boldly conceived and gracefully, sometimes eloquently expressed. But in detail, the book is uneven; it suffers from a superficiality in historical explanation and a tendency to substitute assertion for argument. In part, the difficulties stem from Lasch's unwillingness fully to acknowledge his cultural conservatism. He clings to some of the honorable values in Victorian culture—moral discipline, parental authority, the work ethic—without making his allegiance explicit. As a result, his critique loses polemical focus; sometimes it degenerates into a repetitive tirade. In short, while *The Culture of Narcissism* is an exciting and suggestive book, it could have been a vastly more persuasive one. (p. 91)

With [his] bleak picture of capitalism's corrosion of values, Lasch updates *The Communist Manifesto*. Under capitalism, Marx wrote, "All that is solid melts into air, all that is holy is profaned. . . ." To Lasch, "all freedoms under capitalism come to the same thing, the same universal obligation to enjoy and be enjoyed." It is the cry of the outraged moralist, and it derives its power not from analytical rigor but from the emotional intensity behind it. Yet *The Culture of Narcissism* is more than a *cri de coeur;* it is a complex argument, with some serious shortcomings.

The most obvious difficulty involves a lack of evidence. Lasch makes so many illuminating connections (such as those between politics and sports, between success ideology and *avant-garde* theater) that I am sometimes tempted to overlook his book's sketchiness. As he points out, most social science has degenerated to the measurement of trivia; it is to Lasch's honor that he has chosen to risk speculative generalization. But Lasch does not acknowledge the speculative quality of his work and much of his argument is flawed by his argumentative, assertive style. Some chapters seem pasted together; entire sections are at best tenuously related to the "culture of narcissism" framework. And worst of all, the historical explanations often race breathlessly from point to point, collapsing complex developments into a paragraph or sentence; the subsection called "The Battle of the Sexes: Its Social History" is two pages long. In general, Lasch fails to provide the kind of dense

historical matrix that would have immeasurably strengthened his argument. (pp. 91-2)

[The] transformation of American Christianity is crucial to understanding the culture of narcissism—and Lasch virtually ignores it. From the liberal humanism which preaches "self-realization" to the resurgent evangelicalism which offers conversion as a cure for anxiety, American Christianity has surrendered to therapeutic ideals. Lasch could have extended his range from the likes of Jerry Rubin to some of the "born-again." For many ordinary Americans as well as countercultural radicals, religion often has become little more than a quest for self-fulfillment. As supernatural frameworks of meaning have weakened, religious emphases have shifted from salvation to peace of mind. The culture of narcissism has many social roots, but it also stems from the personal anxieties engendered by secularization.

Lasch's insensitivity to secularization may derive from his determination to preserve some hope for radical reconstruction of society. If a cultural crisis has social origins then it may yield to social solutions. He suggests that a "thoroughgoing transformation of our social arrangements remains a possibility" and that a socialist revolution might well abolish the "new paternalism" which degrades both work and domestic life. But if the nonmorality of consumer capitalism is imbedded at the deep and nearly inaccessible level of the unconscious, prospects for revolution are bleak. More important, if secularization has played a major role in creating the culture of narcissism, how does one undo its effects in attempting to recreate frameworks of meaning outside the self?

One of the most difficult problems facing critics of capitalism is the need to create alternative unities of belief in a culture which has dissolved nearly all higher loyalties—to particularist ideals of family or community, to universalist ideals of fraternity or humanity, to God. While Lasch has insufficiently clarified his commitment to those older values, he has acutely (though unevenly) analyzed the process of their dissolution. His insights undermine his hopes for reconstruction. He himself seems unconvinced that any measures can reverse the corrosive impact of capitalism on morality. But if capitalism's hour is far from late, there are still honorable alternatives to accommodation—not only the attempt to alleviate suffering or promote political resistance but also the effort to keep values alive in a valueless society. This last is the task of moralists in exile, who can find few stronger exemplars than Christopher Lasch. (p. 92)

> Jackson Lears, "Therapy's Triumph," in The Nation (copyright 1979 The Nation magazine, The Nation Associates, Inc.), Vol. 228, No. 3, January 27, 1979, pp. 91-2.

ROBERT BOYERS

[In *The Culture of Narcissism* Christopher Lasch] directs attention most emphatically to the emergence of a character type designated by Philip Rieff some years ago as Psychological Man. What had seemed to many of us a bewildering diversity of life patterns and cultural deformations are now persuasively explained as the products of an ethos for which the instant gratification of limitless desires is the only certain human value. As an historian, Lasch knows that no theory explains everything, and that individual behaviors often defy patterns to which most people conform. He does not pretend to describe everyone, but he has gone well beyond Rieff and other theorists in detailing the confusions and shifting identity images that disturb ordinary people. Where Rieff had largely limited himself—in *The Triumph of the Therapeutic* (1965) and *Fellow Teachers* (1972)—to an examination of intellectuals as a class in American society, Lasch is interested in the much larger population that consumes and is exploited by a great range of creature comforts. What Lasch loses in perfect organizational coherence he gains in diversity and immediacy of implication. Rieff's gifts as prophet-philosopher are nicely complemented by Lasch's eye for telling detail and his pointed distaste for the delusional thinking of current radicals. If Lasch is negative and angry, as hostile critics will say, he yet stakes out a position with the kind of clarity and consistency that will be hard to impugn. Liberals and social reformers especially will have to wonder, reading Lasch, how it is possible to see so much of the current situation without resorting to the meliorist and programmatic optimism that routinely informs the statements even of legislative and journalistic skeptics. (p. 29)

Lasch has made himself the most punishing and persuasive social critic we have by insisting that more than common sense is required to determine what we should and should not be doing. To think of him as a man with or without a detailed blueprint—thus, as optimist or pessimist—is to miss the intention of his work entirely. Lasch thinks of the past not because he is consumed by an effete nostalgia but because he needs some standard by which to judge the results of present practice. He isn't concerned to choose one in place of the other, but to work out a comparative analysis in which no present option seems perfectly fixed or inevitable. To see that events might well have conspired to produce alternative dispensations is to understand how fateful certain choices can seem when people pretend they could never have chosen any other way.

If there is any part of Lasch's account that makes me more than usually uneasy, it is his adaptation of a psychoanalytic vocabulary to the purposes of the social critic and cultural historian. The psychoanalytic theory of culture, as elaborated by Freud and modified by very different critics like Rieff and Herbert Marcuse, has its genuine uses, but there has always been a danger that local insights and explanatory schemes would too readily be pressed into the service of broader perspectives on less precisely focused clinical objects. (pp. 29-30)

Still, Lasch is committed to the psychoanalytic models only insofar as they permit him to do the work of cultural historian and social critic. Which is to say that he returns to these models only briefly and intermittently in the course of a work that has a great many areas to cover. And when the theory of narcissism is permitted to operate without specific clinical content—without the need to argue that individual pathologies constitute the key to every institutional disorder—the theory seems utterly persuasive. (p. 30)

It may be objected that, in pointing an accusatory finger at "society," Lasch makes it all but impossible to fix blame in a precise and helpful way. But Lasch means to show in this work that no political or social institution stands apart from the others at this moment, and that before we try to fix blame we need to appreciate how it is possible to try to maximize human freedoms and satisfactions while at the same time making them meaningless. To preach "not self-denial but self-fulfillment" would seem to most of us a humane and charitable gesture; it is not easy to accept that "self-fulfillment" is an unlikely and frustrating goal for people who have not been taught respect for limits and for goal-determined activities. Similarly, to be asked to entertain "modest fantasies" in place

of the more stirring developments promised by advanced liberationist ideologies is perhaps to feel that we should settle prematurely for second best, before we've had a chance to reach for better. Like Rieff, like Freud, Lasch is quite ready to speak in terms of competence, modesty and restraint, though many feel that they are promised greater things by a society built on the view that consumption is the key to every human pleasure.

Full appreciation of Lasch's book depends upon familiarity with the major texts in the tradition to which he belongs. When he speaks of social control he describes a process that has been evoked with stunning urgency in Herbert Marcuse's *One-Dimensional Man* and in less theoretically ambitious works like Philip Slater's *The Pursuit of Loneliness*. Not that Lasch wishes to follow these forebears in an explicit way or to support their conclusions. He does, though, expect that his reader will have some basis from which to respond to his arguments even when he cannot take the space to work out a given point in detail. This expectation will seem unreasonable to those who believe that Lasch's responsibility is to provide practical suggestions and to avoid demoralizing a constituency already anxious and confused. But Lasch writes in a tradition for which criticism is itself a life-enhancing act. The adversary relation between intellectuals and others seems to him the only proper relation under present conditions, and he is loath to pretend there are less abrasive relations that will do.

In fact, it is precisely the "softening" or "eliminating" of the adversary relation in our culture that he generally holds responsible for many of our problems. Marcuse may have gone too far in his critique of liberal tolerance as the central mode of social control in the West, but one hears him all the same in Lasch's less categorical denunciations. "Society no longer expects authorities to articulate a clearly reasoned, elaborately justified code of law and morality," he argues; "nor does it expect the young to internalize the moral standards of the community. It demands only conformity to the conventions of everyday intercourse, sanctioned by psychiatric definitions of normal behavior." And, we might add, by convention, according to which each is entitled to act out as expressively as he likes provided only that nothing fundamentally troubling is raised to a level of consciousness that will provoke open conflict. People may be nominally free to say or to think what they like, but few are likely to go against the grain in a serious way when nothing is taken seriously. When the only threat that matters is a threat to one's own immediate satisfactions, what wide-ranging argument is likely to seem important? People may quarrel over this item or that, but all are conditioned to feel that they are likely to get whatever they think they want if only they can come up with an effective way to ask for it.

Lasch's study raises the central questions so forthrightly that it ought to touch off important debates in the academy and in our better journals of opinion. (pp. 30, 32)

Robert Boyers, "Books Considered: 'The Culture of Narcissism: American Life in an Age of Diminishing Expectations'," in The New Republic *(reprinted by permission of* The New Republic; © *1979 The New Republic, Inc.), Vol. 180, No. 7, February 17, 1979, pp. 28-30, 32.*

DENNIS H. WRONG

The main thematic chapter of *The Culture of Narcissism* examines the psychoanalytic clinical evidence showing the increasing frequency of a narcissistic personality type very different from the older kind of neurotic identified by Freud and his early followers. Drawing on the theories of Melanie Klein and Otto Sternberg, Lasch argues that the new type does not suffer from specific hysterical symptoms rooted in sexual repression but from more general "character disorders" consisting of lack of a sense of purpose in life, confused identity, and inability to form permanent satisfying relations with others. . . .

I could not agree more with Lasch's claim for the general social and cultural significance of the psychoanalytic evidence. . . . (p. 309)

But Lasch scarcely resolves any of the difficulties that have long plagued efforts to relate "personality and culture." On the issue of how or whether psychiatric patients are representative of the total population, Lasch observes that "every age develops its own peculiar forms of pathology, which express in exaggerated form its underlying character structure." Patients, in short, suffer from ailments that are more widely prevalent in milder forms. The discussions of sports, education, crime, and other subjects that make up the bulk of [*The Culture of Narcissism*] can therefore be regarded as diagnoses of expressions or manifestations of a general "culture of narcissism," although Lasch neglects to trace the precise links between these areas and underlying characterological dispositions. (p. 310)

The question of social and historical causation is a more troublesome one than the problem of representativeness. Presumably, celebrity cults, "how to" manuals, and recent avant-garde fiction—all discussed by Lasch—reflect rather than shape the narcissistic personality, or at most contribute to its secondary reinforcement. The narcissistic personality is primarily the effect of the disintegration of the family recounted at length in *Haven in a Heartless World*. But the evidence in that book for changes in the family comes itself from the clinical data of psychiatry and from the putative impact of the injunctions of the therapeutic professions against which Lasch directs such heavy fire. The "classical" bourgeois family has unmistakably disappeared, but Lasch, with his focus on deeper psychic constellations, claims considerably more than this. Even if he is right, his argument is suspiciously circular, for he fails to present any evidence independent of clinical material that the family is in so parlous a state.

One may readily doubt that the family is actually as weakened as Lasch contends even among the educated and affluent who are receptive to the advice of applied social science, let alone among workers and most sections of the middle class. Parents still control almost exclusively the child's life and growth for his or her first three or four years, the crucially formative period according to psychoanalysis. If the decline of the extended family was exaggerated by Parsons and his followers, as indicated by several sociological studies Lasch cites, it is even less credible that the nuclear family itself has been fatally debilitated, however much this outcome may have been desired by the advocates of "liberated life-styles" abetted by family sociologists and "permissive" therapists. The family is a tough and resilient social formation not likely to succumb to the shafts of trendy shrinks and pop sociologists.

There is also a problem of historical timing. Reading Lasch's cultural criticism, one is frequently reminded of the attacks on "mass culture" so prominent in the 1950s, of C. Wright Mills's exposés of the degeneration of the goal of success into crass self-salesmanship, of the alarm regularly expressed by educators over the increasing anti-intellectualism and semiliteracy of the young, of philippics against romantic escapism in popular entertainment going back to the 1930s, of familiar diagnoses of American fears of aging and documentations of cruel and indifferent treatment of old people. I have the impression, in fact, that I have been listening to Lasch's bill of indictment for most of my life and I wasn't born, alas, yesterday. Even the recognition that character neuroses were displacing symptom neuroses dates back to the late 1930s and was invoked then by neo-Freudians to justify their modifications of Freudian doctrine.

Lasch is much too good a historian not to know all this. Indeed, he frequently cites earlier critics of American culture and often perceptively shows their limitations, arguing, for example, that the complaints in the 1950s against conformism and the decline of individualism overlooked the survival of a Hobbesian world of narcissistic egoism beneath the mask of pretended warmth and other-direction (in Riesman's phrase). The familiarity of Lasch's complaints certainly in no way reduces their cogency, but it does cast doubt on the up-to-the-minute contemporaneity with which he introduces his case. The subtitle of *The Culture of Narcissism*, for example, is "American Life in an Age of Diminishing Expectations." The first sentence of the Preface refers to the end of the confidence expressed in the phrase "the American Century," and Lasch goes on to enumerate the fiscal woes of New York City, Vietnam, and the exhaustion of natural resources, as well as sundry other crises afflicting other "capitalist countries." But his trend toward narcissistic decadence obviously peaked when American "expectations" were still high and on his own evidence long antedates these recent events. Maybe the present really does indicate that "bourgeois society . . . has lost both the capacity and the will to confront the difficulties that threaten to overwhelm it," but, except perhaps for a few years in the late '50s and early '60s, rhetoric to that effect has been around as long as I can remember. (pp. 310-11)

I share Lasch's dislike for narcissism and the therapeutic ideology that legitimates it as well as his respect for the bourgeois values of self-help and the work ethic. But a future American socialist movement would probably demand more not less help from the "helping professions." A movement chiefly animated by Lasch's values would in practice be more likely to resemble George Wallace's right-wing populism rather than one centered on traditional socialist ideas. I recently heard Bennett Berger describe a father he had interviewed in a revivalist Christian commune in California who remarked with self-satisfaction that since becoming a "Christian" he had beaten his son over a thousand times and that both of them were "the better for it." Mass acceptance of Lasch's outlook might multiply that father by millions. Lasch would certainly deplore such an outcome, but ideas as well as actions often have unanticipated consequences.

The therapeutic professions have scarcely seen themselves as providing new support for capitalism, for they have often been in the vanguard of what anticapitalist tendencies have existed in America and, for that matter, elsewhere. Possibly they are victims of the cunning of the "dialectic." But Lasch's Marxist brand of functionalism or systems theory is as tautological as other versions. Because new doctrines and reforms displacing traditional values and practices have managed peacefully to coexist with capitalism, they are therefore defined as expressions of capitalist class interests. Yet this could not help but be true of *any* changes falling short of the total revolutionary elimination of capitalism. Lasch's intransigent radicalism is a familiar posture, although his targets are less saliently political than the reformist parties and trade unions toward which that posture had often been adopted in the past. In any case, the enemy is by now securely ensconced within: Lasch himself notes that recent years have witnessed a "protestant" revolt against the priestly psychiatric profession. If the end result is that everyone aspires to be his or her own therapist, the power of the helping professions is undermined. . . .

In claiming a basic continuity between the initial separation of home and work and the allegedly contemporary expropriation of child-rearing skills by the experts, Lasch seems to be looking back not merely to the heyday of bourgeois values but to the traditional society disrupted by capitalism and all the other modern revolutions. His identification of "socialism" with decentralization and local community control points in the same direction. (p. 312)

But why then does Christopher Lasch fail to go beyond early capitalism as a standard by which to judge our own fallen times? He scornfully dismisses a pair of "revisionist" sociologists for their naiveté in believing that it is possible to revive the social solidarity of the medieval village . . . "without sacrificing equality, individuality, and personal freedom," but it is not really clear just how or why Lasch differs from them. If the invasion of the family began with the birth of the modern world, why look back for an alternative image to present no further than to the halfway house of the bourgeois family? (pp. 312-13)

I am not objecting, let me make it plain, to Lasch's combination of cultural conservatism with a politics of the left. This is an honorable position that I largely share myself. Lasch is clearly right to argue against the "devaluation of the past" and to insist that it is "a political and psychological treasury from which we draw the reserves (not necessarily in the form of 'lessons') that we need to cope with the future." What is questionable is Lasch's weird amalgam of all the groups he dislikes—capitalists, corporation executives, bureaucrats, New Left students, psychotherapists, humanistic psychologists, educational radicals, hippies, and feminists—on one side of the barricades—confronting on the other side, well, it's not quite clear just whom: presumably, a few radical intellectuals of Lasch's kidney and perhaps the workingman resentful of a "middle-class liberalism that has already destroyed his savings, bused his children to distant schools, undermined his authority over them, and now threatens to turn even his wife against him." The student revolutionaries of the '60s were unusual in that, as Barrington Moore, Jr. remarks in his most recent book, they were "the first revolutionary hedonists," but Lasch avoids full acknowledgment of the left's traditional commitment to collectivism in whose name so many of the trends he most dislikes have been justified. Lasch is actually upholding what Marxists have long derided as "bourgeois individualism," while claiming that it has degenerated into narcissistic egoism and minimizing the responsibility of anti-bourgeois political and cultural movements for this development.

The narcissistic search for gratification that Lasch sees as the terminal phase of a "dying culture" indeed represents what Philip Rieff calls a "remissive" casting off of the "interdicts" of the old culture rather than evidence of the birth of a new one. But are sexual repression, the sovereignty of paternal authority, the subordination of women, and the inculcation of guilt in child-rearing necessarily *intrinsic* to the values Lasch

wishes to revive? Must we be liberated from our liberation from these things in order to overcome the discontents of narcissism? Were not the liberations also at least partially implicit in the values of personal freedom and responsibility themselves? Have these values been totally eroded, to the point of transformation into their opposites, by the remissive excesses of the culture of narcissism?

Some of these excesses seem to me to amount to a kind of acting out, a testing of extremes, rather than to the final dissolution of the old culture. The public response to *The Culture of Narcissism* itself, which, like its predecessors in the 1950s, has made the best-seller lists and received enormous attention, suggests as much. I understand that it has even been taken quite seriously in psychotherapeutic circles. Doubtless, this is a manifestation of the very oversensitivity to fashion that Lasch indicts, but not every idea becomes fashionable. (pp. 313-14)

I, too, would like to see the sort of revival that Lasch envisages, but I doubt that his affectation of a Marxist vocabulary is sufficient to ensure against a "praxis" with the potentiality of breaking through the limits assumed by his "theory." That child-beating father in California worries me. There have been popular radical movements affirming traditional values before. "Fascism" was the name they were known by between the two world wars. (p. 314)

Dennis H. Wrong, "Bourgeois Values, No Bourgeoisie?: The Cultural Criticism of Christopher Lasch," in Dissent *(© 1979, by Dissent Publishing Corporation), Vol. 26, No. 3, Summer, 1979, pp. 308-14.*

MICHAEL FISCHER

The Culture of Narcissism is important in part because it challenges the assumptions underlying the uncritical dismissal which it will doubtless receive from many readers. When Lasch uses the past as "a political and psychological treasury from which we draw the reserves (not necessarily in the form of 'lessons') that we need to cope with the future," he will seem to many readers to pass off as radical thinking what is actually reactionary nostalgia. But perhaps this judgment exposes not his backwardness but the imprisonment of much social criticism in a culture that despairs of the future because it is severing its links with the past. Similarly, when he appeals to "earlier traditions of local action," Lasch will appear to be pretending that a make-believe constituency is a potential political base. But maybe this criticism points not to his naivete but to the helplessness of those who make it, whose mutual distrust keeps such traditions from thriving. Finally, when he ties the need for a "socialist revolution" to such values as reason, compassion, and restraint, Lasch will seem to many critics to be anchoring his politics in airy nothing. But perhaps this retort, too, brings to light not his simplemindedness but the skepticism of a society which habitually assumes that "reason" is instrumental calculation, "authority" amoral power, and "freedom" the fleeting self-gratification that comes from outwitting or pleasing those who we keep in power.

The agony of the American left, to use the title of one of Lasch's best books, has always stemmed from its isolation from collective support and from a tradition of social criticism that would make opposition to capitalism not just a quixotic possibility but a cumulative program on which one could build. Understandably desiring influence, leftists have often modified the principles that isolate them, dignifying as "radicalism" what is actually the line of least resistance. *The Culture of*

Narcissism makes no such concessions: Lasch unabashedly bases his comprehensive indictment of American culture in what will seem to many a non-existent alternative. What makes his book vulnerable to quick rejection is precisely what makes it so valuable. Lasch makes sense out of American society at a time when many of us routinely despair of mastering its ''complexity'' and so surrender the task of understanding it to ''educators'' and ''experts,'' who splinter knowledge into expertise and thus perpetuate the very awareness of complexity that heightens dependency on their ''services.'' He sees connections, especially between capitalism, work, and culture, where others see baffling ''contradictions.'' He questions what conservatives unthinkingly assume is necessary and also what leftists just as dogmatically insist is radical. Challenging conventional ideas of liberation, he arrives at what may be the only way out of our present troubles. (pp. 172-73)

> *Michael Fischer, ''Criticizing Capitalist America,''*
> *in* Salmagundi *(copyright © 1979 by Skidmore College; reprinted by permission of the publisher), No. 46, Fall, 1979, pp. 166-73.*

CHRISTOPHER LASCH

Not only its detractors but even some of its admirers have misread *The Culture of Narcissism* as a ''jeremiad,'' an ''iconoclastic'' exposure of our moral decay and self-seeking, a ''sermon'' on the evils of self-absorption and the baneful influence of special-interest groups. Although I have no intention of disavowing the ethical dimension of the book, I regard *The Culture of Narcissism* as a contribution to social theory and social criticism, not to the literature of moral indignation. Rooted in my earlier work, it attempts on the one hand to carry on and deepen the criticism of the American left begun in *The New Radicalism* and *The Agony of the American Left,* and on the other hand to show how changes in the American family, analyzed in *Haven in a Heartless World,* have produced a new type of personality structure, one that exhibits in varying degrees the characteristics of secondary or pathological narcissism.

In its concern with personality and the family, *The Culture of Narcissism* not only continues my own previous work but grows out of a long tradition of culture-and-personality studies, which have tried to establish links between the organization of culture and the psychological mechanisms through which culture is reproduced in individuals. The book derives also from a tradition of social criticism—the tradition of Herbert Marcuse, Max Horkheimer, the early Erich Fromm, and before them Marx and Freud—that has concerned itself with problems of authority, with the internalization of prevailing patterns of domination, and with the cultural and psychological devastation brought about by industrial capitalism.

My attack is directed not against selfishness or the pursuit of gain but against capitalism itself, which in its twentieth-century phase, often in spite of the best intentions of those who preside over its destiny, has steadily eroded the capacity for self-help and self-discipline, reduced large numbers of men and women to a condition of dependence, and has recently begun to encourage psychological traits associated with dependence and with unresolved conflicts dating from infancy. As more and more people find themselves disqualified, in effect, from the performance of adult responsibilities, the psychology of narcissistic dependence begins to pervade American culture, to replace the pursuit of gain with the more desperate goal of psychic survival, and to encourage a strategy of living for the moment, keeping your options open, and avoiding moral or emotional commitments.

In order precisely to forestall the temptation to misread my book as a moralistic indictment of self-seeking or as another protest against the ''me decade,'' I have cited a large body of clinical evidence which suggests that grandiose illusions of omnipotence originate in early feelings of loss and deprivation, more precisely in defenses against a boundless rage, and that narcissism must therefore not be confused with normal rapacity and greed. Far from reflecting the ''alarming growth of ego''— the ''obvious'' fact of our social life which several reviewers accuse me of belaboring at unnecessary length—narcissism signals a loss of ego, an invasion of the ego by social forces that have made it more and more difficult for people to grow up or even to contemplate the prospect of growing up without misgivings bordering on panic. To readers unable to master the distinction between individualistic egoism and narcissism, between self-seeking or self-absorption and the far more serious disorder in which the self loses its boundaries and merges with its surroundings, a psychological argument of this kind will appear to restate the ''obvious'' and to force commonplace observations, as a reviewer complains, into the ''fashionable containers'' of psychotherapeutic jargon. It is true that our therapeutic culture psychologizes everything and thereby trivializes everything, but this does not mean that we can dispense with the insights of psychoanalysis and fall back on common sense. Psychoanalytic theory not only provides indispensable insights into a therapeutic culture and the narcissistic personality who thrives in such a culture; it also serves, strangely enough, as the best innoculation against a psychologizing mode of thought. Those who have entered most fully into the study of psychoanalytic theory best understand its limits and have least inclination to generalize psychoanalysis into a cure-all or into a set of universal explanatory principles. Although psychoanalysis to be sure has been misused, distorted, and absorbed into a therapeutic culture that invokes medicine and psychiatry to justify a permanent suspension of the moral sense, Freud's theory still tells us more than any other about the inner workings of the mind, about the recreation of culture in unconscious mental life, and, indeed, about the crippling effects of a therapeutic culture on the individuals who have absorbed it.

The Culture of Narcissism, then, employs psychoanalytic ideas not to make a ''sermon'' more palatable to readers brought up on therapeutic jargon or to disguise ''obvious'' facts in obscure terminology, but to uncover patterns, both cultural and psychological, that remain far from obvious and largely inaccessible to common sense. Aware of the intricate, convoluted character of the links between culture and personality, painfully conscious of the pitfalls in studying them, and having no wish in any case to add to the outpouring of books claiming to offer highly personal and blindingly original statements about the sorry state of American society, I have relied heavily on the work of my predecessors in the sociology of culture. Risking the predictable rebuke that I look at American society ''behind a barricade of books,'' I have tried to carry on a dialogue, both here and in *Haven,* with a long line of sociologists, anthropologists, psychoanalysts, and social critics. My efforts to revise the work of Riesman, Fromm, and the Frankfurt school— and elsewhere that of Talcott Parsons, Margaret Mead, Ruth Benedict, and Edward Sapir—should not obscure the extent of my indebtedness to those thinkers. I stress it here not merely to set the record straight (for the benefit of readers who can't spare the time to consult footnotes) but to dissociate my work, in the strongest possible way, from those ''book-length diagnoses of our nation's maladies,'' those pseudo-critical confections, neither honest journalism nor honest sociology, which the publishing industry likes to pass off as profound social commentary. This work of dissociation becomes doubly important now that the publisher of the paperback edition has begun to advertise *The Culture of Narcissism* as a book that ''ranks with four of the greatest books on society's changing values''—*Future Shock, The Greening of America, Passages,* and *My Mother Myself.* In view of this ill-conceived promotional campaign, I must repudiate more emphatically than ever the suggestion that my book represents the ''latest addition to the 'what's wrong with us' bibliography,'' as one reviewer has characterized it. Pop sociology was exactly what I proposed to avoid by rooting criticism of American society in a well-established theoretical tradition, in doing which I deliberately rejected, moreover, the idiosyncratic, satirical, self-consciously provocative, iconoclastic style that has been the characteristic vice of American social criticism—even the best of it, as exemplified by the writings of Thorstein Veblen, Willard Waller, and C. Wright Mills. (pp. 194-96)

Christopher Lasch, ''Politics and Social Theory: A Reply to the Critics,'' in Salmagundi *(copyright © 1979 by Skidmore College; reprinted by permission of the publisher), No. 46, Fall, 1979, pp. 194-202.*

PETER HOMANS

Lasch's concern [in *The Culture of Narcissism*] with the Protestant work ethic is entirely moral, as is his sense of the cure for narcissism, which, because it lacks a psychology of imagination, degenerates into moralism as the book closes. (p. 197)

Both Lasch's unmasking and his decrying of the culture of narcissism, with its strong doses of moral condemnation, along with his solution, which is also predominantly moral, lack a deeper, psychological appreciation of the self and its intrinsically imaginative features. At bottom, Lasch simply distrusts the self. His diagnosis and cure convey the brimstone-ethos of the Protestant work ethic which he so admires. The ethic, with its powerful legitimations of repression and sublimation, was at best an uneasy solution to the problem of narcissism. . . .

We need not bend, in the final moment, to Lasch's desperate pleas for morality in order to admire his brilliant and courageous analysis of contemporary culture. (p. 198)

Peter Homans, ''Introducing the Psychology of the Self and Narcissism into the Study of Religion,'' in Religious Studies Review *(copyright © 1981 by the Council on the Study of Religion, reprinted by permission of the Council on the Study of Religion, Wilfred Laurier University, Waterloo, Ontario, Canada), Vol. 7, No. 3, July, 1981, pp. 193-99.**

Bernard-Henri Lévy

1949?-

A French philosopher, social critic, and editor, Lévy is the most prominent of a group of disaffected 1960s leftists known as the "new philosophers." As an editor at the Grasset publishing house in Paris, Lévy has published a host of books by these young writers, including his own *Barbarism with a Human Face* (1977), a forceful critique of Marxist thought and practice. Featured prominently in the French mass media, the new philosophers' anti-Marxist polemics have stirred widespread debate. Critical commentary has ranged from dismissing Lévy and his associates as "disc jockeys of ideas" to praising their "passionate challenge" to the Marxist academic orthodoxy in France.

Photo by Jeff Vinson

Excerpt from *BARBARISM WITH A HUMAN FACE*

I am the bastard child of an unholy union between fascism and Stalinism. I am the contemporary of a strange twilight when the clouds above are dissolving amid the clash of arms and the cries of the tortured. The only revolution I know, the one which may grant notoriety to this century, is the Nazi plague and red fascism. Hitler did not die in Berlin. Conqueror of his conquerors, he won the war in the stormy night into which he plunged Europe. Stalin did not die in Moscow nor at the Twentieth Congress. He is here among us, a stowaway in the history that he still haunts and bends to his mad will. You say the world is doing well? It's certain in any case that it keeps on going, since it isn't changing. But never before has the will to death been so nakedly and cynically unleashed. For the first time the gods have left us, no doubt weary of wandering on the plain of ashes where we have made our home. And I am writing in an age of barbarism which is already, silently, remaking the world of men.

If I were a poet, I would sing of the horror of living and the new Gulags that tomorrow holds in store for us. If I were a musician, I would speak of the idiot laughter and impotent tears, the dreadful uproar made by the lost, camped in the ruins, awaiting their fate. If I had been a painter (a Courbet rather than a David), I would have represented the dust-colored sky lowering over Santiago, Luanda, or Kolyma. But I am neither painter, nor musician, nor poet. I am a philosopher, one who uses ideas and words—words already crushed and macerated by fools. So, with the words of my language, I will do no more than speak of the massacres, the camps, and the processions of death, the ones I have seen and the others, which I also wish to recall. I will be satisfied if I can explain the new totalitarianism of the smiling Princes, who sometimes even promise happiness to their people. This essay should thus be read as an "archaeology of the present," carefully retracing through the fog of contemporary speech and practice the outline and the stamp of a barbarism with a human face.

I will soon be thirty and I have betrayed the dream of my youth at least a hundred times. Like everyone else, I believed in a new and joyful "liberation"; now, without bitterness, I live with the shadows of my past hopes. I believed in revolution, a faith that came from books, no doubt, but all the same I believed in it as a good, the only one that counted and was worth hoping for. Now, feeling the ground give way and the future disintegrate, I wonder not if it is possible but if it is even desirable. I wished to and sometimes did get involved in politics, howling with the wolves and singing in the chorus. I can do so no longer, and I feel like a gambler who has lost hope of winning or like a soldier who no longer believes in the war he is waging. I even believed in happiness, and I love sensuality above all, sensuality that you neither pursue nor beg for, like a blessed respite in the parenthesis that is life. But anguish is stronger and there is no way out of the unholy despair in which men grow fat. "Happy," they say. What do they mean by that?

If I were an antiques dealer, I would like to be able to stuff the glorious remains, the emaciated carcasses that were and still are enthroned in the heaven of optimism. If I were an encyclopedist, I would dream of writing in a dictionary of the year 2000: "Socialism, *n.*, cultural style, born in Paris in 1848, died in Paris in 1968." If I were a surrealist, I would wish to say, like Aragon, that I am, we are the new defeatists of Europe, surrounded by crumbling monuments and newly dug graves which we violate once a year, out of habit. But I am obviously neither a surrealist, nor an encyclopedist, nor an antiques dealer. I am only an "intellectual" who has decided

413

to speak his mind to the experts of progressive thought; a shamelessly irresponsible person who will not easily tire of hunting down philistines and impostors; and especially a pitiful politician who believes in the impossible and in radical evil, but who sticks with the simple thesis that the intolerable also exists, and that we must resist it with every breath. Am I a *moraliste?* Why not? I have attempted nothing in this book but to think through to the end the idea of pessimism in history.

As the tenant of my name and a journeyman of passing time, I have no claim to write except as a witness. Since I am absent from the making of history and have been formed into the little bit of humanity that I am, I know that I have no right to preach and to prophesy. And yet I have decided to write because I have a passion to persuade. Even so, certain things should be made clear. To my sorrow, I am addressing the left here, the institutionalized left; my target is the left in its passion for delusion and ignorance. I am thinking of those socialists who, in these times of armed vigilance and politicians' fantasies, have the courage and the dignity to call themselves "beautiful souls" and to hold high the torch of lucidity. I write for them, for they are the sentinels of a world that would be worse without them. I am thinking of those political men who know, more and more each day, that the course of events is indecipherable, and who are wise enough to think within the form of history without beliving that it has a definite purpose. They are the ones I want to disturb, or at least to question, for they will soon have our fate in their hands. (pp. ix-xii)

> *Bernard-Henri Lévy, in his* Barbarism with a Human Face, *translated by George Holoch (translation copyright ©1979 by Harper & Row, Publishers, Inc.; reprinted by permission of Harper & Row, Publishers, Inc.; originally published as* La barbarie a visage humain, *Editions Grasset & Fasquelle, 1977), Harper & Row, 1979. 210 p.*

ROGER KAPLAN

Lévy's *Barbarism with a Human Face* is probably the most accessible of the "new-philosophical" works, partly because the precious and inbred style which all the "new philosophers" share is kept within reasonable bounds by his cold and lucid elegance. In this book, Lévy goes back to what is for him, as indeed it is for so many intellectuals, the beginning: the optimism of the 18th-century Enlightenment. He finds there a solitary and misunderstood Rousseau, alone against his times (*"Emile* says only this: the idea of a good *society* is an absurd dream"). From here, Lévy takes on every leftist dogma and finds it false, in particular the notions that history is progressive and that the state (when in the right hands) can be an agent of progress. Socialism, the central leftist myth, with its philosophical premises, with its cultural connotations, with its eschatological project, is nothing but an "encyclopedia of lies." As optimism is the surest opiate which despotism can invent, socialism, perennially optimistic, over and against all its failures, is the best trap despotism can devise.

Indeed, the notion of progress is really a deeply reactionary idea, says Lévy, because it always leads to a strengthening of the state. Nor is there such a thing as a "proletarian" state; the whole concept of the proletariat as an elected class is the most stupendous myth of our times. . . . Lévy believes it is high time for intellectuals to proclaim themselves *anti-pro-*gressive, opposing the state's invariable tendency toward absolute power. They must give up the search for the good society and return to the older quest for the good life, becoming "moralistic, in the classic sense of Kant, Camus, or Merleau-Ponty."

Although Lévy's book assails the mentality of the French Left as mendacious and tendentious, its attack is more sweeping than deep. Brilliantly suggestive, it is novel somewhat in the manner of Albert Camus's *The Myth of Sisyphus,* saying out loud what was rapidly becoming a widespread rumor. (p. 75)

> *Roger Kaplan, "France's 'New Philosophers'," in* Commentary *(reprinted by permission; all rights reserved), Vol. 65, No. 2, February, 1978, pp. 73-6.**

WILLIAM BARRETT

Bernard-Henri Lévy, the author of ["**Barbarism with a Human Face,**" an] exciting but exasperating book, was 20 at the time [of the French uprising of May 1968] and a student leader in the rebellion. Now, a decade later, he has reversed all his fundamental beliefs of that earlier period. The gist of Mr. Lévy's position, so far as it can be summarized, runs something as follows: The Gulag prison camps are not an accidental excrescence upon Marxism, a wart on its smiling face, but a cancer that follows from its very nature; indeed, they follow from the nature of socialism itself. And the dictum that socialism leads to Gulag is pounded at us again and again. One wishes that Mr. Lévy had traced the links here more thoroughly, but one can discern their outline in any event. To change society as it wishes, socialism must secure an extraordinary concentration of power in the state; and power, given its usual momentum, must ever extend and deepen itself as the reigning bureaucracy tightens its grip in order to stay on top. This process, if it does not end in the physical horrors of Gulag, will nevertheless entail a drastic curtailment of liberty. . . .

What caused Mr. Lévy to change his mind? The treacherous turnabout of the Communists may have planted some seeds of doubt, but it was the reading of Aleksandr Solzhenitsyn's "Gulag Archipelago," he tells us, that proved decisive. (p. 3)

Mr. Lévy's book, as the voice of a new generation, and possibly a symptom of a new turn in French thought, is a work of primary historic significance. Read, however, as a serious essay on politics and political philosophy, it is disappointing. Perhaps it is only to be taken as a personal manifesto—indeed as a personal explosion of the ideas that have been pent up in its author—rather than a sober treatise. There is no doubt of Mr. Lévy's brilliance, nor of the power of his eloquence; one can understand why his book should have sold so many copies in France. He shoots off ideas like skyrockets, and into all quarters of the compass; they flare up and dazzle us; then they flare out and leave us bewildered. The ideas are too sweeping and unqualified, and they are dealt with more rhetorically than analytically.

In leaping over connecting links and qualifications in his argument, Mr. Lévy fuses and blurs quite disparate matters, as when he declares that socialism is only capitalism in its last stage, and that the two together constitute a single evil—the principal evil of our time. But in justice to him it might be said that these are the faults and habits of the French intellectual milieu; perhaps he will outgrow them. French writers on philosophical and social themes have too often pursued, in recent years, the brilliance of metaphor and the flourish of a phrase to the point of self-indulgence—and at the expense of more prosaic and cautious thought.

Mr. Lévy does not stop with the rejection of socialism, but goes on to attack all the idols that have surrounded and promoted the socialist ideology: the Enlightenment, with its scheme of universal history as an inevitable pattern for which any given generation of humans might have to be sacrificed; progress, which too often turns out to be technical advance and human regression; technology, and even science, which in the hands of a modern dictatorship can turn into instruments of evil. And if we give up all these grand abstractions that have shaped the civilization of the West during the last two centuries, we find ourselves at a fork in the road where we have to seek a new beginning for Western thought—and one hears faintly in the background of Mr. Lévy's diatribe a distant echo of Heidegger. (pp. 3, 20)

Much as one may sympathize with the general intent behind Mr. Lévy's charges (which, by the way, are not altogether novel), one wishes he had been more discriminating in his points of attack. The Enlightenment, for example, was hardly a simple and monolithic affair. When one reviles it, is one speaking of the Enlightenment of Madison or of Robespierre? Of Adam Smith or of Rousseau? (p. 20)

Mr. Lévy is only 30, and one can wait for his gifts of energy and mind to spell out some of the details of an intellectual program whose scope is so broad that it could take a lifetime to accomplish. But on one matter we cannot wait—and that is where he stands now in the struggle between the Soviet Union and the West, from which Mr. Lévy appears to cultivate an attitude of splendid but lonely detachment. To proclaim a curse on both your houses and stand aside is in effect to play into the hands of the Communists. Perhaps Mr. Lévy is still infected with the insouciance of May 1968—of the intellectual flower child insisting on a purism unsullied by the realities of power. One feels one is back at the beginning of World War II arguing with those Marxist purists who refused to support the war against Hitler because it was being waged by capitalist powers. To pursue the moral life in private while turning one's back on the realities of politics would hardly seem to be consistent with the spirit of his professed guides—Camus and Solzhenitsyn. (pp. 20, 22)

William Barrett, "Nouveau Philosophe," in The New York Times Book Review *(© 1979 by The New York Times Company; reprinted by permission), February 11, 1979, pp. 3, 20, 22.*

RICHARD YESELSON

[One] is surprised to find little [in **Barbarism with a Human Face**] that is "new" or insightful and much that is, at best, obvious—i.e., the Soviet Union is not a socialist paradise. At worst, Lévy's prose is filled with petulant polemic. Lévy's anti-Marxism is not at issue here; rather, the problem is the disappointingly vacuous presentation of his views. . . .

As early as page three, Levy establishes a lugubrious tone: "Life is a lost cause, and happiness an outmoded idea." Why not reach for a cyanide capsule now, instead of turning the page? No answer is offered. Laboring on, one finds Levy describing society as synonymous with Power or the Prince or the Master. . . . Only by destroying society itself, argues Levy, do we destroy the need for power. The Prince does not merely dominate society. He, in effect, creates it, not just eternally

winning the game but also building the stadium and setting the rules as well. Language is also subsumed by the Prince, and rebels can only "repeat the pure name of the unity that establishes [the language]." Like the Prince, the State, which is given a separate chapter—the two are never adequately distinguished—invents itself, perpetually.

At this point Levy's ignorance of history should be mentioned, as demonstrated by his failure to discuss the genesis of the State and the evolution of its different modern manifestations: parliamentary, authoritarian, totalitarian. But he has his answer ready: "History Does Not Exist," he asserts in a chapter heading. Levy then attacks an easy target in the deterministic side of Marxism, its insistence on the "iron-bound laws" of history. But he goes well beyond denying the inevitability of social change, and denies the *possibility* of it, too.

Having tidiliy eliminated the obstacles of perspective and context from the path of his gloomy thesis, Levy uncoils one knockout punch after another. If there is only a "senseless and random labyrinth of mud" and no human history, the proletariat cannot be the historical agent of change. Actually, writes Levy, by their scolding of the ruling class, socialists ultimately provide it with the class consciousness it would otherwise lack. Capitalism thrives upon and survives through its contradictions, and has its roots not in the industrial revolution but in what Levy mysteriously calls "the birth of the West" 2000 years ago. The idea of progress is pernicious and pervasive, ending finally in a socialist nightmare. Even when the proletariat wins, Levy believes it incapable of maintaining power and certain of being crushed, a la Hungary or Czechoslovakia. Modern dictatorships are too powerful to defeated by a people's movement.

Levy calls Solzhenitsyn "the Dante of our time," who forever confirms the unbreakable link between Marxism and coercion. As ideology, Marxism is as secure and unchanging as the Prince. It will sneak up on us, warns Levy, "with a human face"—but behind the mask is the barbarian overseer of the Gulag. With a final nod to his former mentor, philosopher Louis Althusser, he outlines the only choice for the individual in "this twilight of night followed by no dawn"—a metaphysical hope against hope, a faith in the subversive power of art, and an apolitical, Kantian morality. End of book, if not the world. . . .

[Levy's] prose is a combination of the bald assertions noted above tied together by the vaporous allusiveness prevalent in so much French political writing. Even those masters of the recondite, Althusser and Foucault, give us more useful stuff than Levy does. What may be meant as enigmatic is often merely vague. It is not enough to universalize Power. Questions must be raised: Who has power? How did they get it? How is it diffused?

Levy's formulations, however novel and arresting, make no sense. Seeing Capitalism as an outgrowth of the Platonic dialogues distends the word so much that, in effect, it becomes meaningless. Undoubtedly, if one strains hard enough, the roots of psychoanalysis and fast-food chains can be discovered in Ancient Greece, too—but so what? It is critical for Levy's argument to claim such static universality for history, language, and philosophy, because if nothing has ever changed, nothing can ever get better. Yet, if "history does not exist," neither can the thread that, as he would have it, connects Plato with Adam Smith.

Levy's understanding of the dynamics of class struggle is confused as well. The Hungarians and Czechs had no pathological need to "submit" to Soviet tanks, as Levy suggests. They were just massively outgunned. More importantly, Levy makes the same mistake that vulgar Marxists do by attributing to Marx a view of human nature that includes an innately "good" side, suppressed by oppressive institutions, destined to be released by a revolutionary proletariat. Levy denies such a side exists, and thinks he is thereby, in one stroke, rejecting Marx and burying the proletariat (alongside history and language). But Marx never claimed there was a "good" or "bad" human nature. What he said was that man is different from the animals because he has the self-consciousness to create his own history subject to the limitations imposed by prior history and material conditions. Marx may be all wrong—but by misreading him, Levy not only fails to confront Marx's actual argument but also vitiates his own credibility.

Levy's impassioned postures are unimpressive even when he may be right. Perhaps Marxism is bound to Stalinism—Kalakowski makes an arguable case—but Levy's repeated insistence makes his thesis no more true than that Sweden's high suicide rate means that welfare states cause suicide. Further, his arguments frequently reflect the same sense of historical inevitability he abhors in Marxism. It must be small comfort to the former shah that a New Philosopher says dictators never lose. Nothing in history should be termed inevitable. . . .

To be fair, Levy does address an important issue, the relationship between technological development and Marxism leading to a technocracy. Whether social control of technology will free men and women to be the whole persons Marx envisioned, or tie them to a bigger, better color TV while ruining the environment, has to be a critical question for socialists. But then it's back to the muddle. Levy's last paragraph reveals a paradoxical political impotence in a book that describes the present peril as so alarming. Become a *"moraliste,"* advises Levy, and write treatises on ethics. Being a lone *moraliste* is fine and admirable when rescuing a fellow citizen from a mugging. But one *moraliste* writing a letter to his congressperson is likely to be no more effective—though more safe—than another loner demonstrating in the streets of Teheran, Johannesburg, or Moscow. It takes a whole lot of *moralistes* to pass legislation or overthrow an oppressor.

Levy would claim that such solidarity is where our troubles begin. But, *malgre lui*, it seems better to persevere, as Antonio Gramsci wrote, "with optimism of the will and pessimism of the intellect," than to pursue the transient media martyrdom that can be Levy's only reward.

> Richard Yeselson, *"French Twist" (reprinted by permission of* The Village Voice *and the author; copyright © 1979), in* The Village Voice, *Vol. XXIV, No. 9, February 26, 1979, p. 74.*

MARTIN PERETZ

[*Barbarism with a Human Face*] is an angry book, and it has angered many on the French left to whom, in some great measure, it was written. But Bernard-Henri Levy is much more than an angry young man, which is why his *Barbarie* persuaded and persuaded deeply. I am confident, in fact, that it will turn out to be one of those rare works which changes the mind of an entire generation. It certainly has had momentous political consequences. There is little doubt that had Levy, his book and his circle not propitiously emerged on the French scene, France would right now be ruled by an asymmetrical partnership of disciplined *anciens militants* from the still barely de-

Stalinized Communist party and the generally well-intentioned, but unruly dissidence which calls itself the Socialist party. The truth is that Levy helped stave off the long-heralded experiment of Eurocommunism-in-power. Reason enough to be grateful: a nation as social laboratory is not a heartening prospect in our era.

The ire Levy has drawn from the left intelligentsia in France should be readily understandable. He has simultaneously exposed the callousness of its politics and the superficiality of the philosophical rationalizations that underpin that politics. . . . Secular millenarianism, Levy argues, with a calm mastery of its various but not so intrinsically different incarnations, always justifies the oppressor. Deception and self-deception support each other. Here he follows Popper and Talmon, but he is addressing an ambience long immune to their scruples. For Popper and Talmon were appealing to the liberal sensibility against its weakness for the strong and dogmatic. It is not the liberal sensibility with which Levy tangles in France; there is hardly such to tangle with. And his adversaries do not have a weakness for the cult of strength and dogma but a positive infatuation with it. Even if he is less patient than he should be with efforts to rescue socialism from what hitherto has been its destiny in cruelty, it is hard to fault his reading of history. What represents itself as socialism, however distorted or debauched, must be weighed as evidence against the plausibility of the pure ideal.

The raw nerve that Levy has struck among American intellectuals is altogether different from the sensitivities of his own countrymen. It is not, after all, any indigenous American philosophical tradition with which he has engaged. It is something much simpler than that. Although bereft of a supporting structure of coherent ideas, liberal romanticism dies hard. (p. 35)

[The deadened conscience and the atrophied memory] are twin goals of both fascist and communist rule, a coincidence with which Levy begins painstakingly to establish an equation. . . . What especially disheartens Levy is that those mental habits have conquered so much territory among intellectuals in the democracies.

This he traces to the great illusion of modernity: the beneficence of technology. . . . Technology is easily fashioned into administration, not simply of goods and services, but of people themselves. On this he is as withering in his critique of capitalism as he is of socialism—though for the usual dishonest reasons his critics choose to ignore his capacity for political evenhandedness, which is also his passion for truth. His reading of technological rationality, at least as much as his bitter analysis of the baleful imperatives of utopian or messianic thinking, leads him into direct conflict with the enlightenment legacy in the advanced industrialized societies. Scientific discovery and technology were seen as guarantors of glad tidings for distressed humanity. The more the better. Such certainties are permitted us no longer. The proposed alternative to the failed success of mechanical accumulation is the satisfaction of the self. But this too is repressive, false. Hence Levy's pessimism, which has so vexed one of his reviewers: let's be hopeful, however sparse the evidence which may be mustered for hope. . . .

An adept at polemic unmatched in our country, Levy has demonstrated that negativity and pessimism may yet sustain those values which allow us to judge our policies and ourselves. (p. 36)

> Martin Peretz, *"'Barbarism with a Human Face',"* in The New Republic *(reprinted by permission of*

The New Republic; © *1979 The New Republic, Inc.),*
Vol. 180, No. 4, April 7, 1979, pp. 35-6.

NORMAN BIRNBAUM

The fruit of a life of action and reflection which its author has yet to live, [*Barbarism with a Human Face*] combines confusion, obscurity and pretense. Looking left and right but neither behind to history nor ahead to a future that may be different, Bernard-Henri Lévy marches into a conceptual morass. A minimal sense of intellectual workmanship, or a modicum of critical reflection, might have enabled this talented young man to have found his way onto ground not solid but only soggy. Alas, he thrashes on in a desperate struggle to find an idea which would give the impression of intellectual coherence for at least two consecutive pages. Occasionally, he manages two paragraphs of sense, even of insight—and promptly throws away his gains in a new accession of frenzy.

This disordered work defies summary, and even description of it is not easy. A tract against Communism, socialism and social democracy, it is no conventional exercise in conservative or liberal apologetics. Lévy's hatred of oppression extends to fascism. He dislikes capitalism, too, and seems most offended by its erasure of human qualities so valuable that he is quite unable to specify them. In familiar terms, he attacks the idea of progress as a secular myth. He warns against those who, when the world fails to progress, are bound to torment it into desired historical shape. There never was and never can be, he tells us, a dictatorship of the proletariat. The danger is a dictatorship of savants, of intellectuals who would impose ideas upon a recalcitrant humanity. Lévy suggests that the Western European left for the moment serves capitalism by disciplining and integrating the supporters of the Communist, socialist and social democratic parties. None of his ideas are new, of course, and the author's astonished rediscoveries of matters most of us have known for not less than two generations (and in some cases, two millenniums) attest to his exhibitionistic vanity.

Lévy wants to think big, and the heart of the book is a criticism of the idea of the social contract. The difficulty, ignored by Lévy, is that there are any number of versions of the social contract (from Augustine to Freud), each of them different and most of them contradictory. Lévy seems to admire Rousseau, although he intimates that his (Lévy's) idea of social origins is far more profound. That idea equates the origin of society to the emergence of a relationship of domination. Humanity, then, is neither master nor servant but both. Society, it follows, cannot be judged by a communal state of nature which never existed. Indeed, we are not entitled to suppose that humanity has potentialities blocked or deformed by history until now, potentialities which can unfold under the other and more favorable circumstances. That, too, would entail a utopia beyond history, the source of a great deal of political trouble.

At this point, Lévy's argument—if it can be termed that—collapses. All societies and particularly modern societies, he holds, tend to brutal despotism, to a relapse into barbarism. Stalinism and the fascisms are alike, orgiastic indulgences in exploitation and submission. He refuses, however, the notion of a sadomasochistic politics. No propensity in human nature explains what is, in his view, not a catastrophic accident or a terrible phase of our development but an enduring condition. Like Ortega y Gasset (one of the few thinkers he does not cite, which enables him to avoid misspelling his name, or misinterpreting his thought, as he does with many of those cited),

Lévy seems to think that we have no nature, only a history. That history, however, is synonymous with domination. All societies are systems of power, and power tends both to corrupt and to expand. Contemporary power is all the more terrible because it has absorbed the religious residue of the past, and sacralizes itself. On what possible basis, then, does Lévy urge us to resist domination and barbarism—root human conditions?

Lévy's answer is piteous. We must refuse to submit. Has he brought French thought back to existentialism, after a tortuous detour through Marxism? The historical defiance of Sartre's great political novels and dramas, the historiography of Rousset, the marvelous human lucidity of Merleau-Ponty appear not to have influenced Lévy at all. He seems unaware of his own legacy. Perhaps his lack of awareness is feigned. Were he to assume the legacy, he would have to renounce his pretensions to originality—and he would have to do political philosophy instead of proclaiming that he has done it. In the end, he presents us with a set of banalities: that government is best which governs least; the precondition for doing good is a drastic lowering of our expectations as to how much good we can do; a politics which seeks to overcome domination and the necessary division of society is likely to become totalitarian. Lévy castigates everyone else for an activism which rests on a spurious theory of progress. His own political morality in the end presupposes a very old (and extremely truncated) sociology, the argument that things being what they are, they are unlikely ever to be much different. Perhaps—but for someone so insistent on looking history in the face, he proclaims a politics of pure arbitrariness, which depends upon averting our gaze from history's supposed lessons.

Lévy's difficulty is not insuperable. It is his lack of education, and time will give him the opportunity to overcome it. . . . Lévy is ill at ease with ideas more than a decade old, of whatever political provenance. No sense of historical complexity qualifies his terrible simplifications, nor could it do so. His posturing precludes a scrupulous inquiry into an obdurate reality. As for his philosophical method, we are obliged (across all national and conceptual boundaries) to blush for the human mind. (pp. 638-40)

> *Norman Birnbaum, "Humanism with a Barbarous Face," in* The Nation *(copyright 1979 The Nation magazine, The Nation Associates, Inc.), Vol. 228, No. 21, June 2, 1979, pp. 638-40.*

CLIFFORD ORWIN

[In *Barbarism with a Human Face*] Lévy restates in impassioned tones certain criticisms of liberalism with which we in the West have become familiar. His achievement is to have extended the leftist critique of politics to the politics of the Left. Having crawled out to the end of the leftist limb, he has surveyed it and seen that it is unsound. Fortunately for Lévy the journalist, and as unfortunately for Lévy the thinker, he knows no other vantage point.

Lévy would not enjoy his present celebrity if he had not denounced the Left in unmistakably leftist terms. His crucial point of agreement with it, implicit in his endorsement of its terms, is that political power is inherently a radical evil. This is melodrama, and we have a right to wonder why it has not occurred to Lévy to question it. Having exposed the exorcist as a liar he continues to credit its account of the demon. He thus leaves himself with nowhere to go, and no principle of political action other than that of abstention from politics. (p. 128)

Clifford Orwin, "Two French Revolutions" (reprinted with permission of the author and The Public Interest; © *1979 by National Affairs, Inc.), in* The Public Interest (© *1979 by National Affairs, Inc.), No. 56, Summer, 1979, pp. 125-28.**

François Bondy, "God's Own Testament?" in Encounter *(© 1979 by Encounter Ltd.), Vol. LIII, No. 2, August, 1979, pp. 56-7.*

FRANÇOIS BONDY

God's own testament? I suppose that after reading **Barbarism with a Human Face** one could sense a development towards ethical-metaphysical reflection, but hardly towards an impassion monotheism as the only obstacle to totalitarian thought, and within that monotheistic acknowledgement (Islam is apparently excluded) essentially to the Old Testament, to the Hebrew prophets (whom Levy, with emphasis on his name and religious origins, sees as his own forerunners).

In the first book there was a plea—since, as is well-known, Nietzsche reported that God was dead—for an "atheistic spirituality." Now in [**The Testament of God**] evidently Nietzsche himself is dead, and if God himself has not been resurrected still there remains his own testament to be fulfilled, necessarily, irresistibly: in other words He has been "rehabilitated."

What kind of crisis did this young Paris intellectual undergo between his 28th and 30th year, perhaps some sudden illumination like Blaise Pascal's, which turned him from the God of the philosophers to the God of Abraham and Jacob? In any event it has driven [Levy] to a scholarly biblical exegesis, softened by an emotional pathos which leads him to write as if we were actually dealing with three testaments, the Old, the New, and now God's own. (p. 56)

[Much] of what he has been saying is not only brilliant but also quite sound and noteworthy. He points out, for example, that totalitarianism does not merely descend "from above" but comes also "from below", that the People, the "plebeian masses" so praised by populistic intellectuals, are capable of an inhumane fanaticism all of their own; that indeed the drive of the state to identify itself with the whole of society, and to be responsible for the happiness of all citizens, is a fearful trend; that there is at bottom a vital connection between *liberal* and *liberty* which no ideological semantics can impugn.

It is regrettable that the author, moving on to such sobering thoughts, brings so little sobriety to his analysis which is rather put in the ecstatic tones of some new revelation. In many cases what he is trying to say already has a long critical tradition . . . , and he comes to certain well-known suspicions and conclusions as if they were both daring and original. At the grievous root of the matter is perhaps the Camus-like infatuation with the role of the writer as an Artist, which leads to an imprisonment of language within the sounds and colours of words, even when a sober glance at a page suggests that nonsense is being put together. Why, for example, does Levy think that the ancient injunction to turn the other cheek must have been a shock for the Hebrews? He senses an echo from the customs of Nineveh, offers a footnote to Jonah, and goes so far as to deduce that what had been lost was the "difference between left and right"! It is perfectly all right for a young militant spirit who pledges himself to resist all violent authority to put down the doctrine of "Christian humility"; but to associate this with some conceptual political confusion about "right" or "left" is as silly as our Bernard believing he is the Saint Bernard for spiritually lost travellers. (pp. 56-7)

THOMAS SHEEHAN

Springtime, O. Henry once wrote, is the season when young men discover what young women have known all winter long. Lévy's bitter springtime, his discovery of the Gulag that other intellectuals, including Sartre, had known about for over twenty years, has engendered the purple prose, alternately threnodic and dithyrambic, that we find in **Barbarism with a Human Face** and **Testament of God**. "If I were a poet," he writes, "I would sing of the horror of living and the new Gulags that tomorrow holds in store for us. If I were a musician, I would speak of the idiot laughter and impotent tears, the dreadful uproar made by the lost camped in the ruins, awaiting their fate." This is pretty heavy stuff, but, as Husserl observed at the turn of the century, one is most vehement against those errors that one recently held oneself. . . . But Lévy is no easier on his young self: he confesses, with a straight face, "I will soon be thirty, and I have betrayed the dream of my youth at least a hundred times." Such earnestness is enough to make cynics weep, and it just might sustain some of them through the two hundred pages of narcissistic prose that one finds in his philosophical *Bildungsroman* called **Barbarism with a Human Face**. . . .

[The] first principle [of **The Testament of God**] is that politics must be restricted to make room for ethics and for an individual who can resist barbarism. Second principle: such an individual can *not* be found in classical Greek thought, where the individual is subsumed by the general and where the notion of "conscience" was unknown. It can only (third principle) be found in classical Judaism's "wager" on a Totally Other who is never incarnate in the world, in fact is now dead, although somehow goes on living, or partly living, in that "book of resistance" called the Bible. . . .

Little can be said about Lévy's position precisely because so little of it is ever argued. He makes his points by rhetorical tropes, wide-ranging historical references ("Consider the Middle Ages," he advises, or the span of history "from Epictetus to Malraux"), or by citations from books that he evidently hasn't read or has poorly digested (a reference to a work by Stalin in the Russian, which Lévy does not read, a reference to *all* of Clement of Alexandria's mammoth *Protrepticus*, which he has not studied, and so on). . . . (p. 15)

Lévy's sense of history is, to say the least, vague. When asked what he meant by saying that "the West was Christian even when the Scriptures were not read in the countryside"—and *analogously*—"The Greek world was Homeric even if, outside the Mycenaean palaces, the *Iliad* and the *Odyssey* were literally dead letters," Lévy confessed that he hadn't known that the Greek epic poems were written some centuries after the events they recount.

All this may be unfair. There is a long tradition of young scholars carrying out their education in public—Schelling enriched nineteenth-century philosophy by doing so. But it can be annoying when, instead of arguing his case, the young Dr. Lévy invites us, as he constantly does, to correct our intellectual errors by "reading" or "rereading" one or another major figure of Western thought, a task we might undertake if we thought Lévy had done as much. . . . This makes one recall the quip attributed to Abraham Lincoln, "Better to remain silent and be thought a fool than to open your mouth and remove all doubt.'' (pp. 15-16)

Thomas Sheehan, ''Paris: Moses and Polytheism,'' in The New York Review of Books *(reprinted with permission from* The New York Review of Books; *copyright © 1980 Nyrev, Inc.), Vol. XXVI, Nos. 21 & 22, January 24, 1980, pp. 13-17.***

ROGER KAPLAN

[Bernard-Henri Levy's purpose in *The Testament of God*] is to establish the principles of an ''anti-barbarian'' stance.

To do this Mr. Levy anchors himself in two major traditions: political liberalism and ethical monotheism. He wishes to show that there is a political theory available to modern man that offers the means to resist the disastrous consequences of the ''fascist'' ideologies. (He uses the word fascist loosely, but it is clear from the historical examples he refers to that he has in mind Communism and Nazism.) He wishes to show that an ethic is available for the taking in the Bible and in Jewish tradition, in which, allowing for a few contradictions in his text, he includes Christianity.

The discovery of constitutional democracy, the ''formal liberties'' and the importance of private property as bulwarks against totalitarianism may strike Americans as about as exciting as a half-cooked omelet, which is indeed the nonliterary object Mr. Levy's book most closely resembles. And his reduction of the Jewish ethical tradition to a somewhat vague paraphrase of the Noachic code may strike American Jews as jeja-vu—namely, deja-vu in 19th Century Reform Judaism. One is hard-pressed to find anything in this book that has not been said elsewhere more profoundly and rigorously.

Thus one finds himself agreeing with most of what Mr. Levy has to say [in *The Testament of God*] about the institutions of liberal democracy, and at the same time wishing that instead of spending so much time demonstrating how original and clever he is Mr. Levy had simply acknowledged that it is indeed possible to rebel *into* a tradition and that the next step is a respectful and thoughtful study of the basic texts of the tradition. . . .

Mr. Levy's inability or unwillingness to follow through on sound premises prevents him from understanding fully what was wrong with his earlier ideas and leads him to disingenuous attempts at justifying past positions, which serve only to diminish the importance of what he is saying now.

Consider, for instance, his brief comments on Indochina. He believes it was both right to resist the intervention in Vietnam by American ''imperialism'' and right to assist the ''boat people.'' What sort of nonsense is this?

Mr. Levy has meditated approvingly upon the effects of liberal institutions without thinking very deeply, if at all, about what it takes to sustain those institutions. His intention is instead to find the tools with which to ''resist'' the totalitarian evil against which the good man, the good people, are basically always on the defensive. Leaving aside whether this is true, it gives Mr. Levy very little to say about the major force for liberty in the world, which is the United States. Indeed, Mr. Levy has managed to write a treatise on political theory which is liberal in inspiration yet ignorant of most of the basic liberal texts.

The eccentricities of this important book are even more apparent in Mr. Levy's attempt to draw sharp lines throughout the Western tradition between monotheism and polytheistic paganism. It is an extremely important issue in the history of ideas that he has reopened here, with more than a little courage.

The rather tortuous way in which Mr. Levy reaches the conclusion that ''monotheism is the thought of resistance of our age'' reminds us that he is writing against traditions in European political thought that have shown nothing but contempt for liberal political theory. Whether glorifying the ''people'' or glorifying the ''nation,'' these traditions, by vesting in a single party a special legitimacy due to its supposedly extraordinary ability to interpret what is needed (by the ''people'' or by the ''nation''), have no small responsibility in creating the concentration camps and the reigns of terror of our times. These fanatical, secular, absolutist faiths are what we must resist, Mr. Levy tells us. Good.

The genuine significance of this book is that it demonstrates that the ''new philosophy'' (a public relations man's term which Mr. Levy has disavowed) was more than a flash in the Cafe de Flore's pan. The French intelligentsia is belatedly acknowledging that in the great political debates that repeatedly shook it in the years, and now decades, after World War II, it was liberals like Camus and Raymond Aron who were right, who said there were poisonous ideas—based on final readings of history—behind the apologies for the Soviet Union and the subversive critiques of bourgeois institutions. The enemies of bourgeois order almost completely dominated the Parisian intellectual and cultural scenes for many years. It is from the morass which they created that Mr. Levy and others are now painfully extricating themselves.

Roger Kaplan, ''Bernard-Henri Levy: Rediscovering Liberalism,'' in The Wall Street Journal *(reprinted by permission of* The Wall Street Journal, *© Dow Jones & Company, Inc. 1980; all rights reserved), October 1, 1980, p. 32.*

GABRIEL VAHANIAN

Blunt, pithy, and iconoclastic. The very first sentence reads: ''It takes some insolence to continue to speak of hope in the century of the gas chamber and the concentration camp.'' And it takes still greater insolence to title this book *The Testament of God,* even though it reads like a book on God and calls for nothing less than a *new* covenant with God. In an age when our public selves seem to sink even more deeply in a political, religious, as well as cultural environment so vastly different and farther removed from the world of the Bible, this work upsets more than one applecart by simply asking, ''Should we re-read the Bible?''

No less ironic is the fact that the author is not a theologian, much less a biblical scholar. A Jew, not so much because of the name he has inherited as because he wants to wear and live in it as a testimony to God's *testament*, he does not even deem himself worthy of being called a believer. But, then, is not the Bible too significant a book to be left in the sole hands of those whose claims to it rest, and only rest, on their having worked on it longer than this eleventh-hour latecomer? Read his book, and you will not again relegate the Bible to its specialists, whether theologians, preachers, and other archeologists or, for that matter, believers from still another planet. If Cyrus was God's anointed, why could Lévy not interpret the Bible for our time and do so with the boldness that is the hallmark of ll authentic, seminal, and therefore, iconoclastic thinking? (p.102)

Gabriel Vahanian, *"Book Reviews: 'The Testament of God'"* (revised by the author for this publication), in Theology Today (© 1981 Theology Today), Vol. XXXVIII, No. 1, April, 1981, pp. 102-04.

THE CRITIC

[*The Testament of God*] could have been a great book, a classic of political thought, but it falls short for several reasons. Bernard-Henri Levy, the most famous of the French anti-Marxist "new philosophers," argues that socialism and fascism are indistinguishable, and that belief in God is the only thing that enables man to resist the claims of the total state. . . .

It soon becomes clear, however, that the author is himself an atheist, and that if he believes the Bible is a testament of liberty, it is as the legacy of a dead God. Ignoring the fact that the Hebrew idea of liberty collapses without belief in God, Levy holds up the prophets, especially Isaiah and Jeremiah, as models for the enemies of tyranny.

In his attacks on Greek thought, Levy seems unaware that modern Judaism, as well as Christianity, is a synthesis of Hellenism and Hebraism. Athens and Jerusalem were reconciled by Philo and Maimonides, as well as by St. Basil and St. Paul. In spite of his best intentions, Levy's interpretation of the Old Testament is eccentric and isolated from any living tradition.

"In Brief: 'The Testament of God'," in The Critic (© The Critic 1981; reprinted with the permission of the Thomas More Association, Chicago, Illinois), Vol. 39, No. 15, April 1, 1981, p. 6.

FRANÇOIS BONDY

[In *L'idéologie française* Bernard-Henri Lévy] smites friend and foe on both Left and Right, and perhaps most of all the "Myth" of France, the mythology of its democratic universalism, its *"rayonnement"*, its pretence of a radiating enlightenment. The debunking argument is based in part around Gobineau, whose notorious "Essay on the Inequality of Human Races" established a disastrous form of European racism; and in part around the true correlation of forces in the affair of the Dreyfus case, with Church and Army and even a section of the French Left stooping to anti-Semitic abuse as the good Captain gets condemned as a spy and sent off to Devil's Island. And, in part, it is about Marshal Pétain who was responsible for a Vichy law about the Jews which pre-empted Nazi occupation policy and even went beyond what Hitler had in mind at the time. As for the so-called Left opposition, it has to be recalled that the French C.P. was for a while pro-Vichy and helped to denounce its Popular Front allies when Léon Blum and Edouard Daladier came up for Pétainist assault.

All traditions go; little remains, and there are no excuses allowed. Lévy has little patience with the rationalisations that would blame the influence of party bosses in Moscow or the power of the Nazis in Berlin. France herself is the source of the fascist, anti-democratic potential in the nation.

As a piece of intellectual and cultural history the book has obvious weaknesses. There was another tradition which criticised Gobineau, defended Dreyfus, resisted Pétain; but it is not one which interests the author at the moment when bombs destroy synagogues, police round up foreign workers, and of-ficial censorship stealthily increases. Can one distortion ever serve to rectify another distortion? (pp. 60-1)

François Bondy, *"French Ideology,"* in Encounter (© 1981 by Encounter Ltd.), Vol. LVI, No. 5, May, 1981, pp. 60-1.

RAYMOND ARON

An author who readily employs the adjectives *infâme* or *obscène* to describe men and ideas is asking his critics to respond in kind. I shall do my best to resist that temptation, much as Bernard-Henri Lévy's *L'idéologie française* . . . contains some of the defects which grate on my own nerves—an overblown style, cut-and-dried verdicts on the merits and demerits of both the living and the dead, the ambition to remind a forgetful nation of the buried part of its own past, and the use of quotations torn from their context and arbitrarily interpreted. Worse still, having read the book one is left with a lingering doubt as to whether the violent tone which is kept up throughout the pamphlet reflects genuine indignation or a love of scandal and publicity.

More than that, the book does not lend itself to objective discussion in the academic sense. It does not offer the reader any fact, text, or document which may not be found in the handful of books from which Bernard-Henri Lévy has lifted and rehashed the bulk of his material. What belongs especially to Lévy is the introduction of a certain vocabulary of words or phrases, a process so subordinated to the author's argument than one wonders whether it is worthwhile holding any debate with a *"philosophe"* who arrogates to himself the role of judge and jury.

What does the argument amount to? First, an indictment of Pétainism and the "National Revolution", and in particular an inquisition into the review *Esprit* and the group "Uriage." And arising out of this, the definition of *l'idéologie française*— no "a" but "the"—whose persistence and underground strength were revealed by Vichy, and which is all the more dangerous today because indigenous French fascism was not stamped out with the Liberation. (pp. 51-3)

What irritates me is the manner in which Bernard-Henri Lévy recalls those tragic moments in the history of France [during the German occupation] without the slightest understanding of the moral dilemmas which faced any number of good Frenchmen. Those who, like [Emmanuel] Mounier, spent long months in jail, accused of representing a certain spirit of *résistance*, and the supporters of Uriage who set off as one man into the *maquis*, gun in hand, have the right to at least a degree of respect. It is legitimate to criticise the decisions they made and the texts they wrote and published between 1940 and 1942 (or 1945); but it is also proper to criticise them seriously, without overlooking the circumstances and without outlawing Péguy's nationalism or communal thinking, no matter how one may judge them in the final analysis.

We in France had known for a long time that racism and anti-Semitism were not a German monopoly. Which of the two countries was ahead of the other? Which of them was more influential? On all these questions there are lessons to be learned from serious accounts, but not from the more or less haphazard utilisation of the historical works from which Bernard-Henri Lévy has borrowed his documentation.

I want to confine myself to one really basic point. What is this *idéologie française* which this book attempts to disclose by giving it a name? French ideology is multifarious and mercurial; it is present everywhere, as much on the Right as on the Left. Proudhon was ferociously anti-Semitic, and so was Charles Maurras, at the other end of the spectrum. Money gets confounded with Judaism, and both can be found condemned in near-identical terms in both socialist and counter-revolutionary literature. ("The Jewish Question", Karl Marx's most anti-Semitic essay, illustrates this deliberate confusion.) All this is not new, and not at all characteristic of France.

What is specifically French about this ideology, this "fascism in the colours of France"? What are the features common to Proudhon, Barrès, Maurras, Sorel, Péguy and Bernanos? I do not see any other answer than this, that they detest the individualist democracy connected with capitalism, the "bourgeois, liberal Republic" of Benda (before he turned to communism) and of Bernard-Henri Lévy. "Gut patriotism", "concrete communities" and tendencies towards the "organic" view of the social order are ways of thinking which Bernard-Henri Lévy himself loathes and detests; so he turns inquisitor, and casts into the outer darkness of a "black France" Péguy and Bernanos and many others who would be astonished to find themselves lumped together in such company as part of Lévy's piecemeal reading and quotations. Simone Weil might just as well have appeared in this gallery of "forerunners."

If one were to complain to Bernard-Henri Lévy that he violates all the rules of honest interpretation and historical method, his arrogant reply would be that he doesn't give two hoots for a bunch of university hacks. But perhaps he'd agree to give a moment's consideration to one indisputable fact, namely that fascism has never "taken" in France, just as some grafts do not take. The communitarian, anti-individualistic varieties of 1930s ideology never went outside the closed coteries of the Paris intelligentsia. They came to power as a result of a national catastrophe. There again they remained a mixture of traditionalism and parafascism. (p. 54)

I come now to the epilogue, and this article's *raison d'être*. There is a possibility that some of Bernard-Henri Lévy's opponents are making him pay the price for rapid success (and too great a readership). (pp. 54-5)

And now he is Fouquier-Tinville, forgetful that democracy too can easily become inquisitorial, if not totalitarian. He is a Jew like me, and he proceeds to exclude from France or to expel into his "black France" countless writers or thinkers of our common homeland.

A number of French Jews are feeling dogged by anti-Semitism once again, and the effect of the resulting state of shock is to make them magnify the dangers, greater or lesser, which they confront. What does this book tell them? That there is dire peril everywhere, and that the French ideology condemns them to continual combat against an enemy lodged in the unconscious mind of millions of their fellow-citizens. Frenchmen who are not Jewish will draw the conclusion that the Jews are even "more different" from other French people than they had imagined, since an acclaimed spokesman proves himself incapable of understanding so many expressions of the French mind, to the point of making them outlaws in their own country.

He wants to proclaim the truth so that the French nation may recognise and overcome its past; and he rubs salt into all the unhealed wounds. With his own hysteria he is only going to feed a more general hysteria, wild talk, wild actions. "A work of public interest", so the review in the *Nouvel Observateur*

concluded. One wonders: Public interest or public danger? (p. 55)

Raymond Aron, "The Debate on 'The French Ideology': Anatomy of a Provocation," in Encounter (© 1981 by Encounter Ltd.), Vol. LVI, No. 6, June, 1981, pp. 51-5.

JEAN-FRANÇOIS REVEL

[*L'idéologie française*] expresses, or rather it reveals, that moment in the crisis of Western conscience when all efforts to distinguish between Right-wing and Left-wing totalitarianism should be, and have been, abandoned. . . .

More important than the history of anti-Semitism, which is only one component of the primeval totalitarian magma—though a component common to both Nazi Germany and Soviet Russia—what seems to me even more important in Lévy's book is its attempt to unearth the root-stock in France of a particular totalitarian, "communitarian", illiberal and anti-democratic sensibility, at the early stage when this line of thinking was still undifferentiated, and had not begun to branch out and express itself as black or red fascism. After all, it was possible for Charles Péguy, Georges Sorel, Jacques Drumont and Georges Bernanos to be enlisted, undistorted, by revolutionaries as well as by reactionaries, by *collaborateurs* and *résistants*, socialists and Maurrassians, Christians as well as anticlericals.

It is not enough to say (as Professor François Bourricaud recently remarked) that the Russo-German Pact of 1939 accounts for the collaborationist statements of the greater part of the French Communist Party's leadership after the defeat of June 1940. What is illuminating in the context of our present concern is that the Communist leaders spontaneously gave voice in the same terms as the traditionalist Rightists of Vichy's *Révolution nationale*. These old confusions and entanglements still have their off-shoots in the present day. Large sections of the French Left, not a few famous intellectuals and several great newspapers have made political heroes of the sorry killers in the Baadér-Meinhof gang, and the mindless butchers of the Red Brigades.

Look at the Right wing of the Gaullist Party and the Left wing of the Socialists—and you see the same xenophobia, the same hatred of European solidarity, the same yen for isolationism and Albanian-style state supremacy—in other words, the same Maurrassian viewpoint, whether under the red flag or the tricolour. (p. 52)

All sorts of comparisons are being made at present between "serious" historians and this upstart Bernard-Henri Lévy whose book supposedly teems with misquotations and inaccurate references. When it comes to misquotations and inaccurate references perpetrated by "serious" historians, I have whole cupboards-full which are readily available to the *Centre National de la Recherche Scientifique* and the *Ecole des Hautes Etudes* in the event that these two august institutions should want to venture into self-criticism.

It is odd that these minor oversights only become mortal sins when they are not committed with the aid of subsidies from the Republic. And it is striking that it is only the really unsettling arguments that make an author suddenly liable to be brought to heel in the name of a scientific rigour which it is usually considered ill-mannered to require on the part of tenured academics. Judged on the qualities required of a guerrilla, how many marshals would reach so much as a corporal's rating? (p. 53)

Jean-François Revel, "The Debate on 'The French Ideology': French Ambiguities," in Encounter *(©1981 by Encounter Ltd.), Vol. LVI, No. 6, June, 1981, pp. 52-3.*

DOUGLAS JOHNSON

[*L'idéologie française*] is about fascism and racism, and it claims that both are endemic in modern French thought. Echoing Georges Marchais's proclamation of a communism which will be truly French, "un communisme aux couleurs de la France", Lévy claims that there is "un fascisme aux couleurs de la France". What might appear as accidental happenings which give rise to explosions of antisemitism—such as the arrest of a junior officer who is Jewish on the charge of selling military secrets to the Germans, or the racist laws proclaimed by the government of Vichy in the wake of the greatest military defeat in French history—are made to appear an integral part of French culture. Doubtless the facts that in December, 1980, the communist mayor of Vitry personally took the lead in the destruction of an immigrant hostel in his commune, and that in the following February the communist mayor of Montigny-lès-Cormeilles publicly denounced a working-class Moroccan family for drug-pushing, are not to be seen merely as examples of electoral tactics. Racism is ingrained in French attitudes.

When a French intellectual wishes to prove anything these days, he reaches for the opinion polls, and Lévy comes up with some good statistics. After the violent bomb attack on the synagogue in the rue Copernie in Paris in October 1980, a poll published by *L'Express* reported that 49 per cent of French people thought there were too many "North Africans" in France. In 1943, Levy points out, 51 per cent of French people replied "no" when asked "Do you like the Jews?" Thus there is, he claims, a constant in French attitudes which can be shown statistically, as well as in other ways.

The other ways which Lévy sees in order to demonstrate the existence of a "real" France which is both fascist and racist are dominated by his love of quotation. He takes a whole series of writers and, by giving extracts from their works, demonstrates their ideas. . . .

But does all this add up to a culture of fascism and racism? Lévy justifies his selection of quotations by comparing it to Foucault's "archáeologie du savoir", as if he were cutting into successive layers of significance. But the isolated quotation is misleading. More often than not Lévy is playing a verbal game. Because someone thinks it essential that France should have strong government, he is not necessarily a fascist (and Lévy avoids the issue of whether Bonapartism or Gaullism can be called fascist), any more than if he uses the word "race" or describes some aspect of thought as "Jewish", he is necessarily a racist. . . .

Some of Lévy's argument is simply bizarre. "Péguy nationaliste? Péguy socialiste?" he asks, and then dismisses the questions as being of little interest. What is important, he claims, is that the two come together, and one discovers "un national-socialisme à la française"—one is reminded of Mr. Pickwick's acquaintance who was reputed to have prepared for his article on Chinese Metaphysics by consulting the encyclopedia first under "China" and then under "Metaphysics."

Lévy's other method of studying "notre pensée réactionnaire" is historical, but no less controversial. The Dreyfus affair, he writes, divided France into two camps, and practically led to civil war—an obvious exaggeration. Then there was Vichy, and it is on this period that Lévy bases the greatest part of his case, as he lists examples of how Vichy chose, of its own free will, to initiate the persecution of Jews, of how the Communist Party sought at certain times to cooperate with the Germans and to assist in the trial of the Third Republic's leaders (such as Léon Blum), and of how a collection of well-educated and able technocrats and civil servants came together at the Ecole des Cadres d'Uriage (near Grenoble) in order to prepare for the national revolution in which the new France would be closely associated with Nazi Germany.

Objections can be made to all these arguments. The Vichy government (as Lévy readily admits) was a varied and shifting group of people, and was far from being united in antisemitism. The Communist Party had for a time (from 1929 to 1933 for example) chosen to treat the Third Republic as a fascist organization, and if the logic whereby such imprisoned communists as Alfred Coste and François Billoux sought to join in the work of the Cour Suprême de Riom is curious, it can hardly constitute what Lévy calls "le Pétainisme rouge". Lévy admits that the whole of the École d'Uriage joined the Resistance movement in November 1942, but he should also recall that many of the technocrats who were associated with Vichy, such as Gabriel Le Roy Ladurie, Barnand and Pucheu, had started their careers with the Maison Worms and were denounced by more extreme collaborators as members of an Anglo-Jewish syndicate, and that such an unbalanced antisemite as Pierre Constantini was, during these years, denouncing the Jewish synarchy which was seeking to control the Vichy administration.

Things are never so simple as Lévy claims. And yet when all his mistakes are pointed out, and all the defects of his reasoning allowed for, one wonders whether there is not something in his argument after all. It remains true that France has shown enthusiasm for racial persecution, and this cannot always be explained away in terms of foolishness. . . .

Bernard-Henri Lévy is short on explanations and short also on recommendations. In his earlier books he regretted the existence of totalitarianism but failed to suggest what could be done to avoid it, other than to change the nature of man and thereby get rid of "la barbarie à visage humain". Those who led, and who were led by, the events of 1968, have always been strong starters and disappointing finishers. But, like 1968, *L'idéologie française* cannot be dismissed lightly. It remains in the mind and its challenge cannot be ignored.

Douglas Johnson, "Liberty, Equality, Fascism . . . ," in The Times Literary Supplement *(© Times Newspapers Ltd. (London) 1981; reproduced from* The Times Literary Supplement *by permission), No. 4087, July 31, 1981, p. 879.*

Simon Leys

1935-

(Pseudonym of Pierre Ryckmans) A Belgian art historian and sinologist, Leys is the author of three controversial books about the People's Republic of China. In *Chinese Shadows* (1974), best known of the three, he forcefully criticizes Communist party totalitarianism in Maoist China and denounces China-watchers whom he feels often obscure the real conditions there behind a veil of myths. Leys argues that Western observers use China as a "utopia which allows them to denounce everything that is bad in the West without taking the trouble to think for themselves." First published in France, his works reflect the disillusionment with political conditions in China felt by French sinologists in the middle 1970s. Some critics insist that Leys too easily discounts China's extreme material disadvantages as a factor in its political situation and ignores the many economic gains achieved in the last three decades. Others, however, praise Leys's forthright criticisms of totalitarian rule. (See also *Contemporary Authors,* Vols. 85-88.)

Excerpt from *CHINESE SHADOWS*

In place of the *real* class struggle in China—which in fact opposes those who are led to leaders, masses to bureaucracy—party propaganda has substituted a fictive struggle between the so-called "proletariat" and the so-called "bourgeoisie." "Proletariat" has been redefined to encompass the top as well as the base, the masses as well as the people, and thus conjures away the real conflict between oppressors and oppressed. As for the "bourgeoisie," this mythical scarecrow at whom the masses are periodically invited to vent their anger and frustration—in a way that leaves intact the powers and privileges of their true exploiters—the "bourgeoisie" is actually comprised of disgraced bureaucrats. The ruling class is torn in a perpetual merciless power struggle; the winning group always gives the unlucky losers a "bourgeois-capitalist" label and then abandons them to popular fury. Thus are two birds killed with one stone: the winners get rid of its rivals, and popular discontent is allowed to vent itself safely.

The oppression and exploitation of the Chinese masses is too real, too deeply felt and universally experienced for the regime to claim that it does not exist. So the masses are encouraged, *up to a point*, to expose their grievances from time to time. However, the identification of guilty parties remains the exclusive preserve of the authorities. And since the struggle for power goes on endlessly without truce, there is no chance of running out of scapegoats: yesterday Liu Shao-ch'i and his clique, today Lin Piao and his lieutenants, tomorrow somebody else. Since all these targets are members of the ruling class, the masses recognize readily that they are true oppressors, and lose no time in vigorously denouncing them. But at this point the authorities must very carefully guide and control the popular anger and prevent it from fulfilling its logical development, which would be to denounce the oppressors *as members of the ruling clique and the group in power*, because this would mean an accusation not against individuals but against the bureaucratic class as a whole, bringing into question the basic principle of the system and showing for all to see the true nature

of the "class struggle" within the regime. To prevent this danger, the propaganda system must forge a criminal identity so fantastic that it will be impossible to confuse disgraced bureaucrats with their colleagues in power. Thus they become spies in the pay of the U.S.A., Kuomintang agents, spies of the Soviet Union, traitors to their country, minions of feudalism, conspirers for a bourgeois-capitalistic restoration. In short, you stick a false nose on Liu Shao-ch'i so that nobody notices how much he looks like Mao Tse-tung.

The "class struggle" as understood in the Maoist system—that is, the denunciation by the masses of guilty parties who have been singled out for them by the powers that be—is the regime's safety valve, its basic hygiene, a periodic bloodletting that allows it to eliminate the toxins in its organism. For the masses, this ritual exercise gives a very convincing appearance of reality. The violence and the blood that always flows in these operations, the high positions and broad powers that had once been the preserve of the bureaucrats now found guilty—all this seems to show that a true revolution is occurring. In fact, the double cross is perfect, for the essence of the bureaucratic system is the interchangeability of bureaucrats, and no mere change of personnel could alter the nature of the regime. After a while, when the masses realize that "while the bottle may be different, it holds the same purgative,'' the people in power have only to throw to the wolves another cartful of ''bourgeois,'' found guilty of a new capitalist ''restoration.'' The great advantage of the ''bourgeois'' created by the regime over the authentic kind is that while the latter variety is practically extinct in China, the supply of the first exactly matches the demand. (pp. 189-91)

Western ideologues now use Maoist China just as the eighteenth-century philosophers used Confucian China: as a myth, an abstract ideal projection, a utopia which allows them to denounce everything that is bad in the West without taking the trouble to think for themselves. We stifle in the miasma of industrial civilization, our cities rot, our roads are blocked by the insane proliferation of cars, et cetera. So they hurry to celebrate the People's Republic, where pollution, delinquency, and traffic problems are nonexistent. One might as well praise an amputee because his feet aren't dirty.

This starry-eyed admiration for all that is done, or not done, in China, with no effort at critical scrutiny—is it really the best service one can render a despotism that already has too much of a propensity to believe in its own infallibility (''Long live the great, glorious and always infallible Chinese Communist Party!'')? Would it not be more useful to call: ''Stop! Watch out!'' when one sees China rushing headlong into deadends that the West, to its cost, has already explored? If China is still relatively free of pollution and traffic problems, it is not for lack of trying. It does not yet have the industrial means to poison the urban air as efficiently as we do, but it is certainly going in that direction, choosing ancient cities, filled with art, and historical landmarks as sites for industries that could have worked just as well—and probably better—elsewhere. Thus, southeastern Peking is already polluted by a steel complex. And in Soochow, the guides proudly repeat this cliché to visitors: ''The countless pagodas of our city have given way to a forest of smokestacks!'' The Maoist government, made up of old men with a nineteenth-century psychology in such matters, would be ashamed of its backwardness if it did not manage to pollute *at least* two or three of China's most venerable cultural metropolises. Western capitals, under the stupid and inhuman pressure of a motor traffic we are unable (or unwilling) to control, have destroyed their beauty to widen their streets and make parking space. They did better in Peking: whole neighborhoods were razed to make vast macadam wastes that in the future will furnish the arena for automotive madness. Right now, the emptiness is dotted with bicycles and donkey carts—making the destruction more odious still, since it was pointless. (pp. 201-02)

Simon Leys, in his Chinese Shadows *(translation copyright © 1977 by Viking Penguin Inc.; reprinted by permission of the publishers; originally published as* Ombres Chinoises *(© Union Generale d'Editions, 1974), Union Générale d'Editions, 1974), Viking Penguin, 1977, 220 p.*

MARTIN BERNAL

According to . . . Simon Leys [in *Ombres Chinoises*], the vast variety and colour of China have been reduced to a few monotonous 'models'. He points out that virtually all foreign delegations go to the same dozen communes, the same dozen factories, schools and hospitals. Even when it comes to individuals they meet a selection of the hundred or so who are thought to be suitable for contact with foreigners. Although Leys—as he admits—exaggerates the situation, there is a good deal of truth in his description, as can be seen in the remarkable monotony of most books about trips to China. . . .

[Leys] completely disregards all descriptions of progress and of loyalty and love for the regime as meaningless conformity, putting all his emphasis on complaints and deviance. He also inclines towards another fallacy of Western 'communist studies': that if the 'communists' admit something bad about themselves 'it must be true and ten times worse', the frequently misleading image of the iceberg. This comes, I think, from the old belief in monolithic totalitarianism, and fails to take into account that all political systems have splits and rivalries and that from time to time these lead to the publication and even exaggeration of unpleasant truths. The fantastic reports during the cultural revolution of massive battles, uprisings and massacres are only an extreme example of this.

The fundamental reason for Leys's overemphasis on the hidden is, I suspect, the desire to stress the importance of esoteric knowledge not available to others. Leys, who has been to China frequently and speaks good Chinese, is obsessed with the notion that he knows China more intimately than anyone else. The self-importance that 'inside dope' gives to its possessors means that they over-emphasise it so that it becomes a serious menace to balanced perception. In nearly all cases one does far better to rely on public information. (p. 599)

Martin Bernal, ''Invisible Men,'' in New Statesman *(© 1975 The Statesman & Nation Publishing Co. Ltd.), Vol. 89, No. 2302, May 2, 1975, pp. 598-99.**

NANCY DALL MILTON and DAVID MILTON

In his opening pages [of *Chinese Shadows*], Mr. Leys states that he knows nothing of Chinese politics, that he learned nothing on his trips to China, and expects to be criticized for a lack of information, the skimpiness and disjointedness of his book. It is precisely because of these inadequacies, however, he tells us, that he felt impelled to take on the thankless job of writing it. In a way that can only be described as embarrassing, Mr. Leys presents himself as spokesman for and protector of the Chinese people and the culture of ''the country I love more than my own.'' . . . Stating that ''under the conditions in which foreign residents and visitors now live in the People's Republic of China, it is impossible to write anything but frivolities. . .,'' he proceeds to do just that, all the while huffing mightily under his white man's burden of giving the Chinese people the China he thinks they should have. The frivolities he describes include the ritual activities now familiar to all China readers of the 1970s—state banquets, statistical briefings by the hundreds and the returning to the visitor of discarded socks, pens or razor blades from vacated hotel rooms. Although Mr. Leys's frustrations and criticisms are expressed with particular venom, they are hardly original. . . . (p. 21)

Nancy Dall Milton and David Milton, ''Understanding China: The Long March,'' in The Nation *(copyright 1977 The Nation magazine, The Nation Associates, Inc.), Vol. 225, No. 1, July 2, 1977, pp. 21-4.**

BENJAMIN I. SCHWARTZ

[Simon Leys provides us in *Chinese Shadows*] with what is probably the most spirited and witty hostile report ever written.

He speaks of Chinese "shadows" yet it is quite obvious that what he attacks is in his own mind not shadow but substance. (p. 40)

[One] comes away from the book with the feeling that the achievements [of the Maoist regime] are fairly well obliterated by the shadows. Some of his most trenchant pages deal with the techniques and rituals for handling foreign guests; with the behavior of the foreign guests themselves, with Maoist cultural and artistic policies and with the life-style of the bureaucracy. He also provides some sensitive evocations of the subtle differences in the atmosphere of various local regions and urban centers.

He makes no secret of his vehement hostility to Maoist cultural and artistic policy. Current official art is *not* popular art in spite of the fossilized folk elements embedded in it. It is rather "petty bourgeois academicism" full of "cloying hideousness, breathtaking saccharinity and viscous, suave vulgarity" similar in spirit to totalitarian art elsewhere. His fury at the esthetic destruction of Peking knows no bounds.

It would be easy to dismiss Leys's cultural rage by setting it against the achievement of a government which has managed to provide for the basic life needs of 900 million people with a fair degree of distributive justice. Yet we must remind ourself that this facile patronizing humanitarianism on our part is based on the assumption that any government which can fill the peasant's rice bowl has the natural right and wisdom to shape every aspect of his cultural-spiritual life. After all, how can his cultural needs be compared to ours?

Leys's total rejection of Maoist cultural policies is linked to his radical disbelief that these policies represent the achievement of a thoroughly egalitarian "mass participatory" society. It is, on the contrary, his view that China is ruled by a highly hierarchized and privileged "military-bureaucratic" ruling class. It does not seem to me that this term provides an adequate description of the complex political reality of China but it is a fact that China is governed by a hierarchized ruling class not free (even if one is to believe its own pronouncements) of the characteristics of ruling classes elsewhere—this in spite of (and to a degree because of?) the doctrines of Mao Tse-tung.

Nevertheless, it is a ruling class which has, by Leys's own admission, realized some important and impressive achievements. Yet when Leys subsumes China under an *a priori* model of a "totalitarian regime which has very little capacity for change," when he asserts that all changes which have taken place in China since 1949 can only be considered tactical and superficial he, in effect, denies these achievements since some of them have been realized only over the course of time. . . . The People's Republic is totalitarian in aspiration and practice but there may be much which that term does not explain. It has *not* precluded significant change and uncertain gropings. It does not absolutely preclude the possibility of a shift in the future from a full-blown totalitarianism to a more limited authoritarianism. (pp. 41-2)

Benjamin I. Schwartz, "Books Considered: 'Chinese Shadows'," in The New Republic *(reprinted by permission of* The New Republic; © *1977 The New Republic, Inc.), Vol. 177, Nos. 6 & 7, August 6 & 13, 1977, pp. 40-2.*

JOHN K. FAIRBANK

["**Chinese Shadows**"] is a brilliant polemic that in 1974, as "**Ombres Chinoises,**" blew the whistle on French adulation of Mao and may have a similar effect here. (p. 1)

It must also be said, to the detriment of Leys's case, that "**Chinese Shadows**" almost entirely manages to ignore the material achievements of the People's Republic—rebuilding the country with trees, dams, ditches, pumps, fields, crops and factories; remaking the society with literacy, organization, technical skills, public health, political participation, patriotism, hard work, cooperation and self-respect. If Chou En-lai were still alive to explain it all to the foreigners, he might point out that revolutions zig and zag. He would not be pessimistic, and neither should we. China is not Russia, and the Chinese style of party autocracy is not just a copy of the Soviet. On the contrary, it has deep roots in China's so-called Legalist tradition, which Mao invoked. Perhaps today Leys would see more chance that the alternative Confucian tradition of individual self-cultivation might still ameliorate China's future. (pp. 21-2)

John K. Fairbank, "Mao's War on Culture," in The New York Times Book Review *(© 1977 by The New York Times Company; reprinted by permission), August 28, 1977, pp. 1, 18, 20-2.*

JONATHAN SPENCE

[How, in *Chinese Shadows,* can Leys], who mocks Ross Terrill for calling his book *The Real China,* who spoofs the fellow-travelers re-parroting the Chinese line, sneers at Chinese émigrés who return from comfortable campuses to extoll the communes, and condemns the Western "lyrical illiterates" of Sinology who praised Chinese socialism in Yenan, how can he have learned so much? By seeing so little, is Leys's original and provocative answer, by living a shadow life among shadow people, in which experience of reality is so consistently denied that "it is impossible to write anything but frivolities," and one can only glean glimpses of reality through chance meetings with a cook, a waiter, a railway attendant.

I wonder if there is not a basic inconsistency behind Leys's attitudes, because at the same time he seeks (demands even) that he be taken seriously as the carrier of a serious message; he juxtaposes himself repeatedly with George Orwell, and feels that his time in China justifies him in making mordant observations and flights of sarcastic abuse. . . .

Yet just as one grows dubious, something Leys has written hits home. . . . (pp. 16-17)

It is a pity in a way that Leys chose to write under a pseudonym, especially since he tells us that his "cover" has been blown anyway by "the Maoist faithful." One might as well respect his desire not to use his real name, but by depriving the reader of any sense of a living context for Leys's experiences in China he makes it doubly hard for us to assess the worth of his observations. Sometimes he comes across like any bitter and frustrated missionary or merchant in the closing years of the Ch'ing dynasty, excoriating the entire society for refusing to take him as one of its own; at other times he is the spokesman for a truly democratic dream which, he passionately feels, the Chinese leadership have long lost sight of.

Since I must attempt a judgment, I would say that Leys's book fails to be an important contribution to our conceptions of China because it divorces the present so sharply from the past, and thus ducks the hardest questions, despite its appearance of no-holds-barred honesty. The peculiar complexity of the Chinese revolution lies in the immensity of the population, and the terrible dislocations of civil life and economic collapse that spurred the revolution. The incredible poverty that any visitor still witnesses in China must be evaluated in the light of past Chinese famine rather than current affluences elsewhere, if our judgments are not to be totally skewed; and we need not like the regime's jargon at all, may indeed find it absurd, yet must still strive, as Silone put it, to "separate the fatuous from the essential." To put it another way, Leys would be happy to apply to contemporary China Koestler's sardonic view that "to survive, we all had to become virtuosos of Wonderland croquet," yet he lacks Koestler's sense of the true difficulties of extricating the noble from the base in revolutionary contexts: "The passions of that time seem transformed into perversions, its inner certainties into the closed universe of the drug addict; the shadow of barbed wire lies across the condemned playground of memory."

What really was that playground? "A refusal to admit the existence of destiny," adds Silone contrapuntally to Koestler, "an extension of the ethical impulse from the restricted individual and family sphere to the whole domain of human activity, a need for effective brotherhood, an affirmation of the superiority of the human person over all the economic and social mechanisms which oppress him." This is a timeless vision, which Silone and Koestler saw snatched from the Soviet Union, as Leys sees it snatched from the Chinese people: "People. The leaders of China manipulate the people cynically, but the people are still the country's only capital. If, despite all the stupid cruelties of politics, China still remains faithful to itself—subtle, human, so supremely civilized—it is due to them. . . . They have buried twenty dynasties, they will also bury this one. They have not changed. As usual, they are patient; they are not in a hurry: they know so much more than those who rule over them!"

Oh, the patience of the ageless Chinese, with their eternal values! One grows a little weary, for this is out of Hegel by Bloomsbury, yet as in much of Leys there is force behind the attention-catching poses, a force found in the continuity of visions for a happier life, with different options that lead to deeper dignities. (p. 17)

> *Jonathan Spence, "The Chinese Dream Machine,"* in The New York Review of Books *(reprinted with permission from* The New York Review of Books; *copyright © 1977 Nyrev, Inc.), Vol. XXIV, No. 15, September 29, 1977, pp. 15-17.**

FRANCIS B. RANDALL

Leys might have written a less rambling and more comprehensive book [than *Chinese Shadows*]. He might have had more charity for sinners and fools. He might have made greater efforts to keep his spleen from overmastering his balance. But then he would not have written so fine a work of prose, and he would not have been so effective a battler in a time of great need. (p. 1245)

> *Francis B. Randall, "Sinners and Fools,"* in National Review *(© National Review, Inc., 1977; 150 East 35th St., New York, NY 10016), Vol. XXIX, No. 42, October 28, 1977, pp. 1244-45.*

THOMAS MASSEY

Like most broadsides, *Chinese Shadows* has excesses of its own, which are not improved by what comes across in translation as a curiously pugnacious style. The book is marked, too, by an arch and snobbish tone, arising partly from Leys' cultural ostentation . . . and partly from his pose as a man who loves Mother China but feels contempt for those who now happen to tenant her soil. . . .

The horrors of a totalitarian state are many, and pointing them out may not seem like much of an insight. . . . But Leys did it first, and in doing so, his book helps focus on the real problem, which is not the *economic* organization of Chinese society, or that of any other "socialist" state, but the rampant spread of the bureaucratic way of life. (p. 45)

[Leys' description of his visit to a "May 7th" school is the part of his] book that most nearly approaches the universal, for his description of China's officeholders is painfully similar to a profile of the US Department of Agriculture—or, of course, General Foods. But it is also the part in which he misses an important point; for when he regards the May 7th schools as a kind of farce, he misses the insight that led Mao to create them. If Maoist China has created the most ponderous bureaucracy this side of the Kremlin, at least Mao recognized, as his counterparts in the Kremlin have not, that he had something of a monster on his hands. In sending the bureaucrats to the field, in overhauling the universities, in loosing the furies of Cultural Revolution, his prescriptions may have been imprecise, but his diagnosis was perfect. He saw, as we should, that to free his nation meant fighting not only ignorance, hunger, and the revisionist devils of Russia, but also the organizations that choked his people instead of leading them. That is the page from his little red book that deserves to be saved. (p. 46)

> *Thomas Massey, "China and India and Me,"* in The Washington Monthly *(reprinted with permission from* The Washington Monthly; *copyright 1978 by The Washington Monthly Co., 2712 Ontario Road, N.W., Washington, D.C. 20009), Vol. 10, No. 1, March, 1978, pp. 44-7.**

JOHN SCOTT

[In *Chinese Shadows*] Simon Leys has provided the more vulnerable China traveller with a valuable antidote, which should, if taken prior to disembarkation, do something to prevent even the most gullible and enthusiastic brown-ricer from chucking any remaining critical judgment out of the touring-coach window. But apart from documenting some of contemporary China's appalling record of state-decreed vandalism, in the section entitled 'Follow the Guide' the author has supplied a great deal of sound information on the main tourist attractions ranging from what is left of the two ancient capitals at Sian and Loyang, as well as the beautiful city of Soochow to the Dazhai Commune which sounds an ideal holiday camp for any Spartan helot who is tired of rainy Sunday afternoon outings to Slough or East Kilbride.

But it is above all the chapters devoted to bureaucracy, cultural life and the universities that the author excels himself in his own delightfully sardonic manner, and it is this caustic critique which would suggest that the only real 'class crunch' remaining in China exists between the rulers and the ruled, the masses and the bureaucrats, the people and the party apparatchiks. (p. 23)

> *John Scott, "Class Crunch,"* in The Spectator *(© 1978 by The Spectator; reprinted by permission of* The Spectator), *Vol. 241, No. 7827, July 8, 1978, pp. 23-4.*

EDWARD FRIEDMAN

[Pierre Ryckmans] makes some shrewd observations on the privileged position of the military sector in Chinese society in his book, *Chinese Shadows*. . . . Cultural historians may, in addition, find in the work a useful compilation of some of the destruction wrought by the Red Guards during the Cultural Revolution. Sadly, the book fails as a deep analysis of Chinese politics. Its attempt to explicate the real roots of China's political dynamics results only in confusion, contradiction and, most unfortunately, McCarthyism.

Ryckmans contends that virtually all other professional analysts of Chinese politics are fools, flatterers, frauds and apologists. The truth that all others but he supposedly miss is that China is a cretinized, totalitarian, Stalinist, slave society of ant-like people. Ryckmans is not given to understatement.

Since Ryckmans believes he has nothing to learn from academics who do not share his simplistic unidimensional explanation, he never comes to grips with the professional consensus which finds more utility in complex non-totalitarian paradigms related to comparative communism, conflict models, nationalism, interest-group theory, bureaucratic politics and notions of collective action, techno-logic and modernization.

Ryckmans' observations, on contrast to his theory, are more in accord with these non-totalitarian paradigms. He records the obvious facts such as Mao's inability to impose his will on the bureaucracy, the almost permanent factions, the nearness of military coups, the persistence of virtually feudal traditions, the vitality of family and the ease with which some educators got around reforms they didn't like. And he does not invent a secret police which terrorizes the populace, since there is none. Indeed, he reports his observation that workers fearlessly impose their own rules.

Ryckmans then ignores what he observes in the present and proceeds to find the roots of his fictive Chinese totalitarianism in China's past. Supposedly, Maoism grows from and builds on a hypostatized totalitarian tradition instituted by the Ming dynasty some 600 years ago. At the same time, Maoism allegedly destroys the continuing humanist Confucian tradition which long predated the Ming dynasty.

This gross and distant argument which finds the origins and meaning of contemporary Chinese political dynamics in ancient times makes no sense at all to me or to most other political scientists of People's China concerned with party and ideology, modernity and socialism. And Ryckmans has no other explanatory scheme to offer.

Ryckmans' good Confucian past even includes traditional China as a veritable "two party democracy." . . . Meanwhile, the real populist, localist, decentralist facet of Maoism, analyzed by so many scholars, receives not a word. Instead, Ryckmans argues that a supposedly sybaritic past . . . has been replaced by a leveling-down. Apparently, he alone never heard about China's earlier mass starvations. (pp. 1476-77)

Since the bases of Ryckmans' theories conflict at every key point with the professional consensus, it is no wonder that he damns and ignores the contributions of professionals.

In fact, Ryckmans' own evidence is not even congruent with his own theses that most everything is wonderful in the surviving elements of the Confucian past. Evincing no love for the dogmatism of much of Chinese educational methods, Ryckmans' comments that "Chinese pedagogy remains . . . desperately conservative and traditional." . . . In addition, he notes that the "age-old contempt of mandarin society for manual work" persists, as "city dwellers still look down upon a country-side posting as exile or disgrace." . . . One less biased than Ryckmans might almost find in his observations some small justification for Maoism's belief in China's need to undermine some undemocratic aspects of Confucianism.

If the data on Chinese politics and society won't support his thesis of a monstrous present replacing a magnificient past—he dismisses the evils of the past as mere "historical accident'," . . . Ryckmans tries to carry the day with an extraordinary verbal assault of extreme language. Words such as "atrocity," "rape" and "murder" . . . and comparisons with the world's most notorious conquerors and killers are linked to the most ordinary acts of China's modernization such as the removal of city walls, the widening and straightening of streets, clapping at the conclusion of a performance and language reform.

No comparison is ever made with other nations' modernization or earlier moments in China's modernization, although that might permit a serious evaluation of the costs and benefits of China's path. It really isn't serious analysis to idealize China's distant past and demonize the present as Ryckman does.

This demonology combines two theodicies. First there is the reverence of antiquarians and former colonials for the heavenly old days in China. Ryckmans pines for some imagined traditional China with its supposedly "straightforward," "warm-hearted," "simple," "natural," "naive," "courteous," "crafty," "subtle" people. You know, the "patient" ones such as the "devoted" cook of the foreigner. . . .

Second, Ryckmans describes himself as one who once adored the revolution as good and now finds it hateful. . . . The flip-flop not only produces the expected percentages of emotion (maximized) and reason (almost nonexistent), but also the major metaphor of the book: the revolution as a false god.

As a result, the book is full of one major judgment or error after another, each and all characterized by the victory of blinding venom over balance or fact. Whereas respected observers such as Benjamin Schwartz and Wang Gengwu describe Mao as an accomplished poet whose poems stir something in every literate Chinese, Ryckmans has only vile adjectives to describe that poetry. Whereas all Western biographers of Mao are grateful for Li Jui's *The Early Revolutionary Activities of Comrade Mao Tse-tung*, . . . Ryckmans insists that the Chinese are kept completely ignorant of Mao's biography. . . . Whereas Mao wrote reams in criticism of Stalin's way (an English translation of some of this is titled *A Critique of Soviet Economics*), Ryckmans insists that not one such word exists. . . .

What we have from Ryckmans, I fear, is not ordinary ignorance or error, but pure malice. His analysis is at this level: "one can see what is wrong with the left-wing movement by the ugliness of their women.". . .

Worst of all, the book is unforgivably vicious. Typically, Ryckmans begins and ends with a back-handed attack on Harvard's John King Fairbank (who probably contributed more than any other individual to fostering rigorous American scholarship on modern China) as a flattering advocate of Maoism. When I recall the hurtful slanders of Fairbank in this regard in the McCarthy period, when I remember that Fairbank's basic category for People's China is totalitarianism and that he has argued at length to keep Taiwan from the PRC, I conclude that

Ryckmans is so much out for effect that he has forgotten not only facts and history but basic human decency. (pp. 1477-78)

Edward Friedman, "Book Reviews: 'Chinese Shadows'," in The American Political Science Review *(copyright, 1978, by The American Political Science Association), Vol. 72, No. 4, December, 1978, pp. 1476-78.*

KAI-YU HSU

Much as I agree with [Pierre Ryckmans in *Chinese Shadows*] that the Chinese masses are submissive to the manipulation of the Communist party and that the Party is hostage to its contending factions, I sensed in 1973 some degree of improvement; formerly impoverished people were now able to walk down the "fashionable" streets of Peking with their chins up and in proud strides. I recall how in my young days the coolies were kicked by their employers, or just anybody richer than they, and did not dare strike back; the old submissiveness, once so pitiful, was gone. One can say that very little has changed—that the new bosses, the Party and its instruments of power, have only replaced the old oppressors, that the label but not the contents has changed. But what about the young boy who defied the policeman in Hangchow and insisted on leaving his bicycle on the sidewalk, ignoring traffic regulations? One could surmise that the traffic policeman was unarmed; the boy *would* bow to an armed soldier. Nevertheless, it is true that the Cultural Revolution, in spite of its many undesirable acts, *has* fostered some defiance of authority in the young. At the moment when I watched the young cyclist's rude behavior toward the policeman, I had mixed feelings, largely blaming the Cultural Revolution for sowing such seeds of lawlessness and violence, but in calmer reflection, I have to recognize that something close to individualism was being expressed—a spark which might flare in the right climate. (pp. 370-71)

Ryckmans wrote this book when he was most irritated by the ignorance, willful or not, of those China experts too eager to see the good in the Mao-led revolution. This eagerness could be due to "our different *concrete* circumstances," as a close friend in Peking repeated to me many times in 1973 to explain our different viewpoints. Some want to protect their loved ones in the PRC; others want to stay on good terms with Peking in hopes of going there again; still others assign priority to embracing a cause, not to academic objectivity, which they consider to be nonexistent. At any rate, Ryckmans lashed out, and at places, struck back, in his well-documented eloquence. His is an art of letters which I envy. After all, he is a close reader of Lu Hsün. (p. 371)

Kai-yu Hsu, "China: 'Chinese Shadows'," in Journal of Asian Studies *(copyright 1979 by the Association for Asian Studies), Vol. XXXVIII, No. 2, February, 1979, pp. 368-71.*

ARVIN PALMER

Although [*The Chairman's New Clothes* is] not entirely satisfying from a scholarly point of view (as Leys himself admits), the author has the broad historical and cultural perspective that, regardless of its precision, is frequently more knowledgeable of the broad spectrum of events.

Leys states plainly that the Cultural Revolution was a power play by a frustrated Mao Tse-tung who resented being shoved into the background after the Great Leap Forward. He characterizes Mao as an old style Chinese Emperor who, after losing his grasp, surrounds himself with sycophants and calls on the loyalties of old comrades to carry out his spoiling activities. Because of his prestige and the peculiar relationships he had with Lin, Chou and others, he was able to succeed in undermining the established political and economic hierarchy. However, as was ever the case in Communist China, once the floodgates were loosed chaos and economic deterioration set in rapidly. The military, not too well controlled from the center anyway, had to be relied on to salvage any control of the nation at all. This left the military in virtual control of most of the organs of government and society, and most of the potential for orderly development was given over to a more or less repressive leadership. Mao won in his bid to overturn sceince and education in favor of mystical Chinese peasant ingenuity, but Leys feels that China lost all the way around.

Leys' study leaves much to be desired in its structure and form but, as he indicates, the information is there for the reader to judge for himself. His insights are provocative and his conclusions have an air of realistic assessment about them. He deserves a thoughtful hearing. (pp. 147-48)

Arvin Palmer, "Book Department: 'The Chairman's New Clothes: Mao and the Cultural Revolution'," in The Annals of the American Academy of Political and Social Science *(©1979, by The American Academy of Political and Social Science), Volume 442, March 1979, pp. 147-48.*

MELINDA LIU

The searing visions which linger in one's mind after a reading of [*Broken Images*] easily compensate for those observations which have become outdated by the pace of recent developments in the Chinese political scene.

The sophistication of Leys' writing is as impressive as ever in this collection of essays. The most powerful is his title essay which offers a series of vignettes gleaned from conversations with immigrants who had made their way, legally or illegally, to Hongkong. . . .

At a few points, Leys' methodology of relying on a specific example to provide the foundation for a broad generalisation has not stood up over time. He writes that Chairman Hua Guofeng could not affort to give freedom to Li Jengtian, the main author of the revolutionary Li Yije group which called for "socialist democracy and legality," as the writer might some day question whether the "gang of four" could have come into power without Mao. He reports Li Jengtian's 1977 sentence of life imprisonment and the 1978 rumour of his execution. In a comment a few weeks ago, Leys semi-justified the fact that Li was freed and the Li Yije group rehabilitated by saying that Peking's decision was made easier since they are dedicated Marxists who believed in the reform of the party from within.

Leys also asserts in *Broken Images* than Chinese bureaucrats do not ask questions about anything taking place outside China, because they feel they know all they need to know. Such a claim may seem ludicrous to visitors to China who have been plied with queries from curious Chinese about life on the outside.

Even so, the points Leys makes offer important insights into the Maoist milieu, particularly the Cultural Revolution which he describes as "the ruthless cretinisation of the most sophisticated nation on earth.'' More importantly, he writes from an eminently human perspective, without attempting to present himself as a monolithic authority on all that transpires in China. (p. 40)

Leys never intended his commentaries to stand as the definitive word regarding the Chinese political and cultural scene. And so the writer succeeds superbly in presenting a fresh perspective and filling in gaps of knowledge. Moreover, judging from the author's note at the beginning of the book, gradual obsolescence of his essays might well be the optimum result Leys could hope for. (p. 41)

Melinda Liu, ''An Iconoclast in China,'' in Far Eastern Economic Review *(© Far Eastern Economic Review Limited, 1981), Vol. 104, No. 24, June 15, 1979, pp. 40-1.*

DENNIS DUNCANSON

Broken Images is another *Chinese Shadows*; the author apologizes for flogging an old horse again but promises that this will be positively the last time. . . . [The essays are] all of high quality, and highly critical of Mao's attitude to the common people. . . . As in *Chinese Shadows,* the message is the ingenuousness of eminent foreign visitors to China today, picking on Professor Fairbank's partial condonation of Mao's labour camps as ''more efficient, productive and disciplined than the Soviet *gulag*''; as Leys points out, those qualities make them doubly repressive of individuality. Just as the tyranny of contemporary China echoes European tyrannies of the 1930s, especially Hitler's and Mussolini's, so does the wit of the victims' reactions: ''Dr S. had just come back from Shanghai. . . . [On a 'democracy wall'] she saw a daring graffito that changed the slogan *p'i Lin p'i K'ung* ('criticism of Lin Piao, criticism of Confucius') into *p'i ling p'i k'ung* ('criticism zero, criticism nil').''

Dennis Duncanson, ''Far East: 'Broken Images— Essays on Chinese Culture','' in Asian Affairs, *Vol. X, Part III, October, 1979, p. 353.*

Seymour Martin Lipset

1922-

Lipset is an American sociologist, author of books on political sociology, and educator. In his widely acclaimed *Political Man* (1960), an evaluation of the "conditions for stable democracy," Lipset argues that western societies have achieved relative stability largely because they have been able to moderate fundamental social conflicts and because the working class has won its struggle to attain "full citizenship." In *The Politics of Unreason* (1978), Lipset and coauthor Earl Raab contend that extremist movements of the right and left are antagonistic to a pluralist democracy which allows for the amicable competition of diverse groups, interests, and ideas. This position was attacked by conservatives for its characterization of the right as "extremist," and by the left for its assumption that tolerance is a quality of the political "center." Other detractors have criticized Lipset for drawing broad theoretical conclusions from limited empirical data. Nevertheless, Lipset is widely recognized as one of America's leading political sociologists. He is currently the Caroline S. G. Munro Professor of Political Science and Sociology, and Senior Fellow of the Hoover Institution on War, Revolution and Peace, Stanford University; he was president of the International Society of Political Psychology from 1979 to 1980. (See also *Contemporary Authors, Vols. 1-4, rev. ed.; Contemporary Authors New Revision Series, Vol. 1*.)

Excerpt from *POLITICAL MAN: THE SOCIAL BASIS OF POLITICS*

A basic premise of this book is that democracy is not only or even primarily a means through which different groups can attain their ends or seek the good society; it is the good society itself in operation. Only the give-and-take of a free society's internal struggles offers some guarantee that the products of the society will not accumulate in the hands of a few power-holders, and that men may develop and bring up their children without fear of persecution. And, as we have seen, democracy requires institutions which support conflict and disagreement as well as those which sustain legitimacy and consensus. In recent years, however, democracy in the Western world has been undergoing some important changes as serious intellectual conflicts among groups representing different values have declined sharply. (p. 439)

The fact that the differences between the left and the right in the Western democracies are no longer profound does not mean that there is no room for party controversy. But as the editor of one of the leading Swedish newspapers once said to me, "Politics is now boring. The only issues are whether the metal workers should get a nickel more an hour, the price of milk should be raised, or old-age pensions extended." These are important matters, the very stuff of the internal struggle within stable democracies, but they are hardly matters to excite intellectuals or stimulate young people who seek in politics a way to express their dreams.

This change in Western political life reflects the fact that the fundamental political problems of the industrial revolution have been solved: the workers have achieved industrial and political citizenship; the conservatives have accepted the welfare state;

and the democratic left has recognized that an increase in overall state power carries with it more dangers to freedom than solutions for economic problems. This very triumph of the democratic social revolution in the West ends domestic politics for those intellectuals who must have ideologies or utopias to motivate them to political action.

Within Western democracy, this decline in the sources of serious political controversy has even led some to raise the question as to whether the conflicts that are so necessary to democracy will continue. (pp. 442-43)

The thesis that partisan conflict based on class differences and left-right issues is ending is based on the assumption that "the economic class system is disappearing . . . that redistribution of wealth and income . . . has ended economic inequality's political significance."

Yet one wonders whether these intellectuals are not mistaking the decline of ideology in the domestic politics of Western society with the ending of the class conflict which has sustained democratic controversy. As the abundant evidence on voting patterns in the United States and other countries indicates, the electorate as a whole does not see the end of the domestic class struggle envisioned by so many intellectuals. (pp. 443-44)

These opinions do not simply represent the arguments of partisans, since supporters of both the left and the right agree on the classes each party basically represents—which does not mean the acceptance of a bitter class struggle but rather an agreement on the representation functions of the political parties similar to the general agreement that trade-unions represent workers, and the Chamber of Commerce, businessmen. Continued class cleavage does not imply any destructive consequences for the system; as I indicated in an early chapter, a stable democracy requires consensus on the nature of the political struggle, and this includes the assumption that different groups are best served by different parties.

The predictions of the end of class politics in the "affluent society" ignore the relative character of any class system. The decline of objective deprivation—low income, insecurity, malnutrition—does reduce the potential tension level of a society, as we have seen. But as long as some men are rewarded more than others by the prestige or status structure of society, men will feel *relatively* deprived. The United States is the wealthiest country in the world, and its working class lives on a scale to which most of the middle classes in the rest of the world aspire; yet a detailed report on the findings of various American opinion surveys states: "The dominant opinion on polls before, during, and after the war is that the salaries of corporation executives are too high and should be limited by the government." And this sentiment, prevalent even among prosperous people, finds increasing support as one moves down the economic ladder.

The democratic class struggle will continue, but it will be a fight without ideologies, without red flags, without May Day parades. (pp. 444-45)

This book's concern with making explicit the conditions of the democratic order reflects my perhaps overrationalistic belief that a fuller understanding of the various conditions under which democracy has existed may help men to develop it where it does not now exist. Although we have concluded that Aristotle's basic hypothesis of the relationship of democracy to a class structure bulging toward the middle . . . is still valid, this does not encourage political optimism, since it implies that political activity should be directed primarily toward assuring economic development. Yet we must not be unduly pessimistic. Democracy has existed in a variety of circumstances, even if it is most commonly sustained by a limited set of conditions. It cannot be achieved by acts of will alone, of course, but men's wills expressed in action can shape institutions and events in directions that reduce or increase the chances for democracy's development and survival. Ideology and passion may no longer be necessary to sustain the class struggle within stable and affluent democracies, but they are clearly needed in the international effort to develop free political and economic institutions in the rest of the world. It is only the ideological class struggle within the West which is ending. Ideological conflicts linked to levels and problems of economic development and of appropriate political institutions among different nations will last far beyond our lifetime, and men committed to democracy can abstain from them only at their peril. (pp. 455-56)

Seymour Martin Lipset, in his Political Man: The Social Basis of Politics *(copyright © 1959, 1960 by Seymour Martin Lipset; reprinted by permission of the author), Doubleday & Company, Inc., 1959, 1960, 432 p., (and reprinted in an expanded form by The Johns Hopkins University Press, 1981).*

Excerpt from *THE POLITICS OF UNREASON: RIGHT-WING EXTREMISM IN AMERICA, 1790-1977*

At its most general, extremism is a self-serving term. It may mean going to the limit, which can often be justified; or it may mean going beyond the limits, which by self-definition is never justified. But, the "limits," as defined by the basic institutions of society, have never been static. In terms of specific issues, extremism most simply means the tendency to go to the poles of the ideological scale. In its more pejorative sense—in the sense in which it is linked to such terms as "authoritarianism" and "totalitarianism"—as an absolute political evil, extremism is not so much a matter of issues as one of procedures. In this sense, extremism means going beyond the limits of the normative procedures which define the democratic political process. Many of these procedural norms are themselves constantly being redefined. . . . But the unchanging heart of the democratic political process, as it is generally understood, is, T. V. Smith notes, a "state of mind"; and his collaborator, Eduard C. Lindeman, describes "proposition one" of that state of mind in these words: "Persons striving to adapt themselves to the democratic way of life are required to discipline themselves to one variety of unity, namely unity which is achieved through the creative use of diversity. A society which is by affirmation democratic is expected to provide and protect a wide range of diversities." There have been numberless variations of this formulation, but, however expressed, such a pluralism remains commonly accepted as the fixed spiritual center of the democratic political process, around which the more mutable rules and mechanisms revolve.

At its most general, pluralism describes a society which tends to protect and nurture the independent coexistence of different political entities, ethnic groups, ideas. More specifically, pluralism describes the kind of societal structure which can sustain such a system of coexistence.

"Liberalism," writes Edward A. Shils, "is a system of pluralism. It is a system of many centers of powers, many areas of privacy and a strong internal impulse towards the mutual adaptation of the spheres rather than of the dominance or the submission of any one to the others."

The kind of spheres to which Shils refers are the political, the economic, the religious, the kinship. Without an accommodating balance among them a society could become plutocratic, theocratic, or politically totalitarian. The mutual "separation of church and state" is one mark of a pluralistic society. But so is the mutual separation of business and state, family and state, university and state. These spheres all influence each other, have mutual responsibilities, and, at best, respect each other. But none of them takes over. This pluralistic principle can extend down through all the subspheres in society, such as the various major branches of government.

The concept of pluralism has another level. A pluralistic society is composed of a number of different interest groups and communities with which the individual can identify. This contrasts with the image of a society as a mass of individuals who connect directly somehow to the total society. Where there are many such groups and spheres, there are operative cross pressures among them which not only allow for more effective advocacy of private conflicting interests but also deter that total society from taking on a more extremist, nonaccommodating shape. And when an individual belongs to a number of different effective groups and spheres with cross interests, he is less likely to act out extremist nonaccommodating attitudes.

This, of course, is a dynamic concept of pluralism, not just the description of a society in which there is static diversity. Lindeman's formulation suggests this when he refers to the fact that diversity is not only to be protected but to be *provided;* that is, a working pluralism foments change and *new* diversity. . . . Pluralism, then, embraces both diversity and change. The procedures which guarantee that condition are the normative democratic procedures whose breach constitutes extremism. The conceptual heart of those procedures is nothing less than the open market place of ideas.

By that token, extremism basically describes that impulse which is inimical to a pluralism of interests and groups, inimical to a system of many nonsubmissive centers of power and areas of privacy. Extremism *is* antipluralism or—to use an only slightly less awkward term—monism. And the operational heart of extremism is the repression of difference and dissent, the closing down of the market place of ideas. More precisely, the operational essence of extremism, of monism, is the tendency to treat cleavage and ambivalence as *illegitimate*. This is a critical aspect of extremism because of certain premises that underlie the concept of "the open market place." (pp. 4-6)

> *Seymour Martin Lipset and Earl Raab, in their* The Politics of Unreason: Right-Wing Extremism in America, 1790-1977 *(reprinted by permission of The University of Chicago Press; © 1978 by The University of Chicago), second edition, The University of Chicago Press, 1978, 581 p.*

JOEL SEIDMAN

[One union is an outstanding exception to Robert Michels' iron law of oligarchy] in both the local and the national organizations: the International Typographical Union. Far from having developed oligarchical tendencies in its national political life, it has witnessed the development and institutionalization of a two-party system over almost half a century. Lipset, Trow, and Coleman have studied the ITU intensively [in *Union Democracy*], focusing on it precisely because it was a deviant case, seeking to discover what made it different, in order to throw light on the reasons for the general rule to which the ITU is an exception. (pp. 627-28)

[Lipset and his colleagues have made a] major contribution to our understanding of political processes within unions. They have been careful in their methods and precise in their observations and have shown imagination and insight in their interpretations and conclusions. Theirs is, in short, an excellent piece of work.

The writers argue that democracy in the ITU is the product of a number of factors. For one thing, the decentralization of the industry—the small size of the shops plus the fact that the industry is not competitive from one city to another—has allowed decentralization of power within the union. . . .

[Printers] depend upon one another to an unusual degree for society and recreation and have developed a network of occupation-centered organizations. These secondary bodies between the members and the union officials, together with the chapel offices, provide abundant opportunities for the development of leadership skills, which, in most unions, can be learned only in political office, controlled by the administration. . . .

Added to all this is a belief in the legitimacy of political opposition and norms to protect it, which is shared by ITU officers and members alike. . . . (p. 628)

The conclusions of Lipset and his colleagues . . . are that the functional requirements for democracy cannot be met most of the time in most unions. . . . Even more, going far beyond their empirical evidence, they argue that democracy is possible only if the interests of the members are homogeneous. For an industrial union to survive, the union head must assume the power of a dictator in order to arbitrate the various conflicts of interest that will arise, paralleling the union's internal stratification. . . . Even in the case of a multiple craft union they are skeptical of the chances of democracy; since interest cleavages are inflexible, the majority will tyrannize over the minority, democracy will break down, and internal unity is likely to survive only under the rigid discipline imposed by a one-party political system. . . . Surely these are drastic and far-reaching generalizations to base upon the scanty evidence of craft differences, such as those with the mailers, in the history of the ITU.

The authors think that the differences within a union hold most promise for a two-party system and therefore for democracy when based on ideological cleavage between right and left, between those who urge militancy against employers as against those who argue for conciliatory tactics. For this to appear, they argue, in effect, that two conditions are needed: (1) the membership must be homogeneous, approximately at one level of skill and pay, or the difference will be in terms of interest rather than ideology; and (2) the union must define its functions broadly, since if it restricts its role narrowly to collective bargaining there is little room for controversy. . . .

Yet one might expect differences to continue to arise within unions, as in national political life; some will want to extend the power of the central organization, while others will want to keep power in the local groups; some will want to enlarge the functions of the union, as in the political sphere, while others would restrict it to collective bargaining. Moreover, there will be those who would widen the differentials between workers of various skills as against those who would narrow them; those who would use the bargaining power of the union to increase employment or provide fringe benefits, such as pensions or welfare funds, as against those who would increase direct wages; those who would keep dues and services at high levels as against those who would prefer to save money; and so on, down to those who are merely for or against the policies or the personality of a particular union officer or candidate for office. It is hard to conceive of a union that would run out of issues or that would long stay out of them, nor can one believe it desirable to have political differences based on ideology and undesirable to have them based on interest. (p. 629)

It is unfortunate that Lipset and his colleagues do not consider the possibility of state action to protect union democracy. Union leaders, needless to say, do not welcome such proposals, since no one likes to be regulated and since labor has abundant reason to challenge the impartiality of the state. Yet the state may intervene now, if the unionist has the time and money to go to court to protect his rights. The Railway Labor Act, the Wagner Act, and the Taft-Hartley Act have all affected internal union matters, as well as relations between unions and employers. Rights to get and keep jobs, to gain admission to a union and enjoy self-government within it, are too important to be left to chance or economic pressure or to be intrusted to the good will of union officers or of a union majority. In this reviewer's opinion there has been enough limitation of democratic rights within unions to justify public action.

Even an autocratic union is better than none, since it interposes its power between the worker and the employer and gives the former the benefits of collective bargaining, a grievance system, and representation before state agencies. Yet there is no reason why workers or public opinion should accept as inevitable a high degree of autocracy within an organization whose social justification rests in large part on its contribution to democracy in the larger society.

The present volume, one might point out, raises the question as to the meaning of democracy within unions. If union democracy is equated with a stable two-party system, as Lipset and his colleagues appear to do, then it is not common. However, they evidently are of the opinion that a union would be called democratic if the members retain final authority and have the power to exercise if when they desire. This requires not only the formal guaranties of democracy—regular meetings and conventions, honest elections, and the like—but also the very practical provisions, such as are found in the ITU, that permit an opposition freedom to organize without penalty and assure it means of communication to the members. Even at the present time there is a vast amount of political activity, often sporadic in large numbers of locals, bringing democratic vigor, locally, in unions dominated by one-party machines at the national level. Given freedom to organize in safety, means to reach the membership, and honesty of elections, the members would have the means to change the officers and therefore policies.

This preoccupation with democracy, however, is beside the point for those who reject democracy as a proper objective for unionism and makes pertinent the question as to what we want unions to be. If they are to be merely effective striking and collective-bargaining agencies, then it is best for them to be disciplined bodies aided by experts in the negotiation of contracts. If they are to be efficient service organizations and nothing more, then a bureaucracy to prosecute grievance cases, represent members before welfare or other government agencies, and the like is enough. . . . It is wholly different, however, if democracy is a desired goal in itself, to be sought in voluntary organizations as well as in the larger society; if one is concerned not merely about the value of a union in protecting a worker from the arbitrary acts of management but also with means to protect him from the arbitrary actions of union leaders; and if one is concerned not merely with a union's effectiveness in collective bargaining but with it as an agency responsive to the desires of its members and subject to their control. (pp. 629-30)

> *Joel Seidman, "Book Reviews: 'Union Democracy: The Inside Politics of the International Typographical Union'," in The American Journal of Sociology (reprinted by permission of The University of Chicago Press; © 1956 by The University of Chicago), Vol. 61, No. 6, May, 1956, pp. 627-30.*

A. H. RASKIN

[In *Union Democracy* Seymour Martin Lipset, Martin Trow, and James Coleman] try to explain why the ITU [International Typographical Union] has not capitulated to the "iron law of oligarchy," laid down by Robert Michels forty-five years ago. It was his cheerful thesis that voluntary organizations, whether unions, professional societies, or business associations, nec-

essarily give rise to self-perpetuating oligarchies, in which the elected assume dominion over the electors, no matter how many democratic safeguards are erected.

The study is an absorbing one, but the more intriguing it gets the less applicable it appears to any other organization. The conditions fostering democracy among the printers seem so distinctive that unions generally will find easy comfort in the notion that it is much more important for them to be attentive to the economic welfare of their members than to provide them with a functioning two-party system of internal government on the ITU model.

> *A. H. Raskin, "Fresh Looks at Labor and Its Ways," in The Saturday Review, New York (copyright © 1957 by Saturday Review; all rights reserved; reprinted by permission), Vol. 40, No. 7, February 16, 1957, p. 18.**

SAMUEL LUBELL

In evaluating the "conditions for stable democracy" [in "**Political Man**"], Mr. Lipset shrewdly recognizes the high value of monarchies as symbols of governmental legitimacy. He also wisely observes that the degree of stability shown by different Western democracies largely reflects their success in moderating basic social conflicts.

As he points out, democracy has been strongest in countries where the conflict of church and state was resolved relatively early and where workers were admitted to full suffrage and union rights without too much opposition. Where one or both of these social struggles were never put to bed, as in France, Spain and Austria, the cause of democracy has had rough going.

"**Political Man**" also effectively demolishes the myth that the "working class" is the special carrier of the so-called "liberal" virtues. The inner workings of trade unions are shown to be anything but democratic; ample evidence is cited that many workers tend to be "intolerant" on racial issues, immigration and other "liberal" causes. But the author is less successful when he analyzes the allegedly "anti-democratic" and "extremist" tendencies of different social classes. His norm of democratic, non-extremist man seems limited to people who share the ideals of New Deal liberals.

More disturbing is the sometimes skillful but often loose jumbling together of the concepts of psychiatry and "the class struggle." Applying the ideas of Marx and Freud to politics can yield exciting insights, but it is also a treacherous exercise which requires one minimum safeguard determining the limits beyond which these concepts do not apply.

For example, Mr. Lipset contends that conditions of "lower class life," such as low education, "isolation, a punishing childhood and economic and occupational insecurities" produce a "rigid, intolerant approach to politics." Presumably then, intellectuals should be much more flexible politically. But in a later chapter he shows that American intellectuals have been perhaps the most rigid of all voters in their unchanging support of the Democratic party and usually simplify political issues into a pro-business or anti-business black and white.

The case has still to be proved that professors are more rational in their politics than ditch-diggers. Again, Mr. Lipset's interpretation of McCarthyism as reflecting "primarily the reactions of small business men" is a truly weird throwback to the Hitler-era stereotype that fascism grows out of the frustrations of the middle class. . . .

But other parts of "**Political Man**" are quite rewarding—for example, the provocative appraisal of democratic prospects in the newly independent countries of Asia and Africa. In Western Europe industrialization with a sizable middle class came first, and the winning of democratic rights largely coincided with the struggle of the masses to gain a better share of the national income. . . .

Mr. Lipset tries to cover too much ground too quickly, and the parts of his books do not form a unified whole. He is weakest when trying to support psychiatric hunches with opinion polling data. He is most stimulating when examining the workings of democratic processes in a historical perspective.

> Samuel Lubell, *"Patterns of Government," in* The New York Times Book Review *(© 1960 by The New York Times Company; reprinted by permission), January 10, 1960, p. 6.*

DENNIS H. WRONG

The fact that [*Political Man*] might with equal appropriateness have been entitled "The End of Political Man" gives it an importance and a unity which are not immediately apparent. In form it is a collection of studies of Western political movements and voting patterns which were undertaken independently of one another and most of which have been previously published. I do not mean to suggest that such a collection is to be regarded as a minor achievement: the author's talents, some of which are rare among professional sociologists, preclude that in any case. As a matter of fact, the book is, in my view, the most important single volume on the sociology of voting yet to appear in the United States or anywhere else. The breadth of Professor Lipset's comparative range, his complete lack of national parochialism, is likely to impress the reader most of all. He rarely says anything about voting habits in one place without telling us whether or not the same habits prevail in an array of other places which may include Finland, New Zealand, and the Canadian prairie provinces as well as those major Western nations whose politics have been intensively studied. Moreover, he is quite free of the chief vice of the professional sociologist: the tendency to lose sight of the problem and become bogged down in methodological details and conceptual digressions. His documentation is always copious and far-ranging, but it is invariably relevant and never seems pedantic or needlessly padded.

But what really gives the book its unity and focus is less the kind of empirical data considered (largely statistics on voting and on the socioeconomic composition of parties and movements), or the comparative approach, than the dominance of a common theme. The theme is the attenuation of class conflict. (p. 265)

The view that yesterday's political struggles no longer have much meaning is, of course, fairly prevalent these days. Lipset's massing of the electoral evidence revealing the decline of the Left and the success of the Right once it has been converted to the support of policies it formerly opposed should, however, convince the last diehard who denies the depth and consistency of this trend (although he is still at liberty to dislike the trend and to object to the rather complacently determinist view Lipset sometimes takes of it). (p. 266)

At times Lipset is insufficiently aware of the limitations of his special approach. Political differences are not entirely reducible to differences in the social bases of parties and movements. Even if one agrees that McCarthyism and Poujadism both expressed the frustrations of small business men (and when it comes to the evidence in the case of the former I am not convinced that Bennington, Vermont, is America), they were surely very different kinds of movement, making very different kinds of ideological appeal. The shakiest essay in the book is, I think, the much-discussed . . . case made for the view that American intellectuals are far more highly regarded by their nonintellectual fellow-citizens than they believe. Professor Lipset seems to think that intellectuals feel they are not sufficiently deferred to, as if this were all that they were complaining about.

Yet while I think he fundamentally misses the point in this essay, there is enough substance to it to invite discussion and the mustering of contrary evidence. The combination of a sense of what is significant, a historically sophisticated theoretical awareness, and the "hardest" sort of empirical data is the book's special virtue. (pp. 266-67)

> Dennis H. Wrong, *"Reviews: 'Political Man'," in* Political Science Quarterly, *Vol. LXXVI, No. 2, June, 1960, pp. 265-67.*

ARNOLD S. KAUFMAN

When [in *Political Man*] Lipset moves from the analysis of evidence to the expression of opinion broadly philosophical, his thinking does move off the rails. He tells us that democracy is not only or even primarily a means to some end; "It is the good society itself in operation." And the definition of democracy is one thing about which Lipset himself expresses little perplexity. Democracy in a complex society is two things: (1) a set of constitutionally established procedures for replacing one group of governing officials with another; and (2) a social mechanism which permits the largest part of the population to participate in this choice of governing officials.

Now this definition is neat, realistic and, above all, methodologically sound (than which there can be no greater virtue for most contemporary sociologists). Lipset's priorities are fine for some parts of sociology. But when they are imported into moral discussion they are enervating and misleading. To call the implementation of his conception of democracy "the good society in operation," is simply absurd. To offer his definition as *the* best definition of democracy is morally outrageous.

Procedures for selecting governing officials are certainly indispensable in a good society, but the identification of the two ideas is grotesque. The good society has ultimately to do with the aesthetic and fraternal dimensions of human experience, and with the extent to which respect for the human being and his natural potentialities are reflected and advanced by *all* our social institutions (not just the political, but, for example, the medical, the housing and the penal institutions).

And the best definition of "democracy" is surely to be determined not by our beliefs about what happens, presently, to be the case, but by our aspirations for something which is not and may never be the case. "Democracy" is not just another word, to be subjected to the sterilizing prescriptions of methodologically passionate social scientists. It is the focal concept around which revolves a constellation of opinions ranging from highest aspiration to most practical policies. If we see democracy as a means of developing human potentialities, then one definition and one set of implementing institutions are indicated. If we see democracy as primarily a means of maintaining social order (as do Schumpeter and Lippmann, for example), then another definition and an alternative institutional emphasis is dictated.

It is Lipset's failure to tear himself loose from the parochial moorings of so much of contemporary sociology that seriously impairs an otherwise provocatively brilliant assessment of the conventional wisdom about democracy. (pp. 496-97)

Arnold S. Kaufman, "Evidence and Absolutes," in The Nation *(copyright 1960 The Nation magazine, The Nation Associates, Inc.), Vol. 190, No. 23, June 4, 1960, pp. 496-97.*

S. J. ELDERSVELD

There is much in [*Political Man*] to commend it—the publication of new research into European political behavior, the re-examination of the ideas of many writers, and the author's own political theories. But this is also a book which generates uneasiness. For it epitomizes the dilemmas and dangers of a certain type of social science writing today. Some distinguishing marks of this trend are: an impulse to generalize in some limited factual setting; impatience with the rigorous testing of theory; nonchalance in the appropriation of non-equivalent, comparative data; and the difficulty in collating interdisciplinary knowledge. The result may be a theoretical synthesis, but with only the appearance of evidential validation. *Political Man*, while admirable in many respects, still must be judged in this genre. It is supposed to test theory. (pp. 737-38)

The chapter on "legitimacy" is a suggestive theoretical piece. Legitimacy is defined as the "capacity of the system to engender and maintain the belief" in itself. However, Lipset falls into a serious contradiction here by failing to integrate the political-institutional arrangements of a society into this concept. He makes the arbitrary value judgment that the multiparty system, PR, and the unitary state weaken democracy, although in many democratic societies these institutions are part of the belief structure and through them cleavage is "managed" and legitimacy maintained. . . .

The preoccupation of the author with the "class struggle" in the United States is certainly not borne out by the data here reviewed, nor by the work of others who have analyzed meticulously the voting behavior of the 1952 and 1956 elections. The concept of "cross-pressures," heavily relied on, leads sometimes to peculiar interpretive paradoxes. For example, we are led down the following path of reasoning: the "open society" is good; it is a society which increases cross-pressures; cross-pressures "serve democracy"; but cross-pressures reduce political participation; and "high participation . . . normally has higher potential for democracy." In this connection, perhaps a re-examination of the data on the effects on participation of upward social mobility would help.

There is much in this book which is perceptive. The synthesis of data was needed. . . . But there is some conceptual fuzziness . . . and empirical juggling here which mars the acceptability of interpretations. This is no doubt due in part to the difficulty in the juxtaposition of hypotheses with the kinds of comparative data on politics available today. But, while one must be cautious in applying the analytical findings and interpretations of this work, it is still a good book in social and political theory. (p. 738)

S. J. Eldersveld, "Book Reviews: 'Political Man'," in The American Political Science Review *(copyright, 1960, by The American Political Science Association), Vol. LIV, No. 3, September, 1960, pp. 737-38.*

RALPH SAMUEL

[*Political Man*] should serve as a warning of what happens when plausible sociological generalisation displaces serious discussion of politics and society.

For it is a parody of true scholarship. The parade of sources, the muster of authorities, the disciplined array of footnotes, indicate not so much the range of [Professor Lipset's] enquiry as its predatory nature: a *chevauchée* into the territory of historians, philosophers and social researchers, a series of raids to carry off their most fruitful insights as hostages for his analysis. Whether claiming Tocquevillian inspiration for his theories, or citing 'the British journalist Richard Hoggart' to sustain the view that working class people are 'exposed to punishment, lack of love and a general atmosphere of aggression since early childhood', Professor Lipset seems grotesquely insensitive to the authors whose work he so freely plunders.

Lipset claims that his method—what he calls 'multi-variate analysis'—is a sophistication of Weberian sociology. It would be truer to see it as an elaborate mechanism for the construction of self-validating hypotheses. Once possessed of a generalisation, he seems to believe that almost *any* fact, drawn from his card index file, is sufficient to support it. In place of judgment, he offers tests of 'statistical significance', so that even the most fugitive statistic or slightest correlation prompt him to formulate, or confirm, a law of political behaviour: a Norwegian by-election poll inspires a theory about voting for 'transvaluational alternatives'; the suicide rate in France—correlating inversely with the Commune, the Boulanger crisis and the Dreyfus affair—'clearly indicates' the (not very surprising) law that 'crises increase interest and involvement with politics.' Where the categories lie readily to hand, the facts slide obediently into place; where they do not, Professor Lipset, in place of qualification, merely elaborates a new, often more fanciful theory. (p. 983)

Facts thus, in Professor Lipset's hands, lose any autonomous existence, and come to be entirely at the mercy of his 'theoretical anticipations'. Countries, epochs and ideologies are reduced to a uniformly servile level where, as 'data', they can be manipulated and correlated at will. Turkey and Lebanon are proved—by 'multiple coefficients' of modernisation—to enjoy conflict-free constitutions, Cuba and Venezuela to be 'stable dictatorships'; the Reformation and Industrial Revolution are treated as contemporaneous; Norway becomes a bastion of revolution in 1920, Iceland a 'dictatorship', and Israel a 'backward democracy' characterised by 'the retention of political legitimacy by Conservative groups.' The argument then proceeds by the juxtaposition of utterly heterogeneous material in which even contradictory facts—listed as 'major exceptions'—manage somehow to be endowed with the character of additional proof. (pp. 983-84)

Everything, in fact, turns out to correlate disproportionately with something else to produce, through Lipset's fecundity of generalisation, what amounts to an essay in systematic overproof. Almost everyone, in his description, seems to vote Conservative—parents ('children serve to restrain any propensity for deviant behaviour on the part of their parents'), the young and the old, the upwardly mobile and the downwardly mobile, people living in stable poverty, people experiencing prosperity; and so exhaustive is his list of 'nonvoters', that in the end it is the voter who appears to be deviant. Some of the generalisations that result stand plainly in opposition to each other: anti-semitism correlates disproportionately with Labour voters [at one point,] with Conservatives—a different survey supporting a different hypothesis—[at another]. More commonly, however, they are pitched at a level so general that they seem designed less to illumine the processes they purport to describe, than to accommodate almost any possible contingency. . . .

His real failure, however, lies less in the book's particular insensitivities than in the crippling effect of so purely sociological a discussion of 'political man'. Never considering the actual character of political movements, confusing referents with determinants, and causation with equation, he sees politics as a mere reflex of status. His study begins and ends with the location of the status bases of political support, so that movements totally different in spirit and purpose—liberalism, fascism, communism, even received religion—appear in his pages as no more than alternative solutions to status discontents, 'ameliorating the strains of the stratification system', while the politics of the American South are found, in a lengthy study, to have been diverted from their 'natural'—*i.e.* sociological— course by the 'confusing' and 'emotion-laden' issues of slavery and Negro rights.

Professor Lipset thus creates a dark and unfamiliar world, peopled with working-class authoritarians and self-employed totalitarians, a world where men are driven by prestige urges to seek perilous outlets of status gratification. Indeed, so frightened is Professor Lipset by the world his theoretical imagination has conjured into being, and so alarmed at the 'aggression' and 'emotion' he finds latent in every political allegiance (even 'nineteenth-century liberals' are found to have strong fascist propensities), that he comes close to condemning voting, participation and political division—the central institutions of the democracy his book ostensibly sets out to protect. (p. 984)

> Ralph Samuel, "Lipset's Nightmare," in New Statesman (© 1960 The Statesman & Nation Publishing Co. Ltd.), Vol. 60, No. 1553, December 17, 1960, pp. 983-84.

PAUL PICKREL

What Lipset has tried to do [in *The First New Nation*] is to define the values that Americans have lived by, and he has tried to do it by asking a series of fairly concrete (but very large) questions: What did the American colonists believe in that enabled them to throw off the imperial yoke and establish a successful independent nation? What can today's new nations learn from that crucial time in American history? Have America's values changed since the era of its newness? How have its values made this nation different from others? Probably no reader will agree entirely with his answers to these questions, but in his attempts to deal with them Lipset calls on some fascinating material (his reading is immense) and sets in motion some ideas of great importance. . . .

Lipset has probably succeeded in locating the critical moment in a new nation's history; it is the moment when the "charismatic" leader—its Washington or Nehru or Nkrumah—surrenders power and a successor administration is peacefully acknowledged as legitimate. . . .

In his discussion of the continuity of American values, Lipset is in part replying to the books of David Riesman and William H. Whyte, who have of course argued that with the emergence of the "other-directed personality" and the "organization man" American values have undergone a major transformation. Lipset sees no such break with tradition. Rather, he believes that throughout American history there has been a conflict between what he calls equality and achievement. . . .

[The] conflict lies between those who believe that everyone should be more or less like everybody else and those who believe that everybody should be free to become whatever he is capable of becoming, with great inequality among individuals as a result. Lipset attempts to reconcile the two sets of values through the old formula of equality of opportunity, but, useful as it has been, it no longer is very convincing, in view of our present knowledge of individual differences. (p. 118)

Probably equality and liberty are irreconcilable values, and American society will be considerably vitalized by the tension between them as long as neither wins a clear victory. Though this is not the way Lipset puts it, the change that Riesman and Whyte were so concerned about may have been less in the American people than in the intellectual community of which they are distinguished representatives. In a general way, American intellectuals in the 1930s had a strong commitment to equality, because they were concerned about the economically and racially disadvantaged. That concern they have not abandoned now, but they have been appalled by the equality of the affluent (otherwise known as conformism) which has appeared since the war. They desire equality for those who cannot afford it and deplore it in those who can. That does not make them fools; it only makes them Americans. In helping us to understand just how American such a paradoxical position is, Lipset has made his most important contribution. (p. 120)

> Paul Pickrel, "New Nations and Old Problems" (reprinted by permission of the author), in Harper's, Vol. 227, No. 1362, November, 1963, pp. 118, 120.*

DAVID MARQUAND

[*The First New Nation*] is an invaluable, if unintentional, piece of evidence [of the theoretical inadequacies of the American Left]. For it is clear that Professor Lipset believes himself to be on the Left, and that in American terms he actually is on the Left. Yet it is equally clear that his conception of what Left-wing politics are about makes no sense outside an American context; and that, so far from recognising the limitations of contemporary American liberalism, he has tacitly assumed that it is the right model for the rest of mankind. It is as though a caged bird had set out to persuade his cousins in the forest that they would be better off in an aviary.

Professor Lipset's propagandist intentions, it is fair to say, are not explicit and may not even be conscious. His ostensible purpose is not political, but academic. He has set out to provide a sociological explanation of the long and subtle process which transformed the United States from "the first new nation," wracked by the tensions and insecurities of its ex-colonial status, into a mature and stable democracy. At the same time he has tried to compare the American "value-system" with those of the stable democracies in the British Commonwealth, and also with those of the notably unstable policies of France and Germany, partly in order to illuminate his first theme and partly to examine what contribution a sociological analysis of this sort can make to the study of a nation's political institutions.

The important point about this exercise, however, is that it is a resounding failure, though in many ways a magnificent one. And the important point about the failure is that it is due, to a very large extent, to the political assumptions and prejudices which have distorted the author's vision.

But these assumptions and prejudices are not explicitly formulated. Professor Lipset does not present us with a coherent ideology, and invite us to inspect it. Indeed, if he were told that he has an ideology to present he would probably rebut the suggestion as a foul and shocking calumny. His political attitudes have to be inferred piecemeal from stray hints and half sentences, distributed at random through the book. To force them into the straitjacket of a theoretical system would necessarily be to misrepresent them, if only by making them seem sharper and more clearly defined than they are. (pp. 60-1)

[The] explanation arrived at in the end is hopelessly circular. The United States, we discover, became a stable democracy because American "values" were such as to promote a stable democracy. Britain did the same because British "values"—although very different from American values—also promoted a stable democracy. France, on the other hand, did not become a stable democracy because its system of values, although in some respects closer to the American pattern than to the British, contained elements antipathetic to democratic stability.

The danger in this exercise is not just that it tells you little which you did not know before. A much more fundamental danger is that it tells you something which is positively debilitating. Although Professor Lipset says at one point that he does not want to put forward a sociological equivalent of the economic determinism of vulgar Marxism, it seems to me that he falls into just that trap. For one of the central messages of his book is that a nation's values do not change. American values, in particular, are alleged to be substantially the same now as they were at the beginning of the nineteenth century; and although British values are not analysed in the same detail, Professor Lipset makes it fairly clear that he thinks that they have changed equally little. But if a nation's political history merely reflects its system of values, and if its system of values is more or less unchanging, it follows that a determined and purposive attempt to transform society is doomed in advance, and that political developments can only occur within a given framework. To some extent, of course, this is true—though not exactly novel. But it is not a doctrine which needs new emphasis in the complacent climate of the western world today. What we need to learn now is not how little society can be changed, but how much. (p. 63)

> David Marquand, "New Nations, Old Nations," in *Encounter (© 1964 by Encounter Ltd.), Vol. XXIII, No. 2, August, 1964, pp. 60-3.*

TALCOTT PARSONS

[Professor Lipset in *The First New Nation* has] succeeded in notably integrating his materials so as to present a very impressive picture of some of the most important aspects of our society. It seems that the focus on the one particular society has helped him greatly in this achievement. But equally important to my mind is the fact that he has not presented just another historical essay on the United States, but has taken the method of comparative and developmental analysis with the greatest seriousness. The comparisons, first, of early American society with the contemporary new nations, and second, with the other variants of Western democratic society, first in the English-speaking world and then in other European societies, are both genuinely illuminating and furnish the most important empirical control on the arbitrariness of his own interpretive judgments of the immensely complex material. (p. 374)

It is of particular interest to the present reviewer that Lipset has taken the concept of values as a constitutive part of the structure of the society as the focus of his theoretical analysis. He delineates a broad pattern for the American case which involves taking account of both the religious background along the lines of Max Weber's analysis of the values of the ethic of ascetic Protestantism, and the values expressed in the documents of the founding period of the Republic. Then, particularly by judicious use of the comments of foreign observers at different periods, he is able to build a strong case for the essential constancy of the main pattern through all the immense structural changes the society has undergone. Related to this in turn is his mobilization of evidence that many of the traits currently adduced to demonstrate a change of values, notably "other-directedness" and an emphasis on conformity, are as old as the society itself, as many observers have noted.

In terms of content Lipset's analysis turns on the balance between two primary components, those of equality and of achievement, both, of course, against the background of a basic individualism. The important point here is the analysis of a *balance* of components that are partly inherently linked with each other but at the same time partly in conflict in such a way that behavior interpreted as a way of dealing with the conflict provides some of the most important clues to understanding otherwise puzzling features of the American scene; for example, a certain exaggerated social snobbery among Americans is interpreted as dynamically related to our equalitarian values under the conditions of competition for opportunity and at the same time, valuation, of individual achievement. (pp. 374-75)

It goes almost without saying that such a book will also take an important position in the current debate among American intellectuals—and their brethren in other countries—about the nature of American society in relation to the conflict between what in some sense are "conservative" and "revolutionary" values. Here Lipset takes a definite and explicit stand, which he backs with an immense accumulation of evidence, that the basic American orientation not only has been, but remains, liberal if not revolutionary. Indeed it is his view that American radicalism, if one may use that term, is more authentically at the core of the main liberal trend of modern society than is the Marxist version. A most important point noted by Lipset in this connection is that the only seriously "alienated" large group in American society is the radical right, the "dispossessed," as Daniel Bell calls them.

In sum, this is an impressive and a very challenging book. It will certainly be sharply attacked by the group that basically disagrees with its diagnosis of American society, but its level of both empirical and theoretical competence and achievement is such as to present a formidable task to him who would refute its main generalizations. (p. 375)

> Talcott Parsons, "Book Reviews: 'The First New Nation: The United States in Historical and Comparative Perspective'," in *The American Journal of Sociology (reprinted by permission of The University of Chicago Press; © 1964 by The University of Chicago), Vol. LXX, No. 3, November, 1964, pp. 374-75.*

TOM BOTTOMORE

[In *The Politics of Unreason* Lipset] reverts to a preoccupation with "stable democracy," in the context of a study of right-wing extremist movements in America. The stage is set by defining democracy as "pluralism," and extremism as "that impulse which is inimical to a pluralism of interests and groups." From this point of view, left-wing extremism and right-wing extremism are "very much the same," since they both have an anti-pluralistic orientation. . . .

Like all conservative thinkers, he is anxious to emphasize the formal structure of checks and balances in a democratic system (without inquiring too closely into how it actually works), and to obscure or eliminate the more radical idea of democracy as a political movement of subject classes and groups against their rulers, which seeks to establish as fully as possible government *by* the people. . . .

Lipset and [coauthor Earl] Raab . . . follow the conservative interpretation of Populism in which the antiindustrial, anti-liberal elements in some sections of the movement are given excessive prominence, and so they include Populism among their "extremist" movements. . . . (p. 22)

The results of a study conceived on these lines are predictable. Since left-wing and right-wing movements are equated as enemies of democracy the distinction between left and right vanishes; the important question of how some popular movements of opposition to the ruling minority become perverted into supporters of the established order is never even formulated; the "American political system" is restored as the model of a democratic order; and the growing disaffection with the two established parties in the United States is regarded as dangerous and undemocratic extremism, which threatens the supreme values of pluralism and stability. The idea of pluralism itself is treated on a curious fashion which seems to imply that every interest group which happens to exist in American society—from commercial television to the Mafia—must be preserved as an element in a democratic order.

What has happened, then, to the challenge presented, in the heady days of 1968, by the "violent eruption of new forces"? What has become of Lipset's recognition of a pressing need for a revaluation of concepts and methods in political sociology? One is tempted to answer by saying that Lipset has behaved rather like the ideal social system imagined by the functionalists. He has restored his equilibrium by integrating an interpretation of the new radical movements into his established scheme of thought, with a few minor adaptations, and in this way has warded off any fundamental change in his outlook. With the balance thus re-established he can take the field once more as a leading defender of the American *status quo.* (pp. 22-3)

> Tom Bottomore, "Conservative Man," *in* The New York Review of Books *(reprinted with permission from* The New York Review of Books; *copyright ©* 1970 Nyrev, Inc.*), Vol. XV, No. 6, October 8, 1970, pp. 22-3.**

ALLAN P. SINDLER

As a political phenomenon, extremist-right movements are regarded by [Seymour Martin Lipset and Earl Raab in *The Politics of Unreason*] as responses to the exacerbation of social strains accompanying periods of change. They are expressions of disaffection born of fear, anger, resentment, or desperation, ul-timately channeled into backlash hostility toward those who are blamed for the nation's ills. Susceptibility to right-wing extremism is thus basically a function of status anxiety or deprivation among population sectors that feel themselves declining in importance, influence, and power, and that then seek to alter society's course through political action. (pp. 23-4)

The present book is distinctive in its insistence on a certain casual explanation [of extremism]. Status anxiety induced by social change is held to be the prime impetus for extremism, which then takes the public form of conspiracy theory and bigotry, political moralism and repressive ideology. When status-deprived groups enter politics they speak less of their status anxieties and prerogatives than of the prime cultural characteristics they value and presume themselves to represent. . . . Yet, in spite of the key place of status deprivation in their interpretation, Lipset and Raab assert its role as a primary cause rather than demonstrate it. Their repeated arguments on behalf of the status-stress explanation are always plausible and often persuasive, but that is not the same thing as testing it for confirmation, rejection, or amendment. (p. 24)

Even [a] cursory run-through of specific movements serves to flag some problems of analysis. If one deals only with actual movements, played against the American backdrop of continuous change, then a connection between change and extremism, as mediated by status anxiety, can always be plausibly asserted. More systematic testing of the proposition is required to establish its validity and refine relationships. Measurements of change and of status deprivation are needed, and then determination of their co-relationship. Were there periods of social stress that did *not* produce the right-wing extremism predicted by the model of status anxiety? Did all right-wing movements attract and repel the "correct" proportions among and within population groups?

The application to particular movements of the monistic model defining extremism also raises problems. By the model's terms it is not clear why [George] Wallace qualifies as a right-wing extremist. If his promises of autocratic action as President, implicitly rejecting the democratic process, so qualify him, then how can Huey Long, the autocratic Kingfish of Louisiana, be excluded? On what basis is the Liberty League, the non-fascist organ of economic royalists fulminating against FDR and the New Deal, included? McCarthyism is shrewdly dissected as a marginal case, but precisely why it is ultimately assigned to the ranks of extremism remains obscure.

The social basis of support of various right-wing groups is also explored by the authors through analysis of many survey and election materials. (pp. 24-5)

[The] followers of an extremist movement, whether joiners, supporters, or passive approvers, are not uniform in their views of the movement and its core doctrines. Many people, particularly among the poorly educated, comprehend neither the range of a movement's policies nor its most salient themes. Those with fuller understanding may endorse the movement because it provides an expressive outlet for their frustrations, or because they agree with some of its positions and are indifferent or at least not intensely opposed to the remainder. The authors effectively examine many important implications of this insight on followership, but they neglect the serious question it raises about the appropriateness of the evidence they use to determine whether a movement is extremist. That evidence consists essentially of quotations selected from spokesmen and the official literature of the movement, which ostensibly delineate its fundamental doctrines. Leaving aside the not unimportant problem of the degree of subjectivity of the analyst in his appraisal of themes, the point here is the method's restriction of scope. If members of the audience hear a movement's messages differently, can movements be classified as extremist solely on the basis of an examination of what was said, neglecting what was heard? (pp. 25, 34)

> *Allan P. Sindler, "Closed Marketplace of Ideas," in* Saturday Review *(copyright © 1971 by* Saturday Review; *all rights reserved; reprinted by permission), Vol. LIV, No. 2, January 9, 1971, pp. 23-5, 34.*

M. STANTON EVANS

Lipset and Raab are Social Democratic types under subsidy from the Anti-Defamation League of B'nai B'rith to explore the antisemitic and other disreputable characteristics of "rightwing extremism" in America [in *The Politics of Unreason*]. All the root assumptions of this effort appear, to the present reviewer, highly questionable—that the Right rather than the Left is the sector which needs investigating, that an "extremist" is somebody who believes in fixed as opposed to fluid value standards, that American conservatism can best be explained by reference to status anxiety, and so forth. . . .

Lipset and Raab have in places risen above the fallacies of the genre. They are, to begin with, generally fair and informative. If they do not always explain the factual material, they do not attempt to twist it. And they reach some conclusions that will prove uncongenial to others in the liberal community—e.g., that the American Right is *not* characteristically antisemitic, and that, just maybe, some scholarship should be devoted to a study of extremism on the Left.

> *M. Stanton Evans, "Notes on the Election of '72," in* National Review *(© National Review, Inc., 1971; 150 East 35th St., New York, NY 10016), Vol. XXIII, No. 7, February 23, 1971, p. 205.**

MILTON MANKOFF

[In *Rebellion in the University* Seymour Martin Lipset] claims to believe in the universal validity of democracy, and he supports mass movements for democratic social change; however, [he] tends to show most enthusiasm for mass protest when it occurs in Communist and underdeveloped societies, which he characterizes as inherently reactionary because of their undemocratic political and economic systems. However, he fears mass political action in the United States and other "Western democracies," particularly if it goes beyond the realm of legality. Ideologically charged politics is presumably inappropriate in advanced capitalist society.

Lipset's work attempts to place the American student movement in a theoretical framework that traces its sources and permits us to estimate its significance in the nation's historical development—as well as its implications for the future of the university and the larger political system in the United States. In the major portion of the volume, he draws upon historical accounts and public opinion polls to demonstrate that the recent wave of extralegal student protest has not been unique in the nation's experience, does not reflect a widespread radicalization of today's younger generation, and is likely to weaken the university while failing to bring about progressive social transformation. . . .

[Lipset's] belief in historical continuity leads to an unfortunate unwillingness to seriously consider whether contemporary student revolt could have greater import for democratic change than did campus unrest in the 18th, 19th and early 20th centuries, when the university, society at large, and their interaction were so different.

Lipset fails, for example, to appreciate the degree to which the modern "multiversity" plays a crucial role in maintaining the stability of parliamentary capitalism through the nature of the research it carries on, by training skilled manpower to meet the requirements of our economic, political and military hegemony over the world, and by developing essentially conservative solutions to pressing social problems. Moreover, although he is aware that professional and semi-professional workers have greater potential power as the "service" sector of the economy grows, he makes only passing reference to the possibility that radicalized graduates could disrupt the normal operation of the communications media and the educational, welfare, medical and legal bureaucracies—and in the process forge vital ties with new constituents.

It is also necessary to criticize Lipset's unexamined assumption that international and domestic economic, political and social forces will continue to provide a favorable context for American institutional stability. There is not the slightest hint in his analysis that the erosion of America's open-door empire, the stagnation of workers' real income coupled with a regressive incomes policy projected for the indefinite future, the increased concentration of militant blacks in urban centers, and the undermining of the Protestant ethic among students and young blue-collar workers alike, might exacerbate domestic conflict to the point of political upheaval. Although Lipset believes in the pluralist interpretation of America's power structure, he does not examine the possibility that the absence of a totally unified elite could prevent precisely the kind of dramatic reform needed to assuage growing discontent. It is at least imaginable that a student insurrection, under conditions of class and racial polarization and national political paralysis, could set the stage for direct political activity, as it did in France during May 1968, with less likelihood of a return to the *status quo ante*.

Perhaps the primary reason why Lipset feels it unnecessary to engage in a detailed examination of the structure and workings of major American institutions is his reliance on public opinion polls as valid indicators of political stability. Lipset cites numerous attitude surveys to suggest that only a tiny proportion of students and nonstudent youth and adults profess to be radicals. Yet, while ruefully admitting that the *behavior* of small minorities of militants can create institutional crises, he still implies that the *attitudes* of all citizens provide the best litmus test of mass insurrectionary possibilities. But the historical record indicates that the majority of people remain passive spectators even in periods of turmoil, despite their ideological sympathies. Moreover, mass movements which culminate in social revolution do not generally depend on revolutionary sentiment so much as on a strong desire for reform that coincides with a loss of legitimacy on the part of inflexible or inadequate authority. Lipset's own analysis of student unrest bears out this contention. Radicals on campuses have always been a minority, but their activism was often supported by more moderate students who shared their short-run goals—and occasionally outdid them in militancy.

These remarks do not imply that a social revolution, inaugurated by student riots, is imminent. I am concerned, rather, to point out that Lipset's evidence in support of the "banality of revolt'' thesis is unsatisfactory. It has been just such reliance on opinion polls that has blinded social scientists to the emergence of the civil rights and student movements in the past.

Lipset's underestimation of the possibilities for radical social change, and the positive role of a militant student movement in such a process, is related to his exaggerated fears of a rightwing back-lash—another perennial bogy. The evidence he adduces is mixed at best, since it is based on a one-sided interpretation of polls and the results of recent elections. (pp. 794-95)

Given Lipset's overall perspective, it is to be expected that his thoughts on the university and the social role of the scholar will be anything but pointedly critical. As in the case of so many defenders of the academy, the author emphasizes the ideals which are presumed to motivate it and glosses over the less flattering reality. For one who believes it is the scholar's duty to bend over backward in presenting evidence contrary to his own biases, his performance in this area is poor.

The contrast between Lipset's search for evidence to discredit the American student movement and his uncritical celebration of the university suggests that *Rebellion in the University* is as much a personal defense as a treatise in social science. Much of what the book presents is valuable—particularly its summary of the literature on the multiple sources of student protest—and Lipset's moderate tone is welcome. But when one steps back and examines the author's assumptions and method, and the distorting effect of his biases on his findings, one is forced to conclude that the balance sheet on *Rebellion in the University* is negative. (p. 795)

> *Milton Mankoff, "University, Si: Students, No," in* The Nation *(copyright 1972 The Nation magazine, The Nation Associates, Inc.), Vol. 214, No. 25, June 19, 1972, pp. 294-95.*

WILLIAM PETERSON

To one who does not share the leftist orientation typical of university communities, Lipset's [*Rebellion in the University*]—however cogent in its own terms—is strangely one-sided. There is no reckoning of the number of persons killed in the bombings [of university buildings], of the careers destroyed, of the millions of dollars of property damage. There is no account even of the damage to the university's educational function through continual accommodation to militants' blackmail. Nothing is said of university administrators who, through ineptitude and moral cowardice, often permitted the institutions in their charge to degenerate, in the worst cases to the edge of total destruction.

Lipset's book, in part a report on the campus revolt, is more fundamentally an attempt to justify himself those more radical than he. Militants have repeatedly accused him and other leftist professors of hypocrisy, and "it becomes necessary for the liberal faculty to explain themselves to their students." This defensive stance begins by granting the high motives, the "idealism," of the vandals who wrecked the campuses. Some activists deserved the appellation; most, I would judge, were simply delinquents (who steal hubcaps not in order to sell them but as an expression of adolescent bravado); the leaders were greedy not for money but, more insidiously and dangerously, for power; some were criminals *tout court,* including seven of ten on the FBI's most-wanted list. In Lipset's long chapter on opinion polls, he takes what may be the rationalization of high

spirits or destructive impulses as genuinely, in all cases, the reasons for the revolt. But don't you see, he argues, that these actions—against the Vietnam war, for example—are "counterproductive"?

Rebellion in the University is written with a completely different tone from the same author's writings on protofascist movements. Significantly, the book's only defense of democracy against totalitarian leftists consists of a quotation from *The Politics of Unreason,* a book on right-wing extremism that he wrote with Earl Raab. Yet American democracy today, I hold, is in danger principally from the left, in large part because the universities that train tomorrow's leaders deviate so markedly from the country's democratic norm. They do so not merely because a minority of faculty members hold antidemocratic views, but because most of those on the democratic left halfsympathetically understand and tolerate such views. (p. 433)

> *William Peterson, "'Rebellion in the University'," in* Social Forces *(copyright © 1974, Social Forces), Vol. 52, No. 3, March, 1974, pp. 432-33.*

STANFORD M. LYMAN

A fine example of a structural-functionalist political sociology—containing its most salient elements and illustrating nearly all of its faults—is that carried out by Seymour Martin Lipset. From his studies of the United States as the "first new nation" through his commentaries on trade unions, intellectuals, nativism, the race question, and the student revolt, and to his most recent commentary on Watergate, Lipset has presented a comprehensive analysis of the structure and processes of what he believes is a social system developing in accordance with its internal dynamic and becoming the progressive democracy destined in its origins.

Combining the functionalist's organic imagery with Max Weber's famous dictum analogizing societal origins to the throwing of loaded dice, Lipset has tried to show [in *The First New Nation*] that certain values and predispositions established at the outset of any society's history become determinants of the channels and directions of social change. He thus explains how the progressive democratic republicanism of the United States works and why it perseveres on its steady and relatively unturbulent march to the fulfillment of its original promise. (pp. 732-33)

The structural-functional approach, in the hands of an able and perceptive sociologist such as Lipset, promises to explain all variations, changes, and eruptions in American society by reference to the complex dialectical operation of its value system. This system is said to persist through a constant but precarious balancing of contradictory values embedded in a network of interlocking institutions. However, as race inequalities persist, students revolt, and, finally, after Watergate challenged the optimistic vision of progressive development, the structuralfunctionalists are at greater and greater pains to account for these apparently discrepant events within the framework of systemic stability that should persist in the midst of these changes. If we . . . examine the works of Seymour Martin Lipset we will see that the excess of disturbing changes begins to overflow the theoretical boundaries which are expected to contain it. (p. 739)

[Lipset asserts] that "the poison of anti-Negro prejudice is a part of American culture, and almost all white Americans have it, to a greater or lesser degree," and that the Negro's problem is more difficult to solve than that of immigrant groups. . . . The legacy of slavery and the less-than-equal treatment of blacks since 1865 have impaired Negroes' capacity to achieve in a suddenly opened market of opportunities or to benefit immediately and significantly from a recently desegregated school system. In order to break the vicious circle of discrimination, deprivation, and demoralization, Lipset argues, "it is necessary to treat the Negro *more than equally,* to spend more money rather than equal amounts for Negro education, to have smaller classes with better teachers in predominantly Negro schools, to enlarge the scope of counseling and recreation facilities available for Negro youth, and the like."

However, Lipset's earlier comments on the balancing of tendencies toward excessive achievement or superfluous egalitarianism would seem to suggest that a move to treat the Negro more than equally would be met by a backlash. Although he does not in fact say so, his subsequent discussion hints at the enormous obstacles to the solution that he has proposed. For the achievement of more-than-equal treatment, Lipset insists, "white Americans today should be prepared to assume responsibility for the educational and economic development of the descendants of those whom earlier white Americans dragooned from Africa to serve them as slaves." But Lipset is only exhortative at this point. Predictions about ultimate equality cannot be made. Instead, a plaintive plea and a peculiarly misplaced observation about the American image abroad follows: "Unless whites are willing to take up their cause in order to force politicians, businessmen, labor organizations, and other relevant groups to support the necessary measures, Negro inequality will remain a blot on the American claim to be democratic and will prevent foreigners from recognizing how real and significant is the national commitment to equalitarianism, as is evidenced in other spheres of American life." While American democracy is stabilized by the shifting balance of achievement and equality, Lipset's solution to the race question requires an *unbalancing* of that system. Although such an imbalance is not impossible, Lipset's *general* systemic analysis would seem to argue that it is not only improbable but also dangerous. Lipset's plea for guilt-directed altruism and his appeal to the sentiments that whites *ought* to feel, while admirable, suggest that the limits of his approach have been passed when he attempts systemic analysis of the race question. (pp. 739-40)

Lipset's discussion of the American stratification system in general and the race issue in particular strains his explanatory scheme almost to the breaking point. Despite all of his qualifications and his genuine sympathy with the plight of America's blacks, Lipset wishes to retain his model and image of American society as one that originated in equality and achievement and is dedicated to the ultimate realization of these ideals through the mechanism of its own systemically balanced tendencies. The strategies Lipset employs to keep his model together are most adroit. First, he separates his analysis of the black problem from the central thesis of *The First New Nation* by placing it in an epilogue entitled "Some Personal Views on Equality, Inequality, and Comparative Analysis." The designation of this excursus as "personal," its compartmentalization away from his general and more sanguine discussion, and the remarkable harshness of his indictment of inequality indicates that he distinguishes the race problem as an exception to the otherwise model democracy he attributes to the United States. Second, the emphasis on the recent educational breakthough of blacks in his later analysis, together with his careful qualifications about the insufficiencies of education, the threat

of older alien norms of equality, and the dysfunctions of meritocratic systems suggests that the "exceptional" nature of the race question is temporary and that it too can be "absorbed" by a dynamically equilibrating social system. By not closing his eyes to the imperfections and inequalities in the system, Lipset has proved to be one of the most perceptive and passionate critics of the social system he champions. By forcing his materials into the systemic mold, however, he unwittingly illustrates not only the weakness of its institutional structures but also, and perhaps in the long run more significantly, the debility of its heuristic value for social science. (pp. 741-42)

Similar problems beset Lipset's analysis of the student revolt. As student revolts began to intensify, Lipset modified his view of American society from one which held out a seemingly unlimited future of pendular shifts between egalitarianism and achievement to one which countenanced a fracture in the social system. His argument reassesses the history of American youth and higher education, and points to the boundary-breaking elements that imperil social systems in general and that of the United States in particular.

There is almost no end of causal explanations for the student revolts of the 1960s. Among the "motivating forces" for student unrest in the sixties, Lipset is able to enumerate no less than nine; while among the "facilitating factors" he finds five. His comprehensive analysis of these fourteen forces and factors, together with his historical analysis, tends to indicate that a severe strain has long existed on the dynamic equilibria and balance of forces in America. Unintentionally, it also reveals inherent weaknesses in the structural-functional model itself. Although Lipset recognizes the significance of the motivating forces and facilitating factors that make up the causal complex for student revolts, he places greater emphasis on those that are more specific and directly related to campus unrest (such as the marginal status of students, the demands of youth culture, the roles of university and faculty) than on those which are so broad and vague as to be incapable of explaining the student revolts (such as rapid rates of social change, a factor which might be used to explain all manner of events). Similarly, when analyzing the five facilitating factors—low commitment of youth; the fact that most college youth are not yet linked to a job, occupation, or career; the fact that most college youth have less responsibilities than parents, workers, or their age-peers not enrolled in college; the peculiar opportunity that a campus provides for mobilizing a social movement; and the significance of current events for arousing the interest, consciousness, and conscience of young people—Lipset regards all but the last as permanent features that, alone, cannot explain the sudden explosion in college campuses across the nation. (pp. 742-43)

Lipset's perception of the fragile structure of the American social and political system reveals itself in his predictions about the immediate future. Whatever the resiliency and potency of social systems in general, whatever tensile strength still exists in a system marked at one time by pushes toward equality and at another by pulls toward achievement, the American social system might crack if it cannot find a way to accommodate itself to the demands of radical and liberal student activists. (p. 744)

By the time the student revolts had run their course, Lipset had lost more than his faith in the unwavering dynamic progressivism of American society. The events of a decade had nearly smashed the model American society he had espoused in 1963. Even more serious, however, his belief in both the comprehensive and predictive capacities of the social sciences had been chastened as well: "The brief look presented here into the history of campus-related unrest and protest," writes Lipset, "should force us to be humble both about our ability to understand and to predict waves of discontent." Lipset had at last recognized that students—an inherently unstable and disturbing element—had to be admitted into the American social system. (pp. 744-45)

To Lipset and [Earl Raab, in their article **"An Appointment with Watergate,"** *Commentary,* September, 1973], Watergate is the extension of the conspiratorial paranoid style of American politics from American backwaters to the White House. They take seriously the statements of Magruder, Dean, Huston, and Mitchell that Nixon and his colleagues acted as they did out of a sincere reaction to "all those activities of the late 1960s ticked off by the Watergate witnesses: disruptive demonstrations, riots, violence, bombings, flag-burnings, civil disobedience." Like the moralists of the 1920s who bitterly resented the looser morals, alcoholic excesses, and revealing clothing of the newly emergent urban cosmopolitans, the Watergate conspirators represented all those who were appalled by the drug, sex, and student revolutions, and resentful of the fact that the United States with all its might could not "defeat a small and underdeveloped Communist enemy in Southeast Asia." In behalf of these beliefs Nixon and his cohorts embarked on a massive attempt to reorganize the security, intelligence, and surveillance apparatuses of the United States and committed a number of illegal, extralegal, and improper acts. Yet Lipset and Raab observe that Watergate was a "pale and tepid . . . expression of extremist action." The "plumbers" operation "was neither massive nor very efficient." . . . Nevertheless, Lipset and Raab assert, the seriousness of Watergate is not minimized by its ineptitude. Most significant, and unlike the backlash demagogues of the 1920s, the Watergate conspirators acted in secret. The secrecy, and especially the cover-up, are, according to Lipset and Raab, "a measure of the restraining power of the cosmopolitan climate not only within the administration but in the nation at large—in, that is, the growing cosmopolitanization of the American people."

Lipset's and Raab's contention is that secrecy became the mode of Watergate operations because the emergence of a more cosmopolitan nation forbade open activities that would have resonated with the more provincial outlook of Americans a half century ago. In support of their belief that cosmopolitanization is on the upsurge, Lipset and Raab point to the fact that American public leaders no longer express themselves in racist terms, that anti-communist rhetoric no longer arouses uncritical fervor, and that internationalism and détente have been accepted by most Americans. However, the linkages of Watergate to backlash politics and Watergate secrecy to growing cosmpolitanism are tenuous. Certainly Lipset and Raab have not provided what a serious social scientist would accept as evidence of this thesis. Rather, all the characteristic features of functionalist historicism are pressed into service to show that Watergate was the inevitable outcome of certain contradictory operations in the American value system. A conjectural history of these operations is presented, the logic of Nixon's election and its aftermath is linked to a chain of developments, and, in conclusion, exhortative messages tell us what is necessary to forestall another such debacle. Lipset's system is now very loosely structured, but, although he will not admit it, his analysis suggests that America as a social system is coming apart at the seams. (pp. 747-48)

"Begin with an individual, and before you know it you find that you have created a type; begin with a type, and you find

that you have created—nothing." F. Scott Fitzgerald's perceptive comment provides a pertinent epigraph to a critique of Lipset's sociology. Precisely because it proceeds from the point of view of a formal type, a totally integrated social system, Lipset's analysis of American society cannot contain the irruptive events and innovative institutions that actually mark its history. The essence of systemic dynamics is the absorptive and integrating process. The facts of recent history, however, suggest that absorption and integration are not occurring, that social classes, ethnic groups, and voluntary associations move in a manner not decipherable by a system model, and that supposedly democratic governments proceed in ways not anticipated by societal values or public purposes. In short, the much vaunted homogeneous cosmopolitan American system is a utopia from which sociological theory must be liberated. (pp. 748-49)

Lipset has peopled America with puppets and presented American history as a puppet show. The ordinary member of a polity is conceived almost exclusively in his capacity as, respectively, a voter, a respondent to public-opinion polls, or a victim of the *voces populi.* The politician in a democratic society is a representative of voters and polled opinions. All are creatures on a string, or rather, on a number of strings, propelled into political participation by pressures. These pressure-strings in turn are moved by the basic mechanisms to which they are attached—class, ethnic, racial, age, and sex groupings. Everywhere there are strings—pulling, pushing, crisscrossing one another in an attempt to move political man in their own way.

Who operates the strings? In Lipset's sociology, there are two distinct but related answers to this question. Quite obviously what order there is must obtain at the outset from the balance of thrusts and counterthrusts of the several invisible pressures. Hence the Punch and Judy aspect of Lipset's political drama: As Punch goes too far, Judy counterpunches with a frying pan on his head, hard enough to knock him down but not out. Lash and backlash—for example, the pendulum swings of equality (Punch) and achievement (Judy) keep one another in line. But this internal order requires that neither Punch nor Judy will go too far. However, as Lipset shows, each sometimes—in fact, often—does just that. How can order be kept if Punch overwhelms Judy, or Judy hits Punch too hard? Enter Lipset. Like a technical consultant, he advises the actors to reduce the invective and armament that each employs against the other, and warns against future failures to act according to the script. In brief, the puppet-show dramaturgy of structural-functionalism is possible because this kind of sociology permits neither the humanistic individual nor the self-correcting group to be the center or the source of political orientations. Instead, in Lipset's perspective, individuals and the groups to which they belong are creatures of sociological habit. The immediate milieux—represented in age, sex, race, religion, nationality, ethnicity, social class—provide pushes, pressures, and pulls and also give off an illusion of self-control. The concept of society composed of self-correcting and shifting interest groups and formations, however, would suggest that the sociologist look not for a fixed source of legitimacy, consensus, and order but rather for the temporary constellation of coordinate interests that, at any one moment, permits a sense of stability and routine to prevail. (pp. 752-53)

The essence of Watergate is the covert criminal practices of a political group that had already achieved power. The actual activities—burglaries, bribery, subornation of perjury, misprision of felony—were carried out by persons who had also at least considered other and more venal crimes. Although at the level of the actual dirty work the motivations of the perpetrators would appear to support elements and strands of the backlash theory offered by Lipset, it is questionable whether these same motivations are also applicable at the level of executive planning and conspiracy. It is doubtful whether we shall ever obtain an accurate statement of the real intentions of Watergate's originators. Nevertheless, their political character is perhaps comprehensible. Nixon's administration did proclaim a hatred of "effete intellectual snobs," war resisters, and counterculture groups. Elected by such a landslide that they could claim a mandate, Nixon and his cohorts utilized that fact to increase their civil and legal distance from the electorate. Developing the power and maximizing the discipline of their own inner circle, Nixon and his fellow planners dissociated themselves from the rules of political conduct expected from men of their station. The Nixon apparatus included circles within circles of conspiratorial actors. The circles struggled with one another for power in the regime. At the center was the corps of planners and executives who plotted what to do and how to cover it up. Believing because of its mandate that it was *the* agency of the state and above and beyond all danger of interference and surveillance, the inner circle almost succeeded in monopolizing control over the investigation of its own malfeasances in office. Secrecy was of the essence—the secret of its real aims, of its methods, of the cover-up of both—and the conspirators attempted to wield the instrumentalities of domestic administration and foreign policy to carry out and cloak their aims with impunity. Government by secrecy is not new, but the recognition that secrecy and dirty work are an inherent part of governments of any kind may be. Recognizing that democratic regimes also burgle, bribe, trespass, and kill without license or right speaks volumes not only to a reconsideration of the philosophy of governance but also toward a revision of the sociology of public administration. (pp. 755-56)

Ironically, it is Lipset's own analyses that do so much to expose the weaknesses in "the first new nation" and indicate how precarious is its "stability in the midst of change." The events of recent history that he has so painstakingly researched suggest that American society is far more unstable and much less secure than the society *manqué* described by a model social system. Structural-functional analysis requires the transposition of events into processes—a most difficult task under the best circumstances. The events that Lipset chose to study—racist acts, student revolts, presidential crimes—do not lend themselves to easy translation. As examples of balanced processes, equality and achievement or provincialism and cosmopolitanism, they seem contrived.

Is there an alternative view? Perhaps. Let us begin with values. Elsewhere I have suggested that racism—the idea that one's membership in an involuntary hereditary aggregate, a "race," is a reasonable criterion to take into account in the political, economic, educational, religious, social, and personal organization of a society—is a value that became embedded in postsixteenth-century Euro-American social organization. The historical evidence that would support this thesis is being adduced more and more. Of course, racism had to compete with other values that contradicted it—among these, the enlightenment values of equality, achievement, and democracy. And such competition lent itself to the rhetorical and political expression of all value commitments in the social construction

of ideologies, utopias, reactions, reforms, and rebellions. Various groups could lay claim to valuable societal resources by couching their appeals in the language of one or another or some combination of these values. Moreover, unscrupulous groups, including the Watergate conspirators, could justify their unlawful acts, and cloak the real reasons they undertook them, by appealing to threats to the value system. A structure of competing and contradictory values has a certain free-floating quality about it. This quality, in turn, lends itself to group efforts to capture, monopolize, and attain mastery over the entire social organization. Totalitarianism is a possible but not necessarily likely outcome of these efforts. (pp. 756-57)

The idea of America as a social conglomerate is perfectly compatible with an overarching structure of values. The latter serve as dramatic devices, rhetorics of competition, preservation, complaint, and legitimation as social groups struggle for moral and material goods. However, it must not be assumed that groups have internalized these values or that they adhere to them without reservation and qualifications. For the sociologist, acculturation needs to be demonstrated in the face of powerful group pressures against it. Moreover, some groups—indeed, perhaps most—will find ways to enjoy and exploit the "cognitive dissonance" that is supposed to prevail when individuals and groups simultaneously countenance contradictory ideas. Finally, it should be noted that groups will form, dissolve, and reestablish themselves in different form or with different aims and procedures as occasion, chance, opportunity, or desperation demands. The contents of the conglomerate are not stable; its structure is dictated by the relations among units that happen to prevail at any moment.

Lipset's analysis of American society as a social system is both a testimony to the imagination and a signification of the failure of the predominant sociological paradigm. Yet, despite its faults, it has located a number of sensitive issues for discussion, attempted a form of comparative and historical sociology, and displayed a passionate regard for the procedures and problems involved in maintaining a just and rational social democracy. Its ultimate problem is conceptual and rooted at the base of sociological theorizing. Commitment to the structural-functional models foils any attempt to come to grips with the crucial happenings and decisive events that shape and modify society. Since the teleological underpinnings of the model assure a strain toward homeostasis and equilibrium, the actual occurrences must be pressed to produce stability in the midst of change. What happened to Lipset's analysis of America is bound to happen to any analysis—regardless of ideological content—that adopts the structural-functional mode: it is undone by its own data.

Only a fundamental paradigmatic shift will prevent sociologists from remaining mired in the systemic morass. As a first step toward this shift, sociologists should abandon the social-system approach, resist the modern revivals of organic and mechanistic analogies, and eschew the uncritical acceptance of developmentalist orientations toward change. All of this has been said before and with much greater vigor and critical discussion. Unfortunately, "systems," "functions," and "evolution of societies" persist as familiar conceptualizations of both radical and conventional sociology, East and West. (pp. 758-59)

Stanford M. Lyman, "Legitimacy and Consensus in Lipset's America: From Washington to Watergate," in Social Research *(copyright 1975 by New School for Social Research), Vol. 42, No. 4, Winter 1975, pp. 729-59.*

(William) D'Arcy McNickle

1904-1977

A Native American anthropologist, novelist, and administrator, McNickle was an advocate of tribal autonomy for American Indians. McNickle's anthropological research on Indian culture, his administrative post with the Bureau of Indian Affairs, and his directorship of American Indian Development, Inc. provided him with a multifaceted perspective on the problems of Indian life. His *Indians and Other Americans* (1959), coauthored with Harold E. Fey, chronicles the long history of failure by the U.S. government in the administration of Indian affairs and suggests a reorientation of policy based on the encouragement of cultural diversity and "the adaptive self-direction of Indian communities." A revised and updated edition of *The Indian Tribes of the United States: Ethnic and Cultural Survival* (1962), *Native American Tribalism* (1973) is a history of the relationship, past and present, between Indians and whites. McNickle argues that presently there is a renewed tribal and traditional awareness among Indians which portends their growing cultural and political autonomy vis-à-vis the white world. Despite some disagreement over specifics, most critics have acknowledged the quality of McNickle's scholarship and the wisdom of his programmatic suggestions. (See also *Contemporary Authors*, Vols. 9-12, rev. ed.; obituary, Vols. 85-88; *Contemporary Authors New Revision Series*, Vol. 5.)

Excerpt from *NATIVE AMERICAN TRIBALISM: INDIAN SURVIVALS AND RENEWALS*

After these many years of inter-ethnic contact in the New World, it is not yet possible to say that the relationship between white man and Indian is free of the presumptuous bias that marked its beginnings. Indians may no longer be expected to vanish before a competition "they had not the means of sustaining," but their moral right to remain a separate and identifiable people is far from assured.

The safeguards against oppression founded in the humanistic traditions of the Western world were time and again ignored or denied by the dynamics of conquest. Pope Alexander enjoined peaceful conversion, but the Spanish invaders in establishing New World dominion slaughtered and enslaved as suited their purposes. The crown of England declared a boundary separating Indian country from the settled areas of colonial North America but could not contain the energies that drove men westward in quest of wealth and power.

The pattern of affirmation and denial established in the first years of contact has never been outlived or outmoded. Men in the dominant society who labored to defend the interests of tribal people were invariably matched by men who resented the existence of "savages," particularly if they controlled landed property and presumed to autonomy in the conduct of their affairs. A John Marshall, speaking out for the right of an Indian tribe to exercise jurisdiction over its native homeland, was matched by an Andrew Jackson who swept the tribes out of the southeast rather than defend their right to determine where and how they wished to live. Bringing the antithetical pattern down to modern times, the effort of the John Collier administration to restore tribal primacy in internal rule was all but

destroyed by the negativism of the United States Senate in the Eisenhower years.

For the Indians of Canada, so little of what they once owned was confirmed to them and so much denied as to leave their future in precarious balance. Only recently have they been aroused to the peril in which they live as tribal people.

It remains to be determined whether in North America self-determination for an indigenous people is to have ideological acceptance and thereby attain enduring political sanction. Certain events discussed in this brief historical review, and some not yet mentioned, would seem to favor an emerging policy of sanctioned self-determination.

One of these is the confirmation of aboriginal land titles in Alaska. While the settlement was achieved in response to the urgings of industrial conglomerates wholly indifferent to and possibly inimical to native interests, as noted above, nevertheless the Natives have assurance that they may now pursue their accustomed lives in communities of their own making. Change will come to those communities, but choice can be exercised as to what changes are accepted. (pp. 166-67)

All through North America, from the Arctic to the Florida peninsula, the long submerged Indian minority has been discovering the value of the published word, and this may prove to be the decisive force in bringing into being an enduring policy of self-determined cultural pluralism. Surveying publications at the beginning of the 1970s, the Smithsonian Institution reported more than a hundred items currently published by Indian and Indian interest organizations. Some of these dealt only with local news, but others carried information and critical articles dealing with national issues. One such publication, *Akwesasne Notes,* carried news stories and editorial comment from all over North America, Mexico, and South America. Its outspoken editorial policy quickly established it as a major voice in telling the Indian point of view in causes at issue.

Indian expression was not limited to social protest. The Kiowa-Pueblo novelist, N. Scott Momaday, won the Pulitzer Prize for fiction in 1969. Indian poets and songwriters are appearing in print. Indian painters, who had to overcome the stereotype of two-dimensional, non-perspective compositions which won them early praise from a patronizing public, now move boldly into the art market. The themes are traditional, but the execution is personal and evocative. In the professions, in social science especially, Indian scholars bring fresh insight in discourses on the condition of man in the modern world.

In all of this, the orientation is notably tribal and traditional, either newly discovered or reaffirmed. The Indian political voice as well as their creative expression reject the values of the dominant society and turn inward for individual and group support. Indian nationalism, pan-Indianism, Red Power—terms used with some degree of common meaning—indicate a growing sense of shared problems, shared goals, and a shared heritage. Such terms are likely to be rejected outright by the older generation, but it should not be inferred from this that the old and the young are at odds; it means only that the grandfathers are not at ease with new English words. However, while words may confuse the elders, they are not confused about who they are. It is this certainty of self which the young proclaim, sometimes loudly. There is no such certainty for them in the white man's affluent society.

Finally, it can be noted in closing that the spokesmen of earlier years who tried to accept what an alien world offered their people, seeing no other choice open, are now silent. If the Indian race is to be destroyed, the new voices avow, the destroying agent will have to contend with an integrating tribal people, not with isolated individuals lost in anonymity. (pp. 169-70)

> *D'Arcy McNickle, in his* Native American Tribalism: Indian Survivals and Renewals *(copyright © 1973 by Oxford University Press, Inc.; reprinted by permission), Oxford University Press, New York, 1973, 190 p.*

STANLEY VESTAL

Mr. McNickle's **"They Came Here First"** . . . attempts to give an authentic account of how the Indian first came here, of his institutions and government, and of the inner world of his mind. . . .

Mr. McNickle writes well. But too frequently one finds a trace of bitterness, a tendency to blame the white men for all the Indians' difficulties. He seems to be trying to set Indians apart as an abused minority, instead of seeing them as one of many contributing elements of the American stock. Such an attitude is false. First, because it no longer fits the facts; second, because it must inevitably delay the obvious solution—the acculturation of the Indian. Yet in spite of those who would rouse group against group, we find the Indians thoroughly loyal to the American way. (p. 21)

> *Stanley Vestal, "Redmen Today and Tomorrow," in* The Saturday Review of Literature *(copyright © 1949, copyright renewed © 1977, by* Saturday Review; *all rights reserved; reprinted by permission), Vol. XXX, No. 42, October 15, 1949, pp. 20-1.* *

CLYDE KLUCKHOHN

I know no other single volume that contains so much trustworthy information on the American Indian [as does **"They Came Here First"**]. From the geology of the Pleistocene to the Indian Reorganization Act of 1934 Mr. McNickle has discriminatingly surveyed the evidence. Nor is the work merely that of critical compilation from monographs and secondary works. Particularly in the historical and literary fields, Mr. McNickle has dug up original sources not previously exploited by writers on the American Indian. His results are excellently organized and presented with force and clarity. Readers of his brilliant and moving novel, **"The Surrounded,"** will not be surprised at the sensitiveness of the prose nor at the restrained passion which underlies the writing and gives a sweep to the book in spite of dates, figures, and an immense amount of sheer data. . . .

The final part [of **"They Came Here First"**], **"Supplanting a People,"** is devoted to a candid examination of the not always glorious record of the dealings of the United States with its Indian population. Mr. McNickle is peculiarly qualified for this task because he has worked in the Office of Indian Affairs since 1936, and he grew up on the Flathead Reservation in Montana. His treatment shows not only a mastery of the historical facts but equally that kind of intuitive familiarity with the problems which can only come from first-hand experience.

> *Clyde Kluckhohn, "They Made This New World," in* Book Week—New York Herald Tribune, *November 13, 1949, p. 30.*

RICHARD L. NEUBERGER

[Harold E. Fey] and D'Arcy McNickle have written a moving and eloquent book [**"Indians and Other Americans"**] which synthesizes the dark deeds that characterized our past dealings with the original owners of America. "Americans have an uneasy awareness of the red brother," they write. And this, of course, is true. By stirring such awareness, the Messrs. Fey and McNickle hope to arouse sentiment for a more generous and open-handed Indian policy in the future.

Alas, it is easier for humanitarians like Harold Fey and his collaborator to record earlier wrongs than to propose future redemption. Their book bristles with indignation against the Federal policy of so-called "termination" which Congress adopted in 1953 at the behest of the Eisenhower Administration. This policy meant, in essence, that "at the earliest possible time" the Indian tribes of the United States "should be freed from Federal supervision and control and from all disabilities and limitations especially applicable to Indians." In other words, reservation Indians were to be turned loose and the reservation divided up like a pie. If the Administration selected for the first such experiment those reservations with valuable timber and mineral resources—well, why be so suspicious and skeptical? Does the white man still covet the Indians property? . . .

In so many such instances, regrettable though it may seem to social-minded men like Harold Fey and D'Arcy McNickle, the Indians themselves have urged that they be liberated from both the protection and restraints of the Federal reservation.

In the beginning, nearly all the greed was on the white man's side. He wanted the Indians' domain and he took it. But now, intruded into the acquisitive culture of his conquerors, the Indian occasionally is not without his own cupidity. (p. 14)

In their indignant treatise, Harold Fey and D'Arcy McNickle charge that the United States provides a far more democratic and adequate Point 4 program for nations overseas than for American Indians. They make the point that any economic program on an Indian reservation is stuffed down the throat of its recipients and beneficiaries, whereas "a Point 4 program is not undertaken unless the people of a country request it. . . . Management is shared jointly, with the requesting country having full authority to veto any items within a proposal."

The authors of **"Indians and Other Americans"** favor expunging from the statute books the resolution of the Eighty-third Congress which heralded "termination" of Federal responsibility for our Indians as the basic policy of the Government. They advocate, instead, the kind of Point 4 program which has been provided for Iran, including "assistance in health and sanitation, education and training, student assistance, industry, sugar importation, transportation, community housing, natural resources development, communications, land distribution, public administration, agrarian development, and land reform."

The proposal has much to commend it, particularly from the standpoint of emotions and sentiment. Yet, would it really be the ultimate answer? Are most Indian reservations susceptible of such development, or was the original theft so thorough that the soil will not accept the seed? How much could it cost the taxpayers of the country? This may be an unpopular question in so emotional an atmosphere; yet I try to be aware of the Treasury chart which shows that some 69 percent of Federal income taxes are paid by Americans with net incomes of $4,500 a year or less. These people need succoring in many instances, too.

Then there is the alternative of going through with "termination" and providing the Indian with thorough training and education to survive in the white man's world. This originally was contemplated. But neither the Administration nor Congress has yet provided the $3.5 million annually, which was recommended in the act of 1955 that sought to encourage vocational preparation for Indians so they could become mechanics, engineers, court reporters, brakemen, barbers, linotypers, etc.

Nearly five centuries after the landing of the Admiral of the Ocean Sea in the New World in 1492, the question of justice for the descendants of the original owners of the realm that he discovered is still to be solved. I recommend a careful reading of **"Indians and Other Americans"** for any and all who want to help us confront this vexing problem. (p. 15)

Richard L. Neuberger, "A Senator Surveys the Land of the Braves," in Saturday Review *(copyright © 1959 by* Saturday Review; *all rights reserved; re-*

printed by permission), Vol. XLII, No. 19, May 9, 1959, pp. 14-15.

GALEN R. WEAVER

Throughout [*Indians and Other Americans* Harold E. Fey and D'Arcy McNickle] contrast two viewpoints that have been struggling against each other in the minds of the non-Indian majority ever since the beginnings of white-Indian contact. The generally predominant one is that Indians are a small primitive group for whom decisions must be made and whose inevitable destiny is to become either extinct or culturally and biologically absorbed. The other viewpoint, which was somewhat prevalent in the 20 years after 1928—"the period of fresh hope," is that Indians are capable of exercising their inherent right to self-management and to the undisturbed use and protection of their "homelands." . . .

The arresting statement is made that "there has been no administration of Indian affairs deserving of that description until within the last thirty years." . . . The authors document this appraisal well. No government rooted in European traditions has done a truly constructive job in relation to subordinated groups of a different cultural background. With new insights and resources from the social and psychological sciences, there is at least a chance that the United States may conceive and carry out a creditable, long-term program within the framework of our democratic faith and institutions.

In the opinion of this reviewer the volume should be assigned reading for members of the U.S. Senate and House of Representatives of state legislatures and state Indian commissions; for the staff of the Bureau of Indian Affairs; for all those who write and speak on Indian Americans; for social welfare workers; for social action committees in churches; and for all those whose consciences are troubled by our unhappy record and the sad present state of many Indian communities and who wish they knew what could be done to solve the problems involved.

Galen R. Weaver, "Information, Stimulation," in The Christian Century *(copyright 1959 Christian Century Foundation; reprinted by permission from the May 20, 1959 issue of* The Christian Century), *Vol. 75, No. 20, May 20, 1959, p. 616.*

KIMMIS HENDRICK

["**Indians and Other Americans**"] is particularly useful because it balances current problems with historical background explanation. It traces the beginnings of Indian culture on this continent. It discusses the idealism John Marshall established for the United States in his judicial interpretations of Indian rights and the "realism" with which Andrew Jackson neutralized ethics by insisting on settlers' rights. It explores the wonderful era of Quaker Indian Commissioners Charles J. Rhodes and J. Henry Seattergood. It tackles indignantly the expediency of much current government legislative and administrative action affecting Indians. . . .

[Dr. Fey and Mr. McNickle] make a team of authors keen with conscience and soundly knowledgeable. They may appear sentimental—too eager to right wrongs, and too hopeful that government action can do it somehow. But in view of this country's record of tragic mistakes and the growing readiness of Indians to assume responsibility for themselves, this kind of sentimentality may not be a fault.

Kimmis Hendrick, "'Indians and Other Americans'," in The Christian Science Monitor *(reprinted by permission from* The Christian Science Monitor; © 1959 The Christian Science Publishing Society; all rights reserved), June 18, 1959, p. 13.*

RUTH UNDERHILL

[Provocative is the special pleading in *Indians and Other Americans*] on what should be done in the future. The Indians' claim that they should receive Point Four assistance seems justifiable, but there arises a further problem which the book does not face. The Collier administration instigated and fostered the incorporation of Indian tribes or groups on reservations with the aim of giving them more self government and self respect. Selling of Indian land was forbidden, and some successful cooperatives were built up. The operative laws for these activities have since been repealed. With the proposed termination of government control, land and enterprise would be turned over to the Indians to do with as they like. Would a cooperative which supports a whole tribe be continued if certain individuals choose to take their share and pull out? The book pleads earnestly that such a situation would mean poverty for the majority and therefore that government supervision should be continued. It could not be done with whites. What is the part of wisdom here? (p. 1164)

Ruth Underhill, "Book Reviews: 'Indians and Other Americans: Two Ways of Life Meet'," in American Anthropologist *(copyright 1959 by the American Anthropological Association; reproduced by permission of the American Anthropological Association), Vol. 61, No. 6, 1959, pp. 1163-64.*

JOSEPH G. JORGENSEN

[In *Native American Tribalism* the] reader gets the impression that Indian policy was usually hammered out by non-Indians—in and out of government—who had the best interests of Indians at heart, but who made awful mistakes. Then, with the advent of Roosevelt's New Deal, Indian policy was hammered out by smart men within government, and those policies brought good times with prospects of even better times. In the early 1950s, however, federal policies reverted to their old form, and the good work of the 1930s and 1940s was undone. Unsaid about the major vehicle of Indian administration in the 1930s and 1940s was that the Indian Reorganization Act of 1934 (Wheeler-Howard Act) gave the secretary of the interior more control over tribal and individual Indian affairs than previously and stripped individual Indians of the "consensual" government referred to in the book.

It is McNickle's opinion that precontact Indians were everywhere governed by consensus and that strategic resources and territories were held in communitarian fashion and were open and available to all. These generalizations, when attributed to Iroquois, Cherokee, Coast Salish, Yokut, Yurok, Tlingit, Tewa, Hopi, and River Yuman—to name some tribes—are non sequiturs. Nevertheless, McNickle both attributes these customs to all Indians in the past and alleges that these customs have persisted. Furthermore, McNickle interprets all Indian responses to federal legislation as responses conditioned by these tenacious customs. It is unfortunate that the communitarian and consensual customs and ideologies of many Indian tribes are lumped together and attributed to all tribes.

The colonial-like government formed under the Indian Reorganization Act, the political and economic forces that created the bulk of federal Indian legislation after 1787, and the political and economic forces that have influenced events from the civil rights movement of the early 1960s through the siege of Wounded Knee in 1973 receive little treatment here, although Wounded Knee certainly receives some attention. Indeed, I get the impression that federal-Indian relations history was shaped more by capricious ideological positions held by whites and by the persistence of consensual governments and communal property, than by federal and state politics, agribusiness, the mining industry, and the railroads. In his desire to explain the widespread phenomenon of Indian generosity and respect for individuals and with a vision of the reemergence of pan-Indian ecumenism from its dormant state, McNickle has written a good book on the ugliness of federal Indian policy and the ability of Indians to endure that ugliness, but he has also written quite a bit about some Indians who never were. (pp. 465-66)

Joseph G. Jorgensen, "Book Reviews: 'Native American Tribalism: Indian Survivals and Renewals'," in The Western Historical Quarterly *(copyright 1974 by The Western Historical Quarterly), Vol. V, No. 4, October, 1974, pp. 465-66.*

NANCY OESTREICH LURIE

[*Native American Tribalism*] adds a valuable comparison of American and Canadian policies as these developed in both similar and divergent ways out of the British colonial Proclamation of 1763, which attempted to establish a pattern of negotiation and administration regarding Native Americans. The inclusion of Canadian data is also an indication of the recent directon of events covered under the subtitle, *Indian Survivals and Renewals*. The pantribal movement transcends the Canadian-American boundary and perhaps the next sequel will have to deal with a global pantribal movement of which there are already intimations in the now extensive Indian news media. (p. 399)

McNickle is to be commended for providing a comprehensive introduction to a highly charged and complex situation. Readers should also appreciate, in view of the fact that McNickle is himself an Indian long active in the struggle for Indian rights, that the author is able to take the long view from initial European contact on into the future with both charity toward the oppressors and optimism—optimism that while matters are still far from perfect, the last decade has seen immense improvement over the preceding centuries. (p. 400)

Nancy Oestreich Lurie, "Reviews of Books: 'Native American Tribalism: Indian Survivals and Renewals'," in Pacific Historical Review *(© 1975, by the Pacific Coast Branch, American Historical Association), Vol. XLVI, No. 3, August, 1975, pp. 399-400.*

MARTHA C. KNACK

Native American Tribalism is the long awaited and timely second edition of D'Arcy McNickle's basic 1962 history, *The Indian Tribes of the United States: Ethnic and Cultural Survival*. The brief original work has been significantly expanded and updated, with new chapters constituting nearly 30% of the volume. . . .

Never blandly historical, McNickle's prose is more partisan than in the original volume, employing the conflict terminology characteristic of modern Indian journalism.

At a time when books about Indian history are vastly popular, it is refreshing to have a new edition by this eminent Flathead scholar. As a brief, coherent introduction to North American history from a point of view different from that of the usual college texts, one which will put students in a better position to understand current Indian problems, tensions, and political behavior, this volume would be hard to beat. Its primary weakness lies in its brevity which requires extensive generalization and selection on the part of the author. At the same time, this brevity permits it to be used in conjunction with other texts in course development and widens the number and types of courses in which it can be used. (p. 444)

> *Martha C. Knack, "Book Reviews: 'Native American Tribalism'," in* American Anthropologist *(copyright 1976 by the American Anthropological Association; reproduced by permission of the American Anthropological Association), Vol. 78, No. 2, 1976, pp. 444-45.*

ALFONSO ORTIZ

Through the unobtrusive grace of his writing, D'Arcy followed the path of the ancient and original Native American explorers of this hemisphere, whom he . . . characterized in these words: "With their singing voices they becalmed the wilderness." D'Arcy, too, becalmed a wilderness with his writing—the wilderness of bigotry and ancient racial fears that lurked in the hearts of many who did not know of the fundamental authenticity and reasonableness of Indian visions of life. . . .

D'Arcy struck one theme, well worthy of reflection, throughout the last four decades of his life. He observed that, despite what seemed on the surface to be massive and rapid breakdown in Indian cultures across the continent, an essential core of cultural integrity was being maintained. He was dismissed for that particular view as an incurable romantic by some and as overly defensive about the inevitability of "progress" by others; very few believed him to be a wise man, in touch with the deepest currents of Indian life. Yet, he has been borne out by the history with which he made his peace so early and which he embraced in his professional writing. (p. 633)

> *Alfonso Ortiz, "Obituaries," in* American Anthropologist *(copyright 1979 by the American Anthropological Association; reproduced by permission of the American Anthropological Association), Vol. 81, No. 3, 1979, pp. 632-36.*

Margaret Mead

1901-1978

Mead was an anthropologist, psychologist, lecturer, and museum curator whose researches in native Pacific and Western cultures produced landmark studies in social anthropology. In *Coming of Age in Samoa* (1928) and throughout her career, Mead applied her knowledge of primitive cultures to contemporary society. For Mead, the relativity of our cultural organization and social mores is revealed in the rich diversity of primitive societies; an appreciation of other ways of life can allow us to "judge anew and perhaps fashion differently the education we give our children." In *Male and Female* (1949) she employed this maxim in a cross-cultural study of sex roles which criticized sex-role ideals in the United States as too constrictive. Though some of her colleagues have criticized Mead's studies for lack of rigor and overgeneralization, others have applauded her ability to write books of scholarly merit which are popular best sellers as well. In her later works Mead focused most of her attention on the social problems of Western society, particularly those related to the young. In *Culture and Commitment* (1978) she argued that the generation gap of the 1960s, troubling as it was, "nevertheless gave us a unique opportunity to face change in a new way"; in the present crisis, the young could "learn enough about change itself to be able to bring up children who are really ready for change." In *Letters from the Field 1925-1975* (1977) Mead provided a record of fifty years of field work as an anthropologist. (See also *Contemporary Authors*, Vols. 1-4, rev. ed.; obituary, Vols. 81-84; *Contemporary Authors New Revision Series*, Vol. 4; and *Authors in the News*, Vol. 1.)

Excerpt from *COMING OF AGE IN SAMOA: A PSYCHOLOGICAL STUDY OF PRIMITIVE YOUTH FOR WESTERN CIVILISATION*

[In *Coming of Age in Samoa* I have described the lives of adolescent Samoan girls], the lives of their younger sisters who will soon be adolescent, of their brothers with whom a strict taboo forbids them to speak, of their older sisters who have left puberty behind them, of their elders, the mothers and fathers whose attitudes towards life determine the attitudes of their children. And through this description I have tried to answer the question which sent me to Samoa: Are the disturbances which vex our adolescents due to the nature of adolescence itself or to the civilisation? Under different conditions does adolescence present a different picture?

Also, by the nature of the problem, because of the unfamiliarity of this simple life on a small Pacific island, I have had to give a picture of the whole social life of Samoa, the details being selected always with a view to illuminating the problem of adolescence. . . . I have tried to present to the reader the Samoan girl in her social setting, to describe the course of her life from birth until death, the problems she will have to solve, the values which will guide her in her solutions, the pains and pleasures of her human lot cast on a South Sea island.

Such a description seeks to do more than illuminate this particular problem. It should also give the reader some conception of a different and contrasting civilisation, another way of life, which other members of the human race have found satisfactory and gracious. We know that our subtlest perceptions, our high-

est values, are all based upon contrast; that light without darkness or beauty without ugliness would lose the qualities which they now appear to us to have. And similarly, if we would appreciate our own civilisation, this elaborate pattern of life which we have made for ourselves as a people and which we are at such pains to pass on to our children, we must set our civilisation over against other very different ones. . . . Here in remote parts of the world, under historical conditions very different from those which made Greece and Rome flourish and fall, groups of human beings have worked out patterns of life so different from our own that we cannot venture any guess that they would ever have arrived at our solutions. Each primitive people has selected one set of human gifts, one set of human values, and fashioned for themselves an art, a social organisation, a religion, which is their unique contribution to the history of the human spirit.

Samoa is only one of these diverse and gracious patterns, but as the traveller who has been once from home is wiser than he who has never left his own door step, so a knowledge of one other culture should sharpen our ability to scrutinise more steadily, to appreciate more lovingly, our own.

And, because of the particular problem which we set out to answer, this tale of another way of life is mainly concerned with education, with the process by which the baby, arrived cultureless upon the human scene, becomes a full-fledged adult member of his or her society. The strongest light will fall upon the ways in which Samoan education, in its broadest sense, differs from our own. And from this contrast we may be able to turn, made newly and vividly self-conscious and self-critical, to judge anew and perhaps fashion differently the education we give our children. (pp. 11-13)

Margaret Mead, in her Coming of Age in Samoa: A Psychological Study of Primitive Youth for Western Civilisation *(copyright 1928 by William Morrow & Company, Inc.; copyright renewed © 1955 by Margaret Mead; reprinted by permission of The Institute for Intercultural Studies), Blue Ribbon Books, 1928, 297 p.*

Excerpt from *MALE AND FEMALE: A STUDY OF THE SEXES IN A CHANGING WORLD*

The differences between the two sexes is one of the important conditions upon which we have built the many varieties of human culture that give human beings dignity and stature. In every known society, mankind has elaborated the biological division of labour into forms often very remotely related to the original biological differences that provided the original clues. Upon the contrast in bodily form and function, men have built analogies between sun and moon, night and day, goodness and evil, strength and tenderness, steadfastness and fickleness, endurance and vulnerability. Sometimes one quality has been assigned to one sex, sometimes to the other. Now it is boys who are thought of as infinitely vulnerable and in need of special cherishing care, now it is girls. In some societies it is girls for whom parents must collect a dowry or make husband-catching magic, in others the parental worry is over the difficulty of marrying off the boys. Some peoples think of women as too weak to work out of doors, others regard women as the appropriate bearers of heavy burdens, "because their heads are stronger than men's." The periodicities of female reproductive functions have appealed to some peoples as making women the natural sources of magical or religious power, to others as directly antithetical to those powers; some religions, including our European traditional religions, have assigned women an inferior rôle in the religious hierarchy, others have built their whole symbolic relationship with the supernatural world upon male imitations of the natural functions of women. In some cultures women are regarded as sieves through whom the best-guarded secrets will sift; in others it is the men who are the gossips. Whether we deal with small matters or with large, with the frivolities of ornament and cosmetics or the sanctities of man's place in the universe, we find this great variety of ways, often flatly contradictory one to the other, in which the rôles of the two sexes have been patterned.

But we always find the patterning. We know of no culture that has said, articulately, that there is no difference between men and women except in the way they contribute to the creation of the next generation; that otherwise in all respects they are simply human beings with varying gifts, no one of which can be exclusively assigned to either sex. We find no culture in which it has been thought that all identified traits—stupidity and brilliance, beauty and ugliness, friendliness and hostility, initiative and responsiveness, courage and patience and industry—are merely human traits. However differently the traits have been assigned, some to one sex, some to the other, and some to both, however arbitrary the assignment must be seen to be (for surely it cannot be true that women's heads are both absolutely weaker—for carrying loads—and absolutely stronger—for carrying loads—than men's), although the division has been arbitrary, it has always been there in every society of which we have any knowledge.

So in the twentieth century, as we try to re-assess our human resources, and by taking thought to add even a jot or a tittle to the stature of our fuller humanity, we are faced with a most bewildering and confusing array of apparently contradictory evidence about sex differences. We may well ask: Are they important? Do real differences exist, in addition to the obvious anatomical and physical ones—but just as biologically based—that may be masked by the learnings appropriate to any given society, but which will nevertheless be there? Will such differences run through all of men's and all of women's behaviour? Must we expect, for instance, that a brave girl may be very brave but will never have the same kind of courage as a brave boy, and that the man who works all day at a monotonous task may learn to produce far more than any woman in his society, but he will do it at a higher price to himself? Are such differences real, and *must* we take them into account? Because men and women have always in all societies built a great superstructure of socially defined sex differences that obviously cannot be true for all humanity—or the people just over the mountain would not be able to do it all in the exactly opposite fashion—must *some* such superstructures be built? We have here two different questions: Are we dealing not with a *must* that we dare not flout because it is rooted so deep in our biological mammalian nature that to flout it means individual and social disease? Or with a *must* that, although not so deeply rooted, still is so very socially convenient and so well tried that it would be uneconomical to flout it—a *must* which says, for example, that it is easier to get children born and bred if we stylize the behaviour of the sexes very differently, teaching them to walk and dress and act in contrasting ways and to specialize in different kinds of work? But there is still the third possibility. Are not sex differences exceedingly valuable, one of the resources of our human nature that every society has used but no society has as yet begun to use to the full?

We live in an age when every inquiry must be judged in terms of urgency. Are such questions about the rôles and the possible rôles of the sexes academic, peripheral to the central problems of our times? Are such discussions querulous fiddling while Rome burns? I think they are not. Upon the growing accuracy with which we are able to judge our limitations and our potentialities, as human beings and in particular as human societies, will depend the survival of our civilization, which we now have the means to destroy. Never before in history has mankind had such momentous choices placed in its hands. (pp. 7-10)

To-day we live in another world, a world so closely knit that no smallest group can go down to disaster—by plague or revolution or by foreign aggression or famine—without shaking the structure of the whole world. No matter how much they may wish to do so, it is no longer possible for a people to keep inventions like gunpowder to use in firecrackers rather than in cannon. We are approaching the place where every step we take not only *may* be important for the whole world and for the whole of future history, but where we can almost say it *will* be important for the whole world. As the culture of each small human society in the past grew, changed, blossomed or decayed, vanished or was transformed into some other culture, and no act within that structure was wholly insignificant for the whole, so to-day the culture of the world is becoming *one*—one in its interdependence, though far from one in the contrasts and discrepancies within it.

The decisions we make now, as human beings, and as human beings who are members of groups with power to act, may bind the future as no men's decisions have ever bound it before. We are laying the foundations of a way of life that may become so world-wide that it will have no rivals, and men's imaginations will be both sheltered and imprisoned within the limits of the way we build. For in order to think creatively, men need the stimulus of contrast. We know by sad experience how difficult it is for those who have been reared within one civilization ever to get outside its categories, to imagine, for instance, what a language could be like that had thirteen genders. Oh, yes, one says, masculine, feminine, and neuter—and what in the world are the other ten? For those who have grown up to believe that blue and green are different colours it is hard even to think how any one would look at the two colours if they were not differentiated, or how it would be to think of colours only in terms of intensity and not of hue. Most American and European women simply cannot imagine what it would be like to be a happy wife in a polygamous family and share a husband's favours with two other women. We can no longer think of the absence of medical care as anything but a yawning gap to be filled at once. Inevitably, the culture within which we live shapes and limits our imaginations, and by permitting us to do and think and feel in certain ways makes it increasingly unlikely or impossible that we should do or think or feel in ways that are contradictory or tangential to it.

So, as we stand at the moment in history when we still have choice, when we are just beginning to explore the properties of human relationships as the natural sciences have explored the properties of matter, it is of the very greatest importance which questions we ask, because by the questions we ask we set the answers that we will arrive at, and define the paths along which future generations will be able to advance. (pp. 12-13)

[When] we ask the very urgent questions we must ask about the differences and the similiarities, the vulnerabilities and the handicaps, of each of the sexes, we must also ask: What are the potentialities of sex differences? If men, just because they are men, find it harder to forget the immediate urgencies of sex than do women, what are the rewards of this more urgent remembering? If little boys have to meet and assimilate the early shock of knowing that they can never create a baby with the sureness and incontrovertibility that is a woman's birthright, how does this make them more creatively ambitious, as well as more dependent upon achievement? If little girls have a rhythm of growth which means that their own sex appears to them as initially less sure than their brothers, and so gives them a little false flick towards compensatory achievement that almost always dies down before the certainty of maternity, this probably does mean a limitation on their sense of ambition. But what positive potentialities are there also? If at each step we ask, consciously and articulately: What are the limitations, and what are the potentialities, the lower limits and the possible upper limits, of the fact that there are two sexes, and of the differences between them? then not only may we find answers that are in themselves rewarding about the place of the sexes in our present changing world; we shall do more. We shall make a contribution to the belief that on every question involving human beings we must concern ourselves not only with limitations, and not only with aspirations and potentialities,

but with both. We will increase our faith in our full humanity—rooted in our biological ancestry that we dare not flout—capable of rising to heights of which each living generation can only glimpse the next step in the ascent. (pp. 20-1)

> *Margaret Mead, in her* Male and Female: A Study of the Sexes in a Changing World *(copyright 1949, copyright renewed 1976, 1977 by Margaret Mead; abridged by permission of William Morrow & Company, Inc.), William Morrow, 1949, 477 p.*

Excerpt from *LETTERS FROM THE FIELD 1925-1975*

These letters from the field are one record, a very personal record, of what it has meant to be a practicing anthropologist over the last fifty years.

Field work is only one aspect of any anthropologist's experience and the circumstances of field work—the particular circumstances of any one occasion—are never twice the same nor can they ever be alike for two fieldworkers. Yet field work—the unique, but also cumulative, experience of immersing oneself in the ongoing life of another people, suspending for the time both one's beliefs and disbeliefs, and of simultaneously attempting to understand mentally and physically this other version of reality—is crucial in the formation of every anthropologist and in the development of a body of anthropological theory. Field work has provided the living stuff out of which anthropology has developed as a science and which distinguishes this from all other sciences. (p. 1)

[Only] in this century have we attempted systematically to explore and comprehend the nature of the relationship between the observer and that which is observed, whether it is a star, a microscopic particle, an ant hill, a learning animal, a physical experiment or some human group isolated for hundreds, perhaps thousands, of years from the mainstream of the world's history as we know it. Throughout my lifetime the implications of the inclusion of the observer within the circle of relevance have enormously widened and deepened. (p. 2)

For the anthropologist living in the midst of a village, waking at cock crow or drum beat, staying up all night while the village revels or mourns, learning to listen for some slight change in the level of chatter or the cry of a child, field work becomes a twenty-four-hour activity. And everything that happens, from the surly refusal of a boatman to take one across the river to one's own dreams, becomes data once the event has been noted, written up, photographed or tape recorded.

As the inclusion of the observer within the observed scene becomes more intense, the observation becomes unique. So the experience of each fieldworker on each particular field trip differs from all other comparable experience. This, too, must be part of one's awareness. And the more delicate and precise the methods of recording—and I have lived through all the improvements from pencil and notebook and still photography to video tape—the more fully these unique experiences become usable parts of our scientific data. Equipped with instruments of precision and replication that were developed to meet the requirements of natural scientists for objectivity and replicable observations, human scientists are able to bring back from the field records of unique, subjectively informed experience which can be analyzed and later re-analyzed in the light of changing theory. (pp. 6-7)

Over the years I have come to realize that each generation of young anthropologists can only build on the present. They can't go back and they can't do it over again. They have to go on in a world that has changed, making observations and developing theory in ways that were not yet possible before their own teachers went to the field and that will no longer fully satisfy their own students when they, in turn, begin their field research. Books and monographs record the outcome of field experience. But we have very few records, written for others to read, of field work in process.

These letters constitute such a record. For from the very first letter, written when the whole adventure of my field work was still before me, to the most recent ones, which incorporate in some sense all my changing field work experience, they were designed to be read by a group of people, and a very diverse group at that, to whom for various reasons I wanted to remain explicable. (pp. 7-8)

These letters . . . are one record of the way modern anthropological field work evolved—a record, based on the experience of one fieldworker, of what goes into the making of a modern anthropological theory, which is both holistic and based on the analysis of the patterning of the finest detail. When the early letters were written, we did not even have a name for what we were doing, except the very general term "field work." The major shift came when anthropologists went to live in the community and shared, twenty-four hours a day, in the sights and sounds, the tastes and smells, the pace and rhythm of a reality in which every detail was not only different in itself but was differently organized as a perceptual scheme.

Only very slowly did we begin to take into account that we ourselves change with each step of the journey, with each day in the field as we learned the language and as nonsense syllables and meaningless gestures resolved themselves into elaborate patterns of behavior. The development of intensive photography made it possible to record some of these changes in our ability to see and understand in the contrast between photographs and films made the first day and the last. (p. 15)

After an interval of forty years, when I found my Arapesh villagers again, reassembled at Hoskins Bay in New Britain, where they were participating in the development of a modern oil palm enterprise, there were only two women who had known me as adults. The others, children when we were in Alitoa, knew of me only as a myth. But in my own memory, in photographs and in works, those I never saw again live on, transfixed in time. In the mind of one who studied them as children, they became more than friends, much more than babies who were dosed and nursed back to health. For even the small children were collaborators in an undertaking that transcended both me and them—the attempt to understand enough about culture so that all of us, equally members of humankind, can understand ourselves and take our future and the future of our descendants safely in our hands. (p. 16)

Margaret Mead, in her Letters from the Field 1925-1975 *(copyright © 1977 by Margaret Mead; reprinted by permission of Harper & Row, Publishers, Inc.), Harper & Row, 1977, 343 p.*

Excerpt from *CULTURE AND COMMITMENT: THE NEW RELATIONSHIPS BETWEEN THE GENERATIONS IN THE 1970s*

In the 1960s young people, the first young people of the new generation, believed they could make the world new overnight. Children of electricity and electronics, they were accustomed to pushing buttons so that there would be light. And, as their instant aspirations erupted at a hundred universities and colleges all over the world, we, their elders, were forced to respond with violent opposition and coercion. In some places youngsters with long hair were forbidden to attend school or were threatened by motorists on the streets of American towns. Traveling youngsters with beards were deported from some countries they visited. Some youngsters, faced with opportunities to sit in the councils of their elders, screeched obscene words in total rejection. Dropping out became routine, and truant officers threw up their hands.

Some older people greeted the new order with varying degrees of enthusiasm and identification; some proclaimed the coming of the counterculture, the greening of America, and dressed and spoke like those much younger than themselves. Hope and fear dominated them, as fear of the past and hope for the immediate results of their protests dominated the articulate young. Now, in more sober retrospect, we can take stock of what has happened since the 1960s, assess what is left of those hopes and fears, and take another long look at the present, realizing even more acutely, just how unpredictable the future was. (p. 95)

It continued to be very difficult for people to comprehend a generation gap that ringed the earth, a gap that separated all those born and reared before the mid-1940s and all those reared since. When this book was first published, angry critics wrote letters pointing out how much more they knew than the young, thinking that I was speaking of knowledge or wisdom, rather than of difference in experience. First-generation Americans, who, once they have become truly committed Americans in feeling, are the least critical of the country they have adopted, explained loftily, "I didn't get on with my father, he didn't get on with his father, and I don't expect to get on with my son, but there is nothing new about that." My French friends, forgetting their exuberance in the year of the May 1968 extravagances, said a greater gap had been created in France by World War I.

At the beginning of the 1970s the student movements seemed to be dying out. The adults who had shared the students' hope that the world might be made new overnight were disgruntled and disappointed; others were secretly gleeful because they believed the enemy had been routed. In the summer of 1970, after the last great outbursts in the United States of youthful outrage over Cambodia and the Kent State and Jackson State massacres, the newspapers began to announce the end of student activism as a death of the spirit. They did not realize that the Generation Gap no longer coincided with the years of undergraduate study.

What was happening was very like what happened in 1945 when the atomic bomb first became part of our consciousness. We were beginning to domesticate the Generation Gap, to ignore its importance, to rob it of meaning, just as twenty-five years before, we had managed to ignore and domesticate the bomb. (pp. 96-7)

Now, in the 1970s, instead of becoming the responsible guardian of world peace, the United States, its allies, and its adversaries all participate actively in the irresponsible and competitive merchandising of arms, nuclear-energy plants, and weapon-quality nuclear materials. Where the atomic bomb presented a clear-cut possibility for deterrence and the partial reassurance of control, the proliferation of commercially used plutonium today presents a kind of danger so diffuse, so unmanageable, that the nightmares of the British novelist Nevil Shute's *On The Beach,* published in 1957, become again a believable depiction of ultimate catastrophe.

But what do the dangers of nuclear power in the late 1970s have to do with the Generation Gap? Ten years ago the Generation Gap could be stated as clearly and simply as the atomic dilemma in the summer of 1945. An unprecedented situation had arisen. As the world became one intercommunicating whole, the experience of all those, everywhere on earth, reared in the post-World War II world, became a shared experience and differentiated them from all their elders. The colleges and universities had exploded under the pressure of their fresh vision. Empowered by this freshness and by the new ethics of shared responsibility, sufficiently alienated from the Establishment—from all establishments—the postwar generation demanded a changed world. It demanded this as surely as the prewar generation's recognition of the bomb demanded a changed world in 1945. The new generation was in fact, the product of the twenty years of grace we had asked for in 1945 when the first atomic explosions changed the world forever.

The Generation Gap, as it occurred in the mid 1960s was both a historical event irreversible in time and a biological event, as it occurred to human beings who would inevitably age. Placed against the background of all known history of *Homo sapiens* on this planet, it was a unique event and could not be expected to happen again. The uniqueness lay in its simultaneity. (pp. 100-01)

[With] the explorations and inventions of the 1940s, the world [became] one, each people subject to the actions of other peoples; a plague developed in one part could now spread to the whole, and all were now exposed to the dangers of total nuclear catastrophe.

In hailing the Generation Gap of the mid-1960s as a moment of opportunity, a moment that would never recur in quite this form again, I was in a sense repeating the response of those of us who were early concerned about the bomb. I was proclaiming that the Generation Gap, tragic as it was for the isolated older generation, frightening as it was to the young who must work without models, nevertheless gave us a unique opportunity to face change in a new way. I realized, of course, that each year the Gap would involve a fresh break between different ages—as the old died off, a new host of infants were born and those who were then disturbing our universities became adults. This meant, and that was clear enough, that the proportions would change each year, until all of those who had been reared before the mid-forties finally died and the unique gap would disappear. During this period, before that happened, while the older generation still held the reins, I and many others hoped we might develop new forms of communication between young and old which would become models for future generations. There would, of course, continue to be vast changes to adjust to. But, we hoped children reared on the other side of the Generation Gap would have an understanding of change which would differ quantitatively and qualitatively from that of their elders. When young people asked, "Will we be as alienated from our children as we are from our parents?" I answered, "I don't think so. There will be no such world-wide gap which will include everyone at once. Change will probably again be more piecemeal, some parts of the world will change at different speeds, and during the present crisis you can learn enough about change itself to be able to bring up children who are really ready for change." (pp. 101-02)

In the 1960s we were also witnessing the explosive change that came with the acceptance of the idea that there were other high religions besides Judeo-Christianity and that all the peoples of the world, physically differentiated into what are called "races,"

were equally capable of learning and using what other peoples of different physiques had invented or discovered. Prejudices were being stripped away. Would it not be possible to use the explicitness of the Generation Gap to go even further than the great religious and ideological systems which have swept the world since time immemorial to form the basis of ever-widening communication with partially shared values?

This was the hope at the end of the 1960s, expressed in many contradictory ways. It was expressed in the flaming belief that the irresponsible consumer society would disappear. This was the hope that the young, the promising gifted young, the cream of their generation, would stem the inevitable dulling and bureaucratizing of the first revolutionary generation in Communist China. This was the hope, expressed very differently, by those Japanese industrialists who recruited future executives from among the most forceful young insurgents.

In the universities, it was the hope of those staff members who knew how moribund and inadequate our university systems had become, as professors droned out their notes, year after year, as if printing had indeed never been invented. It was the hope of those who realized how many of our high schools had become prisons just to keep teen-agers off the streets and our elementary schools places where imagination was stifled but necessary skills no longer learned. The mature members of the older generation realized, differently but often as acutely, the deficiencies and inadequacies and injustices of the societies that had developed in ramshackle, unthinking fashion during the industrial revolution. In the fresh accusing eyes of the young, they saw reflected their own doubts and uncertainties and repudiations. And so all over the world there were strange and sudden capitulations by the perceptive, responsible, and concerned elders, as well as angry, often vicious reactions from those who felt that the very essence of all they held dear was being completely destroyed.

The hopes and the fears were equally extreme. The aftermath has been excessive also. The press decided in the summer of 1970 that the youth movement was over; this again was not a planned campaign of destruction, but born of disappointed hopes when the announcement came from the Nixon White House that nothing the young, or those who sympathized with their aspirations, could do or say would influence the President in any way. Even those college presidents, who had shared the hope of the young, were not received in Washington. And the American media had begun to exploit—and destroy—the more vocal and picturesque of young "leaders" extracted from a movement that was trying to escape from conspicuously fragmented leadership into groping and temporary consensus.

But something else was happening, something that we had allowed for intellectually, but for which no complete provision had been made in our thinking. We knew that the position of the Generation Gap would move up each year, with one more age group included on the other side. But it was not until the gap between the prewar and postwar generations began to appear, not only among the students but among the teachers, that the full implications were clear. The first harbinger came in 1970 with teaching assistants who struck, not as students against the Establishment, but as junior members of the faculty. Where only a few years before, all faculty were on the other side, now the Gap was *inside* the faculty group—young and weak as the members of the new generation were. (pp. 103-06)

As the first generation of American college students who had tried to solve the problems of the world by demonstrations in deans' offices or in the streets of Washington left the campuses and became the first generations in older age groups—in law schools, medical schools, and business schools—the intensity of conflicts on the campuses faded. Students, no longer feeling the full burden of change resting on their pioneer shoulders, were relieved by the end of the Vietnam War in April 1975 from the ever present problems of the draft and decisions of conscience. But they now came under new and unfamiliar pressures as an economic recession deepened and the proportionate number of younger students shrank. Jobs became scarcer because there were so many more contemporary contenders. It became harder than ever to get into medical schools and law schools. The grim business of making a living intruded for the first time on the children of the upper middle class who had felt free to choose whatever course they wished, assured that there would always be money enough.

So the students of the country in the 1970s buckled down to work again, to the unsatisfactory and outmoded methods of learning, once so recently repudiated, now again to be endured. The urgency their predecessors had felt in the mid-sixties has almost completely gone. Activists are almost as rare as they have traditionally been on American campuses. Undergraduate life is again seen as a perpetuation of adolescence, a postponement of choice, or where a professional choice has been made, for a determined pursuit of its academic requirements. Saving the world, like earning a living, can be postponed until later—when once out of law school, one can take up advocacy or out of medical school, one can work for free clinics. Later, the concerned can go to Washington and get jobs in the Environmental Protection Agency, or join Ralph Nader's crusaders, or go to work overseas in a Peace Corps that is today much more sober and more demanding of skill. The new graduates will not retire to the suburbs any more than their predecessors did. The campuses look more like the 1950s, but the questioning generated on the campuses of the 1960s is still with us. (pp. 106-07)

> *Margaret Mead, in her* Culture and Commitment: The New Relationships between the Generations in the 1970s *(copyright © 1970, 1978 by Margaret Mead; reprinted by permission of Doubleday & Company, Inc.), revised edition, Anchor Press, 1978, 178 p.*

RUTH BENEDICT

[In **"Coming of Age in Samoa"** Margaret Mead answers the question as to whether or not the psychological experiences of adolescents are universal.] And the upshot of the matter is that it is precisely at adolescence that the Samoan girl is at peace with the universe.

It is not any one simple variation of our own schemes that has brought about this different result. As Dr. Mead shows, some of the forces that have been at work, like the low evaluation of personality differences, are distasteful to us; and the most fundamental one of all, the simplicity of the choices open to the Polynesian girl, we could recapture only at the price of civilization itself. But the placing of the girl in the economic scheme, the systematic lowering of the effect of decisions, the handling of sex, are all full of that illumination that comes of envisaging very different possible ways of handling invariable problems. . . .

Dr. Mead has sketched the suave and gracious background of Polynesian culture as it was interpreted in Samoa, but she has sketched it as it affects the life of the growing girl. It is culture not as a strange static scene, catalogued for reference, but existence as the individual lives it out and modifies it by his own life history, and readers who have rejected many accounts of primitive peoples may find this one to their liking.

Certainly those who are interested in the way in which the social environment can select and underscore now one, now another, of human potentialities, will find here much illustrative material intelligently presented. Is it possible, we ask ourselves, that a people can exist all of whose virtues are the social graces, who have in themselves so little violence, are so little concerned with mystery, with supernatural forces? For the Samoans live in the well charted seas of social amenities, and they take no notice of the regions that lie outside.

Not only is **"Coming of Age in Samoa"** challenging to the educator and to the parent of growing children, but the anthropological student of psychological problems among primitive peoples should not miss the program of research in the appendix with its due weight given to differences in culture, and the student of sex problems will find here an example of consistent cultural behavior in a society that develops no neuroses in its members. It is a book for which we have been waiting.

> *Ruth Benedict, "The Younger Generation with a Difference," in* The New Republic, *Vol. 57, No. 730, November 28, 1928, p. 50.*

ROBERT REDFIELD

The description of Samoan adolescence [in *Coming of Age in Samoa*] leads to an analysis of those cultural differences which make adolescence different from what it is in America. They are "the general casualness of the whole society," and the absence of conflict situations for the growing girl. There is but one thing for her to do, one attitude to take; and all the other girls are doing and taking just that. Further, she is largely spared the hazards of having a father or a mother, so diffuse is parental authority and affection; and she is always a child in the middle of the series, for she is but one of many sisters and cousins.

From this Q.E.D. Miss Mead passes to a consideration of "any conclusions which might bear fruit in the training of our adolescents." And here the limitations of her viewpoint become apparent. The home "must cease to plead an ethical cause. . . . the children must be taught how to think, not what to think." The family is evidently to relinquish any lingering claims to being a cultural group and is to become a seminar in ethics. This looks, we are told, to a happy time "when no one group claims ethical sanction for its customs."

For all the intimate association with Samoans the book is somehow disappointing. There are exceedingly interesting pages. Why do the Samoans, with whom love is merely one of a hundred unstressed values, and who are cynical of fidelity, follow romantic conventions of courtship in speech and song? How is it that in spite of extreme license in word and conduct there nevertheless remains a residue, apparently quite like our own, of what is salacious and obscene? But Miss Mead is interested, one feels, in problems and cases, not in human nature. There is no warmth in her account. A little Malinowski, stirred in, would have helped, perhaps. (pp. 729-30)

Robert Redfield, "Book Reviews: 'Coming of Age in Samoa'," in The American Journal of Sociology, *Vol. XXXIV, No. 4, January, 1929, pp. 728-30.*

ROBERT H. LOWIE

Miss Mead's graphic picture of Polynesian free love [in *Coming of Age in Samoa*] is convincing. It falls in line with the reports of earlier travellers; it is supported by Dr. Handy's evidence from the Marquesas; and from another Oceanian area we have Dr. Malinowski's Trobriand observations. Nevertheless, this is not the whole story. (p. 532)

On the one hand, we are shown licensed freedom precluding mental derangements; on the other, we see all girls of rank originally subjected to the defloration rite and the *taupo* liable to the death penalty for unchastity. If it is only modern Samoa that connives at free love, it may still remain true that adolescence is not necessarily a quasi-pathological condition; but the *social* applications become banal. . . . [It] is one thing to have a community treat the individual's sex life as an individual matter when the society is in a normal state; quite another, to find it unconcerned with his amours when abnormal contacts destroy old standards and fail to impose substitutes. The reformer must face the question whether any *normal* society can and will practice that lofty detachment found in Samoa nowadays.

But Dr. Mead's pedagogical theses, whether sound or not, should not obscure her solid contributions to ethnographic fact and method. Her picture of child life is among the most vivid I know. . . . Along with other records from the same general area Dr. Mead's account . . . throws doubt on a proposition I have hitherto vigorously maintained, viz., the universality of the individual family. The question involved is not at all that of consanguinity, but of a differential bond between a restricted group—mother, child, mother's spouse—as against the rest of the universe. In Polynesia this bond does seem to be exceptionally loose and to be superseded by more widely diffused ties.

On some points made by Dr. Mead I must frankly avow skepticism. It is hard to believe that all but the youngest boys and girls should fail to use ordinary kinship terms correctly . . . ; or, in an absolute way, that Samoan children do not learn to work through learning to play. . . . It is hard to understand how certain conclusions could have been arrived at. Says Dr. Mead:

> The Samoan girl never tastes the rewards of romantic love as we know it. . . .

Query: What, never? And: Who are "we"? Unless the Samoans are different from other Polynesians, they indulged in the luxury of romantic love precisely like other folk, to wit, in their fiction. Only after the most thoroughgoing search in Samoan folk-literature had yielded no trace of the sentiment, should I feel disposed to accept a negative result. Finally, perhaps from a Plains Indian bias, I am not convinced by Dr. Mead's picture of the "low level of appreciation of personality differences." . . . With due regard to the insolence of seniority and of caste, I suspect that here, too, the normal aspect of ancient Samoan life has been blurred by the blighting contact with European civilization. (pp. 533-34)

These reservations should not be taken to obscure the value of Dr. Mead's achievement. Dealing with problems incomparably subtler than those which usually engage the ethnographer's attention, she has not merely added much in the way of illuminating information but also illustrated a new method of study that is bound to find followers and to yield an even richer harvest. (p. 534)

Robert H. Lowie, "Book Reviews: 'Coming of Age in Samoa'," in American Anthropologist, *Vol. 31, No. 3, 1929, pp. 532-34.*

ISIDOR SCHNEIDER

If ["**Growing Up in New Guinea**"] had appeared as a modern "Gulliver's Travels," the description of Manus society would have sounded like a bitter satire on American life.

Trade obsesses this people. Every social occasion, from birth to marriage, is made an opportunity for investment through gift exchanges. Respect for property is the first and one of the only two social obligations taught to children. Property even acts as a determinant of personality, the man of property being aggressive and overbearing, while the poor man is humble and shamefaced. . . .

As is to finish off the satire, the Manus are the Puritans of Oceania. Adultery is uncommon; prudery is joined with respect for property as the only social instruction given to children. Frigidity among women is taken for granted and the sexual relation is a secret act comparable in offensiveness to evacuation. . . .

This is adult life among the Manus. The life of the children is completely apart. They lead spoiled, selfish existences. They can make any demand upon their parents and they give nothing in return, run no errands, perform no household tasks. Mothers have no part in their lives, for, as soon as they are weaned, the fathers monopolize the right to play with them, to dote on them, and even join in spitefulness against the mothers. The attitude of the children is one of contempt for adult life. They mock the ceremonies, and their intrusions go unpunished. No attempt is made to initiate them into adult life, yet inevitably, as they grow up, they enter into it, and become bitter, quarrelsome business men like their fathers. The sheer absorbent power of example and tradition overcomes their repugnance and rebellion.

The coercive power of Manus life does not lie in its own organization but in a watchful spirit world. Every household has a pot swinging from the rafters in which is kept the skull and other important bones of an ancestor's skeleton. In this way a home is provided for the spirit who is expected to protect the family in return. Seances are held at which he is appealed to for services and advice. The spirits are censorious. They punish moral lapses and lack of business enterprise by sickness and death.

The opportunities presented by such a society for analogies with our own are well used by Miss Mead. It was a task which she had good excuses for evading, but she regarded it as a responsibility of the anthropologist. She undertakes it with intelligence and courage and without prophetic self-consciousness. (p. 330)

Isidor Schneider, "Manus and Americans," in The New Republic, *Vol. 64, No. 831, November 5, 1930, pp. 329-30.*

FLORENCE FINCH KELLY

This Margaret Mead is a dangerous person. She goes down to New Guinea, studies primitive tribes for two years and comes back with a book like a bomb that she drops into the complacent, fundamental conviction of the Occidental world, both scientific and social, that the sexes are innately different in their psychological attributes and that the male is dominant by right of brain and brawn. Her bomb explodes and scatters fragments over all the surrounding area and the first thing she knows some indignant voice will be crying out that this is an outrage and there ought to be a law. . . .

["**Sex and Temperament in Three Primitive Societies**"] delves even deeper into the roots of life and shows a more confident grasp of the significance of her findings [than "**Coming of Age in Samoa**" or "**Growing Up in New Guinea**"]. Whether or not one is disturbed by them, one must admire the fearlessness with which she challenges approved scientific principles and universally sanctioned social usage. For what Margaret Mead has brought back from the South Seas is a demonstration which she believes warrants her conclusion that there is no inherent psychologic difference between the sexes and that the differences that seem and are believed to be inherent are merely the result of social environment and training. . . .

In the final chapters, keenly and clearly thought out and brilliantly written, Miss Mead reviews her findings, comes to her conclusions and casts her challenge to the theory and practice of the civilized world. She shows that "we are forced to conclude that human nature is almost unbelievably malleable, responding accurately and contrastingly to contrasting cultural conditions" and that "only to the impact of the whole of the integrated culture upon the growing child can we lay the formation of the contrasting types."

In no other way, she believes, can the contrasts she found in these three tribes of New Guinea, all within the same culture area, be explained—the Arapesh with both men and women gentle, cooperative, responsive to the needs of others, the Mundugumor with both sexes ruthless, aggressive, positively sexed; the Tchambuli with the woman the dominant, managing partner and the man the less responsible, the emotionally and financially dependent person.

She comes to the conclusion that the distinctive male and female personalities civilization believes to be inherent are "socially produced," that in America, "without conscious plan but none the less surely," social conditioning is doing away with the idea of male dominance, while in Europe, by the same means, fascism is forcing women back into an older and extreme type of subservience, while communism is endeavoring to make the two sexes as much alike as possible. Miss Mead would have civilization achieve a richer culture, with many contrasting values, by weaving, "a less arbitrary social fabric, in which each diverse human gift will find a fitting place" and in which no individual will be forced by artificial distinctions, such as that of sex, "into an ill-fitting mold."

Florence Finch Kelly, "A Challenging View of the Sexes," in The New York Times Book Review *(© 1935 by The New York Times Company; reprinted by permission), May 26, 1935, p. 2.*

JOSEPH WOOD KRUTCH

Miss Mead has a thesis to prove [in "**Sex and Temperament in Three Primitive Societies**"]. Her fellow anthropologists will have to argue it with her, and it will be up to them to decide whether or not her three case histories furnish a broad enough base upon which to rest so sweeping a generalization. Indeed, even the layman can hardly help feeling a certain surprise at the readiness with which all the facts discovered in the course of her investigation seem to play into her hands, or fail to find something almost providential in the fact that the three primitive societies perfectly calculated to support her contention should be found cheek by jowl on the same Pacific island. But whatever other anthropologists may have to say—and Miss Mead is of course an observer of repute who has earned every right to credence—one thing is certain: her book is among the most thoroughly entertaining works in any genre to be published in a long, long time. Very soon the reader will find himself forgetting anthropology as a science and chuckling with pure delight over a book which combines the charm of "Gulliver's Travels" and "Erewhon" with that of "Alice in Wonderland." Miss Mead is a scientist, but it so happens besides, not only that she has fallen upon some extraordinary material, but also that she writes with a full appreciation of its human interest and with what seems like a delight in logical topsy-turvydom for its own sake.

What could be more according to the method of Swift or of Samuel Butler than a voyage which takes you, first, to a land where everybody is womanly; then to a land where everybody is manly; and, finally, to one where the men are womanly and the women manly? . . . Miss Mead concludes that those traits which our culture is inclined to refer to as "masculine" and "feminine" have no real basis in sex difference. Two types of character do exist, but either may be officially encouraged by society, and it is a mere arbitrary convention which regards one or the other as appropriate or natural to one sex or the other. All this seems inherently not improbable and abundantly supported by these facts at least, though one may take it for granted that not all anthropologists will allow the contention to stand unchallenged. Meanwhile ["**Sex and Temperament in Three Primitive Societies**"] deserves to be a best-seller by virtue of its entertainment value alone. Man is an extremely variable creature and this book, like all books of sound anthropology, amusingly demonstrates again how completely absurd was the old assumption that the primitive man was a "natural man." Miss Mead's Arapesh and Mundugumor are at least as tradition-ridden as any European and at least as far as he from that theoretical state of nature in which actions are regulated by either animal impulse or the uncorrupted reason which was once supposed to be the birthright of the noble savage. Perhaps civilized man on a camping trip gets close to nature; primitive man certainly is not.

Joseph Wood Krutch, "Men and Women", in The Nation, *Vol. 140, No. 3647, May 29, 1935, p. 634.*

MALCOLM COWLEY

[In "**Sex and Temperament in Three Primitive Societies**" Margaret Mead concludes that masculine and feminine traits are social rather than biological.]

In the argument leading to this radical conclusion there are some links of which the weakness is obvious even to a non-anthropologist and non-sojourner among the Papuan aborigines. Thus, on the basis of Miss Mead's own records, it is not true that "neither the Arapesh nor the Mundugumor have made any attitude specific for one sex." The attitude of restlessness, of continually seeking new distractions, is a trait of the Arapesh men; their wives call them "Walk-Abouts" or "Never-Sit-Downs." Among the Mundugumor, the attitude of reckless self-exposure in warfare is specifically male. Among all three tribes, even the women-ruled Tchambuli, it is taken for granted that the men will have a monopoly of hunting, trading, fighting, painting and wood-carving, whereas the women will stay at home and preserve the continuity of tribal life. If all the researches of all the anthropologists were added together, it might be shown that a few male and female characteristics have prevailed everywhere. After all, the men are stronger than the women and are unhampered by pregnancy. The matriarch has to be gentler and more conniving than the patriarch. Even the Tchambuli women are careful not to rule their husbands too openly, for, as the men say, "We might become so ashamed that we would beat them."

Yet it seems to me that Miss Mead is essentially right in her principal conclusions about sex and temperament and the lack of a real connection between them. She is right in saying that most of the traits connected with social classes are also non-hereditary, are roles invented as if by a dramatist and imposed as if by a dictator. There is no more biological basis for class distinctions than there is for the belief of the Mundugumor that only a child born with the umbilical cord wrapped round its neck can become an artist. And Miss Mead is justified in her emphasis on the infinite adaptability of human nature. This, indeed, is the lesson pointed by the studies of almost all the modern anthropologists. After scattering over the world for thirty years, they are now carrying home the results of their studies. They have to report that nothing is humanly impossible, that there is certainly no inferno in which man has not managed somehow to live and probably no Utopia toward which he might not rise.

> *Malcolm Cowley, "News from New Guinea," in* The New Republic, *Vol. 83, No. 1070, June 5, 1935, p. 107.*

GERALD W. JOHNSON

The subtitle of ["**Keep Your Powder Dry,**"] "An Anthropologist Looks at America," naturally suggests to a reviewer the retort that America should now look at this anthropologist, for she is an astonishing spectacle, in several ways. In the first place, although she is an anthropologist, she writes English that any high school student can understand with only an occasional reference to the dictionary; in the second place, although she is an idealist, she doesn't drop a single tear throughout nearly three hundred pages; in the third place, although her book is frankly didactic in spirit, it is downright jocund in tone. Miss Mead understands as well as any one, and far better than most, the magnitude of the present crisis, but she can see nothing whatever to be gained by becoming hysterical; so she doesn't. . . .

[The] technic of investigation [Miss Mead] had developed in studying eight primitive tribes she now turned upon the American people, and this book is her report. (p. 1)

Some of her assumptions are questionable and some of her reasoning is tenuous, but her conclusions as to the psychological make-up of the American people are always striking and usually shrewd. The racial factor she dismisses briskly and completely—an understandable attitude in view of the grotesque overemphasis laid upon it by Hitler, but not one which all of Hitler's enemies will accept. However, her aim was to discover the strength of this people, and that certainly is not to be found in racial strains.

Perhaps the most debatable point she makes is her assertion that the American people are not well qualified to stand up under a long series of disasters. Everything depends, of course, upon the definition of the word "disaster"; but the experience of the last eleven months has not been exactly happy. Up to Nov. 7 almost every new arrival was a Job's messenger bearing a tale of fresh calamity; but the American people took it pretty well. In the Civil War the North stood twice as bad a battering for twice as long without going to pieces. The evidence that we can't take it is not impressive.

So Miss Mead comes to consider what contribution this nation may make when the time comes for rearranging a shattered world after the fighting is over. Americans, of all people, ought to be the first to recognize the valuable elements in disparate cultures, for it is a problem with which we have been dealing throughout our national existence. Americans ought to be able to devise the best means of making those valuable elements reinforce each other, rather than neutralise or destroy each other; if not, what is the use of being ingenious? The fact that the mechanical structure of a reasonable world order does not exist should be regarded, not as a handicap, but as the opportunity of the inventor nation.

This cheerful thesis Miss Mead defends with great cheerfulness. She has delightful facility in illuminating a completely serious argument with an occasional spark of wit, and she writes with lucidity that cannot be too much praised. Above all, she is not in the least afraid. She knows that the menace is great, that the time is short, that losses are bound to be heavy at best, but still she is not afraid. Her estimate of the situation convinces her that the American people, although they may be badly battered, are not going to be destroyed. What she urges is not a program to save the nation, because the nation is already saved, but a program for exploiting its moral and intellectual resources efficiently for the benefit of the world and therefore for the benefit of the United States.

It may be that her estimate is too optimistic, but at any rate it is stimulating to encounter a writer whose theme is not, "flee from the wrath to come," but instead, "Keep your powder dry." (pp. 1-2)

> *Gerald W. Johnson, "A Chuckling Anthropologist Studies Us," in* New York Herald Tribune Books, *November 22, 1942, pp. 1-2.*

DAVID RIESMAN

Margaret Mead begins "**Male and Female**"—after a brilliant introductory discussion of the meaning of scientific questions and anthropological methods of posing and answering them—with a description of how the different ways of handling boy babies and girl babies in seven South Sea cultures help to determine sex roles and sex expectations in the children. Her field work, in its subtlety, is far removed from the "diaperology" about which her school of anthropology is often kidded by people unsympathetic with the beginning steps of a science. For she sees that what matters is not so much what is done to the child in strict terms of a formula for feeding or toilet training as how the formula is mediated to the child of each sex through the parent of one sex—and how this in turn reflects the parent's and creates the next generation's whole style of life, particularly its acceptance or rejection of or its anxiety about its sex role.

Moreover, Dr. Mead further complicates her account by suggesting that differences in temperament—that is, in body type or constitution—may cut across differences in stylization of sex roles; so that a boy whose temperament is similar to that of boys in some other class or culture and atypical in his own may be stamped as "feminine," and seek either to become more of a "man" by dissociating himself from his body and the native gifts that go with his body-type, or move altogether in the opposite direction toward homosexuality or transvestitism. Had such a boy been born in a culture which built its picture of maleness on different temperament clues, he might never have doubted his sex, or resented or envied the other sex, but might have elaborated his native potentialities more fully and at less cost.

Underneath, however, the variations and restructurings of sex roles accomplished by culture and temperament, Dr. Mead sees certain biological clues as tending to produce different outlooks in men and women. It is characteristic, she suggests, for women to *be* women simply by growth through the definite stages of menarche, loss of virginity, motherhood, and menopause: a girl has merely to await these stages in her body's cycle for them to come about. As against this, men have no such time-bound indices of being; for them the problem is one of *becoming* male by constant reassertions of potency, of achievement. They must make their own time-divisions, their own climaxes—possibly, Dr. Mead declares, this may be connected with men's historically greater gift for music and mathematics, as well as their greater interest in ceremonies of initiation. While men must achieve, or rather learn, parenthood, women have it thrust upon them; they must learn to want to achieve in other spheres. Indeed, each sex must *learn* what the other *is*. However, in modern monogamous societies, where women outnumber men and the birth rate has fallen, the situation is somewhat different, for many women must learn how to be women without being wives and mothers.

The material from the South Seas is used to prove with concrete illustrations the point made by John Stuart Mill in "The Subjection of Women": that if one sex defines too narrowly the role of the other, it also cramps its own role. This holds for the roles assumed in sexual intercourse, in the family, and in occupations. (p. 376)

Dr. Mead finds her cross-cultural material useful in getting away from the continuing battle in the United States between those surviving feminists who are concerned with proving that women have qualities virtually identical with men and those whom, to coin a word, one might term "feminine-ists," soured on feminism and concerned with proving that women are basically dependent creatures who, as in romances of the ante bellum South, were happier before "emancipation." By pointing to the mild Arapesh—or the violent Mundugumor—Dr. Mead has good case studies of the monotony of an "equality" between the sexes based on likeness rather than the cultivation of difference. On the other hand, by pointing to the Iatmul, she can show the strain put on men—and, derivatively, on their wives—by a culture that exaggerates the differences by keeping women at home and assigning to men the performance of bombastic ceremonial.

In each case she deals with each sex only in its relation to the other and thus avoids the almost inevitable traps of oversimplification that are met when one starts out, like Lundberg and

Farnham, to study women as the "lost sex" or, like Kinsey, to describe male "outlets" in one book without bearing in mind the female "receptacles" of the next book. Likewise, she avoids the trap of studying only a single role, such as the leisure role of romantic love so hated by De Rougemont; her effort is to grasp at once the variety of work-and-play relations between the sexes. While of course every author and every book has to start somewhere and cannot cover everything, still the point where one begins in this field—with men, with women, or with both; with work, with play, or with both—matters enormously.

When Dr. Mead brings these notions and comparisons to the study of contemporary American patterns of sex roles and sex training, she does so not to suggest that solutions to American problems can be found by adopting the sex stylizations in vogue among the Arapesh, or even among the sex-happy Samoans. She uses the knowledge of other cultures as a tool of insight into her own, not as a prescription. (pp. 376-77)

Indeed, Margaret Mead sees the sexes in contemporary America caught in vicious circles of mutual emulation, manipulation, and fear. She also observes that the ideal that each conjugal family should have a separate home of its own condemns many women who attain it to being more isolated than they would like, while the families who must live with relatives or in crowded quarters feel somehow wrong or wronged. This physical freezing of living arrangements into a single ideal—in which unimaginative city planning and the housing industry, or lack of an industry, cooperate—both symbolizes and reinforces the freezing of ideals of sex role and family life by which Americans try to cope with their fluid social system.

Though Dr. Mead has her own ideals—she has gone beyond the cultural relativism so necessary to the development of anthropology—she is terribly aware of the dangers of idealism for Americans, who are apt to bridge the gap between ideals and current practice either by cynical kicking of the ideal or ruthless kicking of the practice. And this danger is especially great in the field of sex roles, where Americans have often abused the findings of psychological and sociological studies—not to speak of the myths of love presented in novels in which no one ever has a cold, a contraceptive, or complications—to make impossible demands on themselves and on others, without regard to individual constitution or, often, to the mood of the moment. Yet Dr. Mead believes that Americans are still sufficiently experimental to be capable of building new patterns of male and female roles that exploit the wisdoms of the body and the wisdoms of all relevant cultural experience.

Any book that attempts so much runs into difficulties. As Dr. Mead is aware, her readers will find it hard to keep straight the threads of seven South Sea cultures, or the seven times seven threads in the American pattern, even though this is limited to the middle class in the East and Midwest. In my opinion there is not sufficient accent on a limited number of themes, but instead a too-great receptivity to concepts from the whole panorama of the human sciences. But perhaps that is the male in me speaking, wanting to order the data around while Dr. Mead is still listening to them. Dr. Mead herself does the very useful thing, in an appendix, of saying where and from whom she learned what; so that the reader can appraise her perspective. Not for anything would she so standardize vantage points that one could not tell whether a book, or a review, was written by a man or a woman. (pp. 377-78)

David Riesman, "Of Men and Women," in The Nation, *Vol. 169, No. 16, October 15, 1949, pp. 376-78.*

ASHLEY MONTAGU

A significant contribution of [*Male and Female*] is the demonstration that cultural response to sexual difference is in some respects universally similar, and in other respects frequently dissimilar. Is the male's creativeness and greater dependence upon achievement a response to the shock of recognition that he can never have a baby, that this is unalterably the birthright of woman? Is this true of men in all societies? Is the female's sense of ambition limited by a rhythm of growth which initially makes her feel less secure than her brothers, plus the tolerable certainty of maternity? These are typical of the questions raised and critically answered in this important volume.

The purpose of the book is not to discover how the sexes differ, but rather how they complement one another. The peculiar qualities of the female have even yet not been allowed their full development. The analysis of what these qualities are, and how they may best be encouraged to develop, is a large part of the purpose of the book. Women see the world in different ways from men—by utilizing that vision the human race may learn to see itself more completely. This is an argument long overdue in the universe of science, and it is a matter for general congratulation that it should have found a contemporary advocate in so sensitive and able an anthropologist as Margaret Mead. The discussion throughout is kept on a high scientific plane and—it is very necessary to say it—nowhere is there the faintest odor of dust suggesting the dragging skirts of the feminist. (p. 152)

In a work which is so chock-full of insights, penetrating critical analyses, and heuristic suggestions Mead's references to homosexuality seem to me somewhat naive and uninformed. . . . As it is, Mead obfuscates the facts by offering what seems to me an ingenious though demonstrably unsound explanation of the infertility of unmarried females in non-literate societies. . . . When Mead writes that genetic theory has again dignified the paternal role to a genetic contribution equal to the maternal, it is obvious that she misses an excellent cue. Her statement is correct for the female offspring only. The male receives an *unequal* contribution, in the form of a deficient (Y) chromosome, from the father. This fact should have provided Mead with much rich grist for her mill. I, for one, am exceedingly sorry that she missed it. It is difficult to believe that Mead is serious when she states that the implied expectation of the permanency of marriage in the United States is "still based of course on statistics." . . . Surely that expectation is based on grounds rather more profound than a knowledge of the statistics relating to divorce and the permanency of marriage?

The chapter on marriage in America is one of the most original and stimulating in the book, and is destined to arouse much beneficial discussion. And so it is with the whole book. *Male and Female* is a substantive contribution to the understanding of the sociology of the status and relations of the sexes in the United States. (p. 153)

> *Ashley Montagu, "Book Reviews: 'Male and Female'," in* American Sociological Review, *Vol. 15, No. 1, February, 1950, pp. 152-53.*

C. E. M. JOAD

[*Male and Female*] is badly written, the style is obscure and it is unnecessarily overlaid with technical jargon. Miss Mead, in fact, has not mastered the art of saying what she means clearly, simply and shortly. As a result it is often extremely difficult to tell what her sentences mean. . . .

So much having been said by way of disparagement, it would be ungracious not to come out handsomely with the avowal that the book represents a great achievement; indeed, for originality of material, freshness of treatment and wisdom of conclusion, there has been nothing like it in the anthropological field since the days of Rivers and Malinowski. (p. 221)

The lessons to be drawn from this important book are, I think, two. First, that if you trace the way in which children grow to be men and women—if you note what they are taught, and particularly what they are taught about their bodies and the mysteries of birth, of marriage and of death, consider the behaviour which at different periods of their lives is expected of them and the ideals of maleness and femaleness which are put before them—you cannot but conclude that our civilization lays the worst possible foundation for happy, easy sexual relations in maturity. Secondly, that over the last fifty years standards of behaviour, and more particularly of sexual behaviour, have changed so rapidly and so radically that it is harder than it has ever been for young people to adjust themselves. How, indeed, can people be expected to adjust themselves to an environment which is always changing? (pp. 221-22)

> *C.E.M. Joad, "Courtship and Mating," in* The New Statesman & Nation *(© 1950 The Statesman & Nation Publishing Co. Ltd.), Vol. XXXIX, No. 990, February 25, 1950, pp. 221-22.*

GEORGE P. ELLIOTT

[In *Continuities in Cultural Evolution* Margaret Mead is] presenting her philosophy and prophesying, with recommendations for actions which would fulfill the prophecies. At best her book is a rationalist dream of salvation. To an anti-rationalist like me, it reads like a nightmare.

Here is a comparison so inexact as to obscure its meaning (which meaning, once got to, turns out to be based on an appalling assumption): "Just as it is important to recognize that such constancies as greater male size, strength, or locomotor ability, may be reversed in some species, it is also important to recognize that there may be many exchanges of models within a learned transmission and innovation system like human culture." To explain the term "exchange of models" she cites the various kinds and uses of houses which men have developed. But, in her sentence, the *biological* fact that in some species of animals the female is stronger than the male is treated as being logically coextensive with the *human* fact that people build and use houses for a wide variety of purposes.

The assumption behind this thought is the key assumption of the book: what men do makes sense and is justified only when seen as an evidence of that same evolution which makes bowerbirds, carrots, and bacilli do what they do. In this view, man is the living creature with the best tool, his conscious intelligence, and this intelligence is not the agent of his will (which assumes a soul) so much as it is a very superior, portable high-speed computer. Also, in this view, the furtherance of the evolutionary process is the reason for man not to exterminate himself but instead to see to it that he makes ever more efficient social arrangements. God is in His monument, and we had better take it upon ourselves to improve on evolution quick before we make The Big Mistake. Our highest duty is to keep on evolving.

In this book Miss Mead asks the big, unanswerable questions, like an earnest sophomore at a bull session. But because she cares whether life has a meaning and what gives it its meaning, and cares so much, she enlists the reader's sympathy. She is neither a nihilist fashionably saying that nothing matters, nor a Jehovah's Witness whose one desire is for the end of the world, nor a Julian Huxley envisaging a race of super-hominids produced by manipulation of our genes. She is an anthropological lady of good heart, and she is looking for a hope great enough to contain her fear that man may exterminate himself. She is a friend. The trouble is that she adopts one of the adversary's philosophies, and so she can also be considered an enemy.

To begin with, she has answers to unanswerable questions. Anybody who completes the sentence beginning "The purpose of life is to . . ." is already in trouble, no matter what he thinks the purpose may be. The intellectually scrupulous say it is a pseudo-problem. The religious say that only God can know the ultimate answers. Ordinary folk shrug uneasily and say it is all very mysterious. But the zealous cannot rest without pat answers, and Miss Mead is in this respect a zealot.

Indeed, she is and always has been a zealous missionary from one of the cults of Science to the illiberal or the not liberal enough, and like any missionary she is chiefly concerned to change our method of educating the young. She has been preaching improved methods of child-rearing for 45 years, but now that the urgency for improvement has become desperate, her remedies have become desperate too. For a long time her educational recommendations were aimed to improve our illiberal hominid minds; now she seems to think nothing less will serve than changing human nature radically. In other words, she wants the same ends as Julian Huxley but she is more practical about how to attain those ends. Which makes her an enemy of mine at least; I want my children to be people.

She has a fixed notion that, after the holocaust (which she takes to be probable), the human beings most likely to survive are some pre-literates living in out-of-the-way corners of the world. From my reading in the atomic scientists, I would guess that her notion has more to do with Rousseauistic fantasies than with the actualities of the next war, resistance to radioactivity not being one of the observed advantages of savagery.

Be that as it may, Miss Mead has a plan by which evolution may continue to work itself out through whichever group survives—whether all mankind, pockets of savages, or just some odds and ends of people. The human contribution to evolutionary progress she identifies with advances in civilization.

Not being a lunatic, she does not suppose that the progress of civilization is determined and irreversible, as, from what she says by the way, many of her colleagues apparently believe it is. Also, she knows that alterations in the condition of human kind come about through the decisions and actions of extraordinary individuals who happen to come along at the right time and to be working with the right little group of fellows.

This last point is apparently revolutionary in the circles in which she moves, though to anyone who has read many novels—Balzac, for example—it seems platitudinous; she spends scores and scores of pages arguing it eagerly, like a good-hearted sophomore fallen into a den of Humes refusing to grant that he is really there. The anthropological company she keeps is sometimes odd indeed. She quotes a Professor Leslie White as saying, "cultural processes can be explained without taking human organisms into account."

Roughly, her plan for saving us is this:

There should be conferences of the best. (In a polite, anemic way, she includes theologians and poets among the best, but she really means physical and behavioral scientists.) "A conference would provide a guaranteed opportunity to meet some vividly first-class people in a non-competitive and intense atmosphere. The conversation would come to an end and would be resumed. There would be freedom to talk and freedom to listen, and the web of meaning would be woven as we talked, making a new pattern before our eyes."

Among this selected group of intellectual aristocrats will be found the geniuses whose ideas will disseminate through the others and thereby alter, if anything can, human destiny for the better, that is to say, in the direction of evolutionary progress.

At these super bull sessions, the geniuses might figure out how to alter the minds of some primitives—perhaps by introducing certain changes in their technical or linguistic patterns of behavior—so that these potential survivors might re-evolve up to our level and charge ahead beyond where we are now, having learned from our errors how to avoid suicide. And, hopefully, the conferees can figure out ways by which to alter us now so that we will save ourselves from the danger we are in.

Since we ourselves created the danger, it follows, by my logic, that we can save ourselves from it only by changing ourselves. But Miss Mead does not mean a religious change of the human spirit; she means a biological improvement of the species—not through direct genetic tampering, since civilized people strongly resist that, but through a sort of cultural manipulation to which they are accustomed, and which makes Madison Avenue's practices seem to me old-fashioned and humane.

It is a rosy picture, till one begins to wonder how evil fits into it, or how it accommodates to evil. One begins to wonder how to keep an Edward Teller out of such a conference. He certainly has a first-class intellect and is greatly concerned about the big problems—to which he too has answers. Then one realizes that she had said "vividly first-class people," and included herself among the elect ("as we talked"). So she would probably leave Teller out because she would not think him a first-class person—which he surely isn't. And he would leave her out of *his* conference of destiny-arrangers, because he would not think hers a first-class intellect—which it surely isn't.

As for myself, I would leave them both out of *my* conference, because I think they are dangerously wrong. In fact, I think that such conferences, whoever chooses the members, are not likely to be attended by pure-hearted saints with right philosophies and so should not take place anyway. My trouble is that I think brains less important than souls.

So where does that leave destiny? Mostly right in the hands of premiers, parliaments and people, where it always was. Still, reality is shaped by dreams, by even the worst dreams. You should know about Miss Mead's dream at Yale, for it has a better chance than most of shaping your future, or, if not yours, that of your super-children. (pp. 4, 8)

George P. Elliott, "Coming of Age in Seminar," in Book Week—The Washington Post *(© I.H.T. Corporation; reprinted by permission), Vol. 1, No. 42, June 28, 1964, pp. 4, 8.*

JOHN R. PLATT

[In *Continuities in Cultural Evolution* Margaret Mead calls for the setting up of] research and development teams for social problems. . . . Such a manifesto, with its buttressing arguments and analysis of the conditions for success, will make this, I believe, one of the two or three most important books of the year for anyone interested in the process of social evolution and in the possibility of directing it more effectively to meet human needs.

Certainly at this time, when many of us have increasing feelings of helplessness or pointlessness and alienation, Dr. Mead's thesis is salutary. (p. 25)

Vico showed that social structures are made by man. The authors of the U.S. Constitution went on to show that new integrative structures could be rationally designed in advance, so as to combine stability with freedom and so as to bring prosperity and hope out of conflicting sovereignties and disorder. The atomic scientists, led by Leo Szilard with his faith in applying intelligence to social problems, have shown by a long series of innovations that this is still possible today, in areas as diverse as energy development, international stabilization, and population control. Margaret Mead supports this faith with her anthropological and social analysis of change, showing that history is indeed on the side of the creative innovators. Her book will give a rationale, and perhaps a new hope and confidence, to those who want to design better cultural patterns to enable all our children to enjoy their coming world of science and education and leisure. She challenges us urgently to lead, to act, to innovate; and most urgently of all, to begin to set up regular structures where innovations can continually be developed in response to developing human needs. (p. 26)

> *John R. Platt, "Physicist Reviews an Anthropologist's Analysis of Change," in* The Bulletin of the Atomic Scientists: a magazine of science and public affairs *(reprinted by permission of* The Bulletin of the Atomic Scientists: a magazine of science and public affairs; *copyright 1964 by the Educational Foundation for Nuclear Science, Inc.), Vol. XX, No. 10, December, 1964, pp. 25-6.*

MELVIN MADDOCKS

Miss Mead is in a bind [in *Culture and Commitment*]. . . . Anthropology advises her that there are no absolute values, only "customs," "traditions," "tribal patterns." Her observations persuade her that in her own "tribal pattern" the power is passing from the old to the young—and Miss Mead is not young.

Yet she is a teacher, and against her logic she has the impulse to teach. But What? She has postulated that only the young really know the New World and that "experience" is not only becoming useless but possibly misleading. Surely nothing is more dispensable than an obsolete relative value.

What gives this unblinking book its considerable worth is that its very existence contradicts Miss Mead's premises. Her scrupulousness leaves her the thinnest of margins to stand upon. In effect she says: "I cannot teach a commitment, but I can teach the need for one. I cannot teach values, but I can teach the value of values."

In practice she does more. She embodies the most specific values; a very particular—old-fashioned, if you will—integrity, curiosity and rationality. "Humanism" is what the old tribesmen called it.

One teaches finally by being. By the passion of her concern Miss Mead stands for commitments she might not dare to voice.

> *Melvin Maddocks, "That Gap Again," in* The Christian Science Monitor *(reprinted by permission from* The Christian Science Monitor; © *1970 The Christian Science Publishing Society; all rights reserved), February 19, 1970, p. 10.*

EDGAR Z. FRIEDENBERG

Miss Mead's heuristic approach to generational conflict [in *Culture and Commitment*] does not involve her in a discussion of the "politics of pot," or the politics of anything else. Her "postfigurative," "configurative" and "prefigurative" cultures—themselves highly reminiscent of David Riesman's societies in stages of "tradition direction," "inner direction" and "other direction"—say nothing at all about the moral or political content of intergenerational conflict. The result is wholly noncontroversial and makes no specific demands; in structure *Culture and Commitment* resembles "A Christmas Carol," with Margaret Mead suggesting that Scrooge be benign, but offering no explanation of or response to the despair of the young that the world has become as loveless, commercial and tawdry as Christmas itself. (p. 25)

> *Edgar Z. Friedenberg, "'Culture and Commitment'," in* The New York Times Book Review (© *1970 by The New York Times Company; reprinted by permission), March 8, 1970, pp. 1, 25, 29.*

PETER CLECAK

The crucial failures of Mead's analysis and prognosis [in *Culture and Commitment*] follow from her inability to demonstrate the actual bases for the prefigurative model. By contending that "our present situation is unique, without any parallel in the past," she tries to distinguish herself from other critics who interpret the current generation gap as merely an intensification of older, co-figurative patterns. But the best evidence she musters is the vague and innocuous claim that "the generation gap is worldwide." (p. 374)

[For Mead], "it is necessary to strip the occurrences in each country of their superficial, national, and immediately temporal aspects." Mead summarizes her essentialist thesis neatly: "The desire for a liberated form of communism in Czechoslovakia, the search for 'racial' equality in the United States, the desire to liberate Japan from military influence, the support given to excessive conservatism in Northern Ireland and Rhodesia or to the excesses of communism in Cuba—all these are particularistic forms. Youthful activism is common to them all."

Essentialist criticism ought not be summarily dismissed. The method of abstracting essential relationships from the bewildering mass of concrete particulars can yield impressive results (as, for example, in the case of Marx). But only if the critic selects the "right" features of the social whole and then proceeds to modify his initial abstractions with a series of qualifying assumptions based on detailed empirical investigation. Mead fails on both counts. She assumes (mistakenly, I think) that *a common* element is *the essential* element. Though it is probably too sweeping to claim that it happens "everywhere," "youthful activism" does occur on a global scale but with obvious and important national and cultural differences. So do a lot of other spectacular phenomena, including rapid technological change, revolution and counterrevolution.

Why, then, defoliate the global social landscape to focus on the "worldwide youth rebellion" as "the explanatory principle"? The reasons are too complex to sort out here. But two considerations strike me as fundamental. The increased awareness of the interdependence of people and nations requires that social critics grasp problems on a global scale. The main issue of our time *is* human survival and the creation of a decent world. Since the world now actually presents itself as Hegelian, the critic requires global vision: "The truth is the whole," as Hegel declared.

Paradoxically, however, the truth remains inaccessible, since the individual critic's vision of the whole is hopelessly inadequate to the complex and enormous realities. He lacks the categories of structured vision as well as the means to demonstrate hypotheses as sweeping as Mead's. While the essentialist mode still serves as a beginning of social analysis, it often leads the critic toward myth rather than toward science. Instead of being tested and qualified, the highly abstract hypotheses are fashioned into myths that explain—in a highly simplified fashion—the sources of individual and social unrest.

If the analyses drift toward myth, so do the solutions. As Mead suggests at the outset: "The prophet who fails to present a bearable alternative and yet preaches doom is part of the trap that he postulates." Typically, when the global problems of the present seem—and are—overwhelming, critics either withdraw into private despair or imagine solutions in—*and by*—the future. For a number of contemporary social critics—including Herbert Marcuse, Theodore Roszak, N. O. Brown, and to a lesser extent, Mead—youth has taken on the mythical role of a modern cavalry galloping to the rescue of an embattled world civilization. As the living embodiment of an unknown future, young people become the missing element in an otherwise hopeless characterization of the world. They are also the moving element; hence, Mead focuses on the current generation gap as the potential engine of "rapid, revolutionary" change. In spite of her intentions, she finally posits a *deux ex machina*.

Only the young—especially the rebellious minority—fully realize that the old ways of solving major social problems no longer work: "The past for them is a colossal, unintelligible failure, and the future may hold nothing but the destruction of the planet. Caught between the two, they are ready to make way for something new by a kind of social bulldozing. . . ." Now, Mead points out at least two crucial flaws in her alternative that make it unbearable, or at least impractical. "The young do not know what must be done, but they feel that there must be a better way." Secondly, their lack of power matches their lack of knowledge: "those who have no power also have no routes to power except through those against whom they are rebelling."

Instead of pursuing a new direction from this impasse, however, Mead presents the contradiction as a conclusion: "Effective, rapid revolutionary change, in which no one is guillotined and no one is forced into exile, depends upon the cooperation of a large number of those in power with the dispossessed who are seeking power." Her prefigurative model is designed to serve as a bridge between the old and the young, the powerful and the powerless, the dark present and a brighter future. The young represent an unknown and unknowable future. If there are to be massive revolutionary solutions to massive problems, the young must discover them. And the elders who have failed must redeem themselves by facilitating the transfer of power.

In an obvious sense, of course, Mead is right: the young *do* embody the future. Moreover, in advanced Western countries (and probably elsewhere as well), they are poorly equipped—at home and at school— for their difficult roles as inheritors of an unstable world. But surely they cannot create a wholly new reality. Nor should they be expected to. The problem of human survival may not be solvable. It is certain that whatever partial solutions emerge will not depend on one generation of social bulldozers backed up by a chorus of elders cheering on the side lines of a global construction site.

Though stated in social terms, Mead's analysis and prescriptions finally become parts of a quasi-aesthetic document. The critical terminology partially disguises the mythical content, lending it an air of credibility. But the force of the myth comes *via* the aesthetic form in which the terrors of the present modulate into a hopeful, though highly tentative, vision of the future.

The myth, however, is not very convincing, if only because of the thin social surface of the book. For example, Mead claims to go beyond others who see the future as no more than an extension of the past. Yet the entire schema she presents— of post-, co-, and prefigurative patterns—has its own inner logic and conventional symmetry. Although it allows for an unknowable future, the prefigurative model constitutes a quasi-aesthetic extension and resolution of the previous two patterns. It may be an emotionally satisfying form imposed on a confusing world. It may give the illusion that the present impasse will end. Yet when one tries to imagine translating the solution into social practice, the myth loses its power.

Perhaps my criticism only confirms one of Mead's leading assumptions—the impossibility of imagining the future in terms of the past. Still, she illustrates her own assumption while claiming to escape its implications. And in the process, the present virtually disappears from her sparse critical landscape. It becomes a nightmare between a secure post-figurative past and an unknown prefigurative future. Masking as social criticism, the myth of youth presumably exorcises the nightmare. Finally, however, the unconscious aesthetic dimension fails. For men live and act in the present—in the "superficial, national, and immediately temporal aspects" of things. And it is in this crevice between past and future that men must try to survive and flourish. Mead's post-figurative and co-figurative schema yield many important insights before they dissolve into an unproductive and, for me, unsettling myth. (pp. 374-76)

> *Peter Clecak, "Immigrants in Time," in* The Nation *(copyright 1970* The Nation *magazine, The Nation Associates, Inc.), Vol. 210, No. 12, March 30, 1970, pp. 373-76.*

FRANK F. FURSTENBERG, JR.

Culture and Commitment [is] both a hypothesis and a conclusion with little evidence to connect the two.

The process of cultural transmission has become disintegrated in contemporary societies. (p. 243)

Mead's prescription is to "create new models for adults who can teach their children not what to learn, but how to learn and not what they should be committed to, but the value of commitment." . . . Many will find the argument plausible and the conclusion appealing. However, other readers who are more familiar with existing empirical evidence will question Mead's premise and be skeptical of her answer.

They will wonder whether there is, as Dr. Mead suggests, a single universal explanation for generational conflict. It might be said that a cross-cultural perspective is most useful when it illuminates historical and structural differences between societies, and least satisfactory when it insists on discovering common patterns in all societies. In any case, it remains to be shown that generational conflict in New Guinea or Latin America emanates from the same sources as conflict in the United States.

Furthermore, locating this conflict in the family obscures the political stakes that are being contested. Youth are not trying to wrest power away from their parents but from political, economic, and social institutions that have long been accustomed to having and doing things their own way. The family may be one of these institutions, but it is hardly the only one, or the most important one. The conflict then is less over who teaches whom, than what is taught, and how knowledge is to be used.

Finally, Mead's argument that youth lack commitment is particularly questionable. One might assert just the opposite— generational conflict began when youth became committed. If this is true, then the problem is not a deterioration of values but a competition of values, and viewing it as simply generational makes it appear to be little more than a family squabble. (pp. 243-44)

> *Frank F. Furstenberg, Jr., "Book Department: 'Culture and Commitment: A Study of the Generation Gap',"* in The Annals of the American Academy of Political and Social Science *(© 1970, by The American Academy of Political and Social Science), Vol. 391, September, 1970, pp. 243-44.*

COLIN CROUCH

There is something of value in [Margaret Mead's] anthropological perspective on the current situation [in *Culture and Commitment*]. Essentially the generation which enters this world of the future is seen as a pioneer generation, entering a world in which existing knowledge and institutions are incapable of dealing with the problems, incapable of subjecting to human control the developments which men themselves have set in train. . . .

[An] analysis of this kind is important when explaining the present alienation of youth, and it is for this purpose that Margaret Mead develops her argument. But although she seems to be arguing that these persepctives of modern youth have a positive contribution to make, it is difficult to discover precisely what it is meant to be. (p. 305)

[What] forms of 'world order' are advocated by a group which is distinguished chiefly by its rejection of institutions at virtually every level? . . . [The] author suggests that the old must admit the young to participation in power so that 'the young, free to act on their own initiative, can lead their elders in the direction of the unknown'. The superiority of the young, then, would seem to consist, not in their possessing a knowledge relevant to their times, but in their having no knowledge at all apart from a certainty of the failure of their elders.

Doubtless, Mrs. Mead has captured in her concept of a prefigurative culture much of the essence of the contemporary youth culture: the rejection of institutions as soon as they achieve some measure of structure and routine, the total rejection of inherited ideas, the cult of transience and spontaneity. But are these the elements from which a successful approach to the management of modern technological society can be forged? Are there perhaps dangers in emphasising the novelty of our situation to the extent that we reject certain lessons of the past which, properly adapted, may be vital points of stability amidst the novelty? (pp. 305-06)

> *Colin Crouch, "Young Leaders and Old Wisdoms,"* in New Statesman *(© 1970 The Statesman & Nation Publishing Co. Ltd.), Vol. 80, No. 2060, September 11, 1970, pp. 305-06.*

ALICE B. KEHOE

A Way of Seeing is a record, as Mead remarks in her foreword, of "personal responses to events at different moments in time." Thus she considers student riots, the generation gap, and couples who flee the anonymity of the city. Mead claims, however, that her responses are more than merely personal: "It is the anthropological viewpoint that gives focus and continuity to these many different essays on our contemporary life." This anthropologist, for one, cannot accept that statement.

In this book Mead calls for two kinds of legal marriage, one intended for cohabitation without the production of children, the other intended for parenthood—more difficult to enter into and to dissolve. . . . A legalization of cohabitation with no expectation of offspring is, to my knowledge, a unique invention by Mead and quite counter to the anthropological generalization that marriage is basically a means of ensuring the physical support and proper socialization of children.

Mead urges the universal adoption of the language of a small literate nation as a second language for all peoples to facilitate the evolution of a true world community. Her argument, following an excellent short exposition of the principle of redundancy in language, is that artificial languages lack redundancy and therefore lack richness, while the major spoken languages now threaten to exterminate the linguistic heritages of the politically unimportant peoples. (Emphasizing the desirability of all peoples learning a second language would presumably protect the minor ones against linguistic imperialism). Anthropological experience would suggest that the strong but subtle link between language and cognition renders the learning of a language without a true immersion in its associated culture a superficial and transient exercise. Teaching Albanian or Andamanese to every child in the world would simply fill the world with people who briefly memorized and then forgot Albanian or Andamanese, as the United States is filled with people who took French in high school but are wholly unilingual. If Mead were thinking this problem out as an anthropologist, she might suggest Liverpudlian English as a universal language because the popularity of the Beatles gives that dialect an emotional effect and an experiential background promising true fluency among millions of youths.

Mead believes households should contain more than one woman, partly to accustom children to various personalities and sources of care, partly to facilitate the careers of those mothers who wish them. Again, anthropologists may be familiar with multi-woman households; but such polygynous or extended households contain only many women doing the same tasks. It is here that the true source of Mead's way of seeing becomes apparent. Mead's own mother was a sociologist, and both as a child and as a mother herself she has lived in the household type she recommends. An anthropologist notices that Mead, like nearly all her fellow humans, holds values reflecting the cultural pattern in which she matured.

The sum effect of Mead's collected essays is Margaret Mead, vigorous, intelligent, sincerely desirous of bettering the world. (pp. 538-39)

> *Alice B. Kehoe, "Book Reviews: 'A Way of Seeing',"* in American Sociological Review *(copyright © 1971 by The American Sociological Association), Vol. 36, No. 3, June, 1971, pp. 538-39.*

WILL DAVISON

Several broad themes stand out [in **"Hope and Survival"**]—science and technology, religion and spirituality, culture and civilization—but, typically, all are important to [Margaret Mead] only as they relate to man past, present and future.

The greatest, and most interesting, part of the book deals with culture, which is, of course, the author's forte. **"Cultural Man"** . . . is a brilliant essay on the meaning of anthropology and how it can be used to enhance and reinforce Christianity. And with what knowledge and delight she writes not only about children but also about the aged!

The book's longest chapter, and perhaps its finest, **"The Future as the Basis for Establishing a Shared Culture,"** . . . anticipates (and is, in some measure, probably responsible for) innovations like: the development of glyphs, which are graphic representations, each of which stands for an idea (male, female, water, etc.); our adaptation of the metric system; education through the use of documentary films; the creation of a common second language. . . .

[Here] in abundance are the now familiar earmarks of Margaret Mead's work: disinterested observation; wisdom and understanding; hopeful anticipation; liberal open-endedness. The book is an interesting journey through the evolution of her thought over the last two decades.

> *Will Davison, "Twentieth Century Faith," in* The New York Times Book Review *(© 1973 by The New York Times Company; reprinted by permission), January 7, 1973, p. 37.*

SHEILA K. JOHNSON

[If] one looks carefully at [Margaret Mead's] early work—and Mead says without a trace of false modesty that by the age of thirty-four, "I had what amounted to a lifetime of completed work behind me"—it becomes obvious that there was never a sharp break between her scientific research and her punditry. Even her earliest book, *Coming of Age in Samoa,* contains two rather preachy concluding chapters about the implications of Samoan education for our own society. Her later columns in *Redbook,* lectures on the generation gap, and raps on race are no more than an extension of this early propensity to moralize. In fact, one would have to say that only a minuscule proportion of Mead's output is truly scientific. Her monographs about the Arapesh, the Omaha, and the Manus kinship system are competent—if not very original—works of social science. *Coming of Age in Samoa* is aimed at a popular audience and written in an anecdotal style, but still deals with an interesting and important theoretical question. Significantly, it was a question not chosen by Mead herself but set for her by her teacher, Franz Boas. (p. 71)

Today scientists laugh at such a categorical, one-sided resolution of the nature-nurture problem; but in 1928 Mead's demonstration of the cultural impact on adolescent behavior was as important as Malinowski's demonstration that the Oedipus complex did not exist in a matrilineal society. Mead subsequently modified her views about the impact of inborn traits—particularly with reference to male and female roles and temperament—but her work on this subject remained anecdotal and illustrative at a time when other social and biological scientists were turning to experimental or carefully controlled research. As a result, her books *Sex and Temperament in Three Primitive Societies* and *Male and Female* have been misunderstood and attacked from all sides. *Male and Female,*, for example, has been criticized by Diana Trilling for ignoring Freud's insights into the psychological impact of being male or female; at the same time it was roasted by Betty Friedan for being a sexist tract urging women to have babies and be "feminine." The problem, I think, is that Mead's discursive approach often permits her to stand on all sides of all issues and leaves her open to such attacks.

A different but related case is the current controversy over Mead's views about the generation gap. As the anthropologist Cora du Bois has pointed out, Mead has long been interested in sociocultural change viewed as generational interaction. That is to say, in several books and articles—most notably in *New Lives for Old* . . . , her restudy of the Manus people whom she first described in *Growing Up in New Guinea*—Mead has focused upon various generations as they are simultaneously exposed to rapid social change. Again, because she favors an anecdotal approach, one is treated primarily to descriptions of incidents in which a father and son disagree or a young middle-aged man states proudly to the visiting anthropologist, "We used to do things this way, but now we do them differently." It is all very persuasive, but no evidence is provided to indicate the prevalence of the habits or traits she describes, and—more serious for an anthropologist purporting to deal with personality change in response to social change—she offers no psychological data, such as depth interviews or responses to psychological tests. In the case of her second field trip among the Manus, such tests were administered in great profusion, but—as Mead admits in the Appendix of *New Lives for Old*—they had not yet been analyzed when she wrote her book.

Her [assertions in *Culture and Commitment*] about social change as a generational phenomenon are so broad as to defy the rules of scientific evidence altogether. . . . Mead's thesis is that children born post-1945 are living in a world in which they feel at home but which their elders can barely cope with, let alone comprehend. . . .

One may well ask what sort of relevance Margaret Mead herself, at age seventy-one, can have for the trackless young; but she has explained that in addition to having been raised almost seven decades ahead of her time (which puts her back at the culturally innocent age of one) the generational crisis we are facing "is, in fact, perceived most accurately not by the young, but by their discerning and prophetic elders." A somewhat less apocalyptic explanation, which has a long and honorable history in anthropology, is that there is always a generation gap of sorts between parents and their children in response to which children often form alliances with the grandparental generation against the middle, power-holding group. According to this view, the young and old ends of the age-spectrum are hostile to the middle sector because they lack the status that an achievement-oriented society awards those who are productive. This view also assumes that the situation is natural and resolves itself: the young become middle-aged and find the world less easy to understand than they once thought; the old eventually die off.

I raise these points about Mead's work not because I dislike popularized anthropology: it is, in fact, my favorite bedtime reading. But I am disturbed when a famous popularizer tries to pass himself, or herself, off as scientifically beyond reproach. And though it may be admirable for some individuals to attempt to act as bridges between the worlds of hard science and popular culture, there is a great temptation to use the cachet acquired in one area to enhance one's status in the other. Thus while Mead is not so highly regarded as an anthropologist by other anthropologists, she is often deferred to by them (particularly at large and public meetings) because of her non-academic reputation; and when she testifies or speaks out publicly on matters she knows little or nothing about (marijuana, arms control, space flight), she is listened to because of her supposed expertise as an anthropologist, I am reminded, in this connection, of a Berkeley cocktail party I once attended in honor of C. P. Snow. At one end of the room several literary critics and novelists were saying, *sotto voce,* "Well, he's really a terrible novelist, but I hear he's quite a good physicist," while at the other end of the room a group of famous physicists were saying to each other, "Of course, he's no good as a physicist, but I hear he's written some nice novels." It was the first time it had occurred to me that the outcome of attempting to bridge two worlds might be simply a pratfall between two stools. (p. 72)

> *Sheila K. Johnson, "A Look at Margaret Mead," in* Commentary *(reprinted by permission; all rights reserved), Vol. 55, No. 3, March, 1973, pp. 70-2.*

LISA PEATTIE

Field work is itself a social process. Like other social processes it constitutes a set of interactions which restate and redefine reality, and which articulate and structure values. It is a process as worth understanding as any of the social and cultural phenomena on which the field worker reports.

Yet on this process, it must be admitted, Mead sheds very little light [in **"Letters from the Field"**]. These letters from the field, are, perhaps, not the place to look. Mead says that she began to write them for a small group of friends; as time went on, knowing that they were passed to others she adapted to "an audience at one step removed from intimacy." They are in tone, vivid, chatty and personal—but with limits. "It would have made no more sense to broadcast one's miseries than to have cast messages onto the waters of the wide Pacific . . . nor would it have made sense to write in detail about the day-to-day intricacies of field work."

It also seems to be true that it took the evolution of field work practice itself, with various anthropologists commenting on each other's work, to generate among professionals a degree of self-awareness about the problems of "disciplined subjectivity." It is only in the later letters that Mead reveals herself as musing on these issues.

Yet even these musings are at a general level, and seem to carry no freight of troubling introspection. Introspection seems not to be Mead's mode. She tells us that while she kept a journal in the field, it was a bare chronology of events, helpful for sorting field notes. What would Doris Lessing make or Anaïs Nin have made of this extraordinary person? (p. 49)

> *Lisa Peattie, "Samoa: Visited and Reported," in* The New York Times Book Review *(© 1978 by The New York Times Company; reprinted by permission), January 8, 1978, pp. 1, 49.*

NANCY McDOWELL

Margaret Mead was one of the best ethnographers in the American cultural anthropological tradition: her fieldwork and published reports stand as models for any beginning field-worker to follow even today. Though most of her major fieldwork was done in the 1920s and 1930s, her descriptions read as thoroughly modern and contemporary. . . .

Apparent throughout her writings is her fascination with cultural diversity. Clearly, her first fieldwork in Samoa, her first encounter with another human tradition, had a profound and lasting impact. One need only compare *An Inquiry into the Question of Cultural Stability in Polynesia* . . . , a thesis written predominantly before her first trip, a lackluster exposition of traits (canoes, houses, tattoos) and their travels, with anything written later to see the extent to which human beings and their lives, their cultural creations, became her central concern. This focus is what gives life to her ethnography, a vividness unmatched and unrivaled in the professional anthropological literature. (p. 278)

The fundamental premise that data are always raw material to be used to further understanding of human behavior and to improve the quality of life is explicitly behind all of Mead's work and explains its dual nature. Simply, data can be used in two ways: (1) to enlighten nonanthropologists, educated laypeople, and professionals in other fields, and to inform social-policy decisions; (2) to provide the material for professional scientific work and theory-building on the nature of human behavior.

Many of Mead's ethnographic publications are specifically designed for use by the general public . . . ; they are meant to inform and enlighten, to educate on the nature of human cultural diversity. Further, she holds the mirror in which we, specifically Americans, might see and understand ourselves better. In *Coming of Age in Samoa* . . . , for example, she informs us that adolescence need not be traumatic, that such a stormy period is a cultural creation. (p. 279)

Mead is also keenly aware of the scientific use of data. She frequently makes reference to other societies as "natural laboratories" . . . but goes beyond by explicitly ensuring that her data are of use to other, perhaps later, scholars with more advanced theories. . . . She once chided participants in a conference for being inadequately aware that data must be in a form useful to researchers in the future. . . . She directs readers to alternative ways of using and analyzing the data she published . . . , and frequently suggests areas needing future investigation. . . .

Most significant is her concern for the precision and accuracy of the data she gathered; unsound and weak data are of use to no one. . . . (pp. 279-80)

Mead is acutely aware that data derived from the study of primitive societies are indeed a precious commodity; never again might field-workers have access to such human creations, and each person is obligated to report with scientific precision and completeness. She presents her material in such a way that it is not only clear but useful to others. . . .

One of the most striking characteristics of Mead's work is that every major body of ethnographic material (except the Mundugumor and Tchambuli in *Sex and Temperament* . . .) contains an *explicit* statement of methodology. She clearly delineates assumptions, aims, and major questions being asked. . . . The focus of each report is clear and the reader knows what, if any, aspects of the society were ignored or discussed superficially, and why. . . . The methodological statement is sometimes a simple description of participant observation with additional detail, such as whether formal interviews were conducted. But, because Mead used so many new techniques in the field, her discussions of methodology are occasionally elaborate and complex. (p. 280)

In presenting her material accurately and precisely, Mead is a careful and exceptionally honest ethnographer. She describes the conditions within which fieldwork was conducted, including the extent to which the presence of the investigator might warp the material. . . . (p. 281)

Mead's deft use of individual examples is also of note. Actual people appear repeatedly in all of her work; she thought it important to know not only what was done but also who did it. Often the example is designed to illustrate some general principle but more frequently it involves a deviation, a person or behavior "out of the ordinary." Such examples are always well chosen and, further, are clearly labeled and analyzed as deviants. They always serve to further the reader's understanding of how the culture actually works. One of Mead's greatest talents is using individual situations and people to illustrate the complexity of how general principles work and how the same concept can have differential impact on people depending on their personalities, histories, or situations. . . .

If Mead's data were only useful and accurate, she would be a good ethnographer. What makes her more than that is the keenness of her observation and insight, the deftness of her description. The ease and grace of her style often mask the subtlety of her perception, but the observations and perceptions are always insightful. . . . It is this combination of perception with professional attention to accuracy and detail that makes for superb ethnography.

One of Mead's major interests is in pattern, the regularities in human cultural life. Although she is concerned with the individual, it is the relationship between individual and pattern that is of special importance. Child rearing is one aspect of the process by means of which people incorporate the pattern and thereby become cultured beings. Her keen sense and use of personality and individual differences only serve to heighten our awareness of the pattern, its complexity, and the relationship between it and deviation. (p. 283)

The continual interplay between pattern and individual relates to another striking characteristic of Mead's ethnography: the extent to which her concern is predominantly with process and system. Her descriptions are never static, always dynamic. Whether she is discussing the development of personality or the workings of the social structure or indeed the interaction between the two, she sees a fluid, dynamic, processual system, something we are only now beginning to appreciate fully. She perceives human cultures to be very complex systems composed of a variety of elements: social, political, and economic structures, personality and ethos, eidos, ideology—all aspects of sociocultural life are combined in a web of interconnect-

edness. . . . Because her conception of system is more far-reaching and inclusive than mere social structure, she is able to perceive subtle and fascinating relationships between diverse elements. She delineates connections, for example, between the symbolic richness of a culture and the way in which the stages of child growth are recognized and organized . . . ; between discontinuities in child maturation and a people's ability to change . . . ; between the way in which the Balinese conceptualize their bodies and the way in which they build their houses. . . .

Mead's continuing interest in the discrepancy between ideal cultural formulations and what actual people do is a significant element in her conceptualization of the system as a whole. (pp. 283-84)

Mead clearly recognizes that time is also an important dimension in these dynamic systems. Her discussion and analysis of the Samoan council or *fono,* for example, demonstrates that ". . . the ideal fixity is continuously subjected to reinterpretation and change." . . . She examines the complex operation of the *fono* through time and isolates, as one important variable, the divisiveness of childhood peer groups and allegiances: this early factionalism is carried into adult life and provides the germ for *fono* fission. What she suggests here is something akin to a developmental cycle for *fono* division. . . . (p. 284)

Mead never neglects the influence of Western contact and colonialization . . . ; change of this sort is a primary interest. There is a considerable range of variation in her ethnographic treatments of change. On the one hand, there are relatively circumscribed accounts of change in one particular aspect of the culture, such as the analysis of the profound impact of Western markets on Balinese art. On the other, there is the exhaustive, detailed study of radical changes on Manus spanning almost fifty years. . . .

Always attuned to fine cultural differences, Mead carefully differentiates the group specifically studied from its close neighbors, and thus provides minute and detailed comparisons. The differences between Manua and the rest of Samoa are explicit . . . ; the Manus culture is clearly a variant within the Admiralty Island group . . . ; Beach, Mountain, and Plains Arapesh are differentiated and described. . . .

Mead's recognition of, and interest in, regional networks leads her to exacting comparisons within a culture area, an approach especially appropriate in the Pacific. Her foremost concern is with influence, relationships, and variations on a general pattern. . . .

The most significant use of comparative material is to highlight cultural variation by contrasting diverse constellations and to evolve theories and generalizations about human behavior. For these purposes Mead often uses her own field materials (surely the juxtaposition and comparison in *Sex and Temperament* . . . is striking) or other Oceanic data, but she does not restrict herself to one area. If one is to ". . . think comparatively in terms of systems" . . . , then the systems being used are not geographically defined or restricted. She compares, for example, Arapesh "affective coherence" with Murngin "cognitive coherence." . . . Such insightful comparisons are interwoven throughout her ethnography.

Mead does not hesitate to make theoretical comments whenever appropriate; indeed, she is continually aware of the very close interplay between data and whatever we conclude from them. Critical theoretical points, of course, are her emphasis on process and system; the discrepancy between the real and the ideal; ethos, eidos, and the relationships among these within the context of system. And there are others.

Mead is among the first to emphasize the importance of network and to question the validity of basing ethnographic work strictly on a "society" or "community." (p. 285)

Although economic systems were certainly not a primary interest to her, she makes significant observations about their nature, especially Melanesian ones. She draws an analogy between Manus marriage payments and investing . . . , discusses the significance of "compulsive barter" in the Manus scarcity economy . . . , and suggests similarities between Arapesh exchange partners *(buanyin)* and banking. . . . In what almost seem to be tangential asides, she makes considerable contributions to the study of kinship. She asserts that behavior, not genealogical position alone, defines Manus kinship . . . and tries to grapple with the nature of complementary filiation without the concept. . . . She offers insights into the continuing "extension" versus "category" controversy surrounding kinship terminology: in Manus, the extensionist argument is appropriate but the categorical approach meshes better with the Samoan data. . . .

One of the most interesting theoretical contributions Mead makes in her ethnographies is the recognition that human cultures may indeed be integrated systems but that they may also embody tensions and internal contradictions. She compares Samoa, Tonga, and Fiji in terms of the way in which each manifests a tension between two contrasting principles, locality and descent group, and maintains a delicate (but different) balance between the two. . . .

Mead's data provide grist for a variety of theoretical mills but her own use of the data is often sophisticated and frequently avant-garde. (p. 286)

One of the goals of ethnography must be that of cultural translation; no one has yet surpassed Mead's abilities to communicate the essence, the touch, smell, and feel of the totality of another way of life as well as its structure and organization. An intuitive empathy pervades her work and conveys a sense that the people are indeed living human beings deserving of respect and concern. It is not only the ethnographer who ". . .

becomes entranced with the beauty and integration . . ." or the aesthetic creation of another people, but the reader as well. (p. 297)

> *Nancy McDowell, "The Oceanic Ethnography of Margaret Mead," in* American Anthropologist *(copyright 1980 by the American Anthropological Association; reproduced by permission of the American Anthropological Association), Vol. 82, No. 2, 1980, pp. 278-303.*

DORIS GRUMBACH

["**Aspects of the Present**"] demonstrates the variety and depth of [Margaret Mead's] interests: She cared passionately about the shape and direction of American culture (in the same way that she had cared in her anthropological studies about the cultures of the South Seas), about peace, the problems and rights of women, the survival of the American family, the health and education of children, about clean air, about the values of the American past and its rituals of celebration—Christmas, Halloween, the Bicentennial and other events.

But the most interesting of these thoughtful pieces (on which she collaborated with anthropologist and friend Rhoda Metraux) are the most radical ones. In 1927 she wrote: "The time has come, I think, when we must recognize bisexuality as a normal form of human behavior." At 74 her acute and sympathetic "way of seeing" (to use the title of her earlier collection of essays) made it possible for her to acknowledge "our human capacity to love members of both sexes." Her views on crime and punishment are equally "mind-expanding" (her term for changing traditional attitudes toward taboos and cultural beliefs). She writes: "We make our own criminals"—and later: "We have concentrated too much on criminals . . . instead of asking what needs they serve and what general attitudes in our society—or in the whole of modern society—are reflected in their actions." . . .

[Margaret Mead's is] a rich and humane vision of the freedom possible in our lives.

> *Doris Grumbach, "Nonfiction in Brief: 'Aspects of the Present'," in* The New York Times Book Review *(© 1980 by The New York Times Company; reprinted by permission), July 27, 1980, p. 13.*

C(harles) Wright Mills

1916-1962

An American sociologist and educator, Mills was one of post-war America's leading radical critics. In *White Collar* (1953) he examined the "new middle classes"—the managers, professionals, office workers, salespeople, bureaucrats, and technicians—and analyzed the social and political implications of their growing prominence. Mills argued that these groups—whom he called "the managed personnel of a garrison state"—represent a new kind of citizen who is powerless and subservient. *The Power Elite* (1956) shifts focus to the "elite" whose members, according to Mills, control the major organizations of modern society. A challenge to pluralist assumptions about the structure of society, this book is particularly controversial because it contests both the dominant view in the social sciences and the self image of most Americans. Though Mills has been criticized for his theoretical position and methodology, his admirers consider his work a challenge to the prevailing conceptions of how sociological study should be undertaken, and regard him a major exemplar of the tradition of critical scholarship.

Excerpt from *WHITE COLLAR: THE AMERICAN MIDDLE CLASSES*

America is neither the nation of horse-traders and master builders of economic theory, nor the nation of go-getting, claim-jumping, cattle-rustling pioneers of frontier mythology. Nor have the traits rightly or wrongly associated with such historic types carried over into the contemporary population to any noticeable degree. Only a fraction of this population consists of free private enterprisers in any economic sense; there are now four times as many wage-workers and salary workers as independent entrepreneurs. 'The struggle for life,' William Dean Howells wrote in the 'nineties, 'has changed from a free fight to an encounter of disciplined forces, and the free fighters that are left get ground to pieces . . .'

If it is assumed that white-collar employees represent some sort of continuity with the old middle class of entrepreneurs, then it may be said that for the last hundred years the middle classes have been facing the slow expropriation of their holdings, and that for the last twenty years they have faced the spectre of unemployment. Both assertions rest on facts, but the facts have not been experienced by the middle class as a *double* crisis. The property question is not an issue to the new middle class of the present generation. That was fought out, and lost, before World War I, by the old middle class. The centralization of small properties is a development that has affected each generation back to our great-grandfathers, reaching its climax in the Progressive Era. It has been a secular trend of too slow a tempo to be felt as a continuing crisis by middle-class men and women, who often seem to have become more commodity-minded than property-minded. Yet history is not always enacted consciously; if expropriation is not felt as crisis, still it is a basic fact in the ways of life and the aspirations of the new middle class; and the facts of unemployment *are* felt as fears, hanging over the white-collar world.

Photograph by Yaroslava Surmach Mills

By examining white-collar life, it is possible to learn something about what is becoming more typically 'American' than the frontier character probably ever was. What must be grasped is the picture of society as a great salesroom, an enormous file, an incorporated brain, a new universe of management and manipulation. By understanding these diverse white-collar worlds, one can also understand better the shape and meaning of modern society as a whole, as well as the simple hopes and complex anxieties that grip all the people who are sweating it out in the middle of the twentieth century.

The troubles that confront the white-collar people are the troubles of all men and women living in the twentieth century. If these troubles seem particularly bitter to the new middle strata, perhaps that is because for a brief time these people felt themselves immune to troubles.

Before the First World War there were fewer little men, and in their brief monopoly of high-school education they were in fact protected from many of the sharper edges of the workings of capitalist progress. They were free to entertain deep illusions about their individual abilities and about the collective trustworthiness of the system. As their number has grown, however, they have become increasingly subject to wage-worker conditions. Especially since the Great Depression have white-collar people come up against all the old problems of capitalist society. They have been racked by slump and war and even by boom. They have learned about impersonal unemployment in depressions and about impersonal death by technological violence in war. And in good times, as prices rose faster than salaries, the money they thought they were making was silently taken away from them.

The material hardship of nineteenth-century industrial workers finds its parallel on the psychological level among twentieth-century white-collar employees. The new Little Man seems to have no firm roots, no sure loyalties to sustain his life and give it a center. He is not aware of having any history, his past being as brief as it is unheroic; he has lived through no golden age he can recall in time of trouble. Perhaps because he does not know where he is going, he is in a frantic hurry; perhaps because he does not know what frightens him, he is paralyzed with fear. This is especially a feature of his political life, where the paralysis results in the most profound apathy of modern times.

The uneasiness, the malaise of our time, is due to this root fact: in our politics and economy, in family life and religion—in practically every sphere of our existence—the certainties of the eighteenth and nineteenth centuries have disintegrated or been destroyed and, at the same time, no new sanctions or justifications for the new routines we live, and must live, have taken hold. So there is no acceptance and there is no rejection, no sweeping hope and no sweeping rebellion. There is no plan of life. Among white-collar people, the malaise is deep-rooted; for the absence of any order of belief has left them morally defenseless as individuals and politically impotent as a group. Newly created in a harsh time of creation, white-collar man has no culture to lean upon except the contents of a mass society that has shaped him and seeks to manipulate him to its alien ends. For security's sake, he must strain to attach himself somewhere, but no communities or organizations seem to be thoroughly his. This isolated position makes him excellent material for synthetic molding at the hands of popular culture—print, film, radio, and television. As a metropolitan dweller, he is especially open to the focused onslaught of all the manufactured loyalties and distractions that are contrived and urgently pressed upon those who live in worlds they never made.

In the case of the white-collar man, the alienation of the wage-worker from the products of his work is carried one step nearer to its Kafka-like completion. The salaried employee does not make anything, although he may handle much that he greatly desires but cannot have. No product of craftsmanship can be his to contemplate with pleasure as it is being created and after it is made. Being alienated from any product of his labor, and going year after year through the same paper routine, he turns his leisure all the more frenziedly to the *ersatz* diversion that is sold him, and partakes of the synthetic excitement that neither eases nor releases. He is bored at work and restless at play, and this terrible alternation wears him out.

In his work he often clashes with customer and superior, and must almost always be the standardized loser: he must smile and be personable, standing behind the counter, or waiting in the outer office. In many strata of white-collar employment, such traits as courtesy, helpfulness, and kindness, once intimate, are now part of the impersonal means of livelihood. Self-alienation is thus an accompaniment of his alienated labor.

When white-collar people get jobs, they sell not only their time and energy but their personalities as well. They sell by the week or month their smiles and their kindly gestures, and they must practice the prompt repression of resentment and aggression. For these intimate traits are of commercial relevance and required for the more efficient and profitable distribution of goods and services. Here are the new little Machiavellians, practicing their personable crafts for hire and for the profit of others, according to rules laid down by those above them.

In the eighteenth and nineteenth centuries, rationality was identified with freedom. The ideas of Freud about the individual, and of Marx about society, were strengthened by the assumption of the coincidence of freedom and rationality. Now rationality seems to have taken on a new form, to have its seat not in individual men, but in social institutions which by their bureaucratic planning and mathematical foresight usurp both freedom and rationality from the little individual men caught in them. The calculating hierarchies of department store and industrial corporation, of rationalized office and governmental bureau, lay out the gray ways of work and stereotype the permitted initiatives. And in all this bureaucratic usurpation of freedom and of rationality, the white-collar people are the interchangeable parts of the big chains of authority that bind the society together.

White-collar people, always visible but rarely seen, are politically voiceless. Stray politicians wandering in the political arena without party may put 'white collar' people alongside businessmen, farmers, and wage-workers in their broadside appeals, but no platform of either major party has yet referred to them directly. Who fears the clerk? Neither *Alice Adams* nor *Kitty Foyle* could be a *Grapes of Wrath* for the 'sharecroppers in the dust bowl of business.'

But while practical politicians, still living in the ideological air of the nineteenth century, have paid little attention to the new middle class, theoreticians of the left have vigorously claimed the salaried employee as a potential proletarian, and theoreticians of the right and center have hailed him as a sign of the continuing bulk and vigor of the middle class. Stray heretics from both camps have even thought, from time to time, that the higher-ups of the white-collar world might form a center of initiative for new political beginnings. In Germany, the 'black-coated worker' was one of the harps that Hitler played on his way to power. In England, the party of labor is thought to have won electoral socialism by capturing the votes of the suburban salaried workers.

To the question, what political direction will the white-collar people take, there are as many answers as there are theorists. Yet to the observer of American materials, the political problem posed by these people is not so much what the direction may be as whether they will take any political direction at all.

Between the little man's consciousness and the issues of our epoch there seems to be a veil of indifference. His will seems numbed, his spirit meager. Other men of other strata are also politically indifferent, but electoral victories are imputed to them; they do have tireless pressure groups and excited captains who work in and around the hubs of power, to whom, it may be imagined, they have delegated their enthusiasm for public affairs. But white-collar people are scattered along the rims of all the wheels of power: no one is enthusiastic about them and, like political eunuchs, they themselves are without potency clarigy his and without enthusiasm for the urgent political clash.

Estranged from community and society in a context of distrust and manipulation; alienated from work and, on the personality market, from self; expropriated of individual rationality, and politically apathetic—these are the new little people, the unwilling vanguard of modern society. These are some of the circumstances for the acceptance of which their hopeful training has quite unprepared them.

What men are interested in is not always what is to their interest; the troubles they are aware of are not always the ones that beset them. It would indeed be a fetish of 'democracy' to assume that men immediately know their interests and are clearly aware of the conditions within themselves and their society that frustrate them and make their efforts misfire. For interests involve not only values felt, but also something of the means by which these values might be attained. Merely by looking into himself, an individual can neither clarify his values nor set up ways for their attainment. Increased awareness is not enough, for it is not only that men can be unconscious of their situations; they are often falsely conscious of them. To become more truly conscious, white-collar people would have to become aware of themselves as members of new strata practicing new modes of work and life in modern America. To know what it is possible to know about their troubles, they would have to connect, within the going framework, what they are interested in with what is to their interest.

If only because of its growing numbers, the new middle class represents a considerable social and political potential, yet there is more systematic information available on the farmer, the wage worker, the Negro, even on the criminal, than on the men and women of the variegated white-collar worlds. Even the United States census is now so arranged as to make very difficult a definitive count of these people. Meanwhile, theorizing about the middle class on the basis of old facts has run to seed, and no fresh plots of fact have been planted. Yet the human and political importance of the white-collar people continues to loom larger and larger.

Liberalism's ideal was set forth for the domain of small property; Marxism's projection, for that of unalienated labor. Now when labor is everywhere alienated and small property no longer an anchor of freedom or security, both these philosophies can characterize modern society only negatively; neither can articulate new developments in their own terms. We must accuse both John Stuart Mill and Karl Marx of having done their work a hundred years ago. What has happened since then cannot be adequately described as the destruction of the nineteenth-century world; by now, the outlines of a new society have arisen around us, a society anchored in institutions the nineteenth century did not know. The general idea of the new middle class, in all its vagueness but also in all its ramifications, is an attempt to grasp these new developments of social structure and human character.

In terms of social philosophy, this book is written on the assumption that the liberal ethos, as developed in the first two decades of this century by such men as Beard, Dewey, Holmes, is now often irrelevant, and that the Marxian view, popular in the American 'thirties, is now often inadequate. However important and suggestive they may be as beginning points, and both are that, they do not enable us to understand what is essential to our time.

We need to characterize American society of the mid-twentieth century in more psychological terms, for now the problems that concern us most border on the psychiatric. It is one great task of social studies today to describe the larger economic and political situation in terms of its meaning for the inner life and the external career of the individual, and in doing this to take into account how the individual becomes falsely conscious and blinded. In the welter of the individual's daily experience the framework of modern society must be sought; within that framework the psychology of the little man must be formulated.

The first lesson of modern sociology is that the individual cannot understand his own experience or gauge his own fate without locating himself within the trends of his epoch and the life-chances of all the individuals of his social layer. To understand the white-collar people in detail, it is necessary to draw at least a rough sketch of the social structure of which they are a part. For the character of any stratum consists in large part of its relations, or lack of them, with the strata above and below it; its peculiarities can best be defined by noting its differences from other strata. The situation of the new middle class, reflecting conditions and styles of life that are borne by elements of both the new lower and the new upper classes, may be seen as symptom and symbol of modern society as a whole. (pp. xiv-xx)

> *C. Wright Mills, in his* White Collar: The American Middle Classes *(copyright 1951 by Oxford University Press, Inc.; renewed 1979 by Yaraslava Mills; reprinted by permission of Oxford University Press, Inc.), Oxford University Press, New York, 1953, 378 p.*

Excerpt from *THE POWER ELITE*

The powers of ordinary men are circumscribed by the everyday worlds in which they live, yet even in these rounds of job, family, and neighborhood they often seem driven by forces they can neither understand nor govern. 'Great changes' are beyond their control, but affect their conduct and outlook none the less. The very framework of modern society confines them to projects not their own, but from every side, such changes now press upon the men and women of the mass society, who accordingly feel that they are without purpose in an epoch in which they are without power.

But not all men are in this sense ordinary. As the means of information and of power are centralized, some men come to occupy positions in American society from which they can look down upon, so to speak, and by their decisions mightily affect, the everyday worlds of ordinary men and women. They are not made by their jobs; they set up and break down jobs for thousands of others; they are not confined by simple family responsibilities; they can escape. They may live in many hotels and houses, but they are bound by no one community. They need not merely 'meet the demands of the day and hour'; in some part, they create these demands, and cause others to meet them. Whether or not they profess their power, their technical and political experience of it far transcends that of the underlying population. What Jacob Burckhardt said of 'great men,' most Americans might well say of their elite: 'They are all that we are not.'

The power elite is composed of men whose positions enable them to transcend the ordinary environments of ordinary men and women; they are in positions to make decisions having major consequences. Whether they do or do not make such decisions is less important than the fact that they do occupy such pivotal positions: their failure to act, their failure to make decisions, is itself an act that is often of greater consequence than the decisions they do make. For they are in command of the major hierarchies and organizations of modern society. They rule the big corporations. They run the machinery of the state and claim its prerogatives. They direct the military establishment. They occupy the strategic command posts of the social structure, in which are now centered the effective means of the power and the wealth and the celebrity which they enjoy.

The power elite are not solitary rulers. Advisers and consultants, spokesmen and opinion-makers are often the captains of their higher thought and decision. Immediately below the elite are the professional politicians of the middle levels of power, in the Congress and in the pressure groups, as well as among the new and old upper classes of town and city and region. Mingling with them, in curious ways which we shall explore, are those professional celebrities who live by being continually displayed but are never, so long as they remain celebrities, displayed enough. If such celebrities are not at the head of any dominating hierarchy, they do often have the power to distract the attention of the public or afford sensations to the masses, or, more directly, to gain the ear of those who do occupy positions of direct power. More or less unattached, as critics of morality and technicians of power, as spokesmen of God and creators of mass sensibility, such celebrities and consultants are part of the immediate scene in which the drama of the elite is enacted. But that drama itself is centered in the command posts of the major institutional hierarchies. (pp. 3-4)

> *C. Wright Mills, in his* The Power Elite *(copyright © 1956 by Oxford University Press, Inc.; reprinted by permission), Oxford University Press, New York, 1956, 423 p.*

JOSEPH A. LOFTUS

[In **"The New Men of Power"** Professor Mills] tackles the thesis that America's labor leaders lead the only organizations capable of stopping the drift towards war and slump. Will they rise to the opportunities to reorganize modern society, or will they continue preoccupied with their own petty power domains in the established order?

This is a major project. The author has done some highly valuable research work on the background and thinking of the labor leaders. The result is a collective portrait, not a series of individual personality sketches. He examines the "politically alert publics" and, to some extent, the politically passive, mass public. The labor leader has to know these people and what they think of him if he is going to do an effective job. . . .

Labor leaders, by and large, fall into the liberal center. Professor Mills warns them that there is something more evil than the practical conservative who wants to break the power of business unionism. It is the sophisticated conservative who has appropriated liberal rhetoric to lure labor into a trap of cooperation. The sophisticated conservatives, he maintains, are geared to the main drift; their program, war-boom slump. It means connivance with the military and the diplomats, and domination of government in crisis.

Comes the crisis, the liberal center would be the natural converging point for all leftist groups. The people will demand action as they demanded it in Italy, Germany and Spain. Will labor leaders be ready to supply the leadership or will they be so ensnared by cooperation that their functions will be expropriated by a government over which they have no control?

Cooperation, key word of the liberal rhetoric, may work in an expanding economy, but in slump, he warns, the emphasis is on the political, and the fight is not merely for dollars but for power. There must be a labor party, in his opinion, but on a broader base than the unions' present membership. The "underdogs" are still unorganized; the huge middle-class population is a natural ally. Labor has failed to analyze these people and doesn't know how to approach them.

The ideas available on the left are less a program than a collective dream, he admits. A new society with a truly independent left would mean a politically alert mass public. Everyone vitally affected by a social decision, regardless of its sphere, would have a voice in that decision and a hand in its administration. Power won by election, revolution, or deals at the top will not be enough to accomplish this. In the day-by-day process of accumulating strength, as well as in times of social upset, the power of democratic initiation must be allowed and fostered in the rank and file.

Professor Mills tells the union leaders what they must do to realize their full potential. He is utterly realistic about them. His program involves so much work and thought for men who are comfortable and ill-prepared for the task that he seems discouraged about prospects of action. . . .

The book is charged with ideas for lively debate, but the professor himself is quite calm. He can smash images with fine detachment. He has delivered us a swift kick in the status quo. There is much solid information about labor, carefully documented. . . . The results of his questionnaires directed to 500 labor leaders are among the most important part of the book, if not the most readable. The effort to remove the statistical curse did not quite come off.

> *Joseph A. Loftus, "Labor Leaders and Trade Unions—Two Studies," in* The New York Times Book Review *(© 1948 by The New York Times Company; reprinted by permission), October 3, 1948, p. 6.* *

PETER F. DRUCKER

As demonstrated in *The New Men of Power,* C. Wright Mills'] personal understanding of the internal politics, the internal stresses and strains, the dynamic forces operating within a labor union is excellent. The incidental comments and asides scattered through the book are vivid, penetrating, and sensitive.

The research material on the structure of labor leadership in the United States which forms the core of the book is largely new. A good many of the facts, such as those relating to age structure and origin of our union leaders, will probably come as a surprise to most leaders as will the figures showing that the educational level of union leadership is conspicuously higher than that of the population in general. (p. 221)

In his main purpose, however, Mr. Mills has unfortunately failed, and failed conspicuously. He does not reach a single one of the goals he has set himself. The book tells us nothing about the labor leader as a political factor. It does not tell us how he behaves or why he behaves as he does. Least of all does it tell us, as the author claims, how the labor leader is likely to behave in the future and why.

There are two main reasons for this failure of so promising a book to attain its goals. In the first place Mr. Mills has fallen victim to his own public-opinion-survey technique. He shows convincingly that the American labor leader, by and large, does not act according to a thought-out, long-range ideology but according to the pressures and problems of the moment. He is also convinced that a major change in national affairs such as a new depression or another war is likely to bring about a large-scale turnover in union leadership. Yet he builds a whole sky-scraper of conclusions on the answers given to him by labor leaders in 1946 and 1947 to the question whether they are in favor of a Third Party—not even taking into account that these answers were given when "Third Party" in every labor leader's mind stood for only one thing: Henry Wallace. Altogether he bases qualitative conclusions regarding a hypothetical future on grossly quantitative data regarding the past.

But the major weakness of the book is its rigid dogmatism. Mr. Mills' dogmatism is not of a crude party-line type; but this makes it only the more doctrinaire. While uncompromisingly anti-Communist, he is nonetheless a doctrinaire Marxist in his assumptions and in his method, though one saddled with a sociological vocabulary and confused by the stubborn refusal of the facts to fit into his preconceived pattern. Altogether he is only too close to the "disillusioned liberals" of the "little magazines" whom he despises so much. Perhaps it would be more accurate though hardly more flattering to say that Mr. Mills' book reminds the reviewer vividly of the discussions of continental European, especially of German, Social Democrats 25, even 40, years ago.

As a result, the book discusses neither the actual political behavior of the American labor leader nor how he is likely to act in the future but soars off into political speculation which has little if anything to do with American reality or with the problems and dangers of our future. (pp. 221-22)

> Peter F. Drucker, "Survey of Books for Executives: 'The New Men of Power'," in The Management Review, Vol. 38, No. 4, April, 1949, pp. 221-22.

D. W. BROGAN

[It is the thesis of **White Collar** that the stereotypes of the nineteenth century] still cloud the American mind. The greater part of the American people have no chance and not even much hope of acquiring a real economic independence. The old middle classes, the merchants, the lawyers, the doctors, the more prosperous farmers, the small manufacturers had this chance and took it. The view that they still have it and are taking it still survives. It is under cover of the interests of the small businessman that the big businessman operates. It is under the cover of the old, independent family doctor that the real unit of medical practice, the large, costly, exclusive, restrictive hospital, operates. Abraham Lincoln hanging up his shingle distracts attention from the great corporation law firms. The existing independent small economic unit can only work in the interstices of the great corporations. And they know this. The small businessman may shout for free competition; but he means "fair" competition, that is, he doesn't mean competition. The American big and middle farmer who gets hot under the collar at the mention of state control or Socialism is too shrewd not to know that his profits come as much from government subsidy and price manipulation as from skilled farming or good or bad harvests. . . . Whether we like it or not, economic power is concentrated, and the answer to that concentration is concentration, political action, the big union—politics in the widest sense.

True, not all white-collar workers see this. The myth of the opportunity to rise, to become one of the big shots is still appealing. Yet Professor Mills suggests that it is losing its old appeal. (p. 19)

The white-collar class is economically giving ground for many reasons, and one is that it is too big. It is a commonplace now that the simple Marxian process that was to produce a conscious proletariat hasn't worked out that way in the advanced industrial countries. It is the clerical, public relations, and selling sections of the employed public that have been growing. Nor is it surprising to learn that the economic spread between white collar and manual worker is narrowing; in some cases and at some times the wage is better than the salary and the white-collar worker has to be satisfied with the diminishing asset of superior social prestige, the prestige of the class in general, the prestige of the kind of job. . . . But as general education spreads the cash and, in the not very long run, the intangible rewards of the comparative scarcity of "educated" people shrink. (pp. 19-20)

Sociologists are notoriously given to jargon, and it is a pleasure to report that Professor Mills eschews the mere trade patter. Only when he comes to the department store does the influence of the environment overcome him and some of the literary habits of copywriters infect his style. But even when he is pushing his points as hard as he can (and he is a vigorous point-pusher) he writes clearly and plausibly (often convincingly as well). Of course he is not always quite convincing or right (I mean he doesn't always agree with me), but this is a book very well worth reading. . . . Professor Mills has suggested, to me at least, lots of themes for reflection. I wish he had given more material for reflection on the symbolism of "white-collar" status, the role of class language . . . , of social status in work indicated by clothes. (p. 20)

> D. W. Brogan, "Rise and Decline of a Class," in The Saturday Review of Literature, Vol. XXXIV, No. 37, September 15, 1951, pp. 19-20.

H. M. KALLEN

[C. Wright Mills'] mid-century portrait of the species *homo Americanus* and of its varieties [in **"White Collar"**] seems a sort of ecology of finance-industry, taking for the prepotent environmental constant the procession of machines—starting with farm and mine and factory and mounting to the gargantuan city concentrations of dwellings, schools, hospitals, department stores, offices, places of entertainment and recreation.

The men and women whose existence is conditioned to the machine-at-work are Mills' "new middle classes." They are all job-holders who are attached to some machine when they have jobs, removed from it when they haven't. On the job they make up the ranks of a hierarchy of diverse bureaucracies, from executive vice presidents to file clerks. Off the job they have little or nothing of their own, and are little or nothing on their own. They are the hollow men, whom the nation's "managerial demiurge" distributes in an occupational pyramid, with themselves at the apex and the true workingmen at the foundation.

The demiurges are the trustees of the owners of the nation's business. They plan, they fix, they rationalize, they manipulate. They serve as the Government's dollar-a-year men. The workers produce and automatic machinery makes fewer needful to produce all that more and more require for their "standard of living." The "new middle classes" fill in the levels between. . . .

Mills limns each category and type. Together they make up a mass of individuals learning to be resigned to their condition. Their true avatar is the "little man" alienated from himself in both his labor and his leisure, swaying to all the doctrinal winds that blow from the mechanic arts of the press, the movie, the radio, the video.

He has graduated from high school, probably from college. Yet he is "bored at work, restless at play," has no roots in the culture of the past, no plan for the future, no true communion or community. He is only a unit in an aggregation, mass-man incapable of organic action, seeking refuge from anxiety and futility in a struggle to keep up appearances. All his values are of the fashions of consumption instead of the arts of production.

As a citizen he is a member of an inert rear guard. As a liberal he is one in a compliant populace of a nation whose "main drift [is] toward a society in which men are the managed personnel of a garrison state." His insignia, one might say his totem, is the white collar. . . .

I get the feeling that Mills has exaggerated what he hates in the class of which he is himself a notable figure and has ignored and minimized what is constructive and praiseworthy. Perhaps, like every caricaturist with a social conscience, he is employing exaggeration for the purpose of reform. Perhaps he desires, by bringing the most unappetizing features of his own class into sharp visibility, to generate the awareness that is preliminary to purposeful alteration.

I think his book would have been better for some attention to the positive, creative developments in his new middle classes that may be transforming them into still newer ones. As it stands, the book conveys a feeling of hopeless disillusion. Yet there are also grounds for hope through disillusion. That Mills does not consider them even in order to refute them makes him an authentic voice of the futility he portrays.

Even so, **"White Collar"** is a book that persons of every level of the white-collar pyramid should read and ponder. It will alert them to their condition for their better salvation.

> *H. M. Kallen, "The Hollow Men: A Portrayal to Ponder," in* The New York Times Book Review (© *1951 by The New York Times Company; reprinted by permission), September 16, 1951, p. 4.*

IRVING HOWE

Mills displays large gifts for social description [in **"White Collar"**], often of a kind one expects from the superior novelist. He is very keen in distinguishing the effects of occupation upon status, and the grueling psychological cost of what he calls "the status panic." With quick, bright strokes he portrays the numerous strata of the new middle class. . . . (p. 309)

[Mills's] descriptions must, of course, be taken with a little salt; Mills often resorts to the economy of caricature, his portraits suggesting tendencies rather than fully accomplished facts. But his mordant book does hit upon the main drift of our society. . . .

Mills concludes that the new middle class will follow "the panicky ways of prestige" in the short run and the pulls of power in the long run; it will, he says, choose only after its "choice" among contenders for power has won. Doesn't such an analysis underestimate the significance of political programs? The German experience indicates that in moments of

crisis this class, or parts of it, will turn to the movement which seems to offer the most dynamic solutions of the problems of society. . . .

Otherwise, I have only minor criticisms. Unaccountably, Mills says nothing about the school teachers, surely a most important section of the new middle class. To balance his sketch of the fixer in industry, he might have added a page or two on the "think-man" in the unions, usually an ex-radical selling verbal fluency and guilty memories. It would have been good if he had included comments on the reasons why the Communist Party found its strongest support in America among the lower ranks of the new middle class, and the reasons why these lower ranks have been swept by a pathetic eagerness for the purchase of culture. Sometimes Mills is too sweeping in his statements: from his rather crude section on the professors one would hardly gather that there are still many dedicated people in the universities doing their work for limited rewards.

And I must quarrel a bit about his style. He writes far better than most sociologists or, for that matter, most literary people; but he lets his genuine gift for the striking phrase run wild and neglects the larger units of composition. **"White Collar"** is exciting to read; but exhausting. Mills's occasional tone of tough, professional power-consciousness is also disturbing; after all, white collars are worn by people, and when one sees how those collars tear into human flesh it would not be amiss to give way to a little grief.

But it is not these weaknesses, I suspect, which will trouble some of the academic sociologists. **"White Collar"** is likely to be attacked for its strengths: Mills will be accused of being an "impressionist"—he does not hesitate to use his imagination or to quote Balzac—and, worse yet, of not being "objective"—he resists the modish acquiescence in the status quo.

For **"White Collar"** is thoroughly radical in its point of view. It is a pleasure to come upon a book rebellious in its political values and entirely free of both Stalinism and that professional anti-Marxism so much the rage these unhappy days; a pleasure, as well, to find a political writer who has enough wit not to take the flush of war economy as evidence of social health. If a few more voices as strong and bold as that of Mills were raised, one might hope for the revival of a free radical wing, which is today the greatest need in American intellectual life. (p. 310)

> *Irving Howe, "The New Middle Class," in* The Nation (copyright 1951, copyright renewed © 1979, The Nation *magazine, The Nation Associates, Inc.), Vol. 173, No. 15, October 13, 1951, pp. 309-10.*

DAVID RIESMAN

[The] mood of *White Collar* is as drab and lacking in hope as the picture of the assorted salespeople, file clerks, intellectuals, and other professionals whose portrait Mills draws. . . .

To [the near-vanished world of the small entrepreneur Mills] manifests a curious ambivalence of attitude, reminiscent of Marx's feeling for the feudal-pastoral world. On the one hand, with his historicist preoccupation with the main drift, he dismisses competitive capitalism and economic liberalism generally as ghosts who have no right to haunt today's ideology and politics and do so only as a cover for big business. But, on the other hand, he uses the values of independence, craftsman-like work, and media-free leisure to damn without mercy or possibility of redemption the ways of today's middle class.

In some degree, perhaps, such ambivalence of attitude cannot be avoided; it represents, in part, the Populist or Wobbly heritage in Mills's outlook. (p. 513)

[Mills's] vignettes convey what goes on in a big-city department store with exceptional force. Less convincing is the discussion of the file clerks and office workers and the steady growth of mechanization and rationalization among them, for here the author draws rather on the literature about the clerks, both German and American, than on direct observation. He may possibly underestimate their powers of sabotage, accommodation, and even *joie de vivre* at work, as he certainly underplays the intellectual skills involved in many filing and other office jobs which can be challenging and demanding despite their low prestige and pay. Just as the intellectual is apt to see the factory assembly line as robotization and to neglect the ways in which the workers adjust the machines to their own rhythms and enjoy their skills in restricting production (a high-skilled operation even on so-called semiskilled jobs), so Mills may miss some of the ways in which even a group of office girls maintains some control over their working day. By opposing to white-collar routines and self-salesmanship the ideal of pre-industrial craftsmanship (and he does consciously present this as an ideal and not as a nostalgic picture of what once was), Mills leads the reader to a verdict on modern industrial society not many steps away from Orwell's *1984*—both books breathe a similar hopelessness. (p. 514)

Obviously, to say that his view is depressing . . . is to say nothing about its correctness; even if it is not correct, it may be a symptom of partial truth, or even an entrant in the stream of self-confirming prophecies. This reviewer, however, feels the view is somethat askew. For one thing, Mills pays almost no attention to the ethnic coloring of attitudes to white-collar work. He does not discuss, for instance, how much it means to the Irish Catholic that he is able to leave the factory and enter not only the lower office ranks but the upper reaches of utility, manufacturing, and government bureaucracy, putting the seal of Americanization on his Catholicism in this way. With different overtones, the Italians are engaged in a similar migration, with the result that a job of teaching school or selling has a meaning for the Italian girl that it may lack for the Anglo-Saxon in terms both of status and of the pains and pleasures of dealing with clients and colleagues at work. By robbing the white-collar people who appear in his book of any ethnic, religious, or other cultural dye, the white collar itself assumes a more wan and celluloidal look than is, on the whole, probably warranted.

For another thing, I believe that the mass media are less exploitative and insipid, and certainly less antirevolutionary in effect, than they appear in Mills's account. Even in soap opera there is considerable variation; some have a good deal of sharpness and bite. Moreover, passivity in the face of the media, documented in the stereotype of the listless TV-viewer, cannot be taken for granted. While very possibly the media are insufficiently challenging and demanding, we would have to learn a lot more about what different media mean to different critical intelligences in their audiences before we can rest discontented with this image.

It is hard to find indexes, of course, to test such issues. But it might be possible to see who are the readers today of self-improvement fiction and true fable, who attends Dale Carnegie sessions, etc. Perhaps these are the marginal hangers-on, going from misfit job to misfit job—people whose reading matter does not tell us too much about the adjustments made to the

personality market by the majority of white-collar folk who, whatever the poverty of their lives from the point of view of the outside observer, may not take the slogans with full seriousness. Similarly, it would be important to see how many white-collar workers, like even the extravagantly alienated Willie Loman, enjoy puttering about the house and garden and have them to putter in.

True, Mills would hardly think better of white-collar life for such small blessings. He is greatly concerned with the white-collar role in politics, and the last part of the book is devoted to the theorems and stratagems that have been proposed for alerting the lower ranks of the salaried strata and for overcoming the illusions or false consciousness that now animate their sporadic political interest. . . . I think that Mills holds against the white-collar "proletariat" not only the actual banalities and miseries of its life but also its uselessness in political insurgency, its lack of a rip-roaring decisiveness, and that this in turn leads him to see even more banality and misery than are really there. (pp. 514-15)

Mills is grappling resourcefully with the big questions of our day, and even if this reviewer is inclined to give somewhat less portentous answers to some of them, he agrees that the questions are central, the research methods fundamentally sound. (p. 515)

> *David Riesman, "Book Reviews: 'White Collar: The American Middle Classes'," in* The American Journal of Sociology, *Vol. LVIII, No. 5, March, 1952, pp. 513-15.*

A. A. BERLE

The American "power elite," C. Wright Mills tells us [in **"The Power Elite"**], is that group of men who command the major organizations in our society. . . .

[Mills] makes a case for that claim. Then, with restrained bitterness, he tears into the resulting structure. . . .

[Mr. Mills] presents our "power elite" as a merger of three interlocked groups with interchangeable members: (1) "big rich" combined with "corporate rich"—company executives; (2) military and naval men ruling the Pentagon and its works; (3) high political figures in government. Mills maintains all are products of a more or less common environment. Unlike Marx, he thinks the "big economic man" is no longer controlling alone; he has merged with "war lords" and "selected politicians." Organization and mass media do the rest. This elite has no dogma, accepts no standards, works in a system of "organized irresponsibility," in a frame of "higher immorality."

More impressive is the author's analysis of the underlying "mass society." There he has a point. American increase in population and the rise of large organizations did, without doubt, shatter the individual communities in which men lived in town meeting days. Big organizations do push their leading figures so far from the bottom millions that communication is hard, or perhaps lost.

Contemporaneously came problems that do not yield to popular discussion. The man in the street knows he does not understand nuclear engineering, intricate financing, economics or complex international problems. He can only give confidence to men he thinks do understand. Increasingly he is in the hands of experts or representatives. His only recourse—if he has any—is to fire them when results are bad.

Information and appraisal he must get through "mass media" which, Mills suggests, are oftener instruments for manipulating than for informing the public. Educational institutions which should help to produce disciplined and informed minds, "bold and sensible individuals who cannot be overwhelmed by mass life," translating "troubles into issues, and issues into terms of their human meaning," aim rather at "life adjustments," encouraging happy acceptance of mass ways rather than struggle for individual or public ascendancy. This hurts. It has a considerable content of truth.

There are no values. The "conservative mood" has no basis in ideas, merely maxima straight out of Horatio Alger. "Liberalism" skirts mindlessness, enshrines a set of administrative routines and defends rather than exercises civil liberties. Freedom (Mills quotes Archibald MacLeish) is no longer something you use, it has become something you "save," something you protect like your other possessions. Liberalism, now "painless to the rich and powerful," no longer defines issues or proposes policies.

In sum, Mills concludes we have arrived at a "higher immorality"—a mindless vacuum with no elaborated justification of ideas and values. Elite members are not the product of virtue or ability, of a sensitive civil service, of responsible national parties, nor are they held in check by a plurality of voluntary associations. "Commanders of power unequaled in human history, they have succeeded within the American system of organized irresponsibilty." (p. 3)

If the American command is as accidental, mindless, amoral, undogmatic, irresponsible, disconnected with the mass as all that, how come it hangs together—and, despite defects, provides people with the highest content of economic, esthetic and intellectual opportunity yet offered a population-block of 165 million?

There is, nevertheless, an uncomfortable degree of truth in Mills' attack. It is not the whole truth. It is weakened by sematic slant. American business executives are not "corporate commissars"; American high officers are not fairly described as "war lords": American high government officers are politicians but to be good they must be something more. Some "big rich," corporate executives and Army officers do act as Mills records. Others run museums of modern art, foreign aid programs, civic services *ad infinitum*. Mills' portrait is an angry cartoon, not a serious picture.

There are also errors of fact. He is wrong in asserting a general "coincidence of interests between military and corporate needs as defined by war lords and corporate rich"; and corporate capitalism is not a "military capitalism," save in a few specialized fields. Nor does the social system move in an intellectual vacuum; Einstein and Oppenheimer could match the "power elite" and defeat it. But the need of a solid value system is great. (pp. 3, 22)

The author insists the characteristic member of higher circles today is an "intellectual mediocrity"—perhaps conscientious but still mediocre. Probably. So were most top groups in history. Perhaps not in Pericles' Athens, or at the founding of the American republic; but social structures are usually run by second-rate men with mixed motives doing the best they can. Probably one test of a society is whether it can carry on with

mediocrities. If it depends on quantity production of first-raters, it is precarious indeed.

Mr. Mills rejects a suggestion made by this reviewer that corporations are gradually developing standards of conduct amounting to a "corporate conscience." Not convincing, he says; corporations live up to standards only because this makes "good public relations." Fair enough: St. Peter will settle whether the creditable things we did were motivated altruistically or by self-interest. Social students must be content with results. If the Pentagon, corporations and political parties do good because they think it good policy, good policy has to serve.

This book is so carefully documented, it deals with such real problems, it hits so many sore spots that it deserves to be read, also to be supplemented. The indictment of the power elite by Mr. Mills is, for lack of a system of values, in need of a guiding philosophy. But that requires the accuser to posit some value system as a take-off point. To indict for social anarchy assumes some form of social law. "Higher immorality" predicates some moral order. Objectively the American structure is not a failure. You cannot condemn it as a "bad society" unless you at least conceive a "good society." . . .

[It] is not true to say that men who reach the top are more unthinking or less moral than usual because they do not spell out intellectual credos. If he believes what he writes, Mr. Mills has cut out his next job. He must tackle the problem of elaborating the values and the institutional forms that can lead to the society he believes to be good. (p. 22)

A. A. Berle, *"Are the Blind Leading the Blind?"* in The New York Times Book Review (© *1956 by The New York Times Company; reprinted by permission), April 22, 1956, pp. 3, 22.*

ROBERT S. LYND

The architecture of [*The Power Elite*] leads up rather gently and discursively to the hard-hitting middle group of chapters, and then glides down again so as to deposit the reader on familiar ground in scarcely more ruffled mood than he might experience after reading one of the occasional critical articles on American institutions in *Harper's*.

This point on the book's over-all structure is relevant because it explains the reader's growing uneasiness over the possibility that perhaps the analysis—all this significant documentation and good thinking—was not intended to get anywhere. Whether a book cumulates in meaning towards the point of joining its several strands in an interlocked body of conclusions, however tentative, is a matter of choice for the author. But not to do so in a book of such weight and potential importance on this subject seems peculiarly unfortunate.

Mills's failure to deal with the meanings for democracy of the impressive power trends he analyzes is the colossal loose-end of *The Power Elite*. He simply fades out on the expectation his pages encourage that this crucial arc in the analysis will be closed before the book ends. The book's opening paragraph stresses the central importance of this problem. . . . This invites the hope that the pages to follow will provide a confrontation between the purposes of the powers-that-be and the efforts of men in democracy to affirm other purposes for which democracy stands. But, curiously, the potentially crucial chapter on The Mass Society is deferred until the third from the end, when the book is already tapering off, and then contents itself with describing what mass societies are and how they happen. Mills tells us that "The United States today is not altogether a mass society"; but he describes a movement towards a mass society that is in full tide, and the power setting of the rest of the book implies that it is to continue unchecked. If Marxism encourages distortion through viewing society from the bottom up, it may be the characteristic distortion of elite analysis that it looks from the top down, and not very far down at that.

This leaves one wondering whether the great bulk of modern society is to Mills but fodder for his elite. If so, he may be correct; but, if so, this becomes the most momentous unstated and unexamined conclusion of his book. If this is what things add up to, then reading about the who's and why's of elites is for us like reading about the scurry of ants zigzagging under the feet of a herd of elephants. Again, this may be correct for our generation. But such a conclusion simply repeats the bankrupt scarcity theory of power: that some people have it, and because they have it none is available for the rest of us. And, over longer time, does what the democratic idea intends provide nothing for man to fight for, and with?

The book has a hit-and-glide quality which derives, I think, from its central effort to instate elites as the master key in the analysis of power. Elite analysis is popular among sociologists nowadays. Its popularity derives, I believe, quite as much from the things it enables an analyst to avoid, as from the things it enables him to do. Most important, it provides a glittering focus above common, troublesome things like capitalism and the class structure of a capitalist society. (p. 409)

[Mills's elite analysis] leaves important questions unanswered. Mills correctly stresses the need to bring the diversity represented by the several elites together, to see the resulting American elite as a whole. The simplest unity may be seen in the fact that, though they come up from different institutions, these diverse members of the elite do arrive at concrete, agreed-upon policies. This poses the question: what is responsible for the readiness of these top persons to agree? I see three possible answers: (1) Men who rise that high in society may be counted on to be seasoned administrators who by long experience recognize the need, through adjustment and compromise, to reach some workable agreement about things to be done. This answer, correct as far as it goes, bases the tendency to agree upon nothing more substantial than influence and expedient bargaining among individuals. (2) Elites from different institutions act together and reach common agreements because one institution represented in the total American elite has power and rewards enough to force other institutions and their respective elites to act in the main in ways compatible with its interests. If this is the answer—as it is in part—Mills would need to assess and to identify the relative weights of his three institutions. This he does not do. (3) Elites from different institutions act together because the same influential class in society spreads across all institutions and controls them in a common general direction. This answer—which includes the relevant parts of the two preceding—provides much the broadest and soundest basis for the analysis of power in American society.

By locating the cohering factor in the elite superstructure, Mills leaves other weighty factors unlashed in and flapping like loose sails. He does not hold steadily in focus the massive continuities involved in the fact that ours is a capitalist society; the factor of class is belittled; the relative weights of his three institutions

in a capitalist society go unassessed; and an unwarranted autonomy is imputed to the several institutions.

Capitalism appears intermittently in the analysis. The author knows that we live in a capitalist society; and I am sure he is aware of how important it is in our system of power. . . . The trouble is not that the author fails to deal with capitalist power. He does so explicitly in the chapters on the very rich and on corporate big business. But he reserves property as a basis of power for one discrete set within the elite, and makes no solid effort to appraise the relative weight and the diffused spread of the power of property throughout all institutions under capitalism. He holds back on such unifying tendencies in order to reserve this dramatic role for his elites.

Mills is correct in insisting that power does not inhere in persons, and that it is not prevailingly a conspiracy. To analyze power under capitalism as a conspiracy of persons, rather than the weighted movement of circumstances in a given society, belittles the realities of power. But can one escape facing the reality that, historically, capitalism means and has always meant that the whole institutional system has become weighted so that, like loaded dice, events tend to roll with a bias that favors property?

There is a similar in-and-out vagueness about class in the book. Through most of the pages one tends to assume that the author takes the presence of classes for granted. . . . He even refers to "the elite as a social class." But three-quarters of the way through the book it turns out that he does not really mean "class," as class is historically identified. By confining the term to the economic sphere . . . and by forcing the term class into the extreme meaning of economic determinism, he limits the involvement of class so defined in the totality of his elite to the immediate representatives from the strictly economic sphere. This enables him to reserve for the elite as a whole the spreading, unifying tendency long identified with class as it operates across the institutions of a capitalist society. But then he must qualify his reference to "the elite as a social class" by differentiating it from a "ruling class." If "'Class' is an economic term; 'rule,'" he says, is "a political one." So he prefers to identify the imputedly non-class character of his "elite as a social class" simply as a "power elite." If the reader has difficulty in following these sophistications, so did I.

Since when has the concept "class" been only "an economic term" and ceased to refer to social aggregates? Along with Mills, I, too, dislike the term "ruling class." But if we dislike its over-inclusive implications, surely we may not overlook the fact that the essence of power under capitalism is ability to exercise continuing influence, to the point of control where that is deemed necessary, over major decisions. Does one dispose of such upper-class power under capitalism by fleeing to the term "power elite"? "Who or what," Mills asks, "do these [elite] men at the top represent?" He wrestles to explain why it is that the elite exhibit such unity of interest and direction of policy, why they tend to have "codes and criteria in common." And he forsakes the social and institutional level and resorts to the psychological level in such explanations as that "There is a kind of reciprocal attraction among the successful." Agreed. But what is it in our society that gives such emphasis to "success"?

All of this confusion stems from Mills's effort to give to his elite an independence and a diversity in outlook uncomplicated by the solid realities generally associated with class membership and interest and with the desire of those marginal to economic power to get under its tent. If Mills's reasoning does not appeal to historically-oriented social scientists, it should permit members of the American "power elite" to sleep better nights.

If Mills does, by main strength and awkwardness, hold his elite somewhat apart from our society's upper class, he has more trouble in keeping institutions apart. Of course he does not intend or imply that institutions are actually sharply separated; the issue is, rather, are institutions and the elites that represent them sufficiently autonomous under capitalism so that, for instance, the economic elite may be expected to have interests and commitments markedly different from the elites representing other institutions? Of corporate business and government he says: "We should . . . be quite mistaken to believe that the political apparatus is merely an extension of the corporate world, or that it has been taken over by the representatives of the corporate rich." Of course. His saving word here is "merely." But the question is—and this is the kind of question he repeatedly avoids: how much big-business control is enough to give it preponderant control? (pp. 409-11)

The questions that all but ask themselves from [Mills's arguments] are: If the contemporary trends in corporate business power and its influence in government are as here suggested, why pretend that government and business are any longer importantly apart? Do such statements imply, when taken with the present increasing dependence of the political sphere upon business prosperity, that big business is increasingly in the position to dominate political democracy? Is the increasingly mass character of our society prevailingly traceable to the serviceability of a mass society to capitalist mass production?

These are weighty questions, and one has no right to insist that a man who writes a book shall answer them. But if that man sees warrant for making such judgments as the above quoted passages imply in a book devoted to the appraisal of power, is one justified in asking that he go on to ask the questions that then become unavoidable, to attempt to answer them, and that his answers—however guarded and tentative—be made the explicit basis for whatever else he thinks is relevant enough to the problem of power to be discussed in his book?

I am indebted to Professor Mills for much that he says in his book, particularly for his straightforward documentation at a number of points. But the basis of my criticism, as the above suggests, runs deep. The book reads as though it were written by two people: one with a relatively sure grasp of the realities of a capitalist society, and the other bewitched by the plausible appeal of a book on elites; and that the two never got together, but the man at work on elites succeeded in blurring and impairing what the other had to say. (p. 411)

> *Robert S. Lynd, "Power in the United States," in* The Nation *(copyright 1956* The Nation *magazine,* The Nation Associates Inc.*), Vol. 182, No. 19, May 12, 1956, pp. 408-11.*

MICHAEL HARRINGTON

Mr. Mills does not stop with a simple analysis [in *The Power Elite*]. He evaluates. The values in which he believes are those of democracy, of increasing the real popular participation in decision, of deciding on the basis of rational debate. And he finds his values opposed at every turn—for him, America is now "a conservative country without any conservative ideol-

ogy," a center of "crackpot realism," its power system is one of "organized irresponsibility."

These are harsh words. Witness, for example, the anguished response of A. A. Berle in his New York *Times* review of *The Power Elite* [see excerpt above]. And yet, one must choose between Mr. Berle's dream of the development of a corporate conscience and Mr. Mills impressive documentation of a very contrary reality. Whatever the choice, Mr. Mills' book is one of the most important to have appeared in many years. It is a refreshing, honest, angry relief from the mood of the American celebration. (p. 306)

> *Michael Harrington, "A Ruling Class," in* Commonweal *(copyright © 1956 Commonweal Publishing Co., Inc.; reprinted by permission of Commonweal Publishing Co., Inc.), Vol. LXIV, No. 12, June 22, 1956, pp. 305-06.*

PHILIP RIEFF

To the ironic critics of the age, the militancy of C. Wright Mills [in *The Power Elite*] . . . is suspect. Annoyed, as by a gadfly who insists on landing somewhere, Mills' fellow critics have fixed on the exaggerations to which his militancy has led—the partisan use of evidence, the unrelieved gloom. In American social letters, Mills is bracketed as a naïf, a pure dissenter in an agreeable time. If this were all, if Mills were accused of nothing worse than being naïve, of remaining narrowly negative in a period of ideological as well as material abundance, the charges should of course be dismissed. He is, however, vulnerable to the more serious charge of posturing. As Christianity, following the death of Christian belief, multiplied its armchair apologists in the universities, so socialism has its professional and passionate academics, transforming their socialism into sociology. Mills must be ranked as one of these caretakers of the socialist polemical tradition. He incites without hope; he offers not a single saving myth—no hope from the proletariat; nor from the engineers; and certainly not from a cultivated and responsible upper class, that fantasy-compliment of the conservative critics to themselves. Further, it is hard to see what group of readers Mills can hope to move. Literate *and* committed audiences are as scarce these days as salvation-bearing social classes. Mills' sympathetic reader is, I suppose, that stable *Partisan Review* type, culturally rather than politically committed—the literary son of socialist fathers, who takes over the tatters of liberal belief and becomes the moralizing man in an immoral society. (p. 464)

The mass society which is rapidly overtaking our inherited liberal one has no explicit faith, and its implicit faith is so diffuse that it can digest any virtuoso heretic striking blindly at where dogma used to be.

The dogma at which Mills strikes has become so shadowy that he never locates it explicitly as his target. Briefly, it is the classical liberal thesis that the institutions of government are distinct from the institutions of property. Mills' antithesis, also not stated explicitly in this book, is the classical socialist denial: power is not separate from property; corporate property cannot be realistically or legitimately considered private. By submitting the present American situation to an essentially socialist analysis, Mills demonstrates (successfully, I think) how irrelevant to American reality liberalism has become. Property, and the hidden privileges and flow of opportunity that go with it, does not exist antecedently to government. Indeed, in our present social arrangement, the major institutions of government and the major institutions of property tend openly to merge. The primitive stuff of institutions are the humans who staff them, and Mills goes about the theoretically simple but polemically complex task of spotting the men who circulate among the merging institutions, therefore occupying what he calls the "command posts" atop American society.

Mills perhaps credits the old liberal dogma of separate and balancing institutions with too much life, so that he fatigues the reader with lengthy parades of tycoons in Washington, generals at ease in executive suites, and the new hybrid politicians, with business hearts and military heads. But the book is no mere exposé of money lords, or of the vested interests of our military economy. Indeed, Mills says too little of the movement of funds that is sapping the economic potential of America, and talks mainly about the movement of men that is sapping our civic potential. For this alliance, between the high officers of executive government and the chief managers of corporate property, Mills finds a new name: the power elite. Despite the fact that such an alliance is the staple of socialist theory, Mills holds that this new name for it is necessary. For a third institution, the armed services, has become the mortar holding the two familiar old institutions of rule together, and has come to personify for a politically illiterate public the idea of political and economic stability: a permanent war economy based on a negative ideology of an absolute enemy.

Mills has written as fine an obituary notice on liberal society as any lover of the genre could hope to read. . . . The liberal principles of a government instituted and operated separately from property, against which the propertied classes had rights and toward which the powers of government were limited—these principles have been quietly abrogated. . . . [When] the historical carriers of liberalism were no longer served by it, the liberal principle of autonomous and mutually limiting political and economic orders was scuttled. In America the scuttling is so recent that Mills takes almost all of his examples of it from the Eisenhower years, though of course it began in the Roosevelt war-preparedness period.

To explain why there has been so little serious opposition to the scuttling of American liberalism, Mills resorts to the obvious tautology that American society is, anyway, in process of transition from liberal to mass form. And, as a result of this trend, the classes and the masses grow together. If anything, I should say that the elites Mills studies are farther along toward the psychology characteristic of a mass society than large segments of the population. The elites are incapable of contemplating serious questions steadily; they have a few fixed ideas and no fixed morality. This much Mills confirms. But the intellectual and moral condition of the many is scarcely better than that of the ruling few. . . . Being so unsentimental as to label the "people" of nineteenth-century liberalism and socialism alike as a "mass," Mills is at a loss to find a sharp angle from which to criticize the higher immorality of the elite. Unwittingly, he demonstrates that the powerless mass and the power elite complement each other perfectly. The lower immorality differs only in size and import from the higher. Such essential agreement creates a major problem of approach for Mills. As a serious critic, who will allow neither his socialism nor his respect for the liberal civilization of an earlier America to bemuse his vision of the present, Mills is unable to moor the repugnant facts of American public life against the pier of American values. In a manner no critic has yet adequately described, the pier has somehow torn loose and floats around like another fact on the calm, oily surface of American life.

Of course to defend is to be conservative, as Mills points out. But just at its best, as an attack, Mills' performance is purely negative. Against the conservative mood of the liberals, Mills offers a mood of vague resentment. He has looked into the faces of the American elite and realized with dramatic pleasure that they are blank. It is the misfortune of the socialist critic in our time, equipped with better social psychology than his forebears, to look into the faces of the mass and see that these too are irremediably blank. Masses are merely the poorer relations of elites. For all Mills' middle-western devotion to the idea that American power is won on the playing fields of Exeter, and other such eastern places, the fact is that the elites are quite as mindless as the mass and share a similarly empty inner life. False consciousness is here to stay; it is the happy psychic condition of a mature and still dynamic industrial civilization that has worked back through a religion of transcendence to a religion of immanence based on a supra-primitive fetishism of infinitely variable commodities. Criticism, when it serves no religion of transcendence, not even a secular one, such as socialism, becomes another bright and shiny thing, to be admired and consumed. All the same, even if blame can be bought like praise nowadays, he who blames is still to be preferred to he who praises. (pp. 464-67)

Philip Rieff, "Socialism and Sociology," in Partisan Review *(copyright © 1956 by Partisan Review, Inc.), Vol. XXIII, No. 3, Summer, 1956 (and reprinted in* The Partisan Review Anthology, *Holt, Rinehart and Winston, 1962, pp. 464-67).*

STUART CHASE

The class struggle as a key to the social structure has been in disrepair since Roosevelt's Hundred Days. It almost seems as if Mr. Mills had resolved [in *The Power Elite*] to rebuild it singlehanded, fortified by a blinding array of scholarly citations. Most of this research, unfortunately, does not seem to be objective scientific study, following facts wherever they may lead, so much as the systematic collection of material to buttress a preconceived argument.

Despite the impressive documentation, and my own chronic distrust of Big Wheels, I cannot make Mr. Mills' structural hypothesis fit the facts of change. . . . It does not fit recent social science research or my own observation over the years.

Americans, say the anthropologists, strive for power and prestige, but the struggle is fluid. W. Lloyd Warner, in his analysis of Newburyport, found six roughly defined classes, but reported that Irish, Jews, Italians, Poles, who started with the "lower-lowers," were already closing in on the "upper-uppers." The elite, as Mills portrays them, cement their position and property over the generations. He cites the astonishing trust funds of the Proper Bostonians, but neglects the Boston Irish—who have had Beacon Street on the ropes for decades.

Berle and Means showed how the owners of our great corporations have a right to a conventional dividend, and a waste basket into which to throw their proxies. Mr. Mills seems to confuse owners and managers. He does not understand Big Business—but then nobody else understands it very well either, not even its managers. It has developed into something brand new in the world, beyond all easy generalizations about ruling circles. Peter Drucker, David Lilienthal, E. H. Chamberlin, among others, could enlarge his view. . . .

Where is any proper appreciation of the graduated income tax as a gigantic sausage machine, taking billions of income away from the rich and the well-to-do, and shovelling it into the bottom? . . .

Another mammoth and unprecedented machine is the Federal Security Agency, which protects the "wage slaves," as they were called in 1910. The "welfare state" is so firmly entrenched that the Eisenhower administration would risk political disaster by any attempt to dismantle it. . . . This is not to say that poverty has been abolished, only that no nation in all history has ever carried material prosperity so far toward the lower depths.

"The Power Elite" has some excellent things to say about civil liberties, the antics of McCarthy, the wizards of Madison Avenue; it has some interesting facts about the behavior of zillionaires from Texas and points East. But its central thesis, that the rich, the big politicos, and the war lords, run America today, bears little relation to any America I know.

> Stuart Chase, "Do Rich Folks, Bosses and War Lords Run America?" in New York Herald Tribune (© I.H.T. Corporation; reprinted by permission), July 1, 1956, p. 7.

LEONARD REISSMAN

Mills' outstanding fault [in *The Power Elite*] is the uncritical acceptance of his own position. The brilliance and conciseness he shows in ferreting out the weakness of a position held by others is not as apparent when he is setting down his own views. He is almost frenetic in piling up his own substantiation. The reader is more overwhelmed than convinced; more entangled, than forced to inescapable conclusions by steady logic and hard fact. Much of this comes, of course, from the polemical character of Mills' writing and observations. Much of what he says, too, rings true but is often pushed to a distant point. The judgment to be made of Mills is never that what he says is true but unimportant, as can be said for much of the reporting in the social sciences; rather what he says is clearly important but not unquestionably valid. The *Power Elite* is without a question a reading experience that should not be allowed to pass. To those who believe that the *Lonely Crowd* is the final perspective of American social structure, the *Power Elite* is strongly recommended as a powerful antidote. To those who have been too long buried under picayune facts and research exercises, Mills should prove properly upsetting. Finally, to those whose appreciation for the larger consequences of social existence and commitment to the hard demands of scientific social analysis have not waned, the *Power Elite* will be both stimulating and frustrating. (pp. 513-14)

> Leonard Reissman, "Book Reviews: 'The Power Elite'," in American Sociological Review (copyright © 1956 by the American Sociological Association), Vol. 21, No. 4, August, 1956, pp. 513-14.

PAUL M. SWEEZY

Perhaps the greatest merit of *The Power Elite* is that it boldly breaks the tabu which respectable intellectual society has imposed on any serious discussion of how and by whom America is ruled. . . . For the first time in a long while, the literate public has been exposed to a serious discussion of social power and stratification at the national—as distinct from the local—level, and currently fashionable theories of the dispersal of power among many groups and interests have been bluntly challenged as flimsy apologetics. This is all to the good. . . . (p. 117)

Mills performs a very valuable service in insisting, emphatically and at times even dogmatically, that what happens in the United States today depends crucially on the will and decision of a relatively very small group which is essentially self-perpetuating and responsible to no one but its own membership. And in upholding this position, he earns our gratitude by a forthright attack on the social harmonics of our latter-day Bastiats such as J. K. Galbraith and David Riesman. Galbraith and Riesman are able social scientists and keen observers of the American scene, but their overall "theories," for which they have received so much praise and fame, are childishly pretentious and superficial. It is high time that a reputable member of the academic community should say so. Some day American social scientists will acknowledge the debt they owe to Mills for having been the first among them to proclaim in no uncertain terms that the king is naked.

I do not mean to imply by this any blanket endorsement of Mills' theoretical contributions. As I hope to show immediately, Mills' theory is open to serious criticism. But he has the very great merit of bringing the real issues into the open and discussing them in a way that anyone can understand; and he refuses to condone the kind of slick cover-up job that so many of his academic colleagues have been helping to put over on the American and foreign publics in the years of the "American celebration."

It is not easy to criticize *The Power Elite* from a theoretical standpoint for the simple reason that the author often states or implies more than one theory on a given topic or range of topics. Sometimes, I think, this arises from haste in composition and a certain intellectual sloppiness or impatience which seems to characterize much of Mills' work. Sometimes it seems to result from acceptance of the substance as well as the terminology of a kind of "elitist" doctrine which is basically antithetical to the general trend of his thought. And sometimes, no doubt, it arises from the fact that Mills, like most of the rest of us, has not made up his mind about all the problems of American social structure and finds himself with conflicting ideas rattling around in his head. (pp. 121-22)

Mills starts off with a concept of the power elite which is disarmingly simple. Those who occupy the "command posts" of our major economic, military, and political institutions constitute the power elite—the big shareholders and executives of the corporate system, the generals and admirals of the Pentagon, and the elected and appointed officials who occupy political positions of national significance. But this of course tells us nothing about the men who stand at these posts—how they got there, their attitudes and values, their relations with each other and with the rest of society, and so on—nor does it provide any but an admittedly misleading clue to these questions; Mills himself repeatedly rejects the notion that the power elite in his sense constitutes some sort of natural aristocracy of ability and intelligence, in spite of the common connotation of the term "elite."

Having in effect defined the power elite as composed of the big shots of industry and government, Mills' next task is to devise a theoretical scheme within which to locate them and to guide his empirical investigations into their characteristics and habits. Two general approaches readily suggest themselves, and Mills follows them both without ever clearly distinguishing them, without asking how far and in what respects they may be in conflict, and without any systematic attempt to reconcile their divergent results. The first approach is via social class: the hypothesis can be put forward and tested that those who occupy the command posts do so as representatives or agents of a national ruling class which trains them, shapes their thought patterns, and selects them for their positions of high responsibility. The second approach is via what Mills variously calls the "major institutional orders" . . . , the "major hierarchies" . . . , the "big three domains" . . . , and other more or less synonymous terms. This assumes that there are distinct spheres of social life—the economic, the military, and the political—each with its own institutional structure, that each of these spheres throws up its own leading cadres, and that the top men of all three come together to form the power elite.

Now there may be societies, past or present, in which this idea of more or less autonomous orders, hierarchies, or domains has enough relevance to make it a fruitful approach to problems of social structure and power. But it seems perfectly clear to me that the United States is not and never has been such a society. Moreover, the cumulative effects of the empirical data presented by Mills is decisively against any such interpretation of the American system. He adduces a wealth of material on our class system, showing how the local units of the upper class are made up of propertied families and how these local units are welded together into a wholly self-conscious national class. He shows how the "power elite" is overwhelmingly (and increasingly) recruited from the upper levels of the class system, how the same families contribute indifferently to the economic, military, and political "elites," and how the same individuals move easily and almost imperceptibly back and forth from one to another of these "elites." When it comes to "The Political Directorate" (Chapter 10), he demonstrates that the notion of a specifically political elite is in reality a myth, that the crucial positions in government and politics are increasingly held by what he calls "political outsiders," and that these outsiders are in fact members or errand boys of the corporate rich.

This demonstration in effect reduces "the big three" to "the big two"—the corporate and the military domains. There is no doubt at all about the decisive importance of the former, and Mills makes some of his most useful and interesting contributions in discussing the wealth, power, and other characteristics of the corporate rich. But the evidence for an autonomous, or even semi-autonomous, military domain of comparable importance is so weak that it can be said to be almost nonexistent. (pp. 123-25)

[The militarization of the civilian higher circles] has nothing in common with the rise to power of a military order headed by an elite of "warlords," though it is in these terms that Mills describes what has been happening in the United States since the beginning of World War II, and indeed *must* describe it or else abandon the whole theory of a composite power elite made of separate "domainal" elites. . . . (p. 125)

But Mills really relies much less on facts than on a sort of unstated syllogism to back up his warlord-military ascendancy theory. The syllogism might be formulated as follows: the major outlines of American policy, both foreign and domestic, are drawn in terms of a "military definition of world reality" which has been accepted by the power elite as a whole; this military definition of reality (also referred to as "military metaphysics") must be the product of the professional military mind

("the warlords"); *ergo* the warlords now occupy a decisive position within the power elite ("the military ascendancy"). This may look impressive and convincing at a first glance, but a moment's reflection will show that it explains nothing and constitutes no support whatever for Mills' theory. Professional military people naturally think in military terms and have doubtless always tried to persuade others to see things their way. Throughout most of United States history, they have succeeded, if at all, only in wartime. The real problem is to understand why it is that since World War II the whole "power elite" has come to think increasingly in military terms and hence to accord a place of greater honor and power to the military. Without an answer to this, all the facts that seem to Mills to add up to the "military ascendancy" of the "warlords" remain quite unexplained.

Now Mills himself never faces up to this question, and the only relevant answer I can find is that the United States now, unlike in the past, lives in a "military neighborhood" (the phrase is used on a number of occasions), which presumably means that the country is under constant threat (or potential threat) of attack and military defeat. This is more sophisticated than saying that we live in mortal danger of red aggression, but its explanatory value is exactly the same: in either case the increasing militarization of American life is the result of external forces. The rise of the warlords, then, is seen as the outcome of a world historical process for which the United States has no responsibility and over which it has no control, and not, as Mills clearly wants to prove, as the outcome of *internal* forces operating in the military domain.

Thus, while Mills appears to have little in common with the cold-war liberals, and in fact rather generally holds them in contempt, his theory of the role of the military leads to very much the same conclusions. I believe that this is no accident. "Elitist" thinking *inevitably* diverts attention from problems of social structure and process and leads to a search for external causes of social phenomena. . . . Semi-elitists like Mills— people who think they can adopt the terminology without any of the basic ideas of elitist theory—tend to get bogged down in confusion from which the only escape is to borrow the most banal ideas of their opponents.

It is too bad that Mills gets into this kind of a mess, because, as I indicated above, his work is strongly influenced by a straightforward class theory which, if he had stuck to it and consistently explored its implications, would have enabled him to avoid completely the superficialities and pitfalls of elitist thinking. The uppermost class in the United States is, and long has been, made up of the corporate rich who directly pull the economic levers. . . . The picture of "warlords" exercising a "military ascendancy" is fanciful: *our* warlords have no fundamental values or purposes different from those of their corporate colleagues; many of them perform virtually indistinguishable jobs; and the crowning achievement of a military career today is the board chairmanship of a billion-dollar corporation. At the same time, we have nothing even approaching a unified military order or caste seeking to impose its "military metaphysics" on the nation. (pp. 126-28)

No, the facts simply won't fit Mills' theory of three (or two) sectional elites coming together to form an overall power elite. What we have in the United States is a *ruling class* with its roots deeply sunk in the "apparatus of appropriation" which is the corporate system. To understand this ruling class—its metaphysics, its purposes, and its morals—we need to study, not certain "domains" of American life, however defined, but the whole system of monopoly capitalism.

A large part of Mills' theory and most of his facts support this view. This, indeed, is why his book, for all its weaknesses, is such a vital and powerful document. Let us hope that in the future he will drop *all* the elitist nonsense and make the contribution he is capable of making to deepening our theory and understanding of the American class system. (p. 129)

Paul M. Sweezy, "Power Elite or Ruling Class?" in Monthly Review *(copyright © 1956, by Monthly Review, Inc., reprinted by permission of Monthly Review Press), September, 1956 (and reprinted as "Power Elite or Ruling Class?" in* C. Wright Mills *and "The Power Elite," edited by G. William Domhoff and Hoyt B. Ballard, Beacon Press, 1968, pp. 115-32).*

D. W. BROGAN

[In *The Causes of World War III*] Professor Mills emphasises things that we don't see or that we ignore. Confronted with the sight of human folly on a cosmic scale, he does not throw up his hands; he spits on them and gets down to the job. For him, history is not a governing condition, neither is past theory. The rational course of action is obvious and if enough people get to work in the right spirit and with the right degree of intelligence, the world will escape the doom of 'World War III.' But unless there is this brisk stocktaking and house-cleaning we will blunder into the final catastrophe. . . .

It would be unjust to reproach Professor Mills with being simply a panacea-monger. He is rather an angry radical shocked and frightened by what he sees in America. He sees an alliance by the great corporations and the Pentagon designed to keep international tensions acute. That way, the present exorbitant expenditure on defence can continue, and a great part of the American economy depends on that expenditure; and, equally important, the managers of the economy depend on the tension-based boom for the rise in stock prices which is their material reward. It should be said that Professor Mills does not depend for the force of his argument on the imputation of motive. Given their training, their natural bias, their defective education, it is natural that, in good faith, the managers and the generals should behave this way. And they are encouraged to do so by a mass culture in which certain fundamental questions are not asked. Much of Professor Mills's anger is directed against the American educated classes, who accept the necessity of the cold war and of the domination of the American scene by the Pentagon and the corporations. They have been content to be treated as second-class citizens and to say ditto or keep their traps shut. They must now speak up.

With much of what Professor Mills has to say it is hard to disagree. Although the extent to which free thought and free speech were threatened in America was exaggerated, there was, in some measure there is, a refusal to face the facts of Soviet power (a refusal punctuated by panic) or the claims of the Soviet Government or of its allies like Communist China. There is still a dangerous addiction to wishful thinking, to an expectation of the inevitable decline of so un-American a society as the Soviet Union, still too much easy and delusory classification of countries and regimes as pro- or anti-Russian. Any fresh voice—and Professor Mills's voice is fresh and loud—is welcome. So are some of his suggestions. I am all for the series of international centres scattered round the world 'containing restaurants and sleeping quarters, multilingual stenographic pools and conference rooms of various sizes.' These are to house 'qualified cultural workmen of all nationalities.' The suspicion with which the American Government regards contact with Communist societies *is* silly and reflects a dangerous state of mind. Then the allocation of great funds (whether taken from the existing U.S. military budget or not) for grants in aid to backward countries like India is most desirable. So is the cessation of atom-bomb tests. So is, as a guiding line, the assumption that 'war not Russia is now the enemy.' . . .

[But] the situation is not as simple as Professor Mills supposes. His tract, for all its virtues, reveals that illusion of American superiority which critics have found so maddening. Although there are a few harsh words for the rulers of the USSR, this is an *American* programme, that is what the US should do. But suppose the USSR doesn't play? . . . A good deal of the present tension has been contributed by the US, but a lot more by the USSR. And it will take two to make peace. Yet, as a shock administered to the dominant American theory of world affairs, this is a most valuable book. It is often, too, a shrewd book. . . . Americans would be rash to adopt all the bold programme advocated here, but they would be wise to re-think some of their principles and practices. . . .

D. W. Brogan, "New Worlds," in The Spectator *(©1959 by* The Spectator; *reprinted by permission of* The Spectator*), Vol. 202, No. 6812, January 16, 1959, p. 82.**

EDWARD POSNIAK

In *The Causes of World War Three* C. Wright Mills projects his earlier analysis of our society as ruled by a "power elite" into the realm of foreign policy. (p. 615)

Paradoxically, while Mills stigmatizes the role of the power elite in what he regards as "the drift and thrust toward World War III," he also believes that "the rise of the power elite . . . opens up new opportunities for the willful making of history." The old international balance of power among many relatively equal nation-states has been replaced by a polarized world; the decisive interplay is now between two super-states. Events have become less subject to fate, more subject to human decision. And while the power elites may be "both dogmatic and incompetent," the concentration of power both within and between nations may open the way to a greater role for reason in human affairs.

While Mills thus perceives some hope in the power elite, he sees little hope indeed in the people: "They are not radical, not liberal, not conservative, not reactionary. They are inactionary. They are out of it. If we accept the Greek definition of the idiot as an altogether private man, then we must conclude that many American and many Soviet citizens are now idiots. . . . The prevalence of mass indifference is surely one of the major political facts about the Western societies today." Speaking of this "time of moral somnabulence," Mills concludes, in a phrase reminiscent of Albert Camus, that "the individual becomes the spectator of everything and the human witness of nothing."

For a self-professed radical, this disbelief in the "masses" and implicit hope in the "power elite" is an interesting deviation from orthodox dogma. But this heresy does not affect Mills' main thesis, which may be summed up as follows: The immediate cause of World War III is the military preparation for it. The immediate causes of the arms race are the official definitions of world realities clung to by the elites of the United States and the USSR. The official theory of war—"the military metaphysic"—is itself among the causes of the thrust toward war. . . . The economic and military causes of war are allowed to operate because of the political apathy of the public and the moral insensitivity of the masses in both Communist and capitalist worlds—and because of the political inactivity and abdication of "leading intellectual circles" of these worlds.

But, Mills emphasizes, the thrust toward World War III is *not* a plot on the part of the elite—adding, with generous impartiality, "either that of the USA or that of the USSR." Among both, he believes, there are "war parties" and "peace parties," and among both there are what he calls "crackpot realists." (pp. 615-16)

While much of Mills' analysis is both relevant and revealing, he weakens his case by oversimplification, particularly by his almost total identification of the characteristics of "the power elites of the USA and the USSR." Surely, it is far cry from the "administrative elite" in control of critical decisions in the United States, subject to at least occasional "interference" from Congress, the press, and the public, to the totalitarian control of the USSR by the Kremlin. To equate the pluralistic society of this country with the monolithic power structure of the Soviet Union is to evade realities. The acid test is that books like *The Power Elite* and *The Causes of World War Three* are published in this country; they are not published in the USSR.

Mills' strongest points are made in the analytical portions of his essay, the parts entitled **"Do Men Make History?"** and **"World War Three."** The last two parts—**"What Then, Ought We to Do?"** and **"The Role of the Intellectuals"**—are much weaker by comparison. Both his "guidelines" for a new foreign policy and his exhortation to intellectuals suffer from a fatal naiveté due in large part to the forced parallelism between the United States and the USSR. In his own terms, Mills' definition of reality seems less than adequate.

Nevertheless, this angry little book, though likely to provoke equally angry retorts, should also stimulate more thought on a subject of literally vital concern. (pp. 616-17)

> *Edward Posniak, "New Books in Review: 'The Causes of World War Three',"* in The Yale Review *(©1959 by Yale University; reprinted by permission of the editors), Vol. XLVIII, No. 4, June, 1959, pp. 615-17.**

EVERETT C. HUGHES

[*The Sociological Imagination*] is primarily an essay on political philosophy. . . . The earlier chapters are a vigorous attack upon what Mills considers the wrong, even dangerously wrong, ways of doing social science, and especially sociology. The more widely practiced of the wrong ways he dubs Grand Theory and Abstracted Empiricism. And what is wrong with them? It is that they not only fall short of the promise of social science, but that they get in the way of it. Indeed, they incapacitate people for developing that "sociological imagination" which "enables us to grasp history and biography and the relations between the two within society." . . .

Mills' complaint (if so vigorous an attack may be called by so mild a word) is that social scientists—again more especially his own colleagues, the sociologists—will not help the young

man [attempt to make his knowledge and insights serve the end of gearing his and others' personal problems into the public, historic processes—with a belief that history can be made]. The Grand Theorist builds systems in useless jargon (Mills translates some examples into simple English) which tell one little about human variety. By a hidden bias in favor of stability, the Grand Theory takes attention away from the struggle for power. The Abstracted Empiricists, the people who make sample surveys of opinions—Mills says—elevate their particular way of working into a general and presumably the only true theory of science; only that knowledge is worth gaining which can be got by their techniques. Since their techniques ignore social structure and the very concept of history, the Abstracted Empiricism breed a generation of a-historical, anti-structural sociologists—technicians and bureaucrats of the new research. Since their surveys are thought useful by businesses and government agencies, they can and do prosper. Their work, too, ignores larger issues and encourages use of talents for minor bureaucratic ends—or at least for ends not of the social scientists' own choosing.

From time to time, Mills takes back some of his hard words, by allowing—in a footnote or aside—that some of the people working in the wrong way are doing good work; or that the older Abstracted Empiricists who have learned classical social science in their youth are better than their disciples, who have only the new training.

Mills' own use of the sociological imagination in analyzing what is going on among his brethren is uncanny. But as with so many good things, enough is too much. Mills seems a bit enamored of his very great powers of analysis and rhetoric; he is rather obsessed with power as a factor in society. He loves to rub power into every wound. It is this just-a-bit-too-muchness that makes it so hard to tell possession by the divine spirit from possession by the devil.

I do not subscribe to all of Mills' strictures on his (and my) fraternity of sociologists. He gives comfort to those who welcome any excuse to attack social science from either the left or the right flank; to those who, having read his chapters of criticism with glee, will go no further. Yet I cannot but welcome the main points of his criticism; and even more one must both welcome and take to heart his plea for "classical social science" brought up to date. For classical social science—as he defines it—gears the small problems to the large, the private to the public; it attacks the problem of freedom and reason with courageous, passionate objectivity. It makes its methods suit the problem, instead of cutting the problem to suit one's favorite technique. If we who are sociologists have enough of the sociological imagination, we can take the criticism, and devote more time to doing our job than to correcting errors of detail in Mills', or other attacks.

> *Everett C. Hughes, "Can History Be Made?" in* The New Republic *(reprinted by permission of* The New Republic; *© 1959 The New Republic, Inc.), Vol. 140, No. 25, June 22, 1959, p. 19.*

W.J.H. SPROTT

What ought sociologists to do, and what is their function in society? To these questions Professor Mills addresses himself [in *The Sociological Imagination*]. His answers are not merely of parochial interest to the sociologist; they are of general significance because of the political role to which, in his view, sociologists should aspire. They are to be the "carriers of reason in human affairs." . . .

Professor Mills notes that . . . piecemeal inquiries into "problems" distracted the sociologist from an examination of the social structure in which they arose. Admirable as they were—and are—these investigations have also led to a preoccupation with method and an accompanying lack of concern about the significance of the topics on which increasingly elaborate methodological devices are brought to bear. Professor Mills launches a devastating attack on what he calls "abstracted empiricists." He accuses them not only of "pretentious triviality" but—worse—of becoming the servants of bureaucratic institutions that can afford to pay for their "projects."

As a reaction, maybe, to the trivialities of much meticulous fact-gathering, we have "grand theory," an attempt to develop an interpretative framework, derived from the very nature of human interaction, which will be applicable to all societies. Unhappily this involves the omission of such empirical data as economics and political systems which are, after all, important structural features of any actual society. Talcott Parsons, the natural target for Professor Mills's attack in this direction, is easy meat. . . .

There is, however, another charge against the theorist—a charge which corresponds to the one launched against the "abstracted" empiricists. The stress on order may serve as an ideological justification of authority. It is here that we come to Professor Mills's most important contention: the moral involvement of the social scientist. Since he is dealing with the affairs of men, his action and his inaction have moral implications. He is never *wert-frei*. By the very choice of his research projects he is either a critic or a half-conscious supporter of the regime in which he works or else he displays a culpable indifference to it which is tantamount to support. This is the real burden of Professor Mills's manifesto. The social scientist must face up to his duties. (p. 55)

[Professor Mills], unlike so many of our Cassandras, appreciates the point that those who cry out about the "crisis of our times" are more concerned with "what is to men's interests" than with "what men are interested in." They are, in fact, infuriated by apathy. Men ought, they say, to be in a position to make rational choices; the social order is such that they can't. This is all wrong—but what if they like it that way? There is, as Professor Mills admits, a concealed hypothesis about human nature in all these criticisms of our Western society. Nevertheless, he would appear to argue that even if people choose what he would call "alienation"—a pejorative word—they must be clear about what they are choosing.

He clearly thinks that the choice will go the other way and this is where the sociologist as "carrier of reason" comes in. It is his job to address the public on the facts of power, to show them what sort of person our bureaucratic society produces—to relate personal problems to structural context—and to put Western man in a position of choice. He holds out no high hopes but he gives the social scientist something worth doing. (pp. 55-6)

> W.J.H. Sprott, "The Ethics of Sociology," in The Nation (copyright 1959 The Nation magazine, The Nation Associates, Inc.), Vol. 189, No. 3, August 1, 1959, pp. 55-6.

CHARLES MADGE

Much as I sympathize with much of [C. Wright Mills's argument in *The Sociological Imagination*], I cannot go all the way with Professor Mills in his feeling that the sociological imagination, as he explains it, is becoming 'the major common denominator of our cultural life'. In the complex division of labour at the level of creative imagination, we have no reason to assume that the social scientist is about to supersede the artist. It is quite true that 'the serious artist is himself in much trouble'; he may even be on his last legs. But I personally resist the suggestion that he could 'well do with some intellectual and cultural aid from a social science made sprightly by the sociological imagination'. Part of the 'trouble' of the artist is the dead weight of undigested sociology that pulls him down. Sociology is necessary, sociology is good. If sociology is imaginative, so much the better. But for myself I would no more put it at the summit of imaginative activity than, with Comte, at the summit of scientific activity. It is the kind of inquiry most characteristic of the sensibility of this epoch; we have to live with our epoch and we have to live with sociology. (p. 282)

> Charles Madge, "The Politics of Truth," in New Statesman (© 1959 The Statesman & Nation Publishing Co. Ltd.), Vol. LVIII, No. 1486, September 5, 1959, pp. 281-82.

TAD SZULC

[In "**Listen, Yankee,**" an] emotional, hurriedly gathered and written volume, C. Wright Mills . . . undertakes to present the Cuban version of the "truth about Cuba" as it seems to stand today and announces that he finds it "compelling" and "persuasive."

The theme running through Mr. Mills' eight "letters," written to a hypothetical "Yankee" in the name of Cuban revolutionaries (and reiterated through the introduction and epilogue) is that Americans, deprived by their own press of anything remotely resembling honest truth about the Castro phenomenon, simply have no understanding of what is happening in Cuba. What is more, Mr. Mills and his composite Cubans say, Americans fail to grasp the responsibility of Wall Street, big United States corporations, Yankee imperialism and the State Department, for the turn of events in Cuba, including Castro's acceptance of Soviet and Chinese military and economic aid. (p. 30)

To restore the United States position in Cuba and Latin America—and Mr. Mills argues that Cuba is our "Big Chance"—he proposes that it forget all the nonsense about communism in Cuban Government and that it help the Castro revolution instead of hindering it. Simultaneously, he writes, the United States should "actively help Latin Americans destroy the vested interests inside their own countries as well as the vested interests of United States corporations now operating in these countries."

Mr. Mills has written a most disturbing and useful book. Through its pages his Cuban letter-writers mercilessly pound on the Yankee for his stupidity, blindness and intellectual sloth before the emergence of social revolutions in a hungry world, and for the criminal venality of his money-mad big corporations. Catching superbly the color, flavor and intensity of the revolutionary thinking and emotion, he has presented with fine accuracy what Castro and his friends think and what makes them act the way they have been acting toward the United States.

Whereas the author has been eminently successful in putting across this "voice of the Cuban revolution," he seems to have overlooked the merits of the old academic tenet about free inquiry and the dictum that there may be two sides to any question. In fact, in the sections in which he undertakes to summarize and speak for himself, he becomes the victim of the evil he so outspokenly ascribes to United States newsmen: total one-sidedness. (pp. 30, 32)

[Mills] renders a long list of final verdicts and pontifications which, he admits at the outset, are based on only one month's stay in Cuba. . . .

Perhaps because his time in Cuba was limited, Mr. Mills did not find it possible to hear opinions at variance with the official line. He, therefore, submits that "all" Cubans are for Castro. He dismisses those who may no longer be for him, including some of the top revolutionary fighters of 1956-58, as counter-revolutionaries or milktoasts. He proclaims flatly that there are no Communists in the Cuban leadership and that the land reform has been a smashing success in all its aspects. He passes lightly over such Cuban realities as denial of freedom and expression and only briefly acknowledges that a reign of terror could develop in Cuba.

Most observers of the Cuban scene will admit that grievous United States errors occurred in relation to Cuba before the revolution and continue to occur. There is much to be said for many of the social reforms of the Castro movement. But it is undeniable that the portrait of Cuba here drawn is only in black and white. It paints total United States guilt and total Cuban righteousness. To right the harm that he says American newsmen have done Cuba and, at the same time, to bow a bit toward objectivity, Mr. Mills might have achieved a better balance had he let the "voice of the revolution" speak for itself—and withheld his conclusions. (p. 32)

Tad Szulc, "Cuba Si, Yanqui No," in The New York Times Book Review *(© 1960 by The New York Times Company; reprinted by permission), December 4, 1960, pp. 30, 32.*

PETER CLECAK

The controversy since [C. Wright] Mills's death over the precise character and structure of the American governing class illuminates, in microcosm, his major strengths and weaknesses as a sociologist and social critic. That he undertook *White Collar* and *The Power Elite* in the 1950s testifies to his intellectual courage and independence. That these books precipitated a serious and fruitful controversy reveals his intellectual boldness: a master of the broad stroke, the sweeping generality, Mills accomplished more than most of us, not only because he worked harder but also because he was able to cut to the center of massive problems swiftly, generally without undue simplification. The controversy also illuminates Mills's corresponding defects, chiefly an inability to sketch out qualifying assumptions and details, which in turn marred his more abstract generalizations. The interrelated strengths and weaknesses of Mills's intellectual character and craftsmanship permeate his work of the early and middle fifties. The deficiencies, especially his theoretical carelessness, also contribute to the most pervasive fault that runs through all his postwar work: a tendency to transform social criticism into a myth of personal consolation.

The confusion between elites and social classes identified by [Paul] Sweezy illuminates the larger tension that Mills acknowledged from time to time but never carefully worked out. He recognized that the main structural tendencies in American society of the 1950s ran counter to his own values and hopes: power was divorced from knowledge and moral vision; powers of individual rationality and purposeful action beyond the personal sphere had been largely arrogated by major institutions. Thus, without the concept of elites at the top, Mills would have been unable to account for the conscious role of men— even the wrong men—in the making of postwar history. Both Sweezy's notion of a ruling class and [G. William] Domhoff's conception of a power elite primarily dependent on the economic system reduce the element of will in the making and remaking of history. Or they implicitly relocate the capacity for radical change in some combination of individuals and classes that Mills considered powerless. But the partially accurate concept of elites enabled Mills to explain the powerlessness of most men and the irrational direction of society without submitting wholly to the mood of despair.

By preserving the power elite as an essentially anthropomorphic category of explanation, Mills retained the hope that history was not necessarily at a dead end. Though currently under the direction of the irrational few, it could theoretically be made democratically by the many: reason and freedom might be linked up with power. As a matter of historical fact, Mills argued, concentration and centralization of power were causally associated with the decline of democracy and freedom in America; this was the historical "drift," the reason for despair. The corollary potentialities for rational, democratic control of man's fate constituted the slim hope, the myth of consolation. Rather than implying a political way out of the historical impasse, however, these theoretical potentialities only preserved the hope that one might be found through a transfer of power from elites to publics. Moreover, Mills's supreme faith in the history-making power of one public, the radical intelligentsia, created a serious moral tension in his developing political philosophy. Substituting a myth of elites for the discarded Marxian notion of the masses as creators of history, he came perilously close to subverting his belief in democracy. "'Every man,'" Mills frequently remarked, quoting his grandfather, "'should have one gun, one vote—and one woman at a time.'" Yet it is as a pragmatic elitist who also believed in participatory democracy, rather than as an unyielding democrat, that Mills admired Lenin, Trotsky, and Castro: in contrast to the old Left groups in the West, these men successfully pursued power—and shaped history—at least for a time.

Although social critics should not be expected to "solve" the theoretical puzzle of the ratios of freedom (chance and choice) and determinism in history, they can be expected to offer lucid statements concerning the mixture as a preliminary context for detailed discussions of concrete situations. In turn, specific analyses should reveal ways of qualifying initial abstractions. By muddling the first task in the fifties, Mills ensured failure at the second. It is not that he was unaware of tensions between the apparently irreconcilable facts of power and the unrealized potentialities of democracy and freedom. He articulated them at the highest level of abstraction. By mingling the concepts of elites and classes, however, he placed both elements—reason and irrationality, power and powerlessness, fate and will, freedom and determinism—in a larger and politically paralyzing construct of hope and despair. At this level, Mills represented the actual elements of "drift" as reasons for pessimism, and the potential "thrust" of publics as the cause for hope.

The only problem was that the wrong people monopolized power, adding their thrust to the historical drift toward oblivion.

In his desire to perceive the making of history as an increasingly conscious activity, Mills probably assigned too much weight to the elites at the top. Having done this, he was committed to overexplaining the powerlessness of other groups. The myth of consolation appealed to powerless individuals, but it implicitly subverted the creation of a new politics. Convinced of this stark version of radical paradoxes—a version bordering on myth—Mills was often unable to write convincingly about domestic politics or about international problems. (pp. 62-4)

Despite the potential safety valves that Mills built into his analyses of the American present, he remained unable to show how sane forces might fill the political void. In fact, he was unable to invest the mythic dimension of his criticism with political credibility, if only because the implied advocates of a new turn no longer existed in significant numbers. In his criticism of the fifties, the nostalgic image of the rational and free man served mainly as a rhetorical device to illuminate ominous social trends. It was also an ideal self that Mills projected into his work, making him alternately the hero and victim of his own symbolic world. At this mythic level, the conflict between elitist and democratic selves takes on a kind of inner consistency. He believes that rational and free men—men like himself—ought to shape history democratically. But he also considers himself part of a small minority, a moral elite that might yet achieve power. Like those of other plain Marxists, Mills's response to the ethical dimensions of radical paradoxes contains an authoritarian undercurrent: in order for history to be made democratic, it cannot be made democratically.

As he became increasingly absorbed with the problems of action, Mills was bound by the mythic dimensions of his social vision to project this old image of a new man as the human agent of progressive change. Ironically, then, the fragmentary and contradictory political philosophy toward which he was groping in his last years depended upon the very social type which, according to his earlier work, had become nearly extinct in contemporary American society. As with other plain Marxists, Mills's concrete hope for a viable Left finally rested on a symbolic construct, a "new" man who, were he not politically lifeless, might enact a genuinely radical program. In the end, the less ambitious personal myth of consolation—the abstract hope that men could still shape history rationally and democratically—allowed Mills to continue his own work: that and no more. (pp. 66-7)

> *Peter Clecak, "C. Wright Mills: The Lone Rebel,"
> in his* Radical Paradoxes: Dilemmas of the American
> Left, 1945-1970 *(copyright © 1973 by Peter Clecak;
> reprinted by permission of Harper & Row, Publishers, Inc.),* Harper & Row, 1973, pp. 31-71.

JOSEPH A. SCIMECCA

Mills offers us [in his writings a "working model of a social system"] that is liberating, while still possessing an adequate conception of social structure—one that does not sacrifice the volitional, active nature of man. Mills points out a path toward freedom. Because of his early training in Pragmatism, Mills never gave up the notion of the autonomous individual who could use his reason to gain and secure his freedom. Like Marx, Mills believed man was alienated given the society he lived in, but where Marx saw alienation as a result of the irrationality of production, Mills saw it coming from man's perception of and adaptation to a society which results from blind drift. In order to be free the individual had to make the connection between "private troubles" and "public issues." He had to be aware that structural problems were the key to his malaise. Only by seeing the interconnection of biography and history could man begin to gauge the limits of his potential. This was the fundamental message of *The Sociological Imagination*, and it is explicit in Mills' working model approach. The social scientist must look at the structure of society as a whole, and at the ways in which the institutions which comprise it shape the character of individuals. But more than this, Mills argued, he must "study the structural limits of human decision in an attempt to find points of effective intervention, in order to know what can and what must be structurally changed if the role of explicit decision in history-making is to be enlarged." . . . The possessor of the sociological imagination should study historical structures in order to find ways which can insure the freedom of individuals. Beyond this locating of where the structure could best be changed lay the political problem of decision-making and the intellectual problem of discerning the structural limits of man's basic nature. (pp. 188-89)

Mills offers a picture of man as free, but constrained by power relations. In this view some men are freer than others and are thereby responsible for their acts. History is made behind most men's backs, not behind all men's backs. There are varying degrees of freedom. Through the use of the model, power and those in positions of power, not necessarily economic elites, can be located. Who they are, as well as why they are powerful, is a problem for investigation by the sociologist. What we have in Mills' model is not an "invidious doctrine" of free-will which can be used to justify punishment and repression when men are perceived as responsible for their actions, as a Scientific Marxist might say, but a doctrine of moral responsibility in the face of societal constraint. Man is free, but some men are freer than others. (p. 189)

My position, quite simply, is that Mills' "working model of a social system" is one of the most important theoretical frameworks developed by a contemporary American sociologist. While it is in no way as grand an undertaking as the system of Parsons, it may very well be, because of its limited scope, a viable alternative to the Parsonian trans-historical theory of man and society.

C. Wright Mills provided a working model of a social system which enables its users to analyze just how much the individual is constrained by his social structure. In doing so Mills left a cohesive, systematic, historical sociology—a model that can provide the structural perspective radical sociology currently lacks. . . . Mills left us a sociological map in the form of a general model of a social system, a model that offers a viable notion of social structure without sacrificing the active, volitional side of man. (pp. 194-95)

> *Joseph A. Scimecca, "Paying Homage to the Father:
> C. Wright Mills and Radical Sociology," in* The Sociological Quarterly *(© Midwest Sociological Society, 1976), Vol., No., Spring, 1976, pp. 180-96.*

Juliet Mitchell

1940-

Mitchell is a New Zealand-born English feminist author and lecturer. She is the author of *Psychoanalysis and Feminism* (1975), a forceful defense of Freud's psychoanalytic concept of femininity. Some critics charge that Mitchell's reliance upon psychoanalytic concepts precludes a practical resolution of the problem of women's subjugation. However, many agree that her ideas are a significant contribution to feminist thought. (See also *Contemporary Authors*, Vols. 45-48.)

Excerpt from *PSYCHOANALYSIS AND FEMINISM*

No understanding of Freud's ideas on femininity and female sexuality is possible without some grasp of two fundamental theories: firstly, the nature of unconscious mental life and the particular laws that govern its behaviour, and secondly, the meaning of sexuality in human life. Only in the context of these two basic propositions do his suggestions on the psychological differences between men and women make sense. It is necessary to make sure of their meaning before any specific theses can be comprehended and assessed.

It is also, I would suggest, a characteristic of most attacks on Freud's work that, though the criticism *seems* to be over specific issues, what is really being rejected is this whole intellectual framework of psychoanalysis. Most hostile critics pay tribute to Freud's discovery of the nature of unconscious mental life and of infantile sexuality, and of the importance of sexuality in general. Most politically revolutionary writers would outbid Freud in their stress on the final indivisibility of normality and abnormality, forgetting that this was one of Freud's starting points. There is a formal obeisance to Freud's theories, yet behind most criticism of details there lies an unacknowledged refusal of every major concept. Time and time again, one dissident after another has repudiated singly or wholesale all the main scientific tenets of psychoanalysis. For the same reason that these critics unconsciously deny the unconscious, it is difficult to offer an explanation of it: it *is* unconscious. But, obviously, it would be worse than inadequate just to suggest that we take Freud's word for it, that we just *believe* in its existence. Although we *can* have a subjective knowledge of our own unconscious mental life, it is only in its random expressions that we can recognize it. Symptoms of the unconscious manifest themselves in latent dream-thoughts, slips of pen and memory, etc., and these are all we can ever know of it in this subjective sense. But Freud, in systematizing these manifestations, offers objective knowledge. We can see how it works and understand the need for it to exist to explain what is happening in the symptom. In one sense, Freud found the unconscious because nothing else would explain what he observed—and he certainly tried everything anyone could think of first. Once, after much doubt, he had postulated its existence, he set out to determine how it worked. This makes the process sound too sequential: an instance of how it worked, of course, would also help convince him of its existence. In other words, unlike the poets and story-tellers to whom he always gave credit for their recognition of the unconscious, Freud could not *believe* in the unconscious, he had to *know* it.

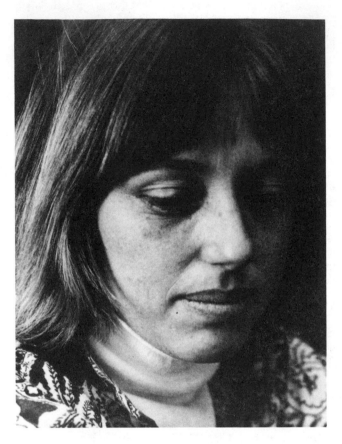

Courtesy of Deborah Rogers Ltd.

To be convinced of his knowledge, we cannot believe it either, but if the laws by which he claimed it operated can be shown to have an internal consistency, then we can give up a faith for a science—imperfect as it may be.

The unconscious that Freud discovered is not a deep, mysterious place, whose presence, in mystical fashion, accounts for all the unknown; *it is knowable and it is normal*. What it contains is normal thought, utterly transformed by its own laws (which Freud called the primary process), but nevertheless only transformed and hence still recognizable if one can deduce the manner of the transformation, that is, decipher the laws of the primary process to which the thought is subjected. For instance, an unconscious wish originating in infancy becomes attached to the wish in the present time which has evoked it, but if it is unacceptable to consciousness, it is pushed down (repressed) into the unconscious where it is transformed and where it remains—until re-evoked, or until it breaks out (as a symptom), or until it is analysed. The point for our purpose here is that unconscious thoughts are repressed and thus transformed 'normal' ones, and that they are always there, speaking to us, in their way.

It is within the understanding of the unconscious that all Freud's observations are made—even those that seem not directly to impinge on it. Leaving aside again those questions that relate to his other great discovery, the role of sexuality, what he is therefore saying, for instance, about the nature of femininity, relates to how femininity is lived in the mind. (pp. 5-7)

[Radical] feminist critics have told Freud he is a fool for not applying the standards of reality to repressed psychical structures; by doing so, they have misunderstood his language. Freud found that an understanding of neurotic mechanisms gave him an understanding of normal mental processes (in other words, they were not different); because both the symptoms of neuroses (in particular in the early days, hysteria) and the normal-psychoses, in other words, dreams, were his 'royal' road to the unconscious (though he used the phrase only of dreams), it was their language they had to use—this was the currency of the land he was mapping.

The snag with Freud's presentation of his discoveries and, therefore, of any attempted simplification and re-presentation of them, is that a description *reverses* the analytic procedure. Freud was listening to the *recollected* history of his patients, he reconstructed infantile life from the fragmentary stories the patient told in which time past and time present are one. He read the history of the person *backwards*—as it is always essential to do; but in retelling it, he describes it as a march forwards, a process of development where it is in fact a multi-level effort of reconstruction. This distinction becomes very important when, as I believe, post-Freudian analysts of femininity continued to describe a process and forgot the historical nature of the events—their work is thus developmental, not analytical. This was a dilemma too, faced later by child analysis. Again, what can be forgotten is that at every moment of a person's existence he is living and telling in word, deed or symptom the story of his life: a three-year-old child has a past that he lives in his present, just as does the octogenarian. It is the crucial acquisition of the story of his life that that person is undergoing at the Oedipal moment, and that repeats itself in different ways throughout his time on earth—or rather within his days in human culture. Freud's discovery of infantile sexuality, and of sexuality as a key factor in mental life, is a perfect example of this difficulty: the person *does* develop and change sexually, but not with ruthless sequential logic and never so that the past is 'past'; even a person's account of his change is a coherent story of himself, it is the way men and women and children 'live' themselves in the world. (pp. 14-15)

> *Juliet Mitchell, in her* Psychoanalysis and Feminism *(copyright © 1974 by Juliet Mitchell; reprinted by permission of Pantheon Books, a Division of Random House, Inc.), Pantheon Books, 1974, 456 p.*

RICHARD SENNETT

[Juliet Mitchell's analysis in *Woman's Estate* of the unequal conditions of men and women] is made on three levels. It is, first, what American sociologists—with typical awkwardness—would call a "structure-functional" approach. Second, it is a method for showing how the injustices women face are a necessity, if the institutions of present-day society are to stay knitted together. Third, the analysis makes a prediction that the bonds of society need not hold, that change of a radical sort is possible, if both women and men act in a certain way. (p. 24)

Mitchell sees the estate of women in society as based on four "structures" or processes: production, reproduction, socialization, and sexuality. None of these processes is a "root," a first principle. . . . Take the increasing percentage of women in the American labor force as an example: what Mitchell would explore about that change in production is how it relates to changes in child-bearing, child-raising, and the relations between men and women at home. If women laborers in factories are increasing, and the size of their families is decreasing, there needs to be, in Mitchell's theory, a connection; such changes in social processes don't happen at random. But she also thinks it useless to try to arrive at a general theory of whether production "determines" reproduction or the other way around.

In the hands of many American sociologists, such analysis has become a liberal instrument: if nothing causes anything else but is only related to it, coherent radical social change seems impossible. If society is unjust, well, no one part of it can be held to blame.

The originality of Mitchell's book is that she uses structure-functional analysis for entirely different ends. She doesn't think you can describe a connection between production and reproduction, for instance, and then argue about whether the connection is just or unjust; it is not enough simply to state the fact that more women are becoming factory laborers and that these women are having smaller families. In Mitchell's view, one cannot understand the possible connection between the two facts without also understanding the loss of freedom the connection causes women: birth control pills give women less family responsibility but *of necessity,* in her view, the production system grows so that these women will be employed in new kinds of very low status factory labor.

The idea of necessity is the critical issue in Mitchell's theory. She is not an economic determinist; nor is she interested in analyzing, either theoretically or empirically, the meaning of terms like "class" or "capitalism." . . . For Mitchell, society must necessarily oppress women because of a characteristic that, according to her hypothesis, all four structures share.

Each of the structures contains an internal contradiction. In her theory, men do not simply dominate women. Sexually, men and women engage in all sorts of subterranean exchanges and compromises, and Mitchell is acute enough to see that the timidity of husbands with their wives is as common as the opposite case. The only way these tensions of sexual life can be dealt with, in Mitchell's view, is for the pressure to be relieved by exerting domination and clear-cut authority in another social process, like raising children. This is why today fathers often acquire certain "rights" over their children and women others. Similarly, contradictions in the productive order that push corporations to seek ever new sources of low level labor can only be relieved by such innovations as birth control pills that seem on the surface to promise women freedom. The image that comes to mind is that of a hydraulic machine.

This image is, I think, the major theoretical achievement of the book, even though it is only stated and illustrated rather than "proved" in an empirical way. Mitchell . . . is a dialectical thinker. According to her, as contradictions in each of the four social processes occur, they interact with the others so that an uneasy equilibrium of oppression is maintained. Mitchell has found a way to show why social changes, such as increasing contraception, that, considered in isolation, seem to promise so much for human freedom, nonetheless have little impact on society. Unlike Herbert Marcuse, she does not subscribe to an idea of "repressive tolerance" to explain this. The paradox she proposes is that, precisely by the turmoil of its parts, precisely by the contradictions within each of the four social processes that prompt interaction with the others, does society remain knit together.

Again unlike Marcuse, Mitchell believes this uneasy equilibrium can be exploded in advanced capitalist countries such as Britain and the United States. "A revolutionary movement must base its analysis on the uneven development of each structure, and attack the weakest link in the combination. This may become the point of departure for a general transformation." Although her text could be clearer at this point, I gather that she sees the family as potentially that "weakest link in the combination" of the four social processes. For her the family is the most important social unit in which society molds human feeling. She makes brilliant use of Freudian as well as structure-functional theory to show a contradiction facing the family at the present time.

The nuclear family, she asserts, is "ideologically" a private unit; it is thought of as a refuge from the larger society, a place where people recover from the terrors and the necessities they encounter in the outer world. But the social function of the nuclear family is in direct conflict with this privacy. The nuclear family cuts people loose from the ties of tradition and allegiance found in the old extended families. No longer are decisions about jobs based largely on what is best for the family, as in the old immigrant families. Rather, the simplicity and small size of the nuclear family make it possible for people to think of regulating the family according to the needs of the job market.

A nuclear family can be much more easily uprooted than an extended one, for instance, if the father is promoted by agreeing to work for his corporation in another city. The nuclear family accustoms people to think of themselves as individual creatures each with "careers" to follow and "success" to achieve. The family adapts them to a productive order where they are supposed to fend for themselves under ever-changing economic conditions; in turn, such people tend to assimilate into the intimacies of the home the patterns of dominance and control they have learned at work.

What results from the celebration of privacy and the practice of individualism, Mitchell points out, echoing R. D. Laing and Philippe Aries, is the eclipse of real sociability and long-standing intimate ties which people can trust. Since trust and intimacy are emotional necessities, this traumatic contradiction in the family ought to be the "point of departure" for a more general movement of liberation.

If I read Mitchell right here, I cannot help reacting with some misgivings. . . . (pp. 24-5)

Nobody can argue that the injustices of family life are a good thing, but a program for radical change is unrealistic if it doesn't take account of the complex experiences and emotional compromises that people squeeze out of bitter and frustrating and crippling circumstances, even out of cooking or cleaning. If Mitchell wants purposeful social action to flow as a logical consequence of the theory, then the theory has to account for the intricacies of the ways people live with and need one another.

This limitation on Mitchell's theory is evident in her analysis of women's groups themselves. She writes, ". . . we try not

to imitate the style and structure of male-dominated radical groups. The refusal to allow leaders to arise is the most obvious aspect of this. A good instinct this—nevertheless it presents problems. . . . Leaders are rarely ousted by anyone other than would-be leaders. In not wishing to act like 'men,' there is no need for us to act like 'women.'" There is no need, but her theory is not constructed to show how to avoid the danger. The title of the book is in this sense exact: to speak of women's estate is to speak of a place where one has mapped contours of the landscape, noting certain obstacles and certain avenues of escape. Yet to draw a map is not to explain how people move on the terrain. (p. 26)

Richard Sennett, "Women: What Is To Be Done?" in The New York Review of Books *(reprinted with permission from* The New York Review of Books; *copyright © 1972 Nyrev, Inc.), Vol. XVIII, No. 7, April 20, 1972, pp. 22-6.**

EDNA G. ROSTOW

[In **Woman's Estate** Juliet Mitchell] confronts us with a paradox. It is a work of intelligence and insight. Miss Mitchell perceives the complexity of the psycho-social forces which are changing women's place in modern society. She seems also to be aware that there are driving needs in both men and women, as well as deeply rooted patterns of attitude, thought, and behavior, which cannot be altered instantly—by wish or will, or even by command. She distrusts easy formulae either to explain the past or to govern the future.

In the end, however, she . . . succumbs to the yearning for a formula. Anxious as she is to avoid the pitfalls and polemics which characterize so much of the literature, one can almost hear her plea from the midst of the jungle of life—"O, God, please let there be an answer—one answer,—some answer— somewhere." The formula she has grasped is that women will not be free until socialism replaces capitalism. Intellectually, it is a simpler answer than we had been led to expect from her, and we are let down.

Her book is, nonetheless, an extraordinary exercise. We watch with fascination as a sensitive mind takes its way past a series of social, economic, emotional, psychological, and biological problems, by clinging to a single thread which she knows will give her safe passage through a formidable intellectual maze to the promised land. That thread is her security. One has the impression that it permits her the critical freedom she exercises on friend, ally, and opponent alike, because she is certain that it will always lead her to a satisfying—because predictable— end.

Miss Mitchell's book has two goals: to achieve a systematic view of the history of women's place in society; and to articulate a program of social change that would enable women— and men as well—to reach true freedom and equality. She concentrates, of course, on the changes which must occur first in women's sense of identity and women's position in order to bring them to an equality with men, even in the conditions which she recognizes as being far from what she would wish in terms of true liberation for both sexes. In her view, that freedom will be denied both to men and women in capitalist democracies: human beings can hope to find full equality and individual freedom only under the economic conditions of socialism. (pp. 629-30)

[Her] deepest need is to indict the Women's Liberation movement for being taken in by the ideological premises of capitalist democracy, which claims to regard freedom, equality, and liberty as rights of the individual, but "which in fact, allow none." (p. 630)

According to Miss Mitchell, women are the victims of their innocence about the true condition of the world. She concedes that there has been change and even progress in the status of women under democratic capitalism. And she is not satisfied with what women have won under socialism as it exists in the world. Yet she believes that capitalism is the less trustworthy of the two: it promises more and gives grudgingly.

Invoking as she does the complexity of social and psychological phenomena to explain the tenacity of attitudes toward women through millennia of experience, and in a wide variety of societies, it is curious that Miss Mitchell wearies of complexity when she turns to remedies. On the one hand, she sees that women have had comparable problems in most societies: rural and urban, agricultural and industrial, tribal and individualistic, and those calling themselves socialist or capitalist. But she seems unable to encompass the notion that women will realize true equality only when there is more than legislation calling for equality between men and women. Legislation is a necessary step in demonstrating that the idea of equality is accepted and prevails in the society as a whole. But nominal acceptance and legislation do not mean full realization of a state of true equality between men and women. That must be experienced in all phases of life. Miss Mitchell has rightly seen that the complexity of this process is what makes women's revolution the "longest." But she rejects these factors in her conclusion. There she falls back on deception, conspiracy, and myth to explain the slowness of social change. The end of innocence, apparently, doesn't bring an acceptance of complexity. (pp. 630-31)

Miss Mitchell remarks on the hopes which women experienced in the various movements of the 'sixties—the civil rights movement, the student movement, the Black Power movement—all of which began with the promise of equality and democratic participation only to bring disappointment. She attributes the beginning of the militant women's movements to these disappointments and frustrations. While she recognizes that leadership is often the realization of an "individual's potential," . . . she deplores any relation between leadership and power, and implies that it would not exist except for capitalism.

One is led to wonder if Miss Mitchell really believes her own interpretations. It may be that she thinks it necessary to be identified with the political left in order to be heard by educated young women on the subject of women's liberation. Certainly the word "liberal" seems now to be past reasonable usefulness. Although Miss Mitchell is aware that it is the imperfect democratic societies, thus far at least, which have permitted the activities lighting up the details of inequality and even of oppression endured by women, she concludes that women need a revolutionary theoretical base in order to succeed in their struggle.

Movement is disorderly at best. Freedom rarely ensures order for any length of time. Does the need to hold to a socialist ideal imply an inability to deal with the complex reality of freedom? Does it reflect a need to intellectualize in the face of the assaults on one's emotional organization?

Miss Mitchell's ideal is a society endowed with a "plural range of institutions which match the free invention and variety of men and women." It is an ideal that many of her readers (including this reviewer) will applaud. But how can she assume that her ideal will be fulfilled naturally in a society where all are employees of the state, and when there is no diversity in the economic or political base? It is too easy to dismiss the existing experience with socialism as inauthentic, and to invoke the ideal of "socialism" only for the perfect form no revolution has yet realized. Perhaps the very act of intellectualization so attracts Miss Mitchell's admirers that they can overlook the simple, fashionable answers provided. Perhaps her vision of pluralist society blinds some to the inflexibility of socialism. But she must assume that many of her followers will ask which kinds of societies now permit unauthorized experiments in pluralism—or anything else. Is it because she acknowledges that the socialist societies of our time are not the Real Thing that keeps her followers from thinking too closely about what she is saying? Or is it the essence of her appeal that she does not describe her ideal socialist world, but vaguely conjures up the political vision of Marx, and makes room for Freud within his political dream? (pp. 631-33)

Miss Mitchell's view of Freud as supplying a useful technique of analysis raises again the question about her need for the idea of revolution. She can see that "basic social formation" and "basic interrelationships between men and women" must change in order to achieve true equality of opportunity and reward for men and women, and to realize true freedom as the milieu in which they live and work. This is a far cry from seeing those relationships simply as a function of economic organization. She sees the combination of factors affecting those relationships—past and present. Can revolution really affect them in a fundamental sense? Or will revolution provide a climax without which the process of change seems dull indeed? And will not that climax recede, leaving "basic" relationships unchanged? (p. 633)

Edna G. Rostow, "Capitalism versus Women's Liberation," in The Yale Review *(© 1972 by Yale University; reprinted by permission of the editors), Vol. LXI, No. 4, Summer, 1972, pp. 628-33.*

NANCY MILFORD

"We should ask the feminist questions, but try to come up with some Marxist answers," Mitchell insists [in *Woman's Estate*]. But why is she so committed to the methods of scientific socialism given the clear discrimination among women experienced in those countries where socialism exists, and which Mitchell herself documents? If socialist ideology is bankrupt, or inadequate, will it not blunt the effectiveness of the emerging feminists? Socialism seems to me no less the invention of men than capitalism is, and neither economic system evolved from the minds of women, as feminism has. Women are working in greater numbers than ever before and in a highly technological society such as ours where sheer muscle power is largely unnecessary. Yet are they any the less oppressed? And if that is true, on what basis are we to assume that woman freed of her reproductive role would be less oppressed? The question before both capitalist and socialist remains: why is she exploited at work as well as in the home? I do not believe that the answer to that question properly involves the sacrifice of her biological self, which I take to be inextricably bound to her identity as a person. I insist upon the prerogative of bearing children as a natural right; the raising of children—what Mitchell calls their socialization—is something which must and can be shared by both sexes. It can be shared, however, only if the structure of values within any given society is open to change; then, working and employment will alter in such a way as to permit not only that sharing, but make it an essential part of a man's, as well as a woman's, definition of self. And there's the hitch. For that is not the case in our own time.

Mitchell says that the family ("like woman herself") while appearing to be a natural object is, in fact, a cultural creation. And she finds the bearing of children as well as raising them a caricature of work in a capitalist society—the child as product. Motherhood becomes a substitute for work, "an activity in which the child is seen as an object created by the mother, in the same way as a commodity is created by a work." ". . . [H]er capacity for maternity *is* a definition of woman. But it is only a physiological definition. Yet so long as it is allowed to remain a substitute for action and creativity, and the home an area of relaxation for men, women will remain confined to the species, to her universal and natural condition." She seems to me guilty of extending the caricature by contributing to it. For unless I have misread her, Mitchell does not accept, or even pay lip service to the "creativity" involved within this physiological self. Why is creativity, or even action, limited to thinking, writing, and political theorizing? And to what else are we to be confined, if not to the species? Are we less limited, less confined if we deny or defy our physiological self; or are we limited in yet another way? I suggest that there is something of unalterable value in woman's experience: the very cyclical motion of her body makes her life marked by upheaval, change, and discharge. I am not willing to say that she is made more vulnerable because of it, but that it is instead a source of potential strength; change need not stun her or threaten her, for she is in constant flux. Her interior territory is not only a protective construct, a sort of psychological metaphor of her sex, for it is from within it that she is capable of nourishing and sustaining and conserving life itself. At the very least its presence gives us options men do not possess.

And are these qualities which may be called womanly of any less moment to a society than those Mitchell implies are to take their place? . . . I am not trying to be poetical about bodily functions; I am suggesting another dimension in which our endowment may be explored.

In the end what Mitchell is after seems modest: the right of women to earn a living wage, the more important right to equal work rather than service jobs which are really only extensions of their family roles. She is not after the abolition of the family. She wants free oral contraception, the abolition of illegitimacy, which will separate marriage from parenthood. Why, she asks, must there be only the mother as "nurse," why "only one institutionalized form of inter-sexual or inter-generational relationship?" She wants a plural range of institutions: "Couples—of the same or of different sexes—living together or not living together, long term unions with or without children, single parents—male or female—bringing up children, children socialized by conventional rather than biological parents, extended kin groups, etc.—all these could be encompassed in a range of institutions which match the free invention and variety of men and women." For Mitchell it is capitalism that has evolved the notion of family that does more than occupy women, it produces, conditions, and isolates them. But isn't there already in this country a plural range of relationships, if not of institutions, which are very like the ones she recommends? Single or divorced people, men and women, raising children; people hired to raise or at the least care for young children who are not their own, privately and in day care centers; black children raised by grandmothers rather than by their biological parents; adopted children brought up by married and single

people who have chosen them; and perhaps a handful of communes with and without children or marriages? And yet doesn't the question remain this one—under what conditions will men change their working lives, will they risk the convention of their jobs and their hours, or even the very definition of themselves to reshape the families they cocreate, and more often than not coinhabit? (pp. 149-51)

Until the destiny of the family is worked out—economically and in terms of its press upon our psychic identity as women— we will stay within it. . . . What we need as women, as people, is a more complex exploration of biological motherhood. What we need even more desperately is the reevaluation of the patriarchal family, capitalist and socialist, which has too often knotted and isolated us within our families, so that it will end with no more damage inflicted upon its women, its children— and even its men. (p. 151)

Nancy Milford, "Out from Under," in Partisan Review *(copyright © 1973 by Partisan Review, Inc.), Vol. XL, No. 1, 1973, pp. 147-51 (revised by the author for this publication).*

PETER SEDGWICK

[In *Psychoanalysis and Feminism* Juliet Mitchell] argues that the female predisposition towards narcissism is laid down in the differing infant-parent relationships experienced by boy and girl babies. Her latest book is the product of a long and ardent search in the Complete Psychological Works of Sigmund Freud: a maze from which she has emerged grasping what she takes to be the clue to the deepest levels of female oppression, concealed in the recesses of personality itself. The Oedipus complex, the castration complex and the fierce pre-Oedipal attachment to mother occur, we are told, universally in infant experience; and occur with an impact which necessarily differs in the case of the male and the female nursling. . . .

Juliet Mitchell, in fact, makes her entire case stand or fall not simply with the importance, but with the overwhelming preeminence of infant sexual identifications in determining both the psychology of gender and the standards of family behaviour. The centrality of the Oedipus complex and of castration-anxiety among young children, is simply taken as established, and with it the belief that there are two, and only two, major paths during infancy for the formation of male and female identity. The Mitchell-Freud model of the family assigns a constant and unique role to Papa: thus, 'it *is* the father and not the two parents' (her emphasis) that is responsible for the repressive power of the superego in the babe's unconscious. But it remains mysterious how a uniform pattern of childhood complexes could ever be established, given the wide—and probably widening—variety of actual paternal roles in contemporary families: shift-working fathers, runaway fathers, nappy-changing, bottle-feeding fathers, weak fathers and cuddly fathers, as well as the traditional Dads of chastisement and authority. At times Mitchell writes as if no evidence from the current state of nuclear families could count against the existence of the Oedipus complex, which is given the status of a necessary corollary of the universal ban on incest. But more usually (and certainly more in keeping with Freud's own exposition) she discusses it as a real experience undergone and repressed by specific individuals within their particular family context. In which case it is not simply 'empiricist', but a valid scientific objection, to point to family contexts which are quite different from Freud's model. . . . [The] available range both of roles and of families goes well beyond anything that Freud conceived of. Mitchell is correct to emphasise the importance of Freud's discovery that gender consists of learned behaviour, whose mode of articulation is crucially shaped by parental rearing in the early years. But anthropologists have gone on discovering uncomfortable exceptions to the Oedipus complex, the latency period and the passivity of the woman ever since Malinowski caught the Trobriand Islanders at play: there is a contest not merely between Freud and the present state of theory, but between him and the present state of the evidence. . . . (p. 621)

The analysis of the child's psychology is of considerable political import, for if it indeed followed from psychoanalysis that our personalities were moulded by Oedipal and pre-Oedipal identifications, the propagandists of feminism would be quite right to reject Freud as a patriarchal ideologue. The movement to change the condition of women can be organised only by women who are themselves changed and changing. If the causes of womanly passiveness lie so deep in the personal unconscious, if the blind bias of the newly-formed psyche always works to strengthen the colossal power of the reactionary centuries, then how could enough cadres ever be mobilised and retained from the successively disabled female generations? The crucial contradiction in Juliet Mitchell's argument is that she allots to women a political role in the ideological and cultural transformation of society comparable to that of the working class as the agency of capitalism's destruction. Yet, on her showing, liberated womanhood can appear only after the emergence of new structures in the unconscious, and these cannot crystallise until after the ending of the long reign of patriarchal society.

As an event, therefore, *Psychoanalysis and Feminism* is in contradiction with its content. As practice it asserts, demands, exposes alternatives: but its ideas, though incisively couched, have the dead weight of shackles, commemorating the past and foreclosing the future. The critics of Freud in Women's Liberation must refuse, and should refuse, the power of the infant unconscious. 'Femininity' is transcended now, or else never. (pp. 621-22)

> Peter Sedgwick, *"See What You've Done to Me!"* in New Statesman (© 1974 The Statesman & Nation Publishing Co. Ltd.), Vol. 87, No. 2250, May 3, 1974, pp. 621-22.*

ELLEN WILLIS

Psychoanalysis and Feminism is an ambitious attempt to correct [distortions of Freud's theories by feminists]. Psychoanalysis, Mitchell argues, is "not a recommendation *for* a patriarchal society but an analysis *of* one," and as such a valuable tool for understanding women's oppression. With an almost academic detachment—it is no coincidence that this book comes from a British feminist, unbruised by the relentless embrace of America's neo-Freudian culture—she discusses Freud's theory of feminine development in exhaustive detail, takes issue with previous feminist writing on the subject, and dissects the "alternative radical psychologies" of Wilhelm Reich and R. D. Laing, advancing the iconoclastic thesis that Freud's work is ultimately more radical than theirs.

Psychoanalysis and Feminism is an important and provocative work. I sympathize with its purpose and admire its boldness. That said, I have to admit I don't like it very much. It may be that my irritation with the book is another reflection of the culture gap: my basic complaint is that it lacks common sense.

Psychoanalysis, like Marxism, is a theory that cannot be abstracted from its practice without courting irrelevance; it is not only a theory but a therapy that raises questions of profound practical consequence. But Mitchell is almost exclusively concerned with theory for its own sake. The result is that much of her thinking has an air of abstract unreality, and some of her conclusions are just plain obtuse. . . .

Mitchell's central argument is that political objections to or reinterpretations of Freud are based on an implicit denial of his most crucial discovery—the existence of unconscious mental processes that follow their own logic and are not bound by external reality. Thus a feminist who criticizes Freud for talking about penis envy rather than women's justified resentment of male privilege is equating unconscious fantasy with sensible thinking—is in effect assimilating the former to the latter. It's true enough that political radicals, for reasons both pragmatic and temperamental, tend to resist the idea of an autonomous inner life, just as conservatives habitually invoke it to "prove" that social change is either impossible or unnecessary. But in a way Mitchell's criticism simply reflects her lack of interest in practical issues. For whether Freud's constructs are assumed to represent people's actual fantasies or (as Shulamith Firestone would have it) a system of metaphors or (as Kate Millett seems to think) just euphemisms, what really concerns feminists is the relation between those constructs and "real life." Why should a little girl assume that everyone is supposed to have a penis? Suppose she has never seen one? How can a little boy fantasize penetrating his mother if he has never observed intercourse or seen a vagina close up? Is it, perhaps, the adult who in retrospect attaches a specific meaning to the child's inchoate desires?

Mitchell can get quite sarcastic about "realistic" questions of this sort; she sees them as philistine and irrelevant. But if most feminists are guilty of not taking the unconscious seriously, it seems to me that Mitchell misconstrues its nature. She regards unconscious fantasy as a special mode of experience, entirely incommensurable with everyday rational thought; I would argue that experience is experience, and that fantasy is rather a mode of *handling* experience, a response whose meaning can be deciphered and "translated" into ordinary sense. (p. 33)

Predictably, Mitchell gives little attention to the problem of how best to use psychoanalysis—theory and therapy—for feminist purposes. At one point, distinguishing between Freud's work and its perversions, she comments, "It is another question whether or not there is something within Freud's work that leads to this ideological abuse. In a sense it is obvious that there must be . . . whatever it is would not, of course, invalidate what surrounds it, though it should be extracted from it and rejected." I think it is precisely the truth at the core of psychoanalysis that makes it so easily exploitable, and that it is less a matter of extracting and rejecting than of recapturing and supplying a new context. *Psychoanalysis and Feminism* begins a long overdue exploration. I hope other feminists will carry it on. (p. 34)

> Ellen Willis, *"Feminists vs. Freud: Round Two,"* in Ms. (© 1974 Ms. Magazine Corp.), Vol. III, No. 2, August, 1974, pp. 33-4.

CHRISTOPHER LASCH

Juliet Mitchell's attack [in *Psychoanalysis and Feminism*] on Reich, Laing, and the neofeminists is inspired by unflinching loyalty to [Freud's] psychoanalytic concepts, difficult, uncompromising, and seemingly unflattering to women as these concepts are. (p. 12)

Except for its glorification of the vagina, the womb, and motherhood, which many feminists would now find objectionable, [the] early feminist criticism of Freud by [Karen] Horney, [Clara] Thompson, [Ernest] Jones, and others anticipates all the strictures of the neofeminists. The latter, however, because they mistakenly identify psychoanalysis with "reactionary" ideas about women, have not availed themselves of this criticism, relying instead on the seemingly more radical work of Wilhelm Reich and, to a lesser extent, of R. D. Laing. It is against Reich and Laing, therefore, and against the neofeminists themselves, that Juliet Mitchell, after a long and detailed account of Freudian theory, directs the full force of her *Psychoanalysis and Feminism.* (p. 15)

In the last section of her book, Mitchell tries to assess the political implications of her defense of Freud and her refutation of his critics. At first glance, her analysis would seem to make the liberation of women more dubious and remote than ever. If Freud is right, women are deeply disabled by their early experiences. Nor can feminists find much consolation in his assurance that there are of course exceptional women who are more "masculine" than "feminine." Psychoanalysis, moreover, strongly suggests that the subjection of women, like the Oedipus complex, is universal. Without rejecting Freud, therefore, one cannot take refuge in the view that women's subjection is peculiar to certain forms of social organization.

Far from flinching from these conclusions, Mitchell reinforces them with the anthropological theory of Claude Lévi-Strauss, who argues that the exchange of women is the basic fact of cultural life. Human society, according to Lévi-Strauss, originates in the rule whereby fathers and brothers renounce marriage with their daughters and sisters, giving their women—the most valuable gift they can bestow—to other groups, who reciprocate with gifts of their own women. (The Oedipus complex, then, appears as the psychic reflection of this fact—of the incest prohibition which is necessary to institute the exchange of women.)

Patriarchy, in other words, is synonymous with culture, and the feminist myth of a matriarchal stage preceding the present organization of society has to be firmly rejected. So too does the hope that women's liberation can be achieved through technology, which will at last free women from childbearing. Not biology but culture is at the root of woman's degradation. The hope of a technological conquest of biology is "redundant," according to Mitchell, since the transformation of biology is already inherent in culture. . . .

This very fact, however, allows us to hope for a transformation of woman's condition—and not merely to hope, but to see it as a real historical possibility. If the incest taboo and the exchange of women are the historic preconditions of culture, it can be argued that these conditions long ago became obsolete. The "socialization of labor" under bourgeois rule, according to Mitchell, makes the exchange of women irrelevant, a "social non-necessity." Mankind is now for the first time united by the work of modern society and no longer needs such primitive agencies of cohesion as kinship.

Similarly Mitchell argues that the prohibition of incest has become unnecessary in a society where "the mass of mankind, propertyless and working socially together *en masse* for the first time in the history of civilization, would be unlikely, *were it not for the preservation of the family,* to come into proximity

with their kin and if they did, it wouldn't matter." The generous use of italics, here and throughout the last chapters of *Psychoanalysis and Feminism,* seems to betray a dwindling confidence in the clarity and forcefulness of the argument. At this point Mitchell confesses, "These are complex questions that I cannot do more than raise here."

Lévi-Strauss is important to Mitchell's argument not only because his work reinforces the contention that femininity is a cultural rather than a biological category, but because it contradicts the widespread assumption that the family is the basis of society. According to Lévi-Strauss, human society originates not in the biological family but in the establishment of alliances between families (alliances cemented by the exchange of women). It cannot be argued, therefore, that society depends on the preservation of the family. Such at least is Mitchell's contention.

It is unfortunate that the concluding sections of her book are exceedingly sketchy and schematic. To say that the objective conditions for the overthrow of patriarchy have existed for some time does not tell us any more than similar statements about the overthrow of capitalism. What remains to be explained is why capitalism and patriarchy still persist in spite of their historic obsolescence. If the fact of their persistence argues a failure of the subjective conditions for revolution, then we have to undertake an analysis of contemporary culture in order to explain the sources of that failure. It will not do to maintain that patriarchy owes its survival to a strenuous propaganda campaign on behalf of the nuclear family—a suggestion that hardly does credit to the level of analysis sustained throughout the rest of Mitchell's book. In bourgeois society the family still serves not only as an agency that inculcates work discipline and respect for authority but as a bulwark of privacy, in which values opposed to those of the market place retain some vigor, however attenuated. The bourgeois myth of the family as a refuge from an inhuman world cannot be dismissed as pure ideology. Precisely in the degree to which the myth expresses an undeniable reality it constitutes the severest indictment of the bourgeois world.

The weakness of the concluding sections of this work—in which the contradiction between women's emancipation and the history of all previous culture is resolved, it seems to me, in a purely formal and schematized fashion—by no means undermines Mitchell's central claim, namely that Freud tells us far more about women's degradation than the enemies of Freud can ever begin to tell us. In making this claim, Juliet Mitchell has risked accusations of apostasy from her fellow feminists. Her book not only challenges orthodox feminism, however, it defies the conventions of social thought in the English-speaking countries (with which feminist thought is thoroughly entangled)—cultural relativism, historicism, an empiricism hostile to theory in almost any form. *Psychoanalysis and Feminism* is a brave and important book, and its influence will not be confined to feminists. Anyone who thinks Freud's work has been conclusively revised, updated, or overthrown will have to contend for a long time to come with this withering rejoinder. (pp. 16-17)

Christopher Lasch, "Freud and Women," in The New York Review of Books *(reprinted with permission from* The New York Review of Books; *copyright © 1974 Nyrev, Inc.),* Vol. 21, No. 15, October 3, 1974, pp. 12-17.*

CAROL LOPATE

While *Psychoanalysis and Feminism* is long and tedious, and Mitchell's insights are often unrelated to the thrust of her argument, the book's accomplishment lies in its reassertion of Freud's concept of the unconscious and in its criticism of psychoanalysts and feminists following him for misunderstanding or ignoring this central idea. Mitchell emphasizes that contrary to feminist criticisms of his work, Freud was not describing biological differences between the sexes. Rather, in keeping with his interest in the "mental side of phenomena," Freud used the terms "masculine" and "feminine" to describe certain mental qualities which related only to the psychological level of experience. Thus, for Freud, masochism and passivity were feminine mental qualities, not necessarily biologically determined characteristics of women. In fact, as Mitchell shows in great detail, Freud considered women and men as sexes to have both masculine and feminine characteristics; in this sense, bisexuality is the normal state of the psyche. While Freud as an individual may have had a preference for women with "feminine" qualities, the scientific inquiry which he pursued in case histories, and which culminated in his theories of the development of the individual personality, was into the mental processes through which females became women and males became men—that is, the process of socialization—within a patriarchal culture.

Briefly, Mitchell is critical of psychoanalytic thinkers such as Wilhelm Reich and some of the most prominent feminists starting with Simone de Beauvoir. . . . Mitchell's main complaint about Reich, de Beauvoir, and others is that their misunderstanding of Freud's category of mental life leads them either to biological determinism, of which they so often accuse Freud, or to a kind of social reductionism in which individual personalities are mere reflections of a pre-existing "social reality." While their critiques of Freud arise out of radical impulses, Mitchell attempts to show that they end up with far more rigid and deterministic notions of what is male and what female, or feminine and masculine, than Freud ever did. (pp. 55-6)

According to Mitchell, while the feminists starting with de Beauvoir have uniformly charged Freud with sexism, their criticisms have generally been superficial and miscomprehending. Mitchell's review of their works is also relatively superficial; her citations make most of them sound thoughtless, although witty, and not all that worthy of close attention in comparison to Freud, Reich, and R. D. Laing. However, Mitchell does point to several important aspects of feminist thinking which bear repeating.

In several of the authors she notes a rationalist empiricist approach which is emphatic about the importance of "concrete reality" and antithetical to a notion of the unconscious. . . .

Although Mitchell notes several times that when an author's ideas are continually misinterpreted or misused one must look into whether there is something misleading about the ideas themselves, she does not conduct such an inquiry regarding any of Freud's ideas. Nor does she try to analyze the reasons for misinterpretation from the standpoint of the misinterpreters. To try to follow through where Mitchell has left off, it seems to me that the concept of mental life is a double-edged sword. On the one hand, it gives people the opportunity to see that many of the obstacles they face are really based in their own psyches, and that therefore it is possible for them to free themselves and make radical changes. But on the other hand, for individuals whose discontent and misery have long been at-tributed to their own psychic deficiencies and who join together in the new awareness that there are real obstacles out there in the world, a singular focus on mental life is, at least for a time, counterproductive. One of the great contributions of analysis is the idea of self-responsibility. But one of the serious problems with the idea is that sometimes it is not entirely one's own fault that one is unhappy, loveless, confused about one's career, and so on. The problem for feminists and other revolutionaries, I believe, is to be sure of what is out there and what is inside one's head, and to be able to go back and forth fluently. I think, therefore, that too much emphasis on the concept of mental life can be repressive, particularly in a society which denies reality and in which altering consciousness is used as a means of convincing people of the reasonableness of the existing order. However, the concept can be wildly radical when used dialectically with a firm understanding that the injustices one experiences are out there, and have to be changed out there, as well as inside one's own mind. By overemphasizing the role that mental life alone can play in bringing about change, Mitchell does not do justice to this dialectic.

Although she succeeds, I believe, in acquitting Freud of the charge of biological determinism, her own answer to the question of whether women are born or made is less satisfactory. . . . [For] Mitchell, neither a biological explanation nor a Marxist explanation is sufficient to explain the fact that women throughout history have been "the second sex." (pp. 56-7)

Broadly, [Mitchell's] argument goes like this: the resolution of the Oedipus conflict represents the onset of civilization on the individual, and thus social, level because it is with the overcoming of the complex that one sees the triumph of the superego, and thus society. . . . This, for Mitchell, is a basic structure of society, transcending capitalism or the nuclear family. In fact, she asserts that at this stage of development "the structure of patriarchal culture becomes redundant."

But what about the little girl? Following Freud, Mitchell asserts that the situation is not parallel for the growing girl and boy. "On the plane of object-attachment, the boy as he enters into his phallic heritage can at first preserve the mother as the focus of his lust. The girl must shift from her mother-attachment to a sexual desire for her father." On the other hand, says Mitchell, "This transference from mother to father is the girl's 'positive' Oedipus complex and, as it is the first correct step on her path to womanhood, there is no need for her to leave it." While the boy fears his father, who is a rival for his mother, and so must leave this phase of his life quickly before, like Oedipus, he is blinded (castrated), "the girl can linger secure in this phase for life." Those girls who traverse most successfully will receive from their husbands and then from their own male children the penis they wanted from their fathers. Thus women do not develop as strong a superego as do men, and, logically, they are not the carriers of patriarchal culture.

Although this description can be seen as an analytical mythology of the mental life of men and women within patriarchal society, Mitchell attributes to it far greater importance. For her, the mythology signifies real structures embedded in human culture. (p. 57)

Thus, for Mitchell, the answer to the question, Are women born or made? is that they are made, but necessarily so, at least up to this time.

This is the structuralist answer to biology, but, as with most other structuralists, it is biology through the backdoor. What are the origins of these structures? The assertion that the biological base is socially transformed, or that the situation is "determinedly social," is not enough without a concrete examination of the relationship between ideology or mental life, social relations, and the mode of production. And yet Mitchell asserts that "in analyzing contemporary Western society, we are (as elsewhere) dealing with two autonomous areas: the economic mode of capitalism and the ideological mode of patriarchy." As with Freud, mythology remains an objectification of innate structures or instincts.

Since Mitchell postulates that a social transformation of the structures into a nonpatriarchal system is possible, the logic of her position demands a theoretical framework which can help explain this possibility. For Freud, there is no possibility of changing the "unconscious structures," even though he has no theory of how they are biologically linked. On the other hand, Mitchell rejects Marx's belief that with the change in the mode of production of material life all forms of ideology (mental life) will be rapidly transformed. . . . She is left, then, in a box that is not opened by her sweeping statement: "When the potentialities of the complexities of capitalism—both economic and ideological—are released by its overthrow, new structures will gradually come to be represented in the unconscious. It is the task of feminism to insist on their birth." Nagging women have not until now been a theoretical platform for change, even when the general theory of society held more hope for transformation. Nor is her advice that women must conduct "a struggle based on a theory of the social non-necessity at this stage of development of the laws instituted by patriarchy" particularly useful. Is this mind conquering mind? When Mitchell argues, finally, that "no society has yet existed—or existed for a sufficient length of time—for the 'eternal' unconscious to have shed its immortal nature," she has certainly been strangled by her own contradiction.

Juliet Mitchell resorts to a radical separation between ideology and the production of material life because she, quite rightly, reads the history and anthropology of society as expressing the various forms of power men have always had over women. She understands that we have no evidence for Engels's matriarchy. If men have always dominated women, although in differing degrees, no matter what the form of production, then, for Mitchell, at a level of basic structure there must be a separation between the two spheres of social life.

I think this need not be the case. Mitchell's implicit definition of socialism is a minimum definition: workers' control over the ownership and means of production. Such a definition does *not* necessarily imply the equality between women and men, but rather, contains within it the possibility for a hierarchy of labor. There is, however, a more comprehensive definition of socialism which, I believe, does hold within it the condition for an end to patriarchy. This is a socialism which does not merely take over, unself-consciously, existing technology, for the technology of capitalism is embedded in the hierarchical division of labor of capitalism. But it is a socialism which allows no production or reproduction that cannot be accomplished in a nonhierarchical fashion. As Juliet Mitchell says, we have never known a society without some form of patriarchy, but we have also never known a society without a hierarchy of labor. I think a theory that understands that the sexual division of labor is the earliest form of inequality and domination must also understand that it is the last to go and probably the easiest to return under certain conditions. (pp. 57-8)

Carol Lopate, "Book Reviews: 'Psychoanalysis and Feminism'," in Social Policy *(copyright 1975 by So-cial Policy Corporation), Vol. 5, No. 5, January-February, 1975, pp. 55-8.*

MIRIAM M. JOHNSON

Although most Marxist feminists will probably feel that Mitchell has betrayed them [in *Psychoanalysis and Feminism*], she is, nevertheless, quite different from non-Marxist feminists. She seems in some almost perverse way to be accepting "the worst of Freud." Instead of stressing the basicness of the mother for both sexes as have Horney, Mead, Chodorow, and others and arguing that the male's "masculinity" is almost a reaction formation against the "femininity" acquired from the mother, Mitchell asserts with Freud that "masculinity" is basic, that "penis envy" is real, and thus in their view "feminity" becomes a mark of oppression. Although she lays great stress on Freud's recognition of the bisexuality of both sexes, the chief meaning of this for her is that women are at first predominantly "masculine" in their orientation until patriarchy renders them "feminine." Women at first are active and "masculine" but are forced to give up and reconcile themselves to "femininity." (p. 490)

Obviously Mitchell has not solved the riddle of the secondary status of women, but she is perhaps at least looking for the answer in the right place, that is, in the patriarchal structure of the family in all cultures. She is not talking about the structure of any particular concrete family but rather about "the family in one's head"—the system of pure cultural elements (in Schneider's sense) defining the realm of kinship including sex and generational roles. It has become very unpopular of late to talk about structural universals and yet ironically what we have in Juliet Mitchell is a radical feminist talking about precisely that. As she says, her message to women is "know the devil you have got" and that devil is the universality of patriarchy. To *describe* the family and its transmission in the unconscious is not to *prescribe* it forever, it is to understand it, in order to change it. And finally, precisely because human social structure is not a mere reflection of biology, it *can* be changed. (pp. 490-91)

Miriam M. Johnson, "Book Reviews: 'Psychoanalysis and Feminism'," in Contemporary Sociology *(copyright ©1975 American Sociological Association), Vol. 4, No. 5, September, 1975, pp. 489-91.*

SHERYL DENBO

The central thesis of [*Psychoanalysis and Feminism*] is . . . clear. Freudian psychoanalysis is a science; it contains no ideological implications, no value judgments. The post-Freudians and . . . the feminists are sociologists, producing reflective ideology. Why Freud has been so universally misunderstood and why his theories, by Mitchell's own admission, have led to ideological abuse, is left unexplained. (pp. 567-68)

[Mitchell sees] no distinction between natural science and social science. Science is knowledge, Mitchell tells us, taking the side of the positivist while, at the same time, failing to acknowledge the century of mind-body debate that marked the birth and development of the social sciences. The setting and personality of the scientist does not affect his work; if it does, it is not a science. Then, in the very next paragraph she says, "there is a sense in which, of course, Freud was culture bound . . . the degree to which Freud operated within available thought, and changed it, is an index not of his being produced by his culture (that is a self-evident observation, when you come to think of it), but of his distance from it. . . .'' . . . Well, let's see, first she says that if a scientist is affected by his environment then what he is doing is not science, then she says it is, of course, self-evident that the individual is affected by his environment. Are we to conclude then that there is no social science, only disciplines? Neither Freud nor Mitchell would accept that. We must conclude that social science is in fact somewhat different from natural science; or at the very minimum we must acknowledge the existence of the debate. Mitchell, unfortunately, is not alone among the Marxists who have translated the method of dialectical materialism (a method that I believe recognizes the subjective reality of the individual as one important factor in the dialectical process) into nineteenth-century positivism which ignores subjective reality as if it either doesn't exist or, at the very minimum, is not relevant to science. (pp. 568-69)

In her concluding section Mitchell tells us: "The longevity of the oppression of women must be based on something more than conspiracy, something more complicated than biological handicap and more durable than economic exploitation (although in differing degrees all these may feature)." . . . To understand the "longevity of the oppression of women," Mitchell offers a very interesting Freud-Marx synthesis. Freudian theory, Mitchell has insisted throughout the book, is not a recommendation for patriarchy, but an analysis of one. . . . Although Mitchell agrees that the Oedipus complex may take different forms in different socioeconomic settings, she denies that it is specific to any particular economic stage. That is, she rejects the Reichian hypothesis that the Oedipus complex and the patriarchy are essentially related to the economic system of capitalism. The Oedipus complex is specific only to patriarchy and, according to Freud, all cultures are organized around patriarchy since civilization begins with the incest taboo and the exchange of women. . . . Thus it seems that according to Mitchell the incest taboo and its result, the exchange of women, is necessary to civilization because civilization starts with a structural relationship between families. As Mitchell points out, even in the stage of monogamous marriage which Engels posits, inheritance and the original class oppression are coincident with civilization. The primitive communism of group marriage took place under conditions of savagery. Thus Mitchell is claiming that the position of women in society is "a question neither of biology nor of a specific society, but of human society itself." . . . (p. 569)

Mitchell clearly indicates the depth of the problem. She also indicates a possible road to its solution. Mitchell believes that in advanced capitalism, the patriarchal kinship system, though still supported ideologically, is archaic; that the ban on incest and the demand for exogamy are no longer needed; and thus that there is a contradiction between the family and the economy. While the working class is at the center of the contradiction in capitalism, women are at the center of the contradiction of patriarchy. Mitchell wants to see this contradiction analyzed and the analysis used to overthrow patriarchy. Unfortunately Mitchell leaves us unclear as to exactly why the incest taboo and the exchange of women is no longer needed. Mitchell offers us only one hint. She tells us there is a contradiction between patriarchal law and the social organization of work, and that this contradiction is held together by the nuclear family. What is this contradiction? Why does the social organization of work make the laws of patriarchy redundant? If patriarchy is not essential to capitalist economy, why does capitalist ideology support patriarchy? Why is the nuclear fam-

ily at the center of the contradiction? What is the relationship between the nuclear family and patriarchy? These questions remain unanswered.

Remaining true to the school of scientific Marxism, Mitchell tells us that the struggle of women must be based on a theory of the "social non-necessity, at this stage of development, of the laws instituted by patriarchy." . . . She ends by reminding women that although "Socialist societies have had too little time on earth to have achieved anything as radical as a change in man's unconscious," socialism still does not necessarily end patriarchy. Women must wage a specific struggle against patriarchy. Women must effect a change in the ideology of a society that is rooted in the human unconscious. Women must make a cultural revolution.

Although I disagree with Mitchell's dogmatic position on Freud and with her positivistic philosophy of science, it is clear that her book is a significant contribution. She has done an excellent job in explaining the pervasiveness of patriarchy and the importance of Freudian theory as an analytical tool. Most importantly she has offered us a new analytical tool to help us understand the position of women, a new theoretical synthesis between Freud and Marx. (p. 570)

> Sheryl Denbo, "Review-Feature: 'Psychoanalysis and Feminism'," in The Sociological Quarterly (© Midwest Sociological Society, 1975), Vol. 16, No. 4, Autumn, 1975, pp. 560-70.

REBECCA Z. SOLOMON

[*Psychoanalysis and Feminism*] only partially fulfils its promise to demonstrate the relevance of psychoanalysis to feminism. Although some of Mitchell's observations are cogent and astute, her presentation is at times difficult to follow. Her discussion of feminism is flawed by her excessive focus on the role of the father and her failure to adequately consider the importance of preoedipal issues in determining gender role for both women and men. The solutions she offers are as simplistic as some of those she criticizes. She advocates the overthrow of patriarchy but neither her reasons for this recommendation nor her suggestions for its implementation are clear. Her alternation between psychological and sociological issues is contradictory and confusing. On the one hand, she refers to the 'eternal unconscious' in which patriarchy has its roots. On the other hand, she suggests that a different organization of society would change unconscious representations. She advocates major social and economic revolutions that will establish a society in which economic exploitation will disappear and patriarchy will have no place. In the unconscious of children growing up in such a society, she asserts, there will be no representation of patriarchy and, therefore, women will no longer be oppressed.

The author's wishful solutions neglect many important issues, including one of special interest to psychoanalysis. She does not come to grips with the reason for the dominant role of men in society. Is it the unconscious symbolic representation of the penis, in both males and females, as a source of power and strength that accounts for the dominant position of men in society, or can this phenomenon be attributed to biological and social factors such as the superior physical strength of males and the necessity for women in the past to devote so much of their energy to homemaking and child rearing? We do not yet know the relative strengths of unconscious factors and social forces in determining the respective roles and the relationship of men and women. Though Juliet Mitchell does not adequately deal with these and other matters, her book is a useful addition to the literature on feminism as it points up some of the contributions of psychoanalysis to the understanding of women and it raises questions for further exploration. (p. 147)

Rebecca Z. Solomon, "Book Reviews: 'Psychoanalysis and Feminism'," in The Psychoanalytic Quarterly *(copyright © 1976, by The Psychoanalytic Quarterly, Inc.), Vol. 45, No. 1, January, 1976, pp. 145-47.*

JOAN B. LANDES

[In *Woman's Estate*] Mitchell argues for a Marxist approach to feminism. Yet the method which she adopts diverges from a Marxist historical materialist approach to social reality. For example, the true subject of *Woman's Estate* is an abstraction called woman. This woman resists any historical or social definition. She is the same, or rather she is determined in the same way, inside different social classes. She performs the same "functions" within all societies. She is a product of an ideology generated through the socialization processes of the nuclear family. The conceptual model for this family is borrowed from functionalist theory. Indeed Mitchell praises Talcott Parsons, especially for his analysis of socialization processes, adding "no Marxist has provided a comparable analysis."

The female subject of the overlapping structures which compose family life—reproduction, sexuality, and socialization—is herself the product of an ideology which is considered eternal. In other words, Mitchell suggests that the source of women's oppression is to be located first within a universal, atemporal ideology of womanhood which is translated into somewhat different practices in different societies. Both the ideology and the family practices possess an extremely durable character, so that woman, the subject of this ideology, possesses a disturbingly permanent social nature. As Mitchell states: "For though the family *has changed* since its first appearance, it *has also remained*—not just as an idealist concept but as a crucial ideological and economic unit with a certain rigidity and autonomy despite all its adaptations." In this account, woman and the family are the embodiments of certain eternal ideas. The two are inextricably intertwined: "The Family 'makes' the Woman." And one could add, woman is constituted over and over again. As in her second work, *Psychoanalysis and Feminism,* Mitchell is here concerned with the primary interrelationships, especially in the family, "between individual animals that make them human beings" and with the manner in which the little girl grows up in every culture to be "*like* her mother but the boy will grow up to be *another* father." She emphasizes the overlapping nature of ideology, womanhood and family life. She also adopts a methodological orientation to her subject which is consistent with the thesis of eternality. By utilizing functionalist role theory, Mitchell deemphasizes the historical character of social relations. Woman, the eternal subject of an eternal ideology, is an abstraction.

Mitchell subsumes classes within the category of group. This allows her the flexibility she needs to focus her analysis on sexual classes rather than economic classes. . . . Class differences, according to Mitchell, split women off from one another, rather than sex divisions dividing workers. The liberation which Mitchell foresees is bound up with the process which functionalists label social change or modernization. Within a differentiated family of the future, Mitchell envisions the possibilities for a pluralistic situation in which no individual would be tied to a particular role or an ascribed status. No longer will biological motherhood necessarily be equated with social motherhood.

In short, Mitchell wishes to differentiate social roles in the one sphere which most functionalists have considered undifferentiable, i.e., the "natural." However, her argument amounts to a confirmation of what has already been, or is now being, affected by capitalism itself: the extension of market relationships to the sphere of personal life, which in the past provided an important, if insufficient and limited, support for individuals in an alienated social world. (pp. 387-89)

[Within] advanced capitalist society the private and autonomous family unit is undermined more and more by the tendency, arising out of the economy, to dissolve all independent cultural institutions. In other words, the logic of capitalism is to abolish the distinctions within the capitalist totality and to turn against social formations which it initially fostered.

To the extent that the classical bourgeois family was bound up with the oppression of women and children, it has been the object of attack by nineteenth and twentieth century feminists. By limiting themselves to this one issue, however, contemporary feminists fall into the trap of endorsing the system responsible for the destruction of autonomous forms of social life which possess a real, if limited, moment of positive community. Full realization of such autonomy can occur only with the abolition of capitalism itself. Thus, Mitchell's shortcoming is further to affirm the social consequences of capitalist development through an uncritical reliance on sociological modernization theory. She seems to agree with many functionalists that human progress can be achieved only through greater specialization and differentiation of functional social relationships. She poses no alternative to formal equality and rationalization as a basis for a more liberated society. She never asks whether woman's present social existence might not encompass something more than a set of abstract functions. She appears to mistake the division of labor under capitalism for freedom. Finally, Mitchell fails to acknowledge the possibility that in creating a movement for the future which abolishes the alienated division of labor, men and women of the present might look backward as well as forward toward an ideal of community which survives in battered and incomplete form in today's family. Instead, Mitchell sees only one side of the family's multi-faceted character; in her view, it "embodies the most conservative concepts available; it rigidifies the past ideals and presents them as the present pleasures. By its very nature, it is there to prevent the future." (pp. 390-91)

Joan B. Landes, "Women, Labor and Family Life: A Theoretical Perspective," in Science and Society *(copyright 1978 by Science and Society, Incorporated), Vol. XLI, No. 4, Winter, 1977-1978, pp. 386-93.**

Robert A(lexander) Nisbet

1913-

Nisbet, an American sociologist, social historian, and author, is Albert Schweitzer Professor in the Humanities at Columbia University. One of his central concerns is the growth of bureaucratic state power and the consequent erosion of civil society and traditional forms of authority, a condition he diagnoses in *The Twilight of Authority* (1975). Nisbet perceives the idea of and desire for equality as major factors in the unprecedented growth and power of the modern state. He therefore urges that we recognize the beneficient inevitability of "natural hierarchies" in all social institutions. In *History of the Idea of Progress* (1980), Nisbet argues that belief in progress is a constant in the history of Western thought. Some critics have argued that Nisbet is a casual scholar who sometimes distorts the ideas of those he cites. Nonetheless, many consider him to be one of our most original social critics. (See also *Contemporary Authors*, Vols. 25-28, rev. ed.)

Wide World Photos

Excerpt from *TWILIGHT OF AUTHORITY*

I believe the single most remarkable fact at the present time in the West is neither technological nor economic, but political: the waning of the historic political community, the widening sense of the obsolescence of politics as a civilized pursuit, even as a habit of mind. By political community I mean more than the legal state. I have in mind the whole fabric of rights, liberties, participations, and protections that has been, even above industrialism, I think, the dominant element of modernity in the West. To an astonishing degree modern Western society has been *political* society, and this has been made possible only by the growing sense of the state in modern times as being more than a structure of power, as being a cherished form of community.

In a very real sense the political community in the West has been the successor, certainly since the eighteenth century, of the church as the major arena of man's hopes, devotions, and aspirations. One would have to go to religion to find anything comparable to modern Western man's willingness to make sacrifices, of property and life when necessary, in the name of political patriotism. Patriotism through most of the nineteenth century and the first part of the twentieth exercised every bit of the hold upon man's relation to state that piety for so long had to church. Looking back, and reflecting on the innumerable centuries earlier when political government was the object of fear and distrust in so many areas, symbolized in popular consciousness by the policeman, soldier, or tax collector, it is one of history's miracles that from the end of the eighteenth century on in the West populations were willing to entrust so much of their economic, social, and moral life to the supervision of the political sphere. Without question, the political—meaning not merely government and state but a whole way of life, participation, and thought—has had man's trust to a degree no other institution in modern times has had.

It no longer has. A variety of evidences, most of them by now obvious to the layman, suggest that confidence and trust have been replaced by opposite sentiments, that government, from being the protector of the lives of its citizens, has become the greatest single source of exploitation in the minds of a growing number of people. Once political government in the United States signified some degree of austerity of life, of commitment to the public weal, of a willingness to forego most of life's luxuries in the name of service that was for a long time closely akin to what one found in the ranks of clergy and teachers. Today, as scores of surveys and polls reveal, government is perceived by large numbers of citizens as the domain of economic luxury, great personal power, high social status, all symbolized perfectly by the pomp and grandeur of public architecture. It is also perceived, we learn from the same surveys and polls, as being possessed of a degree of arrogance that no corporation could today get away with in the business world, that was once regarded as the privilege of hereditary aristocracy.

A clerisy of power exists that in size and complexity is without precedent since the height of the Roman Empire. This clerisy has deep roots in modern European history, but never before, not even in the post-Renaissance absolute monarchies, has it known the intellectual and economic affluence it knows at the present time. It is composed not only of those who occupy the top elective or appointive positions in our political society, and by their aides and subordinates, all alike preoccupied by the attributes of power, but also, and far from least, by the greater part of the intellectual, especially academic, class. For this class the political state has a sacredness that the church once possessed for its own clerisy. I shall have more to say about the clerisy of power later. Suffice it here to say that it is as vivid a reality in modern democracy as it ever was in any Renaissance monarchy; as vivid, and vastly larger.

We are nevertheless witnessing, as I write, a gathering revolt against this same political clerisy and against the whole structure of wealth, privilege, and power that the contemporary democratic state has come to represent. What we are also witnessing, and this tragically, is rising opposition to the central values of the political community as we have known them for the better part of the past two centuries: freedom, rights, due process, privacy, and welfare.

I say "tragically" advisedly. I find it hard to think that very much of the extraordinary burst of economic, social, and cultural growth we have known during the last two hundred years would have been possible apart from the structure of liberties and rights which were guaranteed by the political community. To lose, as I believe we are losing, this structure of values is surely among the more desolating facts in the present decline of the West. Nevertheless, looked at in historical terms, it would be remarkable if the present combination of political Leviathan and sense of helplessness and impotence in citizenry were not attended by disenchantment and rising hatred.

It would be comforting if the revolt were simply the result of Viet Nam and Watergate. But it cannot be so seen. In the first place the roots of revolt are deeper and older in this country. In the second place, precisely the same kind of revolt is to be seen in other Western countries, those which have known neither Viet Nam nor Watergate. In West Germany, Italy, France, the Scandinavian countries, Holland, Belgium, and even—now especially—England, the reports of citizen unrest, citizen indifference, citizen alienation, and citizen hostility to government do not differ appreciably from what we are given in the United States.

Clearly, we are at the beginning of a new Reformation, this time, however, one that has the political state rather than the church as the central object of its force; a force that ranges from the slow drip of apathy to the more hurricane-like intensities of violence and terror. The first great Reformation, that of the sixteenth century, was also a period of twilight of authority in the West. It was terminated by the rise of the national state and the gradual retreat of church, kinship, guild, and hereditary class. Today we are present, I believe, at the commencement of the retreat of the state as we have known this institution for some five centuries, though what the consequences will be no one can be certain. (pp. 3-6)

Robert Nisbet, in his Twilight of Authority *(copyright © 1975 by Robert Nisbet; reprinted by permission of Oxford University Press, Inc.), Oxford University Press, New York, 1975, 287 p.*

Excerpt from *HISTORY OF THE IDEA OF PROGRESS*

As the year 2000 comes closer, there is certain to be a widening and quickening of interest—scientific, scholarly, intellectual, and popular—not only in the year itself, given its chiliastic overtone, but also in the whole question of human progress. What, it will be—is now being—asked, may be expected of the year, as far as the West is concerned? Does a Golden Age

lie ahead; or, as the result of degeneration, an Age of Darkness? And how will progress or regress be assessed, by what criteria? What *is* progress: basically moral and spiritual, with *absence* of material wealth a better indicator than abundance? There are those in the past as well as in the West today who have so argued. Or is progress inextricably related to the skills and insights proceeding from accumulation of knowledge, as a long line of philosophers commencing with Xenophanes and Protagoras in ancient Greece have insisted? Throughout most of Western history, the Middle Ages included, respect for reason, knowledge, and science was so high that it was almost inevitable that criteria of human progress would be drawn from these values. It is different, however, in the twentieth century. The revolt against rationalism and science, the cultivation of irrationalism in a variety of forms, religious and secular, and the astonishing growth of subjectivism, of preoccupation with one's own self and its pleasures—all of this is different in scale at least from anything the West has before known. Will the historic idea of progress be driven entirely from the intellectual field by the massed forces of pessimism: belief in cycles of civilization, with our own Western civilization even now hastening toward the bottom of the downswing? (pp. 3-4)

No single idea has been more important than, perhaps as important as, the idea of progress in Western civilization for nearly three thousand years. Other ideas will come to mind, properly: liberty, justice, equality, community, and so forth. I do not derogate from one of them. But this must be stressed: throughout most of Western history, the substratum of even these ideas has been a philosophy of history that lends past, present, and future to their importance. Nothing gives greater importance or credibility to a moral or political value than belief that it is more than something cherished or to be cherished; that it is an essential element of historical movement from past through present to future. Such a value can then be transposed from the merely desirable to the historically necessary.

Simply stated, *the idea of progress holds that mankind has advanced in the past—from some aboriginal condition of primitiveness, barbarism, or even nullity—is now advancing, and will continue to advance through the foreseeable future.* In J. B. Bury's apt phrase, the idea of progress is a synthesis of the past and a prophecy of the future. It is inseparable from a sense of time flowing in unilinear fashion. Arthur O. Lovejoy, in his *Primitivism and Related Ideas in Antiquity,* writes that the idea represents "an appraisal both of the historic process in general and of the predominant trend which is manifested in it." The consequence of this awareness of historical process, Lovejoy continues, is widespread belief in "a tendency inherent in nature or man to pass through a regular sequence of stages of development in the past, the present and the future, the latter stages being—with perhaps occasional retardations or regressions —superior to the earlier." To which it is necessary to add only that most often this idea also contains assumptions as to the continuity, the gradualness, the naturalness, even the inexorability, of these stages of development. The idea must not be thought the companion of mere caprice or accident; it must be thought a part of the very scheme of things in universe and society. Advance from the inferior to the superior must seem as real and certain as anything in the laws of nature. (pp. 4-5)

[The] record is not always a clean one for the consequences of belief in progress. Faith in the advance of mankind, stage by stage, to some still unfulfilled end or goal can be, and has been, united with faiths most of us in the West find repugnant and hateful. The kind of absolute military-political power we find in twentieth-century totalitarianisms, left and right, has behind it a philosophy of inexorable progress. So does the kind of racism that flourished in the nineteenth and early twentieth centuries: to a man the Gobineaus, Houston Stewart Chamberlains, and Madison Grants were believers in progress, or at least in its possibility and seeking its cause—which they found in race.

But, corruptions of the idea of progress understood—and the two I have just mentioned do not exhaust the number—I remain convinced that this idea has done more good over a twenty-five hundred-year period, led to more creativeness in more spheres, and given more strength to human hope and to individual desire for improvement than any other single idea in Western history. One may say that what is ultimately crucial, the will to advance or improve, lies in the individual alone, that an unverifiable, paradoxical, cosmic dogma is not needed. The individual's own drives and aspirations will suffice to effect progress, and therefore so comprehensive and abstract a proposition as the Western idea of progress is expendable.

I do not agree. The springs of human action, will, and ambition lie for the most part in beliefs about universe, world, society, and man which defy rational calculations and differ greatly from physio-psychological instincts. These springs lie in what we call dogmas. That word comes from Greek roots with the literal meaning of "seems-good." As Tocqueville wrote, "No society can prosper; no society can exist" without dogma. For the individual also "dogmatic belief is not less indispensable to him in order to live alone." It was Cardinal Newman who wrote: "Men will die for a dogma who will not even stir for a conclusion." The idea of the slow, gradual, inexorable progress of mankind to higher status in knowledge, culture, and moral estate is a dogma, precisely the kind that Tocqueville and Newman had in mind.

Everything now suggests, however, that Western faith in the dogma of progress is waning rapidly in all levels and spheres in this final part of the twentieth century. The reasons, as I attempt to show in the final chapter, have much less to do with the unprecedented world wars, the totalitarianisms, the economic depressions, and other major political, military, and economic afflictions which are peculiar to the twentieth century than they do with the fateful if less dramatic erosion of all the fundamental intellectual and spiritual premises upon which the idea of progress has rested throughout its long history.

Perhaps I exaggerate. But I cannot help but think we shall know shortly whether civilization in any form and substance comparable to what we have known during most of the preceding twenty-five hundred years in the West is possible without the supporting faith in progress that has existed along with this civilization. Our problem in this final part of the twentieth century is compounded by the fact that the dogma of progress is today strong in the official philosophies or religions of those nations which are the most formidable threats to Western culture and its historical moral and spiritual values—one more instance of the capacity for Western skills and values to be exported, corrupted, and then turned against the very West that gave them birth. (pp. 8-9)

Robert Nisbet, in his History of the Idea of Progress *(copyright © 1980 by Basic Books, Inc.; reprinted by permission of Basic Books, Inc., Publishers), Basic Books, 1980, 370 p.*

CURRIN V. SHIELDS

[Professor Nisbet's apparent purpose in *The Quest for Community*] is to sound a warning for all democrats: If you do not want to slip into a totalitarian morass, you must deliberately build a pluralist society. Only in a pluralist society can we have both freedom and democracy. The author elaborates his plea for "pluralist democracy" in the now familiar sociological terms of "community."

Professor Nisbet claims that prior to the advent of liberalism, Western societies abounded in local associations like the family, guild, church, and village. These intimate associations performed meaningful functions in men's lives, and they satisfied the psychological need for "community." But during the 19th century the ties holding men together in these associations were cut by rampant individualism. The prime liberal values were the free individual and the sovereign people. With the realization of these values, the state became the sole association for achieving the goals of individuals, as well as the single locus of allegiance and authority. Standing alone as just one of the masses, the individual was confronted by the impersonal, centralized nation state. But in the context of the mass state, liberal values ceased to have meaning, for even these values depended upon the context of local associations. So we find 20th century man in quest of "community." Yet the only remaining link between the atomized mass of individuals and the total state is the ideology of the absolute political community.

What is to be done? We must regard the "individual" as a member of free associations, and we must regard the "people" as an arrangement of quasi-sovereign groups, with the state merely one of many associations. We must revive the intimate "intermediate" associations by vesting them with functions meaningful in the lives of men today. For it is these plural communities which must curb the authority of the state, if that essential balance between order and freedom is to be maintained in democratic societies. So endeth the lesson.

This thesis—which is familiar to those acquainted with recent political thought of Christian inspiration—is no doubt plausible. Yet the argument has a hollow ring. Perhaps it is because the discourse is admittedly within the realm of morals, and because moral arguments have that unfortunate quality of being unconvincing if you do not agree at the outset, and superfluous if you do. Or perhaps it is because the argument remains throughout at a level of abstraction which approximates pure sound. Such generality may be required to get at the big picture, and the big picture may be important to understand. But to be significant the big picture must portray what it represents, and ten thousand words are no assurance of this.

Beyond these reasons, however, the argument rings hollow because it is almost entirely an enterprise in logic. Logic has its uses, but it is a poor substitute for experience in political analysis. Perhaps individualistic liberalism does logically develop into the absolute political community. But Professor Nisbet has prepared his lesson for warm-bodied democrats, and they must perforce ask: Does our experience show that "individualistic liberalism" was ever more than a dream, or nightmare? Does our experience show that "intermediate associations" were destroyed in democratic societies? Does our experience show that associative life, say in America, is now sparse and sterile? Or does our experience show instead the inadequacy of Professor Nisbet's assumptions? (pp. 598-99)

Currin V. Shields, "Book Reviews: 'The Quest for Community'," in The American Political Science

Review *(copyright, 1953, by The American Political Science Association), Vol. 47, No. 2, June, 1953, pp. 598-99.*

ARTHUR K. DAVIS

[*The Quest for Community*] is essentially a conservative ideological essay. It stresses the social values of localism and familism; it carefully elucidates the "good" (i.e., community-making) aspects of war. Yet it unwittingly documents some leading arguments of the Left. That anxiety and disorganization and a literature of decay are 20th-century characteristics is true. But they are specific features of "old regime" societies, like the Western nations today, preoccupied with war and the imminent dissolution of their world. Nisbet's conception of the modern mass revolutions abroad is unfortunately patterned after Orwell's *1984*. A more Olympian view would reveal that there is confidence and reconstruction in the present era as well as pessimism and destructiveness.

The analysis of family roles and small-group values is brilliant. In its broader aspects the reasoning may seem overdrawn to some readers. Nineteenth century "individualism" has something of the straw man about it, and so too has the so-called twentieth century "atomizing" of the masses. The theory of the primacy of the State in modern social change is surely one-sided. Is it not more useful to conceive of change in terms of a system of elements wherein no single factor leads or lags except for purposes of analysis? Nisbet comes perilously close to a one-factor theory of change.

His identification of freedom with cultural diversity and decentralized groups is philosophically legitimate but sociologically parochial. A sociological definition of freedom valid for any social system would run more like this: freedom is a subjective feeling of personal well-being which results from the objective fact of living in an effectively functioning society. A society functions effectively to the degree that its social structure is integrated, that it successfully meets its problems of internal and external change, that it socializes new members, satisfies or reconciles their needs and expectations, etc. The point is that a number of concrete patterns of societal organization can meet this abstract definition of freedom. It is entirely possible that among them is Nisbet's bogey, the totalitarian community—once the latter has been stabilized or routinized. In transition eras, societies fulfill their functional requirements less effectively; hence their members feel they have less freedom.

Nisbet sees clearly the malintegration between primary groups and large-scale organization, and the resulting primary-group *anomie*. He fails to consider those sources of personal insecurity which originate in large-scale organization, e.g., the overemphasis on competitive upward mobility, the business cycle and overproduction, institutional pressures toward war and imperialism, the persistence of discrimination against minorities, management-labor conflict. Solution of these problems will require more State action, probably nothing less than comprehensive central planning, which in turn may provide a framework for approaching the small-group problems raised by Nisbet. (p. 443)

Arthur K. Davis, "Book Reviews: 'The Quest for Community'," in American Sociological Review *(copyright © 1953 by the American Sociological Association), Vol. 18, No. 4, August, 1953, pp. 443-44.*

PETER L. BERGER

[In *The Sociological Tradition*] Nisbet sees the roots of sociological thought in the 19th century in two related but distinct historical developments, the socio-economic transformations brought on by industrialism and the political transformations inaugurated by the French Revolution. This, of course, is not a new notion, but Nisbet's discussion of the "two revolutions" sums it up lucidly and convincingly. Sociological thought, in other words, was born of the necessity to make sense of the disintegration of the old order of pre-industrial, pre-revolutionary Europe. It goes without saying that different people found different "senses" in these events, but Nisbet suggests (very convincingly) that sociological reflection may be seen as moving between the "poles" of Marx and Tocqueville in the assessment of the new emerging world. He further suggests . . . that most of what has gone under the heading of "sociology" has ratified the victory of the Tocquevillean over the Marxian assessment. Put crudely, this means that sociological thought has tended to conservatism rather than revolution, to a more or less dour contemplation of the modern world rather than to a burning desire to transform it. Nisbet here shares the essential perspective of Marxist commentators on what they call "bourgeois sociology," though, of course, Nisbet does not share their negative evaluation of this characterization.

Nisbet enumerates five "unit ideas"—community, authority, status, the sacred, and alienation. Each of these is coupled with a counter-idea to form five "linked antitheses"—community/society, authority/power, status/class, sacred/secular, alienation/progress. It is not difficult to see, details aside, how each of these can be traced back to the fundamental problem of the disintegration of the old order. (p. 570)

[The value of Nisbet's argument] lies in showing how widely different and even discrepant trends in sociological thought may be related to each other and to a common "existential" situation. It should be emphasized that, in doing this, Nisbet does not associate himself with the position that an objective or "value-free" sociology is impossible. Rather he shows how sociologists have responded to the challenges to human self-understanding posited by the modern situation, challenges that are fundamentally normative, irrespective of the cool detachment that some of them sought and, possibly found in the sociological perspective.

He thus assists the reader in understanding sociology as a very specifically modern intellectual discipline, growing out of specifically modern circumstances—an insight, of course, that is in itself sociological! It may thus be said that what Nisbet does is to turn the lens of sociological scrutiny back upon itself. His book, at least in part, is a sociology-of-knowledge view of the knowledge of sociology. If one may make one general reproach against Nisbet, it would be that he does not seem to be sufficiently worried by the implications of this procedure—or, to put it differently, that Nisbet does not seem to be plagued by the doubt that sociology itself may be not only a product but a force of disintegration. The reproach, though, is probably unfair. A reviewer cannot fairly expect an author to share his vertigoes. (pp. 570-71)

Peter L. Berger, "'The Sociological Tradition'," in Commonweal *(copyright © 1967 Commonweal Publishing Co., Inc.; reprinted by permission of Commonweal Publishing Co., Inc.), Vol. LXXXV, No. 19, February 17, 1967, pp. 570-71.*

J. H. PLUMB

[In **"Social Change and History"** Mr. Nisbet sees the] metaphor of growth as one of the most fundamental concepts in European thought from the days of Hesiod to modern sociologists. The danger of Nisbet's method is that in less scholarly and sensitive hands it might lead to banality. He is aware that societies have twisted the basic metaphor to suit their needs, and he approaches a distinction which should be made, but which he never quite makes—the difference between a "past" and history itself.

All societies manufacture pasts for a variety of social needs, and they vary from the single to the complex. Indeed Mr. Nisbet's book would have been far richer, and much longer, had he indicated more clearly the relationship between the various stages of growth theory and the societies that produced them. He does this admirably with the comparative theory of social evolution in the 19th century, and the book quickens into ever more vigorous life at that point.

Curiously enough, I wish Mr. Nisbet would have ranged a little further. He would have found variations on his metaphor of growth and decay long before the Greeks, in ancient Egypt. China, both classical and imperial, India in Vedic or Buddhist days could have provided him with more. Indeed, there is one aspect of his theme that he never explores—the metaphor of growth and decay as a social anodyne. . . .

The end of this metaphor may be nearer than Mr. Nisbet thinks, for, as we begin to move into a full scientific and technological world, a process that historically speaking has only just begun, it is possible that man's concepts of his destiny will change fundamentally and that old metaphors will die, just as there are signs that the power of socially manufactured pasts with their sanctions for morality and institutions are also dying.

> J. H. Plumb, *"To Cover Two and a Half Milennia in 300 Pages Takes a Brave Man," in* The New York Times Book Review (©*1969 by The New York Times Company; reprinted by permission), June 15, 1969, p. 3.*

BENJAMIN NELSON

[In *Social Change and History* Nisbet has] issued one of the most extraordinary challenges presented by a contemporary social theorist to so-called "forward-looking" modern sensibilities. . . . Nisbet's book has the ring of a prophetic summons to abandon evangelical immanentism as the American public philosophy in favor of a strictly nonethnocentric historical view of social change, one allegedly grounded in superior metaphysical and sociological awarenesses which are luckily found to provide to cultural conservatism the firm foundation too long denied to it by the developmental mysticisms, heedlessly spread among us by the masses and classes alike. (pp. 1498-99)

[Although] I largely share Nisbet's hopes for a reform in our ways of thinking about sociology and historical process, . . . I am put off by the excesses of both his historical and his logical analysis of the situation; above all, I fear that the drastic remedies he proposes threaten more loss than gain. The perplexing turns of his concluding "Reflections" bring to mind the famed paradoxes ascribed to Zeno of Elea, implying the self-contradictoriness of the idea of motion. Can it be that Nisbet is a latter-day Zeno, in whose pages we must expect to find Eleatic paradoxes because his true theme, like that of his

ancient predecessor, is the fearsome price we must all pay for slighting the reality of Being in favor of the appearance of Becoming?

Nisbet is very largely right on his key claim: the study of social change does need to be freed from the power of seductive metaphors hastily plucked from disparate contexts. But the alleged affliction of sociology by the growth and development metaphor is hardly so special a case as he implies. All the sciences—certainly all the social sciences—have regularly drawn metaphors from other sciences with mixed scientific and parascientific effects. And social theory has in its winding career absorbed metaphors at least as problematic as those Nisbet lampoons, metaphors which allowed little or no room for a theory of natural history of persons, societies, cultures, and which always required reference to "intrusions" to account for all human action. Nor have the borrowings of sociology from biology by any means all been noxious. A proper history of biological influence on social thought would make certain to mention not only primitive Social Darwinism and Spencerian excesses but also Claude Bernard, L. J. Henderson, urban ecology, the current school of ethologists.

Nisbet's appeal to "history" is far too simple to produce the desired sociological and intellectual reform. His image of concept-free history hardly represents the prevailing practice of historians, who have often been more immersed in metahistorical and metasociological reifications than have sociologists. It is exactly this situation which forced many historians and historically oriented scholars . . . to move away from that discipline in the direction of theoretically better-grounded historical sociology. It is not sociologists who have been guilty of fathering the personified abstractions that clutter the pages of history books.

Nisbet is right on another major point: the concept of "social change" is in a sorry state. But he need not have written about the systematic literature on social change as though it has never emerged from the cocoon of mythic developmentalism—an effect he achieves by overlooking or underemphasizing discussions that are not within his antecedently fixed frames (the absence of reference to Ogburn's work speaks volumes). In his tendency to polarize ideas, he sacrifices the fruits of discriminating scholarship. Moreover, he might surely have told us more about changes in social arrangement and experience which prompted social theorists after 1775 to see change and development at every turn. The thrust to so-called developmental theories was general in the 19th century; the need to understand and explain the large changes of the time led thinkers and theorists of every sort to look for ways of expressing process. And here I must speak directly to Nisbet's sharp attacks on leading contemporary sociologists and anthropologists in the name of history. Parsons, Steward, and their students are avowedly neo-evolutionists, but they came to their positions, as they tell us themselves, in order to relate to realities of societal process—*histories*—not readily open to analysis in other perspectives. Many of Nisbet's attacks from the side of empirical history of events are in one respect a welcome claim that neither sociology nor anthropology can afford to manufacture history *out of nothing;* but some of his charges imply a claim that these disciplines have no legitimate domain outside of history.

Can we look to Nisbet to become the great peacemaker in the war between sociology and history? The more closely one scans his arguments the more the conviction grows that he has scrambled the message he may have originally intended for the contending parties and has been led into a costly double deflation of the intellectual symbolic and emotional values of both ordinary men and social scientists. The first deflation results from a tacit abandonment of central coordinates of societal and culturological analysis. Structural contexts, cultural settings, ecological scenes of action, complex conjunctures largely escape notice in these pages. In his effort to prove that reference to development always implies illicit metaphors, Nisbet loses sight of patterned probabilities. In his attack on immanentism, he essentially rejects every form of systemic bondedness involved in aggregate process, in effect fracturing the social world.

The second deflation takes the form of the abandonment of historicity in the name of "history." The only history Nisbet truly allows is past history, *res gesta,* as processed by behaviorally oriented (sociological) historians of social behavior, and then only as told from the outside as strings of events largely conceived to undergo change as a result of intrusions from without. In this light, societal movement, cultural experience, symbolic innovations lose their context and import. Individuals and groups are scarcely allowed to have or to make their histories.

Thus although promising to reconcile the differences between sociology and history, Nisbet actually broadens the gap between them. Narrowing the horizon of history, he forces sociology into constricted stances. (p. 1499)

Nisbet asserts that the claimed advances in sociological theory since the heyday of evolutionism of the 19th century are largely illusory. Whether or not he means this statement to be taken literally, he seems to forget that the great advances in the realm of empirical study since those days has been profoundly stimulated by new contexts of inquiry and new kinds of understanding. Our very image of societal and historical process continues to be transformed by new concepts in physics and the biological sciences and new theories of scientific explanation. Except for a few highly selective citations of Ernst Mayr and Thomas Kuhn, Nisbet does not relate in any depth to such recent currents of thought. (pp. 1499-500)

[Nisbet's] challenge will be a continuing reminder that we dare not remain content with our current resources—semantic, empirical, philosophic—if we wish to make progress in the perplexing field of social change. But now, at the very moment when we are caught in the rolling surf of no fewer than a half-dozen world-wide revolutions, few sociologists are likely to be persuaded, even by so sensitive and learned a colleague as Nisbet, that we shall understand our motley histories and truly appreciate social change only if we pay proper respect to Fixity. (p. 1500)

> *Benjamin Nelson, "Metaphor in Sociology," in* Science *(copyright © 1969 by the American Association for the Advancement of Science), Vol. 166, No. 3912, December 19, 1969, pp. 1498-500.*

NORMAN BIRNBAUM

For Nisbet [in **"The Degradation of the Academic Dogma"**], the university is identical with the corporate faculty. This body, however, has allowed itself to be distracted from its sacred task, the cultivation of knowledge for its own sake. The corporate faculty was once quite like a body of knights, an order in the realm. Academic freedoms, indeed, are not derived from liberalism: they are remnants of feudal immunities. Like the medieval knights in their period of decline, university teachers

have become mercenaries. They serve others where they once sought the academic equivalent of the Holy Grail. . . .

Medieval scholars were like medieval artisans: they produced knowledge for society. A sacred society required sacred knowledge. Early modern society needed the knowledge that could guide men through the perplexities of a disintegrating religious system. Nisbet himself attributes the decline of the universities in no small part to the individualized rationalism we find in Descartes's faith in the mind's capacity to judge. He ignores the ways in which university organization (and the thought it produced) has always responded to historical pressures. It is absurd to read the modern history of learning as if it had taken place in a vacuum. Nisbet supposes that textual knowledge still has something priestly about it. Our scientists, in his view, owe their academic good fortune to their association with philologists. This is far from an accurate account of the history of science. Worse yet, it distracts us from an urgent contemporary task: the bridging of the yawning chasm between the two (or three) cultures, a philosophical reconciliation of science with the humanities.

Nisbet is not an apologist for the liberal university as it was on the eve of the student revolt. That university, he holds, was corrupted by "academic capitalism." Specialized institutes, contractual research, academic jet-setting, destroyed the prestige of the scholar-teacher. (These activities also gave the university the funds with which to raise even the traditional professor's salary, stilling his protest.) Nisbet claims that the cash nexus destroyed the traditional academy just as it had undermined medieval society. Is his term, "academic capitalism," correct? The university's critics in the 1950's, like C. Wright Mills, held that it had been devastated by academic bureaucratization. The intellect was mobilized to serve the agencies of power in a technocratic society. Kerr, who found nothing wrong with the process, endorsed this view.

It is surprising, further, that Nisbet should attribute political radicalism to the academics employed in the newer sectors of the university. Generally, opposition to the war and to America's institutions has come from the old fashioned scholar-teachers and not from the new academic technicians. Many of the latter now face unemployment, and some are disturbed by the uses or abuses of their learning by society. Perhaps they will become radicalized. For the moment, the corporate faculty is the source of such critical political rationality as the American left may claim.

Nisbet's remedies for our disorders are simple. The pursuit of pure learning is to become, once again, the university's exclusive concern. This will undermine the power of the academic entrepreneurs, restore society's declining respect for universities, and (a not quite unstated premise of his argument) end the rampant subjectivism of modern culture. The university is no longer to engage in the cultivation of the creative arts, applied or practical activities of any kind, or to pay much attention to the developmental problems of adolescence. As for the students, theirs is to study or to leave. The project requires the restoration of the faculty's authority, and an alliance of the faculty with a central administration restored to power and dignity; neither need be bothered by clamorous demands for participation, or even very much by doctrines of accountability.

Nisbet is entirely unspecific as to how this is to be accomplished. He thinks that the fundamental university unit ought to be, once again, the department. Given his historical perspective, this is a drastically shortsighted suggestion. Departments are not medieval in origin. They are administrative reifications of intellectual processes. We often hear of the "knowledge explosion," but it may be more correct to think of the implosion of knowledge, the creation of new thought structures to deal with problems that shatter the boundaries between the disciplines. In these respects, academic departmentalism is often a tiresome irrelevance, precisely from the viewpoint of the pursuit of pure knowledge.

The demand that the university return to the search for pure knowledge tells us nothing of how to reconcile inquiry with the aim of a liberal education: the communication of a central core of culture to a new generation. We are not at all sure as to what we should transmit or how to transmit it. Our students have rushed into this breach. Their demands for the collegiate prepackaging of experience are ridiculous, but the mistakes of the young do not excuse the old from the effort to rethink the traditional office of the university. In a society that demands knowledge, the university can no longer function as a closed corporation of scholars. The humanization of knowledge will not be attained by demanding a return to an entirely imaginary past. The degradation of the academic dogma will not end until we have not dogma, but clear and compelling ideas to put in its place. (pp. 49-50)

> Norman Birnbaum, "*Up Against the Wall—In Bookcases,*" in The New York Times Book Review (© 1971 by The New York Times Company; reprinted by permission), May 16, 1971, pp. 48-50.*

ROBERT McCLINTOCK

Early in *The Degradation of the Academic Dogma* Robert Nisbet makes a revealing aside about the degradation of literary effort: "Older readers will perhaps remember the luster that once attended the book, before that luster was extinguished in the flood of publication during the past two or three decades, before books became, like steel and automobiles, commodities." . . . Admittedly, I am a younger reader, except as the very, very young would count; but all the same, to me the book, a real book, can still have luster, if written with passion and care to make a significant point. Alas, in this case, the passion has flagged, the care has been compromised, and the point is significant but perfunctory, manufactured from recollections primarily to observe an academic occasion. Dross, not luster, attends this book, for it is a commodity hurriedly produced to capture a share of the market for tracts on the academic crisis. (p. 123)

Ironically, the shortcomings of Nisbet's book will be most manifest to those who agree by and large with the views expressed in it. The university is a *setting* for scholarly and scientific endeavor. The endeavor, however, is not itself corporate; the endeavor is the work of particular scholars and scientists; the endeavor, in the end, depends on whether or not those performing it are willing to take account of what others have said, whether or not they are willing to take pains in their work, whether or not they are willing to accept, not the academic dogma, but its standards. And as an example of the standards that should be upheld by those who believe that knowledge *is* important, Nisbet's book will but further degrade the academic condition.

Nisbet, however, distinguishes between prophecy and scholarship, arguing that the rigor of the latter should not be imposed on the former, for fear of limiting its insight, and perhaps he means with this distinction to excuse the numerous shortcuts that he takes in and with his text. I say "perhaps" because he is ambiguous whether or not he considers his book to be a work of prophecy. He claims not to prophesy, but he writes, as he suggests the prophet may, without explicit interest in the work of others, without concern for the usual academic niceties. Nisbet's distinction between prophecy and scholarship is itself dubious, but even without calling it into question, I have difficulty seeing how a prophet of the academic dogma can rightfully exempt his prophecies from its controlling standards, for a prophet, after all, is a man who gives witness to his doctrine not only by the letter of his word, but equally by the spirit of his example. In this work, Nisbet's example belies a latent disdain for scholarship, for knowledge, for the academic dogma. In substance, Nisbet's diagnosis is not new, although he mentions no predecessors, even though some merit mention. . . . If pressed, however, Nisbet might well claim that the substance of his diagnosis has little originality and that such predecessors are to be taken for granted; his main claim instead concerns his perception of the historic significance that the crisis may harbor, and with respect to his claim, his nonchalance about the work of yet other writers has serious consequences.

An historical assertion concerning the character of the Western university provides the foundation of the book: "The prime point is that a certain distinctive kind of community existed [from the Middle Ages to the recent past], with a distinctive dogma its core, and that this community and this dogma required supporting contexts: contexts which were largely destroyed during the period 1945-1960 by the economic, political, social, and intellectual changes I call the Last Reformation." . . . Evidence? Evidence! Why bother? Vigorous assertion will do, along with a little veneer to impress the half-informed, two passages from Hastings Rashdall and one from Charles Homer Haskins. To be sure, the university had medieval origins, as did the state, as Joseph R. Strayer has recently reiterated. But as the state has had a rather significant history since its medieval beginnings, so too has the university.

To ignore the history that intervenes between the medieval university and that which Nisbet began to experience in the 1930s is an evasion, an unscholarly evasion, for that history raises a number of doubts about Nisbet's prime point, doubts that a spokesman for scholarship ought to take up. To begin, a close reading of Rashdall, and studies by Denifle, Kibre, D'Irsay, Leff, and others, would raise the question whether, in fact, the features of the medieval university that long ago died—a separate civil law for members of the academic estate, the organization of students into nations, and the use of cessation and dispersal—were moe properly characteristic of the institution than the features that Nisbet claims have survived essentially untouched by time.

Second, attention to the work of Paulsen and others concerned with the modern university would suggest the possibility that the university Nisbet reveres, one in which scholarship is at once advanced and disseminated by the integral connection of research and teaching, has little to do with the medieval university and is instead a nineteenth-century, primarily German creation, built sometimes (but not in the all-important case of Berlin) on vestiges of medieval universities.

Third, consideration of the work of Veysey and other students of the American university would raise the suspicion that the causes of the present academic degradation, which Nisbet characterizes as primarily post-war phenomena, have actually been at work from the beginning in the adapting of the German university to the United States; perhaps these causes are intrinsic to both the well-endowed private and the well-financed public institutions that alone were able to appropriate the German ideal. Finally, a fuller reading of the history of scholarship might indicate that the vigor of academic work does not depend, to the degree that Nisbet implies, on the health of the university: after all, in describing the character of scholarship, Nisbet himself appealed to the example of "the great Scaliger, Erasmus, and their innumerable contemporaries" . . . without, that is, noting the implications of appealing to men who largely brought their scholarship to fruition in conscious opposition to the university.

Precisely how these historical questions would be resolved at the end of a full and careful study is immaterial here. The important matter in raising them is rather to indicate that they exist and that they merit serious consideration in characterizing the history of the Western university. For some reason Nisbet was unwilling to give them that consideration; instead he chose to found his defense of scholarship on an historical caricature, without assuming scholarly responsibility for addressing himself to the intellectual difficulties that attend his interpretation. But a defense of scholarship that proceeds via its practical denial is no defense at all. (pp. 124-27)

> Robert McClintock, "Book Reviews: 'The Degradation of the Academic Dogma'," in Teachers College Record (copyright © 1971, Teachers College, Columbia University), Vol. 73, No. 1, September, 1971, pp. 123-29.

THE TIMES LITERARY SUPPLEMENT

[Nisbet's history in *The Degradation of the Academic Dogma*] is wrong. Universities as we now know them are late nineteenth and early twentieth-century inventions; to pretend that Oxford's link with the Middle Ages is much more than architectural is to miss the whole point of nineteenth-century English intellectual history. American universities owe everything to Prussia, and nothing to Newman. As a result, Professor Nisbet's view of English intellectual history is quaint. He is clearly quite unaware of the long ancestry of medicine and law at Oxford and Cambridge and regards them as new subjects.

But if many of his facts are incorrect, his general thesis carries conviction. Professor Nisbet heaves a few bricks at scholarship ("dull, stale, leaden and profitless by any standard"), but in his own way he believes in it. What on earth, he rightly asks, has scholarship, a glory of Renaissance and post-Renaissance culture, to do with our universities, as they are now becoming?

> "The Three E's," in The Times Literary Supplement (©Times Newspapers Ltd. (London) 1972; reproduced from The Times Literary Supplement by permission), No. 3646, January 14, 1972, p. 47.*

GERTRUD LENZER

["Twilight of Authority"] is deeply unsettling. Many readers will share [Nisbet's] fear about the increasing capacity of the modern state to penetrate and control even the innermost recesses of social, cultural and individual life. In particular, Nisbet points to the vast centralizing mechanisms of state power in all its visible and less-than-visible manifestations, to the growth of a pervasive bureaucracy, to the ascendancy and concentration of a military that threatens in one country after another to impose despotism and dictatorship upon an atomized citizenry. (p. 31)

Nisbet's account dramatically represents how since World War I the strategies that were originally directed at foreign enemies have helped to promote what he calls "fascism" and a "war society" at home. "Twilight of Authority" is a radical diagnosis of our condition.

As disturbing as the prospects for Western democratic societies may be, many readers will be almost as dismayed by Nisbet's selection of certain historical processes as the source of our present condition, and by the remedies he prescribes to avert the dangers of military despotism and the destruction of liberty. In these parts of his work Nisbet ceases to write as the "social analyst and prophet" that he aspires to be and turns ideologue. And this work becomes a symptom of the very situation that he has undertaken to analyze.

As it turns out, Nisbet locates "the heart of our problem with the state and its governing agencies" in the cultural and social spheres of modern society. In his view, the idea and the desire for equality "at the present time undoubtedly represents the greatest single threat to liberty and social initiative." In choosing to find the chief source of our present peril in the idea of equality, Nisbet is promoting a point of view that is representative of a particular state of ideological mind.

The particular state of mind that Nisbet represents has in the course of recent years abandoned its former praise of equality as a main pillar of American democracy. In those bygone days of ideological warfare against Communism, the citizens of Western democracies were regarded as enjoying (notwithstanding a few "pockets of poverty" here and there) a degree of equality that inured them against whatever appeals the subversive ideology might offer—or so the counter-ideological argument went. Since then, however, the notion of equality has lost its exalted position and has suffered what amounts to a loss of status as a value. As more and more groups began to insist that their condition in society ought to express in some more adequate measure the equalities guaranteed by law, equality as a principle began to go into an intellectual decline. Nisbet is only one among a large chorus of intellectuals who characterize the idea of equality of condition as a dangerous social egalitarianism or "new equality" which perilously enhances the "centralized power's leveling effects upon the natural hierarchies of all social institutions." (pp. 31-2)

In "Twilight of Authority" the discreditation of equality is undertaken in the immense context of world history, philosophy and culture. Nisbet finds that the roots of our present demise reach back to the sixth century B.C. in Greece; the decline of the West is for him intimately associated with the idea of the *polis*. The decline reaches its culmination in modernity and the modern nation state. In other words, the West began to decline as soon as it began to rise, and the end will probably come next Thursday, as Hegel frequently intimated.

In essence, for Nisbet the great error committed by Western civilization was to locate the interests of society in matters of the most general order; in this way the diverse interests of the individual, of groups, estates and classes were increasingly subordinated to the interests of the whole, as arbitration of social conflicts and affairs was progressively relegated to the political realm. The inexorable growth of the sovereignty of the state in turn "manufactured," according to Nisbet, individualism —and both the state and individualism are equally destructive of the "social bond," which is created by such intermediary institutions as "property, family, local community, religion, and voluntary association." The modern state, instead of attending to its two great historical functions—the maintenance of internal order and the making of war—has taken over tutelary and regulatory powers from all these intermediary and sacred institutions. Hence it is no accident, though it is an inconsistency, that the Middle Ages and feudalism emerge as Nisbet's golden historical age. (p. 32)

No high rhetoric will make Nisbet's ideal self-governing societies of the past into anything but hypothetical constructs, just as the state of nature was for earlier philosophers. Nevertheless, it is this model of society that Nisbet envisages in his program for "genuine social reorganization in the West."

"The restoration of authority" and the "renewal of the social bond" can only come about through a revival of social and economic pluralism, a renascence of kinship, the rebirth of localism, of voluntary associations, and a redefinition of citizenship. And since Nisbet firmly believes that "inequality is the essence of the social bond," social hierarchy together with tradition urgently deserve to be reinstated. Certain signs of an equally important revival of locality and neighborhood in our societies are noted by Nisbet when he reports that despite national-regional conflicts in the United States, "the emotional roots of local loyalties remain strong." (pp. 32, 34)

To be sure, Nisbet rarely departs from the heights of historical and philosophical discourse to touch upon concrete circumstances. However, each time that he does, the results are equally telling. He also welcomes a revival of ethnicity in society and in general advocates a new "laissez-faire" of social groups (though not of the individual) in order to offset politicization, bureaucratization and centralization and to restore diversity, autonomy and cultural creativity.

All these measures are proposed to counteract the "new despotism," which is on the one hand government-bureaucratic-military power and on the other social equality, with which that power works hand in hand. According to Nisbet, the chief engineers of this "new despotism" are the intellectuals, philosophers and men of letters—the "political clerisy" without whom the bad idea of equality could never have gained its prominence nor the state its power. The "new equalitarians," such as Rawls and Christopher Jencks, are merely the contemporary incarnations of a long line of clerics. Plato, Hobbes, Rousseau and Marx lead the way as the arch-perpetrators of philosophies inimical to the social bond. With the exception of Burke and Tocqueville and a handful of conservative, traditionalist thinkers, most members of the intellectual class—from the Greek sophists to the present—are charged with having contributed to, if not causing, almost every conceivable evil Nisbet can think of.

Their love of the state, the services they render to military-political figures and regimes, their hatred of all social institutions that carry authority, from the family up to high culture, are all uniformly condemnable and condemned. . . .

It is difficult to know what to make of this hodge-podge of truth and nonsense. Nisbet has chosen as his enemies most of the major figures in the tradition of Western social and political theory. One handy way of dealing with such formidable opponents is to ignore, distort and parody their arguments. What does it matter if certain lines of argument occur in Rousseau's First Discourse rather than in his Second? What does it matter if Plato said this as well as that? Since Nisbet has made up his mind about this gang of terrorists, it doesn't really matter whether he gets their lines straight.

But he doesn't even get the lines of his allies straight: Freud, Keynes, Weber and Burke would find themselves diminished and distorted here. As a single illustration of how Nisbet uses evidence, I will cite his dealings with his favorite predecessor, Tocqueville. Nisbet naturally chooses passages from Tocqueville that appear to corroborate his indictment of the "new equality." Yet Tocqueville's complex argument is everywhere connected with equality of condition. (p. 34)

Nisbet is a historian of ideas, and in this capacity has a certain intellectual responsibility to the record. Part of this record is the great texts of our tradition. Nisbet's deployment of these texts—in the aid of a current ideological cause—is irresponsible in the extreme. In these excesses he has done no service to his political cause or to the more general cause to which his distinguished career as a scholar binds him.

For all its praiseworthy intentions, Nisbet's work is in almost no measure adequate to the weight and importance of the issues addressed in it. Less prophecy than it is polemic, and less polemic than it is confusion, **"Twilight of Authority"** unhappily falls between all possible stools and darkens the scene it set out to illuminate. (p. 36)

> *Gertrud Lenzer, "The Redecline of the West," in* The New York Times Book Review *(© 1975 by The New York Times Company; reprinted by permission), October 5, 1975, pp. 31-2, 34, 36.*

ROBERT H. BORK

Nisbet can be taken at two levels [in ***The Twilight of Authority***]. The first, which is perhaps a dispensable overlay, consists of the concept of a "twilight age," which parallels previous periods of decline, and the prediction of the militarization of society and the rise of a line of Caesars. I do not say this may not be accurate, only that it is not necessary to the argument, that it may be overly dramatic, and that the demonstration of coming militarization seems rather weak.

But all that may be laid aside and the remaining argument is still compelling and disturbing. Despotism is hardly more welcome if the new governors turn out to be not a clutch of colonels but a supposedly benevolent governmental bureaucracy operating in the name of equality of condition and imposing uniformity because of bureaucracy's own dynamic and requirements. And it is here that Nisbet is at his best: demonstrating the connection between centralization of power and the ideal of equality of condition as contrasted with equality of opportunity; pointing out the affinity of modern left-liberal intellectuals for both central power and egalitarianism; showing the increasing legalization of our culture and our individual relationships, which is a way of replacing social forces with state coercion; delineating the growth of state power in new, softer, and hence less resistible forms; linking the current wave of subjectivism and irrationality, manifested in occultism and the state of the arts, to the decline of the political community; showing the reciprocal relationship between the degradation of language, which is essential to the social bond, and the spread of state power. In these and a dozen other things, Nisbet is insightful, provocative, and, sad to say, probably quite right.

Though pessimistic that the forces of political centralization and social disintegration can be reversed, Nisbet closes with a plea for pluralism and the rescue of the social order from the political order, and he identifies some faint causes for hope. The reader will not be much heartened. (p. 1305)

*Robert H. Bork, "A Dark Future Seen at Twilight,"
in* National Review *(© National Review, Inc., 1975;
150 East 35th St., New York, N.Y. 10016), Vol. 27,
No. 45, November 21, 1975, pp. 1305-06.*

VICTOR LEBOW

What its author has done in [*The Twilight of Authority*] is to begin with a catalogue of all the weaknesses, shortcomings, corruption and disruption of our civilization, and draw from them his critique of the equalitarian doctrines and the mindless radicalism which, in his view, all stem from Rousseau with his worship of equality. Most thinking people will not only recognize but also agree with much of what he finds wrong and even evil in our society, our ways and our political and governmental institutions. (p. 695)

His treatment of "the lure of military society" is most interesting for what it reveals about his insights and his blind spots. To him, the rise of militarism in a society means the twilight of authority in the civil sphere. Moreover, he believes that intellectuals are fascinated by the use of power in times of crisis, and so are attracted to the military and to war itself. Even the social welfare budget expands as the military grow in power—as did the "corn dole" in ancient Rome. He cites Condorcet's suggestion that the rise of the infantry led to the creation of democracy, and for that reason democracy itself is closely related to war. In contrast with these speculations, there is a stark fact: Nisbet appears to see no connection between capitalist enterprise and war. And yet a certain career officer, later president of Columbia University and President of the United States, saw it plainly enough to give it a lasting label. He called it the "military-industrial complex" and his name was Eisenhower.

One must agree with Nisbet's estimate of the erosion of patriotism and the defection of the young—but he sees some hope in their communes. He uses Hobbes's famous words on the state of nature to describe how the American people now live "in continual fear and danger of violent death." No longer is patriotism the force it once was, although it made possible our acceptance of the dominant role which the political state has assumed in both social and economic affairs. He appears to prefer the role of the Church in feudal times, when all were under its sway, to that of the nation states of the past several centuries.

Nisbet considers the women's liberation and the black civil rights movements to be genuinely revolutionary, although it is too soon to tell how far they will go and how great will be their consequences. Then he adds, "I am saying only that . . . [these movements] like all others known to us in history, have to be seen against a background of prior destruction or erosion of key values." How this makes special sense in relation to the demands of both women and blacks escapes this reviewer. Particularly disturbing is his treatment of what he calls "The Pains of Affluence." Agreed, that the middle class is aware of its riches in the face of poverty, and that it wants to keep its hands clean while the bureaucracy handles the dole. However, he insists that the fading of the Protestant ethic and the political commitment to universal welfare are bound to reduce the actual amount of work done by individuals and erode the age-old compulsion to work. In this day of some 10 million or so unemployed—and probably more on the way to join

them—Nisbet writes that the ethic of work "cannot for long have the compulsion it has immemorially had in a society now politically committed to unemployment compensation, food stamps, Social Security and Medicare." (He does agree that some degree of security may be a minimum essential for the human community.)

Nowhere in this work with its astounding fund of references and quotations is there a single mention of the corrosive effects upon our political and social life of that most dominant of all institutions, the system of private enterprise, business, capitalism. In fact, Nisbet berates the intellectuals for their dislike of the businessman and his regard for profits, and finds them grievously at fault in denigrating the feudal society of the Dark and early Middle Ages. For him, apparently, those were the halcyon days. (pp. 695-96)

It is an ironic commentary on Nisbet's careful neglect of the role of capitalism in the deterioration of our society and the corruption of our political system that the magazine *Business Week*, by far the most influential of all business publications after *The Wall Street Journal*, should present in its issue of December 1, 1975, the first of three articles entitled "Egalitarianism: Threat to a Free Market." To this reviewer, who is old and inured to threatening clouds, this still looks like something that might be called the Falange of the Academicians. Yes, Nisbet has a chapter of "positive" suggestions. To my mind, they are unreal and without worth. (p. 696)

*Victor Lebow, "Honoring Rank, Class and Estate,"
in* The Nation *(copyright 1975* The Nation *magazine,
The Nation Associates, Inc.), Vol. 221, No. 22, December 27, 1975, pp. 694-96.*

SHELDON S. WOLIN

While there is little novelty to Nisbet's indictment [in *The Twilight of Authority*], and much, as we shall see, that is overstated to the point of perversity, one would have hoped that a writer of his learning and eminence could offer a perceptive explanation of our predicaments, or perhaps a characterization of our situation that might cast some illumination on the possibilities still open to us. (p. 8)

The problem . . . is defined as a distortion of the relationship between state and society caused by the weakening or destruction of intermediate "communities." The centralization of power in the state and its unchecked extension have resulted from the decline of these smaller centers of authority, affection, and morality. When we ask why and when these developments have come about, it becomes evident that Nisbet offers not an explanation but a series of myths.

The first myth posits an idyllic America that existed sometime between the end of the Civil War and the beginning of World War I. Then there was no Leviathan-state; localism and pluralism flourished; the values of family, work, and the "sacred" were respected; political parties were models of vigor and ideological fervor; and our wars were "proper" ones. It is, of course, a credible myth if one overlooks the fact that this period witnessed the corporate revolution, the corruption of the Republican Party during the Grant era, the bitter industrial conflict represented by the Pullman Strike, the emergence of imperialism during the Spanish-American War, the reimposition of racial servitude in the South, and the maturing of interest-group politics.

It is not so much the suppression of history that matters as the irrelevance of Nisbet's categories for understanding the nature of American pluralism. As we shall see, Nisbet conceives groups and associations in pre-industrial, pre-scientific, and predemocratic ways. His ideal of pluralism is explicitly medieval, which means, among other things, that groups are to be understood in terms of hierarchical authority, moral norms, inequality of membership, and stationary existence. As a result, the three most salient characteristics of American pluralism, the preoccupation with material interests, the expanding and dynamic quality of group activity, and resentment of the kind of preferential treatment which hierarchy and inequality entail, are missing.

The fundamental presupposition of American pluralism, the basic condition which has supported both intense group rivalry and a general acceptance of the "rules of the game," has been an expanding economy. The dominant economic groups of business, finance, agriculture, and, later, labor accommodated themselves to rules which they had the power to change; while excluded groups were pacified by the surpluses periodically available or their more "advanced" elements were absorbed. The irony is that this system has produced its own version of the values touted by Nisbet. Corporate structures, labor unions, agribusiness, universities are resplendent examples of authority, hierarchy, inequality, and status. Nor, despite some recent setbacks, do these groupings lack a legitimating belief. They embody the authority of science—natural, social, and economic—the most powerful miracle-producing belief-system since the Middle Ages.

These realities of American politics and society, which would make good sense to a Hamiltonian conservative, are either ignored or given only perfunctory attention by Nisbet because they cannot be accommodated to his second myth. Pluralistic America was subverted by a combination of power-hungry leaders, a "political clerisy" of intellectuals, and the left. "The West's first real experience with totalitarianism—political absolutism . . . with a kind of terror waiting always in the wings—came with the American war state under Woodrow Wilson." Roosevelt's NRA "was America's first experience with Fascism." Both the Wilson and Roosevelt administrations promoted militarism and socialism, and laid the foundations for today's "new despotism" and "new equalitarianism," a purposeless system dedicated solely to power.

Nisbet believes that in large measure the responsibility for warfare, welfare, and Watergate lies with the left and, more heavily, with the intellectuals or "political clerisy" who have been sapping the political and moral foundations of the nation since the days of Woodrow Wilson. Between them the two components of the left-liberal clerisy have promoted an invidious "transpolitical" doctrine that sanctions any action or means so long as it promotes the ends approved by the clerisy. Nixon's erasures and Ellsberg's disclosures were two sides of the same coin.

Although there may be recognizable elements of truth in Nisbet's sweeping generalizations, they do not add up to an explanation. Too much that was important is left unaccounted for: the growth of corporate power, the reluctance of conservative administrations to reverse liberal trends, the dependence of the domestic economy on a world-wide system, etc. Above all, Nisbet attributes to a "political clerisy" what really is a function of the crucial role that systematic knowledge plays in our society. Every major activity is now related to organizations which are founded upon explicit bodies of knowledge and which

dispense products (cars, health, education, entertainment, "defense," etc.) that knowledge has made possible. In so far as "clerisy" and "intellectual" are meant to imply a calling or commitment to the life of the mind, their existence in America has been tenuous and without much political significance.

On the other hand, it is virtually impossible to corrupt practical knowledge: it begs to be used. Woodrow Wilson's friend Baruch, the brains-trust of FDR, Kennedy's best and brightest were not like Plato's philosophers, incorruptible because their deepest loyalties were to a realm of knowledge beyond politics: instead, they were, in the literal sense, sophists, purveyors of instrumental knowledge. (pp. 8-9)

Nisbet's vision of the future is harmless, both to his allies and to his enemies. He tells us that, despite his pessimism, there will be a revival of a pluralist society. His hopes are based on a curious assortment of elements: the current revival of "ethnic nationalism," "fundamentalist religion," "the commune," "kinship and localism," and what he calls "the still-enigmatic role of the multinational corporation." Without pausing to tell us how these elements are to be translated into "a new laissez-faire" society, he lists the principles of the pluralist philosophy. First, there should be autonomy for the "major functions" in society. These include family, school, economy, religion, and "other great spheres of society." Second, there is to be decentralization and the revival of local institutions. Third, he would want hierarchy and stratification or inequality to be instituted, but not in such a way as to consign "any ethnic, economic, or regional segment to perpetual servitude [*sic*]." Fourth, tradition rather than law should rule.

In so far as Nisbet champions voluntary associations, local initiatives, smaller scales of living and work, his view of the general form that future society ought to take makes sense. In so far as he contends that these future forms require odious inequalities, ill-defined "reverence" for authority, and obeisance to some obscure element called the "sacred," he is trying to palm off, in the name of pluralism, the system which Kant called "tutelage." What is intended as the solemn wisdom of the ages comes out too often as merely condescending and fatuous, as when he commends "inherited class attitudes" for having "restrained" the masses from "indulging" their appetites for material goods or higher status; or criticizes intellectuals for having systematically destroyed the cult of "heroes," thereby depriving the masses of their right to hero-worship; or asserts that "culture" is "inherently feudal" and requires that the many pay deference to the few. (p. 9)

Nisbet is justified in his loathing for the centralized and bureaucratic state; but to identify this perversion of power with the "political" is not only wrong-headed but self-defeating. Throughout most of the history of political theory, the political has not been a synonym for the state but for the common life and fate shared by those who were members of the same collectivity. The greatest threats to political community were, as Nisbet's two favorite whipping-boys, Plato and Rousseau, both recognized, its overextension in space and its uncontrolled increase in population. Since it is Nisbet's hope that in the future many of the functions currently performed by the state will devolve upon groups and associations, there would be more pressing need than ever for public values to counter group egoism. (pp. 9-10)

Sheldon S. Wolin, "The New Conservatives," in The New York Review of Books *(reprinted with permission from* The New York Review of Books; *copyright*

© 1976 Nyrev, Inc.), Vol. XXIII, No. 1, February 5, 1976, pp. 6, 8-11.*

FRANKLIN G. MILLER

Two of the key values of Nisbet's philosophy of pluralism [as expressed in *The Twilight of Authority*] are "functional autonomy" and "hierarchy." By functional autonomy, he means the principle that each basic institution in the social order should be free to carry out its characteristic functions. "Everything must be done to avoid intrusion by some one great institution, such as the political state, into the spheres of other institutions." . . . But what are the "proper" spheres of institutions such as the family, the local community, business corporations, trade unions, professional associations, and the political state? Nisbet offers no framework of principles for answering this basic query. A philosophy of pluralism should include a theory of the legitimate role of government in an advanced society. Nisbet, however, does not even suggest the main points of such a theory.

Hierarchy constitutes his answer to the new equality. All social processes, he maintains, involve hierarchy of some sort, and therefore it is not only futile but destructive to attack all hierarchy in the name of equality. He does not, to be sure, advocate a system of caste or of rigid class divisions, and he favors equality before the law and equality of opportunity. But what sorts of ranking and social differentiation should there be in a pluralistic society? Would such a society rest content with legally open access to positions of power, prestige, and wealth—what is sometimes called "formal" equality of opportunity—or should it take compensatory steps to remedy the disadvantages of deprived circumstances? Nisbet does not deal with these and other issues concerning the just role of hierarchy in society.

In the light of his philosophy of pluralism, Nisbet calls for a new laissez faire—but for functionally autonomous institutions, not individuals. Institutions should be released from the deadening grip of the centralized government. I would not question the claim that American government has grossly abused its power in both domestic and foreign affairs, or that it has engaged in unjustified policies administered with undesirable consequences. But I believe that what we need is not a doctrinaire philosophy of government prescribing an across-the-board dismantling of government programs. Why not an approach which reviews the substantive merits of specific programs with respect to an articulated scheme of political values, assesses the ability of government to carry them out efficiently, and makes a rational judgment of the social consequences of having such programs administered by central government? It is doubtful whether our society can provide a satisfactory solution for such problems as poverty, discrimination, the decay of the cities, and the destruction of the environment without maintaining, if not extending, government initiative and regulation. To adopt a new institutional laissez faire would be to renounce the principle that a modern government should take measures to promote the welfare of its citizens. Nisbet fails to convince us that we should abandon this principle of government responsibility. (pp. 277-78)

Franklin G. Miller, "Book Review: 'The Twilight of Authority'," in Ethics *(reprinted by permission of The University of Chicago Press), Vol. 87, No. 3, April, 1977, pp. 276-78.*

J. H. PLUMB

[Robert Nisbet's concern in *The History of the Idea of Progress*] is to trace the idea that history is progressive, that the story of mankind is one of betterment. He believes that a great deal of the accepted wisdom about this idea is wrong—i.e. that the ancient philosophers believed in the cyclical nature of human life; that death and decay and destruction were as inherent in society's as in a person's life. On the contrary, he believes that many philosophers believed the opposite. He would argue, too, that the idea was not foreign to the Middle Ages in the Western world. For Robert Nisbet the idea of progress is an inherent part of the Western tradition that stretches back to Hesiod. (p. 33)

There is no doubt that Hesiod, Protagoras, Plato, and other great philosophers realized that there had been social development in Greece from more barbaric and primitive societies. Yet the major leaps forward—the control of fire, the discovery of arts and crafts, particularly metal-working—were due not to man but to intervention of the gods, or Titans, Prometheus and Hephaestus; and so it was argued the gods might intervene in the future for the betterment of mankind. However, progress for some Greek writers, it seems, required *a deus ex machina*. . . . Nisbet's treatment of St. Augustine loses, I think, a certain candor in order to make this fit into the projected history of this idea from the Greeks to the 19th century. Certainly St. Augustine believed in the developmental nature of human society, but the image that he used, as indeed Nisbet points out, was physiological—from *infantia* to not only *senior aetas* but also to *senectus*. Hence decay and enfeeblement were an essential part of human society; the ages of mankind depended also not on man but upon God. Indeed God is the prime motive force of St. Augustine's concept of human destiny in time—His will in all things is final, not man's intelligence or capacities. The danger of Nisbet's approach is to extrapolate remarks of St. Augustine on history and the process of time from the matrix of his theology. His historical concepts, his view of man's past, present, and future destiny are components of that theology. That some men were capable of betterment in a secular as well as a spiritual sense should also be offset by St. Augustine's firm belief that some societies and multitudes of men and women were not, and were doomed to destruction and everlasting hell-fire. It is not only with St. Augustine that by tearing some concepts from their ideological matrix a distortion is created; it occurs elsewhere in the book. This is, of course, a pitfall almost impossible to avoid in a book that covers so many centuries, so many different worlds of thought and feeling.

There is, I think, a larger criticism. Voices were raised against slavery from the ancient times onward with little or no social effect. Suddenly in the second half of the 18th century in England, they began to acquire an unstoppable social force that finally ended with the abolition of slavery. Why that happened is much more important than the narrative history of anti-slavery ideas of philosophers and theologians. Similarly the idea of progress acquired little or no social force (if you exclude millenarianism as I certainly would) until the 18th and 19th centuries. And why it did so is not discussed by Nisbet.

Why ideas become social attitudes is one of the great problems for historians of thought and culture. And so is the negative of that statement. Why do ideas cease to remain social attitudes? Nisbet stresses that the advanced, industrial Western world (non-Marxist) is turning, indeed has almost turned, away from the idea of progress as an historical force; but he offers little explanation. Of course it is a complex subject but one factor is important: material progress. The idea of progress was at its most powerful when the vast material progress of man appeared to be achievable in the foreseeable future, but the advanced industrial societies of the West have achieved that material progress. There are great inequalities, but the mass of Western mankind has almost all it wants and needs, particularly in America where history as a subject is dying as quickly as the idea of unstoppable and unending progress. Belief in progress is more of a social attitude in Cuba or West Africa and the world's depressed nations.

In spite of two major faults—the almost alarming elasticity of the concept of progress in Nisbet's hands and his lack of interest in the varying social reactions to the idea—this remains a very impressive book. It seems churlish to criticize so admirable an achievement. (p. 34)

> J. H. Plumb, "'The History of the Idea of Progress',"' in The New Republic (reprinted by permission of The New Republic; © 1980 The New Republic, Inc.), Vol. 182, No. 8, February 23, 1980, pp. 33-4.

J. M. CAMERON

[Professor Nisbet tells us "the actual aim" of *History of the Idea of Progress*] "is that of providing a straightforward history of the idea of progress, from the Greeks to our own day." He knows there is something odd about this proposal, for the learned world is pretty much agreed that the idea of progress is not to be found in European thought much before the seventeenth century. This was the view of—to use Nisbet's own list—Comte, Bagehot, Bury, Cornford, Inge, Collingwood, Hannah Arendt. To announce that he is going to maintain, against these and so many others, that the idea is a commonplace among the Greeks, in Saint Augustine, in the Middle Ages, is surely to announce that he intends to give us some hard argument and a close study, and a radical reinterpretation, of the texts and other historical evidences these others found persuasive. He doesn't argue that there was unanimity, or even a majority view among the ancients or the men of the Middle Ages, for "old and recurrent as this conception is, it is by no means . . . universally held by intellectuals."

(The choice of the word "intellectuals" suggests something worrying about Nisbet's approach to historical questions. The concept of the intellectual is so tied to the nineteenth and twentieth centuries that it seems curious to use it of most of those Nisbet has in mind. Was Plato or Aquinas or More or Bacon or Thomas Hobbes an intellectual? This seems like asking if the Apostle Paul was a clergyman. There are other oddities of the same kind. "The conflict Augustine posited between the two Cities is posited by Chamberlain between Teuton and Jew." This qualifies for the "how's that again?" caption sometimes used in *The New Yorker*. And what is one to make of the statement that a passage of Comte [typically flaccid and empty] "could have been written by Aristotle or Thomas Aquinas, as well as by Leibniz?"')

There is in fact no serious examination of particular texts. Fragments are quoted that bring out the not very contentious claim that the ancients knew that there had been technical and other improvements over historical time and that with the taking of pains they could expect other improvements in time to come. No crucial difficulties are faced. A crux for the Nisbet thesis is *Republic* 545,6, but there is no discussion of it. Thucydides

is quoted in such a way as to give the the impression that he counts in favor of the Nisbet thesis. But the quotation is the famous "I shall be content if [my history] is judged useful by those inquirers who desire an exact knowledge of the past as an aid to the interpretation of the future, which in the course of human things must resemble if it does not reflect it" (Crawley's translation revised by R. W. Livingstone—the translation cited by Nisbet—his own?—makes the passage obscure). Not much comfort for the Nisbet thesis here. Nisbet doesn't distinguish between three quite distinct things: first, a genuinely historical account of the conjectured past, as in Thucydides; then, talk about the past in which things such as the theft of fire by Prometheus and the opening of Pandora's box took place (*in illo tempore*, as Eliade would say, not in a time continuous with ours); and finally, genetic explanations, such as Aristotle's account of the origin of the *polis*. These tend to be run together and it is often not clear just what is being argued for. (p. 38)

> J. M. Cameron, "Sounding Off," in The New York Review of Books (reprinted with permission from The New York Review of Books; copyright © 1980 Nyrev, Inc.), Vol. 27, No. 6, April 17, 1980, pp. 36-8.*

ROBERT BIERSTEDT

One is happy to say that Nisbet has written [in *History of the Idea of Progress*] an engrossing history of social thought, one focused on a single idea. (p. 80)

The vast majority of Nisbet's treatments are stimulating and among them I would mention especially those of St. Augustine, Joachim de Fiore, Leibniz, Marx, and Spencer. Some are too brief to be of any account—those of Gibbon and Heine. Some seem wayward, with the emphases in the wrong places—e.g., Vico, Saint-Simon, Comte, and Malthus. Some few may shock. Nisbet, for example, ranks Hegel with Plato, Aristotle, and St. Augustine as the most influential philosophers of Western history. One yearns to ask him why St. Augustine and Hegel and not St. Thomas and Immanuel Kant. Similarly, I would not agree that Toynbee was vastly more learned than Spengler. But these are all matters of opinion. They add relish to the book, and no one who has the slightest interest in the history of ideas should deny himself the luxury of reading it. (p. 81)

> Robert Bierstedt, "Nisbet on Progress," in Contemporary Sociology (copyright © 1981 American Sociological Association), Vol. 10, No. 1, January, 1981, pp. 79-81.

JOHN A. GUEGUEN

[In *History of the Idea of Progress*] Robert Nisbet has written not a history of the idea of progress but a comprehensive survey of Western thought about "progress," however variously understood. His book is not guided by any interpretive rationale or philosophical reference point which might serve to distinguish one level of meaning from another. Even in the epilogue, where an attempt is made to draw conclusions from the survey, Nisbet preserves a neutrality which respects all theories encountered on this guided tour of the reliquary of great books which mention or imply some notion of "progress" (from Hesiod to Teilhard de Chardin). Rather than working out a critical analysis of these ideas about progress, the author is satisfied to provide a kind of annotated bibliography or catalogue of passages which he believes will demonstrate that Western civilization has been supported throughout its career by "a rarely interrupted conviction that the very nature of knowledge . . . is to advance, to improve, to become more perfect" and that the goal of this advancement is an "ever greater perfection of human nature.". . .

[His] litanies of names and concepts, his frequent citations and quotations (all without the documentation one expects in a work of scholarship) advance no thesis. . . . Apart from any bibliographical purpose this might serve, it is not clear how the author expects us to profit from his survey. . . .

Whatever its aim may be, his history reads like a well-informed conversation one could imagine overhearing at a faculty club, where leisurely relaxation rather than serious scholarship is in progress. Among the hazards of generalization to which the book succumbs, the most serious is its failure to make the necessary critical distinctions about the different meanings of "progress" and their significance for the history of ideas. Just about any kind of positive development or process, any sense of progression in time, any theory of continuity or advancement is sufficient to count as "progress," whether it be human or divine in inspiration, temporal or spiritual in content, physical or moral in effect. Even the Aristotelian doctrine about the movement in nature from potency to act is an idea of "progress." . . .

At the very least, definitional responsibility would seem to call for a clarification of the difference between a sense of progressive development and the presumption of progress (progressivism) one finds in the political ideologies which are the product of modernity in the history of philosophy. (p. 176)

Plato, Aristotle, Augustine, and Dante are all made out to be partisans of temporal progress in spite of the manifest orientation toward permanence rather than change which pervades their thought. On the other extreme, Nisbet fails to discover the progressive spirit of Erasmus, Machiavelli, Bacon, and Descartes which so powerfully helped to lay the foundations of modernist progressivism. . . .

Nisbet closes his survey with contrasting essays on the contemporary persistence of progress and the intellectual questioning of that idea which he finds unique to our own times. The suggestion that our century is unlike all that have preceded it in this respect is weakened by the same flaw which pervades the whole work: "progress" is seen as a general idea of virtually limitless range rather than as a spirit with precise philosophical or ideological tendency against which objections were raised in all times and places. (p. 177)

> *John A. Gueguen, "Book Reviews: 'History of the Idea of Progress'," in* The American Political Science Review *(copyright, 1981, by The American Political Science Association), Vol. 75, No. 1, March, 1981, pp. 176-77.*

R. F. BAUM

In calling Thucydides an early contributor to the progress idea, Nisbet [in *History of the Idea of Progress*] relies on Thucydides' statement that the culture and material conditions of his day had arisen from primitive beginnings. While that statement does accord with the progress idea, does it not accord also with the idea of culture's repeated rise and fall, which some attribute to Greeks of Thucydides' time? The difficulty enlarges when with apparent satisfaction Nisbet quotes a passage that seems to weigh against, not for, Thucydides' alleged progressism.

This is the passage where Thucydides promises that his history of the Peleponnesian War will reveal "the truth of both what has happened and what will hereafter happen again, according to human nature." Is there any intimation of progress there?

Claiming Plato as a progressist, Nisbet again relies on texts referring to a primitive past. But he also and rightly acknowledges that in Plato's thought historical *fluctuation* is axiomatic: "Good cities become bad, bad ones good." He also acknowledges Plato's belief in long term, though not identical, historical cycles. . . .

To bring Vico within the progressist fold Nisbet maintains that Vico augmented his well known insistence on recurring divine, heroic, and human Ages with an assertion that each recurrence of the cycle started from a higher level. A re-reading of Vico's *New Science* fails to uncover that assertion. (p. 110)

In considering thinkers of the modern era generally acknowledged to be progressists, Nisbet corrects some unduly simple exegeses of Hegel, Marx, Adam Smith, and others, but the gravamen of his book does not lie there. As a major revisionist work in the history of ideas the book will stand or fall with its attempt to show the idea of progress a constant concomitant or corollary of Christianity and hence a near permanence in Western thought.

One might expect that attempt to begin with consideration of Christ and the Gospels, where Matthew 24's frightening description of the world's *finale* would require some explanation. In fact, the Gospels receive no mention. Nisbet begins instead with Paul's universalizing of the Christian proclamation and with the millenarianism which Nisbet insists upon as a foremost element in the Jewish contribution to Christianity. "Nothing," he writes, "in the entire history of the idea of progress is more important than, if as important as, this incorporation by Christianity . . . of Jewish millenarianism." Here R. M. Grant and other specialists will surely lift an eyebrow. They have found Jewish millenarianism a source not of Christianity but of the Gnosticism which the early Church anathematized. No trace of millenarianism or of the progress idea appears in the credal statement called the Rule of Faith which the 2nd century Fathers settled on to distinguish Christian sheep from pagan and Gnostic goats.

Nisbet styles his lengthy discussion of Augustine a *"piece de resistance."* He contends that in Augustine's *The City of God* we find "all the really vital, essential elements of the Western idea of progress," and he emphasizes that book's esteem for such earthly goods as health, status, and bodily beauty. Now there is little doubt that the disdain of earthly goods shown by many Christians in the time of persecutions (bishops often had to forbid their flocks from actively courting martyrdom) subsided with the advent of the officially Christian Empire of Augustine's own time. In fact, as Theodore Mommsen detailed decades ago, many Christians had reappraised the kingdom of this world and invested hope in earthly progress and in a man-made city, Rome, deemed under divine protection. The Goth Alaric's entry into Rome in 410 A.D. shook those Christians' faith, and it was in large part to instruct them in their faith's true meaning that Augustine unfolded his vision of an eternally invincible City of God. That historical background seems crucial to grasping Augustine's intention. *History of the Idea of Progress* does not remind us of it.

Although warm in admiration of the good things of this world, Augustine again and again insists upon their fragility, transiency, and infinite inferiority to the goods of the world to come. He does, as do progressists, conceive of time as a linear flow, but that is hardly novel. Nisbet remarks the same in Thucydides a thousand years earlier. Like the rise of culture from primitive beginnings that conception of time seems easily compatible with the idea of non-identical historical recurrence. Augustine himself implies just such recurrence when he calls Babylon the first Rome and Rome the second Babylon.

The above is not to say that Nisbet has no case at all. As he insists, Augustine does emphatically assert that over time human genius has invented much and made admirable advances. Augustine also believes that through the ages more and more spiritual truth has been discovered (though he is far from saying that it has been universally embraced). Plato, he writes, improved on earlier paganism, and Christianity improved on Plato. Moreover, though casting an undeluded eye on the claims of governments, Augustine observes that the peace that victorious empires occasionally impose facilitates the spread of truth. That suggests, as Nisbet says, a concept not unlike Adam Smith's benign "invisible hand." Also, Augustine describes the bliss of the saved in terms of earthly joys. But a reader of *The City of God* discovers that Augustine does not end there. (pp. 110-12)

It may well be true, as Nisbet says, that *The City of God* sets forth the essentials of the idea of progress, but that does not mean that the idea gains approval. Any competent critique of an idea sets forth its essentials. As Augustine tells and, no less, foretells earthly history, all human contrivance "totters through the one transitory instability." (p. 112)

[It] seems more than difficult to conceive the idea of progress with its focus on natural knowledge, politics, and material prosperity as a corollary or consequence of Christianity. Does not the idea's ancient emergence before Christianity had been heard of prove the contrary? Nor does there seem any need to sift medieval thought for the beginnings of the idea's re-emergence in the modern era. Those beginnings meet us not only in Jean Bodin and his successors but earlier in the Renaissance and were often voiced by men of very dubious Christian faith, *e.g.*, Petrarch, Pico della Mirandola, devotees of Hermeticism and Orphism, *illuminati* generally.

The dubiety of the notion that the idea of progress secularized or, as some might say, merely secularized Christian hope of Heaven becomes apparent if we turn the notion around and imagine transcendentalizing Marxism. Would not that elicit a roar of rightful rage from old Karl himself? To transcendentalize the one or secularize the other is to subvert and contradict it. (pp. 112-13)

Titled "Progress at Bay," the closing chapter of *History of the Idea of Progress* takes note of the dissent from the idea voiced by Burckhardt and others in the 19th century, and, in stronger terms, by E. J. Mishan and others recently. That would seem the place for Nisbet to advance a solid argument for the idea's truth as an overview or theory of history. But neither there nor elsewhere does Nisbet claim that the idea is true. Yet his Epilogue deplores its recent fall from favor and, on the ground that it has been a near permanence in Western thought, presents it as a vision without which the West itself will perish. In this reviewer's judgment the idea cannot be shown the permanence we are asked to think it. In the ancient world it came and went, and it seems once more going now. (p. 113)

R. F. Baum, "Progress—A Vision Essential to the West's Survival?" in Intercollegiate Review *(© Intercollegiate Studies Institute, Inc. 1981), Vol. 16, No. 2, Spring-Summer, 1981, pp. 109-13.*

Michael Novak

1933-

An American philosopher and theologian who writes on religious, political, and cultural issues, Novak is a critic of the homogeneity of American culture. In *A Theology for Radical Politics* (1969) he criticizes the hollowness and uniformity of American society and urges a "revolution in the quality of human life." In his later works he examines ethnicity in America from a perspective reflecting his Catholic, Polish-American origins. Novak calls *The Rise of the Unmeltable Ethnics* (1971) his attempt to "come to a better and more profound knowledge of who I am, whence my community came, and whither my son and daughter, and their children, might wish to head in the future." In this book he contends that the American "melting pot" has promoted the ascendancy of white Anglo-Saxon Protestants, resulting in a drably uniform society. There is presently a resurgence of ethnicity in America, Novak argues, which will bring about cultural, spiritual, and political renewal. Novak is a controversial writer; while some critics have attacked the credibility of his observations, others have praised him as a sensitive and insightful interpreter of American life. (See also *Contemporary Authors*, Vols. 1-4, rev. ed.; *Contemporary Authors New Revision Series*, Vol. 1.)

Courtesy of Michael Novak

Excerpt from *THE RISE OF THE UNMELTABLE ETHNICS: POLITICS AND CULTURE IN THE SEVENTIES*

The *wrong* reason to promote ethnicity is out of fear. . . . (p. 69)

The *right* reason to promote ethnicity is that it offers resources to the imagination.

America has never confronted squarely the problem of preserving diversity. I can remember meeting in my youth bitter arguments that parochial schools were "divisive." Now the public schools are attacked for their commitment to homogenization. Well, how *does* a nation of no one culture, no one language, no one race, no one history, no one ethnic stock continue to exist as one, while encouraging diversity? How can the rights of all, particularly of the weak, be defended if power is decentralized and left to local interests? The weak have ever found strength in this country through local chapters of national organizations. But what happens when the national organizations themselves—the schools, the unions, the federal government—become vehicles of a new, universalistic, thoroughly rationalized, technological culture?

The tradition of liberalism is a tradition I have had to acquire, despite an innate skepticism about many of its structural metaphors (free marketplace, individual autonomy, reason naked and undisguised, enlightenment). Radical politics, with its bold and simple optimism about human potential and its anarchic tendencies, has been, despite its appeal to me as a vehicle for criticizing liberalism, freighted with emotions, sentiments, and convictions about humans I cannot bring myself to share. (pp. 69-70)

In my guts I do not feel that institutions are "repressive" in any meaning of the word that leaves it meaningful. The "state of nature" seems to me, emotionally, far less liberating, far more undifferentiated and confining. I have not dwelt for so long in the profession of the intellectual life that I find it easy to be as critical and harsh as seems to be the practice. In almost everything I see or hear or read, I am struck first, rather undiscriminatingly, by all the things I like in it. Only with a second effort can I bring myself to discern the flaws. My emotions and values seem to run in affirmative patterns.

My interest, in fact, is not in defining myself over against the American people and the American way of life. I do not expect as much of it as all that. What I should like to do is come to a better and more profound knowledge of who I am, whence my community came, and whither my son and daughter, and their children, might wish to head in the future: I want to have a history.

More and more I think in family terms, less ambitiously, on a less than national scale. The differences implicit in being Slovak, Catholic, and of lower-middle-class origin seem more and more important to me. Perhaps it is too much to try to speak to all peoples in this very various nation of ours. Yet it does not seem evident that by becoming more concrete, accepting one's finite and limited identity, one necessarily becomes parochial. Quite the opposite. It seems more likely that, by each of us becoming more profoundly what we are, we will find greater unity in those depths in which unity irradiates diversity than we will by attempting, through the artifices of the American "melting pot," and the cultural religion of science or the dreams of radical utopias, to become what we are not.

There is, I take it, a form of liberalism not wedded to universal Reason, whose ambition is not to homogenize all peoples on this planet, and whose base lies rather in the imagination and in the diversity of human stories. . . . (pp. 70-1)

> *Michael Novak, in his* The Rise of the Unmeltable Ethnics: Politics and Culture in the Seventies *(reprinted with permission of Macmillan Publishing Co., Inc.; © copyright 1971, 1972 by Michael Novak), Macmillan, 1971, 321 p.*

FREDERICK R. McMANUS

A succession of adjectives might be properly used to praise [*The Open Church*]: penetrating, thoughtful, absorbing, and the rest. It is a book which completely merits the publisher's puff on the jacket: "A brilliant report of the struggle to open the Church to the modern world."

From the start, however, one point must be made. *The Open Church* is a mature and sound study of the 1963 session of Vatican Council II. Michael Novak is a young writer, and young writers have been subjected recently to intolerable criticism, because of their lack of chronological maturity. Such criticism, sometimes close to abuse, on the basis of a man's age is nonsense. It is a good deal easier to discern the Spirit at work in the writings of the new generation, like Michael Novak, than in tired institutional defenses—often by those who could not write an article, much less a book, of the stature and profound insight of *The Open Church*. (p. 582)

The death of excessive authoritarianism . . . is not the central thesis of this book, as the author seeks to uncover the ultimate meaning of the Council. Rather it is a study of theological differences, in terms of which all the concrete and not-so-concrete developments of the Council may be interpreted. The openness of the Church, in every direction and at every level, is seen as flowing from the "erosion of a school of theology, the theology of the 'prophets of doom.'"

This theology, seen now as only one of many theologies in the Church, is termed "non-historical orthodoxy" by Novak. Some will, of course, disagree with the choice of phrase to characterize the fearful, unbending theology of a very modern "tradition." Some readers will weary of the constant return to this single theme—and phrase—as underlying all the issues of the Council. In fact this is the greatest contribution of the book: its attempt to get at the basic developments in religious thought that, however slowly, will influence the Church's life far more than the twists and turns of ecclesiastical politics or the small successes and failures of the Council's plans.

At the same time, *The Open Church* is a thorough and extremely readable report of all the issues of Vatican II, as well as a lively account of the people and events of the second session. . . . In every chapter there is no question of the author's strong sympathy of the majority position at the Council,

but he is most fair and indeed generous in his treatment of the minority (conservative, non-progressive, closed) arguments and personalities.

The same balance and kindness are evident in the delicate matter of evaluating the role played by the American bishops. The author is honest, certainly more honest than those who confuse loyalty with truth, and he is no pessimist. The chapter on "The Bishops of the United States," which could be written only by a discerning and dedicated layman, might well be developed into another book.

The concluding chapter of *The Open Church* is a valuable interpretation of the great struggle going on at the Council. Novak studies briefly the "four chief weaknesses" in the Church: "an uncritical use of abstractions; the loss of honesty and candor; an undue admiration for uniformity, with a lack of esteem for diversity; and a blindness to the spiritual values promoted in the secular world." Positively, he sees the open society of our time, "the society founded on the concrete rights of persons, rather than on abstract ideas," drawing strength from the same source: "the unrestricted drive to understand, and the quest for insight." In today's society the Church can truly live: "No previous form of life was so well adapted to manifesting the message of the Gospels: the freedom of the act of faith, the free community of believers, the service of believers to their neighbors."

It is the prophetic voices in the Church who shape her growth and the combination of philosopher-theologian and journalist makes a good prophet. Anyone seriously interested in the real meaning of Vatican II should study and reflect upon the interpretations set forth in *The Open Church*. (pp. 582-83)

> *Frederick R. McManus, "The Second Session: Progress," in* Commonweal *(copyright © 1964 Commonweal Publishing Co., Inc.; reprinted by permission of Commonweal Publishing Co., Inc.), Vol. LXXX, No. 19, August 21, 1964, pp. 582-84.*

SIDNEY HOOK

Impressed by the scrupulous restraint with which naturalist philosophers refuse to read their fears or hopes into the universe and by the depths of their tragic humanism, [Michael Novak in *Belief and Unbelief*] has made a fresh attempt to restate the case for Christian theism and to meet the challenge of naturalism without sacrificing or diluting his own faith. He recognizes that the revival of contemporary theology has been due less to an upsurge of religious faith than to a shift in intellectual interest from questions about the truth or falsity of assertions concerning the existence of God to questions concerning the meaning of "God." He is aware, however, that any expression of religious faith or belief presupposes the existence of God— granting that God may be conceived in various ways. What is of greater moment, the truth or falsity of such assertions takes us beyond purely linguistic, psychological, or sociological issues. Epicurus could hardly be called a religious man even though he acknowledged the existence of gods. Since the gods were indifferent to man's lot, they had no more religious significance than objects in the sky. However, Novak would differ with those modernists who maintain that religion can dispense with any kind of theology. God's existence or non-existence makes a difference to the believer.

Nonetheless, there is no more comfort for traditionalists in Novak's views than in Tillich's. He rejects any belief in God that rests on "neat conceptions of design and order in the world'' and that views the supernatural as a ''second story of the observable world.'' The uncritical, naive, literal acceptance of the symbols and myths that have stirred countless millions of worshippers of the great historic faiths, leads inevitably to religious superstition. All such conceptions, Novak writes, ''if maintained, must mean the demise of Christianity among men of intellectual integrity.'' Nor can any legitimate support for believers be extracted ''from the cultural context.'' According to Novak, ''the man in tune with our culture does not believe in God.'' Some would question this as a report of fact. But fact or not, one is puzzled that the author should regard it as relevant. Even supposing that the men in tune with our culture did believe in God, this would still prove nothing about the truth of their belief or even its religious value.

Another seductive approach which Novak resists is that of the men who despair of the whole intellectual enterprise of finding grounds for religious belief and are content to serve God wherever He is to be found in the battle for a better life in this world. . . . This tendency, however, strikes Novak as dangerous. In an age in which non-believers have gone down fighting for universal freedom and justice, the religious becomes all things to all good men: ''. . . one becomes godless to the godless, secular to the secular, pragmatic to the pragmatists, a social reformer to the reformers. But then, all of a sudden, it seems more economical not to be a believer at all. Why not be simply Godless?''

An excellent question! How does Novak answer it? At times he seems to suggest that if atheism were a more consistent ''human policy'' he would be prepared to adopt it. This is a rather obscure, if not dangerous, standard since what may be justified as a human policy may not have any bearing on the question of truth. There are situations in which on humane grounds one is justified in encouraging individuals to adopt a policy in the teeth of evidence that it will fail. But even if the policy leads to fruitful consequences, this is not always sufficient ground for affirming that the evidence warranted belief in the results. Novak is aware of this limitation; ultimately he rests his belief not on policy but on the evidence of experience—the primary awareness of insight, reflection, and especially ''the drive to understand.'' He denies Feuerbach's contention that the secret of theology is philosophical anthropology—the projection of the unsatisfied needs of the human heart in a radically contingent world. He contends instead that the secret of theology is intentionality—''intelligent subjectivity.'' The key to what is other and greater than man in the world is not to be found in man's needful, suffering existence but rather in his insatiable intellectual hunger to understand. In this view God cannot be established as a first cause—He is the presupposition of our tendency to look for causes; His existence cannot be proved—yet it alone makes intelligible the quest for intelligibility.

There are several points to be noted about this curious approach. First it overlooks the depth of Feuerbach's insight. A hunger or drive to understand is just as much a part of man's passional nature as other hungers or drives—less fierce, to be sure, but often more sustained. But why should anyone believe that there must be an answering response to human need, whether emotional or intellectual, except on the basis of a piece of question-begging into which Mr. Novak should be too sophisticated to lapse? That man seeks God clearly shows that man is not God, but why assume that what he seeks must exist? Granting even that the quest is not absurd, that some men's need to understand the world has the same poignancy as other

men's hunger for a great love, in what way does this constitute evidence of what is presumed to be there, waiting to be disclosed? (pp. 95-8)

Secondly, Novak's emphasis on subjectivity is so firm that his leap across it to the Rock of Divine Objectivity is quite implausible. He claims that ''the philosopher's empire is his own inner life'' and that his quest for understanding begins with an interpretation of his own identity. But fidelity to understanding takes the self only partly beyond the bias of self-interest, for the possibility of fully objective knowledge is suddenly seen to require a ''transcendent intelligent subject, God'' as the guarantee of human self-understanding and the locus of human good.

Aside from this puzzling leap from the human to the divine, the entire train of thought rests on the mistaken assumption that the philosopher can understand his own inner life without understanding history, and without reference to complex social institutions such as language. The self is inter-twined with the not-self, but the fact that we can make objective distinctions between them is not an adequate reason for inferring or postulating the existence of a Great Self. Vision is wonderfully and incomparably different from the darkness of the atoms in the void or from whatever the conditions are that produce vision. It cannot be explained only in terms of the structure of the eye. Nonetheless, it is unnecessary to postulate the brooding Vision of a Great Eye to make us see better or to make seeing more intelligible.

As one would expect in a book whose mood of desperate faith suggests the cry, ''Oh Lord, I believe! Help Thou my Unbelief,'' the formal argument is the weakest part of the author's case. It is revealed in the very mode of his expression. Throughout the book there are such statements as, ''If the real is intelligible, then there may well be a God.'' Whatever the conditional clause means, it is obviously compatible with the conclusion that there may well not be a God. There is, to be sure, something appealing about Mr. Novak's tentativeness. It is as if he were not seeking to convince others of the truth of his belief so much as pleading with them to understand his decision to believe with the same generosity of spirit that he understands their decision not to believe. The inconclusiveness of the position cannot, however, be redeemed by its tentativeness where it engages in explicit argument. . . . (pp. 98-9)

Mr. Novak tries to turn the flank of the naturalist position by making it appear that all philosophical positions depend upon initial decisions and commitments. Since he holds that they all start from scratch he faces the problem of how we are to determine which ones are more valid than others. ''Decisions are the root of philosophy,'' he claims. This seems to me to be as questionable as the contention that skepticism is the foundation of knowledge. Decisions, of course, enter into philosophy but it seems to be that when they do, like our doubts in fields of knowledge, they are the crown, not the root, of belief. Philosophical positions cannot be ''proved'' but when they are justified they rest on something which is less a decision than a discovery of a state of affairs, a state of the world, society, or man which we do not *in fact* doubt even when we pretend to. Novak underestimates the strength of the naturalist position which is that all human beings live and die in the natural order, even when they seek to defy it. It is the matrix of human sanity. Whatever is not poetry or myth must shoulder the burden of convincing us that there is another order of experience and existence. This book falls far short of doing so.

Still, naturalistic humanists should welcome Mr. Novak's first steps away from the traditional pieties of dominant Catholic thought. There is implicit in his neo-Protestantism an ethical commitment that makes the entire question of God's existence irrelevant to the specific causes of peace and freedom which concern men most today. When he writes of ''judging man by God's standards'' he can only mean that he is judging man by his own moral standards. He should have an easier time defending them as his own than as God's. (p. 100)

Sidney Hook, Liberal Catholic Thought,'' *in* Commentary *(reprinted by permission; all rights reserved), Vol. 41, No. 4, April, 1966, pp. 94-100.*

J. M. CAMERON

[''**Belief and Unbelief**''] offers serious difficulties to the reader. It is rhetorical in the pejorative sense; it goes in for a certain amount of mystification in the styles of Reinhold Niebuhr and Teilhard de Chardin; and it is eclectic in a curious way, for the many philosophers cited—Lonergan, Polanyi, Wittgenstein, Anscombe, Hampshire, to mention only some of the contemporaries—are used to supply proof-texts or philosophical mottoes to adorn theses that some of them would certainly not accept. In some cases it is not at all clear how Novak can both have read a given philosopher and maintain his own philosophical thesis.

A prime example of this is Novak's account of what it is to know something. Knowing and ''awareness'' are for Novak *experiences*. The only way this could make sense would be to stipulate that every report of what I know is to be taken as a report of an experience. But this would be to make the claim that knowing was an experience analytic and therefore trivial. Otherwise, the claim that knowing is an experience is simply false. . . . Knowing, then, cannot be an experience. Perhaps Novak is confusing ''knowing'' with ''feeling sure.'' Again, Novak would certainly want to say that knowing is an introspectible experience, at least, if one introspects very hard. But this is impossible. . . . But perhaps Novak is concerned not with knowing that something is the case, but with knowing something in the sense of being acquainted with it; this would be consistent with his running together of knowing and awareness as ''cognitive experiences.'' Here again we find ourselves on a wild-goose chase after some mysterious core experience lying behind various cases in which we could properly be said to be acquainted with something. . . . Novak has or betrays a suspicion that there is something a little strange about his doctrine that awareness is an experience, for he exclaims that ''it is difficult to describe in words.'' Yes, indeed.

Novak becomes entangled in a thicket of questions which a more attentive reading of Wittgenstein would have enabled him to avoid or to be more sophisticated about, because fundamentally his approach is Cartesian. ''To justify a theory about what knowing is, one must have a theory about the knower, i.e., the 'self.' No one can decide whether or not he believes in God until he decides what his understanding is and can do.'' (It can scarcely be supposed that Novak really means this, for this would imply that belief in God depends upon going through some prior philosophical exercise; this seems a bit rough on, e.g., the Hebrew prophets.) ''Who am I? At least this: I am a self, conscious and alert.'' ''Inevitably, men understand the universe in terms of cognitional theory by which they understand themselves.'' The Cartesian provenance of such observations is plain enough. It is not therefore surprising that No-

vak's argument for God's existence is a queer version of the ontological argument. ''We name [God] as the goal towards which our unlimited drive to understand is aimed.'' ''Belief in God is rooted in reflection upon one's own intelligent subjectivity.'' Of course, unlike Descartes, Novak does not think there is a knock-down proof of God's existence; he offers us an ontological persuasive, rather than an ontological argument.

Nevertheless it should be added that Novak's book, philosophically confused though it may be, is in many ways a moving and perceptive account of the difficulties of a Christian in the present climate of opinion. . . . It expresses, without mitigating, the perplexities of those Christians—roughly, the ''progressives'' in any Christian establishment—who are faintly astonished to find themselves closer to unbelievers than to their believing fellows on a variety of crucial moral issues, typically today those concerned with civil rights and warfare. He is overimpressed by the pseudo-profundities of fashionable theologians who love to generate a certain hysteria that, let us confess it, we do not find altogether displeasing. Talk about the depths of being, ''frontier'' situations, and what have you is not always out of place, but it is mostly idle chatter and serves as a substitute for, say, crime fiction. One wishes that Novak would simply look at the surviving records of the apostolic preaching and give us a report on what he finds in Paul and Mark and the rest. Philosophical reflection is no more a necessary preparation for this task—and it is *this* task that the Christian intellectual of our day so often sets aside, as not requiring his attention until something else has been done—than it is for a treatise on engineering or the report of a murder. Indeed, what Novak fails to see is that he is duplicating the precise error of that theology, sometimes, though mistakenly, called traditional, against which he is in revolt: the belief that Christianity requires philosophical foundations, as though what God says to man in Christ requires the Imprimature of a committee of philosophers before it can be taken to be authentic. (pp. 3-4)

J. M. Cameron, ''What Is a Christian?'' in The New York Times Book Review *(© 1966 by The New York Times Company; reprinted by permission), May 26, 1966, pp. 3-4.**

STEVE MAX

[In *A Theology for Radical Politics* Michael] Novak starts with the premise that ''the revolution required in the United States is a revolution in the quality of human life, a revolution in the quotient of human freedom realized by each of us. His recurring theme is that ''the coming revolution will be moral or not at all.''

Thus Novak falls into the same error that the New Left made in its early years, the belief that the problem was somehow with man himself, and that while the roots may lie in the political relations under which we live, man must change himself first and then change his environment, a classical utopian formulation. We are treated to a series of theoretical discussions on the proper development of identity, intimacy and community which are offered ''in order to be of further use to the movement.'' The theories of knowledge developed here are far richer and more literate than any to be found in the writing from the New Left of the same period—if only the problem had been correctly identified in the first place.

Try though Novak does to devise one, there is no *political* program for the restructuring of man's identity which does not first require restructuring man's society. Thus when Novak comes to make concrete suggestions for the radical movement, his ideological utopianism leads directly to tactical utopianism. "The point of any realistic political program is to find the lever of power that will promote the liberation of a few more men every minute of every day. . ."

A further need, Novak adds, is to "create institutions in which there is room (for those who so wish) to breathe." To accomplish this he offers "two separate strategies:" the first is to adopt a vocation to "poverty community, freedom and service" in the manner of the Benedictines. The second strategy calls for living in the actual world, in the business world, in the military, in government, etc. Thus, "committed individuals work within whatever corner of the system is given to them in order to wrest from it the closest approximation they can to the values they most deeply cherish."

Notice that the task at hand is not the seizure of the system, its abolition and transformation into a new social order. Rather, we are to commit ourselves to the winning of approximate values. . . .

[In his later essays, Novak, following the development of the New Left, argues for a revolution in America]. Unfortunately reaching this new step has not prevented Novak from repeating his first error in a different way. For while he no longer seeks immediate solutions in the search for identity and community, the problem is still the present nature of man. It is no longer the self, however, but the others. His chapter "Identifying the Enemy" tells us: "The enemy in America, then is the tyrannical and indifferent majority: the good people, the churchgoers, the typical Americans . . . So long as such a majority controls the destiny of America, it appears that the nation will remain racist and counterrevolutionary. . . The revolutionary problem is how to fight the moral sickness of the democratic majority." Henceforth demonstrations, disruptions, draft refusal and confrontation are seen in light of their therapeutic effect on the moral sickness of the majority. . . .

[That there is a great concentration of economic power in a few hands, which] leads directly to a corresponding concentration of political power seems to quite escape Novak. He is left standing on his head next to Hegel, for the enemy is not the democratic majority but the tiny powerful corporate elite. . . .

The most fundamental structural criticism [of American society] that Novak can muster . . . is that the system of representative government "does not go far enough and that is what makes it function as if it were sick." (p. 370)

It is not that Novak isn't sympathetic to the idea of revolution; moral illness aside he supports the New Left here. One suspects that he would also favor a socialist solution although it is never mentioned. He notes however that we now live under a system of "socialist-capitalism," a unique historical conception which is elucidated no further.

Apart from his utopianism, Novak's main problem is that he can see no strategic alternative beyond the revolutionary rhetoric of the New Left. When they propose taking up arms against the state, he counsels that the army and police are so powerful that "no conceivable challenge could be raised against them." This is, of course true at present, but having said so, he is stymied.

Since neither Novak nor the New Left have a program of interim demands and structural reforms which weaken the power of the ruling elite and at the same time build the strength of the popular forces, both reach an impasse. The New Left turns to adventurism while Novak takes to theology. It is within this context that a wide range of theological questions are examined, and those who can participate in such discussions must evaluate this one. . . . .

Along with the New Left Novak now discovers that lower-middle (working) class. "One main task of ours is to overcome class prejudice, to come to sympathetic understanding with the lower middle class, with firemen, gas station attendants, meter men. It can not be that such men are inhuman; and in proportion as they are men of flesh with affections and terrors, loneliness and hopes, they are our teachers." Yesterday's "main enemy" then, is today's teacher. How quickly times change. One would think that this discovery would open a new world of political possibilities for Novak, but he focuses instead on the many real shortcomings and disarray of the New Left. (p. 371)

Seeing the magnitude of the problem but not the agency or direction of change confounds Novak quite utterly as he attempts finally to synthesize his religious and political views:

"Brothers and dreamers, there is reason to take heart. A new mysticism becomes one day a new politics. Later a new mysticism will be required. Politics and mysticism, mysticism and politics."

While such words may comfort the mystics, for the political activist they represent a retreat to the erroneous conception with which Novak started: the problem is within man's mind. Man must be redeemed.

"The revolution cannot be exclusive. Nor can it be victorious. We are not obliged to succeed but to labor." Logically then he closes with the words, "The revolution is in the human spirit or not at all." Once again the lesson of the history of the radical movement has been borne out. Utopianism can only lead to defeatism. For indeed we are obliged to succeed. (pp. 371-72)

Steve Max, "Theology for Radical Politics," in Commonweal (copyright © 1969 Commonweal Publishing Co., Inc.; reprinted by permission of Commonweal Publishing Co., Inc.), Vol. XC, No. 13, June 13, 1969, pp. 369-72.

CHARLES C. WEST

Implicitly what Novak portrays [in A Theology for Radical Politics] is liberal humanism going through one more cycle. Moral outrage at a society which betrays its proclaimed ideals of humanity is not new; neither is the willingness to reject and even destroy people because they are inhuman. . . . What is new in this cycle is the curious introspection and underlying despair of today's revolutionary and his sense of being trapped.

Against this background Novak does his theological thing in the last 30 pages of the book. It is a strange and wonderful performance. The enemy, he says, is history—the idea that man is called to remake his environment, to exercise dominion over nature and to realize a destiny. He also objects to "German ideology"—an objection he shares with Albert Camus—because it sees meaning in the historical drama. He finds belief in Jesus Christ as the source and standard of meaning in human life to be narrow and parochial, and the idea of a God before whom we stand, who leads and judges us, as intolerably repressive.

As an alternative Novak would have us go back to nature. What he means by nature is not quite clear: sometimes it is the biological life, especially the sexual life, of the human body; sometimes it is the universe; sometimes it is the use of four-letter words, drinking, gambling, and exposure of human genitalia; sometimes it is organic growth; at other times it is the mystic Hindu identity of the soul with God. Somehow in and through all this one attains experience of the sacred—and this experience is God. . . .

In what sense is this a theology for radical politics? It rejects, contends Novak, the technical consensus upheld by those strange bedfellows, German ideology and American liberal pragmatism. It also rejects Harvey Cox's secular city in the name of a new inwardness of human experience and a new belief in man which despite all setbacks makes us struggle to change community.

One cannot help but be skeptical. The New Leftists whom Novak describes have already entered upon experiences of sufficient depth that they leave his nature worship behind. As every radical community soon discovers, the problem of human community is not solved by liberating human beings from their inhibitions for the sake of self-discovery. History remains an intractable problem as long as human power exists. And with it remains the question of what power there might be that could, for the sake of justice and peace, overrule the plans of men. Novak promised the New Left a theology to meet problems such as these. What he has given them is a word they could just as well have spoken to themselves—one which the more experienced of them will dismiss as a dream they too once had.

> *Charles C. West, "Returning to Nature," in* The Christian Century *(copyright 1969 Christian Century Foundation; reprinted by permission from the July 30, 1969 issue of* The Christian Century*), Vol. 86, No. 31, July 30, 1969, p. 1021.*

CHARLES FRANKEL

[*The Experience of Nothingness*] is a vigorously written book by a philosopher of the rising generation which makes the effort to explore the current mood of alienation and disorientation, to speak for that mood, and to go beyond it to the expression of an ideal which might turn this mood from a purely negative one into an affirmative program.

Michael Novak is in tune with the style and themes of the so-called counter-culture that is rising among us. He is passionate; he is unbending in his scorn for what exists; he wants to recover individuality, human warmth, and a sense of purpose in life from the ravages of a war-oriented public policy and a runaway technology. He is also unapologetically subjective. Like a good many other spokesmen for the new "revolutionary consciousness," Novak speaks for the rights of idiosyncrasy but makes sweeping pronouncements about what is good for everybody. He takes his point of departure from political and social problems, but his basic concerns are psychological, even mystical, and his basic proposal is for a form of religious conversion. . . .

His thesis is that all sound thinking about our present situation must begin with a recognition that "the experience of nothingness" is the primal experience of man. In the boredom of ordinary human beings, in the alienation and revulsion felt by sensitive spirits at what exists, we have intimations of the nature of this experience. And the process of radical cultural criticism takes us to the very borders of the realization of nothingness.

We start with nothing, and we make everything up—our science and art, our politics, our belief in objectivity, our sense of selfhood. There is no structure in the universe except the structures which men in their illusions create. There is only a surrounding nothingness. Yet in this vertiginous encounter with nothingness we can also discover and reassert the human essence, and thus find, in and through nihilism itself, a victory over nihilism.

Does Novak make sense? I must begin by reviving an inexcusably neglected rule of book reviewing and tell the reader that I am among the writers whom Novak attacks in his book. So it will be no surprise that I do not find Novak's arguments persuasive. They seem to me an effort, quite literally, to make something out of nothing. If men cannot see the world except through the prisms of their myths, then how can any man know whether there is or isn't anything behind these myths? And if a man says that nothing is behind them, then how do we experience this nothing? Indeed, what *is* an experience of nothing? I should think it was a non-experience. To attach the substantive suffix "-ness" to the word "nothing" is a verbal snare which does not convert a negative into an affirmative. If you go into a room and don't find anything, you can report this by saying that what you found was the presence of nothing, but putting it this way doesn't mean that you found anything.

This is not a mere semantic quibble. Novak draws important conclusions from what I think are his tricks with words. He holds, for example, that the belief in science and reason is responsible for the cold, cruelly inhuman technological civilization that exists, and he believes that the root error in the belief in reason is its neglect of the significance of the experience of nothingness. It seems to me that Novak is refuting a straw man. Believers in science and reason like Spinoza and John Dewey have regularly condemned the approach to reason which limits its domain to matters of technology, efficiency or political strategy. Their "rationalism" has consisted in the belief that reason should be extended to the examination of our basic values and purposes, and their complaint, like Novak's, has been that reason is narrow and desiccated when it deals only with means and techniques.

It is only in their diagnosis of the cause and their prescription of a cure that they differ from him. Novak nowhere considers in his book the simple possibility that our present chaotic situation may be due not to the excesses of reason but to the unwillingness of men to use it when their egos and their deepest interests are involved. Nor does he ask whether, in his preference for the subjective and the instinctual, he is not inadvertently endorsing the very evils he seeks to condemn.

Of course, it can be said that all this is merely the statement of my prejudices in opposition to Novak's, since, after all, objectivity itself is an illusion. But I think this is wrong. Consider, for example, what is involved in the simple rule that a reviewer should candidly avow the fact that he begins from premises quite different from those of the author he is reviewing. This is, I think, a condition for his being fair to author and reader, and I strongly suspect that Novak would agree. But if he does, then he has not really rejected the ideal of objectivity, for without that ideal he would have no grounds for criticizing anyone for unfair criticism.

Admittedly, objectivity is an extraordinarily hard ideal to achieve. But this does not destroy its validity as an ideal. Novak's own effort to persuade by marshaling arguments and appealing to evidence indicates that he thinks that he, too, is doing something more than expressing his prejudices. He is saying that his point of view is right in terms of independent standards, just as I am appealing to such standards in replying to him. So he has paid his unwilling tribute to reason, and is not quite the apostle of nothingness that he says he is. More power to him.

> *Charles Frankel, "An Unwilling Tribute to Reason," in* Book World—Chicago Tribune *(© 1970 Postrib Corp; reprinted by permission of* Chicago Tribune *and* The Washington Post*), May 31, 1970, p. 7.*

GARRY WILLS

There is something dismaying about an immoral book written by a very moral man. And ["**The Rise of the Unmeltable Ethnics**" is] very well written at that, full of bright aphorisms and seductive phrases, all put to baneful use. I am as seducible by a well-turned phrase as the next man, and my first reaction is to clap with glee at sentences like this: "The innocence of Johnny Carson's face insults the night." But then I stop to reflect that Mr. Carson's only crime, in this book, is his Wasp genealogy, and the glitter of the words begins to dim. After all, even Archie Bunker resented only the uppity Jews and blacks on the tube (Harry Belafonte substituting for Mr. Carson). But now Michael Novak teaches him new hates. Indeed, the first effect of this book is to extend the already vast repertoire of American resentments: "There is nothing that so infuriates me as the disguised aggressions of a Quaker."

Novak . . . is positively determined to be infuriated. He will outgrowl any discontented Wallace audience, be as articulate with self-pity as the victims of any ghetto. . . . This is known as the new ethnic pride—but why should the proud man whine so? Novak tells us the recent TV show "Mister Novak" helped him rescue self-esteem from the stigma of his name—which prompts a suspicion that he may have waited too long, and help came too late.

An earlier Novak told us to go to the Orient and seek wisdom from gurus. Now he tells us we cannot even cross the street and expect real understanding of each other. . . . We are what we are, and the supreme wisdom is "reconciliation to what we are"—not flights to the Orient (or across the street) to become what we are not.

But America's Wasps tried to make him what he was not, to refashion him in their image, neglecting his "fever" and other forms of creative distemper, and Novak will never forgive them. He lashes out at "the power of WASP culture to enforce oppressive normalcy". . . .

Who wouldn't be angry under this repressive yoke of "normalcy"? Anger at it explains even the devils in "Rusty Calley's blood" as he pulls the trigger over and over: "Against whom or what was his flesh rebelling if not the entire history of a normal life?" Wasp culture has manipulated us lesser and "ethnic" types into doing its dirty work: "The unspoken premise of Wasp culture is violence and madness at a distance."

Better to get the hates out on the table than suppress them immediately and inflict them long-distance. . . . How much healthier the ethnics, openly hostile and honest in their hate. . . . That judgment will come as a surprise to Ulster's citizens, who

practice as "genuine" a political hatred as can be found nowadays.

"A Pole who knows he is a Pole, who is proud to be a Pole, who knows the social costs and possibilities of being a Polish worker in America, who knows where he stands in power, status, and integrity—such a Pole can face a black militant eye-to-eye. A Pole uncertain whether he is American or Polish, WASP or racist, worthy or despicable, feels emotions too confused for compromise, emotions most easily discharged as hate." Substitute "Ulster Catholic" for "Pole" in that passage, and "Protestant" for "black militant," and you will know how that first sentence should have ended—"such a Catholic can face a Protestant eye-to-eye, *and kill him without hesitation*."

Novak holds the pop-classics view of *katharsis,* in which mere expenditure of anger becomes a purification from it: "Why try to pretend that violence doesn't occur, or that oneself is incapable of it? Better to see its effects at first hand and learn its horror, than to try and to keep oneself pure of it through distance." One should *trust* those who flush out their emotions regularly, evacuating every day: "Muskie's temper is related to his being Polish; swift expressions of anger are less repressed among a number of ethnic groups." The best man to have his finger on the button is, therefore, the one most prone to tantrums. Trust Ethnics. (p. 27)

So Novak must now huff and puff to prove his own ethnicity, merrily inventing angers as he goes (good open "ethnic" rages, of course, not mere piddling Wasp discomfitures), working his gentle soul into Zorba-the-Greek exhibitionism. Nothing is quite so strange as a naturally pleasant person who feels it his duty to be unpleasant, to call civility an Anglo-Saxon deceit. Novak tells us he has taken to listening for what his flesh intuits and his blood feels—which can be fun, but does not fool us. We know Mr. Novak's brain is telling his blood what to feel. And what his brain has been saying, ever since Novak got involved in electoral politics (and worked for Senator Muskie), is . . . : "There is no need to concede the ethnic voter to the conservative movement."

Novak dictates the plan: "The election of 1972 can differ from that of 1968 if the professional élite tries to follow rather than to lead; tries to be inclusive rather than exclusive; tries to hear voices and accents against which for too long it has closed its ears; tries to moderate its own ideologically 'hot' interests for the sake of shared interests." In short he suggests to others his own role with regard to ethnics—to be "an intellectual who tries to give voice to their instincts" rather than to preach at them. So quickly does listening to one's blood become a matter of sniffing around after loose votes.

This book is part of a rapidly growing literature on the social uses of hatred. Though it is dangerous to play around with prejudice, those who celebrate "dirty hands" must get down and fight Kevin Phillips (of "The Emerging Republican Majority," 1969) on his own ground—though for a higher purpose, of course. The trick is to work an exorcism of one hate by another, a displacement, a substitution. Novak tells us how:

"The ethnic will not say 'nigger' and the black will not say 'pig' when the two decide that they are not each other's enemy—and when the Left decides that in any humane political strategy both white and black must be helped together. The enemy is educated, wealthy, powerful—and sometimes wears liberal, sometimes radical, sometimes conservative, disguise. The enemy is concentrated power. Lower-class ethnics and blacks, who lack that power, are allies."

This is the Great White Ethnic Politics Hoax. All that growling at the Wasp is meant to distract us from the conflict between blacks and whites—and, ultimately, to rechannel its energies creatively. Anti-Wasp racism will drive out the anti-black kind. Getting worked up against Johnny Carson's face on the screen will at least disguise (if not displace) the distinctive rage against Belafonte's presence there. But one can never be sure the exorcism will "take," that the new enemy will not just be added to old ones instead of substituting for them. Canceling out one hate with another would be a tricky business in the best of circumstances. About all one can hope for, in fact, is temporary cessation of one set of hostilities till another is disposed of; then first hates can be resumed, unforgettable as first love. One thing alone is certain—that ethnic rages stirred and kindled will be a net addition to the nation's angers, no matter how disposed or "redirected." (pp. 27-8)

> *Garry Wills, "New Material for Archie Bunker," in*
> The New York Times Book Review *(© 1972 by The*
> *New York Times Company; reprinted by permission),*
> *April 23, 1972, pp. 27-8.*

ROBERT ALTER

[What is untenable in Michael Novak's position in *The Rise of the Unmeltable Ethnics* is] the implicit tendency to view everything through the prism of ethnic origins, with the social and political contexts of any particular act or statement, the individual psychology of the person or people involved, falling away before the "ultimate" fact of their ethnic identity. Eugene McCarthy's peculiar petulance and negligent manner in the campaigning of 1968 are explained not in terms of his idiosyncratic character but as expressions of his refusal as an Irish Catholic to play the Wasp game of evangelical politics. Norman Mailer's attempt to create a "revolution of consciousness" in his writing (perhaps like that of William Burroughs, whom Mailer has much admired?) is seen not as a function of an individual writer's quirky ambition and imagination but as the reflex of a Jewish sensibility rejecting the images of identity of Wasp America. Even a provocative gesture made by a female student demonstrator to a policeman is viewed not as an attempt to offend an armed representative of the Establishment but as an insult directed squarely at the policeman's ethnic sensibilities. To be fair, Novak's book is by and large more carefully reasoned than these few examples might indicate, but they suggest the inherent danger in making ethnicity the absolute point of departure for all thinking about America. On the level of practical politics, such unrelenting insistence on the primacy of ethnic identity could lead, given the perverse logic of competitive interaction among people, not to a new American diversity but to a Balkanization of political interests and cultural life. At any rate, in regard to the way we think about ourselves, the insistence on ethnicity tends to encourage certain unconstructive simplifications and misdirections of attention.

Thus, a major fault [of Novak's book] . . . is to overstate the case against the already abundantly berated Wasp. To be sure, the Wasp elite has much to answer for in American history, from the virulent Nordic racism it once promulgated to its hypocritical ideology of egalitarian individualism as a mask for privilege and the denial of the dignity of new immigrants implicit in its myth of the melting pot. Nevertheless . . . [Novak offers] what is ultimately a racist reading of American history because, finally, all the ills and wrongs of the nation are traced to some sickness or perversion of the Wasp spirit. Such highly industrialized urban societies as those of France,

Germany, and Japan have done quite nicely in producing social pathologies similar to ours unaided by Wasps of their own. Yet reading . . . Novak, one infers that all we suffer derives from the arid puritanism, the estrangement from life, the competitiveness, the sexual insecurity, the hatred of the body, the emotional frigidity, and atomistic individualism, the mechanistic view of self and society, that are seen by these writers as the very body and blood of Wasp ethnicity.

All this, of course, merely turns discredited ideas around 180 degrees; the nation is still divided into good guys (immigrants from Southern and Eastern Europe and dark-skinned people) and bad guys (the paleface descendants of Englishmen and Northern Europeans). This sort of inadvertently Manichean division seems particularly bizarre in the case of a fundamentally reasonable writer like Novak. He implies that, given the imperative fact of ethnicity, there is no common American standard of discourse and value, but his own book illustrates the vigor of just such a standard. He repeatedly insists that the self is mediated by language, and the primary language for almost all ethnics in this country after the first generation is American English—if they choose to write, generally educated American English at that. Thus, the very categories Novak invokes to defend ethnicity—inner freedom, integration of personality, historical symbolic community, conscience, "imaginative and symbolic thickness"—are conceptualizations rooted in a common Anglo-American idiom of thought, if you will, in the dominant Wasp tradition of discourse. (pp. 71-2)

Novak claims at one point that he is not anti-modern, but the "skepticism" he repeatedly evinces toward modernity is so far-reaching that the line between skepticism and actual rejection blurs and fades. If modernization tends to break down traditional social structures, conceives of individuals as free agents, reduces family, clan, and ethnic group to mere options instead of necessary contexts, it must be viewed as a threatening, negative process: "Modern civilization—urban, fluid, democratic, determined to change history—is a Nordic invention. The men of the south and the east have long been skeptical about its outcome." The statement makes clear not only the grudging attitude toward modernity (including democratic process) but, more embarrassingly, the gross distortion of a racial reading of history.

Repeatedly, Novak imagines modernization as a pulverizing mechanical force that assaults traditional life from without. . . . The metaphor of modernity as a destructive mechanism or a technological "processing" that threatens organic growth recurs elsewhere, and it may make one a little nervous, for it has been invoked before by others in the service not of a tolerant conservatism but of fanatic reaction.

Since intellectuals as a class have been the great catalysts of modernity, the social planners, the spinners of schemes for radical innovation, Novak devotes more than a third of his book to a critique of the intellectuals. It is precisely here that one sees most vividly both the positive value and the ultimate danger of conceiving culture and politics in terms of ethnicity. Novak, let me hasten to say, is not anti-intellectual but fits clearly into the tradition, going back to Burke and Tocqueville, of conservative attack against the excesses of the intellectuals. . . . Novak seems especially sound in his sustained assault on the elitism of the intellectuals, their general failure to imagine as real people large segments of our population unlike themselves, their fondness for abstract schemes of social amelioration that are out of touch with the needs and desires of many of the people whose lives are being planned.

The notorious arrogance of the intellectuals, however, is for Novak merely a secondary manifestation of their primary error, which is nothing less than their adherence to "an image of history favoring the future," an image reflected in the very use of the metaphor of an avant-garde for the intelligentsia. From the ultimate viewpoint of a conservatism that seems theological as well as political, Novak sees this commitment to the future as a kind of anthropocentric heresy: "To be on the side of the future (a benevolent future, safeguarding the continuous progress of man) is the equivalent [for modern intellectuals] of standing in the presence of God." It has of course been a long time since such naive faith in continuous progress was a serious intellectual position, but one wonders why the intellectual aspiration to make the future more humanly livable than the past should be inherently suspect. (p. 72)

The intellectual's indispensable role, whatever his sins, has been to envisage alternatives, to imagine new possibilities. According to Novak, however, "his function is not to lead, in the way an avant-garde leads, or in the way planners, managers, and experts lead," but rather "the intellectual's vocation is to be a voice of the people—to put into words what they already know." Though Novak realizes that not everything in the people is admirable—what the intellectual will put into words will "terrify" as well as "illuminate"—he nevertheless comes disturbingly close here to a mystique of *Volkstum*, which hardly seems what we want to return to after all that has been perpetrated in its name in recent history. The individualistic assertion of self, beginning as far back as the Renaissance (and *not* merely among Anglo-Saxons!) has admittedly been one of the most tortuous enterprises of modern culture, but it also has been heroic, incurring great inner risks in order to realize a new order of inner freedom. In this enterprise, the assertive voice of the intellectual has often been abrasive or disdainful but it has been necessary, and I think one must strenuously resist any suggestion that the time has come for the intellectual to submerge himself in the people, or that the most valid realization of self can come only through the people.

It is simply wrong to say, as Novak does, that individual autonomy and personal authenticity are Wasp concepts, limited to the assumptions of Wasp ethnicity. They are, rather, key concepts of modern culture in general—paradoxically, without them Novak would hardly have written his book. Whatever the enormous difficulties in the realization of these ideals, the very currency they enjoy points to a new horizon of possibility for every human being. That horizon, as Novak justly observes, will scarcely beckon at all to large numbers of people; nevertheless one must be grateful for its mere existence, for the fact that a person can at least in part free himself from subjugation (in some degree it is always that) to the community and the past in order to realize his selfhood according to his own needs. (pp. 72-3)

Ethnicity, to be sure, in no way implies the extirpation of individuality, but one is entitled to be suspicious of any political philosophy that might compromise or circumscribe the individual's scope for discovering his own uniqueness. At this point in American history, it seems less than helpful, and it could be pernicious, to promote atavistic feeling at the expense of reason; to proffer a thoroughly ahistorical ideal of innocent organic community as an attainable goal; to suggest that the highest vocation of the intellectual is to become the voice of the people; and, above all, to insist that the ultimate cause of our present national disarray is an ideal of individualism allegedly deriving from white Anglo-Saxon Protestantism. (p. 73)

Robert Alter, "A Fever of Ethnicity," *in* Commentary *(reprinted by permission; all rights reserved),* Vol. 53, No. 6, June, 1972, pp. 68-73.*

PETER J. OGNIBENE

[In *The Rise of the Unmeltable Ethnics,* Michael Novak] shows little scholarly cool. Castigating Protestants in general and their caricatures of ethnics, he manages a few caricatures of his own. He tells us about the ruthlessness of the Irish who "give much devout respect to the church and then do in politics what they must; their political impulse is tougher and harsher than anything they hear in church." He churns out two more stereotypes as dated as vaudeville: "Jews and Italians, we know, are highly dramatic people. . . . For the Italian, pain, like everything else, is communal; he is happy when people are around, because 'life is with people.' . . . Jews will know symptoms, diseases, drugs, and remedies [chicken soup?] with a precision and detail unmatched by other ethnic groups. Pain is the drama of the self in history, and the Jew loves to enliven it." Then he scoops all ethnics into one large bag and pronounces: "The Irish are pagans like the Slavs, the Italians, the Greeks, but pagans who have allowed their church to make Christianity an agent of order and cleanliness, rather than an agent of mystery. . . ." (Well, at least we know they bathe.)

Novak misses few clichés in his early chapters, and he has done little original research. And yet, his book merits serious, however skeptical, attention. (p. 27)

Peter J. Ognibene, "A Glass of Dago Red," *in* The New Republic *(reprinted by permission of* The New Republic*; © 1972 The New Republic, Inc.),* Vol. 167, No. 20, November 25, 1972, pp. 26-30.*

HERBERT S. PARMET

In **"Choosing Our King,"** Michael Novak's concern with ethnicity becomes an attack upon the arrogant romantics of the New Politics. The failure of reformers to understand the significant symbols that mark American existence, he holds, has demonstrated their political impotence and has helped to condition workers toward the reluctant acceptance of George Wallace. (p. 26)

It could have been called "Choosing Our Pope." The President is described as not merely the head of state, not merely the chief executive or the highest elected official, but the symbolic unifier of the American civil religion. As the head of our state church, he furthers the identification that every ethnic group desires, the legitimization of their credentials as Americans. He also provides "our *internal* images of authority, legitimacy, leadership, concern," Novak argues, and his actions help to establish "a limit to national realism. What he *is* drives us away from American and makes us feel like exiles—or attracts our cooperation." He influences our innermost attitudes. Therefore, choosing a President "is an almost religious task; it intimately affects the life of the spirit, our identity. Who the man is determines in real measure who we are." Priding himself as a "realist," Novak has little patience with purveyors of moralistic platitudes. (pp. 26-7)

In short, romantic reformers have failed, and they should recognize their failure. The American worker is more repelled than attracted. Leadership, to be effective, must graduate to an understanding of the "mature dream," which Novak contends "teaches one to recognize the evil in oneself," rather than the "adolescent dream." The latter "holds that individuals are innocent, while evils come from without—from institutions, from outside agitators, from germs thriving out there in the environment, requiring to be cleaned up, sanitized, isolated, outlawed, or reformed. The mature dream holds that evil lurks in the heart of our own goodness and is never more triumphant than when it dons the trappings of morality.". . .

Novak charges the elitist left with insensitivity. Sneering at the Archie Bunkers, they glorify their own bigotry. . . . Their candidates echo such isolation from reality. McGovern, who receives Novak's most scathing dissection, never did try to understand working Americans. He moralized rather than articulated. The New Politics ignored the mundane but very real problems of the "urban, ethnic, working-class Center." Nixon, meanwhile, "tried to comfort their restlessness by repetition of the fragments of the old national faith." Novak fears that such abdication of the "ethnics" by the arrogance of the intellectual left, having already helped deliver them to Nixon, may make them susceptible to opportunistic populism, i.e., George Wallace.

Mr. Novak does pierce the vulnerability of self-righteous "limousine" liberalism. One wishes its argument were sufficiently solid to prevent approval from being visceral rather than cerebral. (p. 27)

> *Herbert S. Parmet, "The Failure of Reform Politics," in* The New York Times Book Review *(© 1974 by The New York Times Company; reprinted by permission), April 7, 1974, pp. 26-7.*

GEORGE E. REEDY

[When in *Choosing Our King* Michael Novak] refers to the President as king, high priest, and prophet, I can foresee readers who will interpret the words as describing superstitions from which men and women must be emancipated. And many of his "civil religion" categories may appear as a restatement in mystical terms of the world perceived by Sinclair Lewis in *Babbit.*

It is to be hoped that current prejudices against any symbolic language other than FORTRAN will not discourage the political audience from plunging more deeply into the Novak thesis. It is valid in the sense that it opens up a rich vein for analysis. The affinity of religious and political activity has always been clear except to the tone-deaf. Both are characterized by the phenomena of conversion, commitment, unquestioning loyalty, and dedication to a higher cause. . . .

But Novak is probing far deeper than the outer layers of religious symbolism. He is going to the heart of the matter—to the faiths by which men live. He argues that the nation has become a church—or rather a collection of churches that are held together by the mystique of the elected "king." To discuss the Presidency with realism, he argues, brings us "to the edges of theological reflection.". . .

The implications of these secular religions are explored in brilliant detail including an analysis of the 1972 elections. Novak is at his best when his eye is roaming to pick up the significant tidbits. . . .

He is equally fascinating when he explores the distinction between morality (humans as they are in fact) and moralism (humans as they would be "if only . . ."). Both have a time-honored role in American political history and have led to

"high symbolic expectations of the Presidency." As he notes, our reaction to chicanery in high office is far sharper than it would be in other nations. One of his best discussions lies in the chapter on whether a President should have "dirty hands" and, if so, to what extent. (p. 602)

Unfortunately, when Novak proceeds from diagnosis to prescription he too tends to confuse pr images with genuine symbols. The concept of a "single spokesman" for the President's opposition party in Congress reflects a complete lack of experience with an American legislative body. Biweekly accountings by the President "before leaders of the opposition" would require not just constitutional revision but a new Constitution. A Cabinet containing a "proportion of members of the opposition party" would quickly become a nullity. And his final proposal—that we elect one President to exercise "symbolic" authority and one to exercise managerial "power"— is strictly from Madison Avenue. Of course, all these things could be done were we to switch to a parliamentary system but Novak seems to be unaware of this prerequisite or its difficulties.

The prescription, however, only occupies one chapter—not enough to flaw an otherwise brilliant analysis. This is a book which not only makes a lot of sense but which serves the highest purpose of writing—to make people think. Perhaps some day we will be able once again to live in comfort with our symbols but we will not do so until we understand them. (pp. 602-03)

> *George E. Reedy, "Symbols at the Top," in* National Review *(© National Review, Inc., 1974; 150 East 35th St., New York, NY 10016), Vol. 27, No. 21, May 24, 1974, pp. 602-03.*

LAWRENCE H. FUCHS

[*The Rise of the Unmeltable Ethnics*] is rich in insight and passion. The passion gets out of hand occasionally when he is expressing hostility toward the power and life styles of Anglo-Saxon Protestants. But few students of ethnicity of American politics would quarrel with many of Novak's major assertions: political unity depends in part upon cultural pluralism: WASPS have disparaged the cultures of Eastern Europe; Jews and blacks have sometimes failed to recognize and act on the political interests they share with white ethnics; and the substructures of family, neighborhood, community, and church can and should be strengthened by stronger ethnic consciousness and expressiveness. . . .

Novak's resentment sometimes clouds his judgment. . . . Novak charges the "intellectuals" with labeling white ethnics as "pig," "fascists," and "racists." Which intellectuals does Novak have in mind? Not those who write on ethnicity, such as Nathan Glazer, Father Andrew Greeley, Patrick Moynihan, Oscar Handlin, or any others I can think of. (p. 790)

The main point of the book—that politics should draw on "resources other than Anglo-Saxon history and values"—is not only acceptable, but is a fact of life and has been for a long time. . . . (p. 791)

Despite weaknesses in the book, I admire Novak's positive biases. America desperately needs a politics which gives strength to families and communities including WASPS trapped by the cult of individualism; and, as Novak argues, ethnic consciousness and expressiveness do provide one answer to the desperate search for a sense of belonging to America. There can be no strong individuals without strong, loving families. To be strong and loving, families need to be rooted in and supported by communities. Ethnic communities are the only traditional organic communities in the United States. Long live ethnicity! But give the WASPS their due. If it weren't for three of their institutions—religious freedom, universal suffrage, and the right to assemble and petition—the rest of us would be a lot worst off, and, in some ways even less ethnic. (pp. 791-92)

Lawrence H. Fuchs, "Book Reviews: "The Rise of the Unmeltable Ethnics: The New Political Force of the Seventies'," in The American Political Science Review (copyright, 1974, by The American Political Science Association), Vol. 68, No. 2, June, 1974, pp. 790-92.

PAUL H. WEAVER

[Choosing Our King] is not an especially well made book. Novak stitches together a bizarre variety of materials—campaign journalism, moral philosophy, political analysis, and cultural anthropology—in a way that is usually less than disciplined; as one makes one's way through the volume, one often has the feeling of reading the author's notes rather than the book that was to have been written from them. Yet despite this flaw, it is a fascinating piece of work, and not only because of its telling insights into the politics and personalities of 1972. It is also interesting as a report on the political education of a reluctant McGovernite. For Choosing Our King is not so much a campaign history or study in political science as it is a personal confession, and in searching out the lessons of his candidate's nomination and defeat Novak proves to be an honest and mostly unillusioned witness. (p. 89)

[The popularity of George Wallace raises a question about Novak's thesis]. If George Wallace represents the sort of politician who flourishes in the religious-symbolic politics that Novak describes, is it possible that our real problem is not with candidates who don't measure up to the requirements of their craft, but with the religious-symbolic nature of the political environment that determines those requirements in the first place?

Novak resists putting the question this way, but he too is troubled by the implications of his analysis. If the Presidency is a religious-symbolic, plebiscitarian institution; if the symbolic preferences of the American people are largely fixed by historically-determined "civil religions"; if the McGovern ethos is inherently offensive to a large majority of Americans—then it follows that the "conscience constituency" should reformulate its beliefs or resign itself to impotence. Novak, perhaps understandably, resists that conclusion. Instead he parts company with the logic of his analysis and urges a "reconstruction" of American civil religions, as if they were made of nothing more permanent than Tinker Toys. In their place we are asked to erect a "new, dark civil religion"—pluralistic, participatory, anti-materialist, un-moralistic, suffused with a sense of the nation's past failure, yet aglow with a vision of a universalistic future. Otherwise, writes Novak in words suggesting how hard it is to eliminate moralism from the American breast, we will be left with the "narrow, naive, immature," and "inadequate" faith that currently "imprisons" the nation and consigns us all to lives of "emptiness." Or: if they don't agree with us, then they'll just have to change their minds.

This is a pretty unsatisfactory way out of Novak's dilemma, but what is interesting is how he got into it. It has always been true that there is a religious-symbolic aspect to politics; it is also true that this aspect has become more important in recent years, with the advent of TV and the decline of the political party; and it is clear that the Presidency has become the focus of our symbolic passions. But from there it is a long—and I think unwarranted—step to saying that our politics is, and ought to be, essentially religious and expressive in nature. Novak takes that long step, partly out of intellectual enthusiasm for an interesting idea, but partly also, it is clear, because he seeks in American politics the rewards he envisions as flowing from his new, dark civil religion: a "genuine liberation" of the "energies of the heart," and an "obscure joy . . . springing from connection to the unfathomable mysteries and terrors of human life."

If people want a sense of purpose, Harold Macmillan once observed, let them go to their bishops, not to the politicians. Novak cites that statement (mistakenly attributing it to Edward Heath) and instantly dismisses it. He really should have taken it more seriously. Allowing for the fact that a measure of symbolism is natural and proper in politics, it says something that is true and important in a pluralistic liberal democracy, namely, that there are limits to what politics can do without ceasing to be pluralistic, liberal, or democratic. It would be no bad thing if this fact were more widely acknowledged. It is not just that gifted and thoughtful persons like Michael Novak would then not find themselves trapped, despite themselves, in a sterile, either/or, us-versus-them Manicheanism. It might even become possible to reverse the current trend of our politics, which is toward precisely the sort of symbolic passion play that Novak says it is already, or ideally ought to be. The events of 1972 and thereafter bear witness to the damage wrought by this view of the political process. (pp. 90, 92)

Paul H. Weaver, "Politics as Passion Play," in Commentary (reprinted by permission; all rights reserved), Vol. 58, No. 1, July, 1974, pp. 80-90, 92.

JOHN LEONARD

[In "The Joy of Sports"] Michael Novak does go on, and too far: "I have never met a person who disliked sports, or who absented himself or herself entirely from them, who did not at the same time seem to me deficient in humanity." The 43-year-old philosopher and unmeltable ethnic cares passionately about baseball, football and basketball. But he is a serious man, and what he cares about must therefore be of a higher order than mere entertainment. . . .

Thus Mr. Novak is not content with proposing sports as "a form of godliness" and a "civil religion" full of "sacred time" and "sacred space." He must go on to claim that "sports are the highest products of civilization and the most accessible, lived, experiential sources of the civilizing spirit. In sports, law was born and also liberty, and the nexus of their interrelation. . . . Symphonies, statues, novels, poems, dances, essays, philosophical treatises—these are the transpositions of the world of sports into the exercises of higher civilization."

Well. Nor is he through. Not only are sports a civil religion, but "an essential salvific religion in our present madness." That madness, as readers of Mr. Novak's previous books might have guessed, is "the religion of making the world better by our work," "the great Protestant delusion . . . that human existence is shaped by human will." "The spirit of play," says Mr. Novak, "is Catholic, Latin, Mediterranean. The spirit of work is modern, Protestant, Northern, Marxist." And: "Protestant traditions tend to link goodness to duty, obligation, command, and will. Catholic traditions tend to link goodness to beauty, proportion, fitness, achievement.''

This is known as going too far, and not only because one's definition of spiritual playfulness has to be elastic enough to accommodate, along with the traditional cathedrals and pietas, the equally traditional juntas and inquisitions. A meditation on sports turns into one more broadside against work, rationalism, secularism, politics, science, the dreary Protestants and reason itself—for, as Mr. Novak tells us, ''the form of life'' is not ''reason,'' it is ''conflict.''

He reasons his way to this assertion, of course. He marshals evidence and draws conclusions. He works hard at trying to make us understand the significance of play, just as Freud worked hard to make us understand the nature of repression, which should be a brief in behalf of reason as not necessarily repressive and of work as being something more than a ''drug for killing time, making a living, acquiring power, place, and possessions.'' It isn't, for Mr. Novak.

Mr. Novak, who knows better, seems to disapprove of complicated fun, the elaborate games of science and art: Although they are as old as organized sports, he implies that they are less universal because they are less ''accessible,'' somehow undemocratic; one must work harder to grasp the rules, appreciate the excellence. He might as well disapprove of the plasticity of our nervous systems, the elaborations of our curiosity.

Of the sundry civil religions, Mr. Novak professes the one with the most adherents, as though numbers were a proof of grace. . . .

Shakespeare, Beethoven and Freud are my major leaguers; they could hit the tragic pitch, and yet weren't strangers to joy. Am I being as overly serious as Mr. Novak? It's his fault. I love sports as much as he does. . . . When he speaks of ''authenticity and individuality'' and ''heroic modes of behavior,'' I grok. To win a game, to know that you have won it, to know that the fans know that you have won, is indeed to enter a kingdom where, momentarily, light is your sword. And to lose is to die a little.

But Mr. Novak is greedy. He preempts and coopts my enthusiasm. He puts my emotions in a beaker and boils them and calls the steam incense. I am not merely to be entertained; I must worship, and be lectured on the jazziness of basketball, the Anglo-Saxonism of baseball and the corporate myth, the ''socialism,'' of football. He appropriates my pleasure for the purposes of his Catholicism, his ethnicity and his loathing of politics, while, astonishingly, making a series of political proposals—government regulation of the number of leagues and teams, indemnification of universities for the training of athletes, ceilings on salaries for professionals, the inventing of new sports for women, etc. How rational, how utopian, how Marxist goody-goody.

If Mr. Novak needs a civil religion as a sort of spare tire for his argument with the cosmos, why not pick on any one of the many other terminals of the human spirit? Banks, for instance, or airports, or TV sets, or drive-in theaters, or Howard Johnson's, or golf: everywhere, there are ceremonies, myths and Muzak. The landscape is acned with stadia, monuments. The franchise is a civil religion. Access roads are jammed with fans of money, watching, eating, war, escape and organic foods. Richard Nixon, says Mr. Novak, politicized everything he touched, even the metaphors of sports. Michael Novak, say

I, theologizes. Anybody who describes the football season as a ''grueling *asceis*'' needs a remedial giggle.

> *John Leonard, ''Serious Games, Tasty Crabs and a Natural Writer: 'The Joy of Sports','' in* The New York Times Book Review *(© 1976 by The New York Times Company; reprinted by permission), June 13, 1976, p. 6.*

BEN YAGODA

[In *The Joy of Sports*] Novak mucks up what could have been a wonderful accomplishment by consistently overstating his case. Similarly, he cannot seem to resist making objective righteous statements about the joy of sports, his theme. He should have realized that the best sports writing has always been irrevocably and admittedly subjective.

If I may be permitted to violate the New Criticism and introduce biographical data to this discussion, it appears that the distortions have been caused by four of Novak's personal characteristics: He is a sports fanatic, a philosopher, a conservative, and a Catholic. His problem is that the last three won't let the first alone. . . . Novak's head can't appreciate his heartfelt love of sports, feels guilty, and confesses by protesting far too much.

I take it as symptomatic of his extravagance that in an entire apostrophe to sports, he never even mentions the simple value of physical exercise. Moreover, he systematizes feverishly. Faithful to one of his idols, Aristotle, he has given us an Ethnics, Politics and Metaphysics, and thrown in a Thomistic *Summa Theologica* of sports. An Esthetics would have been quite enough.

What is most bothersome about *The Joy of Sports* is Novak's consistent and unadvertised religious framework. One can be tolerant of his loving Notre Dame and using the simile ''like an angel'' three times, but Catholicism forms his whole appreciation of sport. For him the batter's box is an altar, a basketball jersey is a sacred vestment, and a faultlessly executed series of pass completions becomes a mass.

Novak believes that the limits and disciplines of sports, like the formal rituals of religion, can momentarily free us from the irredeemable impurities of earthly life. We are rooted in mortality, and ''the underlying metaphysics of sports entails overcoming the fear of death.'' Football, deeply involved with original sin, ''is an almost revelatory liturgy. It externalizes the warfare in our hearts and offers us a means of knowing ourselves and wresting some grace from our true natures.'' More often than not, man is not good enough for the field of play (just as in Catholicism he is not good enough for God): ''But the failures of human flesh to measure up to the beauties possible in sports should not deter us from pursuing what is in them that so draws our love.''

Such pessimistic notions about human capabilities also lead Novak to a conservative, essentially anti-Enlightenment political stance that disturbingly twists his views. Sports are symbolic rituals, he feels, and most of what seems wrong with them should be left alone, because it mirrors what is wrong with life; who would think of taking the blood out of the mass? He continually lambasts those ''liberals'' and ''rationalists'' who, for example, want to reduce the violence in sports. Football, he gloats, ''gives the lie to those who believe that the human being is fundamentally rational, liberal, peaceable, sweetly cooperative.''

Novak's distortions are particularly unforunate because *The Joy of Sports* has the makings of an excellent book. A genuine love of sports shines through the murky theory, and he has fine, occasionally exciting sensitivity to the rhythms and values underlying our three national games: Football is a union of the corporate myth of organization and power with the strain of violence in America; baseball is a leisurely embodiment of the faith in rules and structure that begat this country; and basketball is more akin to jazz than anything else, a loose forum for brilliant improvisation.

Particularly in a long section called "**The Seven Seals**" (after St. John, not Bergman), Novak is convincing on the wonders sports truly can uncover. We *do* look at the sports page first; there *is* something almost sacred and quite irrational about the way an athlete experiences time and space, the passionate identification of fan with team or player with teammates, the quality of spirit that goes into a superb athletic performance. For the limited and formal arena of play *does* provide an opportunity for competition, nobility and excellence that is simply unavailable in the "serious" world. If only Novak hadn't been quite so serious himself.

What one ultimately takes away . . . from sports, is an appreciation for moments: a boy grabbing a spiral, a team that simply and suddenly clicks, two milers embracing, or, in the words of that great scribe Red Smith, "bases filled, two out, three and two on the hitter and everybody moving with the pitch." Occasionally in sports, such wonderful, inexplicable epiphanies happen. When they do, even Novak's grosser hyperbole seems convincing. (p. 19)

> Ben Yagoda, "*Beauty Discipline and the Outside Shot,*" in The New Leader (© 1976 by the American Labor Conference on International Affairs, Inc.), Vol. LIX, No. 15, July 19, 1976, pp. 18-19.*

GEORGE F. GILDER

[*The Joy of Sports*] is revolting. Here, in this Bicentennial year, when Americans should at last be coming to grips with Serious Matters, with the racism and sexism and violence that pervade our national life; here, in this epoch of burning moral challenge, when the flames of fascism lick—no longer directly, from fiery crosses in the Southern night, but insidiously, from beneath the dark robes of a reactionary Republican Court—ever closer to the sacred palladia of the First Amendment and the Garrity Plan, threatening even the freedom of expression, the liberal golden gorges, of John Gardner and Linda Lovelace; at this time of terrible extremity, Michael Novak has fiddled . . . a book which responds, in effect: Take Me Out to the Ball Game! Let us pray for Notre Dame. Let us worship at a shrine of sports. Let us reject the "constituency of conscience," the responsible citizenship of the adult—which requires us to *keep up*, and participate, and protest in the real world—and return to the crushes and fantasies of childhood, the church and the stadium, synthesized and somehow convergent in a vaporous new transcendence: athletic glimpses of divine grace. (p. 849)

Like many lapsing leftists, [Novak] is in the process of discovering that the moralistic abstractions of his lifelong creed have nothing to do with the life he must lead, its real interests, institutions, and relationships. He has discovered in conceiving the book, for example, that he is more deeply and ardently engaged in the dramas of sports than in the ostensibly more "important" realms of public life. . . . He is bored with suppressing these priorities, tired of being a peeping fan; he begrudges his feelings of guilt and self-deprecation about his addiction to the Dodgers.

He has come to believe, first as an intuition of faith, later as an articles of philsophical conviction, that sitting in a stadium, or even in front of a TV screen, watching a game, rooting for a team, he is closer to God, to ultimate things and meanings, than he is when he listens to a speech of Gerald Ford's. Novak would say, in fact, that in leaving athletics to pursue a career in government, Ford moved from a higher to a lower order of reality, from a realm of ends—of play, valuable for its own sake—to a realm of instruments, useful only in their functions and effects; that he has moved, in other words, from religion to plumbing. The test of politics is how much room it leaves for more important matters, like sports.

Novak's argument is complex and sophisticated, and suffers in synopsis. Since . . . *Choosing Our King* expounds the religious dimensions of politics, it would be a mistake to characterize him as bluntly anti-political. But he does maintain that sports are more purely sacred than most other parts of our lives. Sports events take place in reserved and "sacred" time and space; they are liturgical in their reverent repetitions of specific ceremonies; they supply rites and arenas for displays and definitions of virtue and excellence.

The action, however, does not end in the ritual, but mystically transcends it. The contest is often not decided by pure skill or strength or resolve. It is not held chiefly to compare abilities. It is held, Novak maintains, largely as an occasion for grace. The fan (from *fanum*, Latin for temple) seeks in the victory of his own team—the luck it enjoys, the moments of nearly beatified excellence that athletes at their best uncannily attain—a signal of divine approval; a numinous aura that touches alike the performers and their followers. In language perhaps familiar here, sports provide a symbolic way, far better than politics, to "immanentize the eschaton." (pp. 849-50)

The book does have flaws. Occasionally repetitious or self-indulgent, it is about 75 pages too long. Dealing with the matter of women in sports, Novak hems and haws for pages before making some garbled proposals for affirmative action: for example, touch football games for women to accompany the major college football events. The fact is that most sports, in every human society, are chiefly male rites, and women do not take an equal part or interest in them. The effort to force feed football to little girls is suggestive of the patronizing egalitarianism that is everywhere stultifying and confusing our sexuality.

Novak's ideas for protecting or improving our current sports are little better. He proposes new government commissions or regulatory agencies to control every aspect of athletics, from salaries to broadcasting, but he offers no assurance whatever that these bodies would actually be governed by the high purposes he assigns them. The principle of separating church and state, I should think, applies here. . . .

Novak's reforms collectively would make athletics one more domain of government, embroiled in all the usual political fatuities—from affirmative action to wage and price controls—foreshadowed already by the endless absurdities of government meddling in our colleges and universities. It is genuinely frightening to see how an otherwise bold and sensitive observer can fall for nostrums of government intervention that would likely strangle the thing he loves.

Nonetheless, Novak concentrates most of his officious proposals in one forgettable chapter, while elsewhere he provides what must be the best essay ever written on football, and a potpourri of other, only slightly lesser delights, from vivid anecdotes to provocative philosophy. In general, his is a brave and truthful book that, beginning with a focus on sport, ends by casting rare and penetrating light on the entire crisis of Western culture and politics. In the league of social theory, he is easily this year's most valuable player. (p. 850)

George F. Gilder, "Bring on the Gladiators," in National Review *(© National Review, Inc., 1976; 150 East 35th St., New York, NY 10016), Vol. 28, No. 29, August 6, 1976, pp. 848, 850.*

THOMAS R. BROOKS

[In *The Guns of Lattimer* Michael Novak] has recreated with skill and a painstaking attention to detail the events that led to the tragedy at [Lattimer, Pennsylvania, where in 1887 striking coal miners were shot by sheriff's deputies] and the trial of the deputies and of Sheriff James L. Martin that followed. Though more were killed and wounded at Lattimer (the worst labor massacre in the nation up to that time) than at the Boston massacre, the tragedy has been little noted, even by historians of labor and of the United Mine Workers. Novak argues with justification that this is so because the strikers were Slavs, "the most silent, and most invisible, Americans."

When Lattimer is mentioned, incidentally, it is usually cited in a litany of the violence visited upon American workers over the years by the bosses. It was certainly that, but as Novak makes abundantly clear it was more complex as true tragedies often are. For one thing, the Slavs were frequently as exploited by their fellow miners, the "natives," as by the mine owners. Miners were paid for the coal brought out, as Novak reminds us, and not for the time put in. The miner's assistant, a job usually held by the immigrant newcomers, did the difficult work while the miner, who kept two-thirds of their joint take, merely pointed out the day's work and supervised the cuts or dynamite blasts needed to shake the coal loose. The members of the jury who acquitted the sheriff and his posse were workers, and the fear of the sullen Slavs that sustained the deputies was shared by native workers and the middle class of the coal region alike.

This is not to say that there were no villains. Novak's sympathetic portrayal of Sheriff Martin serves to point them up—the bullies among the deputies, the hard-line coal operators and the Pennsylvanian patricians, men like defense attorney Henry W. Palmer, who viewed the Slavs as "the scum" of Europe. Our tragic destiny is hidden in our virtues, Novak believes. "Anglo-Americans," he writes, "share with other cultures, more than is usually recognized, a strong belief in the efficacy of force, hidden under an admirable respect for law and free institutions. . . . The deputies truly believed that American institutions were uniquely free; that the foreigners were not prepared for them; that the foreigners, having been 'brought up under the lash,' respected only the lash, so that it might be the duty of good Americans to give them their own kind of lesson." (p. 35)

The Guns of Lattimer is a minor classic, a solid contribution to American history and well worth reading. But Novak's masterful command of his material is marred, I think, by his fictional vignettes, an attempt to recreate the feelings, fantasies, and inner lives of imagined participants interspersed at critical points throughout the historical narrative. By themselves, these sections are well done but the fictional technique does not really

work and ultimately detracts from the impact of the history. Moreover, there is a tendency to allow the fictional to slip into the actual sweep of events. . . .

Perhaps I am being picky, but I cannot help but feel that the tragedy at Lattimer can stand on its own without imaginative embellishment. Nonetheless, Novak has accomplished what he set out to do, leaving us "the legacy of simple, weary men, blown back by a sudden explosion on a hot September day." It is no small achievement. (p. 36)

Thomas R. Brooks, "Books Considered: 'The Guns of Lattimer'," in The New Republic *(reprinted by permission of* The New Republic; *© 1979 The New Republic, Inc.), Vol. 180, No. 1, January 6, 1979, pp. 35-6.*

RICHARD KLUGER

["**The Guns of Lattimer**"] is not a rich addition to the library of American ethnicity. Although there is an occasional nugget about, say, Slovak wedding customs or the shoeless state of the matriarchy, we learn too few details about how these sorely tried people ate, dressed, worked, learned, played, prayed, cohabited—in a word, survived. Their destitution is a given condition, and this diminishes the book as testimony of their ordeal and somber heroism.

Nor is this a satisfying piece of historical narrative or social analysis. The author, a philosopher and theologian of established merit, notes at the outset that he is not a historian by trade. But he also insists on the scrupulousness of his research, which was aided by others who helped him mine the raw material. Mr. Novak cannot have it both ways. History is not sacred writ. It is composed by whoever chooses to write it, his or her occupation notwithstanding; it must be judged against the ordering and enlightening demands the form makes.

The book's basic flaw is its indiscriminate use of undigested materials. We are offered an excess of biographical and other extraneous data about people only tangential to the event; a falsely portentous opening vignette about one of the defense attorneys, who does not reappear till the book is nearly done, and then only briefly; unintegrated anecdotal bits on a Slovak boardinghouse owner who turns into a minor heroine after the killings. But there is nothing resembling a fleshed-out portrait of any of the principal figures in the tragedy.

Faced with a shortage of hard detail about the miners themselves, Mr. Novak hit upon the "literary device" of introducing a prototypical but fictitious young Slovak miner who is caught up in the confusion and violence. Although the fellow's fears and hopes, most of them centered on his almost inarticulate courtship of an Irish girl, are no doubt authentic in spirit and not altogether unaffecting, they are intrusive. They bear about the same relationship to a work of historical validity as food coloring and preservatives do to a hot dog—cosmetic if not fatal.

One also misses integrated information on many essential points: the state of labor, organized and unorganized, during that era; the social structure of the town of Hazleton, the company fiefdom at the hub of the story; the complex relationships among all the elements that make up the Slavic community and its relation to other working folk of non-Yankee stock. Not all of us know, as the author supposes, the classforming distinction between, say, Hungarian immigrants who speak Slovak and those who speak Magyar. (pp. 12, 29)

[Novak's] useful, if lackluster contribution to the literature of injustice is a welcome reminder of a profound national bias, no longer defensible in a world in which our main rivals for power are Slavic and Mongol peoples. (p. 29)

Richard Kluger, "An Act of Homage," in The New York Times Book Review *(© 1979 by The New York Times Company; reprinted by permission), January 28, 1979, pp. 12, 29.*

Evelyn Reed

1905-1979

Reed was an American author of feminist and socialist non-fiction. In her major work, *Woman's Evolution* (1975), she posited the existence of a primitive matriarchy and contended that patriarchy is a relatively recent development. A Marxist, Reed argued that by abandoning the evolutionary method dominant in the natural sciences, "most schools of anthropology have gone off in a . . . retrograde direction." Instead, she proposed that anthropology recover the materialist and evolutionary approach of its founders. (See also *Contemporary Authors*, Vol. 102.)

Excerpt from *WOMAN'S EVOLUTION: FROM MATRIARCHAL CLAN TO PATRIARCHAL FAMILY*

The early history of half the human species—womankind—has largely been hidden from view. To bring it to light requires a reinvestigation of anthropology, where the role and accomplishments of women in prehistoric society are buried. This book is a contribution to unveiling that remarkable record.

The resurgence of the women's liberation movement has thrown the spotlight on certain dubious assumptions and disputed questions regarding the past. Foremost among these is the subject of the matriarchy. Was there a period in history when women held a highly esteemed and influential place? If so, how did they lose their social eminence and become the subordinate sex in patriarchal society? Or is the matriarchy, as some say, a myth that has no historical basis?

The matriarchy is one of the most hotly contested issues in a hundred-year controversy between contending schools in anthropology. [*Woman's Evolution*] affirms that the maternal clan system was the original form of social organization and explains why. It also traces the course of its development and the causes of its downfall. (p. xiii)

Since the turn of the century, anthropology has amassed an immense stockpile of information about diverse cultures in various parts of the world. These descriptive studies are extremely valuable. However, this wealth of data has not been matched by an equivalent expansion in theoretical insight. Most academic anthropologists have turned away from the evolutionary viewpoint that launched the science, and reject attempts to systematize our knowledge and ascertain what stages society has passed through. (p. xvi)

This book adheres to the evolutionary and materialist method in utilizing these findings. It also presents a new theory about totemism and taboo, among the most enigmatic institutions of primeval and primitive society. Anthropologists of all persuasions have held the view that the ancient taboo on sexual intercourse with certain relatives, like our own taboo, arose out of a universal fear of incest. This book challenges that assumption. The ancient taboo existed—but it was primarily directed against the perils of cannibalism in the hunting epoch.

The elimination of the theory of a universal incest taboo removes one of the most serious obstacles to understanding other savage institutions, such as the classificatory system of kinship, exogamy and endogamy, segregation of the sexes, rules of

avoidance, blood revenge, the gift-exchange system, and the dual organization of the tribe. It clears the way toward an understanding of how society arose—and why it arose in no other form than the material clan system or matriarchy.

The question of the matriarchy is decisive in establishing whether or not the modern father-family has always existed. The very structure of the maternal clan system precluded it. Instead of being the basic social unit from time immemorial, as most anthropologists contend, it is a late arrival in history, appearing only at the beginning of the civilized epoch. (pp. xvii-xviii)

> *Evelyn Reed, in her* Woman's Evolution: From Matriarchal Clan to Patriarchal Family *(copyright © 1975 by Pathfinder Press, Inc.), Pathfinder Press, 1975, 491 p.*

CHOICE

This lopsided and laborious book ["**Woman's Evolution; from Matriarchal Clan to Patriarchal Family**"] probably needs to be in more libraries than it deserves. Written in the style that

Boas lambasted as "the comparative method," it picks and chooses among data and theories to support a set of notions on the evolution of the family and to put down competing theories. Nonetheless, it supports a current fad, it has some interesting new tenets, and it provides a counter-claim to the fantasies of Lionel Tiger, Robin Fox, Desmond Morris, etc. The nicest of the new thoughts in this tedious tome is that the long-debased relation between *totem* and *taboo* is a kindred prohibition on sex and cannibalism. . . . Another charming section is Reed's reinterpretation of those Greek tragedies that inspired so many of Freud's origin myths. The worst features of the book are the endless excerpts stripped of historical context and the lack of balance in Reed's knowledge of anthropology.

> *"Anthropology: 'Woman's Evolution: From Matriarchal Clan to Patriarchal Family',"* in Choice *(copyright © 1975 by American Library Association), Vol. 12, No. 4, June, 1975, p. 575.*

LILA LEIBOWITZ

Described as "the product of over twenty years of research" it is clear from the bibliography and conceptual framework that these years were concentrated in the second and third decades of this century.

[*Woman's Evolution*] is bound to bother anyone whose training is of more recent vintage—it will be difficult to teach from the book because of its departures from contemporary phrasing and word usages. (Foragers and horticulturalists are called "savages" with "savage minds." Kinship systems include "ours" and "the classificatory system.") The book also resorts to idiosyncratic definitions. These will confuse any anthropologist, no matter when trained. ("Only a sex prohibition that forbids the known members of a family circle from mating can be called an 'incest taboo.' A sex prohibition that forbids a whole community of people from mating . . . is only a sex prohibition." . . .) More important, the book ignores or disregards the contemporary work of paleoarchaeologists and ethologists in building its thesis. (p. 533)

Reed, a self-identified Marxist, derides "instinct theory" as Marxists do. Nevertheless she goes on to accept a cannibalistic stage (for men only) in human evolution, as well as violent sexual impulses among mammalian and primate males generally. Despite her stated disbelief in any sort of innate abhorrence toward committing incest, she rejects the idea that the Egyptian ruling classes (whom she believes were unique) really could have indulged in brother-sister matings. Her commitment to Marxism evidently stems from the central position afforded women in Marxist evolutionary reconstructions and revolutionary anticipations. Her commitment does not lead her into using the uniformitarian socioeconomic model of processes Marx applied to past, present, and future events, however. While she has something to say about technology and economy that may appeal to feminists (women invented everything from fire to pottery to architecture and medicine without communicating much with the men they'd made marginal by incest taboos), her notions are essentially Social Darwinian and a far cry from those of process-oriented Marxists.

Despite all of this, the Reed book has something to offer the specialist. Interesting tidbits from older ethnographies suggest that these are sources we should not neglect. . . . The older secondary sources Reed uses turn up antecedents to current discussions, like that on the "raw" and the "cooked." The book may be a mine of information for advanced students, but it will confuse the naive. (p. 534)

> *Lila Leibowitz, "Changing Views of Women in Society, 1975," in* Reviews in Anthropology *(copyright © 1975 by Redgrave Publishing Company; P.O. Box 67, South Salem, NY 10590), Vol. 2, No. 4, November, 1975, pp. 532-38.*

MARGARET HUMAN

In *Woman's Evolution,* [Evelyn Reed] details a controversial theory in which family structure began with maternal clans or hordes, developed into complex tribes with matrilineal descent, then into the matriarchal family and eventually evolved into the patriarchal family (as the concept of private property developed). She suggests that motherhood and its associated instincts led our ancestors into a form of cooperative and equalitarian social relationships which insured our survival as a species. Her careful description of the manner in which these relationships changed (because of internal conflicts and changing economies), is admittedly based on some conjecture. The premises on which the theory rests are found in Engel's ideas about labor and private property and a work by Briffault entitled *The Mothers.* Although her conclusions may not be accepted by all anthropologists, she makes some important points. She validly illustrates some of the difficulties with anthropological data produced by males using male informants and interpreted through the blinders of our patriarchal society. She does not objectively present data to support both sides of a particular issue, but she does use extensive anthropological research to illustrate her views.

> *Margaret Human, "Cultural Anthropology: 'Woman's Evolution: From Matriarchal Clan to Patriarchal Family," in* Science Books & Films *(copyright © 1976 by the American Association for the Advancement of Science), Vol. XII, No. 2, September, 1976, p. 72.*

CHOICE

Although Reed offers some telling criticisms of the present state of anthropology and a convincing call for new historical perspectives [in **"Sexism & Science"**], her discussions are occasionally strident and often weakly supported. This is an old-fashioned, idiosyncratic Marxist accounting, which ignores contributions such as M. Z. Rosaldo and Louise Lamphere, *Woman, culture, and society* . . . and M. Kay Martin and Barbara Voorhies, *Female of the species.* . . .

> *"Anthropology: 'Sexism & Science'," in* Choice *(copyright © 1978 by American Library Association), Vol. 15, No. 7, September, 1978, p. 918.*

CORA BAGLEY MARRETT

[In *Sexism and Science*] Reed attempts to point out the anti-woman biases in much of the anthropological and sociological literature. Among the writers whose work she challenges are E. O. Wilson, Robert Ardrey, Lionel Tiger and Claude Lévi-Strauss. Her criticisms of Wilson center on more than gender-related issues. She finds particularly disturbing his attempt to suggest parallels between human and animal behavior, for "only humans can produce the necessities of life as well as produce new needs and the means for their satisfaction." . . . In addition to drawing inappropriate analogies, Wilson exaggerates the extent of male dominance in nature, according to Reed. She is even less charitable to Tiger, author of *Men in Groups*, referring to him as a "woman hater." Such attacks occur throughout the book and weaken substantially the effectiveness of Reed's arguments. But the volume has other problems as well. Reed describes Robert Ardrey as an "adroit name-dropper" who reduces science to fiction writing. Unfortunately, she can be accused of the same tendency, for too often she provides only anecdotal support for her own arguments or turns to *The New York Times*, *The Village Voice* and other popular sources for documentation. Rather disturbing as well is the book's repetitiveness. The volume actually is a collection of articles Reed published earlier, and in each article she returns to the same themes and often to the same sources. By the second of the eight papers in the collection, one knows all of Reed's principal points; she simply uses the different writers as foils.

Cora Bagley Marrett, "Cultural Anthropology: 'Sexism and Science'," in Science Books & Films *(copyright © 1979 by the American Association for the Advancement of Science), Vol. XV, No. 2, September, 1979, p. 69.*

Emma Rothschild

1948-

Rothschild is a British writer and associate professor in the science, technology, and society program at the Massachusetts Institute of Technology. She is the author of *Paradise Lost: The Decline of the Auto-Industrial Age* **(1974), a critical examination of the declining fortunes of the American automobile industry.**

Excerpt from *PARADISE LOST: THE DECLINE OF THE AUTO-INDUSTRIAL AGE*

All the troubles and hopes and preoccupations of the automobile business lead back to a pattern of industrial inertia—a pattern of obsolescence in selling and production, in expansion, down to most recent strategies for diversification and for foreign growth, in social location. Even beyond economic behavior, and beyond the characteristic caution of aging businesses, the auto industry faces the direst and least tractable problems of social obsolescence. Like all dominant national industries—and like the British railroad industry in the mid-nineteenth century—the auto business depended for its early, glorious growth on the sustenance of social and institutional partiality. Such support provided roads, a favorable tax structure, a dispersal of cities and jobs. It encouraged the decay of alternative modes of transportation, and suspended rational calculations of the costs of auto development and auto waste: it made possible the great and sustained power of American demand for automobiles.

Automotive growth required the technological priority of Fordist mass production, and the opportunities of mass consumption, and also a favoritism of national development. Yet it is exactly this structure of social support that seems most unreliable in present auto troubles, at once the hope and the nemesis of auto development. The recent difficulties of auto selling are caused in part by the collapse of such institutional support, by new public preoccupation with the irrationality and occasional inconvenience of auto use, with the cumulative costs of past auto excesses. At the same time, the apparent inevitability of auto travel in states and cities designed for automobiles is a major force sustaining auto sales and profits—just as the "inertia of use and wont," which Veblen found in British railroad investment and in the planning of nineteenth-century economic and urban development, was responsible for the lingering successes of the demoralized British rail industry. Meanwhile, in yet another conflicting role, this same social inertia of auto development also contributes to the business immobility of auto corporations, which, expecting continued support and continuing, if depressed, profits, are unable to change their habitual strategies.

Consumer preference for automobiles, in the context of social support for auto use, seems more soberly self-interested than mysterious and absolute. Beyond its evident qualities—in offering freedom, independence, privacy, sensations of power—auto transportation has provided the advantages of participation in a most favored sector of the national economy. There seems no need to propose an unexplainable "affinity" between Americans and automobiles: rational consumers would in any case

choose to travel on socially subsidized highways, in socially favored cars. (pp. 245-47)

Social partiality made possible auto domination and the extraordinary profits of the auto industry. Yet because it was supported by quite specific partiality, auto power is comprehensible, contingent, reversible. It required national sustenance, which will be reduced as auto ascendancy declines. Auto sales and profits were able to expand not only because of the opportune efficiency of auto companies, but also because the costs of auto development were ignored or deferred. The 1940s, 1950s, and 1960s brought a consequent overinvestment in auto transport, whose costs now seem ever more apparent. As with the auto companies' industrial decline relative to newer businesses, so an increased national investment in auto support would amount to throwing good resources after bad. The economic troubles of the auto industry are tied to its social troubles: as the industry's rise changed national life, so its decline will bring dislocations barely imaginable in modern, auto-centered cities.

In the present situation of auto difficulty, social support for increased auto use is already fractured and disintegrated. Commuters still find it cheap to travel by automobile—but such travel may also be inconvenient and frustrating, and may soon be increasingly expensive. The discontent of some consumers, particularly in large cities, where the disadvantages of auto-based planning are first apparent, seems in part a reaction against past extremes of auto enthusiasm. More concretely, modern auto consumers are in fact paying a price, in money and convenience, for the past distortion of national development, for decades of overinvestment in auto institutions. In the next ten or twenty years, the real costs of the present and historical structures of automotive support will become ever more evident—and ever more disruptive of auto expansion.

The waste left by auto development will seem less and less tolerable—a waste which is integral to the ways in which cars are made and sold and used. (pp. 247-48)

Such costs, and such waste, are not trivial relative to national development. People will continue most evidently to waste money and resources and energy; the question will be, rather, whether auto civilization is what people want to waste their chances on. Automotive arrangements are not absolute, or absolutely appealing, but depend on a particular conjuncture of social and historical partiality—a conjuncture which has had the most serious national costs. As the social partiality which supported auto expansion erodes, it will become possible to see auto transport as one way among many, a particularly costly way, of spending and wasting resources. (p. 250)

> *Emma Rothschild, in her* Paradise Lost: The Decline of the Auto-Industrial Age *(copyright © 1973 by Emma Rothschild; reprinted by permission of Random House, Inc.), Random House, 1974, 264 p.*

ROBERT SHERRILL

There is an orderliness and elegance [in **"Paradise Lost"**] that is deceptive; it's almost quaint, a kind of "I am now going to tell you why auto executives think the way they do. . . . I am now telling you why they think the way they do. . . . I have now told you why, and this is the import of it" style that is usually associated with 19th-century German philosophers. Sometimes, too, [Emma Rothschild] contemplates her topic with such intensity that she repeats herself. But extra orderliness and repetition of themes are, in Rothschild's hands, not only charming and persuasive but highly practical; they permit her to cram all sorts of complexities and sly extravagances into a simple mold, and permit the reader to enjoy her endless examples of psychoses (of advertising departments that, in despair, turn to lap robes to sell the 1973 Cadillac) without fearing that he will forget the point she set out to make.

You will cheat both yourself and Rothschild if you take **"Paradise Lost"** only for what it at first appears to be, a sober sociological study; it is much livelier and richer than that, almost cinematic, and one can hear in the background the mindless wheezings and clankings and gurglings of some great industrial tragicomedy like Alec Guinness's "The Man in the White Suit" or Chaplin's "Modern Times." (pp. 1, 14)

What Rothschild uncovers at the top of the auto industry is what you might find inside the skull of a 13th-century monk: old faiths petrified and rattling around like agates. And that, says Rothschild, is why the gates of Eden are closed forever to the auto executives. They are apparently incapable of surrendering their faith in outdated Fordism and Sloanism—one

equating the worker with a machine, the other seeing the customer only as a fickle and easy mark for gewgaws. (p. 14)

And so the once mighty Detroit, its feet locked in F. & S. concrete, begins to sink. Some auto executives talk candidly of going "down the drain." Rothschild sees a possible analogy here with the great textile and rail empires of England in the last century, to which that nation had committed itself too deeply and from whose decline it never fully recovered. (p. 16)

> *Robert Sherrill, "'Paradise Lost'," in* The New York Times Book Review *(© 1973 by The New York Times Company; reprinted by permission), October 28, 1973, pp. 1, 14, 16.*

DAVID SANFORD

As Emma Rothschild sees it [in **Paradise Lost**] there is little if anything to be said in favor of the automobile, and no reason whatever to buy stock in Ford or General Motors. Americans once loved cars, there was at least some enthusiasm for work on the assembly line, and great cheer in the board rooms of Detroit. Now the industry is in decline, following a course comparable to that of the British railroads in the late 19th century. The dreams of Henry Ford (in the efficiency and economy of mass production) and of Alfred Sloan (in annual styling changes and constant upgrading of cars to make people lust after a new car or two every year or so) have soured. The market is saturated, highways are clogged and dangerous, the air is foul, workers are disgruntled, parking lots full, profit margins down, gas scarce and auto executives depressed and bereft of innovative ideas to reorganize the industry. And the worst surely is yet to come. . . .

This is the basic and rather familiar story Emma Rothschild has to tell but she does it brilliantly and with the sort of perspective and detachment (attributable I suppose to the fact that she is British) that justifies Jane Jacobs' rave on the jacket: "Emma Rothschild's book . . . explains more than all the highway (pro and con), auto safety and air pollution books put together; it made me feel as if they had all been diddling around on the fringes of the subject, while she has driven straight into it."

Rothschild's analysis may be almost perfect but her way out is less clear, I think, as of course the future always is.

The automobile manufacturers are intent, though without much zest, on persisting in old ways, in forcing mistreated unskilled labor to be more pliant and productive, in pushing the meretricious frills and furbelows that Alfred Sloan believed would enhance growth and hence profits. They have resisted the obvious opportunity to make new safety features a selling point for new cars. (If next year's car is safer than this year's wouldn't consumers be likely to want the new model just as they are now thought to want the latest in vinyl tops?) But traumatized as they have been by auto safety criticism pioneered in the research of men like Daniel P. Moynihan and William Haddon and publicized by Ralph Nader, they have slight interest in auto safety as a way to market automobiles. Rather they are looking for new growth opportunities like making mobile homes and recreational vehicles. (p. 24)

Rothschild isn't certain, nor is Detroit, how the industry will adapt to inevitable change, but obviously it is not in control of events. The current energy crisis . . . , the decline in auto sales . . . , the rising tide of worker discontent, the disillusionment of consumers—all of these things support the thesis that the industry is in very big trouble, and that dependent as we all are on the automobile, it's trouble we share. (p. 25)

David Sanford, "Shared Trouble," in The New Republic (reprinted by permission of The New Republic; © 1973 The New Republic, Inc.), Vol. 169, No. 25, December 22, 1973, pp. 24-5.

ELLIOTT ABRAMS

[The] chief interest of *Paradise Lost* lies less in its conclusions than in the analytic method by which it reaches them—a peculiar blend of the most recent styles of cultural analysis with the most antiquated prejudices of British syndicalism. For all one knows, Miss Rothschild may never have read Charles Reich's *The Greening of America* or the many similar works that came in its wake, but their approach is her approach, one that eschews the careful marshaling of facts and arguments for bold, intuitive generalization. (p. 79)

Instead, Miss Rothschild's main concern seems to be the "greening" of the auto industry, and her chief criticism the fact that this process has so far failed to take place, and shows no signs of taking place in the future. She is far more interested in talking about what might be called the spiritual aspects of car manufacture than about such boring issues as industrial organization, unemployment, and wages.

Perhaps the best example of this predisposition is to be found in the book's attitude toward factory work. As everyone knows, assembly-line jobs are grueling and monotonous for auto workers, as they are for workers in almost any other industry that comes to mind. People take these jobs not because they are pleasant, but because they pay relatively well. To Miss Rothschild, however, factory work is not merely unpleasant, it is also "degrading," "dehumanizing," and "repressive." The increasing mechanization and trend toward automation in auto assembly work she calls "Fordism," and she considers it to be the root of nearly all industrial evil, leading management to the unconscionable attempt "to increase the intensity and precision and predictability of work."

Short of pure Luddism, this analysis leads nowhere. One wonders in fact whether the author is aware that the function of factories is first of all to produce goods in large quantities. Since enough of them do so in America with great efficiency, the country enjoys a level of prosperity which most of its inhabitants do not find degrading, repressive, or even dehumanizing. If the alternative to the assembly line is a return to cottage industries, and the standard of living they entail, most factory workers would no doubt prefer to keep their present jobs. There is something anachronistic in the sight of a presumably knowledgeable observer railing against mass production as a kind of plot devised by the Bosses to make life hard for the Workers.

But it is not only the modern industrial system that incurs Miss Rothschild's distaste. She also seems to dislike cars themselves, and finds it hard to believe that there are others who actually like them. Thus, she speaks of the attempt to persuade consumers "to buy more cars than they need," implying not only the existence of some sinister, manipulating force, foisting desires upon us, but also her own superior qualification to judge the genuineness of the consumer's needs. As a student of economics she recognizes, of course, that the development of various stages of production is determined by "objective" forces (an overused term in *Paradise Lost*), yet she cannot refrain from excoriating the Bosses for their sins. In a manner that seems more quaint than revolutionary, she describes the "ruthless aggression" General Motors executives direct toward their employees, and goes on to picture a world in which the degradation and repression of workers seem very nearly a conscious goal of management. There is "one, American, law outside the plant, and a GM law inside," we are told, quite as though there were no judicial system in the country and, more to the point, no United Auto Workers either.

Miss Rothschild's harsh judgment of the auto executives seems to rest on the fact that, unlike her, they are concerned with profits and production. Auto company management is "intransigent," for it uses "tight managerial control" to cut production costs, and evaluates plans "continuously and competitively." As with her criticisms of mass production itself, one is tempted to ask here what precisely the author is advocating as an alternative. Loose controls? Cost overruns? Irregular and noncompetitive evaluations? Unlike universities or philanthropic foundations, corporations do not aim at seeking truth or raising consciousness, but rather at earning profits by producing and selling goods and services; Miss Rothschild seems to have difficulty remembering this. (pp. 79, 82)

[The] rule that each year's model must look different from last year's is hardly of divine origin, and Miss Rothschild is quite right in attacking this particular marketing principle.

Yet this and other very sensible criticisms of the giant auto industry contained in her book are all but lost in the fervor of Miss Rothschild's romantic distaste for mass production and her outmoded notions of class warfare in American industry. The book has already earned a certain popularity, corresponding as it does to widely-held current notions about the malevolence of American industrial practices. What it proves ultimately, however, is that the anti-industrialist ethos, even when combined with a substantial number of interviews and fairly wide reading in the field, cannot produce the kind of serious study required by the subject. Instead, *Paradise Lost* is part moral fable, filled with heroes and villains and lessons to be learned, and part weary political tract, likely to convince only the true believers. (pp. 82, 84)

Elliott Abrams, "The Greening of Detroit," in Commentary (reprinted by permission; all rights reserved), Vol. 57, No. 3, March, 1974, pp. 78-9, 82, 84.

THE TIMES LITERARY SUPPLEMENT

Paradise Lost is about the rise and fall of the American automobile industry. Sometimes Emma Rothschild implies—with Agnelli, of Fiat—that the world industry as a whole is also doomed. Sometimes she hints that the Japanese, Swedes and Italians do things better (the unfortunate British motor industry is never mentioned, although much is made of a possible parallel with the general decline of Victorian industry). She maintains that because the American industry is so stuck in its own "ways"—persistent upgrading, outdated and inhuman production methods—the technology for more rational methods of urban transport may have to come from other industries. Her argument is that, whatever they say or claim to do, contemporary American automobile executives will be incapable of developing a simple utility car. . . .

Miss Rothschild underestimates the extent to which the suburban way of life, the over-developed car, and all the things that go with them, resulted not only from encouragement and manipulation by industrialists but also from the latent desires or dreams of the people. Of course, the numerous indirect costs—pollution and all that—were inadequately reflected in the price; of course, as the author well illustrates, the organized philosophy of the industry can be blamed for much of what went wrong. But if the consumer had not greatly enjoyed the package (the large, quiet, opulent car, the suburban house), no amount of salesmanship could have put it across. By the same token, Miss Rothschild also underestimates the scale of the problems involved in unravelling the puzzle.

Nevertheless, she tells an interesting tale and tells it well. But she makes no pretence of objectivity. She is interested only in those facts that support her theme. She adjusts figures for inflation only when it suits her. Similarly she accepts uncritically the conventional wisdom that the modern car is exceptionally unreliable. She points out that the car serves both as a luxury and a necessity, a duality that causes both conflict and irritation. The consumer is represented as a mainly passive sufferer. Of course, cars are very much used for essential journeys but many people like to drive about in a vehicle that also gives them pleasure. Indeed, it could well be argued that the basic fault of policy has been to let the car-consuming public get away with too much of what they wanted, rather than the other way about.

"End of the Road," in The Times Literary Supplement *(© Times Newspapers Ltd. (London) 1974; reproduced from* The Times Literary Supplement *by permission), No. 3768, May 24, 1974, p. 544.*

WILLIAM PLOWDEN

[The inevitable decline of the auto industry seems to be the theme of *Paradise Lost*.] Seems, because in fact throughout the book two rather different interpretations are put on the same chain of events. The 'moderate' interpretation envisages that parts at least of the industry might adapt to changing times by developing new technology, new products and new markets—although the process could be painful. The 'apocalyptic' interpretation, featuring phrases such as 'mortal mutation' and comparisons with 19th-century railways or textiles, sees the process of change as so uncertain and so traumatic as to mean the end of the motor industry in its present form. . . .

The case for the moderate line is strong. Undoubtedly the world's motor manufacturers are in difficulties. For GM, British Leyland, Citroen, Fiat and Volkswagen, 1973-74 is not a happy time. . . . The apocalyptic interpretation is much harder to sustain. Treating the oil crisis, as one must, as a special and

exogenous factor, it is hard to see all the other troubles of the motor industry as constituting some inevitable syndrome. How far do its economic problems reflect a long-term trend rather than the current cycle? Violent consumer reaction to defects in cars is surely a sign less of the industry's decline than of the strong hold, emotional and economic, that cars have on people.

More important, extrapolation from GM to the industry at large, which seems to be part of Miss Rothschild's argument, involves the fallacy of composition. Whatever the fate of its individual units, an industry as a whole can sustain massive changes without 'mortal decay', as agriculture shows. . . .

Signs that the world at large may reject the motor vehicle and all its works are even harder to perceive. It may be difficult, if not impossible, to show that the motor vehicle has made the developed countries, all in all, happier places. The empty roads and market squares of Eastern Europe are as remote and as attractive as a pre-war Baedeker. But Miss Rothschild moves almost imperceptibly from the proposition that the developing countries ought to avoid our motorised fate to the prediction that they probably will do so. The recent huge growth in the South Korean car population suggests to her not that South East Asia is a fertile and promising market but that there too disenchantment with the motor vehicle may be just round the corner. But have other polities besides Sark yet firmly turned their backs on the automotive revolution? . . .

In any case, what matters is not only how many cars there are in a community but also how, when and where they are used. Consumer and environmental protests do not threaten the motor vehicle. Their effects in civilising it and its uses are likely, if anything, to remove constraints on its continued growth; if cars were smaller, quieter, safer, less polluting, less oil-consuming and more tightly restrained in urban rush hours (and they could be all these things), their prospects would look even better than they do. The rate of growth of traditional cars may now have passed the mid-point on the S-curve; but there must be a lot of 'environmental' vehicles still to come.

This is where Miss Rothschild applies her Catch-22. It is basic to her apocalyptic thesis that existing major firms in the industry, such as GM, and their natural allies, such as the oil or roads lobbies, are incapable of adapting themselves to produce and provide for cars of this sort. Even if this is correct, it is very unlikely to be true of every major firm in the industry. It seems inevitable that, for better or worse, something not totally unlike the motor vehicle will be with us, in increasing numbers, for a long time yet. (p. 772)

William Plowden, "Car Sick," in New Statesman *(©1974 The Statesman & Nation Publishing Co. Ltd.), Vol. 87, No. 2254, May 31, 1974, pp. 771-72.**

Carl T(homas) Rowan

1925-

Rowan is an American journalist, syndicated columnist, and radio commentator known for his coverage of civil rights struggles in the United States. He has held several positions in the State Department and was appointed director of the United States Information Agency by President Johnson, thus becoming the first black to be a member of the National Security Council. In *Go South To Sorrow* (1957) Rowan examines the status of school desegregation in the South after the 1954 Supreme Court ruling prohibiting segregation, criticizing both Democratic and Republican leadership at the national level for their "moderate" approach toward ending segregation. In *Just Between Us Blacks* (1974) Rowan provides a survey of his ideas on the condition of blacks in America as originally presented in one hundred of his radio commentaries. Rowan's detractors claim that his civil rights coverage is marred by his bitterness and anger. Most critics, however, regard him as an intelligent and diligent reporter whose books are factual and objective. (See also *Contemporary Authors*, Vols. 89-92.)

Photograph by Roy Lewis

Excerpt from *GO SOUTH TO SORROW*

In [*Go South to Sorrow*], I intend to show what has happened since that May day in 1954 when so many Americans beamed proudly over the Supreme Court ruling [*Brown vs. Board of Education*]. I think the record will show that we have invited crisis after crisis by our cowardliness, by falling victim to a national sickness—for which the germ carriers are both Democrats and Republicans—that I can describe only as gutlessness in the name of "moderation." The record may even show that much of the press that exulted so loudly over the ruling, spawning great editorial phrases about freedom and justice, and those government officials who before the ruling expressed such alarm over our relations with the dark peoples abroad, have been the major forces lulling the nation into a slumber of meekness during which the agents of darkness have grabbed the initiative.

For all the noble words in its decision of May 17, 1954, the United States Supreme Court left a vacuum—a dangerous vacuum that represented a calculated gamble. The court was firm in its opinion, but it as much as confessed weakness as to how to secure the application of its ruling. It had to count on the American public for implementation. So the court left a "cooling-off period" of more than a year before issuing the final decree that was legally necessary to provoke any steps toward compliance in the areas affected. The justices obviously hoped that in the months between their dramatic ruling outlawing segregation and the final decree giving orders as to how and when the segregating areas would have to comply, responsible citizens of both races would sit together and chart a course of orderly change. But was the court's delay a practical move firmly founded on the belief that the cries of defiance would die out in time, or was it a needless and dangerous concession to hate peddlers who know no compromise? There were a few Americans who commented unhappily that "justice delayed is justice denied," who observed that those Negro plaintiffs who actually filed the suits asking for judicial relief from state-imposed segregation would finish school without receiving re-

lief, without receiving the justice to which the court now said they were entitled. But at the time there was no great debate on this point, for even the most militant leaders of the NAACP appeared happy to win the legal principle. Negro leaders joined with the Supreme Court in hoping that time would show the South to be law-abiding and amenable to change.

But for the uncompromising racists, the court-ordered delay was a bonanza—a time in which to organize, to harangue, to frighten, to conduct a venomous racial campaign of a magnitude never before experienced by Americans, even in the heyday of the Ku Klux Klan. Thousands of pamphlets, booklets and handbills spewed from the sewers of the National Citizens Protective Association in St. Louis and from a handful of other "hate" organizations that had struggled along in near-obscurity during a decade when a few men of courage in high places were vigorously attacking the American cancer of racism. But many of these courageous men, who had helped produce the Supreme Court decision, fell silent after the ruling, or became absorbed in the cult of "moderation" and left the Supreme Court "holding the bag." (pp. 17-18)

On July 11, 1954, less than two months after the Supreme Court decision, fourteen men met in Indianola, a community in Sunflower County, and formed the first White Citizens Council of Mississippi. These fourteen men circulated a letter suggesting that economic penalties be imposed upon both whites and Negroes who failed to go along with efforts to maintain segregation in Mississippi. Said the letter: "We can accomplish our purposes largely with economic pressure in dealing with members of the Negro race who are not co-operating, and with members of the white race who fail to co-operate we can apply social and political pressure." (p. 20)

Over much of the Deep South this was the process: Bankers refused to refinance mortgages or to grant group loans; supply houses and wholesalers denied the usual credit extended to merchants and small businessmen, or they simply refused to deliver supplies; insurance policies, especially on automobiles, were canceled; Negro farm tenants were forbidden by their employers to patronize Negro doctors, dentists—and even plumbers and carpenters—who spoke for integration. (p. 21)

Economic pressure—this was the weapon of "leading citizens" dedicated to opposing the law "by every lawful means." But the pattern of defiance included more than economic pressure. Militant Negroes received anonymous warnings to leave town; some received death threats; some received fake telephone calls in the night, declaring, "your mother is dead," or, "you'll find your husband in his wrecked automobile three miles out of town"; other Negroes were plagued with character assassination and fake charges of law violations; bricks and bottles were hurled through windows. (p. 22)

Slowly the nation—and sadly enough, the rest of the world—began to see that even in our day of miracle drugs, there would be no easy cure for Achilles. (p. 23)

The nation slumbered, drugged with a complacency pill called "moderation." So I moved across the South filled with worry and roamed the North in disgust, for I saw that while danger rockets flashed bright all about us, the nation was making "moderation" a cult, was adopting the motto, "When in doubt, do nothing," was rationalizing its way into believing that we would not face a racial crisis today if only we had thought to do more of nothing sooner.

But what is this "moderation"? The *American College Dictionary* defines "moderate" as "kept or keeping within due bounds; not extreme, excessive, or intense." In past years, in the field of race relations, some Americans called it "gradualism," a term that was adopted by those basically honest men and women who are constitutionally able to accept only small doses of change at a time. (p. 198)

In 1956, however, I saw that millions of southerners and a sickening number of northerners were embracing this new "moderation" without asking if it still meant the same thing, if it still left room for change while "keeping within due bounds." These Americans were yielding before a new wave of fear, and few of them seemed to care that now the word "moderate" was being misused to cloak economic oppressors, cowardly politicians, men who openly preached defiance of the nation's highest court, confirmed racists, and many more Americans seeking refuge from society's demand that all those with democratic and religious convictions stand up and be counted.

Thus that great middle mass, which must "go along" with social change even if it will not lead, was maneuvered into a position where its camp of gradualism was infiltrated and overwhelmed by fake "moderates" who turned the word, and all who endorsed it, into weapons against progress. (p. 199)

This area concerning the rights of minorities is the only area of our national life where the public and those entrusted with the law of the land sit meekly by, waiting for time to produce justice. I know one person whose life was wrecked by imprisonment because he allegedly stole a monkey wrench. Yet what greater thief is there than one who robs a man of his right to earn a decent living? Is he not stealing food and clothing from that man's children? What greater thief than he who robs me of my right to vote? Has he not stolen my basic form of expression, indeed, my only real protection, in a democratic society? When will my country understand that time alone does not heal the wounds of hatred; that it often petrifies the mind in its narrowness and fear? (p. 216)

We need Negroes who understand that no people ever got freedom on a silver platter, and that the Negro will be no exception—Negroes who understand that black men must suffer and sacrifice to close those cultural and educational gaps, to erase age-old insecurities and jealousies, to make it possible for today's little black boys to enter tomorrow's race of life without handicap. And we need white men who understand that even a great nation's freedom never is finally won, that succeeding generations must fight for it and struggle to secure it for future generations—and that this must be done with a passion and a zeal that rules out even the dictionary version of moderation. Our children will not welcome "moderate" freedoms, nor will they welcome a schizophrenic society in which a citizen of color must always journey south to sorrow. (p. 246)

Carl T. Rowan, in his Go South to Sorrow *(copyright © 1957 by Carl T. Rowan; reprinted by permission of Random House, Inc.), Random House, 1957, 246 p.*

Excerpt from *JUST BETWEEN US BLACKS*

I kid myself, of course, in even pretending that this book can be a private dialogue between one uneasy and frequently angry black American and the millions more who languish out there somewhere between hopelessness and despair. In this era of Watergate venality and general intrigue, no man can speak even with his wife with total certainty that their utterances are private. Yet this book had its beginnings in one hundred radio commentaries in which one black man spoke as honestly as he knew how to other blacks about the hopes and horrors, the pains and promises, of being black in America in an era when power was in the hands of Richard Nixon, Spiro Agnew, John N. Mitchell, H. R. (Bob) Haldeman, John Ehrlichman and the rest of those wonderful people who brought us Watergate. (p. xiii)

But I don't really mind a few whites eavesdropping inside these pages. I know better than most Americans that for all the racial segregation and isolation that exist and persist in this troubled society, there is no separate black world to which anyone can speak exclusively. Nor is there any white world, however rich, arrogant, bigoted, that is not touched, or whose children will not be affected, by the issues and problems that are discussed in these essays. (pp. xiii-xiv)

It is hard to believe that more than nineteen years have passed since the Supreme Court outlawed racial segregation in public schools. In fact, so many minority-group children are still being Jim Crowed that they will not believe that the court ever ruled at all.

Let's take a look at some of the results of that historic decision known as *Brown vs. Board of Education*. The Department of Health, Education and Welfare will drown you in statistics showing that the old dual system of public education has been wiped out in this country. But the figures don't tell the whole truth. A lot more black children are in schools where there are whites. Blatant attempts to maintain "separate but equal" schools *are* generally a thing of the past. But the equality of educational opportunity that the Supreme Court mandated in 1954 is almost as far from reality today as it was nineteen years ago. (p. 24)

Richmond, Virginia, is typical of what has happened North and South. Whites have fled to suburban Chesterfield and Enrico counties, leaving Richmond city schools predominantly black. They have used the technical barrier of jurisdictional boundaries to maintain separation, and the Supreme Court recently divided 4 to 4 on the question of whether the counties could be forced to merge schools with the black inner city.

Even where effective integration has taken place, blacks have been forced to pay a high price for it. The usual pattern of integration has been to destroy everything black and merge it into whatever was white. That made it easy to get rid of black principals and administrators, and fire thousands of black teachers.

It has taken years for the courts to face up to this injustice and require the retention of teachers on the basis of seniority. Where glaring racism has been manifest, courts have decreed that the black-and-white ratio of teachers must be the same as the racial ratio of the student body. Still, many thousands of dedicated black teachers have been ousted as the price for desegregation that the white bosses did not want.

Some blacks look at the pain, the bitterness, the trauma of the last nineteen years and they say that *Brown vs. Board of Education* wasn't worth all the misery it caused. So they talk about a reversion to the dual school system, or neighborhood control of schools. In the general frustration, all sorts of cowardly cop-outs are proposed.

But the truth is that that 1954 Supreme Court decision opened the door to fantastic changes in the South. Blacks live in infinitely greater dignity today. The humiliation and the physical danger are mostly gone. And children are better educated, better able to compete.

Still, we must struggle to see that the next nineteen years bring a lot more compliance with *Brown vs. Board of Education* than the last nineteen years have brought. (pp. 24-5)

Blacks keep asking me, "Where did the civil rights movement go wrong?"

My reply is that the movement is not what went wrong. Blacks simply have been outpropagandized these last few years. And they are not going to make any great new strides until they develop more clout in the field of communications.

Over the last few years there have been great public debates over law-and-order, busing to achieve racial balance, welfare costs, job quotas for minorities. In every instance, the debate wound up with black Americans cast as the villains. And this pointed up with bitter clarity the weak position blacks hold in the communications industry.

Are you aware that until a few years ago minority-group individuals owned fewer than 10 of the 8,000 or so radio stations in this country? Even today only some 30 stations are owned by blacks, Indians, Chicanos or other minorities.

The television situation is even worse. Black ownership is virtually nonexistent, and only one commercial television station has a black general manager. (pp. 47-8)

On only a handful of stations in America is a black free to give commentary on the top issues in the news. And almost nowhere does a black help decide what goes into the news, or into TV documentaries.

The situation is much the same on daily newspapers. The black who helps decide editorial policy is rare indeed. And there are only two or three black columnists who can sound off freely on a national basis.

One reason the Jewish people have fared well in this society is that they understand the value of communications. They know the dangers of being outpropagandized, so Jews have concentrated on the writing skill, on broadcasting, and publishing. We black people simply must train our children to write well, to speak articulately if not eloquently. That, too, is critical to the struggle for equality. (pp. 48-9)

I stirred up a lot of brothers and sisters recently with a column in which I said: "Hair ain't where it's at." I was scolding young blacks (and old ones) who go around bulling themselves with the pretense that wearing their hair a certain way proves they have black pride. For a long time it was the Afro, or the "bush," that was supposed to symbolize pride of African heritage. Now they've turned to cornrows, with both men and women sporting this supposedly ancient African hairdo of checkerboard parts and lots of little braids.

The point I want to make is that you can wear your hair any way you please, but it won't guarantee you pride. Only honest achievement can do that. Show me a black college student who makes the honor roll and I'll show you a proud black—even if his head is shaved as clean as a billiard ball. Show me the young black woman who wins top honors in the conservatory of music and I'll show you a proud sister—and it won't matter whether she wears a "fro" or has ironed her locks till they're straight as baling wire. (p. 54)

We simply cannot delude ourselves with fads about hair styles, or clothing, to the point that we ignore the reality that we must rely on trained intelligence. Jews have stood up against centuries of discrimination because they have pursued brainpower with relentless zeal.

Let me emphasize that it *is* progress when black people stop being *ashamed* of being black, or of having kinky hair. It is only when blacks go on to the nonsense of pretending that cornrows or dashikis prove something that the fad becomes self-defeating. (pp. 54-5)

One of the simplest lessons of life is that there is no pride in failure. No kind of hairdo, no so-called African robe, can give genuine self-respect to a young black who goofs off for four years of college and discovers that he or she is unprepared to compete in this society.

So my plea to young blacks is this: think less about hair and more about how to use your brains and skills to guarantee a brighter future for black people—and all of mankind. (p. 55)

There has been a mean campaign to heap shame upon Americans who are on welfare. I call it a mean campaign because it inspires fortunate Americans to hate the unfortunate. It is designed to blind the average American to the truth that American business, not poor people, is the real benefactor of our welfare system. (p. 73)

[Some] 15 million Americans receive some kind of welfare payment; the total welfare tab may reach $19 billion this year. But does this mean that the poor are riding a gravy train, dragging overtaxed businessmen to the poor house? Not hardly. The welfare program is a beautiful bonanza for businessmen.

That $19 billion dollars won't stay in the hands of welfare recipients long enough for them to recognize the picture of George Washington. During the worst period of the Nixon recession, welfare money was a lifesaver for thousands of businessmen operating in and around neighborhoods of the poor. In 1970 and 1971, those abused poor people spent $30 billion of welfare money for bread, butter, milk, meat, socks and sheets.

Donald M. Kendall, who is Mr. Pepsi-Cola and a close friend of President Nixon, spoke the unspeakable in 1970 when he told the Whittier, California, Chamber of Commerce that the welfare program is a delightful prop for American business. Kendall was arguing for a welfare program that would double the number of recipients as well as the amount of money going to them. He said to those businessmen: "If we wanted a better prop under our economy we couldn't find one."

Kendall knows that when the government gives $200,000 in cotton price supports to Senator James Eastland of Mississippi, that money may help almost no one but Eastland. He can bury it in the backyard or stuff it in his mattress. But every dollar handed to the poor is spent so fast it is like a direct deposit in some businessman's bank account.

Maybe Mr. Kendall can't think of a better prop for business than the welfare program, but I can.

The government can spend money to provide training for people who cannot earn a living because they were denied an education in the past; because they were being brutalized when the era of advanced technology passed by.

The government can ensure that the children of welfare families are able through education to break the cycle of ignorance, poverty and more ignorance. Then they will become earners contributing far more to the national economy. (pp. 73-4)

Wherever I meet with blacks these days, especially young blacks, the inevitable question is whether blacks have a decent future in this society. They refer to unyielding job discrimination, lingering abuses in housing, the vicelike grip of poverty, hostility and bigotry in all things social, and many of them seem on the verge of despair.

I make it clear that the future will be rough, especially the years immediately ahead. But I also make it clear that we black Americans are not without hope.

Some cynicism on the part of blacks is healthy. Too many times in the past we have celebrated what we thought were lasting victories, only to have our dreams shattered. In the Reconstruction period following the Civil War, blacks who were thrust into positions of power no doubt thought they had achieved lasting roles in the political life of the Deep South. They soon were back in bondage.

When the Supreme Court outlawed racial segregation in public schools in 1954, millions of us rejoiced at the thought that Jim Crow was dead. We know, sadly, what a tough, tricky old bird he is.

During the demonstrations of the late fifties, the great civil rights march of 1963, some blacks truly believed their chant, "We shall overcome. . . ."

Now years of fighting hard just to stand still have made it clear to us that the price of our liberation must be constant struggle and eternal vigilance.

Perhaps nothing is a more pointed commentary on the feeble magnitude of black participation in their federal government than the gallery of photographs that was spread across the front pages of most newspapers on March 2, 1974. A grand jury had indicted seven of the most powerful former members of the Nixon Administration on charges of conspiring to cover up the Watergate crimes—and every man indicted was white. (pp. 201-02)

Now, some would call it racial progress had the power grabbers included a few blacks among the plotters, schemers, burglarizers. But I regard it as racial progress that this overweeningly powerful, lily-white group, with all its appeals to racism and snobbery, could not completely bamboozle the American people.

If we black people develop some new goals that we can share; if we help each other to seize educational and employment opportunities; if we discard slovenly indifference and move with pride, to use the tools and powers that we have, we shall yet find an army of white allies.

And we shall breathe new life into the old dream that "We shall overcome." (p. 202)

> *Carl T. Rowan, in his* Just Between Us Blacks *(copyright © 1974 by Carl T. Rowan; reprinted by permission of Random House, Inc.), Random House, 1974, 202 p.*

ROBERT R. BRUNN

[Rowan's desire in writing **"South of Freedom"**] was to report "what it means to be a Negro in America." Only a Negro can do this with sensitivity and accuracy, but to do it he must achieve a certain sense of detachment that is most difficult to attain under the circumstances. This Carl Rowan does.

He travelled 6,000 miles through his native American South to make this study of discrimination and segregation between Negroes and whites. What he found was not a "New South," but this. . . .

[In **"South of Freedom"**] he reports the state in the South of what is known in every living room in America as "the Negro problem." And before he is through he does not excuse the rest of America its more subtle discriminatory practices. Knowing the problem as only a Negro can, he concludes that all over the United States what the Negro wants and needs is simply put. Dignity. . . .

Mr. Rowan has no sympathy with the gradualist doctrine which he describes as "Be patient, democracy will come to you later." He believes that segregation and other forms of discrimination against Negroes in employment, education, and community life must be met head-on with the force of the federal law whenever possible. Of all people, he is hardest on those Negroes in the South and elsewhere who have profited from segregation and its freedom from white competition and so defend it.

Carl Rowan has known that this problem existed from the time he was a humiliated small country boy in a big city who was sent to the kitchen of a large restaurant to eat while his fellow (white) winners of a newspaper contest ate in the dining room.

It is due to his humility and balance that this is not an embittered tract nor a bland glossing-over but an intimate and convincing view of America's most deplorable social problem.

Robert R. Brunn, "Not Embittered Nor a Bland Glossing-Over," in The Christian Science Monitor (reprinted by permission from The Christian Science Monitor; © 1952, copyright renewed © 1980, The Christian Science Publishing Society; all rights reserved), August 4, 1952, p. 9.

WILLIAM A. BROWER

Perhaps Mr. Rowan has said nothing new about one of the nation's most grievous problems—the so-called Negro problem. Perhaps, even, there is little novelty in the way he has said it. Yet **"South of Freedom"** is a book every American should read.

Mr. Rowan is a Negro. He has experienced, in a hundred different ways, the emotional hell that harasses Negroes simply because they are Negroes. Undoubtedly as a reporter for a metropolitan daily newspaper, the Minneapolis *Tribune*, Mr. Rowan has also had a taste of what we call equality of opportunity. As a result he is a discerning analyst of our schizophrenic democratic personality. . . .

To those inclined toward a cowardly, queasy outlook on the issue of Negro rights today, Mr. Rowan's scalpel-like report will not bring much comfort. All the sorry ingredients of second-class citizenship—segregation, personal humiliation, physical peril, stereotype characterizations, economic exploitation, intermarriage taboos, Jim Crow paradoxes—are here incisively diagnosed. Segregation, Mr. Rowan declares, is the South's god. Some white Southerners are willing to admit that the Negro's life and opportunities are not the same as the white man's. But few if any, in his opinion, will concede that segregation itself is a basic cause of the existing injustices. (p. 176)

In discussing the ticklish issue of communism and the Negro, Mr. Rowan cites the pathetic case of Willie McGee, the Laurel, Mississippi, Negro who was given the kiss of death by the Communists. McGee was executed in May, 1951, for the alleged rape of a white woman. Communists, Rowan remarks, bled the "last drop of propaganda" from this case of one-sided justice, but he points out that there is a more important and deeper lesson than the patent one of Communist exploitation. "Nobody seemed to remember," he writes, "that Communists magnified an issue because one-sided application of the law gave them an issue to magnify. Had Willie McGee been given a 'white man's sentence,' the case might have died in the same obscurity that once engulfed McGee, and the Communists would have had to work much harder for their symbol."

Mr. Rowan has no kind words for Negro appeasers, who invariably paint the rosier aspects of racial discrimination. He lists George Schuyler, associate editor of the Pittsburgh *Courier*, the nation's largest Negro weekly, as an eminent example. . . . He condemns Schuyler for pointing out, for instance, that Negroes are better off in America than in South Africa. "Is it an American test by which we decide that what the American Negro gets is more satisfactory because Negroes in South Africa get something worse?" he asks. "Americans can only judge America by the American standard, and that is the standard of democracy."

In the final analysis, this is the standard by which the Negro American, like every other American, judges his country and

his rights. He wants everything that any other American wants. And he feels, as Rowan concludes, that he is entitled to nothing less. (p. 177)

William A. Brower, "The Single Standard," in The Nation, Vol. 175, No. 9, August 30, 1952, pp. 176-77.

HAROLD FLEMING

Had [Carl Rowan] been less honest or less perceptive, [*South of Freedom*] might easily have been another "exposé" exhibiting Jim Crow in all its one-dimensional ugliness. Fortunately, it is something considerably richer and more rewarding.

The South, as Rowan observed it, still worships its old god, segregation, but with growing doubt and defection, occasionally amounting to open heresy. . . . He found a few white Southerners who were willing to suffer ostracism for their belief in racial equality. But he found many more who feared to speak out for decency, and some who would do violence to preserve white supremacy. . . .

Here are the paradoxes, the big injustices, the startling signs of hope which characterize today's South. Within the limits of his investigation, Rowan has caught their complexity and reported it honestly and effectively.

But much the best passages in the book are those in which Rowan ceases to be a reporter and draws freely on memory and reflection. His return to the South was a profound personal experience, and he communicates that experience to the reader with unusual skill. We share his anger and hurt at discriminations practiced as a matter of course, accepted unthinkingly by a whole society. And, finally, we join in his desire for "a simple little thing called dignity," which is neither simple nor little, but the essence of equality.

Harold Fleming, "A Negro in the South," in The New Republic, Vol. 127, No. 12, September 22, 1952, p. 28.

A. T. STEELE

Mr. Rowan went to India in the dual role of lecturer and reporter. Out of his experiences has come [**"The Pitiful and the Proud",**] a book of great value to perplexed Americans seeking an intelligent appraisal of Asian attitudes toward this country. . . . Mr. Rowan is not given to sweeping generalizations. His word picture of India is rich in informative and colorful detail with a very fair representation of the various points of view.

Mr. Rowan's trip grew out of an invitation from the State Department to go to India and tell Indian audiences something about the United States as he knew it. . . . The job was tougher than he expected. Talking to clubs and youth groups, Mr. Rowan sometimes found his hearers more intent on pouring out their bitterness toward the United States than in listening to his views. . . . After repeated experiences of this kind, especially at meetings of young people, Mr. Rowan was obliged to conclude that Indian Communists and their sympathizers were making a calculated effort to embarrass him.

Being a Negro, Mr. Rowan was subjected to considerable needling on United States racial tensions. Most Indians he met wanted to believe that the United States was incurably racist. Throughout his book Mr. Rowan maintains remarkable objectivity, considering the racial and political passions that swirled about him on his Asian tour. . . .

Behind India's distrust of the West Mr. Rowan finds many reasons, some rational, some irrational. Among the former stands colonialism—still very much alive in Africa and parts of Asia. Among the latter he mentions such things as India's thin-skinned pride, her assumption of spiritual superiority and the tendency of nationalist Indians to see only the rosy features of the Communist world and only the worst features of the West. He makes no attempt to minimize the Communist danger in India and other parts of southern Asia. He was surprised at the extent to which Communist-inspired phrases have become a part of everyday conversation for many Indians. The Communist co-existence line, he notes, has had a strong appeal in Asia. Indeed the Reds have succeeded in convincing many Asians that the Communists are for co-existence, while the Americans are not. Mr. Rowan believes the United States will have to play the Asian game to some extent if it is to make any headway against Communist propaganda in Asia. . . .

Leaving India and moving on into other south Asian lands, Mr. Rowan is depressed by the poverty in Pakistan, the corruption in Thailand, the Communist problem in Malaya. He hangs a big question mark over Indo-China, the Philippines and Indonesia. He counts Burma, despite its many problems, as "one of Asia's best gambles for democracy." Mr. Rowan's thumbnail surveys of these countries are informative as far as they go, but they seem anticlimactic after the author's top-notch report on India. . . .

In the main, however, he must be credited with a fact-filled, intelligently written book that answers many of the questions Americans would like to ask about conditions and attitudes in Asia.

> *A. T. Steele, "An American Negro's Thoughtful Report on South Asia," in* New York Herald Tribune Book Review *(©I.H.T. Corporation; reprinted by permission), April 29, 1956, p. 4.*

JOSEPH McSORLEY, C.S.P.

[Mr. Rowan] gives us the impression [in *The Pitiful and the Proud*] that the evils prevalent in India are practically ineradicable; and although he believes in the need for a campaign to diminish over-population by the policy of contraception, he doubts that the program could be made effective. . . . He records his hearty dislike of President Ngo Dinh Diem of Vietnam, alludes several times to the fact that he is a Catholic, calls him unqualified as a leader, prudish, stubborn, an introverted egotist; and he adds—apparently as a disqualification—that he practices chastity. The book contains a surprisingly large number of references to Senator Joseph McCarthy who, in the eyes of the author, is a "demagogue," a "scoundrel," a "disgrace to the Senate and American democracy." We find no criticism of Alger Hiss, or of Harry Dexter White, or of the Rosenbergs; and no praise is given to any anti-Communist. More than one reader will close this volume convinced that its author does not—possibly cannot—write objectively.

> *Joseph McSorley, C.S.P., "Other New Books: 'The Pitiful and the Proud'," in* Catholic World *(copyright 1956 by The Missionary Society of St. Paul the Apostle in the State of New York), Vol. 182, No. 1095, June, 1956, pp. 237-38.*

MARGARET PARTON

The first encounter with India is for most Westerners a considerable shock. There is the shock of poverty, always far worse than had been imagined. . . .

Carl Rowan had few shocks of misunderstanding—although his assumptions, recorded in his book **"The Pitiful and the Proud,"** that an old man peacefully sharing a mud hut with a cow is necessarily unhappy, or that a naked boy riding a water buffalo into a mud hole is a "squalid" scene, might be put into the categories of misunderstanding. But for him there was a greater shock, the shock suffered by a literate and sensitive American Negro who discovers that India is probably the most racially-conscious country in the world today. . . .

His conclusions are bitter: ". . . this concern with color had become close to an obsession and I was convinced that for many years to come race would be an important factor in India's foreign policy. . . . Now it seemed that India itself was strolling on a bitter road named Racism in Reverse. . . . Asian questions about racism in America are not asked out of a deep concern about the American Negro. Basically they are an expression of the Asian's concern about *himself*, of *his own* quest for status and dignity."

He attributes much of this situation of course to the sinister activities of the Communists. . . . [He] found the Red menace greater and more frightening than he imagined it would be. Unless the arrogant intellectuals of India turn their attention to the pitiful poor of their own country, he concludes, the Red tinge will become reality.

Mr. Rowan is a brilliant and diligent reporter. He also travelled through Burma, Thailand, Malaya, Indonesia, Indochina, Hong Kong, the Philippines, and covered the Bandung Conference. It is a big book.

One wishes, though, that Mr. Rowan had not been quite so thoroughly the diligent, serious reporter. If he had taken time to relax and enjoy himself in India he might better have caught the tempo of time, of timelessness. . . . If he had visited the community projects, the laboratories, the Gandhian ashrams, or the Himalayas his notable book might have acquired the dimensions it now lacks—the dimensions of gentleness and hope.

> *Margaret Parton, "An Asian Obsession," in* The Saturday Review, *New York (copyright © 1956 by Saturday Review; all rights reserved; reprinted by permission), Vol. XXXIX, No. 31, August 4, 1956, p. 26.*

JANE CASSELS RECORD

Three years have passed since the Supreme Court declared public school segregation unconstitutional; two years, since the Court ordered desegregation "with all deliberate speed." Some communities have complied—others have taken a posture of open defiance. . . .

Carl Rowan's ["**Go South to Sorrow**"] is an indictment of the national leadership—both Democratic and Republican—which practices "gutlessness in the name of moderation," of the Southern press which practices "cowardice" in the name of objectivity, of decent folk who practice silence in the face of indecencies. . . .

The outlander finds it difficult to understand Southerners, with their contradictions of graciousness and violence, warmth and cruelty, patriotism and rebelliousness. Tennessee-bred Carl Rowan catches and sets down their manner of speaking, their way of thinking, the nuances of their interrelationships. . . .

Mr. Rowan writes with passion, yet also with a remarkable compassion that extends beyond the downtrodden Negro to the downtrodden poor white, caught in a web of ignorance and fear and needing desperately to feel better than somebody. The author's compassion stops short, however, of demagogues who make political capital of ignorance and fear. . . .

Courage is not a geographical commodity. The silent liberals of the South are no more censurable than Northern liberals who knuckled under to McCarthyism. And it is easier for Southern expatriates to be brave and bold about integration than for their confreres left behind. Yet is is none the less true that Southern progressives and other decent folk, by their abdication of leadership, set the stage for a reign of terror.

Mr. Rowan regards the "cooling-off" period between the first and second Court decisions as a mistake; into the vacuum move the "merchants of hate" to organize what had been a rather formless resentment. He criticizes the national administration for its failure to use the tremendous personal prestige of the President, or to call a White House conference which would give support to and provide a vehicle of communication for reasonable men. Certainly firm evidence that the Federal government intended to prosecute and punish violations of personal liberty would have discouraged atrocities.

But though such measures might keep Delta rednecks from throwing colored boys into the bayous, how can the people of Tchula, Miss., be made to take these children into their white schools next fall or the year after? What kind of force are we prepared to use? These are the difficult questions. Perhaps the Court should have set up a timetable and spelled out sanctions. This is a moot point. Carl Rowan has offered no blueprint. But then neither has anybody else.

Jane Cassels Record, "The South Since the Supreme Court Spoke," in New York Herald Tribune Book Review (© I.H.T. Corporation; reprinted by permission), April 21, 1957, p. 6.

MARK ETHRIDGE, JR.

["**Go South to Sorrow**"] is the book of the flaming militant, and the angels are most certainly on his side. [Carl Rowan] decries the injustices that have refused to yield before the dicta of the Supreme Court. He shudders alike at Southern paternalism that gives the Negro "the easy side of the law" and at Southern brutality as displayed in the cases of Emmett Till and Autherine Lucy. He is revolted at the demagoguery of such politicians as Senator James C. Eastland of Mississippi. He is moved by the quiet courage of the Reverend Martin Luther King in the Montgomery bus boycott. Rowan's reporting is frequently high-quality stuff which makes it easy to see how he has compiled an enviable record of journalism awards.

But too often bitterness and anger force even the most sympathetic reader to discount much of what he has to say. He succumbs to the temptation to oversimplify; he praises his heroes unqualifiedly; he damns his villains unmercifully. Because he feels that it is impossible for such a creature as a "moderate" to exist, the Southern moderate bears the brunt of Rowan's anger. Yet the truth is that the moderate not only exists in the South, but must continue to exist as a vital force in gaining Southern acceptance of the court's decision.

"**Go South to Sorrow**" is not so much a report on the South today as it is a blind confirmation of noble prejudices. It adds little to the cause of justice or of journalism.

Mark Ethridge, Jr., "Books: Angry Man in the South," in The Saturday Review, *New York (copyright © 1957 by Saturday Review; all rights reserved; reprinted by permission), Vol. XL, No. 26, June 29, 1957, p. 15.*

ROBERT H. AMUNDSON

[*Go South to Sorrow* is] 246 pages of hard-hitting, penetrating and incisive reporting which will find some readers nodding in assent, others squirming on the horns of the "moderation" dilemma, and still others in open defiance and total condemnation of the facts reported. It is on the latter two groups that Mr. Rowan trains his journalistic artillery.

The term *moderation,* much like the word *liberal,* can be defined in many ways. When applied to the implementation of the Supreme Court decision, there seem to be two groups of "moderates." The first group concedes that segregation is wrong and must be ended, and cautions moving slowly but surely. The author does not voice serious concern about these moderates, although he may not agree with their timetable. Most of his wrath is directed against the "self-styled moderates"— the do-nothings—who insist that time alone will solve the segregation issue. (p. 398)

[Mr. Rowan] courageously outlines in detail how the champions of white supremacy first intimidated the Negro, then manipulated many white moderates into a do-nothing party either by threats and coercion or by brainwashing them with the fear of intermarriage. The next step was a series of attacks on philanthropic foundations, corporations, and organizations such as the NAACP, and the National Urban League, which in any way tried to present the Negro in a favorable light. The demagogues were then prepared to take the final step—open defiance of the highest tribunal in the land.

Despite the scant progress made since 1954, the author still sees hope that in a democracy based on the Judaeo-Christian concept of the intrinsic worth and dignity of the individual person, black and white Americans together can still solve the American dilemma. To do so, however, the initiative must be wrested from a few defiant men, lest the real meaning of the Supreme Court decision in 1954 be dashed into incomprehensibility upon the Procrustean bed of acquired behavior patterns. (pp. 398-99)

Robert H. Amundson, "Other New Books: 'Go South to Sorrow'," in Catholic World *(copyright 1957 by The Missionary Society of St. Paul the Apostle in the State of New York), Vol. 185, No. 1109, August, 1957, pp. 398-99.*

SAMUEL F. YETTE

In [*Just Between Us Blacks*], Rowan is an author in the rare true meaning of the word, that of being an *authority* on his subject, i.e., Black people, high and low, in varying stages of confusion and flux, and, in a time when Rowan, himself, as journalist-diplomat, is at the pinnacle of his specialty—observing the American scene. . . .

Just Between Us Blacks is a personal book, more subjective than either of Rowan's previous books, except, perhaps, his first, *South of Freedom*. . . . (p. 213)

To an author who is also a journalist, it matters whether the first person or third person is employed. The object of third-person objectivity is a credibility based on an ability to see clearly and find the truth through personal *non*-involvement. In Rowan's case, he has achieved a credibility through first-person approaches that might not have been attainable otherwise.

There are times when he equivocates; at other times he lays it on the line. When he equivocates, he leaves the reader to ponder, perhaps, even to question. When he lays it on the line, he has few peers, and leaves even fewer questions.

The book's most glaring equivocation, perhaps, is the author's view of the so-called "Black Power" militancy of the 1960s, particularly the role and effect of Dr. Martin Luther King, Jr.

"The Montgomery boycott succeeded," Rowan acknowledges. "But let us not delude ourselves into believing that Gandhian tactics of nonviolence caused those Dixiecrat racists to knuckle under. It was a Supreme Court decision that finally gave Dr. King and his colleagues victory."

Rowan's deeper look at those developments reflected what he would likely regard as a necessary balanced view, though others might read into it a certain ambivalence Dr. King's movement stirred in the author: . . .

> Some students of Dr. King say that pressures from . . . militants forced him to change his style. They say he felt forced to adopt some of the angry rhetoric that became so popular among young blacks, even though he sensed that wild rhetoric and senseless violence would only infuriate and militarize oppressive forces within "the establishment" that he had half won over.
>
> We know the result. The forces of hatred, bigotry, oppression did rise up. Dr. King was slain. This country was thrown into a "white backlash" that dominates this nation even today.

This "balancing" or "equivocation"—whichever—was more noticeable in the context of the author's unmitigated praise of other public men of that period, including Black Senator Edward Brooke (R-Mass.), NAACP Executive Secretary Roy Wilkins, and President Lyndon B. Johnson, whose senseless and unconstitutional devastation in Southeast Asia was opposed by Dr. King, but was given no notice in the book.

But Rowan is clearly at his best when he is either laying it on the line (without divided loyalties) or interpreting the foggy figures he digs out of federal budgets to prove his point on behalf of Blacks in need.

Rowan's pragmatic approach to desegregation is gut-level. Mixing your company racially, he argues, simply means that you then have a better chance at a job that you otherwise would never even hear about. (pp. 213-15)

Long before the reader completes this personal tour of Rowan's broad experience and expansive mind, there is a coming together of Rowan, the man, and the book. The book becomes what he is, pretty much: an unapologetic pragmatist, laced with flourishes of old-fashioned wit, and steeped in the common sense ethics of his native backwoods Tennessee. (p. 215)

Samuel F. Yette, "'Just Between Us Blacks'," in The Journal of Negro Education, *Vol. 44, No. 2 (Spring, 1975), pp. 213-16.*

Bayard Rustin

1910-

Rustin is an American nonfiction writer, civil rights leader, and administrator. A key organizer of the 1955 Montgomery, Alabama, bus boycott led by Martin Luther King, Rustin was also instrumental in organizing the 1963 March on Washington and has since sought to build a coalition of blacks, liberals, and labor for progressive social change. *Down the Line* **(1971) is a collection of Rustin's writings on civil rights over more than three decades. Rustin is executive director of the A. Philip Randolph Institute in New York. (See also** *Contemporary Authors,* **Vols. 53-56.)**

Excerpt from *DOWN THE LINE: THE COLLECTED WRITINGS OF BAYARD RUSTIN*

There are two Americas, black and white, and nothing has more clearly revealed the divisions between them than the debate currently raging around the slogan of "black power." Despite—or perhaps because of—the fact that this slogan lacks any clear definition, it has succeeded in galvanizing emotions on all sides. Many whites see it as the expression of a new racism, and many Negroes take it as a warning to white people that Negroes will no longer tolerate brutality and violence. But even within the Negro community itself, "black power" has touched off a major debate . . . , and one which threatens to ravage the entire civil rights movement. Indeed, a serious split has already developed between advocates of black power like Floyd McKissick of CORE and Stokely Carmichael of SNCC, on the one hand, and Dr. Martin Luther King of SCLC, Roy Wilkins of the NAACP, and Whitney Young of the Urban League, on the other.

There is no question, then, that great passions are involved in the debate over the idea of black power; nor, as we shall see, is there any question that these passions have their roots in the psychological and political frustrations of the Negro community. Nevertheless, I contend not only that black power lacks any real value for the civil rights movement, but that its propagation is positively harmful. It diverts the movement from a meaningful debate over strategy and tactics, it isolates the Negro community, and it encourages the growth of anti-Negro forces.

In its simplest and most innocent guise, black power merely means the effort to elect Negroes to office in proportion to Negro strength within the population. There is, of course, nothing wrong with such an objective in itself, and nothing inherently radical in the idea of pursuing it. But in Stokely Carmichael's extravagant rhetoric about "taking over" in districts of the South where Negroes are in the majority, it is important to recognize that Southern Negroes are in a position to win a maximum of only two congressional seats and control of eighty local counties. . . . Now there might be a certain value in having two Negro congressmen from the South, but obviously they could do nothing by themselves to reconstruct the face of America. Eighty sheriffs, eighty tax assessors, and eighty school board members might ease the tension for a while in their communities, but alone they could not create jobs and build

low-cost housing; alone they could not supply quality integrated education.

The relevant question, moreover, is not whether a politician is black or white, but what forces he represents. Manhattan has had a succession of Negro borough presidents, and yet the schools are increasingly segregated. Adam Clayton Powell and William Dawson have both been in Congress for many years; the former is responsible for a rider on school integration that never gets passed, and the latter is responsible for keeping the Negroes of Chicago tied to a mayor who had to see riots and death before he would put eight-dollar sprinklers on water hydrants in the summer. I am not for one minute arguing that Powell, Dawson, and Mrs. Motley should be impeached. What I am saying is that if a politician is elected because he is black and is deemed to be entitled to a "slice of the pie," he will behave in one way; if he is elected by a constituency pressing for social reform, he will, whether he is white or black, behave in another way. (pp. 154-55)

The winning of the right of Negroes to vote in the South ensures the eventual transformation of the Democratic party, now controlled primarily by Northern machine politicians and Southern Dixiecrats. The Negro vote will eliminate the Dixiecrats from the party and from Congress, which means that the crucial question facing us today is who will replace them in the South. Unless civil rights leaders (in such towns as Jackson, Mississippi; Birmingham, Alabama; and even to a certain extent Atlanta) can organize grass-roots clubs whose members will have a genuine political voice, the Dixiecrats might well be succeeded by black moderates and black southern-style machine politicians, who would do little to push for needed legislation in Congress and little to improve local conditions in the South. While I myself would prefer Negro machines to a situation in which Negroes have no power at all, it seems to me that there is a better alternative today—a liberal-labor-civil rights coalition which would work to make the Democratic party truly responsive to the aspirations of the poor, and which would develop support for programs aimed at the reconstruction of American society in the interests of greater social justice. The advocates of black power have no such programs in mind. What they are in fact arguing for (perhaps unconsciously) is the creation of a *new black establishment*.

Nor, it might be added, are they leading the Negro people along the same road which they imagine immigrant groups traveled so successfully in the past. Proponents of black power—accepting a historical myth perpetrated by moderates—like to say that the Irish and the Jews and the Italians, by sticking together and demanding their share, finally won enough power to overcome their initial disabilities. But the truth is that it was through alliances with other groups (in political machines or as part of the trade union movement) that the Irish and the Jews and the Italians acquired the power to win their rightful place in American society. They most certainly did not make isolation their primary tactic.

Negroes are once again turning to nationalistic slogans. And "black power" affords the same emotional release as "Back to Africa" and "Buy Black" did in earlier periods of frustration and hopelessness. This is not only the case with the ordinary Negro in the ghetto; it is also the case with leaders like McKissick and Carmichael, neither of whom began as a nationalist or was at first cynical about the possibilities of integration. It took countless beatings and twenty-four jailings—and the absence of strong and continual support from the liberal community— to persuade Carmichael that his earlier faith in coalition politics was mistaken, that nothing was to be gained from working with whites, and that an alliance with the black nationalists was desirable. In the areas of the South where SNCC has been working so nobly, implementation of the Civil Rights Acts of 1964 and 1965 has been slow and ineffective. Negroes in many rural areas cannot walk into the courthouse and register to vote. Despite the voting rights act, they must file complaints and the Justice Department must be called to send federal registrars. Nor do children attend integrated schools as a matter of course. There, too, complaints must be filed and the Department of Health, Education and Welfare must be notified. Neither department has been doing an effective job of enforcing the acts. The feeling of isolation increases among SNCC workers as each legislative victory turns out to be only a token victory— significant on the national level, but not affecting the day-to-day lives of Negroes. Carmichael and his colleagues are wrong in refusing to support the 1966 act, but one can understand why they feel as they do.

It is, in short, the growing conviction that the Negroes cannot win—a conviction with much grounding in experience—which accounts for the new popularity of black power. So far as the ghetto Negro is concerned, this conviction expresses itself in hostility, first toward the people closest to him who have held out the most promise and failed to deliver (Martin Luther King, Roy Wilkins, etc.), then toward those who have proclaimed themselves his friends (the liberals and the labor movement), and finally toward the only oppressors he can see (the local storekeeper and the policeman on the corner). On the leadership level, the conviction that the Negroes cannot win takes other forms, principally the adoption of what I have called a "no-win" policy. Why bother with programs when their enactment results only in sham? Why concern ourselves with the image of the movement when nothing significant has been gained for all the sacrifices made by SNCC and CORE? Why compromise with reluctant white allies when nothing of consequence can be achieved anyway? Why indeed have anything to do with whites at all?

On this last point, it is extremely important for white liberals to understand what, one gathers from their references to "racism in reverse," the President and the Vice-President of the United States do not : that there is all the difference in the world between saying, "If you don't want me, I don't want you" (which is what some proponents of black power have in effect been saying), and the statement, "Whatever you do, I don't want you" (which is what racism declares). It is, in other words, both absurd and immoral to equate the despairing response of the victim with the contemptuous assertion of the oppressor. It would, moreover, be tragic if white liberals allowed verbal hostility on the part of Negroes to drive them out of the movement or to curtail their support for civil rights. The issue was injustice before black power became popular, and the issue is still injustice.

In any event, even if black power had not emerged as a slogan, problems would have arisen in the relation between whites and Negroes in the civil rights movement. In the North, it was inevitable that Negroes would eventually wish to run their own movement and would rebel against the presence of whites in positions of leadership as yet another sign of white supremacy. In the South, the well-intentioned white volunteer had the cards stacked against him from the beginning. Not only could he leave the struggle any time he chose to do so, but a higher value was set on his safety by the press and the government— apparent in the differing degrees of excitement generated by the imprisonment or murder of whites and Negroes. The white person's importance to the movement in the South was thus an ironic outgrowth of racism and was therefore bound to create resentment.

But again: however understandable all this may be as a response to objective conditions and to the seeming irrelevance of so many hard-won victories to the day-to-day life of the mass of Negroes, the fact remains that the quasi-nationalist sentiments and no-win policy lying behind the slogan of "black power" do no service to the Negro. Some nationalist emotion is, of course, inevitable, and black power must be seen as part of the psychological rejection of white supremacy, part of the rebellion against the stereotypes which have been ascribed to Negroes for three hundred years. Nevertheless, pride, confidence, and a new identity cannot be won by glorifying blackness or attacking whites; they can only come from meaningful action, from good jobs, and from real victories such as were achieved on the streets of Montgomery, Birmingham, and Selma. When SNCC and CORE went into the South, they awakened the country, but now they emerge isolated and demoralized, shouting a slogan that may afford a momentary satisfaction but that is calculated to destroy them and their movement. Already their frustrated call is being answered with counterdemands for law and order and with opposition to police review boards. Already they have diverted the entire civil rights movement from the hard task of developing strategies to realign the major parties of this country, and embroiled it in a debate that can only lead more and more to politics by frustration.

On the other side, however—the more important side, let it be said—it is the business of those who reject the negative aspects of black power not to preach but to act. Some weeks ago President Johnson, speaking at Fort Campbell, Kentucky, asserted that riots impeded reform, created fear, and antagonized the Negro's traditional friends. Mr. Johnson, according to the *New York Times,* expressed sympathy for the plight of the poor, the jobless, and the ill housed. The government, he noted, has been working to relieve their circumstances, but "all this takes time."

One cannot argue with the President's position that riots are destructive or that they frighten away allies. Nor can one find fault with his sympathy for the plight of the poor; surely the poor need sympathy. But one can question whether the government has been working seriously enough to eliminate the conditions which lead to frustration-politics and riots. The President's very words, "all this takes time," will be understood by the poor for precisely what they are—an excuse instead of a real program, a cover-up for the failure to establish real priorities, and an indication that the administration has no real commitment to create new jobs, better housing, and integrated schools.

For the truth is that it need take only ten years to eliminate poverty—ten years and the $100 billion Freedom Budget recently proposed by A. Philip Randolph. (pp. 160-63)

Today, with the spiraling thrust of automation, it is even more imperative that we have a legally binding commitment to [the goal of fair and full employment].

Let me interject a word here for those who say that Negroes are asking for another handout and are refusing to help themselves. From the end of the nineteenth century up to the last generation, the United States absorbed and provided economic opportunity for tens of millions of immigrants. These people were usually uneducated and a good many could not speak English. They had nothing but hard work to offer and they labored long hours, often in miserable sweatshops and unsafe mines. Yet in a burgeoning economy with a need for unskilled labor, they were able to find jobs, and as industrialization proceeded, they were gradually able to move up the ladder to greater skills. Negroes who have been driven off the farm into a city life for which they are not prepared, and who have entered an economy in which there is less and less need for unskilled labor, cannot be compared with these immigrants of old. The tenements which were jammed by newcomers were way stations of hope; the ghettos of today have become dead ends of despair. Yet just as the older generation of immigrants—in its most decisive act of self-help—organized the trade union movement and then in alliance with many middle-class elements went on to improve its own lot and the condition of American society generally, so the Negro of today is struggling to go beyond the gains of the past and, in alliance with liberals and labor, to guarantee full and fair employment to all Americans.

We must see, therefore, in the current debate over black power, a fantastic challenge to American society to live up to its proclaimed principles in the area of race by transforming itself so that all men may live equally and under justice. We must see to it that in rejecting black power we do not also reject the principle of Negro equality. Those people who would use the current debate and/or the riots to abandon the civil rights movement leave us no choice but to question their original motivation.

If anything, the next period will be more serious and difficult than the preceding ones. It takes very little imagination to understand that the Negro should have the right to vote, but much creativity, patience, and political stamina are demanded to plan, develop, and implement programs and priorities. It is one thing to organize sentiment behind laws that do not disturb consensus politics, and quite another to win battles for the. redistribution of wealth. Many people who marched in Selma are not prepared to support a bill for a two-dollar minimum wage, to say nothing of supporting a redefinition of work or a guaranteed annual income.

It is here that we who advocate coalitions and integration and who object to the black-power concept have a massive job to do. We must see that the liberal-labor-civil rights coalition is maintained and indeed strengthened, so that it can fight effectively for a Freedom Budget. We are responsible for the growth of the black-power concept because we have not used our own power to ensure the full implementation of the bills whose passage we were strong enough to win, and we have not mounted the necessary campaign for winning a decent minimum wage and extended benefits. "Black power" is a slogan directed primarily against liberals by those who once counted liberals among their closest friends. It is up to the liberal movement to prove that coalition and integration are better alternatives. (pp. 163-65)

Bayard Rustin, in his Down the Line: The Collected Writings of Bayard Rustin *(copyright © 1971 by Bayard Rustin; reprinted by permission of Times Books, a Division of Quadrangle/The New York Times Book Co., Inc.), Quadrangle Books, 1971, 355 p.*

THOMAS R. BROOKS

Down the Line opens with a simple account of an incident that took place in the summer of 1942. Refusing to go to the back of the Louisville-Nashville bus, Rustin informed an angry, frustrated driver, "If I were to sit in back I would be condoning injustice." Beaten and arrested, he responded to Jim Crow with a lesson in nonviolence. It ended, he recalls, with the assistant district attorney of Nashville saying, "very kindly, 'You may go, *Mister* Rustin.'"

In subsequent chapters, he describes the theory of nonviolence, indicates the conditions for its success, and evokes what the Quakers call "witness." Robert Penn Warren once noted that Rustin's appearance is "a strange mixture of strength and sensitivity." Both qualities are present in his prose, which is lean, sinewy, spare as his lanky frame, yet grows in complexity as his ideas and tactics become increasingly concerned with the difficulties of mass action, the uses of the ballot and the necessity for coalition politics. His book reflects a journey from individual affirmation to collective effort, infused all the way with moral purpose.

"I reject the idea of working for the Negro as being impractical and immoral," Rustin said in 1965, "if one does that alone." But much earlier he and his pacifist colleagues had begun teaching brotherhood and nonviolence by their actions as well as their words . . . knocking down segregated interstate travel.

This approach reached its climax in the 1963 March on Washington.

Later in the '60s, when the focus shifted "from protest to politics," as Rustin puts it in the pivotal essay of the book and of his career, he insisted that the country could settle for no less "than the radical refashioning of our political economy." (p. 17)

Rustin vigorously opposed the trend toward black separatism. A handful of blacks may integrate a lunch counter or even force the hiring of black workers at construction sites *if there are jobs,* he argued, but they cannot independently create jobs, tear down our slums or rebuild our cities; that requires political power. . . .

First advanced in 1964—before Watts, Newark, Detroit and all the other riots and confrontations of the years since—this argument holds with even greater force today. . . .

I regret that his book lacks a summation, a reflective, analytical explanation of the direction his life—the most political of journeys—has taken. His early compulsion to witness sits uneasily with his later assumption of the imperatives of the class struggle. Rustin clearly has resolved any conflict in his own mind. It would be valuable to have him tell us how he has done so in his own words. (p. 18)

> *Thomas R. Brooks, "Record of a Pacifist's Progress," in* The New Leader (© *1971 by the American Labor Conference on International Affairs, Inc.), Vol. LIV, No. 23, November 29, 1971, pp. 17-18.*

DAN LACY

[*Down the Line* records] the wisdom and maturity of a man who has been able to harness both love and anger with a steady and clear-eyed realism. Rustin may well emerge as the most creative and constructive of the black leaders of our generation. These essays, often written in haste and to deal with immediate problems, still manage to capture the essential qualities of a great man. (p. 212)

> *Dan Lacy, "Reflections on Being Black in America," in* Commonweal (copyright © *1972 Commonweal Publishing Co., Inc.; reprinted by permission of Commonweal Publishing Co., Inc.), Vol. XCVII, No. 9, December 1, 1972, pp. 211-12.*

THE NEW YORKER

[In *Strategies for Freedom*] Bayard Rustin reviews the black struggle of this century and argues for the principles of integration, nonviolence, and coalition politics. He is convinced that his race has generally suffered when it has followed the call of separatism, and that only a concern for both the class and the racial bases of inequality can produce long-lasting effects. His principles place him at odds with other spokesmen for his race, but he pleads his case lucidly. . . .

> *"Briefly Noted: 'Strategies for Freedom: The Changing Patterns of Black Protest'," in* The New Yorker (©*1976 by The New Yorker Magazine, Inc.), Vol. LII, No. 18, June 21, 1976, p. 120.*

ROBERT L. ZANGRANDO

[*Strategies for Freedom*] contains three or four factual errors, mostly incorrect date citations in the overview of historical events. Examining **"The Early Years"** (1900 to 1950), **"The Protest Era"** (1950 to the mid-1960s), and an **"Agenda for the Future"** (post 1965) in abbreviated but provocative fashion, [Rustin] asserts that justice for black people in America must spring from programs dedicated simultaneously to integration, nonviolence, and coalition politics. (p. 141)

Rustin correctly argues that the civil rights movement failed to shift sufficiently from legal to economic issues in the mid-1960s, but he offers no convincing explanations. Indeed, his most promising points are frequently underplayed and too little developed. Although employing each theme, he provides no definition of the New Left, no discriminating identification of those who strayed from nonviolence, and no explication of the hazards of relying upon political power brokers and their business allies. Opportunities to enlighten and rally his readers fade before allusive and occasionally misleading generalizations. Unfortunately for Rustin, when such assertions fail to bear the full weight of historical analysis they may actually jeopardize prospects for the widely structured coalitions he advocates. (pp. 141-42)

> *Robert L. Zangrando, "Book Reviews: 'Strategies for Freedom'," in* The Journal of Southern History (copyright © *1977 by the Southern Historical Association), Vol. XLIII, No. 1, February, 1977, pp. 141-42.*

JOSEPH ELIOT PATTISON

[The subtle economic and political realities which lay at the root of black problems, and the tactics required to overcome them, form the heart of *Strategies for Freedom.*] Writing authoritatively as a participant in the major civil rights struggles of the last half-century, Rustin's sensitivity to these realities and his commitment to their downfall lends a moral and intellectual vitality to this [book]; . . . indeed, between the lines of this concise, well-formed historical commentary lies also the deep moral fiber and concern with humanity which so clearly characterizes the national Social Democrats chairman. Rustin is able to cast refreshing vigor into the phenomenon of being at once black and American.

Rustin identifies three primary beliefs which led his movement to success, ultimately firing the nation's conscience: a realization that racial progress could only be achieved "in an integrated framework", a commitment to nonviolent programs, and a belief that broad changes necessitated "coalition politics." (p. 109)

Why did the nation blind itself to the lynchings of 1927 and yet respond so emphatically to the protests of the Sixties? Rustin finds one answer in the qualitative difference between the kinds of violence practiced in these decades. The bombing of Dr. King's home and murder of civil rights workers "was no longer just mob violence; it had become political terrorism," a terrorism which could not be condoned by American society. Another reason, says the Notre Dame board of directors' member, was the influence of television, which brought glimpses of bombed churches and howling mobs into every home. Without the television cameras, Martin Luther King would never have become a national spokesman, Rustin maintains, of black Americans.

Strategies for Freedom is a valuable book. Although it occasionally suffers from sweeping unsubstantiated criticisms or demands stemming from Mr. Rustin's socialist persuasions, ultimately it is a provoking historical analysis which lends color and depth to the civil rights struggle. While it acts as an affirmative documentary to the credo of nonviolent racial equality it is in a larger sense a testament to that marvelous phenomenon, constructive and peaceful social change. (p. 110)

Joseph Eliot Pattison, "Book Reviews: 'Strategies for Freedom: The Changing Patterns of Black Protest'," in American Notes and Queries, *Vol. XV, No. 7, March, 1977, pp. 109-10.*

P. M. WILLIAMS

[In *Strategies for Freedom* Bayard Rustin] provides a capsule history of the Civil Rights Movement and its twentieth-century forerunners; gives a sophisticated analysis of the strategic adaptations required, but not always met, when the target changed from legal discrimination in the South to economic deprivation in the North; and pleads eloquently for the old fundamentals—non-violence, integration, mass protest, alliance with white sympathizers—against the revival of black supremacy and revolutionary rhetoric in the last decade. Rustin . . . argues that today's problems imply conflict over bigger social and economic changes which blacks alone cannot hope to achieve. He hits many nails on the head, particularly in his richly deserved criticism of President Eisenhower, and in his justified (though to some no doubt surprising) tribute to the labor unions as the blacks' most reliable ally. Unkindly, he also suggests that it was when they found the going becoming too hard that the New Left deserted the cause for more fashionable novel issues.

P. M. Williams, "Comparative Politics: 'Strategies for Freedom: The Changing Patterns of Black Protest'," in Political Studies *(© Oxford University Press 1978), Vol. XXVI, No. 2, June, 1978, p. 282.*

Phyllis Schlafly

1924-

Schlafly is an American conservative social activist, politician, and writer on social and political issues. She is best known as the leader of the movement to prevent passage of the Equal Rights Amendment. Through her speeches and writings, and as chairman of the national organization Stop ERA, Schlafly has consolidated anti-ERA forces and is in large part credited with the almost-certain defeat of the amendment. Her first book, *A Choice Not an Echo* (1964), an attack on moderate Republicans, gained her national attention and is credited with helping Barry Goldwater win the 1964 presidential nomination of the Republican party. In *The Power of the Positive Woman* (1977) she argues for a traditional view of womanhood and against feminism and the ERA which, she contends, are undermining the family and the privileged position of women in American society. (See also *Contemporary Authors*, Vols. 25-28, rev. ed., and *Authors in the News,* Vol. 1.)

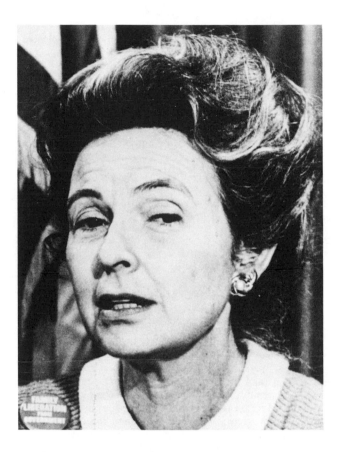

Wide World Photos

Excerpt from *THE POWER OF THE POSITIVE WOMAN*

The first requirement for the acquisition of power by the Positive Woman is to understand the differences between men and women. Your outlook on life, your faith, your behavior, your potential for fulfillment, all are determined by the parameters of your original premise. The Positive Woman starts with the assumption that the world is her oyster. She rejoices in the creative capability within her body and the power potential of her mind and spirit. She understands that men and women are different, and that those very differences provide the key to her success as a person and fulfillment as a woman.

The women's liberationist, on the other hand, is imprisoned by her own negative view of herself and of her place in the world around her. This view of women was most succinctly expressed in an advertisement designed by the principal women's liberationist organization, the National Organization for Women (NOW), and run in many magazines and newspapers and as spot announcements on many television stations. The advertisement showed a darling curlyheaded girl with the caption: "This healthy, normal baby has a handicap. She was born female."

This is the self-articulated dog-in-the-manger, chip-on-the-shoulder, fundamental dogma of the women's liberation movement. Someone—it is not clear who, perhaps God, perhaps the "Establishment," perhaps a conspiracy of male chauvinist pigs—dealt women a foul blow by making them female. It becomes necessary, therefore, for women to agitate and demonstrate and hurl demands on society in order to wrest from an oppressive male-dominated social structure the status that has been wrongfully denied to women through the centuries.

By its very nature, therefore, the women's liberation movement precipitates a series of conflict situations—in the legislatures, in the courts, in the schools, in industry—with man targeted as the enemy. Confrontation replaces cooperation as the watchword of all relationships. Women and men become adversaries instead of partners.

The second dogma of the women's liberationists is that, of all the injustices perpetrated upon women through the centuries, the most oppressive is the cruel fact that women have babies and men do not. Within the confines of the women's liberationist ideology, therefore, the abolition of this overriding inequality of women becomes the primary goal. This goal must be achieved at any and all costs—to the woman herself, to the baby, to the family, and to society. Women must be made equal to men in their ability *not* to become pregnant and *not* to be expected to care for babies they may bring into the world.

This is why women's liberationists are compulsively involved in the drive to make abortion and child-care centers for all women, regardless of religion or income, both socially acceptable and government-financed. Former Congresswoman Bella Abzug has defined the goal: "to enforce the constitutional right of females to terminate pregnancies that they do not wish to continue."

If man is targeted as the enemy, and the ultimate goal of women's liberation is independence from men and the avoidance of pregnancy and its consequences, then lesbianism is logically the highest form in the ritual of women's liberation. Many, such as Kate Millett, come to this conclusion, although many others do not.

The Positive Woman will never travel that dead-end road. It is self-evident to the Positive Woman that the female body with its baby-producing organs was not designed by a conspiracy of men but by the Divine Architect of the human race. Those who think it is unfair that women have babies, whereas men cannot, will have to take up their complaint with God because no other power is capable of changing that fundamental fact. On some college campuses, I have been assured that other methods of reproduction will be developed. But most of us must deal with the real world rather than with the imagination of dreamers.

Another feature of the woman's natural role is the obvious fact that women can breast-feed babies and men cannot. This functional role was not imposed by conspiratorial males seeking to burden women with confining chores, but must be recognized as part of the plan of the Divine Architect for the survival of the human race through the centuries and in the countries that know no pasteurization of milk or sterilization of bottles.

The Positive Woman looks upon her femaleness and her fertility as part of her purpose, her potential, and her power. She rejoices that she has a capability for creativity that men can never have.

The third basic dogma of the women's liberation movement is that there is no difference between male and female except the sex organs, and that all those physical, cognitive, and emotional differences you *think* are there, are merely the result of centuries of restraints imposed by a male-dominated society and sex-stereotyped schooling. The role imposed on women is, by definition, inferior, according to the women's liberationists.

The Positive Woman knows that, while there are some physical, competitions in which women are better (and can command more money) than men, including those that put a premium on grace and beauty, such as figure skating, the superior physical strength of males over females in competitions of strength, speed, and short-term endurance is beyond rational dispute. (pp. 11-13)

If sex equality were enforced in professional sports, it would mean that men could enter the women's tournaments and win most of the money. Bobby Riggs has already threatened: "I think that men 55 years and over should be allowed to play women's tournaments—like the Virginia Slims. Everybody ought to know there's no sex after 55 anyway."

The Positive Woman remembers the essential validity of the old prayer: "Lord, give me the strength to change what I can change, the serenity to accept what I cannot change, and the wisdom to discern the difference." The women's liberationists are expending their time and energies erecting a make-believe world in which they hypothesize that *if* schooling were gender-free, and *if* the same money were spent on male and female sports programs, and *if* women were permitted to compete on equal terms, *then* they would prove themselves to be physically equal. Meanwhile, the Positive Woman has put the ineradicable physical differences into her mental computer, programmed her plan of action, and is already on the way to personal achievement. (p. 14)

Despite the claims of the women's liberation movement, there are countless physical differences between men and women. The female body is 50 to 60 percent water, the male 60 to 70 percent water, which explains why males can dilute alcohol better than women and delay its effect. The average woman is about 25 percent fatty tissue, while the male is 15 percent, making women more buoyant in water and able to swim with less effort. Males have a tendency to color blindness. Only 5 percent of persons who get gout are female. Boys are born bigger. Women live longer in most countries of the world, not only in the United States where we have a hard-driving competitive pace. Women excel in manual dexterity, verbal skills, and memory recall. (p. 15)

Does the physical advantage of men doom women to a life of servility and subservience? The Positive Woman knows that she has a complementary advantage which is at least as great—and, in the hands of a skillful woman, far greater. The Divine Architect who gave men a superior strength to lift weights also gave women a different kind of superior strength.

The women's liberationists and their dupes who try to tell each other that the sexual drive of men and women is really the same, and that it is only societal restraints that inhibit women from an equal desire, an equal enjoyment, and an equal freedom from the consequences, are doomed to frustration forever. It just isn't so, and pretending cannot make it so. The differences are not a woman's weakness but her strength. (pp. 15-16)

The new generation can brag all it wants about the new liberation of the new morality, but it is still the woman who is hurt the most. The new morality isn't just a "fad"—it is a cheat and a thief. It robs the woman of her virtue, her youth, her beauty, and her love—for nothing, just nothing. It has produced a generation of young women searching for their identity, bored with sexual freedom, and despondent from the loneliness of living a life without commitment. They have abandoned the old commandments, but they can't find any new rules that work.

The Positive Woman recognizes the fact that, when it comes to sex, women are simply not the equal of men. The sexual drive of men is much stronger than that of women. That is how the human race was designed in order that it might perpetuate itself. The other side of the coin is that it is easier for women to control their sexual appetites. A Positive Woman cannot defeat a man in a wrestling or boxing match, but she can motivate him, inspire him, encourage him, teach him, restrain him, reward him, and have power over him that he can never achieve over her with all his muscle. How or whether a Positive Woman uses her power is determined solely by the way she alone defines her goals and develops her skills.

The differences between men and women are also emotional and psychological. Without woman's innate maternal instinct, the human race would have died out centuries ago. There is nothing so helpless in all earthy life as the newborn infant. It will die within hours if not cared for. Even in the most primitive, uneducated societies, women have always cared for their newborn babies. They didn't need any schooling to teach them how. They didn't need any welfare workers to tell them it is their social obligation. Even in societies to whom such concepts as "ought," "social responsibility," and "compassion for the helpless" were unknown, mothers cared for their new babies.

Why? Because caring for a baby serves the natural maternal need of a woman. Although not nearly so total as the baby's need, the woman's need is nonetheless real.

The overriding psychological need of a woman is to love something alive. A baby fulfills this need in the lives of most women. If a baby is not available to fill that need, women search for a baby-substitute. This is the reason why women have traditionally gone into teaching and nursing careers. They are doing what comes naturally to the female psyche. The schoolchild or the patient of any age provides an outlet for a woman to express her natural maternal need.

This maternal need in women is the reason why mothers whose children have grown up and flown from the nest are sometimes cut loose from their psychological moorings. The maternal need in women can show itself in love for grandchildren, nieces, nephews, or even neighbors' children. The maternal need in some women has even manifested itself in an extraordinary affection lavished on a dog, cat, or a parakeet.

This is not to say that every woman must have a baby in order to be fulfilled. But it is to say that fulfillment for most women involves expressing their natural maternal urge by loving and caring for someone.

The women's liberation movement complains that traditional stereotyped roles assume that women are "passive" and that men are "aggressive." The anomaly is that a woman's most fundamental emotional need is not passive at all, but active. A woman naturally seeks to love affirmatively and to show that love in an active way by caring for the object of her affections.

The Positive Woman finds somebody on whom she can lavish her maternal love so that it doesn't well up inside her and cause psychological frustrations. Surely no woman is so isolated by geography or insulated by spirit that she cannot find someone worthy of her maternal love. All persons, men and women, gain by sharing something of themselves with their fellow humans, but women profit most of all because it is part of their very nature.

One of the strangest quirks of women's liberationists is their complaint that societal restraints prevent men from crying in public or showing their emotions, but permit women to do so, and that therefore we should "liberate" men to enable them, too, to cry in public. The public display of fear, sorrow, anger, and irritation reveals a lack of self-discipline that should be avoided by the Positive Woman just as much as by the Positive Man. Maternal love, however, is not a weakness but a manifestation of strength and service, and it should be nurtured by the Positive Woman. (pp. 16-18)

Another silliness of the women's liberationists is their frenetic desire to force all women to accept the title *Ms* in place of *Miss* or *Mrs*. If Gloria Steinem and Betty Friedan want to call themselves *Ms* in order to conceal their marital status, their wishes should be respected.

But that doesn't satisfy the women's liberationists. They want all women to be compelled to use *Ms* whether they like it or not. The women's liberation movement has been waging a persistent campaign to browbeat the media into using *Ms* as the standard title for all women. . . .

Finally, women are different from men in dealing with the fundamentals of life itself. Men are philosophers, women are practical, and 'twas ever thus. Men may philosophize about how life began and where we are heading; women are concerned about feeding the kids today. No woman would ever, as Karl Marx did, spend years reading political philosophy in the British Museum while her child starved to death. Women don't take naturally to a search for the intangible and the abstract. The Positive Woman knows who she is and where she is going, and she will reach her goal because the longest journey starts with a very practical first step. (p. 19)

Where man is discursive, logical, abstract, or philosophical, woman tends to be emotional, personal, practical, or mystical. Each set of qualities is vital and complements the other. (p. 20)

An effort to eliminate the differences by social engineering or legislative or constitutional tinkering cannot succeed, which is fortunate, but social relationships and spiritual values can be ruptured in the attempt. Thus the role reversals being forced upon high school students, under which guidance counselors urge reluctant girls to take "shop" and boys to take "home economics," further confuse a generation already unsure about its identity. They are as wrong as efforts to make a left-handed child right-handed. (p. 21)

> *Phyllis Schlafly, in her* The Power of the Positive Woman *(copyright © 1977 by Phyllis Schlafly; reprinted by permission of Arlington House Publishers), Arlington House, 1977, 225 p.*

W. F. RICKENBACKER

Although [Phyllis Schlafly's and Chester Ward's *The Gravediggers*] was prepared for use in the recent election, it is far more than a political squib. The résumés of the programmed ebb of American military force around the world and of the simplistic extremism of McNamara's strategic planning are the most concise I've seen. The point is, of course, that Khrushchev was confident he would "bury" us only because he understood the essentially suicidal significance of the Liberal ideology of the West; and for every theorist who digs ideologies by the shovel, there's a drone who uses his shovel for drone's work—in this case, digging his, and our, grave. They, the Liberals, the appeasers, are our gravediggers. Against a shelf of books on the psychological, historical, and political "realities," it is well to have a volume or two like this one, dealing with the hard facts and remorseless logic of military weaponry. Despite the gratuitous mention of "Bilderbergers" and "New York financial interests," whose presence adds nothing to an already powerful argument, the book deserves the currency it has gained.

> *W. F. Rickenbacker, "Books in Brief: 'The Gravediggers',"* in National Review *(© National Review, Inc., 1965; 150 East 35th St., New York, NY 10016), Vol. XVII, No. 4, January 26, 1965, p. 73.*

CHOICE

[*Kissinger on the Couch*] is the major attack thus far from [Henry Kissinger's] enemies on the right. The title implies a psychobiography by trained psychiatrists. Not quite. . . . The flavor is well suggested by the 48 itemized slurs and loaded questions on the back dustjacket, including: "Young Kissinger goes to Harvard—turns left. . . . Did Kissinger purposely deceive the President? . . . The oil crisis: Henry's baby?" Just about the only arrow typically aimed by rightwingers at their enemies which is not here thrown at K is an allegation that he is part of "the international Jewish conspiracy." But the book contains some useful items. Most serious students of American diplomacy will want to use this book as a checklist of virtually all conceivable criticisms—the legitimate along with the phony— which can be leveled at Dr. K.

"Political Science: 'Kissinger on the Couch'," in Choice *(copyright © 1975 by American Library Association), Vol. 12, No. 3, May, 1975, p. 451.*

JOHN R. COYNE, JR.

[By] pulling together nearly every cogent criticism ever made of our defense posture, *Kissinger on the Couch* will provide an invaluable supply of ammunition for anyone who in the '76 campaign decides to take on the Administration's discredited concept of detente, should Gerald Ford continue to try to defend it.

Unfortunately, the book also has serious flaws. It is too long, too repetitious, its tone and therefore its effectiveness flawed by polemical overkill. Kissinger, the villain of the piece, is variously depicted as a loon, a coward, a Svengali, a liar, and a traitor whose policies "constitute a sellout of the United States to the Communist Party of the Soviet Union."

But *why* the sellout? And here the going gets sticky. Embarrassing pop-psychology aside, the Schlafly-Ward thesis seems to be that Kissinger is a sort of Manchurian Candidate, planted in government by Pugwashers and members of the Council on Foreign Relations. He totally subscribes, say the authors, to the CFR one-world, better-Red-than-dead philosophy, and believes that since the Russians won't make concessions to us, we must surrender to them in order to bring about world peace. Kissinger, in short, is the willing tool of conspirators bent upon disarming us unilaterally.

Perhaps. Admiral Ward is, after all, a CFR member, and therefore must know what they're up to. And it's no longer quite so fashionable to sneer at conspiracies.

But the problem is that the Pugwash-CFR conspiracy theory explanation is simply not necessary here. It will, of course, be received joyously by already-converted members of the old hard Right. But it will also undercut the book's persuasiveness among those who are made uneasy by such theories. And that's a shame, for the factual material in *Kissinger on the Couch*—really, Kissinger's *policies* on the couch—should be widely aired and nationally debated before we strike further imperfectly explained SALT bargains with the Soviets. But because *Kissinger on the Couch* is guilty of personal and ideological overkill, this is unlikely to happen.

I can't, of course, refute the Schlafly-Ward thesis. There may be a carefully managed conspiracy to make us relinquish our national sovereignty. For that matter, Satan may be alive and living in Zurich, conspiring there to buy up our souls at bargain rates. But I don't quite think so. And I can't quite buy the Schlafly-Ward CFR thesis, given the lack of hard evidence presented here. There is another explanation for Kissinger's policies that might strike the unconverted as more plausible. (p. 624)

Conspirator? I don't think so. More likely, a brilliant academic possessed of a driving ego, determined to validate an unworkable abstract academic blueprint for peace on earth. (p. 625)

John R. Coyne, Jr., "Overkilling Kissinger," in National Review *(© National Review, Inc., 1975; 150 East 35th St., New York, NY 10016), Vol. XXVII, No. 24, June 6, 1975, pp. 624-25.*

A. JAMES McADAMS

Gerald Ford was ambushed at Vladivostok. This, at least, is the conclusion of Phyllis Schlafly and Chester Ward, who argue in [*Ambush at Vladivostok*] that the 1974 SALT II accords marked yet another dismal passage in the history of American strategic emasculation. "Ambush" is indeed a reasonable choice of terms for, as the authors demonstrate, the President was taken by surprise and out-maneuvered in the fast-paced talks which constituted the treaty conference. (p. 109)

According to Schlafly and Ward, Kissinger is to be held principally responsible for the Vladivostok debacle; he knew about the nature of the conference beforehand, and he consciously led Ford into the ambush. SALT II, the authors insist was but another manifestation of the Secretary's "sick" and "defeatist" foreign policy through which he has "*deliberately* brought the United States down from a position of overwhelming power to the brink of strategic surrender." As key evidence for this controversial contention, the authors cite a statement which Kissinger supposedly made to Admiral Zumwalt—"The day of the United States is past and today is the day of the Soviet Union. My job as Secretary of State is to negotiate the most acceptable second best position available"—a statement which Kissinger denies that he ever made. In their attempt to impute next to treasonous actions to the Secretary, the authors go to great lengths to prove that the statement was made and cite speculative psychological evidence to suggest its probability. Yet, as far as this reviewer can discern, their case remains unfortunately problematic, for they fail to provide specific motivations on Kissinger's part under which his policies can be construed as acts of "deliberate surrender" rather than as simple (perhaps egregious) errors in judgment. Nevertheless, it is quite easy to agree with Schlafly and Ward that Kissinger's actions, the pessimism underlying his foreign policy and his passion for "preemptive concessions," attest to qualities which make him eminently unqualified for the management of American strategic diplomacy. (pp. 109-10)

According to Schlafly and Ward, Ford could make [the astonishing statement that SALT II had maintained an "essential equivalence" in strategic arms] because he sincerely, albeit naïvely, believed that SALT II limited the number of MIRV warheads allowed to both sides. As the authors are quick to demur, the agreement actually limited only the number of missiles on which MIRVs could be mounted. Under the agreement Ford thought he signed, the Soviets would have been allowed to MIRV only 165 of their missiles, whereas under the *real* agreement, they were guaranteed 1320 missiles with multiple warheads. Yet, and this is the irony of Ford's quest for "equality," even if MIRVs had been limited, the Soviet's overwhelming superiority in terms of nuclear throw weight (app. 3 megatons per Soviet SS-18 vs. app. 170 kilotons per U.S. Minuteman III) would have given them 3960 megatons of explosive power to counter a puny American assault of 222.4 megatons.

These are *prima facie* staggering figures, but what do they really mean? According to Schlafly and Ward, they imply that the U.S. is at "the brink of strategic surrender," that we would be powerless to counter any possible Soviet initiative. One wonders, however, whether American strategic capability has been as thoroughly weakened as the authors appear to believe. Wars may be fought partly in terms of throw weight and megatonnage, but not solely in those terms. There are other factors involved—weapons technology, missile accuracy and kill ratios, missile and deployment obsolescence, geographical distribution of weapons—and until these are considered in concert, it is quite difficult to determine who would win the next war, were such a confrontation to arise.

This is not to say that the central thrust of Schlafly's and Ward's account is in any way misconceived. To the contrary, their book is important and valuable because it exposes the current American policy trend—its concessionism and its unrealistic trust in Soviet good will—as courting calamity. (p. 110)

> *A. James McAdams, "A Far Eastern Ambuscade," in* Modern Age *(copyright © 1977 by the Intercollegiate Studies Institute, Inc.), Vol. 21, No. 1, Winter, 1977, pp. 109-10.*

MORTON KONDRACKE

Most of Schlafly's major arguments against ERA are outrageous fabrications, but they are so artful and so brazenly repeated that Schlafly has put ERA proponents on the defensive in state after state. ERA will legalize homosexual marriages and permit gays to adopt children, Schlafly charges, when it is obvious that ERA simply will require the law to discriminate against lesbians and male homosexuals equally. Congressional sponsors of ERA made it clear six years ago that ERA would not supersede rights of privacy, but Schlafly is still convincing people that the amendment means unisex toilets in public buildings and co-ed college dormitories, prison cellblocks, military barracks and gymnasium dressing rooms. Schlafly also persists in scaring housewives with the prospect that they will lose legal rights to support during marriage, alimony after divorce and death benefits in case of widowhood. In fact, the legislative history of ERA firmly establishes the principle that, where laws bestow desirable benefits and protections, they would simply have to be extended to both sexes on an equal basis.

Not all of Schlafly's arguments are totally groundless. Sports teams in public schools might have to be co-educational, probably to the detriment of girls' basketball and the complication of tackle football. Men and women would be equally subject to the draft if it were reinstituted, and some males in a combat unit surely would sue if women were being exposed to less risk in military assignments than men. But Schlafly has not come so close to beating the Equal Rights Amendment merely by winning debating points. She has clearly tapped elemental currents of resentment, fear and anger running beneath the surface of American society. (p. 14)

Schlafly's anti-ERA movement is based on the notion that the traditional homebody role for women is rightful, ordained by God and part of the natural order of things, and that ERA somehow will undermine it. In fact, it seems long since undermined, without ERA, by the free enterprise system that Schlafly and other anti-ERA militants also espouse. Only 34 percent of two-adult families in the United States now observe the classic husband-breadwinner, wife-homemaker pattern that prevailed in the country until the 1950s. Though she is hardly one of them, Schlafly represents the stay-at-homes who look at women's liberation and the working lifestyle as a threat and a rebuke. The old rules decreed that women got married and had babies, and millions of women dutifully followed the pattern. Now the rules are suddenly being changed, and these women are being told they have wasted their lives. They won't sit for it. They are taking it out on ERA, and Schlafly is leading the way. (p. 15)

> *Morton Kondracke, "End of an ERA?" in* The New Republic *(reprinted by permission of* The New Re-

public; © *1977 The New Republic, Inc.), Vol. 176, No. 18, April 30, 1977, pp. 14-16.*

REV. JOSEPH P. SANDERS, S.J.

[*The Power of the Positive Woman*] is an interesting, although somewhat predictable, piece of writing if for no other reason than that, under the guise of describing the characteristics of "The Positive Woman," Phyllis Schlafly describes herself. Thus she is also describing the personality roots of that power which has helped to bring about the present situation in which [passage of the Equal Rights Amendment is in jeopardy]. . . .

It seems a shame that a book which advances some solid arguments against the adoption of the ERA . . . should so often use intemperate language against those whom Schlafly sees as the ERA's main proponents, the members of the women's liberation movement. . . .

In my judgment this book is overly ambitious. It would have been much improved if it had totally omitted the characteristics of the Positive Woman, which at times are over-generalized, and even naive. Instead it should have presented the arguments against the ERA as a more calm refutation of the women's liberation movement's arguments on behalf of the amendment.

Despite these reservations, however, the book is certainly worth reading since it not only helps to understand the substance of the opposition to ERA, but also shows us what makes Phyllis Schlafly tick.

> *Rev. Joseph P. Sanders, S.J., "Women: 'The Power of the Positive Woman'," in* Best Sellers *(copyright © 1977 Helen Dwight Reid Educational Foundation), Vol. 37, No. 7, October, 1977, p. 223.*

JENNIFER DUNNING

[In "**The Power of the Positive Woman**" Phyllis Schlafly] deals with issues raised by the "femlib fanatics," among them the role of women in the home and business worlds and the effects, as she sees them, of the Equal Rights Amendment, the passage of which she helped to defeat in 20 states as a leading spokesman for the conservative viewpoint. Less conservative thinkers than she have entertained doubts over some of those issues, chief among them perhaps the implications of affirmative action programs determined by gender and race.

The reader is spared one or two standard red herrings like the presumed post-E.R.A. enforced use of unisex toilets. And Mrs. Schlafly raises some provocative questions.

But the book is a perfect example of the game of quoting in-house statistics and authorities, though it is not confined to the author's end of the political spectrum. Her silly notion that obscenity is part of the "every-day language of the women's lib movement" and her horror that one Federal regulation may keep colleges from "refusing to admit prostitutes, homosexuals and lesbians" do Mrs. Schlafly's cause no good. Neither do unsubstantiated and snide attacks on the motivation of movement supporters, some not even named. And her pleased disclosure of the fact that Agatha Christie thought up the plots for her mysteries while washing the dishes is the stuff of the most outrageous feminist satire.

This is a book for the confirmed "positive woman." But she presumably does not need it. The "libber" will pass it by.

And Mrs. Schlafly's smug self-approval and lack of charity are likely to alienate the rest of the population.

Jennifer Dunning, "Books: Unequal Rights Advocate," in The New York Times *(© 1977 by The New York Times Company; reprinted by permission), October 14, 1977, p. C25.*

LUCINDA FRANKS

[*The Power of the Positive Woman*] is a strange little book. It would probably merit scant attention were it not for the fact that Mrs. Schlafly has succeeded, to the consternation of the women's rights movement, in galvanizing thousands of housewives to lobby against the Equal Rights Amendment. . . .

Whatever the secret of Mrs. Schlafly's appeal, it certainly does not lie in the lucidity of her mind. The book, her ninth, reads like a medieval morality play in which the characters are called White Knight, Black Demon, and so on. The hero (or heroine) here is The Positive Woman. We are told what she does, what she does not do. (p. 44)

Mrs. Schlafly's main point is that women do not want equality, and in any case they have enough already. Any more would destroy the family and rend the fabric of American society, she thinks. The women's movement has tempted mature women to fly from the nest in search of some elusive identity, only to find themselves in "cold, lonely apartments" without love or money. It has driven indulgent husbands, disgusted with this display of ingratitude, to the taverns; forced neglected children to drugs and fornication; been responsible for risqué textbooks, socialized medicine and the demise of the Bible. If a woman is unfulfilled these days, she says, the best thing she can do is to stay away from women's magazines and remember that the key to being loved is to lavish admiration on her husband, to make him feel like a man. But then, Mrs. Schlafly's own choice of metaphor reveals more about her ideas than any paraphrase could: "Marriage," she says, "is like pantyhose: It is what you put into it that makes the difference." Much of the book is spent presenting arguments against the E.R.A., which she dubs the "Extra Responsibilities Amendment." She maintains that the legislation will bring more, not less discrimination against women. Women will lose the right to be full-time homemakers and enjoy the financial support of their husbands. They will lose their right to alimony and to child support. (pp. 44-5)

In fact, however, the existing laws designed to protect housewives and mothers financially are rarely enforced. Courts have been reluctant to interfere in marriages and to force negligent husbands to support their families. In divorce cases a smaller percentage of women are awarded alimony, and more judges are giving husbands alimony if the wife is earning more than her spouse. In child-support cases the payments awarded usually cover less than half the actual cost of supporting offspring, and over 60 percent of fathers ordered to pay child support pay little or nothing in the first year after divorce. Thus, the laws which Mrs. Schlafly lauds are more myth than reality.

What *is* real, however, is the fact that existing legislation barring sex discrimination is inadequate. . . .

Mrs. Schlafly's theories are overgrown with contradictions, distortion and sophistry. This is a pity, because buried beneath the thicket of her thinking is some good sense. It is true, as she says, that the E.R.A. is going to deprive women, at first anyway, of some special rights. Much protective legislation designed to regulate working conditions for women (protecting them from having to lift heavy weights and work overtime, for instance) will be put in jeopardy. E.R.A. supporters contend that protective laws designed to hold women back will perish under the amendment while those that are beneficial can, with the help of union agitation, be extended to men.

This will take time, however, and there will undoubtedly be a long period in which working women will suffer an abridgment of their existing rights. And it is true that if the draft were reinstated, the Constitution would require that women be placed in the same kind of military service as men.

Moreover, one of Mrs. Schlafly's essential points—and this is something that the women's movement is just beginning to come to grips with—happens to be indisputably true. There *are* basic emotional, physical and psychological differences between the sexes that dictate a variation in life styles. Biology may not have to be destiny, but it seems that these days women who have stepped into the traditional male role are no more fulfilled than those who have chosen a female role, while those who have combined the two most often admit that they have given their best to neither.

What is most disturbing about her book is its undertone of contempt for everyone. She is basically anti-woman; wives can only get the upper hand over their husbands with sexual favors, and any woman who gets divorced, she says, has relinquished her rights and does not deserve to be supported. And she is also anti-men. Although she stresses that men are more rational, analytical and capable than women, she paints them as primitives who would run amok if not kept within the restraining walls of the home. (p. 45)

Lucinda Franks, "How to Keep Your Man," in The New York Times Book Review *(© 1977 by The New York Times Company; reprinted by permission), October 30, 1977, pp. 44-5.*

M. STANTON EVANS

[*The Power of the Positive Woman* is] a comprehensive, cogent answer to the Steinem-Abzug liberationists. As the title suggests, the book is a clarion statement in behalf of traditional womanhood, stressing the creative, civilizing role of women, the centrality of home and family, and the profound distinctions between the male and female psyches which the radical feminists would deny.

Mrs. Schlafly attacks head-on the radical view that traditional female roles as helpmeet, mother, and homemaker are demeaning to women or the result of masculine conniving. Her reprise of the Equal Rights Amendment, as one might expect, is annihilating and, to this reader, conclusive. She provides detailed responses to all the arguments for ERA and demonstrates that it would subvert the family unit as Western society has understood it.

M. Stanton Evans, "Dark Horses," in National Review *(© National Review, Inc., 1978; 150 East 35th St., New York, NY 10016), Vol. 30, No. 5, February 3, 1978, p. 169.*

E(rnst) F(riedrich) Schumacher

1911?-1977

Schumacher was a German-born British economist who became something of a folk hero in the mid-seventies for his advocacy of small-scale technology in *Small Is Beautiful* **(1973). This book became a best seller and its "less is more" philosophy found many followers, perhaps the best known being California Governor Jerry Brown. A Christian humanist, Schumacher in his economic policy places material ends subservient to moral, humanistic ends.** *A Guide for the Perplexed* **(1977) and the posthumously published** *Good Work* **(1979) make explicit the ethical and religious basis of his thought. He was founder and director of the Intermediate Technology Development Group, which promoted the use of small-scale technology in the Third World; he also served for twenty years as economic advisor to the British Coal Board, which under his administration adopted a decentralized structure; and he was chief economic editorial writer for** *The Times* **of London. (See also** *Contemporary Authors,* **Vols. 81-84; obituary, Vols. 73-76.)**

Excerpt from *SMALL IS BEAUTIFUL: A STUDY OF ECONOMICS AS IF PEOPLE MATTERED*

The hope that the pursuit of goodness and virtue can be postponed until we have attained universal prosperity and that by the single-minded pursuit of wealth, without bothering our heads about spiritual and moral questions, we could establish peace on earth, is an unrealistic, unscientific, and irrational hope. The exclusion of wisdom from economics, science, and technology was something which we could perhaps get away with for a little while, as long as we were relatively unsuccessful; but now that we have become very successful, the problem of spiritual and moral truth moves into the central position.

From an economic point of view, the central concept of wisdom is permanence. We must study the economics of permanence. Nothing makes economic sense unless its continuance for a long time can be projected without running into absurdities. (pp. 30-1)

The economics of permanence implies a profound re-orientation of science and technology, which have to open their doors to wisdom and, in fact, have to incorporate wisdom into their very structure. Scientific or technological 'solutions' which poison the environment or degrade the social structure and man himself are of no benefit, no matter how brilliantly conceived or how great their superficial attraction. . . . Wisdom demands a new orientation of science and technology towards the organic, the gentle, the non-violent, the elegant and beautiful. . . . We must look for a revolution in technology to give us inventions and machines which reverse the destructive trends now threatening us all. (p. 31)

The neglect, indeed the rejection, of wisdom has gone so far that most of our intellectuals have not even the faintest idea what the term could mean. As a result, they always tend to try and cure a disease by intensifying its causes. The disease having been caused by allowing cleverness to displace wisdom, no amount of clever research is likely to produce a cure. But what is wisdom? Where can it be found? Here we come to the crux of the matter: it can be read about in numerous publications but it can be *found* only inside oneself. To be able to find it, one has first to liberate oneself from such masters as greed and envy. The stillness following liberation—even if only momentary—produces the insights of wisdom which are obtainable in no other way.

They enable us to see the hollowness and fundamental unsatisfactoriness of a life devoted primarily to the pursuit of material ends, to the neglect of the spiritual. Such a life necessarily sets man against man and nation against nation, because man's needs are infinite and infinitude can be achieved only in the spiritual realm, never in the material. Man assuredly needs to rise above this humdrum 'world'; wisdom shows him the way to do it. . . . (pp. 35-6)

The modern world has been shaped by its metaphysics, which has shaped its education, which in turn has brought forth its science and technology. So, without going back to metaphysics and education, we can say that the modern world has been shaped by technology. It tumbles from crisis to crisis; on all sides there are prophecies of disaster and, indeed, visible signs of breakdown.

If that which has been shaped by technology, and continues to be so shaped, looks sick, it might be wise to have a look at technology itself. If technology is felt to be becoming more and more inhuman, we might do well to consider whether it is possible to have something better—a technology with a human face.

Strange to say, technology, although of course the product of man, tends to develop by its own laws and principles, and these are very different from those of human nature or of living nature in general. Nature always, so to speak, knows where and when to stop. Greater even than the mystery of natural growth is the mystery of the natural cessation of growth. There is measure in all natural things—in their size, speed, or violence. As a result, the system of nature, of which man is a part, tends to be self-balancing, self-adjusting, self-cleansing. Not so with technology, or perhaps I should say: not so with man dominated by technology and specialisation. Technology recognises no self-limiting principle—in terms, for instance, of size, speed, or violence. It therefore does not possess the virtues of being self-balancing, self-adjusting, and self-cleansing. In the subtle system of nature, technology, and in particular the super-technology of the modern world, acts like a foreign body, and there are now numerous signs of rejection.

Suddenly, if not altogether surprisingly, the modern world, shaped by modern technology, finds itself involved in three crises simultaneously. First, human nature revolts against inhuman technological, organisational, and political patterns, which it experiences as suffocating and debilitating; second, the living environment which supports human life aches and groans and gives signs of partial breakdown; and, third, it is clear to anyone fully knowledgeable in the subject matter that the inroads being made into the world's non-renewable resources, particularly those of fossil fuels, are such that serious bottlenecks and virtual exhaustion loom ahead in the quite foreseeable future.

Any one of these three crises or illnesses can turn out to be deadly. I do not know which of the three is the most likely to be the direct cause of collapse. What is quite clear is that a way of life that bases itself on materialism, *i.e.* on permanent, limitless expansionism in a finite environment, cannot last long, and that its life expectation is the shorter the more successfully it pursues its expansionist objectives. (pp. 138-39)

The threefold crisis of which I have spoken will not go away if we simply carry on as before. It will become worse and end in disaster, until or unless we develop a new life-style which is compatible with the real needs of human nature, with the health of living nature around us, and with the resource endowment of the world. (p. 144)

It is almost like a providential blessing that we, the rich countries, have found it in our heart at least to consider the Third World and to try to mitigate its poverty. In spite of the mixture of motives and the persistence of exploitative practices, I think that this fairly recent development in the outlook of the rich is an honourable one. And it could save us; for the poverty of the poor makes it in any case impossible for them successfully to adopt our technology. Of course, they often try to do so, and then have to bear the most dire consequences in terms of mass unemployment, mass migration into cities, rural decay, and intolerable social tensions. They need, in fact, the very thing I am talking about, which we also need: a *different* kind of technology, a technology with a human face, which, instead of making human hands and brains redundant, helps them to become far more productive than they have ever been before.

As Gandhi said, the poor of the world cannot be helped by mass production, only by production by the masses. The system of *mass production,* based on sophisticated, highly capital-intensive, high energy-input dependent, and human labour-saving technology, presupposes that you are already rich, for a great deal of capital investment is needed to establish one single workplace. The system of *production by the masses* mobilises the priceless resources which are possessed by all human beings, their clever brains and skilful hands, *and supports them with first-class tools.* The technology of *mass production* is inherently violent, ecologically damaging, self-defeating in terms of non-renewable resources, and stultifying for the human person. The technology of *production by the masses,* making use of the best of modern knowledge and experience, is conducive to decentralisation, compatible with the laws of ecology, gentle in its use of scarce resources, and designed to serve the human person instead of making him the servant of machines. I have named it *intermediate technology* to signify that it is vastly superior to the primitive technology of bygone ages but at the same time much simpler, cheaper, and freer than the super-technology of the rich. One can also call it self-help technology, or democratic or people's technology—a technology to which everybody can gain admittance and which is not reserved to those already rich and powerful. (pp. 144-46)

I have no doubt that it is possible to give a new direction to technological development, a direction that shall lead it back to the real needs of man, and that also means: *to the actual size of man.* Man is small, and, therefore, small is beautiful. (p. 150)

E. F. Schumacher, in his Small Is Beautiful: A Study of Economics as if People Mattered *(copyright © 1973 by E. F. Schumacher; reprinted by permission of Harper & Row, Publishers, Inc.; in Canada by Blond & Briggs, Ltd), Harper & Row, 1973 (and reprinted by Harper Colophon Books, 1975, 290 p.).*

Excerpt from *A GUIDE FOR THE PERPLEXED*

The progressive elimination of "science for understanding"—or "wisdom"—from Western civilization turns the rapid and ever-accelerating accumulation of "knowledge for manipulation" into a most serious threat. . . . The steadily advancing concentration of man's scientific interest on "sciences of manipulation" has at least three very serious consequences.

First, in the absence of sustained study of such "unscientific" questions as "What is the meaning and purpose of man's existence?" and "What is good and what is evil?" and "What are man's absolute rights and duties?" a civilization will necessarily and inescapably sink ever more deeply into anguish, despair, and loss of freedom. Its people will suffer a steady decline in health and happiness, no matter how high may be their standard of living or how successful their "health service" in prolonging their lives. It is nothing more nor less than a matter of "Man cannot live by bread alone."

Second, the methodical restriction of scientific effort to the most external and material aspects of the Universe makes the world look so empty and meaningless that even those people who recognize the value and necessity of a "science of understanding" cannot resist the hypnotic power of the allegedly scientific picture presented to them and lose the courage as well as the inclination to consult, and profit from, the "wisdom tradition of mankind." (pp. 55-6)

Third, the higher powers of man, no longer being brought into play to produce the knowledge of wisdom, tend to atrophy and even disappear altogether. As a result, all the problems which society or individuals are called upon to tackle become insoluble. Efforts grow ever more frantic, while unsolved and seemingly insoluble problems accumulate. While wealth may continue to increase, the quality of man himself declines. (p. 56)

If we cannot achieve a real ''meeting of minds'' with the people nearest to us in our daily lives, our existence becomes an agony and a disaster. In order to achieve it, I must be able to gain knowledge of what it is like to be ''you,'' and ''you'' must be able to gain knowledge of what it is like to be me. . . . Since we know that very little knowledge comes naturally to most of us and that the acquisition of greater knowledge requires effort, we are bound to ask ourselves the question: ''What can I do to acquire greater knowledge, to become more understanding of what is going on inside the people with whom I live?''

Now, the remarkable fact is that all traditional teachings give one and the same answer to this question: ''You can understand other beings only to the extent that you know yourself.'' Naturally, close observation and careful listening are necessary; the point is that even perfect observation and perfect listening lead to nothing unless the *data* thus obtained are correctly interpreted and understood, and the precondition to my ability to understand correctly is my own self-knowledge, my own inner experience. In other words . . . : there must be *adaequatio*, item by item, bit by bit. A person who had never consciously experienced bodily pain could not possibly know anything about the pain suffered by others. The outward signs of pain—sounds, movements, a flow of tears—would of course be noticed by him, but he would be totally *inadequate* to the task of understanding them correctly. No doubt he would attempt some kind of interpretation; he might find them funny or menacing or simply incomprehensible. The *invisibilia* of the other being—in this case the inner experience of pain—would remain invisible to him. (pp. 82-3)

To be able to take the inner life of my neighbor seriously, it is necessary that I take my own inner life seriously. But what does that mean? It means that I must put myself in a condition where I can truly observe what is going on and begin to understand what I observe. In modern times there is no lack of understanding of the fact that man is a *social* being. . . . At the same time, however, the cultivation of self-knowledge has fallen into virtually total neglect, except, that is, where it is the object of active suppression. That you cannot love your neighbor unless you love yourself; that you cannot understand your neighbor unless you understand yourself; that there can be no knowledge of the ''invisible person'' who is your neighbor except on the basis of self-knowledge—these fundamental truths have been forgotten even by many of the professionals in the established religions. (p. 84)

The moment we recognize that there are two different *types* of problems with which we have to deal on our journey through life—''convergent'' and ''divergent'' problems—some very interesting questions arise in our minds:

> How can I recognize whether a problem belongs to the one type or to the other?
> What constitutes the difference?
> What constitutes the solution of a problem in each of the two types?
> Is there ''progress''? Can solutions be accumulated?

The attempt to deal with questions of this kind will undoubtedly lead to many further explorations.

Let us begin then with the question of recognition. With a convergent problem . . . , the answers suggested for its solution tend to converge, to become increasingly precise, until finally they can be written down in the form of an instruction. Once the answer has been found, the problem ceases to be interesting: A solved problem is a dead problem. (pp. 124-25)

The moment we deal with problems involving the higher Levels of Being, we must expect *divergence*, for there enters, to however modest a degree, the element of freedom and inner experience. In them we can see the most universal pair of opposites, the very hallmark of Life: growth and decay. Growth thrives on freedom (I mean healthy growth; pathological growth is really a form of decay), while the forces of decay and dissolution can be contained only through some kind of order. (p. 125)

Divergent problems cannot be killed; they cannot be solved in the sense of establishing a ''correct formula''; they can, however, be transcended. A pair of opposites—like freedom and order—are opposites at the level of ordinary life, but they cease to be opposites at the higher level, the really *human* level, where self-awareness plays its proper role. It is then that such higher forces as love and compassion, understanding and empathy, become available, not simply as occasional impulses (which they are at the lower level) but as a regular and reliable resource. (p. 126)

The pairs of opposites, of which *freedom and order* and *growth and decay* are the most basic, put tension into the world, a tension that sharpens man's sensitivity and increases his self-awareness. No real understanding is possible without awareness of these pairs of opposites which permeate everything man does. (p. 127)

Man's life can thus be seen and understood as a succession of divergent problems which must inevitably be encountered and have to be coped with in some way. They are refractory to mere logic and discursive reason, and constitute, so to speak, a strain-and-stretch apparatus to develop the Whole Man, and that means to develop man's supralogical faculties. All traditional cultures have seen life as a school and have recognized, in one way or another, the essentiality of this teaching force. (p. 128)

Many people today call for a new moral basis of society, a new foundation of ethics. When they say ''new,'' they seem to forget that they are dealing with divergent problems, which call not for new inventions but for the development of man's higher faculties and their application. (p. 131)

The first Great Truth . . . is the hierarchic structure of the World: at least four great Levels of Being, with new powers added as we move up the Chain of Being. At the human level, we can clearly perceive that it is open-ended. . . . The human being, even in full maturity, is obviously not a finished product, although some are undoubtedly more ''finished'' than others. (p. 132)

The second Great Truth is that of *adequatio*—that everything in the world around us must be matched, as it were, with some sense, faculty, or power within us; otherwise we remain unaware of its existence. There is, therefore, a hierarchic structure of gifts inside us, and, not surprisingly, the higher the gift, the more rarely is it to be found in a highly developed form, and the greater are the efforts required for its development. To enhance our Level of Being, we have to adopt a life-style conducive to such enhancement, which means one that will grant our lower nature no more attention and care than it requires and will leave us with ample free time and attention to pursue our higher development.

A central part of this pursuit is the cultivation of the Four Fields of Knowledge. The quality of our understanding depends decisively on the detachment, objectivity, and care with which we learn to study ourselves—both what goes on inside us (Field 1) and how we appear as objective phenomena in the eyes of others (Field 3). Instruction on cultivating self-knowledge of this dual kind is the main content of all traditional religious teachings but has been almost entirely lacking in the West for the last hundred years. That is why we cannot trust one another, why most people live in a state of continuous anxiety, why despite all our technologies communication becomes ever more difficult, and why we need ever more organized *welfare* to plaster over the gaping holes torn by the progressive disappearance of spontaneous social cohesion. (pp. 133-34)

The "inner world," seen as fields of knowledge (Field 1 and Field 2), is the world of freedom; the "outer world" (Field 3 and Field 4) is the world of necessity. All our serious problems of living are suspended, as it were, between these two poles of freedom and necessity. They are *divergent* problems, not for solving. Our anxiety to *solve* problems stems from our lack of self-knowledge, which has created the kind of existential anguish of which Kierkegaard is one of the early and most impressive exponents. The same anxiety to *solve* problems has led to a virtually total concentration of intellectual effort on the study of *convergent* problems. (p. 134)

While the logical mind abhors divergent problems and tries to run away from them, the higher faculties of man accept the challenges of life as they are offered, without complaint, knowing that when things are most contradictory, absurd, difficult, and frustrating, then, *just then,* life really makes sense: as a mechanism provoking and almost forcing us to develop toward higher Levels of Being. The question is one of faith, of choosing our own "grade of significance." Our ordinary mind always tries to persuade us that we are nothing but acorns and that our greatest happiness will be to become bigger, fatter, shinier acorns; but that is of interest only to pigs. (pp. 134-35)

The art of living is always to make a good thing out of a bad thing. Only if we *know* that we have actually descended into *infernal regions* where nothing awaits us but "the cold death of society and the extinguishing of all civilised relations," can we summon the courage and imagination needed for a "turning around," a *metanoia.* This then leads to seeing the world in a new light, namely, as a place where the things modern man continuously talks about and always fails to accomplish *can actually be done.* The generosity of the Earth allows us to feed all mankind; we know enough about ecology to keep the Earth a healthy place; there is enough room on the Earth, and there are enough materials, so that everybody can have adequate shelter; we are quite competent enough to produce sufficient supplies of necessities so that no one need live in misery. Above all, we shall then see that the economic problem is a convergent problem *which has been solved already:* we know how to provide *enough* and do not require any violent, inhuman, aggressive technologies to do so. There *is* no economic problem and, in a sense, there never has been. But there is a moral problem, and moral problems are not convergent, capable of being solved so that future generations can live without effort.

No, they are divergent problems, which have to be understood and transcended. (pp. 139-40)

E. F. Schumacher, in his A Guide for the Perplexed *(copyright © 1977 by E. F. Schumacher; reprinted by permission of the author's agent, C & J Wolfers Ltd),* Harper & Row, Publishers, *1977, 147 p.*

THE ECONOMIST

[Dr Schumacher's title, *Small is Beautiful: A Study of Economics as if People Mattered*], a kind of Godspell alternative to the teutonic multisyllables that adorn economics books, is refreshing but indicative. For he rambles happily over an enormous amount of ground. But the strange thing about Dr Schumacher's tour de force is that it is presented as a challenge to economists and other specialists. In fact, he does little more than pick up one aspect of the theory of comparative costs. As generations of economics students have been taught, countries will not necessarily specialise in those production fields in which they are more efficient than other countries, but more likely in those in which they are relatively the most efficient compared with the alternatives available to them.

Yet Dr Schumacher writes not only as if this were novel, but with contempt for other economists. "Virtually all experts, the captains of industry, the economic managers in the governments of the world, the academic and not-so-academic economists, not to mention the economic journalists" all agree that "the problem of production has been solved". If they actually held the views ascribed to them, they would, of course, be wrong. But Dr Schumacher ought to know better than to make such generalisations about the views and intelligence of his fellow men. Messianic books have a noble purpose; but it is not the conversion of the converted.

"One-Horse Theory," in The Economist *(© The Economist Newspaper Limited, 1973), Vol. 247, No. 6773, June 23, 1973, p. 113.*

THE TIMES LITERARY SUPPLEMENT

[Does] "The Modern World" have a workable future before it? And if so, is it a future that anybody wants?

So we take sides, as "people of the forward stampede" or as "homecomers", to use E. F. Schumacher's useful terminology; and those of us who are homecomers tend to feel rather helpless, since the politicians and the power-men and the experts all tend to be people of the forward stampede. [*Small is Beautiful*] goes some way towards a redressing of that imbalance. . . . The book has been carpentered together rather crudely, out of many self-contained articles and lectures, and it does not add up to a single progressively-reasoned argument; but as the manifold and most vigorous statement of a homecomer's philosophy, it carries weight and deserves close attention.

Much of it goes over fairly familiar ground: the environmental crisis, the energy crisis, our folly in neglecting coal in favour of soon-to-be-gone oil, our greater folly in plunging ahead with nuclear energy without first solving the insoluble problem of wastes; the dehumanization of industrial work; the flight from the countryside, the breakdown of the cities; the negativism of the humanities as currently taught, the consequent ethical vacuum, the consequent despair; the moral squalor of any society which drives itself on by avarice, greed, envy, and a contemptuous bullying of the natural environment; the need to establish a simpler, more decentralized, more permanently viable sort of life-style and economy.

About a great many such matters, Dr Schumacher has good things to say, a proportion of them already familiar from Chesterton and Tawney and *Blueprint for Survival* and other sources, but here argued with remarkable force, well supported by hard facts and figures, and stated so apothegmatically as to tempt a reviewer to immoderate quotation.

Dr Schumacher's most distinctive contribution concerns aid to the developing world. Here, he argues very cogently that we miss the point: thinking in terms too crudely economic, we offer rich men's answers to poor men's problems; this means that our "aid" only exacerbates the disease, which is one of rural decay coupled with a cancer of unviable urbanization. The solution proposed—and in Dr Schumacher's energetic practice, not merely in this book—is "Intermediate Technology": intermediate in its capital cost per work-place, available therefore to poor societies; labour-intensive rather than capital-intensive, ordered to the multiplication of useful and decentralized employment and the recovery of human dignity rather than to mere output, sharply relevant therefore to the actual needs of real people.

Such a programme is open to an obvious political objection: the Third World—or its politicians and power-men at least—can reply that like so much else that is said about environment, it is merely a White man's patronizing plan for holding the poor Niggers down at the romantic-savage level. . . .

A wider difficulty is that Dr Schumacher writes by implication, and, quite frankly in places, as a moralist and almost a theologian. This is fair enough, since it is certainly an ethical and religious sort of problem. But should we therefore not drop all this technical stuff about economics and environment and ecology, and get back to the simply religious preaching of a quasi-Franciscan—or perhaps Buddhist—revolution? Otherwise we shall just be fiddling around with symptoms. . . .

In a sense, this book cuts its own throat: it speaks so emphatically about our need to "seek first the Kingdom" as to make its other and more particular themes—economic and ecological—seem almost irrelevant. Arguably, that lesson is the one we really need to learn: meanwhile Dr Schumacher offers stimulation and plenty of nice knock-down arguments for the distressed homecomer who can take comfort.

> *"A Homily for Homecomers,"* in The Times Literary Supplement (© *Times Newspapers Ltd.* (London) *1973; reproduced from* The Times Literary Supplement *by permission*), No. 3734, September 28, 1973, p. 1108.

RALPH HARRIS

I fear [*Small is Beautiful: A Study of Economics as if People Mattered*] is a most perverse collection of essays, with a tantalising mixture of profound insights and superficial commentary which must drive a conscientious reviewer near to schizophrenia in trying to decide whether to pronounce a benediction or a curse on Dr Schumacher. Since his final solution is wrongheaded (and has therefore attracted rave notices in all the usual places—with whole pages or features in *New Society, Observer, Times, Peace News*).

The central thesis is that a combination of market forces and modern technology has conscripted a growing proportion of the population into larger factories and towns, because profits take precedence over people. Even if some readers were tempted to fall for this diagnosis, they would surely pause before accepting that the outcome can be adequately described as alienation, despair, misery, ugliness, escapism, vandalism, crime, violence and all the other ills (not forgetting "spiritual death") the flesh is heir to.

It is not merely exaggeration which strains credibility, but the touching error of always blaming instrumentalities and missing the worse culprit of poor old human nature. I personally accept the relevance of Dr Schumacher's frequent quotations from the Bible; but to his "Man shall not live by bread alone," I would reply with Anselm: "Not yet has thou considered the gravity of sin." And I would add that sin may be most vicious of all when masquerading in political garb as 'the national interest'.

This brings me to my central quarrel with the author. The market economy, he says, is "propelled by a frenzy of greed and indulges in an orgy of envy . . . which destroys intelligence, happiness, serenity, and thereby the peacefulness of men." Do we recognise ourselves or our friends—or even our enemies—in this grotesque caricature? If any category of humanity comes near this pathological state, it is not the competitive entrepreneur but the monopolistic, political power-monger who would most likely supplant him.

But is the *competitive* market to blame for the "giantism" our author so valiantly assails? As economic adviser to the National Coal Board for 20 years, why does Dr Schumacher fail to grapple with the truth that of the eight largest companies (by employment, not profits!) in the non-Communist world, four are the major British nationalised industries. . . .

Patiently turning to manufacturing industry, we find that for all the spectre of mass-production, in the US, Britain, France, Germany, Japan (though *not* in USSR), between one-half and three-quarters of the labour force work in plants with under 500 people. Further evidence that the author has misdirected his indignation is that the size distribution of British public companies did not change appreciably from 1900 right up to the 1960s—when such non-market forces as Wedge-Benn, MinTec, IRC got busy overruling the private judgments of investors and entrepreneurs. Who are the high priests of the superstition 'twice as big, twice as good' but the politicians who since the 1930s have manipulated the market and suppressed competition in the name of 'rationalisation,' 'modernisation' and 'growth.'

It is such sizeable motes in Dr Schumacher's eye which lead him to the earnest error that socialism might be part of the cure—instead of being most of the disease. Of course, he acknowledges, socialism would have to change; and here we run across the author's engaging other-worldliness. Socialism, for him, "is of interest solely for its non-economic values. . . ." Tell that to Mr. Wilson—and to the marines! . . .

But then on nationalisation the former economic adviser to the NCB is a true reactionary who simply retreats into innocent quotations from Tawney. The level of critical analysis is fairly indicated by a trio of quotations. Having written off the market on page 40 as "the institutionalisation of individualism and non-responsibility" he proclaims as "The Principle of Motivation" on page 232 that "people act in accordance with their motives" and acknowledges that in large bureaucracies "motivation is the central problem". Yet on page 251 he calmly asserts that nationalised industries should have a statutory obligation to serve "the public interest *in all respects*."

What more question-begging, incoherent, truly "non-responsible" basis could there be for leaving fallible, political appointees free to exercise their arbitrary judgement? Recalling those words of wisdom on motivation, imagine the scope for corrupting politicians and their creatures still further. Picture Mr Wedgwood Benn—or Mr Peter Walker—judiciously weighing the "public interest" against the pressures from marginal constituencies before deciding where the biggest subsidies are to go.

Certainly, Dr Schumacher is right in wishing to elevate human conduct and in preaching against the worship of forecasting GNP, growth and material wealth. But all that our Fabian author rightly spurns has been aggravated by the politicisation of every aspect of life by Labour—followed, alas by Conservatives and Liberals.

I conclude with two pieces of advice, the first to the market men whom the author castigates for thinking economics is all. My text would be from the Book of Proverbs: "Where there is no vision, the people perish. . . ."

My advice to Dr Schumacher is that in his laudable effort to subdue human sin—his real target—he should cease making the market system his scapegoat.

> *Ralph Harris, "Tell It to the Marines," in* The Spectator *(© 1973 by* The Spectator; *reprinted by permission of* The Spectator*), Vol. 231, No. 7581, October 13, 1973, p. 483.*

PETER BARNES

[*Small Is Beautiful: Economics As If People Mattered*] is a most unusual economic treatise, enormously broad in scope, pithily weaving together threads from Galbraith and Gandhi, capitalism and Buddhism, science and psychology. The reader is left wishing that somehow an economist of Schumacher's vision could be scooped from his subterranean hideaway and ushered into the White House disguised as Arthur Burns.

Schumacher's point is that the foremost concern of economics should be people, not goods. People do need goods, of course, but they need much more to utilize and develop their facilities through meaningful work. If this sounds like a simple—indeed almost simplistic—premise, its implications are nonetheless far-reaching. (p. 30)

Schumacher is persuasive precisely because his theories are grounded in long experience. At the British Coal Board the problem was to convert an enormous government-owned monopoly into a confederation of human-scale units. Self-contained "quasi-firms" were set up for 17 separate mining regions. Additional "quasi-firms" were established for transport, brickworks and other diverse activities. . . . If all is not bliss at the Coal Board—the recent miners' strike would indicate that it is not—the fault, Schumacher would presumably argue, lies with national leaders and their policies rather than with the decentralized structure of the enterprise. . . .

The trick, as with any vision of a better society, is getting from here to there. . . . For large-scale industries Schumacher proposes that the public convert its present right, embodied in the tax laws, to 48 percent of corporate profits, to half ownership without a corporate income tax. He warns, however, in some strong criticism of doctrinnaire British socialists, that public

ownership, or public half-ownership, is not an end in itself but merely a means to the end of a humanized economy. In addition Schumacher urges a much higher degree of indicative planning, so that economic decisions are not made entirely on the basis of what is best for each individual enterprise, but incorporate elements of a broader wisdom.

It would be easy to nitpick at many of the details and ramifications of Schumacher's *tour d'horizon*. I choose instead to nominate him for a prize of some stature. (p. 31)

> *Peter Barnes, "Wise Economics," in* The New Republic *(reprinted by permission of* The New Republic; *© 1974 The New Republic, Inc.), Vol. 170, No. 24, June 15, 1974, pp. 29-31.*

BURTON G. MALKIEL

[The major theme of **"Small Is Beautiful"** is] that growth, once unquestioningly accepted as the proper goal of civilization, is the root cause of the current crisis. . . .

Schumacher believes that continued growth is undesirable. . . .

But without economic growth how can we ever provide minimally decent living standards for the billions living in the less developed world? The answer is apparently "income redistribution." (p. 19)

But even if the developed nations shared their wealth with less-developed ones (which they have shown little inclination to do) the result would simply be that everybody had an income that was only a fraction of the poverty level. And it is painfully clear that our electorate is less likely to redistribute part of its own income to the poor than it might be to allocate a larger share of a growing total. . . . Practically, continued economic growth (together with control of world population) offers the only prospect for a better life for Americans. (pp. 19-20)

[Is] Schumacher correct that the inevitable companion to growth is pollution, which threatens to bury us in a billowing cloud of smoke and sludge? The problem here lies in defective public policy that allows us to despoil the environment and escape without paying for the costs we impose on others. The answer given by most economists is to impose "effluent charges" on those who pollute the air or water. . . . Such a program would probably strike Schumacher as immoral—as selling to industrialists a license to pollute. But that is surely better than giving it away free. And by varying the tax it would be possible to lower pollution to any level desired. . . .

Apart from the effect of economic growth on the quality of life is the issue of whether continued growth is possible. . . . Schumacher [is] filled with Malthusian forebodings. [He assures] us that we are rapidly using up our limited natural resources and further growth will soon be impossible. (p. 20)

What [his] argument misses is the possibility of continual increases in the productivity of the natural resources. . . . [As] natural resources become scarce and expensive, firms will be increasingly induced to invent ways in which to economize on their use and to develop substitutes for them. In addition, the price of products that make intensive use of scarce resources will rise. Consumers will then be induced to switch to other products that use less of these inputs—providing further resource savings. The invisible hand of free enterprise will not inevitably lead us to all the goals we desire as a society, such as clean air and water; but we should not forget the automatic self-correcting mechanism of market economy, which allows us to react and adjust to scarcities. (pp. 20-1)

Burton G. Malkiel, "What to Do about the End of the World," in The New York Times Book Review *(© 1975 by The New York Times Company; reprinted by permission), January 26, 1975, pp. 19-21.**

ADAM MEYERSON

As one might expect from its voguishness, [*Small Is Beautiful*] is neither sophisticated nor imaginative. But the astonishing thing is that in its simplistic way the book is really rather sensible.

To be sure, it has its share of crackpot ideas. The reader might profitably skip the last two chapters, in which Schumacher puts forth a silly and poorly argued proposal for partial public ownership of corporations. It is also best to pass over Schumacher's unthinking screed against nuclear energy, for, though his fears of nuclear power are not altogether unjustified, he makes no attempt to weigh its costs and benefits, or to compare its risks with those of the sources of energy he prefers, such as coal. On the contrary, one suspects a self-serving bias in his anti-nuclear vitriol: Schumacher was for twenty years planning director of the British National Coal Board, yet he does not mention the threats to health and the environment posed by increased reliance on coal, threats which many scientists and environmentalists regard as more serious than those from nuclear energy.

Put aside these sections, however, and you will find *Small Is Beautiful* to be eminently reasonable and even conservative. Schumacher may quote Gandhi and appeal to Buddhist principles more than ethnocentric Westerners will care for, but he also quotes Etienne Gilson and papal encyclicals, and his sensibilities are fundamentally those of an old-fashioned Christian moralist dissatisfied with the materialistic preoccupations of modern civilization. . . . [He] articulates a number of familiar conservative themes—the advantages of decentralized power, the need to preserve resources for the future, and the overriding importance of strength of character and human dignity.

Antagonistic as he often is to industry and technology, Schumacher is no Luddite. Both the title of the book and Theodore Roszak's introduction are a little misleading in this regard, for they imply an anarchistic impulse to break down large organizations and curtail economic growth. Actually Schumacher is more thoughtful. Though his ideas on organizational size are remarkably shallow, he at least recognizes the need to have both large *and* small organizations, and in particular "to achieve smallness *within* large organizations." . . . Still, one of Schumacher's major aims is to inveigh against the "idolatry of giantism"—having big cities, big companies, and big countries just for the sake of bigness. In so doing, he makes two valuable contributions.

The first is his distinction between renewable and non-renewable resources. . . . [Some] of our most fundamental resources—including our present sources of energy—are quickly running out; and Schumacher argues cogently that to the extent our economy depends on non-renewable resources, we must, for the sake of future generations, place voluntary limits on our economic growth.

Of course, just as it is best to ignore his section on nuclear energy, so it is best not to take Schumacher's every word on resources. In condemning the industrial world, and specifically the United States, for consuming much more than our fair share of energy, he forgets that we *produce* much more than our share as well—and that our high consumption has encouraged better exploration and production methods, which have benefited the whole world. . . . Schumacher is also partly mistaken in his attack on the marketplace: isn't it shameful, he asks, that we should equate a dollar's worth of valuable energy with a dollar's worth of any other product? He forgets that a product's value—including, to some degree, its long-term value—is already reflected in its price. For all his oversights, however, Schumacher's distinction is vital (although by no means original): we must guard our non-renewable resources as precious treasures, and we must shift the basis of our economy to renewable resources if we wish to sustain our standard of living.

Schumacher's second contribution is his discussion of Third World development, which is informed by a refreshingly old-fashioned view of poverty. Conventional wisdom tends to blame Third World poverty on Western exploitation and a failure of Western governments to grant enough foreign aid. Not Schumacher. "The primary causes of extreme poverty," he writes, "are immaterial. They lie in certain deficiencies in education, organization, and discipline." Therefore, he argues, showering money on the problem won't solve it; the task is rather to provide work opportunities, however menial, that will encourage the habits and skills which alone will lead to development. And here is where Schumacher's critique of "giantism" is most enlightening. So long as the developing countries concentrate on showplace technology—on building steel mills and modern automobile plants and so on—they will be unable to advance more than a small sector of their populations. It is foolish, he contends, to expect that poverty and backwardness can be eliminated all at once; development takes patience and hard work, and it would be much better to concentrate on what he calls "intermediate technology"—small-scale industries in rural areas with tools and machines simple enough for unskilled villagers to work with and learn from.

The domestic implications of Schumacher's argument are startling, for, if the causes of Third World poverty are to be found in education, organization, and discipline, so perhaps are the causes of domestic poverty. (pp. 1415-16)

[Conservatives] should rejoice that *Small Is Beautiful* is becoming so popular; however diluted its message, in many ways it is our own. (p. 1416)

Adam Meyerson, "Even Conservative," in National Review *(© National Review, Inc., 1976; 150 East 35th St., New York, NY 10016), Vol. XXVIII, No. 49, December 24, 1976, pp. 1415-16.*

MARTIN MAYER

[*Small Is Beautiful*] is a peculiar performance, some of it interesting and cogently (if rather abstractly) argued, some of it highly emotional, uninformed, and self-contradictory to the point of incoherence. Unfortunately, the latter sections seem to have drawn for the book its following. (p. 232)

A lot of [Schumacher's arguments are] appealing, and plausible on first sight, though not always on consideration. Schumacher notes the old saw that you help a man more if you teach him fishing than if you give him fish—and expands it to argue that you help him more if you teach him to make his own fishing tackle than if you give him the equipment. But what if he's a carpenter and would rather sell chairs for cash and buy fish?

Do we really have to do without the productivity of the division of labor to practice Schumacher's "economics as if people mattered"? Worse—what if this white man's burden and his family are hungry right now? It takes time to make fishing tackle.

When Schumacher suggests that instead of sending bulldozers to build a road we teach natives about wheelbarrows and help them create the back-up shops they will need to make wheelbarrow parts, what he is really saying is that these fellows don't need that road for another generation. (He doesn't like roads anyway; they're part of the damnable modern transportation technology that makes men "footloose.") These people may not have that much time—they certainly don't think they do. For all his insistence on the need to take a dynamic view and relate the parts of the problem, Schumacher ignores entirely the impact of public health technologies that, by reducing the death rate, created a population explosion. Neither cultures nor technologies come as snap-together independent parts; we are dealing with conflicts not of technique or attitude, but of commitment.

The desire to believe Schumacher is ultimately eroded by his bad manners as a controversialist (he is forever putting into the mouths of unnamed antagonists things nobody worth arguing with would ever say, like "People talk freely about 'machines to foretell the future'"), and by an astonishing absence of specificity. *Small Is Beautiful* does not offer a single example of the recommended "intermediate technology" or, as its author coyly puts it, "technology with a human face." (Lord knows what that is supposed to mean, other than "good.") (pp. 232-33)

Schumacher ventures some nice *aperçus*. My favorite is the observation that if Germany had conquered Denmark in the 1860s or if Napoleon had not been forced from Belgium, we would now regard an independent Denmark or Belgium as nonviable, and Danish or Belgian separatist movements as foolishly romantic. Mostly, though, the book is rhetoric, and when dealing with contemporary life in the rich countries it is simply hysterical. . . .

Steady-state philosophers like Schumacher get into trouble because they claim radical credentials for an intensely conservative, even reactionary, attitude. No significant ideational or technological advance may be dreamed in their philosophies; the problems they see can be solved only by turning back. Schumacher is fairly explicit about this, concluding with a call for rededication to the cardinal virtues (in Latin, too). (p. 233)

> Martin Mayer, *"The Closet Conservatives," in* The American Scholar *(copyright © 1977 by the United Chapters of Phi Beta Kappa; reprinted by permission of the publishers), Vol. 46, No. 2, Spring, 1977, pp. 230, 232-33, 236-37.**

HARVEY COX

["A Guide for the Perplexed"] begins literally where ["Small Is Beautiful"] ended. It is small, only half the length of the previous one. Whether it is beautiful, however, is open to question. I found parts of it wise, much of it hard to follow, and some of it not at all convincing. "A Guide for the Perplexed" is a call, more like a plea, for a radical turn toward self-awareness, something about which the author believes only the great religious traditions of the world, not science, have something to teach us. . . .

The trouble is that Schumacher violates his own best advice. He goes big. He pours on too much and therefore is not persuasive. . . .

I kept feeling that something urgent was being said about how the reductionist logic of modern science has indeed misled us and is useless when it comes to the most perplexing questions we face. Ironically, however, the man who has taught so many of us the virtues of modesty and restraint has resorted to a kind of scattershot and overkill. Not only has he tried to do too much in one small book—repudiate scientism, reinstate the hierarchical mode of thinking, reclaim the perennial philosophy—but the firepower he has concentrated is so mixed and so massive that his original point frequently gets lost.

I hope not completely lost, however. Schumacher surely has something important to say. He knows that the really serious issues facing us today cannot be "solved" but must, as he says, "be grappled with" and that such grappling will require us to learn more than most modern people want to from the great religious traditions. He feels very strongly that the modern experiment of living without religion has failed, and without a certain kind of self-knowledge all our knowledge of the outside world will be worse than useless. So, behind the prolixity lies a truth that a very thoughtful man is trying to get through to us: In order to survive as a species, we must change in ways that will exact much more from us than we now anticipate, and if we want to survive, we had better get on with it.

> Harvey Cox, *"A Subtreasury of Traditional Wisdom," in* The New York Times Book Review *(© 1977 by The New York Times Company; reprinted by permission), October 2, 1977, p. 10.*

ERIC KORN

Small Is Beautiful is a book to change the lives of people and nations. Its virtue is in its practical suggestions for alternatives to loutish ravening growth; its stampede of powerful ideas and asseverations leaves little time to question even some of his oddly precise prescriptions for what he believes are unchangeable human needs: no city must exceed half-a-million inhabitants, no workplace must cost more than $5,000 per employee to establish. . . . This suggests a wholesome metaphysical horror of bigness: Schumacher seems to see no benefit from the television transmitter, the electron microscope or the giant printing press. The ideal is the hand-press, the well-equipped workbench.

Despite his socialism, however, he is closer to Chesterton and Gill than to William Morris; there is an undercurrent of obscurantist medievalism in his curiously intemperate attack on economics: 'something is uneconomic when it fails to produce an adequate profit in terms of money. The method of economics does not and cannot produce any other meaning.' But surely even the most reverently organic homesteader uses economic calculus in deciding what to do with his seed potatoes: practical problems cannot be solved exclusively by the application of *a priori* wisdom. 'Man is far too clever to survive without wisdom,' wrote Schumacher, and *A Guide for the Perplexed* sets out to chart that wisdom, showing a certain haste to abandon cleverness in the process. Yet we need both . . . , and Schumacher, quick to detect false antitheses in others . . . , sets up a few of his own.

The most significant contours on his world map are Aristotelian, 'the four levels of Being'—mineral, plant, animal, man;

material, living, sentient, rational; unhelpfully pseudo-quantified as 'm +x +y +z'; and startlingly equated with the physical body, the etheric body, the astral body, and the spirit. Between them are 'ontological discontinuities': Man is, under God, supreme in the natural order, and must rule it wisely and lovingly, while striving to raise his level of awareness by prayer or yoga. The enemy is reductionism in any guise: relativism, positivism, Marx, Darwin, Freud. (p. 481)

Schumacher makes an untenable distinction between instructional sciences, which are permitted to be modestly useful, and descriptive sciences like biology, which has got above itself. . . . It is loudly proclaimed, says Schumacher, that 'man is nothing but a complex biochemical mechanism'. But is it? The quotation is not from a reductionist but from a hostile critic: 'nothing-butism' is largely fictitious, surviving only among a dwindling but important clique of psychologists. Biologists do not say 'nothing but', rather 'and all this also'.

If the life sciences debase us, what does Schumacher offer to raise levels of consciousness? Though he denounces modern occultism, he proposes the exemplars of Therese Neumann, the stigmatist, Edgar Cayce, the automatic writer, and Jakob Lorber, to whom an inner voice dictated 'the *New St John's Gospel* in ten big volumes'. If this seems a depressing prospect, Schumacher's arguments are invigorating, provoking, and often dramatic. (pp. 481-82)

> Eric Korn, "Small Is Small," in New Statesman (©1977 The Statesman & Nation Publishing Co. Ltd.), Vol. 94, No. 2429, October 7, 1977, pp. 481-82.

DENIS HAYES

During the last two years of his life, Fritz Schumacher devoted much of his energy to a book that, he felt, would be much more important than *Small is Beautiful*. Published posthumously, *A Guide for the Perplexed* is Schumacher's final word. He uses the volume to set forth his views on the "big" issues: the existence of God and the meaning of life.

As with his earlier work on technology run amok, Schumacher is exploring a theme of great current interest to persons 40 years his junior. His purpose in writing this book is to sketch an intellectual "map" of the terrain he has travelled so that others may follow the path to his conclusions without first spending a lifetime exploring dead-end streets. Schumacher believes in a higher order of being. As a consequence, he believes that the Good Life is not the one extolled in Pepsi ads but rather a life of spiritual elevation guided by experience and faith.

In essence, *Guide* is one man's statement of belief. It draws eclectically from many religions and mystics and imposes a loose structure on the resulting array of quotations. The result is a sometimes odd blend of Thomas Aquinas and Nyanaponika Thera, of Dante and Edgar Cayce.

Many who enjoyed the crisp logic of Schumacher's earlier work will be disappointed, and even embarrassed, by elements in the new book, which appears unlikely to become the sort of bible for the newly religious that *Small is Beautiful* has become for appropriate technologists. But as the summation of an unusual man with a vast range of interests, it could be a useful touchstone for some who are perplexed by the inability of western materialism to satisfy a nagging void in the soul. The "map" will be of interest even to those who don't find the treasure where Schumacher says it is buried. The book is an

appropriate final note for a man who always wore a human face behind his economist's mask.

> Denis Hayes, "E. F. Schumacher: Charting the Way," in Book World—Washington Post (copyright © 1977 by The Washington Post Company), November 27, 1977, p. 4.

ROBERT LEKACHMAN

Schumacher's 1973 **"Small Is Beautiful"** continues to be a sacred text for opponents of nuclear energy, massive technology, chemical farming and the huge public and private organizations that administer these spiritually devastating varieties of human labor. The most attractive of Schumacher's concepts, particularly in developing societies, has been the idea of intermediate technology. . . .

What counted for Schumacher in [**"Good Work,"**] this posthumous volume based on lectures delivered in the last years of his life, as in his previous writings, was the quality of human experience, not the quantity of the items meaninglessly summed up in Gross National Product comparisons. . . .

In **"Good Work,"** whose tone fluctuates between pessimism about what technology has done to deform the human spirit and optimism about the chances of personal and social renewal that have against all odds survived, he levies a severe four-count indictment of modern technology. Its gigantic scale discourages community and individual imagination. Its complexity separates the educated from the rest of the population. Its enormous cost discourages progress in poor societies. Finally, it violently assaults the natural environment.

Even in the richest communities, advanced technology drains meaning and satisfaction out of work. Yet, urges Schumacher, good work is essential to the fulfillment of the Creator's three intentions—fulfillment of our own potentialities, aid to others and aspiration to the divine. How can human beings advance toward even the first and most self-centered of these goals within the crushing context of infinitely subdivided tasks that are the common experience? (p. 12)

The message here, as in Schumacher's previous volumes, is a call, not for class or economic warfare, but for the improvement of individual behavior and activity and the transformation of industrial society into a humane residence for creative and consequently happy men and women. It is not at all difficult to comprehend Schumacher's immediate and enduring appeal. He asks us to start where we are—with ourselves and our immediate environment. Let each cultivate his own garden and by so much reduce the pollution of the universe. (pp. 12, 24)

> Robert Lekachman, "Between the Hoe and Tractor," in The New York Times Book Review (© 1979 by The New York Times Company; reprinted by permission), May 20, 1979, pp. 12, 24.

JOHN NAUGHTON

Good Work is addressed to a question with strong metaphysical connotations: what is the purpose of human work? To this [E. F. Schumacher] gives three answers: to produce goods and services which are both necessary and useful; to enable us to perfect our gifts and skills; and to serve, and collaborate with, other people in order to liberate ourselves from our inborn egocentricity.

Inevitably, any collection of speeches, if published in unedited form, is likely to be uneven. This is certainly the case with *Good Work*. . . . On the credit side there are three impressive chapters: a succinct summary of the events which led up to our current energy predicament; an excellent exposition of the idea on which Schumacher's main claim to fame rests—the notion of "Intermediate" or "Appropriate" technology . . . ; a third chapter presents some evidence, culled from practical successes in implementing intermediate technology, for the view that we do not have to remain intellectually paralyzed in the face of our global difficulties. These chapters show Schumacher at his best—marshalling the complex facts of life into a coherent and compelling order, making a sophisticated analysis look simple and "obvious".

The remaining three chapters of *Good Work* are less satisfactory, largely because the author's exposition and style of reasoning are not really suited to metaphysical speculation. "On Appropriate Forms of Ownership and Action" presents an unduly simplistic picture of the possibilities for alternative forms of organizational structure, and underestimates the complexity of the forces which shaped conventional structures. "Education for Good Work" sets out to identify some features of an educational process which might prepare people for meaningful work, but comes to no very obvious conclusion. "The Party's Over" starts out as a tirade against the tyranny of GNP and ends up with a biblical exhortation to purge ourselves of the slavish adulation of scientism.

The trouble with these chapters is that they promise more than they deliver. They are presented as unpretentious, Mark Twain-type exploration of troubling questions about human priorities and aspirations, but are in fact engaging expositions of personal conclusions which are rigidly determined by their author's religious and ethical premises. No doubt this is partly a reflection of the deficiences of the popular-lecture format. But it is also a reminder that a gift—such as Dr Schumacher possessed in abundance—for clear thinking about issues such as energy is no guarantee of success when the subject of discussion lies submerged in the murky waters of the soul.

John Naughton, "The Appropriate Alternative," in The Times Literary Supplement *(© Times Newspapers Ltd. (London) 1979; reproduced from* The Times Literary Supplement *by permission), No. 4005, December 21, 1979, p. 148.*

Gay Talese

1932-

An American essayist, journalist, and editor, Talese is one of the best-known practitioners of New Journalism, the genre that combines the descriptive techniques of the novel with the realism of nonfiction. Talese provides an exhaustive analysis of the power structure of the *New York Times* in *The Kingdom and the Power* (1969), a book enlivened by the many personal anecdotes he relates about his former employers. *Honor Thy Father* (1971) contains a unique picture of the family life of a mafia member, Bill Bonanno. Following the publication of *Honor Thy Father,* Talese began searching for a new, sweeping topic for a book. He found that "what most intrigued him was America's new openness about sex, its expanding erotic consumerism, and the quiet rebellion that he sensed within the middle class against the censors and clerics that had been an inhibiting force since the founding of the Puritan republic." In 1980, after nine years of researching and writing, Talese published *Thy Neighbor's Wife,* a "participatory history" of the sexual revolution. This controversial book contains portraits of such people as Hugh Hefner, founder of *Playboy,* and Alex Comfort, author of *The Joy of Sex,* as well as reports of the author's own experiences working in a massage parlor and visiting group sex communes. Although the more sensational aspects of Talese's book have received the most publicity, *Thy Neighbor's Wife* also contains factual reports of landmark literary obscenity cases and amendments regarding community standards. (See also *Contemporary Authors,* Vols. 1-4, rev. ed., and *Authors in the News,* Vol. 1.)

© *Jerry Bauer*

Excerpt from *THE KINGDOM AND THE POWER*

Most journalists are restless voyeurs who see the warts on the world, the imperfections in people and places. The sane scene that is much of life, the great portion on the planet unmarked by madness, does not lure them like riots and raids, crumbling countries and sinking ships, bankers banished to Rio and burning Buddhist nuns—gloom is their game, the spectacle their passion, normality their nemesis.

Journalists travel in packs with transferable tension and they can only guess to what extent their presence in large numbers ignites an incident, turns people on. For press conferences and cameras and microphones have become such an integral part of the happenings of our time that nobody today knows whether people make news or news makes people—General Ky in Vietnam, feeling no doubt more potent after his sixth magazine-cover story, challenges Red China; after police in New York raided the headquarters of young hoodlums, it was discovered that some gang leaders keep scrapbooks; in Baltimore, a day after the Huntley-Brinkley Report mentioned that the city had survived the summer without a race riot, there was a race riot. When the press is absent, politicans have been known to cancel their speeches, civil rights marchers to postpone their parades, alarmists to withhold their due predictions. The troops at the Berlin Wall, largely ignored since Vietnam stole the headlines, coexist casually, watching the girls go by.

News, if unreported, has no impact. It might as well have not happened at all. Thus the journalist is the important ally of the ambitious, he is a lamplighter for stars. He is invited to parties, is courted and complimented, has easy access to unlisted telephone numbers and to many levels of life. He may send to America a provocative story of poverty in Africa, of tribal threats and turmoil—and then he may go for a swim in the ambassador's pool. A journalist will sometimes mistakenly assume that it is his charm, not his usefulness, that gains such privilege; but most journalists are realistic men not fooled by the game. They use as well as they are used. Still they are restless. Their work, instantly published, is almost instantly forgotten, and they must endlessly search for something new, must stay alive with by lines and not be scooped, must nurture the insatiable appetites of newspapers and networks, the commercial cravings for new faces, fashions, fads, feuds; they must not worry when news seems to be happening *because* they are there, nor must they ponder the possibility that everything they have witnessed and written in their lifetime may someday occupy only a few lines in the plastic textbooks of the twenty-first century.

And so each day, unhaunted by history, plugged into the *instant,* journalists of every creed, quality, and quirk report the news of the world as they see it, hear it, believe it, understand it. Then much of it is relayed through America, millions of words a minute, some thousands of which penetrate a large fourteen-floor fact factory on Forty-third Street off Broadway, the *New York Times* building, where each weekday afternoon at four o'clock—before it is fit to print, before it can influence the State Department and perplex the President and irritate David Merrick and get the ball rolling on Wall Street and heads rolling in the Congo—it is presented by *Times* editors seated around a conference table to one man, the managing editor, Clifton Daniel. (pp. 1-2)

Gay Talese, in his The Kingdom and the Power (*reprinted by permission of Candida Donadio & Associats, Inc.; copyright © 1966 by Gay Talese*), World Publishing Co., 1969, 555 p.

CHRISTOPHER LEHMANN-HAUPT

[**"The Kingdom and the Power"**] is beguilingly gossipy, intimately anecdotal, exhaustively and sometimes irrelevantly detailed. It gives a sense of the scope of the Time's history from its founding in 1851 to the events of last year.

It catches the vast complexity of the paper's operation and gives some dimension to the personalities who have occupied its seats of power. I confess that I read it hungrily as if it were the manual of instructions to a grand game. Every so often I was even moved by it (to laughter, to awe of the complexity of power). But when all is said and done it leaves the old lady her dignity. And the reason that it does is, in a peculiar sense, what's wrong with the book.

There is something illusory about Mr. Talese's epic. Not that he hasn't dug very deep; he has. I'm not referring to minor errors of fact. . . .

I'm not suggesting that he has been unrealistically kind to the paper and its people: as you know if you read any of the magazine installments, there are petty and ugly episodes, although placed in the larger framework of the book they seem understandable, even to be sympathized with.

But in trying hard to keep his long history alive and immediate, Mr. Talese has resorted to artificial techniques. He has built his story out of dramatic episodes placed within dramatic episodes, all of which he leaves unresolved for interminable stretches while he wanders from one subject to another, scooping up huge quantities of background material and filling you up with it until you've forgotten what you're waiting for. . . .

The dramatic question that spans the whole book and supports its shaky superstructure is: will the editors of 43d Street ultimately succeed in bringing the independent Washington Bureau to heel? Great importance seems attached to the answer by everyone, although Mr. Talese never quite makes it clear why. There are hints, but they are too diffuse for either analysis or drama.

Even that superproblem is never resolved satisfactorily, but builds instead into a melodramatic fiasco—a bloodless uncoup. Of course, that's the way real life is—an endless round of dramatic fizzles. But if you portray real scenes by artificial means and then pretend to be honoring real life, what you end up with is something like a promotional film with scenes from "The Brothers Karamazov." That's what **"The Kingdom and the Power"** finally boils down to—a grand epic that personalizes the impersonal and turns monolith to flesh—an advertisement for our times.

Christopher Lehmann-Haupt, "Advertisement for Our Times," in The New York Times (© *1969 by The New York Times Company; reprinted by permission*), May 21, 1969, p. 45.

DAVID BERNSTEIN

[*The Kingdom and the Power*] is the ultimate inside story. . . . Talese's effort reads . . . like a Who's Who in the Zoo, and has all the fascination of such accounts for other members of the animal kingdom. His book is long, often lyrical, sometimes disjointed, with the faintest touch of voyeurism and a seasoning of mischief. While newspapers are notoriously reticent about themselves, everybody who worked for the *Times* seems to have talked to him with awesome candor.

Although *The Kingdom and the Power* apparently grew out of a magazine article Talese wrote several years ago, the marks of haste and repetition abound in the final product. Yet even this has a peculiar charm. It is as if some staffer who knew everything unfit to print about his bosses were sitting over a drink in a midtown bar, measuring out anecdotes with a liberal hand, one incident reminding him of another, a name mentioned casually at one moment picked up the next and limned from babyhood to eminence.

The story of managing editor Clifton Daniel is an example. It threads through the narrative with touches of grandeur and pathos, moving from his first encounter with Margaret Truman . . . to the horrendous day when he learned that James Reston had consolidated his domination over the *Times* once and for all ("Daniel turned pale and swallowed his drink").

Does all this matter? Is it really vital to know the people behind the prestigious by-lines, inside the dignified masthead on the editorial page, covering the events, editing the copy, deciding what goes on the front page? The answer, quite truthfully, is yes. For the *Times* wields a power over public opinion and public figures that no other newspaper, no television network, no individual except the President himself, can possibly match. (p. 28)

Gay Talese is quite right to place his emphasis upon all this when he describes the kingdom that is the *Times*. What might appear at first glance to be a frivolous book is in fact a serious and important account of one of the few genuinely powerful institutions in our society. (p. 29)

David Bernstein, "Behind the 'Times'," in The New Leader (© *1969 by the American Labor Conference on International Affairs, Inc.*), *Vol. LII, No. 10, May 26, 1969, pp. 28-9.*

BEN H. BAGDIKIAN

[**"The Kingdom and the Power"**] concentrates on The Times from the mid-fifties to the present. It was a time of traumatic change in the world and therefore in journalism and most particularly in The New York Times. . . .

The events turn on the shock waves of new leadership, new rivalries, new styles, new philosophies of reporting and the infighting of editors in New York trying to increase their influence over the powerful outlying duchies of Times bureaus in Washington and abroad.

But this is not just another book about organization men scheming to reach the top. Men lust for power in newspapers as they do elsewhere, but with a difference. An organization like The Times has unique stakes compared with General Motors or Proctor & Gamble. The outcome of the Times's conflicts will not influence the design of radiator grilles or detergent containers but of public policy in the United States. Every public and private leader in Washington and New York, and every newspaper editor reads a paper like The Times before he starts his day, and adjusts to the version of reality created on Page One by the men who struggle in this book. During the period Talese describes these men and their views were the subject of intense, almost obsessive concern by the most powerful policy-makers in the country.

So the hero (heroine? villain? victim?) of the book is The Times itself, "a rather delicate and sensitive monstrosity," that envelops the men who struggle to control it and in the end influences their lives more than they influence it.

It is a fascinating book, compelling for those addicted to newspapers, and to anyone else who lets himself get caught up in the interplay of the characters, whether or not he recognizes the bylines. . . .

His writing is lively, aided by an eye for irreverent detail that reminds you constantly that this is not an official biography. Frederick Birchall, a former acting managing editor, is introduced in one scene, "one day while driving his car with one hand on the steering wheel and the other on the Baroness's leg.". . .

The book is rich in intimate detail, personal insights and characterization. While The Times turns its face to the world with a stiff upper lip and all the news that's fit to print, in this book the men of The Times emerge not as godlike models of intrepid journalism but as unique individuals who, in addition to other human traits, have trouble with their ambitions, alcohol, wives and analysts.

But this is the book's weakness. It implies value in professional newspapermen on the basis of personal idiosyncrasy. Individual tastes are important, but so is man's perception of reality, of issues, and of public events, which, after all, are the substance of his trade. It is interesting to learn the kind of woman and clothing that turns on a particular editor, but there is more to judgments of journalists than bedmates or haberdashers.

Inevitably, much has to be taken on faith, like the author's descriptions of men's inner thoughts and motives. And there are times when this faith is shaken by unfairness including that toward the late publisher, Orvil Dryfoos, and toward James Reston. Talese depicts Dryfoos as a rather precious agent of the Establishment, criticizing him and Reston because they ordered the story of the Government's preparations for the Bay of Pigs "toned down, moved to a less prominent place on the page, its headline minimized, and any reference to the imminence of the invasion eliminated" (which I agree was a bad decision).

While Talese uses this incident as a key to Dryfoos's chacrater, he does not credit the same character for making courageous anti-Establishment decisions that offended important people at The Times. . . . (p. 8)

Talese is least convincing in areas he does not know well— Washington and foreign affairs—not a small failing in a book about The Times. . . .

Despite its flaws, the book creates moving scenes and personalities. Seldom has anyone been so successful in making a newspaper come alive as a human institution. It is a story that many ambitious newspapers would wish their best writers to produce—about someone else. (p. 30)

> Ben H. Bagdikian, " 'The Kingdom and the Power'," in The New York Times Book Review (© 1969 by The New York Times Company; reprinted by permission), June 8, 1969, pp. 8, 30.

A. J. LANGGUTH

Dozens of times [in *The Kingdom and the Power*] Talese recreates in absorbing detail the conflicts between one man and another, between writer and editor, the New York office and the bureau in Washington, the Sunday department and the weekday. But somehow the substance of these debates hardly seems to matter and real differences of policy are reduced to a series of petty squabbles.

Yet the book is fascinating, laden as it is, behind a genial facade, with adroit and ill-natured tattle. Talese is a romantic who can find glamour in that drab factory on 43rd Street and excitement in dissecting its cautious managers. (p. 29)

Except for a nod to [David Halberstam, Talese ignores many important stories reported by *The Times*]. He omits, too, any discussion of the areas in which the paper may have exerted real power within its own city. Little is said about whom *The Times* has supported politically through the years less about what a *Times* endorsement means in coverage or contributions. To his cursory mention of Claude Sitton's fine reporting from the South Talese adds no clue as to what, if anything *The Times* was telling its readers about Harlem during those same years.

To judge from Talese, the editors are not so much interested in publishing a paper as securing a higher spot on the masthead. Harrison Salisbury's trip to Hanoi was interesting, Talese would grant that, but he manages to convey that its real importance was in forestalling attempts to dislodge Salisbury from his post as assistant managing editor.

The same technique that makes the book so readable adds to Talese's problems in capturing the essence of his characters. Taking material from extensive interviews, Talese has fashioned a narrative that tells, in Talese's words, what each editor thought and felt at his moment of bureaucratic crisis. Since Talese seldom quotes them directly, the reader hears mostly a smooth omniscient voice that sees all, tells all, but misses in its crystalline high style any distinctive rough edges. (pp. 30-1)

> A. J. Langguth, "Tales of the Times," in The New Republic (reprinted by permission of The New Republic; ©1969 The New Republic, Inc.), Vol. 160, No. 26, June 28, 1969, pp. 29-33.

C. H. SIMONDS

It is as an institution that Talese examines the *Times* [in *The Kingdom and the Power*], but he stops regrettably short. He has written, he tells us, "a human story of an institution in transition . . . a factual story of several generations of *Times*-men and the interplay within [among?] those generations, the internal scenes and confrontations and adjustments that are part of the vitality and growth of any enduring institution." Fine as far as it goes, but there is too little consideration of the sources, extent and effects of the *Times*' considerable power; too many scenes and confrontations, too much novelistic scene-setting and picture-painting. . . . Such gobbets of information are mildly interesting in a ladies'-magazine way, but when troweled on, to the extent that Talese trowels them on, they get in the way.

Of what? Well, of the Big Drama, which, one gathers, is the "depersonalization" of the *Times* between the early 1950s and today; the process by which the one-man rule of Adolph Ochs and then his son-in-law, Arthur Hays Sulzberger, was supplanted by a regime of bankerish executives. (p. 811)

Such a chronicle of executive maneuvering might be interesting; in Talese's hands it is tiresome for two reasons. First, there is the *Times'* pace: There are no lightning coups at the *Times,* everything moves with the speed of erosion; it may take a decade to ease a man upstairs, or downstairs, or over to an obscure desk behind a post. Second, there is Talese's pace; more precisely, his inability to follow the main line of the story and dovetail in the background, asides and subplots so that they support instead of obscure. . . . Quite plainly, Talese is under the influence of Truman Capote's "nonfiction novel" and the highly personal reportage of Norman Mailer; quite sadly, he is not up to their level. The stream of consciousness is muddied. The juxtaposition of events does little to enlighten, much to confuse.

Talese is under another influence as well: that of the writers of what he himself calls "bad novels about big business." His book has heroes and villains; chosen capriciously. To judge from his portraits of [Clifton Daniel and Harrison Salisbury], they are the modern-day equivalents of Chateaubriand's Fouché and Talleyrand, "crime leaning on the arm of vice." (pp. 811-12)

Occasionally Talese tiptoes up to the questions about the *Times* that need to be answered; always, he hiccups and runs away. *Why* is the *Times* important, respected, revered? Because it is "necessary proof of the world's existence, a barometer of its pressure, an assessor of its sanity." That won't do. Why is the *Times* powerful? Because it is close to the Establishment: "The two forces [are] both committed to essentially the same goals, the preservation of the democratic system and the established order." This too-hasty identification of the *Times* with the Establishment leads Talese to strain, as when he lays the internal conflicts in the two institutions to the deaths, within months of each other, of John Kennedy and the *Times'* publisher, Orvil Dryfoos. And for all that the *Times* had Lyndon Johnson to lunch at a table decorated with red, white and blue carnations "set in transparent glass bowls so that the Secret Service men could be certain that they were bomb-free," one wonders what LBJ would make of Talese's charges of hand-in-gloveism. (p. 812)

> *C. H. Simonds, "Printed to Fit," in* National Review *(© National Review, Inc., 1969; 150 East 35th St., New York, NY 10016), Vol. 21, No. 31, August 12, 1969, pp. 810-12.*

SAUL MALOFF

"Fame and Obscurity" is a collection of representative work spanning much of Talese's career: Esquire profiles of tabloid and neon celebrities; all of "The Bridge," his short book on the mighty race of bridge-builders; and all of "New York—A Serendipiter's Journey," glimpses and oddments culled from the streets and alleys of the city. There are good things here, very good, details which in themselves give pleasure, attract light and take on color, assume dimension in isolation and distinctiveness because they are well seen—especially in the vignettes of city life.

It is noteworthy that here Talese tries for nothing grand; he is gathering and arranging found objects for a setting, but not populating or activating it with characters and actions. When he does—as in the profiles—the results are quite different: the larger the ambition, the smaller the success.

Rendering some plausible version of what makes Sinatra run, what drives Joshua Logan, what it is with Peter O'Toole—that is another matter. And here, where it counts, is where Talese slips, in some instances badly. (pp. 6-7)

[The] insights are too easily won, they emerge too creamily from the insight-machine that manufactures such stamped and certified knowledge. Somehow none of it is convincing; it rings hollowly of instant psychoanalysis, pop psychologizing. Talese is too unwary, too incautious, too ready to accept at-hand conveniences, gladly presented by the subjects themselves as the hard, bitter truths of their interesting lives. These are the "truths" of bad-to-middling fiction.

This, precisely, is what the good novelist rejects, refusing all kinds of offers to help generously bestowed, knowing that truths are to be found elsewhere than at home, waiting to be picked up for the asking. And this is what the New Journalist—compelled to write at restrictive length for an audience that demands familiar formulas above all and has no more tolerance than he for loose, tattered ends, bewildering inconsistency, apparent contradiction, surprise and enigma, the elements that steadfastly resist the false coherence of imposed pattern—apparently cannot acknowledge, settling instead for the flat, varnished tale, the kind that goes down so easily, and is as easily forgotten. (p. 7)

> *Saul Maloff, "Creamy Insights, Pop Psychologizings," in* The New York Times Book Review *(© 1970 by The New York Times Company; reprinted by permission), August 2, 1970, pp. 6-7.*

COLIN MacINNES

The flaw in "Honor Thy Father" seems to me to be that Gay Talese has become so seduced by his subject and its "hero," that he conveys the impression that being a mobster is much the same as being a sportsman, film star or any other kind of public "personality".

The "hero" in question is Salvatore "Bill" Bonanno, son of the more celebrated Joe, who is chiefly remembered for his being mysteriously kidnapped for 18 months in 1964-66 and for the subsequent "Banana War" between the remnants of the Bonanno "family" and its rivals. Mr. Talese became friendly with Bill Bonanno as a consequence of these events, and his book chiefly consists of the life story of the junior Bonanno, and of the relationship of him and his father to other distinguished characters of what used to be called the "Mafia," was then called "Costa Nostra," and which it is now apparently tactless—for fear minority sensibilities be offended—to call anything at all.

A splendid opportunity, then, for an "inside story" of a bizarre and significant sector of the American scene; yet I am sorry to say Mr. Talese fails to seize it. It is doubtless impossible for any outsider, however intimate his connection with one member of this society, to learn many of its real secrets; and certainly the disclosures of Joseph Valachi, an insider though a minor one, and the F.B.I. recordings of criminal conversations are far more revealing than are these pages. Yet even so, I feel Mr. Talese might have made more of the material that was available to him.

For what we have, in the first place, is a lengthy recapitulation of American gangster history that is by now quite generally known. There are also enormous chunks describing the day-to-day life of Bill Bonanno which, apart from his being who he is, are of no particular interest. The portrait of a minor mobster in decline has a certain melancholy fascination, though what is said in pages would often be better put in paragraphs. The whole tone of the book is rather sentimental, and curiosly snobbish: one is reminded, at times, as the author evokes his alarming and deplorable characters, of the voice of a gossip columnist.

Most disconcerting of all is Mr. Talese's attitude in describing these events and personalities. Bill, he implies, is a nice guy and a victim of circumstance, and at no point does the author assess him and his world from any clear standard of personal opinion. I am not, of course, saying it is a writer's business to "judge" any other human creature, but it certainly is to measure him by some identifiable code of human conduct. . . .

Perhaps the most interesting sections of **"Honor Thy Father"** are not those where Mr. Talese is rather cosily describing Bill and his devoted family, but where he tries to assess the financial structure of organized crime in the United States. He is also excellent on the historical origins of the Mafia, and does well to remind us that it was originally a secret society founded to defend Sicilian rights against their oppressors. The sections on the recent emergence of major black gangsters have an unfortunate relevance here, since this is also in part a consequence of the oppression of a minority group by the majority.

If I have been damning with faint praise, I would conclude by saying I do think the book will interest many readers. Perhaps the public as a whole is not so different from artists in its preoccupation with crime and criminals. The themes of so much fiction, films and television are proof of this; and Mr. Talese's book at least has the advantage of dealing with real, and not invented, personalities and social problems. (p. 18)

> *Colin MacInnes, "Does the ----- Really Exist?" in* The New York Times Book Review *(© 1971 by The New York Times Company; reprinted by permission), October 31, 1971, pp. 2, 18.*

PETE HAMILL

In some strange way, it doesn't really matter that the major characters in this splendid book *Honor Thy Father* actually exist. In the world of newspaper headlines and whirring television cameras, there really are people named Joseph, Bill, and Rosalie Bonanno; usually we see the two men posed in front of courtrooms, flanked by lawyers, smiling, offering nothing to their auditors beyond a certain sullen civility. They are Mafia, which is to say, their lives have been publicly offered to us as entertainment or moral tale. Their women are mysteries to us, black-veiled at funerals, white-veiled at weddings, but existing behind the walls of male silence, extensions in space only of the men who rule their lives. Their lives, until now, hardly exist because figures in morality tales have no history, not even that form of history known as the past; the men have

police records and the women go to Mass and there is nothing else.

In this long, finely-detailed book Gay Talese has changed all of that forever. In telling the story of Bill Bonanno, his father Joseph, and his wife Rosalie, Talese has constructed one of those sturdy Victorian novels that take us beyond the curtains to look at human lives; that the story he tells is about actual people makes the feat somewhat more compelling, but that is not crucial. After the principals are all gone, the book will remain, a family saga as important as any we've seen in this country. It is a book about fathers and sons, about trust and betrayal, about the old style and the new; it is, of course, a tragedy, because the genre of the family saga, real or imagined, always seems to turn out that way. But the book is also a stunning comment on America and the failure of its romantic promise. (p. 4)

Along the way, the reader has learned more than he had expected and the people in the Mafia are suddenly human beings. Talese, who did the reporting for this book over a five-year period, has been careful to keep himself out of it, but its completeness, its driving force, its compassion and care come from his own obsessions about being Italian-American. The book is as good as anything Balzac wrote out of his obsessions, and anything that the Victorian novelists constructed out of theirs. (p. 10)

> *Pete Hamill, "Bonanno and Son," in* Book World— Chicago Tribune *(© 1971 Postrib Corp.; reprinted by permission of* Chicago Tribune *and* The Washington Post), *November 7, 1971, pp. 4, 8, 10.*

WILFRID SHEED

Gay Talese has been criticized for writing [in *Honor Thy Father*] what amounts to promotional material for the Bonanno family, but his book is an invaluable document and I don't know how such books can be obtained without some compromise. It is a lot to ask of an author that he betray the confidence of a Mafia family. As with a tapped phone call, one must interpret the message. *Honor Thy Father* conveys at least what the Bonannos would like you to think of them, or what they wouldn't mind you thinking of them. Talese signals occasionally to his educated audience—dull, aren't they? Almost pathetic. But that's all he can do. Our language differs from theirs about a few words like "dull." (God knows, they would find Sidney Hook's life dull.) But beyond that, Talese must play it straight.

His account of Bill Bonanno's thought processes is therefore all the more illuminating for being precisely the way Bill would like you to get it. When I add that it reminded me of Yogi Berra reading Gospel comics, this is not to indicate that Bill seems stupid. On the contrary. He is stupid only in the one area where he can't afford to be intelligent, that is, in questions of moral legitimacy. Here he becomes like a scientist hanging onto a fundamentalist religion. He argues like a well-drilled child, going over the same responses again and again, and never moving forward an inch. We're only doing what everybody else does, the Banana war is nothing compared with Vietnam (that mighty mother of excuses), we're only providing for needs that society is too hypocritical to recognize—fair enough if you include listening to the juke box and hauling grain among these. The Mafia uses legitimate businesses to "dry clean" its money—and apparently its members' consciences. (pp. 24-5)

Unfortunately the author cannot follow Bill all the way to the trenches. Talese's role was like that of a Mafia child, or, as Bill Bonanno might say, like a US citizen under Johnson, assured that the other guy started it and that daddy detests violence. Talese's account of the Banana war seems disingenuous even on a reading of texts. Nicholas Gage states categorically that Joe Bonanno had contracts out to kill the archdukes of the Luchese and Gambino families and that the contracts fell into the wrong hands—Joe Colombo's, as it happened—lighting the whole string of crackers. Talese ascribes the contracts to a loyal but muddled lieutenant of Bonanno's, acting for once in his life without orders. (This lieutenant died shortly afterward of heart failure, the Mafia's No. 1 killer.) And during the war itself, according to Talese, we are not to suppose young Bill did any actual killing. Some days he went to work like a Jane Austen gentleman who does something or other in the City; other days, he hid out and worried about his weight, every fluctuation of which is carefully recorded; but in neither case was he anything but passive.

Some critics have found mischief in this apparent whitewash, but the writer as Mafia child has an interesting vantage point. With the violence down to a dull roar off stage, we get a better look at the way of life all that blood is paying for. There is a brooding sense of self-pity and injured innocence in the Bonanno household that infects even their pleasures. . . .

Talese's book has a further peculiar advantage of a kind that can only happen once. The method he has chosen, that of the nonfiction novel or new journalism or whatever it's called this month, would be, at least as practiced here, an unfortunate strategy for most subjects. Talese uses the resources of fiction all right—but what fiction! For instance, to vivify scenes where he was not present himself, he decorates with things that are *likely* to have happened, those lifelike things we all do—i.e., Bill loosens his tie when he boards his plane, stretches his legs, etc.—little wax flowers of description that give off the same unreality as bad Victorian novels. But this proves to be weirdly right for the subject. The prose matches the stiff watchful facade of the Mafia. One is reminded of a touched-up country wedding photo, with the cheeks identically rouged and the eyes glazed, of the kind the Bonanno family might have ordered for themselves back in Sicily. (p. 25)

Wilfrid Sheed, "Everybody's Mafia," in The New York Review of Books *(reprinted with permission from* The New York Review of Books; *copyright © 1972 Nyrev, Inc.), Vol. XIX, No. 1, July 20, 1972, pp. 23-7.**

PAUL ROBINSON

Thy Neighbor's Wife is a better book than its inauspicious beginning would lead one to expect. For all its minor annoyances and substantial heft, it makes interesting, informative, and sometimes even titillating reading.

I should note immediately that its subject is much narrower than the advance publicity has suggested. Talese himself calls it "a book about sex in America," and he describes its theme as "the redefinition of morality." But in reality, he treats only limited aspects of American sexual life. . . .

The book's strengths and limitations derive from a single intellectual predilection: like any good reporter, Talese conceives of the recent history of sexual customs as a "story," or, as he puts it himself, as "one of the most important stories of his lifetime." Stories display certain characteristics: they have shape and drama, they are dominated by personalities, and, at their best, they express a point of view. The most successful parts of Talese's book are precisely those that lend themselves to "storial" treatment. (p. 105)

Talese's second theme—the new style of infidelity—gives him more trouble. Unlike the vicissitudes of the Playboy empire or the history of censorship, it is not a story. It can't be adequately encompassed through an account of individual characters; it lacks clear dramatic contours; and it raises moral questions that only the most poised and rigorous intelligence can negotiate successfully. The subject best lends itself to two possible approaches: the sociological, such as Alfred Kinsey pursued in his monumental studies of 1948 and 1953; or the novelistic, such as one finds in, say, John Updike's *Couples*. Talese's procedure falls, none too happily, between these stools.

He begins by accepting the sociologist's rigorous empirical premises: "The names of the people in this book are real, and the scenes and events described on the following pages actually happened." Everything about the book argues that Talese, save for isolated rhetorical extravagances and an occasional lapse into self-deception, has been faithful to his word. Nevertheless, he isn't willing to express his findings in the highly abstract statistical form that a commitment to historical realism usually implies. Rather, he wants to convey something of the concrete feeling and nuance of changing sexual mores—in other words, he wants to convey just those things that are inaccessible to the sociologist because they don't allow of systematic treatment.

He attempts to escape this predicament by way of autobiography and what might be called projected autobiography. To his credit, Talese has the frankness to acknowledge this tactic and even to introduce it explicitly into his text. He ends with an explanation (in the third person) of how he came to write the book, which leaves no doubt that the new style of infidelity he describes is in large measure his own infidelity. . . .

Talese is too intelligent to generalize blithely from his limited data. For the most part, he is satisfied merely to intimate that his own experience and that of the Sandstone [Retreat commune] habitués prefigure America's sexual future. His procedure is self-consciously impressionistic, and he seldom makes bolder claims for his findings than would a good novelist. Still, one does not come away from this book, as one did from the Kinsey volumes, with the confident sense of having found out how things really are.

Judged, then, as a work of gentle introspection and astute but essentially casual social observation, *Thy Neighbor's Wife* must be counted a success. Within its own self-imposed limits, it has only two important shortcomings. First, it is infected by a subtle overinflation. In order to heighten the sense of drama, the characters are lent a weightiness that they can't always bear. Each dalliance, it seems, must have existential resonances and reflect profound psychological shifts. People aren't simply horny, they are dissatisfied with their lives. They don't just want to get laid, they are seeking escape from bourgeois conformity. Talese's refusal to let his characters be the prosaic and insipid figures that they sometimes must have been soon grows tiresome.

A more serious fault is the author's moral diffidence. He is not certain in his own mind exactly how he feels about the sexual changes he describes. On the one hand, he appreciates the case for liberation. Indeed, he has benefited from it in his own life. But he is sensitive enough to recognize that something valuable has been endangered in the process. . . . One might argue that he has the courage to expose his own moral confusion. Yet it seems fair to expect those who make a public matter of their sexuality to demonstrate a firmer grasp of the issues than the rest of us bemused creatures. (p. 106)

Paul Robinson, "The Talese Report," in Psychology Today (copyright © 1980 Ziff-Davis Publishing Company), Vol. 13, No. 11, April, 1980, pp. 105-06.

ROBERT SHERRILL

The publicity [surrounding *Thy Neighbor's Wife*] has been extraordinary—"landmark book," and so forth—but the product is not. *Thy Neighbor's Wife* is constructed mostly from the sort of intellectual plywood you find in most neighborhood bars: part voyeurism, part amateur psychoanalysis, part six-pack philosophy.

Arthur Bremer failed to achieve orgasm in a New York massage parlor, and a month later he shot George Wallace in a Maryland parking lot. (Get it, huh?) A woman who finally became convinced that her genitalia were as good-looking as the next woman's gained so much confidence that "she demanded a raise—and got it." The only essential difference between nude art and nude porno is that one is created for the wealthy and the other for the common man.

There you have three accurate paraphrases of Talese. I stick them in here at the beginning so you'll know you can unbuckle your seat belts. *Thy Neighbor's Wife* never takes off. At best it is little more than expansion of what any semiconscious newspaper reader already knows: that the establishment is a pretty clumsy monitor of morality, that there is a great deal of money to be made by those persons clever and daring enough to circumvent the establishment's strictures, and that society's sex taboos are falling like an aged lothario's ardor.

Although Talese is practical enough to admit that money is the chief motivation of the sex industry, he also seems to be arguing that virtually all purveyors of erotica are created by childhood oppression. (pp. 1-2)

Unfortunately for Talese, he brings such titillations to the marketplace too late to shock. Descriptions of sex clubs have been finding their way into print, even in family newspapers, for years. . . .

[The] most irritating aspect of *Thy Neighbor's Wife,* aside from the bad psychiatry, is the bad writing. Talese smothers you in clichés and soap-opera language. . . .

For a book that pretends to be a broad survey, there are some strange omissions. Where's Bob Guccione of *Penthouse,* who pushed the pink much farther into mass circulation than Hefner ever dared to do? And why is there not one mention of the whorehouse industry? Has it disappeared?

Still, there are pluses. Talese does an excellent job reviewing the court battles between bluenoses and freethinkers over the past century or so. And he does come up with some fine folk trivia. . . .

It's just too bad that Talese has to be so heavy-handed. In trying to get a good grip on sex he squeezes it to death. In trying to make kinky sex seem ordinary he only succeeds in making ordinary sex seem kinky. *Thy Neighbor's Wife* offers sex without elegance or mystery and—most dread defect of all—without even a touch of humor. (p. 2)

Robert Sherrill, "Selling Sex in America," in Book World—The Washington Post (© 1980, The Washington Post), April 27, 1980, pp. 1-2.

ELIOT FREMONT-SMITH

I think *Thy Neighbor's Wife* is a perfectly worthy, even brave endeavor, and that it is an achievement of sorts on its own real—not claimed—terms. I also think that thematic and structural grandiosity . . . is . . . transparent and deterimental.

The intention seems hard-core commercial and is certainly time honored: to neaten and elevate the book, as if programmed receptivity were all. The result is not only a kind of gridlock, but intimations of large conclusions about sexual nirvana that the book cannot support, and indeed, at times, belies. . . . [Talese] is a seemingly inexhaustable interviewer of others and himself, a listener and recorder and arranger, but not a complicated questioner. The assumption that he is, and that this book more than scratches the surface (or underside) of "the social and sexual trends of the entire nation," has led and will continue to lead to much critical effluvia. (p. 40)

The fault—and it is first of all the book's—is that it pretends to be more encompassing and coherent that it is. In fact, its substantive materials are quite modest. What's our fault is the enormous premium we place on the big and unifying theme . . . and our willingness to equate organizational dramatics with analytical break-through. One can't really get around the determined structure of *Thy Neighbor's Wife* (certainly part of what took nine stamina-filled years), but that doesn't excuse the critical failure even to recognize that Talese's structure far from complementing thematic coherence, points up its absence.

Talese has very little to say, of broad and substantive interest, about the whyfores and whithers of changing American sexual mores. What he does do is weave together a bunch of stories that would have remained isolated but for his own *physical* enterprise of traveling around the country and then organizing a narrative suspense. (pp. 40-1)

There is no question that the country has undergone an enormous shift of attitude about sexual behavior, but Talese's concentration is on specific tales, mostly fringe, and on spinning connections between them, both as writer and researcher/experiencer, that seem to widen their scope and significance and reveal new fact—that monogamy, for instance, is on the way out and that that's a good thing. . . .

At the end, Talese seems to glimpse the difficulty, the void at the center of the book. Try as he does, he cannot really pull it together in the big and meaningful way intended; the incidents are one place, their true effects somewhere else. . . .

I don't know about thee, but this seems to me an achievement of sorts—circa many years ago, but touching all the same. It shouldn't destroy marriage, or drive critics crazy. (p. 41)

Eliot Fremont-Smith, "Thy Neighbor's Old Lady" (reprinted by permission of The Village Voice and the author; copyright © News Group Publications, Inc., 1980), in The Village Voice, Vol. XXV, No. 17, April 28, 1980, pp. 39-41.

BENJAMIN DeMOTT

We've leaped forward . . .—in Talese's view—from shame to happy expressiveness, from unacknowledged burning to relaxed acceptance of our pleasures, from superstition to light. Therefore—inevitably—a book about sex in America [*Thy Neighbor's Wife*] must take the form of a paean to Progress.

It's a mindless form, in my opinion, far out of touch for much of its length with the best current thinking about the behavior and attitudes it presumes to describe. I know of few historians, anthropologists, or semiologists nowadays who don't consider it a mistake to seal off change in sexual attitudes and behavior from the broader structures of life, as though such change occurred in some inviolable theater of ideas, Benightedness and Enlightenment wrestling each other, one on one, for domination of the human future. Some experts take as a starting point the assumption that true liberation for humankind necessarily entails a struggle for recovery of a sense of human solidarity—a recovery hard to achieve not because of prudery but because of divisions rooted in property and class. Others stress that the new sexual permissiveness—"repressive tolerance," as Herbert Marcuse called it—is simply one of a hundred instruments of social control guiding the consumer economy. But no writer of consequence in the field shares Gay Talese's vacuous faith in the autonomy of the so-called sexual revolution.

The reason this vacuity isn't fatal to *Thy Neighbor's Wife* is partly that Talese is journalistically adept at ferreting out undernoticed intricacies of overpublicized events—sexual curiosities past and present, revelatory details of the personal life of celebrities, numberless other items of "feature interest." (p. 99)

In the end, though, it's merely the author's alertness to piquant sidebar material that distracts attention from his weak intellectual scaffolding. The case is that, lodged in the middle of his book, as utterly unpredictable and unassimilable as a sermon on *radix malorum est cupiditas* would seem if encountered midway through, say, *How You Can Become Financially Independent by Investing in Real Estate,* is a narrative of liberation that's extraordinary in its crude emotional power, and that burned off, for me, swiftly and irresistibly, much of the jungle of progress-prattle surrounding it. . . .

Nightmares, . . . garish and sensational—as many as a half-dozen—are distributed throughout the Bullaro-Williamson chapters of the book. Soap, chatchpenny lubriciousness, and sideshow chills jostle each other in these scenes. Repeatedly as one reads one finds oneself wanting to hoot at the extravaganza, the spectacle of lordly, half-educated Faustians, self-styled Ayn Randian Leaders, imagining themselves as instructors to nature, exhorting their presumed inferiors to break every chain of attachment to the past, to common humanity, ordinary trust, ordinary shame. What have we here but a hideously farcical reduction of the decent aspirations of democratic individualism? What response to such madness could be appropriate except a chortle?

But loss is not mocked—not substantial human loss, not when accompanied by deep and intense awareness that it is self-caused, and that alternatives existed. Two hundred pages before the end of *Thy Neighbor's Wife* we see John Bullaro contemplating the wreckage of his days, recalling in despair the "first sexual encounter with Barbara at the insurance convention in Palm Springs, the emergence of John Williamson as a problem solver, the nude evenings in the Williamsons' house on Mu-

llholland Drive . . . '' That teasing time, rich in intimations of holiday release, seemed "so exhilarating and liberating"—and now Bullaro understands it as nothing other than "a preamble to destruction and chaos." Whatever love and order had been the stability of his life he had "sacrificed to the whim of experimentation and change." (p. 100)

I can imagine a reader of taste and good sense refusing sympathy to this victim, stiffening against the current of sentimentality. But the refusal is difficult; I was moved.

The author himself seems not to have been. The entire hundred-page Bullaro *exemplum* seems indeed to have had minuscule impact, psychological or otherwise, upon him. After dutifully running it through, he returns to the upbeat chronicle of Reason Triumphant, as though no real interruption had taken place. . . .

Thy Neighbor's Wife says a good deal, I'd argue, about the impacted condition of moral discourse in the late twentieth century. A fair conclusion is that we can bear reminders of the profound historical admonitions agains covetousness and betrayal only if they're spotted into alien surroundings, allowed to peep out through the scrim as though by accident, claiming no more than an impatient and reluctant attention. Cameo appearances. Yet I remain impressed that Gay Talese, eyewitness, represented so fully the pathetic anguish of his experimenting couple. Despite chic obtuseness and intellectual naiveté, he possesses, as a good reporter, the ability to recognize (if not to understand) a whole story when it's proffered. Beyond this he has an honorable sense of obligation: whole stories, assimilable or no, deserve to be passed along in their fullness. Thanks to these gifts, nourished in this instance by a purely professional code (what besides purely professional codes survives?), the paean to Progress in *Thy Neighbor's Wife* may self-destruct. (p. 101)

Benjamin DeMott, "A Sexual Pilgrim's Progress," (copyright © 1980 by The Atlantic Monthly Company, Boston, Mass.; reprinted with permission of the author), in The Atlantic Monthly, *Vol. 245, No. 5, May, 1980, pp. 98-101.*

ROBERT COLES

[Gay Talese] offers us a report [in "**Thy Neighbor's Wife**"] . . . on just how far some of us have willingly, gladly strayed not only from 19th-century morality, but from the kind that most of the 20th century has taken for granted. His method of inquiry is that of "participant-observation"; as a matter of fact, I doubt any so-called "field worker" can claim to have surpassed Mr. Talese with regard to personal involvement. He talked with men and women who had embraced uninhibited or unconventional sexuality, but he also became a distinct part of a world he was trying to comprehend. That is, he not only worked in Manhattan's massage parlors, he became a beneficiary of their favors. He joined, briefly one gathers, a nudist camp. He did not fail to get at least some pleasure out of the activities ("communal sex") that took place at Sandstone, near Los Angeles.

Yet this long narrative will probably disappoint those with prurient interests. It is not an exhibitionist's confession. . . . Mr. Talese has a serious interest in watching his fellow human beings, in listening to them, and in presenting honestly what he has seen and heard. He writes clean, unpretentious prose. He has a gift, through a phrase here, a sentence there, of making important narrative and historical connections. We are given, really, a number of well-told stories, their social message cumulative: A drastically transformed American sexuality has emerged during this past couple of decades. . . .

The heart of Mr. Talese's book is the life stories he presents—factual accounts of men and women not provided disguises: Hugh Hefner of Playboy; Dr. Alex Comfort ("The Joy of Sex"); Barbara Cramer and John Williamson, the founders of Sandstone; Al Goldstein, the founder and editor of Screw magazine; and the most compelling of all, couples such as John and Judith Bullaro, he an insurance salesman, she a housewife and mother, ordinary people who gradually became part of the quite new sexual life such places as Sandstone have offered.

The tone of the book varies—a reflection, surely, of the author's complicated, if not ambiguous responses to what he witnessed and sometimes took part in (now gingerly, one surmises, now with few if any reservations). Mr. Talese is at his best when he is away from the high-pitched cosmopolitanism of California—in the Midwest or the rural South. . . .

But no matter the geography, Mr. Talese pays attention to more than sex; we get, repeatedly, the textures of a given social scene. He can be a controlled but touching writer, anxious to convey the melancholy, the hurts of a particular life, yet able to stop short of sentiment. I had not expected to feel anything but repulsion for some of the people described in this book; yet as is often the case when a good writer looks beneath the surfaces of life, even the kind that seems cheap or tawdry or twisted or just plain foolish, strangely compelling proofs are discovered—reminders that here, too, is a moment of important human truth. (p. 3)

What Mr. Talese claims is that the "polymorphous perverse" of Freud has now become enough a part of our everyday social life to merit a study that took a long time to do and to write up. His evidence—the range of his informants, the geographic and cultural spread of his investigation—seems to bear him out. Whether he is describing a rising tide or one now already at ebb (as with some descriptions of "youth" and their "behavior" made in the recent past) is hard to know. But one thing comes across loud and clear: The people who embraced sexuality for various reasons—be they mainly personal, or for commercial profit—are still, like the rest of us, slouching toward Jerusalem; that is, are as mean and self-centered and vain and ungenerous and nasty, from time to time, as the rest of us "unliberated" ones. . . .

What kind of ethical responsibilities are at work in such lives? One wonders, too, about the moral sensibility presumably at work in this book. The author is quick to scorn our hypocrisies and self-serving pieties. He mocks some of our Supreme Court Justices. He confesses his various lusts. He mentions his wife and children—the troubling effect his work had on them. But exactly what does he think of Hugh Hefner, of the life he lives—all those oiled and powdered women, an endless succession bought by a demanding millionaire in the service of his sexual megalomania? Does Gay Talese want such a fate for any woman—for his daughters? And what about the women who give all those Manhattan massages—why the reluctance to look at their lives, to comment on their situation? Has this shrewd journalist, this acomplished storyteller not once been inspired by the abovementioned to a cautionary tale he can share with us—maybe even to shed his "cool" with an outburst of disgust? Who ought to get "love" (if that is the right word here) from whom—and at what cost of human dignity? What happens to a culture, a civilization, when sexual fantasies become for increasing numbers a reigning preoccupation—one

vast Id, with the Ego and Super-Ego mere straws in the brisk wind of a given social history?

I don't think those are the questions of a few sexual puritans, or for that matter, a few narrow-minded influential burghers, anxious to stifle the physical aspirations of others. Ordinary men and women all over the world wonder about such matters; do so not necessarily because they are "inhibited," because they have yet to become "liberated," but out of their humanity. As philosophers once knew to put it—and would that they did so more often these days: what is the meaning of life, and how ought one to live it? (p. 39)

> *Robert Coles, "Transforming American Sexuality," in* The New York Times Book Review *(© 1980 by The New York Times Company; reprinted by permission), May 4, 1980, pp. 3, 38-9.*

DOUGLAS HILL

Talese's assumptions [in *Thy Neighbor's Wife*] often seem paralysingly traditional when set against his ambitions: he has entertained few possibilities for sexual existence beyond the conventionally orgasmic. The book is primarily male-oriented despite some lip service to feminism. The male organ, Talese tells us, is "rooted in man's soul, and without its potence he cannot truly live." It follows that liberation (free love) is better than constraint. Coupling, even with constraints (like marriage and children), beats masturbation. Masturbation is a good deal better than nothing. It took nine years to come up with *this*?

Talese is a dogged and honest reporter, even if his biases and limitations prevent a reader's full sympathy with his earnest conclusions. If one believes that acquaintance with the phenomena of a situation is valuable in and for itself, then *Thy Neighbor's Wife* can provide at least that starting point for understanding and change. The book never fails to be thought-provoking. It might just do for sexual enlightenment what television is accomplishing for the proceedings on Parliament Hill. It won't provide the truth, and what it does provide is less fun and more banal than we ever imagined, but at least for the moment, through the magic of the medium, we're *there*.

> *Douglas Hill, "A Pageant of Sexual Obsession" (reprinted by permission of the author), in* Maclean's *Magazine, Vol. 93, No. 19, May 12, 1980, p. 60.*

ALEXANDER COCKBURN

Though [*Thy Neighbor's Wife*] purports to be a saga of sex liberation, of society's journey upward toward the light, Talese is not interested in sensuality, the erotic, or the perverse.

In fact the book is terribly sedate. He has a concept of sex as "recreation," rather like the other great postwar bourgeois obsession, tennis. Singles, or doubles, a good fast serve, netplay, game, set and M-A-A-A-T-C-H. Then back to the nuclear nest and more deeply felt, improved netplay with the Missus.

The dark god can be found in the index, wedged between, "Peeping Toms" and "Pennsylvania." This is Mr. "Penis" who has the modest distinction of getting three references. Talese's normally lackluster prose takes on a modicum of energy when dealing with Mr. P. . . .

Talese's book, though purportedly about liberation and the escape from the Puritan heritage, is not about the liberation of women or of Mrs. V [Vagina] into emancipated hunter-gatherers of sexual gratification. Mr. P is the hunter, home from the hill to the womb. . . .

The overall assumption of the book is that Mr. P is having a better time these days. Talese noticed this almost a decade ago and thought he would write a book explaining how and why.

Various techniques are mustered for the enterprise. Least successful is Talese's nonchalant blend of instant-history, which crops up intermittently—reeking of scissors, paste, and the hot breath of the editor. . . . (p. 6)

Talese deals with Hefner at length. His function in the book is twofold, as illustration of how Americans were provided a better class of wank in the postwar years, and as emblem of the great success story; how Mr. P shook aside his early inhibitions, grew rich and successful, lived in a lovely home, possessed Mrs. Vs by the hundreds, if not thousands, without truly paying the price demanded by nineteenth-century morality. (p. 8)

Sandstone was a sex resort dedicated to the refutation of [the double standard], where every P could merge with every consenting V and vice versa, and Talese devotes much space to the intentions and adventures of its original inhabitants.

Put in elemental terms the story tells what happens when the insurance business meets up with the military-industrial complex. (p. 10)

The truth is that there are two Taleses hard at work, telling two stories at cross purposes to each other. Advanced, "recreational sex" Talese hawks the free fuck/freer world line of goods, with plenty of bouncy stuff about the joys of $P^2 = V^2$ and the merry times enjoyed by all down on the old sex farm. Ur-Talese, New Jersey Catholic with a size 16 superego, comes lumbering along behind with intimations that Bullaro wanted to kill Williamson; that Williamson was Mr. P(rimus) inter P(are)s, group guru and power fucker; and he hints that unlike John Humphrey Noyes's boast about the nineteenth-century experiment in P/V multiple equations at the Oneida Colony ("We made a raid into an unknown country, charted it, and returned without the loss of a man, woman or child") there were some psychic victims of Sandstone. Oneida was a manufacturing facility with an emphasis on eugenics, hence was the self-confident progeny of nineteenth-century industrial capitalism, whereas Sandstone was, in the appropriate late capitalist mode, devoted to sex servicing (voluntarily engaged in by the adepts), being finally bought in 1974 by an ex-marine and social worker whose first act was to double the couples-club rates. Surplus sex = surplus value. Neither manufacturing nor eugenics was of interest to the Sandstonistas. Talese's book is almost devoid of any mention of children. The P/V reportage steers clear of them, presumably on the grounds that recreation and re-creation are not the same thing.

Ur-Talese and Advanced Talese, toiling through the nine-year travail of *Thy Neighbor's Wife,* never quite sorted things out between themselves on matters of basic attitude, but they are at one in extolling the book's high importance. (p. 11)

The shabbiest thing about this sad book is Talese's view of it as pioneering because it tells what "real people" do in real bedrooms. It is as though the prime sexual discourse of the twentieth-century—psychoanalysis and "the case study"—let alone the far older juridical confession—had never been Talese's function as a journalist in this particular project is quite other than he proposes. His ambition was to describe a struggle

against puritanism, and his belief seems to be that though puritanism still threatens and menaces the liberation of Mr. P and Mrs. V, all will be well and at least the middle classes will evolve to more natural sexual mores, confounding the repressive instincts of the state and other powers that be. Back to Reich and the crazies: freer fuck means freer world.

Reich was wrong, and Michel Foucault right when he said, "We must not think that by saying yes to sex, one says no to power." (pp. 11-12)

[Talese] should have pondered his actual achievement as a journalist here. In his meandering package tour he has ratified the fresher forms of subjugation of Mr. P and all his friends in these late capitalist days. With the same true instincts of the social-issues liberal he touts the trip as a journey toward liberation and a better world, with "real life" stenciled on the side of the suitcase. (p. 12)

*Alexander Cockburn, "Mr. P, Mrs. V, and Mr. T,"
in* The New York Review of Books *(reprinted with permission from* The New York Review of Books; *copyright © 1980 Nyrev, Inc.), Vol. XXVII, No. 9, May 29, 1980, pp. 6-12.*

HERBERT I. LONDON

The publication of Gay Talese's book, *Thy Neighbor's Wife,* is an important statement about this nation and its values circa 1980. This, I should hastily add, has nothing at all to do with the value of the book. In character and in content this work is lubricious. Its only redeeming quality is in the author's seemingly endless ingenuity in making sex passionless. In many respects Talese is like a contemporary Lucretius. He mistakes the mechanics of sex for the celebration and the mystery of love in the same way Lucretius mistakes energy for the transcendence and the majesty of God. This book, which supposedly deals with sex in America, reads like directions for an Erector Set. What I find particularly baffling is the author's view that descriptions of massage parlors, Al Goldstein's enterprises, Hugh Hefner, and Sandstone—a commune for casual sex—constitute an examination of sex in America. Where is the discussion of sex as a dimension of fulfilling and binding relationship? Is Talese prescient? Are we evolving to a time when sex is exchanged like handshakes?

Thy Neighbor's Wife is much less a description and more a prescription of what sexual morality should be. Talese is not a dispassionate journalist. He arrives at conclusions based on his own experiences. When the evidence doesn't suit him—as is the case with one sexual pioneer whose activities in Sandstone end in divorce, therapy, loneliness, and despair—Talese drops the matter as an unwelcome exception to the generally blissful generalization of promiscuous sex. One gets the impression that the enemy in the book is inhibition. Whether the inhibition is caused by Anthony Comstock's crusades against sex or by bourgeois morality seems unimportant. The only distinction that counts is whether you are for or against casual sex.

This argument, which appears as ingenuously as Candide facing the verities of life, ignores the totality of human experience. It is as if Gay Talese thinks he has discovered Somerset Maugham's "New-Found-Land" only to find it is Sodom and Gomorrah. By accepting the adolescent belief that doing what you want makes what you want worth doing, Talese preaches a standard for anything goes. At Sandstone, for example, conventional morality is subordinated to feelings of satisfaction. . . .

Where is the so-called liberation in this setting? Can one be a dissenter at Sandstone without a psychic price being extracted? Talese tells us that his generation was "uptight" about sex; it was caught in the bourgeois trap of religious and moral standards which cause shame, guilt, anxiety, and neurosis. I won't attempt to explain to the sybarites why there is a societal need for guilt. But what I find baffling is Talese's total insensitivity to the psychological demands of contemporary liberationists. How can one ignore the role that sexual freedom has played in destabilizing family relationships and sinking sexual pioneers into a cesspool of loveless sex and depression? (p. 415)

Talese writes solely to the drum beat of sexual awareness. His human awareness is not discernible. For him the good life is the one free of commitments, open to sexual adventures, and severed from the bond of bourgeois constraints.

There is a curious irony to this argument that has obviously eluded Talese. If man should free himself from the shackles of middle class morality, why associate with those who, by virtue of this union, limit that freedom? The logical concomitant of this reasoning is that those who are free are also without associations, except, of course, those associations that gratify immediate desires. Since any relationship assumes some degree of commitment, autonomous man must guard against a genuine involvement with others. One result is a divorce rate that soars to the level of newly discovered free spirits who had once promised to love, honor, and obey. Institutions such as Sandstone are then created for free spirits to come together or massage parlors open in direct response to the need for companionship. All the while liberationists contend that nirvana has been found in a hot tub or that the range of human experience has been enhanced through casual sexual encounters. But they protest too much. All one has to do to discover the vacuousness in the claims is causally chat about loneliness with the recently liberated. The vacant stares reveal more than any words of satisfaction.

Nonetheless, the publicity for new lifestyles (whatever happened to a life?) continues unabated. . . . But when the noise is subdued and people have a chance to consider the consequences of sexual liberation, they may find that human relationships have lost some of their loveliness. We may find that the mystery of sex has been unraveled and in the process human sensitivity and concern have diminished as well. And, alas, we may come to believe that love is a maudlin preoccupation that represents a bygone era. I suspect that even Talese won't like that time very much. (p. 416)

Herbert I. London, "A Contemporary Lucretius," in Modern Age *(copyright © 1980 by the Intercollegiate Studies Institute, Inc.), Vol. 24, No. 4, Fall, 1980, pp. 415-16.*

Alvin Toffler
1928-

Toffler, an American futurist writer, was formerly an associate editor of *Fortune* magazine. The title of his first best seller, *Future Shock* (1970), has been transformed into everyday usage to mean the "inability of people to cope with very rapid social and technological change." Toffler is admonitory but essentially optimistic in both *Future Shock* and his latest book, *The Third Wave* (1980), in which he sees society moving towards decentralization and profound economic diversity. Some critics have faulted his method, arguing that he inundates the reader with a mass of undigested data, from which he draws fairly simplistic conclusions. Most critics agree, however, that his futurist books are readable and have contributed some genuinely original concepts to future studies. (See also *Contemporary Authors*, Vols. 13-16, rev. ed.)

Excerpt from *FUTURE SHOCK*

Future shock is a time phenomenon, a product of the greatly accelerated rate of change in society. It arises from the superimposition of a new culture on an old one. It is culture shock in one's own society. But its impact is far worse. For most Peace Corps men, in fact most travelers, have the comforting knowledge that the culture they left behind will be there to return to. The victim of future shock does not.

Take an individual out of his own culture and set him down suddenly in an environment sharply different from his own, with a different set of cues to react to—different conceptions of time, space, work, love, religion, sex, and everything else— then cut him off from any hope of retreat to a more familiar social landscape, and the dislocation he suffers is doubly severe. Moreover, if this new culture is itself in constant turmoil, and if—worse yet—its values are incessantly changing, the sense of disorientation will be still further intensified. Given few clues as to what kind of behavior is rational under the radically new circumstances, the victim may well become a hazard to himself and others.

Now imagine not merely an individual but an entire society, an entire generation—including its weakest, least intelligent, and most irrational members—suddenly transported into this new world. The result is mass disorientation, future shock on a grand scale.

This is the prospect that man now faces. Change is avalanching upon our heads and most people are grotesquely unprepared to cope with it.

Is all this exaggerated? I think not. It has become a cliché to say that what we are now living through is a "second industrial revolution." This phrase is supposed to impress us with the speed and profundity of the change around us. But in addition to being platitudinous, it is misleading. For what is occurring now is, in all likelihood, bigger, deeper, and more important than the industrial revolution. Indeed, a growing body of reputable opinion asserts that the present movement represents nothing less than the second great divide in human history, comparable in magnitude only with that first great break in

historic continuity, the shift from barbarism to civilization. (pp. 11-12)

Alvin Toffler, in his Future Shock *(copyright © 1970 by Alvin Toffler; reprinted by permission of Random House, Inc.), Random House, 1970 (and reprinted by Bantam Books, 1971, 561 p.).*

Excerpt from *THE THIRD WAVE*

A new civilization is emerging in our lives, and blind men everywhere are trying to suppress it. This new civilization brings with it new family styles; changed ways of working, loving, and living; a new economy; new political conflicts; and beyond all this an altered consciousness as well. Pieces of this new civilization exist today. Millions are already attuning their lives to the rhythms of tomorrow. Others, terrified of the future, are engaged in a desperate, futile flight into the past and are trying to restore the dying world that gave them birth.

The dawn of this new civilization is the single most explosive fact of our lifetimes.

574

It is the central event—the key to understanding the years immediately ahead. It is an event as profound as that First Wave of change unleashed ten thousand years ago by the invention of agriculture, or the earthshaking Second Wave of change touched off by the industrial revolution. We are the children of the next transformation, the Third Wave. (p. 3)

Humanity faces a quantum leap forward. It faces the deepest social upheaval and creative restructuring of all time. Without clearly recognizing it, we are engaged in building a remarkable new civilization from the ground up. This is the meaning of the Third Wave.

Until now the human race has undergone two great waves of change, each one largely obliterating earlier cultures or civilizations and replacing them with ways of life inconceivable to those who came before. The First Wave of change—the agricultural revolution—took thousands of years to play itself out. The Second Wave—the rise of industrial civilization—took a mere three hundred years. Today history is even more accelerative, and it is likely that the Third Wave will sweep across history and complete itself in a few decades. We, who happen to share the planet at this explosive moment, will therefore feel the full impact of the Third Wave in our own lifetimes.

Tearing our families apart, rocking our economy, paralyzing our political systems, shattering our values, the Third Wave affects everyone. It challenges all the old power relationships, the privileges and prerogatives of the endangered elites of today, and provides the backdrop against which the key power struggles of tomorrow will be fought.

Much in this emerging civilization contradicts the old traditional industrial civilization. It is, at one and the same time, highly technological and anti-industrial.

The Third Wave brings with it a genuinely new way of life based on diversified, renewable energy sources; on methods of production that make most factory assembly lines obsolete; on new, non-nuclear families; on a novel institution that might be called the "electronic cottage"; and on radically changed schools and corporations of the future. The emergent civilization writes a new code of behavior for us and carries us beyond standardization, synchronization, and centralization, beyond the concentration of energy, money, and power.

This new civilization, as it challenges the old, will topple bureaucracies, reduce the role of the nation-state, and give rise to semiautonomous economies in a postimperialist world. It requires governments that are simpler, more effective, yet more democratic than any we know today. It is a civilization with its own distinctive world outlook, its own ways of dealing with time, space, logic, and causality.

Above all, . . . Third Wave civilization begins to heal the historic breach between producer and consumer, giving rise to the "prosumer" economics of tomorrow. For this reason, among many, it could—with some intelligent help from us—turn out to be the first truly humane civilization in recorded history. (pp. 4-5)

> *Alvin Toffler, in his* The Third Wave *(copyright © 1980 by Alvin Toffler; abridged by permission of William Morrow & Company, Inc.), William Morrow, 1980, 544 p.*

THEODORE ROSZAK

Those to whom it comes as no news that "change is avalanching upon our heads and most people are grotesquely unprepared to cope with it," may not find much more in the first 300 pages of [*Future Shock*] than a fresh supply of evidence. . . . Too much, too soon, too big, too fast: Toffler wraps it all up in the blanket term "future shock": "the distress, both physical and psychological, that arises from an overload of the human organism's physical adaptive systems and its decision making processes."

Toffler becomes far more interesting when he gets round to suggesting remedies for the pathological impermanence of contemporary life. Now, you would think that a book calling impassionedly for better social planning would have something to do with sociology and politics, would you not? Would it not seem that getting a grip on the fluidity and fragmentation around us required some discussion of who controls the dynamics of change? Yet Toffler devotes not a page to the analysis of social power. As if future shock were nobody's fault in particular. As if indeed there were not power, privilege, and profit in abundance to be had from keeping industrial society in its chronic state of bedazzled dislocation. The politics of vertigo, it might be called. (p. 596)

Nonetheless, he, like all his colleagues in this strange and suspicious enterprise called the "futures industry," prefers not to see social change as a political issue. For that requires naming names and stepping on toes; . . . which futurologists seem to regard as bad professional manners. Best, then, to regard "acceleration and transience" of our lives as a conveniently impersonal force of nature. It is an "avalanche," a "storm," a "vortex," an "upheaval." The change-freighted future just somehow "arrives" . . . "prematurely" . . . like a spring flood. Future shock is a "disease"; but there seem to be no known germ carriers. Little wonder, then, that the only hard knocks Toffler deals out are directed, not at the corporation elites and industrial commissars of the world, not at the military-industrial axis and its vast and various liveried brains trusts; but rather at "the angry and recalcitrant minorities" of "superindustrial society": "Rousseauan romantics," hippies, "technophobes," "young radicals" . . . indigestible types who irk Toffler by opting for such things as "'free societies,' cooperatives, pre-industrial communes, few of which have anything to do with the future."

Ultimately, Toffler is sold on a Flash Gordon vision of things to come; there is no mistaking the zest with which he writes about the technical tricks and gimmicks the future promises. But he would have them work their way painlessly into our lives. The prescription that follows from this is what one would expect: cunning techniques of adaptation, the social extension of the psychology of adjustment. Thus, he suggests "personal stability zones" in the privacy of our own homes. . . . For those who cannot keep up, there might be "enclaves of the past" where they can indulge their atavistic tastes without getting in the way of industrial necessity. . . . What are these but so many psychic lubricants, the better to oil the wheels of officially defined progress?

To be sure, Toffler gives required lip service to democratic values. For the "future consciousness" of the millions, he offers "social futurism." He envisages "social future assemblies" in every locality where all of us may, as amateur "imagineers," brainstorm "probable . . . possible . . . and preferable futures." Thus, "a continuing plebiscite on the future," which is what I would have thought politics has always been about.

Ah, but what Toffler wants is a *responsibile, sophisticated* debate. Meaning, there must be much red-hot and appreciative talk about technological marvels. Meaning, above all, that the participants must take their cues from those who *really know* about the future: the professional futurists whose "scientific futurist institutes" and "future data banks" must be "spotted like nodes in a loose network throughout the entire government structure." Here will be "top calibre men and women from all the sciences and social sciences" especially skilled in esoteric methodologies of predictive evaluation. . . . (pp. 596-97)

Such knowledgeable folk will run our popular deliberations through a "filtering process" for "merciless screening." They will work full time at "the collection and systematic integration of predictive reports by scholars and imaginative thinkers in all the intellectual disciplines all over the world.". . . [They] will watch over "special switchboards and computers" that "tabulate the yes-no votes and pass them on to the 'decision-makers'."

What nonsense this is. And yet what prophetic nonsense. For what could be more inevitable if one is determined to maintain the scale and centralism of the superindustrial machine, and to keep the power where it is? . . . Toffler makes a great point of stressing that "social futurism" is "post-technocratic." But he is dead wrong. It is the perfection of technocracy: the subtle subversion of citizenly competence by beneficient expertise; the obliteration of politics. (p. 597)

> Theodore Roszak, "*Flash Gordon of the Future*" (© New Society; *reprinted by permission of the author*), *in* New Society, *Vol. 16, No. 418, October 1, 1970, pp. 596-97.*

FRANCIS HOPE

[Mr Toffler is] an honourable recruit to the mentally second-best army of American best-sellerdom. Like Vance Packard, he has chosen a good subject. Like David Riesman, he radiates social concern. Like William H. Whyte, he never tells one illustrative anecdote where five will do. Like Daniel Boorstin, he will do better than he deserves. There is a great future for *Future Shock.*

On the other hand to compare Mr Toffler with J. K. Galbraith (as Raymond Fletcher does on the dust-jacket) is an injustice to the elegant sage of Massachusetts. Mr Galbraith was an intellectual being funny; Mr Toffler is an ex-journalist being deadly serious. He is really very concerned that we may not be able to adapt to the pace of change in our century. 'Future shock'—a term coined by analogy with 'culture shock', the extreme disorientation felt by a peasant pitchforked into industrialism or an Eskimo working on a US airbase—really is a threat. The banality of expressions like 'everything changes so fast these days' is a proof of their validity. Can we really cope with disposable marriages, vocational retraining every five years, brain transplants, underwater cities, computer judges and the rest? Or will the whole society, as some critics warn, have a collective nervous breakdown? . . .

Every such work of pop-sociology contains one good idea, wrapped in a catchy phrase. . . . Mr Toffler's contribution is 'The Adhocracy'. Instead of a rigid class of rulers and decision-makers, he argues, modern industry and politics rely more and more on the task force or the special commission, a group of experts in related fields who are convened to solve a particular problem and then go their separate ways. . . .

[His] notion of 'modular' change . . . is really a smart way of describing flexibility: houses with movable walls or machines with adaptable extensions and parts, where the overall framework has a longer life because each component has a shorter one. But his attempt to carry this through into the field of human relations leads him into shallow optimism: a quick turnover of friends and marriage partners is not so easily absorbed as a preference for renting cars rather than owning them, or using a throwaway ballpoint instead of a durable goose-quill. 'Men, in short, seem to be more skilled at breaking off relationships than women,' is Mr Toffler's summing-up of social mobility: not entirely a value-free statement, and one of doubtful value. Suppose we said that women, in short, seem to be more skilled at maintaining relationships than men—would we be condemned to hopeless nostalgia or a double dose of shock?

In the same way, much of Mr Toffler's empirical research contradicts his breezy optimism. (p. 419)

But it is in his proposed remedies that Mr Toffler falls most obviously short of his own grandiose plan. To avoid future shock, children should read science-fiction at school; they should also acquire, not dull old data, but the three basic skills of Learning, Relating and Choosing. (A more pompous and less original definition of the aims of humanistic education would be hard to find.) We need contemporary rituals. 'Certainly, July 20, the day Astronaut Armstrong took "one small step for man, one giant leap for mankind", ought to be made into an annual global celebration of the unity of man.' We need a technology ombudsman. . . . Finally, of course, we need much more and better-paid research in the field of futurology, and governments must pay more attention to it. Mr Toffler conducts such research himself.

It would be difficult to quarrel with the book's main thrust: that rapid change causes psychological problems, that it is also inevitable (though not uncontrollable) and that we shall therefore have to change our ideas, not only about this and that particular problem but about all perceptions, habits and values. (Our idea of an idea, for example, may not survive third-generation computers.) What is disappointing is the mass of energy that goes into specifying these platitudes, without ever questioning their universal truth. For example, the striking inequalities in rates of change worry Mr Toffler not at all. A growing world population is not just one more 'plus' in the list of changes: it cancels out several others, leaving the bigger population no better fed, no more richly provided with commodities than before. . . . Man is still, obstinately, the measure of all things, clothing old impulses of lust, affection and curiosity in the latest available gear. This counter-platitude never figures in Mr Toffler's work, any more than the historical sense which would show him how many innovations are in fact reactions to an earlier pattern. It may yet be the subject of another best-seller—to be called, perhaps, *The Constant Matrix*—which will demonstrate, with many examples and in racy prose, how little has changed on this planet of ours. The nub of such a book might be the 'expectation gap': a boy reads in the papers that everything is changing, and then finds himself doing the same job as his father did, marrying the same kind of girl, eating the same food, travelling equal (psychological) distances for work and pleasure, and bored out of his mind just as the old man was. In a curious way, such a book could coexist happily with *Future Shock*. Like ecumenical faiths, best-sellers never contradict each other; perhaps because they are not saying enough. (pp. 419-20)

Francis Hope, "Whatever Next," in New Statesman (© 1970 The Statesman & Nation Publishing Co. Ltd.), Vol. 80, No. 2063, October 2, 1970, pp. 419-20.

JEROME ZUKOSKY

Hardly anybody will quarrel with [*Future Shock*'s] starting point that great changes have taken place in American society during the past generation. Toffler explores these changes—in family and community life, the organization of work, education, communications, leisure—with a good feel for the stresses induced by alterations in familiar patterns and the human strains involved in adapting. He raises once again the persistent questions that afflict any adult who is socially, economically, and physically mobile: How do you establish and maintain roots, preserve ties with friends and family, obtain satisfaction from job, career, marriage, parenthood? These are the familiar parameters of the "life is a rat race" quandary one finds treated in so many printed pages nowadays, and those worried about it will find the same unexceptional advice in *Future Shock*. . . .

Beset by this total, overwhelming change. . . , many Americans have been unable to adapt. They suffer from "the disease of change," namely "future shock." Like some other terms in the book, "future shock" is subject to variable definitions. At one point it is "the dizzying disorientation brought on by the premature arrival of the future," and at another, "the response to overstimulation." . . .

Taxing the author of *Future Shock* with imprecision or inconsistency, however, is somewhat like taxing a surrealist painter with failure to represent objects realistically. *Future Shock* primarily appeals to emotions, not intelligence. It can best be understood as a secular, modernistic version of a salvationist tract. The format is somewhat like that of an old-time fundamentalist sermon. (p. 195)

Toffler's hell is the future descending upon us, the accelerating torrents of change impelled by technology, "that great growling engine of change." Every imaginable human woe and social stress is attributed to change and technology in an effort to create an impression of onrushing doom. Change, indeed, is *all* that happens in Toffler's society. The process, however, is spurious, a flashing of images outside the self, which exists, it appears, only to be impinged upon. Change consists of movement from one unreal stereotype to another. A disquisition on change in relations between the sexes, for example, takes off from the observation that totally new kinds of arrangements are appearing "as conventional marriage proves itself less and less capable of delivering on its promise of lifelong love." One may wonder when conventional marriage, or any other kind, was ever capable of delivering on such a promise. Not alone among those who write about the future, Toffler seems to lack any sense of the past. He seems unaware that all generations have had to bear the burdens of the human condition; that the human past, at least as much as the present, was full of blood, sweat, and tears, none of which stain the pages of his book.

Future Shock bristles with trivia presented as revelations. . . . We learn, among other things, that a paperback book appears simultaneously "on more than 100,000 newsstands" in the U.S. and disappears thirty days later. . . . (pp. 195-96)

There are many pages of such snippets, accompanied by an obbligato of portentousness, from which we are supposed to gather that something awful, or at least ominous, is happening. Then, well along in the second hundred pages, we begin to get a whiff of brimstone. As Toffler limns the technological novelties to come—"packaged experiences," genetic manipulation, babies produced in laboratory jars—the reader may well be inclined to murmur, "Stop the world, I want to get off." . . .

As a fantasy of doom and salvation, *Future Shock* is designed to appeal to those who are possessed by a powerful itch to believe in their own helplessness, and who externalize their feelings of rage or impotence by blaming "society" and "conditions" for their personal difficulties. The "real problem," Toffler assures them, "lies outside ourselves." This view is a fundamental tenet of the prevailing intellectual orthodoxy, of course, but it is nonetheless at least half wrong, and much mischief has flowed from it.

Future Shock has a perverse quality, for Toffler calls upon the reader to gain salvation by becoming hollow, like those whose emptiness is the principal cause of the social and psychic ills he has taken pains to try to depict and diagnose. The widespread sense of emptiness and rootlessness that he points to as a cause and symptom of "future shock" is attributable less to the acceleration of change than to the cumulative effects over time of voices telling us, in one context or another, that our heritage from the past is outworn and irrelevant. Toffler is only the latest of many.

As for devoting more thought to the future, making more effort to guide it rather than just letting it happen, that may be good advice, but whether the net results turn out to be beneficial will depend on who does the thinking and guiding, and by what criteria, and to what ends. And whatever our efforts to manage the future, it will, of course, remain unpredictable—which to the mature adult is one of its delights. (p. 196)

Jerome Zukosky, "Antidotes for 'Future Shock'," in FORTUNE (© 1970 Time Inc.; all rights reserved), Vol. 82, No. 5, November, 1970, pp. 195-96.

ROBERT CLAIBORNE

Alvin Toffler's *Future Shock* assays as unmistakable schlock, albeit of superior quality. His style is lively and readable—his chapter and section headings, in particular, glitter with such gems as "The Paper Wedding Gown," "The Modular Man," "Communes and Homosexual Daddies" and (my favorite) "Twiggy and the K-Mesons." And, to do him full justice, he has come up with an absolute dilly of an Insight: Future Shock, "the shattering stress and disorientation that we induce in individuals by subjecting them to too much change in too short a time." Future shock is in effect a subdivision of cultural shock—"what happens when the familiar psychological cues that help an individual to function in society are suddenly withdrawn and replaced by new ones that are strange or incomprehensible." Toffler deserves our gratitude for having the wit to see that culture shock can occur not only in space but also in time. (p. 117)

Given an Insight of this potency, it doesn't much matter that Toffler's account of its origins is overlong and exaggerated, or that his discussion of the physical and psychological ills it entrains is overshort and scientifically inconclusive. Future shock is a reality that most of us can feel in our guts. . . .

Yet for all that, the book . . . still comes out schlock. As regards documentation, we note that Toffler's bibliography includes no less than 358 books, plus seven "consulted" periodicals, in half a dozen languages including the Scandinavian. They range from *A Social Psychological Interpretation of the Udall, Kansas, Tornado* to John Barth's *The Floating Opera*. Less than half of them are listed in the footnotes, engendering the suspicion that at least some of the remainder are padding. Suspicion is strengthened when we notice a tendency common among schlock sociologists: citation of other schlock or quasi-schlock authorities. As a rule of thumb, suspicion of mutual schlock-scratching exists when an author cites more than six works by Vance Packard, Buckminster Fuller, David Riesman, Marshall McLuhan, B. F. Skinner and Margaret Mead, singly or in combination. Toffler cites fourteen. . . .

It is when we examine Toffler's analytic methods, however, that the suspicion of schlockiness becomes certainty, for he consistently uses most of the half-dozen ploys by which the schlock sociologist obfuscates the problem he is ostensibly elucidating. To begin with, the Evasive We, invaluable for shifting the responsibility for a social problem from somebody to nobody. Thus (my emphasis) "*We* have created the disposable person: Modular Man"; "*We* are forcing people to adapt to a new life pace". . . . To make certain that an author is employing the Evasive We, replace "we" with "I and my friends"; if the result is gibberish, you are being conned.

Sometimes, however, the Evasive We won't do; only a fool would expect to get away with saying that "*We* are making new scientific discoveries every day and *we* are putting them to work more quickly than ever before." Toffler therefore adopts the Plausible Passive: "New scientific discoveries are being made every day. . . . These new ideas are being put to work more quickly. . . . "—thereby rather neatly obscuring the fact that scientists and engineers (mostly paid by industry) are making the discoveries and industrialists (often with the aid of public funds) are putting them to work. . . .

[Something] is surely causing social change, and Toffler is too expert a schlockmeister to ignore this fact. He therefore resorts to yet another ploy, Rampant Reification, in which conceptual abstractions are transformed into causal realities. Thus he speaks of "the roaring current of change" as "an elemental force" and of "that great, growling engine of change—technology." Which of course completely begs the question of what fuels the engine and whose hand is on the throttle. One does not cross-examine an elemental force, let alone suggest that it may have been engendered by monopoly profits (especially in defense and aerospace) or accelerated by government incentives. . . . (p. 118)

Space does not allow a detailed discussion of all Toffler's schlock ploys. . . . Two devices, however, must be singled out for special attention because they bear on the substance—if that is the word—of Toffler's argument.

The first is the Things Are Usually What They Seem caper. Toffler gets into this because, while deploring the headlong pace of change in general (Goldbrick Generality), he fights shy of attacking specific kinds of changes, and in fact seems to feel that in most areas change is a pretty Good Thing. Thus he finds traditional bureaucracy changing to a looser-structured (and presumably less dehumanizing) arrangement that he calls Ad-hocracy. This is obviously a Good Thing—so long as one

ignores the fact that the new Ad-hocracies somehow end up doing the same manipulative, self-serving and often stupid things as the old bureaucracies. . . . (pp. 118-19)

Again, he sees modern technology as by and large a Good Thing; it does not (as suggested by some) lock us into a rigid, dehumanized existence but rather enormously expands the choices open to us. As an example of these choices, he quotes McLuhan (who else?) on the various "combinations of styles, options and colors available on a certain new family sports car"; the total works out at some 25 million "choices." Unfortunately, every goddamn one of the 25 million pollutes the atmosphere, dents if you lean on it too hard and is unsafe at any speed. . . . Schlock sociology, like schlock everything else, focuses on the package, not the contents.

Yet despite his evident reluctance to indict any specific changes as dispensable, Toffler has made too powerful a case against future shock to drop the matter there. Indeed, he concedes that both future shock and most of our other problems "stem not from implacable natural forces but from man-made processes that are at least potentially subject to our control." Taken together with his previous citation of the "elemental force" of change, this is of course a Now I Say It Now I Don't, and simultaneously a Goldbrick Generality, since it leaves hanging the central question of what men are in fact making these man-made processes.

Insofar as he makes a stab at answering the question, in passages scattered throughout the book, Toffler resorts to perhaps the most basic maneuver of all liberal schlock sociology: All Men Are Guilty—and So What? Manufacturers are guilty—"many of the annual model changes . . . are not technologically substantive." Well then, should we—meaning I and my friends—try to force manufacturers to dispense with trivial changes? Deponent sayeth not. Manufacturers are guilty—and so what?

Advertising is also not blameless: "Madison Avenue frequently exaggerates the importance of new features and encourages consumers to dispose of partially worn-out goods to make way for the new." Should we perhaps do something about Madison Avenue—say, a truth in advertising law, or a limit on the amount of advertising that can be charged off as tax-deductible? Toffler doesn't tell us.

Consumers, too, are guilty: often the consumer "has a vague feeling that he wants a change." This statement is undocumented and, in my own case, untrue. . . .

Obviously, tackling the problem of unnecessary change from any of these directions, let alone all three together, would involve a long, hard and dubious battle. Toffler, as a partisan of the "nothing much need be done about it" school, wants none of this. What he proposes is not struggle but a series of Mad Tea Parties. Thus he recommends "the construction of highly intricate models, games and simulations, the preparation of detailed speculative scenarios" to descry the alternative futures open to us. . . . Having told us that we are being psychologically raped by change, Toffler finally concludes that with just a bit of painless social tinkering we can relax and enjoy it.

A meaningful, non-schlock analysis of the future-shock problem would have to begin with Toffler's own unexceptional conclusion: "Change rampant, change unguided and unrestrained, accelerated change, overwhelming not only man's physical defenses but his decisional processes—such change is the enemy of life.'' It would continue with the recognition that most changes in our society—at a guess, something like 80 per cent—are unnecessary (in the sense that they make no contribution toward meeting human needs or improving the human condition) and often actively inimical. (p. 119)

We do not have to put up with these changes. We do not have to have an SST or an Everglades jetport; we do not have to have the annual spate of new, ''improved'' models in everything from automobiles to skirts; we do not have to have conglomerates, nonreturnable bottles, paper wedding gowns or any of the other innovations which simultaneously foul up our natural, our social and (as Toffler has made clear) our psychological environments. We do not have to have schlock.

But to set bounds to these changes, be they inimical or merely spurious, involves facing up to the nature of their source. Toffler himself, in one of his few non-schlock passages, says of technological change what could equally be said of change in general: ''In the West, the basic criterion for filtering out certain . . . innovations and applying others remains economic profitability.'' If we are to seize control of our own future, we must confront the long, difficult problem of restructuring social institutions so that they march to a different drummer, making man, not Mammon, the measure of all things. And if, bemused by the agile evasions and trendy catchwords of schlock sociology, we fail to do this, then we—meaning I and my friends and all the rest of us—will deserve what we get: both future shock and a schlock future. (pp. 119-20)

> Robert Claiborne, ''Future Schlock,'' in The Nation (copyright 1971 The Nation magazine, The Nation Associates, Inc.), Vol. 212, No. 4, January 25, 1971, pp. 117-20.

JOHN GREENWAY

Future Shock is only rhetorically about the future. . . . Its subject is really what we know in an undifferentiated sense as culture shock, but extended brilliantly from its traditional synchronic dimension to a diachronic concept. Anthropologists have studied group psychological trauma almost exclusively as a phenomenon occurring when an advanced civilization collides with a backward society; but with its primitive competitors destroyed, the advanced society is in shock from colliding with its own advancement. Toffler's thesis is not thoroughly sound, however; by drawing his data from his own society, he frequently mistakes vagaries for verities. He is correct in seeing our future as a busted play with Americans scrambling frantically for a way to be saved—but cultural shock is lethal only to a society whose soul is corrupt. My own experience studying the Paleolithic aborigines of Australia brings into question the principal thesis of *Future Shock*—that the limits of change the human organism can absorb are discoverable and are therefore controllable. I have seen these Old Stone Age people move ten thousand years in a day with scarcely any culture shock, for the soul of their society is strong. Anthropology, with a rich storehouse of evidence from hundreds of cultures, could have given Toffler the comparative information to improve his ideas, but the study of man has been allowed to slip into the hands of mere bearded youths who waste the substance of their heritage by sifting coprolitic nuggets from the middens of their minds to build therewith a new anthropology. They no longer admit qualitative differences between cultures, so they cannot show why one society succumbs to the shock of change while another survives. The anguish of our own state they attribute

to sins we have committed upon the weak, the poor, the ''ecology,'' and the nonliterate peoples with whom we share our mischievously polluted planet.

In the most important last section of his book Toffler shows that this is nonsense, that the most serious credibility gap is academic rather than political. Our intellectual guides tell us we must reconstruct the world they say we have ruined. Toffler argues that the only remission for uncommitted sins is in changing ourselves. Without guidance our efforts to make accommodations with this impossible situation lead us into the crazy behavior the first half of *Future Shock* entertainingly describes. Toffler does not pretend that by taking thought, lobsters can grow wings within a year and fly, but he does show how each of us can accomplish a commensurate miracle—to adapt ourselves to cope with a world we cannot change. If this sounds like Eric Hoffer, it is because *Future Shock* is the most perceptive analysis of the ordeal of change since *The True Believer*, though these two social analysts disagree about the path to our salvation. Toffler believes social evolution to be irreversible, like biological evolution, but I have been into the past, and have seen the aborigines of Australia's western deserts remain fundamentally in the Old Stone Age after two centuries of violent contact with the future. They take the new and imprison it in the past. So too may we, when we have had our fill of prophets urging us forward. (pp. 179-80)

> John Greenway, ''Book Reviews: 'Future Shock','' in The American Journal of Sociology (reprinted by permission of The University of Chicago Press; © 1971 by The University of Chicago), Vol. 77, No. 1, July, 1971, pp. 179-80.

SAMUEL McCRACKEN

One of the best-known recent examples of apocalypse disguised as journalism is Alvin Toffler's *Future Shock*. Toffler's thesis has just enough simple grandeur to provoke skepticism: change dizzily accelerates (this proven by an endless succession of statistics and other examples); such acceleration in turn makes people physically and psychically sick (this demonstrated by summaries of some recent research correlating change and illness); and to avoid an apocalyptic crisis, the earliest stages of which are upon us (demonstrated by attributing practically anything objectionable in the culture to incipient future shock), we must raise up a breed of futurist cicerones who will peer into the abyss and lead us into it. All this is set forth in a highly Lucid style . . . in which the words ''incredible'' and ''fantastic'' appear often enough to last this reader a twelve-month, sandwiched in between repeated dark statements to the effect that ''it is no accident that'' or ''it is not by chance that'' this or that is the case, to the effect, if not with the intent, that once one has said what a relationship is *not*, one is absolved from saying what it *is*.

An author who writes on so many topics ought, doubtless, to be reviewed by a committee, but even the narrowly educated reader will note some difficulties. Thus, surveying the history of speed, from camel to rocket, Toffler observes an impressive and accelerating rate of acceleration, from 8 to 18,000 mph, the increment having been 12 mph the first 4½ centuries, 80 mph in the next 3½, 300 mph in the next six decades, 400 mph in the next two, and 17,200 mph in the next two or three years. *Gee-Whiz!* one is tempted to chorus in harmony with Toffler's characteristic tone, until one recalls that only a handful of people on earth have experienced 18,000 mph, which (so I am told) is in free-fall much like any other speed you'd care to mention; of lay Americans only a minority have experienced 600 mph; of the world at large, only a tiny minority. (pp. 61-2)

Even more traumatic than such increases in personal speed ought to have been those attained by information, the telegraph, like the railway, having become available by mid-century. The telegraph annihilated of a sudden the geographical imperative with which man had lived from the rise of the camel until its minor amelioration by the railway. If change be in principle traumatic, the sudden increase in the range over which there might be knowledge of nearly simultaneous action—from the distance to the horizon to thousands of miles—and in the speed of transmission—from 8 mph to 186,000 mph—ought to have been a real shocker. Why then did the Victorians not suffer from future shock? . . .

Toffler presents a great deal of evidence for the assertion that we live in a wildly transient age: the rise of the disposable, the mobile, and the rentable; the increasing evanescence of the family; and the like. Some of this material is quite striking, although Toffler is often very naive in his handling of it, as is the case with the linguistic argument he advances: from the unwarranted assumption that the English lexicon was as large in the 16th century as now, and the undoubted fact that a great many words have been coined since then, he draws the ludicrous conclusion that at least 200,000 words, perhaps several times that many, have dropped out of the language since Shakespeare. The most obvious test of this theory, one would think, would be reading Shakespeare to see whether he is intelligible. Apparently the expedient was not resorted to. Further, slang terms out of immediate fashion are presumed by Toffler to have become unintelligible. Here, as elsewhere, he fails to array, let alone confront, any contrary evidence. A good deal of the slang of the 1920's notoriously remains with us, in a sort of museum permanent-collection, as well as such syntactic medievalisms as "willy-nilly." (p. 62)

While Toffler is aware that technology has its problems, his cheery assurance that it will all work out if one takes the long view is enough to make some schools of Neo-Luddite pessimism look tolerable. It is, he says, slanderous to accuse technology of wanting to standardize everything, for standardization is an artifact of primitive mass production, whereas the super-industry now benevolently cradling us has learned to produce the unique as cheaply as the uniform. Our only problem is going to be resisting a paralysis of the will in the face of a stultifying *embarras de richesses*.

Perhaps so, but not on the basis of the evidence adduced. The bellwether of the coming diversity, sprung on us by Toffler with all the earnestness of a Ford ad, is the Mustang, available, so it is pointed out, in *x* bodies times *y* engines times *z* transmissions, not to mention variations in color and trim. . . . Technology's idea of diversity, as explicated by Toffler, is to give you tulips with the widest choice possible of streak-color. He attains self-parody in another example of the New Diversity: cigarettes. Well, maybe if someone came out with a *square* cigarette, or a *safe* one. (pp. 62-3)

[Toffler] proposes some home remedies for the disease of future shock, among which is the curious advice that one learn to forget information for which one is not going to have any further use. Both future shock and runaway technology, however, will best be treated, Toffler thinks, by public-health programs, primarily the establishment of Councils of the Future, which will operate in a variety of organizational contexts and provide advice on probable futures. . . .

Of any serious thought about the social and governmental structures which will apply the wisdom thus generated, the book is innocent. Society even now does a certain amount of futurizing, and there is not yet any consensus as to what is to come and what is to be done about it. . . .

Finally, Toffler's work is charged with a fatal contradiction inherent in pop futurism. In order to show that disaster is staring us in the eyeball, or that the future is going to be very different, or whatever, it becomes necessary to rely on the notion of accelerating change so heavily that prescription becomes increasingly risky. If the present is to be altered all out of recognition, then there is no guarantee as to the rate of change which will be characteristic of the remote future. Even the celebrated but not terribly helpful remark of Heraclitus, to the effect that nothing endures but change, leaves the futurist with the difficulty of treating a patient whose sole symptom is that his symptoms are in flux. Long-term planning becomes difficult, if not indeed impossible, for those committed to the notion of apocalyptic change. (p. 63)

> *Samuel McCracken, "Apocalyptic Thinking," in* Commentary *(reprinted by permission; all rights reserved), Vol. 52, No. 4, October, 1971, pp. 61-70.**

HUGH STEPHENSON

[The thesis of *The Eco-Spasm Report*] is that the whole global system is going into spasm and the prognosis is not good, because the doctors are only able to think in terms of sovereign remedies suitable for Weimar-type hyper-inflation or 1929-type hyperdepression. In as much as there is hope, it lies in early recognition of the fact that the spasm bears little or no relation to anything in past experience, coupled with the adoption of new attitudes and policies.

Mr. Toffler is not, however, as specific as he might be in prescribing new remedies. He appears to be saying that we are in the process of related economic and social changes as great as those associated with the original Industrial Revolution. In his analysis we are moving from an "industrial" past and present into a "super-industrial" future. . . . In order to reach the new stage without being totally overwhelmed, Mr Toffler suggests some general courses of action. These include devising some means of controlling the activities of international companies . . . ; the creation of global reserves of foods and raw materials; the decentralization of employment and industrial policies, so that people can work out for themselves what they want; and the decentralization of the democratic process so that people become involved in and responsible for the success of what they are doing.

The book is an expansion of an article that appeared in *Esquire* and it reads like it. There is, for example, an annoying amount of repetition for a book that is only 105 paperback pages long. In the author's own words, he is dealing with serious and complex issues "in a . . . reportorial form and in a futurist perspective"—i e, this is a piece of journalistic speculation about the future. The serious-minded will not find in it much in the way of original work. . . .

At its own level, however, the book brings together several important insights about our present economic and moral plight. . . .

But Mr Toffler (as do others like him) exaggerates his case for the sake of effect and an arresting title. Exaggerates, first, on the level of evidence. The fact that housewives hoarded sugar in 1974 is held to prove eco-spasm, but few historians would take the view that panic hoarding was a phenomenon that first emerged in the mid-twentieth century. . . .

At the level of analysis, the flaw of this class of book is that, at a time when established relationships are certainly changing rapidly, it projects present trends indefinitely into the future, thus forecasting eco-spasm, or worse. But, as someone once put it: "A trend is a trend is a trend. The question is will it bend." Social and industrial change will no doubt continue at a pace that could be called revolutionary. It is very doubtful, though, whether those who experience it will conclude that they have been living through an eco-spasm.

> *Hugh Stephenson, "Trends and Speculations," in* The Times Literary Supplement *(© Times Newspapers Ltd. (London) 1975; reproduced from* The Times Literary Supplement *by permission), No. 3830, August 8, 1975, p. 894.*

RICHARD A. WRIGHT

The Eco-Spasm Report constitutes futurist Alvin Toffler's . . . pompous appraisal of the 'animated Armageddon' into which he believes industrial societies are plunging. Representing an apparent attempt to reconcile the current economic instability evinced in advanced nations with his 'future shock' theme, this new monograph merely substantiates some of the fundamental weaknesses of Toffler's earlier work. As a consequence, the author's latest exercise in futurism may eventually achieve a sort of negative notoriety as a common starting point from which to assail the substantive body of Toffler's theoretical propositions.

The major motif of this book is that traditional economic solutions applied by federal regulatory agencies in the past to curb financial crises are no longer suitable for postindustrial societies. Instead of inflation and recession, advanced nations are currently suffering from 'eco-spasm'—or, wild oscillation between inflation and recession produced by rapid social change characteristic of increasingly complex systems. Eco-spasm is accentuated by underproduction resulting from shortages in such natural resources as uranium and oil. These recent social developments render Keynesian economics bankrupt in advanced industrial societies, according to Toffler.

Besides yielding few insights not more succinctly phrased by such authors as J. K. Galbraith, Herbert Marcuse, Daniel Bell, and S. M. Lipset, Toffler's eco-spasm concept produces an intolerable schism in his future shock paradigm. For, it must be queried, can a society suffering from the peril of eco-spasmic underproduction produced by natural resource shortages simultaneously maintain the increasingly rapid technological expansion originally projected by Toffler in *Future Shock*? The answer is, of course, that it cannot. Future Shock is an illness of abundance, while our current eco-spasmic economic malaise, as Toffler correctly suggests, is a sickness weaned on shortage. (p. 191)

Assessing *The Eco-Spasm Report* on its own merits, and not as a mere extension of Toffler's future shock theory, numerous flaws still emerge that make this monograph second-rate social science. First of all, Toffler tends to derive broad generalizations from either selective references or undocumented assertions. At one point, for example, the author suggests that reshuffling of sex roles will culminate in significant economic change, yet he neither supports this generalization with em-

pirical data, nor does he explain the style of economic change that he envisions.

The author also tends to employ catchy phrases that, while superficially appearing profound, nevertheless mask rather trite concepts. The outdated tenets of Keynesian theory transforms into 'Maginot economics' for Toffler, while rapid social change converts into a 'metabolic burst' and economic planning becomes 'economics of acceleration.' The social sciences were already infused with too much superfluous conceptual baggage before the advent of Toffler's needless terminology.

Finally, as previously intimated, most of Toffler's grand 'new' ideas have been part and parcel of social science for many years. Emile Durkheim recognized the disturbing qualities of 'future shock' in his 19th century writings on anomie, while J. K. Galbraith and Daniel Bell have for sometime acknowledged the inappropriate characteristics of Keynesian economics in advanced industrial systems. (pp. 191-92)

These remarks have indeed treated *The Eco-Spasm Report* harshly by measuring a monograph of social commentary against the more meticulous standards of academic social science. If however, advanced nations actually are threatened by such specters as 'future shock' and 'eco-spasm,' rigorous empirical scholarship—and not weak armchair speculation performed by authors like Toffler—will be demanded of social scientists to spare us from Armageddon. (p. 192)

> *Richard A. Wright, "Book Reviews: 'The Eco-Spasm Report',"* in Social Science, *Vol. 51, No. 3, Summer, 1976, pp. 191-92.*

LANGDON WINNER

A follow-up study to **"Future Shock,"** . . . **"The Third Wave"** contains the same kind of titillating but slipshod analysis, the same way of playing fast and loose with history and current events.

Changes in society, Mr. Toffler explains, take place in great waves that wash over both the physical and the human landscape, leaving nothing untouched. So far there have been two such waves—not all that many, if you think about it. The first occurred about 10,000 years ago, the agricultural revolution that established civilization on a firm footing. Then about 300 years back, another wave began sweeping over us—the Industrial Revolution—bringing fundamental alterations in material production and social structure. Didn't anything happen in the centuries between those two events? Mr. Toffler does not have time to ask. There's another wave about to roll in, and it looks as though it's going to be a real lulu. . . .

The book's evidence for these brash claims is considerably less than systematic or convincing. Mr. Toffler's method involves gathering a mass of personal anecdotes, magazine article references and fragmentary data from widely scattered sources and assembling them in a colorful, fast-moving pastiche. (p. 3)

Mr. Toffler offers many provocative observations about contemporary social trends, especially on patterns evolving in work and family life. But he's in such a hurry to package his ideas in flashy conceptual wrappers that he seldom completes a thought. A string of neologisms—"prosumer," "technorebel," "econsciousness," "infosphere," "practopia"—are concocted to help master the buzzing chaos of rapid change. . . . Unfortunately, the book announces new terms with such dizzying frequency that the reader soon learns to distrust them.

Why is this Third Wave about to transform our way of life? How can one explain these astonishing developments? Mr. Toffler dismisses these queries by saying, "Nobody knows." He correctly points out that the biosphere can no longer withstand industrial civilization's limitless assault and that the age of nonrenewable energy is over. Beyond this, he has little to say. Those who worry about cause and effect and explanation are, in Mr. Toffler's eyes, hopelessly mired in a Second Wave linear mentality.

Even if we grant that the trends the book identifies are enduring rather than ephemeral, it is still doubtful that all of this would constitute a transcendence of industrialism. Many of the specific economic and technological innovations Mr. Toffler forecasts are radical extensions of the industrial mode of production into areas previously untapped. The oceans, outerspace and even the gene pool itself are going to be exploited for a great leap in production and profit. With the coming of the home computer and the "information society," each household will be transformed into an "electronic cottage" workshop—in my view an apparent throwback to the cottage industries and putting-out system of the earliest stages of the Industrial Revolution. Mr. Toffler warns that a terrible struggle will take place, pitting the forces of industrialism against the advocates of the Third Wave. What he does not make clear is how we'll be able to tell the losers from the winners.

Throughout his writing Mr. Toffler employs the favorite device of futurists and fortunetellers everywhere—the marvelous auxiliary verb "will": "The role of the secretary will be transfigured as electronics eliminates many old tasks and opens new opportunities." The verb brings with it not only the future tense but also strong connotations of likelihood or necessity. These things *will* happen—that is, they *must*.

Concealed in this way of talking is a not-so-subtle form of advocacy. Mr. Toffler predicts that we will adapt to every new gadget, junk our traditional social structures, trade in old personalities for new ones and dismantle our political system. He also believes that we ought to do these things. (pp. 3, 22)

Personally, I look forward to a Fourth Wave, which I can see looming in the distance even now. It will install a wonderful new epoch in which sociological popularizers stop counting history in threes and our visions of the future contain more than cheap thrills. (p. 22)

> Langdon Winner, "Postindustrial Man," in The New York Times Book Review (© 1980 by The New York Times Company; reprinted by permission), March 30, 1980, pp. 3, 22.

FRANK TRIPPETT

In *The Third Wave* Toffler promises a spanking new civilization. Global. What's more, as an added attraction, he offers a "quantum jump" in history. The quantum jump is one of the most intriguing feats in futurist gymnastics.

"This new civilization," Toffler declares, "brings with it new family styles; changed ways of working, loving, and living; a new economy; new political conflicts; and beyond all this an altered consciousness as well."

There may be a temptation to say gee whiz. The impulse can be resisted, however, by anyone who remembers that the present civilization has been repetitiously producing every last one of those items—and without invariably pleasing everybody. It has contrived families so new in style and composition they scarcely seem like families. It has turned much work into a romper-room drill. While it has not done much for the timeless arts of loving and living, it has contributed more than is easily digested to sexual indulgence and those ephemeral posturings called lifestyle. A new economy? The present civilization has been giving us a new economy every generation or so—even though everybody (including the folks at Chrysler) has continued to call it the free-enterprise system. As for consciousness, it has been hard lately to walk an entire city block without getting it altered, retreaded, or razed. Toffler's vision calls not for awe but for closer inspection.

He appears to be conveniently putting Third Wave labels on many of the changes engendered by the industrial civilization he assiduously decries. The rise of multinational corporations, for instance. The spread of computers and the elaboration of computer technique. The burgeoning electronics industry. Even to an ordinary untrained eye, it must seem that those developments have arisen out of industrial society or the Second Wave. No, says Toffler, they are Third Wave manifestations. (p. 110)

Toffler reprises it all, and nimbly applies the Third Wave stamp wherever it assists his argument. Still, in this frequently polemical work, the dream is the thing, his coming civilization. . . .

Who knows but what it might be a nifty world? Toffler admits it will not simply happen. It will entail some effort and even difficulties. . . .

Is that to say that the Third Wave looms far, far away in the future? Perhaps. In fact, it may not be in the future at all. Toffler acknowledges just incidentally that it is not "inevitable." Still, in many ways it is already here, and it is coming soon in many others. In fact, Toffler says, disclosing something that has escaped pedestrian journalism, "the most important political development of our time is the emergence in our midst of two basic camps, one committed to Second Wave civilization, the other to Third."

Who forms these camps? Toffler never says. But he offers a confusion of clues. (p. 113)

Any reader of this book is bound to stay busy wondering about much else. "Blind men everywhere are trying to suppress" the Third Wave. Who are they? Toffler does not say. Third Wave advocates are warned to be ready for "fighting off the idea-assassins." The *who?* Toffler does not say. . . . There's more yet to mystify. Toffler early establishes that only two significant "waves" were ever on earth at the same time, yet he gravely goes on to point out the disturbances to be expected "when a society is struck by two or more giant waves." Finally, one wonders why Toffler is so repetitiously inattentive to himself. On page 448 he gushes about the "far-reaching power of the multinational corporation," but on the very next page declares that "we are witnessing a fundamental decentralization of production and economic activity." (p. 114)

[It] is amazing that he fell so short of precision in his reports from the front lines of what he considers the most important political struggle in history. How goes the battle? Witness:

The Third Wave is in its "dawn" on page 25, is "emerging" on page 26, is "challenging" the Second Wave on page 27, is "thundering in" on page 28 . . . , is "drastically altering" the Second Wave on page 174, merely "foreshadows" the end of the Second Wave on page 346, but is "gaining momentum with every passing hour" on page 366. Et cetera.

The Second Wave? It is "dying" on page 28, "has not entirely spent its force" on page 30, is "diminishing" on page 32, is simultaneously "dying" and "declining" and "sinking" and in its "last days" on page 33. . . . By page 390, however, the Second Wave merely has "widening cracks."

Battlefield reports are notoriously confused, true. But good grief!

Toffler's feverish belief in a highly improbable future can be shrugged off as par for the futurist course. It is not as easy to forgive his gushy imprecision about the existing status of a revolution whose terms, after all, he is personally defining. Even so, the sloppiness, like the book it occurs in, is probably best forgiven, forgotten. (p. 115)

> Frank Trippett, "Wiped Out by the Future," in Psychology Today (copyright © 1980 Ziff-Davis Publishing Company), Vol. 13, No. 11, April, 1980, pp. 110, 113-15.

BARBARA AMIEL

Toffler is a master of absolute reduction. In [*The Third Wave*] he manages to dismiss every single idea, event or manifestation in history from Buddha to Freud as mere side effects of his own underlying theories of causation. The real split in history, he proclaims, is between producers and consumers and not, as some of us may have thought, between conquerors and the conquered, pagans and Christians, capitalists and proletarians, perhaps even the living or the dead. This producer/consumer split was caused by market specialization introduced by the Second Wave industrial society, and will be cured by the emergence of the "prosumer" in the Third Wave. This new creature will recombine the roles of producer and consumer in a world of staggered hours and at-home work in the "electronic cottage," possibly growing and eating his own tail as well. (pp. 64-5)

Is this summary unfair? Yes, it is. Beyond his irritating habit of presenting the obvious and trite as his own original discoveries, Toffler does offer some of insight and predictions that may well prove to be correct. As well, Toffler's description of the past is not necessarily inaccurate—what he calls the First Wave has been known to others as the great Neolithic civilization and it did have a profound impact on the Paleolithic cultures that preceded it. But Toffler is a textbook example of what George Orwell called the "nothing but" type of sweeping superficialities. It is perhaps not altogether surprising that Toffler has such an appeal in an age whose very complexity makes people yearn for reductions, even to absurdity. (p. 65)

> Barbara Amiel, "History as Simple as One, Two, Three," in Maclean's Magazine (© 1980 by Maclean's Magazine; reprinted by permission), Vol. 93, No. 15, April 14, 1980, pp. 64-5.

THE ECONOMIST

Grand syntheses of the world's problems present a number of traps for authors and Mr Toffler falls into several of them [in *The Third Wave*]. One trap is the risk of inaccuracy when trying to pronounce on so many subjects. . . .

More important is the danger of over-generalisation, which the author also falls into. For example, vital to the third wave is the exponential increase in the productivity of manufacturing computer components. Mr Toffler frequently extols this productivity but without mentioning the countervailing lack of productivity in writing the computer software needed to make use of all these components.

Indeed, he sometimes gives the impression that he not only used a computer to type his manuscript—as he boasts—but also to select evidence for his hypotheses. The selection shows signs of the sort of uncritical bundling together of all possible evidence that a badly programmed computer would produce. . . .

The author seldom shows signs of having considered alternative interpretations of the facts to the one that suits his hypothesis, a practice that is particularly dangerous when trying to account for the complexities of human behaviour. But, then, anything that does not fit neatly into his second wave or his third wave can be conveniently accounted for as part of the confusion caused by the overlapping of these two waves.

Mr Toffler cites an enormous reading list both of newspaper cuttings and of weightier works. He might have done better by reading less and thinking more. The reader of this volume, having taken heed of all these caveats, can still however enjoy the book for its many thought-provoking forecasts about the future.

> "Enough Said," in The Economist (© The Economist Newspaper Limited, 1980), Vol. 275, No. 7137, June 21, 1980, p. 111.

ROSALIND H. WILLIAMS

Toffler's writing style [in *The Third Wave*] reveals a way of thinking that habitually depersonalizes history. On nearly every page, the waves of history surge, fuse, collide, batter, uproot, and revolutionize. Abstract entities, not human beings, are the active agents of change, according to Toffler. . . . Groups of people "spring up" or "crop up" only afterward to pick up or "integrate" the social pieces "shattered" or "broken" by the waves.

It is by confining human experience and action to neatly defined "waves" that Toffler evades all the problems of historical causation. . . . Toffler praises the elegantly simple typology of three waves that puts familiar facts "in a dazzlingly fresh light." His preference is understandable. The methodology of the ideal type—and the three waves are ideal types—is one of the most useful tools of modern sociology. By generalizing and simplifying complex phenomena, ideal types can indeed put the familiar in a fresh light, if not a dazzling one. But such typologies are static: they do not account for change. And since change is precisely Toffler's grand theme, the vocabulary of the waves is inadequate for his purpose.

As a result, despite Toffler's lip service to multicausal complexity in history, he falls into a crude technological determinism. History is defined primarily as the effects of technology, which is generated independently of human volition according to its own internal processes. He seems to have retained a sort of crude caricature of Marxist ideas regarding historical inevitability and the technological "substructure" as social phenomena.

Toffler's vision of the future is based on the premise that coming technological revolutions will generate radical social change, "a whole new civilization in the fullest sense of that term." But technological change does not automatically trigger meaningful changes in social relations and values, the true stuff of history. Technologies don't just roll in with the tide, they arise not only from internal logic but also from social intentions and priorities. The development of a new technology—while it may carry unforeseen potential for social change—may also reinforce the domination of present values and structures. Most of the technical wonders Toffler foresees would in fact tend to confirm the present order rather than usher in "a whole new civilization." . . .

According to Toffler, there are five major areas of technological development that will bring about major shifts in economic, social, and political structures: renewable and decentralized energy sources and "four clusters of related industries"—space, underseas, DNA, and electronics/computers. Diversifying sources of power, however, does not diversify the economic power that exploits them: oil companies are now buying into a wide variety of energy sources to reinforce their hold on the market. Geothermal, oceanic, and nuclear energy, not to mention electric cars and hydrogen-powered buses, are expensive and complicated technologies that require large capital investments, promise large profits, and invite government regulation. The same goes for sending up space shuttles, mining underseas, and producing new organisms. These developments would prolong the present order, not alter it radically. New markets do not make a new civilization.

Toffler's problem is not that he dares to predict, but that his prophecies overlook possible extensions of the commodity- and energy-intensive civilization of today. For example, he points out that computers will make it possible to produce more individualized goods tailored to consumers' personal needs. But he also admits this trend is already far advanced thanks to "today's savviest businessmen [who] . . . know how to customize . . . at lowest cost . . ." and who do not necessarily use computers to do so. The present code of social values is a major cause of this application of computers, not the other way around, and the use of computers for customizing would in turn reinforce this code. A truly radical change from the present would be a voluntary shift to asceticism.

Toffler displays a Second Wave fascination with seductive gadgetry to aid in production and communication, especially gadgets that facilitate action at a distance. Here . . . he confuses electronic wizardry with a new social reality. He predicts that remote switches will enable customers to pipe product specifications directly into a producer's computer, or even to turn on the productive machinery, and claims that this ability makes the customer as much "a part of the production process as the denim-clad assembly-line worker was in the world now dying." But the essential economic relationships are unchanged: the customer pays the producer for the product, while the denim-clad worker is paid by the employer for the labor. (p. 16)

One way to read *The Third Wave* is as a strategy handbook for businesspeople who want to profit from technological changes. . . . [He] directly addresses "today's elites, subelites and superelites," urging them to tap the "collective imagination" and demonstrate "flexibility and intelligence" so that, unlike past ruling groups, they will not be swept away by the coming tide of history but "go with the flow." According to Toffler, people do not make waves but react to them; human struggle and resolution have only a marginal role in deflecting, diverting, or channeling "the racing currents of change."

But this is not all there is to Toffler or his book. *The Third Wave* contains countercurrents and eddies that portray a future where social relations and values will be genuinely altered. Most of these suggestions involve Toffler's ideal of "prosumption," a reintegration of the activities of production and consumption separated so drastically by Second Wave industrial capitalism. He correctly stresses the importance of overcoming this division. Some of the trends he cites as examples are ludicrous—such as the pumping of one's own gas as representative of consumer involvement in production—and some are just new species of hobbyism. But other proposals involving cooperative ownership would indeed recast present roles of active producer and passive consumer.

Even more significantly, Toffler understands the need to transcend those roles altogether, establish a "transmarket civilization," and reduce the present economic and psychological dominance of exchange activities. Finally, Toffler discusses the human needs for community, structure, and meaning. Although his specific proposals to meet these needs tend to gadgetry (the need for friendship, for example, is to be solved in part by a computerized "pairing service"), at least he takes seriously the unquantifiable dimensions of social life and gropes for ways to improve them. (pp. 16-17)

In addition to being a manual of survival strategies, *The Third Wave* has the important function of a stimulus to the imagination, especially for scientists, engineers, businesspeople, and others who deal with advanced technologies. . . . Scholars will not be impressed with the evidence or analysis, but Toffler has plunged ahead to confront significant issues that more cautious thinkers, all too aware of the complexities, have hesitated to address for fear of being wrong. (p. 17)

> *Rosalind H. Williams, "Making Waves," in* Technology Review *(reprinted with permission from* Technology Review; *copyright 1980), Vol. 83, No. 1, October, 1980, pp. 15-17.*

MAGOROH MARUYAMA

[*The Third Wave*] is based on extensive data gathered from the frontiers of trends in our society, many of which are outside the established categories and are therefore overlooked by most social scientists. But *The Third Wave* is not a mere compilation of data. Its merit lies in the identification of patterns, the interpretation of which requires an interactionist frame of mind instead of the more usual hierarchical thinking.

The book has a few theoretical flaws, ranging from ethnocentrism to conceptual and technical misinterpretations of the characteristics of pattern-generating interactive processes. But it presents many useful insights and data to be taken seriously. (pp. 410-11)

Theoretical flawlessness is perhaps too much to expect from a popular book. However, since Toffler addresses epistemological problems, some theoretical criticisms will not be out of place.

First, his book is ethnocentric in the sense that he is unfamiliar with cultures in which what he calls the "Third Wave" way of thinking always existed with or without industrialization or postindustrialization. Because of this, he talks about some African, Asian, and Latin American countries "bypassing" the

Second Wave industrial patterns and moving directly from the First Wave feudal patterns to the Third Wave patterns. . . .

Second, he repeatedly places the Third Wave way of thinking somewhere between the traditional, familiar opposites: hierarchy and individual. Thus, he speaks of the "balance" between the big and the small, centralization and decentralization, self and community, holism and reductionism, freedom and regimentation, inner drives and outer drives, objectivity and subjectivity. He *fails* to see that the Third Wave principles are based on the concept of *pattern-generating, mutually beneficial* interactions between heterogeneous elements. This concept is shared neither by the hierarchical way of thinking nor the individualistic way of thinking. It is important to realize that the interactions are nonhierarchical; patterns are not mere statistical aggregation of independent individuals; on the contrary, individuals are intersupportive, neither subordinated nor independent; it is not necessary for some to lose in order for others to gain; heterogeneity enables mutual benefit. . . . (p. 411)

Third, he makes several errors in his theoretical chapter (chapter 21) on new causal models which are relevant to anthropological theories of the causes and processes of culture change. Toffler fails to see that it is causal *loops,* not causal hierarchy or randomness, that systematically *generate* heterogeneity and mutual benefit, reinforcement, and further amplification among the heterogeneous elements. Often his notion of heterogeneity is nothing more than that of random, independent, and isolated variations.

There are other theoretical errors in this chapter. He seems to consider nonloop causality as deterministic and loop causality as probabilistic. This is wrong. Many nonloop processes are probabilistic, while many loop models are deterministic. (pp. 411-12)

He also confuses multipath evolution with gaps and jumps. He does not realize that branching usually occurs from a small change which is subsequently amplified, rather than from gaps and jumps; any point along the line of evolution is a potential branching point if it is in a positive feedback process; and, those who consider branching points to be infrequent "singular points" are trapped in the Second Wave mentality of "prime mover."

These misinterpretations are not entirely Toffler's fault because the authors he quotes, including Ilya Prigogine, are themselves partially trapped in the Second Wave epistemology. But Toffler has gone, very faithfully, as far as those he quoted have gone. And, overall, the shortcomings of the book are very minor compared to its contribution in encouraging readers to revise many of their assumptions and patterns of thinking about cultural processes. (p. 412)

Magoroh Maruyama, "Book Reviews: 'The Third Wave'," in American Anthropologist *(copyright 1981 by the American Anthropological Association; reproduced by permission of the American Anthropological Association), Vol. 83, No. 2, 1981, pp. 410-12.*

Barbara W(ertheim) Tuchman

1912-

An American historian and a former foreign correspondent and editor, Tuchman approaches history from a narrative perspective, creating books that are praised for their literary qualities. Using characterization as a major tool, she reconstructs significant eras and events in a highly readable form which has attracted a popular audience. Tuchman compiles facts which support a particular thesis and filters out those which detract; thus she is considered a selective historian. Although some critics debate the validity of this method, Tuchman has been awarded two Pulitzer Prizes: in 1963 for *The Guns of August*, and in 1972 for *Stilwell and the American Experience in China, 1911-1945*. While most of Tuchman's chronicles have dealt with the twentieth century, in a recent book, *A Distant Mirror* (1978), she recreates the fourteenth century and attempts to draw parallels to contemporary events and attitudes. (See also *Contemporary Authors*, Vols. 1-4, rev. ed.; *Contemporary Authors New Revision Series*, Vol. 3.)

Excerpt from *THE GUNS OF AUGUST*

So close had the Germans come to victory, so near the French to disaster, so great, in the preceding days [of August 1914], had been the astonished dismay of the world as it watched the relentless advance of the Germans and the retreat of the Allies on Paris, that the battle that turned the tide came to be known as the Miracle of the Marne. Henri Bergson, who had once formulated for France the *mystique* of "will," saw in it something of a miracle that had happened once before: "Joan of Arc won the Battle of the Marne," was his verdict. The enemy, suddenly halted as if by a stone wall springing up overnight, felt it too. "French *élan*, just when it is on the point of being extinguished, flames up powerfully," wrote Moltke sorrowfully to his wife during the battle. The basic reason for German failure at the Marne, "the reason that transcends all others," said Kluck afterward, was "the extraordinary and peculiar aptitude of the French soldier to recover quickly. That men will let themselves be killed where they stand, that is a well-known thing and counted on in every plan of battle. But that men who have retreated for ten days, sleeping on the ground and half dead with fatigue, should be able to take up their rifles and attack when the bugle sounds, is a thing upon which we never counted. It was a possibility not studied in our war academy."

Bergson notwithstanding, it was no miracle but the inherent ifs, errors, and commitments of the first month that determined the issue at the Marne. Kluck notwithstanding, faults of German command contributed as much as the verve of the French soldier to the outcome. If the Germans had not withdrawn two corps to send against the Russians, one of the two would have been on Bülow's right and might have filled the gap between him and Kluck; the other would have been with Hausen and might have provided the extra strength to overwhelm Foch. Russia's loyal launching of an unready offensive drew those troops away and was given tribute by Colonel Dupont, French Chief of Intelligence. "Let us render to our Allies," he said, "the homage that is their due, for one of the elements of our victory was their debacle."

Other "ifs" accumulated. If the Germans had not committed too much strength to the attempt at double envelopment by the left wing, if the right wing had not outrun its supplies and exhausted its men, if Kluck had stayed level with Bülow, if, even on the last day, he had marched back across the Marne instead of forward to the Grand Morin, the decision of the Marne might have been different and the six-week schedule for victory over France achieved—might have been, that is, except for the first and decisive "if": if the six-week schedule itself had not been based on a march through Belgium. Quite apart from the effect upon the war as a whole of bringing Britain in, and the ultimate effect on world opinion, the addition of Belgium as an enemy reduced the number of German divisions that came up to the Marne and added five British divisions to the Allied line.

At the Marne the Allies achieved the numerical superiority they had not been able to muster at any one point in the Battle of the Frontiers. The missing German divisions were partly responsible, and the balance was tipped by the added French divisions drawn from the Third Army and from the embattled and unflinching armies of Castelnau and Dubail. All during the retreat while the other armies were giving ground, these two held shut the eastern door of France. For eighteen days they fought an almost continuous battle until, finally acknowledging failure too late, Moltke called off the attack on the French fortress line on September 8. If the French First and Second Armies had given way at any point, if they had weakened under Rupprecht's final onslaught of September 3, the Germans would have won their Cannae and there would have been no opportunity for a French counter-offensive on the Marne, the Seine, or anywhere else. If there was a miracle of the Marne, it was made possible on the Moselle.

Without Joffre no Allied line would have existed to bar the German path. It was his impregnable confidence during the tragic and terrible twelve days of retreat that prevented the French Armies from disintegrating into a shattered and fragmentary mass. A more brilliant, more quickthinking commander with ideas of his own might have avoided basic initial errors, but after the debacle the one thing France needed Joffre had. It is difficult to imagine any other man who could have brought the French Armies out of retreat, in condition and position to fight again. When the moment to turn came, alone he would have been insufficient. The stand he contemplated at the Seine might well have come too late. It was Gallieni who saw the opportunity and, with a powerful assist from Franchet d'Esperey, provoked the earlier counter-offensive. It was the broken figure of Lanrezac, allowed no share at the Marne, who in saving France from the original folly of Plan 17 made recovery possible. Ironically, both his decision at Charleroi and his replacement by Franchet d'Esperey were equally necessary to the counter-offensive. But it was Joffre, whom nothing could panic, who provided the army to fight it. "If we had not had him in 1914," said Foch, his ultimate successor, "I don't know what would have become of us."

The world remembers the battle ever since by the taxis. A hundred of them were already in the service of the Military Government of Paris. With 500 more, each carrying five soldiers and making the sixty-kilometer trip to Ourcq twice, General Clergerie figured he could transport 6,000 troops to the hard-pressed front. The order was issued at 1:00 P.M., the hour for departure fixed for 6:00 P.M. Police passed the word to the taxis in the streets. Enthusiastically the chauffeurs emptied out their passengers, explaining proudly that they had to "go to the battle." Returning to their garages for gas, they were ordered to the place of assembly where at the given time all 600 were lined up in perfect order. Gallieni, called to inspect them, though rarely demonstrative, was enchanted. *"Eh, bien, voilà au moins qui n'est pas banal!"* (Well, here at least is something out of the ordinary!) he cried. Each with its burden of soldiers, with trucks, buses, and assorted vehicles added to the train, the taxis drove off, as evening fell—the last gallantry of 1914, the last crusade of the old world.

After the incomplete victory of the Marne there followed the German retreat to the Aisne, the race to the sea for possession of the Channel ports, the fall of Antwerp, and the Battle of Ypres where officers and men of the BEF held their ground, fought literally until they died, and stopped the Germans in Flanders. Not Mons or the Marne but Ypres was the real monument to British valor, as well as the grave of four-fifths of the original BEF. After it, with the advent of winter, came the slow deadly sinking into the stalemate of trench warfare. Running from Switzerland to the Channel like a gangrenous wound across French and Belgian territory, the trenches determined the war of position and attrition, the brutal, mud-filled, murderous insanity known as the Western Front that was to last for four more years.

The Schlieffen plan had failed, but it had succeeded far enough to leave the Germans in occupation of all of Belgium and all of northern France down to the Aisne. As Clemenceau's paper was tirelessly to remind its readers, month after month, year after year, *"Messieurs les Allemands sont toujours à Noyon."* For their presence there, deep within France, the error of Plan 17 was responsible. It had allowed the enemy to penetrate too far to be dislodged by the time the French regathered their strength at the Marne. It permitted the breakthrough that could only be stemmed, and later only contained, at a cost of the terrible drain of French manhood that was to make the war of 1914-1918 the parent of 1940. It was an error that could never be repaired. Failure of Plan 17 was as fatal as failure of the Schlieffen plan, and together they produced deadlock on the Western Front.

Sucking up lives at a rate of 5,000 and sometimes 50,000 a day, absorbing munitions, energy, money, brains, and trained men, the Western Front ate up Allied war resources and predetermined the failure of back-door efforts like that of the Dardanelles which might otherwise have shortened the war. The deadlock, fixed by the failures of the first month, determined the future course of the war and, as a result, the terms of the peace, the shape of the interwar period, and the conditions of the Second Round.

Men could not sustain a war of such magnitude and pain without hope—the hope that its very enormity would ensure that it could never happen again and the hope that when somehow it had been fought through to a resolution, the foundations of a better-ordered world would have been laid. Like the shimmering vision of Paris that kept Kluck's soldiers on their feet, the mirage of a better world glimmered beyond the shell-pitted wastes and leafless stumps that had once been green fields and waving poplars. Nothing less could give dignity or sense to monstrous offensives in which thousands and hundreds of thousands were killed to gain ten yards and exchange one wet-bottomed trench for another. When every autumn people said it could not last through the winter, and when every spring there was still no end in sight, only the hope that out of it all some good would accrue to mankind kept men and nations fighting.

When at last it was over, the war had many diverse results and one dominant one transcending all others: disillusion. "All the great words were cancelled out for that generation," wrote D. H. Lawrence in simple summary for his contemporaries. If any of them remembered, with a twinge of pain, like Emile Verhaeren, "the man I used to be," it was because he knew the great words and beliefs of the time before 1914 could never be restored.

After the Marne the war grew and spread until it drew in the nations of both hemispheres and entangled them in a pattern of world conflict no peace treaty could dissolve. The Battle of the Marne was one of the decisive battles of the world not because it determined that Germany would ultimately lose or the Allies ultimately win the war but because it determined that the war would go on. There was no looking back, Joffre told the soldiers on the eve. Afterward there was no turning back. The nations were caught in a trap, a trap made during the first thirty days out of battles that failed to be decisive, a trap from which there was, and has been, no exit. (pp. 436-40)

Barbara W. Tuchman, in her The Guns of August
(reprinted with permission of Macmillan Publishing

Co., Inc.; © by Barbara W. Tuchman 1962), Macmillan, 1962, 511 p.

Excerpt from *THE PROUD TOWER: A PORTRAIT OF THE WORLD BEFORE THE WAR, 1890-1914*

The Great War of 1914-18 lies like a band of scorched earth dividing that time from ours. In wiping out so many lives which would have been operative on the years that followed, in destroying beliefs, changing ideas, and leaving incurable wounds of disillusion, it created a physical as well as psychological gulf between two epochs. [*The Proud Tower*] is an attempt to discover the quality of the world from which the Great War came.

It is not the book I intended to write when I began. Preconceptions dropped off one by one as I investigated. The period was not a Golden Age or *Belle Epoque* except to a thin crust of the privileged class. It was not a time exclusively of confidence, innocence, comfort, stability, security and peace. All these qualities were certainly present. People *were* more confident of values and standards, more innocent in the sense of retaining more hope of mankind, than they are today, although they were not more peaceful nor, except for the upper few, more comfortable. Our misconception lies in assuming that doubt and fear, ferment, protest, violence and hate were not equally present. We have been misled by the people of the time themselves who, in looking back across the gulf of the War, see that earlier half of their lives misted over by a lovely sunset haze of peace and security. It did not seem so golden when they were in the midst of it. Their memories and their nostalgia have conditioned our view of the pre-war era but I can offer the reader a rule based on adequate research: all statements of how lovely it was in that era made by persons contemporary with it will be found to have been made after 1914.

A phenomenon of such extended malignance as the Great War does not come out of a Golden Age. Perhaps this should have been obvious to me when I began but it was not. I did feel, however, that the genesis of the war did not lie in the *Grosse Politik* of what Isvolsky said to Aehrenthal and Sir Edward Grey to Poincaré; in that tortuous train of Reinsurance treaties, Dual and Triple Alliances, Moroccan crises and Balkan imbroglios which historians have painstakingly followed in their search for origins. It was necessary that these events and exchanges be examined and we who come after are in debt to the examiners; but their work has been done. I am with Sergei Sazonov, Russian Foreign Minister at the time of the outbreak of the War, who after a series of investigations exclaimed at last, "Enough of this chronology!" The *Grosse Politik* approach has been used up. Besides, it is misleading because it allows us to rest on the easy allusion that it is "they," the naughty statesmen, who are always responsible for war while "we," the innocent people, are merely led. That impression is a mistake.

The diplomatic origins, so-called, of the Great War are only the fever chart of the patient; they do not tell us what caused the fever. To probe for underlying causes and deeper forces one must operate within the framework of a whole society and try to discover what moved the people in it. I have tried to concentrate on society rather than the state. Power politics and economic rivalries, however important, are not my subject.

The period of this book was above all the culmination of a century of the most accelerated rate of change in man's record.

Since the last explosion of a generalized belligerent will in the Napoleonic wars, the industrial and scientific revolutions had transformed the world. Man had entered the Nineteenth Century using only his own and animal power, supplemented by that of wind and water, much as he had entered the Thirteenth, or, for that matter, the First. He entered the Twentieth with his capacities in transportation, communication, production, manufacture and weaponry multiplied a thousandfold by the energy of machines. Industrial society gave man new powers and new scope while at the same time building up new pressures in prosperity and poverty, in growth of population and crowding in cities, in antagonisms of classes and groups, in separation from nature and from satisfaction in individual work. Science gave man new welfare and new horizons while it took away belief in God and certainty in a scheme of things he knew. By the time he left the Nineteenth Century he had as much new unease as ease. Although *fin de siècle* usually connotes decadence, in fact society at the turn of the century was not so much decaying as bursting with new tensions and accumulated energies. Stefan Zweig who was thirty-three in 1914 believed that the outbreak of war "had nothing to do with ideas and hardly even with frontiers. I cannot explain it otherwise than by this surplus force, a tragic consequence of the internal dynamism that had accumulated in forty years of peace and now sought violent release." (pp. xiii-xv)

> Barbara W. Tuchman, in her The Proud Tower: A Portrait of the World Before the War; 1890-1914 (reprinted with permission of Macmillan Publishing Co., Inc., copyright © 1962, 1963, 1965 by Barbara W. Tuchman), Macmillan, 1966, 528 p.

Excerpt from *A DISTANT MIRROR: THE CALAMITOUS 14TH CENTURY*

The genesis of [*A Distant Mirror*] was a desire to find out what were the effects on society of the most lethal disaster of recorded history—that is to say, of the Black Death of 1348-50, which killed an estimated one third of the population living between India and Iceland. Given the possibilities of our own time, the reason for my interest is obvious. The answer proved elusive because the 14th century suffered so many "strange and great perils and adversities" (in the words of a contemporary) that its disorders cannot be traced to any one cause; they were the hoofprints of more than the four horsemen of St. John's vision, which had now become seven—plague, war, taxes, brigandage, bad government, insurrection, and schism in the Church. All but plague itself arose from conditions that existed prior to the Black Death and continued after the period of plague was over.

Although my initial question has escaped an answer, the interest of the period itself—a violent, tormented, bewildered, suffering and disintegrating age, a time, as many thought, of Satan triumphant—was compelling and, as it seemed to me, consoling in a period of similar disarray. If our last decade or two of collapsing assumptions has been a period of unusual discomfort, it is reassuring to know that the human species has lived through worse before. (p. xiii)

The interval of 600 years permits what is significant in human character to stand out. People of the Middle Ages existed under mental, moral, and physical circumstances so different from our own as to constitute almost a foreign civilization. As a result, qualities of conduct that we recognize as familiar amid these alien surroundings are revealed as permanent in human nature. (p. xiv)

The fifty years that followed the Black Death of 1348-50 are the core of what seems to me a coherent historical period extending approximately from 1300 to 1450 plus a few years. To narrow the focus to a manageable area, I have chosen a particular person's life as the vehicle of my narrative. Apart from human interest, this has the advantage of enforced obedience to reality. I am required to follow the circumstances and the sequence of an actual medieval life, lead where they will, and they lead, I think, to a truer version of the period than if I had imposed my own plan.

The person in question is not a king or queen, because everything about such persons is *ipso facto* exceptional, and, besides, they are overused; nor a commoner, because commoners' lives in most cases did not take in the wide range that I wanted; nor a cleric or saint, because they are outside the limits of my comprehension; nor a woman, because any medieval woman whose life was adequately documented would be atypical.

The choice is thus narrowed to a male member of the Second Estate—that is, of the nobility—and has fallen upon Enguerrand de Coucy VII, last of a great dynasty and "the most experienced and skillful of all the knights of France." His life from 1340 to 1397 coincided with the period that concerned me, and, from the death of his mother in the great plague to his own perfectly timed death in the culminating fiasco of the century, seemed designed for my purpose. (pp. xiv-xv)

It may be taken as axiomatic that any statement of fact about the Middle Ages may (and probably will) be met by a statement of the opposite or a different version. . . .

Contradictions, however, are part of life, not merely a matter of conflicting evidence. I would ask the reader to expect contradictions. not uniformity. No aspect of society, no habit, custom, movement, development, is without cross-currents. Starving peasants in hovels live alongside prosperous peasants in featherbeds. Children are neglected and children are loved. Knights talk of honor and turn brigand. Amid depopulation and disaster, extravagance and splendor were never more extreme. No age is tidy or made of whole cloth, and none is a more checkered fabric than the Middle Ages. (p. xvii)

Difficulty of empathy, of genuinely entering into the mental and emotional values of the Middle Ages, is the final obstacle. The main barrier is, I believe, the Christian religion as it then was: the matrix and law of medieval life, omnipresent, indeed compulsory. Its insistent principle that the life of the spirit and of the afterworld was superior to the here and now, to material life on earth, is one that the modern world does not share, no matter how devout some present-day Christians may be. The rupture of this principle and its replacement by belief in the worth of the individual and of an active life not necessarily focused on God is, in fact, what created the modern world and ended the Middle Ages.

What compounds the problem is that medieval society, while professing belief in renunciation of the life of the senses, did not renounce it in practice, and no part of it less so than the Church itself. Many tried, a few succeeded, but the generality of mankind is not made for renunciation. There never was a time when more attention was given to money and possessions than in the 14th century, and its concern with the flesh was the same as at any other time. Economic man and sensual man are not suppressible.

The gap between medieval Christianity's ruling principle and everyday life is the great pitfall of the Middle Ages. (p. xix)

Chivalry, the dominant political idea of the ruling class, left as great a gap between ideal and practice as religion. The ideal was a vision of order maintained by the warrior class and formulated in the image of the Round Table, nature's perfect shape. King Arthur's knights adventured for the right against dragons, enchanters, and wicked men, establishing order in a wild world. So their living counterparts were supposed, in theory, to serve as defenders of the Faith, upholders of justice, champions of the oppressed. In practice, they were themselves the oppressors, and by the 14th century the violence and lawlessness of men of the sword had become a major agency of disorder. When the gap between ideal and real becomes too wide, the system breaks down. Legend and story have always reflected this; in the Arthurian romances the Round Table is shattered from within. The sword is returned to the lake; the effort begins anew. Violent, destructive, greedy, fallible as he may be, man retains his vision of order and resumes his search. (pp. xix-xx)

> *Barbara W. Tuchman, in her* A Distant Mirror: The Calamitous 14th Century *(copyright © 1978 by Barbara W. Tuchman; reprinted by permission of Alfred A. Knopf, Inc.), Knopf, 1978 (and reprinted by Ballantine Books, 1979, 677 p.).*

ERNEST S. PISKO

[Mrs. Tuchman's] stupendous knowledge of all the facts and all the persons even remotely involved in the dramatic story [told in **"The Zimmermann Telegram"**] is admirable and her style has verve and wit. The opinions she expresses of high dignitaries on both sides of the Atlantic are often so withering that one reader at least felt she must have for some of her verbal portraits exchanged the typewriter for a ball-point pen. . . .

On a few occasions Mrs. Tuchman forgot her good scholastic manners and wrote not only what some people did or said, but also what they thought or felt. But this is a very minor flaw in an otherwise brilliant exposition of an enormously complicated chain of events which led to America's entry into World War I and, in the author's words, marked "the end of innocence" in the lives of the American people.

> *Ernest S. Pisko, "A Telegram as a Turning Point in World War I," in* The Christian Science Monitor *(reprinted by permission from* The Christian Science Monitor; *© 1958 The Christian Science Publishing Society; all rights reserved), October 2, 1958, p. 15.*

FERDINAND KUHN

[Mrs. Tuchman's narrative in **"The Zimmermann Telegram"**] gallops along whenever it deals with Zimmermann and his message. But it bogs down in the muddy history of the Mexican revolution and civil war, much of which is not relevant to her story. And she oversteps the bounds of scholarship when she deals with American touchiness about Japan in those years.

Was it really true, as she says, that "the Yellow Peril became as popular as the Turkey Trot" during the Taft Administration? When President Taft ordered 20,000 troops to the Mexican border, and said they were on maneuvers, did "everyone else" really say it meant war with Japan? Or, in these judgments, has Mrs. Tuchman been confusing the Hearst press with American public opinion?

She calls the Zimmermann affair "the last drop that emptied Wilson's cup of neutrality"—a debatable statement, perhaps, since he did not finally make up his mind until after the Germans had sunk three American ships in mid-March.

Toward the end the author regains her scholar's balance in assessing the impact of the message on the American people. It stunned the pro-Germans, the pacifists, the waverers, and "awoke that part of the country that had been undecided or indifferent before." For this reason, the blundering telegram was important in history, and for this reason the story is worth telling. (pp. 63-4)

Ferdinand Kuhn, "War by Wire," in Saturday Review *(copyright © 1958 by* Saturday Review; *all rights reserved; reprinted by permission), Vol. 41, No. 42, October 18, 1958, pp. 63-4.*

THE TIMES LITERARY SUPPLEMENT

[The sequence of events described in **The Zimmermann Telegram** makes] a dramatic story—and when Lord Balfour could call the day he handed the telegram to the American Ambassador "the most dramatic moment of my life," we may be sure we are not exaggerating. It has often been told before. . . . Mrs. Tuchman has drawn freely on [earlier accounts] . . . , and also, for the first time, used several unpublished sources. As an American, writing in America primarily for American readers, she has had access to important American manuscripts. . . .

This gives authority to a narrative which Mrs. Tuchman has made as thrilling as an A.E.W. Mason or John Buchan novel.

There is only one doubt. The writer is clearly not among the admirers of Wilson or House, and leaves the impression that Wilson, "a seer whose achievement never equalled his aims," needed to be blown up by Hall's "grenade" to come to the rescue of the Allies at all. The fact that he had broken off relations with Germany before he know of the Zimmermann telegram is stated fairly enough, but it might perhaps have been more just to stress the fact that it was the President who, though so angry at first that he was for immediate publication, on Lansing's advice timed the publicity in America so skilfully that it unified public opinion in the Middle West and the West with that of the Eastern seaboard in supporting an active effort to defeat Germany. Apart from this criticism on a question of emphasis in a realm which still remains one of conjecture— the innermost mind of Wilson—there can only be praise for the writer's mastery of a mass of documents treating all sides of this amazing affair. . . . No historian, even if he does not concede the unique and absolute importance of the telegram in ending America's isolation, will ever again, one feels, be able to put it at the bottom of a page.

"Intercepted Dispatch," in The Times Literary Supplement *(© Times Newspapers Ltd. (London) 1959; reproduced from* The Times Literary Supplement *by permission), No. 2977, March 20, 1959, p. 154.*

CYRIL FALLS

The guns of August were the batteries which opened fire in 1914, beginning what is still to its veterans *the* great war. . . . It is this prelude, roughly the first thirty days of battle, of

which Barbara W. Tuchman writes so brilliantly and inspiringly—yet unevenly [in **"The Guns of August"**]. . . .

Battlefield scenes, strategic problems and the rise and fall of powerful personalities are all part of Mrs. Tuchman's canvas. She has brought before us too, in her vivid manner, the characteristics of the rank and file. The author must be credited for realizing what so many critics forget: that soldiers are only human. There has never been a battle without a blunder on the victorious side, though it may have been small. Big ones of genius abound. Wellington set up outpost defenses at the start of the Waterloo campaign which were very poor, inferior to those of the Prussian General Blucher (certainly no genius) and allowed himself to be thoroughly humbugged. . . .

Mrs. Tuchman has written a lucid, fair, critical and witty account in **"The Guns of August."** . . .

The first Battle of the Marne, Sept. 6-9, is one of the easiest to describe in a single volume devoted to the whole war, because the main features are simple, but it is one of the most difficult to deal with on this scale in the history of war. This is despite the fact that information is so full that in some cases one ought to be able to find out where individual men stood, as in the case of Stonewall Jackson at First Bull Run. When treated in detail the complexities are baffling, and there has been only one James E. Edmonds, the British official historian, whose account the author rightly describes as superb. Yet one can hardly praise too highly Mrs. Tuchman's exposition. Everyone groped toward a solution in this battle. Joffre came nearest to finding one, and so gained a great victory which saved France, but a strategic victory only, like Moltke's victories on the frontier, lacking the prisoners and guns needed for decisive victory. (p. 1)

I think the German atrocities abominable as they were, are somewhat overdone in this account. General von Hansen, commanding the Third German Army in Belgium, was probably the worst villain; it was he who replied to a staff officer's hint that one of the more disgusting episodes would look bad in history, with the words: "But we shall write history ourselves." A good many of the charges launched during the war have since been found grossly exaggerated, if not entirely false.

The errors and omissions of **"The Guns of August"** mount to a formidable total. To begin with, the Schlieffen plan for the German attack into the Low Countries is misrepresented. The sour old genius and hermit, Count Alfred von Schlieffen, demanded the invasion of Holland as well as Belgium—as part of a overwhelmingly strong right flank movement designed to crush France in one lightning stroke. The younger Moltke cut out Holland, not so much to give himself one foe the less as to keep open neutral ports. This is never explained. There is, however, an even graver fault. The great series of battles between Russians and Austrians in Galicia were crucial and fascinating in their intricacy, but they are dismissed in three or four sentences. Why should they not have had as much space as Tannenberg? It is true that the period covered is nominally confined to August, but the fighting in France is described up to September 6th and by that date a decision had almost been reached on the Dniester and the San to the east. . . .

I conclude with an ancient chestnut by declaring that I have been unable to put this book down, but hope that in future editions the author will put this book right; for as I said in the beginning, she writes brilliantly and inspiringly. (p. 26)

Cyril Falls, "And There Was No Turning Back," in The New York Times Book Review *(© 1962 by The*

*New York Times Company; reprinted by permission),
January 28, 1962, pp. 1, 26.*

ERNEST S. PISKO

It seemed hardly possible that anything new of significance could be said about the prelude to and the first month of World War I. But this is exactly what Mrs. Tuchman has succeeded in doing in [**"The Guns of August"**]. Not as to the main facts of the initial campaigns in Belgium, France, and East Germany—these are written with indelible ink into the record. Where she has improved upon her predecessors is in illuminating, practically inch by inch, the roads by which the fateful decisions were reached in Berlin, Paris, St. Petersburg, and London and by transforming the drama's protagonists as well as its immense supporting cast from half-legendary and half-shadowy figures into full-dimensional, believable persons. . . .

There is much of battle orders, of tactical, strategic, and logistical problems in the pages of **"The Guns of August."** But such is the skill of the author that these technical issues become organic parts of an epic never flagging in suspense. She is equally able in painting in the domestic political situation on both sides of the Channel, and she is superb in her portraits of all the leading figures. . . .

Many lessons can be learned from Mrs. Tuchman's engrossing study. . . . Not the least important of them is the tendency of generals to ignore intelligence reports that clash with their preconceived notions or would force them to change their strategy.

Ernest S. Pisko, "Fiction—Autobiography—World War I: Men on the Road to Decision," in The Christian Science Monitor *(reprinted by permission from* The Christian Science Monitor; © *1962 The Christian Science Publishing Society; all rights reserved), February 1, 1962, p. 7.*

BRUCE BLIVEN, JR.

Barbara W. Tuchman has an extraordinary ability to write about war as if the complicated, confusing mess were clear. . . .

Her big point [in **"The Guns of August"**] is that von Moltke's meddling with the splendid von Schlieffen Plan, which he had inherited from his predecessor, explains Germany's failure to defeat France and Great Britain that very first August, and that Joffre's uninspired execution of France's Plan XVII, combined with Sir John French's hesitation about letting the British Expeditionary Force fight, led to the Allies' failure to cripple the Germans on the Marne in September, and that together these lapses produced an enormously influential lack-of-a-decision. . . . There was no better world after the war—the one dénouement that could have justified in some measure its appalling cost. The war's length and the peculiar ugliness of the trench warfare on the Western Front added to the feeling that it had all been in vain. I'd have been just as happy if she had omitted this thesis. She needs no excuse for concentrating on the August battles; it is enough that they were fought and that she can describe them so well. (p. 178)

The last word on historical controversies has often gone to the best writer, which isn't entirely unfair. Mrs. Tuchman leans toward seeing issues as black and white, but her control of her material is so certain and her opinions are so passionate that it would be risky to argue with her. Still, I think it's axiomatic that any military history is no more than a slice or two of the whole truth. Mrs. Tuchman, by virtue of her nearly perfect literary triumph, may outshine all the other accounts of these actions and so obliterate some differing interpretations and some differing perspectives that may be worth saving. I notice that she seems to despise nearly all her generals. Pity might have been equally appropriate. She uses the phrase "the military mind" several times as an insult. I'm not sure I know what it means. Is it the kind of mind good generals don't have? Mrs. Tuchman proves, beyond question, that those August battles were tragedies of error. But I've always understood that every battle, closely examined, was a catalogue of blunders. Perhaps she blames von Moltke, Joffre, French, and the others for some things inherent in the nature of war. She is unduly upset—she mentions it repeatedly—by Joffre's famous insistence on good meals at regular hours. Of all the failures she describes, von Moltke's tampering with the von Schlieffen Plan draws Mrs. Tuchman's iciest scorn; and, indeed, as all R.O.T.C. students are asked to memorize, von Moltke's failure to concentrate more of his strength on his right was a horrible violation of basic principle. Still, he has had several defenders. He was wrong, but his reasons for being wrong were pretty good. Mrs. Tuchman might have included an additional slice of truth by saying more about them. (pp. 181-82)

Bruce Bliven, Jr., "Men of War," in The New Yorker *(© 1962 by The New Yorker Magazine, Inc.), Vol. XXXVIII, No. 8, April 14, 1962, pp. 178, 181-82.*

HENRY STEELE COMMAGER

This is the theme of [*The Proud Tower*]—the contrast between the pomp and the privilege of the rich and the misery and desperation of the poor. . . . And not only the contrast, but the illusion of security in which the rich and the powerful indulged themselves. . . .

Mrs. Tuchman gives us not only the Patricians, but the Anarchists: it is something new to have historians do justice to them. We forget, most of us, that anarchism had its own philosophy, its own justification, even, in a curious way, its own respectability, what with men like Prince Kropotkin and Pierre Proudhon and Professor Reclus all espousing its cause. And to dramatize the logic of anarchism, Mrs. Tuchman gives us a powerful and brilliant chapter on the Dreyfus case—imagine having anything new to say about that well-worn subject! She tells it partly as a detective story, partly as a morality play, and it is a tribute to her literary skill and her historical sophistication that she persuades us that this was an issue which seemed to transcend ordinary politics, ordinary law, ordinary morality. . . . Mrs. Tuchman, whose sympathies, needless to say, are all with the Dreyfusards, is yet able to make us understand how otherwise upright and kindly people could persuade themselves that when the good name of the Army and the Church was at stake justice to one man was of no importance.

There are morals here for our own time which Mrs. Tuchman does not point; there are morals for our own time, too, in the tragic-comic story of the two Hague Conferences—conferences more concerned, it would seem, with frustrating peace and circumventing peace-mongers (we call them peaceniks now) than with their ostensible objectives. Not least interesting here, is the role of the United States—the United States or Roosevelt. . . .

We sometimes imagine that the United States, at least, was a "peace-loving" power, just as today we persist in thinking of ourselves as a "peace-loving" nation. Mrs. Tuchman makes clear that the United States was, if anything, less interested in peace and disarmament than Britain or France or Russia. . . .

The United States was more fortunate than Europe in these fateful years, but not very different morally. . . . The United States, too, developed her own form of imperialism—it was called expansion or manifest destiny here—and her own militarists. Mrs. Tuchman tells this story largely in terms of the conflict between Thomas B. Reed—she brings him to life as has no other biographer—and Albert J. Beveridge and Captain Mahan. Morally and intellectually Reed won all the battles, but Beveridge and Mahan triumphed in the political arena— and the imperial. (p. 17)

> Henry Steele Commager, "The Princes and The Paupers," in Book Week—The Sunday Herald Tribune (© I.H.T. Corporation; reprinted by permission), January 9, 1966, pp. 1, 17.

MARTIN DUBERMAN

"**The Proud Tower**" requires its own evaluation, but first it might be useful to attempt a more general estimate of Barbara Tuchman's accomplishments as a historian, for her work raises some fundamental questions about the nature and purpose of historical inquiry. . . .

Mrs. Tuchman's popularity is due to more than her skill with words. She has two other virtues often lacking in historians trained in the academy: she never loses sight of individuals, and she is not afraid to tell a story. These qualities, no less than her writing style, have led to criticism and misunderstanding. (p. 1)

Mrs. Tuchman believes that individuals are of interest for what makes them unique as well as typical. She believes, too, that "broader forces," though a necessary part of historical explanation, are not in themselves a sufficient explanation. . . . She would never assume that the "logic of events" dictated the course of the Russian Revolution; she would recognize that it might have turned out very differently had not a single man, Lenin, worked his influence, and had not elements of accident and unaccountability played their part.

Such a view of history is sometimes dismissed as "romantic." And in our age of collectivization and system-building, it is always suspect to pursue the individual and the particular. Yet, by her respect for the special nature of each person and each event, Mrs. Tuchman is able to suggest some of that complexity and chaos of historical procedure largely lacking in the work of the pseudo-scientists. What they exclude, she evokes: those irregularities of personality and incident which are in historical events an echo of our own untidy lives.

Mrs. Tuchman's descriptive narrative also serves a more sophisticated end than its detractors are willing to admit. An event's "significance" lies not only in some abstracted essence but in all the disordered detail which surrounds it. The willingness to "tell a story," moreover, and the skill at doing so, can do much to give us a "feel" for circumstances that is essential to our intellectual understanding of them.

The power of literate, narrative history to engage us on the level of feeling and fantasy may explain why historians like Herodotus, Prescott or Macaulay continue to find audiences even after their "facts," even their bases for selecting facts, have been found wanting. It may explain, too, why today so few people read the academic historians while so many read Barbara Tuchman. Without slighting the academic virtues of carefulness and depth research (though her research is almost wholly confined to printed sources), Mrs. Tuchman has filled her pages with individualized human beings subject to luck and whim, rather than with faceless automata carrying out "the spirit of the times." Indeed, she makes the very unmethodical quality of their "stories" an integral part of their significance. In other words, the past she re-creates is recognizably like the present; since we are thereby enabled to identify with the past, it becomes endowed with relevance. This is what most readers want, and they are not wrong in wanting it.

Admiring as I am of Mrs. Tuchman's aims and accomplishments, I was disappointed to find that her new book does not come up to the high level of "**The Guns of August.**" Many of her familiar virtues are in evidence. She can still strike off an epigram as apt in its insight as in its phrasing. . . . She shows, too, a continuing ability to bring clarity (not to be equated with over-simplification) to a welter of detail. (p. 18)

"**The Proud Tower**" also contains additional evidence of her narrative talents; the chapter on Dreyfus manages to separate the central issues of that affair without sacrificing the descriptive detail which does so much to recapture its dramatic intensity. Finally, as in all her books, this one is resplendent with people—not symbols or historical agents (though that, too, when pertinent) but marvels of idiosyncratic fullness. . . .

Yet, for all its rewards, "**The Proud Tower**" is a good way from being an unqualified success—and its deficiencies are of a kind which could give ammunition to those who disparage Mrs. Tuchman's work in general. . . .

There are, first of all, a surprising number of stylistic crudities and clichés for a writer of her power. . . . Sometimes, too, the writing is intrusive, not in service of the material but an end in itself. Mrs. Tuchman will sneak in an anecdote which bears slight or no relation to the discussion at hand, simply because it is amusing and she apparently cannot bear to leave it out. Or, she will allow phrasing to substitute for analysis, leading her into oversimplified statements of causality, which ordinarily she is too sophisticated to sanction. (p. 20)

It is here, in treating personality, that the author's lapses are most disappointing, since she herself so often provides the standard of excellence. . . . Though Mrs. Tuchman continues to be successful in not reducing her personae to abstract symbols, she is less careful about reducing them to their eccentricities. (pp. 20, 22)

The most serious defect of "**The Proud Tower**" is structural. In attempting "**A Portrait of the World Before the War, 1890-1914**," Mrs. Tuchman has taken on an imposing assignment, one which can be accomplished, if at all, only when the historian has a clear conception of what he or she takes to be the central themes of the period. If Mrs. Tuchman has such a conception, she has not made it apparent. The book's eight chapters remain separate vignettes, unconnected by any thematic unity.

She offers an explanation for this, and on its face a plausible one: no tidy generalization, no neat package can or should be made, she writes in her foreword, of an age so heterogeneous. But this is an evasion. Some standard of evaluation did guide her decisions about what to put in the volume and what to leave out. This, in turn, presupposes some model in her head, conscious or not, of what the period was all about. . . .

The subjective element is inescapably involved in the historian's choice of subject matter. But if this is not admitted, especially to himself, if the historian believes instead that the choice of what is representative or important is dictated by the material (and then, into the bargain, denies that the material *does* superimpose patterns), there is little hope that his study will show purposeful design. . . .

If Mrs. Tuchman could have made explicit the subjective bases for her choices in **"The Proud Tower,"** if she could have given them shape and definition, she might thereby have raised them to the level of an organizing principle. As a result, her book could have taken on thematic coherence. But since she remains unaware of or embarrassed by her *modus operandi*, we have instead not a "portrait of the period," but random brush strokes, leaving a canvas unoccupied by any ruling vision. (p. 22)

> Martin Duberman, *"The Past Is Also People,"* in The New York Times Book Review (© 1966 by The New York Times Company; reprinted by permission), January 9, 1966, pp. 1, 18, 20, 22.

OSCAR HANDLIN

The Proud Tower is consistently interesting. [Barbara Tuchman] is a skillful and imaginative writer. She has the storyteller's knack for getting the maximum dramatic effect out of the events which crowd her pages. . . . The effective use of anecdotes and quotations carries the reader effortlessly along.

That Miss Tuchman has not told the whole story she is well aware. The book, she explains, "could be written all over again under the same title with entirely other subject matter." Her vignettes open eight windows through which we catch discontinuous glimpses of the life of a tumultuous era. But we do not thereby arrive at a comprehension of the forces that move the people we observe.

The disclaimer of completeness explains but does not justify crucial omissions. We arrive at the final page to discover the international solidarity of labor dissolved as the worker shoulders his rifle against fellow workers of another land. But there has been no coherent discussion of nationalism, nor indeed of such other major developments as industrialization and technological change.

Miss Tuchman is unwilling to judge some subjects more important than others because she does not aim to arrive at any overall conclusion: "to draw some tidy generalization from the heterogeneity of the age would be invalid." As a result she is content to refrain from asking, and therefore fails to answer, the significant questions. . . . It is a tribute to Miss Tuchman's narrative skill that she can guide the reader's attention away from issues of this sort. But in doing so she misses the opportunity for adding to his understanding. (pp. 130-31)

> Oscar Handlin, *"The Atlantic Bookshelf: Readers Choice,"* in The Atlantic Monthly (copyright © 1966, by The Atlantic Monthly Company, Boston, Mass.; reprinted with permission), Vol. 217, No. 2, February, 1966, pp. 130-31.

JAMES JOLL

In [*The Proud Tower* Mrs. Tuchman] has attempted an ambitious piece of historical painting. She concentrates on internal social and political problems and does not deal with the factors that actually caused the war. This is because she does her best to ignore the final *dénouement;* "it was not a part of the experience of the people of this book." It is only a later generation that thinks of the prewar decades as inevitably ending in catastrophe. . . .

In fact such a refusal to use hindsight is bound to be somewhat artificial and hard to sustain. The irony of history is never far from our thoughts. . . . She is quite right to reject the rosy, nostalgic view of these years as *"la belle époque,"* the last period of untroubled peace and prosperity before the deluge. In so far as the eight chapters of this book have a common theme, and they differ considerably in content and method, it is that, even without the impact of the war, the old values were being challenged, and that in the societies with which the book is mainly concerned, England, the United States, France, and Germany, some sort of revolutionary change was already on the way even before 1914. . . . At the same time, the liberal ideas of peace and progress were being undermined; the Hague peace conferences of 1899 and 1907—to which Mrs. Tuchman devotes her best and most original chapter—showed how the sincere good intentions of the humanitarian propagandists for disarmament and arbitration were exploited by the cynicism of governments and the greed of armament manufacturers. . . .

It will be seen that *The Proud Tower* raises a number of interesting problems, both of substance and of method. It is based on wide reading, especially of contemporary memoirs; it contains a great deal of information, mostly accurate. . . . However, it cannot be said that the book solves all the problems which it raises. This is partly because each of its chapters stands on its own, and the links between them are not made explicit enough; the contrast between the ideals and methods of the Anarchists and those of the Social Democrats would surely be more pointed if the two movements were studied in relation to each other and not as unrelated phenomena in separate chapters.

The author, understandably enough, has been highly selective in the episodes or trends that she discusses, and there are obvious omissions for which no one will blame her, although to leave out Italy means that there is barely a mention of such important formative forces as Croce, d'Annunzio or the Futurists. It is a pity, too, that such few references as there are to Vienna are perfunctory and superficial. . . . However, even within the fields Mrs. Tuchman chooses to cover, there is often too much information and too little analysis. One often has the feeling that, having plucked a fact or a phrase from one of the many books she has consulted, she could not bear to leave it out. One can sympathize with her desire to give an impression of the wide and varied range of phenomena with which she is dealing, but the result is often confusing. . . .

The book, with its crowded vitality, its jumps from one scene to another, its jerky movements, its tantalizing glimpses of figures of whom one wants to see more, often reminds one of those assemblages of early newsreels, in which a rapid flash of the Kaiser is followed by a fleeting appearance of Sarah Bernhardt. . . . At its worst, even the style becomes that of a film commentator. . . . (p. 9)

However, in spite, or even because, of its weaknesses, this book may well have a popular success. Mrs. Tuchman has a narrative gift, and those sections where she is telling a story or describing an individual scene are vivid and often very entertaining. Above all, the book raises the important question of how one is to estimate the values of an age. Is it by the quality of its public life or by its popular culture, or is it by the ideas and movements which outlast it and continue to affect peoples' lives several generations later? . . . [Perhaps] the significance of the decades before 1914 lies less in what was destroyed by the war, than in those movements which were just starting and which are still affecting our lives in the second half of the twentieth century. Seen from this perspective, the years from 1890 to 1914 are not just the end of one century, but the beginning of another, not just years in which old values were being replaced by meretricious or sinister substitutes, but years in which totally new values, intellectual, political, aesthetic, and moral were being created. On this view, it is the people who point ahead who are more important for the cultural historian: Stravinsky and Schoenberg are more interesting than Strauss, Lenin is more interesting than Millerand, Picasso than Sargent, and the Fagus factory than the Petit Palais. It would, in short, be more valuable to write about this period by taking account of the ideas which dominate our own age and not just in a mood of regret for the values which were vanishing by 1914. (pp. 9-10)

> James Joll, "Guided Tour," in The New York Review of Books (reprinted with permission from The New York Review of Books; copyright © 1966 Nyrev, Inc.), Vol. VI, No. 1, February 3, 1966, pp. 9-10.

JONATHAN SPENCE

"Quintessentially American," Barbara Tuchman calls [General Joseph Stilwell] on the first page of [**"Stilwell and the American Experience in China, 1911-1945"**]. Quintessentially American should mean nice things, or things that are nicely meant, and for 100 pages or so Barbara Tuchman's Stilwell seems to be running true to type; he is tough, intelligent, generous, energetic and brave, and if he is acid it is only with the acidity of a man driven to it by the stupidity of others.

But slowly—and it takes time and sifting, for this is a solid book—the portrait thickens layer on layer. Another Stilwell emerges, and if he too is quintessentially American then God help us all. This Stilwell is passionately involved with his own martial career, a constant reminder to us that the ambitious soldier feeds on war. He yearns for chances to prove himself heroic, and will make the opportunity if it does not present itself. He is violently intolerant of weakness, real or imagined, in others. His contempt for someone, flaring at an initial meeting, endures. He overflows with sympathy for the poor and oppressed as long as they live overseas, but has no eyes for the suffering in his own country. He despises Presidents, particularly if they have some idealistic streak: Wilson he calls an "addlepated boob," and F.D.R. "a flighty fool" or, in moments of particular venom, "rubberlegs."

There's no doubt, though, that Stilwell is a stunning subject for a biography. (p. 1)

[This] is an intriguing book for the tenacious reader, but I also found it desperately sad. It is sad because it is a book almost unremittingly about failure. There is the failure of Stilwell to achieve his dearest goals: rated the best corps commander after leading maneuvers in the United States in 1941, he never got the chance to use his talents in action, but ebbed out his life in Chungking diplomacy and the mud of Burma until his recall in October, 1944. And then in 1945 the atomic bombs robbed him of his chance to lead ground armies into Japan, as death from cancer in 1946 robbed him of retirement with his family in his beloved Carmel. There is the failure of Chiang Kai-shek

to wage war effectively or to govern with a trace of imagination or compassion. There is the hopeless failure of the British armies in Singapore and Rangoon. And there is the double failure of American leadership, the failure to make any intelligent preparations for the war they knew was coming, and the failure to comprehend what was happening in China as the war unfolded.

It is sad, too, because it is a book about waste: hundreds of millions of American dollars were used to shore up the hopeless Chinese economy, or were simply stolen by Chinese politicians. . . . The waste of human life was on a colossal scale. . . . (pp. 1, 28)

It is sad, finally, because it is a book about lies, about the gullible people who swallow the lies and the impatient or ruthless people who feed the gullible people lies. The news from the China theater between 1937 and 1943 was distorted beyond all measure, presenting to the American people a picture of a heroic and united China battling under Chiang Kai-shek's leadership for freedom and democracy. (p. 28)

Barbara Tuchman claims, at one point that she is writing "warts-and-all biography," and her title includes the phrase "The American Experience in China." But though she is not shy about warts—and Stilwell made a real fetish of his—this is in no sense a truly analytical biography of Stilwell; and though there are many excellent background sections on Chinese 20th-century history, there is no attempt to fit American experience as a whole into them.

Stilwell was a tough and dominating man, who wrote with brilliance and venom, and Barbara Tuchman gradually succumbs to him. The last 300 pages of the book are mainly through Stilwell's eyes—one sees this in the fact that no one else is allowed a rounded existence, and nobody is allowed to speak in self-defense. F.D.R., Chiang Kai-shek, Chennault, Wavell, Willkie, T. V. Soong, Mountbatten, Stimson, Marshall and the rest of the huge cast are either caricatures etched in with Stilwell's own acid language, or shadow-figures.

Yet even if one has regrets that this is not the great book that might have been written about Stilwell, it is still a fantastic and complex story finely told, and loaded with new information, maps and pictures. It is also a serious book that forces one to think about these moments in history not so long ago. It leaves me convinced (though the author does not pass judgment) that the appointment of Stilwell to the C.B.I. theater was an extremely serious error of judgment by Stimson and Marshall, and also that the refusal to transfer Stilwell at any one of a dozen junctures between June, 1942, and September, 1944, compounded that initial blunder.

The book also prompts more anguished reflections: How could American leaders have acted so confidently when they were so ignorant? How could they have been so sure of their right to manipulate another country, how so quick to praise and so quick to condemn? If the lack of any coherent thinking behind Stilwell's initial appointment in 1942 is understandable in the light of the immediate post-Pearl Harbor chaos, there is surely no excuse for the muddles of 1943, the breaking of the agreements made at Cairo, the insistence in 1944 that Stilwell be made commander of the Chinese armies on Chinese soil; and the intense anger at Chiang Kai-shek's poor performance in 1944 was the overreaction of politicians who had eaten too much of their own propaganda.

How could the same lies have been repeated for so long, with such an arrogant disregard for truth as it might affect either the general public or the staff in key government departments? The systematic pigeonholing of the reports written by such shrewd observers as Service, Davies, Clubb and Barrett—which dealt with both the Kuomintang and the Chinese Communist base-areas—was as stupid as the subsequent pillorying of such observers in the McCarthy period was shameful.

And how on earth could those who lived through this whole tragic, messy, destructive tangle in Asia, and then became leaders in their turn, have learned so little—so incredibly little? (p. 29)

> *Jonathan Spence, " 'Stilwell and the American Experience in China 1911-45',"* in The New York Times Book Review (© *1971 by The New York Times Company; reprinted by permission), February 7, 1971, pp. 1, 28-9.*

JOHN GITTINGS

The first half of [*Stilwell and the American Experience in China 1911-1945*], which covers Stilwell's earlier career up to his wartime appointment, breaks new biographical ground and is of undoubted value in providing a readable account of this period. . . .

Yet when Mrs. Tuchman comes to the period of the Second World War—effectively the last act of Stilwell's life, since he died in 1946—she adds remarkably little, although at much greater length, to the Stilwell Papers as originally edited by [Theodore] White. The circumstantial detail of international and Chinese wartime politics with which she pads out the story is already familiar, at least on the conventional lines which she follows. In spite of its ambitious title—*Stilwell and the American Experience in China*—this book is really successful only as a personal biography.

It is Stilwell's experience in China, not that of the United States, which forms the central theme. There is only an occasional glimmer of understanding that Stilwell the soldier was the instrument of a deliberate and dynamic policy toward China, rather than just the victim of a passive policy which, in the author's words, failed to "adjust" to changing reality. Mrs. Tuchman perceptively describes the postwar decision by General Marshall to help Chiang Kai-shek move his troops to North China (thereby intervening in the incipient civil war) as "essentially a decision for counter-revolution." But her general conclusions show little advance on those expressed in the White Paper which Dean Acheson produced in 1949 to justify the American "loss" of China. American intervention was, she explains, a tragic mistake; it would have been better to have accepted Stilwell's advice that, as he wrote on August 19, 1945, five days after Japan's surrender, "we ought to get out— *now*." It was futile to attempt to sustain the status quo or to delay what Mrs. Tuchman describes as "the cyclical passing of the mandate of heaven"—more usually known these days as the Chinese Revolution.

Exactly why China was so important to the United States never emerges from Mrs. Tuchman's narrative, although she fully recognizes that it was so. . . .

The dimension that is missing here can easily be supplied from the contemporary documents, including those published by the Department of State. There one can find a clear account of both the economic and political rationale for regarding the western shores of the Pacific as America's postwar frontier. It was Vice President Wallace who in July, 1944, after returning

from a visit to China, urged that "the American businessman of tomorrow" should recognize that "the new frontier extends from Minneapolis . . . all the way to Central Asia." His view reflected a widely held belief that the high levels of employment, wages, and production which had been achieved during the war could be preserved only by developing a high volume of postwar exports. Japan was guilty not just of crimes against humanity but—and perhaps this was a much greater crime— of seeking to create a "self-sufficient economic bloc" in East and Southeast Asia which would frustrate the legitimate desires of the world and of the United States for what Secretary of State Hull described as "a system of sound international economic relations." (p. 6)

Mrs. Tuchman makes some interesting comments on [the] lost opportunity for the United States to switch its support from the Kuomintang counterrevolution in China. It was not necessarily naïve, she argues, to regard the Communists—as did Stilwell and many others—as a progressive variety of "agrarian reformers." Agrarian reform was after all what they were principally concerned with at the time, and the future course of the revolution would always be peasant-oriented. Nor was their future alignment in international affairs necessarily fixed.

> What course Chinese Communism might have taken if an American connection had been brought to bear is a question that lost opportunities have made forever unanswerable. The only certainty is that it could not have been worse.

Or is this conclusion itself little more than an updated version of the "Why we lost China" rationale first put forward by Dean Acheson in the 1949 White Paper? In both versions it is the circumstances and accidents of history that are to blame, not the actors—at least not those in the American cast. If only the Kuomintang had been more efficient, complained Dean Acheson. If only the opportunities had not been lost, suggests Mrs. Tuchman.

But why were they lost? Even if the China landing strategy had been pursued, bringing American troops into physical working contact with the Eighth Route Army, and even if some political links had been made with the Communists, would Washington really have withdrawn its support from the Kuomintang when the struggle between revolution and counterrevolution got seriously under way? Even with Roosevelt still in the White House, and Stilwell still in China, the answer would almost certainly have been no, in view of the postwar objectives of American policy which required an assertive US presence in the whole Pacific area. To withdraw support from Chiang Kai-shek would have been, on the contrary, to adopt a policy of neutrality and nonintervention in the Chinese civil war. One suspects that Stilwell's advice after the defeat of Japan "to get out—*now*" could only be offered from the sidelines. If he had still been commander of the US forces in China he would surely have been airlifting Chiang Kai-shek's troops to the north, however much he might swear at Peanuts for making him do his dirty work. (pp. 7-8)

> *John Gittings, "Peanuts and the Good Soldier," in* The New York Review of Books *(reprinted with permission from* The New York Review of Books; *copyright © 1971 Nyrev, Inc.),* Vol. XVII, No. 1, July 22, 1971, pp. 6-8.

HARRY L. COLES

[*Stilwell and the American Experience in China, 1911-1945*] is a model biography: the research is thorough but not ponderous;

the point of view empathetic but not worshipful; the relative emphasis on the man and his times, nicely balanced; and the writing, professional and restrained.

The task of relating the military career of General Joseph Stilwell to the American experience in China, 1911-1945, was a formidable one. United States relations with China have attracted some of the best journalism and some of the worst politics the United States has to offer. There are bulky official histories of the army, navy, and air force to say nothing of mountains of official papers. Yet Tuchman has been able to find hitherto unpublished nuggets in the Stilwell papers in his home in Carmel, California, and in various other collections. Armed with a firsthand knowledge of China gained as a journalist before World War II Tuchman was able to sift and evaluate with rare skill. There is not a dull chapter in the whole book, and on every page there is revelation and insight. Narrative and character development are handled with the skill of a first-rate novelist. (pp. 799-800)

To write meaningfully of great issues and important men is to invite controversy. Tuchman's evaluation of men and her interpretation of events will not go unchallenged. But whoever in the future seeks to unravel the China tangle must reckon with this impressive book. (p. 800)

> *Harry L. Coles, "Book Reviews: 'Stilwell and the American Experience in China, 1911-1945'," in* The Journal of American History *(copyright Organization of American Historians, 1971), Vol. LVIII, No. 3, December, 1971, pp. 799-800.*

LAWRENCE STONE

Mrs. Tuchman has written four books about twentieth-century diplomatic and military history, and has won a Pulitzer Prize for two of them, which is a remarkable achievement. The criteria used for the award of these prizes would seem to be stylistic elegance, vivid descriptive narrative, accurate scholarship, a clear point of view, and a subject of current interest to a wide educated public. The winners of these prizes have been highly respected by the profession for all these qualities, but they have not usually been regarded as path-breaking innovators in the field of history. Very few of them, for example, have received that final accolade of the profession, nomination as president of the American Historical Association. The impressive virtues and the limitations of Mrs. Tuchman's work seem fully to conform to this pattern.

Why has this student of the modern world suddenly decided to throw herself into the fourteenth century? She explains in the preface [to *A Distant Mirror: The Calamitous Fourteenth Century*] that she regards it as a period not dissimilar in character to our own:

> After the experiences of the terrible twentieth century, we have greater fellow-feeling for a distraught age whose rules were breaking down under the pressure of adverse and violent events. We recognize with a painful twinge the marks of "a period of anguish when there is no sense of an assured future."

The premises behind this proposition deserve some scrutiny.

In the first place, it is very doubtful whether contemporary perceptions of the two periods are comparable. Today, although things seem to be drifting out of control, we know that we possess the technical knowledge, administrative skills, and fi-

nancial resources to put most of them right. . . . We know what to do, whereas fourteenth-century man did not, which makes a profound difference, even if in practice we both turn out to be equally ineffective. If it is perception that we wish to compare, and the quotation just referred to certainly suggests that it is, then the two centuries do not bear much relation to each other.

If we are to compare reality, one may seriously question whether either century stands out in history as so unrelievedly and exceptionally black as Mrs. Tuchman makes it out to be.

First take the twentieth century. . . . It is hard to be proud of belonging to a century whose record in the history books will include mention of the Somme and Verdun, Dresden and Hiroshima, Lidice and My Lai, Auschwitz and the Gulag Archipelago, the invention of poison gas and napalm.

On the other hand, it is arguable that all this gloom and doom is based on a lack of sober evaluation of what things were like in the past and also what, given a little luck and some good management, could potentially happen in the future. . . .

Seen in a historical perspective, the atrocities of today seem only larger in scale, rather than different in kind, from those of earlier ages. . . .

If the modern end of Mrs. Tuchman's analogy is at any rate open to question, what about the other, the "calamitous fourteenth century"? The only event which makes that century stand out as fundamentally different from any other in the last thousand years of Western history was the arrival in 1348 of the bubonic plague, which in recurrent outbreaks over half a century reduced the population of Europe and Western Asia by up to a third, and kept it there for another century. Thus its effect was about the same as that which would occur from a limited nuclear exchange between America and Russia today. Mrs. Tuchman first became interested in the fourteenth century in order to find out "what were the effects on society of the most lethal disaster of recorded history," but she soon gave up the attempt, and only one chapter in twenty-seven is devoted to the subject. The result is rather like a production of *Hamlet* that allows the Prince of Denmark no more than a walk-on part. She gave up, she says, because she found that the society was equally tormented by "war, taxes, brigandage, bad government, insurrection, and schism in the Church."

Her central theme is therefore not demographic at all, but political and military, the breakdown of law and order in France. . . . But if the breakdown of law and order and plundering by roving bands of cut-throats are the tests, then the fourteenth century was no worse than the ninth to the eleventh, when Vikings were pillaging and burning around the periphery of Europe, and each noble was an independent petty warlord who terrorized the neighborhood. . . .

Moreover, it is loading the dice to single out France for attention, since it bore the brunt of all this savage devastation by marauding troops. . . . (p. 3)

Apart from devastation of war, Mrs. Tuchman's second major theme is the cat's cradle of marriage alliances and treaties that formed the warp and woof of medieval high diplomacy. Her third is the code of chivalry that theoretically governed the conduct of the knightly class. She looks with a cold eye upon that bizarre mixture of idealism, honor, pride, and courage, combined with folly, hypocrisy, wastefulness, and cruelty. Her emphasis on the activities of the knightly class, to which her documentation among the chronicles leads her, is reinforced by the decision to hang the last half of the book very loosely around the career of one of its most prominent members, the enormously wealthy and powerful French nobleman Enguerrand de Coucy. The trouble is however, that Coucy remains so shadowy a figure, a mere cardboard cutout, prancing fantastically over the surface of great events. . . . It is hard to work up much interest in so dimly documented a figure.

If Mrs. Tuchman has loaded the dice by focusing so strongly on the misfortunes of France, she has loaded it still further by concentrating upon these three themes of the horrors of war, the absurdities of dynastic diplomacy, and the futility of the chivalric code. There is a good deal more to the fourteenth century than that and much of what is left out is positive. . . . Representative institutions were taking hold in many places across Europe, and in England Parliament for the first time reached out for real power to limit the royal executive, and in so doing set critical precedents for the future. Although hard hit by the recurrent plagues, the universities nevertheless became stronger and better organized as great intellectual centers, thus providing a continuity in higher education that no other civilization could offer. The Schism, curiously enough, was a great stimulus to theology.

All these were institutional developments which were to have decisive effects on the long-term future of Western Europe, but they barely get a mention in Mrs. Tuchman's somber picture of the age. Still less in evidence are the cultural developments of the time. . . . The reader gets no hint that already in Florence by 1400 Fra Angelico, Brunelleschi, Ghiberti, and Donatello were laying the foundations of Renaissance art and architecture.

The only promising new development to which Mrs. Tuchman devotes some attention is the heretical program and theology advanced by John Wycliffe, which in many ways provided a foretaste of the Lutheran Reformation of the sixteenth century. Somehow Mrs. Tuchman contrives to treat it both as a part of the general breakdown and disorder, and also as a portent of modernity, to which it has no real claim. (pp. 3-4)

Given these limitations, let us now look at the very substantial merits of Mrs. Tuchman's book. She has done an amazing job in mastering her sources and in getting a feel for the quality of aristocratic life in the fourteenth century, as described by Froissart and the chroniclers. She is entranced, but not deceived, by surface appearances, and her basic theme (although the phrase would not drop from her elegant pen) is the very convincing one that the fourteenth century suffered from a severe case of what we now call "cognitive dissonance." Rarely has the gap between the ideal and the real been so large. . . .

Her pages are filled with descriptions of dripping blood, severed heads and limbs, piles of corpses, hideous tortures, brutal executions. She comments that "accustomed in their own lives to physical hardship and injury, medieval men and women were not necessarily repelled by pain, but rather enjoyed it." She is fully aware that the humanitarian movement against cruelty was still 400 years in the future, awaiting the Enlightenment of the eighteenth century.

There are also other set pieces, crammed with lavish detail about the grotesquely extravagant feasts and ceremonies which accompanied peace negotiations, or the dynastic marriages that endlessly shifted young girls around the chessboard of Europe as pawns in the diplomatic art of constructing political alliances. (p. 4)

There are many . . . gaudy passages, sometimes about food, sometimes about clothing, sometimes about ceremonial; they stun the reader with the precision and intimacy of the detail. Mrs. Tuchman has tried to make sense of all this waste by advancing the theory that

> conspicuous consumption became a frenzied excess, a gilded shroud over the Black Death and lost battles, a degenerate desire to show oneself fortunate in a time of advancing misfortune.

This is an interesting idea, but it does not quite fit the facts, which are that this kind of extravagance can be found at least since the twelfth century, and running on into the eighteenth and beyond. Veblen had a better explanation to offer in *The Theory of the Leisure Class*.

There is no doubt that Mrs. Tuchman is a brilliant descriptive writer. But sometimes, when trying to give a picture of ordinary life, the "pointillist" method at which she excels turns into a potpourri of unconnected facts. (pp. 4, 6)

Mrs. Tuchman covers an amazing amount of ground, while maintaining an equally amazing level of stylistic elegance and verve. She tells us, always accurately, about the weather, the level and means of sanitation, the absence of privacy, the growth of anti-Semitism, the relation of parents to children and of men to women, attitudes toward sex and love, the sources of energy, the limitations of technology (the loom and the cogged gear-wheel, but not the fore-and-aft sail), the speed of communications. She has read the chronicles, looked carefully at the manuscript illuminations, and drawn her conclusions. Her comments are always sensible, often very shrewd, and she is scrupulous never to claim to know more than her sources tell her.

But her world is by and large the world of Froissart, of nobles and battles and feasts and chivalry, and she has not much to say about bourgeois and peasants, and virtually nothing about such mundane subjects as administration, the machinery for collecting taxes, or the rise of a bureaucracy. It has to be admitted that even her lively pen cannot breathe much life into the posturings of those preposterous and murderous kings and nobles. The whole last section of the book, in which Coucy drifts off on a crusade against the Turks, takes part in the well-deserved rout of the Christian army at Nicopolis, is captured, and dies in prison, is something of an anti-climax.

Mrs. Tuchman's historical method does not enable her to work far beneath the surface, to explain *why* the late medieval church was in such decay, *why* changes in military technology and in financial and administrative practice led to the rise of the mercenary companies and the tactics of destroying the civilian population, *why* the peasants and townspeople so often rose in such futile revolt, *why* people were generally so cruel to enemies and indifferent to their families, *why* the French nobles behaved like suicidal idiots on the field of battle at Crécy, Poitiers, and Nicopolis. Yet these are all matters which two generations of medieval scholars have labored to elucidate. Since she does not know too much about the eleventh, twelfth, or thirteenth centuries, she has no yardstick even to be sure that things were really getting worse.

Mrs. Tuchman's book is marred by the very narrow and elitist choice of central themes, the abandonment of the original plan to examine the psychological effects of the Black Death, the neglect of the more positive aspects of the age, and the intellectual shallowness of the "thin description" technique. But it also has great merits. It is beautifully written, careful and thorough in its scholarship, extensive in the range of topics peripherally touched upon, and enlivened by consistently intelligent comment. What Mrs. Tuchman does superbly is to tell *how* it was, to convey a sense of time and place, of what it was like to be a great French nobleman in the late fourteenth century. No one has ever done this better. For the reader who is not interested in the deeper questions I have mentioned, the book offers the most interesting and illuminating work available about life in the fourteenth century. It well deserves the success that almost certainly awaits it. (p. 6)

> Lawrence Stone, *"The Worst of Times?"* in The New York Review of Books *(reprinted with permission from* The New York Review of Books; *copyright ©* 1978 Nyrev, Inc.*), Vol. XXV, No. 14, September 28, 1978, pp. 3-4, 6.*

LACEY BALDWIN SMITH

Barbara Tuchman's *A Distant Mirror* is a magnificent achievement. The book fulfills all of Mrs. Tuchman's dicta for the writing of good history: It must be readable; it must be tied to the present, casting light upon humanity's struggle to survive in a changing environment; it must synthesize without distorting; and above all, it must be selective, stressing (as Macaulay wrote) "such parts of the truth as most nearly produce the effect of the whole." In a phrase, good history is a work of art. And yet the mirror that reflects Mrs. Tuchman's purpose in writing about an "era pregnant with sinister events . . . the grave of good laws and good morals" is flawed.

History, Mrs. Tuchman maintains, is consoling: It is therapeutic to know that humanity has survived the nightmare of the past and that our forefathers somehow struggled through the horrors that beset Europe in the 14th and early 15th centuries. . . .

The proposition that the agonies of our own times are analogous to those of the 14th century does justice to neither era. To ask the reader to equate the pessimism of the 20th century with that of the 14th is to compare prunes and elephants, which have only their wrinkled, unpleasant-looking skins in common. The grave diggers of our own age—overpopulation, pollution, war, and the ultimate horror of the extinction of the species— are different both in kind and degree from the Black Death, which swept away a third of the population of Europe. The Black Death struck capriciously, meaninglessly, and without warning, and hastened, if not necessarily caused, the paranoia and collapse of nerve that settled upon most of 14th-century Europe.

Our own specters are unique, for they need not wear the faces of death. Pollution must be set against technological discoveries that have transformed the utopia from a dream into a potential reality. The atomic holocaust is part and parcel of our conquest of outer space. Overpopulation is the ironic consequence of man's triumph over the very menace that brought the 14th century to the brink of collapse—the Black Death and the myriad of other diseases that turned all other centuries save our own into a torture chamber of pain. And finally, modern war has, as often as not, been the sinister step-parent to man's effort to achieve security and equality for himself and his heirs.

Our dilemma is unprecedented, for our afflictions lie within ourselves, and our pessimism stems from the bitter realization that the sword of knowledge is sufficiently sharp but that the hand that wields it is too frail. . . .

The depression of the 14th century was deeper than our own, for there could be no dawn to the endless night save the light of faith, faith in a God who allowed his believers to die at the hands of either human devils or unseen, incomprehensible bacteria that transformed the strongest body into a convulsion of suffering. . . . There was little that could be done except to suffer either in patience or in anger.

In contrast, the frustrations of our own age stem from the knowledge that we possess the keys to the kingdom but lack the nerve to open the gates. If the calamities of the 14th century have a fascination—as indeed they have—it is not the attraction of consolation but a reflection of our taste for violence, perversion, and horror.

Barbara Tuchman is well aware that equating two centuries has yet another danger: It breeds distortion. In her quest to console us with the miseries of the past, the 14th century appears as a tabloid of atrocities so bloody and mindless that it becomes a caricature of reality, which, after all, is relative to time and place. . . .

The 14th century was indeed "a bad time for humanity," but Barbara Tuchman supplies no answer to the ultimate question— why did war, death, failure of leadership, and natural catastrophe breed necrophilia, fanaticism, violence, perversion, and gloom in the 14th century, yet the same level of disruption and horror produce the dynamism and optimism of the 16th century? . . .

Although Mrs. Tuchman avoids the ultimate questions and answers about historical causation, she does supply her readers with an immensely rich and warm narrative of the age. . . .

The story is given a human dimension by the presence of a remarkable individual around whom the narrative is organized: Enguerrand de Coucy VII, whose life (1340-1397) touched upon almost every major event of the century.

The Sire de Coucy, as he appears in Mrs. Tuchman's pages, was the only sensible, sane, and restrained character on a stage swarming with madmen and butchers. . . .

It is a pity we know so little about a nobleman who seemed to have been the one man whom everyone liked and praised. . . . Coucy's story is marvelous, and whatever reservations the reader may have about Barbara Tuchman's concept of history, he will remain, as always, a delighted admirer of her historical artistry.

> Lacey Baldwin Smith, *"A Splendid History of Bad Luck and Bad Times," in* The Chronicle Review *(copyright © 1978 by The Chronicle of Higher Education, Inc.), Vol. 17, No. 5, October 2, 1978, p. R5.*

GEOFFREY BARRACLOUGH

There was room for a good book on the 14th century; but [*A Distant Mirror: The Calamitous Fourteenth Century*], alas, is not the book we were waiting for. What Mrs. Tuchman gives us is chronicle, not history—not surprisingly, perhaps, since she draws so heavily on the famous chronicler Froissart. In essence her book is a chronicle of the wars between England and France as seen through the eyes of a wealthy French nobleman, Enguerrand de Coucy. . . . (p. 32)

Coucy's career is an odd peg on which to hang what purports to be a history of the entire 14th century. He was not, after all, born until 1340; his first appearance on the stage of history occurs in 1358, when characteristically he is found cutting down peasants "without pity or mercy"; though active earlier, it was only after 1380 that he rose to prominence and only in 1390, at the age of fifty, that he finally emerged as "the leading noble . . . in the royal entourage."

All this compromises a good deal less than half the century and points to one of the critical imbalances in Mrs. Tuchman's book. This is her neglect of the fifty years before 1348. . . . The second imbalance results from her fascination with the knightly class, as exemplified by Enguerrand de Coucy, as though the nobility, with all its inborn prejudices and limitations, was representative of the teeming diversity of 14th-century Europe. And the third imbalance is simply the geographical limitation of her view, as though France was (as, indeed, she seems to think it was) the "favored land of the Western world."

No one reading Mrs. Tuchman could possibly realize, for example, that China also was afflicted after 1335 by popular risings on a scale far in excess of the French Jacquerie, that the Chinese population decreased by 40 percent between 1278 and 1393, or that Japan also was involved in incessant civil war after 1333. But even without going as far afield as Asia, the self-imposed limitations are evident. Germany figures scarcely at all in Mrs. Tuchman's narrative, except when Coucy takes it into his head to go there, and though we hear much of urban unrest in Paris and Rouen, and less of that in Florence, England and Flanders, nothing is said of the ten years of class war and terror in Salonica between 1342 and 1352, of similar movements in the chief cities of Aragon, or, later in the century, of the disaffection in the cities founded by the Teutonic Knights in far away Prussia.

These omissions are important because they preclude the simplistic view, which Mrs. Tuchman has apparently made her own, that the troubles of the 14th century stemmed from the extinction of the Capetian dynasty in 1328, the war between England and France that followed, the pillaging of France by English troops and freebooters, the consequent breakdown of law and order, and the feckless irresponsibility of the French ruling class. If we want to know why the 14th century was (in Mrs. Tuchman's phrase) a "calamitous century," we must look further and look deeper than she has chosen to do.

Troubles which encompassed the whole continent from Ireland to Poland and from the Hanseatic north to the Greek south cannot be explained by a chronicle of events. They require historical analysis. Instead Mrs. Tuchman deluges us with facts and details, piled together higgledy-piggledy from here, there and everywhere. And yet, at a distance of 600 years, what we want—or should I say what intelligent readers want?—is explanation, not narrative. (pp. 32, 34)

Instead of serious historical analysis we are regaled with a kaleidoscopic picture of depraved morals, frenetic gaiety, wild expenditure, debauchery, greed and avarice; but perhaps Mrs. Tuchman concluded (no doubt correctly) that there is not much of a market today for serious historical analysis.

And yet a serious study of the 14th century has much to tell us. It was, put briefly, the time when feudalism broke down—as capitalism is breaking down today—under the strain of its own inherent contradictions. By 1302, when the Flemish weavers mowed down the French cavalry at Courtrai, the feudal

host was an anachronism, and the chivalry which Mrs. Tuchman so lavishly describes, with its jousts and tournaments and orders of knighthood, is not feudalism at all but what historians call "bastard feudalism," an attempt to refurbish the trappings when the body was dead.

But the decline of feudalism was, of course, far more than a military phenomenon. Its roots lay in economic change, in the breakdown of the feudal organization of agriculture and of the manorial system which had been the basic feature of feudal society. To examine these aspects in detail would require far more space than is available here, and all it is necessary to say is that Mrs. Tuchman doesn't do so either, though they are the ultimate source of the malaise she describes. Nor could she do so, given the fact that she starts for all practical purposes in 1348, by which time the essential changes—whose beginnings take us back to the period around 1270—had already occurred.

If we take its pretensions seriously, the only possible verdict on Mrs. Tuchman's book is that it promises far more than it delivers. If we treat it instead simply as a brisk narrative, it can at least be said that she writes with verve and weaves together an amazing amount of information. . . .

But even at the level of story-telling Mrs. Tuchman's book cannot be accepted without reservations. First, as regards her methods—or, more bluntly, her flouting of historical method. Take, for example, the case of Froissart, on whom she draws so lavishly. His story, says the great historian Delachenal at one point, is a "tissue of fables." Mrs. Tuchman trots it out nevertheless, no doubt because, like another "suspect" chronicle, it provides "vivid information." The criterion, it seems, is vividness, not accuracy. . . .

I suppose—since neither Mrs. Tuchman nor her publisher is likely to misjudge the market—that there is a public for this sort of dressed-up history. What is more difficult to understand is what it was that induced Mrs. Tuchman to switch from 20th-century history, where she has an enviable record, to the middle ages; but it is hard to think that her foray will enhance her reputation. What, in the end, she has given us is a very old-fashioned book, the sort of history Buckle denounced over a century ago when he wrote of the "strange idea" that the historian's business is "merely to relate events," occasionally enlivened by "moral and political reflections." (p. 34)

Geoffrey Barraclough, "Books and the Arts: 'A Distant Mirror: The Calamitous Fourteenth Century'," in The New Republic *(reprinted by permission of* The New Republic; © *1978 The New Republic, Inc.),* Vol. 179, No. 18, October 28, 1978, pp. 32, 34.*

DAVID HERBERT DONALD

Wise, witty, and wonderful, *A Distant Mirror* is a great book, in a great historical tradition. It deserves the enthusiastic popular applause it has already received.

Yet it is safe to predict that *A Distant Mirror* will have, at best, a mixed reception from scholars, who have not generally been kind to Mrs. Tuchman. . . .

In part the negative tone of scholarly comment on Mrs. Tuchman's books is attributable to the fact that she—like so many of the other great figures in American historiography—is not a professional historian. (p. 75)

In all fairness, though, it must be said that academic historians tend to resent Mrs. Tuchman not merely because of her success but because of her ability to set her own rules for playing the game of history. Seeking no appointment, promotion, or academic honor, Mrs. Tuchman can afford to move from field to field—from European to Chinese history, from the 20th to the 14th century. A professor who thus wandered over the historical map would be considered at best eccentric and almost certainly would be condemned as superficial. Looking for the approval of a broad reading public, and not that of a handful of her peers, Mrs. Tuchman can boldly undertake a book on the Middle Ages, even though she admits that she is "not fluent in Latin" and for some sources "must depend on quotations and excerpts in English by other historians." No professor could afford to make that admission. Not interested in founding a new school of historical interpretation or in having her name connected with some novel thesis, Mrs. Tuchman is free to retell a story that may be entirely familiar to experts. The academic historian who follows well-trodden paths is likely to be called derivative.

I do not want to be understood as suggesting that Mrs. Tuchman has done no research, has no interest in ideas, and offers no interpretations. Those statements would all be entirely incorrect. . . . [My point is] that Mrs. Tuchman is not fundamentally concerned with the novelty of the facts she presents and she does not particularly care whether previous historians have agreed or disagreed with her interpretation of the facts. She assumes, correctly, that both her facts and her interpretations will be fresh to the large audience to whom her work is primarily addressed.

Even though much of the academic criticism of Mrs. Tuchman's work is niggling and self-serving, some of it points to serious problems in her historical craftsmanship. There is, for example, the matter of the narrative form, to which Mrs. Tuchman, like most other non-academic historians, is deeply attached. . . . It was a technique that worked well in her earlier books, where the sequence of world-shaking events was enormously important. It is far less effective in a study of 14th-century society, which changed slowly and almost imperceptibly. (pp. 75-6)

In writing *A Distant Mirror,* Mrs. Tuchman might also have profited by giving serious thought to the reasons academic historians generally avoid the highly personalized, or biographical, approach. . . . There is no way, Mrs. Tuchman admits, to recreate the thought and character of the typical peasant—yet the huge majority of the whole European population consisted of peasants. In her book, consequently, the peasants "remain mute." . . .

Desirous of tracing "the circumstances and the sequence of an actual medieval life," she has been obliged to choose a figure from the nobility, Enguerrand de Coucy VII. . . .

Yet an academic historian could have alerted Mrs. Tuchman that far too little is known about Coucy, or any other individual, to make him the central figure in the story of the 14th century. (p. 76)

More serious is the literary distortion that the focus on Coucy causes in *A Distant Mirror.* Though Coucy was indeed involved in nearly all the political, military, and diplomatic struggles of his age, his role was always a secondary one, and Mrs. Tuchman's sense of proportion prevents her from exaggerating his importance. In order, then, properly to set forth the actions of her hero, she has been obliged to write a history of the Hundred Years' War nearly as long and detailed as Froissart's *Chronicles.* The result is a bit like a map of the United States drawn

on a scale to show the streets of Cos Cob, Mrs. Tuchman's town in Connecticut. . . .

If Mrs. Tuchman could only write narrative history with a biographical focus, the weaknesses of the last half of *A Distant Mirror* would be easier to accept. But, as she demonstrates in her first six chapters, dealing with the cult of chivalry, with medieval warfare, and with the Black Death, she can write superb social history without having to rely on a chronological framework and without having to drape events around a single individual. It is truly regrettable that a historian of Mrs. Tuchman's genius has not been in close, constant communication with academic scholars, who might have helped her in reconsidering the basic structure of her book.

The moral is, I trust, obvious: academic and non-academic historians need each other. If academic historians ought to emulate Mrs. Tuchman's sweep, grace, and insight, Mrs. Tuchman could learn something from academic historians about technique, focus, and scope. (p. 77)

> *David Herbert Donald, "In the Great Tradition,"* in Commentary *(reprinted by permission; all rights reserved), Vol. 66, No. 6, December, 1978, pp. 74-7.*

MITCHELL S. ROSS

[The fourteenth century] was an age in which war was chronic, engaging the passions in much the same way that sports do in our day; in this, at least, Western Civilization has made much progress: we still fight wars, but not as often, and we do not rely upon them for sport and glory as our ancestors did. By concentrating upon this aspect of fourteenth century history [in *A Distant Mirror*], however, Mrs. Tuchman has not necessarily extracted the most interesting representation of her period. Boccaccio, Petrarch, and Chaucer are all mentioned in passing, but none are treated as fully as a dozen dull warriors; the artists of the era rate barely more than a brief hello. The author never really addresses the economic situation of the times, either. In general, it is often difficult to discern the framework within which her characters are moving. We know that the Catholic Church was a mess, that chivalry was a battered ideal, and that charlatans abounded, but Mrs. Tuchman's narrative leaves a hazy impression of the whole scene.

All of this would be unimportant if her artistry were greater. She is, however, only a good writer, not a great one. She needs to have her events clearly ordered for her, as they were in *The Guns of August* or *The Zimmermann Telegram;* she is better working on small canvases than large ones. Her style has dignity, but little wit. . . . [The] aphorist must sparkle to succeed, and Mrs. Tuchman is in this respect a little dull.

Her greatest difficulty, however, is her own doing; this is the placement of Enguerrand VII de Coucy at the center of the narrative. Another Vinegar Joe he is not, at least as far as anybody knows: although clearly a talented and influential figure, he never comes to life; indeed, there was never any chance that he might do so. The only physical fact known about the man is his baldness. His deeds were chronicled by contemporary writers, particularly Froissart, whom he patronized, but Mrs. Tuchman could hardly have hoped to do more than rewrite her predecessors' work. Moreover, as our author is herself at pains to indicate, the kings of France, and not the nobles, were the central figures in the minds of men; so, if a biographical peg is required, and the historian is determined to have war, politics, and diplomacy as her primary story, then she is being quite contrary to make this shadowy noble, rather than a king, her hero, for her narrative is warped as a result.

Yet, despite these flaws, it can hardly be said that *A Distant Mirror* is a bad book, or that its stupendous success should be regarded as unfortunate. There are barely a handful of American historians alive today who can be read with pleasure as well as profit, and certainly Mrs. Tuchman is still one of them. (pp. 1548, 1550)

Mitchell S. Ross, "Through a Glass Darkly," in National Review *(© National Review, Inc., 1978; 150 East 35th St., New York, NY 10016), Vol. 30, No. 49, December 8, 1978, pp. 1548, 1550.*

MARCUS CUNLIFFE

[In *Practicing History* Barbara Tuchman argues that] the historian's basic mode is that of narration: movement through time, so as to disclose to the reader in a clear, compelling sequence a set of significant events. "Narrative," she declares, "is the lifeblood of history . . . the medium through which the historian communicates what he has to tell. Primarily I think of the historian as a storyteller." In another essay Tuchman implies that historians are mainly concerned with powerful (or in Sidney Hook's term, "event-making") people: "captains and kings, saints and fanatics, traitors, rogues and villains, pathfinders and explorers, thinkers and creators, even, occasionally heroes . . . They may be evil or corrupt or mad or stupid . . . but at least, by virtue of circumstance or chance or office or character, they *matter*." Readers, she continues, "want to see man shaping his destiny or, at least, struggling with it."

The great historians for her, not surprisingly, are Thucydides, Gibbon, Macaulay, G. M. Trevelyan—fine phrasemakers, craftsmen of the narrative act, and as perceptive as novelists in conveying character and motive. She dislikes the distinction sometimes drawn between professional and amateur historians. "The faculty people are professional historians, we outside are professional writers. Insofar as they borrow our function, and we borrow their subject, each of us has a great deal to learn from the other."

In style Barbara Tuchman is certainly a professional. . . . She has a nice wit, as in address on "Generalship" she was invited to give by the commandant of the U.S. Army War College. "No doubt he could safely assume that the subject in itself would automatically interest this audience in the same way that motherhood would interest an audience of pregnant ladies." She has an eye for apposite anecdote, for instance on the Kaiser, recounting with emotion some criticisms of himself in the international press: "a tear fell on his cigar." She pounces upon the discrepant insistence, in Kissinger's memoirs, on *realpolitik* and also upon "honor" or "innocence," in the conduct of American foreign affairs. Sometimes, though, her comments sound orthodoxly middlebrow. (p. 4)

Marcus Cunliffe, "How History Is Written," in Book World—The Washington Post *(© 1981, The Washington Post), September 27, 1981, pp. 4, 7.*

PETER STANSKY

["**Practicing History**"] is a book to celebrate. It brings together some 33 pieces written over 35 years, but mostly in the 1960's

and 70's. . . . Most of the essays are a delight to read, affording glimpses into Mrs. Tuchman's interests, writings and life. Here is the variegated Tuchman, in practice clothes, so to speak, less imposing perhaps than the full-dress historian of her major works, but just as persuasive.

There is some autobiography in these pages—one wishes there were more—and a picture emerges of the historian herself, a common-sensical if somewhat disillusioned liberal. Although she believes in the old idea that the "I" should be kept out of historical writing, in most of these essays one has a firm awareness of the author being present, giving us something of a progress through her life: the making of a historian and woman of letters. (p. 7)

She devotes the first part of the collection to eight essays on "The Craft." Her message is clear: "I believe that the material must precede the thesis, that chronological narrative is the spine and the blood stream that bring history closer to 'how it really was.'" The historian is a narrator, a storyteller; the point is made somewhat repetitiously in the first section. She recognizes that point of view, and explanations are essential to historical narrative. She may be overly optimistic about the degree to which they emerge from the material and not from preconceptions.

The first essay, **"In Search of History,"** should be read by any historian, aspiring or practicing. As she tells us, historians must plunge into primary material, and in due course they must also know when to stop—universities are littered with historians who are doing that last bit of research before they embark on the terror of writing, of making their work available to others. Mrs. Tuchman says about writing: "It is laborious, slow, often painful, sometimes agony. It means rearrangement, revision, adding, cutting, rewriting. But it brings a sense of excitement, almost of rapture; a moment on Olympus. In short, it is an act of creation." This is a rapture she would deny to most historians, usually within the academy, who she feels are more interested in history than in writing it. This leads her—falsely to my mind, but I'm prejudiced—to divide historians from writers. . . .

I fear that Mrs. Tuchman may undervalue the contributions of less traditional historians, particularly the new social historians. In her legitimate emphasis on the *story*, she may neglect ways in which her discussion of history might have been made even more interesting, insightful and complex.

The second group of 13 essays demonstrate "The Practice." Some, such as **"Israel: Land of Unlimited Impossibilities"** and **"Mankind's Better Moments,"** are a little too determined to be optimistic, but most demonstrate the historian's intelligence, "accurate, investigative, and synthesizing." She bravely tells audiences what they may not wish to hear. . . .

The pragmatic, sensible view has been much betrayed in this country, yet here Mrs. Tuchman believes it has the best chance to work. Problems should be faced, as when she argued in favor of impeaching Richard Nixon. . . .

[Hers] is an optimism tempered by an unflinching acceptance of the realities of history. Many of Mrs. Tuchman's books have dealt with war, violence and suffering. These, rather than peace, are likely to define the human condition, which she has explored with a sympathy and understanding that define her achievements as historian and writer. (p. 43)

Peter Stansky, "Variegated Tuchman," in The New York Times Book Review *(© 1981 by The New York*

Times Company; reprinted by permission), September 27, 1981, pp. 7, 43.

CHRISTOPHER LEHMANN-HAUPT

There are a number of high points in ["**Practicing History**"] by the historian Barbara W. Tuchman. Among the brightest spots are two exemplary book reviews—one of Henry A. Kissinger's "White House Years," . . . that fairly crackles with wit and indignation; the other an analysis . . . of the Freud-Bullitt study of Woodrow Wilson that puts psychohistory in its place for the duration—as well as a courageous and sensible commencement address delivered at Williams College in 1972 on why it is irresponsible for young people opposed to war to turn their backs on military service; and an absorbing essay, a little too brief and scant on personal details, on why the career of the author's grandfather, Henry Morgenthau Sr., embodied the dilemma of the Jewish assimilationist. . . .

Elsewhere, at her best, Mrs. Tuchman shows why she is a first-rate popular historian—by practicing what one might call (without intending any derision) the art of animating the obvious: for instance, what it must have been like to live in an age that still believed in the divinity of man (**"Historical Clues to Present Discontents,"** a 1969 address delivered at Pomona). . . .

And in a couple of other places she goads a reader awake simply by raising curious intellectual conundrums—such as when she sums up the argument of the English historian E. H. Carr that "historical facts" do not exist "independently of the interpretation of the history," and then rejects it on the grounds that, for example, even "if Domesday Book and all the other records of the time had been burned, the transfer of land ownership from the Saxons to the Normans would be no less a fact of British history." . . .

But too often while reading these essays, I felt the sort of discomfort one used to feel in school when something important was being said that made one sleepy despite its worthiness.

Part of the reason for this unpleasant torpor is that Mrs. Tuchman has a rather bland way of putting things. Only rarely, as in the Kissinger review, does her prose effervesce. Mostly, it lacks fizz. . . . [Representative of her blandness is] her statement that "Communication, after all, is what language was invented for." One can't argue with that as one begins to snore.

The obviousness of this last suggests another problem with many of these essays. They simply don't surprise us anymore. We know that in 1973 the American Presidency was growing too big for the Constitution's britches, and that Congress should trim President Nixon's sails by proceeding with his impeachment. But Congress did proceed, and though we credit Mrs. Tuchman for taking such a strong position as well as predicting that President Nixon would resign, the fact remains that her conviction, and Mr. Nixon's lack of one, are dated. As for a number of the other essays, which are essentially spin-offs of . . . books by Mrs. Tuchman . . . : they lack the punch of freshness because we happen to have read the books.

The most painful thing about one's torpor is that Mrs. Tuchman's heart and mind are so often in the right place, especially in her essays on Vietnam.

Christopher Lehmann-Haupt, "Books of the Times: 'Practicing History'," in The New York Times *(© 1981 by The New York Times Company; reprinted by permission), September 29, 1981, p. 21.*

WALTER KENDRICK

Tuchman's special skill is the processing of complex historical muddles into narrative that preserves an air of complexity but can be simply read. . . .

In *Practicing History,* she's at her best in essays like **"Pericardis Alive or Raisuli Dead,"** the story of a bizarre 1904 kidnapping which takes its tiny but necessary place on the twisting primrose path that led to World I. In **"The Assimilationist Dilemma"** she's at her best again, describing how all the efforts of her grandfather, Henry Morgenthau Sr., who firmly opposed Jewish separatism, cleared the way for the founding of a separate Jewish state.

Tuchman also excels at a special kind of on-the-spot reporting: journalism combined with a historian's perspective and erudition. *Practicing History* offers several examples of this rare combination, from **"Japan: A Clinical Note,"** explaining "the East for an ignorant West" in 1936, to "Israel's Swift Sword," analyzing the Israeli victory in the Six-Day War of 1967. Other brief essays show her calling for U.S. withdrawal from Vietnam in 1968 and proposing the abolition of the imperial presidency in 1973. . . .

Tuchman makes history read like fiction—no small achievement, given the dust and ashes of her academic rivals—but unfortunately she's not content with this. Knowing that her work is sneered at by academics, knowing that it's too absorbing to seem true, she's felt obliged from time to time to defend it theoretically in essays with titles like **"When Does History Happen?"** and **"The Historian as Artist."** She may call these pieces "thought," but to me they're some of the blindest double think that's ever stained paper. Skip the [thought] part of *Practicing History* ("**The Craft**") if you value your blood pressure.

Tuchman's goal for history is to recreate, in words she quotes from Leopold von Ranke, *wie es eigentlich gewesen*—"how it really was." Fact is fact, she confidently asserts, and fiction is fiction; the one is true, the other is false; the one really happened, the other didn't. Between these ancient opposites she vacillates maddeningly: to omit facts is only a novelist's privilege, she says at one point; but the careful selection of facts is a historian's duty, she says a few pages later. Her [thought] essays explode in your face like trick cigars, each paragraph demolishing the one that went before, leaving nothing behind but stink and astonishment.

None of Tuchman's work gives us anything close to "how it really was," and half of her head knows as much. The other half, however, is equally confident that the ornate, figurative, highly artificial narratives she turns out under the name of "history" are qualitatively different from the fictions they exactly resemble. Two heads are better than one, but two half-heads are worse.

If posterity remembers Tuchman at all, it will be as an entertainer, one who made the past palatable to millions of readers. Academic historians disdain her work now and always will; her opinions have nothing to recommend but the force and fluency of their utterance. When she refrains from "thought," however, and just tells a story, it's hard to beat her.

Walter Kendrick, "Barbara Tuchman on the Q.T." (reprinted by permission of The Village Voice *and the author; copyright © 1981), in* The Village Voice, *Vol. XXVI, No. 40, September 30-October 6, 1981, p. 39.*

JACK BEATTY

The salient literary quality of [the] 33 essays, speeches, and occasional columns [in *Practicing History*] is their high-buffed charm. Mrs. Tuchman describes herself as "a writer first whose subject is history," and as a writer she consistently achieves her aim, "a clear running prose that is simple yet full of surprises." She is succinct, is as attentive to her audience as a great hostess, and is aristocratically casual in the way she makes her points. In short, charming.

Her distinction as a stylist owes more to application than to nature, to judge by the many strategies to "hook" the reader that she catalogues in a brace of essays on her craft. Her trademark is the artful use of arresting detail. (p. 37)

Some of Mrs. Tuchman's reflections on her craft, it must be said, are elementary—for example, her suggestion that the way to infuse the narrative of a past event with suspense is to adopt the point of view of the immediate participants who had no knowledge of the outcome. Still, the essays on craft have the merit of being candid about a subject—the tricks of the writer's trade—that is often etherealized. . . .

Several of these essays—notably **"Mankind's Better Moments,"** the short pieces on Vietnam and Watergate, and the reviews of Henry Kissinger's memoirs and of the Freud/Bullitt psychobiography of Woodrow Wilson—suggest why history written in the Tuchman mold has supplanted the novel as a mode of social understanding: for in each of them Mrs. Tuchman manages at once to accept man in all his imperfections and, conscious of how much the race has achieved between its bouts of destruction, to urge him to do a little better. The novel was once a source of this moral sanity, but it has been a tendency of modernism in the arts to reduce or distort the human image, in order to capture truth in extremity, rather than to present it in this central way. The contemporary novelist typically depicts society as the enemy of autonomy and holds the consciousness of evil a higher thing than the practice of good. By contrast, a historian like Mrs. Tuchman accepts society much as we all do in our daily lives—as a racket, no doubt, but not a complete racket, which does and should have authority with us. She sees her characters' weak spots, but does not look for their essence in weakness. As a historian she knows their sphere of freedom is small, but that does not stop her from celebrating it as a force for renewal. (p. 38)

Jack Beatty, "Brief Reviews: 'Practicing History'," in The New Republic *(reprinted by permission of* The New Republic; © *1981 The New Republic, Inc.), Vol. 185, No. 16, October 21, 1981, pp. 37-8.*

Elie(zer) Wiesel

1928-

Wiesel is an American novelist, journalist, and essayist whose central concern has been to come to grips with the horror of the Nazi Holocaust: to bear witness to his personal experience at Auschwitz, to trace the effect of the Holocaust on Jewish identity, to examine the plight of the individual survivor, to find a meaning in unspeakable atrocity. In *The Jews of Silence* (1966) Wiesel reports the plight of Soviet Jews and discovers their strong desire to preserve their cultural heritage; in *One Generation After* (1970) he examines what the Holocaust means to the world a quarter century thereafter; and in *A Jew Today* (1978) he recounts his personal experience in a Nazi concentration camp and considers the implications of the Holocaust for Jews today. Throughout, Wiesel has struggled with the question of silence: his own, the result of doubt about the propriety and means of conveying these experiences; that of an indifferent world for which "It is as if nothing had happened"; and finally, the silence of six million dead, for whom, despite the inadequacy of words to convey the horror, it is imperative to speak. For Wiesel, it is necessary to seek a language which celebrates life, to be used as a weapon against the meaninglessness which the Holocaust has conferred upon history, upon life. Even if, as Wiesel writes in *One Generation After*, "Nothing has been learned, Auschwitz has not even served as a warning," nevertheless, he concludes, "man owes it to himself to reject despair," for "there is no alternative: one must impose a meaning on what perhaps has none and draw ecstasy from nameless, faceless pain." This "obsession with life rather than death," in the words of Charles E. Silberman, has "lifted [Wiesel] above the ranks of every other writer of the Holocaust" and confirmed the oft-stated judgment that he is "one of the great writers of this generation." (See also *Contemporary Literary Criticism*, Vols. 3, 5, 11, and *Contemporary Authors*, Vols. 5-8, rev. ed., and *Authors in the News*, Vol. 1.)

Excerpt from THE JEWS OF SILENCE: A PERSONAL REPORT ON SOVIET JEWRY

Before I left for the Soviet Union I determined that the purpose of my trip was to discover if the Jews of Russia really wanted to be Jews. I never imagined that the answer would be so absolute and clear. I could never have foreseen that I would stand in a synagogue surrounded by men of all ages, not only the old; that I would be present at a public gathering of thirty thousand youngsters on the night of Simchat Torah and that they would be singing in Hebrew and Yiddish. Who would have thought that teenagers would be dancing the *hora* on a Moscow street, shouting "David, King of Israel, lives and endures"? Who could have dreamed that some of them—perhaps many of them—would be studying the Hebrew language, would be passing slips of paper back and forth covered with Hebrew words?

On that night of Simchat Torah I happened to be in the company of a Jew from abroad who prided himself on his antireligious and antinationalist convictions, a cold, dry, unsentimental, liberated Jew. The youngsters were singing, "Come let us go together, all of us together, and greet the Jewish people." Unable to contain himself, he burst into tears. The next day he appeared at the synagogue. "Don't think I've become religious," he said to me. "It's not that. But they have made me a better Jew."

Who knows—perhaps our salvation, too, will come from them. (pp. 98-9)

It is possible that not all Jews want or are prepared to circumcise their sons or to fight for their synagogues. But there *are* Jews who will under no circumstances let themselves be severed from their people.

That is what I wanted to see, and that is what I saw. It is good for us to know; it is essential that we know, both for them and for ourselves. No matter how often it is repeated, the official claim that, apart from a few old men, the majority of Russian Jews wish to forget their Jewish identity is simply untrue. (p. 101)

One may question whether we have any way of knowing that the Jews of Russia really want us to do anything for them. How do we know that our shouts and protests will not bring them harm? These are very serious questions, and I put them to the Russian Jews themselves. Their answer was always the same: "Cry out, cry out until you have no more strength to cry. You must enlist public opinion, you must turn to those with influence, you must involve your governments—the hour is late."

In Kiev a Jew said to me, "I hope you will not have cause to regret that you have abandoned us." And in Moscow a religious Jew said, "The preservation of human life takes precedence over all six hundred thirteen commandments. Don't you know that? Don't our cries reach you? Or do they reach you but not move you? If that is so, then we are truly lost, because you live in a world wholly guilty, and your hearts have become foul." In every city I heard dozens of cries like these, almost without variation. I was not to forget, I was to tell it all, I was to warn the Jewish communities of the world that their continued indifference would be accounted a horrible crime in the years to come. I promised I would do it, but I wept before them as I promised. I wept because I knew that nothing would help. Our Jews have other problems on their minds. When you tell them what is expected of them in Russia, they shrug their shoulders. It is exaggerated; or, we can do nothing about it; or, we must not do too much lest we be accused of interfering in the cold war. The Jewish brain has killed the Jewish heart. That is why I wept.

I believe with all my soul that despite the suffering, despite the hardship and the fear, the Jews of Russia will withstand the pressure and emerge victorious. But whether or not we shall ever be worthy of their trust, whether or not we shall overcome the pressures we have ourselves created, I cannot say. I returned from the Soviet Union disheartened and depressed. But what torments me most is not the Jews of silence I met in Russia, but the silence of the Jews I live among today. (pp. 102-03)

> *Elie Wiesel, in his* The Jews of Silence: A Personal Report on Soviet Jewry, *translated by Neal Kozodoy (translation copyright © 1966 by Holt, Rinehart and Winston, Inc.; reprinted by permission of Holt, Rinehart and Winston, Publishers; originally published as a series of essays in* Yediot Aharanot), *Holt, 1966, 143 p.*

Excerpt from *ONE GENERATION AFTER*

Twenty-five years. A quarter-century.

And we pause, trying to find our bearings, trying to understand: what and how much did these years mean? To some a generation, to others an eternity. A generation perhaps without eternity.

Children condemned never to grow old, old men doomed never to die. A solitude engulfing entire peoples, a guilt tormenting all humanity. A despair that found a face but not a name. A memory cursed, yet refusing to pass on its curse and hate. An attempt to understand, perhaps even to forgive. That is a generation.

Ours.

For the new one it will soon be ancient history. Unrelated to today's conflicts and arguments. Without impact on the aspirations and actions of adolescents eager to live and conquer the future. The past interests them only to the extent that they can reject it. Auschwitz? Never heard of it.

And yet there is logic in history. The future is but a result of conditions past and present. Everything is connected, everything has its place. Man makes the transition from the era of holocaust silence to the era of communications with remarkable ease. Once walled in by ghettos, man now takes flight to the moon. If today we live too quickly, it is because yesterday we died too quickly. If today we endow machines with increasingly wide powers, it is because the generation before us so foolishly left its fate and decisions in the hands of man.

Spring 1945: emerging from its nightmare, the world discovers the camps, the death factories. The senseless horror, the debasement: the absolute reign of evil. Victory tastes of ashes.

Yes, it is possible to defile life and creation and feel no remorse. To tend one's garden and water one's flowers but two steps away from barbed wire. To experiment with monstrous mutations and still believe in the soul and immortality. To go on vacation, be enthralled by the beauty of a landscape, make children laugh—and still fulfill regularly, day in and day out, the duties of killer.

There was, then, a technique, a science of murder, complete with specialized laboratories, business meetings and progress charts. Those engaged in its practice did not belong to a gutter society of misfits, nor could they be dismissed as just a collection of rabble. Many held degrees in philosophy, sociology, biology, general medicine, psychiatry and the fine arts. There were lawyers among them. And—unthinkable but true—theologians. And aristocrats.

Astounded, the victors find it difficult to accept the facts: that in the twentieth century, man's armor against himself and others should be so thin and vulnerable. Yes, good and evil coexist without the one influencing the other; the devil himself strives for an ideal: he too sees himself as pure and incorruptible. Inherited values count for nothing. Seeds sown by earlier generations? Lost in the sand, blown away by the wind. Nothing is certain, the present erases triumphs and treasures with hallucinating speed. Civilization? Foam that crests the waves and vanishes. Lack of morality and a perverted taste for bloodshed are unrelated to the individual's social and cultural background. It is possible to be born into the upper or middle class, receive a first-rate education, respect parents and neighbors, visit museums and attend literary gatherings, play a role in public life, and begin one day to massacre men, women and children, without hesitation and without guilt. It is possible to fire your gun at living targets and nonetheless delight in the cadence of a poem, the composition of a painting. One's spiritual legacy provides no screen, ethical concepts offer no protection. One may torture the son before his father's eyes and still consider oneself a man of culture and religion. And dream of a peaceful sunset over the sea.

Had the killers been brutal savages or demented sadists, the shock would have been less. And also the disappointment. (pp. 3-5)

> *Elie Wiesel, in his* One Generation After, *translated by Lily Edelman and the author (copyright © 1965, 1967, 1970 by Elie Wiesel; reprinted by permission of Random House, Inc.; originally published as* Entre deux soleils), *Random House, 1970, 198 p.*

Excerpt from *A JEW TODAY*

And then came the Holocaust, which shook history and by its dimensions and goals marked the end of a civilization. Concentration-camp man discovered the anti-savior.

We became witnesses to a huge simplification. On the one side there were the executioners and on the other the victims. What about the onlookers, those who remained neutral, those who served the executioner simply by not interfering? To be a Jew then meant to fight both the complacency of the neutral and the hate of the killers. And to resist—in any way, with any means. And not only with weapons. The Jew who refused death, who refused to believe in death, who chose to marry in the ghetto, to circumcise his son, to teach him the sacred language, to bind him to the threatened and weakened lineage of Israel—that Jew was resisting. The professor or shopkeeper who disregarded facts and warnings and clung to illusion, refusing to admit that people could so succumb to degradation—he, too, was resisting. There was no essential difference between the Warsaw ghetto fighters and the old men getting off the train in Treblinka: because they were Jewish, they were all doomed to hate, and death.

In those days, more than ever, to be Jewish signified *refusal*. Above all, it was a refusal to see reality and life through the enemy's eyes—a refusal to resemble him, to grant him that victory, too.

Yet his victory seemed solid and, in the beginning, definitive. All those uprooted communities, ravaged and dissolved in smoke; all those trains that crisscrossed the nocturnal Polish landscapes; all those men, all those women, stripped of their language, their names, their faces, compelled to live and die according to the laws of the enemy, in anonymity and darkness. All those kingdoms of barbed wire where everyone looked alike and all words carried the same weight. Day followed day and hour followed hour, while thoughts, numb and bleak, groped their way among the corpses, through the mire and the blood.

And the adolescent in me, yearning for faith, questioned: Where was God in all this? Was this another test, one more? Or a punishment? And if so, for what sins? What crimes were being punished? Was there a misdeed that deserved so many mass graves? Would it ever again be possible to speak of justice, of truth, of divine charity, after the murder of one million Jewish children?

I did not understand, I was afraid to understand. Was this the end of the Jewish people, or the end perhaps of the human adventure? Surely it was the end of an era, the end of a world. That I knew, that was all I knew.

As for the rest, I accumulated uncertainties. The faith of some, the lack of faith of others added to my perplexity. How could one believe, how could one not believe, in God as one faced those mountains of ashes? Who would symbolize the concentration-camp experience—the killer or the victim? Their confrontation was so striking, so gigantic that it had to include a metaphysical, ontological aspect: would we ever penetrate its mystery?

Questions, doubts. I moved through the fog like a sleepwalker. Why did the God of Israel manifest such hostility toward the descendants of Israel? I did not know. Why did free men, liberals and humanists, remain untouched by Jewish suffering? I did not know.

I remember the midnight arrival at Birkenau. Shouts. Dogs barking. Families together for the last time, families about to be torn asunder. A young Jewish boy walks at his father's side in the convoy of men; they walk and they walk and night walks with them toward a place spewing monstrous flames, flames devouring the sky. Suddenly an inmate crosses the ranks and explains to the men what they are seeing, the truth of the night: the future, the absence of future; the key to the secret, the power of evil. As he speaks, the young boy touches his father's arm as though to reassure him, and whispers, "This is impossible, isn't it? Don't listen to what he is telling us, he only wants to frighten us. What he says is impossible, unthinkable, it is all part of another age, the Middle Ages, not the twentieth century, not modern history. The world, Father, the civilized world would not allow such things to happen."

And yet the civilized world did know, and remained silent. Where was man in all this? And culture, how did it reach this nadir? All those spiritual leaders, those thinkers, those philosophers enamored of truth, those moralists drunk with justice—how was one to reconcile their teachings with Josef Mengele, the great master of selections in Auschwitz? I told myself that a grave, a horrible error had been committed somewhere—only, I knew neither its nature nor its author. When and where had history taken so bad a turn?

I remember the words of a young Talmudist whose face was that of an old man. He and I had worked as a team, carrying boulders weighing more than the two of us.

"Let us suppose," he whispered, "let us suppose that our people had not transmitted the Law to other nations. Let us forget Abraham and his example, Moses and his justice, the prophets and their message. Let us suppose that our contributions to philosophy, to science, to literature are negligible or even nonexistent. Maimonides, Nahmanides, Rashi: nothing. Spinoza, Bergson, Einstein, Freud: nothing. Let us suppose that we have in no way added to progress, to the well-being of mankind. One thing cannot be contested: the great killers, history's great assassins—Pharaoh, Nero, Chmelnitzky, Hitler—not one was formed in our midst."

Which brings us back to where we started: to the relations between Jews and Christians, which, of course, we had been forced to revise. For we had been struck by a harsh truth: in Auschwitz all the Jews were victims, all the killers were Christian.

I mention this here neither to score points nor to embarrass anyone. I believe that no religion, people or nation is inferior or superior to another; I dislike facile triumphalism, for us and for others. I dislike self-righteousness. And I feel closer to certain Christians—as long as they do not try to convert me to their faith—than to certain Jews. I felt closer to John XXIII and to François Mauriac than to self-hating Jews. I have more in common with an authentic and tolerant Christian than with a Jew who is neither authentic nor tolerant. I stress this because what I am about to say will surely hurt my Christian friends. Yet I have no right to hold back.

How is one to explain that neither Hitler nor Himmler was ever excommunicated by the church? That Pius XII never thought it necessary, not to say indispensable, to condemn Auschwitz and Treblinka? That among the S.S. a large proportion were believers who remained faithful to their Christian ties to the end? That there were killers who went to confession between massacres? And that they all came from Christian families and had received a Christian education?

In Poland, a stronghold of Christianity, it often happened that Jews who had escaped from the ghettos returned inside their walls, so hostile did they find the outside world; they feared the Poles as much as the Germans. This was also true in Lithuania, in the Ukraine, in White Russia and in Hungary. How is one to explain the passivity of the population as it watched the persecution of its Jews? How explain the cruelty of the killers? How explain that the Christian in them did not make their arms tremble as they shot at children or their conscience bridle as they shoved their naked, beaten victims into the factories of death? Of course, here and there, brave Christians came to the aid of Jews, but they were few: several dozen bishops and priests, a few hundred men and women in all of Europe.

It is a painful statement to make, but we cannot ignore it: as surely as the victims are a problem for the Jews, the killers are a problem for the Christians.

Yes, the victims remain a serious and troubling problem for us. No use covering it up. What was there about the Jew that he could be reduced so quickly, so easily to the status of victim? I have read all the answers, all the explanations. They are all inadequate. It is difficult to imagine the silent processions marching toward the pits. And the crowds that let themselves be duped. And the condemned who, inside the sealed wagons and sometimes on the very ramp at Birkenau, continued not to see. I do not understand. I understand neither the killers nor the victims.

To be a Jew during the Holocaust may have meant not to understand. Having rejected murder as a means of survival and death as a solution, men and women agreed to live and die without understanding.

For the survivor, the question presented itself differently: to remain or not to remain a Jew. I remember our tumultuous, anguished debates in France after the liberation. Should one leave for Palestine and fight in the name of Jewish nationalism, or should one, on the contrary, join the Communist movement and promulgate the ideal of internationalism? Should one delve deeper into tradition, or turn one's back on it? The options were extreme: total commitment or total alienation, unconditional loyalty or repudiation. There was no returning to the earlier ways and principles. The Jew could say: I have suffered, I have been made to suffer, all I can do is draw closer to my own people. And that was understandable. Or else: I have suffered too much, I have no strength left, I withdraw, I do not wish my children to inherit this suffering. And that, too, was understandable.

And yet, as in the past, the ordeal brought not a decline but a renascence of Jewish consciousness and a flourishing of Jewish history. Rather than break his ties, the Jew strengthened them. Auschwitz made him stronger. Even he among us who espouses so-called universal causes outside his community is motivated by the Jew in him trying to reform man even as he despairs of mankind. Though he may be in a position to become something else, the Jew remains a Jew.

Throughout a world in flux, young Jews, speaking every tongue, products of every social class, join in the adventure that Judaism represents for them, a phenomenon that reached its apex in Israel and Soviet Russia. Following different roads, these pilgrims take part in the same project and express the same defiance: "They want us to founder, but we will let our joy explode; they want to make us hard, closed to solidarity and love, well, we will be obstinate but filled with compassion." This is the challenge that justifies the hopes the Jew places in Judaism and explains the singular marks he leaves on his destiny.

Thus there would seem to be more than one way for the Jew to assume his condition. There is a time to question oneself and a time to act; there is a time to tell stories and a time to pray; there is a time to build and a time to rebuild. Whatever he chooses to do, the Jew becomes a spokesman for all Jews, dead and yet to be born, for all the beings who live through him and inside him.

His mission was never to make the world Jewish but, rather, to make it more human. (pp. 8-13)

Elie Wiesel, "To Be a Jew," in his A Jew Today, *translated by Marion Wiesel (copyright © 1978 by Elirion Associates, Inc.; reprinted by permission of Random House, Inc.), Random House, 1978, pp. 3-13.*

　　　　　• • • • •

What about the so-called literature of the Holocaust? Novels, poems, films, plays, documentaries seem to indicate that the public is interested and that it wants to be informed.

Well, at the risk of shocking you, I will tell you that as far as I am concerned, there is no such thing as Holocaust literature—there cannot be. Auschwitz negates all literature as it negates all theories and doctrines; to lock it into a philosophy means to restrict it. To substitute words, any words, for it is to distort it. A Holocaust literature? The very term is a contradiction.

Ask any survivor. He will confirm to you that it was easier for him to imagine himself free in Auschwitz than it would be for you to imagine yourself a prisoner there. Whoever has not lived through the event can never know it. And whoever has lived through it can never fully reveal it.

The survivor speaks in an alien tongue. You will never break its code. His works will be of only limited use to you. They are feeble, stammering, unfinished, incoherent attempts to describe a single moment of being painfully, excruciatingly alive—the closing in of darkness for one particular individual, nothing more and perhaps much less. Between the survivor's memory and its reflection in words, his own included, there is an unbridgeable gulf. The past belongs to the dead, and their heirs do not recognize themselves in its images and its echoes. The concept of a theology of Auschwitz is blasphemous for both the non-believer and the believer. A novel about Auschwitz is not a novel, or it is not about Auschwitz. One cannot imagine Treblinka, just as one cannot reinvent Ponar.

If you have not grasped it until now, it is time you did: Auschwitz signifies death—total, absolute death—of man and of mankind, of reason and of the heart, of language and of the senses. Auschwitz is the death of time, the end of creation; its mystery is doomed to stay whole, inviolate.

The survivor knows it; he alone knows it. Which accounts for his obsessive helplessness coupled with guilt.

True, his survival imposes a duty on him: the duty to testify. Offered to him as a reprieve, his future must find its raison d'être as it relates to his past experience. But how is one to say, how is one to communicate that which by its very nature defies language? How is one to tell without betraying the dead, without betraying oneself? A dialectical trap which leaves no way out. Even if he were to succeed in expressing the unspeakable, his truth would not be whole.

And yet . . . In the very beginning, on a continent still in ruins, he forced himself to relent enough to at least lift the veil. Not to free himself of the past; on the contrary, to assert his loyalty. To him, to forget meant a victory for the enemy. The executioner often kills twice, the second time when he tries to erase

Wiesel holds membership in the fellowship of those reconstructionists of faith who have arisen amongst traditional Jewish blasphemers after each major tragedy in Jewish history. After the destruction of the Temple, the Talmud was committed to writing. After the expulsion from Spain, the Kabbalah flourished in an attempt to explain what had occurred. Wiesel is the *Tanna Kama* (master-teacher) of the new Talmud, trying to explain why God's prayers, as well as man's, remain unanswered. He is the *Ari,* the "Lion" of our generation: he roars at God, he purrs at God. Perhaps it would be more correct to say that he is writing a new Bible. For the Holocaust claims Wiesel: though it is the antithesis of Sinai, it is its equal in significance. This new Bible would have as its major theme not God's disappointment with man but man's disappointment with God. (p. 40)

If God's trials of the pious are in some way an expression of His love . . . , then the faithfuls' trials of God are also an expression of their love. The moral challenge to God does not manifest arrogance but profound disappointment in a loving parent. It is an encounter which assumes a deep intimacy with the Divine. As in the lawsuit of the Berditchever against God, for example, Wiesel, too, prays to God to aid him in his unbelief. The trial itself is harsh and legal, but its purpose is not to chastise the defendant but to express the advocate's desire that He at least offer a plea on His own behalf.

Only once in Wiesel is such a plea heard—God's answer is an answer which speaks with silence. The answers come but are not understood. In a way Wiesel is apprehensive of the answer. He yearns to "know God" and is afraid to do so. Here, too, Wiesel is Elisha. He is entering the Garden (*pardes*) of forbidden knowledge, aware that this may bring insanity or apostasy . . . : "You can love God but you cannot look at Him . . . If man could contemplate the face of God, he would stop loving Him."

But Wiesel, having seen God in the face without His mask, continues to love Him in disappointment. Despite all his yearning for God and for an answer, he must condemn God for the most unforgivable crime—useless murder. Man can live with a cruel God, who creates men to murder them, who chooses a people to have them slain on a sacrificial altar, but he cannot live in a world without God. Better to be insane, better to blaspheme, than to be without God. (pp. 41-2)

Second to Wiesel's indictment of God is his accusation of man. Man was created in the image of God, inheriting the cruelty of his Creator. Wiesel, like Camus, insists that no one has escaped the guilt; no one is clean. As Sartre puts it, everyone shares in the crime of the twentieth-century "rummage sale, the liquidation of the human species . . . by the cruel enemy who has sown from time immemorial . . . to destroy him, that hairless, evil, flesh-eating beast—man himself." . . .

Man, like God, is indicted for one crime—being a spectator, being indifferent. Our worst sin is not that of criminal activity but of nonactivity, of apathy, indifference. "Evil is human, weakness is human, indifference is not." It is incomprehensible how humans find it so easy to be inhuman. . . . The spectator is an "it"; only thou's have a claim upon being human.

Wiesel's question and quest while the crime was being perpetrated remained his question after the war. Then the search for an answer began. (p. 42)

The answer has not been found because the question is being relived. The question for Wiesel is not: Where were the Ger-

mans?—but: Where was man? The even deeper question is: Where was the Jew then? Where is the Jew today? Does the Jew, like his God, insist on always hiding?

The deepest and most incomprehensible tragedy for Wiesel is the failure of the Jew, the unprecedented failure of one Jew to care for another. We are indicted with the claim: "The Jewish brain has killed the Jewish heart." The meaning of the Holocaust and its lesson are the cost of indifference. . . . We are each warned: "God wouldn't judge you by your deeds, but by what you haven't dared to do." (p. 43)

All traditional philosophical accounts of evil are rejected by Wiesel as not valid explanations of the tragedy in Europe. From the Kabbalah, however, some glimmer of an answer is obtained. Wiesel expresses a distaste for the dogmatic rigor of classical philosophy and for the enthronement of reason: "On your way throughout life you'll meet men who cling to reason, but reason gropes like a blind man with a white cane . . ." He turns away from philosophy toward Kabbalah with a fervor reminiscent of Rabbi Moses of Burgos who, when he heard philosophers praised, would angrily say: "You ought to know that these philosophers, whose wisdom you are praising, end where we [mystics] begin." So Wiesel, too, denies all three premises in the unique manner of Kabbalistic discourse. (pp. 43-4)

Wiesel's presentation of the notion of the presence of evil in God is biting. If it is blasphemy, it is traditional blasphemy. The notion of evil as a necessary by-product of creation, Wiesel combines with the idea of God's mistake in creation: "After creating the universe, says the Cabalah, God smashed his tools. Why? To avoid repeating himself." (p. 46)

Wiesel, in suggesting a notion of finitude and evil within God, thus follows a respected, well-trodden path in Jewish theology. Perhaps it is our nineteenth-century *haskalah,* neo-Maimonidean attitude which Wiesel affronts; perhaps it is our jolly-old-man-in-heaven-God-idea attacked so harshly by Wiesel that makes us shiver. But perhaps the God of Abraham Azuli, Isaac Luria, Israel Baal Shem, Moses de Leon, Aaron of Starojjele—the God of Wiesel—is closer to being the God of the Jews than the neo-Kantian system of synthetic *a priori's* amongst which the Master of the World seems to have disappeared.

Wiesel has been criticized for obscuring his meaning with continuous paradoxes. In doing this he writes not so much as a novelist but as a Kabbalist. The *Zohar* speaks in paradoxes as its way of rejecting the narrowness of a philosophical system built upon Aristotelean logic. Why waste time debating God's ability to make round squares and to make "A" be "not—A"? For God both can exist simultaneously. The infinite God can exist simultaneously with the finite God; the omnipotent God of spiritual activity can exist simultaneously with the impotent God dependent upon human action; the God who brings redemption can also be the God who awaits redemption.

Rabbi Akiba's insistence that God's presence in the world is determined by the deeds of man and the suggestion that there is a lack of complete divine omnipotence is the thesis of Jewish theology. Rabbi Ishmael's calling God to account is the antithesis. Though the synthesis is yet to be found, the movement of the dialectic in Wiesel is the latst manifestation of a perennial theological dilemma.

As no question can be asked of the infinite, silent God—the *En Sof*—the Unmoved Mover, before whom all man's profoundest questions are only expressions of his pitiful finiteness,

Wiesel turns his attention to the manifested God of appearances, who appears to man in "vestments." Expecting no response from the Unmoved Mover of the Godhead, Wiesel turns to the Most Moved, that aspect of the Godhead which in a way shares in our finiteness. The turning is made especially toward the *Shekhinah*, the "indwelling" presence of God in the world, who, like man, has no substance of its own and is only the reflection of the divine powers above. This is the aspect of God which yearns for man, the aspect of the Divine in need of man and in search of the human attribute of infinity—active concern.

Rabbi Akiba suggested that the fate of God in the world is effected by the fate of man. When man is imprisoned, God joins him. Both share in the redemption from slavery which is yet to come. Man occasionally is complacent with his slavery, but God awaits redemption.

The major purpose of man's existence according to the *Zohar* is to give "strength to God." . . . The *Zohar* also contains the idea that *zeevug* (union) would bring redemption to God and the world through uniting all primordially dispersed elements of divine and material entities. Through man's action, which thus gains a cosmic significance—having an effect on the internal state of the Godhead itself—either redemption, unification, or a sharper disunity and dispersion of the forces occur.

Perhaps the central idea of Kabbalah is this ability, indeed this destiny of man to play a central role in the life of God. Hegel suggests that world history is God's autobiography. The Kabbalah disagrees: world history is God's biography as written by God and man; God supplies the letters—man writes the sentences.

Wiesel expresses this idea of the interdependence between man and God. The freedom of God, the liberation of the divine "sparks," is man's task. "God is imprisoned. Man must free Him. That is the best guarded secret since the creation." The criminals of the world, the forces of evil, know this secret. It is for that reason that they seek imprisonment. For once in prison they can kill God.

God awaits redemption from His confinement. He awaited it in Auschwitz, and He awaits it today as He dwells among the Jews in Russia. The truest Jews share in the plight of God. The truest Jews are those who await the redemption of God and of man. The genuine Jew not only awaits the Messiah but is the Messiah.

Man's suffering gains meaning when it is for a thou, whether the thou be human or divine. The "other" attains his existence through our suffering for him. To the human thou Wiesel suggests: I suffer—therefore you are. Even the existence of God is in a way determined by human suffering. . . . (pp. 46-8)

The legend with which Wiesel concludes *Town Beyond the Wall,* in which man and God change places, expresses the interdependence of human and divine fate and freedom. The corollaries which Wiesel develops from this legend are that man assumes a degree of freedom and infinity surpassing that of the imprisoned God, and that from man's adopted role it follows that God is dependent upon man to assert His existence and reality, which are dependent upon human activity and suffering.

Like Sartre, Wiesel sees a man as condemned to freedom. Sartre's man is free to bring himself into existence. For Wiesel man's freedom brings God into existence. For Sartre man is totally free because there is no God. For Wiesel man is free only in order to free God from His confinement. For Sartre man is totally responsible to himself because there is no God. For Wiesel man is totally responsible to a God whom he must free: Blessed be man who frees Him who is in captivity.

Man is given freedom of action, while this is denied to God. "Freedom is given only to man. God is not free." How is this freedom given to man? Through suffering. The meaning of suffering is its ability to elevate man above God, to secure His redemption from confinement. Suffering and evil are inherent in the processes of redemption as well as of creation.

Wiesel restates the Kabbalistic notion that the internal unity of the Godhead is to be equated with redemption. Unity, the "collection of the sparks," restoring the primordial unity of the divine forces in the cosmos, stressed in Lurianic thinking, is reiterated by Wiesel. . . . (pp. 48-9)

Not only is God's redemption dependent upon man, but so, in a way, is His existence and presence in the world. Wiesel often speaks of God's dying, but he as often denies being a "God is dead" advocate. "God cannot die; He is immortal"—His immortality and His eternity are assured by man's suffering. God is not dead; He is buried alive by man's indifference. Since the destruction of the Temple, the *Shekhinah* has been limited to four cubits. Man, too, is ultimately limited to four cubits—his grave. The God who dies in Wiesel's writings has the face of a child, a face of innocence, helplessness, victimized by human brutality and indifference. God only dies insofar as the image He shares with man, the stamp of divinity, has been erased by apathy—erased from God, erased from man. Only the redemption will herald the return of the image.

The "God is dead" movement, consisting of comfortable American theologians who gained their theological training contemporaneously with Auschwitz, makes its claim after Auschwitz. Wiesel, the messenger of the dead, who gained his theological training in Auschwitz, spends his life thirsting for and seeking the God he lost at Auschwitz. With the loss of innocence the search is difficult, but the farther God hides the greater is Wiesel's yearning. Or as Hasidim would say: "Once one knows that God is hidden, He is no longer really hidden." Wiesel is God-intoxicated. His yearning is fierce. He asks the same question asked by the "God is dead" theologians: "After what has happened to us, how can you believe in God?" While for them the question alone suffices, Wiesel requires an answer: "With an understanding smile on his lips the Rebbe answered: How can you *not* believe in God after what has happened?"

Perhaps Wiesel is the *rebbe*. Perhaps he is our *rebbe*. Perhaps not, for he has been called the "high priest of our generation." If so, was he not made ritually impure by the corpses at Auschwitz? No. Like God, he is a priest who was purified by fire. . . . (pp. 49-50)

A progression from deep pessimism toward a somber but firm optimism is discernible in the chronological development of Wiesel's writings. His earliest book, *Night,* presents a world without mercy, without humanity, without God. It is a world of night and abandonment of responsibility.

This motif, so widely expressed in contemporary existentialist literature, is as old as the Bible. While the Rabbis also compared this world to night, this deep pessimism serves as a minor theme, overlaid by the fervent hope for the future expressed by the Prophets and later by the Rabbis.

Wiesel's second work—*Dawn*—begins the end of night. A glimmer of hope is presented. The meaning of the establishment of the State of Israel begins the end of absolute pessimism for the survivor of tragedy. *Le Jour* is mistakenly translated as *Accident;* it should be called "Day." With the assertion that life has meaning, Wiesel states the assumption to be expounded in his following work, *The Town Beyond the Wall.* In this work meaning in life is understood as found in one's caring for another, in suffering for another, and in preventing another from suffering: I suffer—therefore you are. These ideas are explored more completely in the *Gates of the Forest,* Wiesel's latest novel. Here Wiesel is optimistic. As long as there is man, there is hope. "What is man—dust turned into hope." The theme of care and suffering is expanded. Suffering endows man with the fortitude to work, even in spite of God, for redemption. Remembrance of former suffering and new faith are needed to prevent a reoccurrence of old suffering; the meaning of suffering is to prevent more suffering. The goal of suffering is to ennoble.

Israel waits to whisper the secret of suffering and the secret of survival to mankind. In the face of nuclear holocaust, the suffering of Israel may be a beacon-light to warn mankind of the price of indifference. . . . Said the Besht: *tzarah* (suffering) brings *tzohar* (light). The flames of the crematoria do have a purpose; they are a light to the nations.

Wiesel, in the last analysis, is a hopeful worshiper, not a blasphemer. Like Ibn Gabirol, in fleeing from God, he actually flees toward God (*Kether Malkhut*). He is a novelist and a Kabbalist. In Kabbalah nothing occurs by chance. There is meaning in all hints. Perhaps there is meaning in Wiesel's number at Auschwitz (as he reports in *Night*) having been 7713. In *Gematria*, adding up the sum of the digits, this equals 18—*Hai*—Life. Emerging from a planet of death, Wiesel affirms life. (pp. 51-2)

> Byron L. Sherwin, "Elie Wiesel and Jewish Theology," in Judaism *(copyright © 1969 by the American Jewish Congress), Vol. 18, No. 1, Winter, 1969, pp. 39-52.*

HUGH NISSENSON

"Legends of Our Time" is a continuation of a sacred history of our era that Wiesel began with "Night." It is sacred in the same sense that the Bible is sacred: history is conceived as the interaction of the human and the divine.

Wiesel's vision of the Holocaust is unique among writers because he experienced it as a religious Jew for whom nothing was profane and everything could be sanctified by human endeavor. Each encounter, if properly understood, is a revelation of the sublime. (p. 34)

It is as a mythologizer that Wiesel must be understood. It is a measure of his great artistic achievement that almost alone he has been able to transfigure the anguish of European Jewry into a form that is simultaneously immediate and timeless. Drawing upon the technique of Hassidic tales, he has created his own "midrash Aggadah": a compilation of legends that elucidate not Scripture, but life.

And death. "The secret of the *Maase-B'reshit,* the beginning of all things, is guarded by the Angel of Death. One approaches it only at the risk of losing his last tie to the earth, his last illusion, his faith, or his reason."

Loss of faith, madness and death pervade "Legends of Our Time." They are linked by silence; the silence of the streets of Sighet, on the night when Wiesel returns to that Transylvanian town from which he had been deported, and where he now discovers that it is as if the Jews there had never been. *It is as if nothing had happened.* It is only in the Jewish cemetery that he feels at home, among those graves on which the Jews had thrown themselves to implore the holy dead to intercede with God to save his people.

"The intercession had done no good. God had closed his ears and let it all happen." God is silent. And yet, here too in Sighet, Wiesel encounters a Jew sanctifying the world. He is a *shochet,* a ritual slaughterer who has assumed the burden of serving the few Jews who remain in the area. "If the legend of the Thirty-six Just Men is true, this slaughterer is one of them." He is, perhaps, one of those upon whom the very preservation of this world depends.

The *shochet* remains in the mind. His is, in essence, the Jew whom Wiesel so magnificently celebrates. He is, in fact, the quintessential Jew whose condition is defined by his relationship with God—even a God who has been eclipsed by the shadow of those incandescent clouds of smoke that hung in the air over the chimneys of Auschwitz. It was there, Wiesel suggests, that this immemorial relationship was consummated. And it was that which induced so many Jews to passively accept their fate. To believe, in such circumstances, that God is unjust, if not insane or diabolical, is intolerable. "If I am here," the prisoner reasoned, "it is because God is punishing me; I have sinned and am expiating my sins . . ."

The Germans understood this, and used it: "The system of *Lebensschein* in the ghettos and *Selekzion* in the camps not only periodically decimated the populations, but also worked on each prisoner to say to himself: 'That could have been me, I am the cause, perhaps the condition, of someone else's death.'" Thus death yields up its appalling secret: it is the accomplice of those executioners who by incriminating their victims drove them to embrace their own destruction.

In revealing this, Wiesel has neither gone mad nor lost his faith. He is, to be sure, a witness for whom "no one, neither human or divine" can free from guilt. As God does not respond, they are condemned to pursue a ceaseless monologue with the dead. And yet, with his incomparable lucidity, Wiesel speaks to us as well. It is an act of faith. "Some writing," he says "can sometimes, in moments of grace, attain the quality of deeds." They are equivalent to *mitzvoth,* those injunctions of the Torah performed by religious Jews to sanctify the world. "Legends of Our Time" is exactly that. (pp. 34-5)

> Hugh Nissenson, "A Sequel to the Sacred History of Our Era," in The New York Times Book Review *(© 1969 by The New York Times Company; reprinted by permission), January 12, 1969, pp. 34-5.*

LAURENCE GOLDSTEIN

For Elie Wiesel memory is an instrument of revelation. Each word he uses to document the past transforms both the word and the memory into an act of faith. The writings of Elie Wiesel are a journey into the past blackened by the Nazi death camps where the charred souls of its victims possess the sum of guilt and endurance that mark the progress of man. It is a compulsive, fevered, single-minded search among the ashes for a spark that can be thrust before the silent eyes of God Himself. . . .

This is the substance of legend. Each episode in Wiesel's life marks a portion of a journey that has torn the provincial Jew from the confines of the *shtetl* and set him loose upon the world. Since the fact of his life is a triumph over the indifference of that world, his destiny is dramatically self-contained. He is both the living repository of his people's legends and the sole interpreter of their meaning.

Legends of Our Time is a celebration of the liberation of memory from horror too terrible to be recounted or dismissed. If the holocaust defies analogy, it can be confronted only by an assault of an imagination determined to humanize the bestiality, guilt and fear that have sealed it from human experience. For Wiesel "Auschwitz, by definition, is beyond the vocabulary" of those scholars and philosophers who have had the opportunity to observe the tragedy. And so, for Wiesel, memory and its compulsive, mythic extension into fantasy become probes to search out feelings that remain in the brutalized nerve endings that are the final legacy of the holocaust. . . .

[The] compulsion to return, to understand, to confront his hatred and make it as axiomatic to his values as justice and compassion drives him to revisit Germany. It doesn't work. In **"An Appointment with Hate"** Wiesel realizes the Germans "had started and lost the most ignominious war in history, and afterward had managed to surpass their conquerors in wealth and happiness. Above all, in complacency." Yet knowing there is no forgiveness, knowing that each Jew betrays the dead unless he houses that healthy, virile hate "for what the German personifies and for what persists in the German," Wiesel cannot forge that hatred. He quotes the Israeli humorist Ephraim Kishon: "Logic, too, went up in smoke at Auschwitz."

This ambivalence, the knowledge that irony is as much the servant of sanity as commitment, moves him to see life as a process where each experience affords a double vision "between them and myself, between the self I had left at Buchenwald and the other self that thought it was healed." The possibilities offered by this vision account for the remarkably compassionate tone of Wiesel's work. He writes with that possessive reverence for language that celebrates, as much as describes, experience. The written word becomes a powerful assertion, the triumph of life over death and indifference. To carve words, especially in a graveyard, is to love. (p. 250)

[In] his final **"Plea for the Dead,"** Wiesel begs us to learn that "The lesson of the holocaust—if there is any—is that our strength is only illusory, and that in each of us is a victim who is afraid, who is cold, who is hungry. Who is ashamed."

Words carved on gravestones, legend torn from the pit where millions of broken bodies lie. This is the inheritance which Elie Wiesel brings to us. His voice claims us with its urgency. His vision lights the mystery of human endurance. (p. 251)

Laurence Goldstein, *"Memory and Revelation," in* The Nation *(copyright 1969* The Nation *magazine,* The Nation Associates, Inc.*), Vol. 208, No. 8, February 24, 1969, pp. 250-51.*

THE TIMES LITERARY SUPPLEMENT

[In *One Generation After* Elie Wiesel does not retell his concentration camp] experiences, but examines the world and himself: what does Auschwitz mean one generation after? For the majority of people alive today Auschwitz is just a word, belonging to history, like St Bartholomew's Night. Mr Wiesel admits that the quarter of a century which has elapsed since the prisoners of the Nazi camps were liberated is a long, long time. The Era of the Moon is upon us: the age of Auschwitz is closed. . . .

Mr. Wiesel is somewhere in between [those prisoners who can shake off their concentration camp experiences and bear no visible scars, and those who are haunted by them for the rest of their lives]; he is a thoughtful and sensitive man. His beautifully written book is full of passion and compassion, of bitterness and kindness; it is a cry of despair and a plea of resigned acceptance, as well as a shrug of the shoulders, at one and the same time. Auschwitz remains the central experience of his life. He is not obsessed by it and is free of self-pity. But wherever he may be, he is always in Auschwitz; whatever is in front of his eyes, he also sees Auschwitz beyond the images of reality.

The shock he cannot get over is not the bestial cruelty of the people who ran and guarded the camps but their very ordinariness. . . .

In addition to the title essay, the book contains a number of other essays, prose-poems, snapshots, snippets, sighs, cries and stories. Mr. Wiesel goes back to the village from which he was taken to Auschwitz, digs up his gold-watch, the one he received for his thirteenth birthday, the symbol of his parents' love, the last link with the past. He does find it: it is corroded, covered with dirt and rust, crawling with worms. He buries it again and goes away, this time forever.

Not all the short pieces are on this level. A number were written about Israel—one at its birth, another after the Six Day War. Mr. Wiesel speaks about "the conquerors of Sinai and the liberators of Jerusalem", waxes emotional and writes like a not too skilful propagandist. All this may have been quite good journalism a few days after the events, but hardly stands up to reprinting in book form.

"The Shock of Auschwitz," in The Times Literary Supplement *(© Times Newspapers Ltd. (London) 1971; reproduced from* The Times Literary Supplement *by permission), No. 3619, July 9, 1971, p. 809.*

ALBERT H. FRIEDLANDER

Souls on Fire is a celebration of Hasidic life in which the pietistic fervor and turbulent yearnings of Central and Eastern European Jewry are drawn together into clear images of the great Hasidic teachers and masters, from the founder of modern Hasidism, Israel ben Eliezer (1698-1760)—the legendary Baal Shem Tov—to Menahem-Mendl of Kotzk (1787-1859). Each was a master of the parable, and Wiesel's sensitive evocation of a world that with the Nazi holocaust disappeared into darkness turns their lives into personal parables.

Scholars will disagree with parts of Wiesel's interpretation and with some of the factual details within his work. They may be upset by the loose organization of *Souls on Fire* and occasional repetitions where the bones of the author's popular lecture series show through. Wiesel's theory that the Seer of Lubin, Rabbi Yaakov-Yitzhak's fall out of a window was a second suicide attempt goes counter to the entire Hasidic tradition (which *knows* Satan pushed the Seer) and is less realistic than another suggestion that the Seer was drunk (as were many Hasidim on the eve of *Simhat Torah*, the Feat of Rejoicing in the Law). Wiesel's presentation of Nahman's complex tale of the seven beggars can be challenged since it ignores recently published Hebrew commentaries in Jerusalem—but all of these quibbles are out of place here.

The superiority of Wiesel's work set against that of such scholars as Gershom Scholem or Martin Buber lies precisely in the fact that this book is a testimony and not a study. Hasidism is revealed from within; it is not analyzed from outside. And Elie Wiesel ("I, grandson of Dodye Feig, Hasid of Wizsnitz, . . .") speaks with conscious authority as one who has seen the fire and has heard the story. All he wants to do is to transmit the legend and the world that created it. In this work . . . he achieves his purpose. (pp. 76-7)

The various biographical sketches are linked to form a highly personal account of the Hasidic movement. Its opponents and adherents; the political structure of Eastern Europe and the cometlike appearance of Napoleon; the juxtaposition of poverty and great wealth, love and envy, knowledge and ignorance— all converge in Wiesel's evocation. Polish Hasidism won too easily and degenerated quickly. Lithuania and other areas provided a sterner challenge and demanded scholarship from Hasidic teachers and their followers; and so outside Poland the movement attained greater depth and content. As the institution of the Tzaddik, the "Just Man," developed and leadership became hereditary, negative aspects grew stronger in Hasidic life. All of this is documented by Wiesel—but can be found elsewhere. What remains after his book has been laid aside are the men and their stories, fused in a manner that cannot be forgotten. . . .

The nature of Wiesel's work is such that this account of Hasidism (it is in fact a sourcebook) now becomes part of Hasidic literature. Tales heard in the "kingdom of night" are retold, and past and present merge: Tradition has it that the great leaders of Galician Hasidism—the innocent, humble Zusia and the autocratic Elimelekh—went from the house of the Great Maggid of Mezeritch to found Hasidic centers every place they stayed. The two brothers arrived in a small village near Cracow with the intention of stopping overnight. But they were restless and felt compelled to leave. As dusk fell, they left. It is the grandson of Dodye Feig of Wizsnitz who tells us the name of the village—Auschwitz. (p. 77)

Albert H. Friedlander, "'Souls on Fire: Portraits and Legends of Hasidic Masters'," in Saturday Review *(copyright © 1972 by* Saturday Review; *all rights reserved; reprinted by permission), Vol. 55, No. 9, February 26, 1972, pp. 76-7.*

CHARLES E. SILBERMAN

The judgment has been offered before: Elie Wiesel is one of the great writers of this generation. With the publication of **"Souls on Fire,"** that judgment is confirmed; his work takes on a new dimension that makes comparison with Camus inevitable.

Until now, Wiesel's greatness had rested on the unique role that his life and talents had forced upon him—that of witness to the Holocaust, messenger to the living from the dead. What has lifted him above the ranks of every other writer of the Holocaust has been his obsession with life rather than death. If every literary trail led him back to the Holocaust, it was in a desperate attempt to confer a retroactive meaning on the unrelieved horror of those years. "Who knows," he wrote, "if we can make ourselves heard, man will change. His very vision of himself will be altered. Thanks to illustrations provided by us, he will henceforth be able to distinguish between what he may or may not do . . ."

The effort was in vain. "Nothing has been learned," he lamented two years ago, in **"One Generation After,"** "Auschwitz has not even served as warning." But Wiesel somehow has survived this negation, even as he has survived the Holocaust itself. Like Camus, he insists on being a spokesman for man rather than against him. Running through all of Wiesel's books, therefore, sometimes explicitly, sometimes only barely hinted at, has been another search—a search for sanity in the face of insanity, for faith and commitment in a world that makes faith impossible and absurd. In one way or another, each of his books has addressed itself to the question with which Camus and other existential philosophers have struggled: How can one be, how can one affirm life, after having experienced unrelieved and absolute evil that, as Wiesel wrote in his first book, **"Night,"** "consumed my faith forever" and "deprived me, for all eternity, of the desire to live"?

"Souls on Fire" is the product of that search,,and the answer to it; it should be read by everyone concerned with the existential question, which is to say, by every sensitive and thinking human being. Like a true existentialist, Wiesel is relentless in insisting that man must himself create the meaning he once derived from faith; unlike most existentialists, he is equally relentless in repudiating absurdity. His central theme, in fact, is that "man owes it to himself to reject despair." Difficult, yes, but "there is no alternative: one must impose a meaning on what perhaps has none and draw ecstasy from nameless, faceless pain."

How is this possible? For Wiesel, through an exploration of the Hasidic world in which he was raised. In **"Souls on Fire,"** he takes non-Hasidic readers on a "pilgrimage to the sources of Hasidic experience," weaving together his own retelling of Hasidic tales and legends with portraits of some of the leading Hasidic masters and an account of how the movement developed. . . . [Like] almost all [Wiesel's] writing, the book cries to be read aloud.

But why Hasidism? Does it offer Wiesel anything more than a comforting nostalgia? More to the point, can these 18th-century and 19th-century eastern European Jewish mystics really speak to late 20th-century Americans? Can they offer anything relevant to our concerns . . . ? (p. 1)

What, then, does Hasidism have to offer? Not answers, Wiesel suggests, but a way to live—a way to live joyously—when there are no answers. Part of Hasidism's appeal to Wiesel is that it does not pretend to answer the unanswerable; nor is it a stranger to melancholy and despair, or even loss of faith. . . . To challenge God "is permissible, even required," Wiesel insists. "He who says no to God is not necessarily a renegade. Everything depends on the way he says it and why. One can say anything as long as it is for man, not against him. . . . It all depends on where the rebel chooses to stand. From inside his community, he may say everything."

If belief is difficult or impossible, if there are no answers to the existential question, it is nonetheless possible to draw strength from the despair that is man's lot. (pp. 1, 26)

Like most Jewish mystical movements (and unlike most Oriental), Hasidism is a mysticism that emphasizes the here and now, a search for the invisible and the eternal by way of the mundane and the visible. Above all, it is a mysticism that emphasizes the relationship between man and man. The essence of Hasidism, as Wiesel puts it, is the combination of presence and transformation. . . .

Scholars, to be sure, may quarrel with Wiesel's version of Hasidism, as they quarreled with Buber's, arguing (perhaps correctly) that it is hopelessly romanticized and historically incorrect. No matter; **"Souls on Fire"** is not intended to be a work of historical scholarship; like the Hasidic legends themselves, it is a work of genius and of art—an extraordinary man's extraordinary effort "to humanize fate." (p. 26)

> *Charles E. Silberman, "How to Live Joyously When There Are No Answers," in* The New York Times Book Review *(© 1972 by The New York Times Company; reprinted by permission), March 5, 1972, pp. 1, 26.*

SEYMOUR SIEGEL

[*Souls on Fire*] is sure to attain the status of a classic resource for those who want to understand the soul of the hasidic masters and the import of their teachings. Unlike Buber's evocation of the hasidic teachers which consists of a series of short anecdotes, and unlike the various scholarly historical descriptions of the movement, Wiesel's book weaves together history and legend, tale and chronicle to present full length portraits of the leaders of the hasidic communities. Like all significant portrait painters, Wiesel has put much of himself into the result, interpreting the hasidic spirit in the light of his own very intense, personal experience. (p. 467)

The mystery, the enthusiasm and the sanctified attachment to life which characterized hasidism have a special meaning for us today. *Souls on Fire* will enlighten and warm those who seek to know about a group who "knew how to worship. And trust. They had mastered the art of giving and receiving. Of sharing and taking part." (p. 468)

> *Seymour Siegel, "Book Reviews: 'Souls on Fire'," in* America *(reprinted with permission of America Press, Inc.; © 1972; all rights reserved), Vol. 126, No. 14, April 8, 1972, pp. 467-68.*

FREDERICK GARBER

[Wiesel] can be masterful at a brief, incisive scene of extraordinary pressure and intensity, such as the hallucinatory vision in *Dawn* or Katriel's parable in the otherwise maudlin *A Beggar in Jerusalem*—scenes which are themselves cast in the mold of those same legends that we find [in *Souls on Fire*], and that have been the stuff of his imagination since earliest childhood. In *Souls on Fire,* where he is working at the very source of this material, there are, not surprisingly, a goodly number of such scenes—pungent and resonant with illuminated meaning.

Yet for all the drama and sense of mystery which Wiesel conveys, something is missing at the heart of this book. Wiesel tells us that he has ignored "theories" for the sake of character, but the fact is that character is precisely what the book lacks. Here, as in his novels, Wiesel tends to mistake the amassing of personality traits—Rabbi Zusia's fathomless humility, for example, or the puzzling flamboyance of Israel of Rizhin; the Bratzlaver's egocentricity and astonishing gift of narrative, or the crushing despair of Menahem Mendl of Kotsk—for the creation of a living personality; only rarely does the spark jump the gap and make a character dance with life. The consequence is that we are left only with hearsay about the charisma Wiesel tells us these people possessed and with no living sense of that

blazing power of intellect—its name is religious genius—which dazzled their disciples and antagonists alike.

True, these essays originated as lectures, and it may be that Wiesel's exceptional passion and personal presence lent them that warmth of life which is lacking here. But in print only a very few of the *Tzaddikim* emerge with any degree of conviction; the rest are shackled by varying degrees of sentimentalism.

By sentimentalism in this connection, I mean mainly a tendency to exploit the easier possibilities of the material. For example, dealing as he does here with mystics and individuals of the very highest order of intuition, Wiesel quite appropriately reports what must have been extraordinary incidents of foresight on the part of several *Tzaddikim,* premonitions of the terror beyond imagination which would come to pass in the Holocaust a hundred years later. Yet he can also pass with jarring tastelessness from such cryptic and mysterious episodes to the melodramatic story of Zusia and Elimelekh's vague uneasiness in a village where, sometime in the middle 1800's, they refused to spend the night—the village of Auschwitz.

This tendency to go soft where hardness is required is, I think, the besetting flaw in Wiesel's work generally, and it is perhaps more apparent in *Souls on Fire* than in his earlier books. In the novels one could watch the struggle of the bruised survivor of Auschwitz to make a style out of despair. One had to recognize that the struggle was never totally successful, but one also had to recognize that the events Wiesel was trying to mold into art had brought civilization down so many notches that to make meaningful sense of them was beyond nearly every possibility of prose. *Souls on Fire,* however, takes in other territory, finding food for post-Holocaust souls in 18th-century geniuses. Hence it is especially disappointing to discover that as we reach deeper into the book it becomes vaguer and more shrill, at its core a large blur which belies its surface persuasiveness and the admirable intensity of its passion. (pp. 84-5, 88)

> *Frederick Garber, "Sentimental Journey," in* Commentary *(reprinted by permission; all rights reserved), Vol. 54, No. 3, September, 1972, pp. 84-5, 88.*

HARRY JAMES CARGAS

The questions proliferate in modern literature concerning the meaning of life, the meaning of humanity. There is one genre, however, which, while also positing doubt, if we may say it that way, by questioning God rather than persons, heaven rather than the world, actually concludes with a kind of hope which may be opposed to the despair of a [Yukio Mishima, a Kurt Vonnegut, or an Alain Robbe-Grillet]. This genre has been labeled Holocaust Literature.

The authors of this literature, particularly those who are survivors of the Nazi concentration camps, sometimes demand answers from God, sometimes scold, defy, rebel against God, but most seem to voice their doubts within a context that admits of God's existence. In a way their attitude of faith has been summed up by Elie Wiesel in his cantata *Ani Ma'amin:* ". . . the silence of God is God." Some are more strident, recalling the "atheist" Bendrix in Graham Greene's Catholic novel *The End of the Affair* who, after the woman he loves is lost in death, metaphorically shakes his fist at a God he has been denying and says these words which close the book: "O God,

You've done enough, You've robbed me of enough, I'm too tired and old to learn to love, leave me alone forever.''

We must not conclude, however, that the questions asked of God by Wiesel, Nelly Sachs, Paul Celan, Primo Levi, Jakov Lind, Andre Schwarz-Bart, Emmanuel Ringelblum, Lena Donat, Joset Bor and so many others are necessarily far removed from the doubts of Robbe-Grillet, Nathalie Sarraute, Michael Butor, Jean Cayrol, Robert Antelme, [Carlos] Fuentes, Severo Sarduy, and still others. It may be less than a giant step from doubt in man to faith in God. Perhaps the best illustration of this is found in the work of a man who progressed from the night of Auschwitz to at least the approachables of faith (for, after all, who can say that one truly has belief), Elie Wiesel.

Those who write a type of literature of frustration raise their questions from that frustration. Wiesel and others, on the contrary, see in their queries the very basis of life. Edmond Jabes, a Jew born in Egypt, now writing in Paris, has said so succinctly, ''God is a questioning God.'' Wiesel presents this view in a number of his works. (pp. 594-95)

Because answers divide, are incomplete, are lies, one response to the mysteries of existence is silence. This is not something negative but rather a kind of prayer, a listening to God. Wiesel ends one of his non-fiction volumes by saying that silence, ''. . . demands to be recognized and transmitted.''

The transmission is, of course, of ultimate importance for many survivors of the Holocaust. Eugene Heimler said it remarkably: there were ''messages I had to deliver to the living from the dead. . . . Of their dead, burnt bodies I would be the voice.'' Wiesel too is obsessed with being such a bearer. He feels his responsibility to the dead. He told me, ''I don't have the right not to communicate.'' He fears having said too much, perhaps thus cheapening what he wishes to commemorate; but he nevertheless must not be destructive in a silent way. (In his book *The Jews of Silence* Wiesel distinguishes between constructive silence—illustrated by the praying Jews of Russia—and the destructive silence of Jews throughout the world who refuse to act on behalf of their suffering brothers and sisters.)

This philosophy must inevitably affect the author's style. His has been called a literature of silence. An example or two may be in order. In *Night* Wiesel tells of seeing a young boy hanged. His body was so emaciated that it did not weigh enough to help him to die. For over half an hour he continued swaying, struggling between life and death. About his own reaction the author has but seven words: ''That night the soup tasted of corpses.'' In that same book we read of a cattle car experience. The writer witnesses a son murder his own father in order to steal bread from the old man's mouth. The killer is, in turn, beaten to death by others. Again the reaction: ''I was fifteen years old.'' Silence, for Wiesel, is beyond language, beyond lies. . . .

Not to write, for Wiesel, as for so many other survivors of Hitler's camps, would be a betrayal. How then do they understand this minimal breaking of silence? Again Wiesel provides some clues. He knows what every Jew knows, that for 6,000,000 victims it will be impossible to say the memorial Kaddish at their graves because either the sites are unknown or there are no graves. ''My generation has been robbed of everything, even of our cemeteries.'' . . . So Wiesel says that ''the act of writing is for me often nothing more than the secret or conscious desire to carve words on a tombstone: to the memory of a town forever vanished, to the memory of a child-

hood in exile, to the memory of all those I loved and who before I could tell them I loved them, went away.''

Beyond this, Wiesel would agree with Jabes on the seriousness of the writer's work. (p. 595)

Wiesel's works, then, like those of other important Holocaust writers, be they diarists, chroniclers, playwrights, novelists, or poets, are not so much lamentations as they are deeds. They can be distinguished from the writings of Robbe-Grillet, Ionesco, Beckett, and others because they are acts of faith—*even as questions* because those questions are addressed to God rather than being images of absurdity. We are asked to risk *with* Wiesel and the others rather than despair alone. They live out the teaching of the Rabbi in Wiesel's drama *Zalmen, or the Madness of God:* ''God requires of man not that he live, but that he choose to live. What matters is to choose—at the risk of being defeated.'' (p. 596)

Harry James Cargas, ''Elie Wiesel and the Holocaust,'' in Commonweal *(copyright © 1976 Commonweal Publishing Co., Inc.; reprinted by permission of Commonweal Publishing Co., Inc.), Vol. CIII, No. 19, September 10, 1976, pp. 594-96.*

L. KAHN

In this volume of essays, open letters, dialogues et cetera, [entitled *Un juif aujourd'hui*], Wiesel returns to his main themes: the Holocaust, its theological, political and human implications, the mysteries of Jewish persecutions and survival, man's grappling with a silent, inscrutable divinity. Wiesel delves into some of these questions more deeply than before, and his positions on some have changed, though more in degree than in substance.

Of Wiesel's works to date, the current volume is the most overtly political. Yet he is interested in politics only at the point at which it intersects Jewish and moral questions. . . . Wiesel's power is on the thought and narrative levels rather than in the dramatic sphere.

L. Kahn, ''French: 'Un juif aujourd' hui','' in World Literature Today *(copyright 1978 by the University of Oklahoma Press), Vol. 52, No. 3, Summer, 1978, p. 437.*

ANDREW M. GREELEY

A more appropriate title for **''A Jew Today''** would be ''A Survivor Today.'' A collection of essays, sketches, letters and impressions, **''A Jew Today''** amplifies the passionate cry that rose from the young Elie Wiesel's lips when he was freed in 1945 from a concentration camp. It is a cry not of outrage or of protest or even of horror, but a more elemental cry whose content is ultimately unutterable. . . .

Wiesel . . . relies sparingly on graphic physical descriptions of Auschwitz and achieves his impact rather by describing the effect of the holocaust on people: those who died, those who survived, and now even the children of the survivors. The effect is overwhelming, devastating, appalling. It is as though Auschwitz was yesterday instead of almost 34 years ago—though Wiesel himself would doubtless argue that it not only was yesterday but is today.

There is little that is new here; many of the pieces have appeared before, and Wiesel's cry has been more or less the same since we first heard it—from which it does not follow that we do not need to hear it still.

"A Jew Today" is, finally, less a cry of despair than of defiance. Informed of incidents of persecution against Ukrainian Jews, Rabbi Nahman of Bratzlav protests: "You want me to shout with pain, weep in despair, I know, I know. But I will not, you hear me, I will not. . . . Jews, for heaven's sake, do not despair."

For the present non-Jewish reviewer, the most surprising chapter in the book is the last one, **"A Plea for the Survivors,"** in which Wiesel insists that the world Jewish community does not listen to the survivors and is even contemptuous of them. I am not competent to say whether this is literary imagery, Wiesel's personal reaction, or the feeling of many of the survivors themselves. But there is a temptation to insist that if one is told often enough that one cannot understand, one eventually gives up trying. Is it wrong to suggest that there is more to being a Jew than remembering the holocaust? Can a later generation be expected to hear a cry that has been repeated so often that it has become background noise? But such issues are hardly the author's concern. Pedagogy, theology, even religion in the ordinary sense of the word are not what Wiesel's cry is about. His subject is horror and, astonishingly, hope. For others it will be different. For Elie Wiesel, a Jewish boy dragged away to Auschwitz at the age of 12, horror and hope are what it means to be a Jew today.

Andrew M. Greeley, "Listen to the Survivors," in The New York Times Book Review *(© 1979 by The New York Times Company; reprinted by permission), January 21, 1979, p. 10.*

Appendix

THE EXCERPTS IN *CIC*, VOLUME 1, WERE REPRINTED FROM THE FOLLOWING PERIODICALS:

Acta Sociologica
America
American Anthropologist
The American Economic Review
American Indian Quarterly
American Journal of Orthopsychiatry
The American Journal of Sociology
American Notes and Queries
The American Political Science Review
The American Scholar
American Sociological Review
The Annals of the American Academy of
  Political and Social Science
The Antioch Review
Asian Affairs
The Atlantic Monthly
Best Sellers
The Black Scholar
Black World
Book Week—New York Herald Tribune
Book Week—The Sunday Herald Tribune
Book Week—The Washington Post
Book Week—World Journal Tribune
Book World—Chicago Tribune
Book World—The Washington Post
Books and Bookmen
Bulletin of the Atomic Scientists: a
  magazine of science and public affairs
Canadian Journal of Political Science
Catholic World
Chicago Tribune
Choice
The Christian Century
The Christian Science Monitor
Christianity and Crisis
The Chronicle Review
Columbia Law Review
Commentary

Commonweal
Contemporary Psychology
Contemporary Sociology
The Critic
Dissent
Economic Development and Cultural
  Change
The Economist
Encounter
Esquire
Ethics
Far Eastern Economic Review
Fortune
The Guardian Weekly
Harper's
The Historian
History: Reviews of New Books
The Human Context
The Humanist
Intercollegiate Review
International Affairs
Interracial Books for Children Bulletin
The Journal of American History
Journal of Asian Studies
Journal of Black Studies
The Journal of Conflict Resolution
The Journal of Economic History
The Journal of Economic Literature
The Journal of Interdisciplinary History
Journal of Marriage and the Family
The Journal of Modern African Studies
The Journal of Negro Education
The Journal of Political Economy
The Journal of Southern History
Judaism
The Listener
Maclean's Magazine
Man

The Management Review
Modern Age
Monthly Review
Ms.
The Nation
National Review
Natural History
The New Leader
The New Republic
New Society
New Statesman
The New Statesman & Nation
New York Herald Tribune
New York Herald Tribune Book Review
The New York Review of Books
The New York Times
The New York Times Book Review
The New Yorker
Off Our Backs
Pacific Affairs
Pacific Historical Review
Partisan Review
The Philosophical Forum
Phylon: The Atlanta University Review of
  Race and Culture
Policy Review
Political Science Quarterly
The Political Science Reviewer
Political Studies
The Progressive
The Psychoanalytic Quarterly
Psychology Today
The Public Interest
The Quarterly Journal of Speech
Religious Studies Review
Review of Social Economy
Reviews in Anthropology
Salmagundi

San Francisco Review of Books
Saturday Night.
Saturday Review
Science
Science and Society
Science Books
Science Books & Films
Scientific American
Signs
Sinister Wisdom
Social Casework
Social Forces
Social Policy

Social Research
Social Science
The Social Science Journal
The Social Service Review
The Social Studies
The Sociological Quarterly
Sociology: Reviews of New Books
South Atlantic Quarterly
The Spectator
Studies on the Left
Teachers College Record
Technology Review
Theology Today

The Times Literary Supplement
The Village Voice
The Virginia Quarterly Review
The Wall Street Journal
The Washington Monthly
The Western Historical Quarterly
William and Mary Quarterly
Win
World Literature Today
World Politics
Worldview
The Yale Review

THE EXCERPTS IN *CIC*, VOLUME 1, WERE REPRINTED FROM THE FOLLOWING BOOKS:

Arendt, Hannah. On Revolution. *Viking Penguin, 1963*.

Arendt, Hannah. On Violence. *Harcourt, 1970*.

Berns, Walter. For Capital Punishment: Crime and the Morality of the Death Penalty. *Basic Books, 1979*.

Blassingame, John W. Black New Orleans: 1860-1880. *University of Chicago Press, 1973*.

Bookchin, Murray. Post-Scarcity Anarchism. *The Ramparts Press, 1971*.

Buckley, William F., Jr. Cruising Speed—A Documentary. *Putnam's, 1971*.

Buckley, William F., Jr. Execution Eve, and Other Contemporary Ballads. *Putnam's, 1975*.

Buckley, William F., Jr. God and Man at Yale: The Superstitions of Academic Freedom. *Henry Regnery Company, 1961*.

Buckley, William F., Jr. Up from Liberalism. *McDowell, Obolensky, 1959*.

Carter, Angela. The Sadeian Woman: And the Ideology of Pornography. *Pantheon Books, 1979*.

Chomsky, Noam. American Power and the New Mandarins. *Pantheon Books, 1969*.

Chomsky, Noam. For Reasons of State. *Pantheon Books, 1973*.

Clecak, Peter. Radical Paradoxes: Dilemmas of the American Left, 1945-1970. *Harper & Row, 1973*.

Commoner, Barry. The Politics of Energy. *Knopf, 1979*.

Commoner, Barry. The Poverty of Power: Energy and the Economic Crisis. *Knopf, 1976*.

Dahl, Robert A. Polyarchy: Participation and Opposition. *Yale University Press, 1971*.

Dahl, Robert A., and Tufte, Edward R. Size and Democracy. *Stanford University Press, 1973*.

Daly, Mary. Gyn/Ecology: The Metaethics of Radical Feminism. *Beacon Press, 1978*.

Davis, Angela. Angela Davis: An Autobiography. *Random House, 1974*.

Davis, Angela Y. and others. If They Come in the Morning: Voices of Resistance. *The New American Library, 1971*.

Debo, Angie. And Still the Waters Run. *Princeton University Press, 1940, Gordian Press, 1966*.

Debo, Angie. A History of the Indians of the United States. *University of Oklahoma Press, 1970*.

Domhoff, G. William. The Powers That Be: Processes of Ruling-Class Domination in America. *Random House, 1978*.

Douglas, William O. The Court Years, 1939-1975; The Autobiography of William O. Douglas. *Random House, 1980*.

Douglas, William O. Points of Rebellion. *Random House, 1970*.

Douglas, William O. The Three Hundred Year War: A Chronicle of Ecological Disaster. *Random House, 1972*.

Falk, Richard A. This Endangered Planet: Prospects and Proposals for Human Survival. *Random House, 1971*.

Fanon, Frantz. Black Skin, White Masks. *Translated by Charles Lam Marksmann. Grove Press, 1967*.

Fanon, Frantz. The Wretched of the Earth. *Translated by Constance Farrington. Grove Press, 1965*.

Freeman, Jo. The Politics of Women's Liberation: A Case Study of an Emerging Social Movement and Its Relation to the Policy Process. *David McKay Company, 1975.*

Friedenberg, Edgar Z. Coming of Age in America: Growth and Acquiescence. *Random House, 1965.*

Friedenberg, Edgar Z. The Disposal of Liberty and Other Industrial Wastes. *Doubleday, 1975.*

Friedenberg, Edgar Z. R. D. Laing. *Viking Penguin, 1973.*

Friedman, Milton, and Friedman, Rose D. Capitalism and Freedom. *University of Chicago Press, 1962.*

Friedman, Milton, and Friedman, Rose D. Free to Choose: A Personal Statement. *Harcourt, 1980.*

Galbraith, John Kenneth. The Affluent Society. *Rev. ed. Houghton Mifflin, 1969.*

Galbraith, John Kenneth. The New Industrial State. *Rev. ed. Houghton Mifflin, 1978.*

Geismar, Peter. Fanon. *Dial, 1971.*

Gilder, George. Sexual Suicide. *Quadrangle/The New York Times Book Co., 1973.*

Gilder, George. Wealth and Poverty. *Basic Books, 1981.*

Goodman, Paul. Growing Up Absurd: Problems of Youth in the Organized System. *Random House, 1960.*

Goodman, Paul. Little Prayers & Finite Experience. *Harper & Row, 1972.*

Gwaltney, John L. The Thrice Shy: Cultural Accommodation to Blindness and Other Disasters in a Mexican Community. *Columbia University Press, 1970.*

Gwaltney, John Langston. Drylongso: A Self-Portrait of Black America. *Edited by John Langston Gwaltney. Random House, 1980.*

Habermas, Jürgen. Knowledge and Human Interests. *Translated by Jeremy J. Shapiro. Beacon Press, 1971.*

Habermas, Jürgen. Legitimation Crisis. *Translated by Thomas McCarthy. Beacon Press, 1975.*

Habermas, Jürgen. Toward a Rational Society: Student Protest, Science, and Politics. *Translated by Jeremy J. Shapiro. Beacon Press. 1970.*

Hansen, Emmanuel. Frantz Fanon: Social and Political Thought. *Ohio State University Press, 1977.*

Harrington, Michael. The Accidental Century. *Macmillan, 1965.*

Harrington, Michael. The Other America: Poverty in the United States. *Macmillan, 1962.*

Harrington, Michael. The Twilight of Capitalism. *Simon & Schuster, 1976.*

Hobsbawm, E. J. Revolutionaries: Contemporary Essays. *Weidenfeld and Nicolson, 1973.*

Hofstadter, Douglas R. Gödel, Escher, Bach: An Eternal Golden Braid. *Basic Books, 1979.*

Hymes, Dell. On Noam Chomsky: Critical Essays. *Anchor Press, 1974.*

Jansen, G. H. Militant Islam. *Pan Books, 1979.*

Johanson, Donald C., and Edey, Maitland A. Lucy: The Beginnings of Humankind. *Simon & Schuster, 1981.*

Kahn, Herman. On Thermonuclear War. *Princeton University Press, 1960.*

Kahn, Herman, with the Hudson Institute. World Economic Development: 1979 and Beyond. *Westview Press, 1979.*

Kirk, Russell. Decadence and Renewal in the Higher Learning: An Episodic History of American University and College since 1953. *Gateway Editions, 1978.*

Ladner, Joyce A. Mixed Families: Adopting across Racial Boundaries. *Anchor Press, 1977.*

Ladner, Joyce A. Tomorrow's Tomorrow: The Black Woman. *Doubleday, 1971.*

Laing, R. D. The Divided Self. *Tavistock, 1960.*

Laing, R. D. The Politics of Experience [and] The Bird of Paradise. *Penguin Books, 1967.*

Lasch, Christopher. The Culture of Narcissism: American Life in an Age of Diminishing Expectations. *Norton, 1978.*

Lévy, Bernard-Henri. Barbarism with a Human Face. *Translated by George Holoch. Harper & Row, 1979.*

Leys, Simon. Chinese Shadows. *Viking Penguin, 1977.*

Lichtheim, George. The Concept of Ideology and Other Essays. *Random House, 1967.*

Lipset, Seymour Martin. Political Man: The Social Basis of Politics. *Doubleday & Company, Inc., 1959, 1960.*

Lipset, Seymour Martin, and Raab, Earl. The Politics of Unreason: Right-Wing Extremism in America, 1790-1977. 2d ed. *The University of Chicago Press, 1978.*

Martin, David. The New Left: Six Critical Essays. *Bodley Head, 1970.*

McCarthy, Mary. On the Contrary. *Farrar, Straus and Cudahy, 1961.*

McNickle, D'Arcy. Native American Tribalism: Indian Survivals and Renewals. *Oxford University Press, New York, 1973.*

Mead, Margaret. Coming of Age in Samoa: A Psychological Study of Primitive Youth for Western Civilization. *Blue Ribbon Books, 1928.*

Mead, Margaret. Culture and Commitment: The New Relationships between the Generations in the 1970s. *Anchor Press, 1978.*

Mead, Margaret. Letters from the Field: 1925-1975. *Harper & Row, 1977.*

Mead, Margaret. Male and Female: A Study of the Sexes in a Changing World. *William Morrow, 1949.*

Mills, C. Wright. The Power Elite. *Oxford University Press, New York, 1956.*

Mills, C. Wright. White Collar: The American Middle Class. *Oxford University Press, New York, 1953.*

Mitchell, Juliet. Psychoanalysis and Feminism. *Pantheon Books, 1974.*

Moraga, Cherríe, and Anzaldua, Gloria, eds. This Bridge Called My Back: Writings by Radical Women of Color. *Persephone Press, 1981.*

Nisbet, Robert. History of the Idea of Progress. *Basic Books, 1980.*

Nisbet, Robert. Twilight of Authority. *Oxford University Press, New York, 1975.*

Novak, Michael. The Rise of the Unmeltable Ethnics: Politics and Culture in the Seventies. *Macmillan, 1971.*

Podhoretz, Norman. Doings and Undoings: The Fifties and After in American Writing. *Farrar, Straus & Giroux, 1964.*

Reed, Evelyn. Women's Evolution: From Matriarchal Clan to Patriarchal Family. *Pathfinder Press, 1975.*

Rossi, Alice S., and Calderwood, Ann, eds. Academic Women on the Move. *Russell Sage Foundation, 1973.*

Rothschild, Emma. Paradise Lost: The Decline of the Auto-Industrial Age. *Random House, 1974.*

Rowan, Carl T. Go South to Sorrow. *Random House, 1957.*

Rowan, Carl T. Just Between Us Blacks. *Random House, 1974.*

Rustin, Bayard. Down the Line. *Quadrangle Books, 1971.*

APPENDIX

Sampson, Geoffrey. Liberty and Language. *Oxford University Press, London, 1979.*

Schlafly, Phyllis. The Power of the Positive Woman. *Arlington House, 1977.*

Schroyer, Trent. The Critique of Domination: The Origins and Development of Critical Theory. *Braziller, 1973.*

Schumacher, E. F. A Guide for the Perplexed. *Harper & Row, Publishers, 1977.*

Schumacher, E. F. Small Is Beautiful: A Study of Economics as if People Mattered. *Harper & Row, 1973.*

Simon, James F. Independent Journey: The Life of William O. Douglas. *Harper & Row, 1980.*

Solotaroff, Theodore. The Red Hot Vacuum and Other Pieces on Writing in the Sixties. *Atheneum, 1970.*

Talese, Gay. The Kingdom and the Power. *World Publishing Co., 1969.*

Toffler, Alvin. Future Shock. *Random House, 1970.*

Toffler, Alvin. The Third Wave. *William Morrow, 1980.*

Tuchman, Barbara W. A Distant Mirror: The Calamitous 14th Century. *Knopf, 1978.*

Tuchman, Barbara W. The Guns of August. *Macmillan, 1962.*

Tuchman, Barbara W. The Proud Tower: A Portrait of the World Before the War; 1890-1914. *Macmillan, 1966.*

Wiesel, Elie. A Jew Today. *Random House, 1978.*

Wiesel, Elie. The Jews of Silence: A Personal Report on Soviet Jewry. *Holt, 1966.*

Wiesel, Elie. One Generation After. *Random House, 1970.*

Index to Critics

CRITIC INDEX

CRITIC INDEX

CRITIC INDEX

CRITIC INDEX

Index to Subjects

SUBJECT INDEX

SUBJECT INDEX

SUBJECT INDEX